I0715317

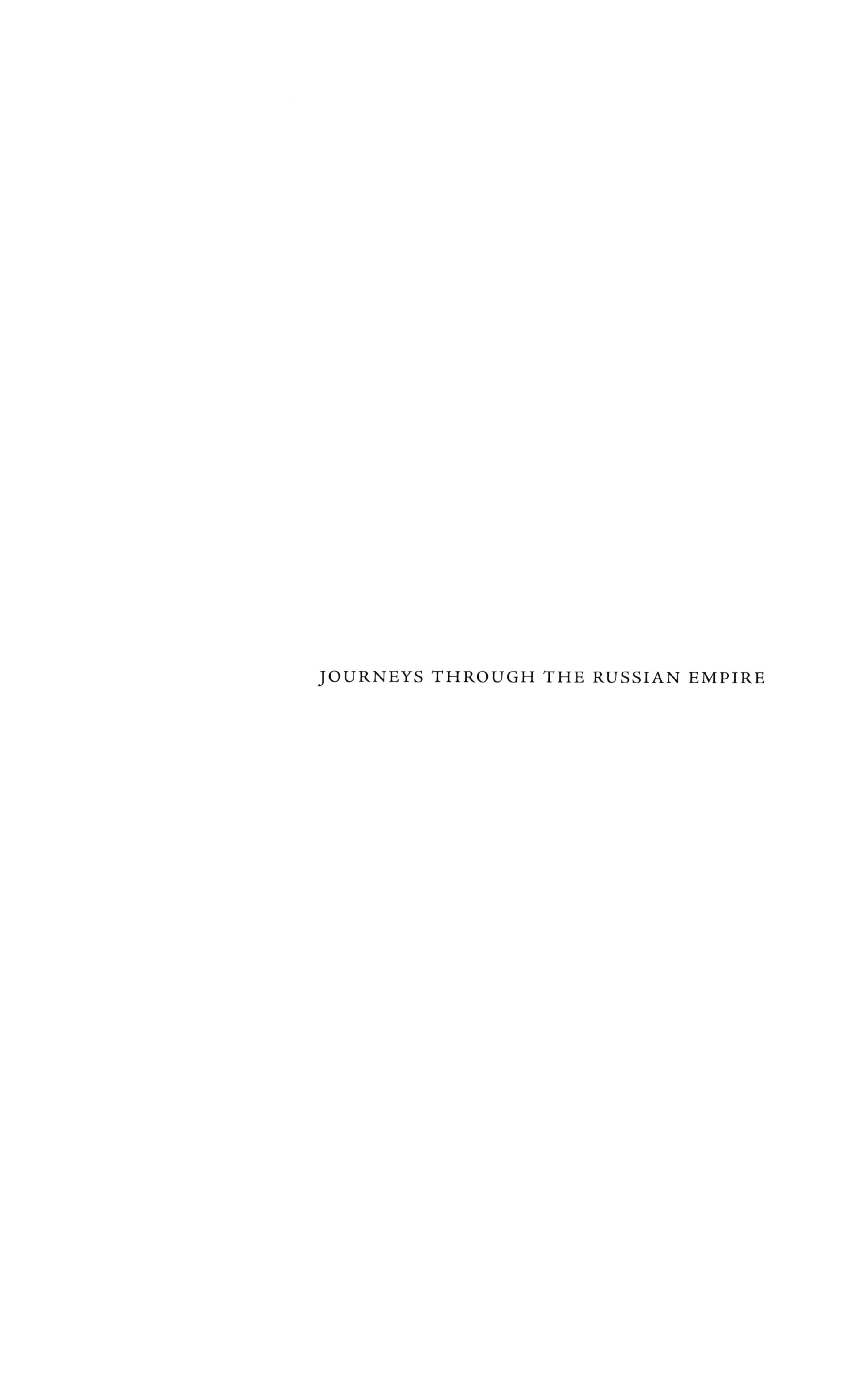

JOURNEYS THROUGH THE RUSSIAN EMPIRE

WILLIAM CRAFT BRUMFIELD

Journeys

THROUGH THE RUSSIAN EMPIRE

THE PHOTOGRAPHIC LEGACY *of* SERGEY PROKUDIN-GORSKY

DUKE UNIVERSITY PRESS · DURHAM AND LONDON · 2020

ACKNOWLEDGMENTS

To write an acknowledgements page for a book that covers five decades of one's work is a questionable exercise. To whom should I express my gratitude? Everyone, figuratively speaking. In Russia, to the hundreds of friends, colleagues, and strangers who made my life and work possible. To editors and publishers, to drivers and museum workers, to people who gave me shelter. Some perhaps remember, others probably do not.

In this country, to everyone who believed in my work, or simply gave me a pass. Friends, colleagues, strangers, institutions, foundations, universities, endowments. My parents, my sister . . . One person I will name is James Billington, Librarian of Congress from 1987 to 2015. The reasons for this would take more than a page.

I am forever indebted to the staff at Duke University Press and to Miriam Angress, my editor for two books. And to Richard and Betty Hedreen, whose generosity in support of my book is surpassed only by their understanding of why it is necessary. And to Tamara, who is always in my memory.

The eight photographic journeys in this book are composites created to give a sense of discrete geographic regions in Sergey Prokudin-Gorsky's work and my own during our many expeditions. The maps at the beginning of each journey will convey the outlines of the respective regions.

In consultation with the editorial staff at Duke University Press, I have decided to reproduce the digital images of Prokudin-Gorsky's photographs without "corrections," that is, without cropping or retouching. They are presented here in the form produced by the Library of Congress during the digitization of the Prokudin-Gorsky Collection at the beginning of this century.

The foundation of this volume consists of the comparison of Prokudin-Gorsky's photographs with my own taken several decades later. Although broad in its scope, the book is not intended as a comprehensive study of Prokudin-Gorsky's life or his work. References to published sources are contained in the "History" section in part I, "Sergey Prokudin-Gorsky: Photographer of an Empire," but there is no bibliography. The information presented in the text that accompanies the photographs is derived from a myriad of Russian-language sources on regional architectural heritage as well as from notes compiled over decades of my documentary research and field work.

Russian words and names have been transliterated with a modified version of the Library of Congress transliteration system for the Cyrillic alphabet.

An Unsentimental Journey

The color photographs of Sergey Prokudin-Gorsky—more precisely, the digital scans of his work made available by the Library of Congress—have launched an extraordinary wave of engagement and soul searching among the Russian public. Websites, blogs, and lavish albums seem omnipresent in Russia. The fascination with his work has led to an examination of virtually each image from a geographical point of view—where he placed the camera, and what is currently at the site that he photographed, or from which he photographed. Internet projects have offered exhaustive research and ingenious interpretations, often involving the participant's personal experience with a specific site. These personal, shared comments represent public expressions of devotion to local history on a national scale. For these participant-commentators, Prokudin-Gorsky's photographs deeply validate the reality of their specific locality in a national—indeed, global—context.

The grand unity of Prokudin-Gorsky's extraordinary productivity has increased a sense that the Russian Empire at the beginning of the twentieth century appears authentically in his photographs. Many photographers had worked in Russia before the revolution, but what is preserved of their work (in black-and-white) seems fragmented and localized in comparison with the scale of Prokudin-Gorsky's photographic sweep. The diversity and geographical range of his collection give the impression that he had captured the essential totality of the empire, although the collection does not

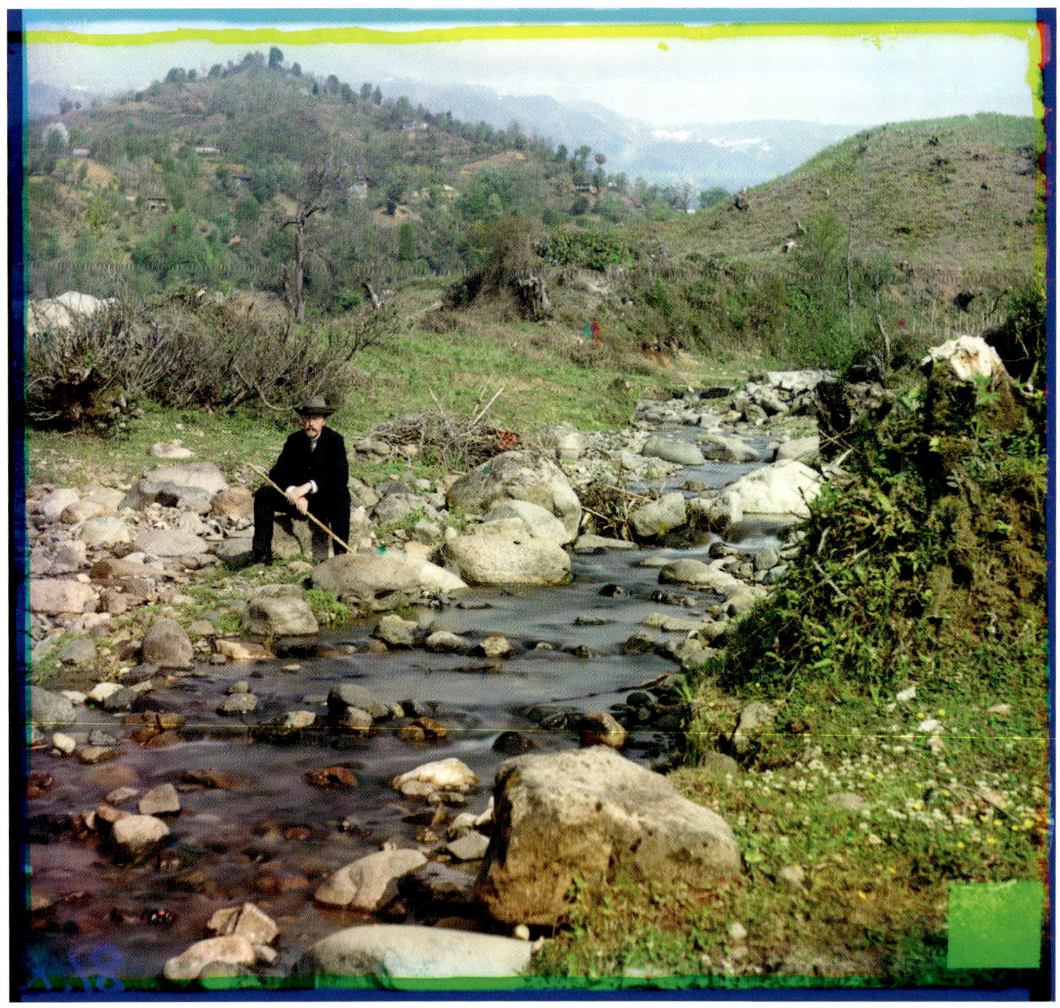

contain the two major cities, Saint Petersburg and Moscow. His purpose was to gather the provinces, both near and distant, in a visual record that could be (and was) presented to the metropoles, a unifying vision of the vast space they controlled—a space defined, as it were, by its periphery.

It could be argued that the trope of imperial "manifest destiny" lies at the basis of his collection, and that assumption must remain in the background of any appraisal of his work. To what extent did the subjects he photographed in Turkestan or the Caucasus consider themselves a part of "Russia"? Even if the collection is selectively limited to the Russian heartland, the current Russian engagement with the Prokudin-Gorsky Collection raises questions about the nature and uses of photographs in collective memory. The astonishment at the lush colors has undoubtedly added

Sergey Prokudin-Gorsky seated by the small Skuritskhali River on the outskirts of Batumi, a Black Sea city located in the Republic of Georgia. PHOTOGRAPH TAKEN IN MARCH 1912 BY ONE OF THE PHOTOGRAPHER'S ASSISTANTS. 21468.

to their impact as viewers struggle to connect with another time, another reality, another conception of Russia.

In a broader sense this struggle has occurred at least since the dissolution of the Soviet Union in 1991. In a period of unsettling transformation many Russians began to contemplate an earlier cataclysm. There is no better example than the provocatively titled book *The Russia That We Have Lost*, published in 1991 by the director and social activist Stanislav Govorukhin. The following year Govorukhin released an impassioned documentary film with the same title. The essence of both can be summarized as an extended commentary on prerevolutionary Russia—its potential, its hopeful progress. Despite the ensuing controversy, the film was credited with opening a post-Soviet comprehension of the twilight years of tsarist Russia—in effect, the era of Prokudin-Gorsky. The polemical resonance of Govorukhin's film has lingered, and his recent death (on June 14, 2018) will undoubtedly extend the commentary.

Some two decades later, the same phrase—"the Russia we have lost"—was used, not coincidentally, in public commentary on a documentary film and subsequent television broadcast about Prokudin-Gorsky created by the television producer Leonid Parfyonov. The title of his widely distributed film, *Tsvet natsii* (2013) can be translated either as "color of the nation" or "flower of the nation," a word play on both Prokudin-Gorsky's color photography and a sense of the country's best representatives. Parfyonov wished to evoke a neglected heritage that promised much for Russia. Indeed, there are moments in the film when the pathos is exaggerated by the framing of views to convey the impression of overgrown monuments, abandoned sacred relics. Having photographed the same sites during a similar period, I can attest that there are other, clearer perspectives that show the sites in relatively good condition. Despite catastrophic vandalism and loss, a careful comparison with the photographs of Prokudin-Gorsky shows that much has indeed remained. To reveal those remnants is the purpose of my work on the following pages.

The hand of fate seems to hover everywhere in this volume. Most of Prokudin-Gorsky's photographic work occurred between two Russian revolutions—1905 and 1917—and between two disastrous wars—the Russo-Japanese and World War I. Born in April 1895, my father fought in the marines as part of the American Expeditionary Forces on the Western Front in that Great War. He was the first person I knew who had seen Russians, soldiers who formed part of a sizeable contingent provided by Nicholas II to bolster the French army. And in August 1918, just as my father's unit

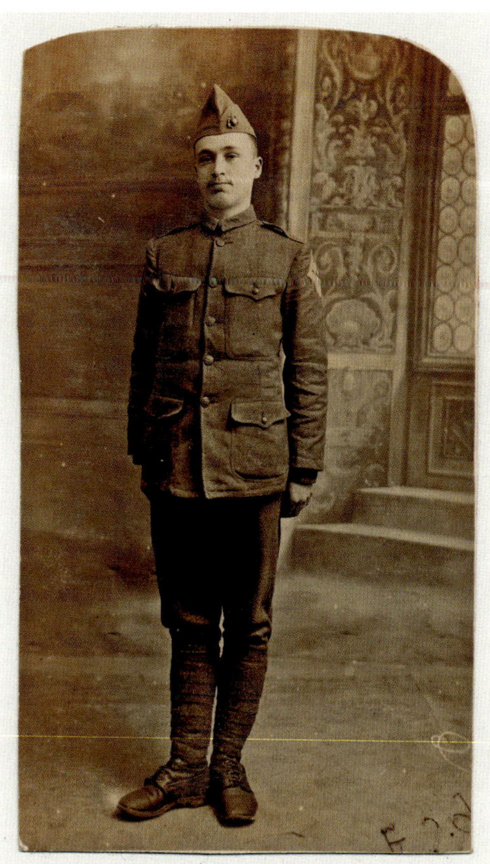

Lewis Floyd Brumfield, private, United States Marine Corps. STUDIO PHOTOGRAPH TAKEN JULY 1918 IN AIX-LES-BAINS, FRANCE.

Sergey Prokudin-Gorsky on handcar with railway official near Petrozavodsk (Karelia). Standing behind them are Austro-Hungarian prisoners of war used as construction labor for railroad to port of Romanov-on-Murman (now Murmansk). PHOTOGRAPH TAKEN IN SUMMER 1916 BY ONE OF THE PHOTOGRAPHER'S ASSISTANTS. 20245.

(6th Regiment, 4th Marine Brigade, 2nd Infantry Division) was fed into the maelstrom on the Marbache Sector of the front as a prelude to the Saint-Mihiel offensive, Prokudin-Gorsky had left his native land, never to return.

After the humiliating Treaty of Brest-Litovsk in March 1918, what was then known (briefly) as the Russian Soviet Republic lost much of the western part of the former Russian Empire. At this point the Russian contingent—formally no longer at war with Germany and probably suspected of Bolshevik contagion—were interned in French camps, where my father saw them in the latter part of 1918. He mentioned this encounter to me in the winter of 1952 (during the Korean War), and I consider these brief but sympathetic words to be the origins of a fascination with Russia that would one day launch me on journeys through the lands traversed by Prokudin-Gorsky.

To contemplate Prokudin-Gorsky's miraculous accomplishment is to summon further encounters with fate. In his driven efforts to photograph over such distances, did he ever sense a premonition that he was recording an empire on the brink of demise? Unlikely, and yet there are intersecting lines that intrigue on a subjective level. Among them are the photographs

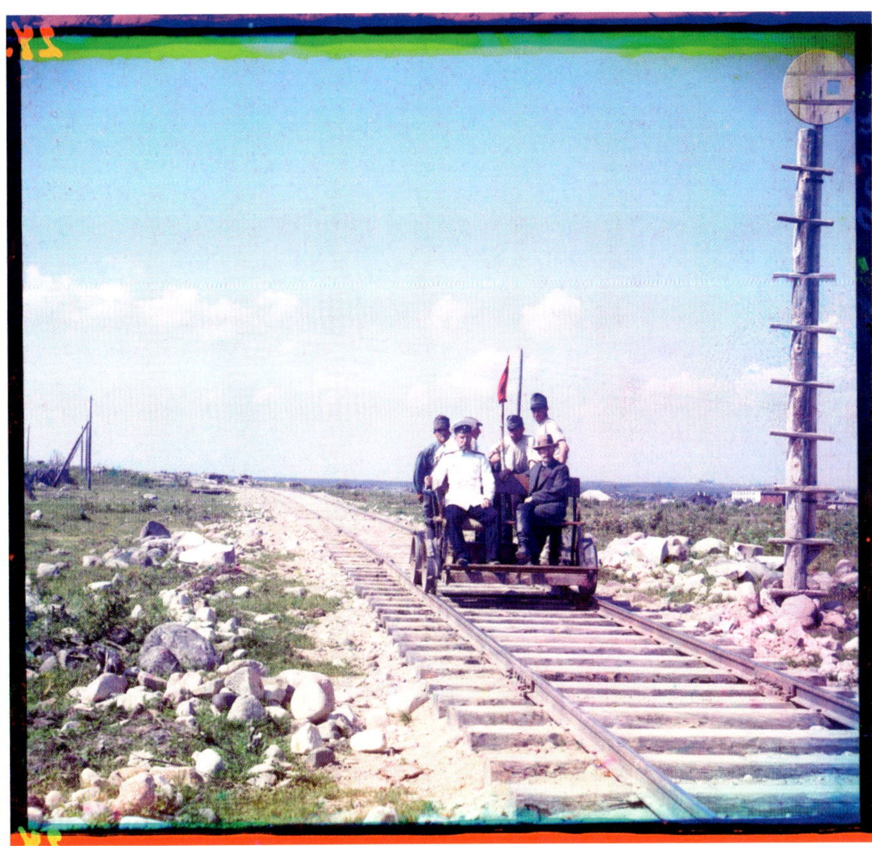

of Solovetsky Monastery taken in 1916 (his last photographic expedition), a half decade before the beginning of the monastery's conversion into the prototypical gulag, the defining monument of the gulag archipelago. As will be seen in Journey Eight, these photographs were taken during Prokudin-Gorsky's documentation of a strategic war project, the building of a railroad north to a new port that would become Murmansk. Labor on that project included many prisoners of war from the Austro-Hungarian army.

Prokudin-Gorsky's documentary work has many components (ethnographic, transportation expansion, land development and amelioration in the Caucasus and Central Asia), but I believe that the heart of his project is historical architecture. Russia's architectural heritage not only gave meaning, value, and energy to the implementation of Prokudin-Gorsky's colossal project but also provided the artifacts and the structures whose existence inspired the creation of a visual record that he and I shared. The individuals that he photographed have long since gone. The development projects—whether northern canals or Central Asian irrigation systems—had little to offer in visual or cultural specificity and have since been transformed. The architectural monuments, however, remain as an expression of history, art, and spiritual culture. For both of us, they have provided an aesthetic frame of reference, constant but subject to many variables: lens, sensitivity of film, angle of view, lighting, time of day, and season. And then there are the marks of human intervention over the decades that separate our journeys.

This book is not intended to be an exhaustive examination of the Prokudin-Gorsky Collection. That is an ongoing project that involves hundreds of participants, particularly in Russia and primarily through the internet. In the following sections I provide an overview of his work, as well as a brief description of the Prokudin-Gorsky Collection at the Library of Congress and my collection at the National Gallery of Art. That material is a prelude to the book's larger purpose: to examine and compare the intersections between Prokudin-Gorsky's photography and my own. To that end I have chosen to focus on the architectural heritage of two great cultural regions — the European Russian heartland and the ancient cities of Samarkand and Bukhara, located in what was then called Turkestan and now is Uzbekistan.

It must be emphasized that my documentation and study of Russian architecture has had its own dynamic and trajectory. It began with photographs taken during my first trip to Russia in the summer of 1970 — long before I had heard of Prokudin-Gorsky. I became involved with the Prokudin-Gorsky Collection precisely because of my field experience in photographing Russian architectural monuments. While surveying his contact albums in the Prints and Photographs Division, I realized how frequently our photographic priorities overlapped. In some cases, this was to be expected for anyone with a serious interest in Russian architectural history — the twelfth-century cathedrals of Vladimir, for example. But other intersections in our journeys were entirely fortuitous, such as my trip to Uzbekistan in May 1972 as a graduate student engaged in dissertation research at Leningrad State University. In surveying Prokudin-Gorsky's photographs I realized that through a twist of fate I had seen and photographed the great monuments of Samarkand and Bukhara (now substantially reconstructed) in something like their condition when he documented them six decades earlier.

Acquaintance with the Prokudin-Gorsky Collection did not lead me to change my field itineraries simply to duplicate his journeys, nor did I set out to replicate his views. Often the visual logic of the location and the specific architectural structure resulted in a convergence of our perspectives. In other cases, the contrast is startling. Whatever the differences, the juxtaposition of our images, separated at least by sixty-five years and in some cases

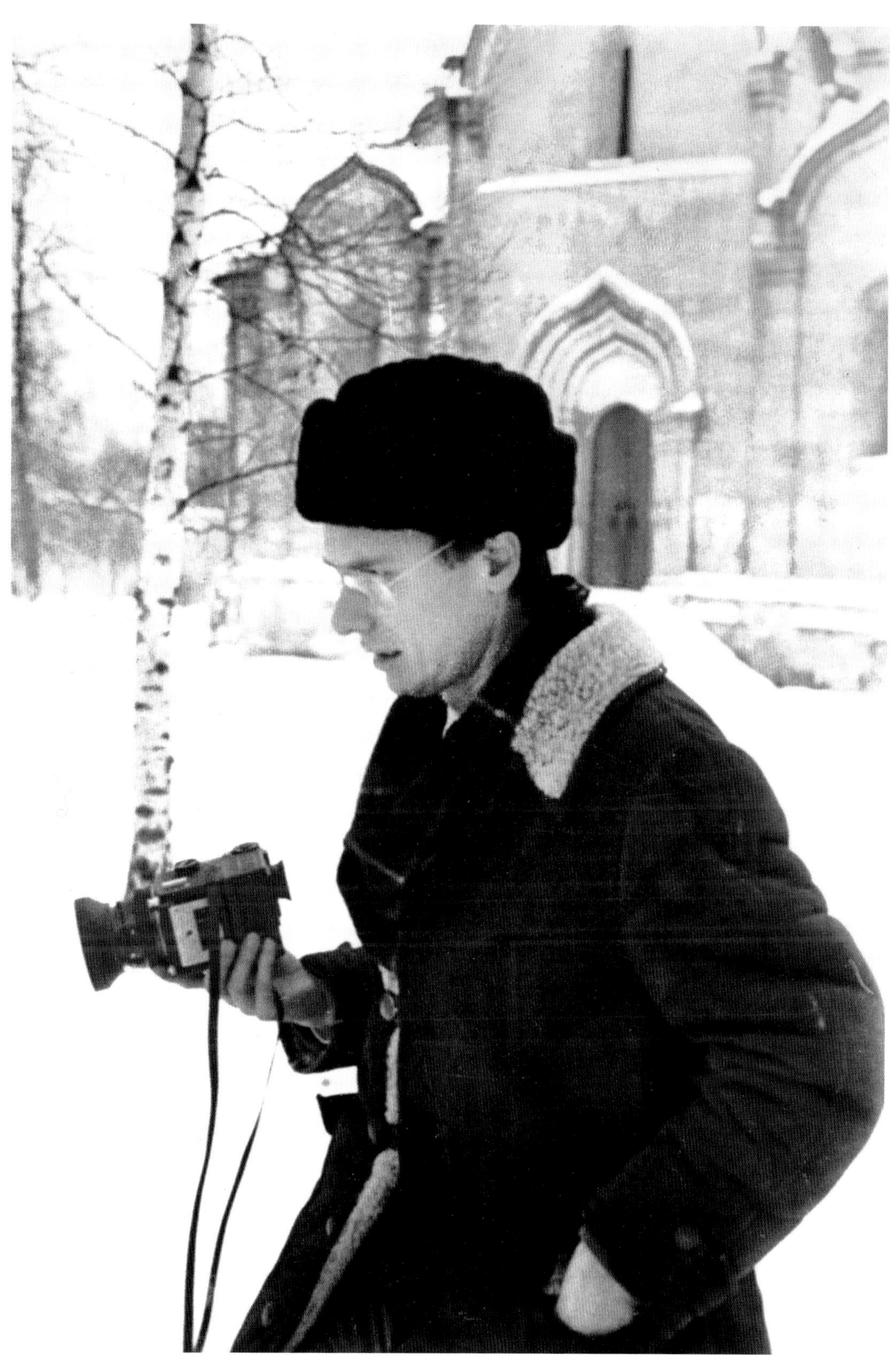

Author at Savior-Andronikov Monastery, Moscow. DECEMBER 21, 1979.

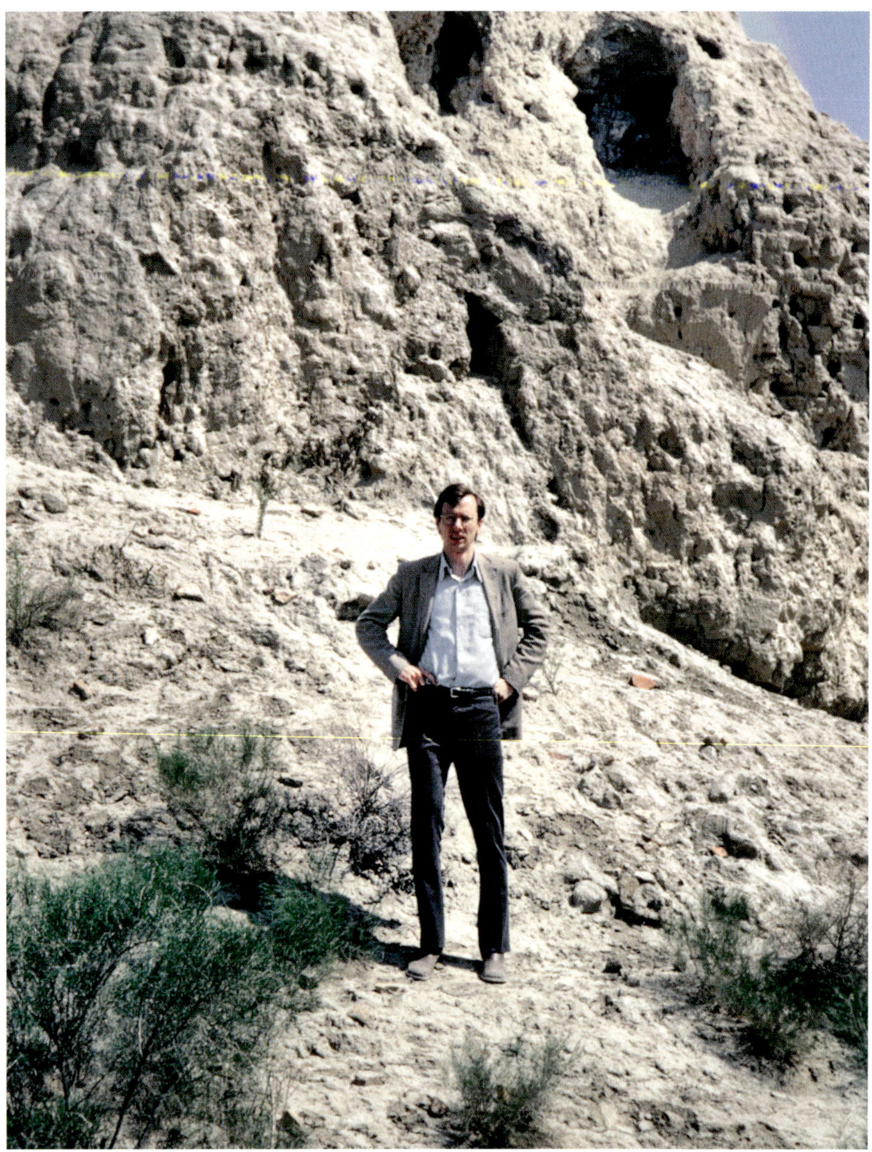

Author at ruins of medieval fort near Bukhara, Uzbekistan. MAY 13, 1972.

by a century, yields telling contrasts in the condition of architectural monuments and the history that surrounds them. It is this play of convergence and contrast that forms the crux of the book.

To illuminate this juxtaposition, I have structured a series of "journeys" through eight geographical regions. These journeys do not necessarily reproduce specific itineraries (either his or mine) but represent composites that allow me to organize the photographs in a logical sequence for the reader. The towns or sites in each journey are concisely described from a historical perspective, and each Prokudin-Gorsky image is placed within that context, including information on the time of his visit. (I have written annotations for most of the images in the Prokudin-Gorsky Collection at the Library of Congress.)

The accompanying text provides commentary comparing his and my photographs. Each of my photographs is precisely dated as a basic means of documenting the differences noted in the comparative analysis of the respective photographs. From the parallels in our journeys through time and space, images and text raise questions about fundamental issues concerning the preservation of Russia's cultural heritage.

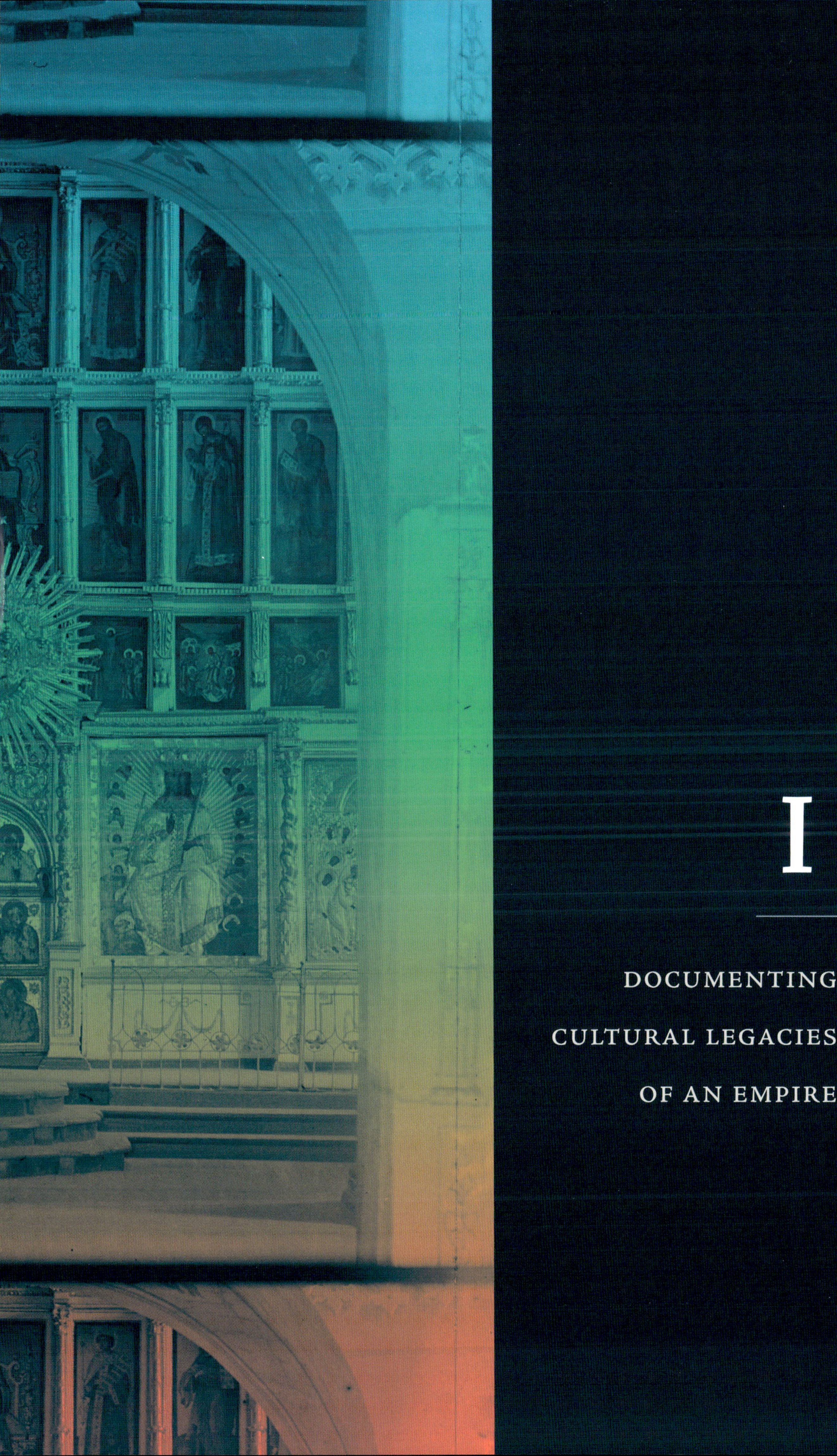

I

DOCUMENTING

CULTURAL LEGACIES

OF AN EMPIRE

Sergey Prokudin-Gorsky

Photographer of an Empire

Between 1907 and 1916 the Russian photographer and inventor Sergey Mikhailovich Prokudin-Gorsky embarked on a series of journeys that resulted in an unparalleled documentary record of the Russian Empire, from Smolensk to Samarkand, during the decade before the revolution. The geographical scope of his photographic work is in itself notable — and characteristic of an age of enterprising photographer-explorers, but the cultural and ethnic diversity captured by Prokudin-Gorsky is all the more remarkable for his development of a camera that produced three-separation negatives that could be recombined to create a color image. This complex process was ultimately not in the mainstream of color photography, yet it provided images capable of being reproduced with a clarity of detail and color unusual by any standards. Indeed, the viewer of these photographs may find it difficult to reconcile the usual perception of prerevolutionary Russia, abundantly illustrated in recent albums of black-and-white photographs, with the quality of color conveyed in Prokudin-Gorsky's work.

The Russia that Prokudin-Gorsky recorded was a land in the throes of great, if fitful, social change. The reforms instituted during the reign of Alexander II (1855–81), had led to substantial economic development in major Russian cities, but growth was uneven, and large parts of the country seemed untouched by the benefits of progress. The inability of traditional methods of land tenure to support a rapidly growing population created massive social dislocation as peasants poured into Moscow, Saint Petersburg, and lesser cities — either as seasonal laborers or to enter the permanent workforce of enormous new industrial enterprises, often funded by foreign capital. Despite the widespread poverty and lack of basic social services in both country and city, by the beginning of the twentieth century an optimistic observer could find reason to believe that Russia was evolving toward a modern economic, if not political, system.

The French in particular invested heavily in Russia's expanding railway network, and nothing symbolized the belated industrial revolution in Russia more clearly that the construction of railroads — which proved indispensable to Prokudin-Gorsky, not only as a means of transportation but also as a primary subject of his photographic work. The social and economic impact of the railroads must have been felt more intensely in Russia than elsewhere in Europe, not simply because of the country's relative backwardness but also in relation to the vast distances that could be linked through the coming of the technological age. By the time Prokudin-Gorsky began his color photography, the greatest of Russia's railroad construction projects — the Trans-Siberian — was approaching completion. The railroad represented the hope of progress, and there were those who saw the new machine as a means of transforming backward Russia.

But the railroad also signified dislocation and chaos. Russian writers in the latter part of the nineteenth century and the beginning of the twentieth registered the effects of the transformation in "post-reform" Russian society (after the liberation of the serfs in 1861), and no literature has explored the effects of rapid social change with a greater sense of drama. Behind the clash of new ideas and traditional belief in the Russian novel during this period, there is the incursion of the machine, the factory, and the railroad into what had been an overwhelmingly rural country, only recently freed from a semifeudal system of master and serf.

From Dostoevsky's *Crime and Punishment* (or any of his other novels) to Chekhov's *The Cherry Orchard*, the wrenching effects of the new order — still in the process of formation — are explored with depth and sensitivity. But perhaps the most profound use of literature to probe the obscure relations between individual destiny and a society in transition occurs in Leo Tolstoy's *Anna Karenina*, whose moral searching unfolds on a background of relentless social change symbolized, again, by the railroad. Although many of the novel's characters endlessly discuss the state of contemporary Russian society, they have little apparent control over its transformation, which they only dimly perceive.

Tolstoy's personal attempts to define the essential, moral relations between the individual and society led to a status approaching sainthood by the time Prokudin-Gorsky photographed him, in 1908, shortly before the writer's eightieth birthday. Yet Tolstoy's enormous moral authority possessed a universal significance that had little tangible effect on the immediate paradox facing Russia: the closer it approached the modern industrial age, the more intractable seemed its problems in creating a just and economically viable social order. The enigma of Prokudin-Gorsky's photographs is that they seem to convey so little of this paradox; and yet for all their portrayal of ancient monuments and a traditional social order, they also reflect a land and people on the brink of cataclysmic change.

Whatever its social contradictions and squandered opportunities during the half century preceding World War I, Russia offered enormous potential for development, and it witnessed extraordinary—if often unrewarded—personal initiative in science, the arts, and technology. Prokudin-Gorsky, born in 1863 to a family of noble origins and limited means, was very much a product of this burgeoning technological age.

After graduation from Saint Petersburg's prestigious Alexander Lycée (founded by Alexander I for children of the nobility), he continued his studies in the natural sciences during the latter part of the 1880s at the Saint Petersburg Technological Institute, and also studied painting at the Imperial Academy of Arts.[1] During this period he came under the guidance of the eminent chemist Dmitry Mendeleev, who taught at the technological institute. As a member of the Imperial Russian Technical Society (founded in 1866), Mendeleev actively supported research in photography, which had first appeared in Russia in the late 1830s and was subsequently included with chemistry as part of the First Department of the Technical Society.

The combination of photography and chemistry in this major scientific society serves as a reminder of the period before "instant" cameras, when even an amateur photographer had to know something of practical chemistry. More to the point, the attention given photography in the Russian Technical Society testifies to its importance as a scientific tool. Although critics in the mid-nineteenth century debated the validity of photography as an art form, there could be no doubts about its usefulness for documentary purposes, especially in a country of such geographic and ethnic diversity. By 1878 Mendeleev, together with the photographers Vyacheslav Sreznevsky and Sergey Levitsky, had established within the technical society a fifth department, devoted solely to photography.[2] Despite its sparse resources, the new section played a leading role in the propagation of photography through exhibits and lectures, and Prokudin-Gorsky would later find it a useful platform from which to discuss his investigations.

Upon leaving the technological institute in 1889, Prokudin-Gorsky studied for two years in photochemical laboratories in Berlin and Paris, where he gained an understanding of the principles and the complexities involved in reproducing color photographically. His work in western Europe also led to a familiarity with the latest techniques and cameras of Adolf Miethe and Edme-Jules Maumené.

After returning to Russia in the early 1890s, Prokudin-Gorsky resumed research into the scientific and technical aspects of photography. In 1890 he married Anna Lavrova, with whom he had three children: Dmitry, born in 1892; Catherine, born in 1893; and Michael, born in 1895. By 1897 he was a frequent lecturer at the Russian Technical Society, which was interested in the results of his work from both a theoretical and a practical point of view. Photography had been used in Russia since the 1860s as an aid to the study of natural sciences and ethnography but increasingly sophisticated techniques permitted its use in other areas such as astronomy and microbiology, and Prokudin-Gorsky conducted courses in the application of photography in scientific research.

The first of Prokudin-Gorsky's published works on photography appeared in 1898: *Printing (Copying) from Negatives* and *Photographing with Instant Hand Cameras*.[3] Both of these publications concentrated on black-and-white photography, and at the 1900 Paris Exposition, Prokudin-Gorsky exhibited his own photographs in that medium under the auspices of the Russian Technical Society. Yet color remained the overriding goal of his work. In 1903 he established in Saint Petersburg a commercial laboratory for color printing and published the booklet *Isochromatic Photography with Instant Hand Cameras*, based on his research in color photography.[4] His resources as a printer were tested the following year, when, after the outbreak of the Russo-Japanese War in February 1904, he undertook a project for a large illustrated volume from the Manchurian battlefields. The published album, which contains only brief captions with almost no text, consists primarily of static or posed scenes that give little idea of the devastation of the fighting, although the sepia photographs convey the vast scale of the battlefields and the unprecedented size of the Russian army's ultimately futile operations.[5]

In February 1905 Prokudin-Gorsky arranged the first major demonstration of his color slides before an audience at the Russian Technical Society. The seventy or so slides included various generic scenes that illustrated the range of color reproduction possible with the photographer's inventions.[6]

With the growing public awareness of the success of his method, Prokudin-Gorsky assumed the editorship of the Saint Petersburg journal *Amateur Photographer* (*Fotograf-liubitel*), published from 1890 to 1909.

Between 1906 and 1909 he used the magazine to inform his readers of technical innovations in color photography. In 1906 he published a twelve-part survey of the theoretical principles of color photochemistry and reported on the design of cameras suitable for photographing in color. This information no doubt exceeded the abilities of amateur photographers, but the articles provide a detailed look at his own approach to a feasible color system with frequent acknowledgment of the work of pioneers such as Miethe and the Lumière brothers.[7]

Amateur Photographer also became a forum for propagating Prokudin-Gorsky's vision of photography as a means of enlightenment, of enlarging the public's view of distant lands and peoples, and of natural phenomena such as the solar eclipse he photographed in Siberia at the beginning of 1907. The Russian Empire seemed particularly suited to such a vision, and Prokudin-Gorsky was tireless in his advocacy of scientific research as a means of advancing Russian photography to a level comparable with that elsewhere in Europe. In 1908 he did much to implement his views by initiating a series of courses on photography at the Petersburg Technological Institute, where he had himself been a student twenty years earlier.

Prokudin-Gorsky's ambitious plans for a color photographic survey of the Russian Empire and its cultural monuments were formulated by 1907. He had perfected a portable camera, based on a model by Adolf Miethe, that allowed him to take in rapid succession three exposures with different filters on color-sensitive plates. Although the process and its resulting three-color separation could be transferred to paper, Prokudin-Gorsky achieved a more dramatic effect by projecting his color image onto a screen for public showing. For this purpose, he designed a projector that could combine light through positives of his three-color separations into a brilliant and precisely focused image.

During 1908 he mounted a series of slide presentations before audiences that included the Russian Technical Society and the Saint Petersburg Photographic Society. In May 1908 he received permission to photograph the writer Leo Tolstoy at his estate, Yasnaya Polyana, and his color portrait of Tolstoy (one of a series taken at the estate) appeared shortly thereafter in the *Notes of the Imperial Russian Technical Society* in celebration of the writer's eightieth birthday.[8] An excerpt from Prokudin-Gorsky's description of the session with Tolstoy gives an idea of the photographer's

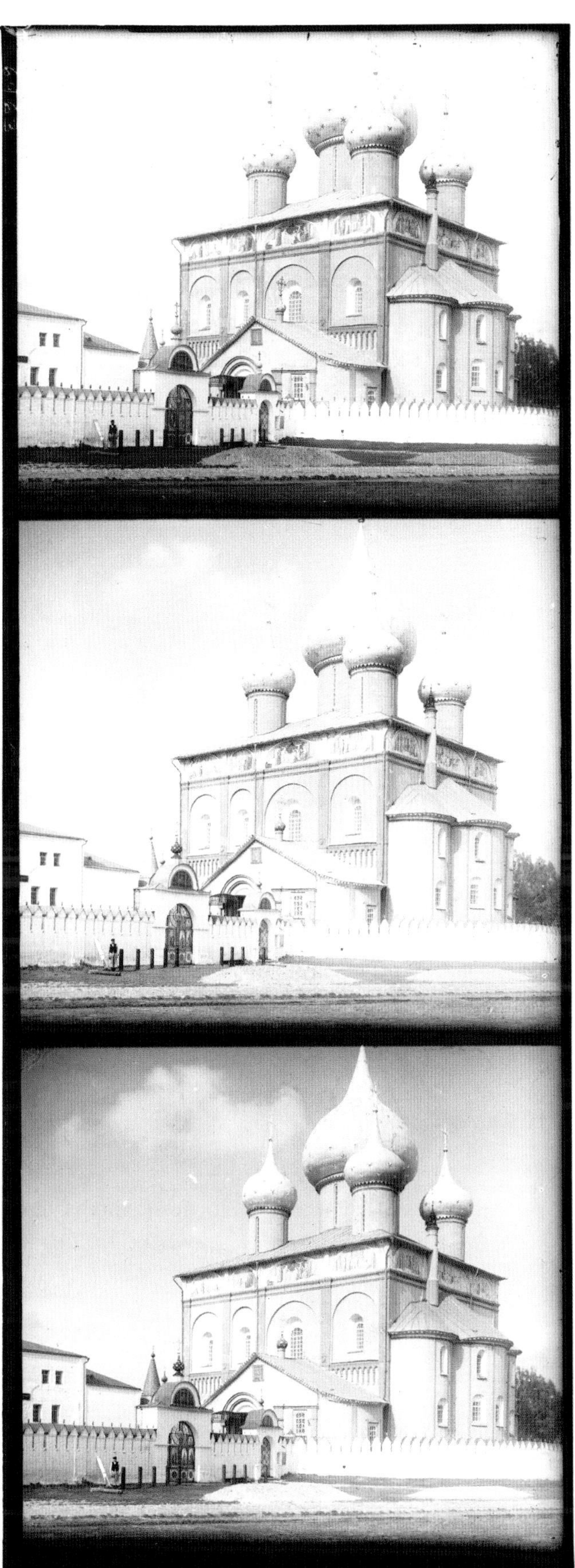

Cathedral of the Nativity of the Virgin, Suzdal. 1912. Three-separation negative on glass plate. ORIGINAL IN THE PROKUDIN-GORSKY COLLECTION, LIBRARY OF CONGRESS. 01256.

method of work: "In order to record the color image, it is necessary to make three separate negatives from the same position and quickly expose one after the other. The portrait of Count Tolstoy took six seconds—a remarkably fast exposure if one considers that during this time the cassettes [with the plates] were shifted twice, and also that the color filters greatly reduce the intensity of the light."[9] By the end of 1908 Prokudin-Gorsky's accomplishments had brought him to the attention of the imperial family, and early in 1909 he was called to give a presentation to Nicholas II. The success of this demonstration before the imperial court enabled Prokudin-Gorsky to surmount a number of the financial and bureaucratic obstacles connected with his plan to photograph monuments of culture and history throughout the Russian Empire.[10] Nicholas no doubt appreciated the loyalty and pedagogical zeal that lay behind the photographer's idea of recording the diversity of a vast land; and there were other, more pragmatic reasons to justify a series of photographic expeditions.

In a creative combination of the logistical with the documentary, it was decided that Prokudin-Gorsky could record the development of Russia's far-flung transportation system with attention to rail- and waterways. In addition to passage by train and boat, the Ministry of Transportation granted him a specially equipped railway car to accommodate his cameras, laboratory, and assistants. In the summer of 1909 Prokudin-Gorsky completed trips along the Mariinsky Canal system (linking the Volga and Neva Rivers) and to industrial areas in the Ural Mountains. During the following three years his travels included the Caucasus and Central Asia, as well as large areas of the Russian heartland.

While this pragmatic agreement with the Ministry of Transportation provided Prokudin-Gorsky with the mobility necessary to accomplish his larger goals, it also led to a curious dual emphasis in his work. On one hand, there are prosaic shots of the transportation system and the industrial enterprises linked by that system (particularly in the Ural Mountains). On the other hand, there are the views of ancient monuments and a bucolic way of life seemingly untouched by the social transformation described above. Each group is meticulously composed with the photographer's usual skill and concern for detail; and indeed, many of the "transportation" shots, especially along the railways, are so perfectly framed as to supersede, at least momentarily, an awareness of the specific functional object in view—a bridge, a factory, a track right-of-way.

During the intervals between his travels Prokudin-Gorsky frequently gave public slide presentations in which he demonstrated the technical splendors

of his method and urged its use in the study and preservation of cultural monuments. The essence of his views is conveyed in the published summary of a lecture titled "Monuments of Antiquity along the Mariinsky Canal System and the Upper Volga, and a Few Words about the Significance of Color Photography," which he delivered in January 1911 to the Fourth Congress of Russian Architects at the Academy of Arts in Saint Petersburg:

> With contemporary progress in the area of color photography and color printing, we have at hand a valuable means for saving many decaying monuments of art from oblivion. This is the great significance of color photography. By using light-sensitive plates to register the creation of artistic inspiration in all its richness of hue, in all the charm of its color, and with all of the subtleties of individual talent, we give to our descendants an invaluable document. Only on the basis of such documents can Russian society—both specialists and people who are simply interested in all that is beautiful—make a proper judgement about the true dimensions and meaning of the artistic riches located in their domains.[11]

Prokudin-Gorskii perhaps overstated the exclusive importance of color photography in the study of artistic monuments. From both an aesthetic and documentary perspective, black-and-white photography has proved to be a fundamental resource. But there can be no doubt that his impassioned plea—accompanied by a show of his slides—for the preservation and recording of national landmarks accurately predicted the enduring public demand for color photographic reproductions of such treasures. In addition, his belief in the need to have reliable color representations for the restoration of damaged or destroyed works of art proved all too prophetic later in the century, as war and revolution wreaked havoc throughout Europe—especially in what had been the Russian Empire.

After 1911 official support for Prokudin-Gorsky's photographic expeditions terminated. In 1910 he had sent an appeal to the Council of Ministers (headed by Peter Stolypin, the last effective Russian prime minister) requesting that the state purchase his collection and provide additional support for his documentary work. Although a special government commission recommended that the collection be acquired and preserved under the auspices of the Russian Museum in Saint Petersburg, the proposal received no support.[12] Had the proposal been realized, the Prokudin-Gorsky plates would presumably be at the State Russian Museum rather than dispersed in various collections, the most notable of which is at the Library of Con-

gress. But with myopic parsimoniousness, the Russian bureaucracy let the matter die.

Undaunted, Prokudin-Gorsky turned to his own financial resources, augmented by income from the Biochrome Company, which he had established to market services in both color photography and photographic printing (black-and-white as well as color).[13] By these means he and his business partner, S. O. Maksimovich, organized a trip in the fall of 1911 to the fabled cities of Bukhara and Samarkand in Turkestan (now Uzbekistan). Not only did the journey to Turkestan produce some of the most spectacular of Prokudin-Gorsky's color photographs, it also served as a stimulus for the demonstration of a color movie camera that he and Maksimovich had devised. No film has been found from the camera, for which Prokudin-Gorsky ultimately received a Russian patent in 1915. His work on behalf of the government resumed briefly in 1916, when he photographed along the railroad being constructed to the port of Murmansk as a means of expediting the shipment of Allied war materiel to Russia (too little, too late).

As World War I lengthened beyond the expectations of any of the combatants, Russia's worsening economic and political situation put an end to Prokudin-Gorsky's extensive plans for further commercial and scientific gains in color photography. Yet not even the October Revolution in 1917 and its attendant chaos prevented him from arranging public slide shows, lectures, and the organization of a new photography institute in June 1918.[14]

Prokudin-Gorsky seems to have been resolutely apolitical and concerned primarily with the development of Russian science in his area, as well as with the pedagogical aspects of his color photography. His activities during the first six months after the Bolshevik revolution indicate that he wished to continue this work, whatever the political regime. Later that year, however, Russia was gripped by an increasingly violent political confrontation, which claimed among its victims in July 1918 Nicholas II, his wife, Aexandra, and their five children. He could not have remained indifferent to the murder of those who had shown him such generosity.

Prokudin-Gorsky went first to Norway—ostensibly on a purchasing trip for the new government—and never returned. In September 1919 he moved to England, where he continued his photographic research and published in journals such as *The British Journal of Photography*.[15] Two years later, in September 1921, he resettled in Nice, France, with his second wife, Maria Shchedrina, with whom he had a daughter, Elena. After an unsuccessful attempt to establish a cinema studio to advance his ideas for color film, he

moved to the Paris area. During this period, he was rejoined in emigration by his first family, concluding in early 1925 with his former wife Anna, their daughter Catherine, and son Dmitry.

Deprived of the Russian milieu to which he had contributed so much as a scientist and as a photographer, Prokudin-Gorsky was able to establish a photograph studio in France that provided employment for himself and his sons. His existence in exile was modest, yet by 1931 he had received through a still unclear turn of events most of his 2,500 sets of negatives. After his death in Paris on September 27, 1944, the collection remained with Prokudin-Gorsky's two sons (by his first marriage) until 1948, when the Library of Congress acquired this extraordinary treasure.[16]

. . . .

A survey of the Prokudin-Gorsky Collection reveals abundant possibilities for the study of his work in itself, as well as within the context of the history of Russian photography before the Bolshevik Revolution.[17] A simple inventory of the photographs suggests that Prokudin-Gorsky omitted certain important subjects and environments. For all the considerable range of his work in the Russian Empire, there is virtually nothing of Saint Petersburg or Moscow. The main purpose of his color photography consisted in bringing the unfamiliar and the remote to audiences in Russia's major cities — a goal reminiscent of the activities of the National Geographic Society in America. The cityscapes of Moscow and Petersburg must have seemed all too familiar, and in any event, they had been well recorded — in black-and-white — by other photographers, whose work should be better known. Yet his superb photographic method could have been used to record the details of Moscow's medieval churches, many of which were destroyed for political reasons in the 1930s. Prokudin-Gorsky had, after all, advocated the documentary use of color photography as a precaution against the destruction of such monuments in his lecture at the Congress of Russian Architects in 1911. It must be admitted, however, that no one at the beginning of the century could have predicted the cause or the extent of the devastation inflicted on Russia's cultural monuments.

In addition to Prokudin-Gorsky's preference for photographing outside of major cities, his color process required a relatively long exposure time, thus excluding many scenes of active daily life in urban areas. His views of provincial towns are almost always taken from a distance (minimizing the effect of motion), and while spectacular for topographical information they

contain, such views also minimize the details of the urban environment. When photographing people at close range, Prokudin-Gorsky required a stability of pose that at times seems to suggest a metaphorical comment on the stability of the social setting in which his subjects exist. This is not, however, to imply that the photographs convey a forced expression. In looking at the faces of these people (many of whom are in traditional peasant dress) photographed between 1909 and 1911, one is drawn to questions about their fate in the ensuing decade—particularly in the Ural region, where some of the most intense fighting of the civil war occurred.

Prokudin-Gorsky also photographed the Russian industrial landscape, particularly in the Ural Mountains but also including areas in central Russia and even along the Black Sea. Here, too, the natural setting and the photographer's artistry seem to contradict the obvious presence of a metalworking factory or a huge foundry belching smoke. In a number of these photographs the only visual rival to the factory is the soaring form of the local Orthodox church, of equally imposing size and usually of recent construction. The building of large churches was a matter of civic pride in many industrial towns in the Urals and Siberia during the nineteenth century, and the government had established a special fund, named after Alexander III, for the construction of churches along the Trans-Siberian Railway.

In Prokudin-Gorsky's photographs the wooden houses cluster between the two polarities of church and factory in towns that seem to have no other point of focus or institutional structure. No doubt there were schools, hospitals, banks, and commercial enterprises within the provincial industrial townscapes that Prokudin-Gorsky photographed, yet his work conveys an impression of rapid industrialization in a setting unmediated by any other social institution than that of the officially sponsored religion. If the people he photographed often seem to exist in a preindustrial world (as many of them undoubtedly did), Prokudin-Gorsky has caught that world in its last fading days. Yet the poise and dignity of his subjects have a universality that both partakes of and transcends that poignant historical moment. There is much still to be read in the photographs of Prokudin-Gorsky, for they have preserved a rare insight into a diversity of cultures that have since changed beyond recognition—as well as scenes that remain much as they were when he photographed them.

It should be emphasized that Prokudin-Gorsky did not make prints from his separation negatives, which were intended to be recombined in a projector for slide shows. Therefore, in preparing prints for an exhibition of Prokudin-Gorsky's work at the Library of Congress in 1986, considerable critical judgment was required in order to reclaim the colors from the information left on the photographer's color-sensitive negatives.[18] The resulting prints are a credit to the soundness and ingenuity of Prokudin-Gorsky's method, as well as to modern phototechnology.

The plates in the present volume are reproduced from these prints, with no retouching or cropping (apart from the frayed edges of certain images). In many cases, however, the negatives are too badly damaged to be used for reproduction. Fortunately, Prokudin-Gorsky made contact prints from one of the separation negatives on each plate and compiled them into albums described in the section below. For the Library of Congress exhibit, as well as for this book, black-and-white enlargements were made from contact prints whose exceptional quality and thematic interest recommend them to the reader. In many of the Prokudin-Gorsky photographs, the color that he so vividly captured is an essential element, yet those prints that can now be reproduced only in black-and-white remind us of his consummate mastery of composition in photography.

NOTES

1. The biographical details in the introduction have been drawn primarily from unpublished archival material in the Library of Congress, and from an article on Prokudin-Gorsky's work by Svetlana Garanina, "Uchenyi, izobretatel', fotokhudozhnik" (Scholar, inventor, photographic artist), *Sovetskoe foto*, no. 8 (1982): 25–27. Some of this information has been previously published in William Craft Brumfield, "The Color Photographs of Sergei Mikhailovich Prokudin-Gorskii," *Visual Resources* 6 (1990): 243–56.

2. A basic history of Russian photography from its beginnings to the twentieth century is Sergey A. Morozov, *Russkaia khudozhestvennaia fotografiia* (Moscow: Iskusstvo, 1955). A more recent publication on the history of Russian photography is Yelena V. Barchatova et al., *Portrait of Tsarist Russia: Unknown Photographs from the Soviet Archives* (New York: Pantheon, 1989). The English translation of the chapters by Russian authors has been filtered through an earlier German edition of the book, and as a result there are numerous errors, particularly in the transliteration of Russian terms. Nonetheless, this volume provides information not previously available in English on the development of Russian photography in the nineteenth century. For its account of the formation of the fifth department of the Russian Technological Society, see 13–15.

3. *O pechatanii (kopirovanii) s negativov* (Saint Petersburg: self-published, 1898); and *O fotografirovanii momental'nymi ruchnymi kamerami* (Saint Petersburg: self-published, 1898).

4. *Izokhromaticheskaia s"emka momental'nymi ruchnymi kamerami* (Saint Petersburg: Samokat, 1903). Prokudin-Gorsky also published a technical guide "for publishers, editors, artists, and printing houses" titled *Fototekhnicheskoe delo: Kratkii ukazatel' dlia izdatelei, redaktorov, khudozhnikov, tipografii, i t. d.* (Saint Petersburg: "Obshchestvennaia pol'za," 1905).

5. *Russko-Iaponskaia voina* (Russo-Japanese War) (Saint Petersburg: Press of the General Command Staff, n.d.). The Library of Congress has a copy of this rare book, which presumably appeared in 1905.

6. See Garanina, "Uchenyi, izobretatel', fotokhudozhnik," 25. A description of the slide presentation was entered into the society's meeting report, now preserved at the Central State Historical Archive in Leningrad.

7. "Fotografiia v natural'nykh tsvetakh" (Photography in Natural Colors), *Fotograf-Liubitel'* 17, nos. 1–12 (1906): 1–12. The Lumière system of producing color transparencies (or autochromes) differed from Prokudin-Gorsky's color photographic method, with its separation negatives.

8. Prokudin-Gorsky's photographic session with Tolstoy is described by Svetlana Garanina, "Portret s natury v natural'nykh kraskakh," *Sovetskoe foto*, no. 9 (1978): 24; and the same author's "Neizvestnye diapozitivy," *Sovetskoe foto*, no. 2 (1983): 40–41.

9. *Zapiski Russkogo Tekhnicheskogo Obshchestva*, no. 8 (1908): 369. Also quoted in Garanina, "Portret s natury v natural'nykh kraskakh," 24.

10. An account of Prokudin-Gorsky's audience with Nicholas II is presented in Robert H. Allshouse, ed., *Photographs for the Tsar* (New York: Dial Press, 1980), xv–xviii.

11. The text of Prokudin-Gorsky's lecture was published in the proceedings of the Fourth Congress of Russian Architects: "Pamiatniki stariny Mariinskoi sistemy i verkhnego Povolzh'ia i neskol'ko slov o znachenii tsvetnoi fotografii" (Monuments of antiquity along the Mariinsky [Canal] System and the Upper Volga and a few words on the significance of color photography), *Trudy IV s"ezda russkikh zodchikh* (Works of the Fourth Congress of Russian Architects (Saint Petersburg: Gosudarstvennaia tipografiia, 1911), 591–94.

12. The relevant archival documents, preserved in the Central State Historical Archive, are quoted in Garanina, "Uchenyi, izobretatel', fotokhudozhnik," 26. The commission noted that the Prokudin-Gorsky negatives could be used to make copy negatives, triple positives for screen projection (from each of the separation negatives), color slides (according to a process of superimposed layers that Prokudin-Gorsky would patent in 1913), and color prints to be made available for sale to the public.

13. His clients as a printer included Russia's major architectural journal *Zodchii* (Architect), with whom he had a contract to print the photographic supplement illustrating current architectural projects at the end of each issue. Indeed, he had been printing both color and black-and-white plates in this lavishly produced supplement since 1904, and would continue to do so until 1917.

14. In March 1918 the People's Commissariat of Enlightenment sponsored a series of presentations titled "The Wonders of Photography," held in the Nikolaevsky Hall of the Winter Palace. According to a published report, two thousand people attended Prokudin-Gorsky's concluding slide lecture. See Garanina, "Uchenyi, izobretatel', fotokhudozhnik," 26.

15. See, for example, the comparison of his color system with the autochrome process of the Lumière Brothers in S. de Procoudine Gorsky [*sic*], "Importance of Colour Photography for Schools and the Community in General," *British Journal of Photography: Monthly Supplement on Colour Photography* 13, no. 161 (April 2, 1920): 13–15, and no. 162 (May 7, 1920): 19–20. In November 1922 the same journal published a description of Prokudin-Gorsky's process for color cinematography, a project that had been initiated some ten years earlier.

16. The acquisition of the Prokudin-Gorsky Collection by the Library of Congress occurred under the auspices of the Russian Translation Project, sponsored by the American Council of Learned Societies. For a published account, see Paul Vanderbilt and Alice Lee Parker, "Prints and Photographs," *Library of Congress Quarterly Journal of Current Acquisitions* 6, no. 1 (November 1948): 37–38.

17. Until the late twentieth century, the study of nineteenth-century Russian photography received little attention either from art historians or from museum curators. In the late Soviet period, popular articles on the history of Russian photography before the revolution began to appear regularly in major Russian periodicals such as *Literaturnaia gazezta* and *Nashe nasledie*.

18. The complicated process of obtaining accurate color values and registration in printing the photographs for the Library of Congress Prokudin-Gorsky exhibit is described in John J. McKeon, "The Empire That Was Russia: The Work of Sergei Prokudin-Gorskii," *Technical Photography* 20 (March 1988): 33–34.

The Intertwining Fates of Two Collections

THE SERGEI PROKUDIN-GORSKY COLLECTION

LIBRARY OF CONGRESS

This book consists of two photographic collections linked to each other by geography and subject over a period of several decades. The earlier collection, created by Prokudin-Gorsky, has since 1948 resided in the Prints and Photographs Division of the Library of Congress, Washington, DC. Unlike other, more practical methods of color photography that relied on chemical emulsion layers on one surface, Prokudin-Gorsky's process required an elaborate box camera capable of registering three sequential exposures with basic color filters on a chemically prepared glass plate. The resulting three sequential negatives could be recombined through an equally elaborate projecting system to display a vivid color image on a large screen for public demonstrations.

Although Prokudin-Gorsky used the process to print a series of commercially available color postcards, he did not extensively engage in reproducing the images on paper as color prints. Nonetheless, his process inherently contained the capability to create lasting color images on paper in a manner analogous to chromolithography. And with the digital revolution at the end of the twentieth century, the same three-color separation process proved ideally adaptable for recreating Prokudin-Gorsky's color photographs. As will be noted below, this revolution exponentially increased the public range and cultural significance of his work.

By 1905 Prokudin-Gorsky was able to demonstrate the images created by his color process to a widening circle of viewers, beginning with professional colleagues. The recognition that accrued to his demonstrations eventually led to interest on the part of Tsar Nicholas II and to support at the highest levels of the state bureaucracy. This support proved critical for the implementation of Prokudin-Gorsky's vision, for he was not content to have invented an ingenious color process with limited (as it proved) commercial application. Rather, Prokudin-Gorsky had a grand concept of using his method to convey the cultural and ethnic diversity of the vast Russian Empire, of using the innovative medium of color photography to convey a message not only about the richness of Russia's history and culture but also about the extension of that richness into the borderlands of the empire.

Motivated by this vision, Prokudin-Gorsky embarked on a series of journeys from 1903 to 1916 during which he covered a remarkable geographic range, from the southeastern shore of the Black Sea and the Caucasus Mountains to the western part of Siberia, from ancient Smolensk on the Dnieper River to the Solovetsky Islands in the White Sea. The diversity of his interests was no less remarkable: architectural monuments, museum objects, sacred relics, portraits (with an emphasis on ethnic diversity), landscapes, natural wonders, panoramic city views, amelioration projects (particularly in Turkestan), waterways, and railroads. Because of the extended exposure times required by his photographic process, architectural monuments such as churches were particularly suited to this project. Architecture also directly reflected his interests in history and culture.

As the number of Prokudin-Gorsky's images increased to over a thousand, negotiations were initiated to acquire the collection for the state as a national cultural treasure. The failure of these negotiations (attributed to the assassination in September 1911 of Prime Minister Pyotr Stolypin, who had ultimate authority to approve the acquisition) left the collection in the photographer's possession. With the worsening political situation following the killing of Nicholas II and his family in July 1918, Prokudin-Gorsky left Russia in August 1918, never to return. Details of the collection's existence during this period until the early 1930s remain uncertain. After his death in Paris in September 1944, a representative of the Library of Congress bought the entire collection from Prokudin-Gorsky's heirs in 1948.

The Prokudin-Gorsky Collection at the Library of Congress contains over 1,900 of the photographer's original glass plates, as well as fourteen albums of contact prints made by the photographer from the magenta separation negative on the glass plates. The negatives themselves are in various states of preservation, ranging from intact to badly damaged or cracked, and are now kept in closed storage. In compiling his contact print albums Prokudin-Gorsky provided brief Russian captions for the photographs, and in some cases noted the expedition year at the beginning of the album. Other albums, however, must be dated provisionally. In some cases many contact prints are missing and were probably confiscated—along with the negatives—after the photographer left Russia in 1918.

The first two albums, numbered 10332 (A and B), contain material from Prokudin-Gorsky's first expedition for the Ministry of Transportation in 1909. Commissioned to survey the Mariinsky Canal system (now known as the Volga-Baltic Canal, linking the upper Volga and Neva Rivers), he photographed bridges, dams, locks, rivercraft, and the people who operated the canals. In addition he photographed peasants and workers, as well as the churches in communities en route (e.g., Belozersk). Despite the prosaic nature of his main task, many of the images from this trip are of considerable ethnographic interest.

Album 10333 is a mixed compilation that includes some of Prokudin-Gorsky's earliest color photographs, taken in 1908 at Tolstoy's estate, Yasnaya Polyana, as well as some pastoral views of the Russian countryside. Album 10334, on the other hand, appears to contain the latest Russian material in the collection, and must have been the result of a final commission from the Ministry of Transportation. Its subject is the Murmansk Railway, under construction as a supply link between Russia and its allies during World War I. Among the photographs is one of Austrian prisoners of war, thus giving a provisional date of 1915 for this album. The area surveyed extends between Lodeinoe Pole (on the Svir River, northeast of Petersburg) to the town of Kem, some four hundred miles to the north. The railway was not finished to Murmansk until late 1916. In addition to his railway views, Prokudin-Gorsky photographed churches and towns, as well as the local inhabitants. From Kem, he journeyed to Solovetsky Island and photographed its great monastery.

Album 10335 (in two parts) returns to 1909, the first year of Prokudin-Gorsky's work for the Ministry of Transportation (cf. albums 10332A and B). As part of his survey of the Ural industrial region he took views of Chelyabinsk, Yekaterinburg, Perm, Ufa, Zlatoust, Minyar, and other communities engaged in mining and metalworking. In addition to these industries and their workers, he also photographed church interiors. This album contains some of his most dramatic landscapes, and conveys the technical ingenuity involved in the construction of new railways through this rugged terrain.

Prokudin-Gorsky's photographs of the Caucasus, in album 10336, seem tame in comparison with his views of the Urals, despite the inherently more impressive landscape of the Caucasus. Rather than focus on the most spectacular scenery, whose distant reaches may have been inaccessible to the photographer, he concentrated on the resort areas and tea plantations in the areas around Batumi, Sochi, and Sukhumi on the Black Sea coast. Also included are views of Tbilisi, as well as numerous portraits of Armenians, Georgians, Greeks, and Daghestan mountaineers in native costume. There is no date given for this album.

Album 10337 is devoted primarily to a survey, commissioned by the emperor in 1911, of Russian battlefields from the War of 1812. Since the campaign covered much of the western part of the empire, the photographs here extend from Borodino (near Moscow) to Vilno and Vitebsk in the west. Also included are Minsk, Smolensk, Polotsk, Vyazma, Mozhaisk, Dvinsk, Kovno, and Maloyaroslavets. In addition to monuments, churches, monasteries, and landscapes associated with the battles, Prokudin-Gorsky took general views of the towns and their surrounding areas.

In 1911 Prokudin-Gorsky traveled to Central Asia (or Turkestan, as it was then called) with the photographer and inventor Sergey Maksimovich. The photographs from this trip, contained in album 10338, are among the most vivid of Prokudin-Gorsky's work. Most were taken in the Uzbek cities of Samarkand and Bukhara, which contain some of the greatest monuments of Islamic architecture. The photographs accurately convey the rich polychromatic tile work of mosques and other buildings from the time of Tamerlane and his successors in Samarkand (from the late fourteenth and fifteenth centuries). Similar monuments in Bukhara are also included, as are numerous views of street life and bazaars, with merchants, school children, beggars, and local potentates.

The subsequent two albums, 10339 and 10340, are the result of Prokudin-Gorsky's journey in 1910 along the Volga River, from its sources in northwest Russia to its confluence with the Unzha River. Both albums contain views of the Volga as it flows past a number of central Russia's oldest cities. Included in the first album are Ostashkov, Rzhev, and Staritsa, as well as Torzhok. The second album (10340) continues the journey past Kalyazin, Kashin, Uglich, Rybinsk, Yaroslavl, Kostroma, Kineshma, and Yurevets on the Unzha River. In addition to city panoramas, there are photographs of the area's churches and monasteries, as well as of peasants and fisherman at work along the river. While portraying the seemingly timeless way of life in this region, Prokudin-Gorsky also captured the incursions of a new industrial order into the heartland, with its river traffic and large commercial enterprises.

Album 10341, dated 1911, probes more extensively into the richness of medieval Russia's centers of culture, such as Vladimir, Pereslavl-Zalessky, Rostov, Yaroslavl, and Kostroma. Some of these towns had been photographed on his previous Volga trip, but the present album contains more cultural and religious subjects. Views of churches and monasteries are supplemented with photographs of items from the Russian Orthodox ritual, as well as icon screens and other religious art in church interiors. Yet even in the ancient city of Vladimir, Prokudin-Gorsky did not neglect to photograph the local train yards, set in the foreground of a broad Russian landscape.

Album 10342, from 1912, contains photographs from a survey of the waterways linking Yekaterinburg (Sverdlovsk) in the Urals with the city of Tobolsk in Siberia. This album can be said to complement Prokudin-Gorsky's earlier work in the Ural region (cf. album 10335) during a trip that had proceeded in a westerly direction from Yekaterinburg. Returning to the same city, the photographer traveled to the east along a network of rivers that link the towns of Dalmatovo, Shadrinsk, Tyumen, and Tobolsk (at the confluence of the Tobol and Irtysh Rivers). The photographs include town panoramas, churches, portraits of the local peasantry, and factories situated in a rugged natural setting.

The final album in the collection (number 10343, dated 1912) is a mixture of technical photographs of hydraulic engineering on the Oka River, together with views of two centers of medieval Russian culture: Ryazan and Suzdal. Since Ryazan is situated on the Oka, Prokudin-Gorsky would have had no trouble in photographing these diverse subjects during the same trip. Suzdal probably required a separate journey, but it too is in the same general area. The Oka links the Moscow River with the Volga, and improvements to its channel were of particular importance to the Ministry of Transportation, the primary sponsor of Prokudin-Gorsky's travels.

At the Library of Congress, however, the collection lay largely unknown until the publication in 1980 of a book edited by Robert Allshouse titled *Photographs for the Tsar: The Pioneering Color Photography of Sergei Mikhailovich Prokudin-Gorskii Commissioned by Tsar Nicholas II*. At this point the Prokudin-Gorsky Collection became—as it remains—a sensation. In 1985 I was invited by the Library of Congress to examine the Prokudin-Gorsky Collection with the goal of creating a public exhibition of his work. That exhibit, consisting of eighty color prints from Prokudin-Gorsky's negatives, was launched at the Library of Congress in the fall of 1986 and traveled to thirteen other venues through 1991.

The reasons for my selection as a curator have a bearing on the current book: a doctorate in Slavic Languages (University of California, Berkeley, 1973) that gave me a thorough knowledge of the Russian language and its literature; parallel graduate training in Russian history; extensive travel and research experience in the Soviet Union; a photographic experience with publications and photography exhibits; and, as it turned out, personal experience with a number of the sites recorded by Prokudin-Gorsky.

This unusual conjunction of interests—specifically the combination of scholarship with professional, documentary photography—led to the publication in September 1983 of my first major book on Russian architecture, *Gold in Azure: One Thousand Years of Russian Architecture*. Illustrated with a large selection of my black-and-white photographs and eighty color plates, the book received many reviews, including a page by James Billington in the *Times Literary Supplement*. Although Billington had yet to be appointed the librarian of Congress, his position as director of the Woodrow Wilson Center for Scholars ensured that the review would be noted by academic specialists at institutions such as the library.

I became involved with the Prokudin-Gorsky Collection because of my field experience in photographing Russian architectural monuments. While surveying Prokudin-Gorsky's contact albums in the Prints and Photographs Division, I realized that he and I had covered much of the same territory. That overlap has greatly increased during the flowing three decades, to the point that the majority of architectural sites photographed by Prokudin-Gorsky are also in my collection.

This confluence of events not only facilitated my exhibit work with some of the best images in the Prokudin-Gorsky Collection (his Turkestan photographs) but also suggested the insights to be gained by comparing his work with mine several decades later. That idea has now borne fruit after a gestation of some thirty years, during which the range of my work has greatly expanded, as has our knowledge of Prokudin-Gorsky's image content.

A major change in the fate of the Prokudin-Gorsky Collection occurred in 2000 with the decision to digitize the entire collection, including the small contact prints in the fourteen albums. Throughout this revolutionary period in presenting Prokudin-Gorsky's photographs to the public, my involvement with the collection has continued. Over the past decade I have written an item-by-item annotation for the color images in the Prokudin-

Gorsky Collection at the Library of Congress. And since the beginning of 2017 I have published a series of articles comparing his photographs of Russian architectural monuments with my own under the heading "Discovering Russia" for the *Russia Beyond* website. For the present book, many categories have been excluded from the Prokudin-Gorsky Collection: the ethnographic studies, the nature "etudes" (as he called them), landscapes, and even entire regions, such as the Caucasus. Nonetheless, the approximately two hundred Prokudin-Gorsky images reproduced here represent a major contribution of his work to our understanding of Russian architecture, history, and culture.

THE WILLIAM BRUMFIELD COLLECTION

NATIONAL GALLERY OF ART

My own photographic odyssey, whose beginnings date to the summer of 1970, has continued with increasing momentum following my switch to digital photography almost a decade ago. The Prints and Photographs Division of the Library of Congress has a collection of some 1,200 of my photographs, but the main archival home for my work is the William Craft Brumfield Collection in the Department of Images Collections (formerly the Photographic Archives) at the National Gallery of Art in Washington. The collection now consists of some 100,000 black-and-white negatives and identified digital images. There are still some seventy thousand color slides and digital images to be identified.

My first trip to the Soviet Union was something of an accident. In the spring of 1970, during the middle of my graduate study at the University of California, Berkeley, a faculty advisor tapped me on the shoulder and informed me of the dearth of applicants for the US-USSR summer exchange of language teachers at Moscow State University. In those years US scholars at whatever level traveled to Russia through negotiated study programs, and gaining admittance to this particular program, sponsored by the International Research and Exchanges Board (IREX), was a significant step—technically speaking, undeserved. At the time I was not an accredited teacher of Russian, but a graduate student with limited classroom experience. Whatever the logic of my unexpected inclusion, those summer months in the Soviet Union transformed my vision of Russia in the most literal way.

In preparation for the trip I bought my first camera, a small fixed lens

Konica, and a few rolls of slow, rich Kodachrome film (ASA 25). Knowing little about camera work, I assumed that a small amount of slide film would be sufficient The excitement at seeing those first photographs of Moscow and Leningrad, and projecting them in a Berkeley classroom, was revelatory. My small audience included the olympian Gleb Petrovich Struve, son of one of pre-revolutionary Russia's most distinguished liberal politicians, passionately devoted to Russian emigre literaure, and utterly opposed to the Soviet system. His compliments on my photographs were as unexpected as they were gratifying, and I immediately applied for an IREX dissertation fellowship at Leningrad State University.

Leningrad during the 1971–72 academic year was not a "soft" environment, what with primitive dormitories, hot water once a week, difficulties with food supplies (particularly fruits and vegetables) and the hostile weather. But the beauty of the city, even in its decrepitude, haunted me — and reminded me of New Orleans, founded fifteen years after Petersburg. The official purpose for my being in Leningrad was to pursue research on a dissertation topic (Vasilii Sleptsov and the radical literary milieu of the mid-nineteenth century), but my deeper motivation was to explore with my camera the urban environment that had so entranced in my reading of Russian literature. I justified these photographic wanderings through the city as a quest of Dostoevsky's milieu, yet it turned into much more than that, not only in Leningrad, but also through excursions and explorations among ancient centers of Russian culture, such as Novgorod, Vladimir, Suzdal, Pskov and Moscow.

The yield from that year was some 1,200 slides, most on dense Kodachrome film shipped out for development via the embassy pouch. The greatest treasure was a final university trip for Western graduate students in May 1972. The itinerary, unimaginable today, included the astounding monuments of Islamic architecture in Uzbekistan, the three Caucasus republics, and the Ukrainian port of Odessa. Giddy at the prospect of going to Central Asia, I was the only American who joined the small group.

The completion of graduate studies at Berkeley in 1973 led to a temporary position at the University of Wisconsin (1973–74) and then an appointment as assistant professor in the Department of Slavic Languages at Harvard University. In 1978 my cover story and photographs on the architecture of St. Petersburg for *Harvard Magazine* drew the attention of the Boston publisher, David Godine. The book that he published, *Gold in Azure: One Thousand Years of Russian Architecture*, began as an idea to produce a lavish album in anticipation of the 1980 Moscow Olympics.

The first challenge was getting back to Russia for a sufficient period to do extensive photography. Although the photographs of 1970–72 provided a superb base, research that I had already done for the project indicated that far more was needed. A fellowship application to IREX failed (why undertake a project that Western art historians barely acknowledged?). My desire to stake everything on the Godine book meant nothing without passage to Russia. Hearing of the situation, a Harvard colleague suggested that I apply to the American Council of Teachers of Russian (now American Councils for International Education) for the position of resident director of their semester program at Moscow's Pushkin Institute. The gambit worked, and a selection of several thousand additional photographs made their way into *Gold in Azure*, which finally appeared in the fall of 1983.

In the meantime, my stay at Harvard concluded in the summer of 1981 (assistant professors were rarely promoted with tenture in those days) and I accepted a position in Russian at Tulane University. The departure from Harvard complicated my ability to print photographs, but the Russian architectural project continued. In 1985 my article "Russia's Glorious Churches," published in *Preservation Magazine* (the National Trust for Historic Preservation), elicited a letter from Andrea Gibbs, curator for architecture in what was then known as the Photographic Archives at the National Gallery of Art. In return for my donation the Photographic Archivese undertook to develop and print the results of my field photography. Thus began of one of the longest ongoing projects the Photographic Archives had ever undertaken, and the largest gift from a private individual to this collection to date. At present the collection has almost 150,000 images, with at least 30,000 more to come.

The relaxation of travel restrictions within the Soviet Union during the late 1980s greatly accelerated the range and pace of my field research in Russia. An equally great leap occurred in 1998 when James Billington, librarian of Congress, designated me the photographer and architectural historian for the "Meeting of Frontiers" project, a grandiose undertaking based on the premise that the Russian move eastward and the American move toward the west created shared boundaries in the Pacific region. My role was to illuminate the Russian movement by photographing historic architecture from the Russian North (the area around the White Sea) to Vladivostok. From 1999 to 2002, Billington repeatedly sent me to Siberia, and the experience fundamentally changed the trajectory of my work. Through the Library of Congress, Prokudin-Gorsky's grand (ad)venture and my own have merged.

The preceding section has drawn on material from the following articles: "Faded Glory in Full Color: Russia's Architectural History (Interview with William Craft Brumfield)," *Kritika: Explorations in Russian and Eurasian History* 17, 2 (2016): 379–404, and Andrea Gibbs, "Treasures in the Cellar: Images of Architecture in the National Gallery of Art Library Image Collections, and Other Highlights for Slavic and East European Scholars," *Slavic and East European Information Resources* 11 (2010): 2, 184–195.

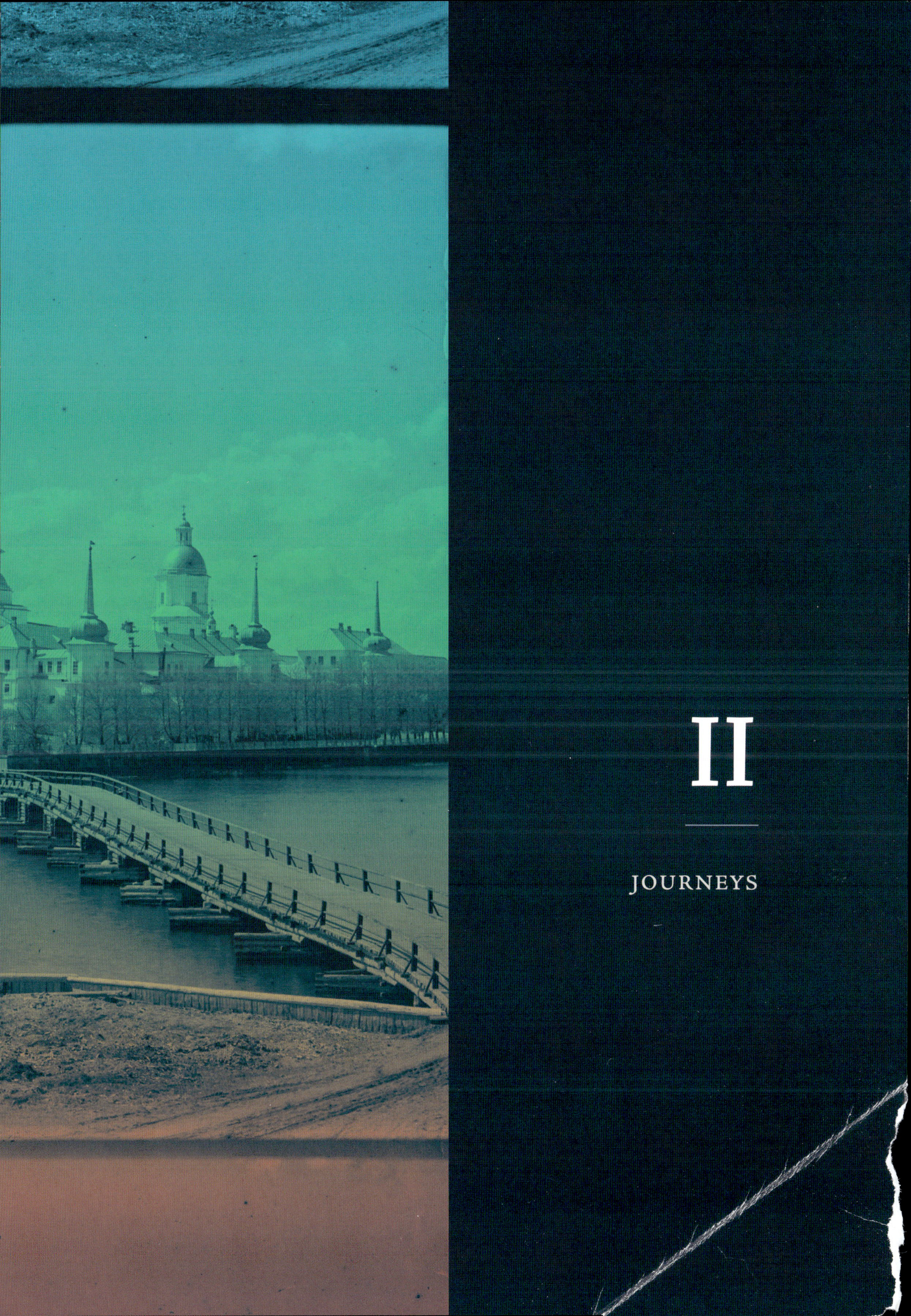

II

JOURNEYS

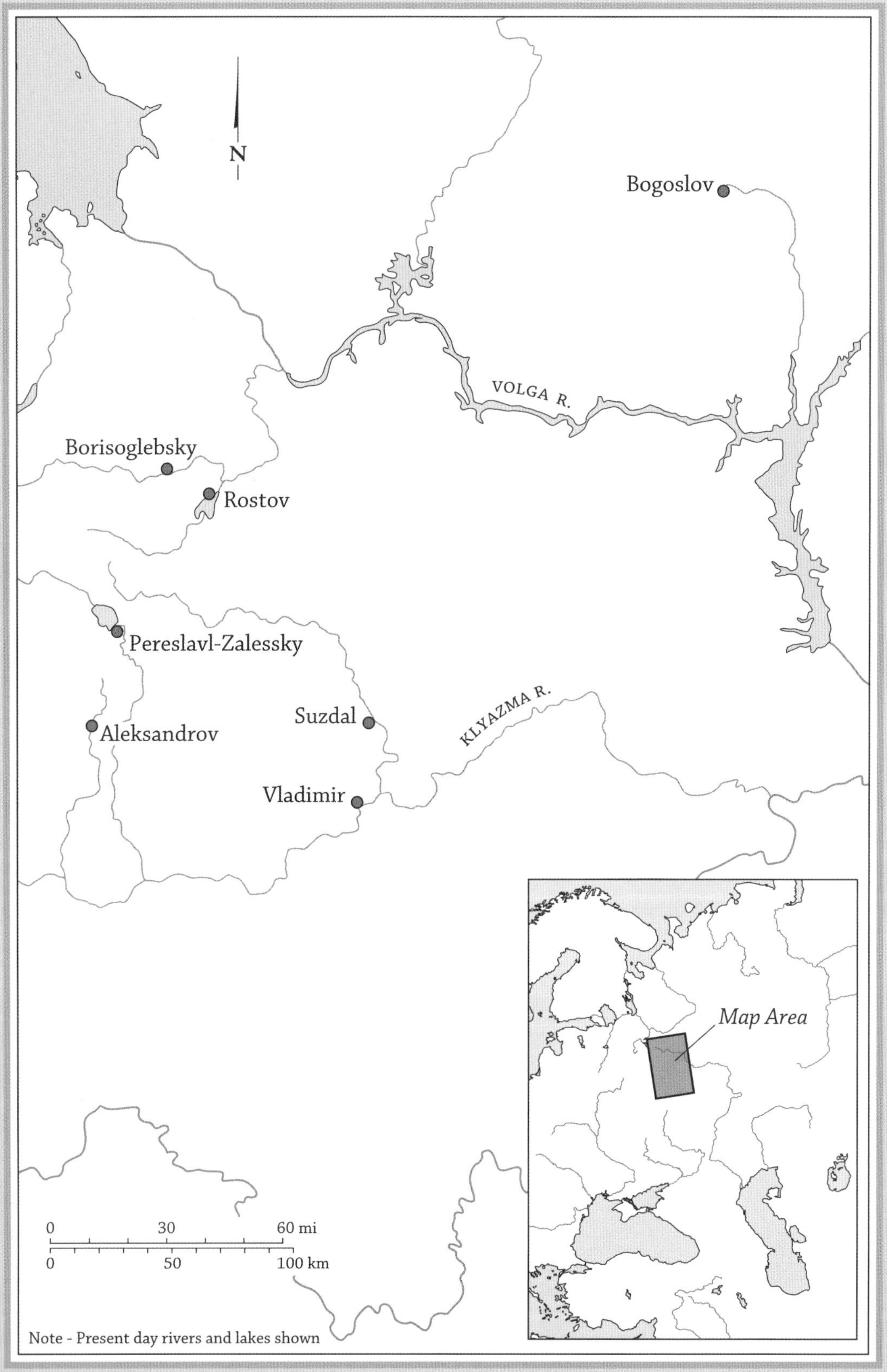

N
Bogoslov
VOLGA R.
Borisoglebsky
Rostov
Pereslavl-Zalessky
Suzdal
KLYAZMA R.
Aleksandrov
Vladimir
Map Area
0   30   60 mi
0   50   100 km
Note - Present day rivers and lakes shown

ONE · The Ancient Heartland

During the thirteen years of Sergey Prokudin-Gorsky's documentary journeys throughout the Russian Empire, his cultural vision unfolded with special clarity in the photographs that he took of medieval architecture in historical settlements northeast of Moscow—Vladimir, Suzdal, Pereslavl-Zalessky, Rostov, and Yaroslavl. In the second half of the nineteenth century photographers such as Ivan Barshchevsky and Mikhail Nastiukov had compiled important photographic collections of architectural monuments, primarily religious and with emphasis on the area along the Volga River. By the early twentieth century, the study of medieval architecture had become an object of increasing interest among Russian scholars, as demonstrated by the appearance of the first volumes of *History of Russian Art*, edited and co-authored by Igor Grabar. Notable for the high quality of their photographic illustrations, these volumes were widely known in educated Russian society.

Although the extent of Prokudin-Gorsky's familiarity with Grabar's magisterial work is undocumented, the existence of *History of Russian Art* provides a context for his interest in recording architectural monuments. He was not trained as an art historian, yet his approach is discerning and knowledgeable in its choice of subjects as well as its approach to documentation—both general views and details. This ability to define the structure through photography is particularly evident in the campaigns that he undertook in the ancient towns surrounding Moscow. These towns form the first part of this photographic survey, beginning with Vladimir, the precursor of Moscow.

Among the most important of the medieval towns photographed by Prokudin-Gorsky was Vladimir, whose central cathedrals he documented in the summer of 1911. Located on the Klyazma River 190 kilometers to the northeast of Moscow, Vladimir is now an industrial and regional administrative center of some 350,000 inhabitants. From the twelfth through the thirteenth centuries it attained status as the political and religious center of the territory that would become Russia's heartland. The date of the founding of Vladimir is usually given as 1108, the year in which Grand Prince Vladimir Monomakh of Kiev established a fortress on the site and consolidated his hold over the nearby lands of Suzdal. Vladimir Monomakh ruled from 1113 to 1125, and his reign is considered one of the most productive in the complex history of Kievan Rus. With his guidance the area around Vladimir accrued political and economic power in the northeastern part of Rus, as the lands of the eastern Slavs were known in the early medieval period. Under the rule of his descendants in the second half of the twelfth century, Vladimir and its surrounding settlements witnessed a surge of church construction in white stone, a form of limestone.

By the 1160s Vladimir had become the political center of the northeastern part of medieval Rus under Prince Andrei Bogolyubsky, founder of the nearby palace compound of Bogolyubovo and ruler of Vladimir from 1157 to 1174. This status was reflected in a series of churches, of which the greatest is the Cathedral of the Dormition of the Virgin (1158–60), one of Russia's defining architectural monuments. The Dormition Cathedral was the first major structure commissioned by Andrei Bogolyubsky in Vladimir itself. Located within the large citadel, or kremlin, it followed a design typical of such structures in Kiev and Novgorod during the same period. However, the building material of smooth cut stone was distinctive to Vladimir's twelfth-century architecture.

The masonry construction launched by Andrei Bogolyubsky was continued by his half-brother, Vsevolod Yurevich, grandson of Vladimir Monomakh. In 1162 Andrei drove Vsevolod's mother, Elena, and her sons into exile in Constantinople. After the death of Andrei, Vsevolod returned to rule in Vladimir from 1174 to 1212 as Grand Prince Vsevolod III. After a fire in 1185 that destroyed much of Vladimir, Vsevolod ordered the rebuilding of the severely damaged Dormition Cathedral. His builders retained the fire-weakened walls of the earlier structure as the core of the cathedral and added aisles on the north, west, and south sides. The eastern part of the structure, containing the apse with the main altar, was rebuilt with a substantial increase in depth. The new walls built by Vsevolod reached two stories, but not to the full height of the original structure. The relation between the old and the new was thus clearly defined. In effect the new structure, completed in 1189, enclosed the earlier one in a brilliant display of engineering skill.

The exterior walls of the Dormition Cathedral are marked at midlevel by an arcade frieze but relatively little carved ornament. The walls themselves possess a lapidary quality and culminate in a curved roofline outlined in decorative metalwork. The new cathedral also had four additional cupolas at the corners. The rebuilding of the Dormition Cathedral produced one of the largest masonry structures in medieval Rus. As the center of religious authority in the expansive domains of Suzdalia, the cathedral also served as a monument to the power of Vsevolod III and to the culture that he fostered.

During his visit Prokudin-Gorsky photographed the Dormition Cathedral from the east in a view that included the regional administrative building (*prisutstvennye mesta*), constructed in a regal neoclassical style in 1785–90. I found the same perspective from the small square in front of the Cathedral of Saint Demetrius during my first visit to Vladimir, in January 1972 — years before I had heard of Prokudin-Gorsky's work.

Soon after the rebuilding of the Dormition Cathedral, Vsevolod commissioned a church attached to his palace and dedicated to Saint Demetrius of Thessalonika (Saint Dimitry Solunsky in the Russian). Built between 1193 and 1197, this structure is smaller than the Dormition Cathedral and similar in plan to the churches built in the 1160s by Andrei Bogolyubsky at his palace compound in nearby Bogolyubovo. The upper part of the structure is covered with carved stonework, testimony to the imagination of anonymous medieval artisans. Prokudin-Gorsky took carefully framed views from the east, south, and west.

As an expression of princely power, the carvings on the facades of the Saint Dmitry Cathedral begin with a depiction of the biblical King David on the upper part of the west facade — the main entrance. Rulers depicted on the south facade include Alexander the Great and a central figure tentatively identified as King Solomon. In addition to these iconic depictions of divinely anointed rulers, the carvings include representations of Christ, as well as an array of saints and figures from the Old Testament. Many of the carved blocks display ornamental figures or heraldic motifs such as lions. The middle of the structure is marked by an arcade frieze whose carved, attached columns frame niches for statues of saints. The order of the carved blocks on the facades has been partially preserved despite renovations over a period of eight centuries.

The origins of this elaborate display have been the subject of extensive scholarly discussion. Romanesque architecture and sculpture in central

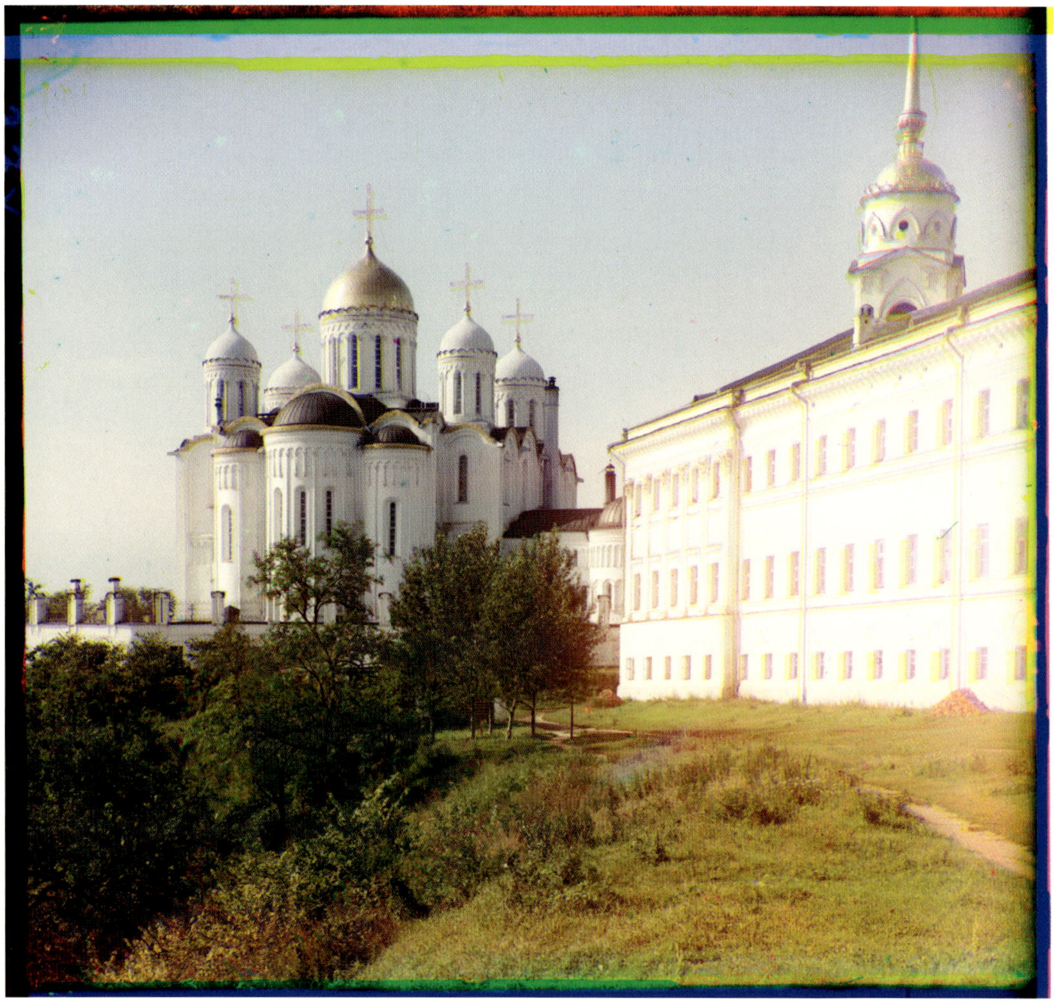

Europe are possible sources, although the specifics of this transfer are unknown. The influence of carved church facades in the medieval Caucasian kingdoms of Georgia and Armenia has also been suggested. Byzantine ornamental motifs (including manuscripts) form another likely source, for Vsevolod had spent several years in Constantinople before returning to rule in Vladimir.

Less than a half century after the completion of these two cathedrals, the Vladimir principality was overwhelmed by the Mongol invasion of Rus. In late February 1238 the city was captured and sacked with great loss of life. The grand prince at that time, Vsevolod's son Yury, was killed a few days later in a final battle with the Mongol armies. When Yury's wife, Agafya, along with other members of the family, took refuge in the Dormition Cathedral, the Mon-

VLADIMIR Dormition Cathedral. East view with regional administration building. PROKUDIN-GORSKY 20028. 1911.

VLADIMIR Dormition Cathedral. East view with regional administration building. BRUMFIELD, MARCH 6, 1972.

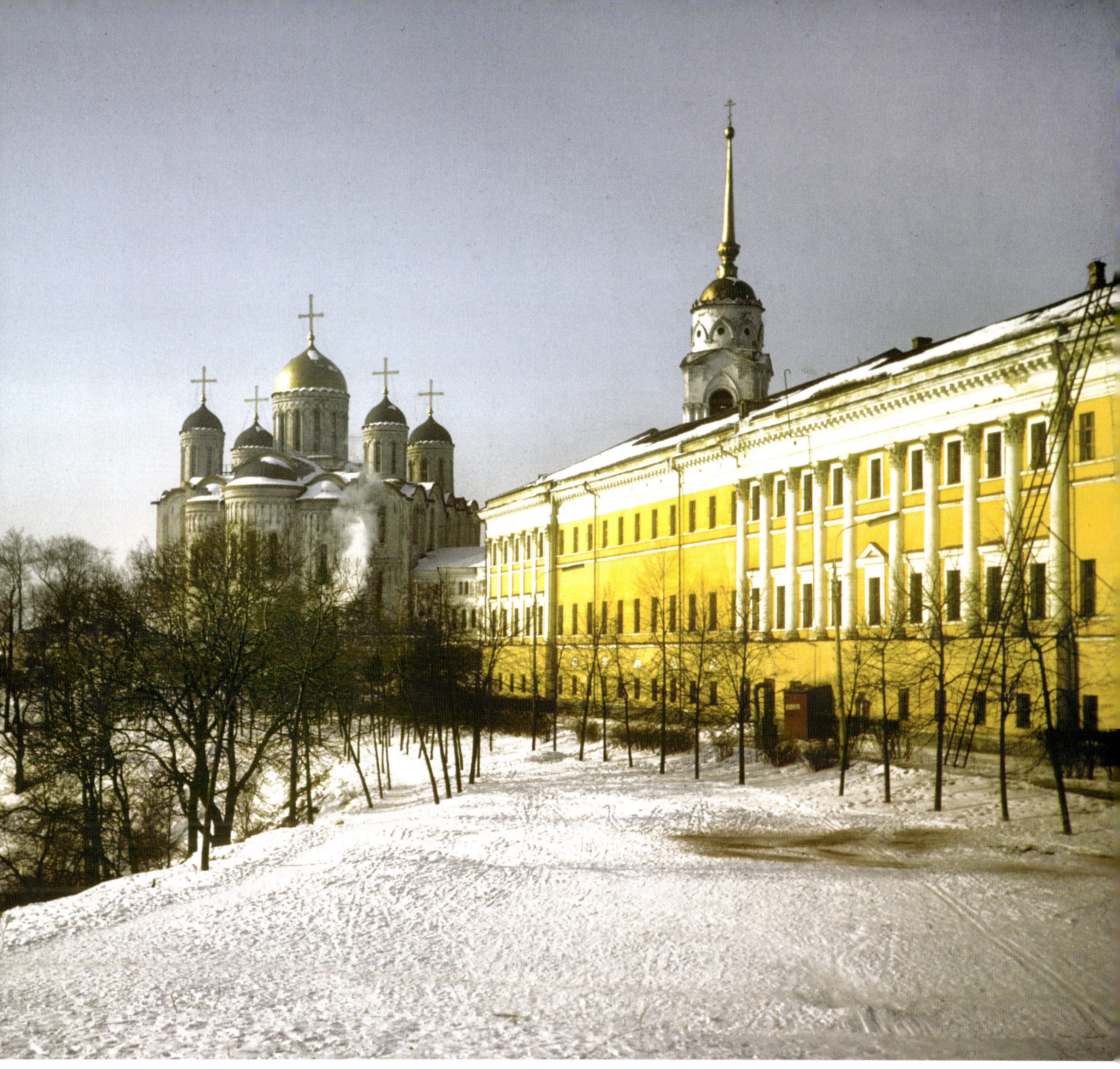

gols placed burning timber against the thick walls, and those inside were asphyxiated. The Dormition Cathedral was again damaged during a large Tatar raid at the beginning of the fifteenth century. Nonetheless, the basic form of both cathedrals remained despite repairs and modifications.

For the Cathedral of Saint Demetrius, a turning point occurred in 1834 during a visit of Tsar Nicholas I. Alarmed by the dilapidated appearance of the Saint Demetrius Cathedral, the tsar ordered a restoration of the shrine to its "original form." That form, however, was determined with less than scholarly rigor, with the consequent demolition in 1837–39 of parts deemed

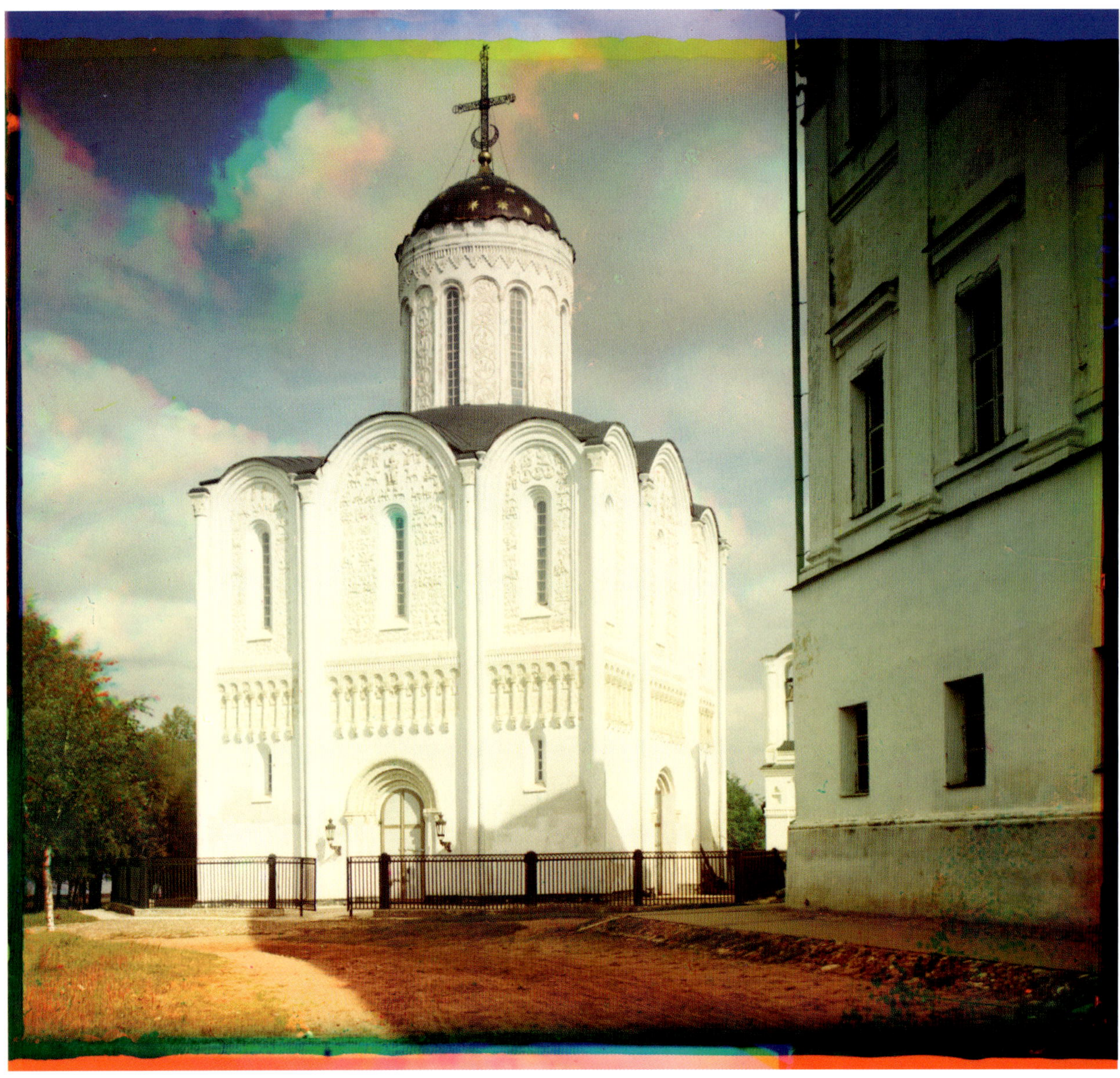

VLADIMIR Cathedral of Saint Demetrius. Southwest view. PROKUDIN-GORSKY 21275. SUMMER 1911.

VLADIMIR Cathedral of Saint Demetrius. Southwest view. BRUMFIELD, JULY 18, 2009.

to be ancillary. These included a bell tower attached to the northwest corner as well as an exterior gallery that contained stairs to the upper level and buttressed the structure on the south, west, and north sides. After this removal, many stone blocks were replaced with new carvings (particularly in the arcade friezes), and the order of some of the blocks was rearranged.

These modifications enhanced the perception of the facade carving, but valuable details were lost for lack of proper documentation. Furthermore, a renovation of the interior in 1840–47 led to the loss or overpainting of early

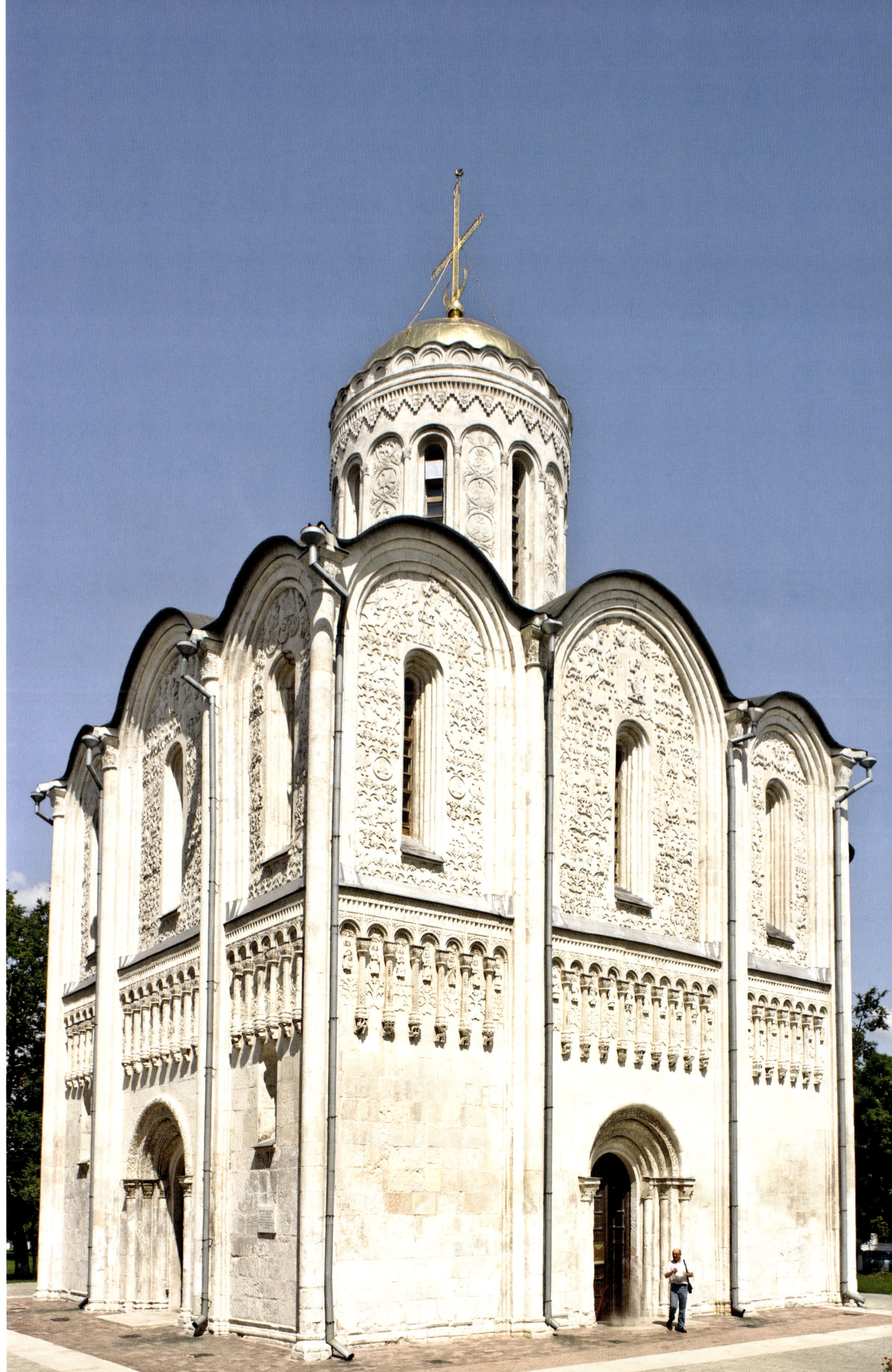

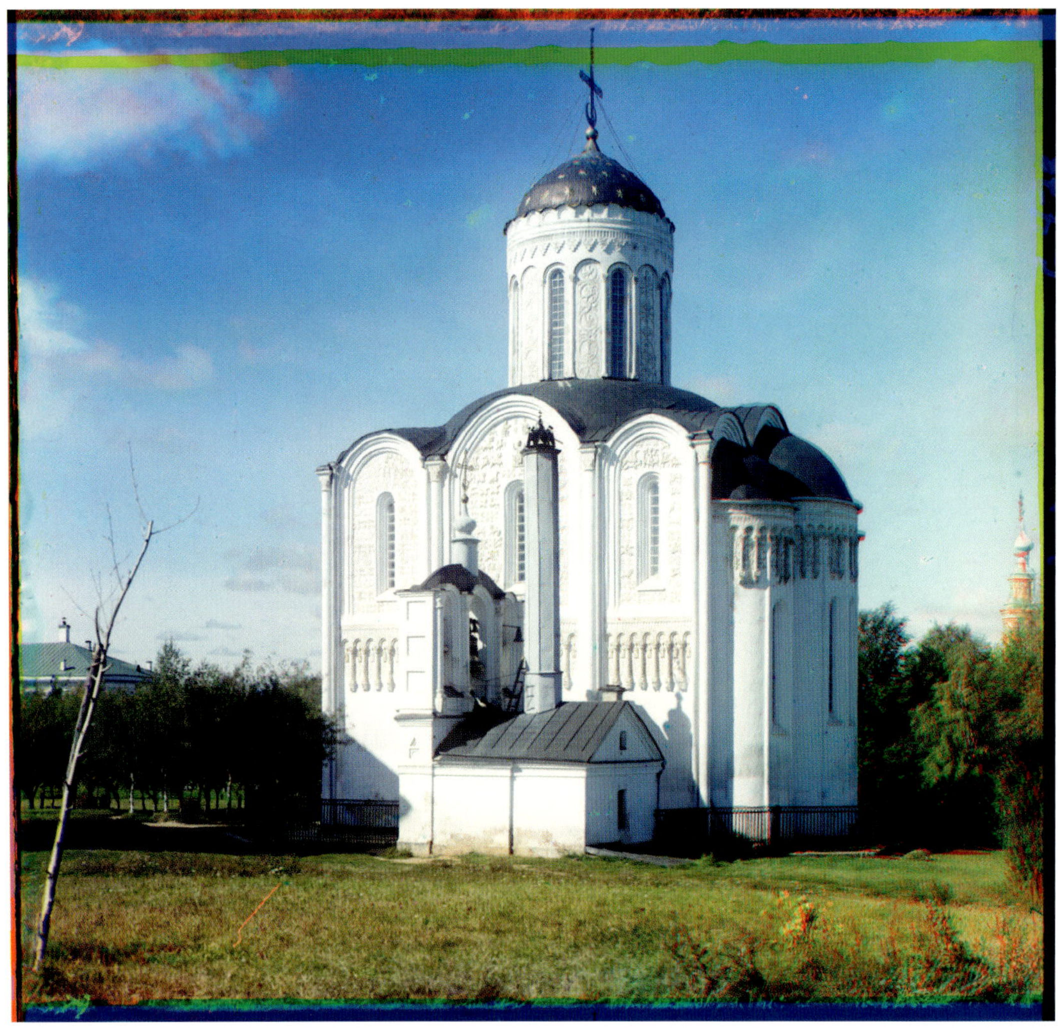

medieval frescoes. In 1883 the installation of a calorific heating system (for winter services) led to the construction of
a service building with a tall chimney just to the south of
the cathedral. This small structure, which also supported a
belfry, is clearly visible in the Prokudin-Gorsky photograph
taken from the southwest. After the revolution, the Saint
Demetrius Cathedral was studied by the prominent art historian Igor Grabar, who in 1918 uncovered some of the valuable late twelfth-century frescoes. In 1919 it was converted
to a museum, but progressive deterioration threatened its
survival. (Removal of the exterior galleries had weakened
the structure.) So grave was the danger to this major monument that measures were taken to stabilize the foundation
in 1941, even as the first desperate months of war raged to

VLADIMIR Cathedral of Saint
Demetrius. Southeast view.
PROKUDIN-GORSKY 21265.
SUMMER 1911.

VLADIMIR Cathedral of Saint
Demetrius. Southeast view.
BRUMFIELD, MAY 25, 1998.

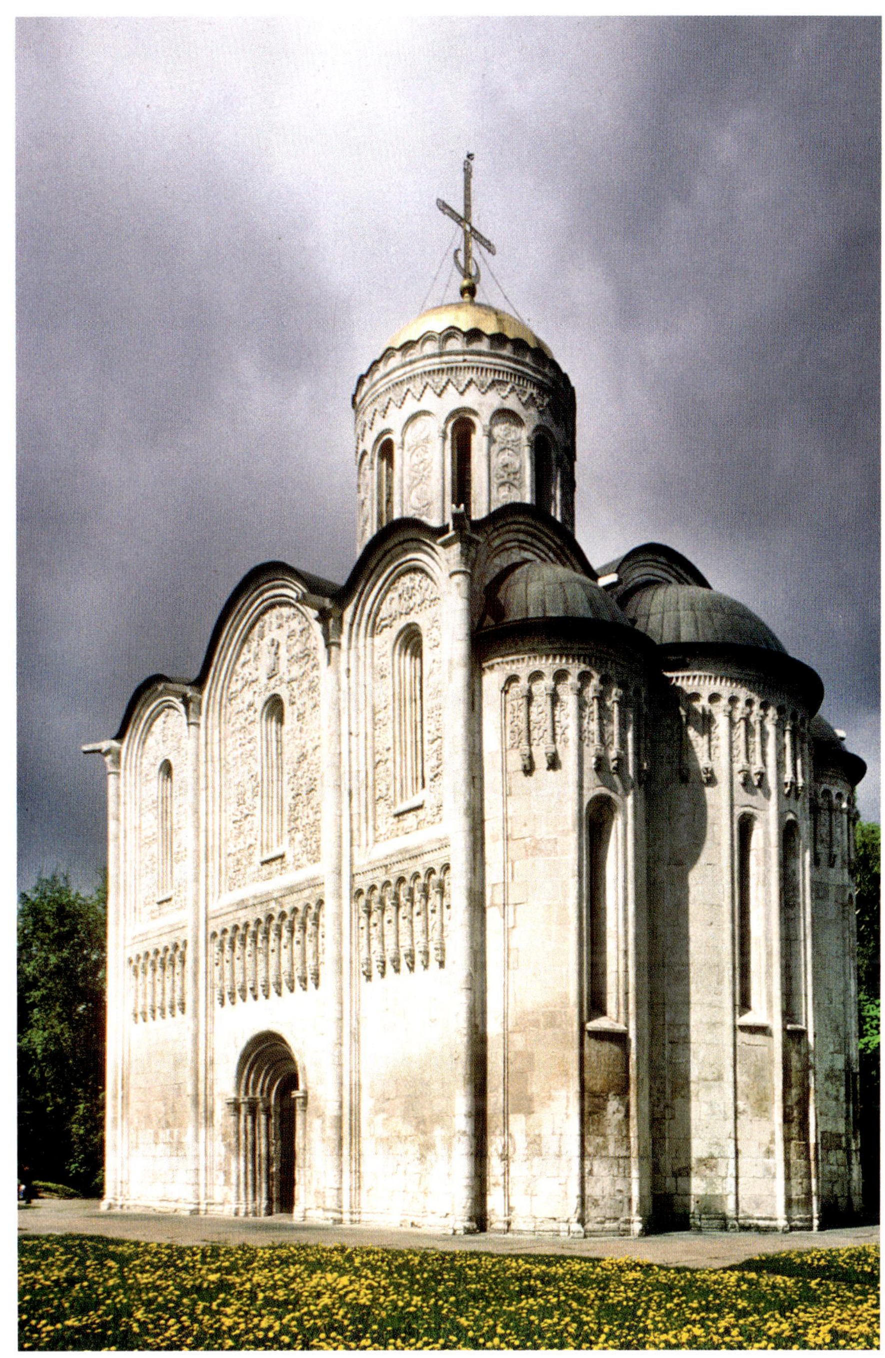

the west of Moscow. The carved limestone facades were also damaged by de-cades of industrial pollution and acid rain. After years of study the exterior was given a special protective coating visible in my photographs from 2009.

Near Vladimir is the town of Suzdal, an important center of medieval Russian princely authority with an exceptionally rich concentration of ar-chitectural monuments. Bypassed by railroad construction and with little industry, Suzdal retained a bucolic atmosphere poignantly conveyed in

Prokudin-Gorsky's photographs taken in the summer of 1912. At the time of his visit the town had about seven thousand inhabitants (current population ten thousand). Isolated for much of the twentieth century, Suzdal endured severe damage to its architectural heritage: fifteen churches were destroyed and many others despoiled. With the declaration of the town as a national cultural landmark in 1967, the process of cultural preservation accelerated.

The first mention of Suzdal in medieval chronicles occurs under the year 1024, yet there were undoubtedly settlements of Finno-Ugric and Slavic peoples in the area by the ninth and tenth centuries. By the early eleventh century, Kiev had extended its political and religious authority into this rich agricultural territory, and at the turn of the twelfth century Prince Vladimir Monomakh of Kiev arrived with a new wave of settlers. Monomakh erected a citadel above the small Kamenka River and began construction around 1102 of the Suzdal cathedral, possibly the earliest major brick structure in the territory of northeastern Rus.

In 1222–25 Prince Yury Vsevolodovich, son of Vsevolod III and great grandson of Monomakh, razed the original church and erected a large cathedral dedicated to the Nativity of the Virgin (Theotokos). The structure was primarily a light tufa, with limestone for the carved details. Prokudin-Gorsky devoted special attention to the Nativity Cathedral, which he recognized as a defining monument of medieval Russian culture. My photographs of the cathedral span a range from March 1972 through May 2009. The exterior was decorated with the ornamental stone carving that is a distinctive feature of stone churches built in the Vladimir area at the end of the twelfth century by Yury's father, Vsevolod III. The carved ornamentation included columns that formed the arcade band as well as lions and female masks at the corners and along the facades. Prokudin-Gorsky recorded these details in a separate photograph of the south facade in 1912.

The Nativity Cathedral withstood the sack of Suzdal by the Mongols in 1238, even though the interior was completely pillaged. Through decades marked by plague, famine, and invasion, the structure stood until 1445, when a raiding force of Kazan Tatars sacked the town and set fire to the cathedral interior. This so weakened the roof vaulting that the upper part of the building collapsed. In 1528–30 Moscow's Grand Prince Vasily (Basil) III rebuilt the Nativity Cathedral as part of a campaign to restore the heritage of the Russian lands under Moscow's protection. During this reconstruction, the remains of the stone walls were uniformly lowered to the level of the "blind" arcade at the top of the first floor. The upper structure and the drums beneath the five cupolas were rebuilt of new brick in the style of large

Muscovite churches. Fortunately, much of the original stone carving was preserved.

In the 1630s Archbishop Serapion repaired structural damage sustained in the early seventeenth century and oversaw the construction near the cathedral of an octagonal bell tower with a small Church of the Annunciation on its second level. Crowned by a "tent" roof, the bell tower was expanded at the end of the seventeenth century by Metropolitan Hilarion. A powerful and cultured prelate, Hilarion also built the third component of the cathedral ensemble, the Archbishop's Residence. Its oldest section, visible on the left in Prokudin-Gorsky's photograph, retained walls from the fifteenth-century bishop's residence. My photograph of 1972 provides a different perspective on the ensemble.

After damage from a major fire that swept through Suzdal in 1719, the upper part of the Nativity Cathedral underwent substantial repairs. Further changes were implemented in 1748, when the five cupolas gained their flaring onion shape, and a sloped roof was placed over the rounded gables (*zakomary*). In 1815 a chapel dedicated to the Nativity of Christ was added to the south facade. In 1895 the cathedral gained a new heating system that required the construction of a tall chimney seen in Prokudin-Gorsky's view.

In the 1950s a capital restoration of the cathedral retained the eighteenth-century onion domes but restored the curved roofline of the sixteenth-century zakomary. The attached chapel visible in Prokudin-Gorsky's photograph was removed to reveal the original limestone porch. The beige-toned aggregate that coated the facades was replaced with whitewash. Prokudin-Gorsky's photograph shows nineteenth-century frescoes on the zakomary, but Soviet specialists considered the paintings historically insignificant and replaced them with whitewash. My photographs show these many changes to a monument that is now included on the UNESCO World Heritage List.

Among other Suzdal monuments that attracted Prokudin-Gorsky's attention, the Intercession (Pokrovskii) Convent is of special importance in Russia's dynastic history. A sweeping view of the convent from the north is provided by the high bluff across the nearby Kamenka River. I used the same view in various seasons between 1972 and 2009. Founded in 1364, the Intercession Convent was built entirely of wood until the early sixteenth century, when it drew the favor of Grand Prince Vasily III. With support from the grand prince, work began in 1510 on the convent's Cathedral of the Intercession of the Virgin, consecrated in 1514 and visible with three cupolas at the center of Prokudin-Gorsky's photograph. The cuboid brick structure combined features of Muscovite churches with devices common

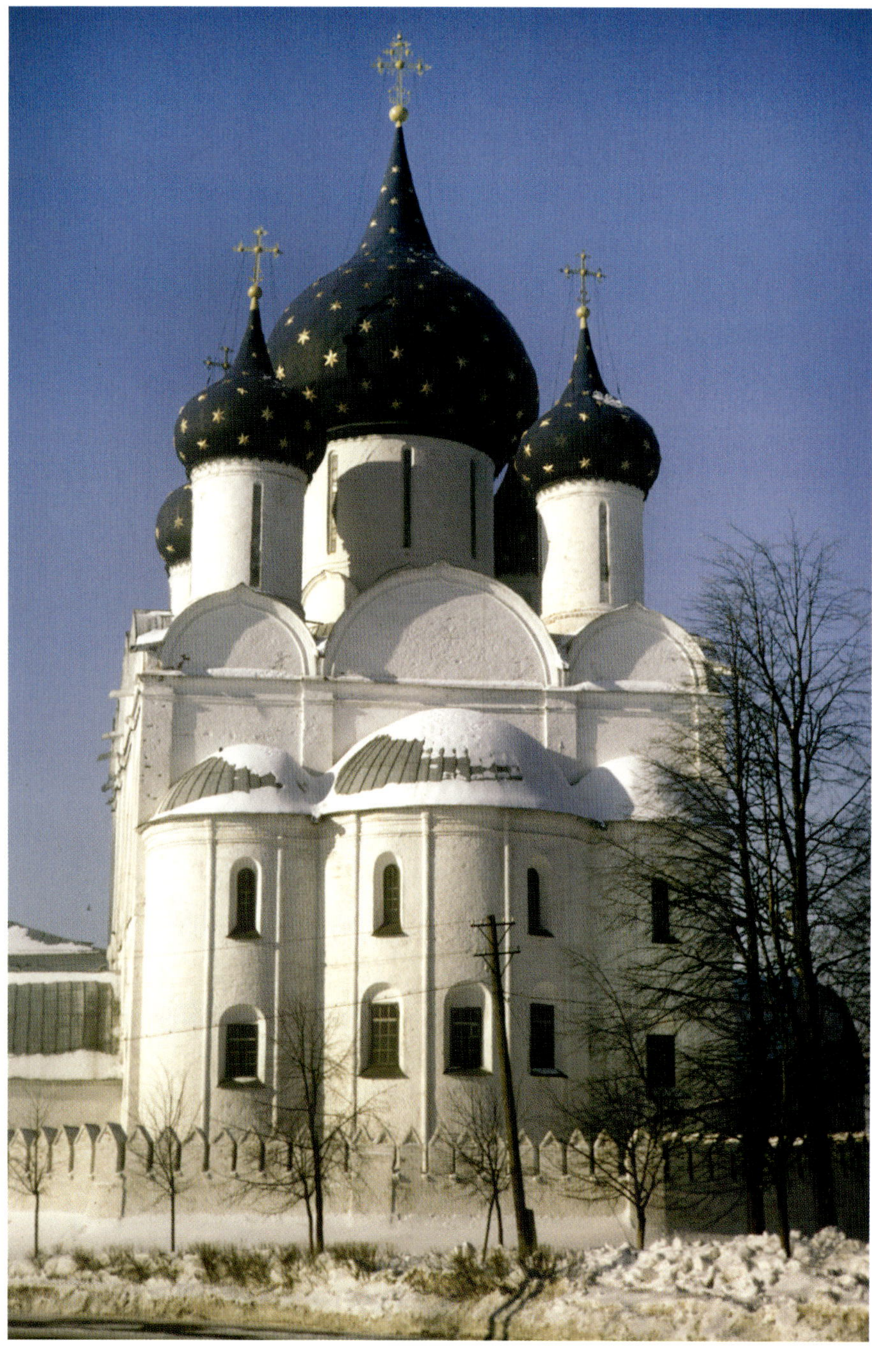

SUZDAL Cathedral of the Nativity
of the Virgin. EAST VIEW.
BRUMFIELD, MARCH 5, 1972.

SUZDAL Cathedral of the Nativity
of the Virgin. Southeast view.
PROKUDIN-GORSKY 21256. SUMMER
1912.

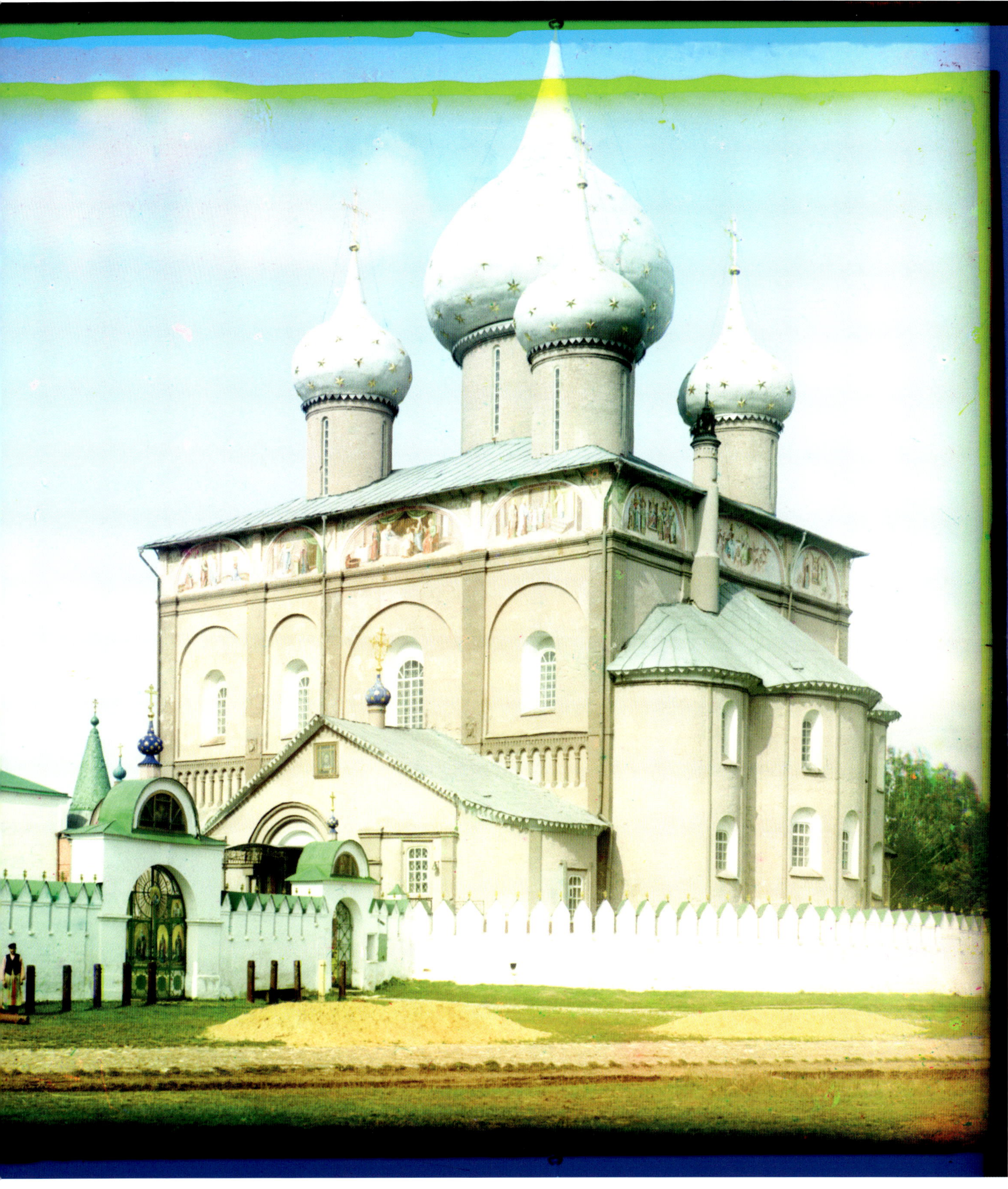

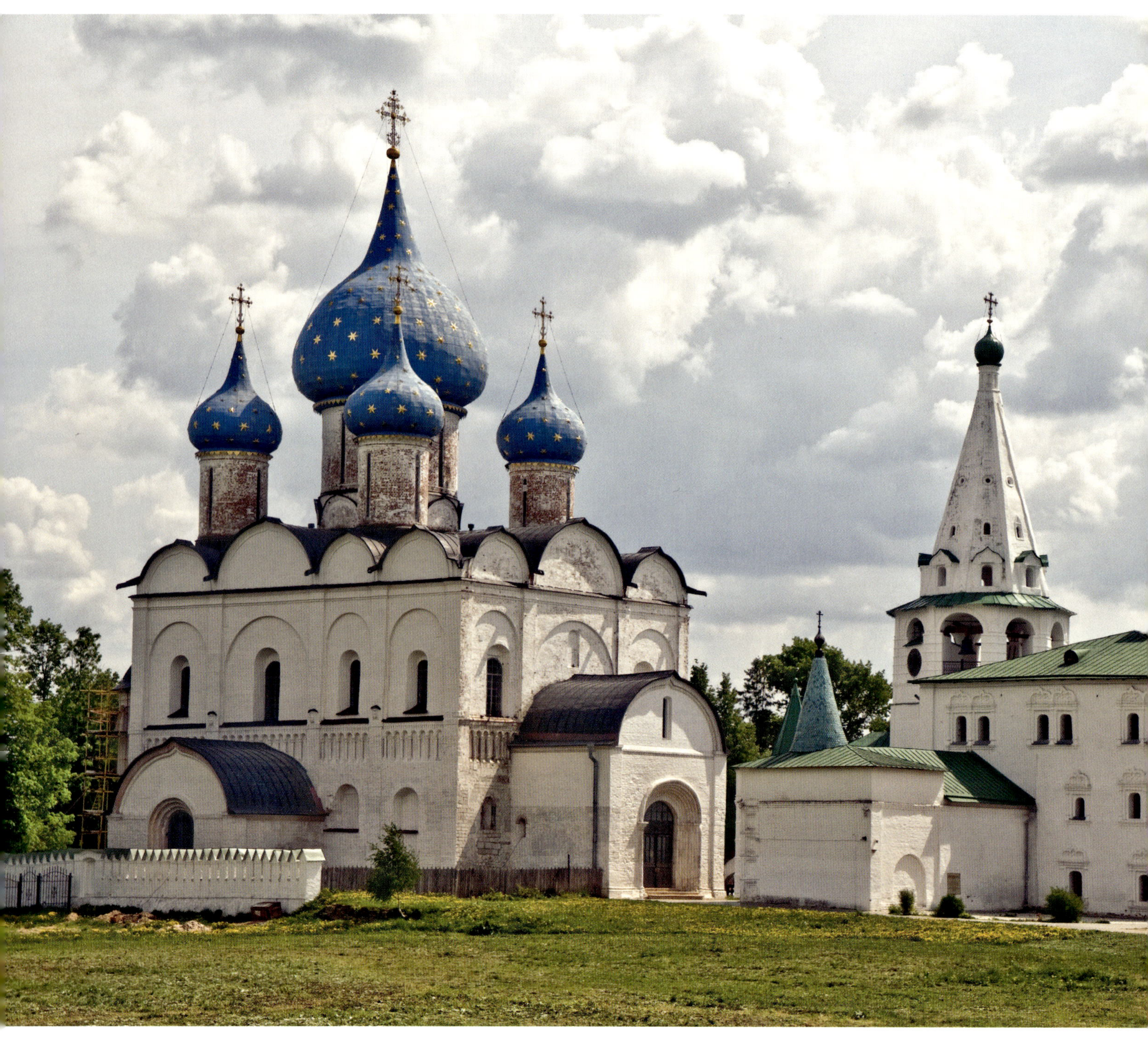

SUZDAL Cathedral of the Nativity of the Virgin bell tower and Archbishop's Residence. Northwest view. BRUMFIELD, MAY 29, 2009.

SUZDAL Cathedral of the Nativity of the Virgin and bell tower. South view. PROKUDIN-GORSKY 20943. SUMMER 1912.

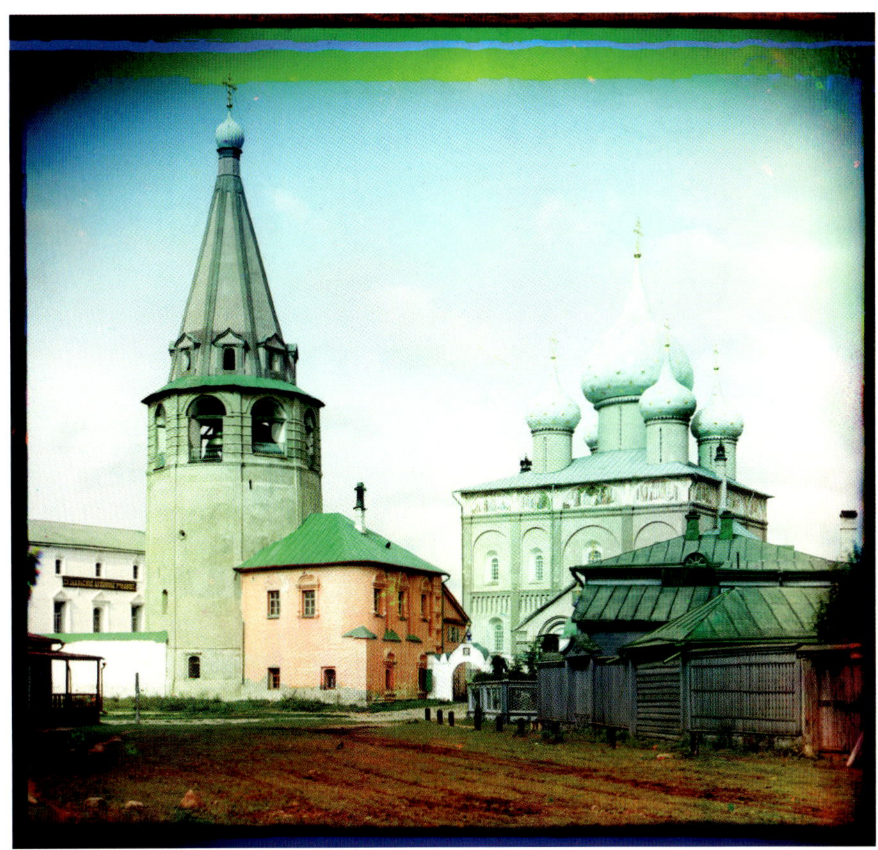

in early Suzdalian architecture. In addition to its main cupola, the Intercession Cathedral has two smaller cupolas over chapels located within the eastern corner bays. In the foreground is the Church of the Conception of Saint Anne, presumably built in the mid-sixteenth century in memory of Ivan IV's daughter, who died in 1551. This elongated archaic structure served as the convent's refectory church.

Kremlin involvement is plausible since many of the structures were associated with a votive offering from Vasilii III and his first wife, Solomoniia Saburova (ca. 1490–1542), in supplication for the birth of an heir. Unfortunately, their prayers were unanswered. Solomoniia, the offspring of a prominent Tatar family, was admired for her good character and beauty, but the passage of years without a child undermined her position at court. By 1525 the continued lack of a male heir and the specter of dynastic instability led Vasilii, with the support of Metropolitan Daniil, to the controversial decision of annulling his marriage. Solomoniia was taken to Moscow's Convent of the Nativity of the Virgin, where she assumed the religious name "Sophia." Shortly thereafter, she was sent to more distant exile at the same Suzdal Intercession Convent that she had known a decade earlier as a suppli-

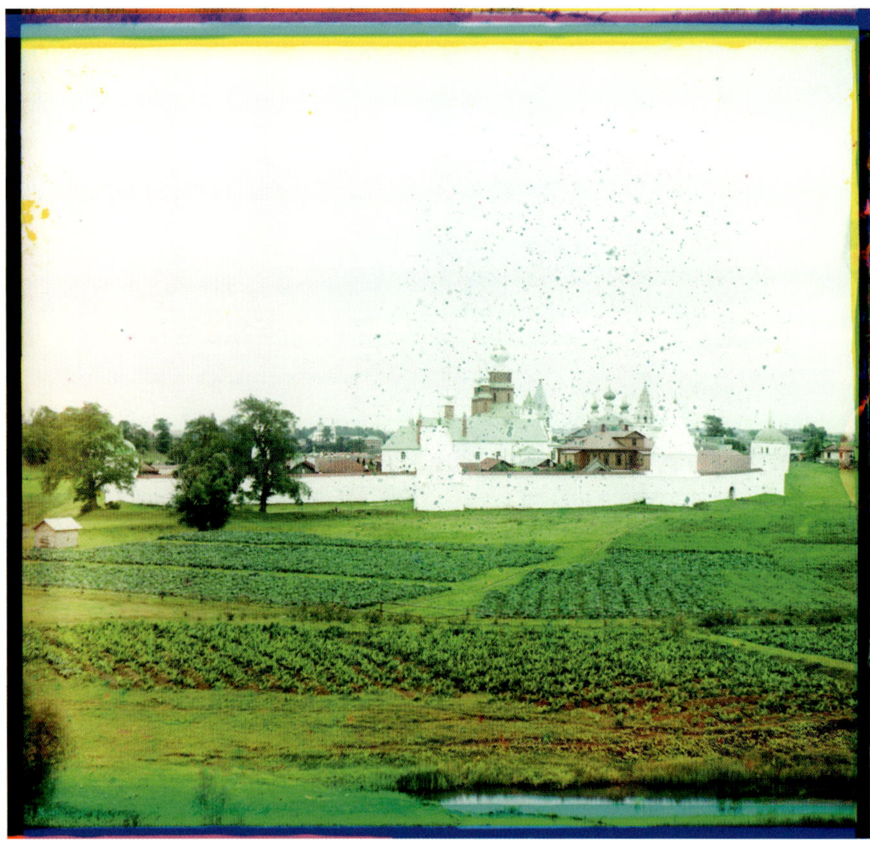

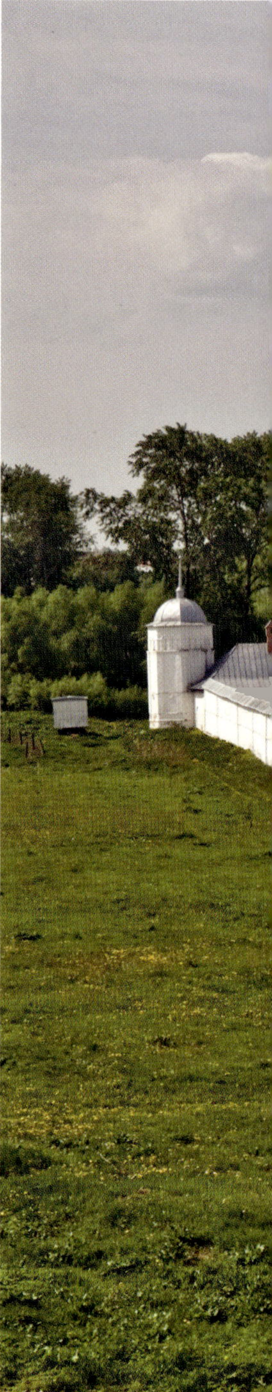

cant. She died there in December 1542. Vasilii's subsequent marriage in 1526 to Elena Glinskaia (ca. 1508–38) finally produced a male heir — Ivan IV — in 1530. Solomoniia's personal tragedy became legendary, and by the latter part of the sixteenth century Solomoniia-Sophia had already become revered as a saintly figure and even martyr. Numerous miracles were subsequently attributed to her power, and in 1650 Patriarch Iosif permitted her local veneration as Sophia of Suzdal, a decision that substantially increased the number of pilgrims to the Intercession Convent.

Solomoniia-Sophia would not be the last women of noble status destined to conclude life sequestered within the Intercession Convent's walls. Among these unfortunates was Anna Vasil'chikova, whom Ivan the Terrible took as his fifth "wife" in 1575. She was soon compelled to enter the Intercession Convent, where she died in 1579. The most notorious case was that of Evdokiia Lopukhina (1669–1731), the first wife of Peter the Great. Their marriage, which produced three sons (two of whom died in infancy), was strained, and the Lopukhin clan had little sympathy for Peter's inclinations toward Western culture. In 1698 Peter demanded that Evdokiia take monastic vows

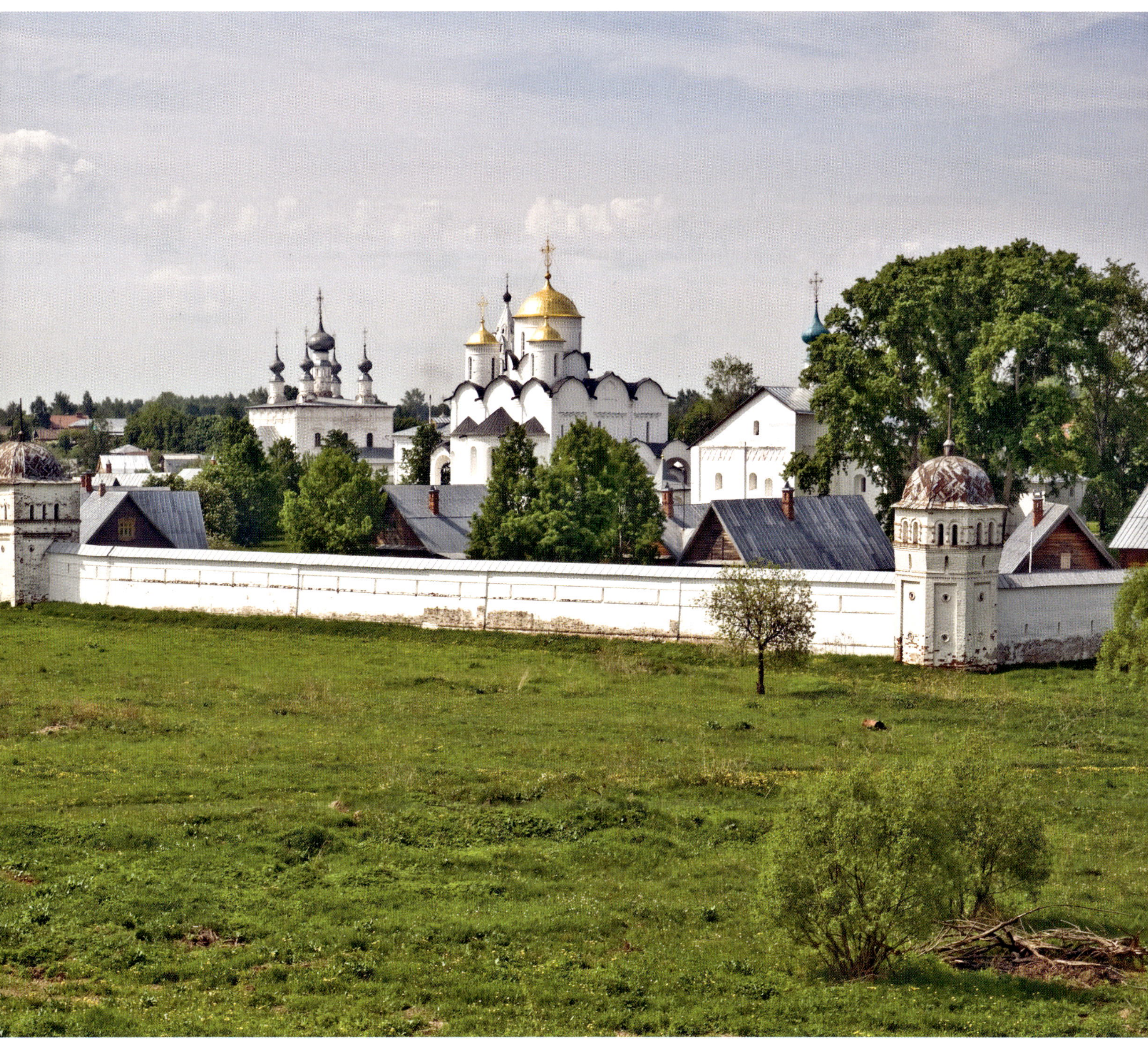

SUZDAL Intercession Convent. North view. PROKUDIN-GORSKY 21434. SUMMER 1912.

SUZDAL Intercession Convent. Northeast view from Savior-Evfimy Monastery. BRUMFIELD, MAY 29, 2009.

(under the name Elena) and sent her to the Intercession Convent, where she spent the next nineteen years of her life.

Prokudin-Gorsky also photographed parts of Suzdal's largest monastic institution, the Savior-Saint Euthymius (Evfimii) Monastery, founded in 1352 by Prince Boris Konstantinovich. Seen as a fortress as well as a religious institution, the monastery benefited in the sixteenth century from gifts by Muscovy's rulers (Vasilii III, Ivan IV). During the reign of Aleksei Mikhailovich (1645–76) the monastery's wooden walls were replaced with a grandiose brick wall twelve hundred meters in length, with twelve towers. The Saint Evfimii Monastery possessed over ten thousand serfs, and the walls perhaps imitated the Moscow Kremlin in an attempt by the church to reassert its political authority. As the burial place of Prince Dmitry Pozharsky (1577–1642)—the commander of Russian forces in 1613 during the Time of Troubles—the monastery had the character of a secular shrine and was much used for purposes of state at the turn of the eighteenth century. The main tower, square in plan and twenty-two meters in height, provided an imposing entrance not only for its size but also for its decorative friezes, including a row of "gothic" ogival window surrounds. Prokudin-Gorsky's view of the tower has been preserved only in the contact print. Over the decades that I have photographed them, the tower and monastery walls have remained in good condition. Inside the monastery Prokudin-Gorsky photographed only two monuments: the north gate church and the archaic form of the monastery bell cot. My photograph of the latter shows the results of a major restoration undertaken after World War II.

A short distance to the south of the Savior-Saint Euthymius Monastery is the Convent of the Deposition of the Robe, known for its brightly festive Holy Gate crowned with twin miniature towers, which Prokudin-Gorsky photographed in the summer of 1912. Founded in the early days of the Suzdal principality in 1207, the convent was dedicated by Bishop Ioann to a Byzantine holiday commemorating the discovery of the robe of the Virgin Mary. The convent was known for one of its first monastics, Saint Euphrosyne

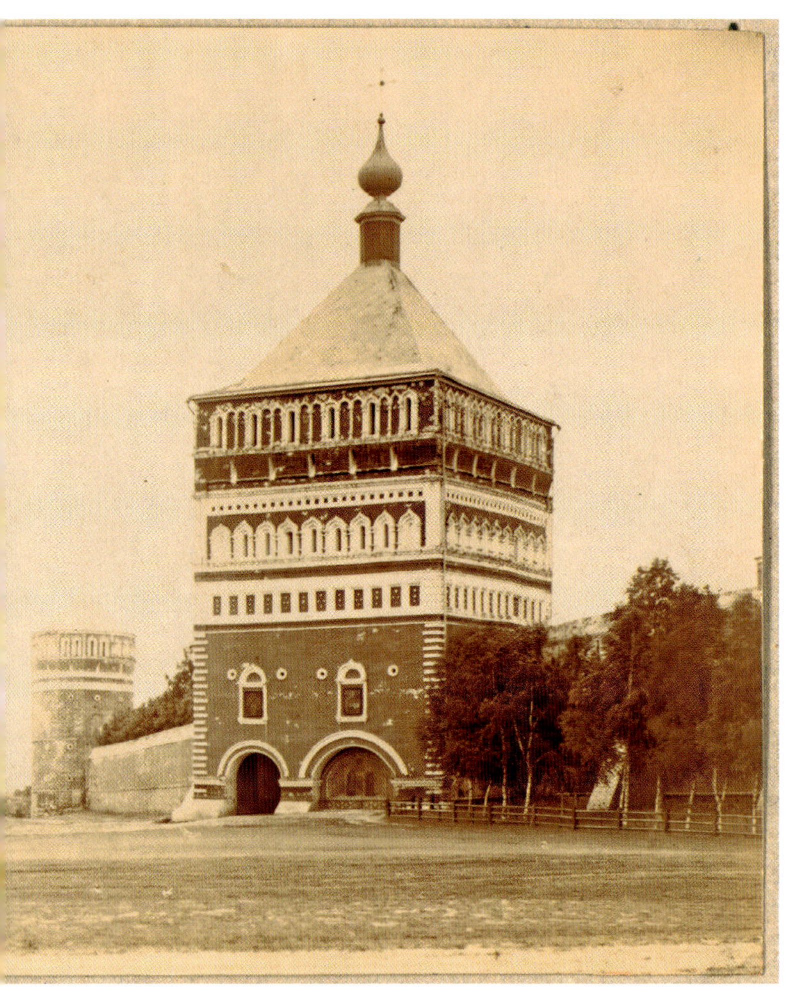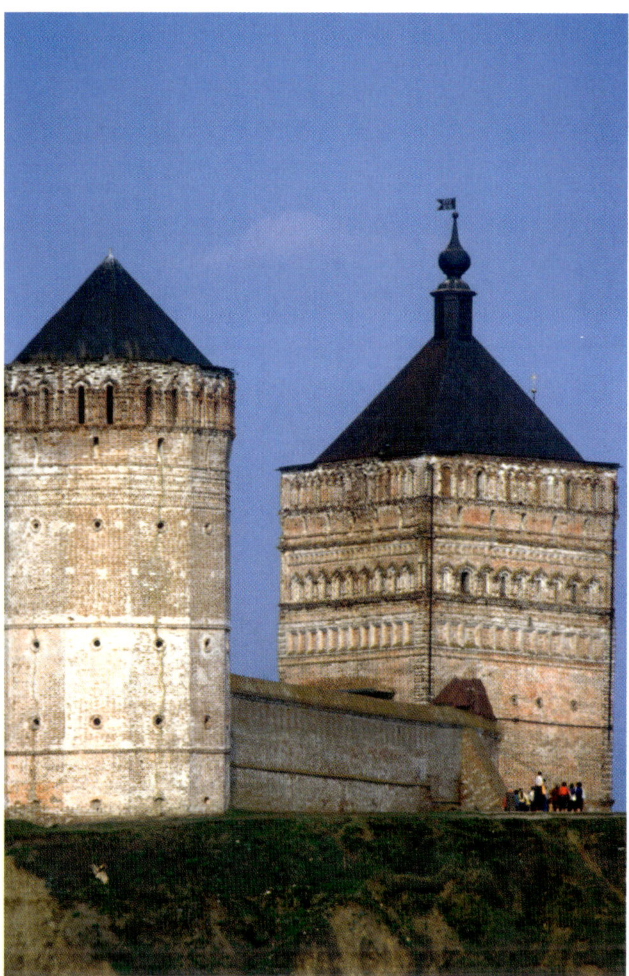

of Suzdal (1212–1250), a princess who took monastic vows after the death of her betrothed. Although she lived at the nearby Intercession Convent, her final resting place was the Convent of the Deposition of the Robe.

For much of its history the convent shared the turbulent fate of Suzdal, which suffered at the hands of invaders from the thirteenth through early seventeenth centuries. Its earliest surviving monument is the Cathedral of the Deposition, visible in the right background of the Prokudin-Gorsky photograph. Erected in the early sixteenth century, the small structure adhered to traditional church forms and had three cupolas. In the nineteenth century the cupolas were modified to the onion domes visible in Prokudin-Gorsky's photograph. They were destroyed in 1929 when the structure was converted to an electric station for security units guarding the prison in the nearby Savior Monastery. In the late 1960s the cupolas were restored to their original "helmet" form seen in my photograph.

The same builders created the Holy Gate seen in Prokudin-Gorsky's

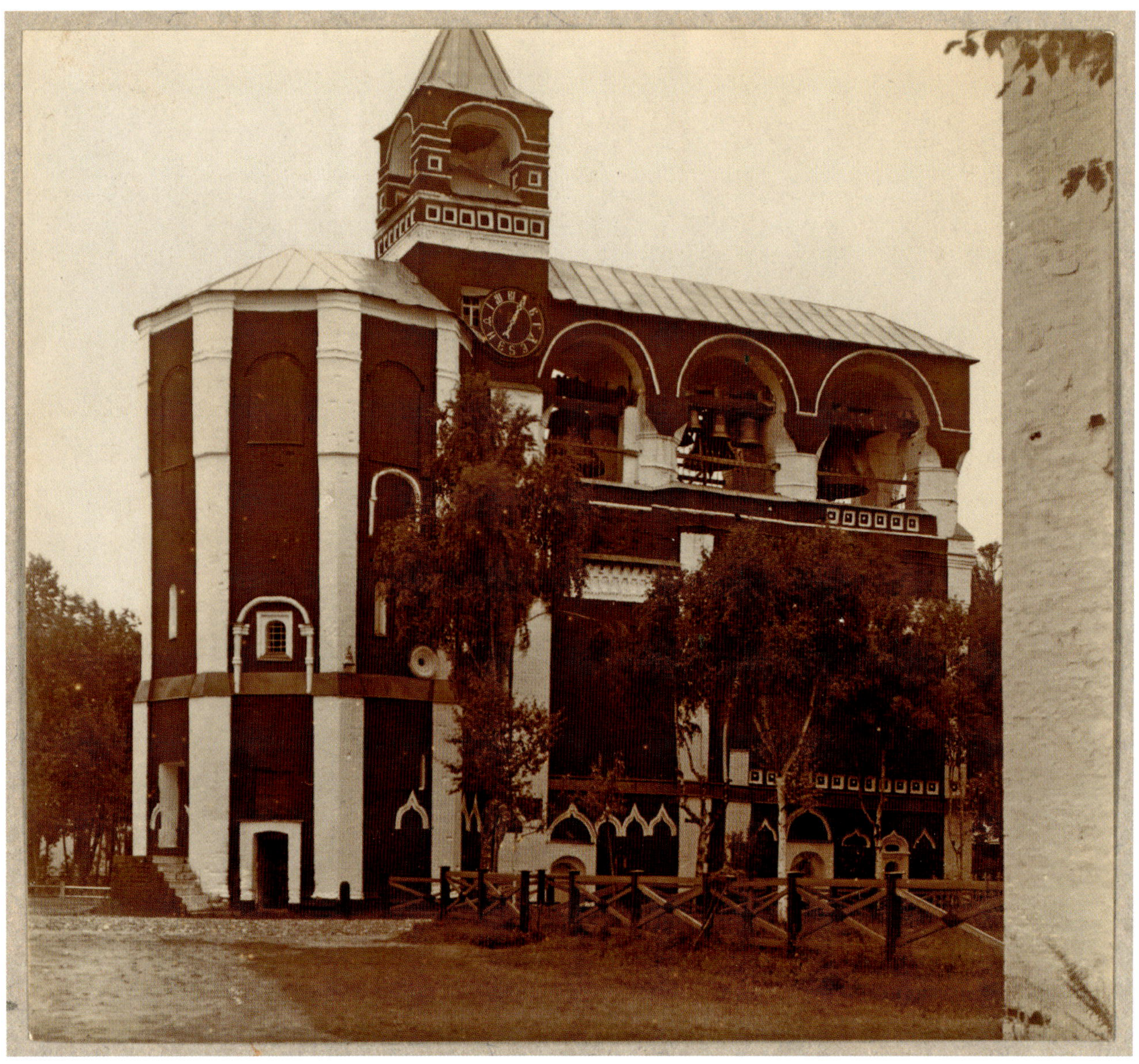

view. With its two arched entrances—one for pedestrians and the other for vehicles—the structure is decorated with recessed panels (*shirinki*) that contain ceramic tiles. The roof supports two octagonal forms, also ornamented with shirinki and miniature windows with decorative surrounds. Above are eight-sided tower caps known as "tents." Their surfaces display two rows of framed blank surrounds that appear to be open in my 1972 photograph. Each "tent" is crowned with a small cupola and cross. In 1999 the Convent of the Deposition of the Robe was returned to the Orthodox Church.

SUZDAL Savior-Saint Euthymius Monastery. Bell tower. West view. PROKUDIN-GORSKY 02620. SUMMER 1912.

SUZDAL Savior-Saint Euthymius Monastery. Bell tower. Northwest view. BRUMFIELD, JUNE 30, 1995.

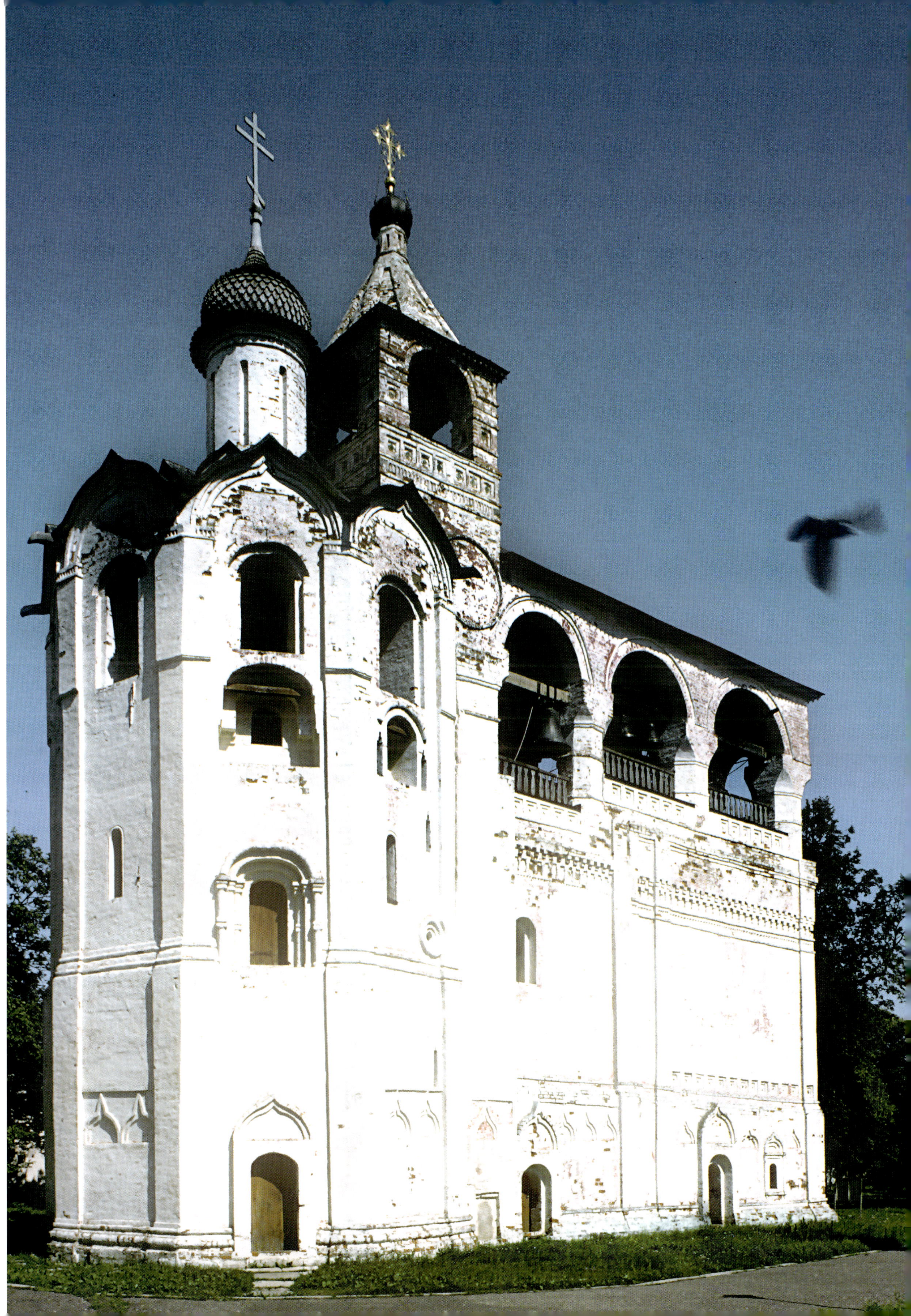

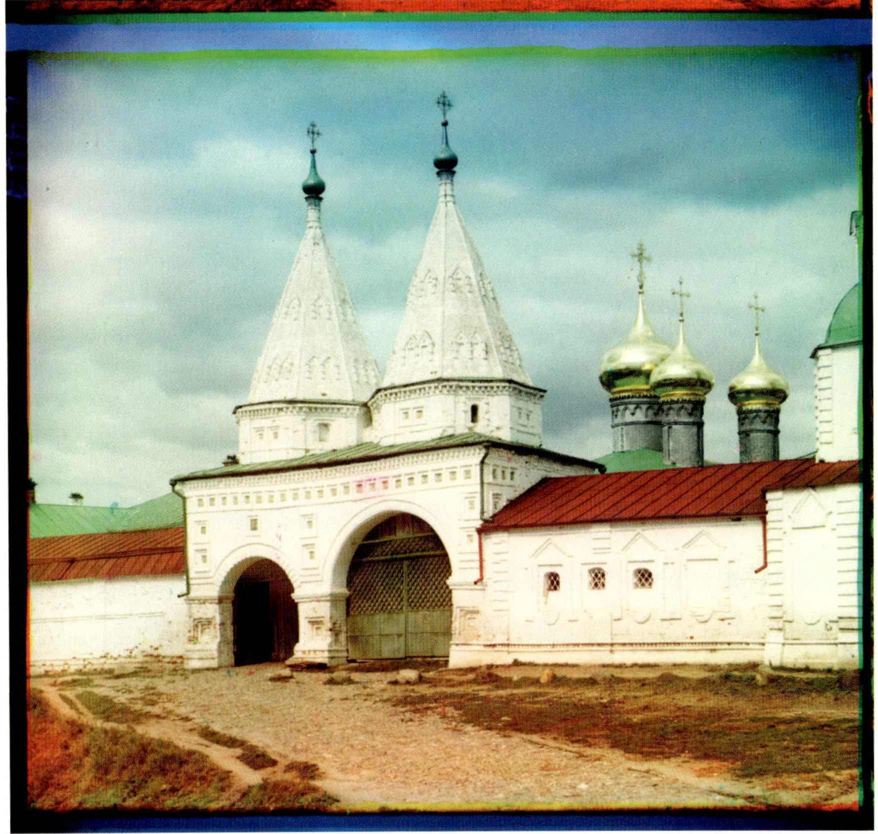

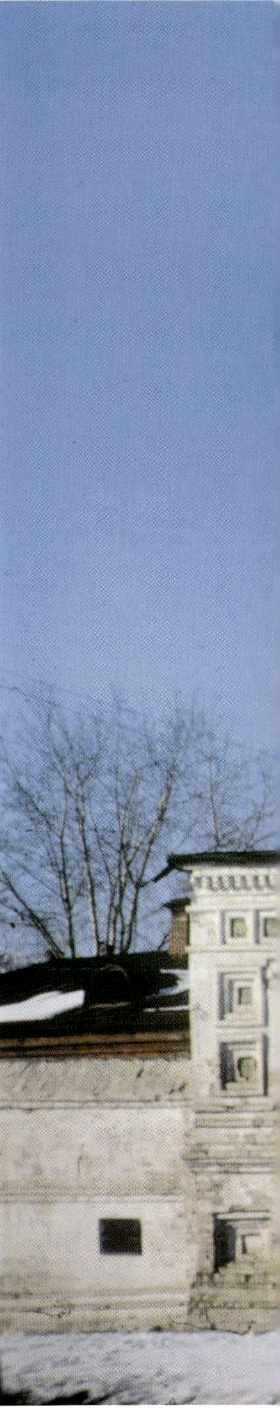

In addition to monasteries, Prokudin-Gorsky photographed parish churches in Suzdal, including the Church of Saints Boris and Gleb, built in the mid-eighteenth century. The view taken from the bell tower of the Church of Saint Dmitry (demolished in 1936) is remarkable not only for the church but also for the fecundity of the garden plots and the tightly organized farmstead in the center. My photograph, taken from a slightly different vantage, shows a spare landscape in early spring with the church exterior intact as a sturdy example of provincial baroque architecture.

Other bucolic scenes include a view up the Kamenka River with pair of churches in the Suzdal tradition: the smaller church, which could be heated for use in the winter; and the larger, more imposing but unheated church for use in the summer.

In this photograph the "winter" is dedicated to the Nativity of John the Baptist, while the summer church is dedicated to the Epiphany. My photograph shows a different perspective across a field, with the grand bell tower of the Convent of Deposition of the Robe in the right background.

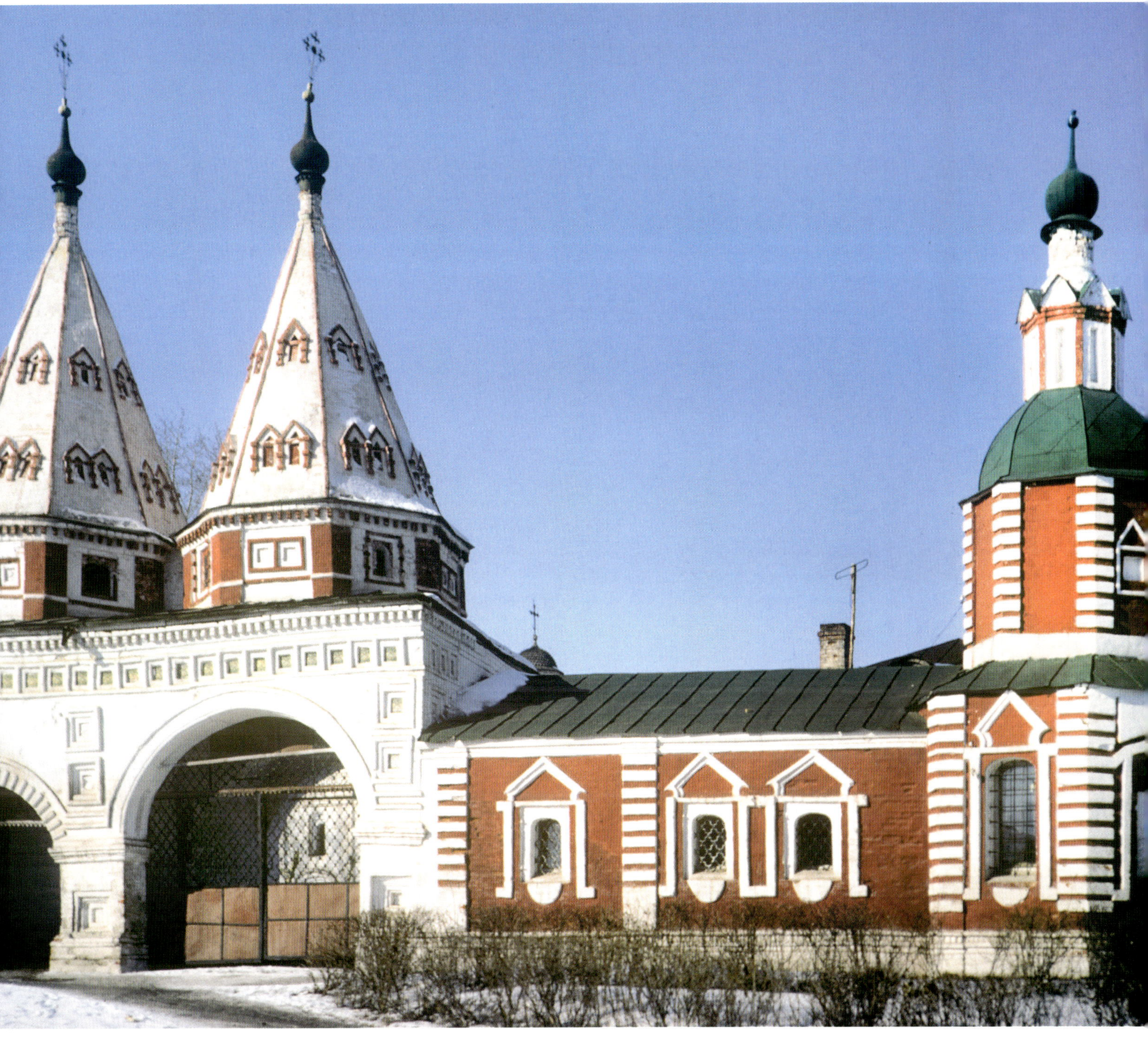

SUZDAL Convent of the Deposition of the Robe.
PROKUDIN-GORSKY 21242. SUMMER 1912.

SUZDAL Convent of the Deposition of the Robe. Holy
Gate and south wall. BRUMFIELD, MARCH 5, 1972.

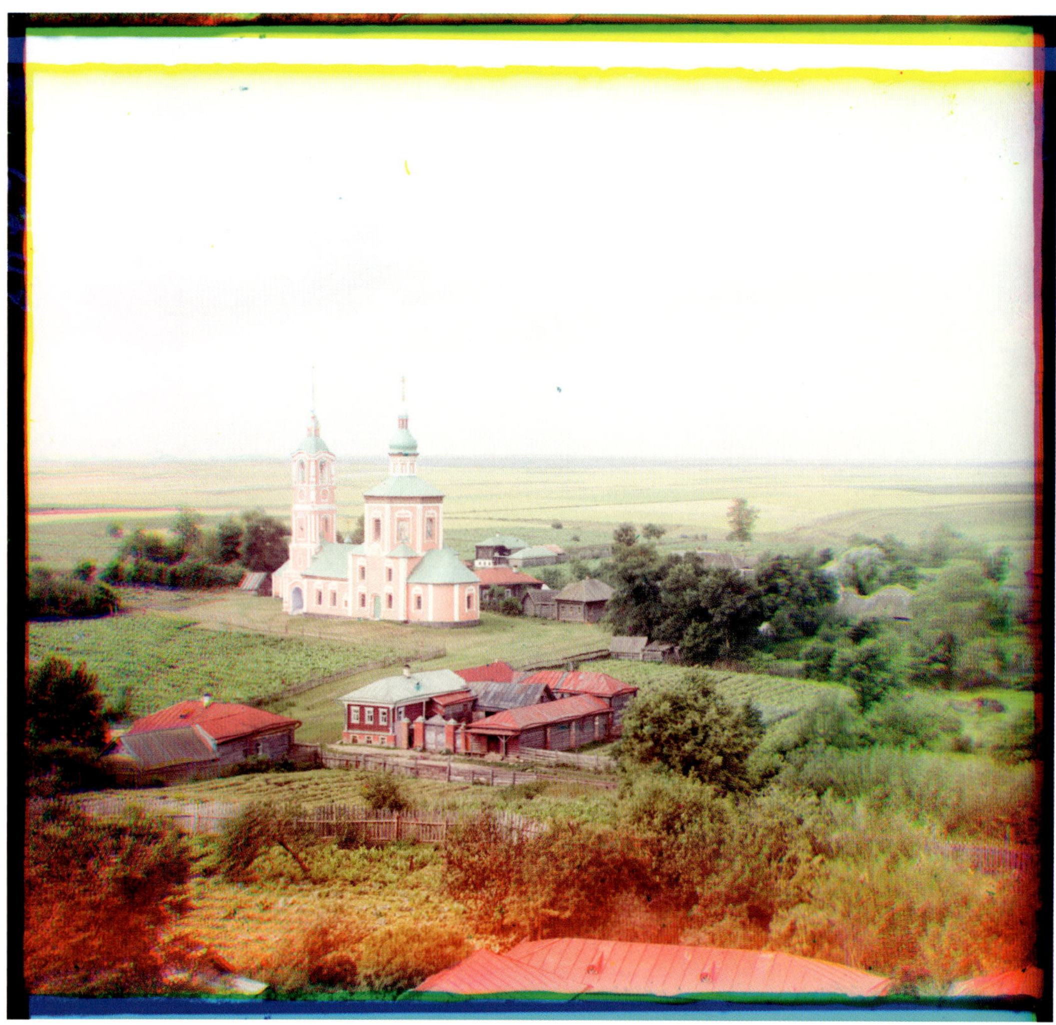

PERESLAVL-ZALESSKY

For centuries, pilgrims, merchants, and ordinary mortals have traveled along the road northeast of Moscow to the great Holy Trinity Monastery at Sergiev Posad (not photographed by Prokudin-Gorsky) and beyond to the medieval towns of Pereslavl-Zalessky, Rostov, and Yaroslavl on the Volga River. Despite the depredations of the twentieth century, their wealth of monuments sheds light on the complex history of medieval Russia.

Located near the shores of Lake Pleshcheyevo, Pereslavl-Zalessky was established in 1152 by Yury Dolgoruky (the Long-Armed), prince of the large territory of Rostov-Suzdal and known as the founder of Moscow in 1147. Settlers from

SUZDAL Church of Saints Boris and Gleb. Southeast view. PROKUDIN-GORSKY 21145. SUMMER 1912.

SUZDAL Church of Saints Boris and Gleb. South view. BRUMFIELD, APRIL 27, 1980.

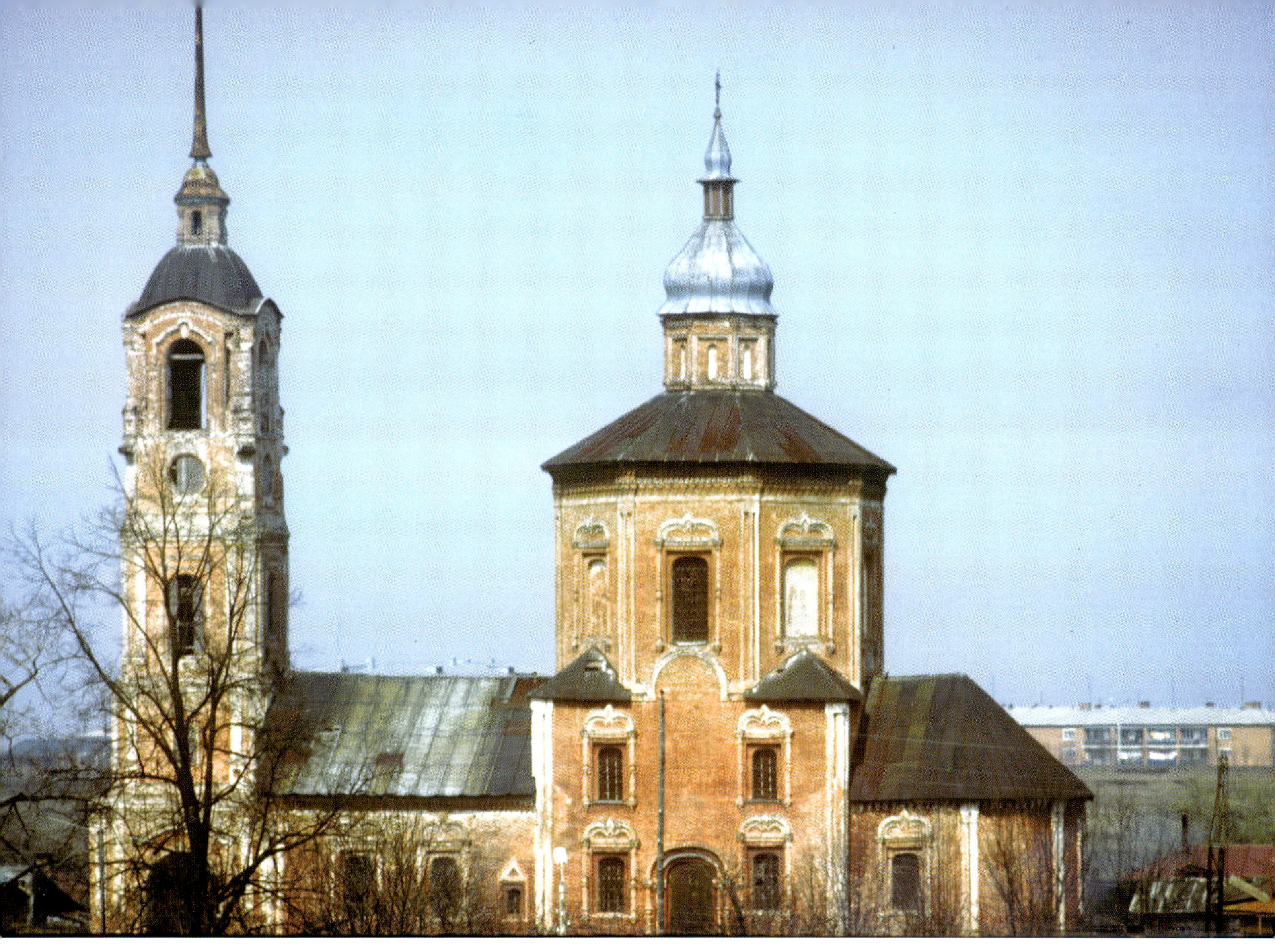

the medieval capital of Kiev had moved to the area since the turn of the twelfth century, and the town's name is thought to derive from the town of Pereyaslavl, near Kiev. The addition of "Zalessky" ("beyond the forests") indicates that the new settlement lay within a forest zone in central Russia. Yury Dolgoruky spent most of his life in a quest for the princely throne in Kiev, and he died within a year of achieving that goal, in 1157. In architecture Dolgoruky's primary legacy is the Cathedral of the Transfiguration of the Savior in Pereslavl-Zalessky, one of the earliest cut stone churches in Russia. Although lacking the design refinements that characterize later churches built by Dolgoruky's sons in Vladimir and Bogolyubovo, its form shows a skillful use of cut limestone. The cathedral is dimly visible in a contact print from the Prokudin-Gorsky albums. (The original glass negative is not preserved.)

Pereslavl-Zalessky had numerous monastic institutions—as many as twelve in the immediate area during the mid-eighteenth century. Their number reflected the town's role as a center of early missionary activity when

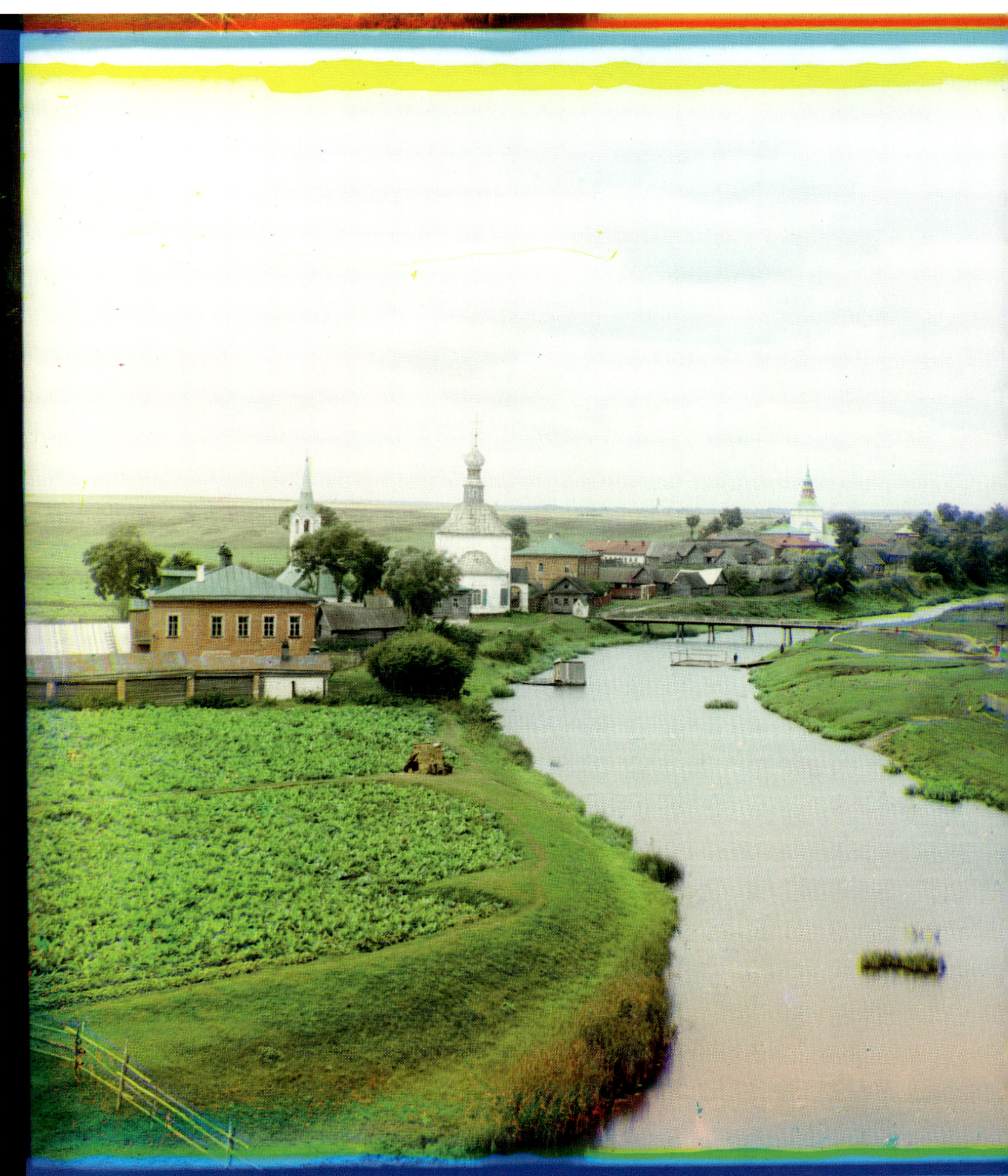

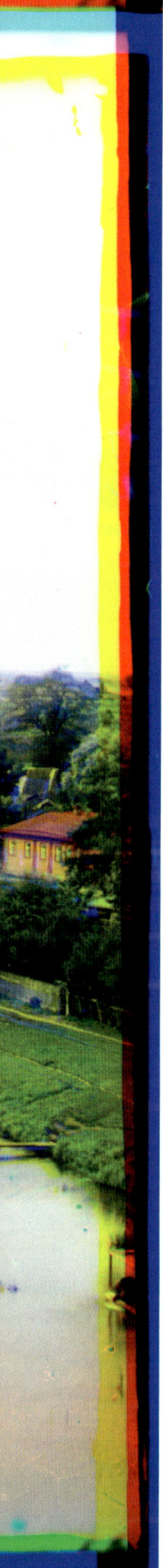

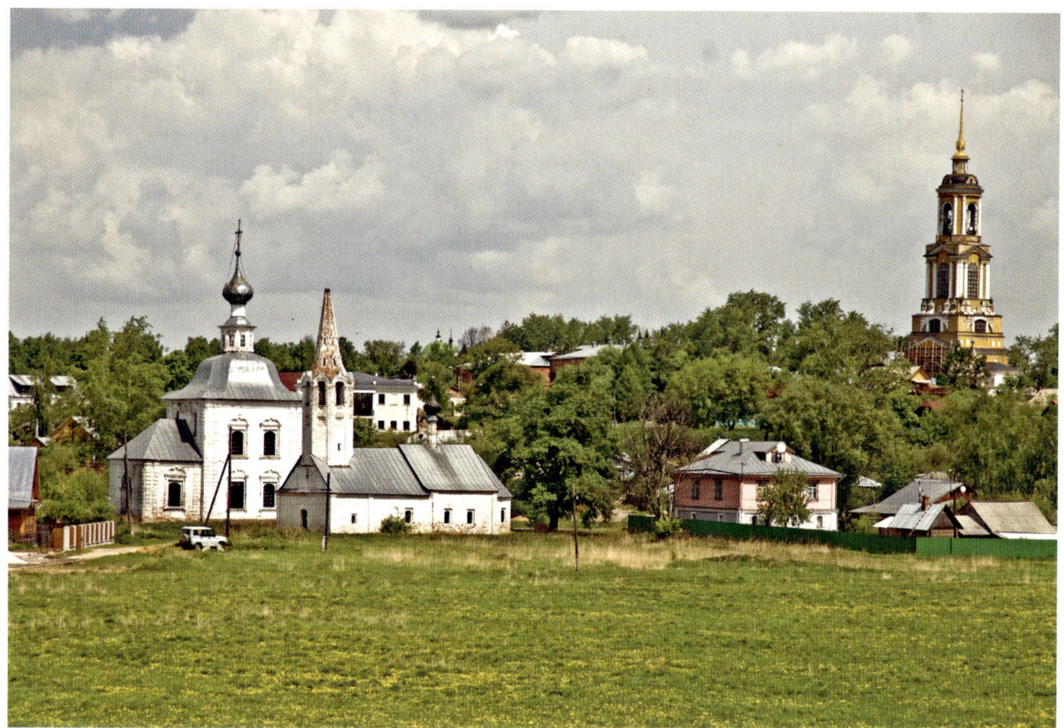

much of the Rostov territory had only nominally accepted Christianity. The monasteries also benefited from the town's position on a major pilgrimage route traversed by the grand princes of Muscovy. Five monasteries still have a presence in Pereslavl-Zalessky.

Prokudin-Gorsky seems to have been especially taken by the Goritsky-Dormition Monastery, situated on a high bluff above the south shore of Lake Pleshcheyevo. There is sparse information about the monastery's origins, but it is known to have existed by the mid-fourteenth century and was perhaps founded earlier in the century by Moscow Prince Ivan Kalita (1283–1341?). Saint Dmitry Prilutsky, one of Russia's most revered monastics, was tonsured at the monastery, rose in the hierarchy, and came to the attention of Sergius of Radonezh, avatar of Muscovite monasticism. Saint Sergius became the spiritual adviser to Grand Prince Dmitry Ivanovich of Moscow (1350–89), and the monk Dmitry assumed a similar role with the prince's children.

Destroyed by the Tatars in 1382, the wooden monastery was quickly rebuilt and became a major religious cen-

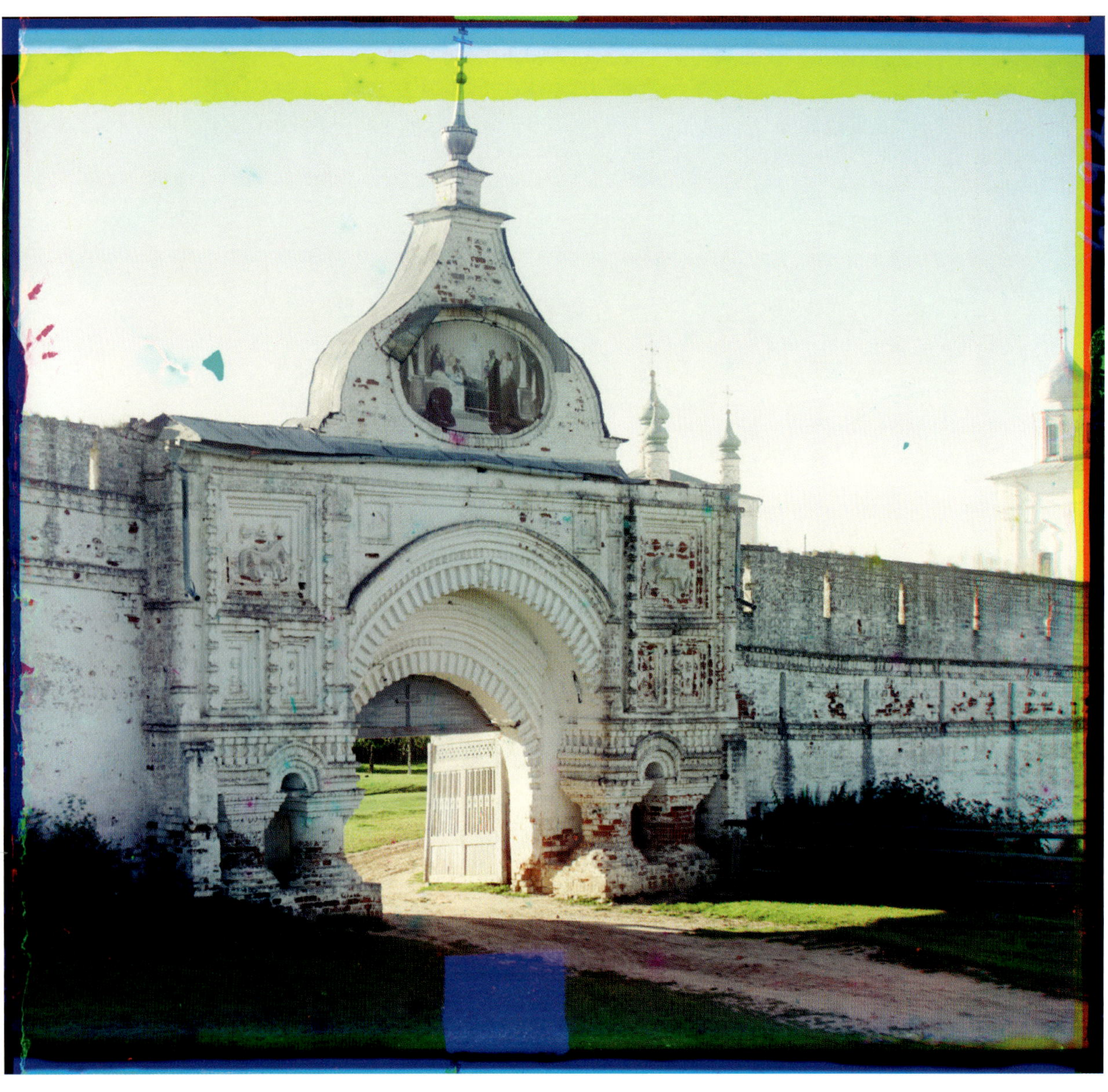

ter. In the late fifteenth and sixteenth centuries, the monastery developed close ties with Grand Princes Vasily III and Ivan IV (the Terrible). In 1608 the monastery was ravaged by Polish-Lithuanian forces during a dynastic interregnum known as the Time of Troubles. With the rest of Pereslavl-Zalessky, the monastery revived over the course of the seventeenth century. During this period the monastery walls were expanded and enhanced by the addition of entrance structures with decorative brick ornamentation. Prokudin-Gorsky photographed the east gate against the setting sun. A comparison with my photograph from 2012

PERESLAVL-ZALESSKY Goritsky-Dormition Monastery. East gate, east view with painting of Dormition of the Virgin. PROKUDIN-GORSKY 21405. SUMMER 1911.

PERESLAVL-ZALESSKY Goritsky-Dormition Monastery. East gate, east view with painting of Dormition of the Virgin. BRUMFIELD, JULY 12, 2012.

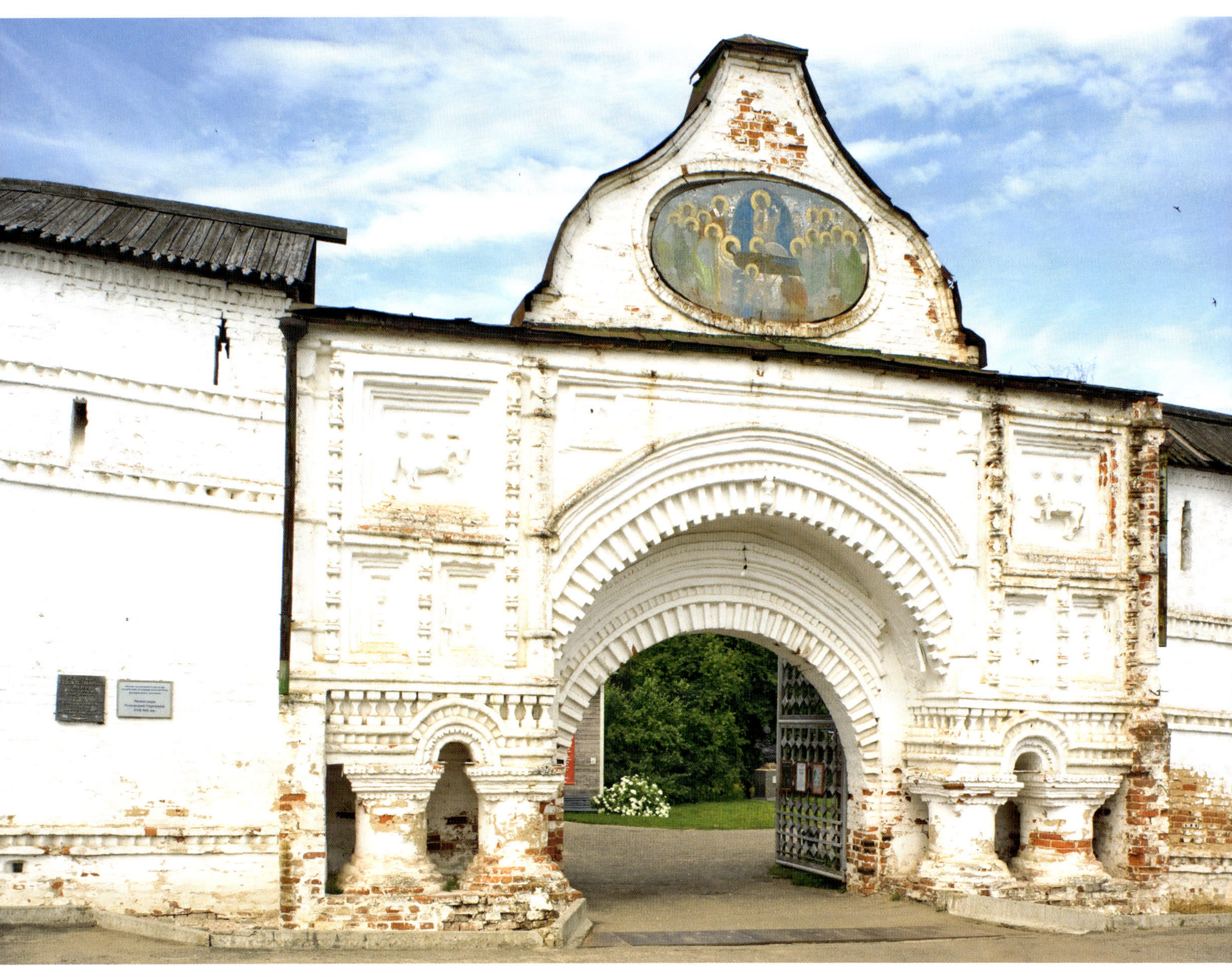

shows modifications to the nineteenth-century crown and painting of the
Dormition of the Virgin.

In 1722 a fire swept through the monastery and destroyed its archive, but
fate unexpectedly brought improved fortunes. An ecclesiastical reorgani-
zation during the reign of Empress Elizabeth Petrovna led in 1744 to the
creation of a wealthy Pereslavl eparchy, or bishopric. Consequently, the Go-
ritsky Monastery was transformed into the residence of the archbishop, an
elevated status that brought resources for the rebuilding of churches on a
grand scale. The most imposing structure from this period is the Cathedral
of the Dormition of the Virgin, begun in the early 1750s and completed in

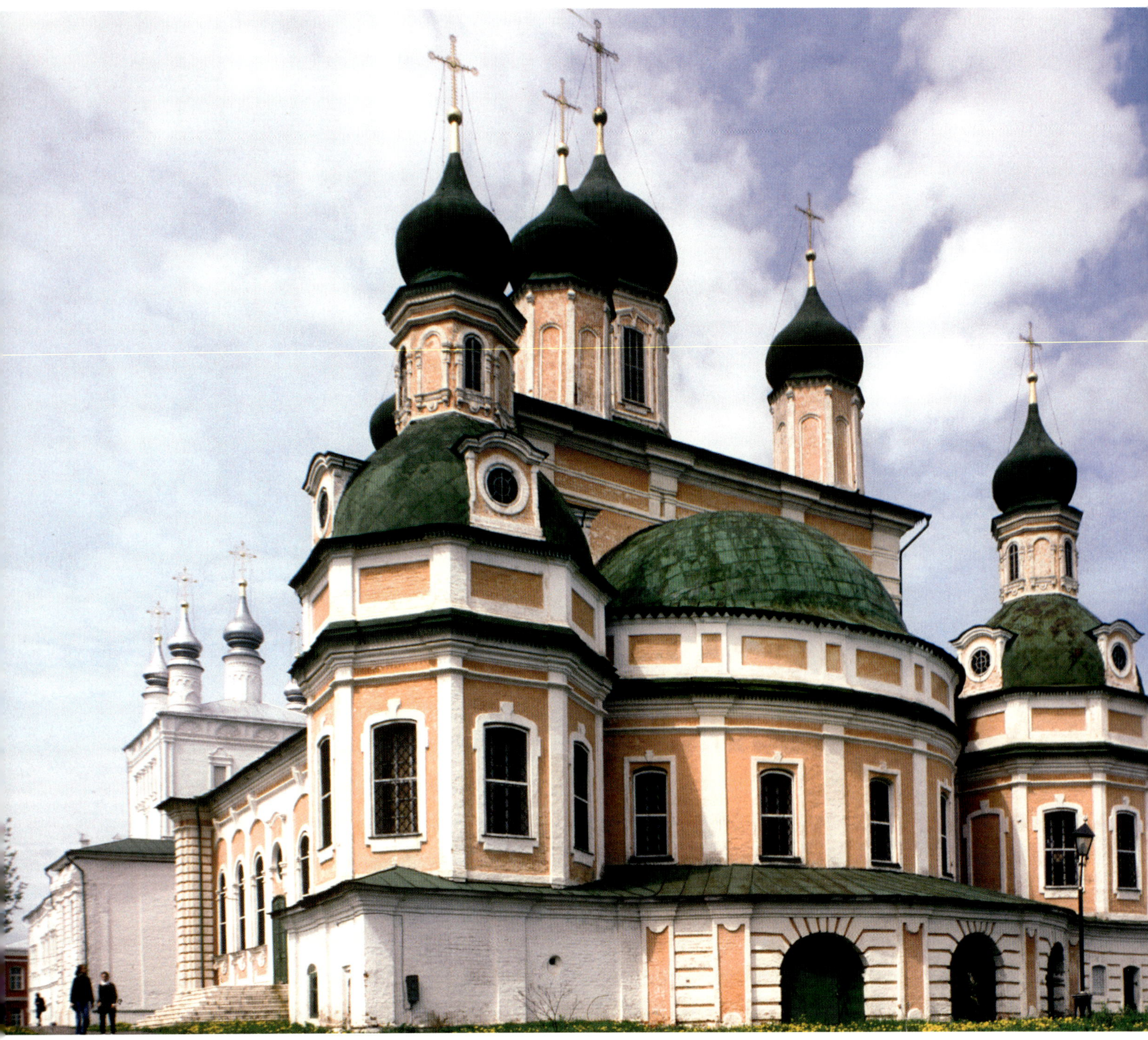

PERESLAVL-ZALESSKY Goritsky-Dormition Monastery. Dormition Cathedral, southeast view. *Left background*: Church of All Saints. BRUMFIELD, MAY 21, 1996.

PERESLAVL-ZALESSKY Goritsky-Dormition Monastery. Dormition Cathedral (*right*) and Church of All Saints, south view. PROKUDIN-GORSKY 21406. SUMMER 1911.

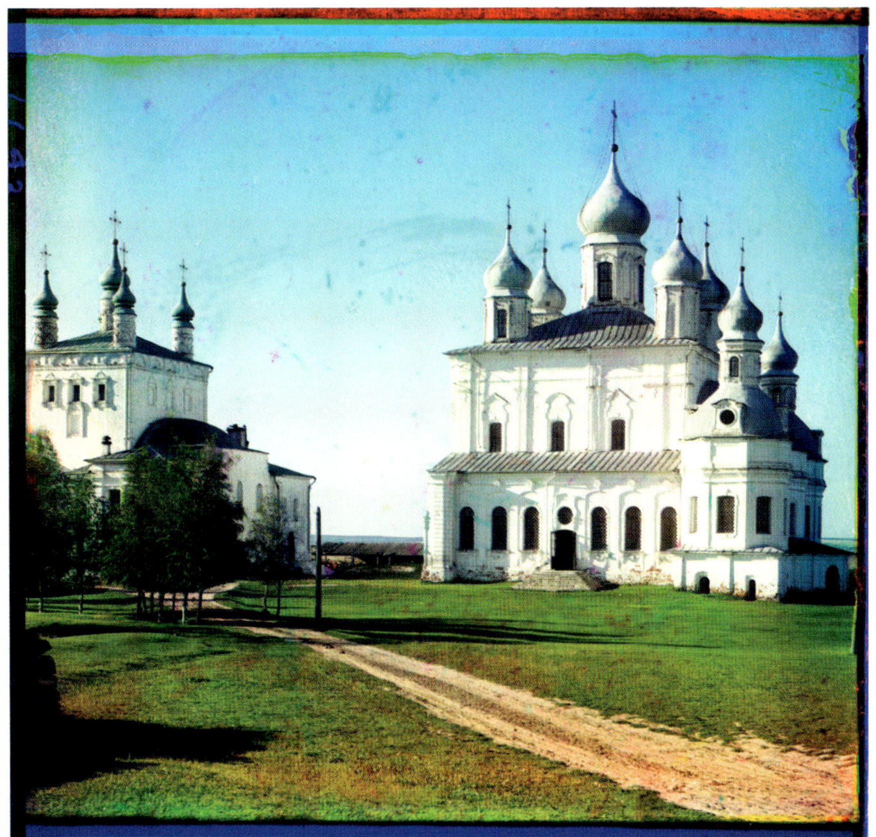

1761 to replace a church built in the 1520s. On the exterior its design consists of a restrained mixture of baroque and neoclassical elements characteristic of the work of the leading Moscow architect Karl Blank. Prokudin-Gorsky's south view of the cathedral, taken in the late afternoon, conveys a sense of abandoned grandeur. My photograph, taken in 1996, shows the structure restored as part of the regional history museum.

The interior of the cathedral displays a decorative magnificence in the late baroque style, epitomized in the work of Bartolomeo Rastrelli, author of the Winter Palace in Saint Petersburg, and Dmitry Ukhtomsky, a baroque master active in the Moscow area. The centerpiece is the magnificent carved icon screen that soars to the ceiling vaults of the main interior space. For technical reasons involving the inability to tilt his large camera, Prokudin-Gorsky photographed not the central iconostasis but instead chose the smaller icon screen in the south chapel. My photograph of the chapel space in 2012 shows a rare example of excellent preservation.

Prokudin-Gorsky also took a general view of the Convent of Saint Theodore Stratelates with the main entrance, or Holy Gate, in the fore-

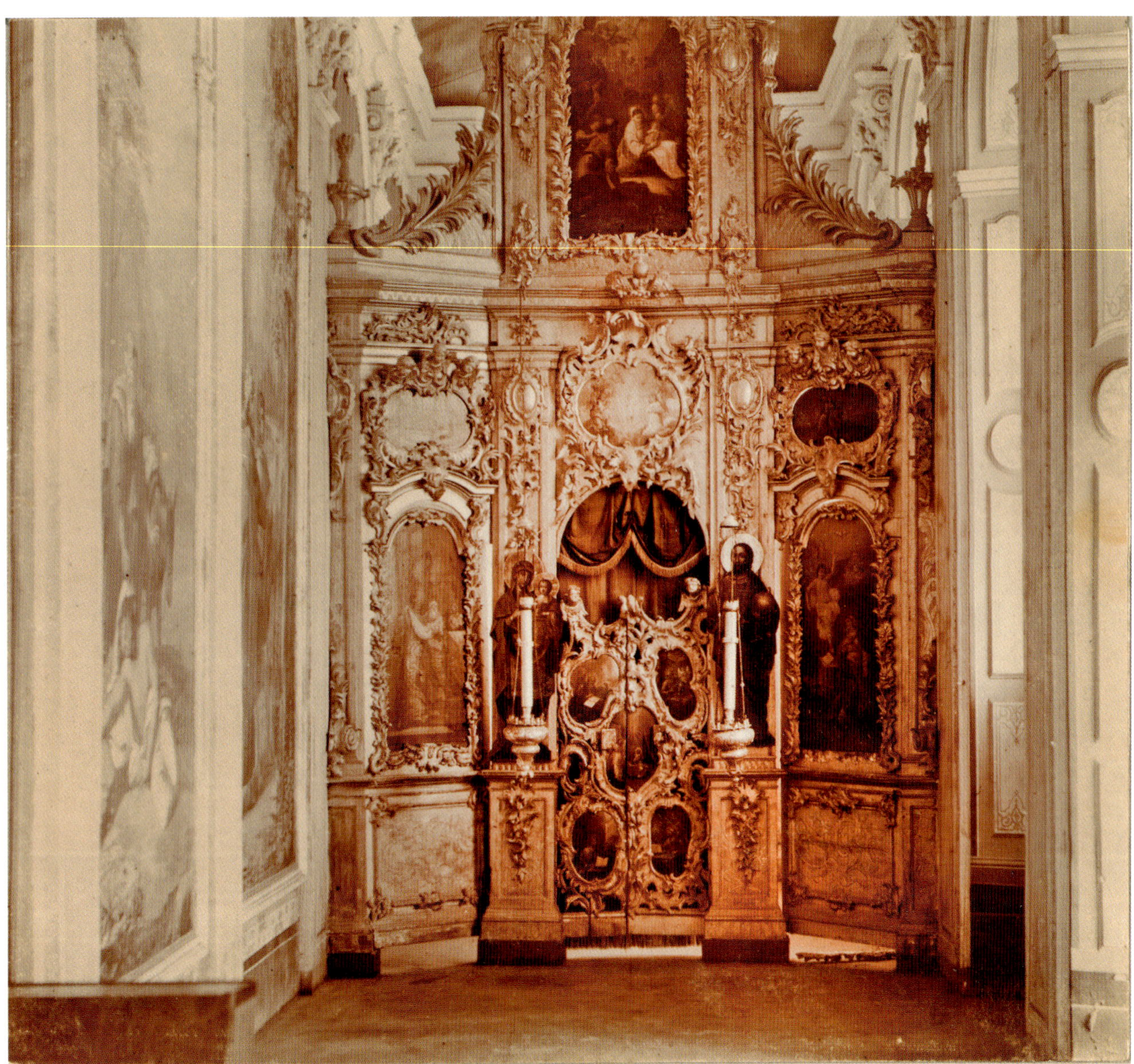

PERESLAVL-ZALESSKY Goritsky-Dormition Monastery. Annunciation Chapel of the Dormition Cathedral. View east toward iconostasis. PROKUDIN-GORSKY 02589. SUMMER 1911.

PERESLAVL-ZALESSKY Goritsky-Dormition Monastery. Annunciation Chapel of the Dormition Cathedral. View east toward iconostasis. BRUMFIELD, JULY 17, 2012.

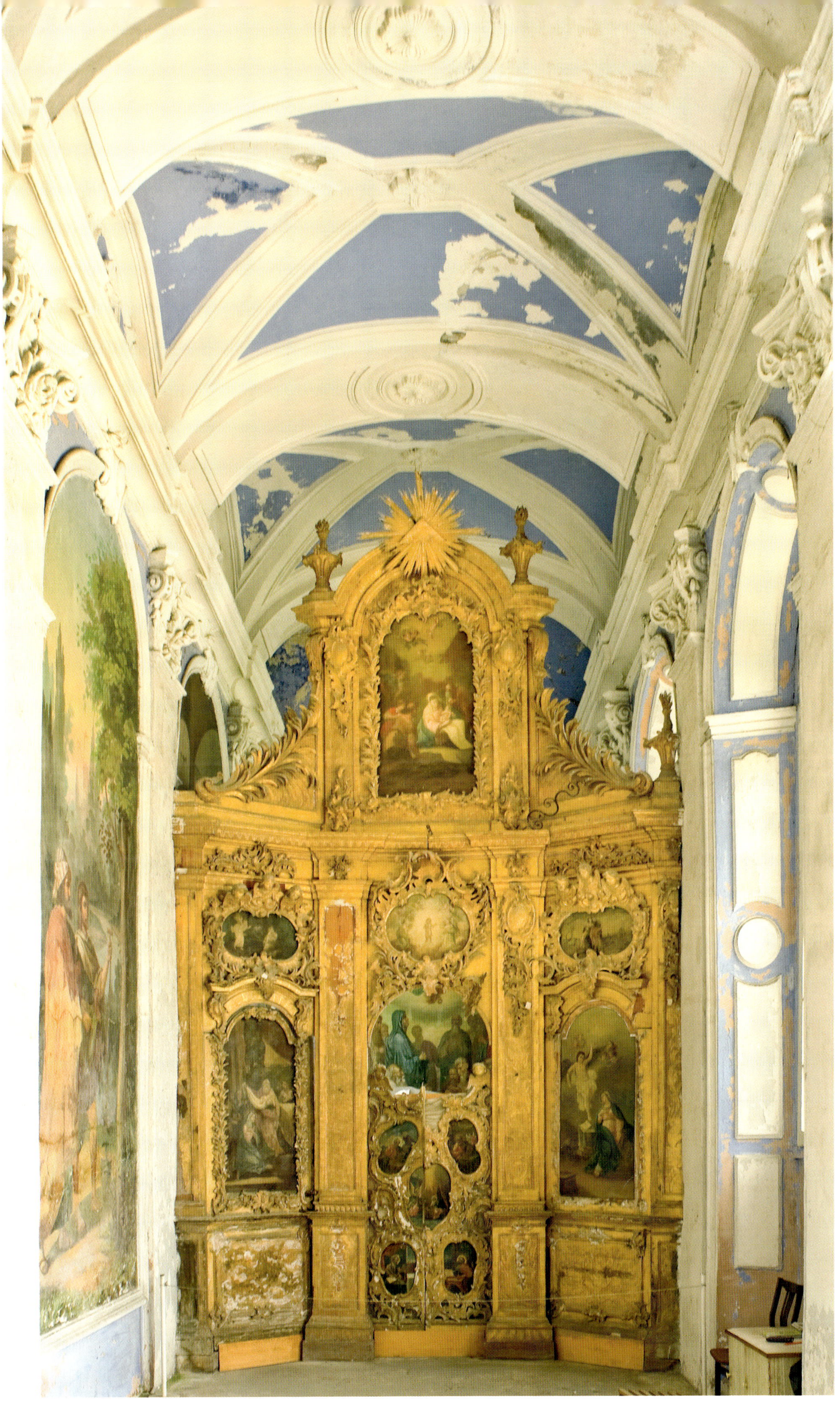

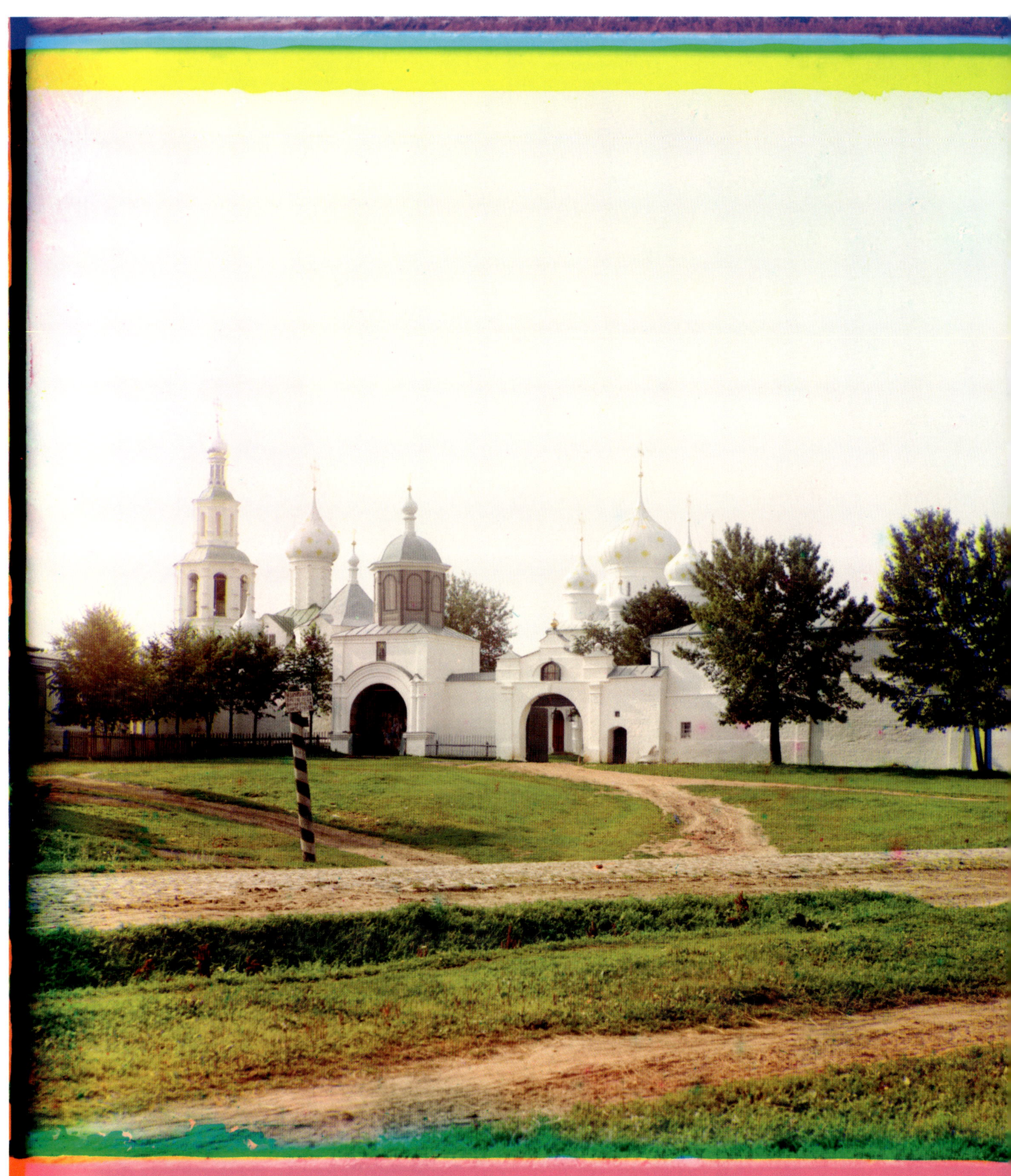

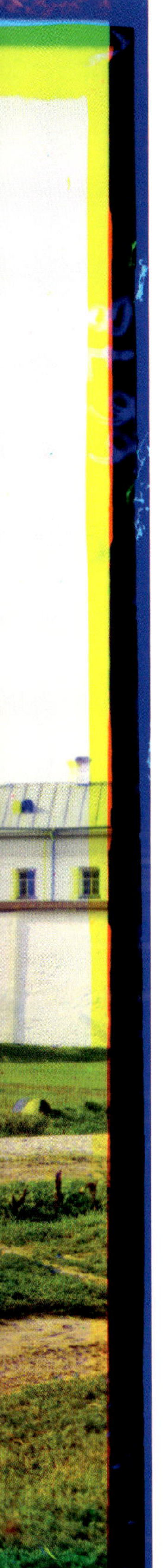

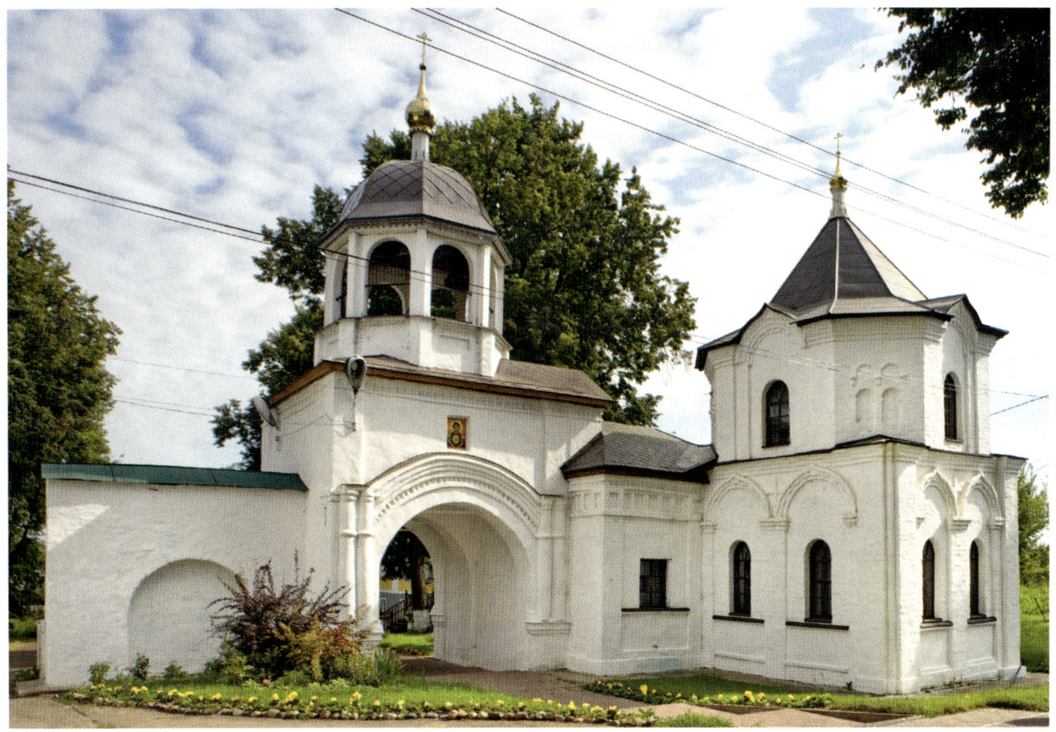

ground and the main monastery shrines hovering beyond. The site on which the convent stands is traditionally thought to have been the field of a battle between the principalities of Moscow and Tver on June 8, 1304. In the Orthodox Church calendar this day is dedicated to Saint Theodore (Feodor in Russian) Stratelates, a Roman officer martyred for his Christian faith in 319 and considered the patron saint of warriors. In the battle the forces of Prince Yury Danilovich of Moscow succeeded in defeating Prince Mikhail Yaroslavich of Tver (1271/72–1318); subsequently he was killed at the Golden Horde and canonized as a martyr by the Russian Orthodox Church. In gratitude for his victory, Prince Yury established the monastery and dedicated it to Theodore Stratelates.

Over a period of almost three decades, I have photographed the transformations in the convent before and after its return to the Orthodox Church. The photograph that I have chosen here shows the small, exquisite Holy Gate ensemble that is also at the center of Prokudin-Gorsky's photograph. Hovering in the background is the Cathe-

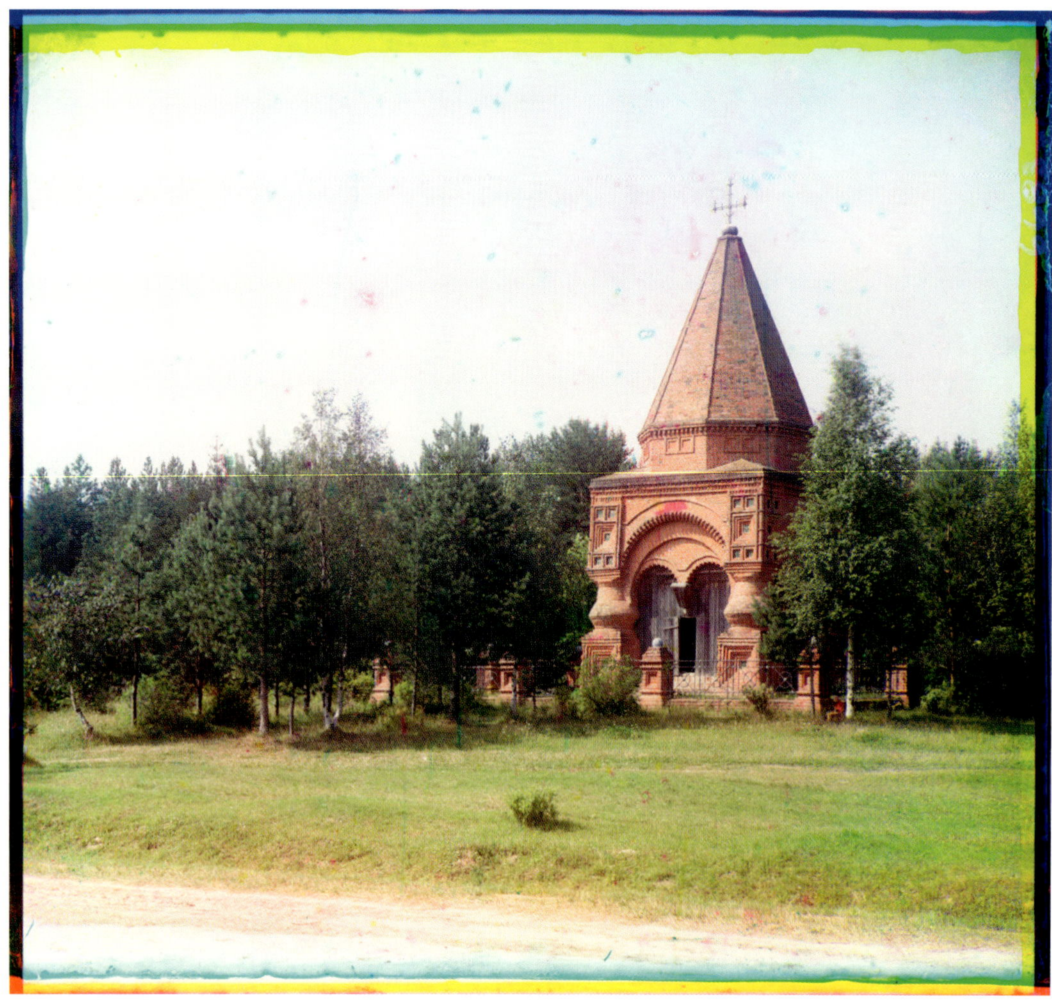

dral of Theodore Stratelates, completed in 1557 with support from Ivan the Terrible to commemorate the birth of his third son, Feodor (1557–98).

Indeed, Prokudin-Gorsky photographed another monument to this royal event, a chapel purportedly at the site where Tsaritsa Anastasia Romanovna, wife of Ivan the Terrible, gave birth to Feodor. Located three kilometers from the Monastery of Saint Theodore Stratelates on the southern approach to the town, the original chapel was apparently built of wood. In the mid-seventeenth century it was rebuilt in brick in an ornate style typical of the period. Dedicated to Saint Theodore, the chapel was known as "The Cross" because of the presence of a large cross within it. The deterioration of the structure in the nineteenth century led to its measurement in the 1880s by the architect Vladimir Suslov,

PERESLAVL-ZALESSKY
(SOBILOVO) Holy Cross Chapel. Northeast view. PROKUDIN-GORSKY 21397. SUMMER 1911.

PERESLAVL-ZALESSKY
Holy Cross Chapel. Southeast view. BRUMFIELD, MAY 24, 1997.

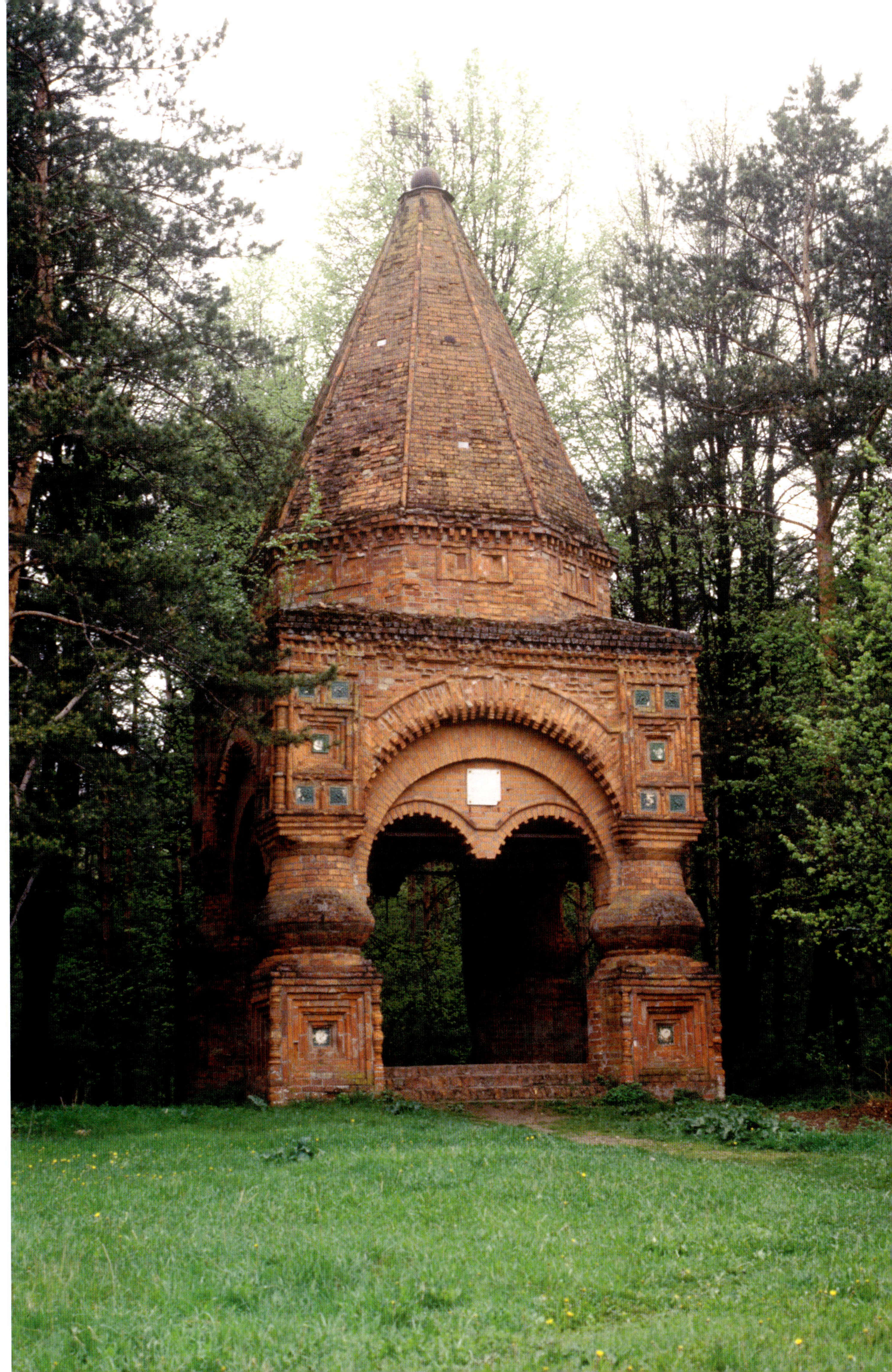

a pioneer in the study of Russian architecture. In 1889 the chapel was disassembled and carefully rebuilt in its present form.

ROSTOV THE GREAT

Although increasingly burdened with traffic, the road from Pereslavl-Zalessky to Yaroslavl occasionally passes through groves of birch, pine, fir, and aspen that convey a sense of the forest in the history of this part of Russia. Along this ancient path there is no sight more imposing than the towers and cupolas of Rostov, often referred to as "Veliky," or Rostov the Great. Prokudin-Gorsky's several photographs provide an excellent survey of the town's rich architectural heritage as well as the antiquities in the local museum, whose august patron was the tsarevitch Nicholas Aleksandrovich, later Tsar Nicholas II.

Rostov is one of the earliest historically attested towns in Russia, first mentioned under the year 862 in the ancient chronicle "Tale of Bygone Years." Throughout the tenth century, Slavic settlers—primarily from the Novgorod lands—moved into this area, sparsely inhabited by Finno-Ugric tribes. In 988 Grand Prince Vladimir of Kiev gave the Rostov territory to one of his sons, Yaroslav, subsequently Grand Prince Yaroslav "the Wise." By the middle of the eleventh century, Rostov had passed to Yaroslav's son Vsevolod, and Christian missionaries intensified their attempt to convert a still largely pagan population.

The consolidation of church authority was symbolized in the mid-twelfth century by Prince Andrei Bogolyubsky's Cathedral of the Dormition of the Virgin, rebuilt by Prince Konstantin Vsevolodovich in 1213. Although the Mongols captured and burned much of Rostov in 1237, the cathedral and monasteries remained, and Rostov gained an increased role in church-supported culture during a time when much else had been destroyed. In the fourteenth century, Rostov continued to be a center of religious learning and propagation of the faith, producing such missionary pioneers as Saint Stephan of Perm and Epiphanius the Wise.

The central monument to Rostov's religious heritage remains the Dormition Cathedral, created in brick on the site of the two earlier limestone versions mentioned above. The rebuilding of the Rostov cathedral, probably begun in the reign of Ivan III and continued by Vasily III and Ivan the Terrible in the sixteenth century, was a demonstration of Moscow's dominant political position and its determination to enhance the ancient centers of Russian religious culture. The cathedral figures in several photographs by Prokudin-Gorsky, with a level roofline created in an eighteenth-century renovation. Particularly evocative is his south view from within the Metropolitan's Court (see below) with the adjacent Gate Church of the Resurrection. My photograph from the same perspective shows a postwar reconstruction of what is considered to be the original roofline. Although this photograph shows the exterior of the Dormition Cathedral in good condition, the interior was severely damaged during the Soviet period. The cathedral wall paintings have since undergone extensive restoration.

In 1589 Rostov's stature as a center of Orthodoxy increased with its elevation from an episcopate to a metropolitanate. This event occurred in the same year that the Orthodox patriarch in Constantinople agreed to bestow the rank of patriarch on the head of the Russian Orthodox Church, thus elevating Moscow's status in the Orthodox hierarchy. Sacked by Polish forces in 1609 during the Time of Troubles, Rostov regained its religious significance and witnessed a dramatic architectural transformation in the second half of the seventeenth century. The building campaign was set in motion by Jonah Sysoevich (ca. 1607–90), an ambitious, dynamic church leader. The son of a country priest, Jonah rose through the monastic structure in Rostov and in 1652 was appointed metropolitan (head) of Rostov by the newly elected Patriarch Nikon in Moscow. During this period, the Russian church embarked on extensive building projects that would be the final expression of church power before the curtailing of its wealth by the state in the eighteenth century. Jonah had at his command sixteen thousand serfs as well as the best craftsmen of his large and prosperous eparchy. Within twenty years—between 1670 and 1690—Jonah's builders erected not only several large churches and other buildings for the Metropolitan's Court and residence but also monumental walls with towers and gate churches situated on the north shore of Lake Nero.

The Dormition Cathedral is linked visually to the Metropolitan's Court by a great belfry, built in 1682–87. In addition to including it in his general views of Rostov, Prokudin-Gorsky photographed the belfry's upper tiers from the compound wall at the northeast corner of the cathedral. The belfry is composed of two adjoining structures, of which the taller contains the largest of the bells—the thirty-six-ton "Sysoy," named after Jonah's father. The other segment of the belfry, with three bays, contains twelve bells with names such as "Swan" and "Ram." Among my several photographs is a general view from the west.

From the belfry, the northern entrance to the citadel is marked by two

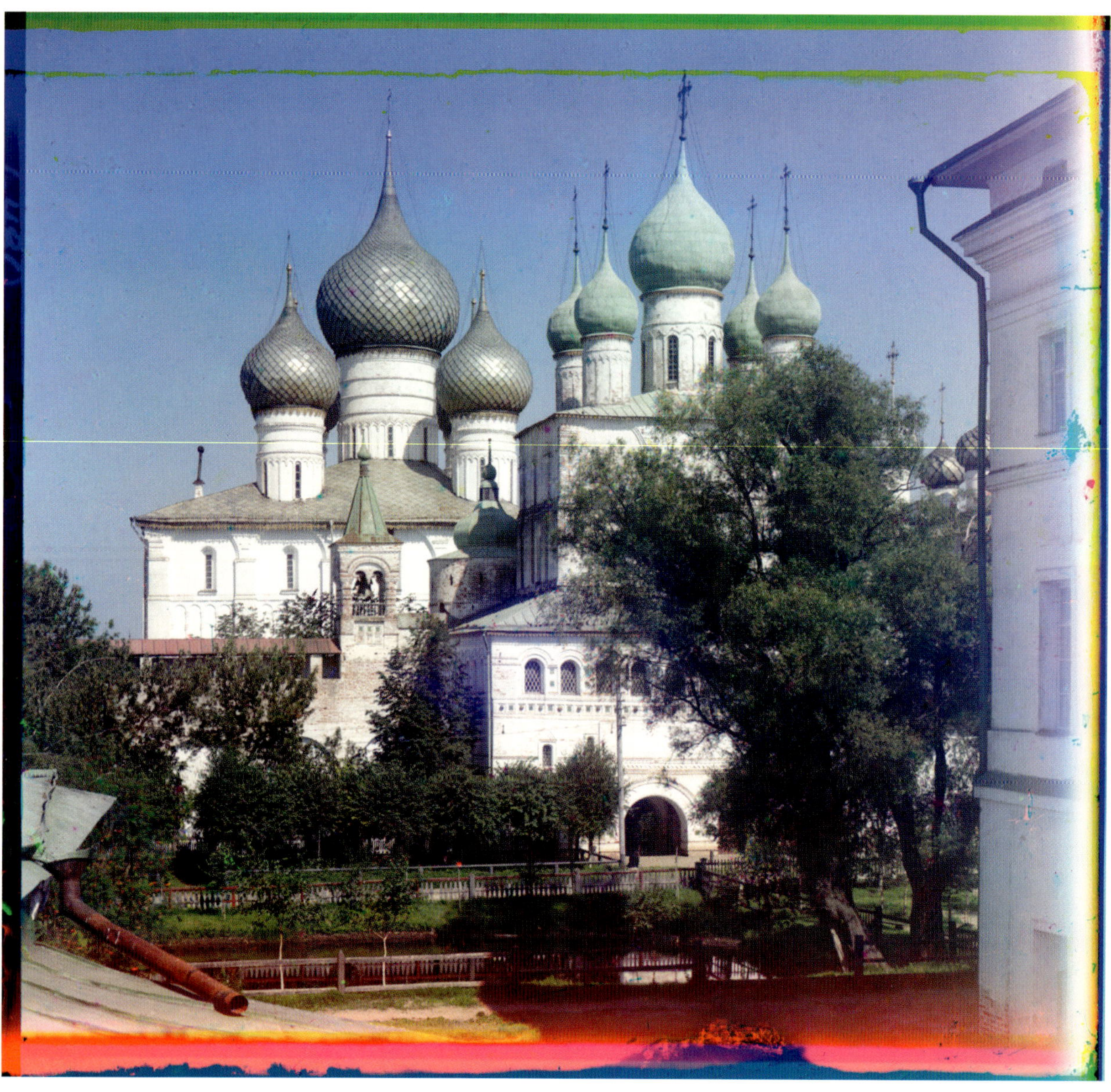

domed towers and the Church of the Resurrection (1670). Prokudin-Gorsky used his perch on the wall of the cathedral compound to record a softly lit north view in the late afternoon sun. My photographs of the north facade over several years show good preservation, although the color has varied according to the type of coating on the brick facades. The main difference is the postwar modification of the roofline to reproduce its presumed original configuration.

The Metropolitan's Court centers on the Red Chambers (1672–80), used as the residence of the prelate. Although Prokudin-Gorsky recorded the structure, the original nega-

ROSTOV Metropolitan's Court. Church of the Resurrection (*right*) and Cathedral of the Dormition. South view. PROKUDIN-GORSKY 21272. SUMMER 1911.

ROSTOV Metropolitan's Court. Church of the Resurrection (*right*) and Cathedral of the Dormition. South view. BRUMFIELD, OCTOBER 4, 1992.

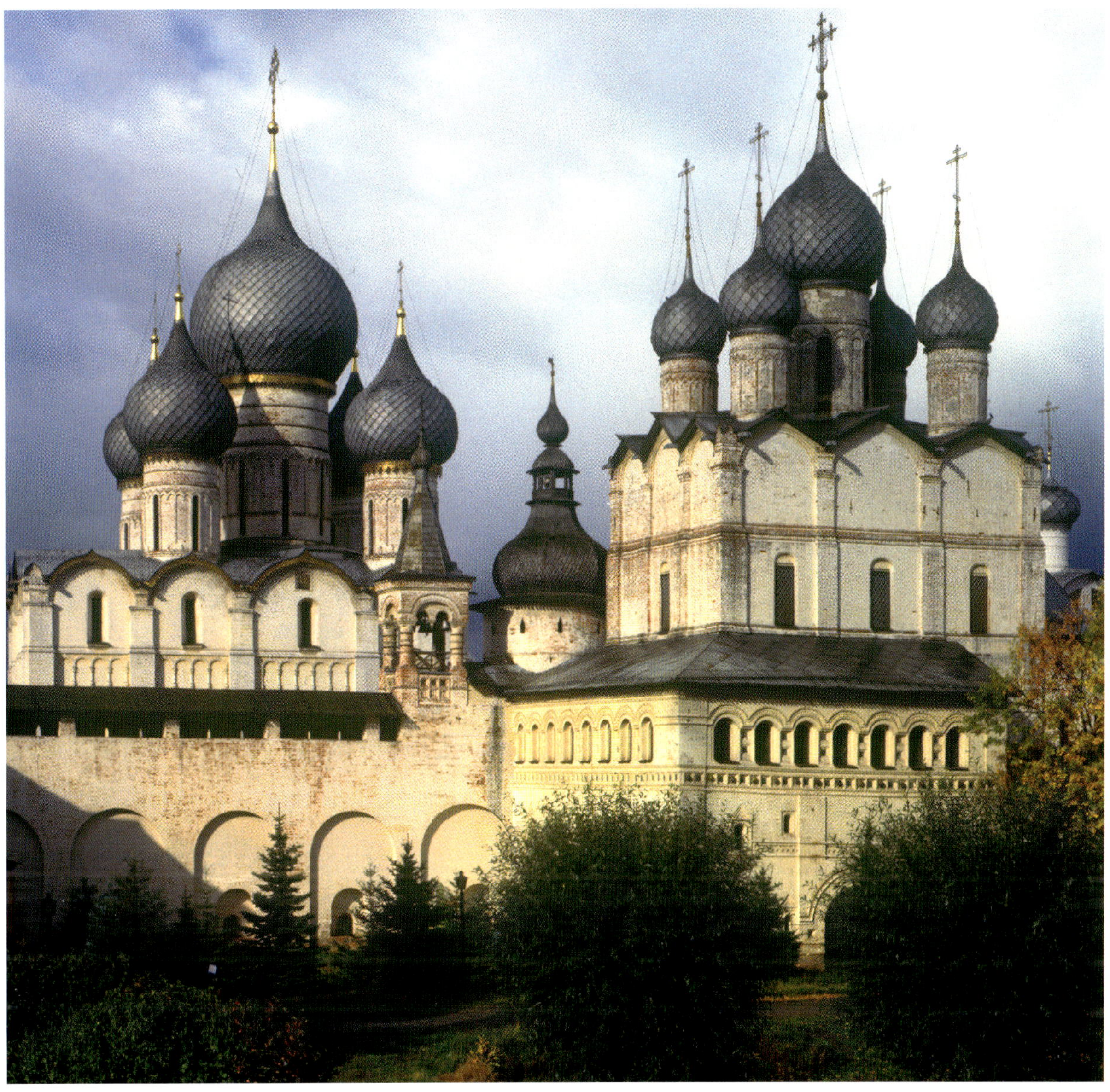

tive has not survived. Near the Red Chambers is the Church of the Miraculous Icon of the Savior on the Vestibule (*na seniakh*), built in 1675 above a provisions cellar. It served as the metropolitan's devotional chapel and for the performance of sacred music. By placing his camera in a meadow to the southeast of the walls, Prokudin-Gorsky was able to encompass not only the church but also the south kremlin wall with its decorative towers overlooking Lake Nero. My photograph shows the same ensemble from the southwest.

The interior of the church was covered with the richest of wall paintings in the kremlin ensemble. Although Prokudin-Gorsky's lens did not permit comprehensive, wide views, his detailed photographs provide essential

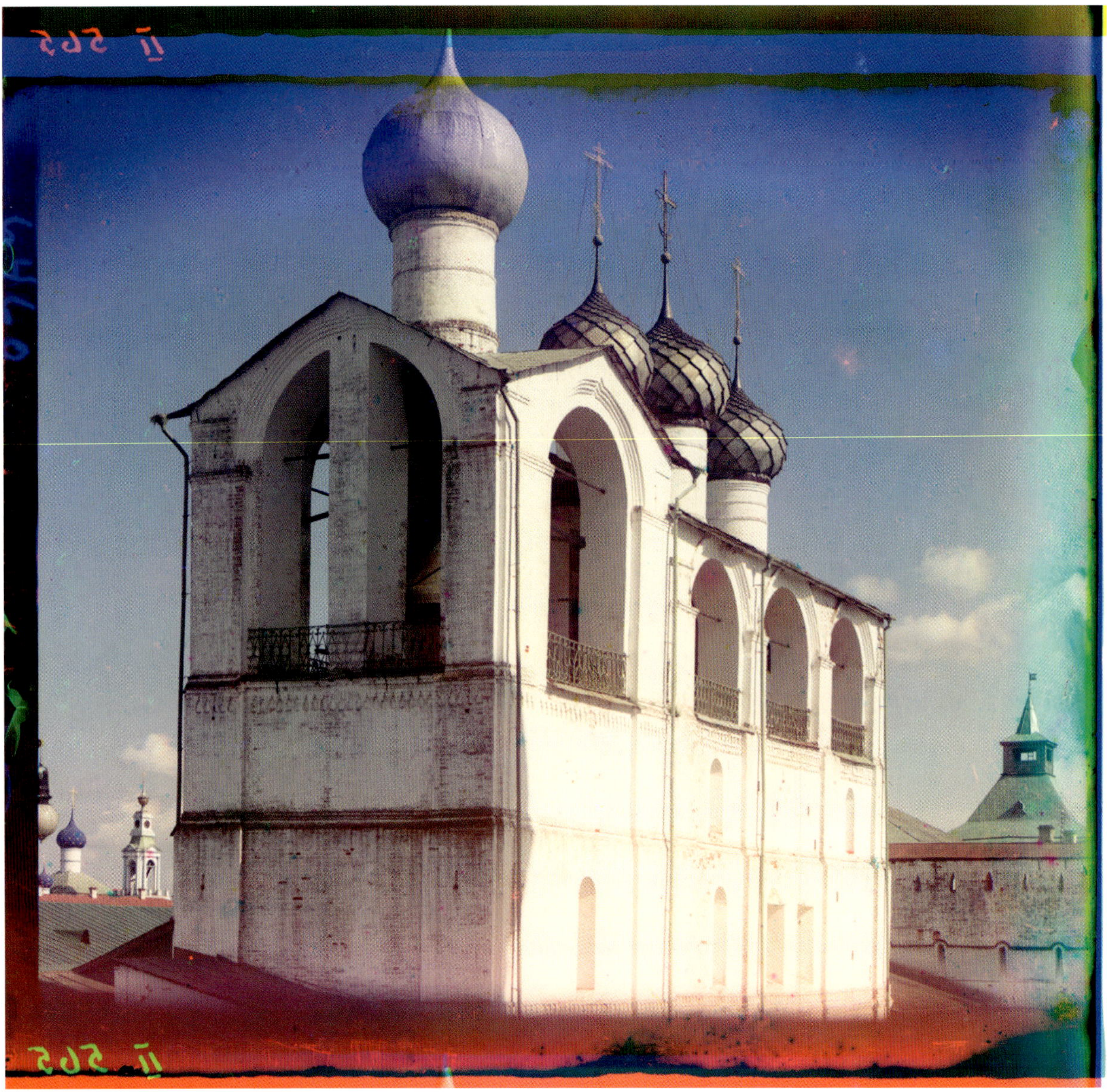

documentation of these paintings. Under complex natural lighting conditions, he took four interior photographs, including a spectacular Last Judgment with a serpent coiling down to hell. Taken with a wider lens in 1997, my photograph shows the same Last Judgment beautifully preserved in a larger view.

Dominating the center of the west kremlin wall is the second major gate church, dedicated to Saint John the Divine and flanked by large towers (1683). Only the contact print exists of Prokudin-Gorsky's northwest view of the church with the west wall and towers, perfectly lit in afternoon summer light. A comparison with my photograph from a similar perspective

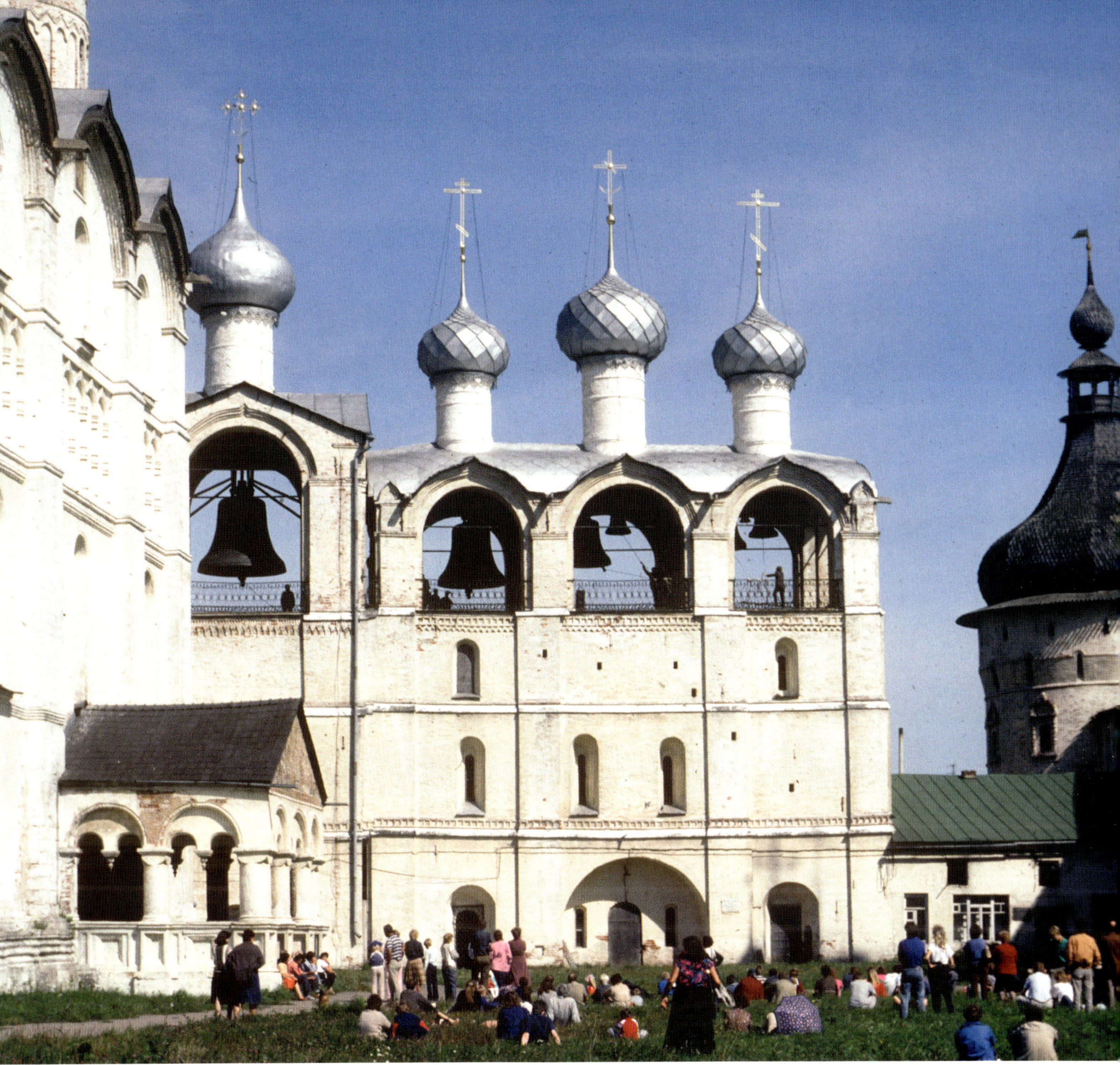

ROSTOV Metropolitan's Court. Bell tower with
Church of the Entry into Jerusalem. Northwest view.
PROKUDIN-GORSKY 21253. SUMMER 1911.

ROSTOV Metropolitan's Court. Cathedral of the Dormition (left), bell tower with Church of the Entry into Jerusalem. West view. Foreground: visitors during demonstration of bell ringing. BRUMFIELD, AUGUST 21, 1988.

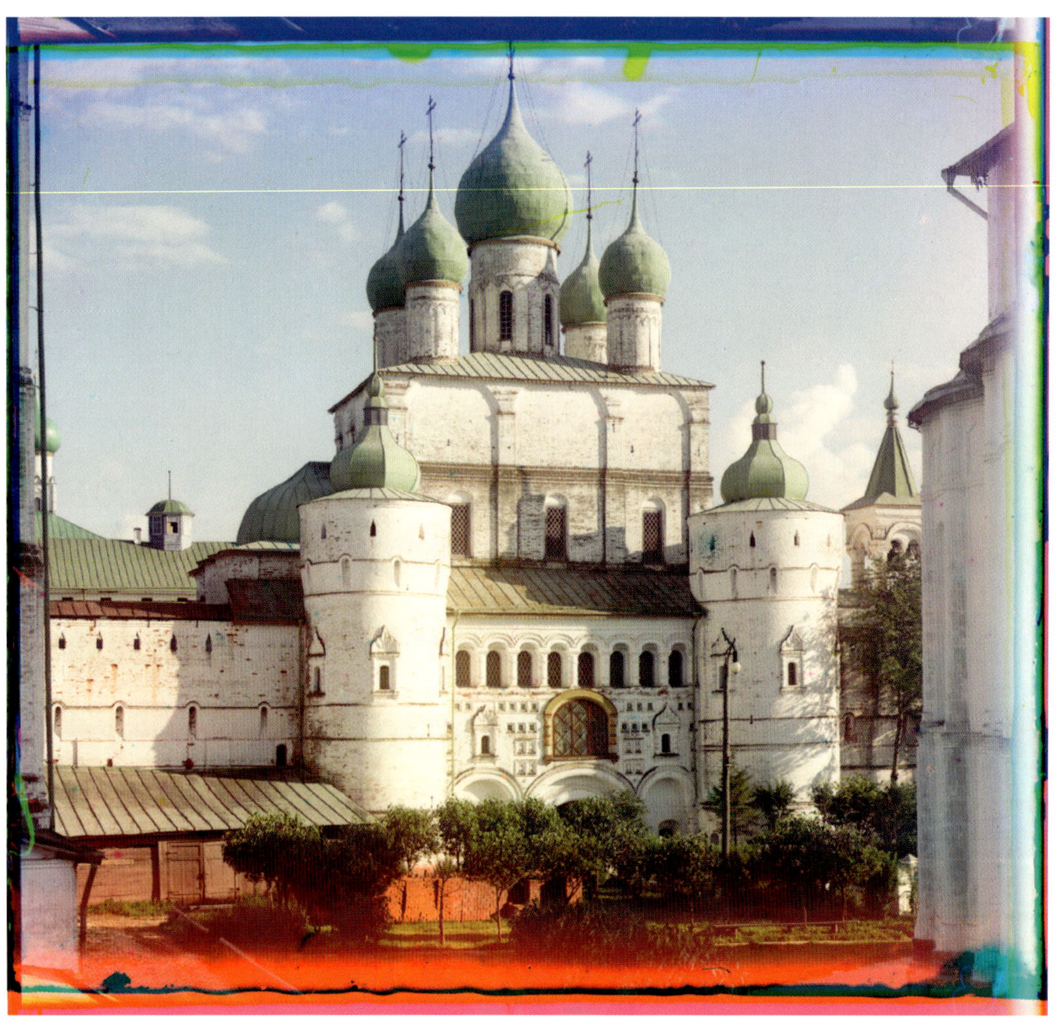

ROSTOV Metropolitan's Court. North Gate and Church of the Resurrection, northeast view. PROKUDIN-GORSKY 21268. SUMMER 1911.

ROSTOV Metropolitan's Court. North Gate and Church of the Resurrection, north view. BRUMFIELD. AUGUST 7, 1987.

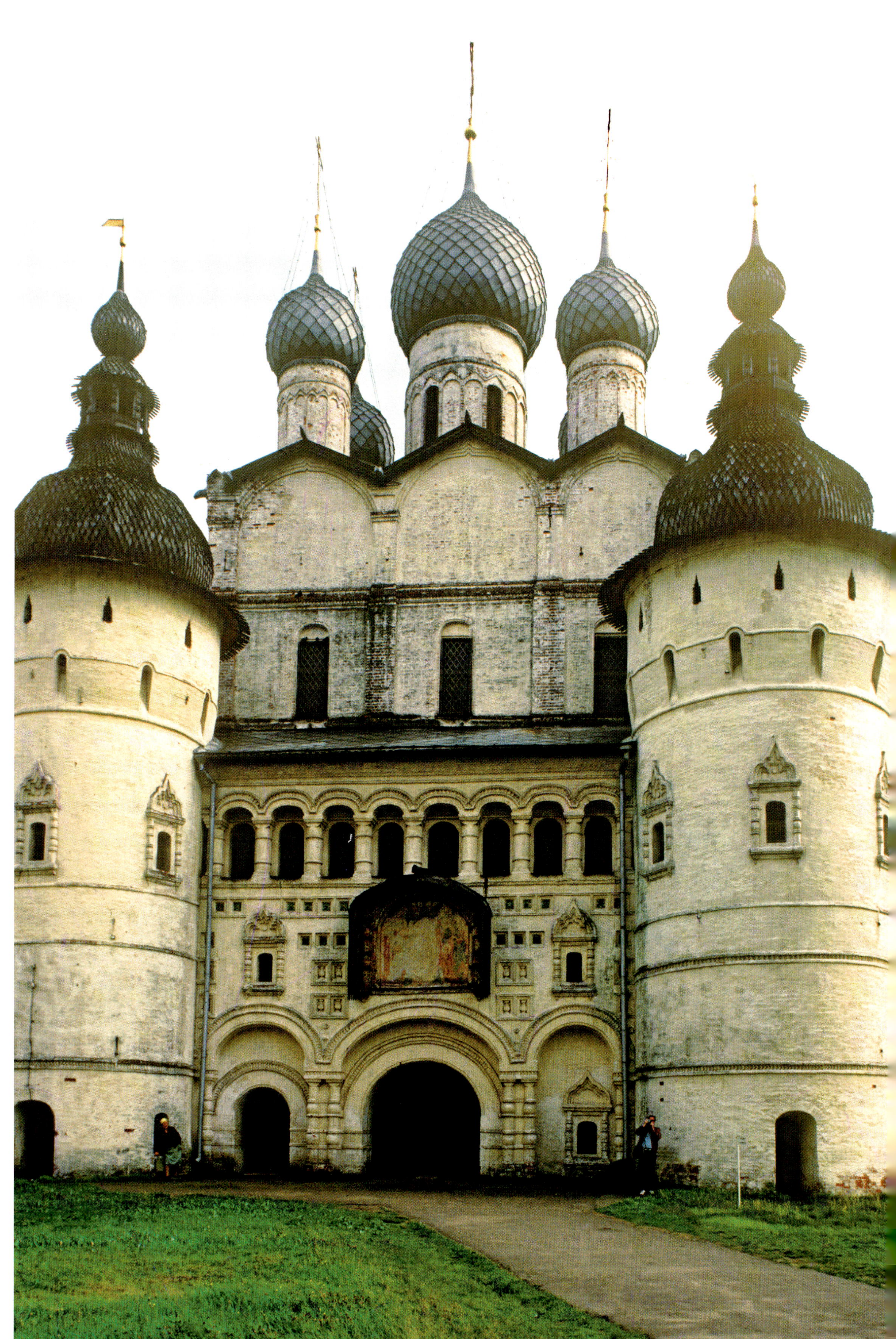

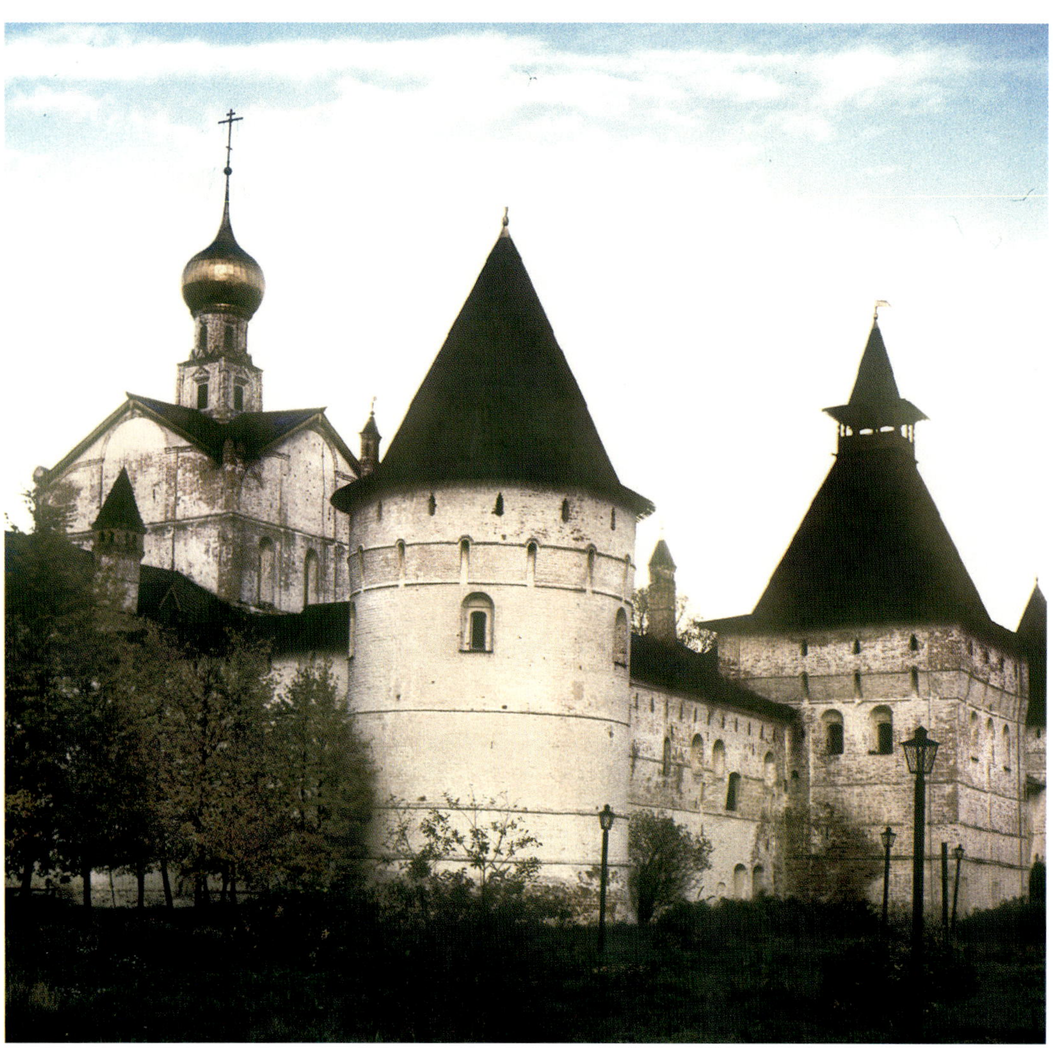

ROSTOV Metropolitan's Court. East wall, south-west corner with Church of the Miraculous Icon of the Savior. *Right*: Garden Tower. Southwest view. BRUMFIELD, OCTOBER 4, 1992.

ROSTOV Metropolitan's Court. East wall, south-east corner with Church of the Miraculous Icon of the Savior on the Vestibule. *Left*: Garden Tower. Southeast view. PROKUDIN-GORSKY 21320. SUMMER 1911.

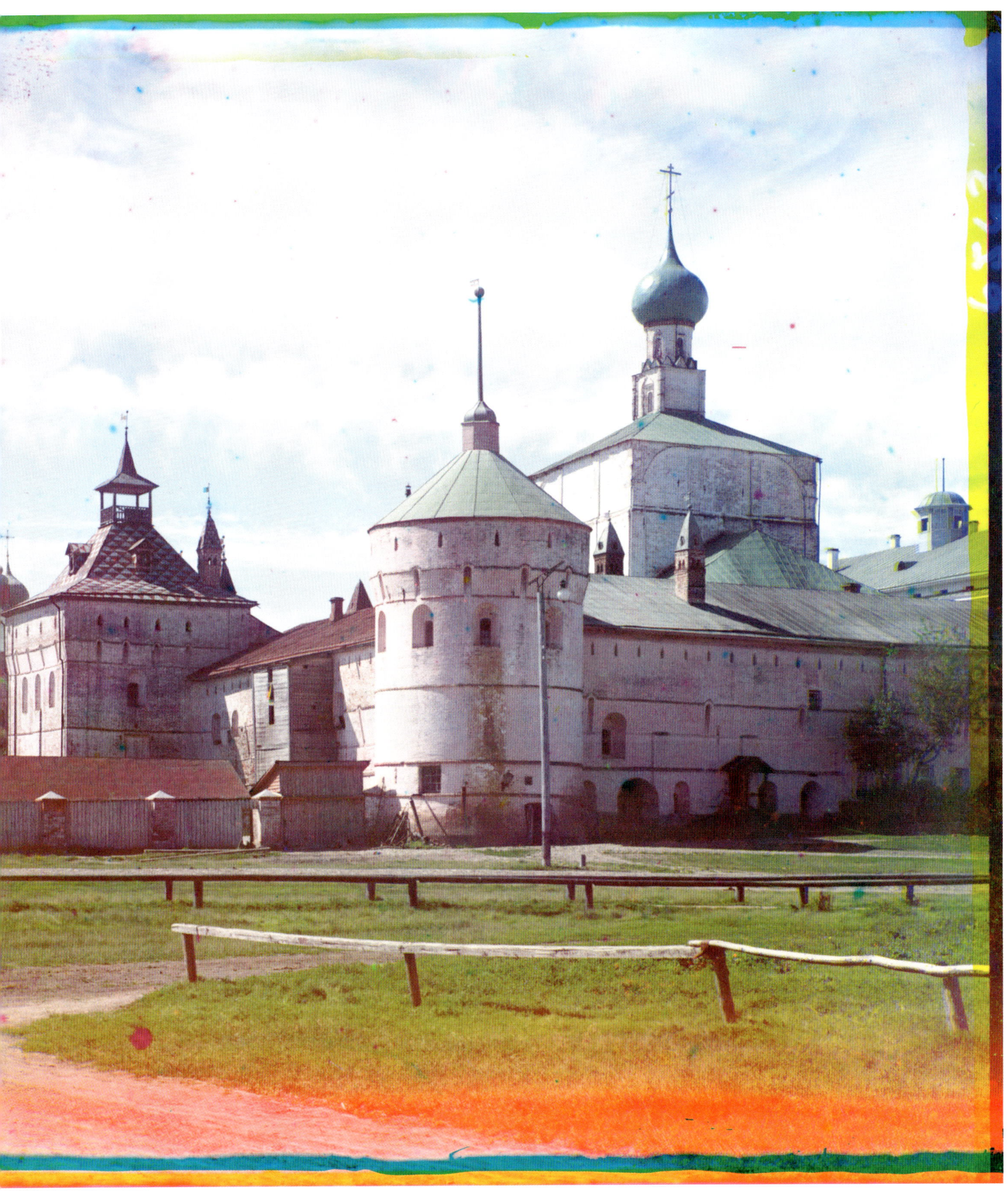

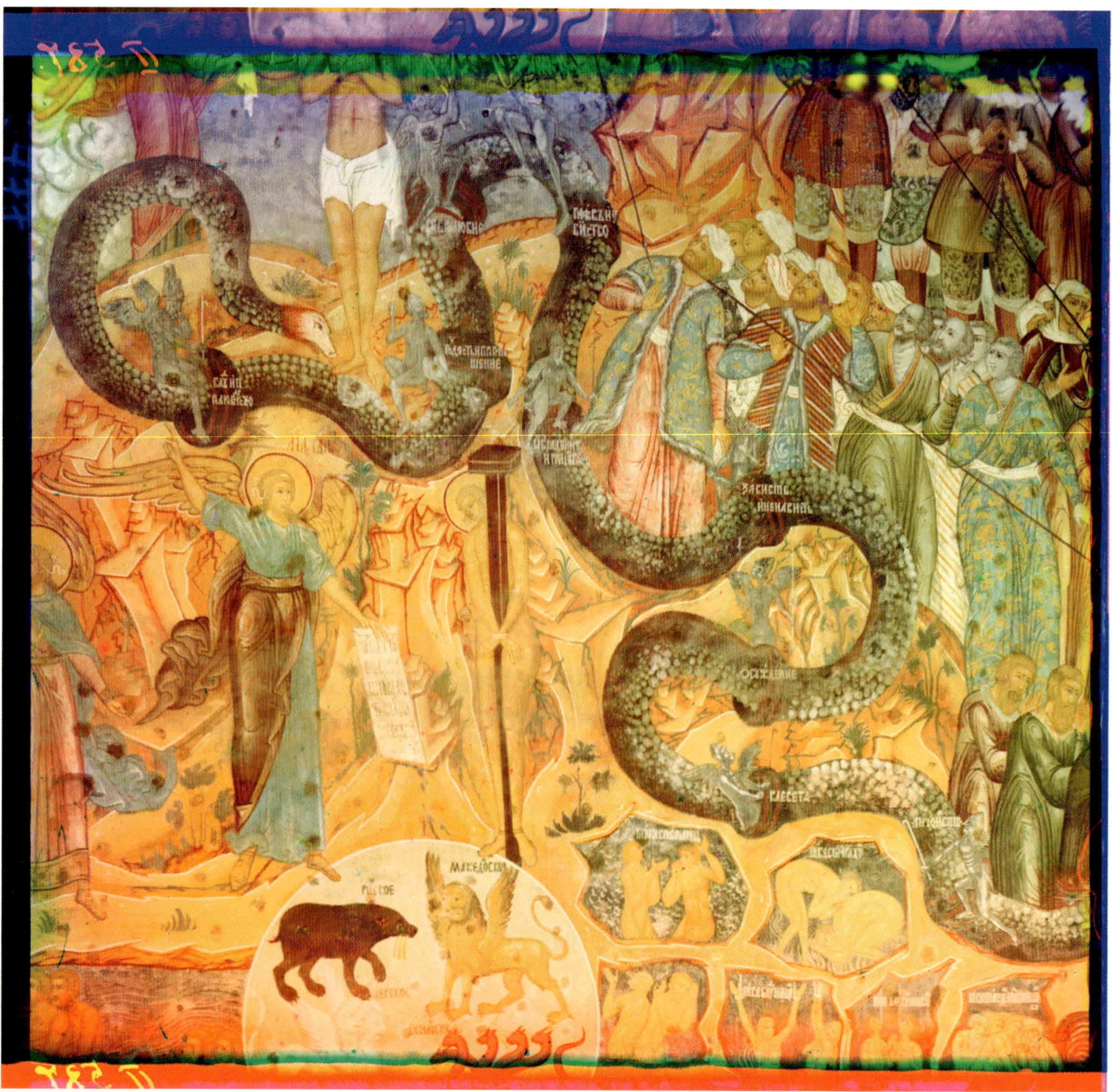

shows the result of a postwar modification of the roofline to return it to its presumed original configuration.

After the death of Jonah in 1690, work on the Rostov ensemble was continued by the Metropolitan Josephat, whose buildings included a church dedicated to the Hodegetria Icon of the Virgin. Completed in 1693 at the northwest corner of the kremlin walls, the Church of the Hodegetria Icon underwent modifications in the eighteenth century. Its basic form, however, remained, with a single cupola and an open gallery on the upper floor. The colorful diamond pattern on its exterior was apparently instigated by Afanasy Volkhovsky, bishop of Rostov from 1763 to 1776 and known to be fond of "Moscow baroque" ornamentalism. The diamond pattern was im-

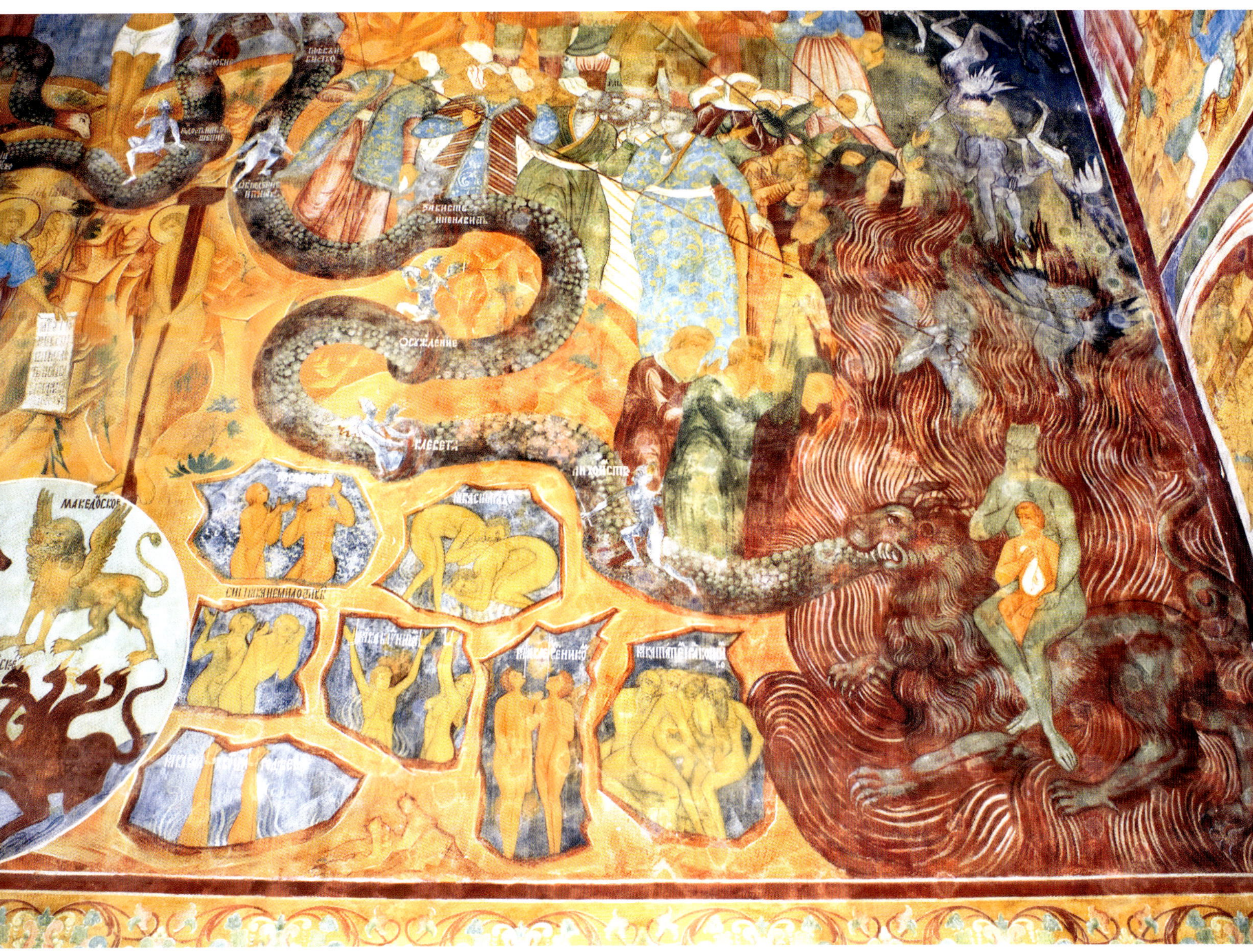

ROSTOV Metropolitan's Court, Church of the Miraculous Icon of the Savior on the Vestibule. Fresco of Last Judgment (the damned). PROKUDIN-GORSKY 21269. SUMMER 1911.

ROSTOV Metropolitan's Court, Church of the Miraculous Icon of the Savior. Fresco of Last Judgment (the damned). BRUMFIELD, JULY 5, 2019.

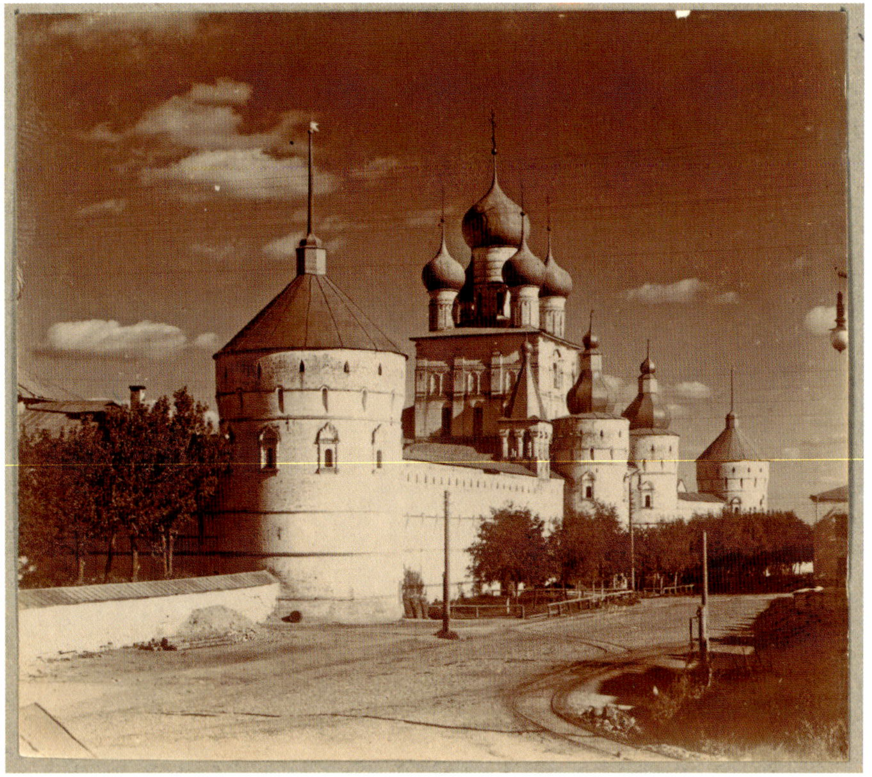

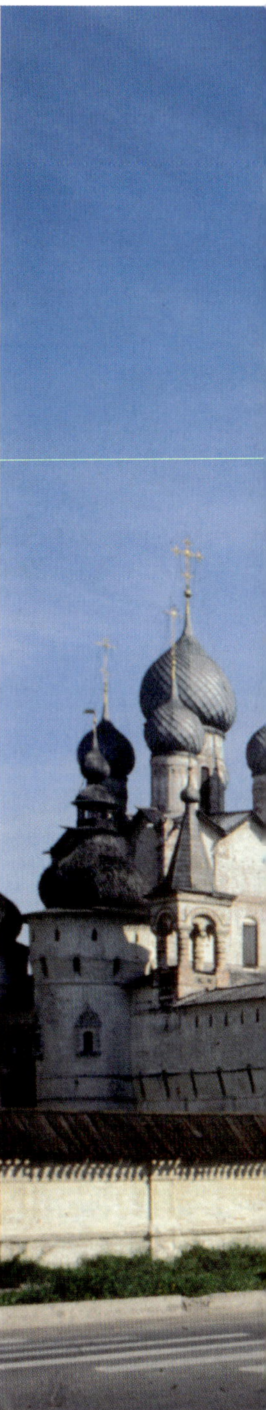

ported to Muscovy by Italian architects at the turn of the sixteenth century. Although the pattern had an enduring appeal in Russia, local builders rarely applied it in carved stone. It was easier to paint the facets on brick walls as a colorful trompe l'oeil. The surge of ornamentalism at the end of the seventeenth century saw a revival of this technique throughout Muscovy, from Kostroma to Sergiev Posad. A comparison of my photographs of the Hodegetria Church with those of Prokudin-Gorsky shows a notable difference: just beneath the roof you will notice the disappearance of a row of iconic wall paintings, with a large image of the Virgin of the Sign (Znamenie) in the middle. It is not clear when they were originally created, but such exterior paintings were usually effaced during the Soviet period.

After the death of Josephat in 1701, little else of note was built in the Rostov kremlin. Skilled masons throughout Russia were drafted into the construction of Saint Petersburg, founded in 1703. With the transfer of the regional metropolitanate from Rostov to Yaroslavl in 1787, the Rostov kremlin began to decay. In the late nineteenth century, however, Rostov merchants gathered funds to maintain the kremlin ensemble, and in 1883 the White Chamber, built as a banquet hall for the metropolitan, opened as a museum of church antiquities that was the predecessor of the current distinguished

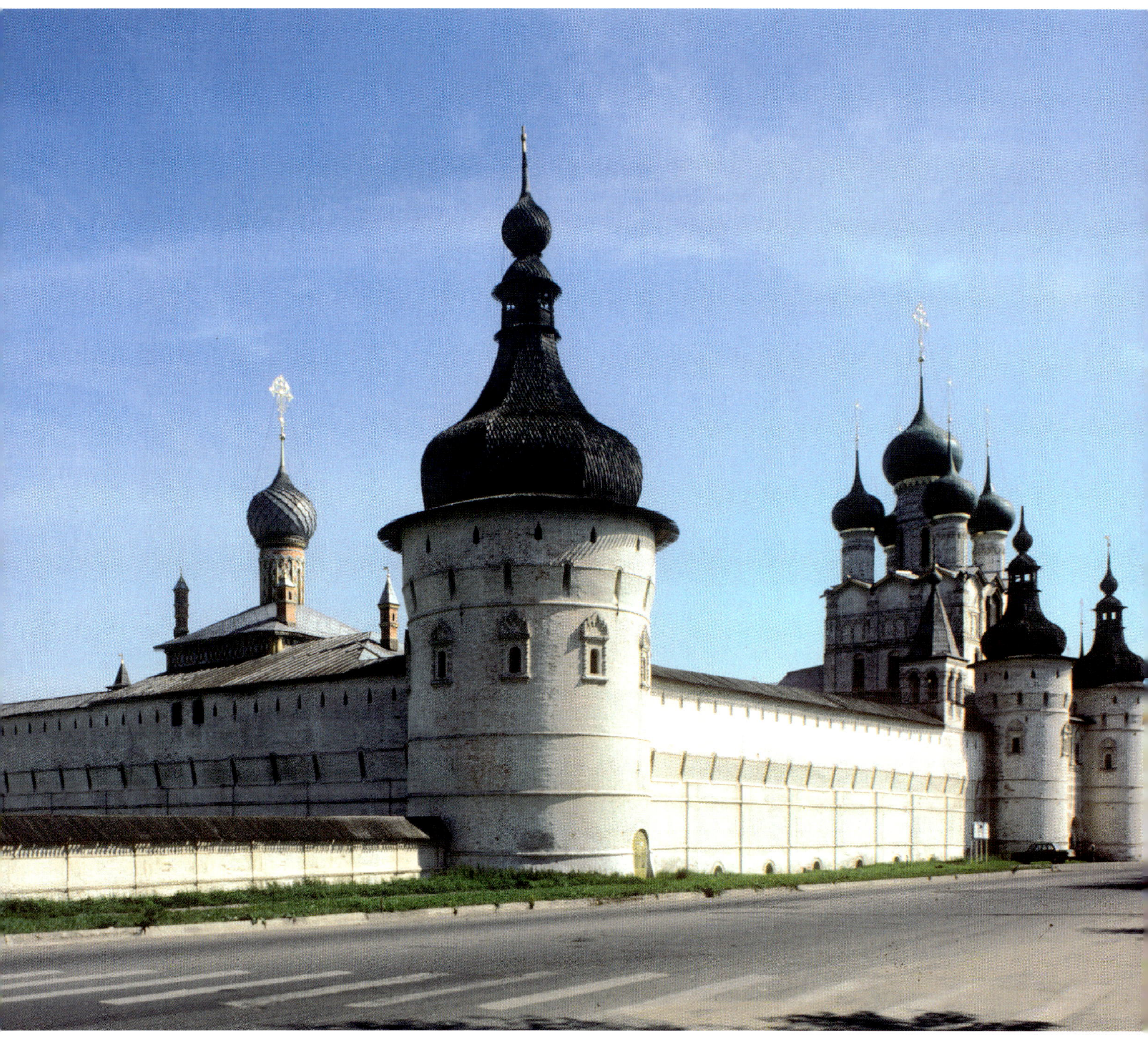

ROSTOV Metropolitan's Court. West wall with Church of Saint John the Divine. Northwest view. PROKUDIN-GORSKY 02566. SUMMER 1911.

ROSTOV Metropolitan's Court. Northwest view. *From left*: Church of the Resurrection, Church of the Hodegetria Icon, northwest corner tower, Church of Saint John the Divine over west gate with flanking towers. BRUMFIELD, AUGUST 21, 1988.

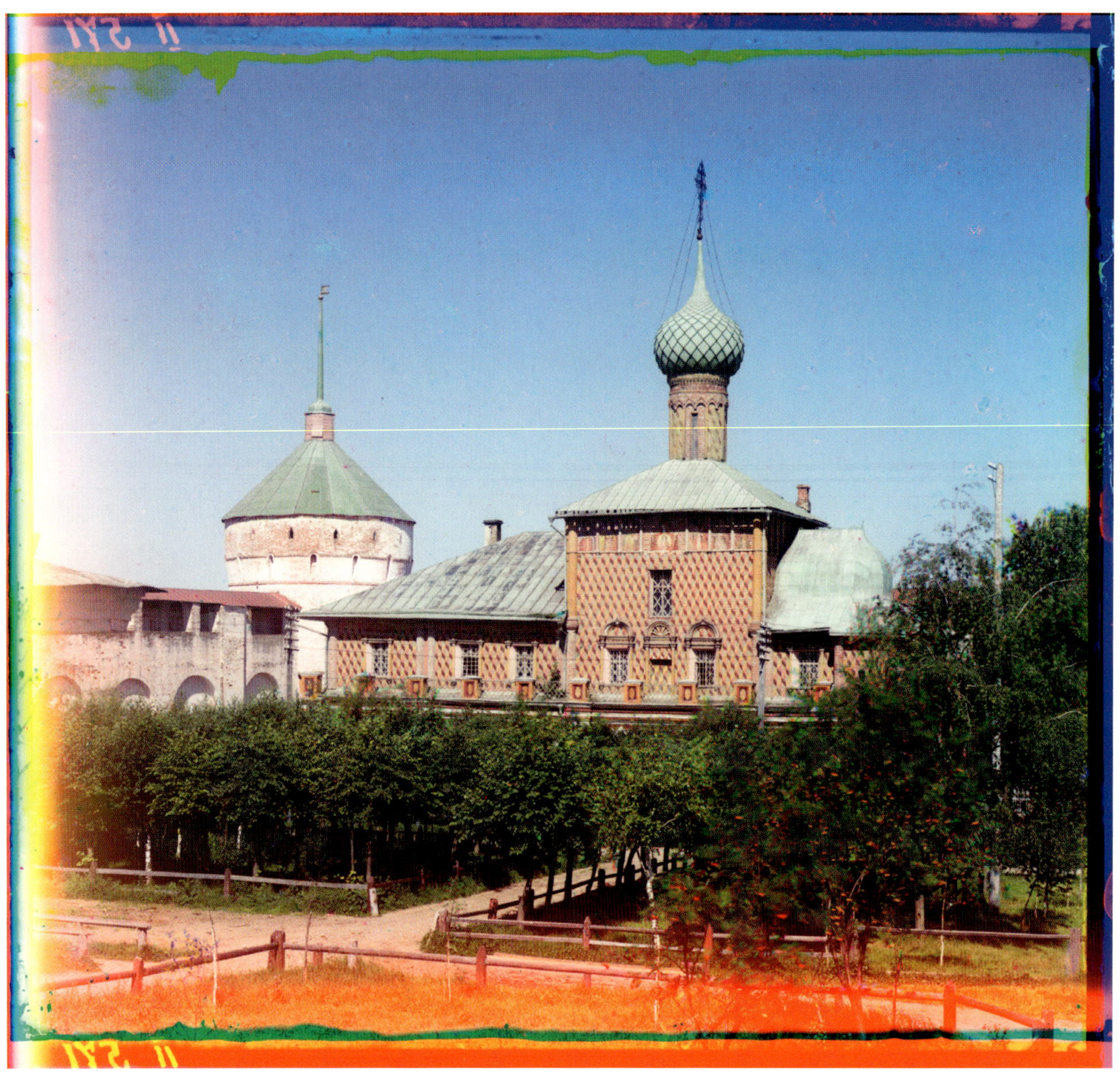

Rostov Kremlin Museum. Through local pride, Metropolitan Jonah's visionary project was preserved for Prokudin-Gorsky and subsequent generations.

In addition to the Archbishop's Court, Rostov has remnants of churches and monasteries that contribute to its imposing silhouette. To the west of the kremlin is the Saint James (Yakovlev) Monastery, founded in the fourteenth century and enlarged by Metropolitan Jonah. In 1709 Bishop Dimitry of Rostov, an energetic supporter of Peter the Great, was buried here, and the monastery became a pilgrimage site patronized by prominent families such as the Sheremetevs as well as by Emperor Alexander I. Most of its large churches were rebuilt in the early nineteenth century. Although the original negative is not extant, Prokudin-Gorsky's contact print gives an excellent

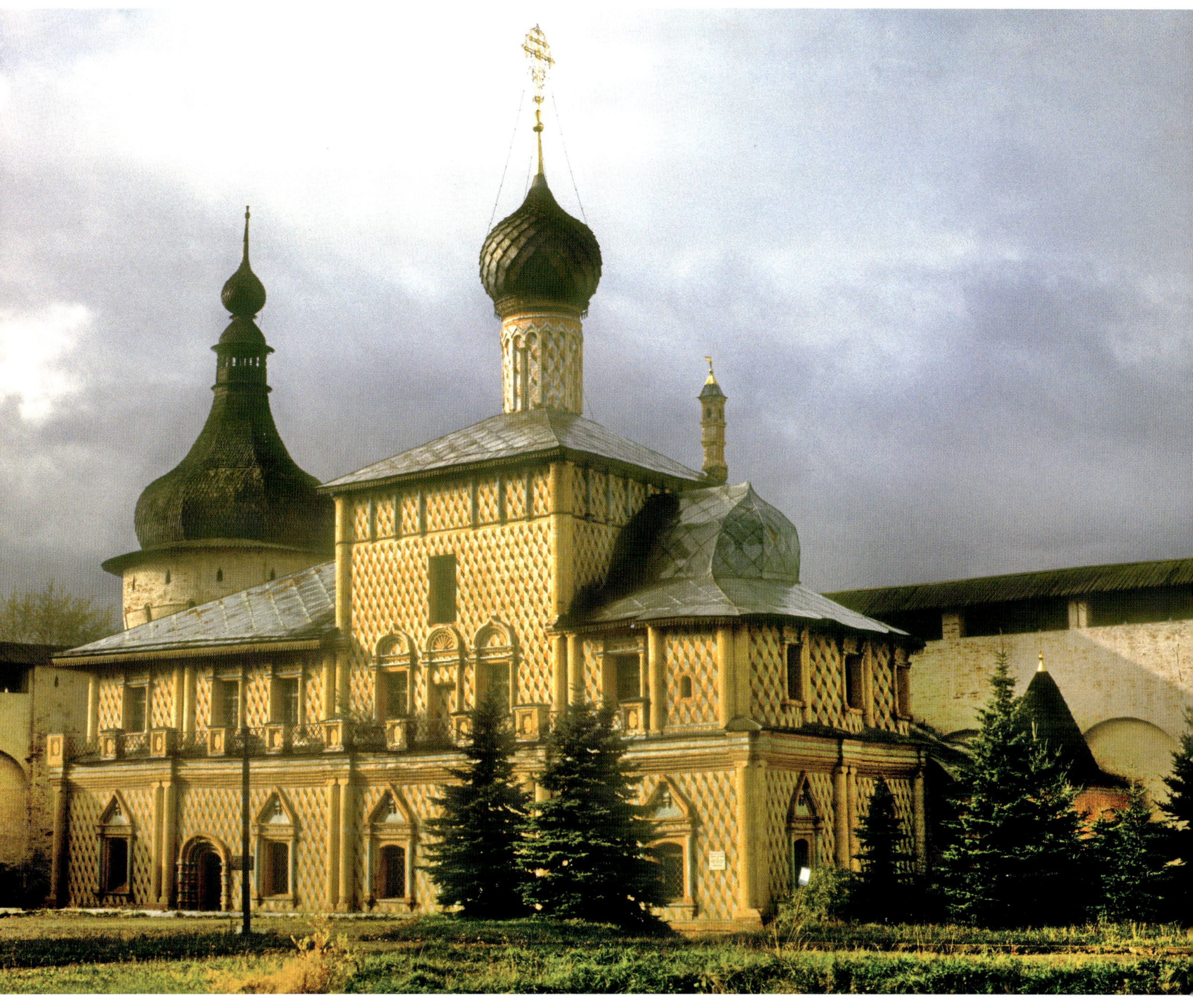

ROSTOV Metropolitan's Court. Church of the Hodegetria Icon of the Virgin and northwest corner tower. South view. PROKUDIN-GORSKY 21324. SUMMER 1911.

ROSTOV Metropolitan's Court. Church of the Hodegetria Icon of the Virgin and northwest corner tower. South view. BRUMFIELD, OCTOBER 4, 1992.

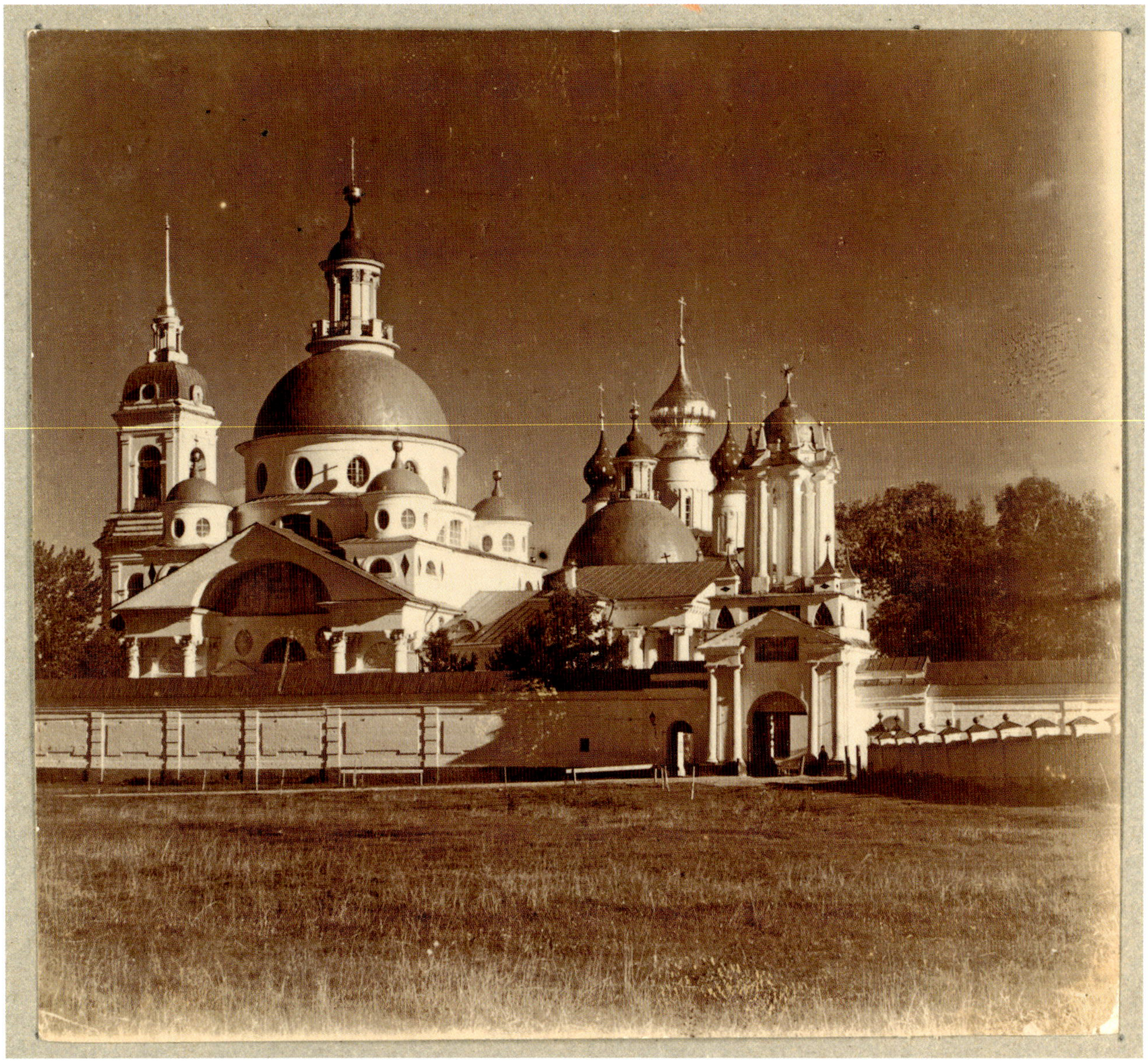

view of the ensemble in morning light. Within the monastery is the Cathedral of Conception of Saint Anne, built in 1686 and originally dedicated to the Trinity. In 1725 a Chapel of Saint Anne was added to the north facade, and in 1754 the main altar was dedicated to Saint Anne. In 1709 Metropolitan Dimitry of Rostov, a noted author of religious texts, was buried in the cathedral. My photograph of the ensemble exterior gives the appearance of preservation; the interiors were vandalized during the Soviet period.

In 1953 a storm caused extensive damage to Rostov and destroyed most of the church cupolas. Restoration experts gathered support and the kremlin was repaired under the supervision of Vladimir Banige, one of the leading specialists in the history of Rostov. In 1970 Rostov was designated a histori-

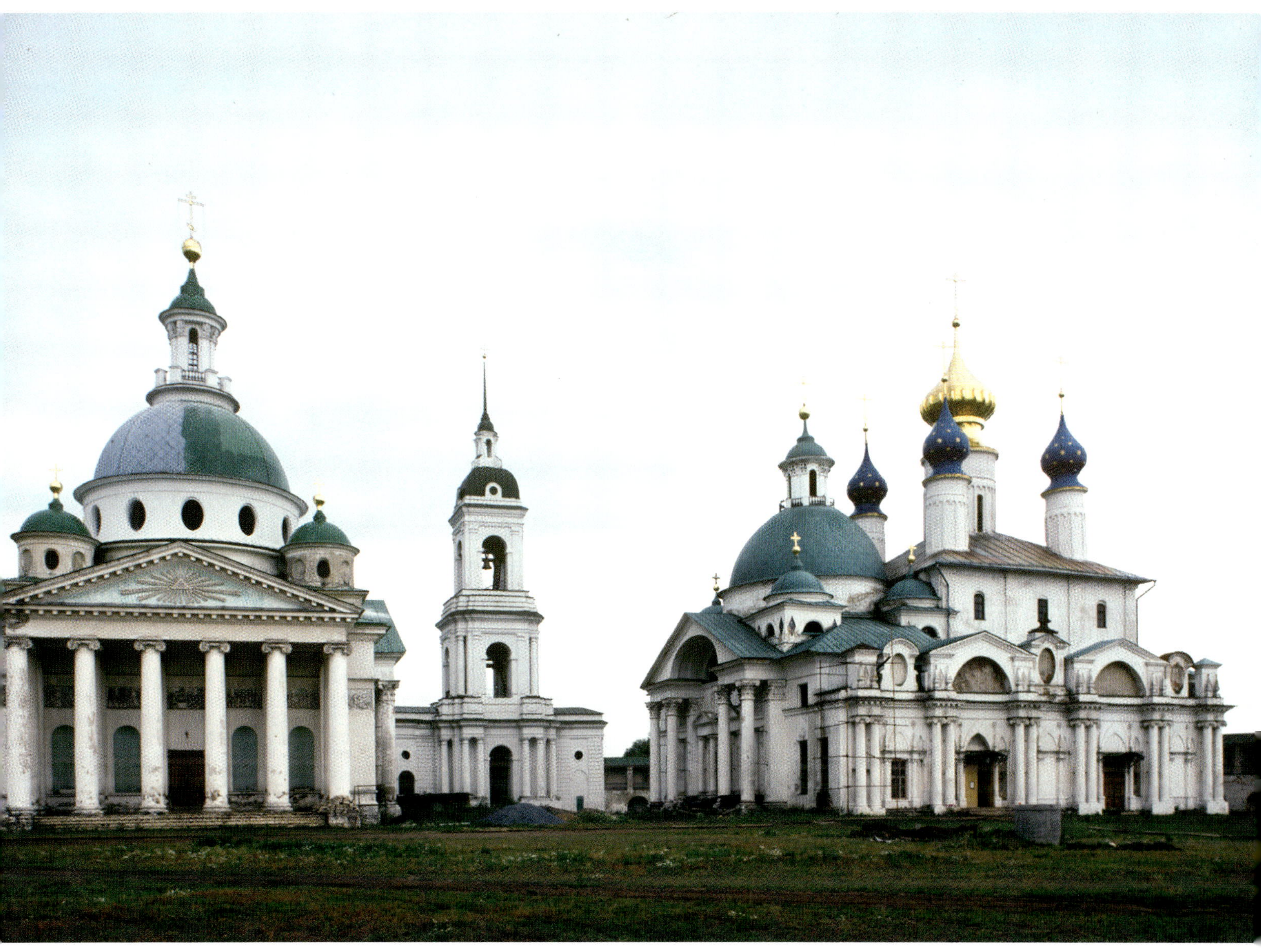

ROSTOV Savior-Saint James Monastery. South view. *From left*: bell tower, Cathedral of Saint Dmitry of Rostov, Church of Saint James and Cathedral of the Conception of Saint Anne. PROKUDIN-GORSKY 02578. SUMMER 1911.

ROSTOV Savior-Saint James Monastery. West view. *From left*: Cathedral of Saint Dmitry of Rostov, bell tower, Church of Saint James and Cathedral of the Conception of Saint Anne (attached). BRUMFIELD, AUGUST 5, 1995.

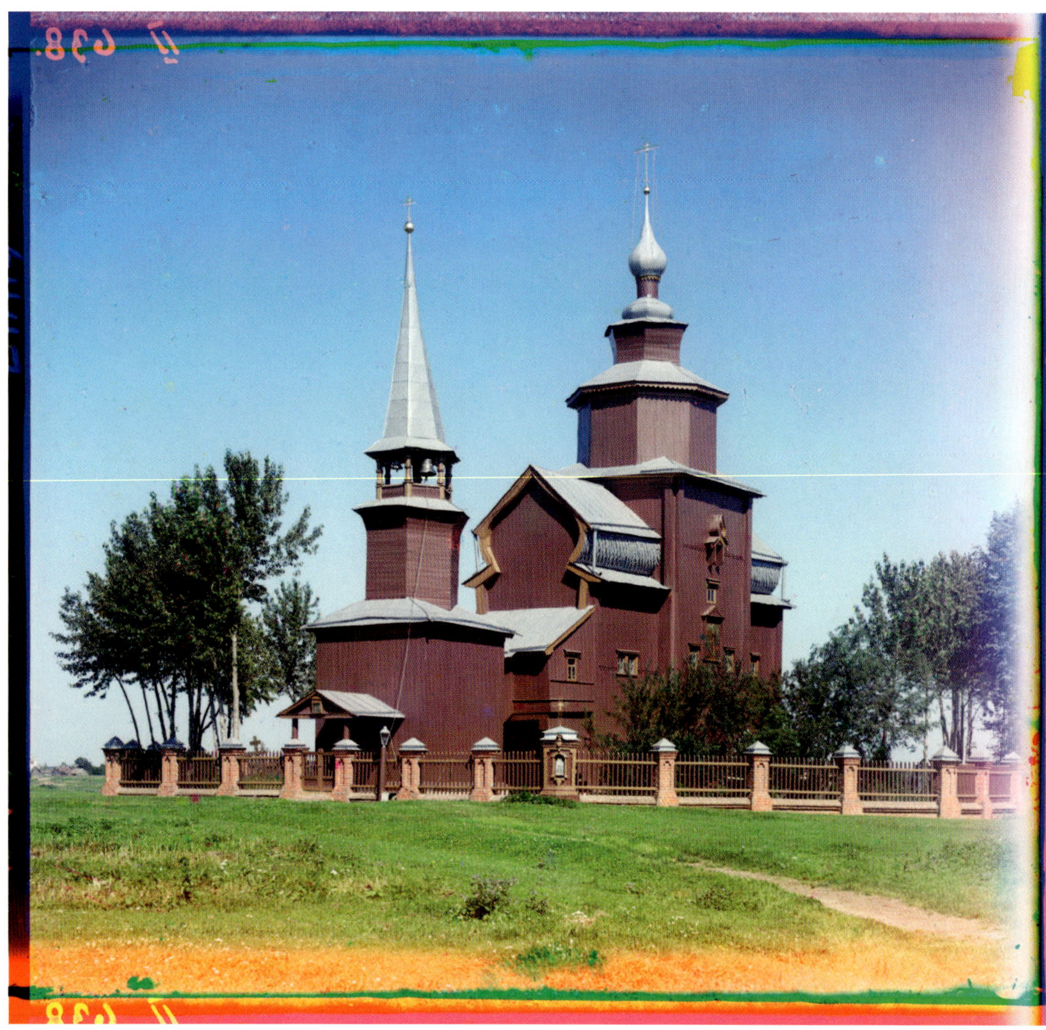

cal preserve with the idea of creating a tourist destination such as Suzdal. Although those plans did not materialize on the envisioned scale, the combined forces of the Orthodox Church and the Rostov Kremlin Museum have maintained much of the architectural legacy.

On the outskirts of Rostov is the village of Bogoslov, located on the small Ishnia River and site of the wooden Church of Saint John the Divine (in Russian "Bogoslov"). The church was built of logs in 1687–89 by Gerasim, archimandrite (abbot) of the Saint Avraamii-Epiphany Monastery, to commemorate a vision of Saint John that appeared to Saint Avraamii at the site. The tall main structure, covered with plank siding and painted dark red, culminates in two octagonal tiers and a cupola. Prokudin-Gorsky's southwest

BOGOSLOV Church of Saint John the Divine on Ishnya, southwest view. PROKUDIN-GORSKY 21240. SUMMER 1911.

BOGOSLOV Church of Saint John the Divine on Ishnya, southwest view. BRUMFIELD, MAY 21, 1996.

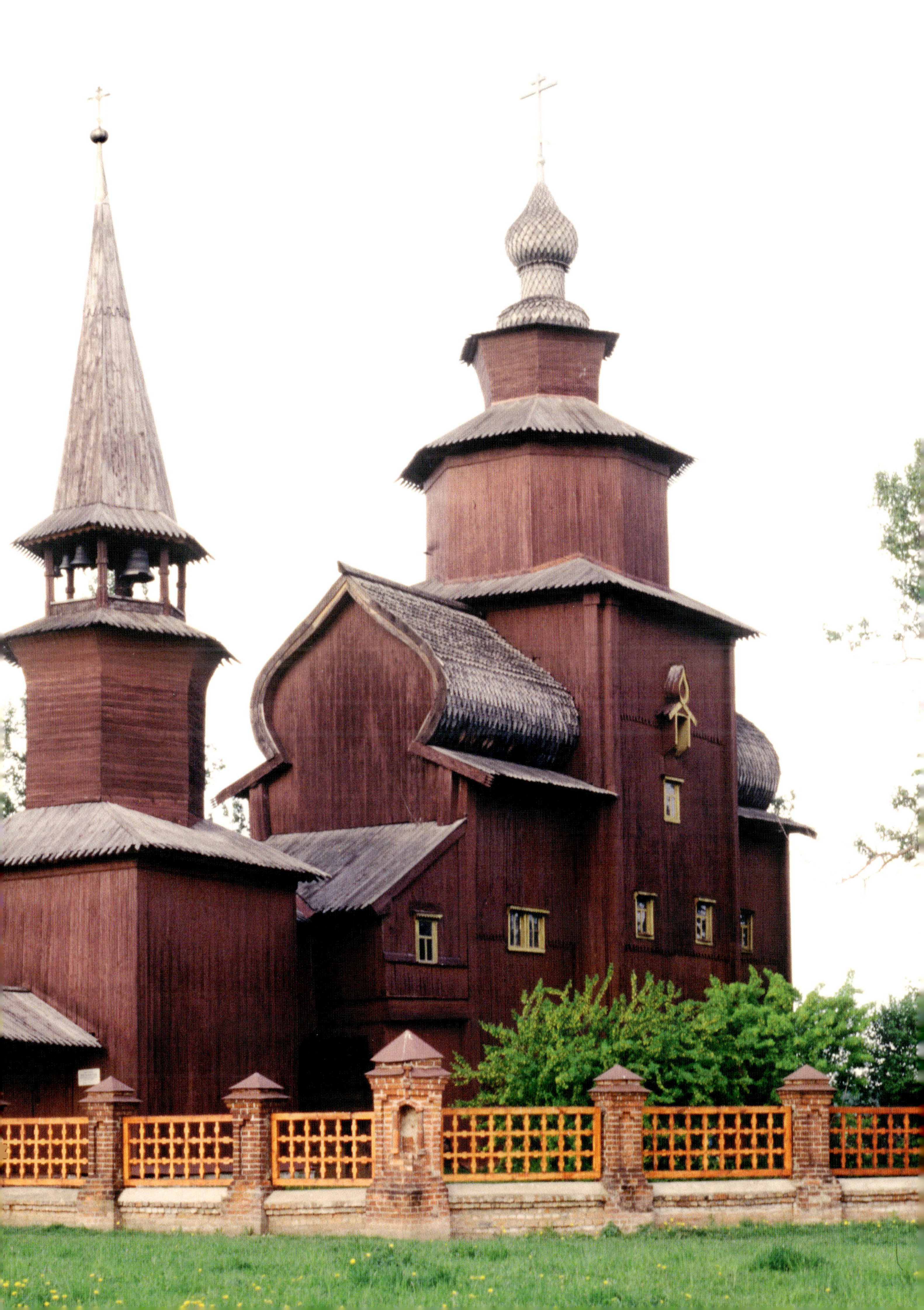

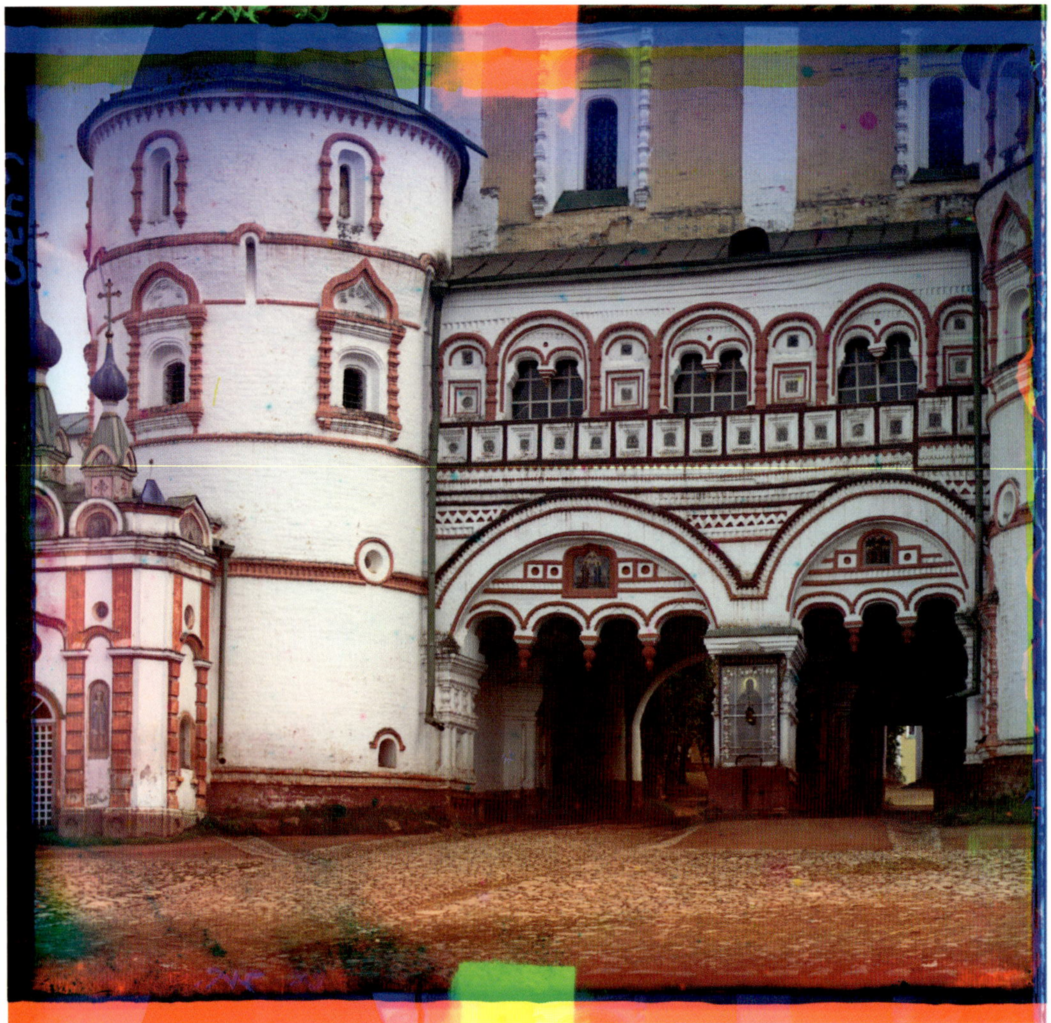

view shows the attached refectory with a covered staircase descending to the entrance structure, which supports the bell tower. To the east is a symmetrical extension, or apse, containing the altar. Each extension has a curved roof clad with "fishscale" shingles. Because of difficulties in maintaining the shingles, the upper part was protected with a plank roof. My photograph shows the exterior preserved in its essentials. The interior, which Prokudin-Gorsky also photographed, was emptied in the Soviet period and the Royal Gate of the icon screen was taken to the Rostov Kremlin Museum.

A significant part of Prokudin-Gorsky's work in Yaroslavl Province during the summer of 1911 occurred in the small market town of Borisoglebsky, location of the Mon-

BORISOGLEBSKY Rostov Monastery of Saints Boris and Gleb. North Gate with Church of the Purification. North view. PROKUDIN-GORSKY 21262. SUMMER 1911.

BORISOGLEBSKY Rostov Monastery of Saints Boris and Gleb. North Gate with Church of the Purification. North view. BRUMFIELD, OCTOBER 4, 1992.

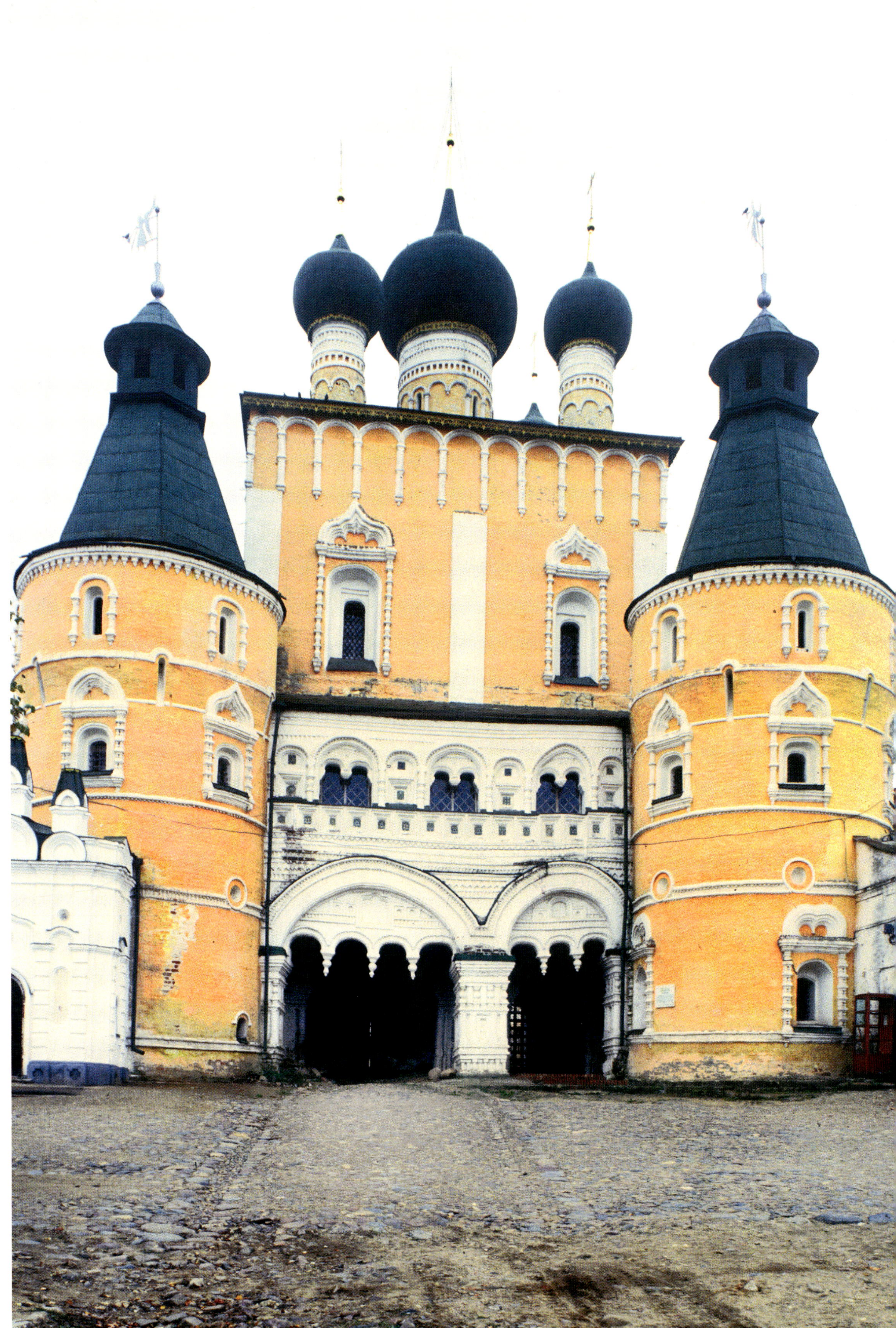

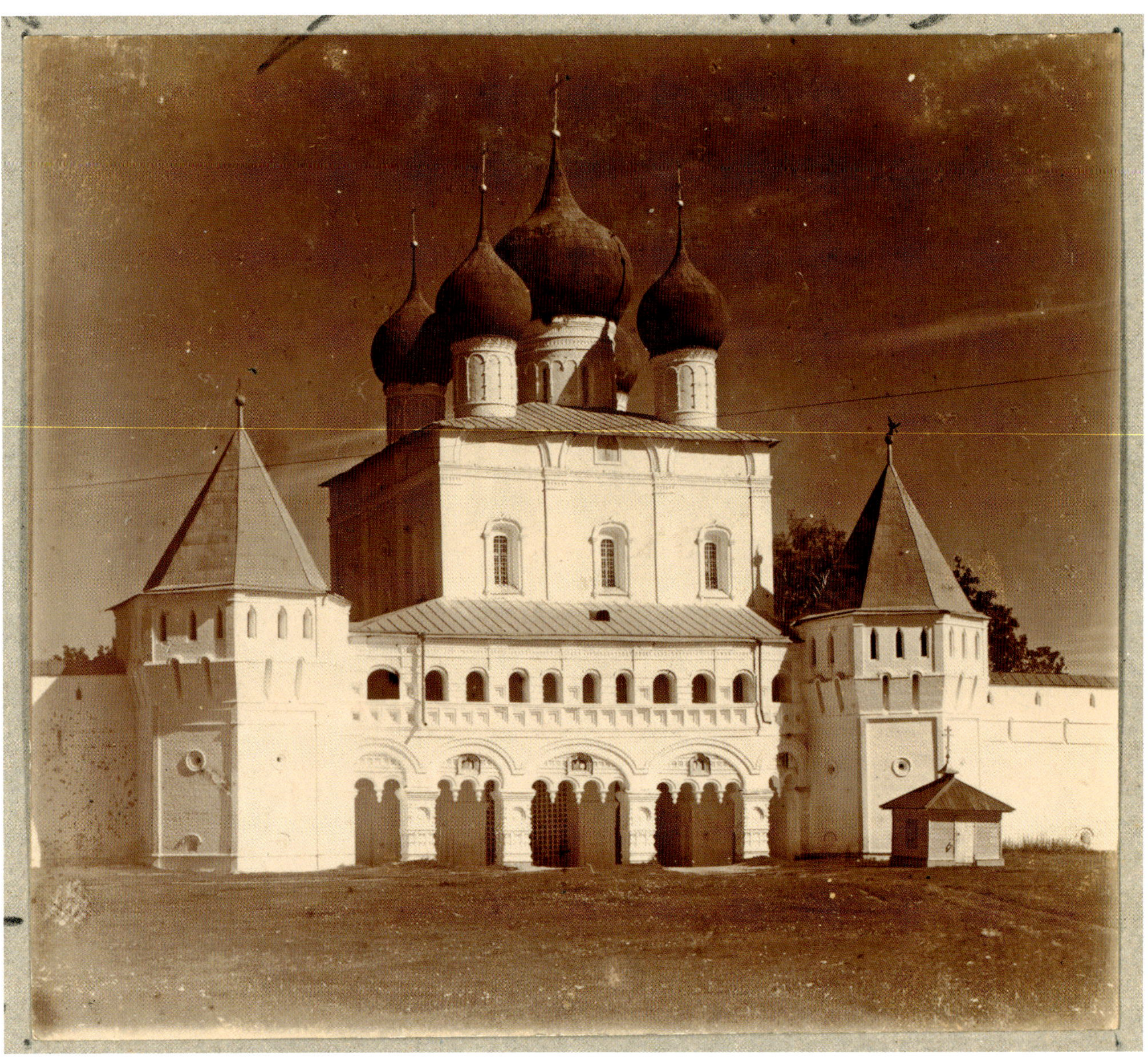

astery of Saints Boris and Gleb. Founded in 1363 with the blessing of Saint Sergius of Radonezh, the avatar of Muscovite monasticism, the monastery was favored by Muscovy's rulers, including tsars Ivan III, Vasily III, and Ivan IV (the Terrible). In the late seventeenth century, a building campaign supported by Metropolitan Jonah Sysoevich included the expansion of its massive brick walls. Among Prokudin-Gorsky's several photographs are close views of the gates in the north wall, with flanking chapels and round towers. The decorative details, including window surrounds and pendants (*girki*) within the gate arches, are outlined in red

BORISOGLEBSKY Rostov Monastery of Saints Boris and Gleb. South Gate with Church of Saint Sergius Radonezh. South view. PROKUDIN-GORSKY 02580. SUMMER 1911.

BORISOGLEBSKY Rostov Monastery of Saints Boris and Gleb. South Gate and wall with Church of Saint Sergius Radonezh. Southeast view. BRUMFIELD, OCTOBER 4, 1992.

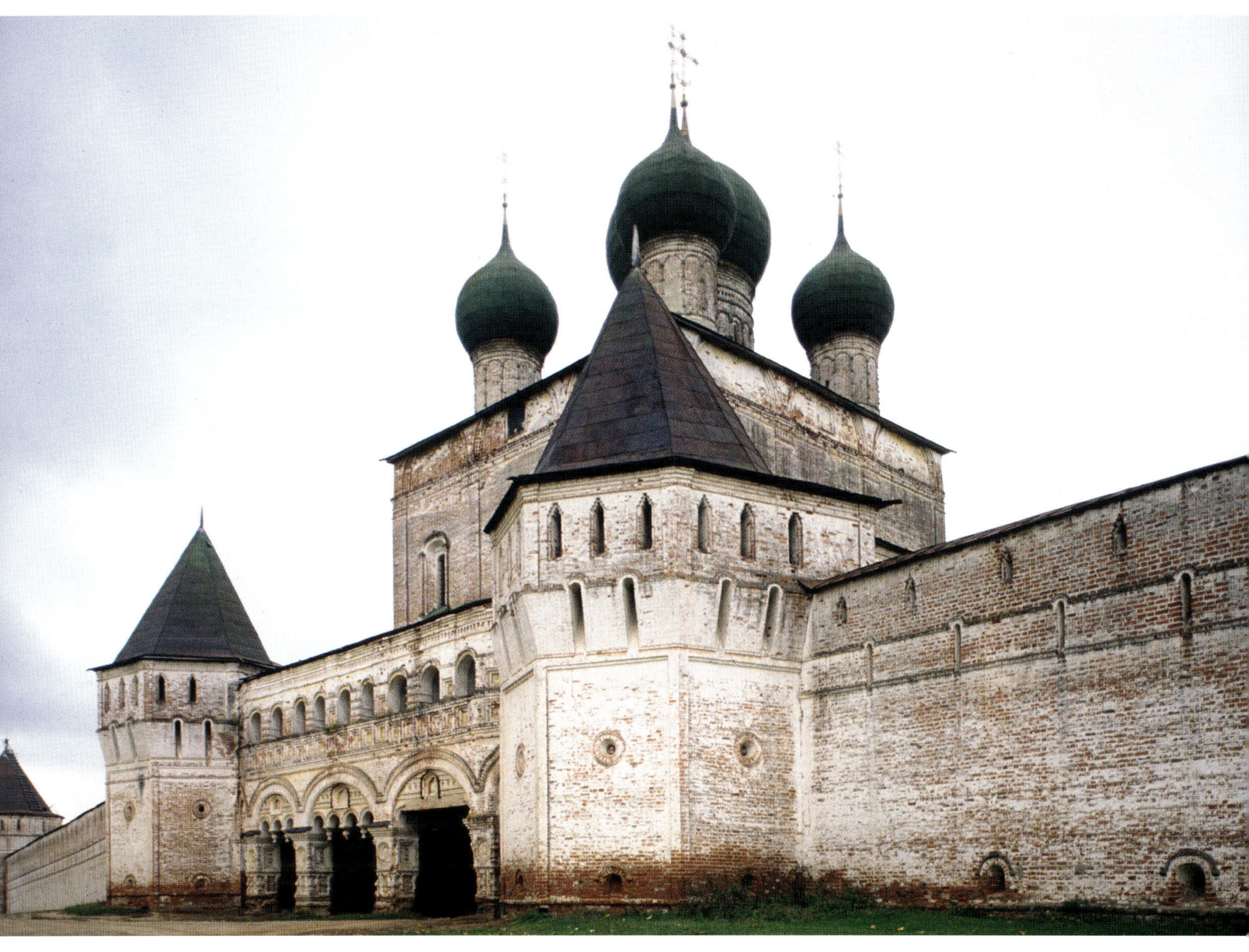

paint. Visible at the top is the lower part of the north facade of the Church of the Purification over North (or Water) Gates. The date usually given for this distinctive structure is 1680, but recent sources place it a decade later. Although the town market lay in the shadow of the gate church, Prokudin-Gorsky found a time when the space, with its cobbled pavement, was empty. My photograph gives a wider view of the structure. Just beyond the North Gate, the monastery center is occupied by the Cathedral of Saints Boris and Gleb, whose cuboid archaic form—constructed in 1522–24 but subsequently much modified—is the oldest in the entire ensemble.

The monastery's south wall is centered on the Gate Church of Saint Sergius of Radonezh, for which we have only Prokudin-Gorsky's contact print.

Although similar in size and form to its counterpart over the North Gate, the South Gate church has less of the imposing frame given to the Church of the Purification over the North Gate, which faced the market square. Nonetheless, the Church of Saint Sergius over South Gate towered above the main road from Rostov to Uglich and could be seen by travelers at a great distance. My photograph takes a close view of the long-abandoned church.

The monuments surveyed in this section reveal architectural traditions formed from twelfth-century Vladimir to eighteenth-century Rostov. From a temporal perspective, this group represents the broadest range of Prokudin-Gorsky's photographs of Russian architecture and the most varied range of architectural styles. Indeed, these traditions extended to the northeast of Rostov in the magnificent seventeenth-century churches of Yaroslavl and Kostroma. Those cities, however, belong to another journey, along the Volga River. Having defined the center, it is now appropriate to turn to the western periphery—Smolensk—and from there to move back across the Russian Empire, from Europe to Asia.

From Smolensk Southward to Ryazan

The towns that Sergey Prokudin-Gorsky photographed to the west of Moscow were primarily part of a project to document sites linked to the centenary of the 1812 Napoleonic campaign against Russia. The extensive series of photographs that he took in Smolensk during the summer of 1911 are among the crowning achievements of his work in architectural documentation. Although Prokudin-Gorsky's views depict a bucolic landscape covered with verdure, Smolensk witnessed rapid urban growth at the turn of the twentieth century. Russia's general economic advance during this period had an impact on the city, and by the time of Prokudin-Gorsky's visit it had become an important railroad hub with a population of some seventy thousand.

Located on the upper reaches of the Dnieper River, Smolensk is one of the oldest settlements in Russia. First mentioned in medieval chronicles under the year 862, it was long a center of the Krivichi, an eastern Slavic tribe. Its river location endowed it with importance for the development of a lucrative trading route between the Baltic and the Black Seas, from "the Varangians to the Greeks." By the late ninth century, the town had entered the orbit of Kiev, center of the Varangian princes of the Riurikovich dynasty on the middle Dnieper River. With the conversion of Kiev's Grand Prince Vladimir to Orthodox Christianity in 988, Byzantine forms in architecture and art came to the Dnieper River basin. In the 1050s, Smolensk emerged

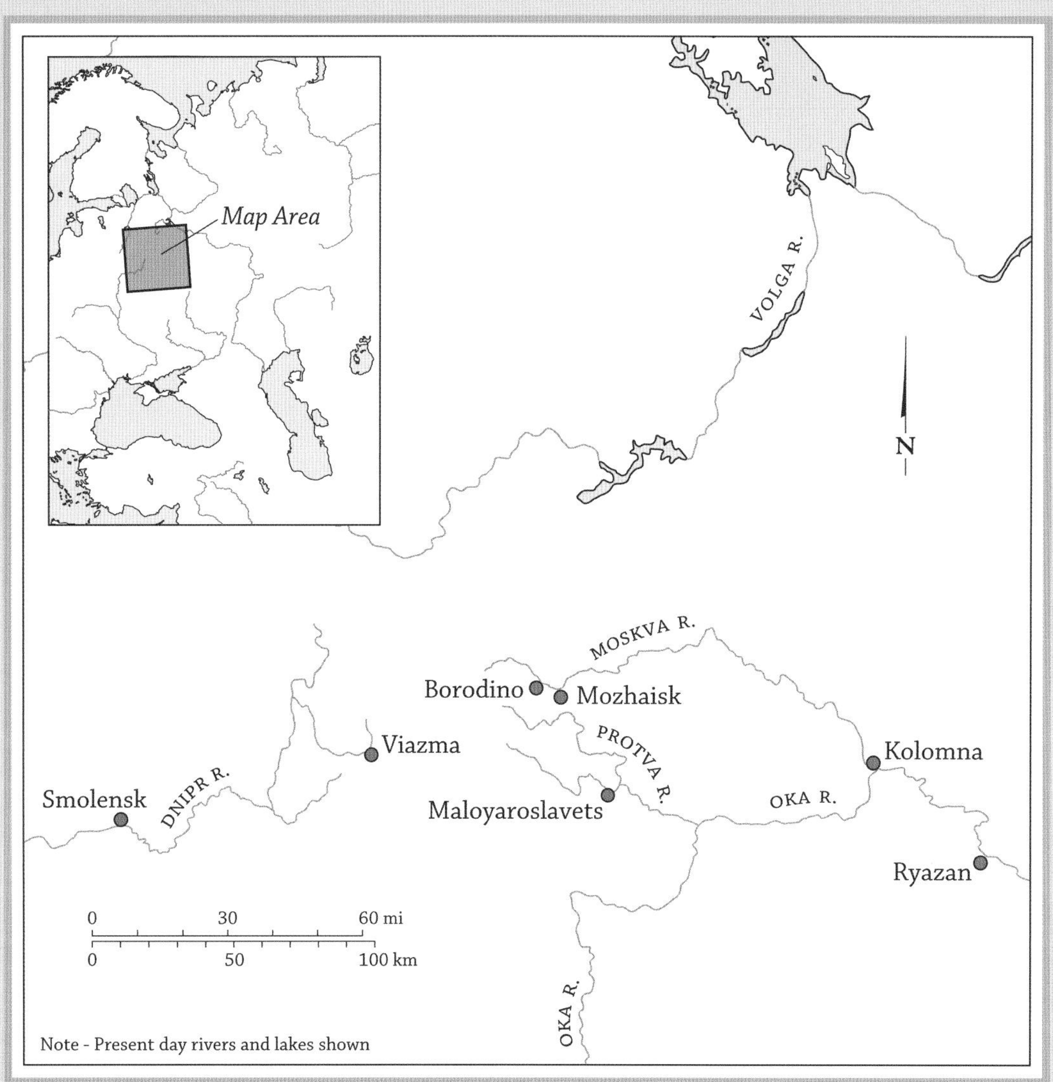

Map Area
VOLGA R.
MOSKVA R.
Borodino
Mozhaisk
Viazma
PROTVA R.
Kolomna
DNIPR R.
Smolensk
Maloyaroslavets
OKA R.
Ryazan
OKA R.
N
0   30   60 mi
0   50   100 km
Note - Present day rivers and lakes shown

as a subordinate principality that eventually came to rival the power of Kiev itself. Fortunately, Smolensk was spared the Mongol invasion of 1237–40. Nonetheless, the general devastation wrought by the Mongols led to a decline in the region's power. For the next four centuries, control over Smolensk would alternate among the Grand Duchy of Lithuania, Poland, and Moscow. The capture of Smolensk by Basil III in 1514 is still considered a major date in Russian history.

The strategic importance of Smolensk was reaffirmed by Tsar Boris Godunov (1551–1605), who saw it as a bulwark against Poland and undertook a massive rebuilding of the city walls between 1595 and 1602. One of the largest Russian construction projects before the reign of Peter the Great, the fortress had thirty-eight towers along a wall perimeter of 6.5 kilometers in length. (By contrast the Moscow Kremlin walls are not quite 2.3 kilometers long.) Construction, supervised by the engineer Fyodor Kon, required a massive mobilization of resources and labor. The production of the 100,000,000 bricks needed for the walls and the great quantity of limestone blocks used for their base was made possible by the standardization of building materials, as well as a centralized organization of the work process. Prokudin-Gorsky photographed large segments of the walls and towers. My documentation of the walls began in 2006 and culminated in 2014.

Despite this grandiose fortification, Smolensk was lost again to the Poles during the Time of Troubles. From Godunov's death in 1605 until the end of the 1610s, Russia was wracked by foreign invasion and brigandage. In June 1611 Smolensk fell to the Poles after a twenty-month siege and would not return to the Muscovite fold until a campaign in 1654. With the Andrusovo Truce of 1667, Moscow's possession was formally acknowledged by Poland, although for another century much of the local nobility adhered to Polish culture. Two centuries later, in August 1812, one of the major battles of the Napoleonic invasion was fought at Smolensk. Described by Leo Tolstoy in *War and Peace*, the Smolensk battle allowed the Russian army to retreat in orderly fashion but at catastrophic loss to the burned city. Only churches and the great walls remained relatively intact.

The city's preeminent shrine is the Cathedral of the Dormition of the Virgin, which Prokudin-Gorsky photographed from distant perspectives that gave a sense of its commanding presence. Begun in 1101 by Prince Vladimir Monomakh (1053–1125), the Dormition Cathedral was completed in the 1140s by Monomakh's grandson, Rostislav Mstislavich (1110–1167), who ruled in Smolensk from 1125 until 1160. Virtually nothing remains of the original cathedral, which was severely damaged during the Polish siege in

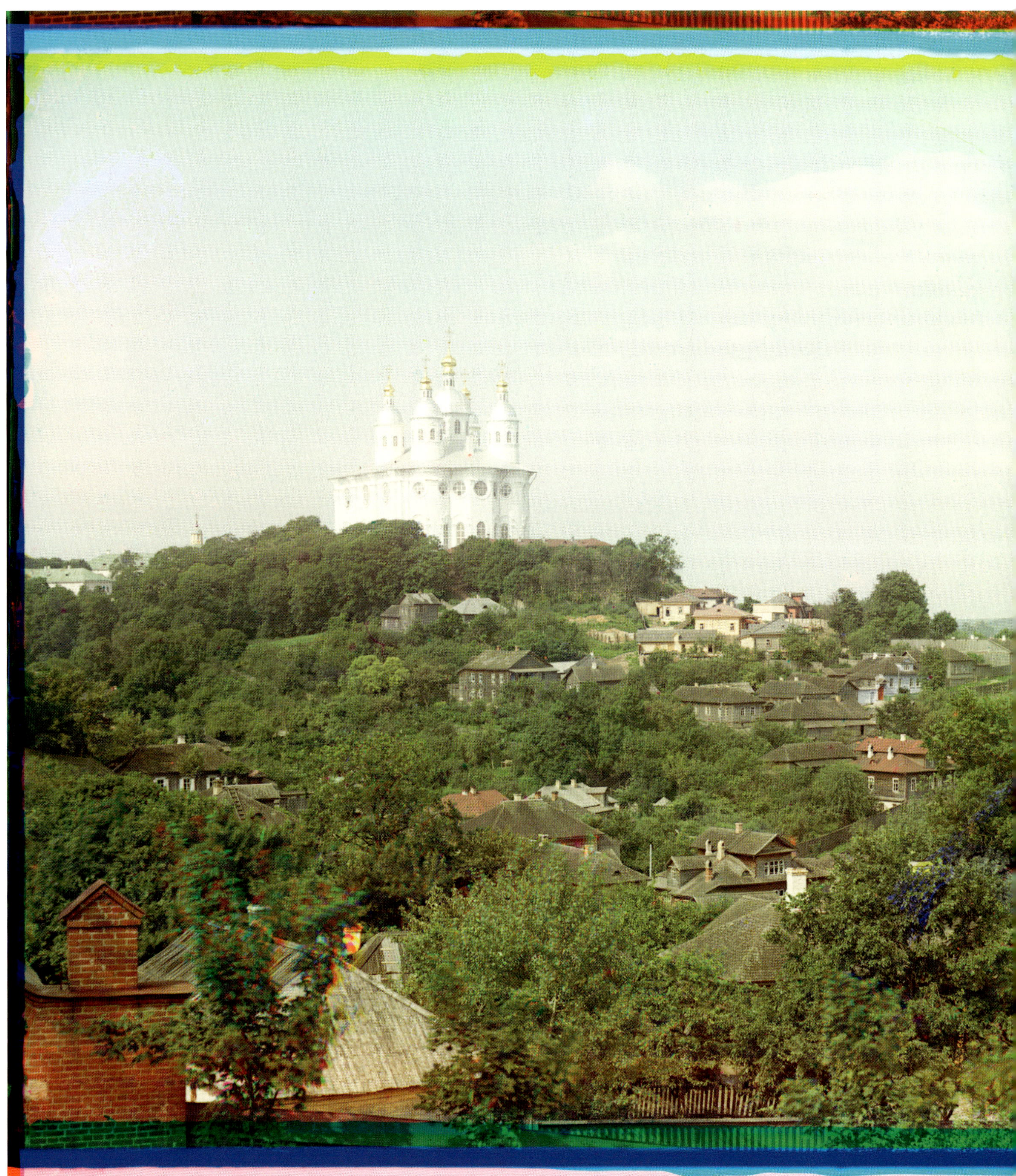

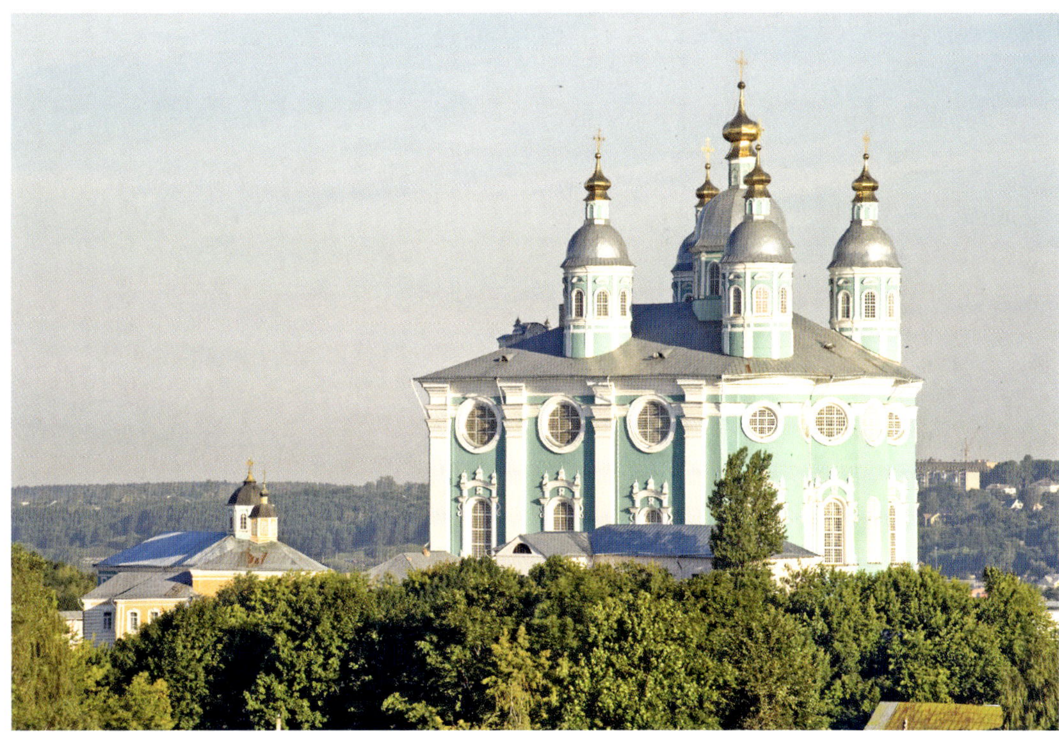

the early seventeenth century. After the return of Smolensk to Muscovite control in 1654, a rebuilding of the Dormition Cathedral began on the same site. Construction difficulties extended the project from 1677 to 1740, with additional work until 1772. Its present baroque form, crowned with five cupolas, was created in the 1730s by Gottfried Schädel.

Prokudin-Gorsky's view from the southeast shows the three segments of the apse, which contains the main altar in the east part of the structure. The facade design reflects the influence of a baroque style that flourished in seventeenth-century Ukrainian church architecture. The upper tier is defined by unusual circular windows, and the low roof is crowned with five ornate cupolas. Against all odds, the cathedral escaped major damage during World War II. My southeast view was taken in 2014 from a slightly different perch on the east wall of the grand Smolensk fortress (near the Eagle Tower). Prokudin-Gorsky's camera lens includes much of the cathedral hill, yet the image of the cathedral is softened by the hazy summer atmosphere. My telephoto lens allowed a tighter focus.

Prokudin-Gorsky also entered the cathedral, where he

photographed its most sacred shrine—the Smolensk Icon of the Virgin. That photograph has acquired exceptional importance, not only because of its technical challenges (a shadowed interior with only natural light) but also because the icon disappeared at some point during the two years of German occupation from mid-July 1941 to late September 1943. Every Orthodox icon is sacred, but the original of Our Lady of Smolensk was especially venerated. Traditional Orthodox narratives state that the icon was among those painted by Saint Luke. It defined the form known as Hodegetria (from the Greek for "She who points the way") in which Mary holds the Christ Child on her left arm and points to the infant with her right hand. Through imperial patronage the image made its way from Jerusalem to the Blachernae Church of Saint Mary in Constantinople under the protection of Empress Pulcheria (398–453), canonized by both the Catholic and Orthodox Churches for her role in consolidating early Christianity. According to church accounts Byzantine emperor Constantine IX Monomachos gave the Hodegetria Icon to his daughter Anastasia (or Anna; the precise name is unclear) in 1046 on her marriage to Vsevolod, son of Kievan Grand Prince Yaroslav the Wise.

After Vsevolod's death the icon was inherited by his son Vladimir II Monomakh (1053–1125; the Byzantine name was inherited from his mother), who would play a fundamental role in expanding the power and territory of medieval Rus. Around 1095 Vladimir transferred the icon from Chernigov, his original principality, to Smolensk, where in 1101 he initiated the construction of the original Cathedral of the Dormition of the Virgin. The icon was eventually installed in the cathedral, which was completed in the 1140s by Monomakh's grandson, Rostislav Mstislavich.

The cathedral and the icon miraculously survived a Mongol attack in 1239. In 1398 the icon was brought to Moscow by Princess Sophia, bride of Grand Prince Vasily I, son of Dmitry Donskoi. The icon remained in the Kremlin Annunciation Cathedral until 1456, when at the request of the Bishop Misail of Smolensk the Hodegetria Icon was returned by Grand Prince Vasily II. (At that time Smolensk was in the domains of the Grand Duchy of Lithuania.) Before the icon's return to Smolensk, a faithful copy at the same size was made for the Kremlin Annunciation Cathedral, where it stayed until 1525, when it was transferred to the newly built Cathedral of the Smolensk Icon of the Virgin at Moscow's Novodevichy Convent.

The icon survived the Time of Troubles and various sieges of Smolensk in the seventeenth century. During the prolonged rebuilding of the Dormition Cathedral, the main work was done in the 1730s and 1740s, when the cathedral acquired its present form influenced by the Ukrainian baroque.

The baroque style is particularly evident in the interior, with a magnificent icon screen, whose carved, gilded frame and tiers of icons were created by a group of artists and craftsmen headed by the Ukrainian master Sila Trusitsky. A portion of the first tier is visible in the background of Prokudin-Gorsky's photograph. My photograph, taken in 2014, conveys a sense of the grand scale of the iconostasis. The interior was further enhanced by the creation in 1743–46 of elaborate baldachins and icon cases (*kiot*) situated at the base of the cathedral's west piers near the icon screen. It was here that the Smolensk Icon of the Virgin remained in regal array.

In early August 1812, the Smolensk Icon was evacuated to Moscow as Napoleon's army advanced. Before the epochal Battle of Borodino, the icon was displayed in a procession at the Kremlin walls, and when Moscow itself was threatened, the Smolensk Icon found refuge in Yaroslavl. Improbably, the Dormition Cathedral remained unscathed during the furious assault on Smolensk and was guarded from looting until the French abandoned Smolensk in October. In November 1812, the Smolensk Icon with its intricate metal overlay was returned to the Dormition Cathedral, where Prokudin-Gorsky photographed it almost a century later.

Defying all odds, the Smolensk Dormition Cathedral survived two prolonged battles in 1941 and 1943. During twenty-six months of German occupation the cathedral was closed and guarded, but its miraculous icon was missing when the largely ruined city was retaken. Not only was this a great loss for Russian culture, but the disappearance also meant that the ancient object was never studied with advanced scientific methods. The space containing the original Smolensk Hodegetria Icon is now occupied by a copy painted in 1602 for the nearby church dedicated specifically to that icon and located in the Smolensk fortress north wall.

The Dormition Cathedral is situated within a network of shrines closely related to the cathedral. Just to the north is the Church of the Smolensk Hodegetria Icon, built over the Dnieper River Gate, formerly the main entrance in the north fortress wall. In 1728 a wooden church was erected to house the eponymous Smolensk Icon in the space created when one of the towers of the city walls was razed. In the 1790s this church was rebuilt in brick in a neoclassical style. In 1811–12 the structure, seen from the south, was modified to serve on its lower level as a passageway (since enclosed). On the opposite, north side is a street along the Dnieper River embankment. Prokudin-Gorsky's photograph shows a still-active passageway and even a tramline. Among my photographs of the church, I have chosen the north view to show its relation to the Dnieper River.

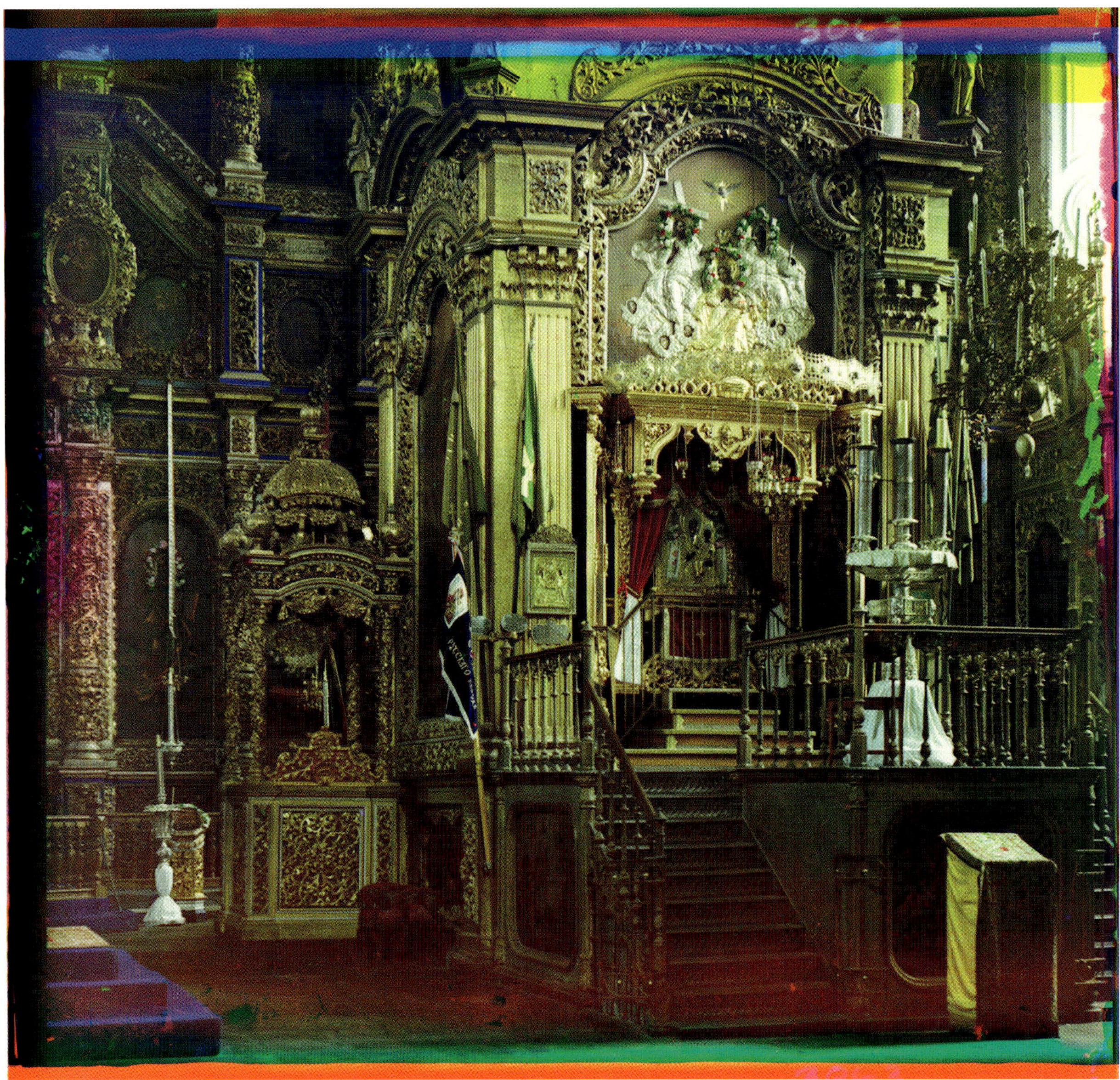

Prokudin-Gorsky also photographed the main gate of the south wall, the Nikolskii Gate Tower, which was the westernmost surviving element in the southeast range of the Smolensk walls. The tower, one of the secondary entrances into the city, was named after the Church of Saint Nicholas, destroyed during the Napoleonic invasion. The tower passage was closed in the nineteenth century, and in 1898–1900 a larger arch was opened in the wall to the east of the tower. In 1901 a tramline was laid through the arch. Visible over the old gate is an icon of Saint Nicholas. The brick walls, built at the turn of the seventeenth century, were periodi-

SMOLENSK Cathedral of the Dormition of the Virgin. Interior, view east with baldachin containing the Miraculous Hodegetria Icon of the Virgin. PROKUDIN-GORSKY 20413. SUMMER 1912.

SMOLENSK Cathedral of the Dormition of the Virgin. Interior, view east toward iconostasis, with south pier and baldachin. BRUMFIELD, JULY 1, 2014.

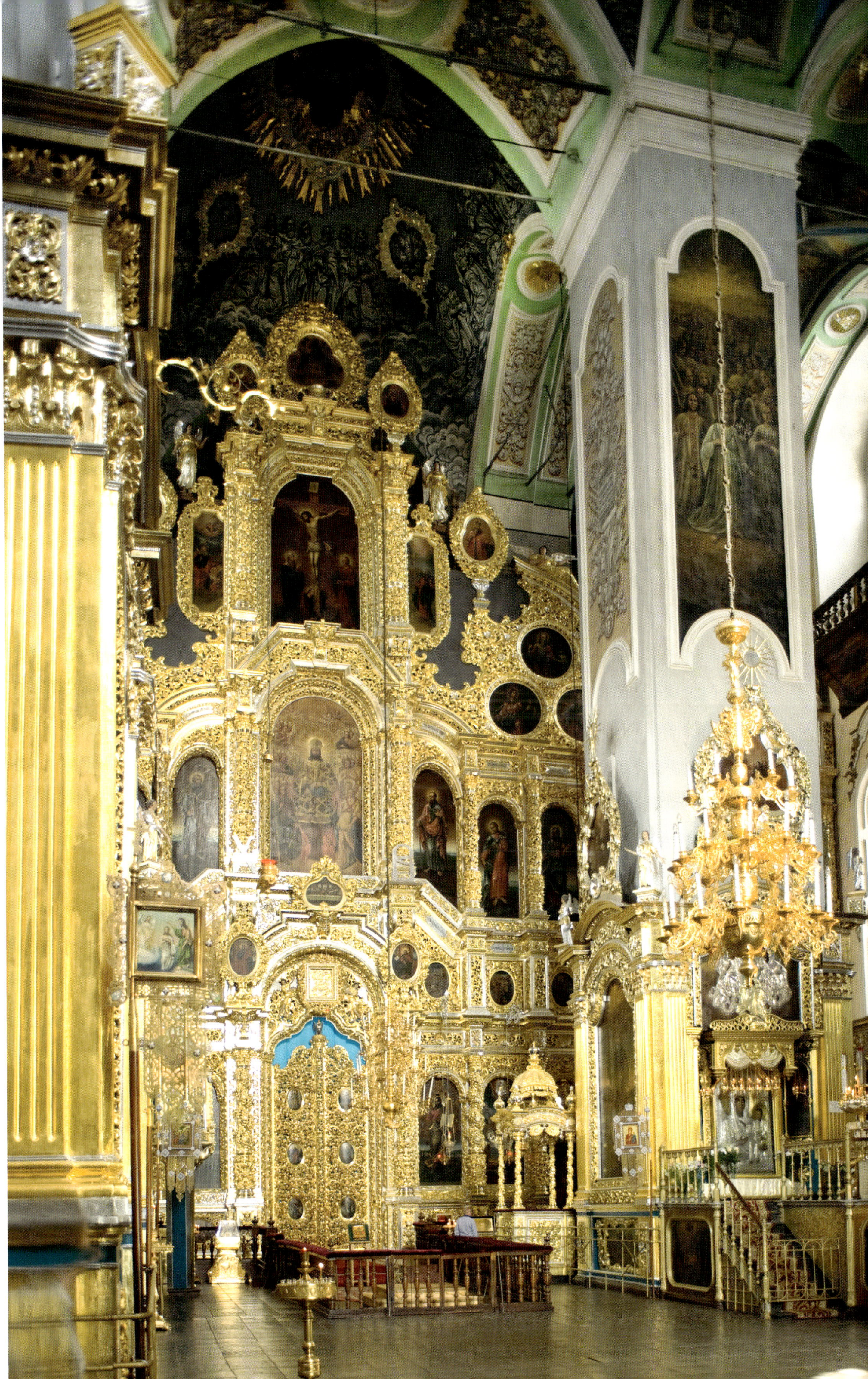

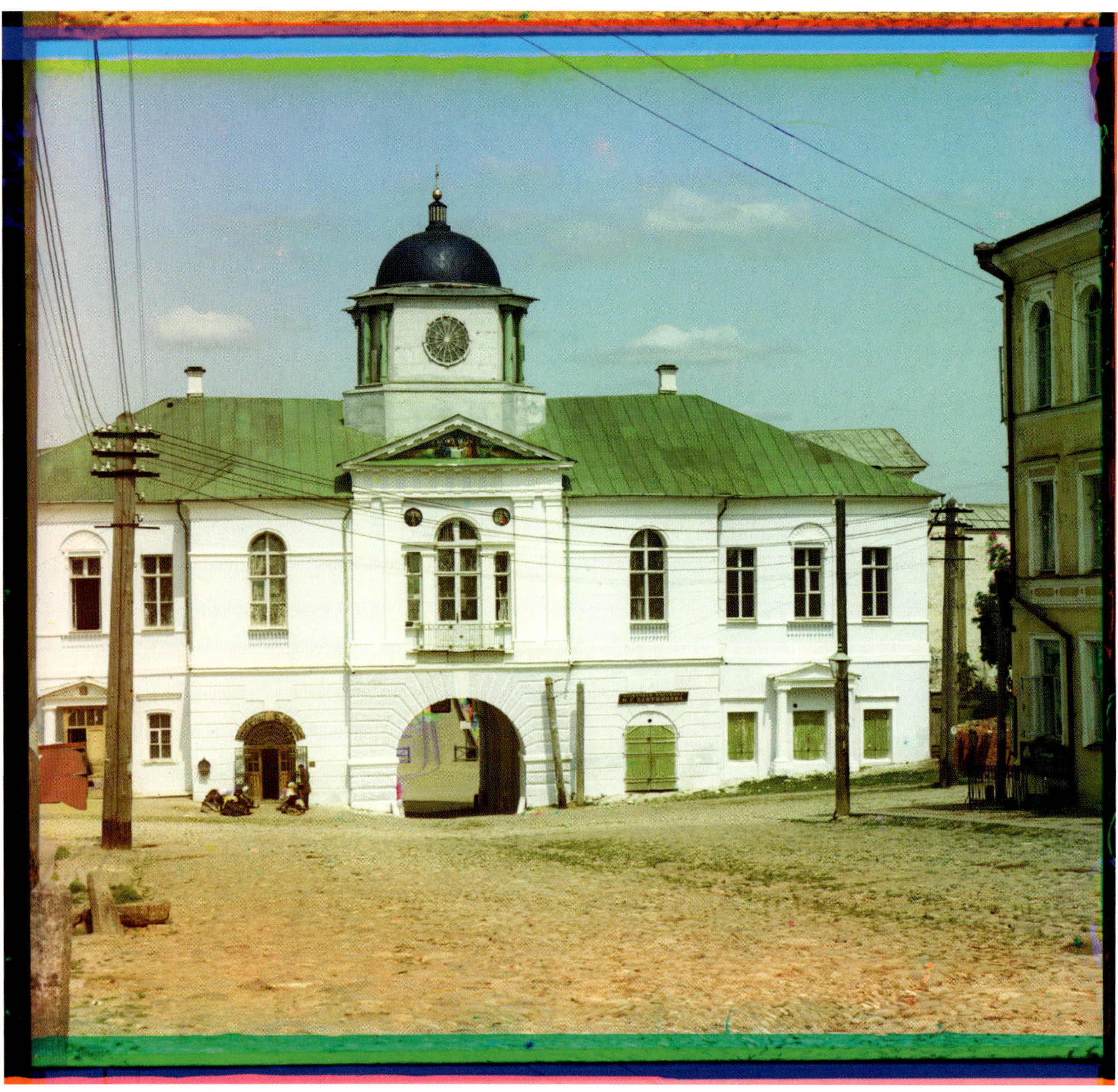

cally whitewashed. The view from the north shows that the old gate was framed by a blue-painted facade. My photograph shows the structure intact.

Near the south gate is the Transfiguration of the Savior-Saint Avraamy Monastery, founded in the early thirteenth century by the monk Avraamy of Smolensk. The monastery was ransacked and turned into a Catholic cloister when the Poles took Smolensk in 1611. After the recapture of the city by Tsar Aleksey Mikhailovich in 1654, the Avraamiev-Transfiguration Monastery gradually revived. One of Prokudin-Gorsky's most lyrical architectural photographs

SMOLENSK North fortress wall and Dnieper Gate with Church of the Smolensk Hodegetria Icon of the Virgin. South view. PROKUDIN-GORSKY 20414. SUMMER 1912.

SMOLENSK North wall, Dnieper Gate and Church of the Smolensk Hodegetria Icon of the Virgin. Northwest view from Central Bridge over Dnieper River. BRUMFIELD, JULY 1, 2014.

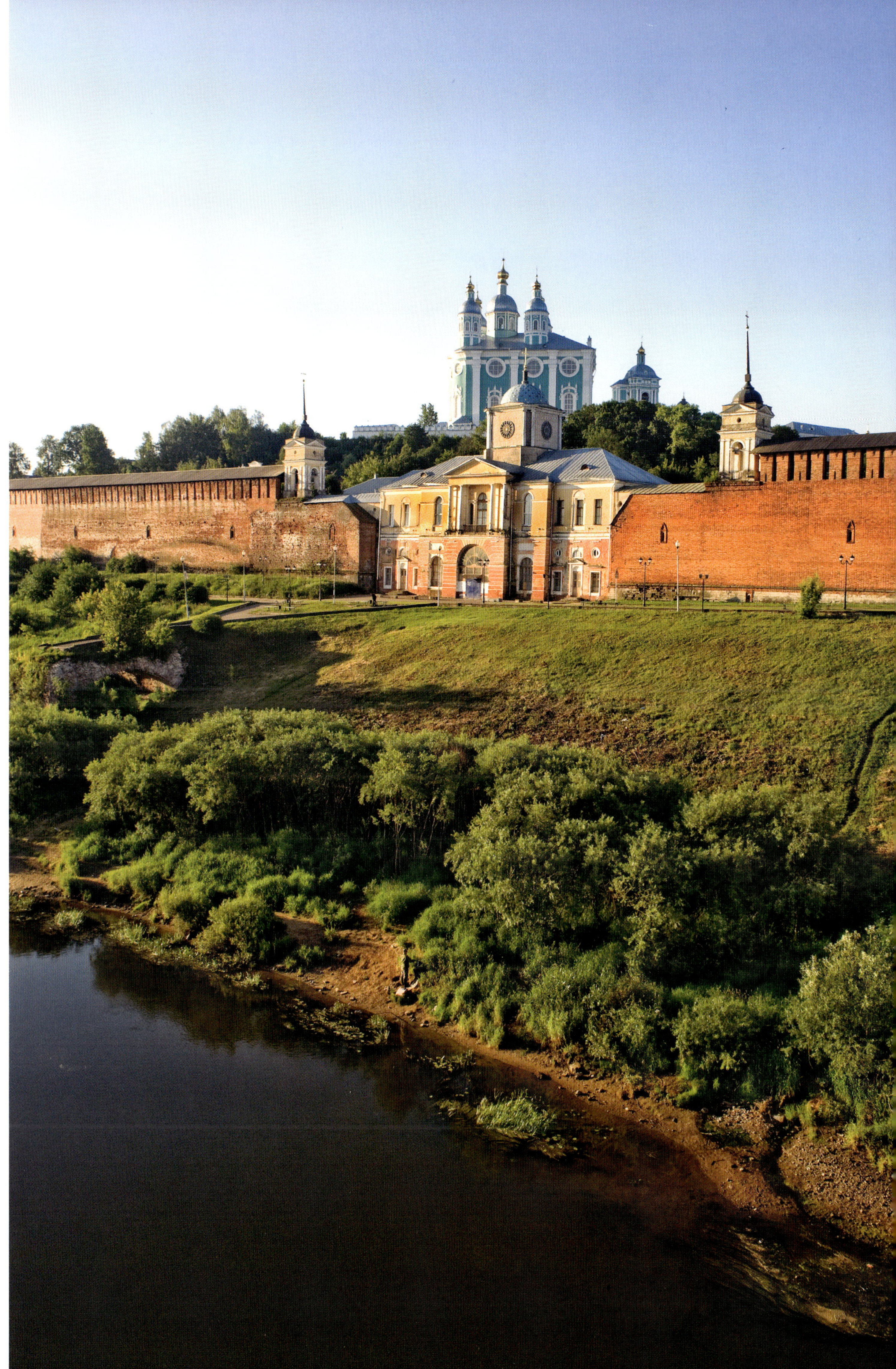

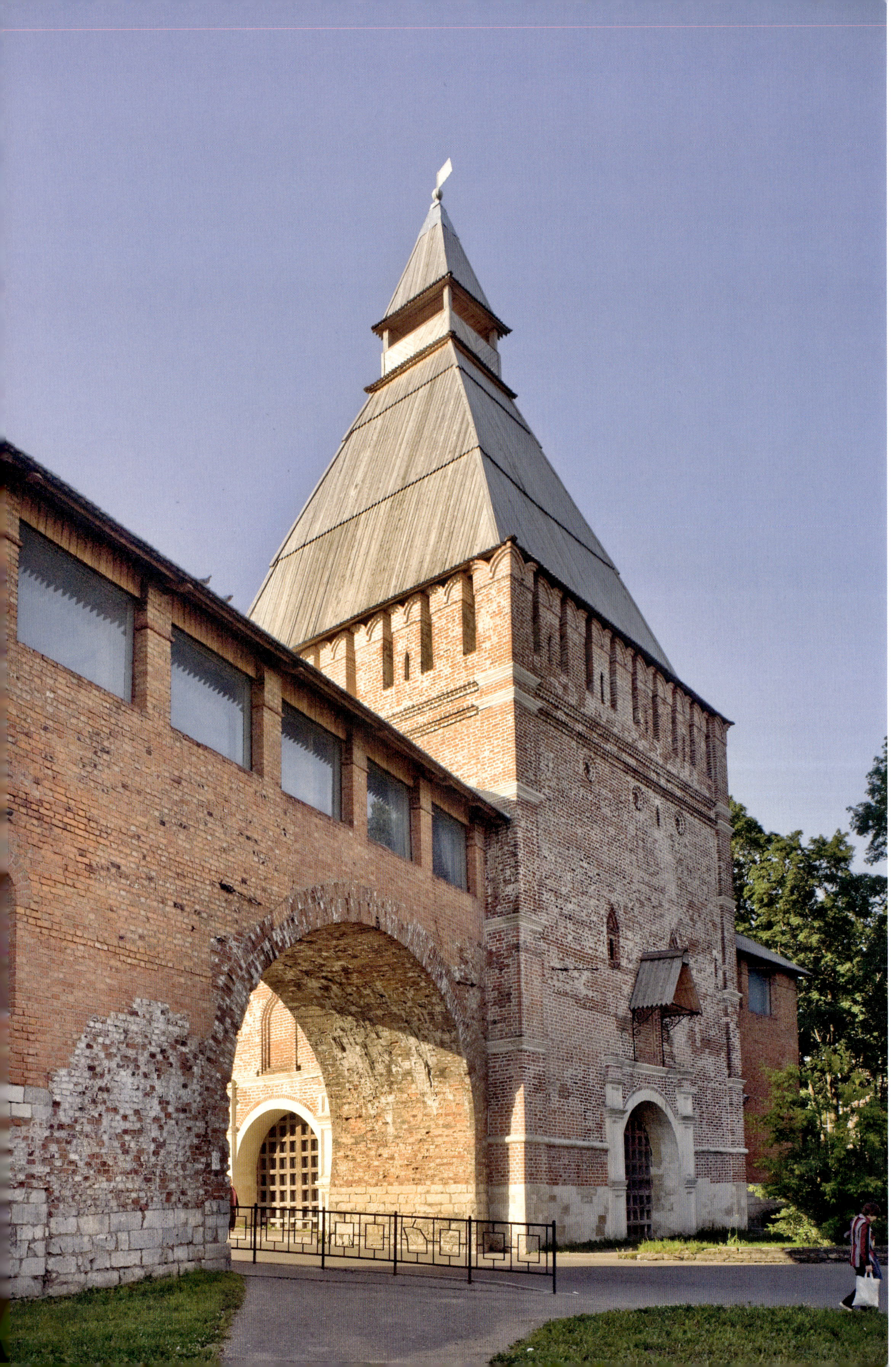

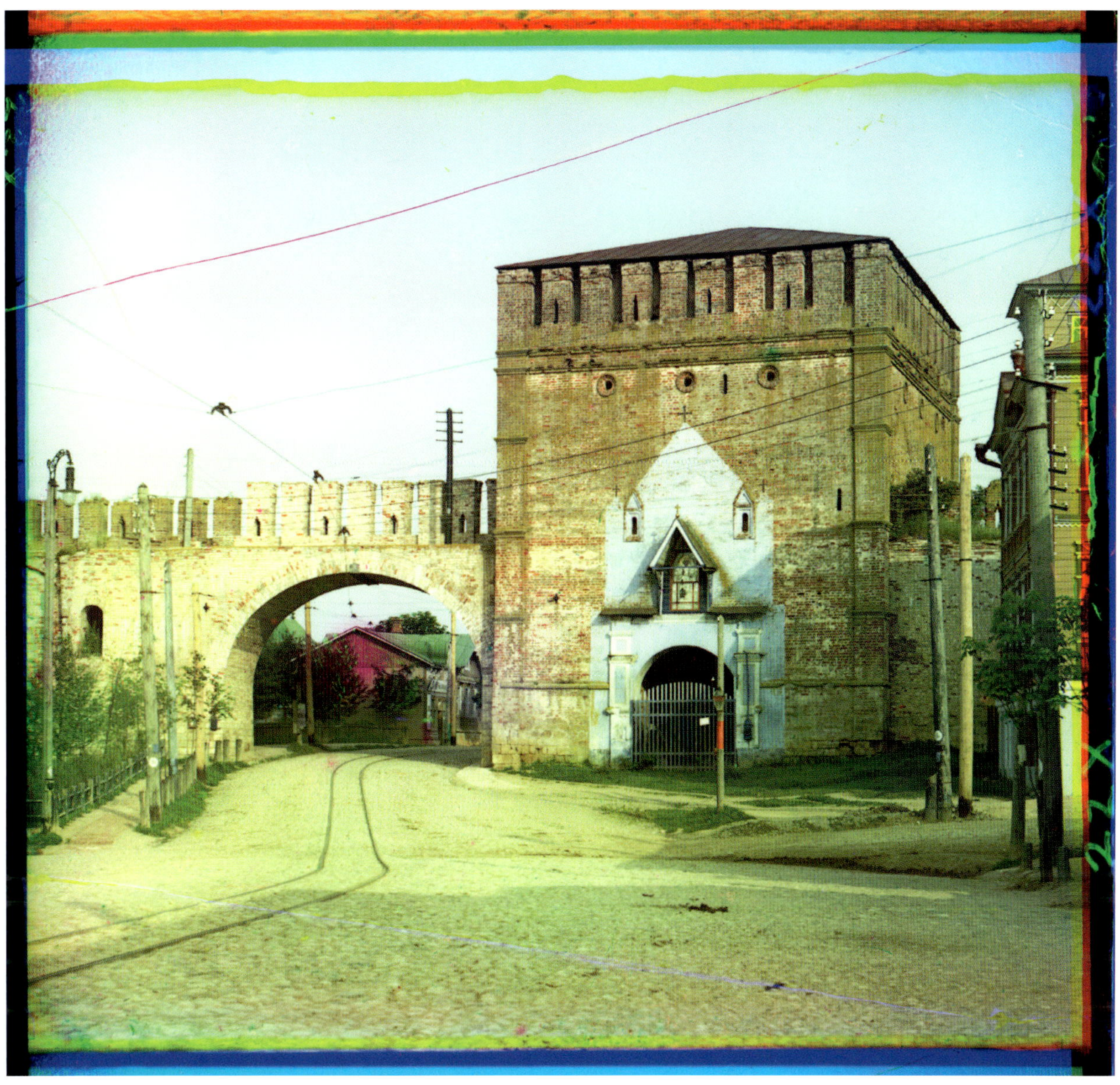

is his view down a cobbled lane leading to the north facade of the monastery's Cathedral of the Transfiguration of the Savior, completed in 1755. My photograph from the same perspective conveys a different sense of a corner whose peace has remained through so many cataclysms.

In addition to religious architecture, Prokudin-Gorsky photographed the fortress walls, whose massive bulk provided an ideal vantage for his large box camera. The largest surviving section is the east wall, with several major towers. Prokudin-Gorsky photographed a segment with the Avraamiev Tower (name after Saint Avraamy of Smolensk) and

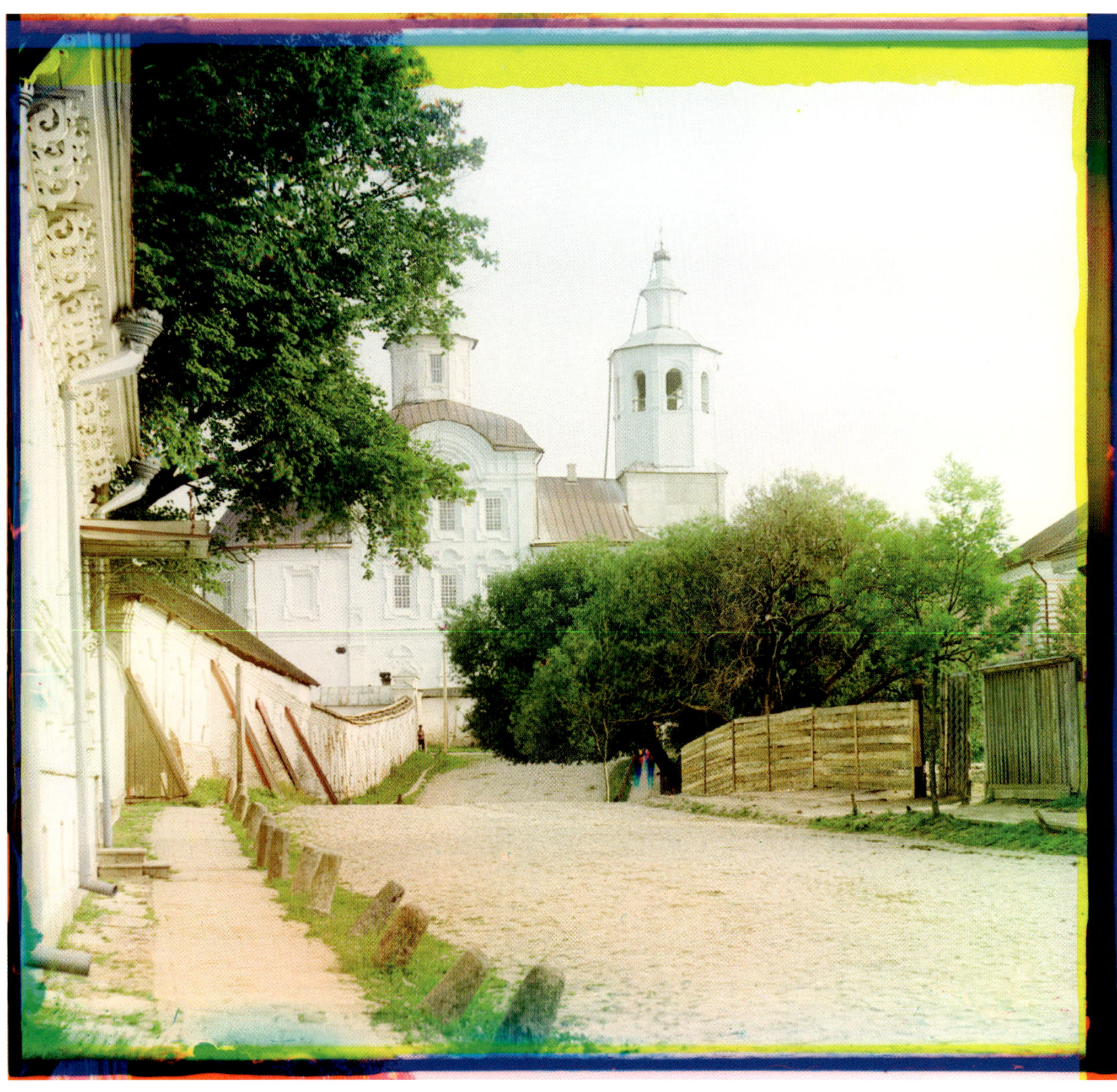

the Oryol (or Gorodetsky) Tower, one of the largest towers. Narrow interior passageways allowed access to the top. Visible in the valley across the Dnieper is the Church of the Elevation of the Cross, and on the hilltop is the Church of the Icon of the Sign. My photographs shows these and other towers well preserved—particularly the massive Oryol (Eagle) Tower.

Beyond the walls to the north lay the main commercial district, the railroad station, and several parish churches, including the Church of Saint Nicholas. My photograph shows the baroque structure (1745–48) reasonably well

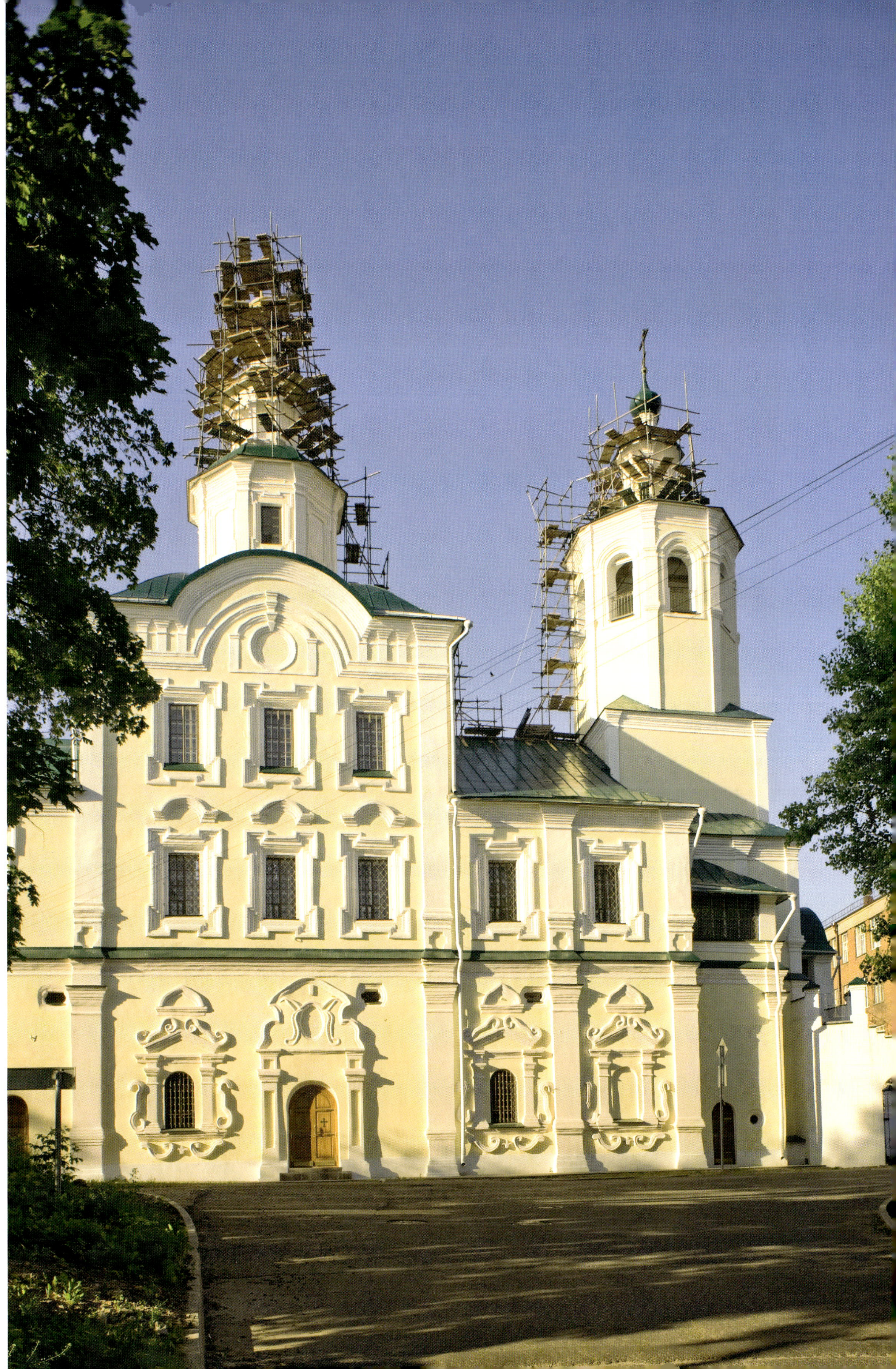

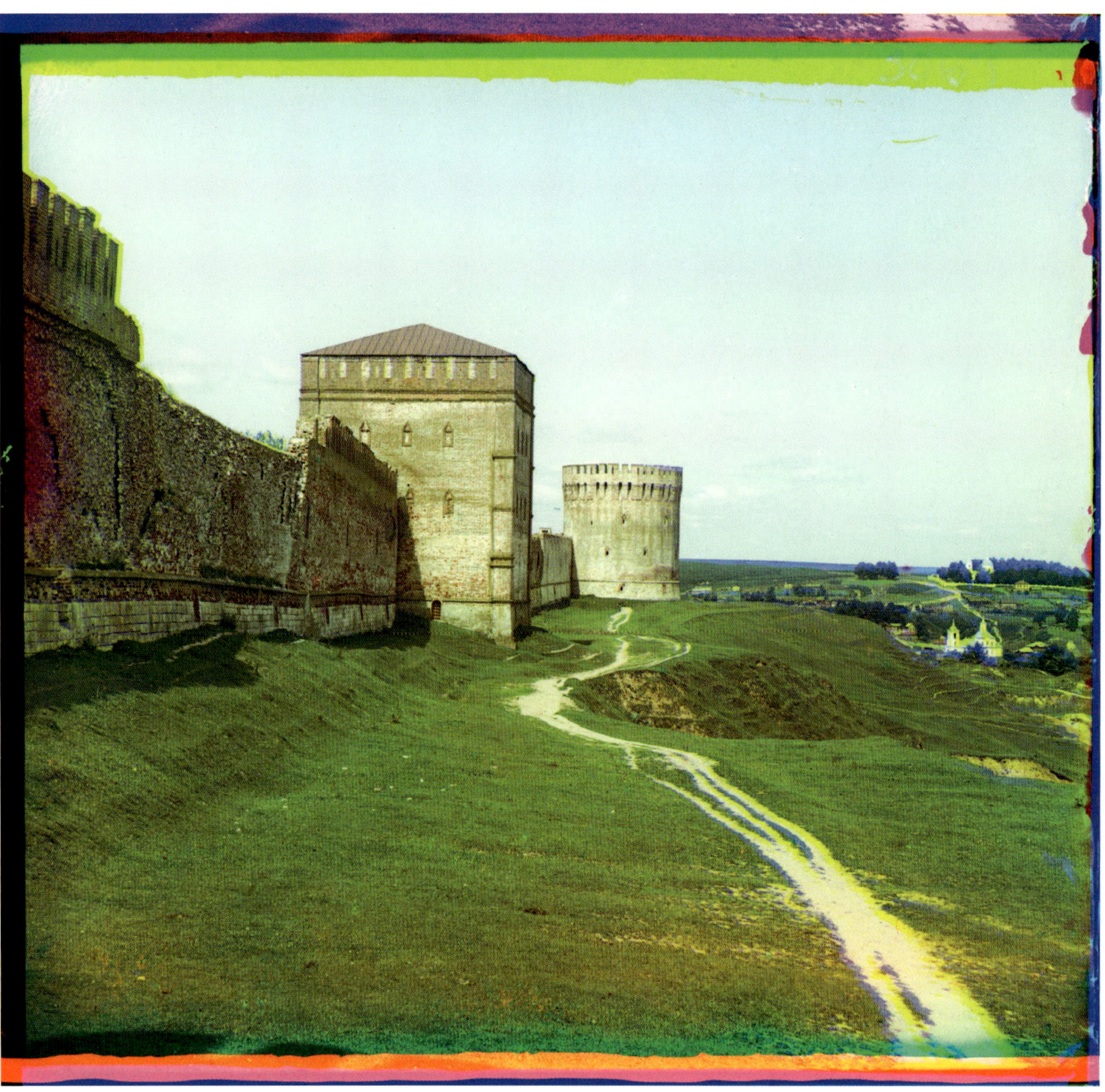

preserved. Prokudin-Gorsky also recorded the Church of Saints Peter and Paul, originally built in the mid twelfth century. He found an unusual close view of the structure across a disheveled lumberyard. Over the centuries the church was substantially modified, particularly during decades of Polish control in the first half of the seventeenth century. At this time the building was used by the Uniate Church, and a residence for the Uniate bishop was added to the west side. With the return of Smolensk to Russia in 1654, the church was returned to Orthodoxy. In 1753–57 the

SMOLENSK East fortress wall with Avraamiev and Oryol (Eagle) Towers. East facade. PROKUDIN-GORSKY 20418. SUMMER 1912.

SMOLENSK East fortress wall with Oryol (Eagle) Tower. East facade. BRUMFIELD, JULY 1, 2014.

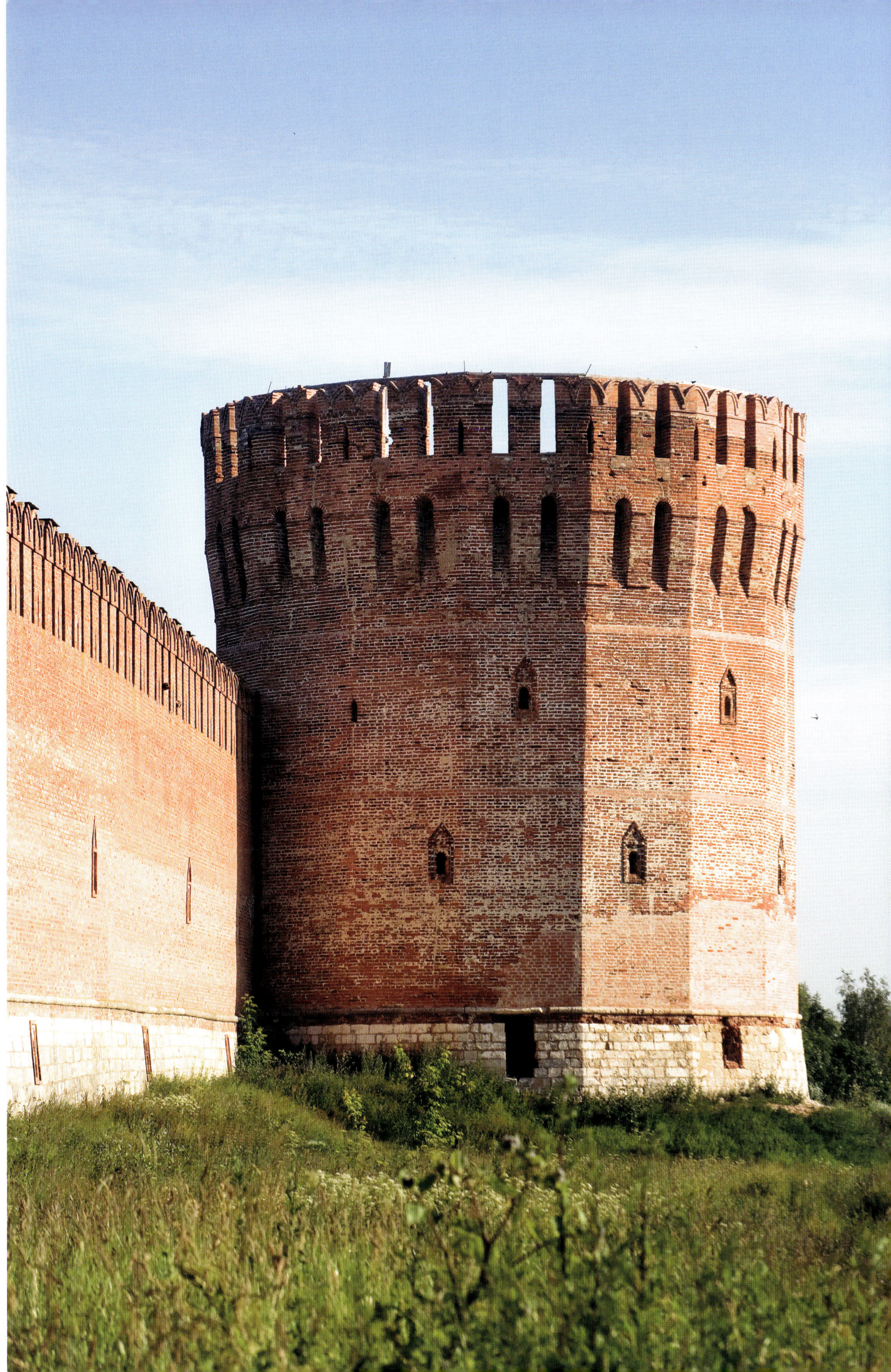

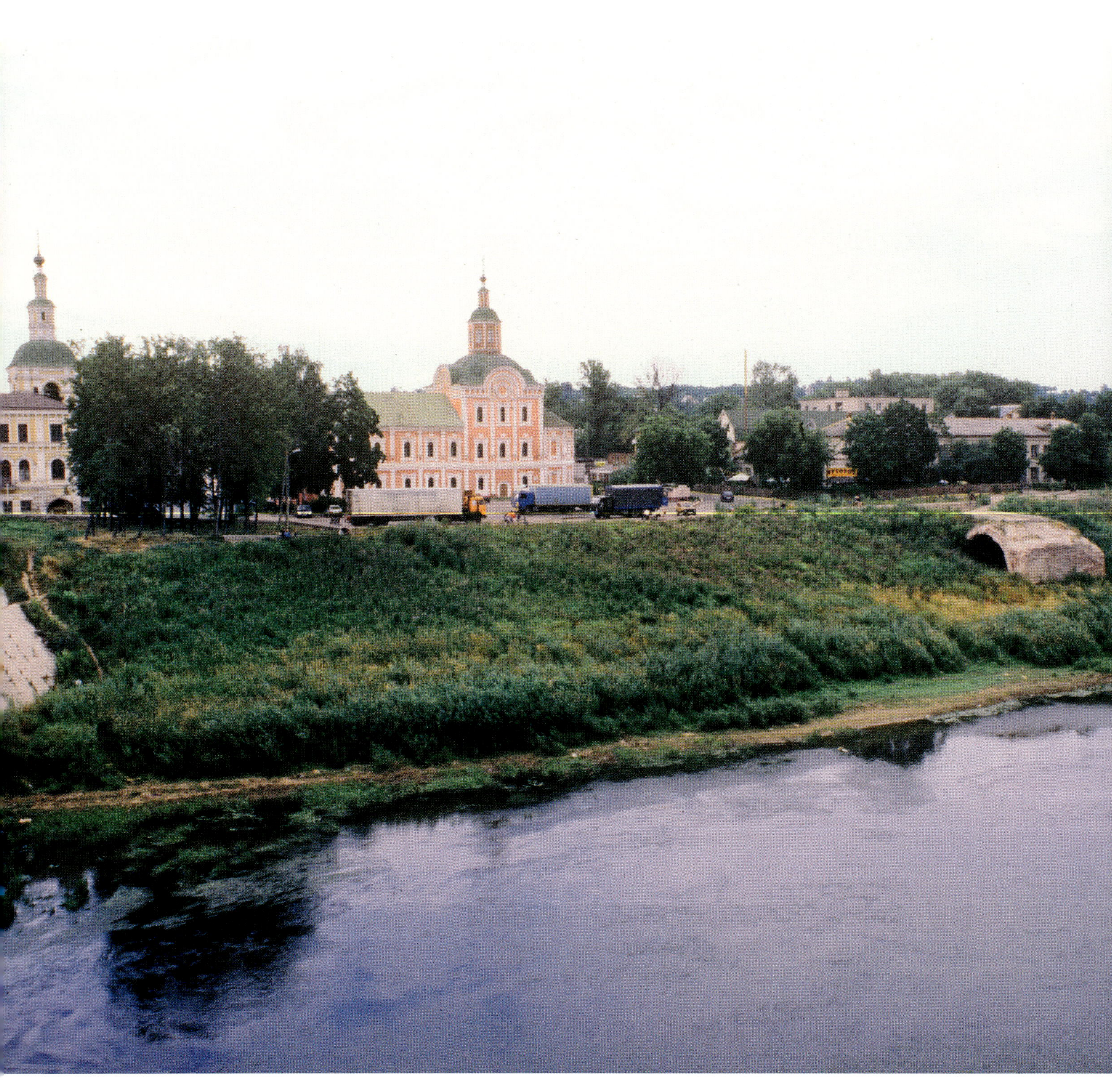

SMOLENSK Left (north) bank of Dnieper River, view northeast from Dnieper River Bridge. *Left*: bell tower and Church of Saint Nicholas. *Right*: remains of abutment for nineteenth-century North Gate bridge over Dnieper (visible in Prokudin-Gorsky's photograph). BRUMFIELD, JULY 16, 2006.

SMOLENSK View north from cathedral bell tower. North wall and Dnieper Gate with Church of the Smolensk Hodegetria Icon. Beyond the two bridges across the Dnieper River is the Church of Saint Nicholas. PROKUDIN-GORSKY 20408. SUMMER 1912.

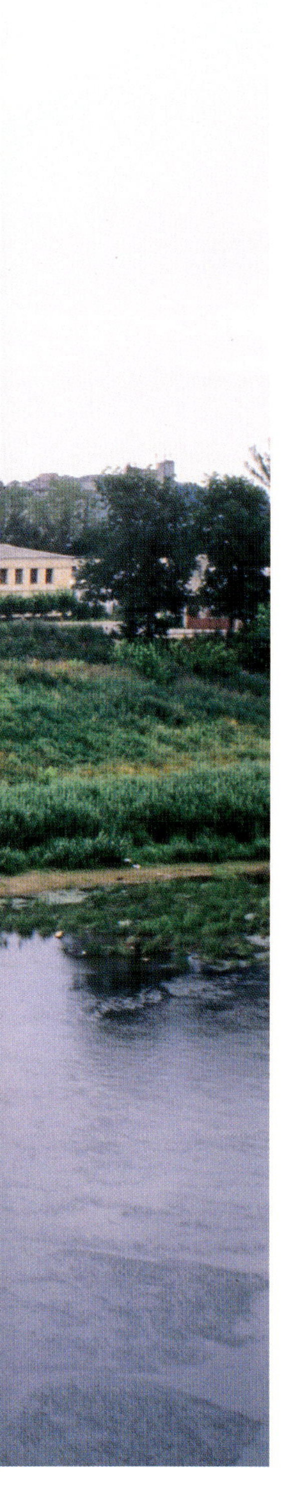

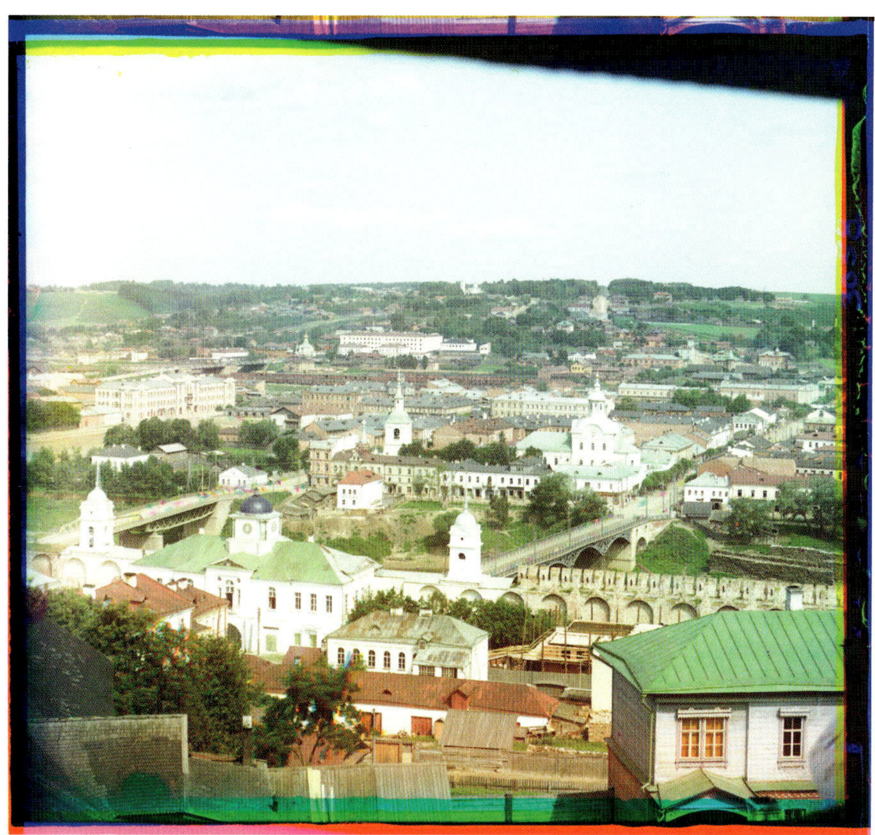

residence was rebuilt in the baroque style as the Church of Saint Barbara, with the ancient Church of Saints Peter and Paul attached. In 1962–63 the church was restored by Peter Baranovsky to what is considered its original form, as seen in my photograph, taken in early light from the station overpass.

A similarly complex history belongs to the Church of Archangel Michael, included in a panoramic view to the northwest. One of the major surviving monuments of late twelfth-century Russian architecture, this church also underwent a major restoration after the war. The church was built during the reign of Prince David Rostislavich (1180–97), who is recorded as frequently visiting it. Although the precise dates of construction are unclear, it is generally accepted that the structure was completed by the late 1190s. The bold plan of the Archangel Michael Church represents a noticeable departure from the cuboid form. Although the core of the structure conforms to the cross-domed plan, the south, west, and north facades have tall extensions that create the impression of a cruciform plan. These extensions also serve to buttress the core structure, which achieves an unusual height especially noticeable in the interior. The corner bays of the main structure were

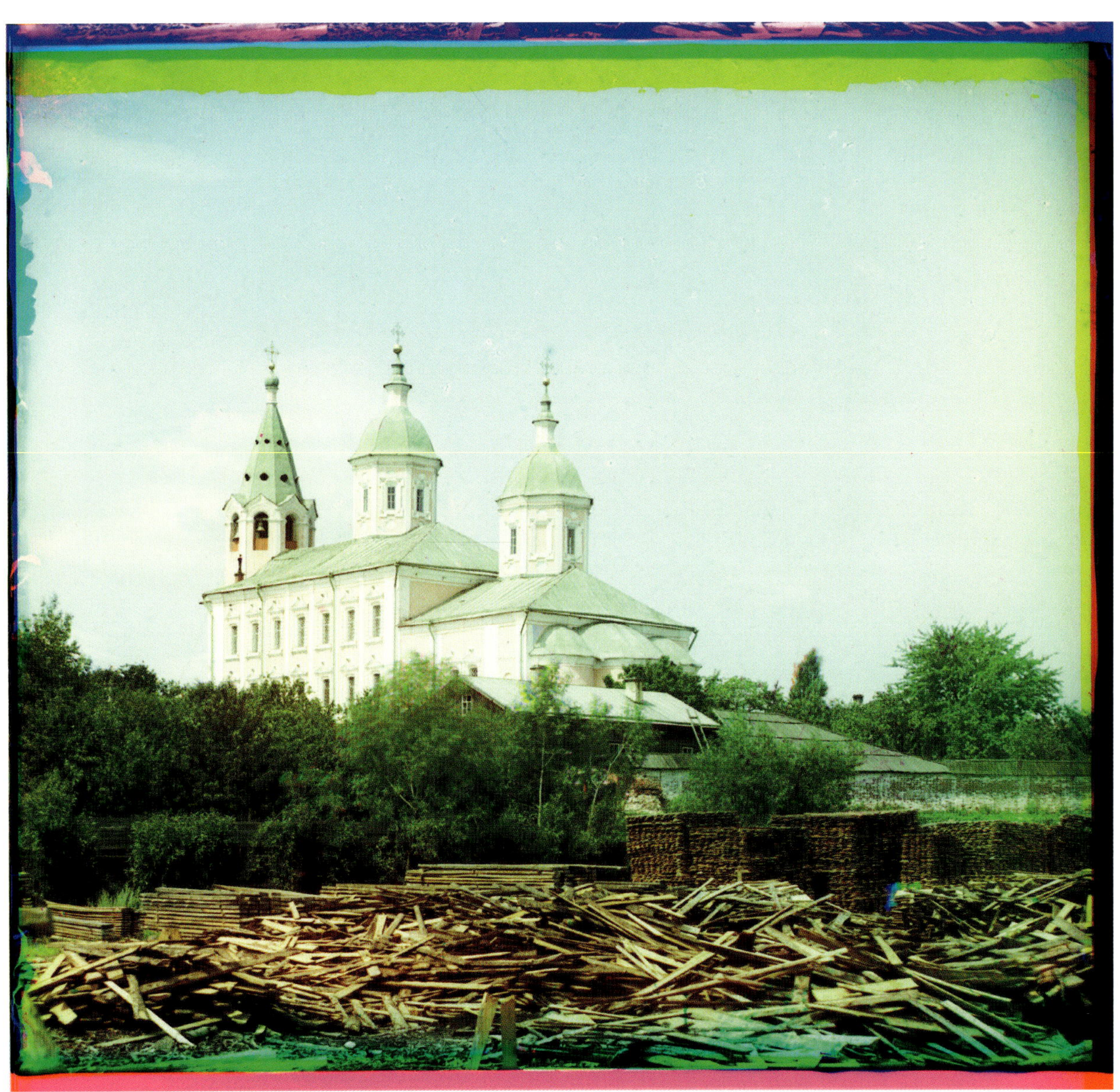

SMOLENSK Church of Saint Barbara with attached
Church of Church of Saints Peter and Paul in Goro-
dianka. Southeast view from lumber yard. PROKUDIN-
GORSKY 20423. SUMMER 1912.

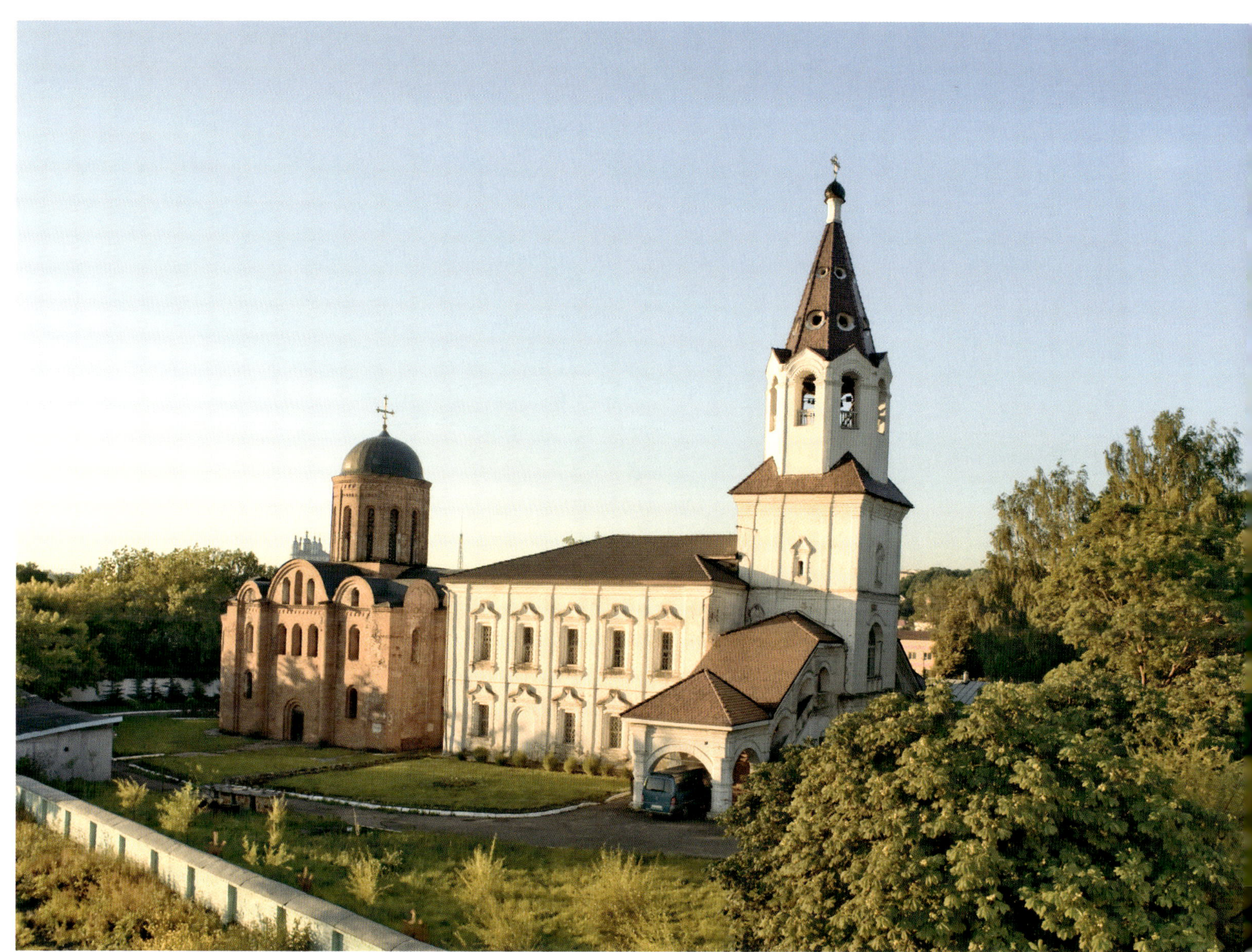

SMOLENSK Church of Saint Barbara with attached mid-twelfth century Church of Saints Peter and Paul in Gorodianka (restored to original form after World War II). Early morning northwest view from railroad station pedestrian bridge. BRUMFIELD, JULY 1, 2014.

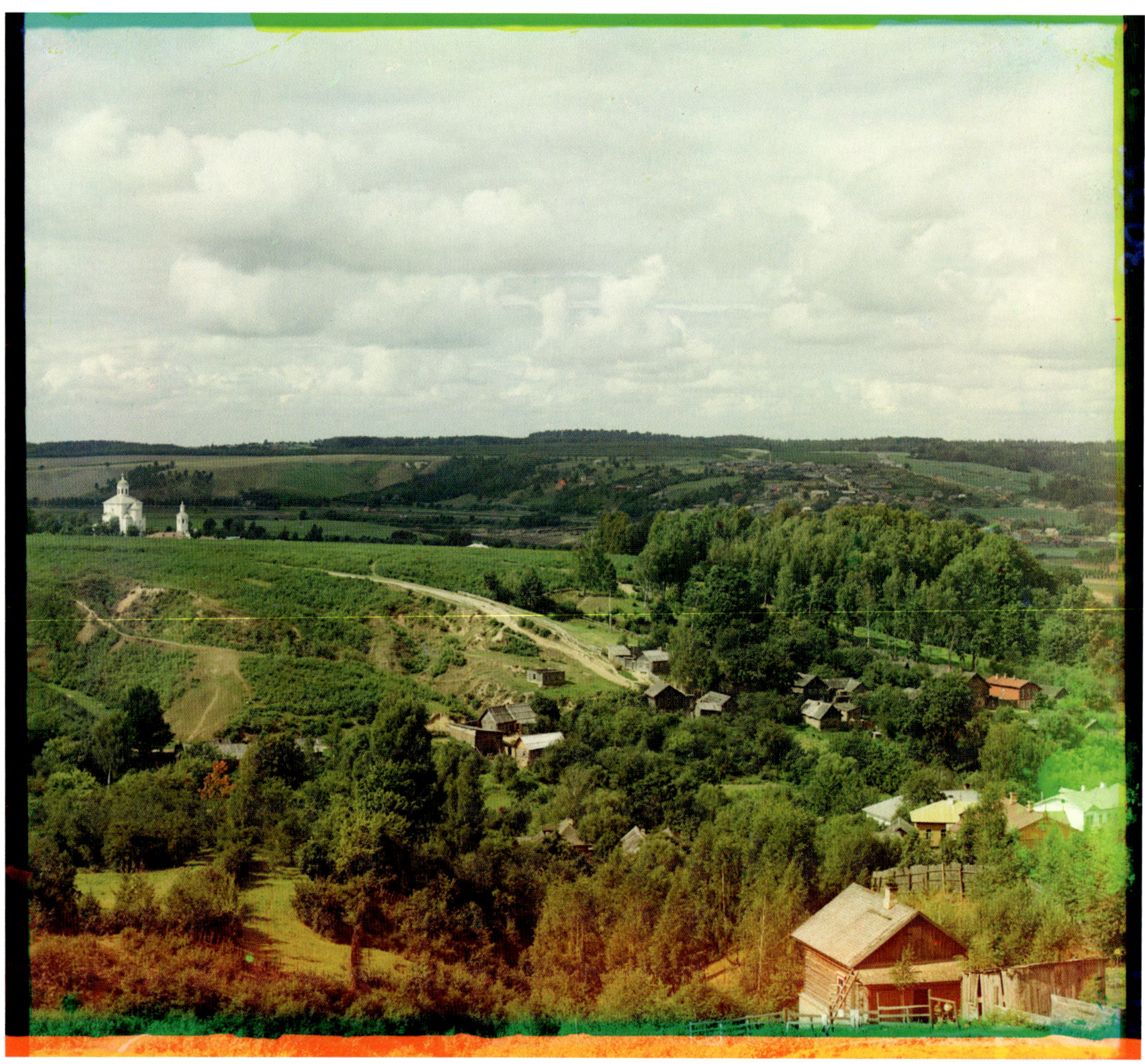

higher than the facade extensions but lower than the central bay of each facade, thus intensifying the verticality of form.

Moving eastward on the main road to Moscow, Prokudin-Gorsky visited Vyazma, situated 165 kilometers to the east of Smolensk and 230 kilometers to the west of Moscow. The first attested mention of Vyazma dates to 1239, a time that coincides with the Mongol invasion and the widespread destruction of an already fragmented medieval Rus. The town remained a part of the Smolensk principality until 1403, when it was seized by the Grand Duchy of Lithuania.

SMOLENSK View northwest from Lopatin Garden near fortress wall. *Left*: Church of Archangel Michael. PROKUDIN-GORSKY 20405. SUMMER 1912.

SMOLENSK Late twelfth-century Church of Archangel Michael (restored after World War II). South view. BRUMFIELD, JULY 17, 2006.

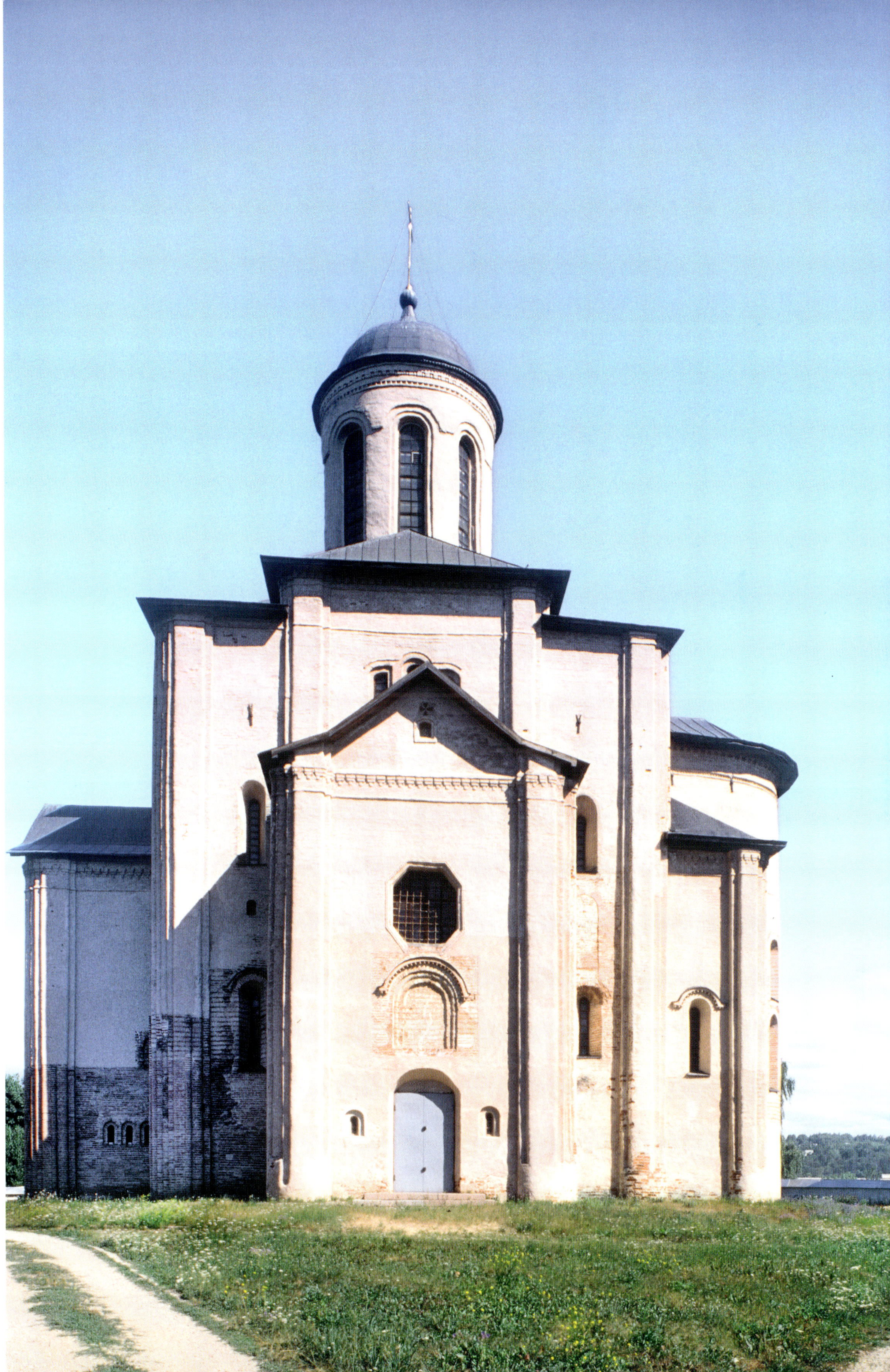

By the end of the fifteenth century, control of Vyazma shifted to Moscow, which gained it through a series of border wars with Lithuania. In the sixteenth century it served as an important western defense point, as Muscovy's western boundary shifted and the much larger, more exposed fortress of Smolensk at times fell to Poland. During the Time of Troubles in the early seventeenth century the town was again caught in a series of shifting allegiances before serving the new Romanov dynasty. Vyazma fell to the French on August 29, 1812. Much of it was burned in late October when pursuing Russian forces commanded by generals Mikhail Miloradovich and Matvei Platov engaged in a sharp battle with a corps of the retreating French commanded by Marshal Davout.

Most of the churches in Prokudin-Gorsky's general view of central Vyazma were destroyed during the twentieth century. An exception is the church dedicated to the Icon of the Most Merciful Savior, built in 1786 at the Saint Arkady Monastery. The only remaining structure from that monastery, the church now serves as the town library. Severely damaged during World War II, the central part of Vyazma is a mixture of postwar Soviet architecture with nineteenth-century buildings rebuilt from the ruins. A picturesque survivor is the Church of the Nativity of the Virgin (1727–28), which Prokudin-Gorsky photographed from the northeast with a parish school and large pile of firewood in the foreground. The church is now surrounded by a park, whose pond offers a reflection of the south facade.

The road east to Moscow passes near the village of Borodino (120 kilometers beyond Vyazma), best known from Leo Tolstoy's *War and Peace*. It was here that the Russian and French armies clashed on September 7, 1812, in an epochal struggle before the gates of Moscow. Known to the French as the Battle of Moscow, the Battle of Borodino is thought to have been the bloodiest in all the Napoleonic wars, exceeding even Waterloo. The French won a tactical victory but failed to destroy Russian forces under the command of Prince Mikhail Kutuzov. Although the retreat of the Russian army after Borodino resulted in the destruction of much of Moscow, the occupation of the ancient capital led not to Russian defeat but to the disintegration of the French Grande Armée.

Of the many battlefield monuments scattered over Borodino Field, most of them (thirty-three) were erected to honor valorous military units during the centennial observance in 1912. In retrospect the centennial had a double meaning, as Europe girded for another massive bloodletting. Prokudin-Gorsky photographed a number of these monuments, as well as landscapes of important points in the vast battle. The field itself is dominated by the large obelisk (27.5 meters in height) that is the primary monument to all Russian soldiers who took part in the battle. Designed by the architect Antonio Adamini, the monument was dedicated in the presence of tsar Nicholas I in July 1839, the twenty-fifth anniversary of the Russian army's entry into Paris (March 1814). The monument also served as the burial place of the remains of general Peter Bagration, a consummate hero who died of wounds suffered in the battle. In 1932 the obelisk was destroyed by the Soviet regime, which during the 1930s demonstrated a virulent hostility to memorials to the Patriotic War—as the war against Napoleon is known in Russia. At that time, these monuments were seen as relics of the tsarist era and closely related to the Orthodox Church. Those attitudes rapidly changed with the onset of the war against Nazi Germany—the Great Patriotic War. Once again, Borodino Field was attacked by an invader (in October 1941), and the spirit of the first Patriotic War was again summoned in defense of Moscow. The monument underwent another restoration in preparation for the bicentennial in 2012.

The center of the battlefield is occupied by the Spaso-Borodino Convent (formally known as the Convent of the Transfiguration of the Savior). This monastic institution evolved from a small religious commune during the 1820s and achieved the status of convent in 1838 through the initiative of Margarita Tuchkova, widow of general Alexander Tuchkov. At the height of battle, Tuchkov died at the head of his Murom and Revel Regiment in a charge to retake a position captured by the French (the central Redan). During the latter half of the nineteenth century the Spaso-Borodino Convent became a shrine to Russian military valor. Prokudin-Gorsky took multiple views, including one from the east.

My photographs include a northeast view with the main cathedral, dedicated to the ancient Vladimir Icon of the Virgin, which is believed to have miraculously caused the retreat of the dreaded Tamerlane from Russia in 1395. Nearby stands the Church of the Decapitation of John the Baptist, considered a memorial to soldiers who perished in battle. Indeed, part of the Borodino fortification system known as the Bagration flèche (after General Bagration) was re-created within and just outside the convent walls. In 1867 Leo Tolstoy visited the convent and stayed overnight at its hostel.

On the eastern approach to Borodino Prokudin-Gorsky photographed the graceful Church of the Smolensk Icon of the Virgin, the image revered as a protector against Russia's enemies from the west. Originally dedicated to the Nativity of Christ, the whitewashed brick structure was built in 1698–1701 on the initiative the owner of the village, Timofey Savyolov, member of

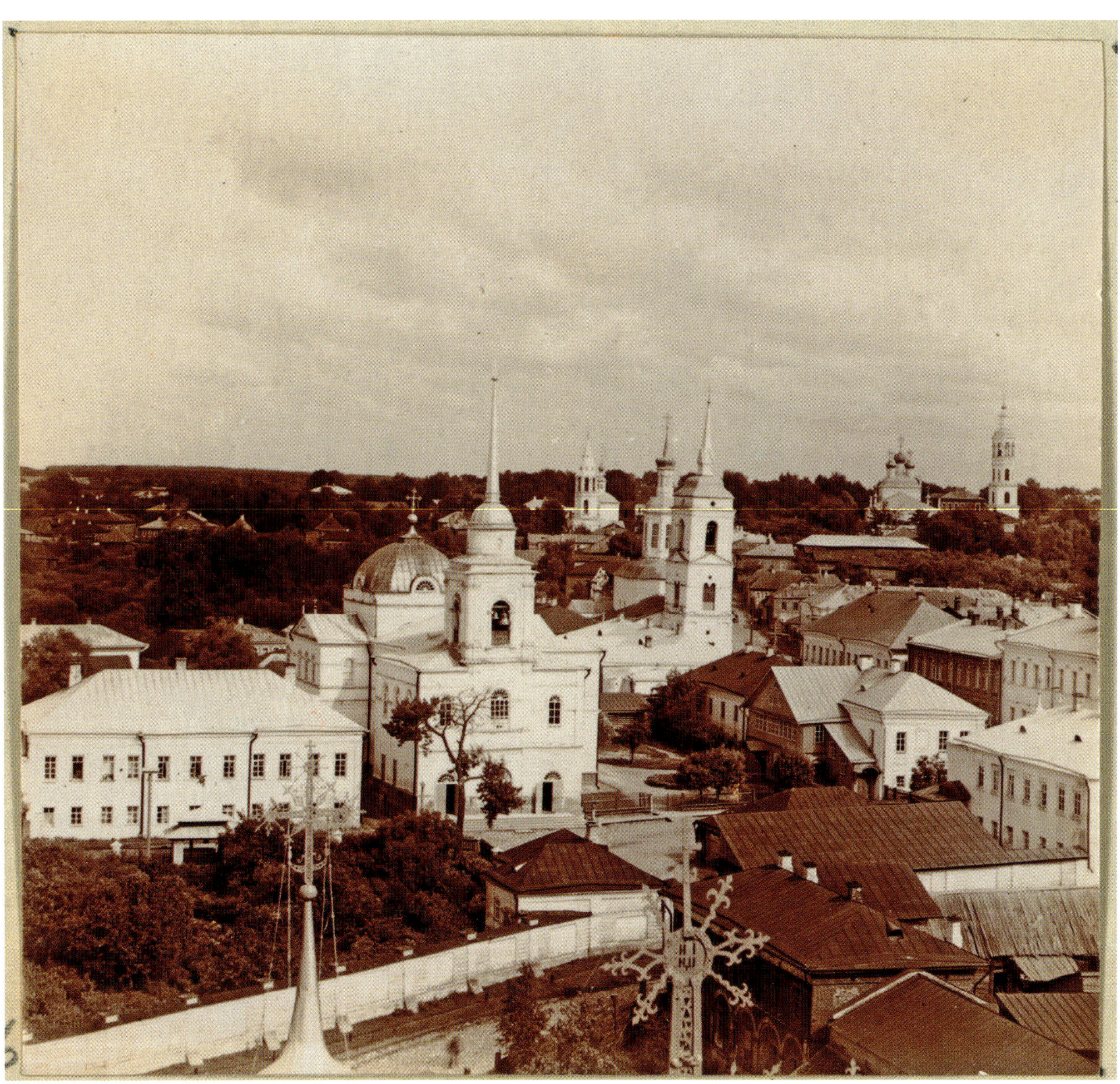

VYAZMA Saint Arkady Monastery. Church of the Icon
of the Most Merciful Savior (*foreground*). Northwest
view. The two churches in the middle, dedicated to
Saint Nicetas and Saint Barbara, were destroyed in the
Soviet period. The transfiguration church in the right
background still stands, but without the bell tower.
PROKUDIN-GORSKY 02250. SUMMER 1912.

VYAZMA Saint Arkady Monastery. Church of the
Icon of the Most Merciful Savior. Northwest view.
BRUMFIELD, AUGUST 22, 2012.

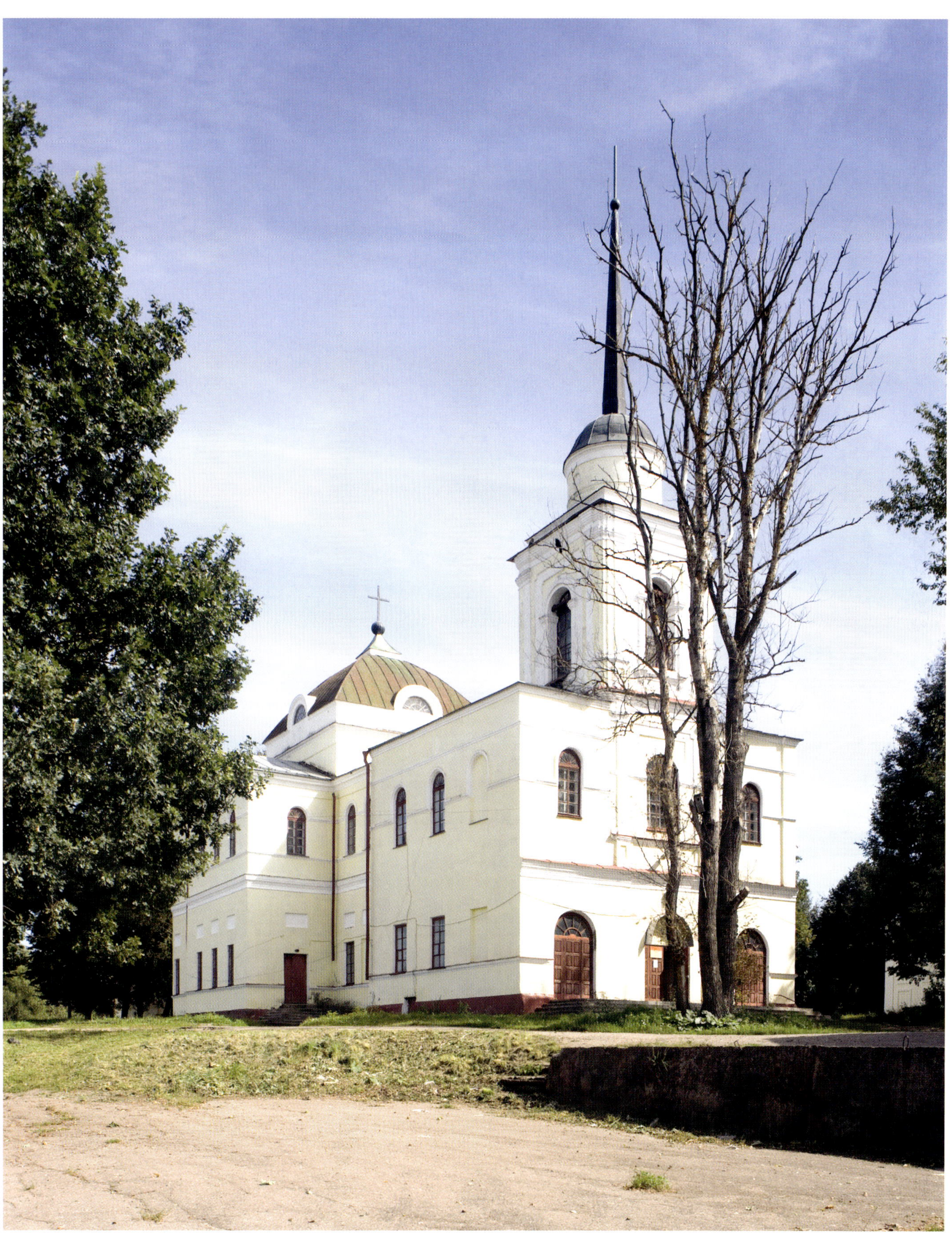

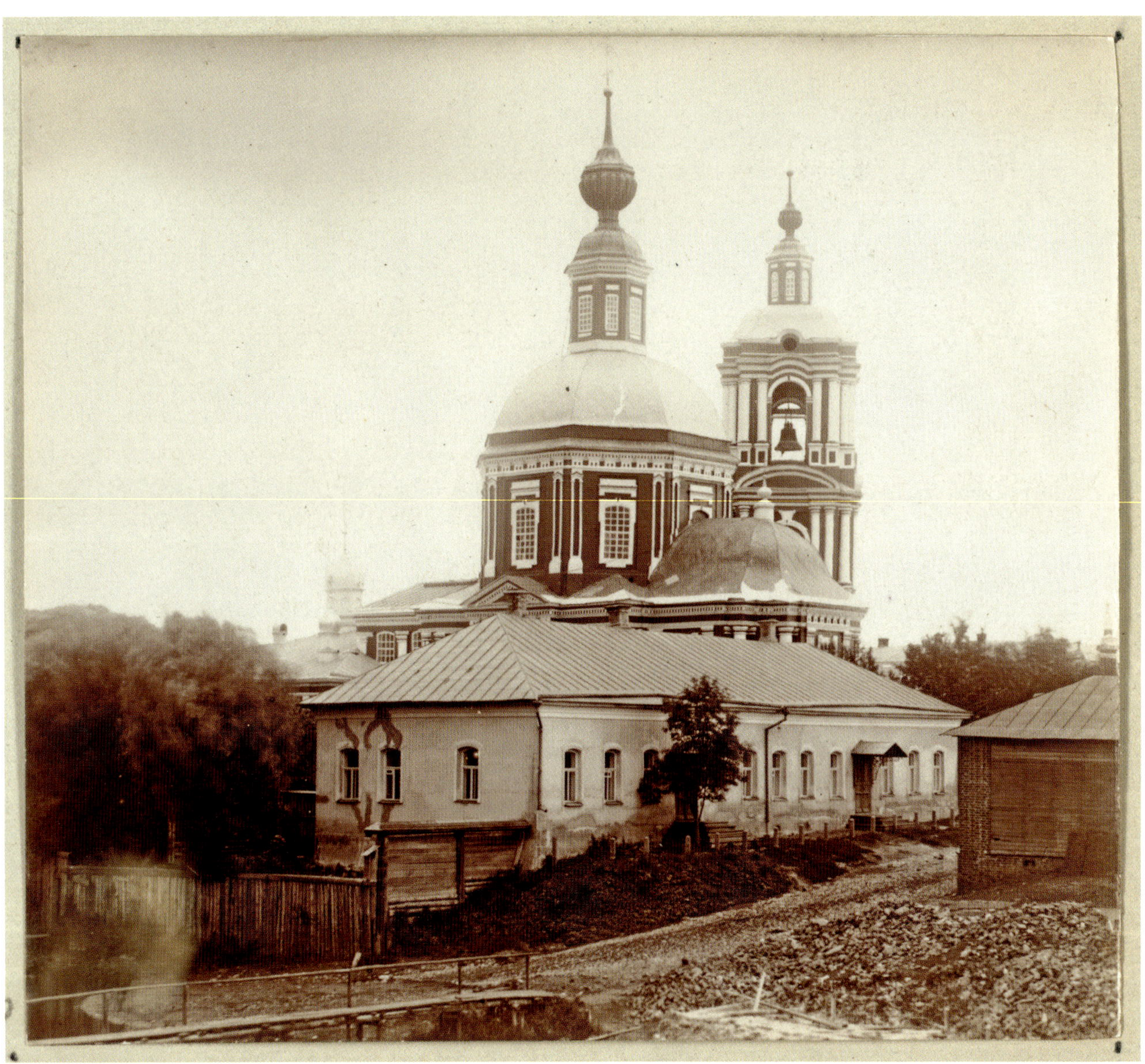

VYAZMA Church of the Nativity of the Virgin. South-east view. PROKUDIN-GORSKY 02252. SUMMER 1912.

VYAZMA Church of the Nativity of the Virgin. South view. BRUMFIELD, AUGUST 22, 2012.

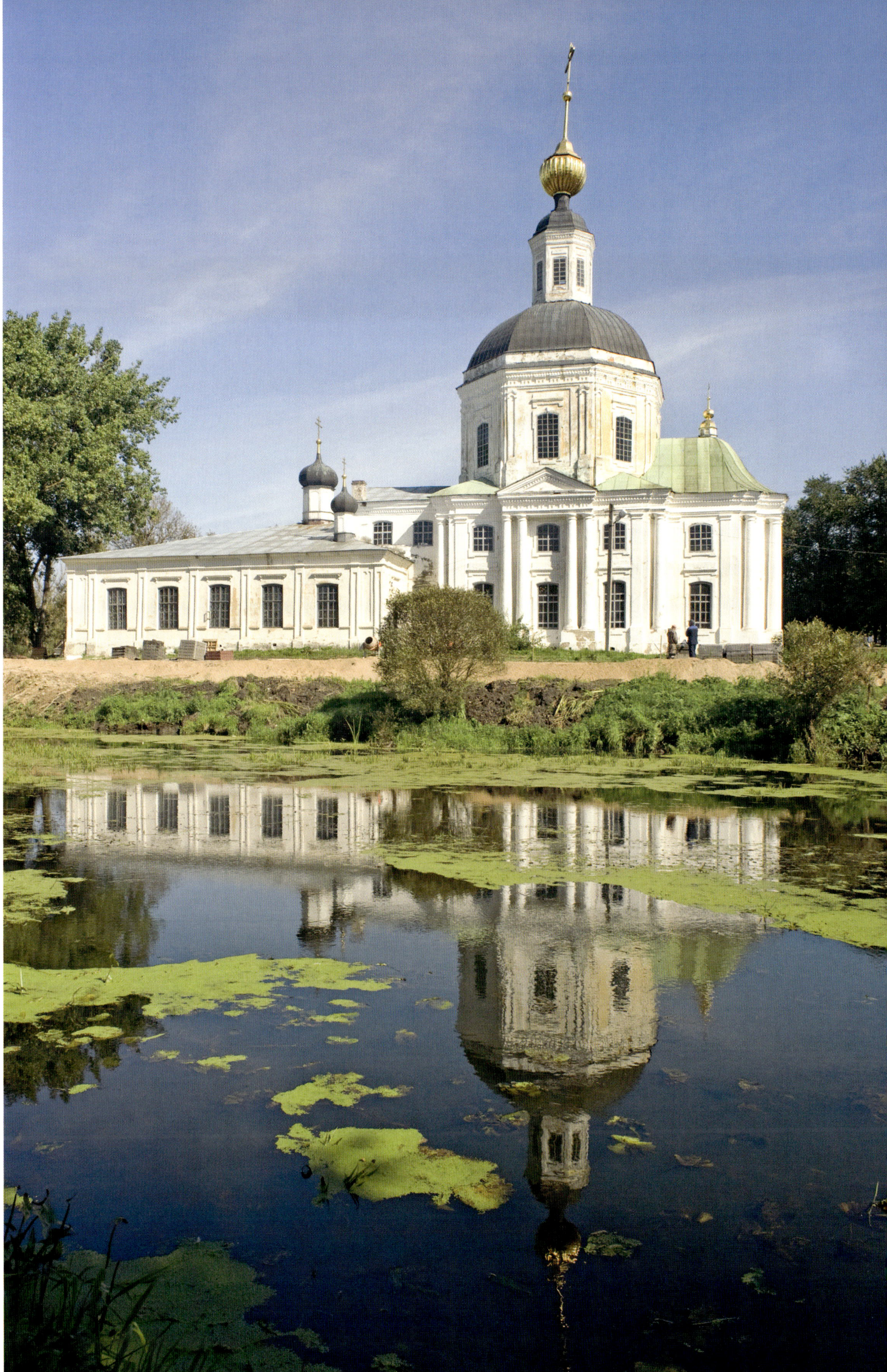

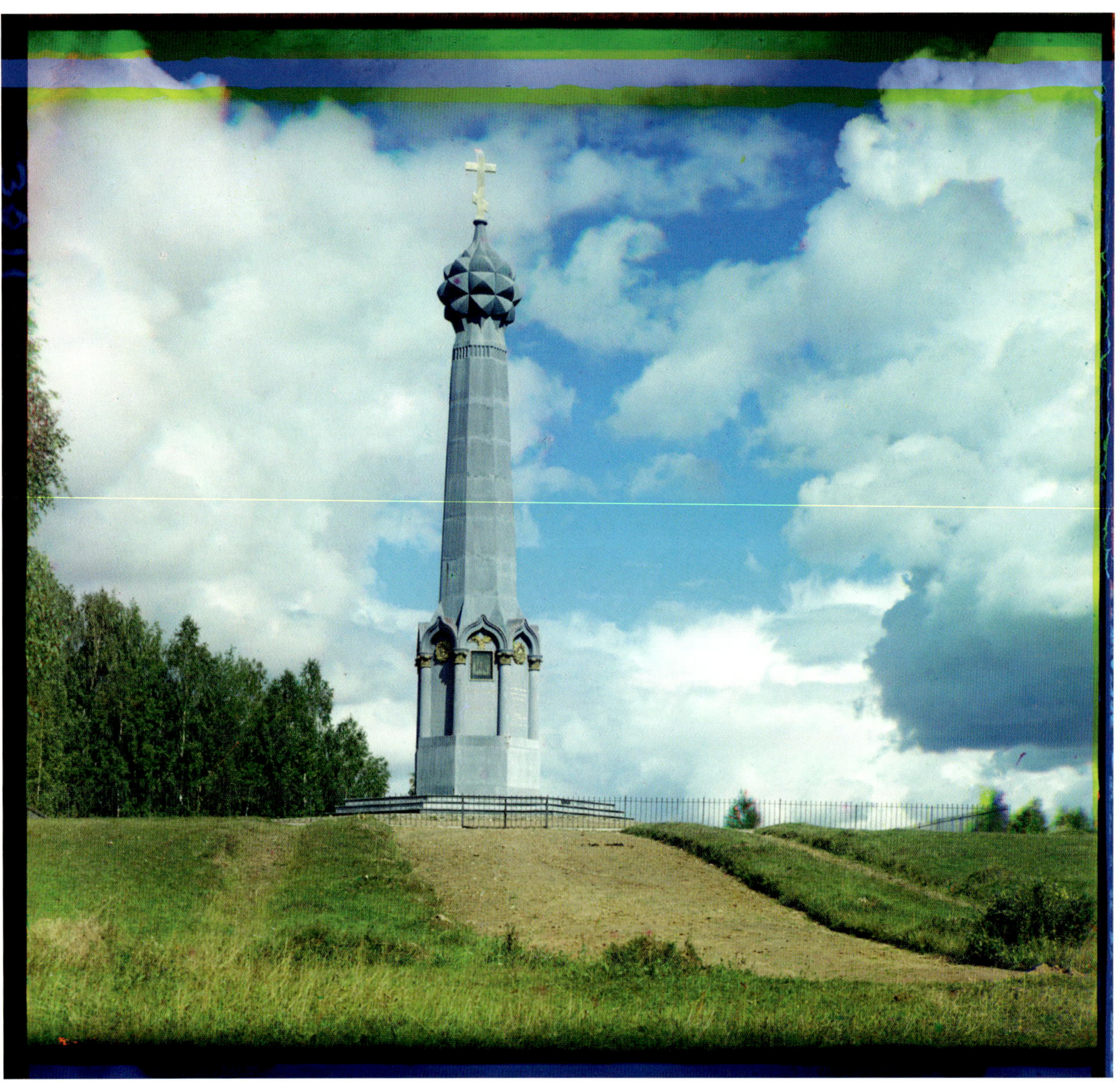

BORODINO Monument at the Raevsky Redoubt.
PROKUDIN-GORSKY 20369. SUMMER 1911.

BORODINO Monument at the Raevsky Redoubt.
BRUMFIELD, AUGUST 21, 2012.

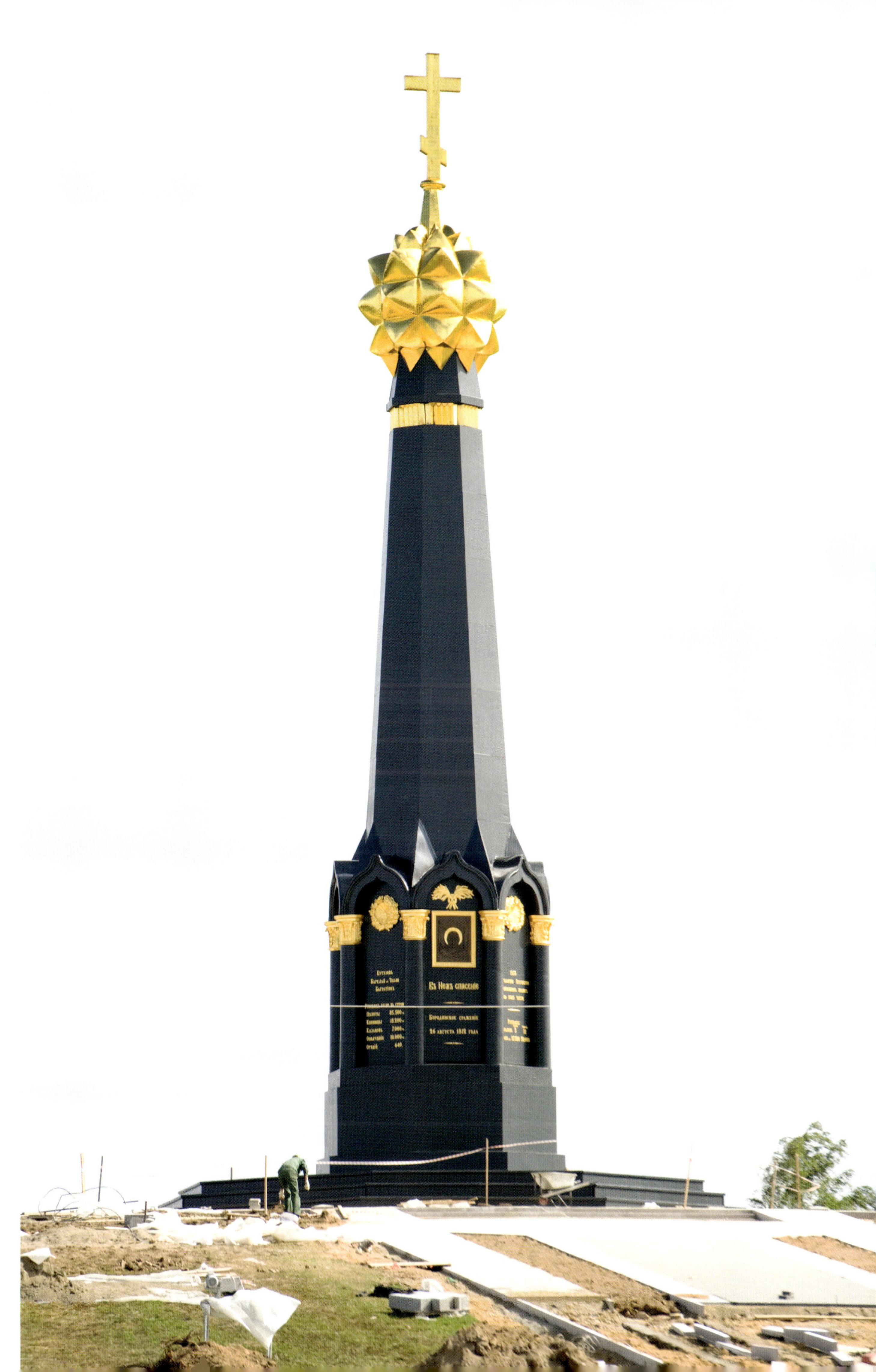

Кутузовъ
Барклай де Толли
Багратіонъ
Въ Немъ спасеніе
Бородинское сраженіе
26 августа 1812 года

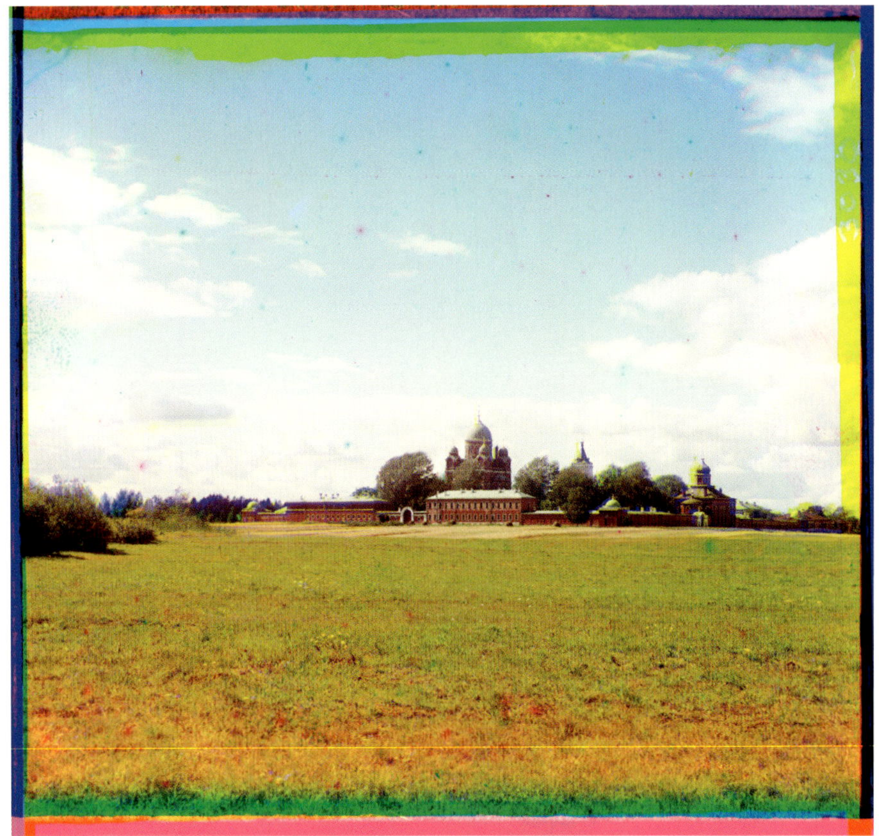

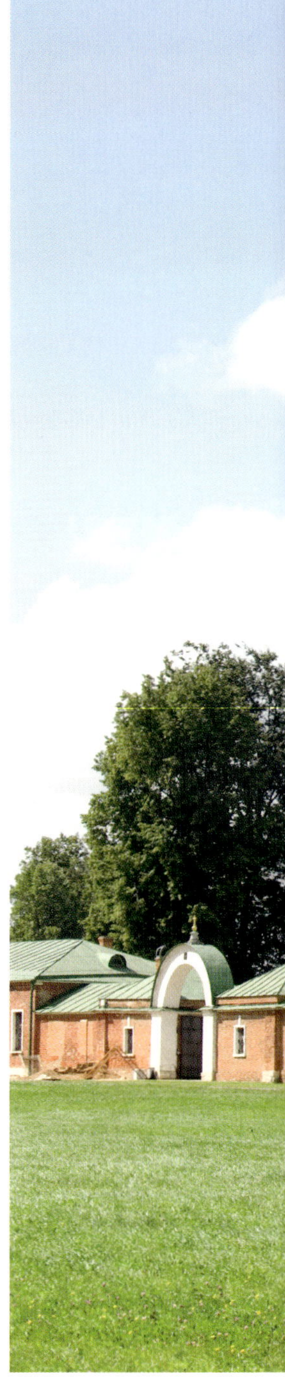

a family closely connected with the tsar's court. (His brother Ivan became Patriarch Joachim, head of the Russian Church from 1674 to 1690.)

The church has two stories, the lower of which contained a secondary altar dedicated to Saint Sergius of Radonezh. With its octagonal upper structure and single cupola, the church represents a simplified version of late seventeenth-century "Moscow baroque" tower churches. On the west is a narthex and bell tower, with a covered stairway to the ground level. A comparison of my photograph with Prokudin-Gorsky's lyrical evening view reveals a small pointed tower instead of the earlier low dome. And his photograph shows the bell tower flanked by two unusual wooden galleries, lost during the Soviet period.

In 1798 the village and church were acquired by retired brigadier Vasily Davydov (1747–1808), father of the poet and war hero Denis Davydov (1784–1839). Denis and his sister Alexandra spent much of their childhood there. During the Borodino battle, the church bell tower served as a Russian observation point and was damaged by French artillery, which also hit the dome of the church. The French occupation of the village resulted in severe fire damage to the church interior. After the war the task of rebuilding the

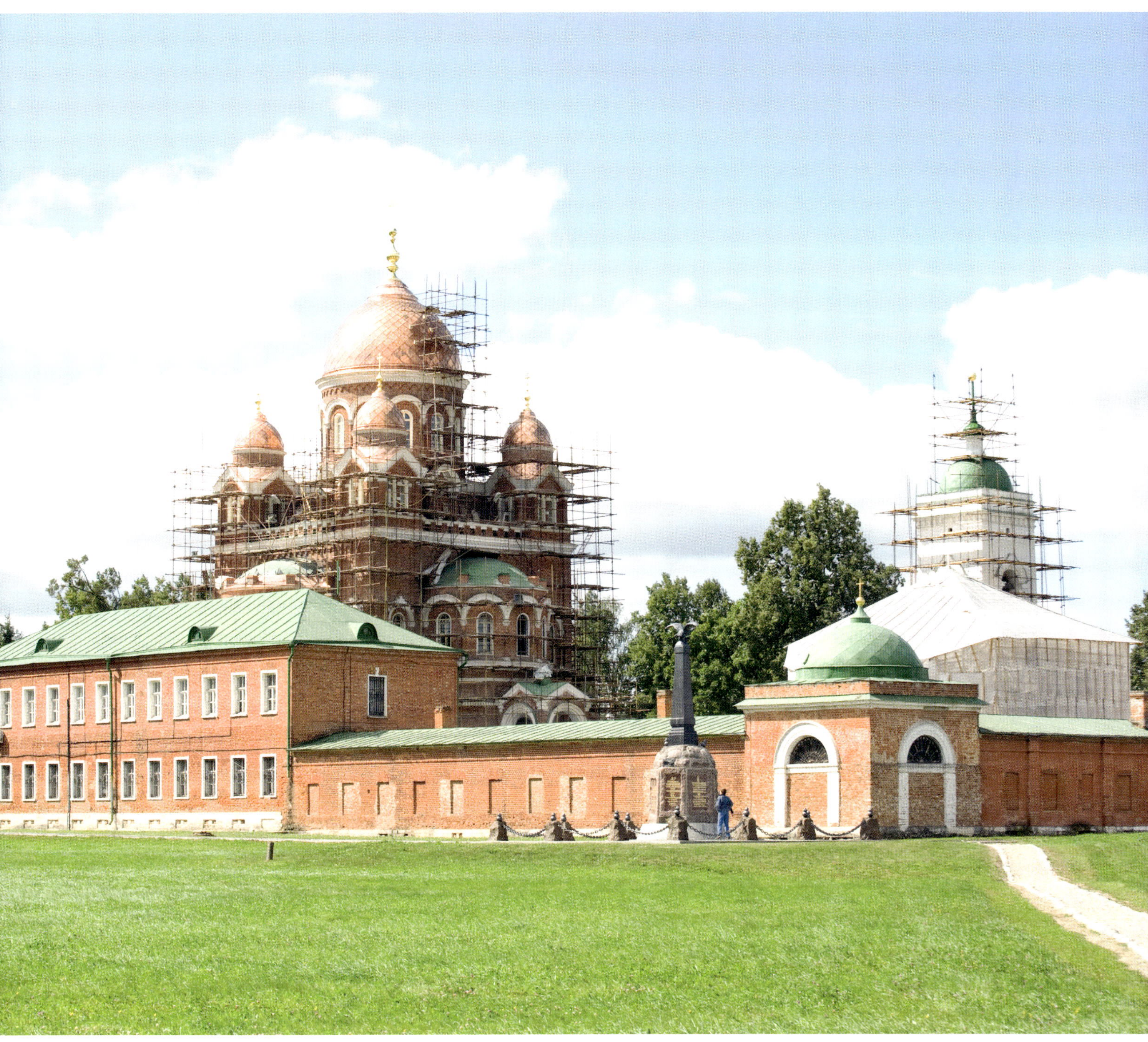

SAVIOR-BORODINO MONASTERY Northeast view.
East wall and cloisters with Cathedral of the Vladimir Icon of the Virgin and Church of the Decapitation
of John the Baptist (*right*). PROKUDIN-GORSKY 20382.
SUMMER 1911.

SAVIOR-BORODINO MONASTERY East wall and cloisters. Northeast view. *Center*: Cathedral of the Vladimir Icon of the Virgin. *Right foreground*: Monument to
Regiments of Second Grenadiers Division, Church of
St. Philaret the Merciful. BRUMFIELD, AUGUST 21, 2012.

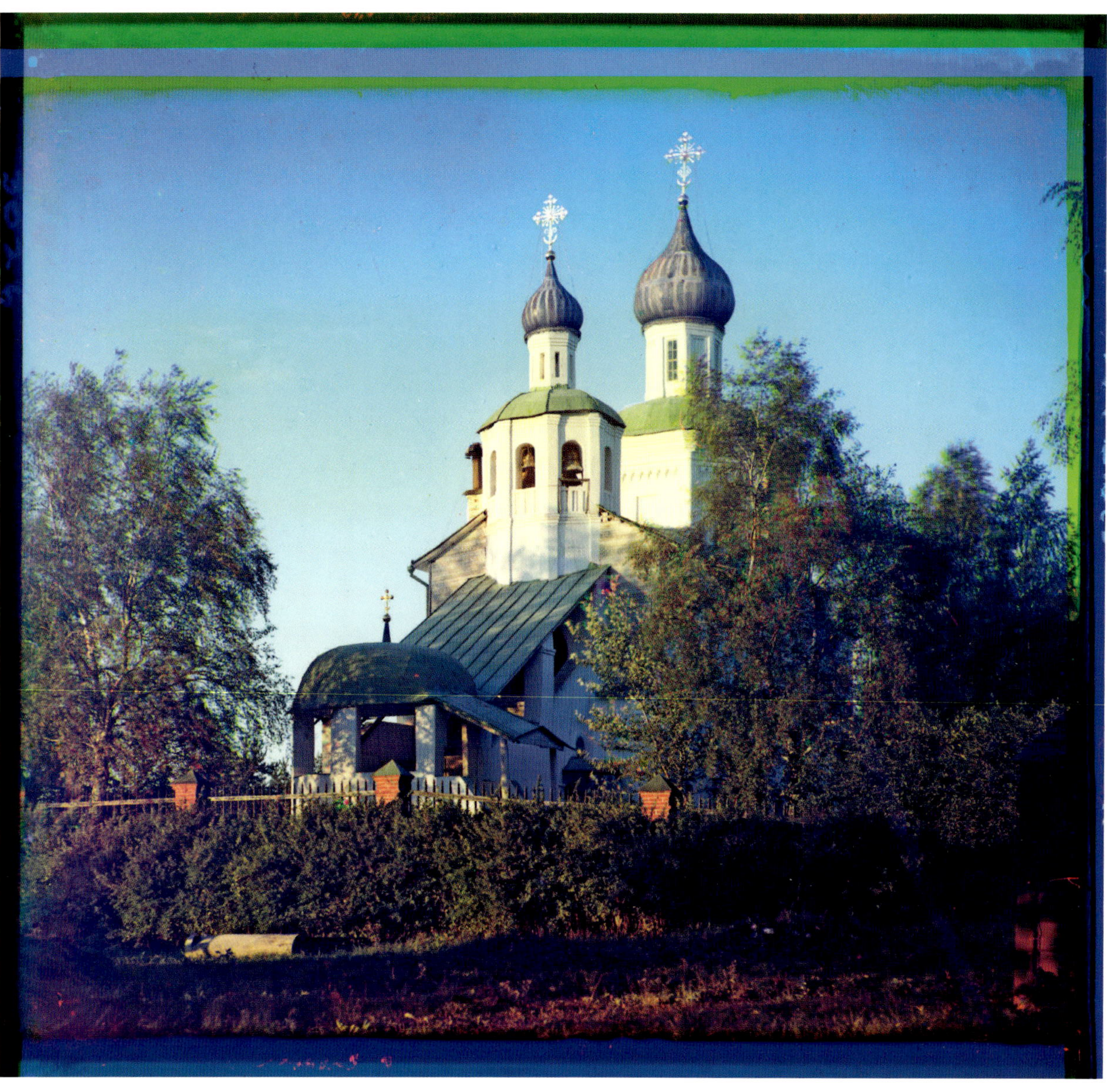

ruined church was beyond the means of the village owners, the widow Elizabeth Savyolova and Alexandra Davydova. In 1816 the lower church, with the altar to Saint Sergius, was repaired on the initiative of Margarita Tuchkova (Naryshkina), widow of General Alexander Tuchkov. In his memory she would establish the Savior-Borodino Convent, which Prokudin-Gorsky also photographed. In 1824 the Borodino church was visited by the distinguished Orthodox prelate, Metropolitan Philaret of Moscow, who provided funds to restore the upper church in 1826. Nonetheless, the upper church remained unfurnished and unconsecrated. In 1830

BORODINO Church of the Smolensk Icon of the Virgin (before 1839, Church of the Nativity of Christ). Southwest view. PROKUDIN-GORSKY 20378. SUMMER 1911.

BORODINO Church of the Smolensk Icon of the Virgin. Southwest view. BRUMFIELD, AUGUST 21, 2012.

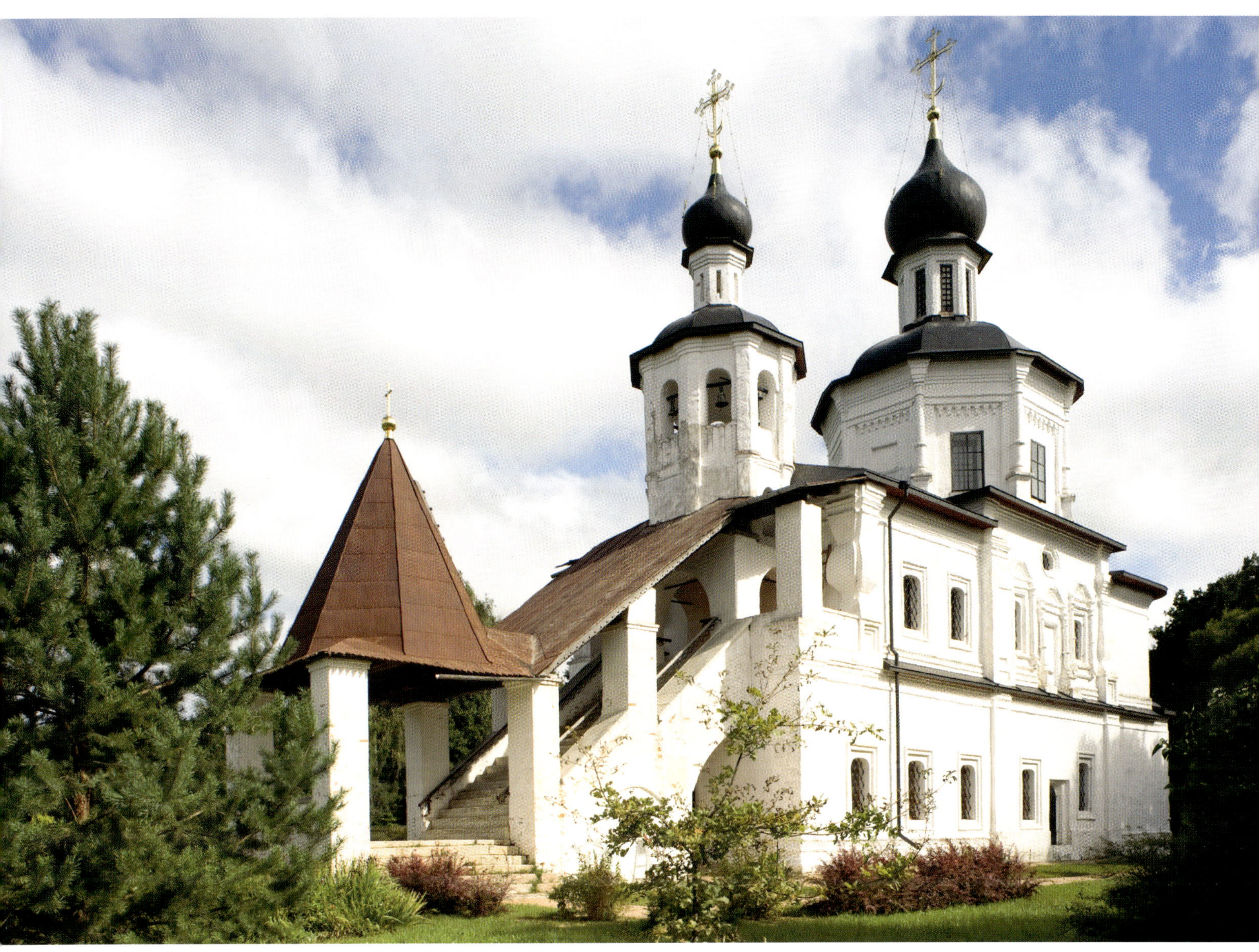

Alexandra Begicheva (formerly Davydova) sold the village to Elizabeth Voyeikova. In July 1837 Tsarevitch Alexander (the heir to the throne) visited Borodino and made a substantial donation to the church.

At the end of 1837 the upper church acquired a remarkable icon screen through a twist of fate. In Moscow, plans were under way to create a national memorial in Moscow to Russian sacrifices in the war with Napoleon. Various sites had been proposed for the Cathedral of Christ the Savior, and in the early 1830s final decisions were made by Emperor Nicholas I as to the architect (Konstantin Ton) and the site, adjacent to the Saint Aleksii Convent in the center of Moscow. In preparation for clearing the site, work began in 1837 on moving the Saint Aleksii Convent to a new location

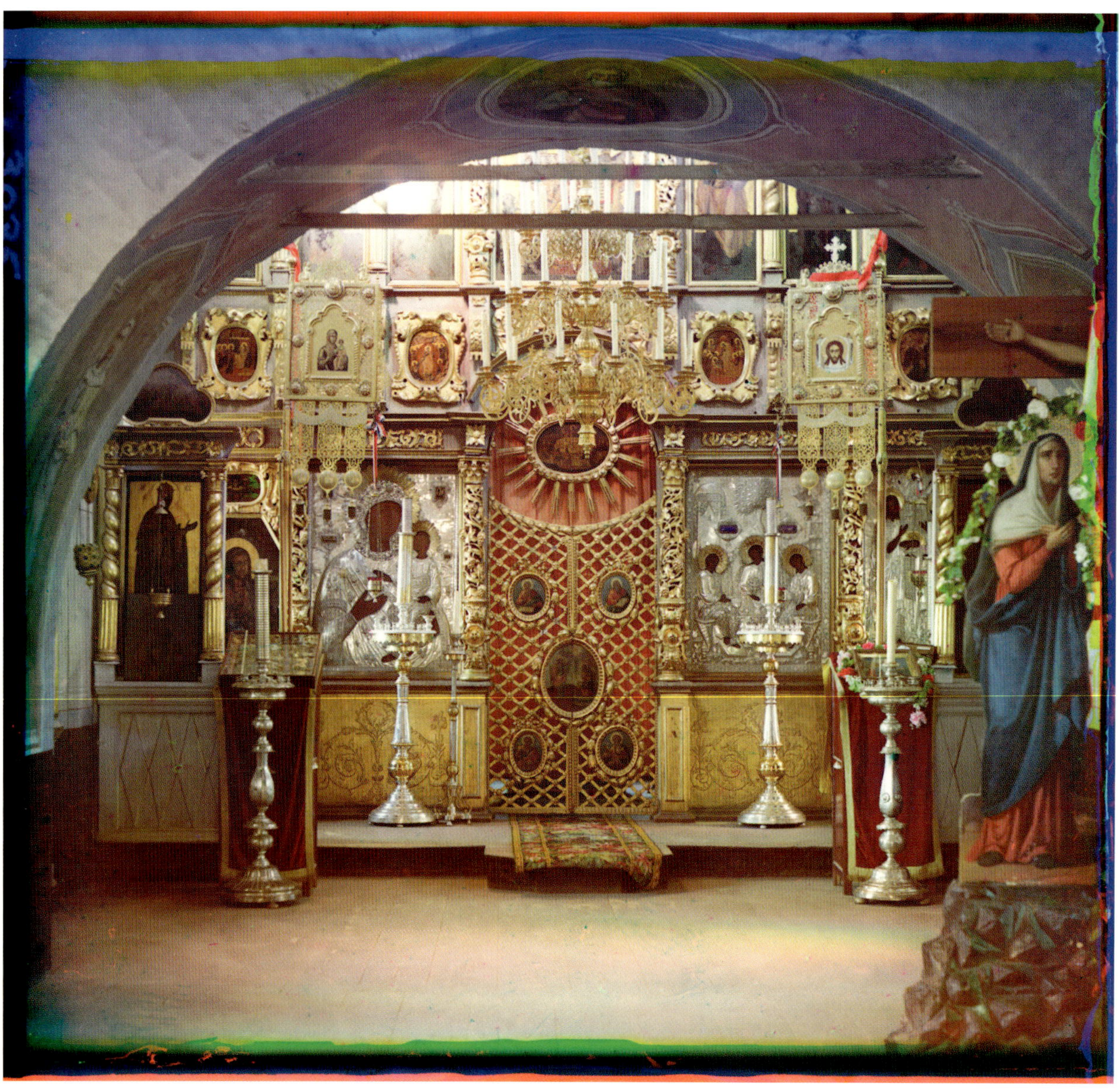

and vacating the original buildings, among which was the early seventeenth-century Cathedral of the Transfiguration and Saint Aleksii. The decision was made to dismantle the cathedral's exquisite late seventeenth-century icon screen and reinstall it in none other than the Borodino church. Its elaborate "grapevine" carving is clearly visible in Prokudin-Gorsky's interior photograph.

In view of its historical significance, the Borodino area was purchased in 1837 by Nicholas I from Elizabeth Voyeikova as a gift to his son Alexander. During a solemn commemoration of the battle, in July 1839 the main altar of the

BORODINO Church of the Smolensk Icon of the Virgin. Interior, upper level. View east from vestibule toward iconostasis. PROKUDIN-GORSKY 20388. SUMMER 1911.

BORODINO Church of the Smolensk Icon of the Virgin. Interior, upper level with new iconostasis. BRUMFIELD, AUGUST 21, 2012.

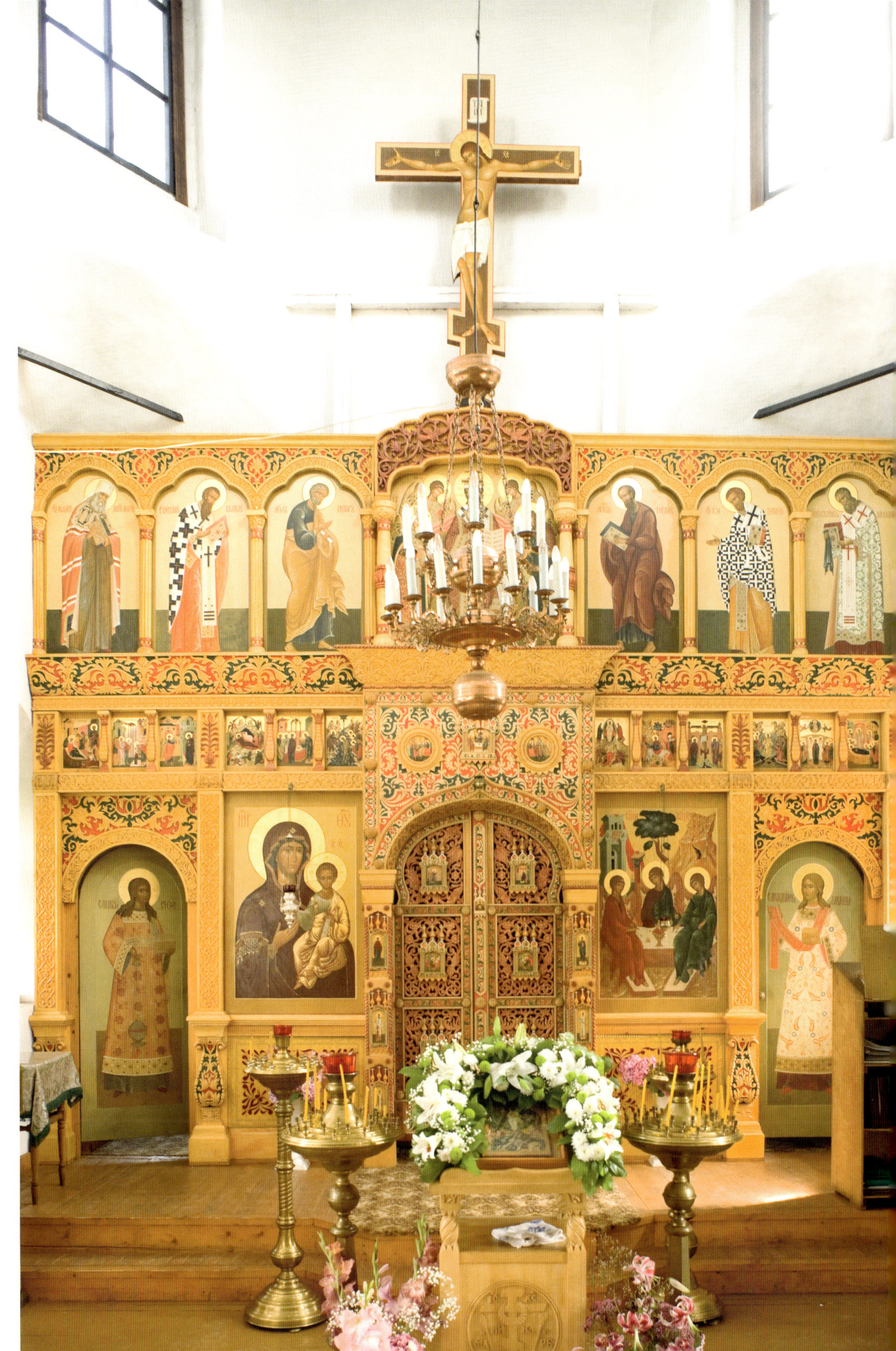

Borodino church was consecrated by Metropolitan Philaret to the Smolensk Icon of the Virgin. This icon in the Hodegetria form was closely associated with Russian valor at Borodino. The sacred image was venerated by both major Russian commanders in the conflict — field marshal Mikhail Kutuzov and general Peter Bagration, who died from wounds suffered in the battle. Indeed, the church treasures included Bagration's personal copy of the Smolensk Icon. In subsequent decades the church continued to be patronized by the royal family. Alexander II, who had long revered the shrine, visited with his wife, Maria, in June 1861. And Nicholas II visited in 1912 on the bicentennial of the battle. In preparation for that anniversary the church was refurbished by the artist Anikita Khotulev. Prokudin-Gorsky's 1911 photographs — exterior and interior — are an indispensable record of the Borodino church before the cataclysm of war and revolution.

During the Soviet period, the church was closed in 1930 and disfigured over the decade by various workshops. A state commission in 1937 determined that there was little justification for an extensive restoration. The Borodino church was again fated to witness the carnage of war in the fall of 1941, during the prolonged Battle of Moscow. When Borodino was retaken on January 21, 1942, little remained of the largely wooden village, which had been burned by the retreating Germans. Yet the church had survived the fighting and three months of occupation. During the years following the war, however, it was subjected to depredations by the local kolkhoz head, who attempted to dismantle the structure for brick. The bell tower was demolished, but resistance from historians and preservationists prevented a complete destruction.

As the Borodino sesquicentennial (1962) approached, renewed efforts to restore the church involved the prominent director and actor Sergey Bondarchuk, who supported the exterior restoration of the church (with rebuilt bell tower) for his gargantuan four-part film *War and Peace* (1965–67). With the making of the film, the restored church was entrusted to the State Borodino Museum. Toward the end of the Soviet period, the museum returned the church to the Moscow eparchy. First services were held in the lower (Saint Sergius) part of the church in 1989, and the upper part was consecrated for services in 1995. A thorough renovation, begun in 1999, involved the creation of new icon screens for both upper and lower churches, as well as wall paintings for the lower church by Peter Stepanov, grandson of the Stalin-era political leader Georgy Malenkov.

Just beyond Borodino in the direction of Moscow is the town of Mozhaisk. Located on high bluffs near the confluence of the Mozhaika and Moscow Rivers, early medieval Mozhaisk developed at the intersection of major trading routes, from Smolensk in the west to Vladimir in the east, and from Novgorod and Tver south toward Ryazan on the Oka River. This geographic advantage in peaceful times would, however, prove a curse to the settlement over the centuries of warfare that defined Muscovite history. Although the fortress at the center of Mozhaisk was defended by natural features such as deep ravines, this did not prevent its frequent devastation by attacking forces.

The first mention of Mozhaisk in medieval chronicles falls under the year 1231 when the settlement confronted attacks both by Novgorod and by Prince Yaroslav of Vladimir. The Mongol invasion later that same decade would in its destruction dwarf anything yet seen in medieval Rus. In 1303 Mozhaisk was seized by Moscow Prince Yury Danilovich, who saw its fortress as a bulwark on Muscovy's western borders. Mozhaisk was again devastated by Khan Tokhtamysh in 1382 during an invasion to reassert the authority of the Horde over Moscow's Grand Prince Dmitry Donskoy, who had defeated the large Tatar army of Khan Mamai near the Don River in 1380.

From 1389 to 1493 Mozhaisk existed as a feudal principality subordinate to Moscow. During this period, the town also became a destination for pilgrims drawn by an account of a miraculous appearance of Saint Nicholas during one of the many attacks on the town. With upraised sword in hand, Saint Nicholas is thought to have protected the besieged fortress. Like Zaraisk, another Moscow regional center, Mozhaisk had its own widely venerated, miracle-working icon of Saint Nicholas. The image was frequently reproduced as a painted wooden statue holding a sword in one hand and a representation of the citadel in the other.

At the turn of the fifteenth century the town gained a masonry cathedral of modest proportions dedicated to Saint Nicholas. With the completion of a new Saint Nicholas Cathedral in the early nineteenth century, the older church, built of limestone blocks, was rededicated to Elijah the Prophet in 1812. In 1844 the dilapidated medieval structure collapsed. It was rebuilt in 1849–53 to a design by Alexander Shestakov that was considered a faithful copy, albeit with brick, rather than limestone, walls. The church was then dedicated to Saints Peter and Paul, although local tradition still refers to it as the Old Cathedral of Saint Nicholas.

The present ("New") Cathedral of Saint Nicholas originally arose in 1680–84 on the foundations of the Saint Nicholas Gate, the main entrance to the medieval fortress and the shrine of the miraculous Mozhaisk Icon of Saint Nicholas. A prolonged reconstruction of the church culminated in 1802–14 with an exuberant pseudo-Gothic display created by Alekse N.

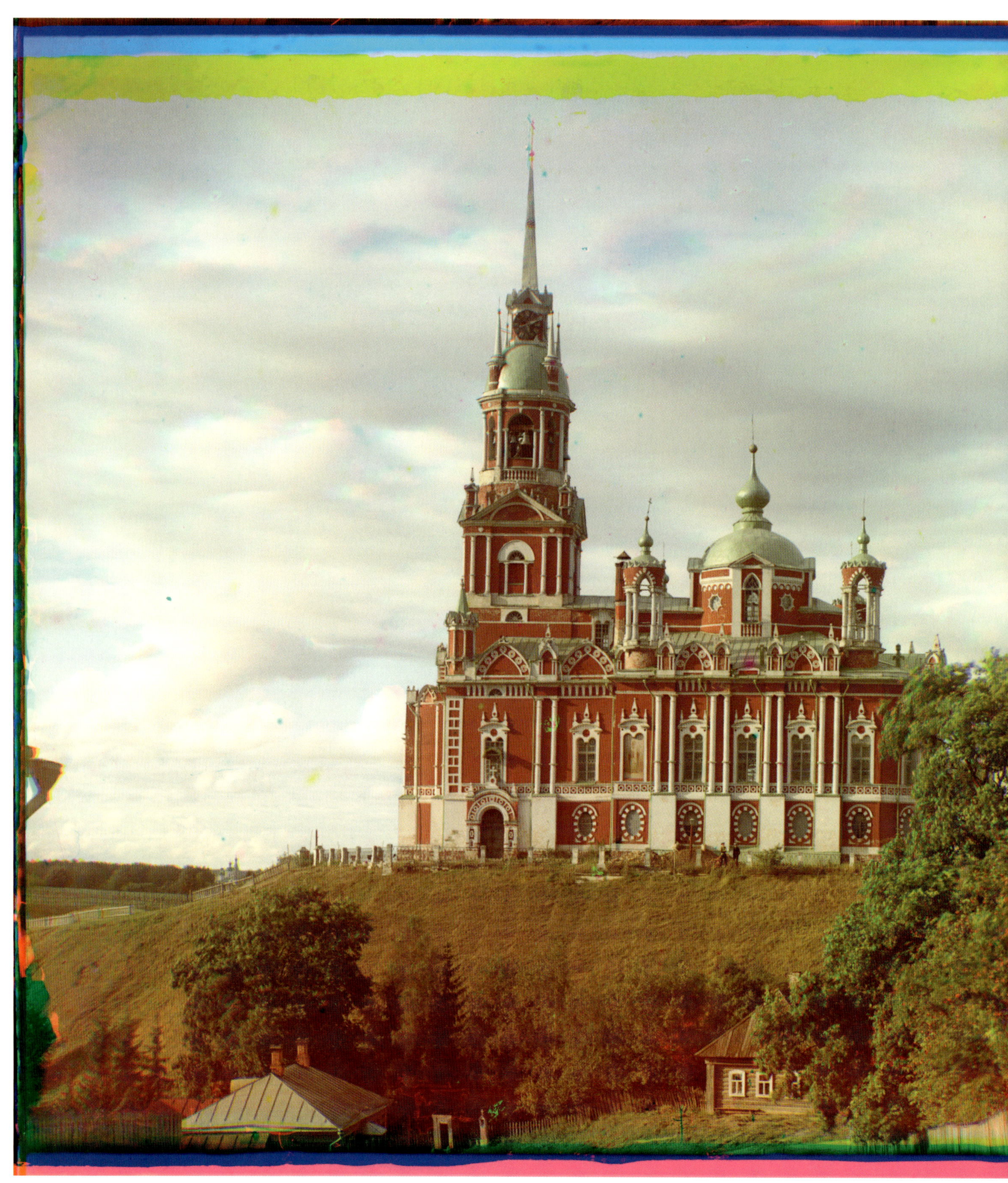

MOZHAISK   Cathedral of Saint Nicholas. South view.
PROKUDIN-GORSKY 20364. SUMMER 1911.

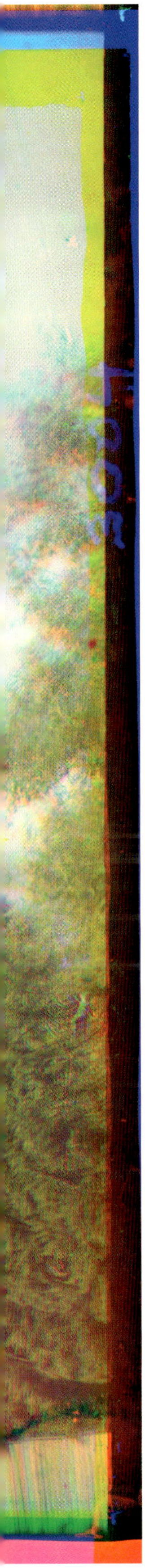

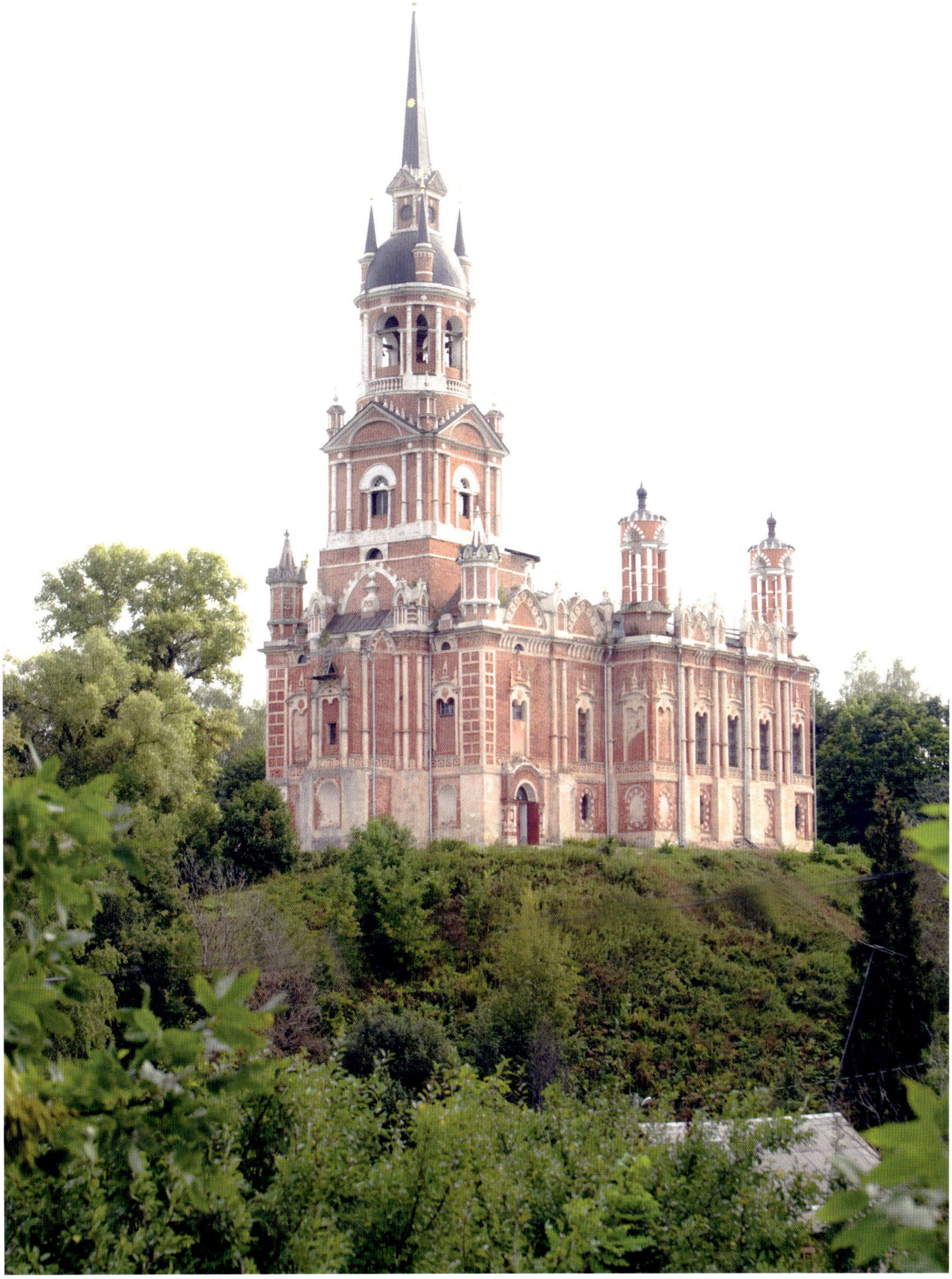

MOZHAISK Cathedral of Saint Nicholas. Southwest view.
BRUMFIELD. AUGUST 21, 2012.

Bakarev, a pupil of Matvey Kazakov, author of much of the pseudo-Gothic fantasy at Moscow's Tsaritsyno estate. Napoleon's troops would have seen this grand display as they sacked the town on the way to Moscow in the fall of 1812. Prokudin-Gorsky's best-known view of the unusual structure is from the south. My photographs provide a similar perspective.

In the fall of 1941 the Mozhaisk area lay squarely at the center of the German attempt to seize Moscow. After sharp resistance, the town was seized on October 18 and liberated on January 20, 1942, as part of the counteroffensive following the Soviet victory in the Battle of Moscow. A comparison of Prokudin-Gorsky's photographs with mine shows the effects of war damage in the roof structure, including a small rotunda that was not rebuilt when the roof was repaired.

Prokudin-Gorsky also photographed the Luzhetsky Nativity of the Virgin Monastery, overlooking the Moscow River on the northwestern fringe of Mozhaisk. Its founder, Saint Ferapont of Belozersk (1330s–1426, canonized in 1549), was a monk of noble origins and a disciple of Saint Sergius of Radonezh, the avatar of Muscovite monasticism. The name of Saint Ferapont is now closely associated with the Nativity of the Virgin-Ferapontov Monastery, which he founded in northern Vologda province in 1398. That small monastery is known for its sublime frescoes, created in 1502 by the Moscow painter Dionisy and his sons.

Ferapont had close connections with the Moscow court, and his reputation had come to the attention of Prince Andrei of Mozhaisk, son of Moscow's Grand Prince Dmitry Donskoy and holder of title to the northern lands around White Lake (Beloozero). At Andrei's request, Ferapont arrived at Mozhaisk in 1408 to establish the Mozhaisk monastery dedicated to the Nativity of the Virgin. The prince supported the endeavor with the construction of a small limestone church, whose foundations are visible at the monastery.

Renewed construction began under the direction of Makary, who served as abbot of the monastery in 1523–26 and continued to support it after becoming the metropolitan of the Russian Orthodox Church in 1542. Of special importance was a new masonry Cathedral of the Nativity of the Virgin begun in the 1520s and consecrated in 1547. Makary subsequently played an important role in both church and state affairs during the early reign of Ivan the Terrible. Prokudin-Gorsky's photographs include an east view with the imposing bell tower, built in the last quarter of the seventeenth century.

The position of Mozhaisk on the road to Moscow brought renewed danger during the Napoleonic invasion of 1812, as great armies converged on the nearby village of Borodino. Following the Battle of Borodino, Mozhaisk was filled with Russian wounded. As Kutuzov's main force retreated toward Moscow, the French occupied Luzhetsky Monastery on August 27 (Julian calendar) and Mozhaisk the following day. When the French abandoned Mozhaisk during Napoleon's retreat in mid-October, the town and the monastery presented a scene of devastation. During the Soviet period, the monastery was again devastated, as recorded in my photographs. My photographs taken within the monastery show the results of restoration after the return of the monastery to the Orthodox Church in 1994.

The concluding link in Prokudin-Gorsky's documentation of sites linked to the French invasion of 1812 is the small town of Maloyaroslavets, whose defense on October 24, 1812, played a decisive role in compelling Napoleon's Grande Armée to return to the Smolensk road in catastrophic retreat. Maloyaroslavets is located some 120 kilometers southwest of Moscow on the Luzha River, a right tributary of the Protva, which in turn flows into the Oka, part of the Volga basin. The town still has the remains of a flattened hillock that served as a citadel for a tribe of Vyatichi, local Slavs who were subdued by Kiev's Prince Svyatoslav in the second half of the tenth century.

The present town was founded at the end of the fourteenth century by Prince Vladimir the Brave of Serpukhov (1353–1410), who named it after his fourth son, Yaroslav (1388–1426). The first written reference to the town occurred in chronicles under the year 1402, which is considered the town's official founding date. At the same time Vladimir established what would become the town's major spiritual and cultural institution, the Saint Nicholas-Chernoostrovsky Monastery, located not far from the ancient citadel. Yaroslav ruled only briefly in the town that his father had founded, for he and two of his brothers succumbed to the plague in 1426. His remains now rest in the Archangel Cathedral of the Moscow Kremlin. Over the next four centuries Maloyaroslavets developed into a modest regional center, a status formalized in 1776 during Catherine the Great's administrative reforms of Russia's vast territory. The town was placed within the province of Kaluga, located 60 kilometers to the southwest.

The placid existence of Maloyaroslavets would be shattered—and most of the town ruined—by the events of late October 1812. Isolated in smoldering Moscow and with no prospects of Russia's suing for peace, Napoleon and his reduced army (about 110,000 troops) began the Moscow exodus on October 19. Because of lack of fodder, the Grande Armée already faced catastrophic limitations in cavalry, artillery, and transport—all horse-drawn. The intention was to replenish supplies by marching southwest toward relatively

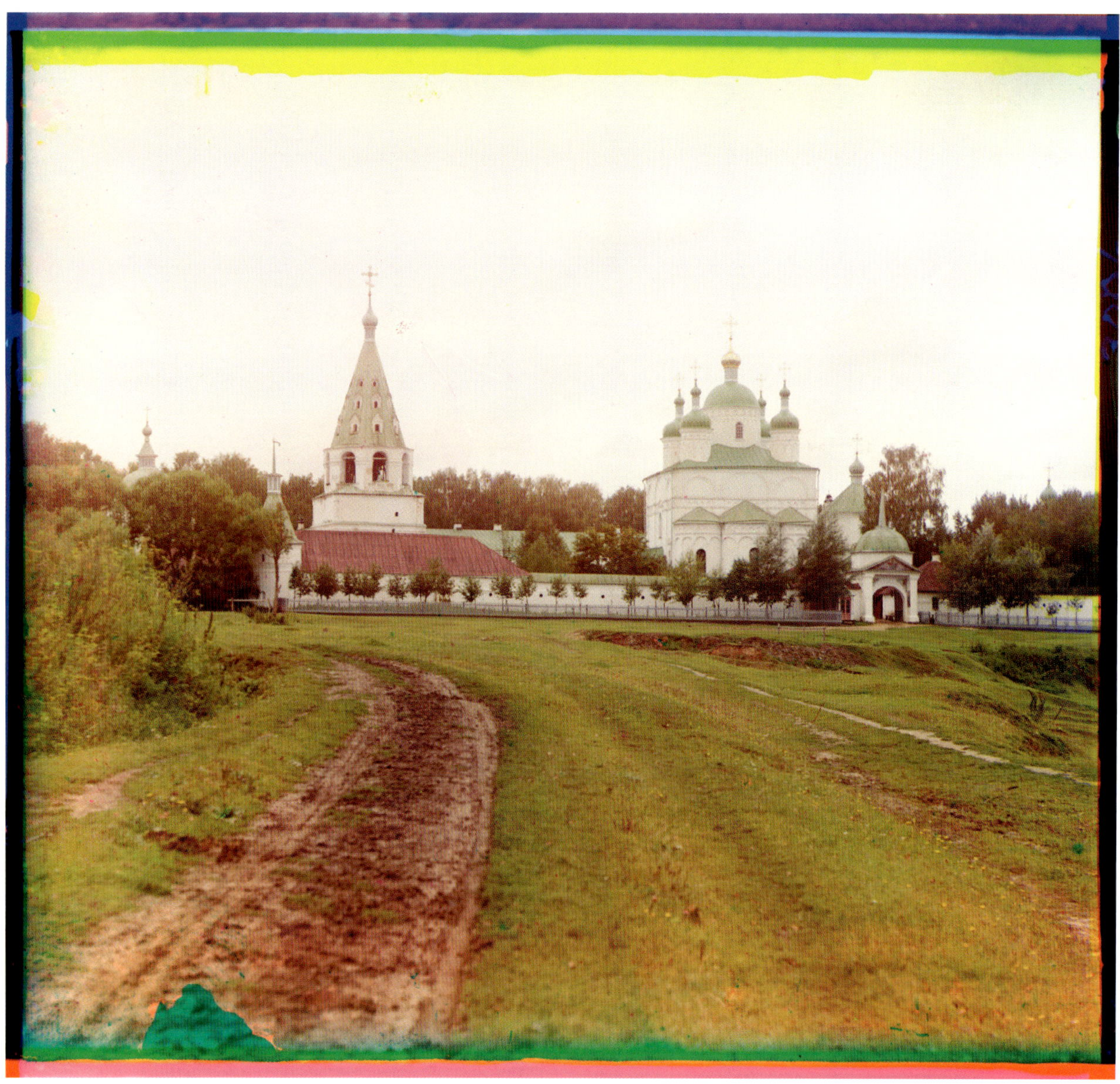

unscathed territory—perhaps as far as Ukraine. However, the path southwest was threatened by the Russian army, preserved as a coherent fighting force by Kutuzov after the Battle of Borodino and the evacuation from Moscow. By establishing his main camp at Tarutino on the Old Kaluga Road to the southwest of Moscow, Kutuzov had artfully covered the main southern routes available to Napoleon.

On October 18, Russian forces inflicted a sharp defeat on a probing operation by Marshal Murat near Tarutino, a sign that Kutuzov's army was full of fight. Switching to the New Kaluga Road, Napoleon's army reached Borovsk by Octo-

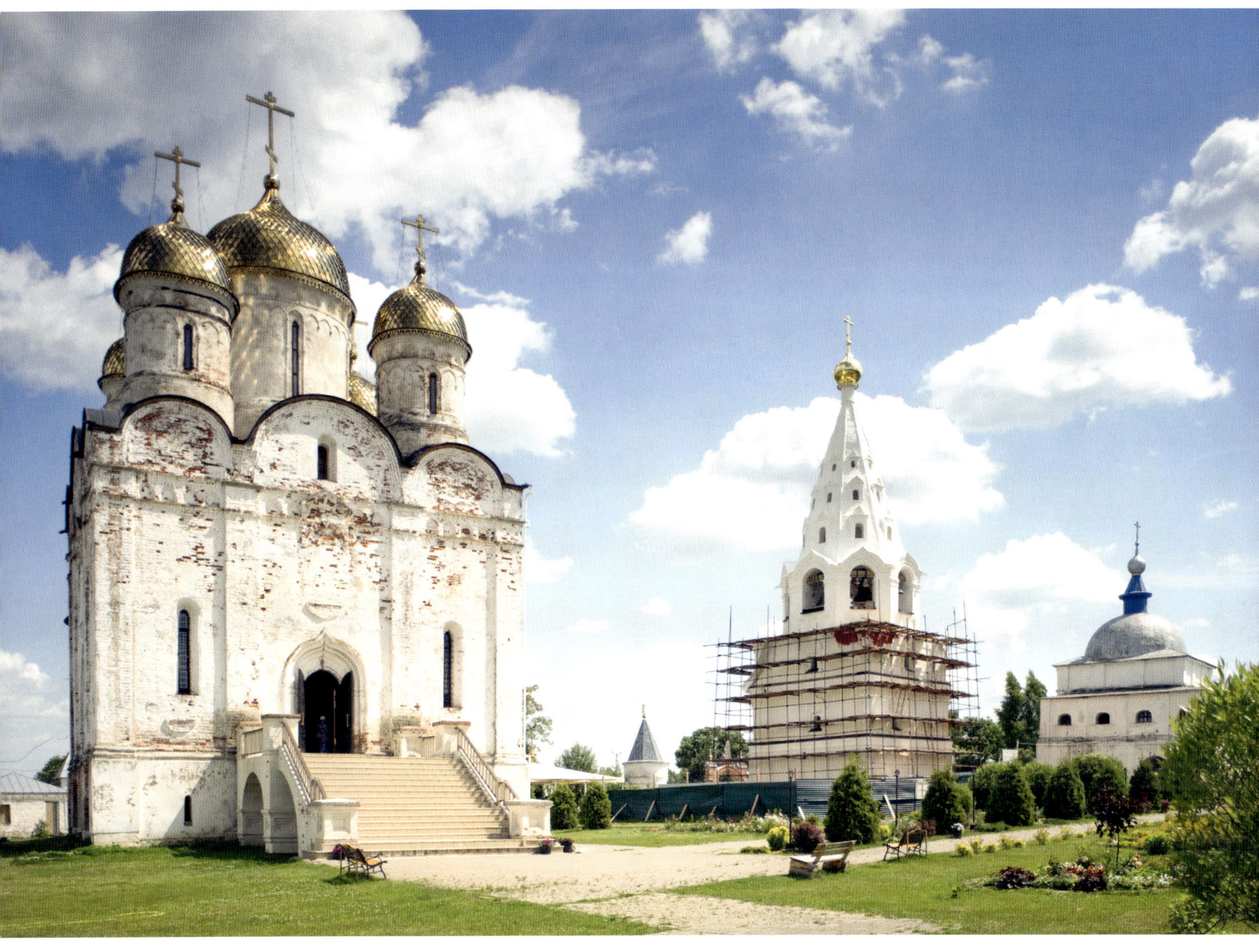

ber 22 and began to move toward Maloyaroslavets on the way to Kaluga. On October 23 both sides were confused as to the precise locations of the main body of opponents. Alarmed by Russian cavalry raids, Napoleon paused and sent his Thirteenth Division, commanded by Alexis Joseph Delzons, ahead to Maloyaroslavets early on October 24. Kutuzov ordered Dmitry Dokhturov, commander of the Sixth Corps, to counter this move, and as the day unfolded, both sides fed more forces into the battle. The French several times crossed the Luzha River at Saint John's Meadow (Ivanovsky Lug) and stormed the heights near the Church of Saint John the Baptist (1770s) and the Saint Nicholas Monastery.

The town itself, which had about fifteen hundred inhabitants, changed

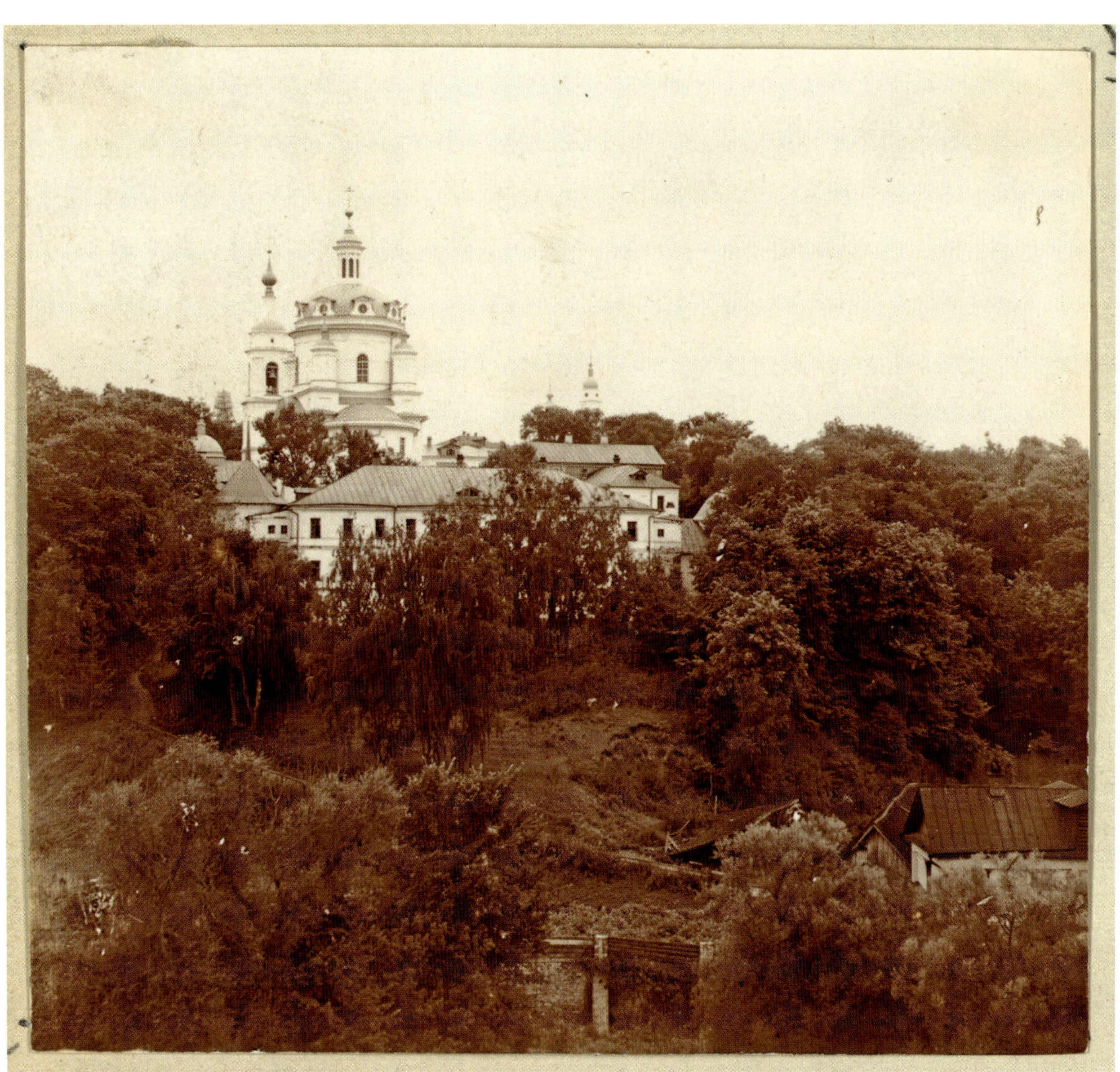

MALOYAROSLAVETS Saint Nicholas-Chernoostrovsky Monastery. East view. *From left*: dome of Church of Korsun Icon of the Virgin, bell tower, Cathedral of Saint Nicholas, east cloisters, Cathedral of the Kazan Icon of the Virgin. PROKUDIN-GORSKY 02256. SUMMER 1912.

MALOYAROSLAVETS Chernoostrovsky Saint Nicholas Monastery. East view. *From left*: dome of Church of Korsun Icon of the Virgin, bell tower, Cathedral of Saint Nicholas, east cloisters, Cathedral of the Kazan Icon of the Virgin, Church of Archangel Michael. BRUMFIELD, AUGUST 7, 2016.

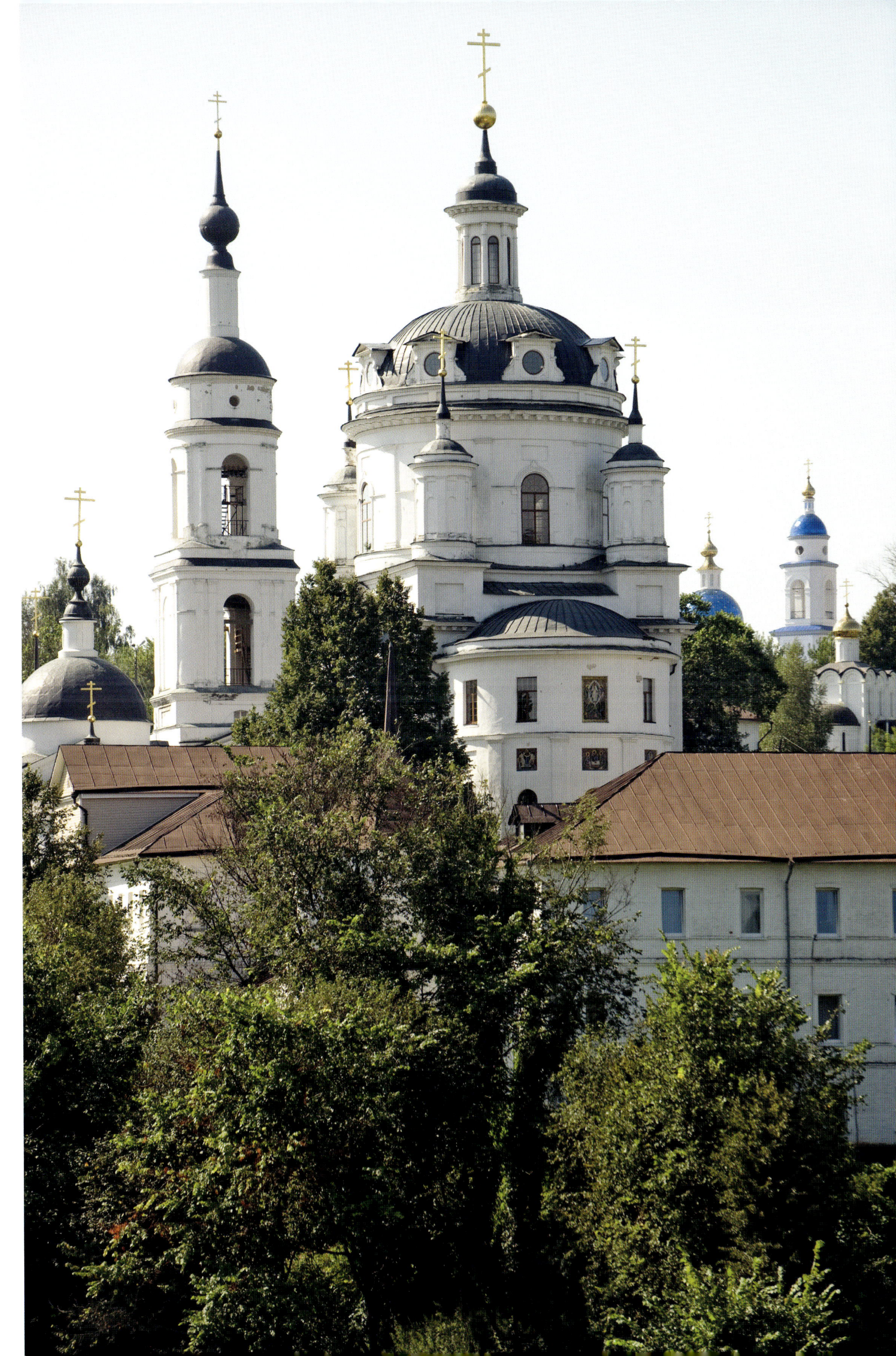

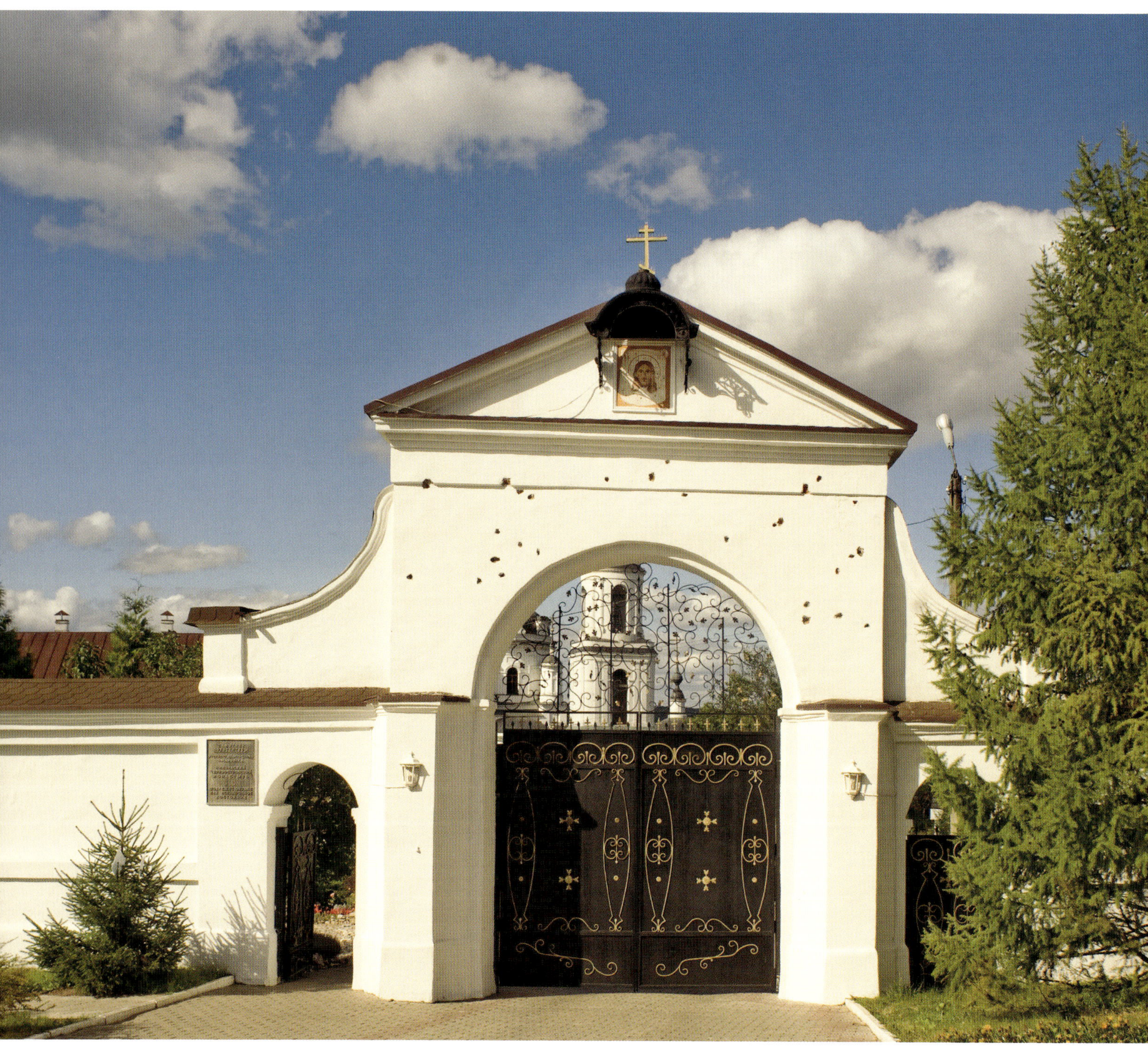

MALOYAROSLAVETS Chernoostrovsky Saint Nicholas Monastery. Holy Gate with traces of battle damage. West view. *Beyond gate*: bell tower and Saint Nicholas Cathedral. BRUMFIELD, AUGUST 8, 2016.

MALOYAROSLAVETS Chernoostrovsky Saint Nicholas Monastery. Holy Gate with traces of battle damage. West view. PROKUDIN-GORSKY 02257. SUMMER 1912.

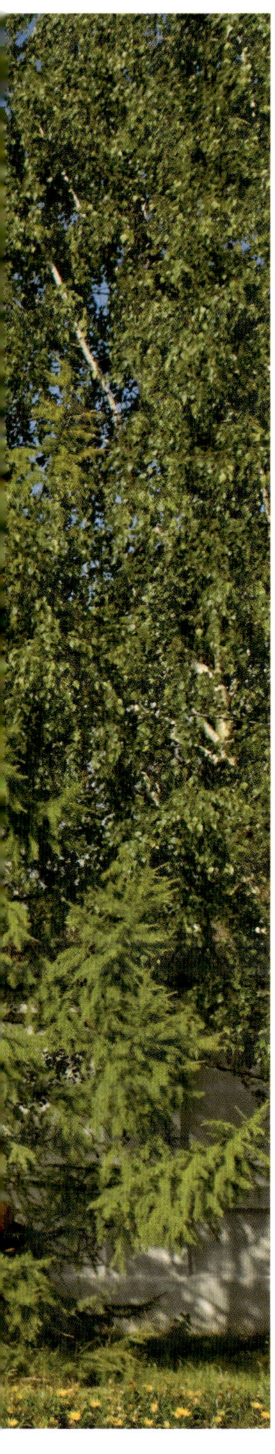

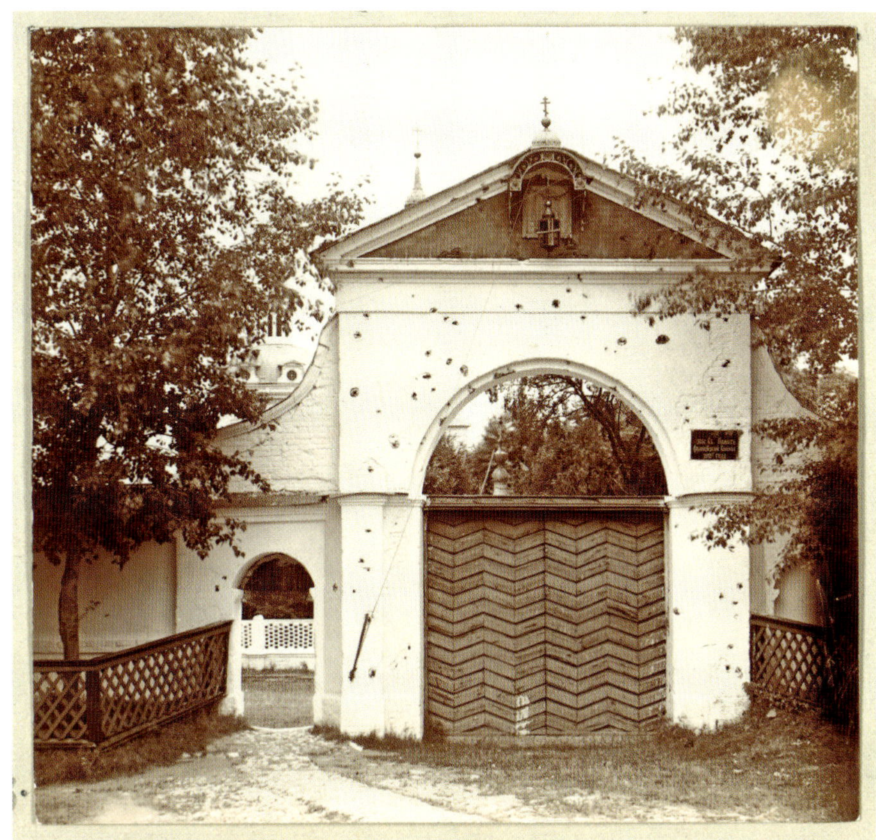

hands eight times during a day of relentless hand-to-hand combat. The few streets were rapidly consumed by flames, and many of the wounded died in the fires. Russian losses were some seven thousand, and the French suffered perhaps as many as six thousand, including General Delzons. As the day waned, Kutuzov abandoned the struggle for Maloyaroslavets and shifted his forces to prepared positions just to the south, thus blocking the road to Kaluga. Left in possession of a small, ruined town, and with reduced cavalry and artillery (for lack of horses), Napoleon made the fateful decision to turn back to the northwest and the already devastated road to Smolensk. Maloyaroslavets proved the culminating clash in a week that would turn Napoleon's Grande Armée toward its agony.

In the following decade Maloyaroslavets recovered and by the middle of the nineteenth century had over 2,500 inhabitants. The Saint Nicholas Monastery was imposingly rebuilt in a neoclassical style, recorded in Prokudin-Gorsky's contact print. My photograph shows a similar view of the recently restored ensemble. The monastery's main gate was left as a memorial, with traces of damage visible in Prokudin-Gorsky's photograph. A comparison of our photographs suggests that little has changed over the past two centuries. Ransacked during the Soviet period, the monastery was returned to the Orthodox Church in 1991 and revived as a convent.

SOUTH OF MOSCOW

Due east of Maloyaroslavets and to the southeast of Moscow lies the town of Kolomna, picturesquely situated at the confluence of the Kolomenka and Moscow Rivers. Kolomna is one of the most appealing of Russia's provincial towns. Its monasteries, which create the historical silhouette of the town, are being restored, and many of its merchant houses from the early nineteenth century have been preserved with their neoclassical charm. The earliest mention of Kolomna in medieval chronicles refers to a clash in 1177 between Vsevolod the Great Nest, Grand Prince of Vladimir, and his rival Prince Gleb of Ryazan. Such struggles were frequent among Russian princes in the twelfth and early thirteenth centuries, but they were soon to be followed by the far more devastating Mongol invasion of 1237–41. Overwhelmed in the initial attack, Kolomna was ravaged in 1237, although not without fierce resistance. Kulkan, the youngest son of Genghis Khan, was killed during the battle for Kolomna.

From the beginning of the fourteenth century Moscow's princes valued Kolomna as a strategic citadel guarding its southern border. Located not far from the point where the Moscow River flows into the Oka (the major western tributary of the Volga), Kolomna was traversed by trading routes from much of central Russia. This movement of goods through the town would create the basis for a lasting merchant culture. Despite its increasing prosperity, Kolomna experienced a full measure of catastrophes in the fourteenth century, including an outbreak of plague in 1363 and looting by the army of Tatar khan Tokhtamysh in August 1382. Yet in the same period Kolomna proved its resilience in 1379 with the construction of its first large church, dedicated to the Dormition of the Virgin. It was in the shadow of this church—since completely rebuilt—that Moscow's Grand Prince Dmitry Donskoi held a prayer service in preparation for the great battle against the Tatar khan Mamai at Kulikovo Pole in September 1380.

Curiously, the Prokudin-Gorsky Collection contains no photographs of Kolomna itself. Rather, he chose to photograph the picturesque Epiphany-Golutvin Monastery, known after 1800 as the Old Golutvin Monastery, located to the south of Kolomna near the confluence of the Moscow and

Oka Rivers. Disfigured and ransacked during the Soviet period, the monastery has been thoroughly restored. Its center is dominated by the boxy Epiphany Cathedral, photographed by Prokudin-Gorsky from the northeast. Originally built at the end of the fourteenth century, the cathedral was rebuilt, expanded, damaged by fire in 1718, and fundamentally rebuilt during the eighteenth century. The most distinctive features of the Old Golutvin Monastery are its wall towers, architectural fantasies built of red brick with limestone details in the style of Matvey Kazakov. Prokudin-Gorsky and I both took multiple photographs of the towers. I have chosen the recently restored northwest corner tower, near the main entrance to the monastery, with the monastery bell tower under restoration to the left.

From Kolomna, Prokudin-Gorsky traveled south by rail to Ryazan, another of the oldest cities of the Russian heartland. Already an important town in the eleventh century, Ryazan was completely devastated by the Mongols in 1237 and eventually revived at another location nearby. Today Ryazan is a growing city with a population of over half a million, located 180 kilometers to the south of Moscow. Among its several distinctions, Ryazan serves as a major administrative center of the Russian Orthodox Church, and the Ryazan kremlin has one of Russia's most imposing cathedrals.

By the middle of the twelfth century Ryazan had become the center of a major principality that held sway over extensive territory in the Oka River basin. It had massive earthen-wall fortifications, portions of which have survived to the present as one of the largest archeological sites in Russia. This period of growth mingled with princely feuds came to a catastrophic end with the Mongol invasion of 1237–41. After a crushing defeat of the Volga Bulgars toward the end of 1236, the Mongols (traditionally referred to in Russia as "Tatars") moved toward the Russian principalities. Because of its southerly location, Ryazan was the first to be conquered, in late 1237. The destruction of Ryazan was complete, and attempts to reestablish settlements in the immediate area were undercut by repeated Tatar raids over the following decades.

By the fourteenth century the local church and political leadership decided to reestablish Ryazan at the better-defended settlement of Pereyaslavl, fifty-five kilometers northwest at the point where the small Trubezh River empties into the Oka. For centuries the town was known as Pereyaslavl-Ryazansky. By the beginning of the fifteenth century Pereyaslavl-Ryazansky had a large fortress (kremlin) whose earthen ramparts are well preserved to this day. Although the threat of Tatar raids waned, the region was afflicted

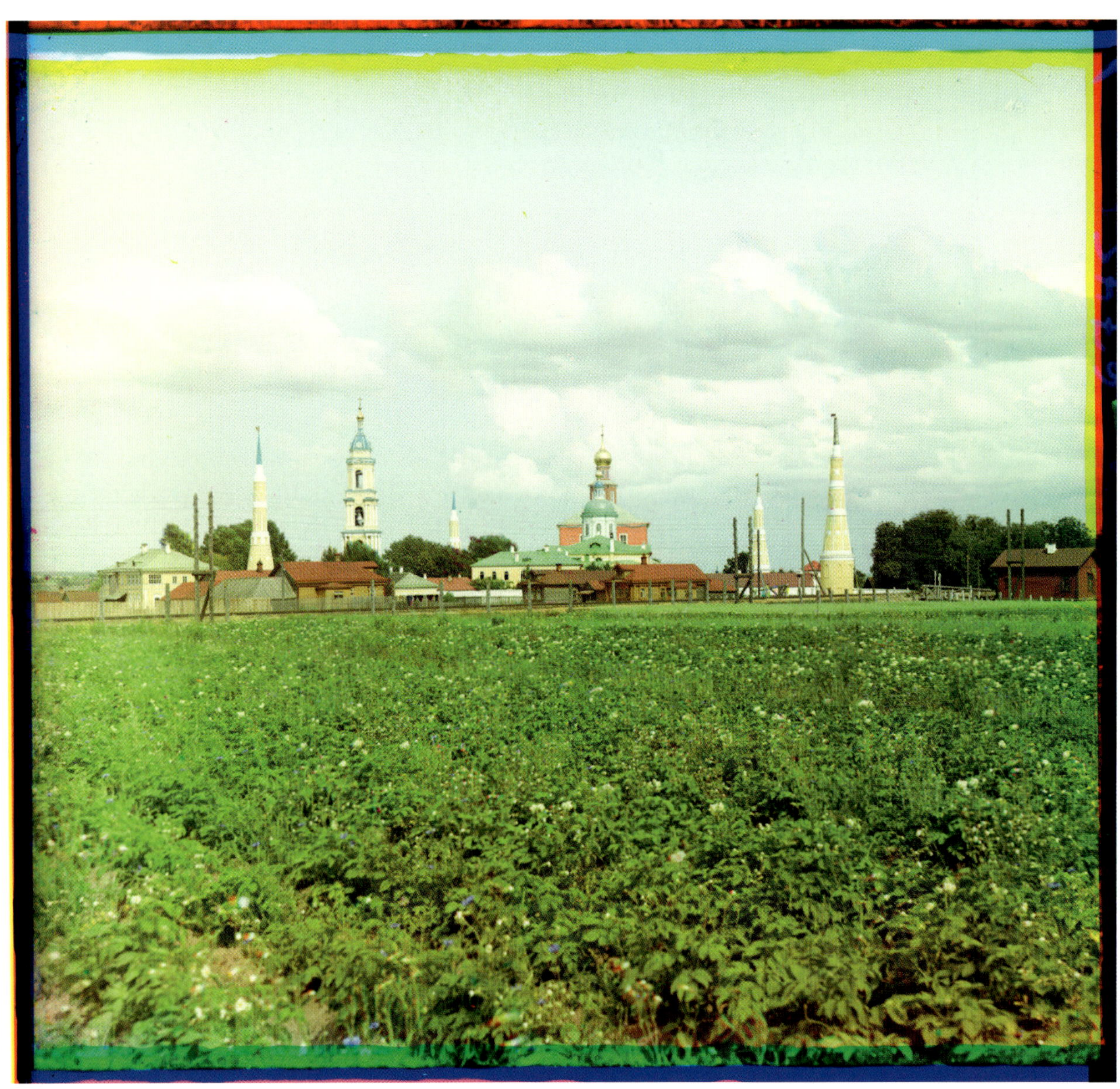

KOLOMNA Epiphany-Golutvin Monastery. *From left*: northwest corner tower, bell tower, northeast corner tower, Church of Saint Sergius of Radonezh, Epiphany Cathedral, southeast corner tower, southwest corner tower. PROKUDIN-GORSKY 21442. SUMMER 1912.

KOLOMNA Epiphany-Golutvin Monastery, northwest corner tower. Northwest view with north wall and bell tower. BRUMFIELD, JULY 21, 2006.

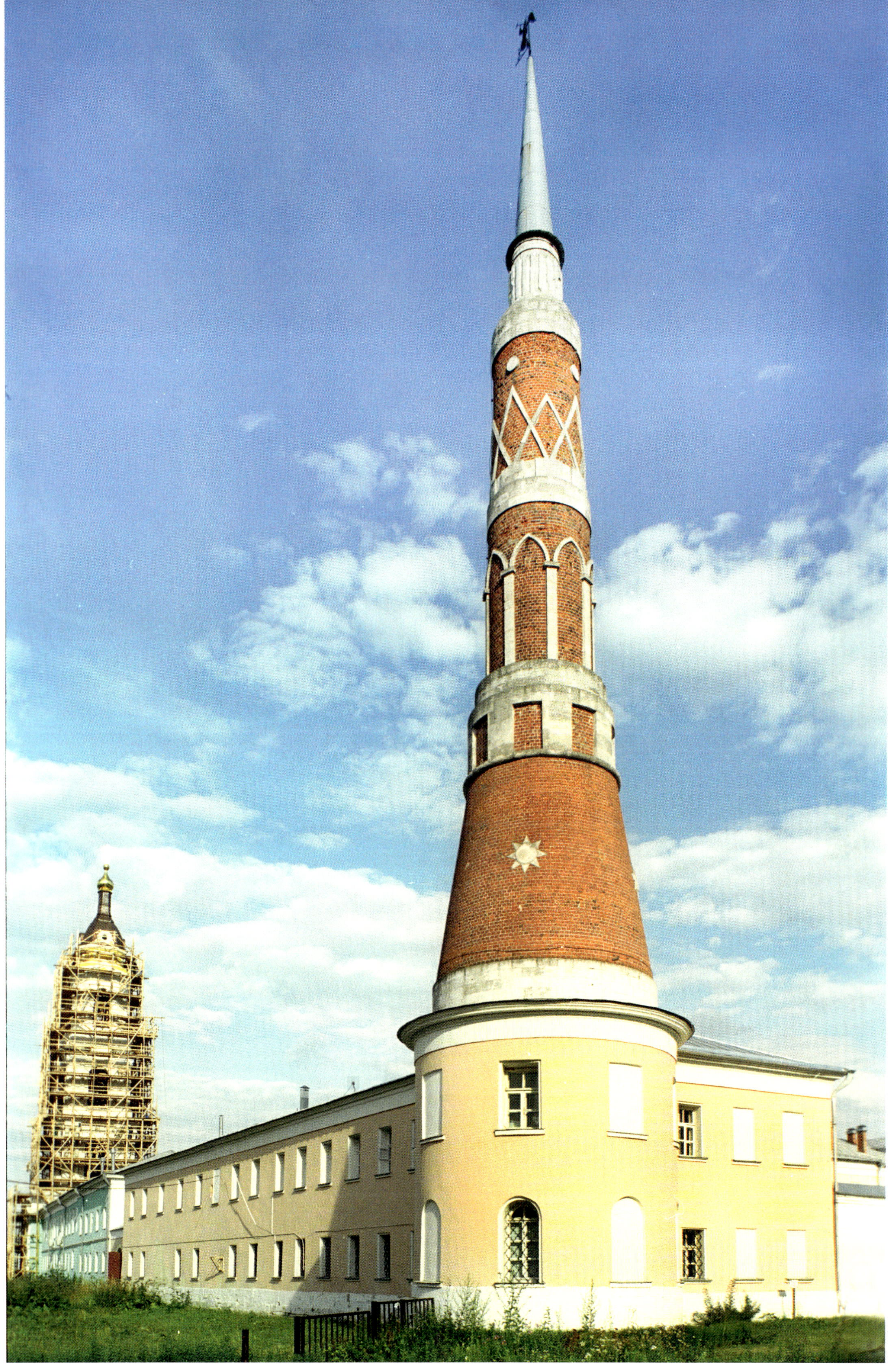

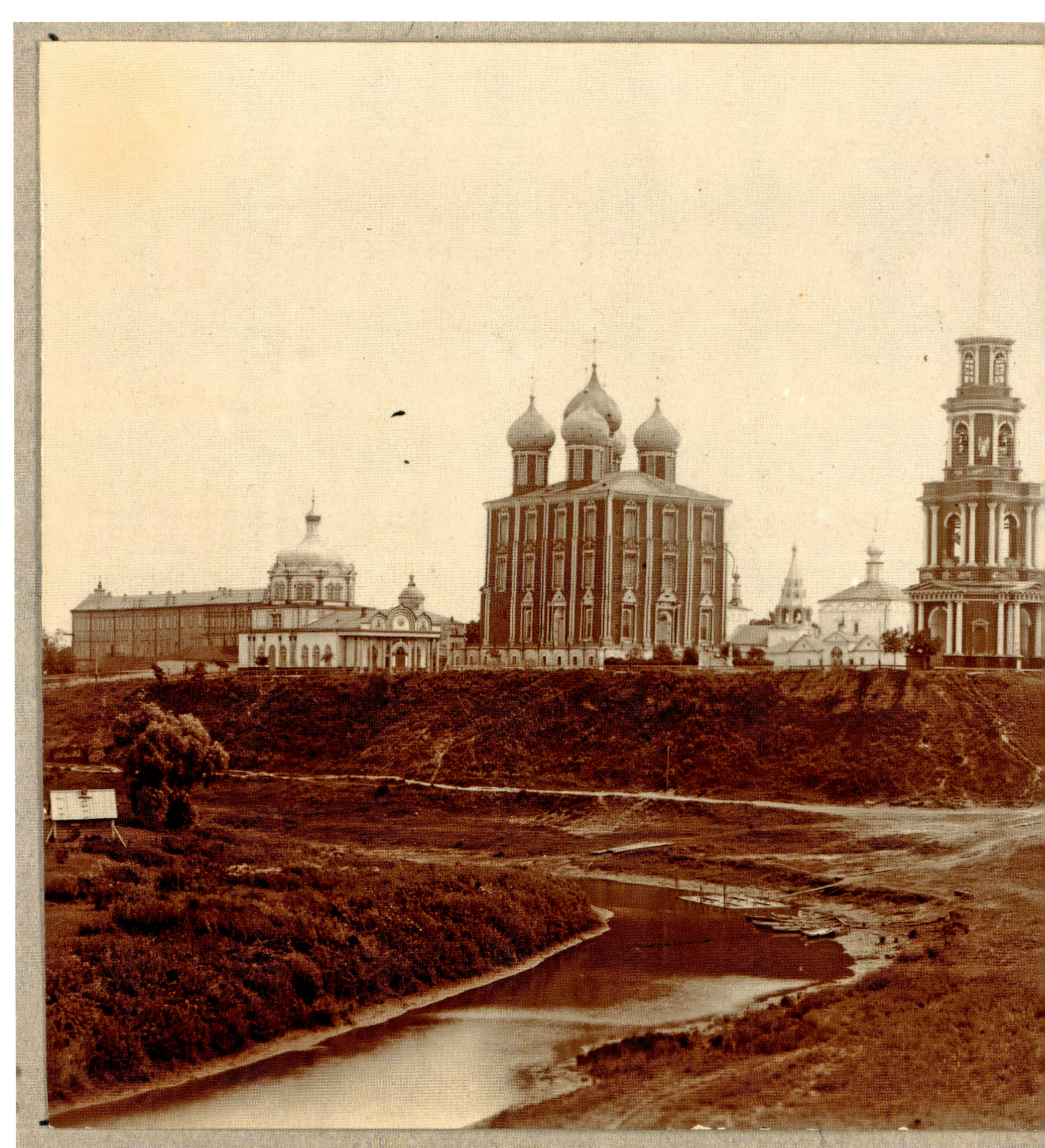

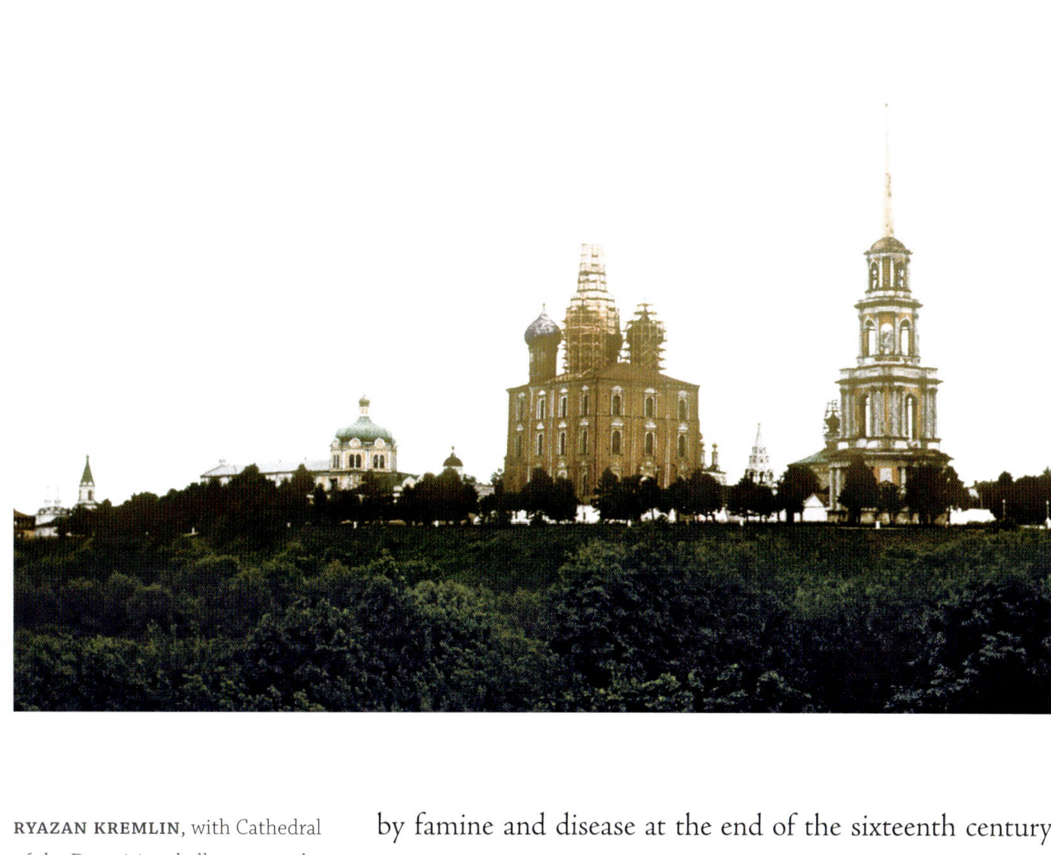

RYAZAN KREMLIN Northwest view. *From left*: Church of the Descent of the Holy Spirit, Cathedral of the Nativity of Christ, Cathedral of the Dormition, Church of the Epiphany, Cathedral of the Transfiguration, bell tower. Trubezh River concealed by trees. BRUMFIELD, MAY 13, 1984.

by famine and disease at the end of the sixteenth century and wracked by violent disorders in the early seventeenth century during the Time of Troubles.

Like most Russian provincial centers, Ryazan gained a new city plan during the reign of Catherine the Great. The plan, preserved to this day, was implemented in 1778, the year in which the town name was changed to Ryazan. The development of commerce in the early nineteenth century led to the construction of neoclassical market rows. In the 1890s Ryazan developed into a major railroad center, and by the time of Prokudin-Gorsky's visit in 1912 had a population of almost fifty thousand.

The city's defining monument is the Cathedral of the Dormition, whose dedication derived from a twelfth-century cathedral in Old Ryazan. At the turn of the fifteenth century a masonry Dormition Cathedral was erected within the fortress of the new location of Ryazan. In the early 1680s Metropolitan Avraamy undertook a much larger cathedral to meet the needs of an expanded diocese. The cathedral was intended to rise above the ramparts and tower

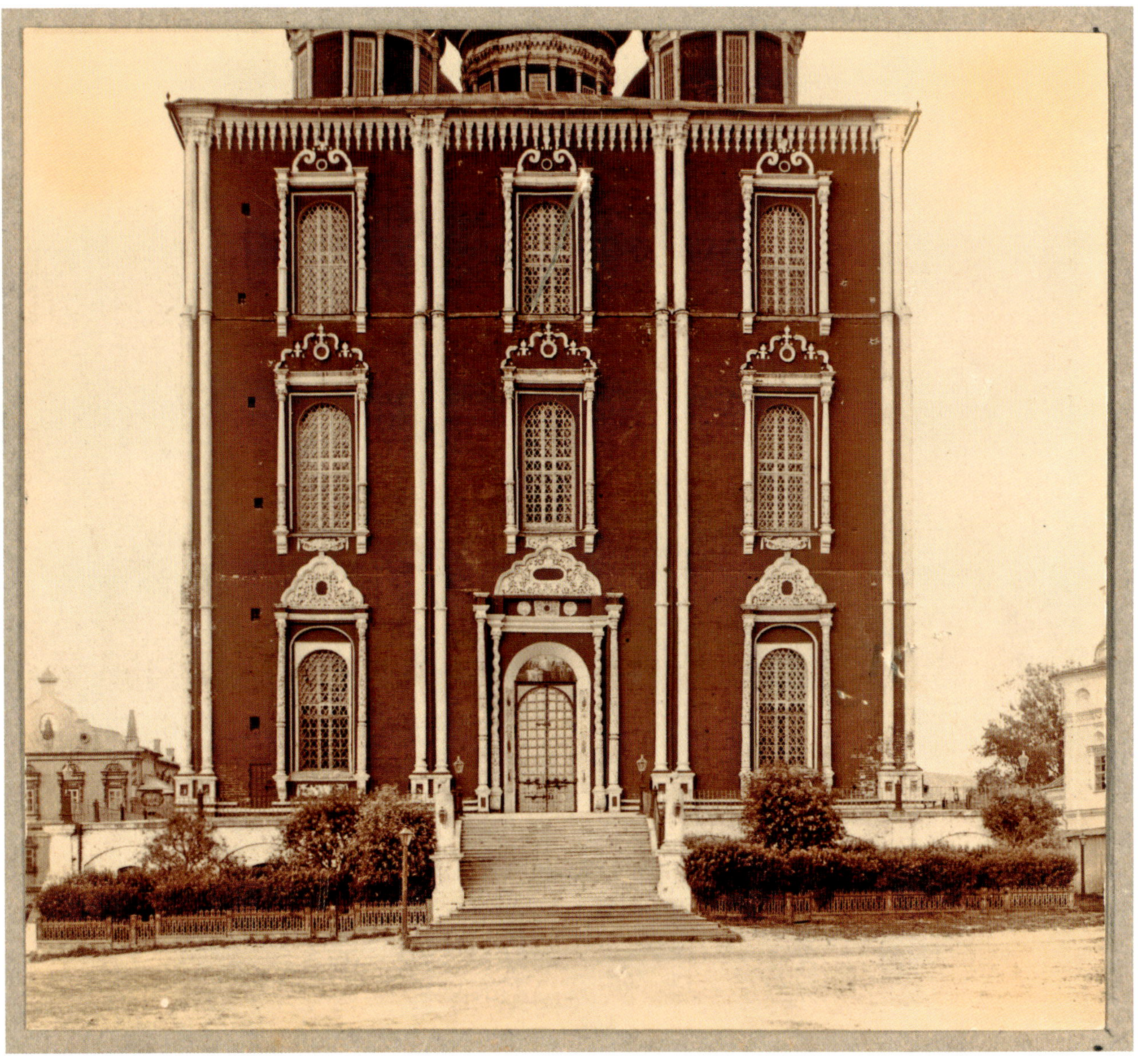

over the town. Although the original glass negative has not survived, Prokudin-Gorsky took a clear view of the kremlin and cathedral that included the Trubezh River in the foreground. My photograph some sixty years later shows little change to this historical ensemble.

Begun in 1684, the cathedral was plagued with structural flaws, and in 1692 the almost completed walls collapsed. After the initial debacle, the project was entrusted to one of the few known Russian architects of the seventeenth century, Yakov Bukhvostov, who also had difficulties with the foundations and the roof vaulting for the immense

RYAZAN KREMLIN Cathedral of the Dormition. West facade. PROKUDIN-GORSKY 02616. SUMMER 1912.

RYAZAN KREMLIN Cathedral of the Dormition. West facade. BRUMFIELD, MAY 13, 1984.

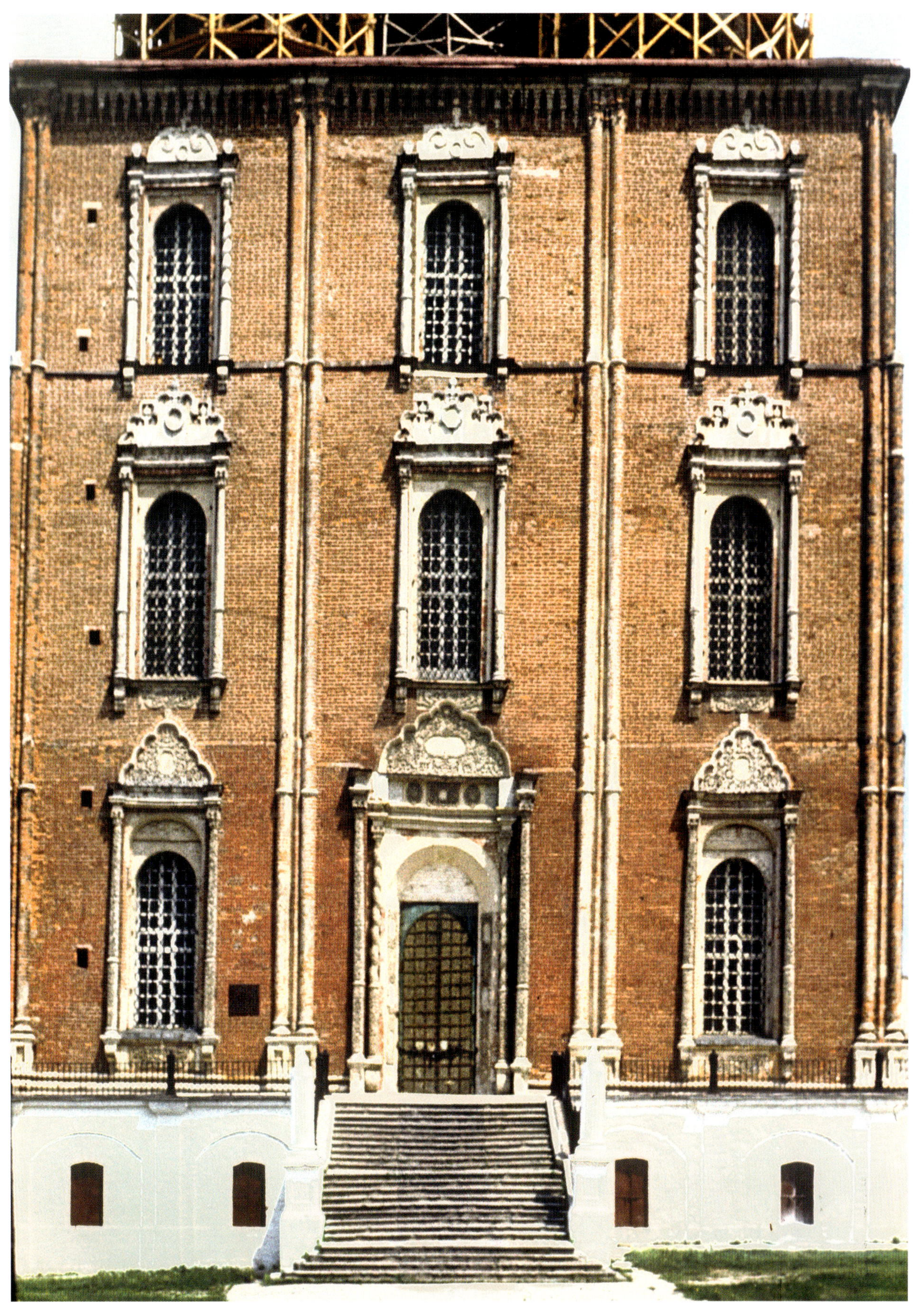

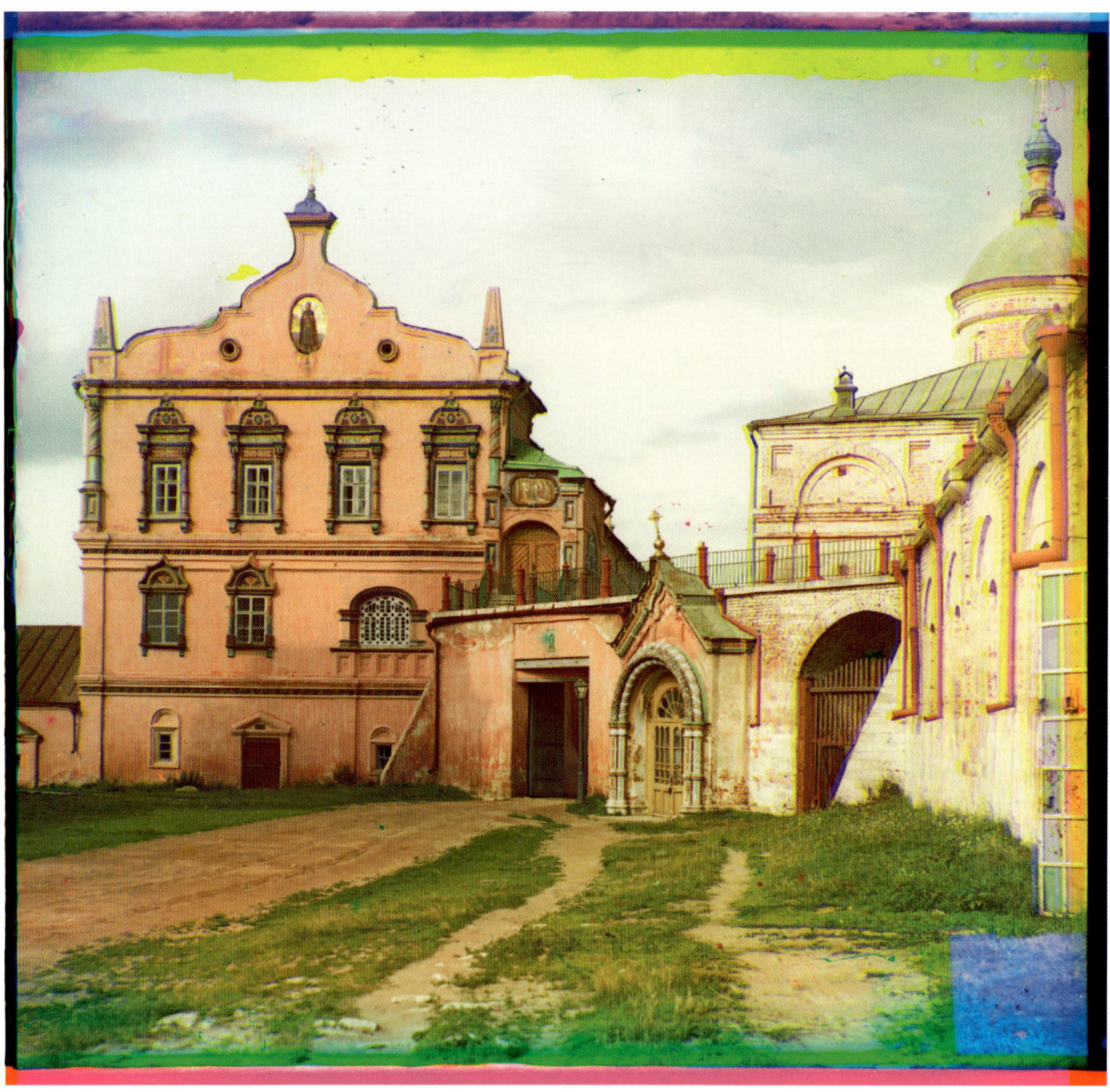

structure. Over forty meters in height, with five large drums and cupolas as well as extensive window space, the structure was balanced on an ingenious system of cellar vaults, which support an imposing terrace platform for the cathedral. Although preserved only in the contact print, Prokudin-Gorsky's direct frontal view conveys with striking clarity the distinctive facade design. The rectilinear segmentation seems designed to provide a backdrop for the intricacy of the carved limestone columns. The cathedral's roofline was designed as a horizontal cornice with decorative brick patterns. The tall windows were framed with carved limestone

RYAZAN KREMLIN Archbishop's Palace. West view. PROKUDIN-GORSKY 21449. SUMMER 1912.

RYAZAN KREMLIN Archbishop's Residence. West view. BRUMFIELD, MAY 13, 1984.

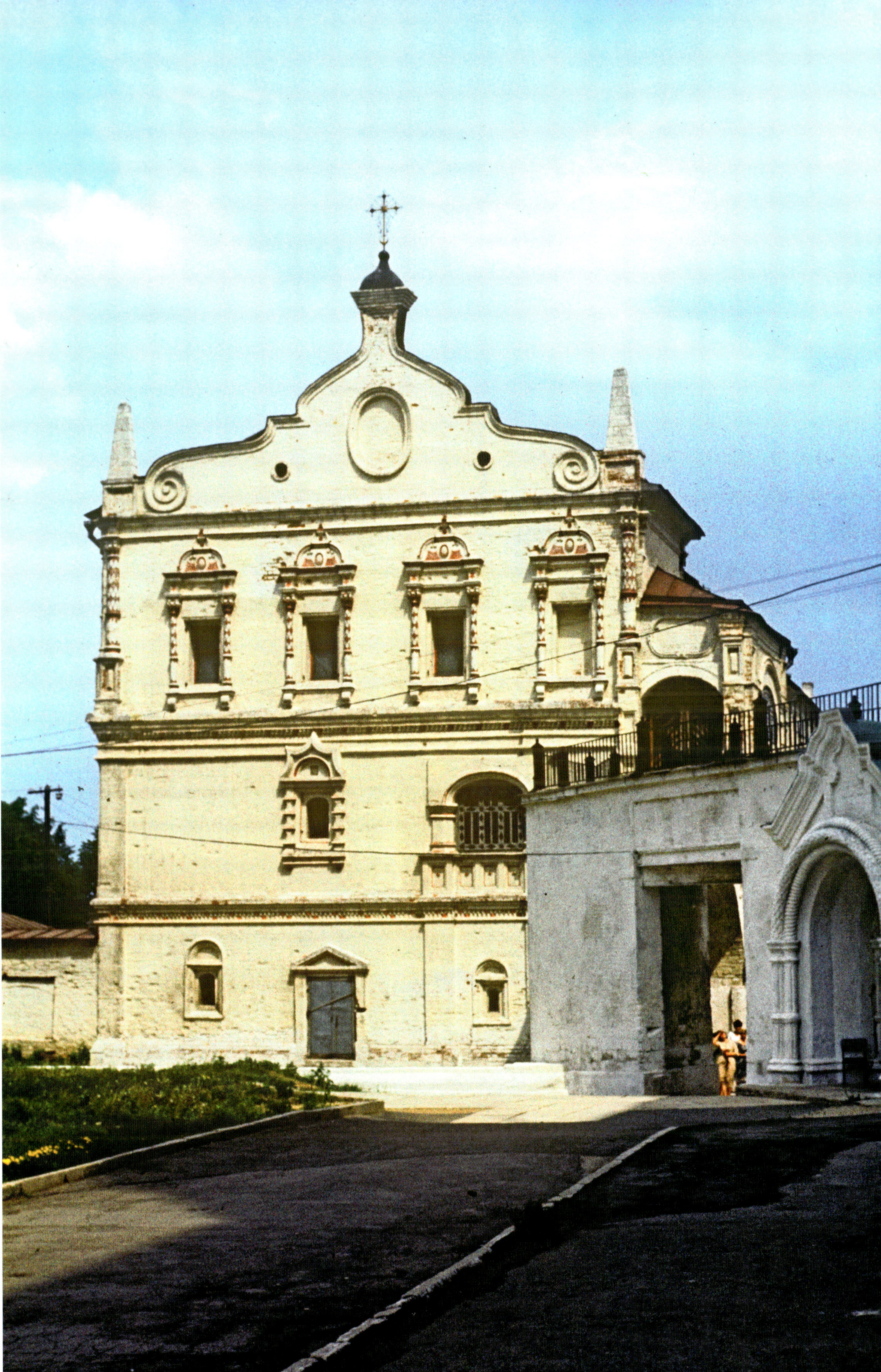

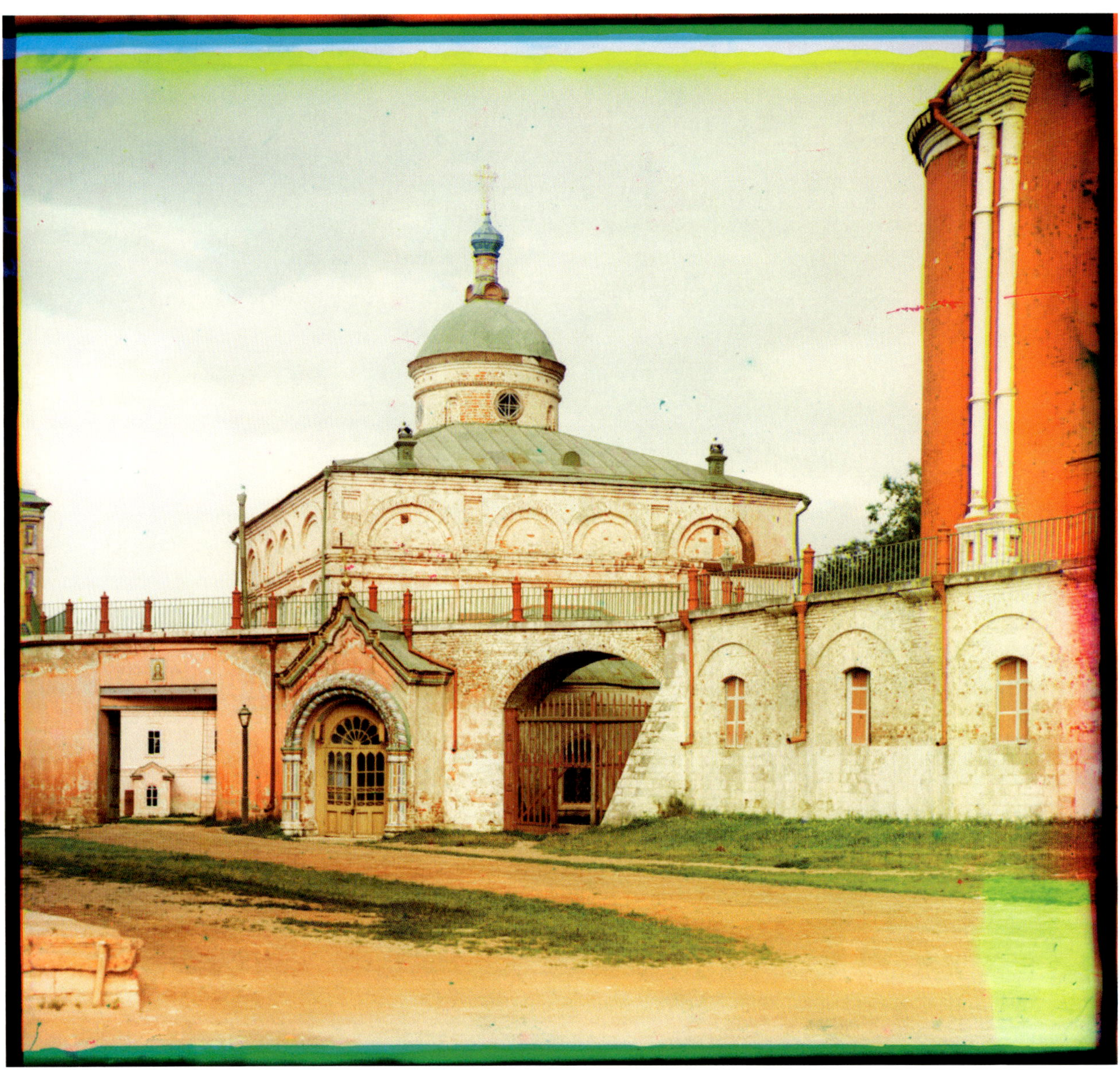

columns and pediments, visible in Prokudin-Gorsky's detailed view of the north facade. My photographs of the west facade reveal the monumentality of the stonework. Some five thousand blocks comprising the limestone details were standardized, thus enabling the architect to complete the structure by 1699, a relatively short period in view of the complexity of the project and Bukhvostov's ongoing work elsewhere. The window surrounds and the paired brick columns (painted white) that vertically divide the brick facades create a palatial ambience in one of the largest churches of

RYAZAN KREMLIN Cathedral of Archangel Michael. Northeast view. *Right*: Dormition Cathedral. PROKUDIN-GORSKY 21444. SUMMER 1912.

RYAZAN KREMLIN Cathedral of Archangel Michael. Southeast view. *Left*: Dormition Cathedral. BRUMFIELD, AUGUST 28, 2005.

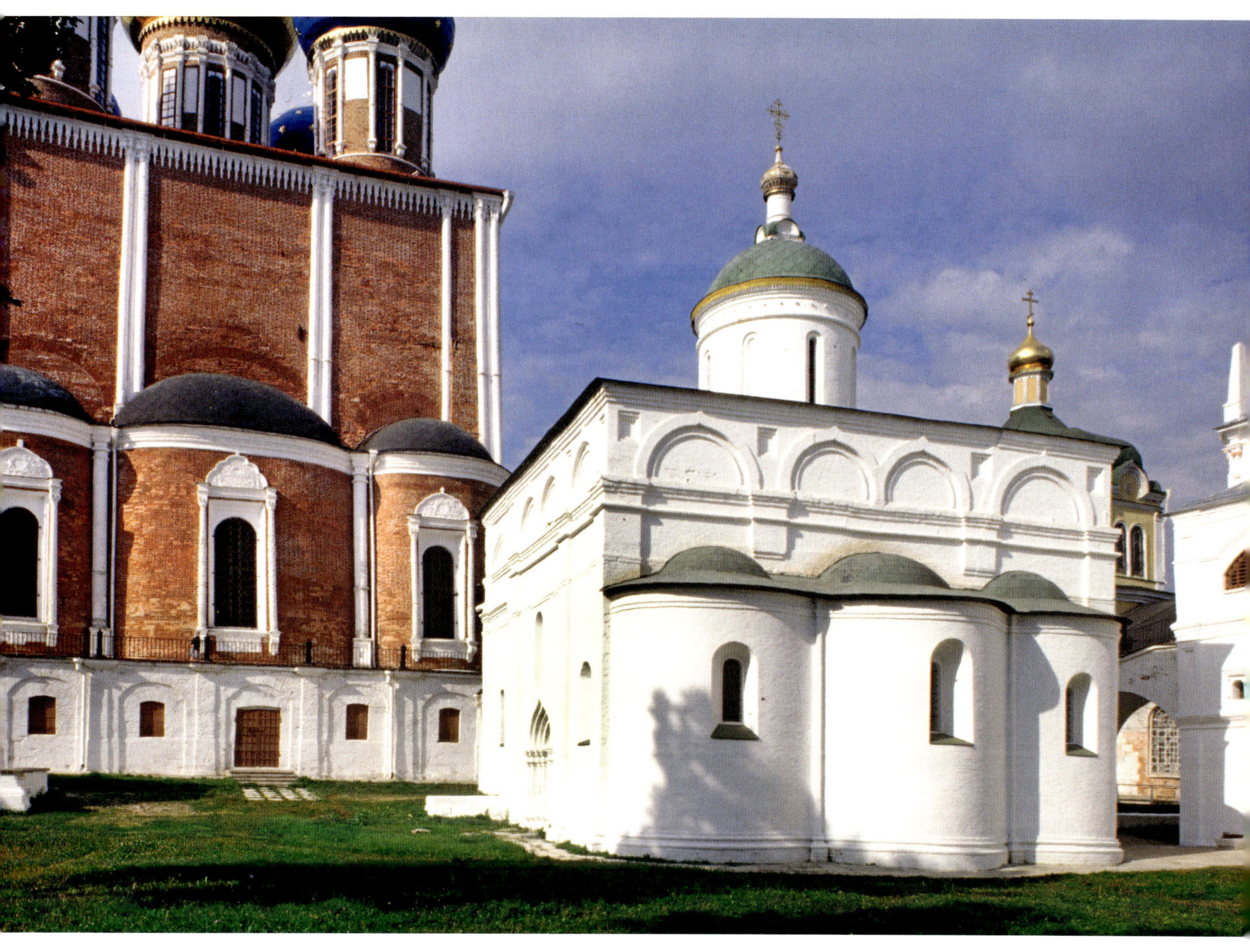

the seventeenth century—larger, in fact, than the Dormition Cathedral in the Moscow Kremlin.

Prokudin-Gorsky also photographed the building commonly known as the Grand Ducal Palace, with a medallion depicting Prince Oleg Ivanovich, a prominent and controversial leader to the Ryazan principality in the latter half of the fourteenth century. (The medallion was effaced in the Soviet period.) In fact, the structure was originally built in 1653–55 for Archbishop Misail and expanded in the late seventeenth and eighteenth centuries. The main facade of the Archbishop's Palace was completed in 1692 with elements of baroque decoration. Visible on the right is part of the Cathedral of

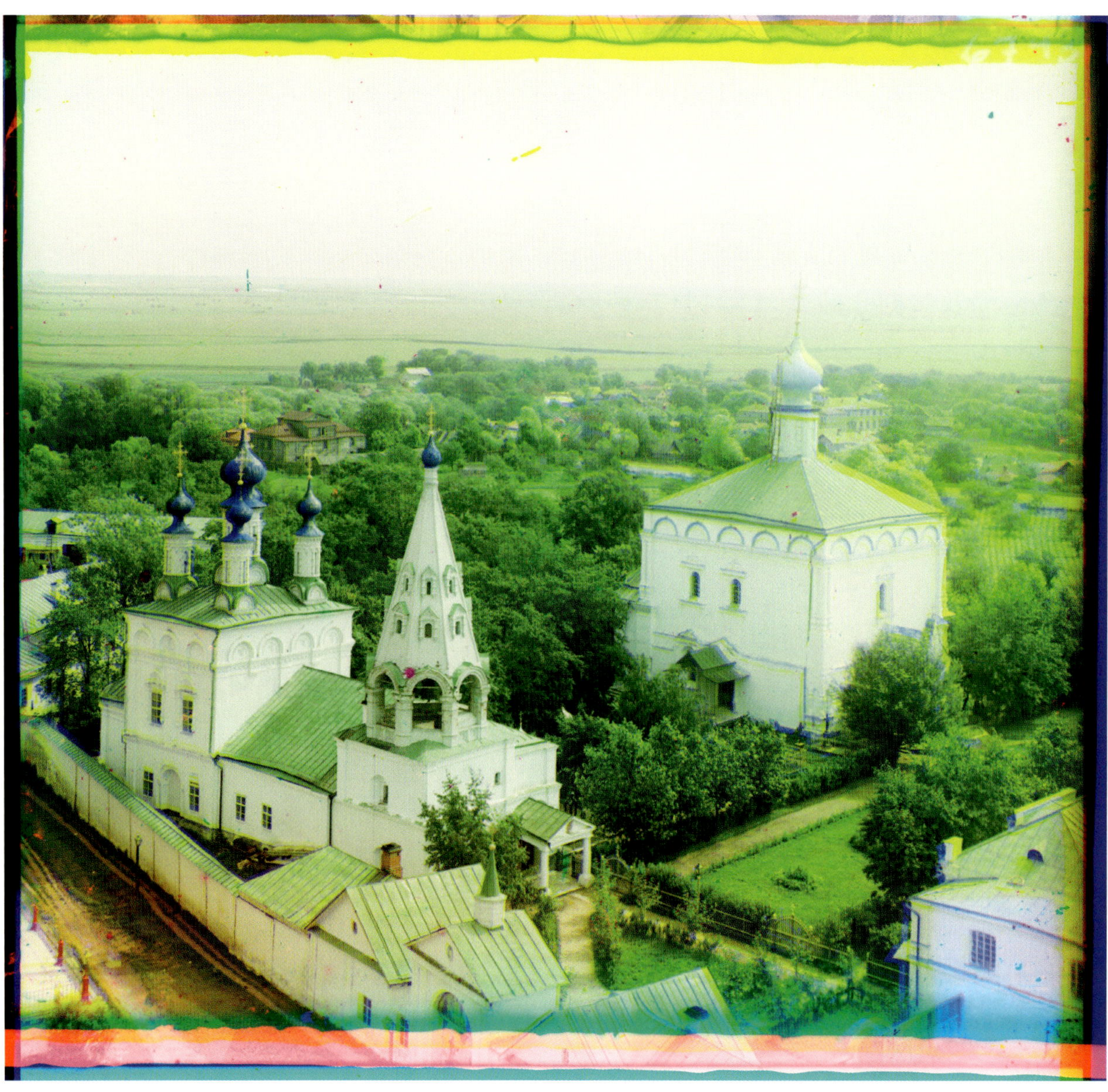

Archangel Michael, whose proposed dates of construction range from the 1470s to the mid-sixteenth century. It was subsequently modified in 1647 and 1865. Prokudin-Gorsky made a closer photograph of the structure from the Dormition Cathedral courtyard. My photograph of the Archangel Cathedral shows fresh whitewash and the effects of a 1970s restoration.

Other monuments in the kremlin complex include the Monastery of the Transfiguration of the Savior, which contained the Transfiguration Cathedral (1702), Church of the Epiphany (1647), and Church of Saint John the Divine

RYAZAN KREMLIN Monastery of the Transfiguration of the Savior. Church of the Epiphany (*left*), and Transfiguration Cathedral. Northwest view from Cathedral Bell Tower. PROKUDIN-GORSKY 21440. SUMMER 1912.

RYAZAN KREMLIN Cathedral of the Transfiguration of the Savior. Southeast view. BRUMFIELD, AUGUST 28, 2005.

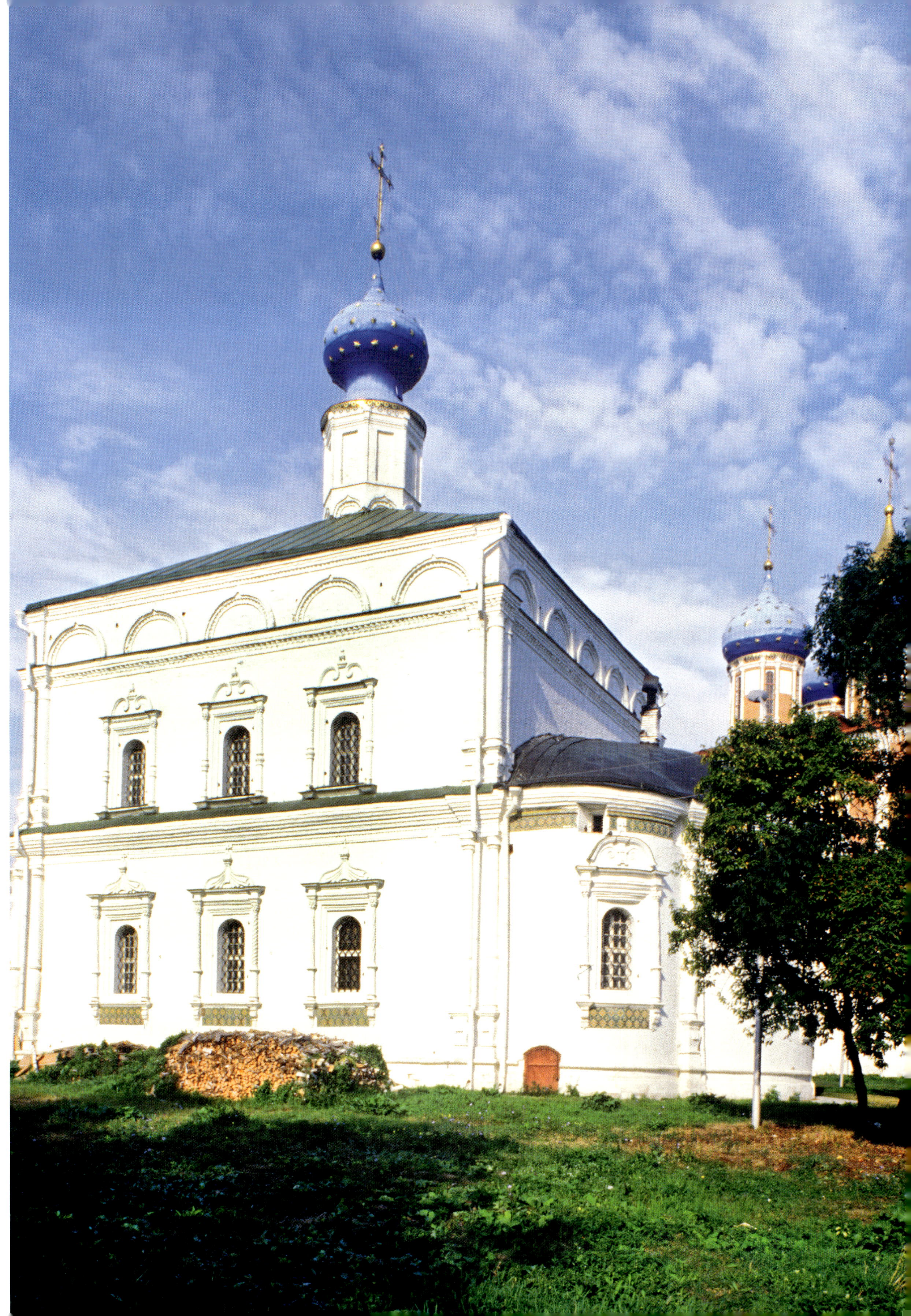

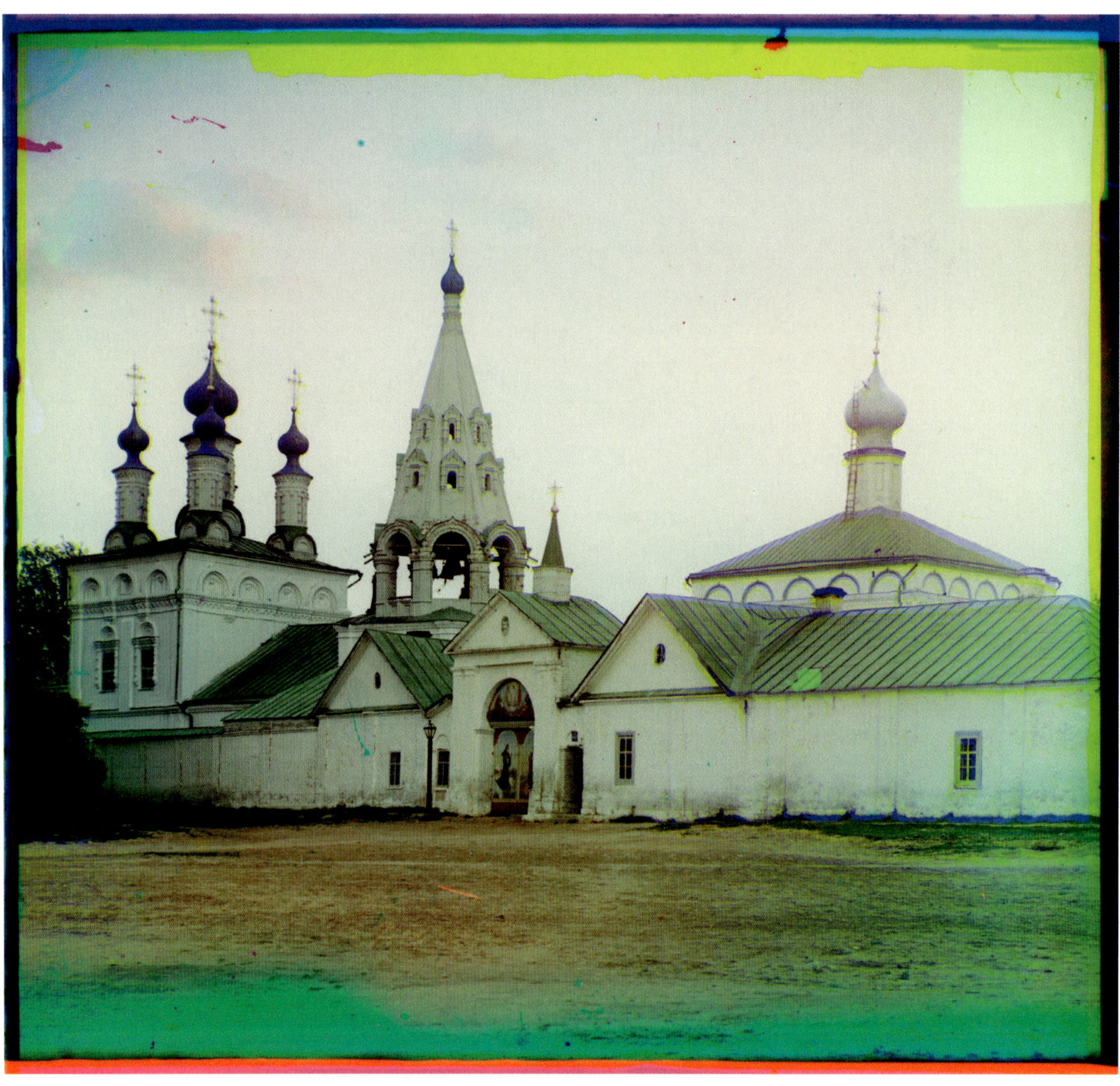

(1904). Prokudin-Gorsky photographed the monastery from the cathedral bell tower, a perspective that he often used for its sweeping views of the surrounding countryside. I have included a closer perspective of the whitewashed cathedral from the ground. Prokudin-Gorsky took an evocative view of the monastery from ground level in soft light, with the Epiphany Church in the foreground. I have chosen a view of the Epiphany Church in sharp summer light, with the monumental Dormition Cathedral in the background.

RYAZAN KREMLIN Monastery of the Transfiguration of the Savior. Northwest view. *From left*: Church of the Epiphany, Holy Gate, Transfiguration Cathedral. PROKUDIN-GORSKY 21465. SUMMER 1912.

RYAZAN KREMLIN Church of the Epiphany. Southwest view with Dormition Cathedral. BRUMFIELD, AUGUST 28, 2005.

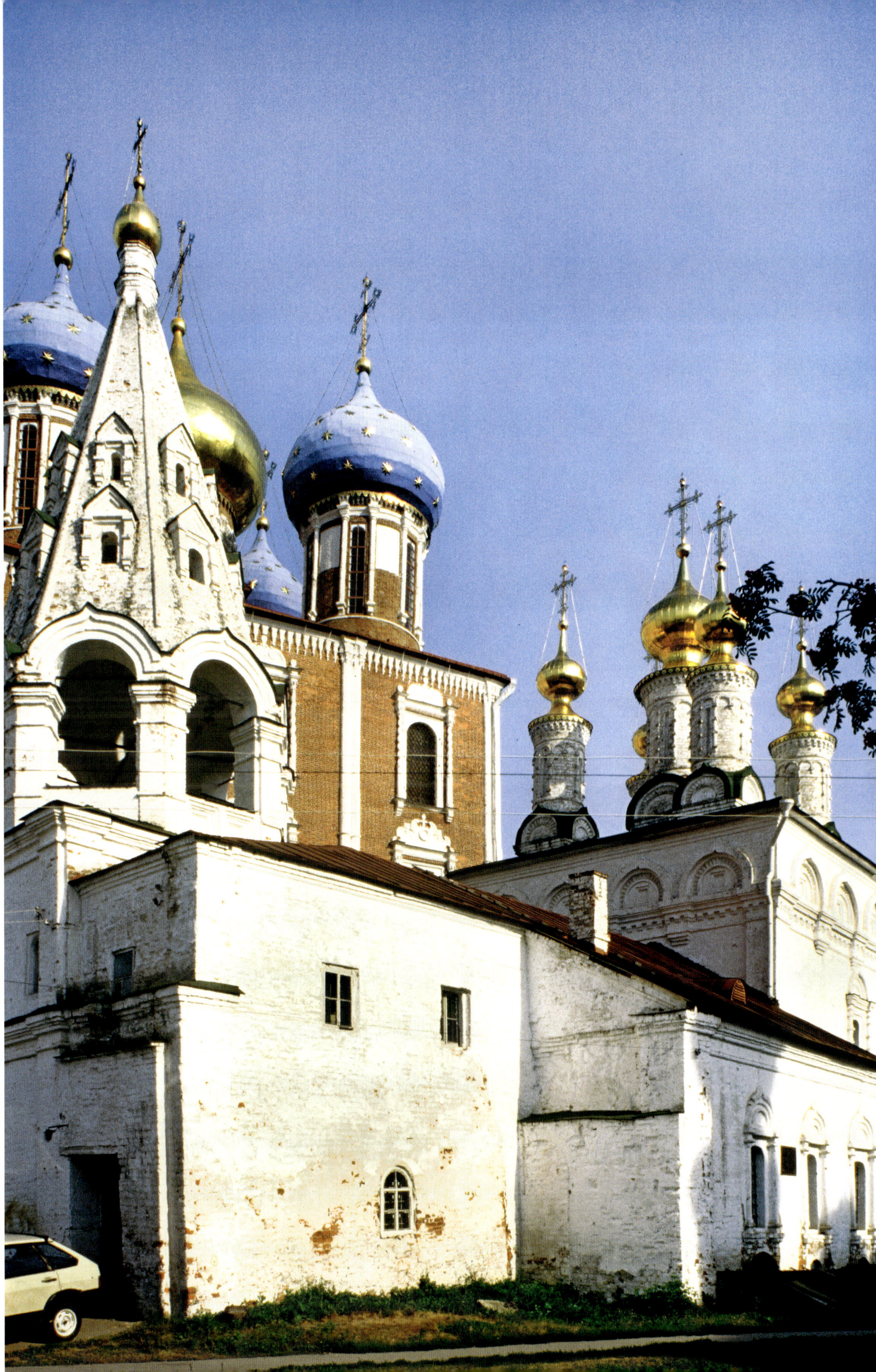

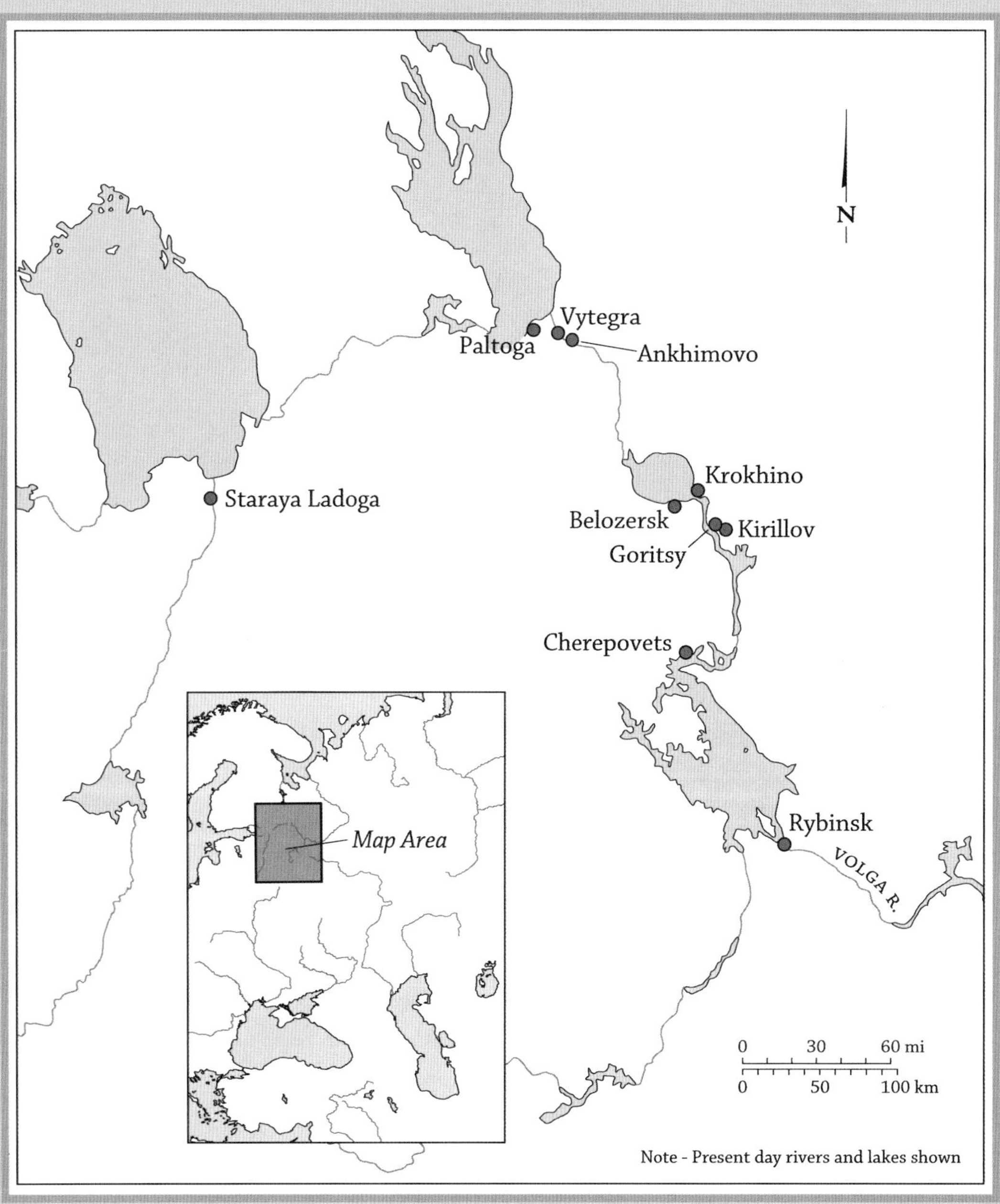

N
Vytegra
Paltoga
Ankhimovo
Krokhino
Belozersk
Kirillov
Goritsy
Staraya Ladoga
Cherepovets
Rybinsk
VOLGA R.
Map Area
0 30 60 mi
0 50 100 km
Note - Present day rivers and lakes shown

THREE · The Northwest

From Lake Ladoga to the Volga Basin

In June and July of 1909 Sergey Prokudin-Gorsky received a commission
from the Ministry of Transportation to photograph along the Mariinsky
Waterway, a decision that proved significant in the development of his documentary project. The route chosen was not only connected with some of
the most ancient archeological sites in northwestern Russia but also illuminated important episodes in the development of Saint Petersburg, founded
in 1703 and designated the capital of Russia in 1712. Faced with the challenge
of linking the new capital to the interior of the country, Peter the Great initiated the development of a canal system eventually known as the Mariinsky
Waterway, which connected Saint Petersburg with the Volga River basin.

A major point in Prokudin-Gorsky's journey along the Mariinsky Waterway was Old (Staraya) Ladoga, one of the oldest known settlements in northwestern Russia. Archeological finds suggest that the site, strategically located
near the southeast edge of Lake Ladoga, was a trading center as early as the
seventh century. In the latter half of the ninth century, the settlement was associated with the rise of the first Russian dynasty, the Riurikovich. The first
fortress on the site, with earthen ramparts, arose during the same period,
while a masonry wall was erected in the early twelfth century. Prokudin-
Gorsky took photographs of the remains of the fortress compound.

The oldest monument photographed by Prokudin-Gorsky in Old La-

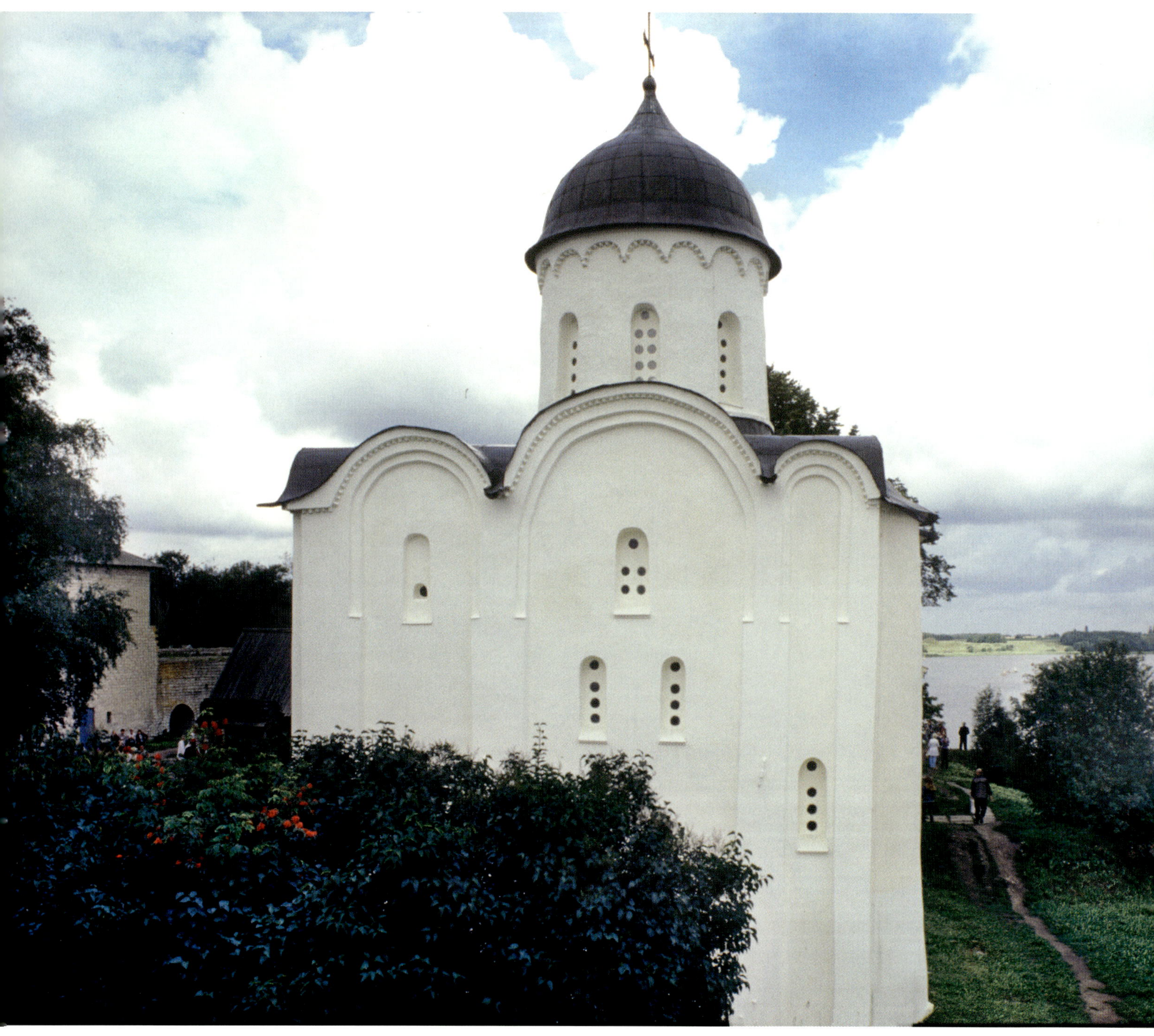

STARAYA LADOGA Church of Saint George. South
view from fortress wall. *Right*: Volkhov River.
BRUMFIELD, AUGUST 16, 2003.

STARAYA LADOGA Church of Saint George. West view
with fortress wall and Ladozhka River. PROKUDIN-
GORSKY 20890. SUMMER 1909.

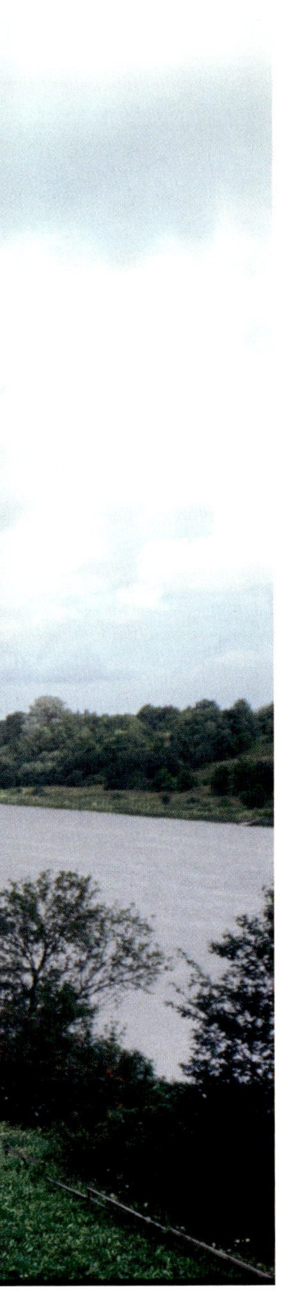

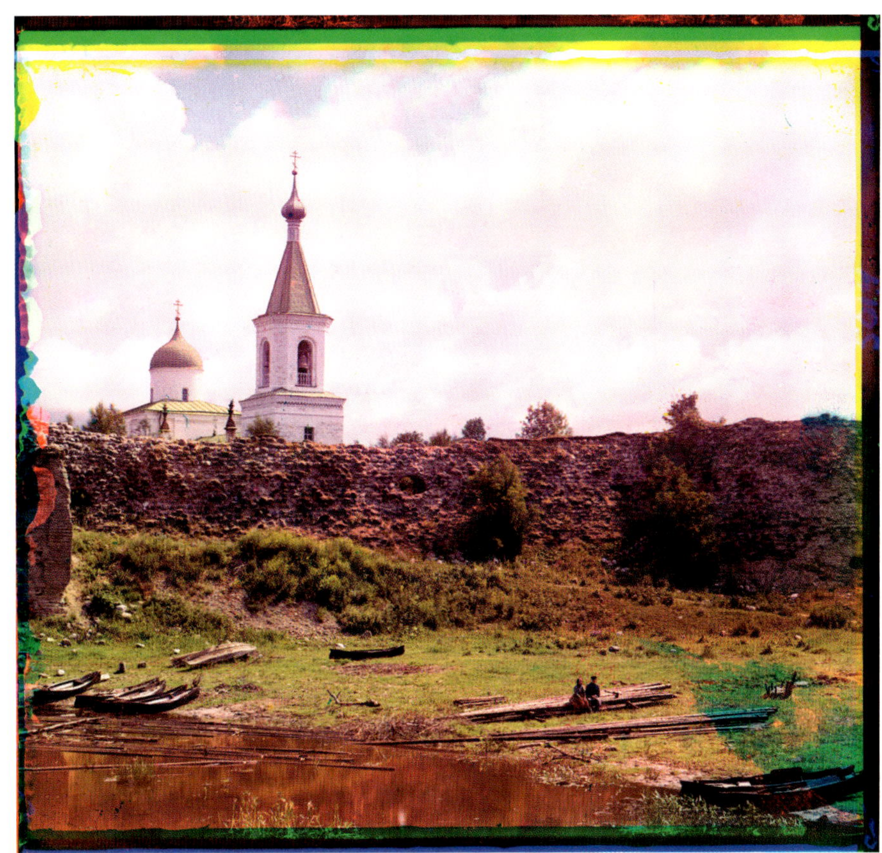

doga was the Church of Saint George, seen over a section of the ancient fortress. Consensus about the construction dates of the monument is elusive, but all versions place it in the second half of the twelfth century, a time when Slavs were fighting with Swedes for control of this strategic territory. The Saint George Church conforms to a basic form common in pre-Mongol Rus: three bays on each side, an apse in the east, and a single dome over the interior crossing of the main bays. In the interior Prokudin-Gorsky photographed fragments of twelfth-century frescoes. The ancient church was restored in various phases during the twentieth century (the 1920s and 1950s) and the nineteenth-century bell tower visible in his photograph was demolished as anachronistic. In the foreground of his view is the small and muddy Ladozhka River. My view shows the beautifully renovated church with the Volkhov River, waterway of the Vikings.

The fickle northern weather cooperated for Prokudin-Gorsky's sharply illuminated south view of the Church of the Nativity of John the Baptist on Malysheva Hill. The original church was apparently built in the late thirteenth century, but little is known of its history. The church was rebuilt in 1695 as part of the small Monastery of John the Baptist. The perspective that

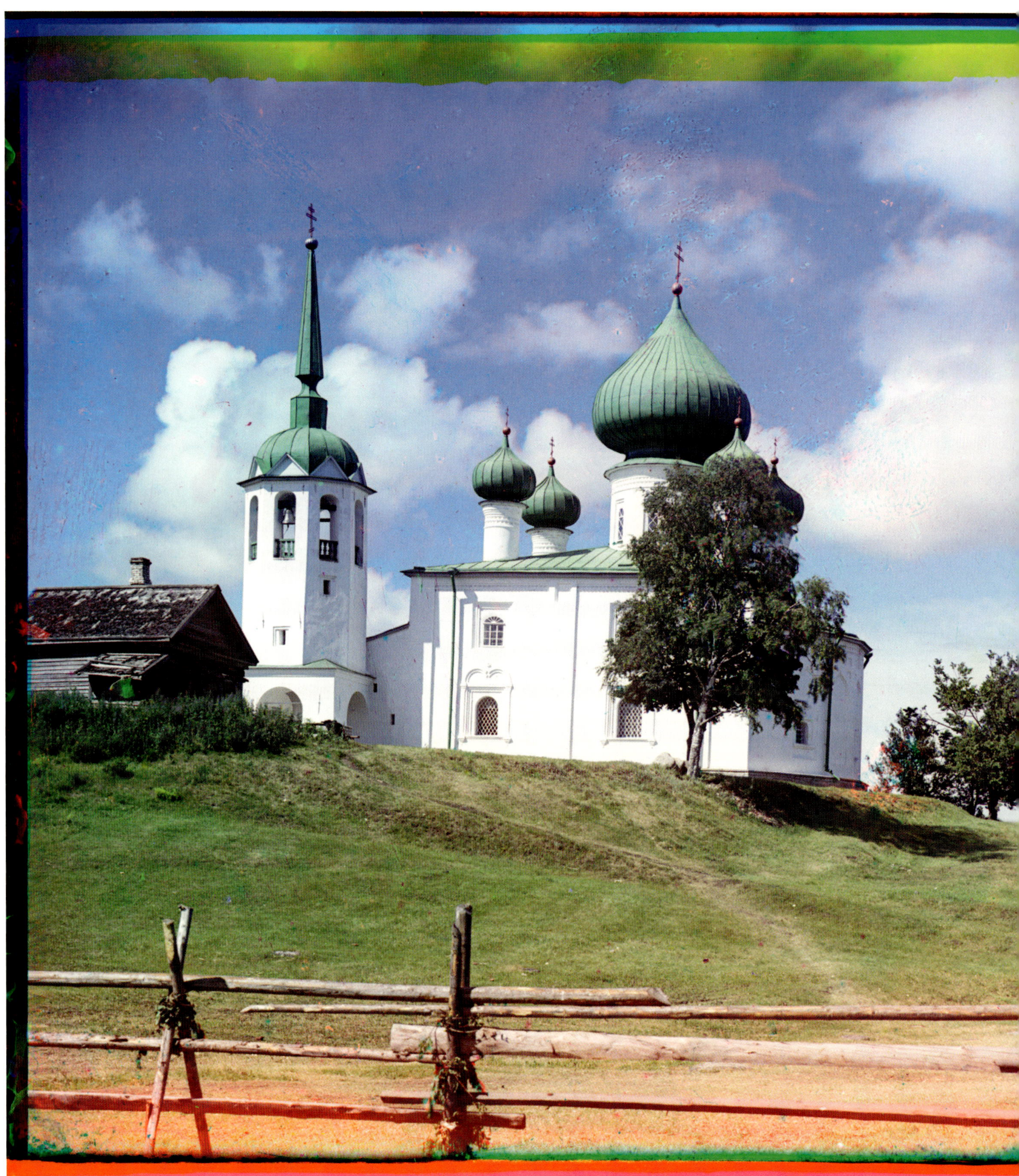

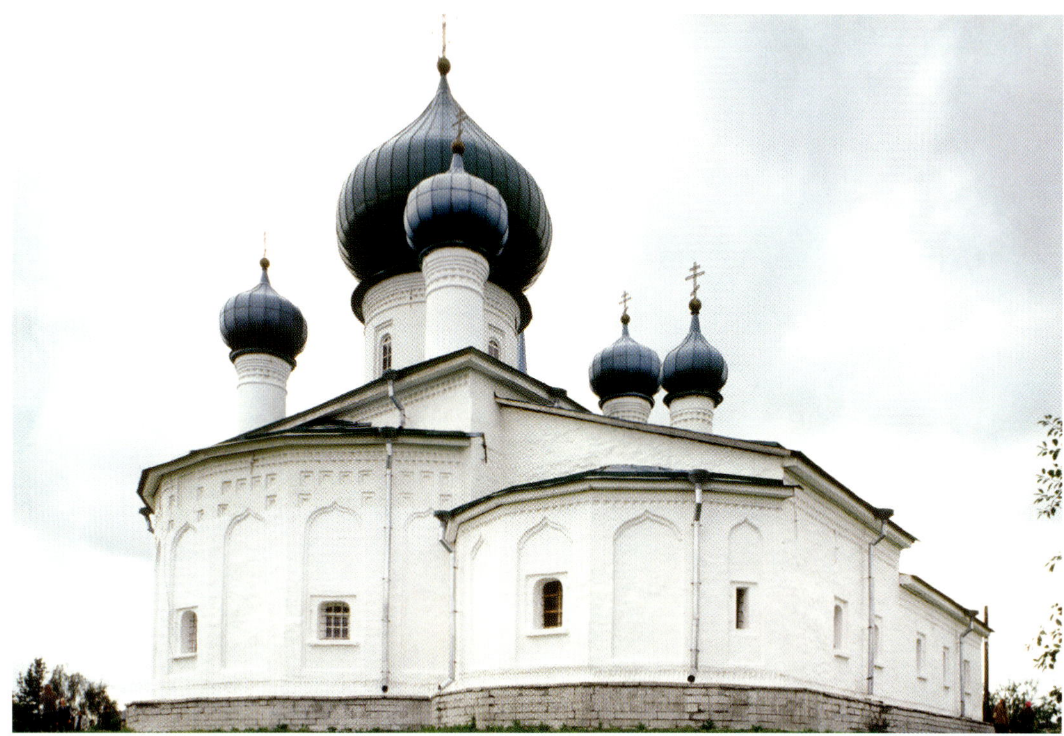

STARAYA LADOGA Church of
John the Baptist on Malysheva
Hill. South view. PROKUDIN-GORSKY
20889. SUMMER 1909.

STARAYA LADOGA Church of
John the Baptist on Malysheva
Hill. Northeast view. BRUMFIELD,
AUGUST 16, 2003.

I have chosen is from the opposite, northeast side. Although
the bell tower (a later addition) is not visible, this perspective gives a sense of the volume of the structure as well as a
clear view of the attached Chapel of Saint Paraskeva.

From Lake Ladoga, Prokudin-Gorsky followed the Mariinsky Waterway system along the Svir River, which con-
nects the two great lakes of northwest Russia: Ladoga and
Lake Onega to the east. On the southeast shore of Lake
Onega, the system enters the Vytegra River, part of a con-
duit leading to the southeast and location of the town of
Vytegra, first referred to in written documents at the end
of the fifteenth century. By the early eighteenth century, the
settlement had become a crossroads for trade between the
northern port of Arkhangelsk and the city of Saint Petersburg. The first major component of the Mariinsky Waterway was a canal that linked the Vytegra River (flowing into
Lake Onega toward Saint Petersburg) and the Kovzha
River, which flows south into White Lake. In 1799 this
segment was named the Mariinsky Canal, and Vytegra—
officially designated a town in 1773—became the canal's administrative center.

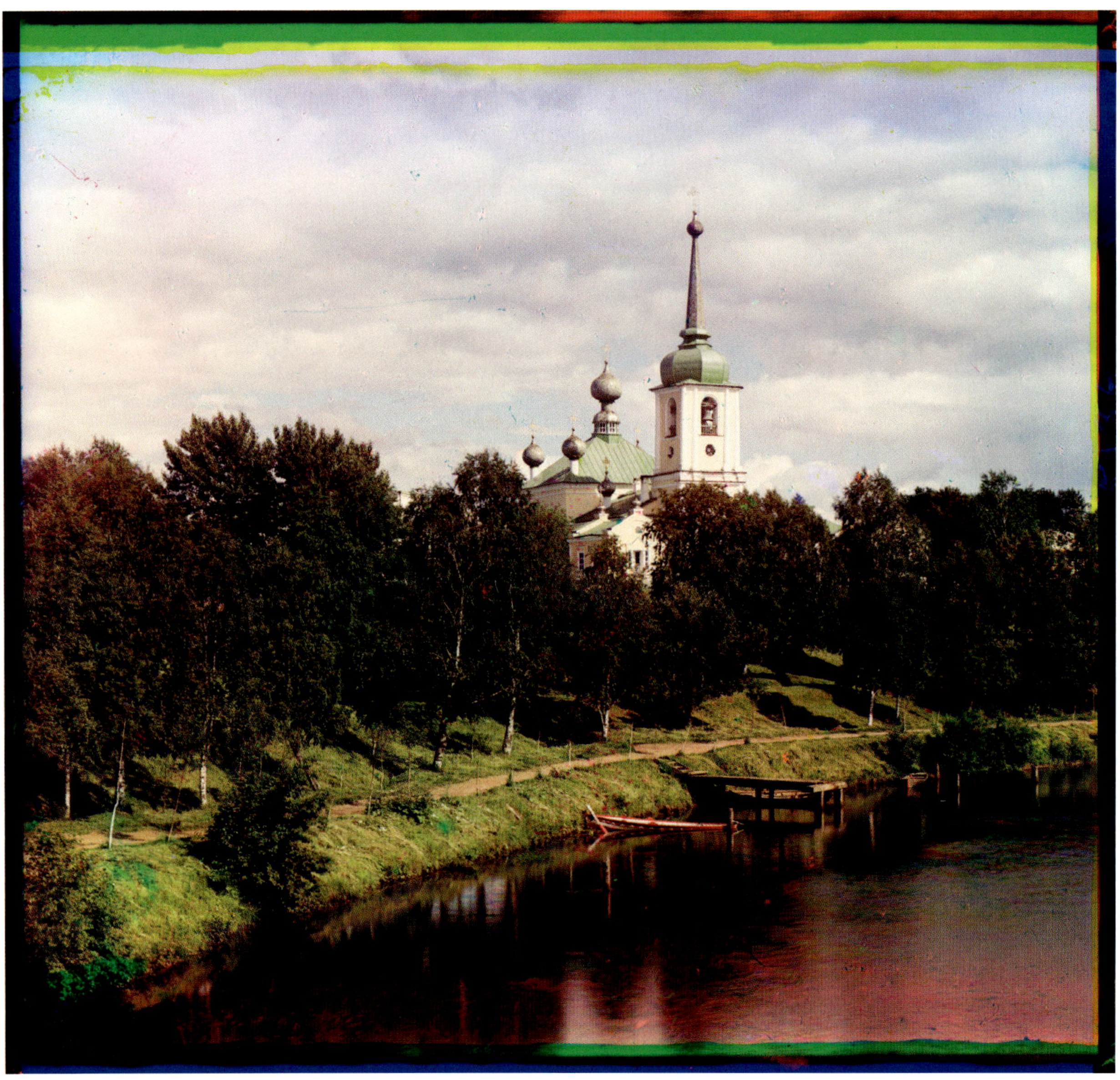

VYTEGRA Cathedral of the Resurrection. West view from Sivers Bridge. PROKUDIN-GORSKY 20951. SUMMER 1909.

VYTEGRA Cathedral of the Resurrection (now House of Culture). Southeast view. BRUMFIELD, AUGUST 28, 2006.

Although Vytegra was built of primarily of wood, the town center had several brick structures at the turn of the twentieth century, including administrative buildings, merchant houses, schools, and churches. Among Prokudin-Gorsky's photographs of Vytegra is the Cathedral of the Resurrection (1796–1800), seen from the west with its bell tower and spire. My photograph from 2006 reveals a typical Soviet-era maneuver for converting churches into clubs: demolish the bell tower and upper structure with cupolas, then enlarge the windows.

The region beyond Vytegra had excellent examples of

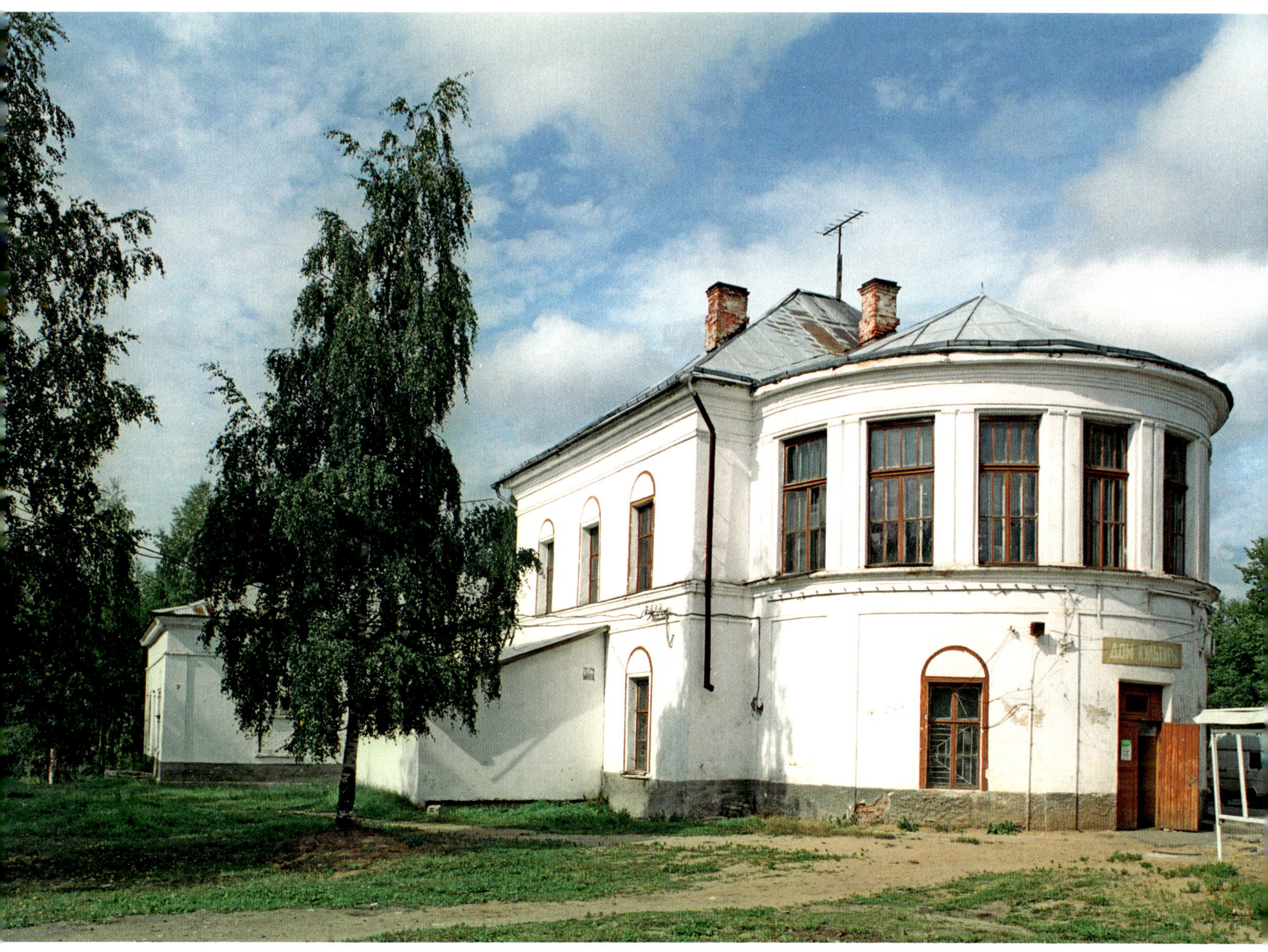

wooden church architecture, most of them now vanished. Prokudin-Gorsky visited the village of Paltoga, just to the west of Vytegra, where he photographed the log Church of the Epiphany (1733), an unusual, beautiful form crowned with five cupolas. Already in a state of extreme disrepair when I photographed it in 2006, this remarkable church collapsed soon thereafter. Efforts have been made to conserve what is left of the lower structure, with hopes for rebuilding the church. Prokudin-Gorsky's view includes the adjacent whitewashed brick Church of the Virgin of the Sign (Znamenie), built in 1810. Taken from a different perspective, my photograph of both churches shows the latter a picturesque neoclassical ruin.

High above the river bank to the east of Vytegra is the village of An-

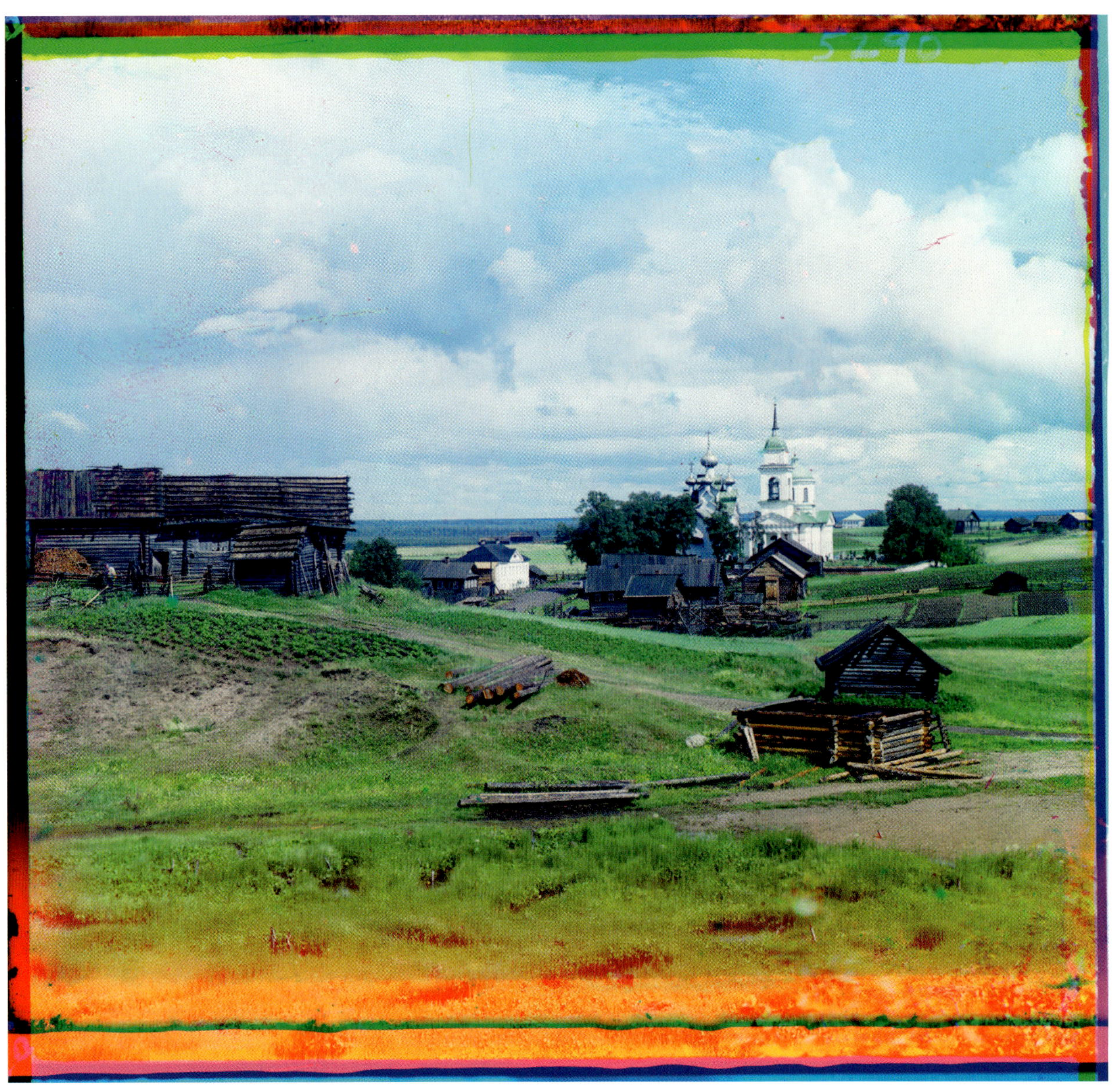

khimovo (also known as Vytegorsky Pogost), whose ensemble includes the Church of the Miraculous Image of the Savior (1780), stripped of its five cupolas and its interior art during the Soviet period. Nearby is the baroque-domed Church of All Saints, built in 1905 as a burial crypt for the wealthy merchant A. F. Loparyov. Prokudin-Gorsky and I photographed both these structures. The main Ankhimovo monument, however, was the soaring form of the Church of the Intercession, built of logs in 1708. With its twenty-five cupolas, it was a predecessor of the famed Church of the Transfiguration on Kizhi Island (1718). Destroyed by a

PALTOGA View east toward Church of the Icon of the Virgin and wooden Church of the Epiphany. PROKUDIN-GORSKY 21082. SUMMER 1909.

PALTOGA Wooden Church of the Epiphany and Church of the Icon of the Virgin of the Sign. Northwest view. After its collapse in 2009, the Epiphany Church is now under reconstruction. BRUMFIELD, AUGUST 28, 2006.

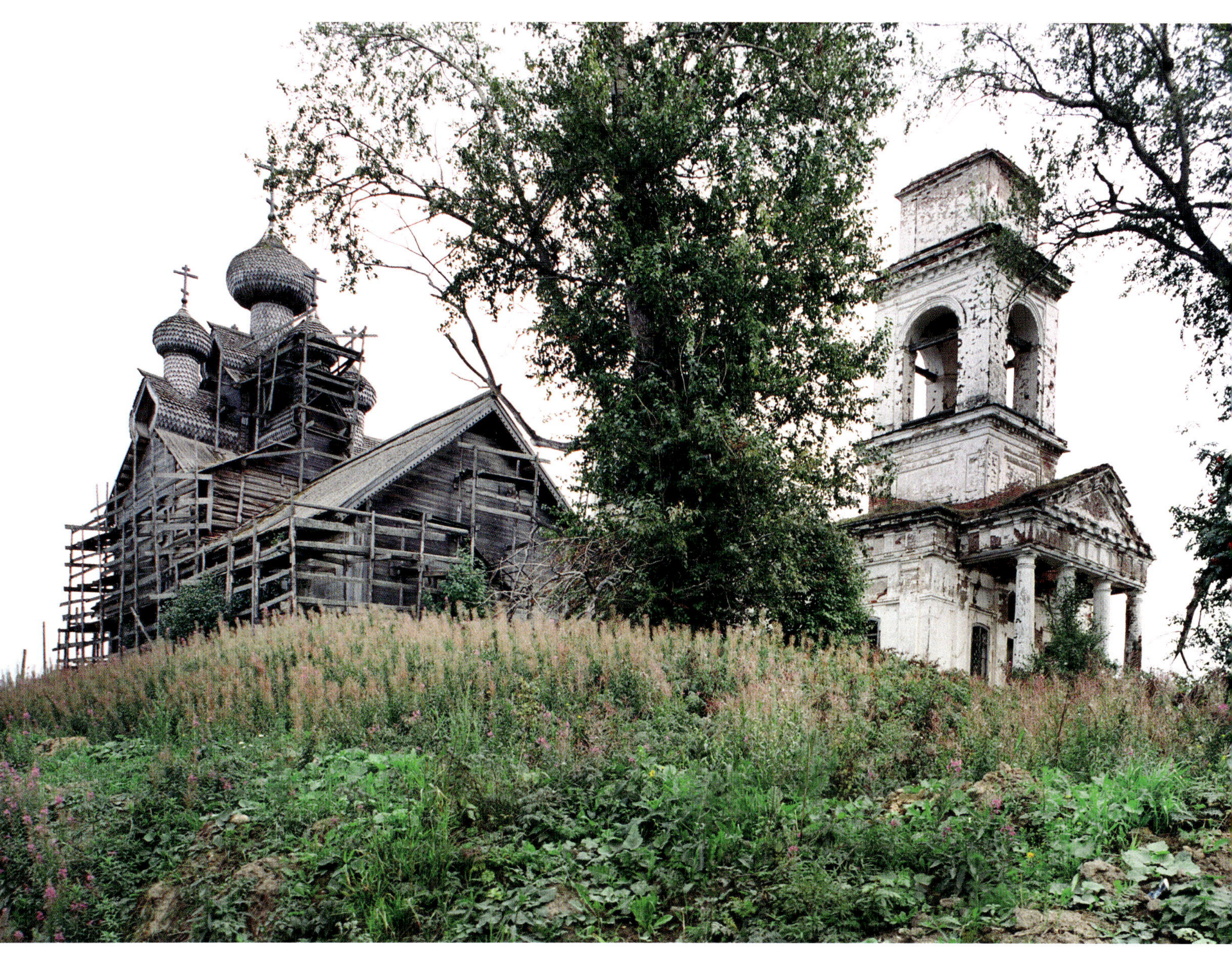

careless fire in 1963, the Intercession Church was reconstructed in 2004–7 for a park near Novosaratovka, a suburb on the Neva River to the southeast of Saint Petersburg. My photograph shows the reconstructed form (without the painted plank siding), now used as a parish church.

From Vytegra the Mariinsky Canal System led south toward White Lake (Beloe Ozero). Although smaller than Lakes Ladoga and Onega, White Lake is a pivotal link between those two lakes and the Russian heartland. Across the lake on the south shore is the town of Belozersk. The origins and early location of Belozersk are uncertain, but "Beloozero" is considered among the oldest recorded settlements among the eastern Slavs. It was mentioned in the *Primary Chronicle* under the year 862 as one of the five towns

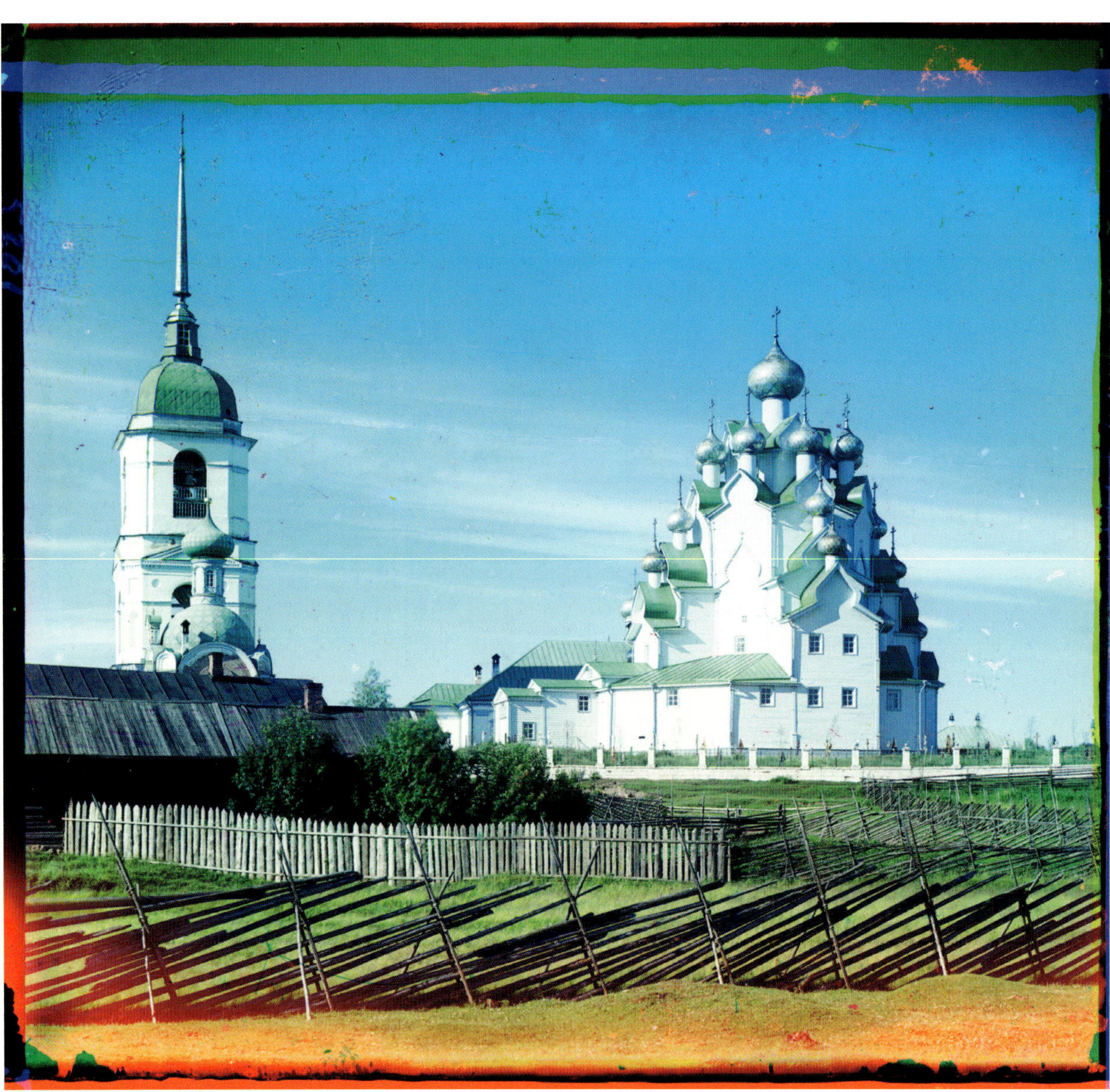

ANKHIMOVO (VYTEGORSKY POGOST) Wooden Church of the Intercession (destroyed by fire in 1963), with Church of All Saints (burial chapel of Loparyov family) and bell tower of the Church of the Miraculous Image of the Savior. PROKUDIN-GORSKY 20993. SUMMER 1909.

NEVSKY LESOPARK (right bank of the Neva River southeast of Saint Petersburg) Copy of the Intercession Church at Ankhimovo erected in 2005–6 without nineteenth-century plank siding. Serves as active church within Bogoslovka Estate complex. BRUMFIELD, AUGUST 17, 2009.

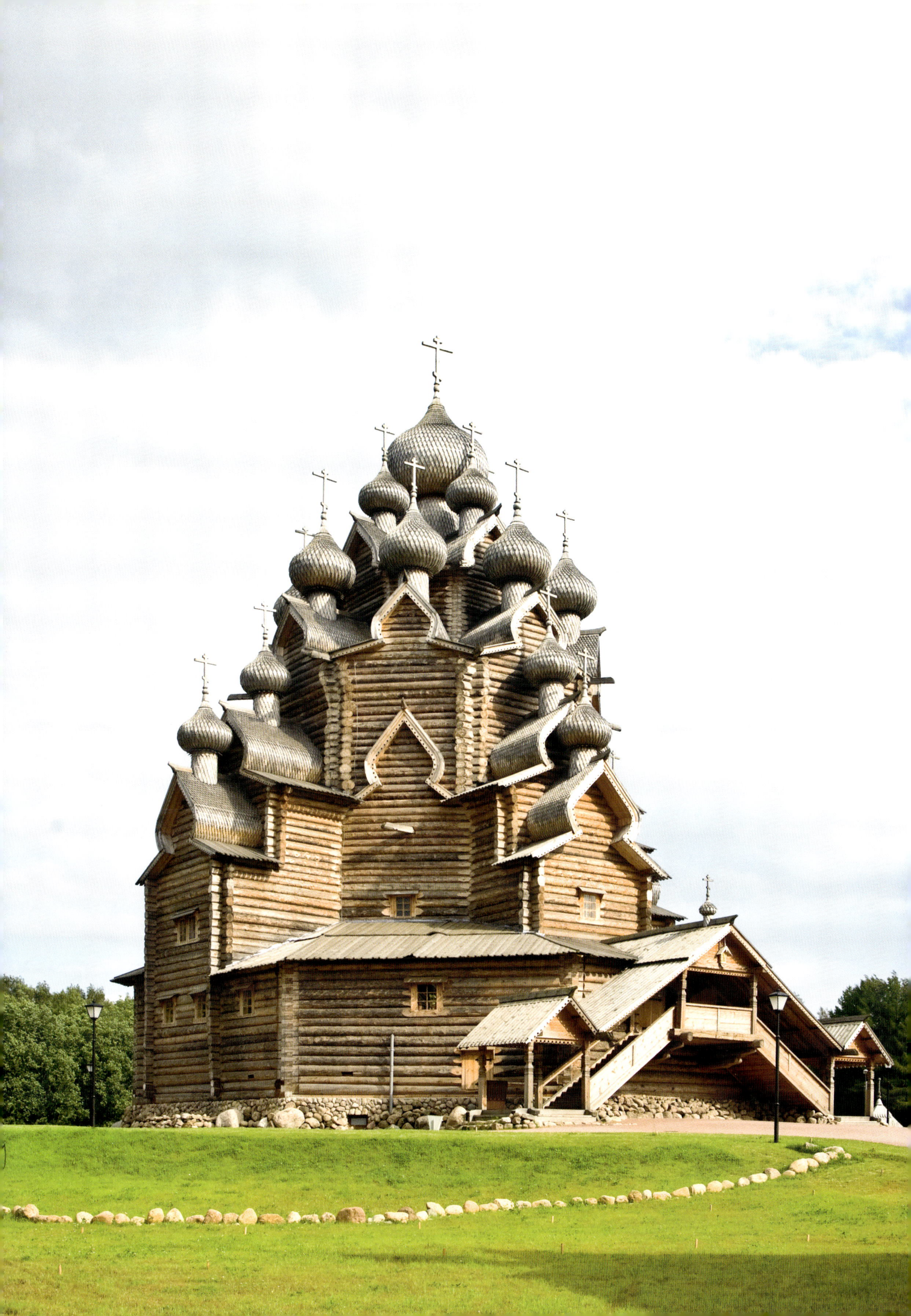

granted to the Varangian (or Viking) brothers Riurik, Sineus, and Truvor, invited (according to the chronicle) to rule over the eastern Slavs in what was then called Rus. Whatever the details of its history, it is clear from the name that the town was closely connected with White Lake (Beloe Ozero).

The early Beloozero—as it was originally called—was at a different location on White Lake, and the town was resettled again until it occupied its current place in the late fourteenth century. As Moscow's power increased in the fifteenth century, Beloozero gained strategic importance as a bulwark on Muscovy's northwestern frontier and its water routes. In 1487 Ivan III (the Great) constructed a large fortress, or kremlin, whose earthen ramparts still stand. This citadel is perhaps the best-preserved example of a type of earthen fortress once widespread among the eastern Slavs. Roughly quadrilateral in shape, the fortress was protected on two sides by a moat. In the late seventeenth century the ramparts were still surmounted with a log wall containing eight towers and two gates—all removed in the eighteenth century.

The town prospered during the middle of the sixteenth century, particularly as a source of iron goods and fish. An impressive visible reminder of that wealth is the fortress-like Church of the Dormition, begun in 1553 on one of the town's highest points. Beloozero witnessed the disruptions of the latter part of the reign of Ivan the Terrible (1547–84), when the town was included in his personal domain (*oprichnina*) and served as a place of exile. The inclusion of Beloozero in Ivan's domains did not prevent it from experiencing the famine and disease inflicted on much of the rest of Russia in the late sixteenth century. And during the Time of Troubles, the year 1612 brought a full measure of devastation with the sack of Beloozero by a marauding force.

With the revival of trade in the seventeenth century, Beloozero's location and natural resources again proved advantageous. During the reign of Aleksei Mikhailovich, the Cathedral of the Transfiguration was built within the kremlin in the 1670s. With the founding of Saint Petersburg in 1703 Beloozero found itself in a pivotal position between the Volga River basin and the large northwestern lakes Onega and Ladoga that led via the Neva River to the new imperial capital. In 1777 the town's name was formally changed to Belozersk, and the next year it gained a new plan as part of Catherine the Great's project to remake Russian provincial life by redesigning regional centers.

Prokudin-Gorsky understood that the best general views of historical Belozersk are from the ramparts of the kremlin. As befitted the regional importance of Belozersk, the fortress interior was arranged around two cathedrals. The surviving Cathedral of the Transfiguration of the Savior was begun in 1668 during the reign of Aleksei Mikhailovich and completed in the late 1670s, with a narthex added in the early nineteenth century. Support for the cathedral's construction came from both Moscow and local sources. The Transfiguration Cathedral follows a sixteenth-century pattern typical for large churches in provincial centers. The facades are each divided into three bays capped by semicircular gables known as *zakomary*. The cathedral is crowned with large cupolas and high ornamental iron crosses visible in my photographs and Prokudin-Gorsky's. The drum, or cylinder, beneath each cupola displays an arched pattern with slender attached columns. Even with tall cupolas the height of the Transfiguration Cathedral seems truncated, due in part to a slight subsidence of the boulder foundations into the soft ground—a common occurrence with medieval churches in northwest Russia. Presumably the builders decided not to risk a taller structure on such a base.

An earlier wooden church, dedicated to the Byzantine theologian Saint Basil the Great, had also existed at the kremlin site. This church was rebuilt in 1738 as the Cathedral of Saint Basil the Great, with a second altar dedicated to Saint Nicholas added on the north side at the turn of the nineteenth century. The Transfiguration Cathedral itself had a secondary altar dedicated to Basil the Great, whose local cult seems to have arisen during the reign of Grand Prince Basil (Vasily) III, ruler of Muscovy from 1505 to 1533. The two cathedrals were visually unified by an octagonal bell tower.

The entire ensemble is beautifully presented in Prokudin-Gorsky's 1909 photograph, taken from the northwest on a summer afternoon. Both the bell tower and Saint Basil's Church were demolished in the Soviet period, leaving only the seventeenth-century Transfiguration Cathedral. His northwest view is now obscured by trees and later structures. My photograph shows clear views from the south rampart of the kremlin. One of the most appealing parts of Prokudin-Gorsky's photograph is the bucolic view of haystacks among carefully tended plots with potatoes and cabbage. The once active fortress, whose ramparts are visible in the background, reverted to the peaceful use of its fertile soil. Over the next three decades this placid scene would be disfigured in the aftermath of revolutionary change.

The cathedral interior was not painted with frescoes, and that allows one to concentrate on one of the most remarkable icon screens in Russia. The main space is defined by two massive square piers faced on their lower level with carved, gilded icon frames. The piers support the west and central cathedral vaults and frame the view of the wondrous icon screen. The typical Russian Orthodox iconostasis forms a grid of two dimensions for

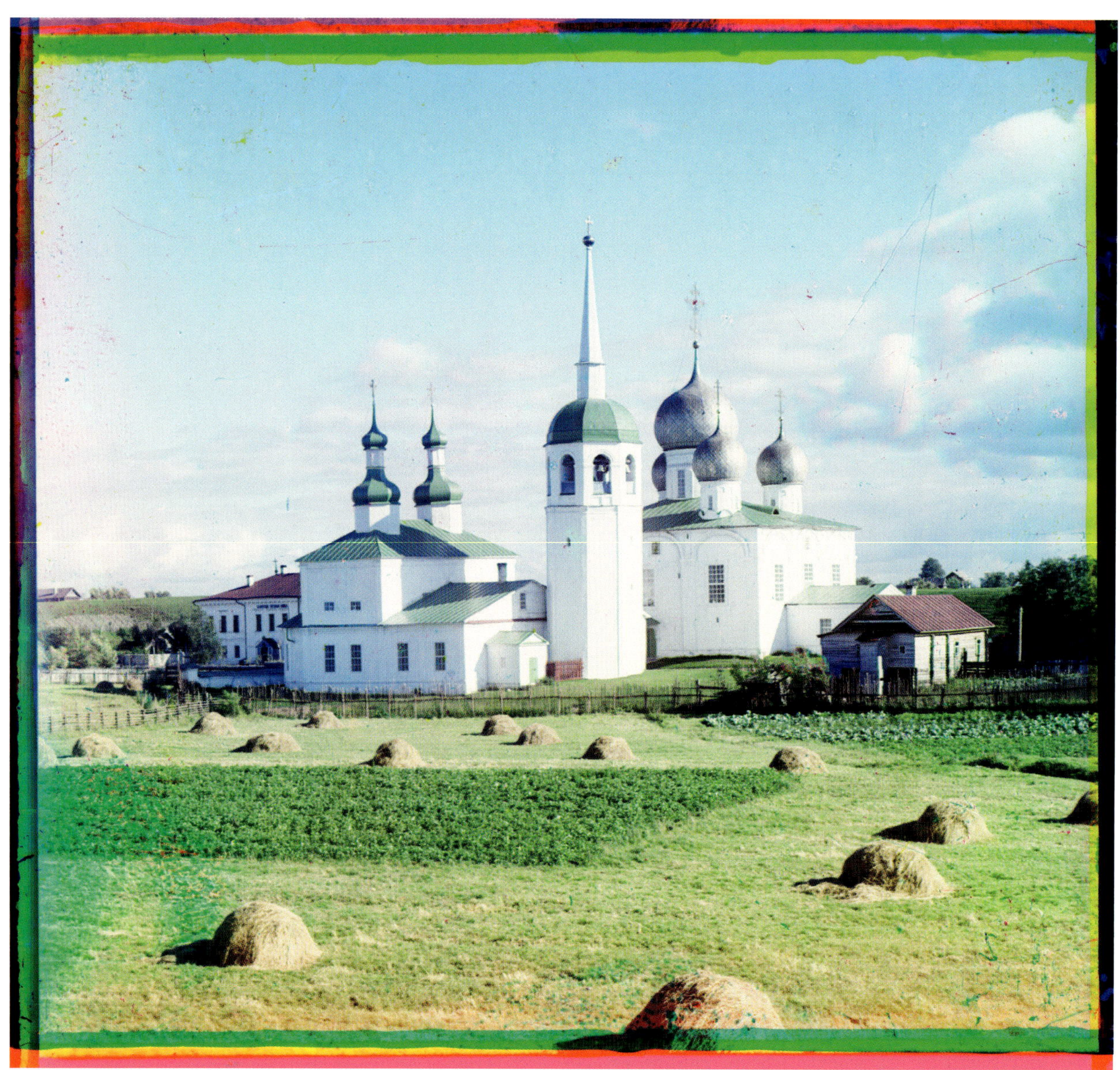

BELOZERSK KREMLIN View toward southeast from fortress rampart with Churches of Saint Basil the Great and Saint Nicholas, and the Transfiguration Cathedral. PROKUDIN-GORSKY 20986. SUMMER 1909.

BELOZERSK KREMLIN View toward northeast from fortress rampart with pond and Transfiguration Cathedral. BRUMFIELD, JUNE 9, 2010.

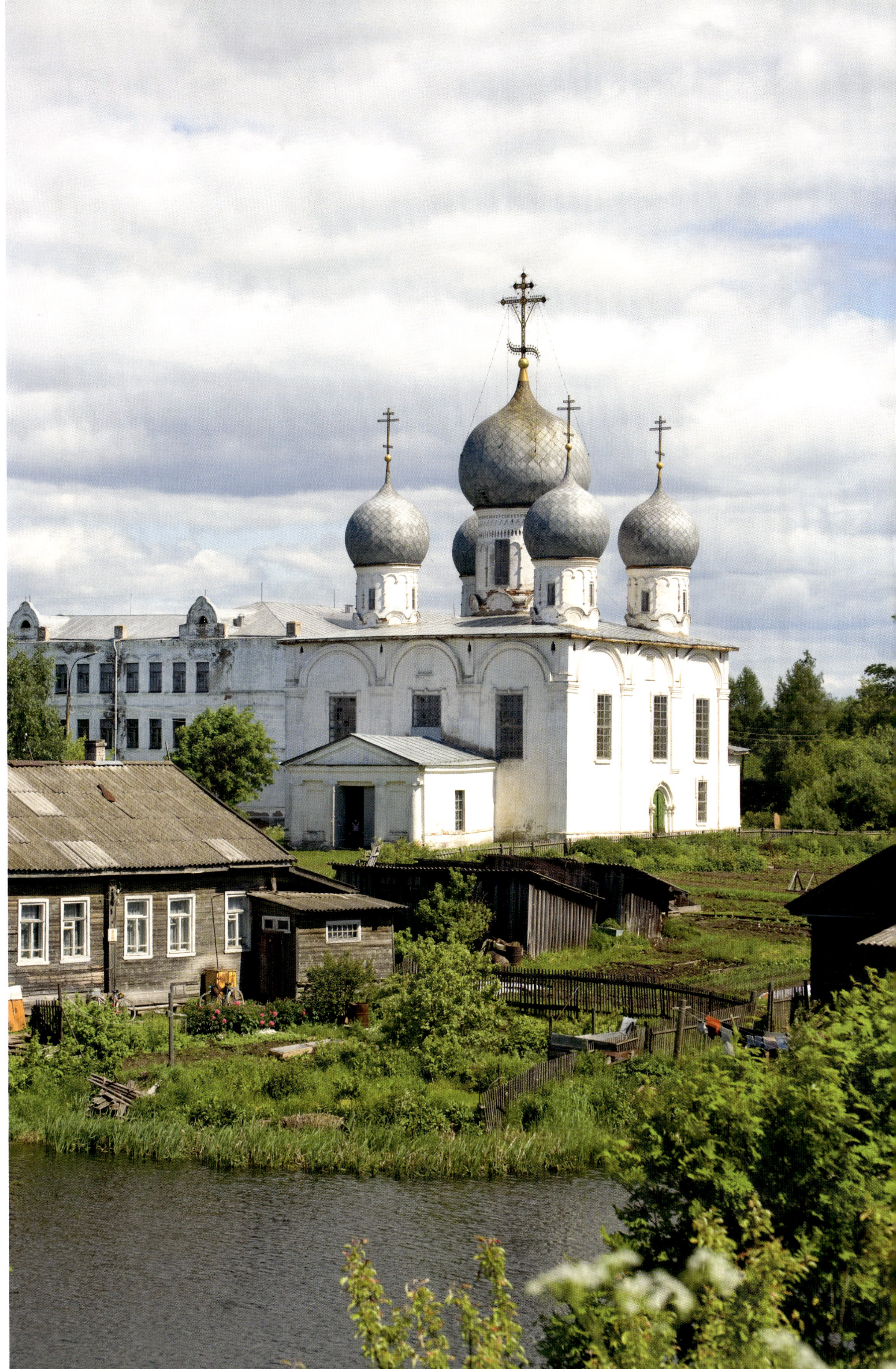

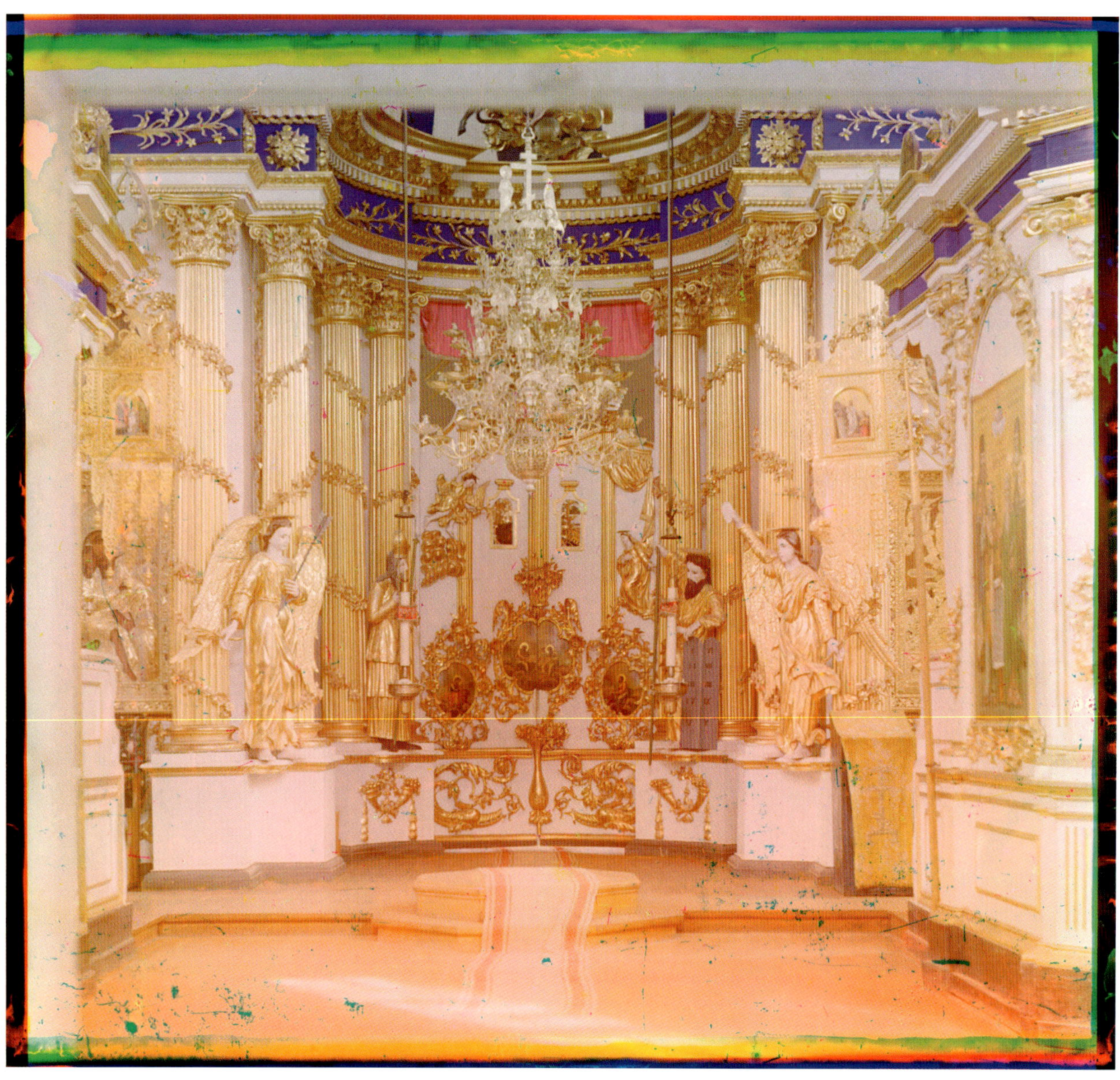

the ascending rows of icons, with the main portal to the altar—the Royal Gate—in the center. At the beginning of the eighteenth century, there appeared a more dynamic form of screen influenced by baroque art and with a greater sense of depth in the center of surrounding the Royal Gate.

Yet the icon screen at the Belozersk Transfiguration Cathedral was created decades after the waning of the baroque, perhaps at the beginning of the nineteenth century. It represents a merger of the baroque and neoclassical styles, of vigorous northern wooden carving with refined elements characteristic of Saint Petersburg. The channeled column

BELOZERSK KREMLIN Transfiguration Cathedral, interior. View east toward iconostasis (lower tier). PROKUDIN-GORSKY 20988. SUMMER 1909.

BELOZERSK KREMLIN Transfiguration Cathedral, interior. View east toward iconostasis (lower tier). BRUMFIELD, AUGUST 8, 2009.

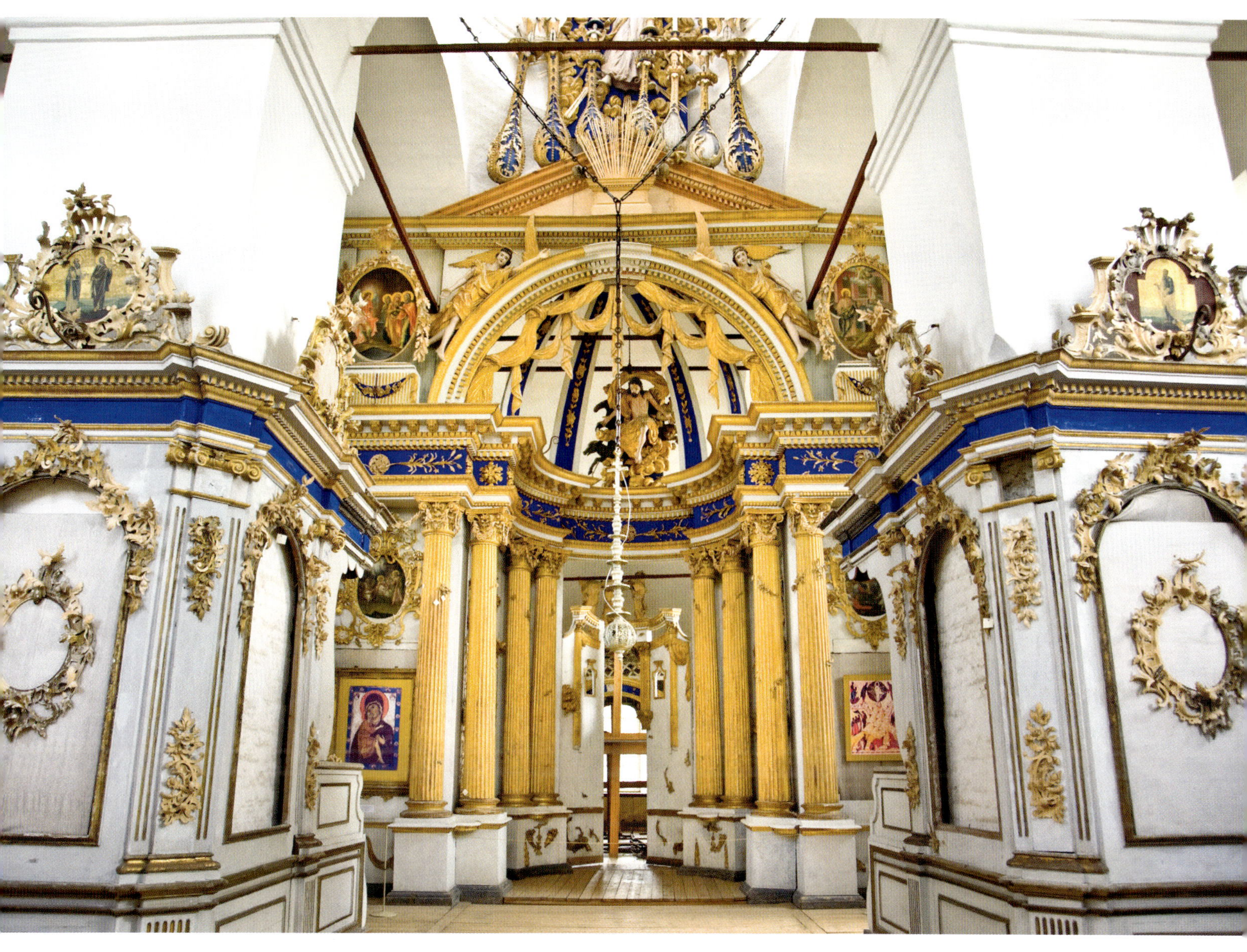

shafts and the elaborate Corinthian entablature, as well as sinuous decorative baroque figures, are highlighted in gold on a white background. Angels and cherubim occupy the flanks of the structure and guard its center. Despite the loss of certain elements during the Soviet period, the iconostasis is relatively well preserved and Prokudin-Gorsky's valuable photograph allows a precise reconstruction of its original form.

On the first level the corners of the central space were occupied by vigorous statues of angels, beyond which the eye discerns the curved walls leading to the Royal Gate. As Prokudin-Gorsky's photograph shows, the original design had statues of Moses, holding the tablets of the Ten Commandments, and his brother Aaron, with the miraculous rod, placed oppo-

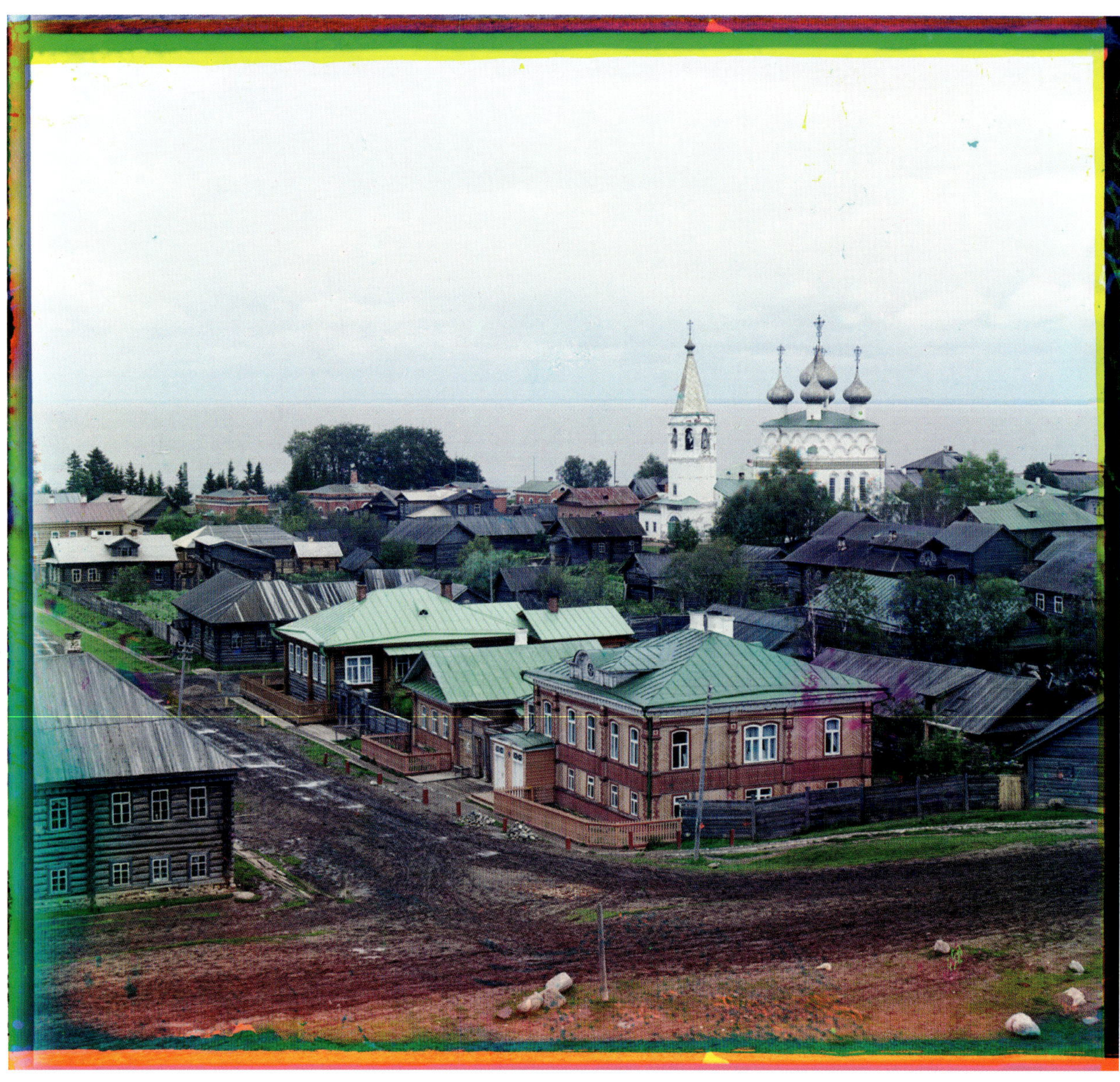

site one another on the curved walls. These two statues prefigure the painted cartouches originally present on the two halves of the Royal Gate: the four Evangelists, the Annunciation, and the Last Supper. For technical reasons involving the drop mechanism of his three-exposure process, Prokudin-Gorsky was unable to tilt the camera sharply upward. Therefore, he left only a view of the lower tier, but because of the missing artwork, that record now has exceptional value.

As one moves toward the center of the iconostasis, which is lit from above by the main cathedral dome, the three-

BELOZERSK Church of the Icon of the Most Merciful Savior. Southwest view from north rampart of fortress. PROKUDIN-GORSKY 20987. SUMMER 1909.

BELOZERSK Church of the Icon of the Most Merciful Savior. Southwest view from north rampart of fortress. BRUMFIELD, AUGUST 8, 2009.

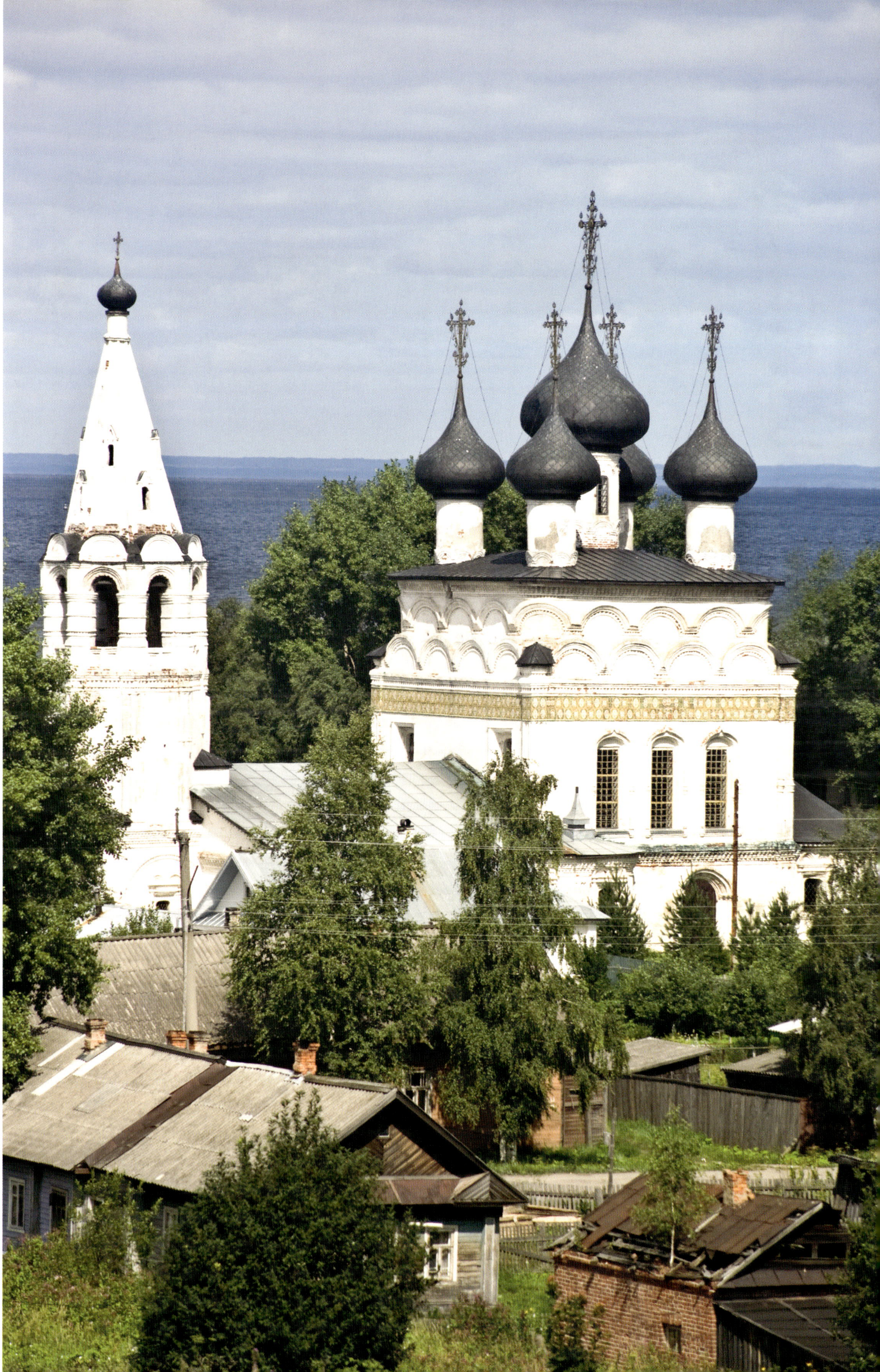

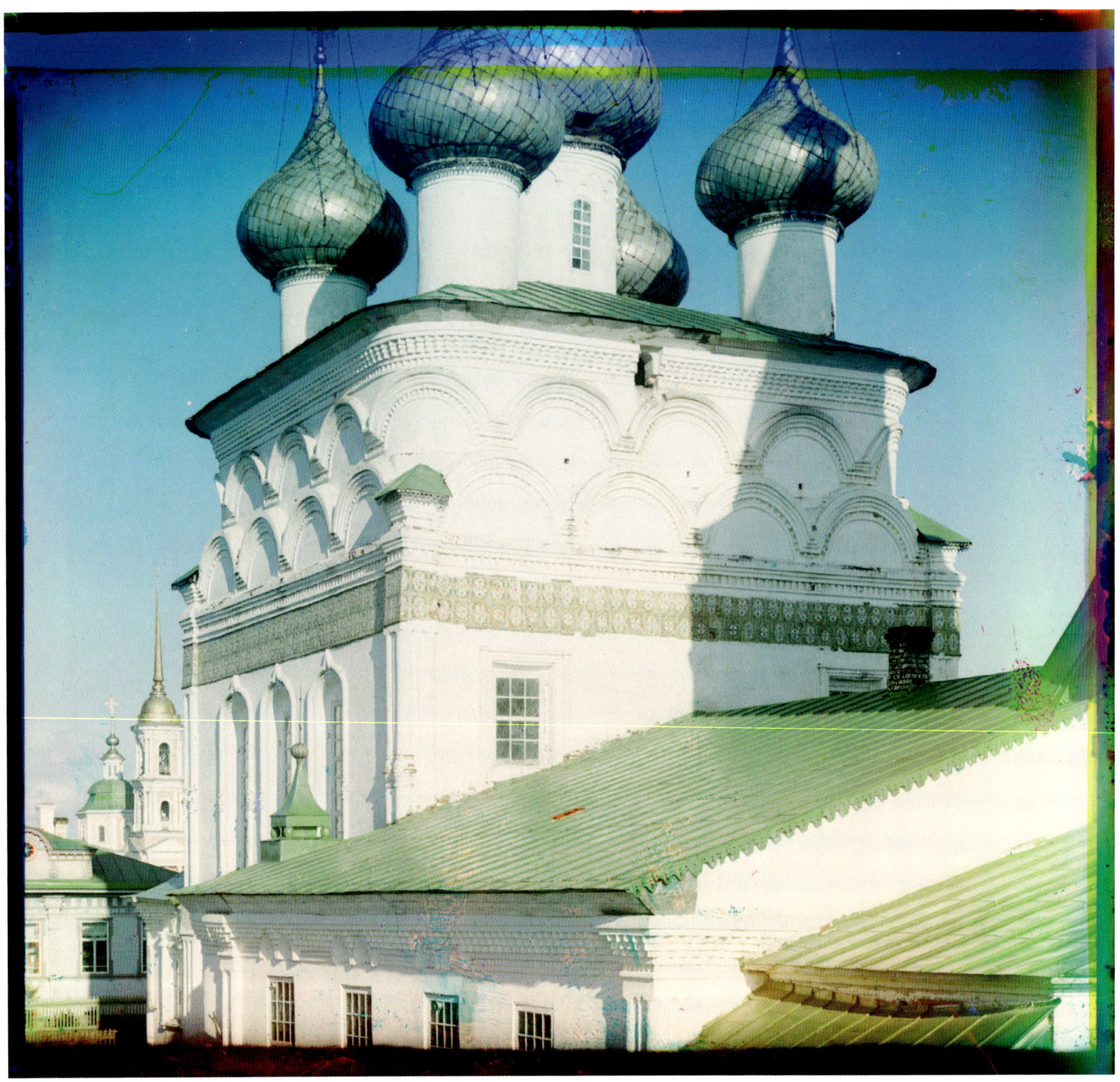

dimensional drama of the central space becomes evident through the placement of an array of sculpted figures seen in my photographs. The frame for the Royal Gate ascends to a massive entablature (gold on white, with a deep blue horizontal border), on which rests the shell of a dome formed by a hemispherical section with ribs in the background and gilded draped bunting in the foreground. This dramatic display envelops a sculpted figure of Christ clad in a loincloth and ascending to heaven in a cloud of glory. On either side of Christ are the four symbols of the Evangelists: the lion of Saint Mark, the angel of Saint Mathew, the eagle of

BELOZERSK Church of the Icon of the Most Merciful Savior. West facade. PROKUDIN-GORSKY 21075. SUMMER 1909.

BELOZERSK Church of the Icon of the Most Merciful Savior. South facade. BRUMFIELD, DECEMBER 29, 2010.

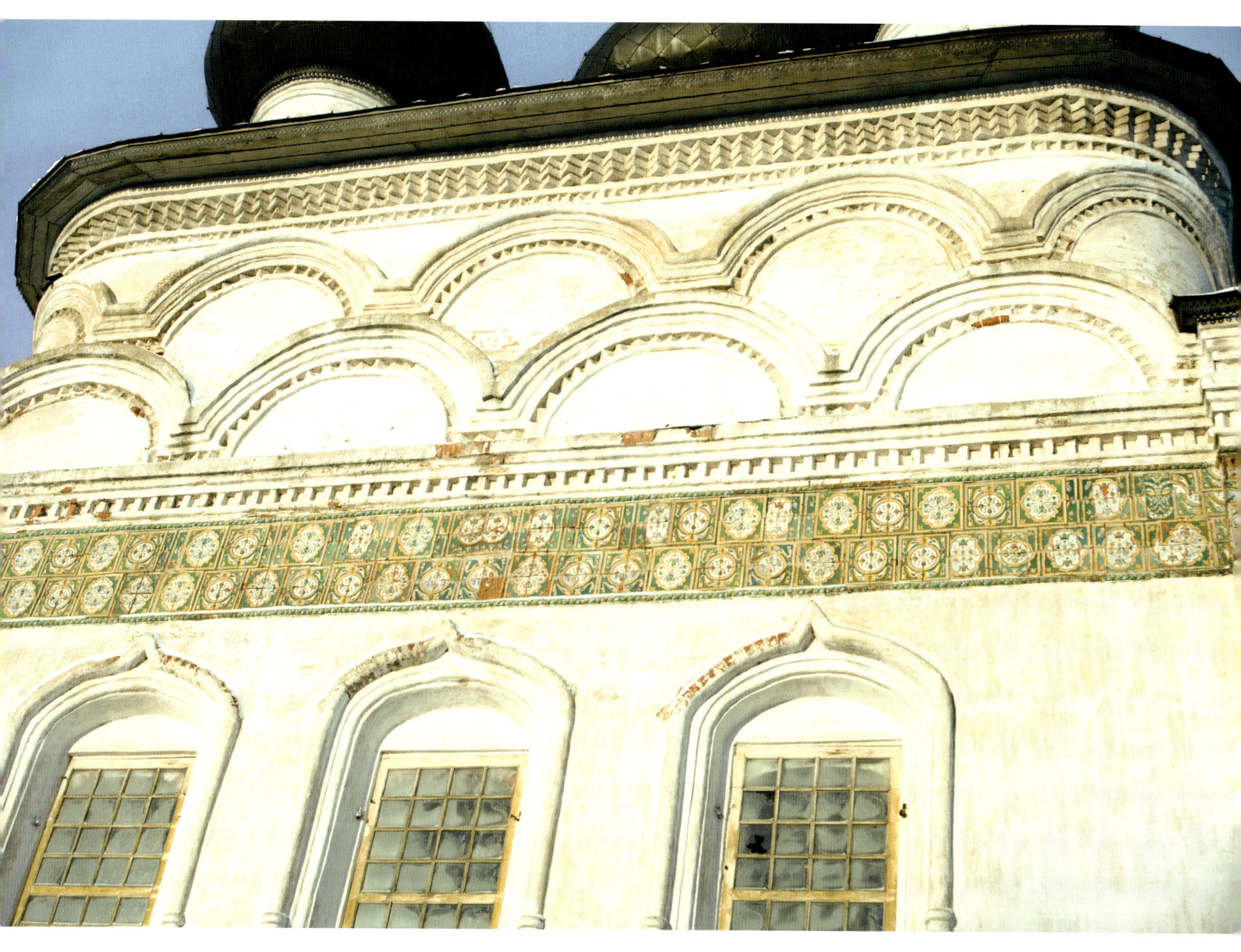

Saint John, and the flying bull of Saint Luke. At the very top of the iconostasis, ascending into the drum under the main dome, is another sculpted figure of Christ resurrected, in a glorious aura with angels, rays of light and massive candles—all associated with the Apocalypse. Although the Orthodox Church generally frowned on fully sculpted figures in church art, these statues continue a distinctive tradition of wooden carving throughout the Russian north. Together with its stylistic exuberance, the structure and the theological significance of the Transfiguration Cathedral icon screen are among the richest in Russia.

Turning toward the town, Prokudin-Gorsky took the northeast view toward White Lake from the north rampart of fortress. The dominant ele-

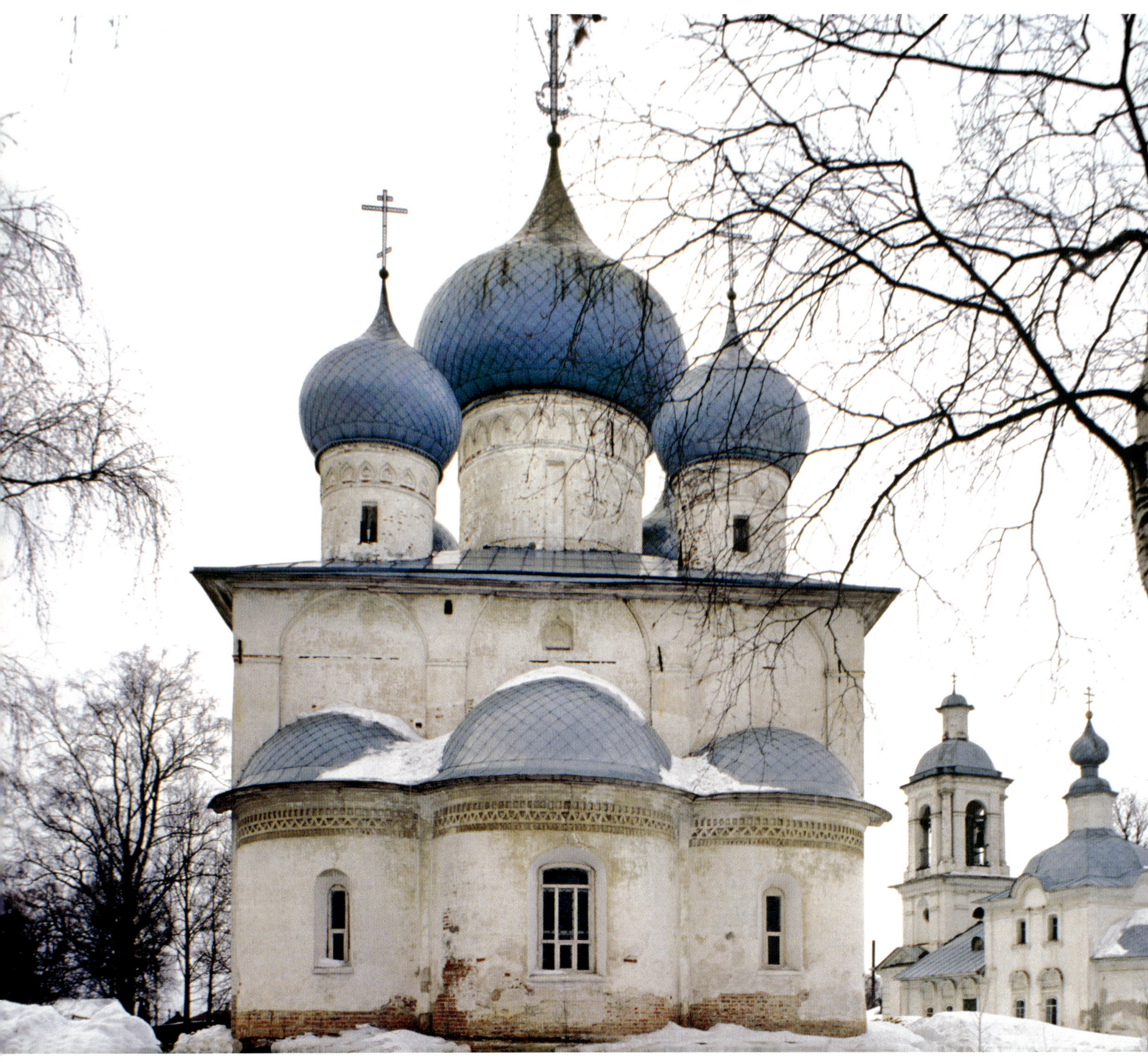

BELOZERSK Cathedral of the Dormition and Church of the Epiphany (*right*). East view. BRUMFIELD, MARCH 3, 1998.

BELOZERSK Church of the Epiphany (*left*) and Cathedral of the Dormition. Northwest view. PROKUDIN-GORSKY 20991. SUMMER 1909.

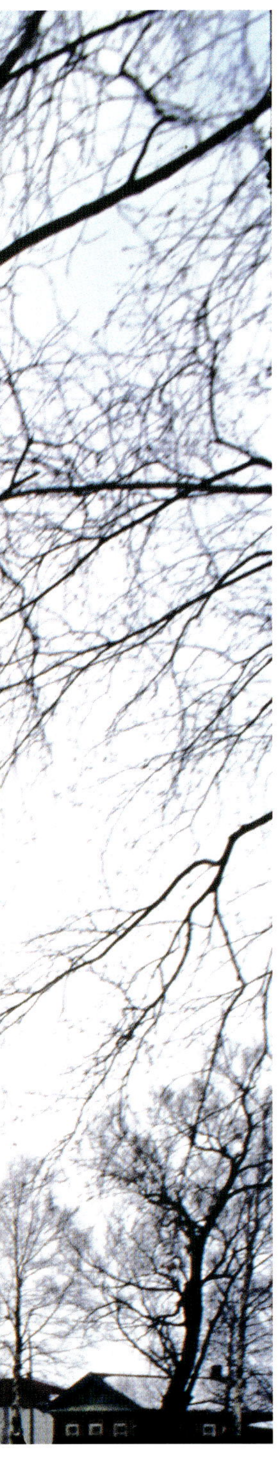

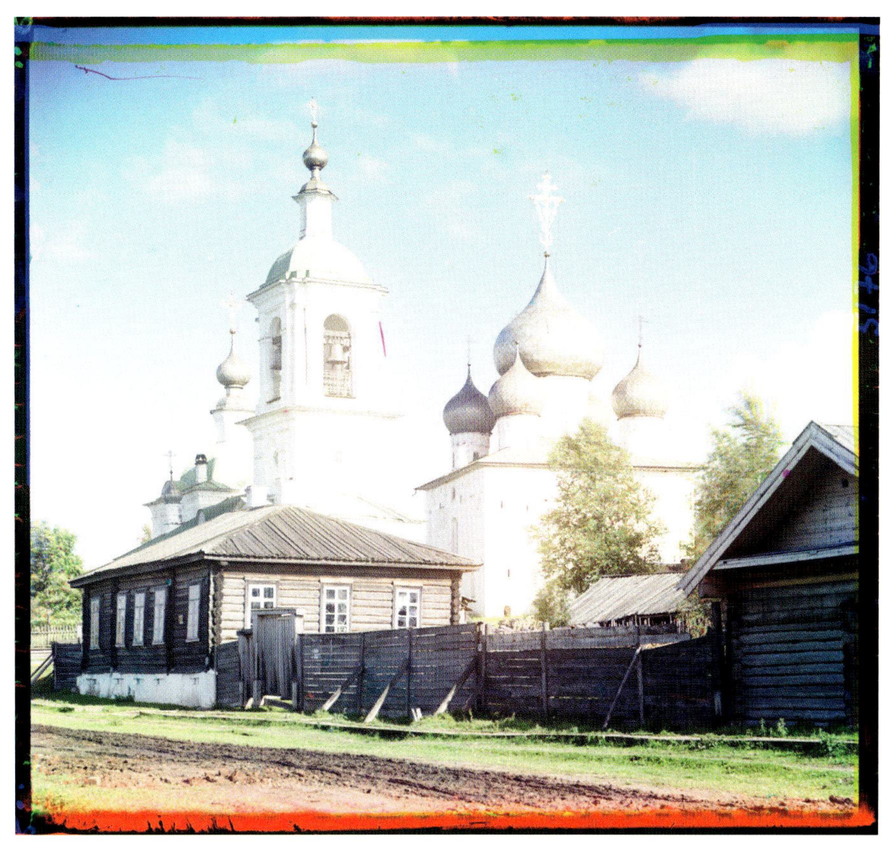

ment is the remarkable Church of the Icon of the Most Merciful Savior. My photograph from the same perspective seems to show all intact, but the interior of the church was ransacked during the Soviet period and now faces the threat of water seepage in the lower part of the walls. Prokudin-Gorsky's closer view of church's west facade shows a band of decorative ceramic tiles beneath the roofline. My photographs portray several perspectives on the facades and the ceramic work.

At one of the town's highest points, Prokudin-Gorsky photographed the church ensemble consisting of the Church of the Epiphany and Cathedral of the Dormition. My photographs over the past decade show that both have survived in good condition. The Epiphany Church, presumably built in the latter eighteenth century, was modest in size and used for worship in the winter, when the larger cathedral could not be heated. It had an unusual secondary altar dedicated to Saint Dmitry of Rostov and placed on a level above the main space.

The main interest in the ensemble is the Dormition Cathedral, which Prokudin-Gorsky photographed from the west. Built in 1553–70 by command of Ivan the Terrible on the site of the former Dormition Convent, it

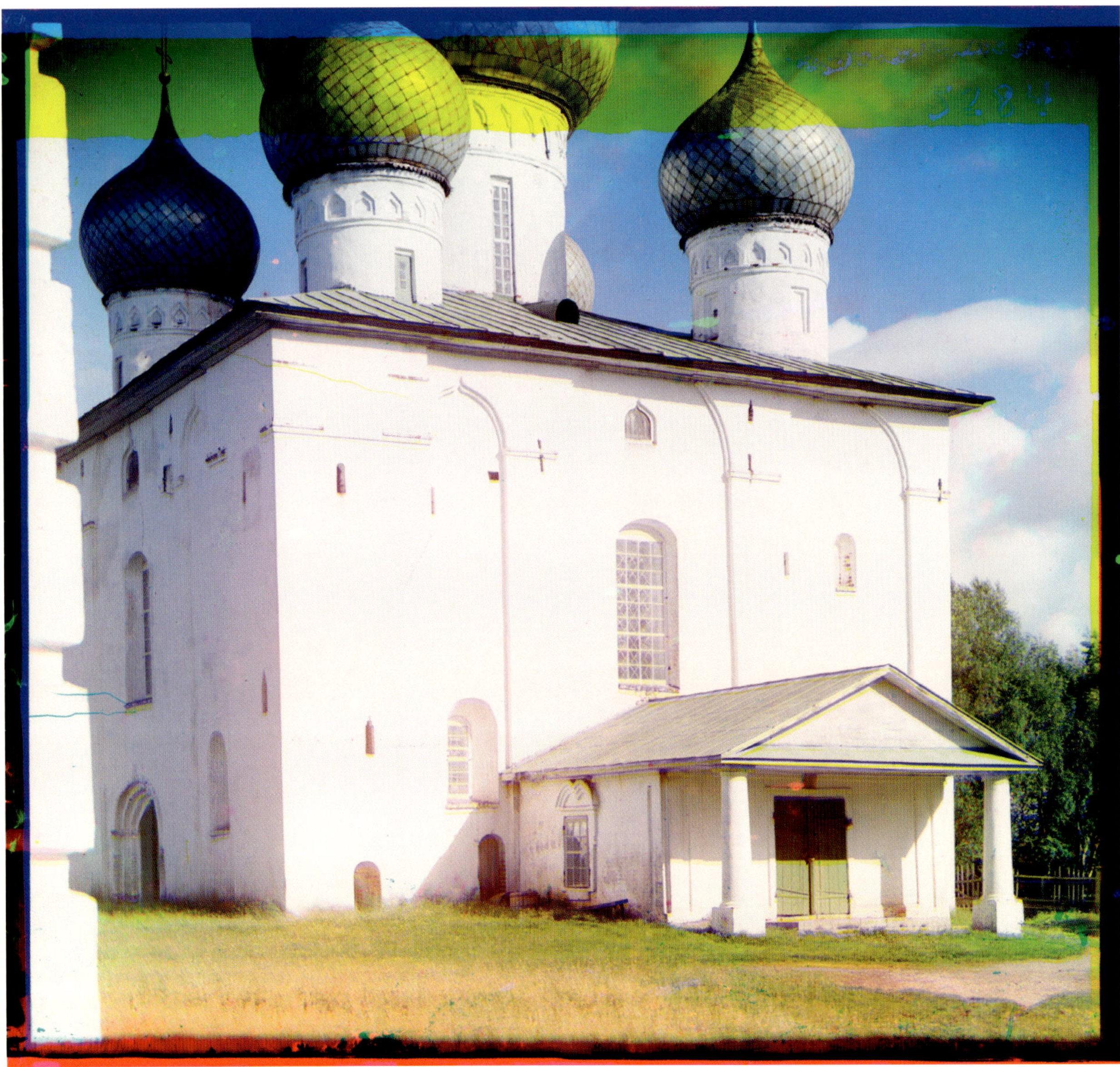

is the town's oldest monument. The structure is crowned by the traditional five cupolas, but its exterior decoration is sparse. The northwest corner, visible in Prokudin-Gorsky's photograph and mine, was constructed with reinforced masonry and might have served as an observation point, particularly in view of the church's location at the highest point in town. My photograph from the same perspective encompasses the cupolas, truncated by Prokudin-Gorsky's lens. Although Prokudin-Gorsky did not photograph the cathedral interior, it has a magnificent baroque iconostasis that stands in sharp contrast to the austerity of the exterior.

BELOZERSK Dormition Cathedral. Northwest view. PROKUDIN-GORSKY 21076. SUMMER 1909.

BELOZERSK Dormition Cathedral. Northwest view. BRUMFIELD, JUNE 9, 2010.

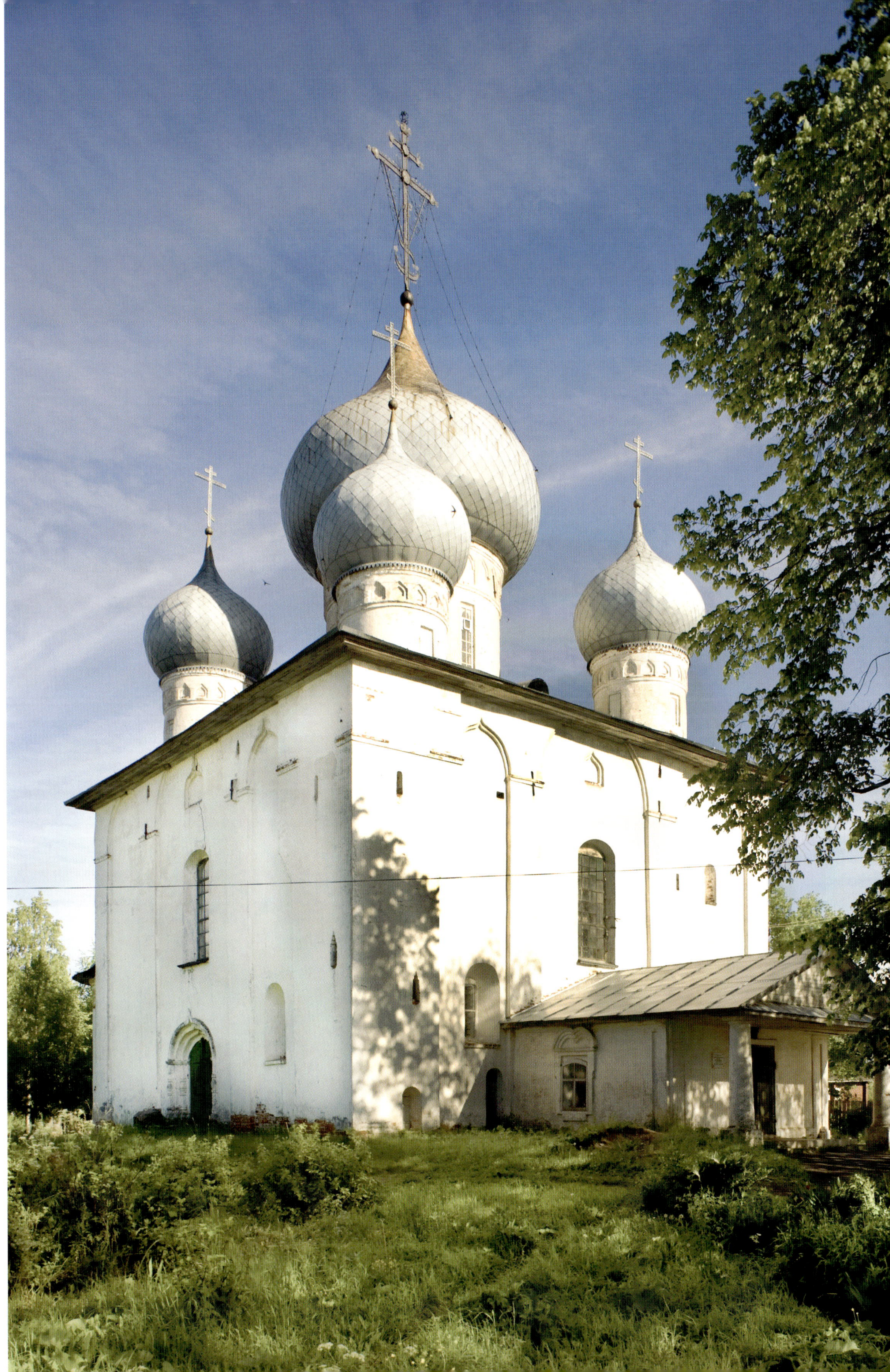

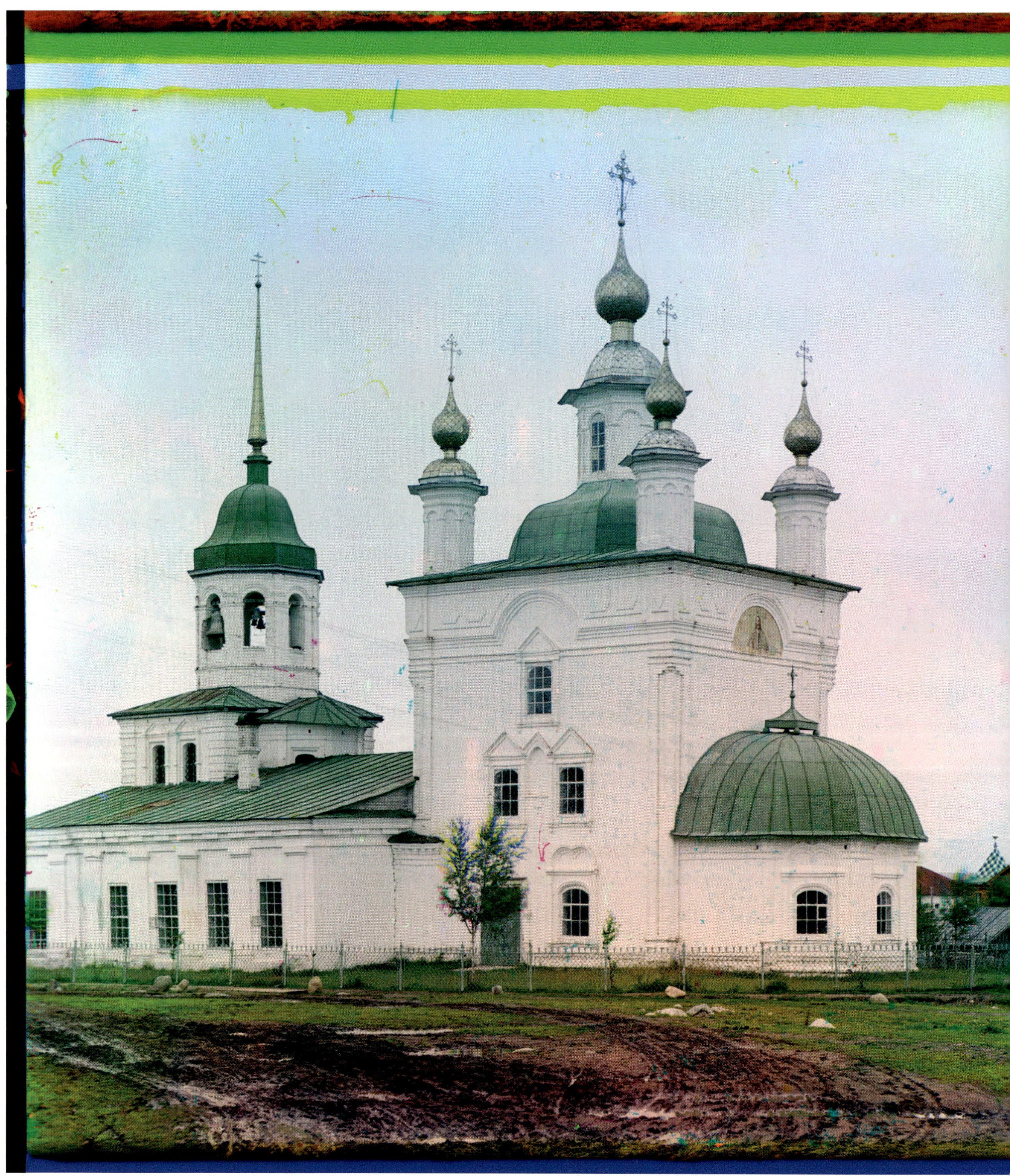

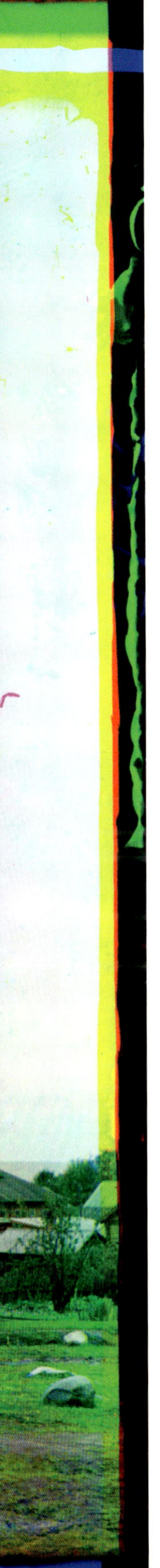

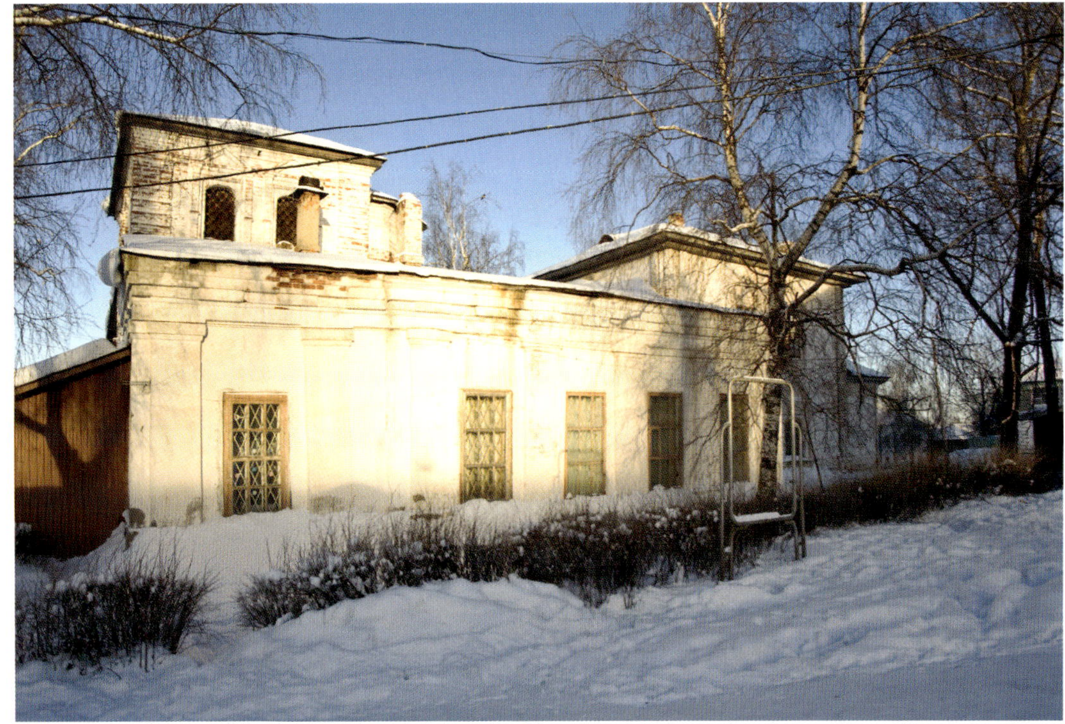

Unfortunately, the preservation of the Dormition Cathe-dral ensemble is the exception in Belozersk. The Soviet period promulgated a general disregard for religious monu-ments, and the small town does not have the resources to restore abandoned parish churches, some of which now exist only in Prokudin-Gorsky's photographs. An example of the vandalism is the Church of Saints Peter and Paul, whose once elaborate form was photographed by Prokudin-Gorsky from the southeast. My photograph shows a much reduced church.

A similar spectacle of neglect is evident in a photographic comparison of one of Belozersk's most distinctive ensembles, the Church of the Intercession and the wooden Church of the Prophet Elijah. Prokudin-Gorsky photographed them together from the southwest, with the Intercession Church in the foreground. Although simple in its provincial ba-roque detailing, the 1740 structure had the most beautiful bell tower in Belozersk. As my photographs show, nothing remains of the tower, and the church itself falls into greater ruin, unlikely to be restored or even conserved.

Hopes were greater for the preservation of the Elijah

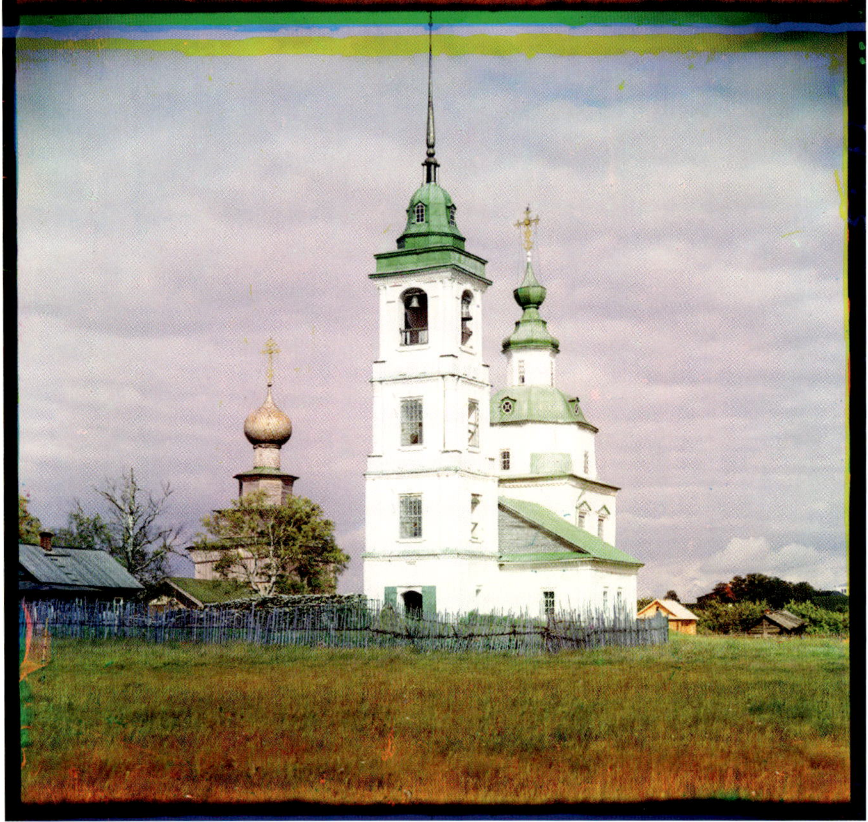

Church, considered a landmark of national significance. Prokudin-Gorsky's view, available only in the contact print, is an invaluable record. Built in 1690, the Elijah Church ascends in three tiers to a large wooden cupola that is clearly visible from the southwest corner of the kremlin. Attached to the west of the cuboid structure are a vestibule and a covered porch. The structure was disassembled in 2012 for a thorough restoration to deal with the threat of seeping ground water. The preservation of this rare and ancient church should have the highest priority, but it now exists in a limbo of competing projects.

One of the most poignant photographs in the Prokudin-Gorsky Collection is a group of children on a grassy bank near the shore of White Lake. The head of the small girl at the bottom is blurred because she moved during the three exposures. Some of the boys are indifferent to the camera, but the children seem sweetly obedient, holding still for the long exposure with the afternoon sun in their faces. One wonders about the fate of these young people over the next decades of war, revolution, famine, and massive social upheaval. The church in background, dedicated to Saint Paraskeva Piatnitsa (1795), is now in ruins. The historical architecture of Belozersk offers mute

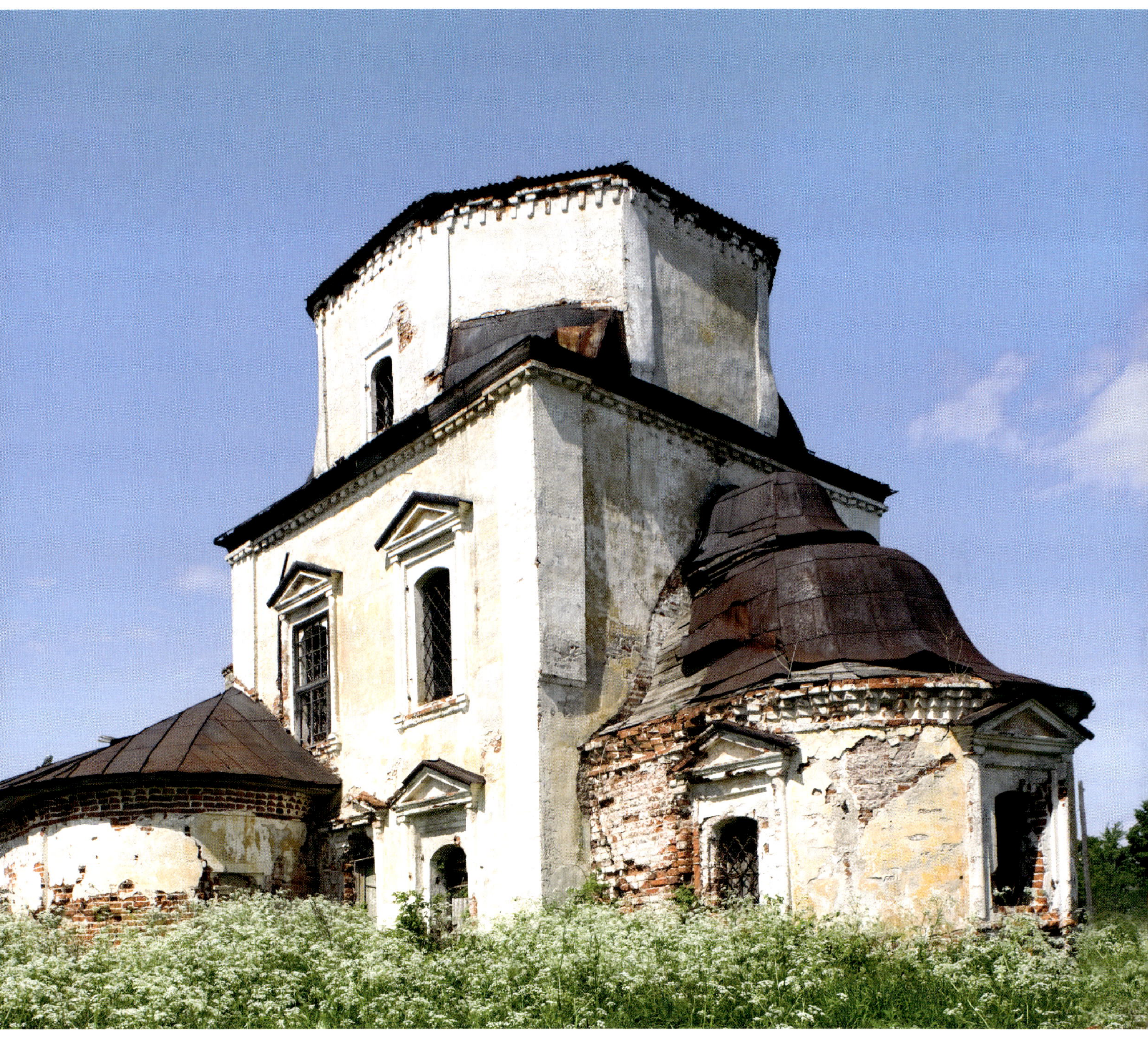

BELOZERSK Church of the Intercession with wooden
Church of Elijah the Prophet (*left*). Southwest view.
PROKUDIN-GORSKY 21064. SUMMER 1909.

BELOZERSK Ruins of the Church of the Intercession.
Southeast view. BRUMFIELD, JUNE 9, 2010.

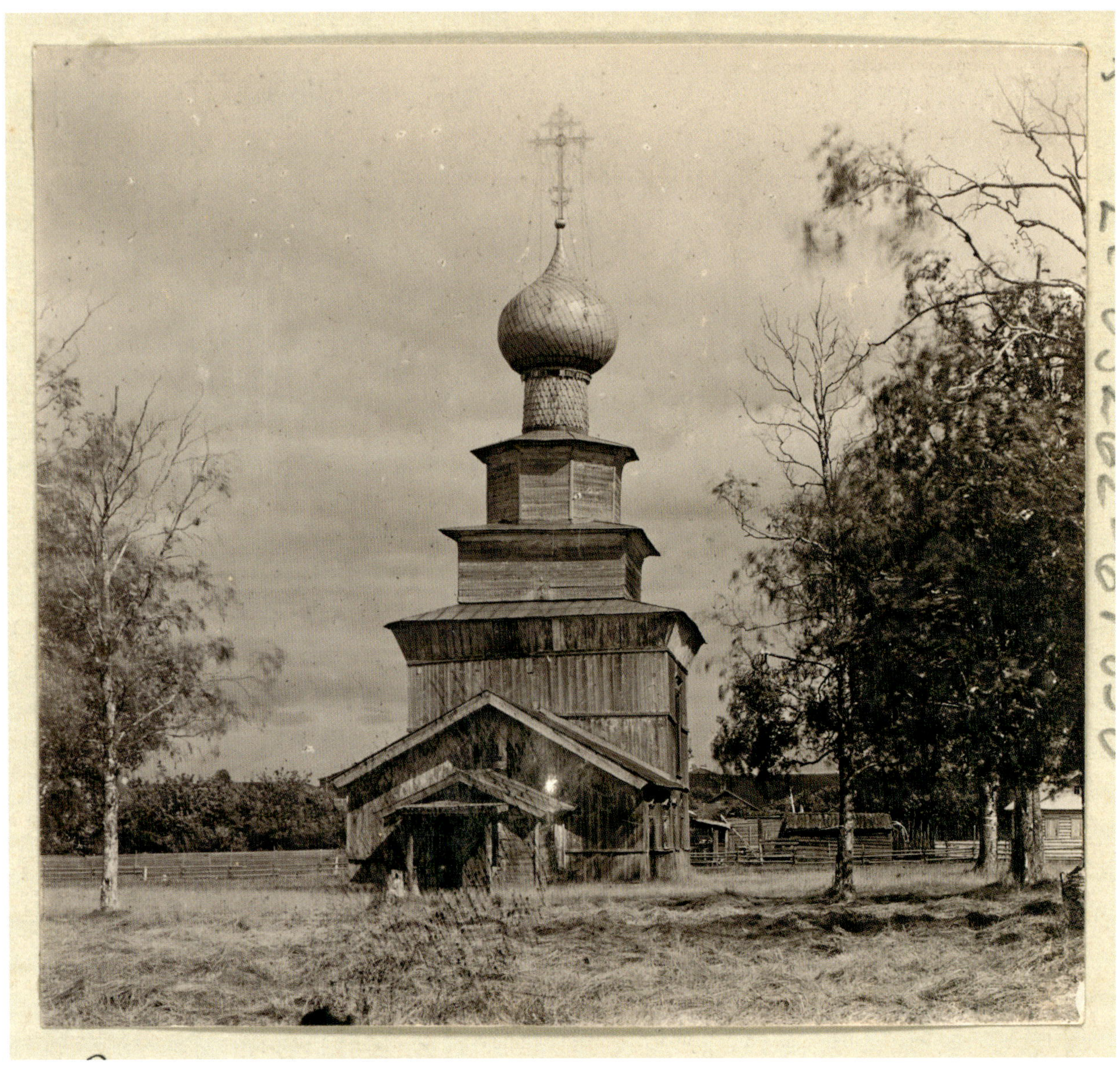

BELOZERSK Wooden Church of the Prophet Elijah. West view. PROKUDIN-GORSKY 01965. SUMMER 1909.

BELOZERSK Wooden Church of the Prophet Elijah.. Southwest view. BRUMFIELD, JULY 23, 1999.

testimony to the price exacted from Russia's regions during the twentieth century.

On the southeast end White Lake drains into the Sheksna, a tributary of the Volga and the route of many summer cruise boats between Moscow and Saint Petersburg, and past the village of Krokhino, with its imposing Church of the Nativity of Christ, which Prokudin-Gorsky photographed from the northeast. The first mention of the village is dated to 1426, when it was listed within the holdings of the Saint Kirill Belozersky Monastery. Although it is likely that the settlement had a church, information is

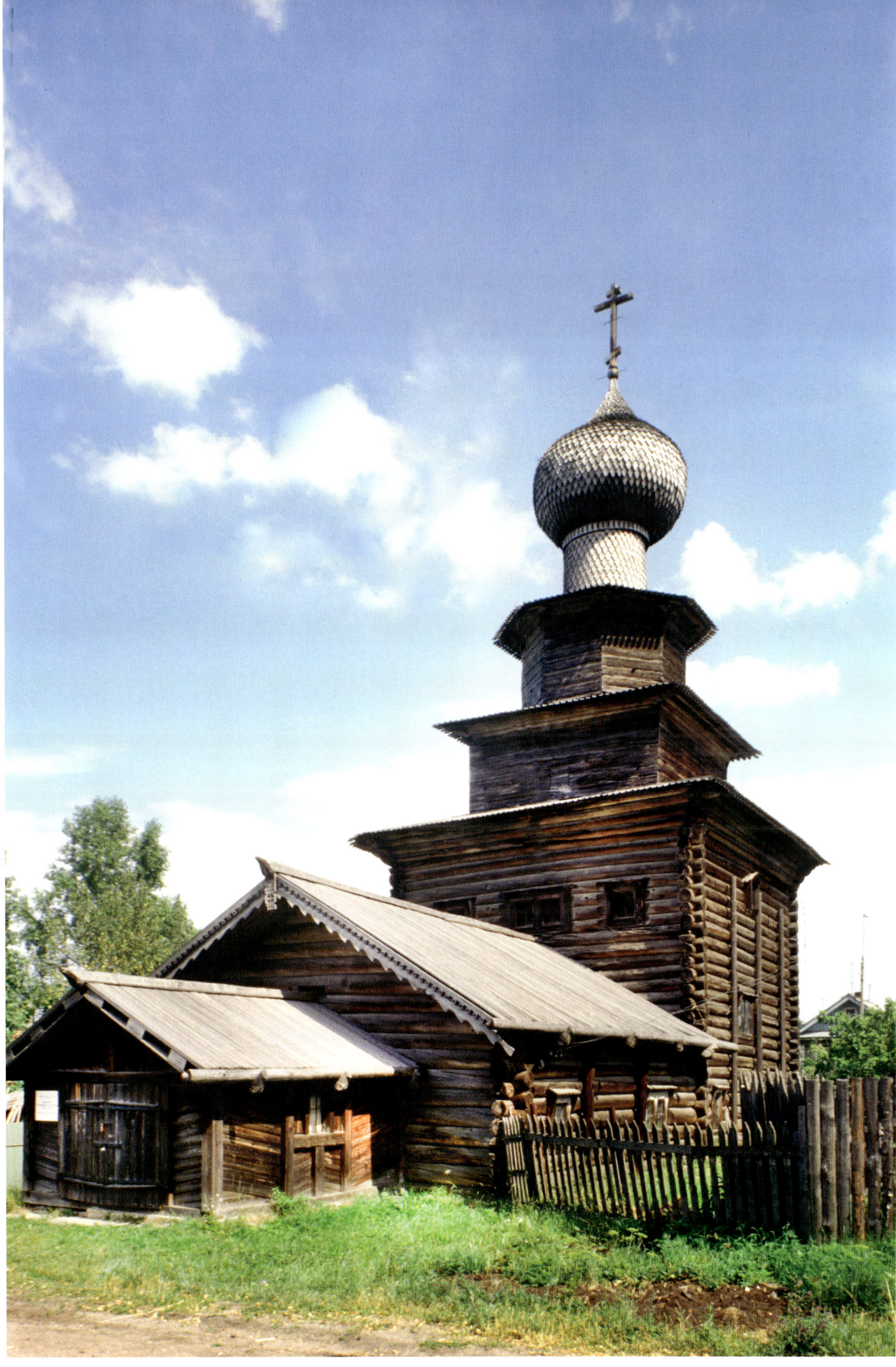

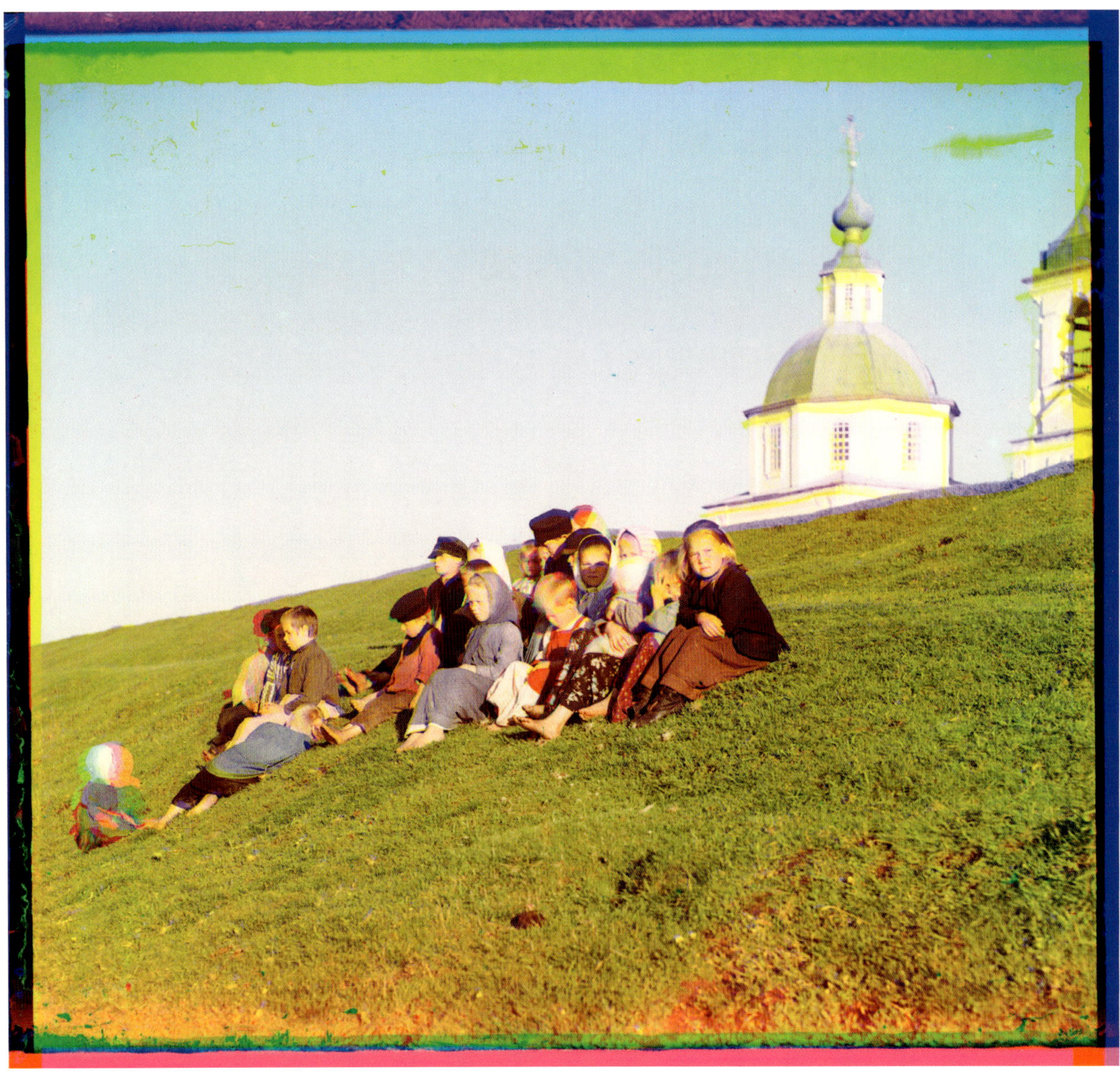

lacking. The church that Prokudin-Gorsky saw was apparently begun in the late eighteenth century and built in stages until completion in 1820, with secondary altars dedicated to Saint Nicholas and Saints Peter and Paul. Its style was a provincial mixture of simplified baroque and neoclassical elements, but its height and the bell tower gave it a commanding presence. With the filling of the Sheksna Reservoir in 1961, Krokhino village was submerged and only the church remained on a slightly higher elevation. Standing just at the water line, the abandoned church was buffeted by waves and the wake from passing boats in the dredged

BELOZERSK Children with Church of Saint Paraskeva in background. PROKUDIN-GORSKY 21067. SUMMER 1909.

BELOZERSK Ruins of Church of Saint Paraskeva. Southeast view. BRUMFIELD, JULY 22, 2010.

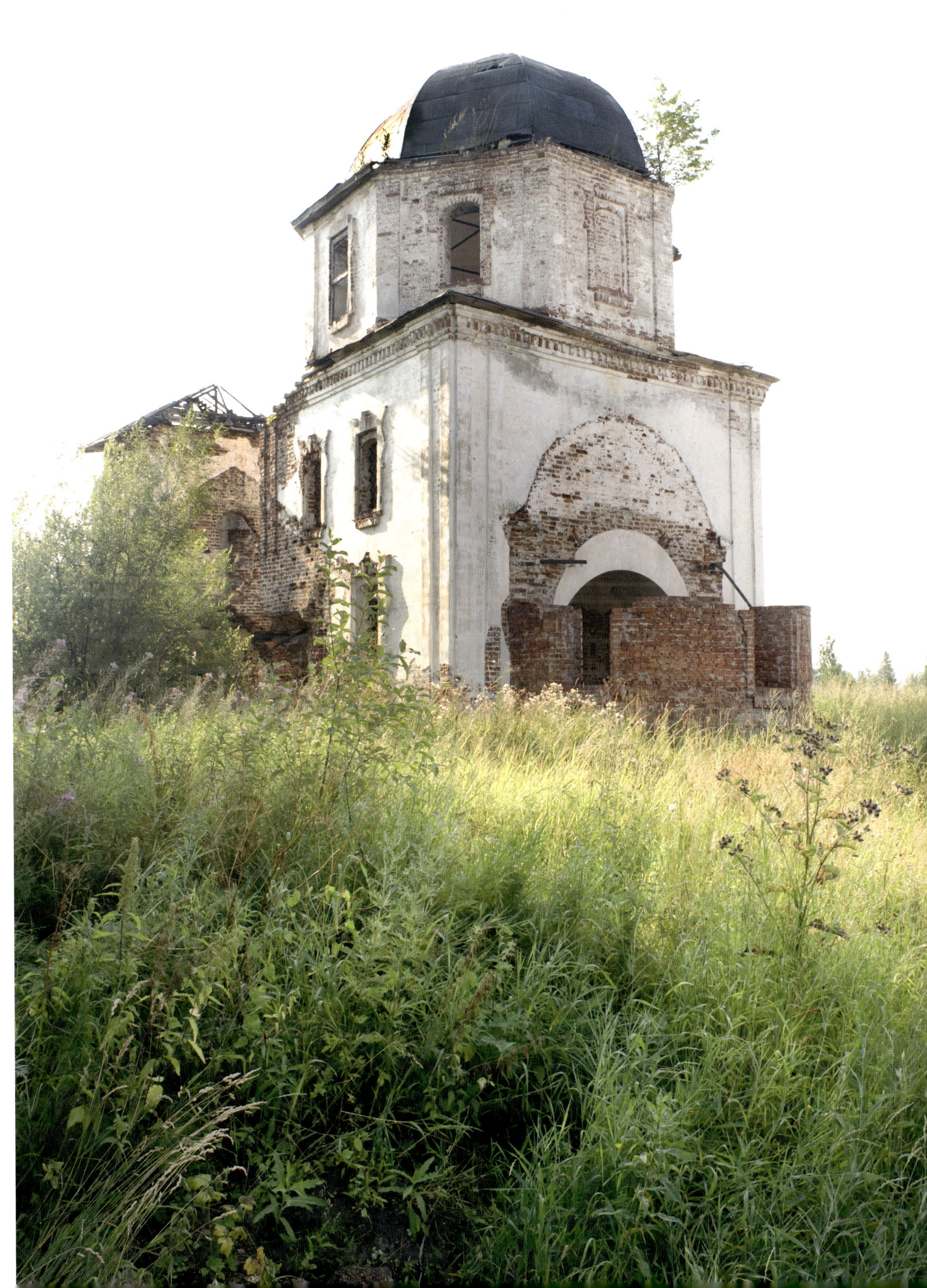

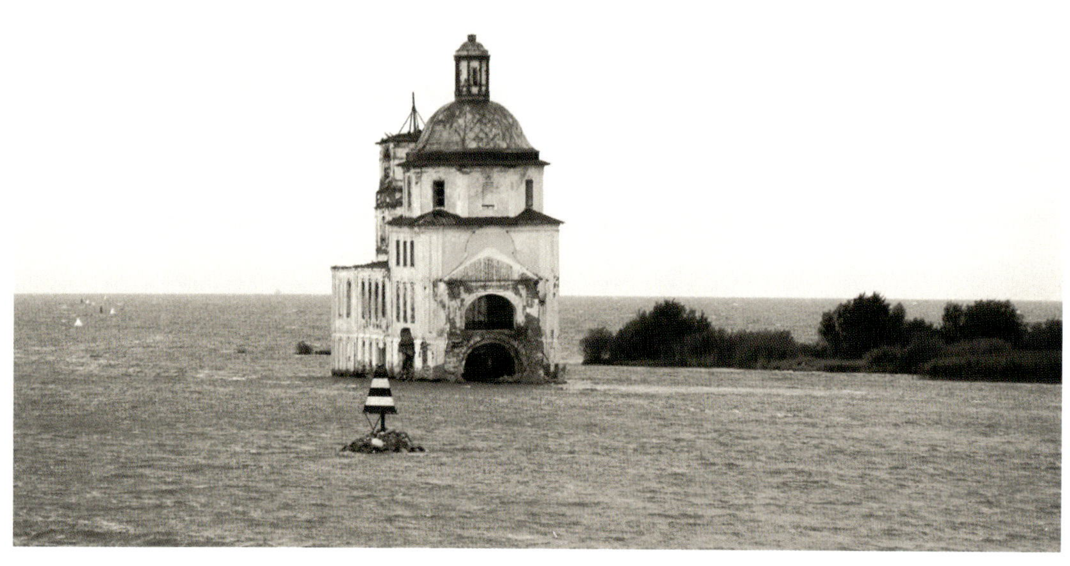

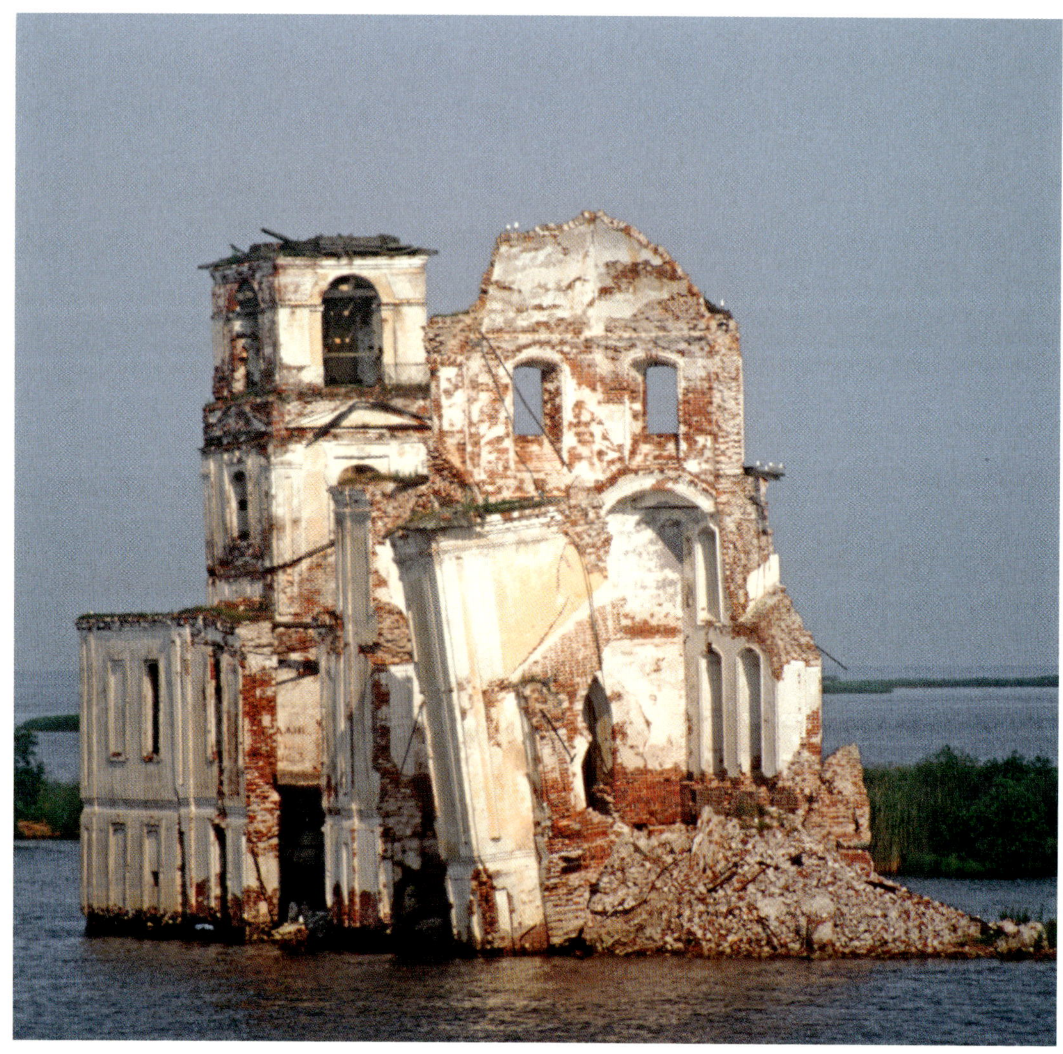

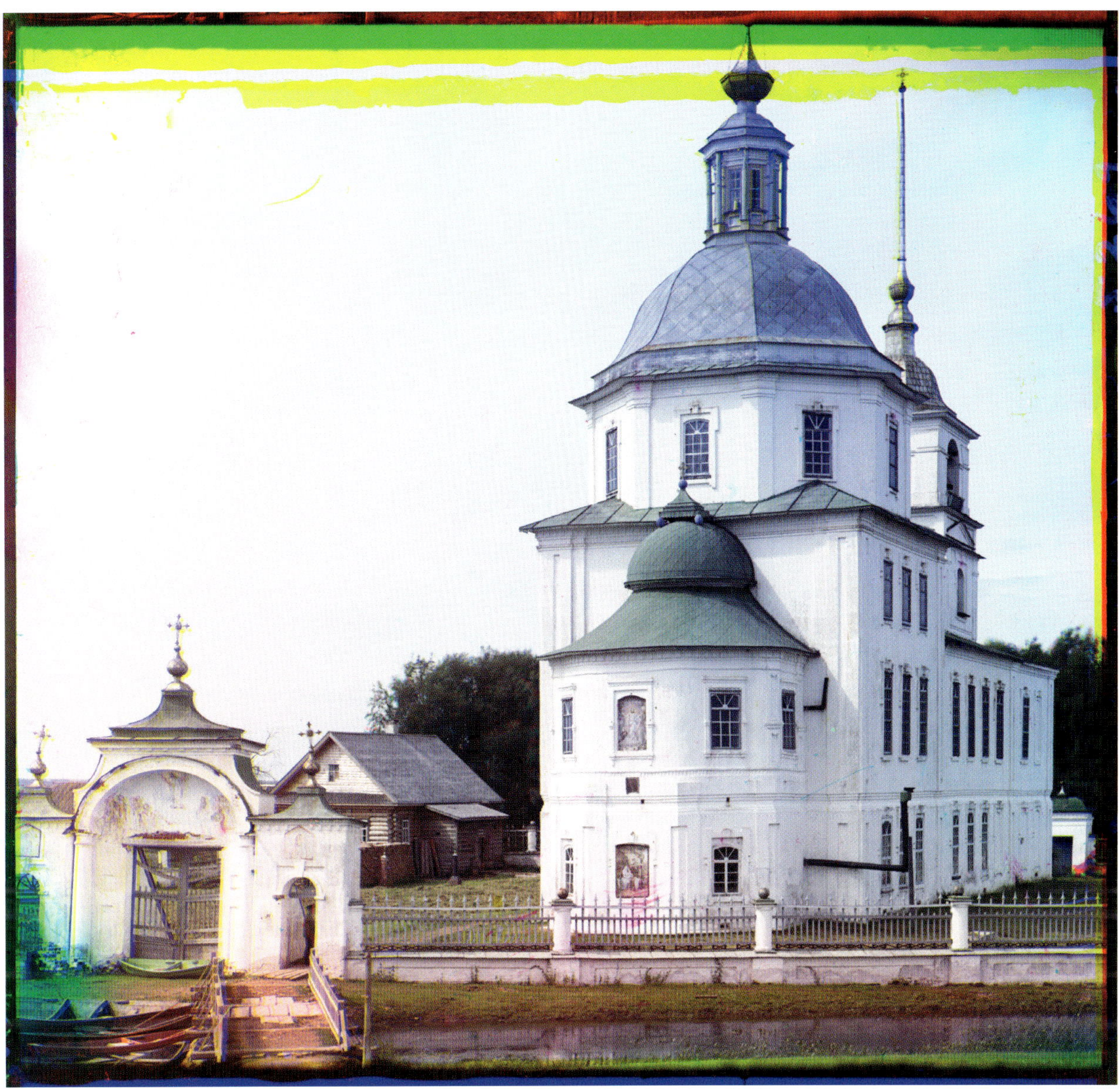

KROKHINO Church of the Nativity of Christ in Sheksna Reservoir. Southeast view. BRUMFIELD, AUGUST 8, 1991.

KROKHINO Church of the Nativity of Christ in Sheksna Reservoir. Southeast view. BRUMFIELD, JULY 14, 2007.

KROKHINO Church of the Nativity of Christ on Shekshna River. Northeast view. PROKUDIN-GORSKY 21061. SUMMER 1909.

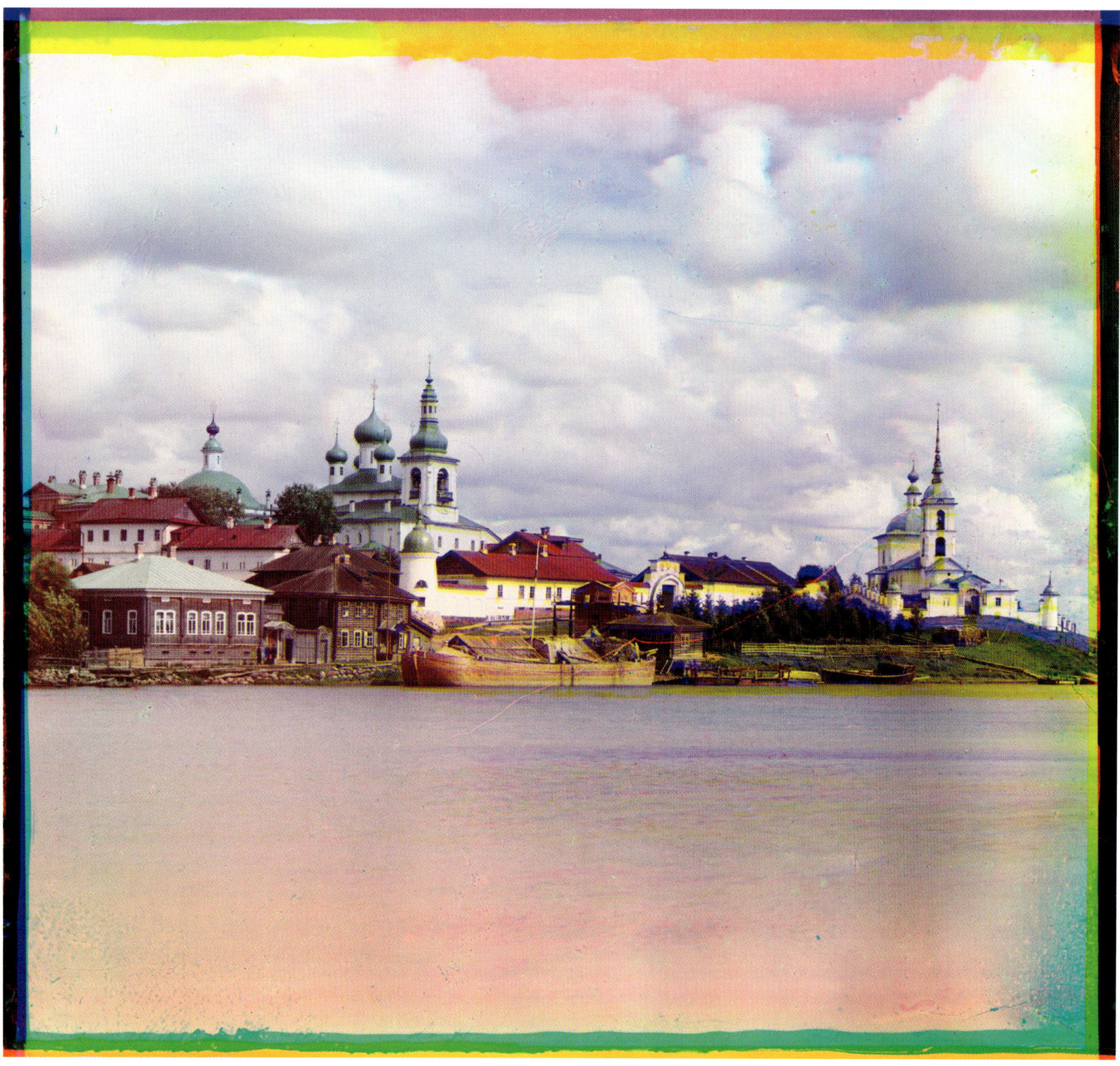

channel. My photographs over an interval of several years show progressive deterioration of the structure.

Modern reservoir and canal construction have much altered the appearance of the Sheksna River, but it still serves as a link in the major transportation route flowing south from White Lake and connecting the Volga River with lake Onega. On the left bank of the Sheksna is the village of Goritsy, with its Convent of the Resurrection, founded in 1544 by Princess Evfrosiniya Staritskaya, widow of Prince Andrei Staritsky, who in turn was the uncle of Ivan the IV (the Terrible). Ivan conducted a deadly feud with the Staritsky clan,

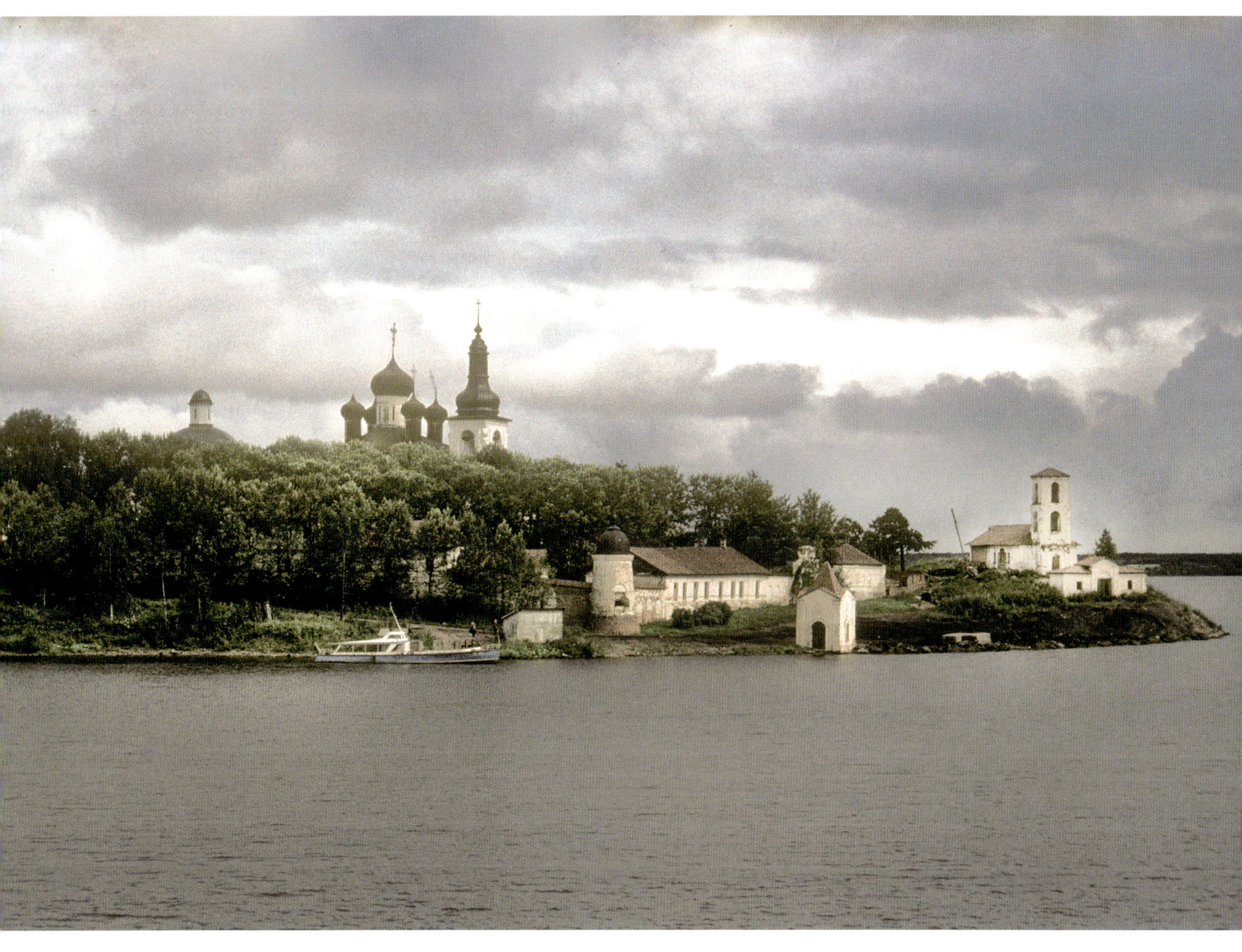

and in 1563 Evfrosiniya was exiled to the convent. In 1569 Evfrosiniya, her small retinue, and several other nuns were killed by Ivan minions. (Apparently they were drowned in the Sheksna.) In 1575 Ivan sent to exile in the convent his fourth wife, Anna Koltovskaya. Other noblewomen exiled there include Maria Nagaya, mother of Tsarevitch Dmitry; and Xenia Godunova, daughter of Tsar Boris Godunov.

In the center of the convent is the Resurrection Cathedral, built in memory of Prince Andrei Staritsky and Evfronsiniya in 1544. The convent has a second cathedral, a large neoclassical structure dedicated to the Trinity and

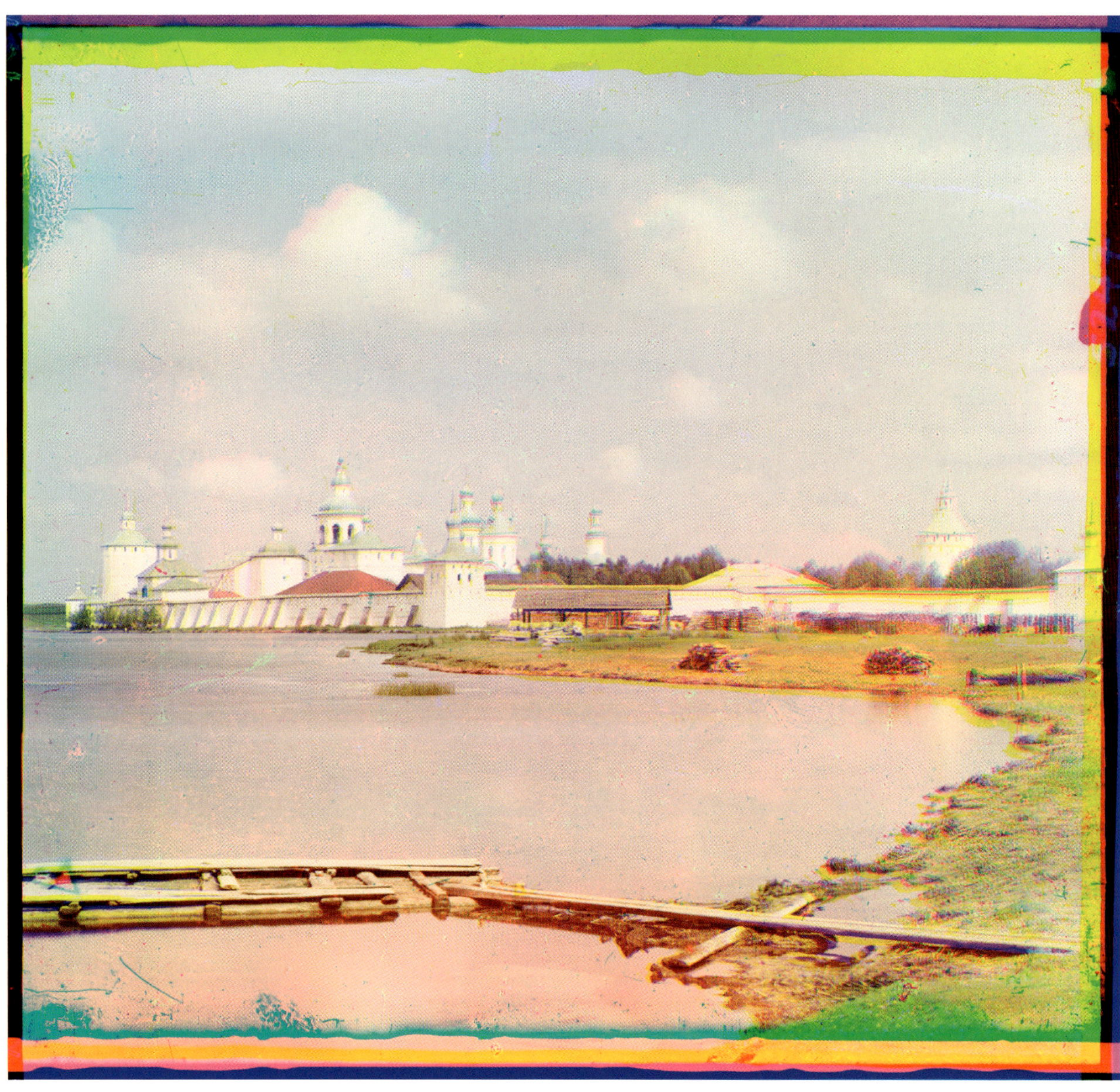

erected in 1821 on the burial site of Princess Evfronsiniya. Prokudin-Gorsky photographed the convent from the Sheksna. My photographs over several years show repairs to some of the convent structures.

Ten kilometers inland from Goritsy is Kirillov, a small town that includes a few streets with nineteenth-century merchant houses photographed by Prokudin-Gorsky. Its main feature, however, is the massive fortress-monastery founded in 1397 by Kirill (Cyril), a Muscovite monk of noble origins. In all of Russia there are few more impressive sights than the walls and massive towers of this monastery, which Prokudin-Gorsky photographed from the shore of Lake Siverskoe. Its location near the Sheksna River was both remote and strategically important. With the revival of monasticism

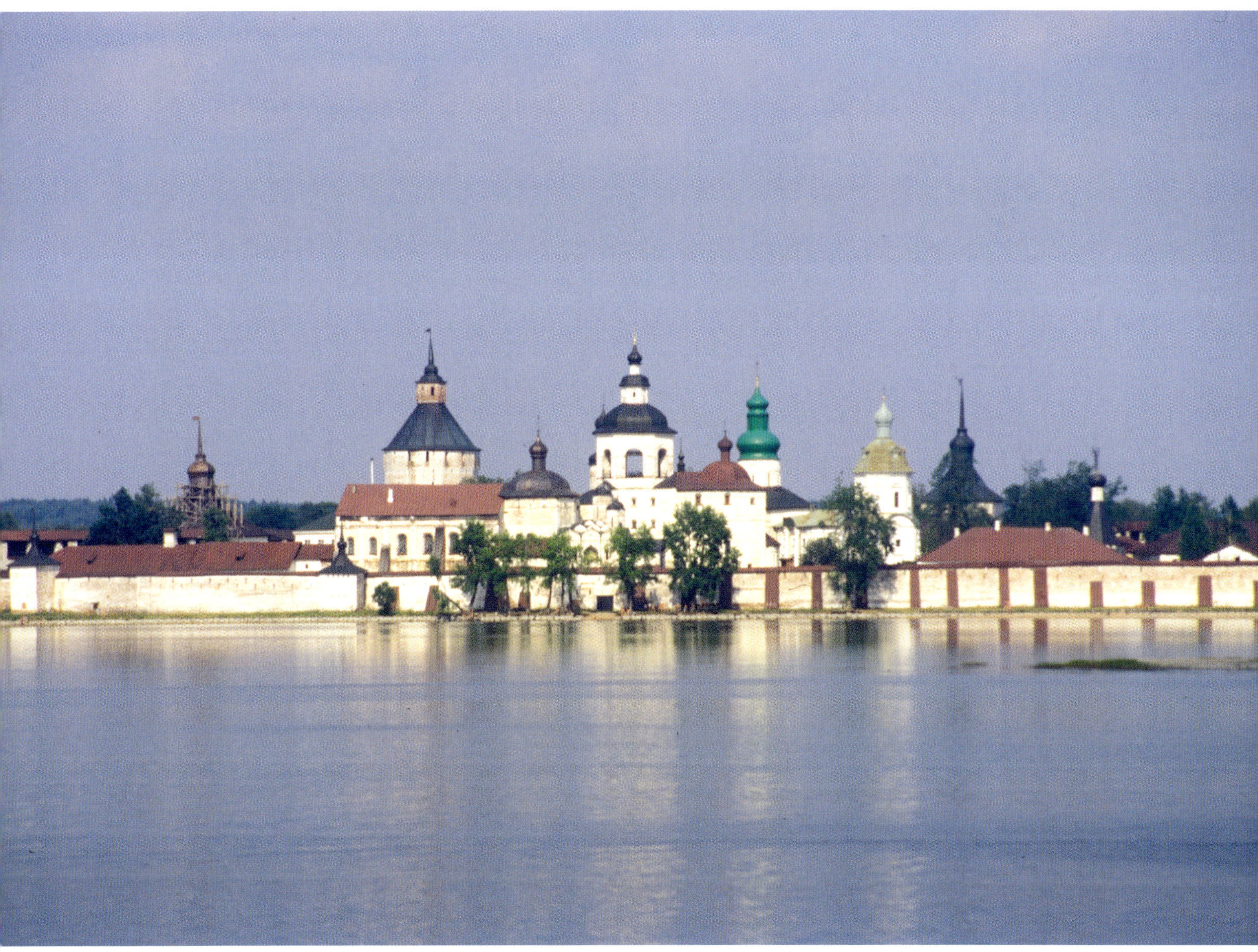

KIRILLOV Saint Kirill Belozersky Monastery, south-east view from Lake Sivers. *From left*: Smithy Tower, south wall and Church of the Transfiguration at Water Gate, Refectory Church of the Presentation, bell tower, Church of Archangel Gabriel, Ferapont (Moscow) Tower (*in background*), Svitok ("scroll") Tower, Dormition Cathedral (*in background*), Church of Saint Kirill, Kazan Tower (*in background*), Church of John the Baptist, Vologda Tower. PROKUDIN-GORSKY 21039. SUMMER 1909.

KIRILLOV Saint Kirill Belozersky Monastery. South view across Lake Sivers. *From left*: south wall and Cook's Tower, west wall and Kosaia ("crooked") Tower (*in shadows*), Bread Tower, scullery, Ferapont (Moscow) Tower (*in background*), Refectory Church of the Presentation, Church of the Transfiguration at Water Gate, bell tower, Church of Archangel Gabriel, Dormition Cathedral (with green dome), Church of Saint Kirill, Kazan Tower (*in background*), cloisters and infirmary Church of Saint Evfimy. BRUMFIELD, JULY 15, 1999.

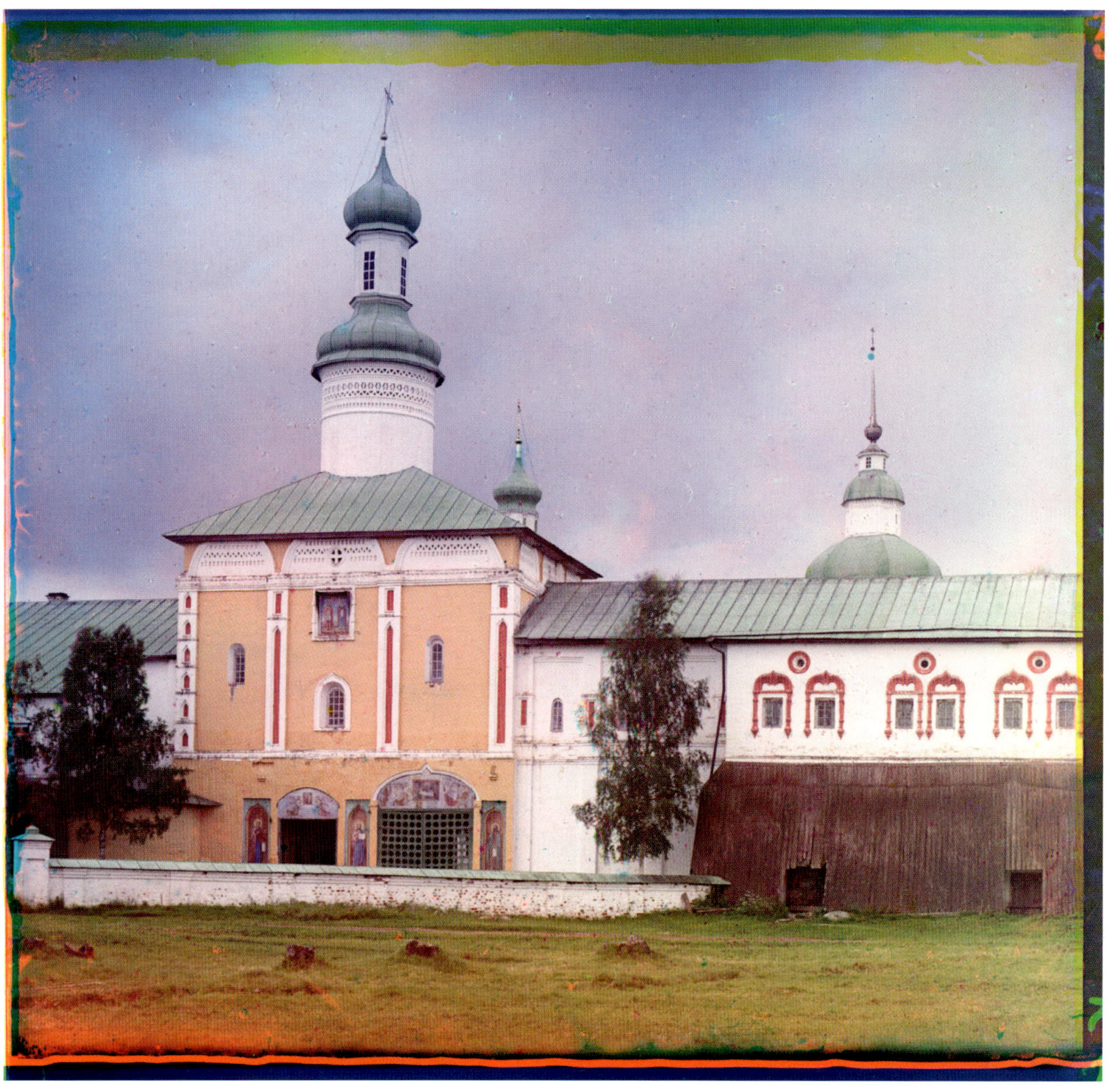

in Moscow during the fourteenth century, pioneer monks sought remote areas as a test of their ascetic faith and dedication. At the same time, Muscovite princes supported these efforts not only to spread and maintain the Orthodox faith but also to consolidate Moscow's territorial expansion into the rich forests of the far north.

In the early fifteenth century, this monastery, formally dedicated to the Dormition of the Virgin, played a major role in supporting Moscow's dynastic stability. Consequently, the monastery received major donations that by the sixteenth century made it one of the largest Russian monas-

KIRILLOV Saint Kirill Belozersky Monastery, Church of Saint John Climacus over Holy Gates. North view with cloisters. PROKUDIN-GORSKY 21023. SUMMER 1909.

KIRILLOV Saint Kirill Belozersky Monastery, Church of Saint John Climacus over Holy Gates. Northeast view with cloisters. BRUMFIELD, APRIL 1, 2001.

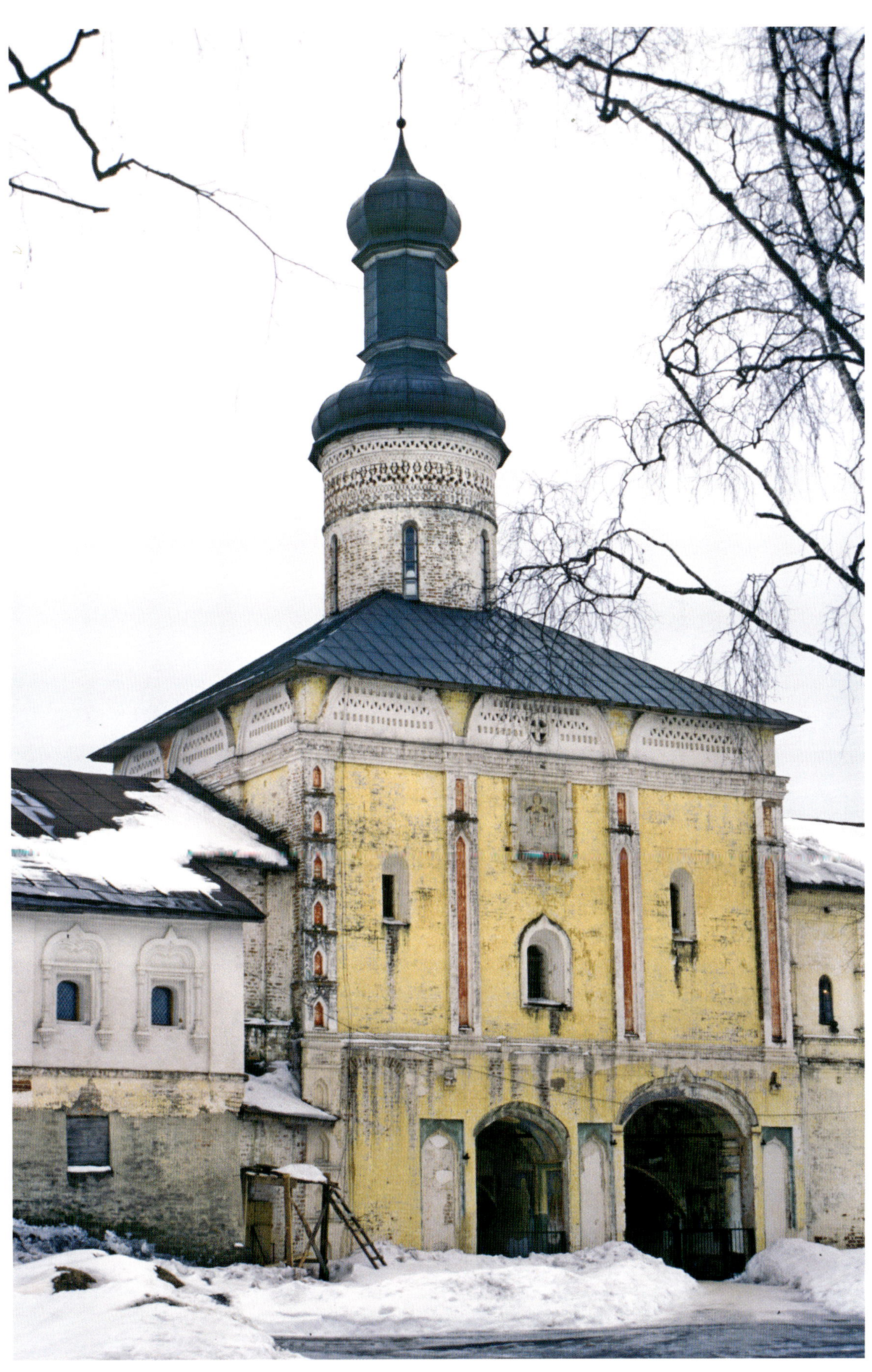

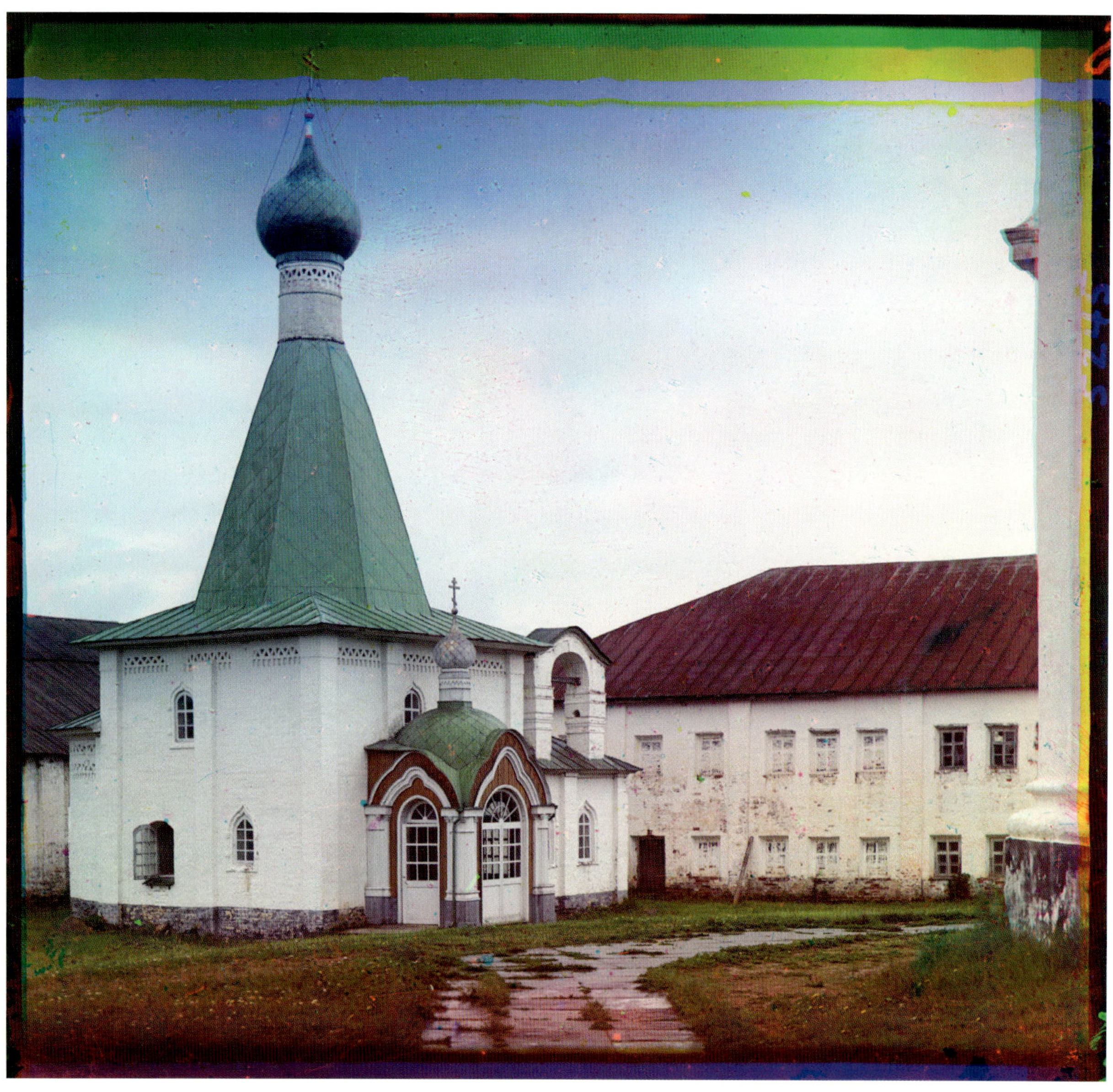

tic institutions, second in size to the Trinity-Saint Sergius Monastery near Moscow. The first church to be built in brick and stone was the Dormition Cathedral, begun in 1496 and expanded with small picturesque attached churches over the next two centuries. The cathedral interior has a grand icon screen and seventeenth-century frescoes that are still under restoration. One of the main patrons of the monastery was Basil III, Grand Prince of Moscow, who in 1528 made a pilgrimage to the monastery with his second wife, Elena Glinskaia, to pray for the birth of a son and heir. In the 1530s Basil sponsored two brick churches in the monas-

KIRILLOV Saint Kirill Belozersky Monastery, Church of Saint Evfimy. Northwest view. PROKUDIN-GORSKY 21037. SUMMER 1909.

KIRILLOV Saint Kirill Belozersky Monastery, Church of Saint Evfimy. West view. BRUMFIELD, JUNE 1, 2014.

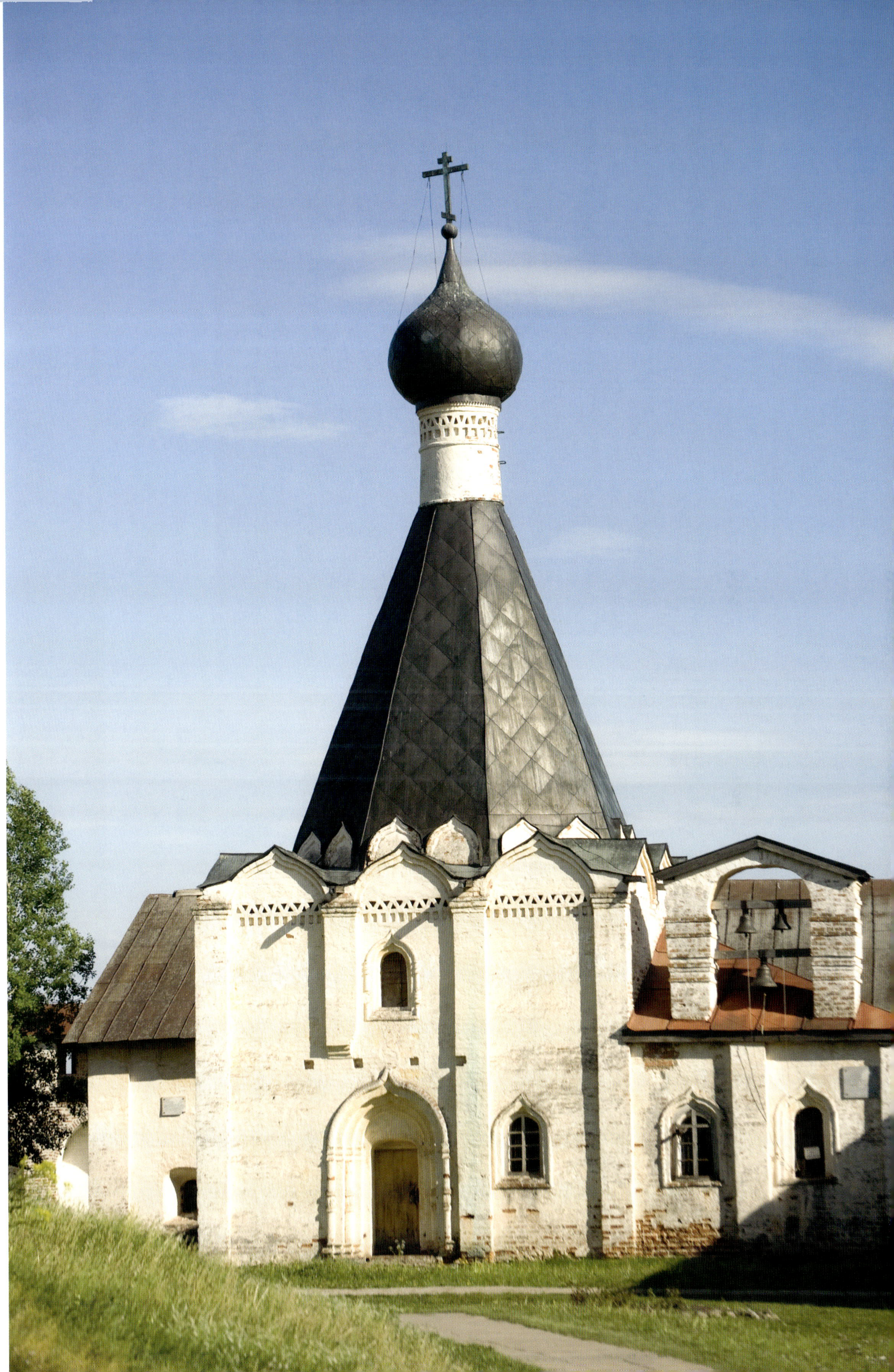

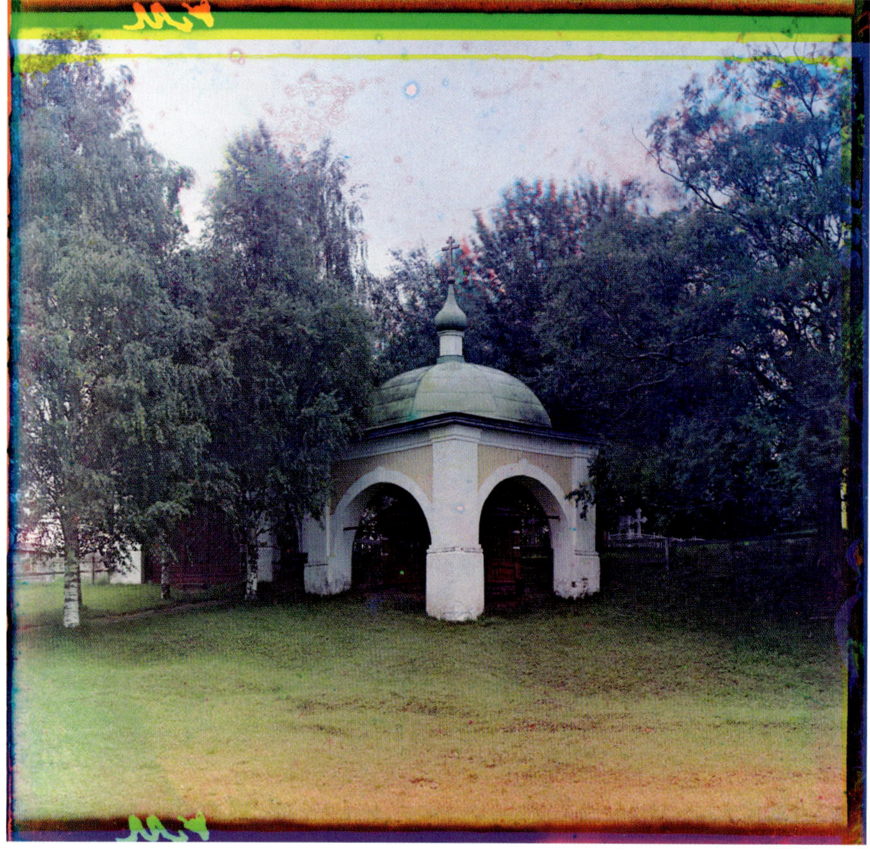

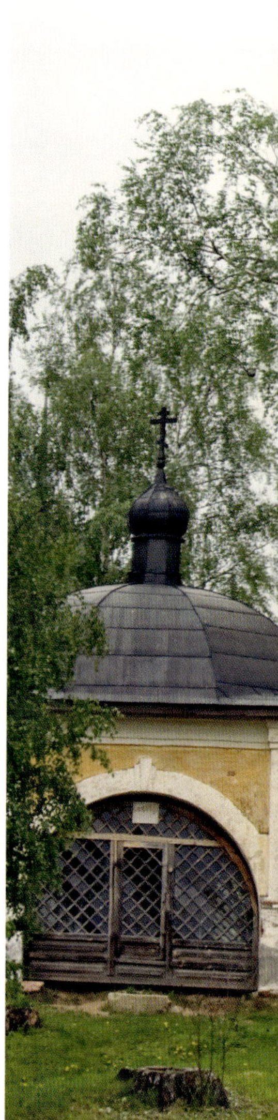

tery, including the Church of John the Baptist, which became the nucleus of another monastery. Thus Saint Kirill-Belozerskii Monastery is composed of two monasteries (the Dormition and John the Baptist), as well as a settlement for lay workers protected by a large system of walls.

Prokudin-Gorsky did not photograph the monastery systematically, but he recorded sixteenth-century monuments such as the Church of Saint John Climacus over Holy Gates (the monastery's main north entrance), built in 1569–72. My photographs of this distinctive monument, with its elongated drum and cupola, show some changes in the roofline. The most idiosyncratic form in the monastery is the Church of Saint Evfimy, built as part of the monastery infirmary in 1653. The modest cuboid structure is capped with a polygonal "tent" tower typical of a half century earlier. The unusual miniature belfry attached at the southwest corner suggests the influence of Pskov, as does the brick ornamentation beneath the roofline. Prokudin-Gorsky's view from the northwest shows a small covered porch that was removed in a postwar restoration, as my photograph shows. In the paired Monastery of John the Baptist, Prokudin-Gorsky photographed a brick canopy chapel

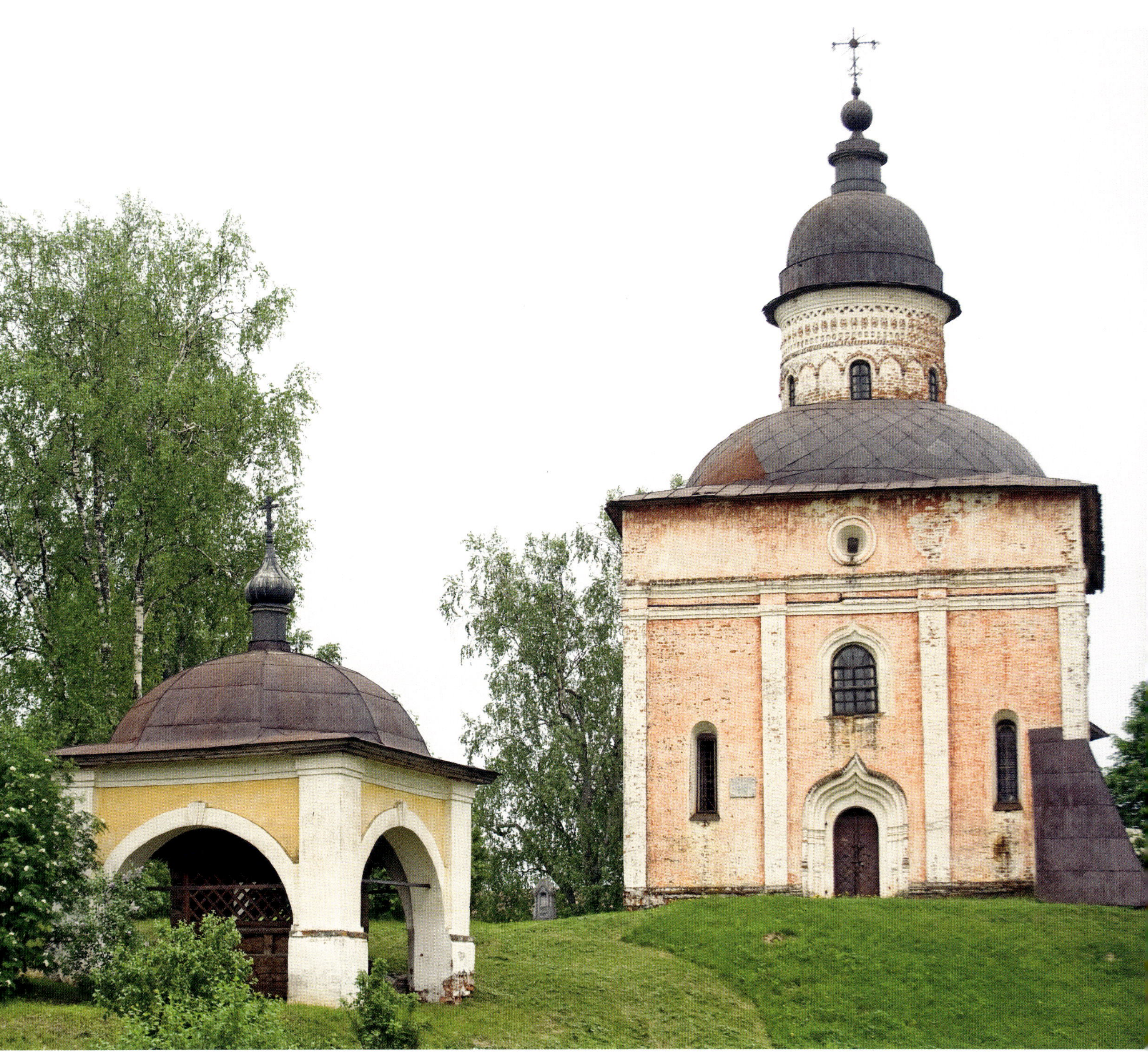

KIRILLOV Saint Kirill Belozersky Monastery. Canopies over the earthen cell of Saint Kirill. PROKUDIN-GORSKY 21034. SUMMER 1909.

KIRILLOV Saint Kirill Belozersky Monastery. Canopies over the earthen cell of Saint Kirill. *Right*: Church of the Decapitation of John the Baptist. BRUMFIELD, JUNE 2, 2014.

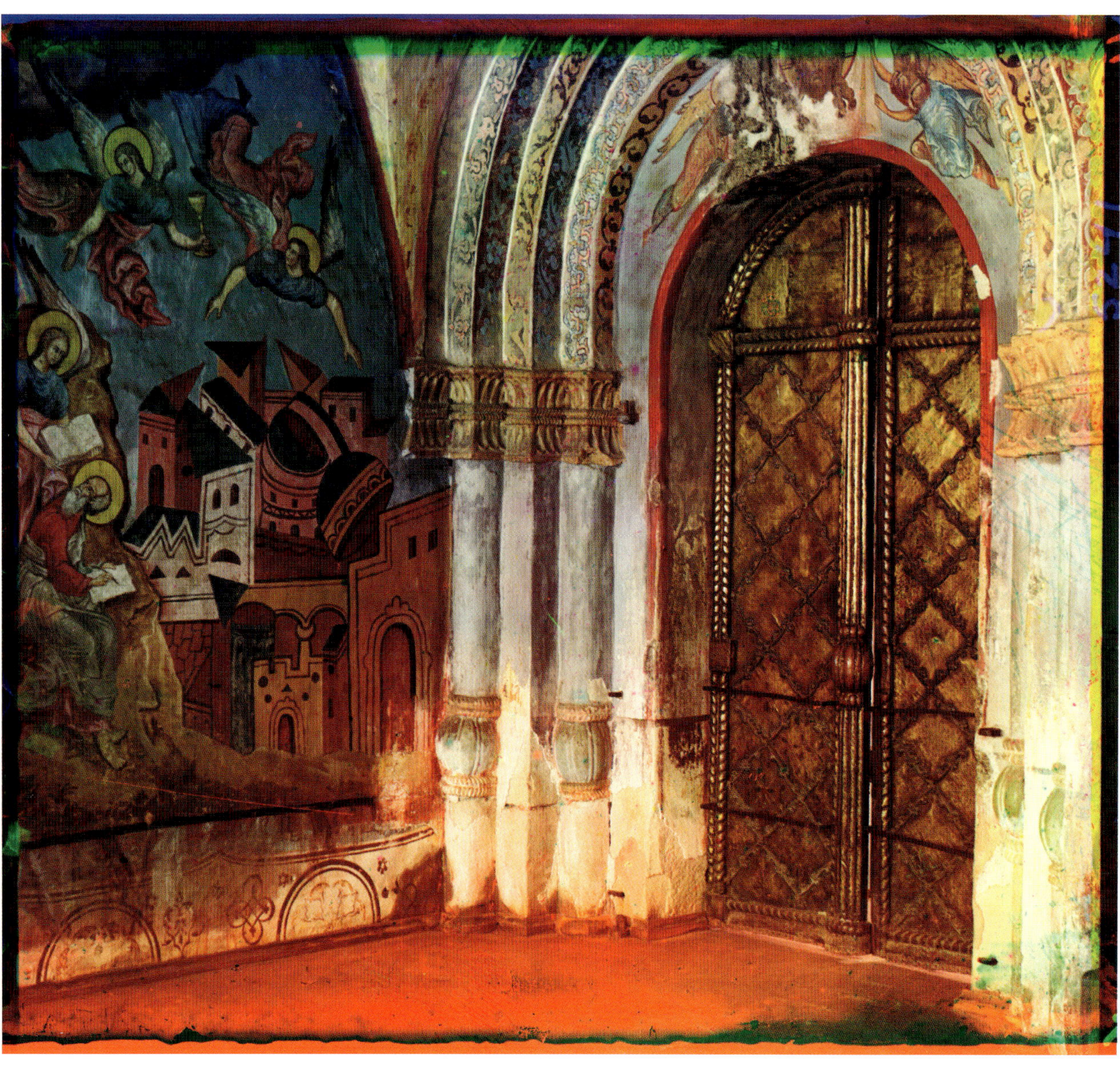

over what had been the earthen cell of Saint Kirill. These simple structures have remained largely untouched.

The one interior photograph taken in the monastery shows the portal to the Church of Saint Vladimir, attached to the north gallery of the Dormition Cathedral. The left part of his photograph also includes part of the gallery's depiction of the Apocalypse, one of the most vivid in medieval Russian art. My photographs give a more comprehensive view of these frescoes, including various hairy devils.

At the beginning of the seventeenth century the fortified Saint Kirill Monastery defended the area against maraud-

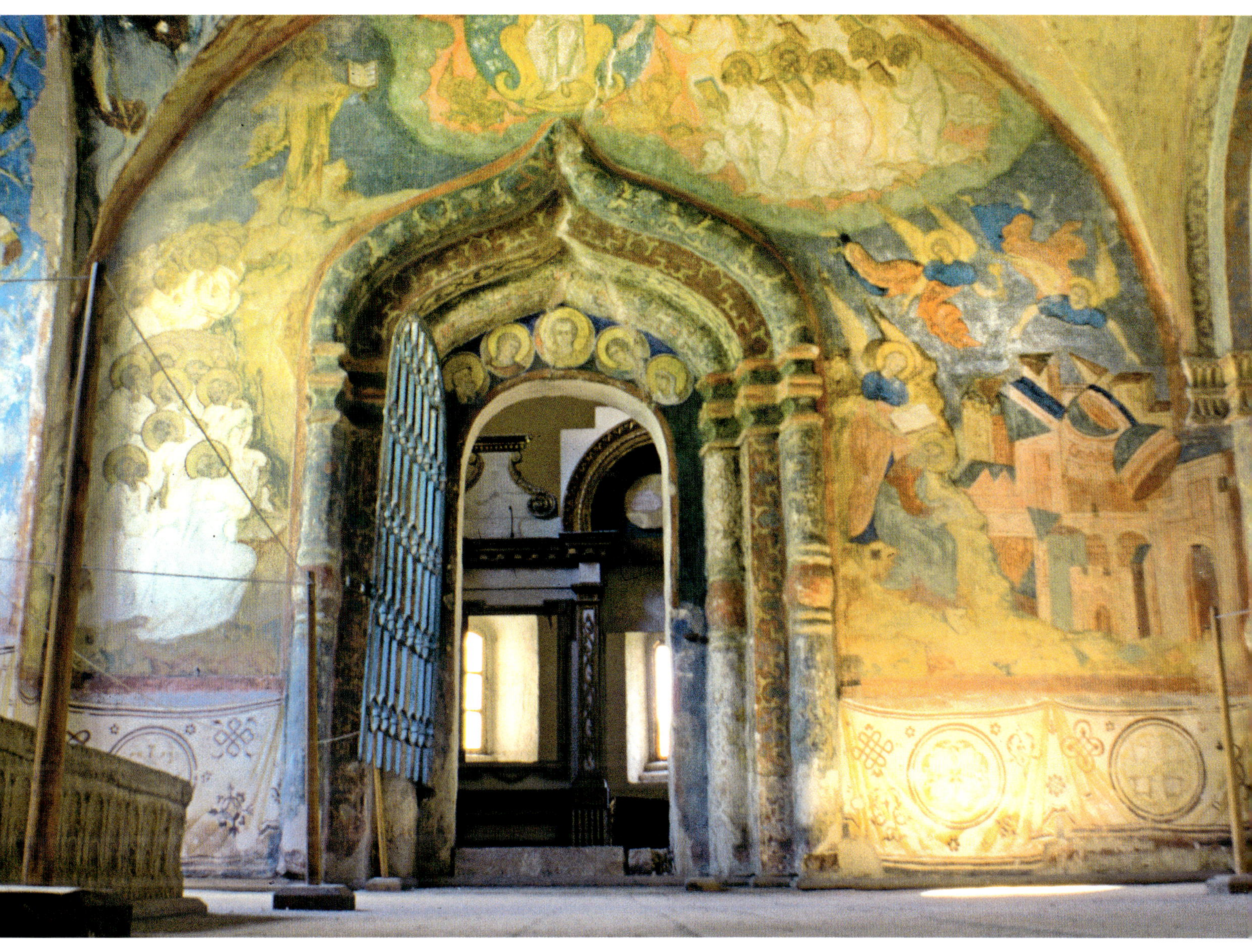

ers during the Time of Troubles. A surge in the monastery's fortunes occurred in the second half of the seventeenth century, when Tsar Alexis Mikhailovich decided to rebuild the monastery walls as a symbol of Moscow's dominance in the north. At that time, the likely enemy was Sweden, which had over the preceding century gained considerable territory held in medieval times by the Russian city-state of Novgorod. In 1653 Alexis decreed the expansion of the walls and towers in a construction project that lasted several decades. Prokudin-Gorsky's one photograph of the walls has survived only in the contact print and includes the massive

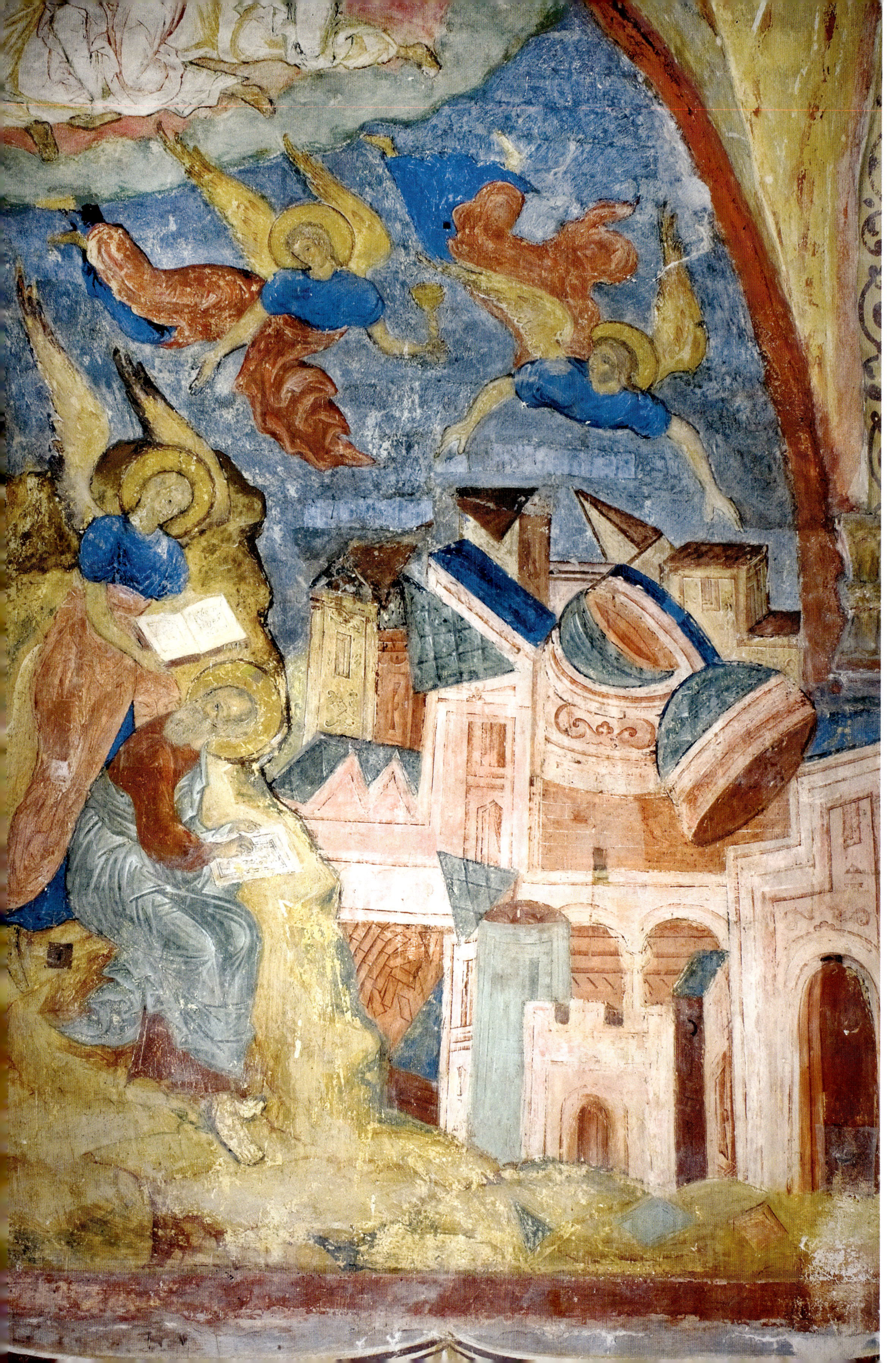

Moscow, or Ferapontov, Tower. My photograph of that tower and adjacent walls gives a broader view of the scale of the walls, with their double gallery.

Yet no hostile army came close to the fortress that had been expanded at such effort. With his victories against the Swedes in the early eighteenth century and the founding of Saint Petersburg (1703), Peter the Great altered the geopolitical position of the Russian north. The declining importance of the Saint Kirill Monastery led to its neglect and decay during the eighteenth and nineteenth centuries. In the late nineteenth century a revival of interest in Russia's medieval heritage led to restoration efforts that continued during the early Soviet period. In 1929 the first museum was established in the monastery. The Stalinist period undercut much of this work and led to substantial material losses, such as the melting down of the monastery's remarkable bell ensemble—one of the most important in Russia. After World War II, the Kirill-Belozersk Museum revived and is now a major repository of Russian cultural treasures with an excellent collection of historical religious art. Part of the monastery has reverted to the use of the Orthodox Church.

Farther down the Sheksna is Cherepovets, situated at the confluence of the Sheksna and Yagorba Rivers and now one of Russia's largest centers for iron and steel production. The earliest mention occurs in the fourteenth century in reference to a Monastery of the Resurrection in "Cherepoves." A major stimulus to Cherepovets occurred with the opening in 1810 of the Mariinsky Canal System. With few other settlements on the long Sheksna portion of the waterway, Cherepovets became a base for boat building and repair in addition to barge hauling. By the time of Prokudin-Gorsky's trip, the population was some eight thousand. Prokudin-Gorsky made two photographs of the small river port from the Sheksna. One view includes the Cathedral of the Resurrection, remnant of the monastery that formed the town's original center. The Resurrection Monastery was founded around 1362 by Feodosy and Afanasy (d. 1392), monks from the Trinity-Saint Sergius Monastery, the primary center of Muscovite monasticism. The impoverished Resurrection Monastery struggled to exist throughout the seventeenth and eighteenth centuries. The monastery's first masonry structure was a rebuilding of the Resurrection Church in 1752–56, with secondary altars dedicated to Saint John the Divine and to Saints Feodosy and Afa-

KIRILLOV Saint Kirill-Belozersky Monastery. Dormition Cathedral. North gallery, east wall with fresco of Apocalypse: Destroying Angels and Saint John writing the Book of Revelations. BRUMFIELD, JUNE 2, 2014.

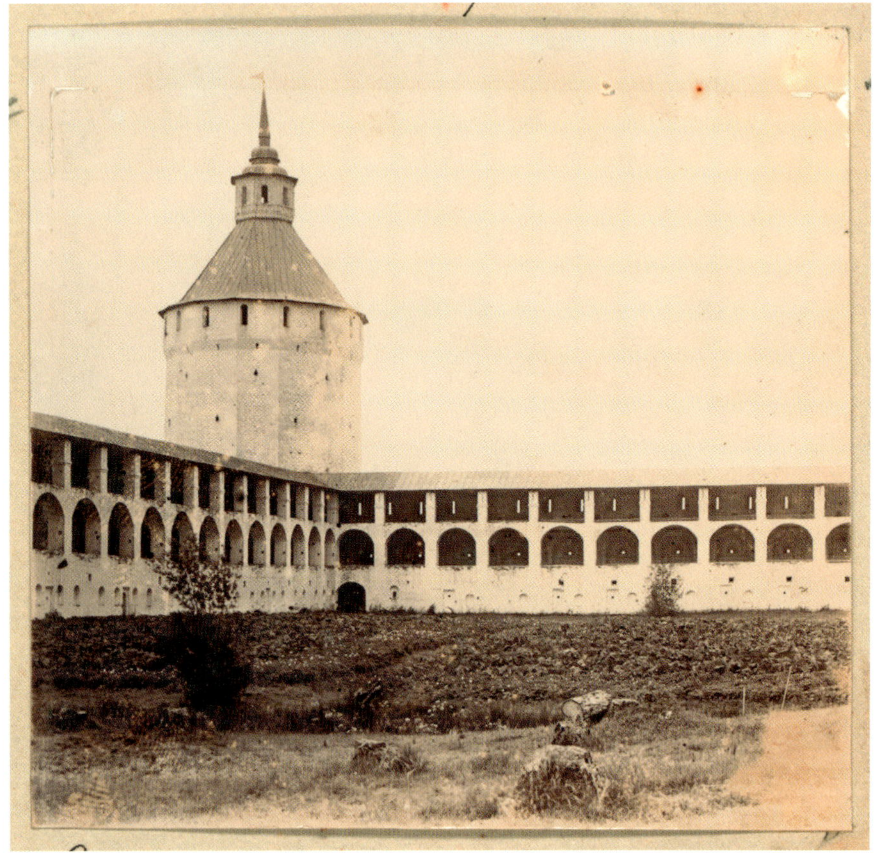

nasy. In 1761 work began on a second brick church, dedicated to the Trinity and to Saint Sergius of Radonezh, founder of the Trinity-Saint Sergius Monastery.

The monastery was closed in 1764 as part of the secularization of monastic holdings by Catherine the Great. Converted to parish use for the settlement that had developed around the monastery, the church became the Resurrection Cathedral following the official bestowal of town status to Cherepovets in 1777. After the cathedral's closure in 1934 its five decorative domes were demolished, but its wall paintings, done in 1851, remained, as did those in a refectory expanded in 1884–85. During the war, the structure housed a repair facility for aircraft engines, but in 1946 it was returned to the Orthodox Church as the city's one functioning house of worship. The domes were restored in the late 1980s.

Down the river from Cherepovets, Prokudin-Gorsky photographed the imposing Convent of John the Baptist at Leushino, one of the largest Orthodox centers in Russia before the revolution. Its monumental buildings are now submerged beneath the waters of the Rybinsk Reservoir, as are the surrounding areas that Prokudin-Gorsky photographed. However,

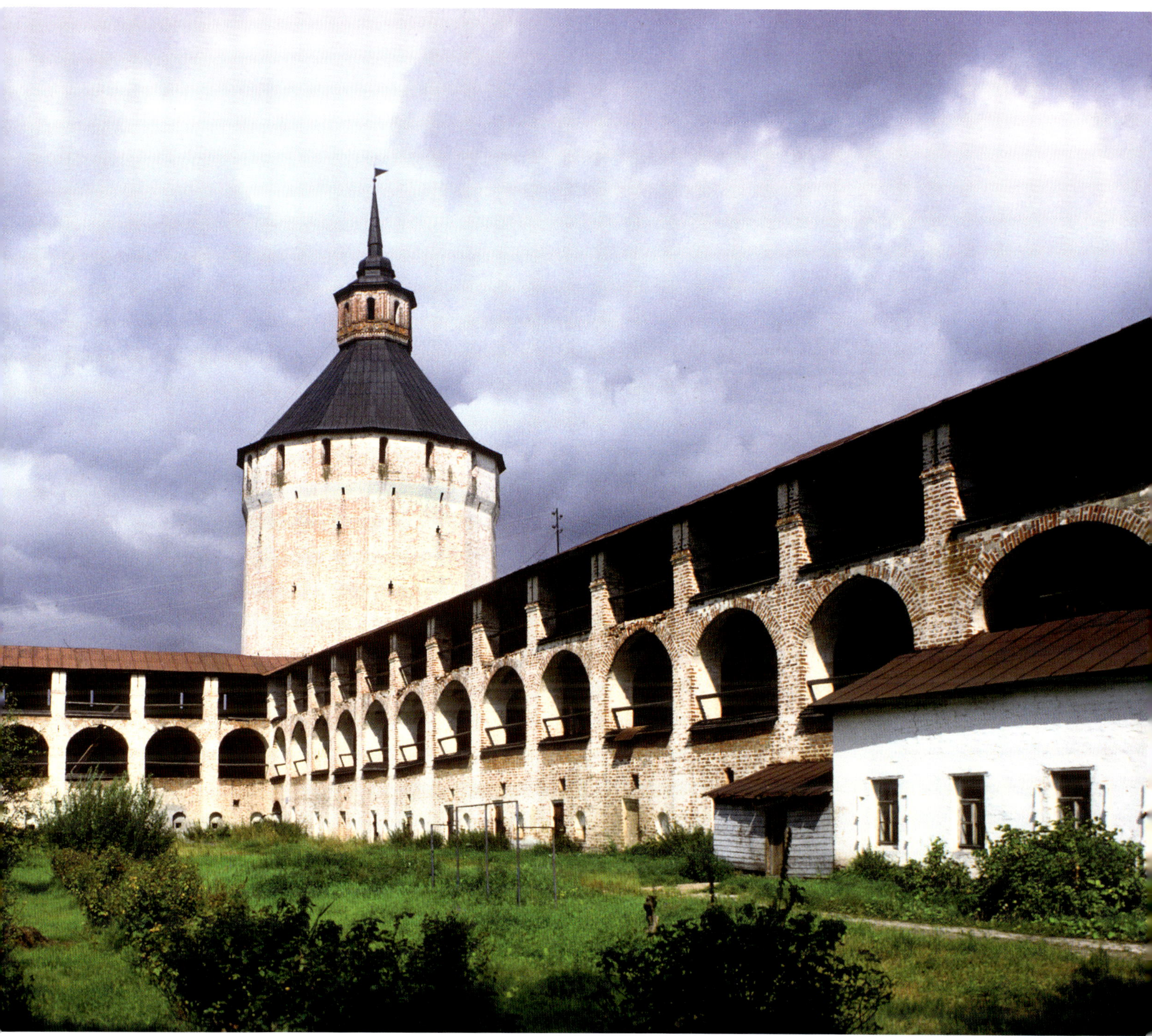

KIRILLOV Saint Kirill-Belozersky Monastery. Moscow (Ferapont) Tower. PROKUDIN-GORSKY 01968. SUMMER 1909.

KIRILLOV Saint Kirill-Belozersky Monastery. Moscow (Ferapont) Tower. Right: north wall. BRUMFIELD, AUGUST 8, 1991.

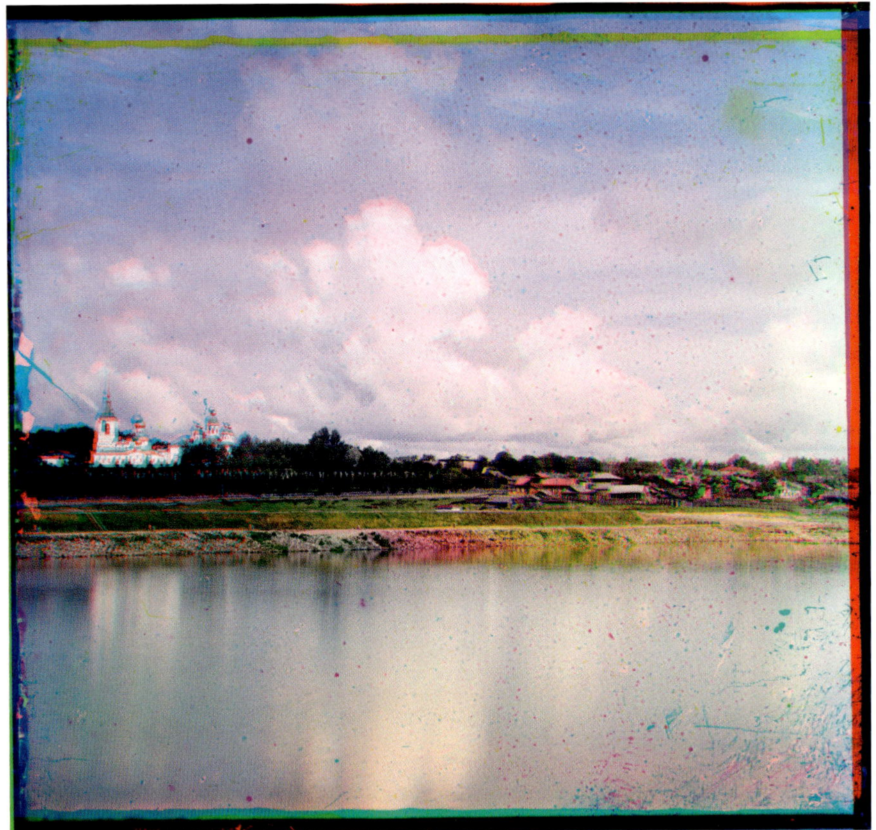

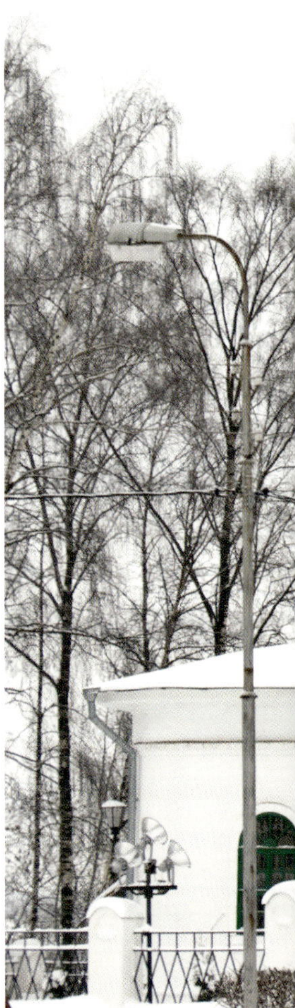

I have included his photograph of a windmill in a field of rye at the village of Leushino because it shows a type of ingenious structure widespread in the Russian north. My photograph of a very similar windmill at the village of Kimzha near the Mezen River in Arkhangelsk territory illustrates the range of this remarkable form.

Prokudin-Gorsky's journey along the Mariinsky Canal System concluded at the town of Rybinsk, where the Sheksna merged with the Volga River. Its resident population of 32,000 at the beginning of the century periodically swelled to over 100,000 with seasonal labor from the countryside. Rybinsk was not only a major grain port situated in a productive agricultural region but was also much involved in the caviar trade. Although the town grew in chaotic fashion, its perspective from the Volga is dominated by the bell tower and Cathedral of the Transfiguration of the Savior. The cathedral, a project of much civic pride, was built between 1838 and 1851 with funds raised by the local merchant community. Its late neoclassical form was typical for the period by the architect Avraam Melnikov, who had designed similar churches—including one in Saint Petersburg. The bell tower, an excellent example of neoclassicism, was constructed in 1802 for the previous

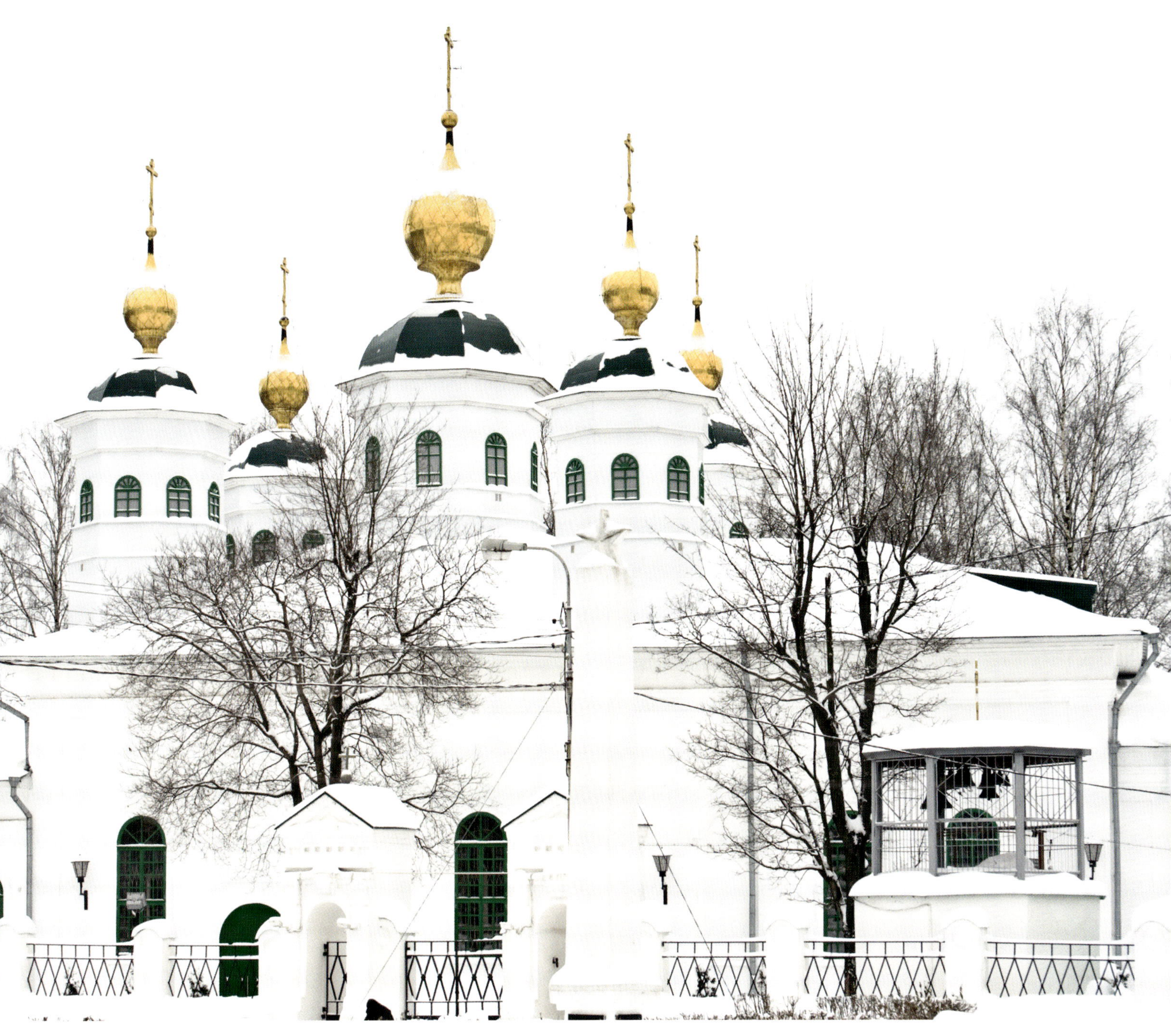

CHEREPOVETS View north across Sheksna River. Trinity Cathedral (not extant), Cathedral of the Resurrection (*right*). PROKUDIN-GORSKY 21013. SUMMER 1909.

CHEREPOVETS Resurrection Cathedral. North view. BRUMFIELD, JANUARY 1, 2010.

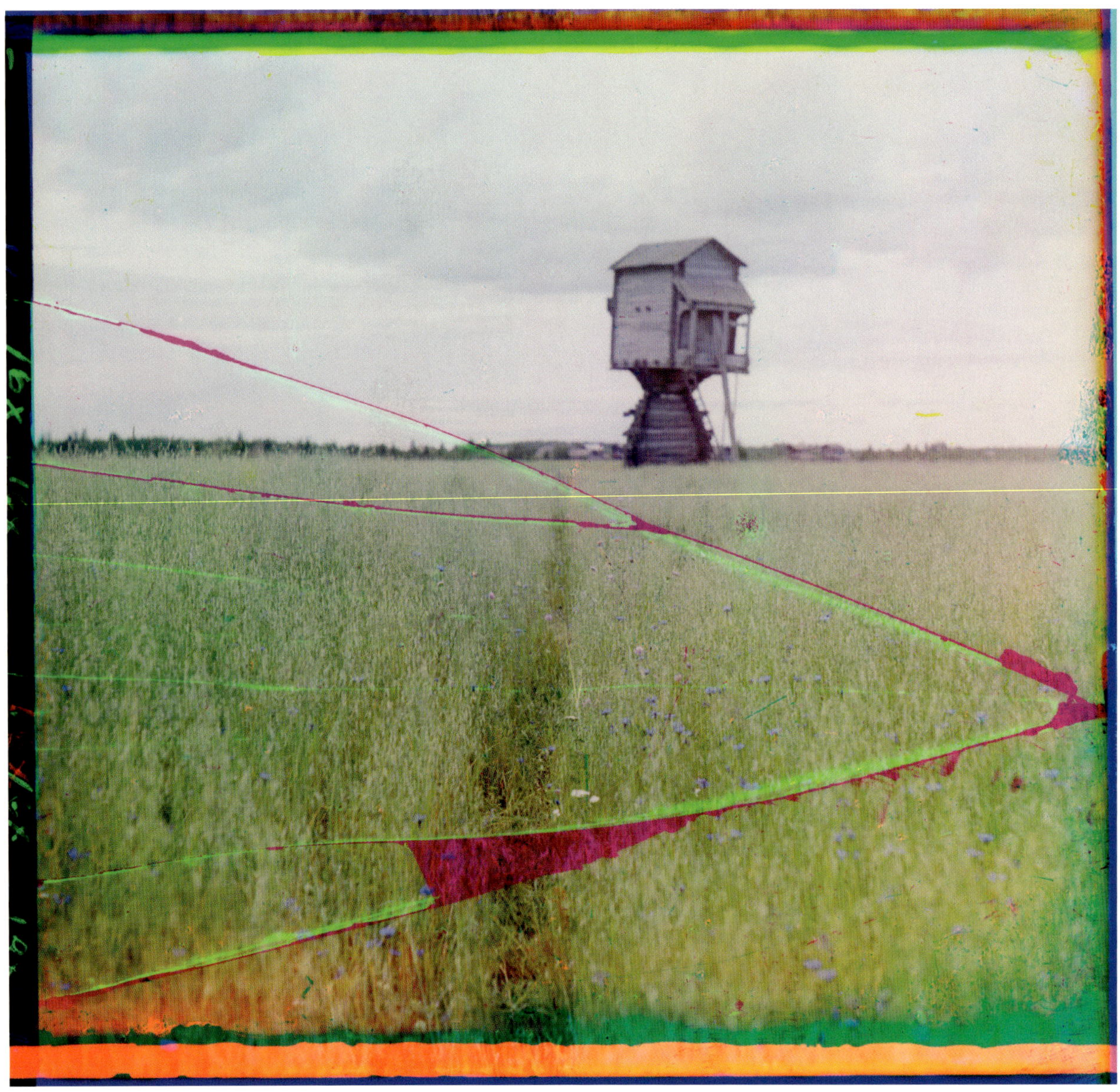

cathedral that had occupied the site since the seventeenth century. Prokudin-Gorsky's photographs show not only these monuments of church architecture but also a bustling river port, crowded with the barges that carried most of the Volga's commerce. (Although the famed Volga boat haulers continued to work the river long after the coming of steam power, they had largely vanished by 1910.)

Prokudin-Gorsky's original glass negatives of Rybinsk are not preserved in the Library of Congress Collection, but contact prints include a northeast view of the dominant architectural monument, the Cathedral of the Trans-

NEAR CHEREPOVETS Wooden windmill in rye field. PROKUDIN-GORSKY 20223. SUMMER 1909.

KIMZHA (ARKHANGELSK PROV-INCE) Log windmill. BRUMFIELD, AUGUST 2, 2000.

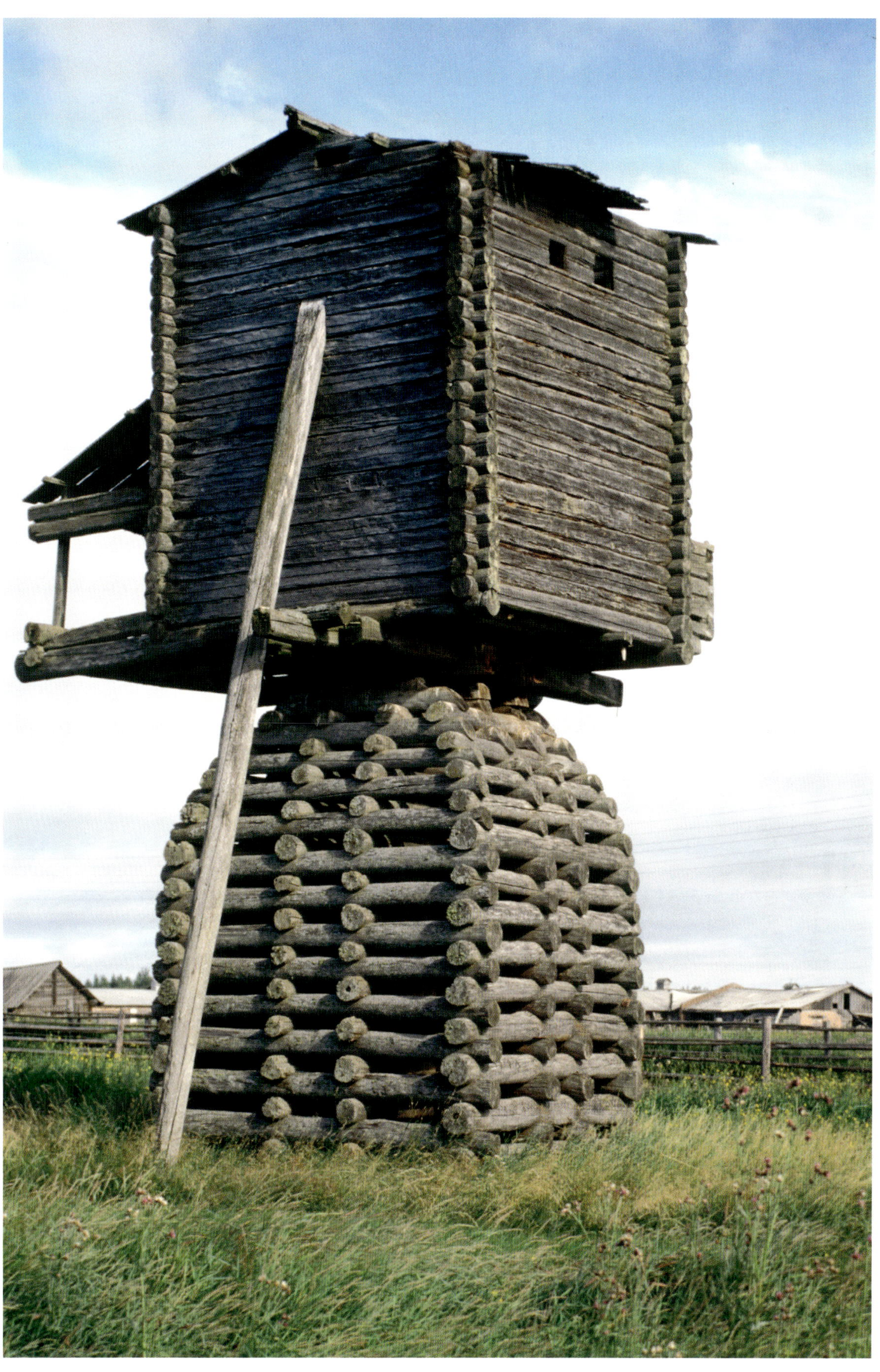

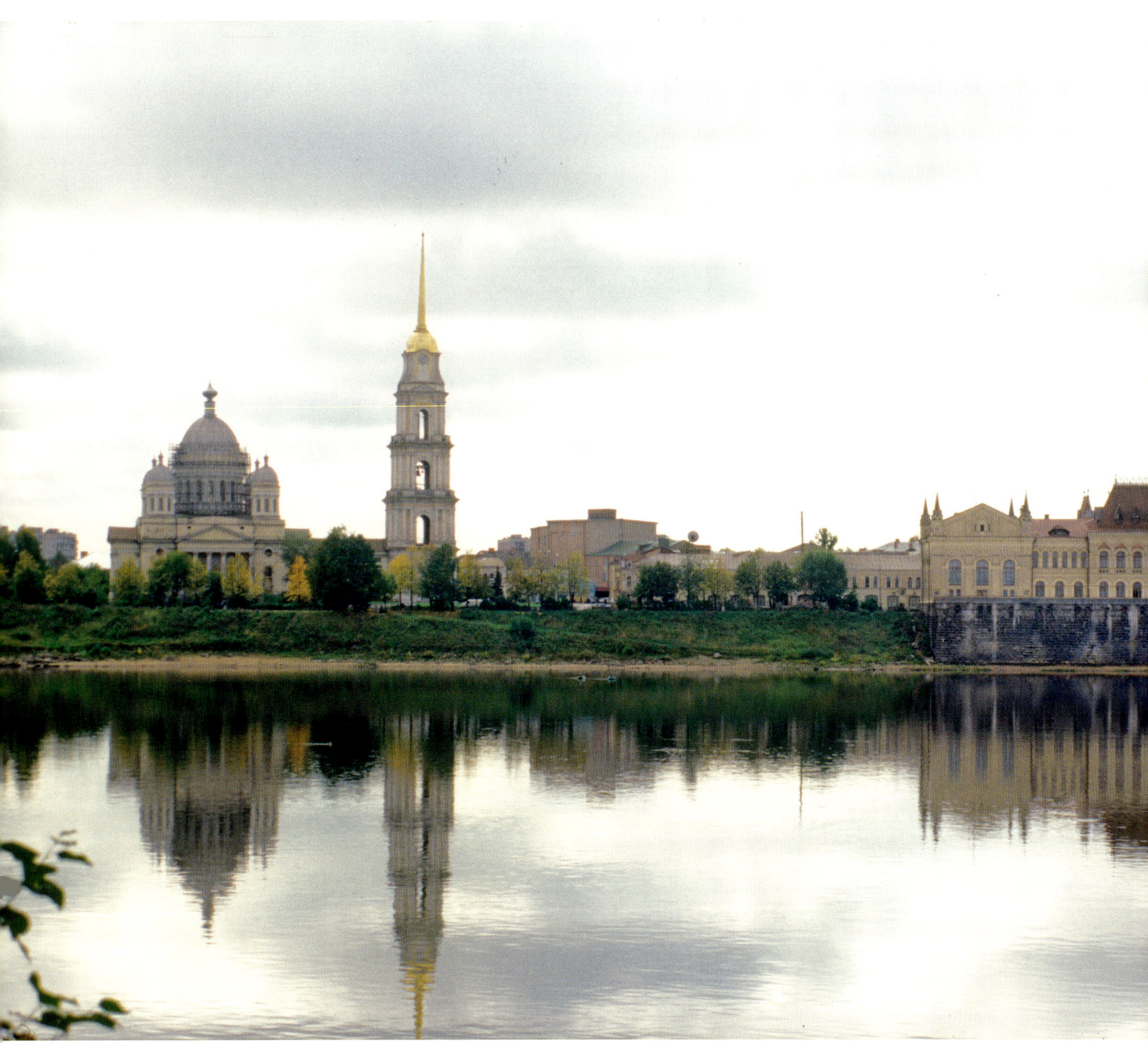

RYBINSK View south across Volga River. *From left*:
Cathedral of the Transfiguration, commercial build-
ings, Grain Exchange Building (now Rybinsk Museum).
BRUMFIELD, SEPTEMBER 14, 2001.

RYBINSK Cathedral of the Transfiguration, com-
mercial buildings. View southwest from Volga River.
Foreground: Cathedral of Saint Nicholas (not extant).
PROKUDIN-GORSKY 02395. SUMMER 1910.

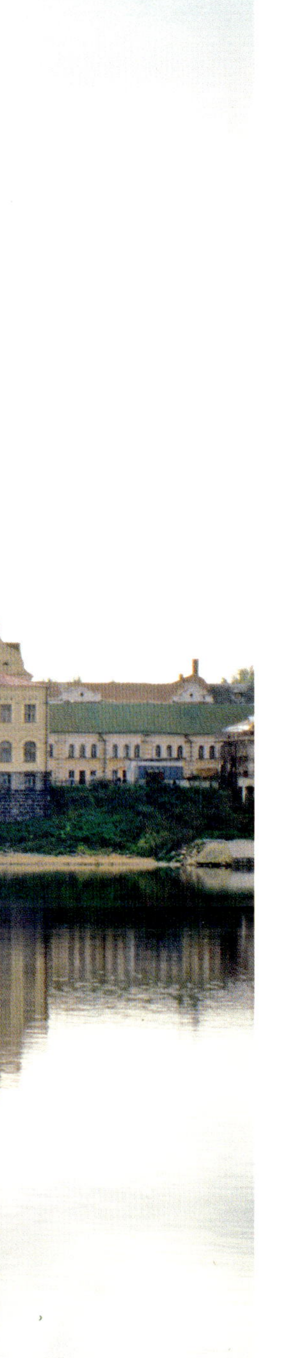

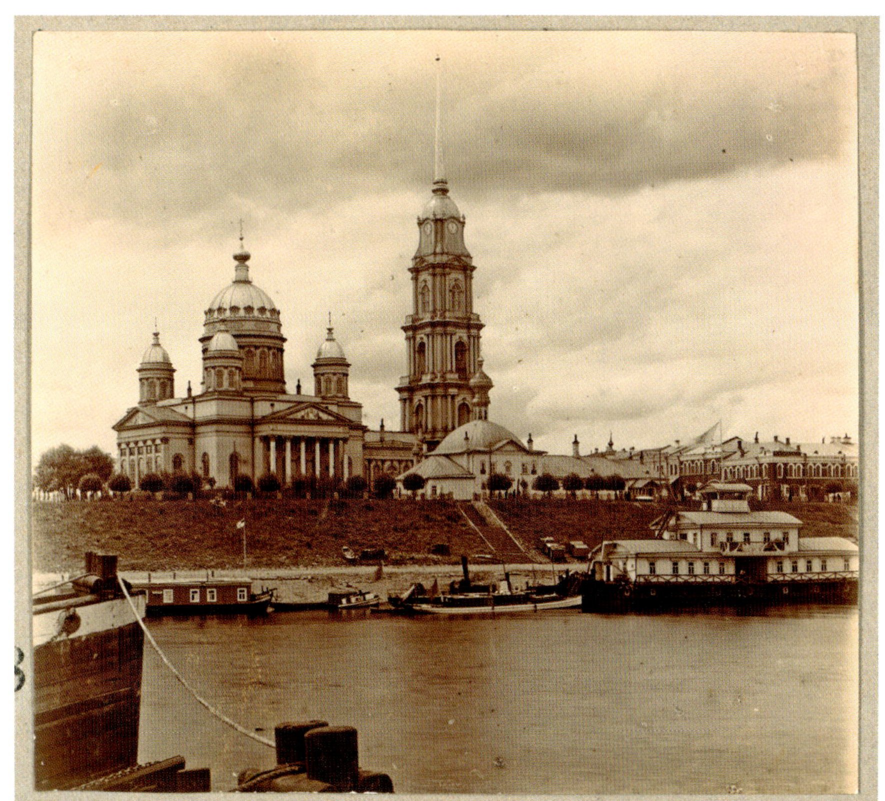

figuration. Built in 1838–51 overlooking the Volga near its confluence with the Sheksna, the grand neoclassical structure combines in its details the two major cathedrals of Saint Petersburg—the Kazan Cathedral and Saint Isaac's. The tall bell tower, which has touches of Petersburg baroque, could be seen for a great distance along the Volga. Above the river dock is the much smaller Cathedral of Saint Nicholas, built in the 1720s and demolished during the Soviet period. Rybinsk was the concluding point of Prokudin-Gorsky's journey along the Mariinsky Waterway in 1909, but during the following years he would return to the mighty Volga River for two of the most productive itineraries in his work.

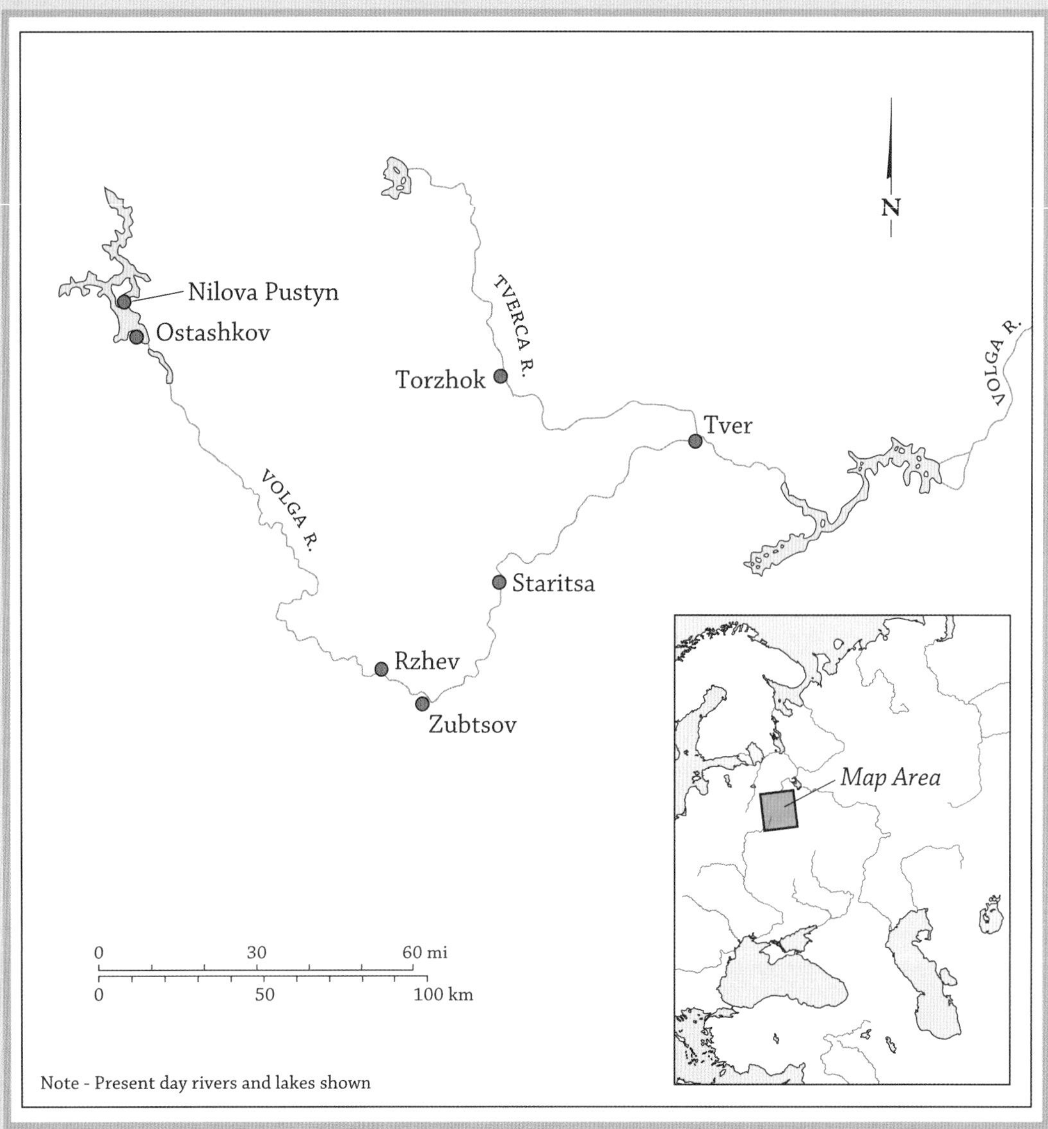

Nilova Pustyn
Ostashkov
Torzhok
Tver
TVERCA R.
VOLGA R.
VOLGA R.
Staritsa
Rzhev
Zubtsov
N
Map Area
0   30   60 mi
0   50   100 km
Note - Present day rivers and lakes shown

FOUR · The Upper Volga

From the Valdai Heights to Torzhok

In 1910 Sergey Prokudin-Gorsky traveled along the upper Volga River, which extends from its source near the town of Ostashkov to its confluence with the Oka River at Nizhny Novgorod. The Volga of 1910 had a very different appearance than it does today, after decades of Soviet hydroelectric and navigation projects intended to regulate the level of a river that in natural circumstances would fluctuate as much as fifty feet between late spring and late fall. Instead of a series of engineered reservoirs, Prokudin-Gorsky's photographs show a river with steep banks upon which are situated medieval monasteries and market towns that had served trade and colonization in east central Russia for some seven centuries.

The Volga originates in an area of primeval forest, lakes, and marshes some 320 kilometers northwest of Moscow. Near the origins of the Volga, and eventually flowing into it, is Lake Seliger, one of the larger lakes in the central part of European Russia. Prokudin-Gorsky photographed extensively in this area, including the great Hermitage of Saint Nilus on Stolobny Island. Founded in the late sixteenth century and named in honor of a renowned eremite who lived on the island, the monastic hermitage flourished in the seventeenth and eighteenth centuries under the patronage of princes, wealthy boyars, and on occasion the tsar himself. By the time its Epiphany Cathedral was rebuilt in a grand neoclassical style between 1821 and 1833, the hermitage resembled a city rather than a modest retreat.

The monastery's guiding spirit, the monk Nilus (Nil in Russian), was born in the Novgorod region in the late fifteenth century. Orphaned at an early age, he entered the Kripetsky Monastery near Pskov and took the name of Saint Nilus of Sinai, a fifth-century Byzantine monastic and theologian. In 1515, with his abbot's blessing, he went into the deep forest for a more rigorous form of monastic isolation. After thirteen years in the forest Nilus made his way to an uninhabited island in one of the many inlets of Lake Seliger near the settlement of Ostashkov. Known to practice extreme forms of self-abnegation, Nilus in his final hours (December 1555) expressed a desire for a monastic community to arise on the island. In 1560 a log chapel was erected over the site of his forest cell. In 1594 Patriarch Job, leader of the Russian Orthodox Church, assented to the existence of the monastery. Locally venerated after his death, Nilus was acknowledged as a saint throughout the Russian Orthodox Church in 1756.

The founder of the Nilus Stolobensky Epiphany Monastery was the monk Herman from the nearby Saint Nicholas-Rozhkovsky Monastery. Inspired by Nilus's example, Herman and others erected a log church dedicated to the Epiphany on the island in 1591–94. Shortly thereafter a monastic community took root with the Patriarch's blessing. The efforts of Herman and his brethren were soon threatened by the Time of Troubles, a dynastic crisis that led to a decade of widespread social and political chaos following the death of tsar Boris Godunov in 1605. In 1610 the small monastery was devastated by marauding forces. Although Herman struggled to maintain the community, little remained after his death in 1614.

Herman's follower, Nektarius (1586–1667), possessed many practical talents and was able in 1622 to erect the monastery's second church, dedicated to the Intercession of the Virgin. His abilities were noted by the Muscovite court, and in 1636 tsar Mikhail Romanov oversaw his elevation to bishop of Siberia and Tobolsk. Exhausted by severe Siberian conditions, Nektarius was permitted to return to his beloved monastery in 1640. In 1647 he resumed control of the community, which began to receive major gifts from Tsar Aleksei Mikhailovich. After a fire devastated the monastery in 1665, Nektarius launched a rebuilding that continued with royal support after his death. However, almost all of the current structures were rebuilt in the eighteenth and nineteenth centuries.

Prokudin-Gorsky's best-known photograph of the monastery was taken across a narrow strait from the village of Svetlitsa to the northeast. My photograph from a similar point shows that outwardly, little has changed over the past century. The monastic ensemble is dominated by the great

Epiphany Cathedral and its bell tower. From the end of the sixteenth century there had always been an Epiphany Church on the island, but over the centuries it had been rebuilt as the monastery expanded. After the visit of Tsar Alexander I in 1820, work began on the present cathedral, a grand neoclassical design originally conceived by Carlo Rossi but completed by another major Saint Petersburg architect, Joseph-Jean Charlemagne. Consecrated in 1833, the new cathedral required several more years of interior work that included extensive wall paintings.

During the first half of the nineteenth century, other components of the ensemble were completed, including the monumental Archbishop's Chambers and south cloisters in a mixture of the neoclassical and Gothic Revival styles. The massive granite building foundations and embankments among the south and east sides amplify the sense of imperial Saint Petersburg. In the midst of this grandeur, the pilgrims in Prokudin-Gorsky's photograph seem minimized. A similar capitoline atmosphere is conveyed in my photographs. An elegant accent to the east embankment is provided by the Archbishop's Landing, built in a refined Doric style in 1814. My photographs show a reasonable state of preservation, although with losses to the embankment.

Within the monastery territory, Prokudin-Gorsky photographs include churches that were rebuilt in the middle of the eighteenth century. An example of this baroque style is the Church of Saint Nilus Stolobensky, built over the Holy Gate (the main entrance on the east) in 1751–55. Prokudin-Gorsky's photograph of this church, taken from the west, includes the south facade and portico of the Epiphany Cathedral. My photograph, taken from a similar perspective in August 2016, shows the results of recent restoration efforts.

Following the Bolshevik Revolution, the Nilus Stolobensky Monastery endured many trials. Closed in 1928, it was used as a place of incarceration, primarily for juvenile offenders. Its darkest moment occurred in 1939, when it was filled with 4,700 Polish prisoners of war (the "Ostashkov Camp"). In the spring of 1940 they were transferred to a prison near Tver (then called Kalinin) and shot in April and May as part of a mass execution of Polish prisoners by the NKVD. Their common grave at the village of Mednoe is now the site of a large memorial.

With the outbreak of war, the monastery and the town of Ostashkov were close to the front line from the fall of 1941 until January 1943. The monastery itself was used as a military hospital throughout the war. From 1945 to 1960 it again housed juvenile delinquents, then for a decade was used as a home

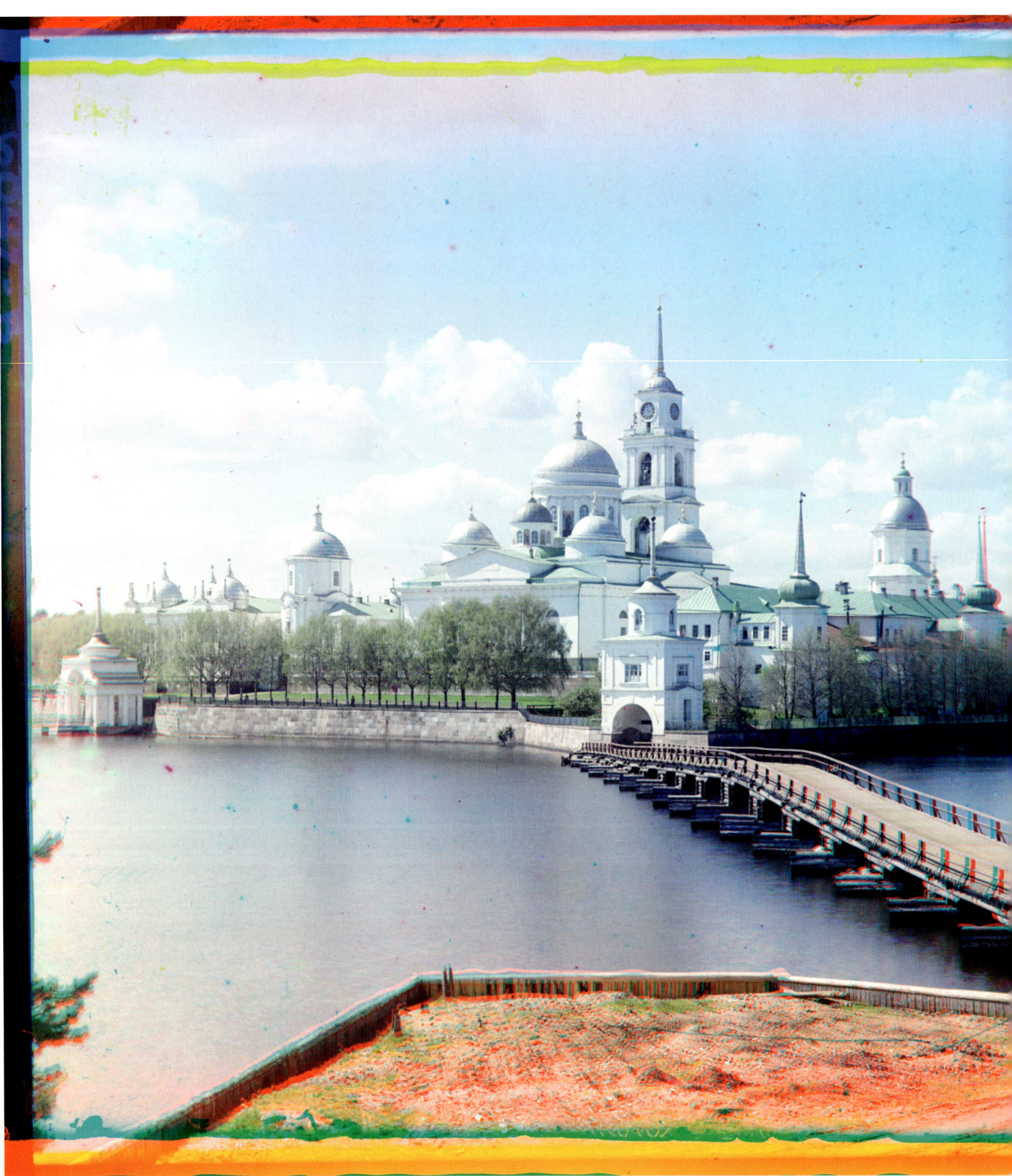

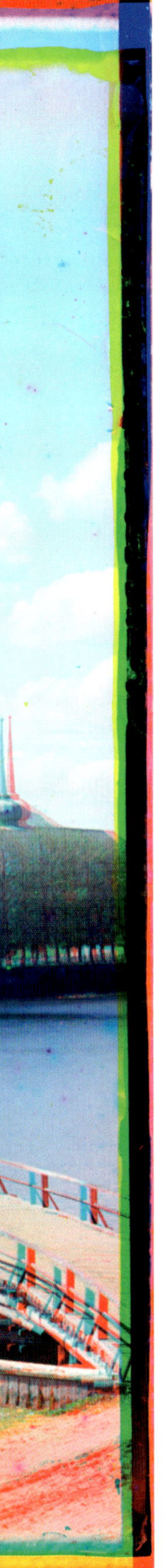

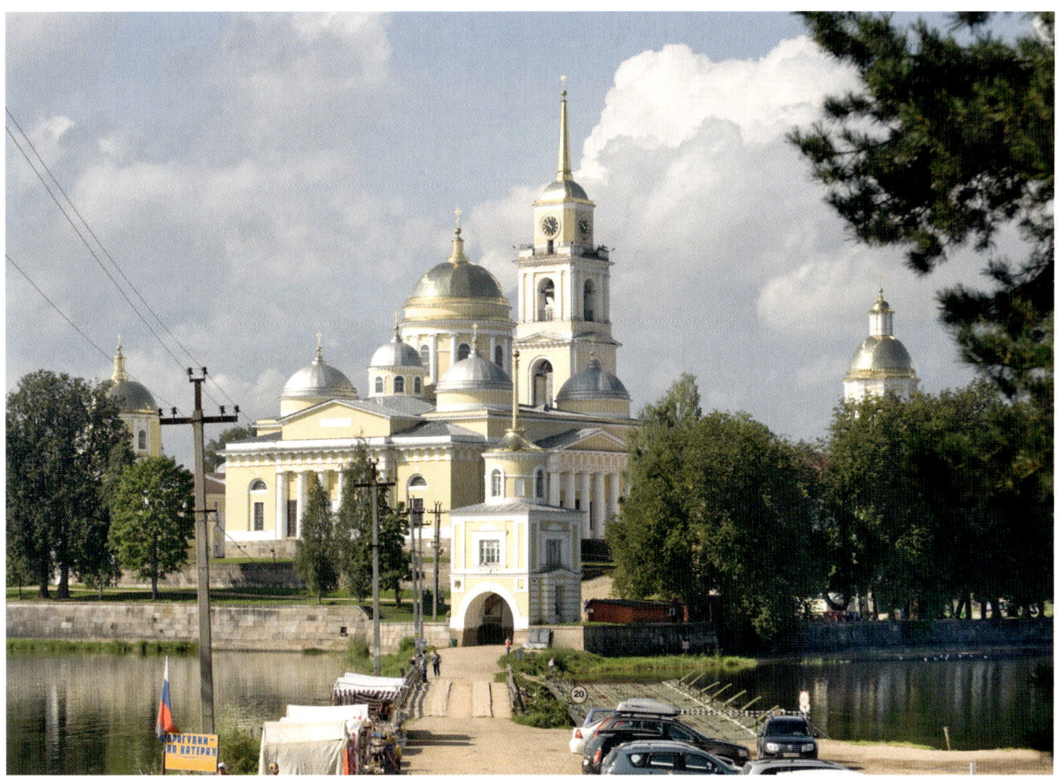

for the elderly. Despite the natural beauty of the location, attempts between 1971 and 1990 to create a tourist base within
the former monastery failed for lack of resources — not to
mention the inherent contradiction within the idea itself. In
1990 the territory of the monastery, with ransacked buildings, was returned to the Orthodox Church. In 1991 the first
liturgy was celebrated in a section of the Epiphany Cathedral. The restoration has required enormous effort and resources, but each year brings significant progress. In 1995
the relics of Saint Nilus were returned from the Ostashkov
Museum to the Epiphany Cathedral, and in 2003 the relics
of Saint Nektarius were elevated.

In May 1910, Prokudin-Gorsky continued his work in
the Volga basin with a trip to Ostashkov, located on a spit
of land extending into Lake Seliger to the south of Saint
Nilus Monastery (Nilova Pustyn). The first references to
Russian settlements at the site date to the late fourteenth
century. Log fortifications erected in 1587 were sufficiently
strong to withstand a Polish attack in 1610, during the Time
of Troubles. Ostashkov's position between Veliky Novgo-

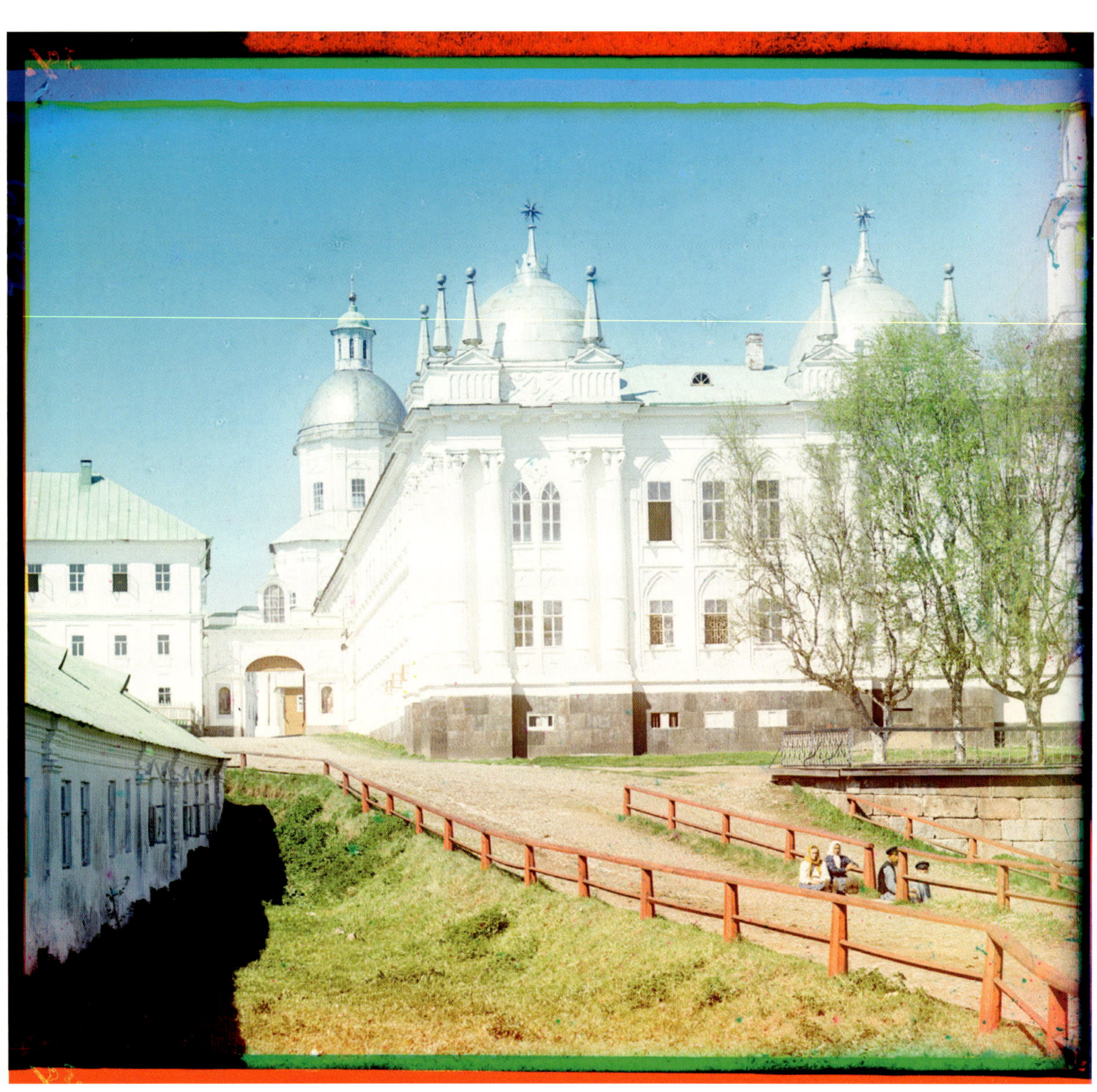

SAINT NILUS STOLOBENSKY MONASTERY

Archbishop's Chambers and cloisters. East view.

PROKUDIN-GORSKY 21111. SUMMER 1910.

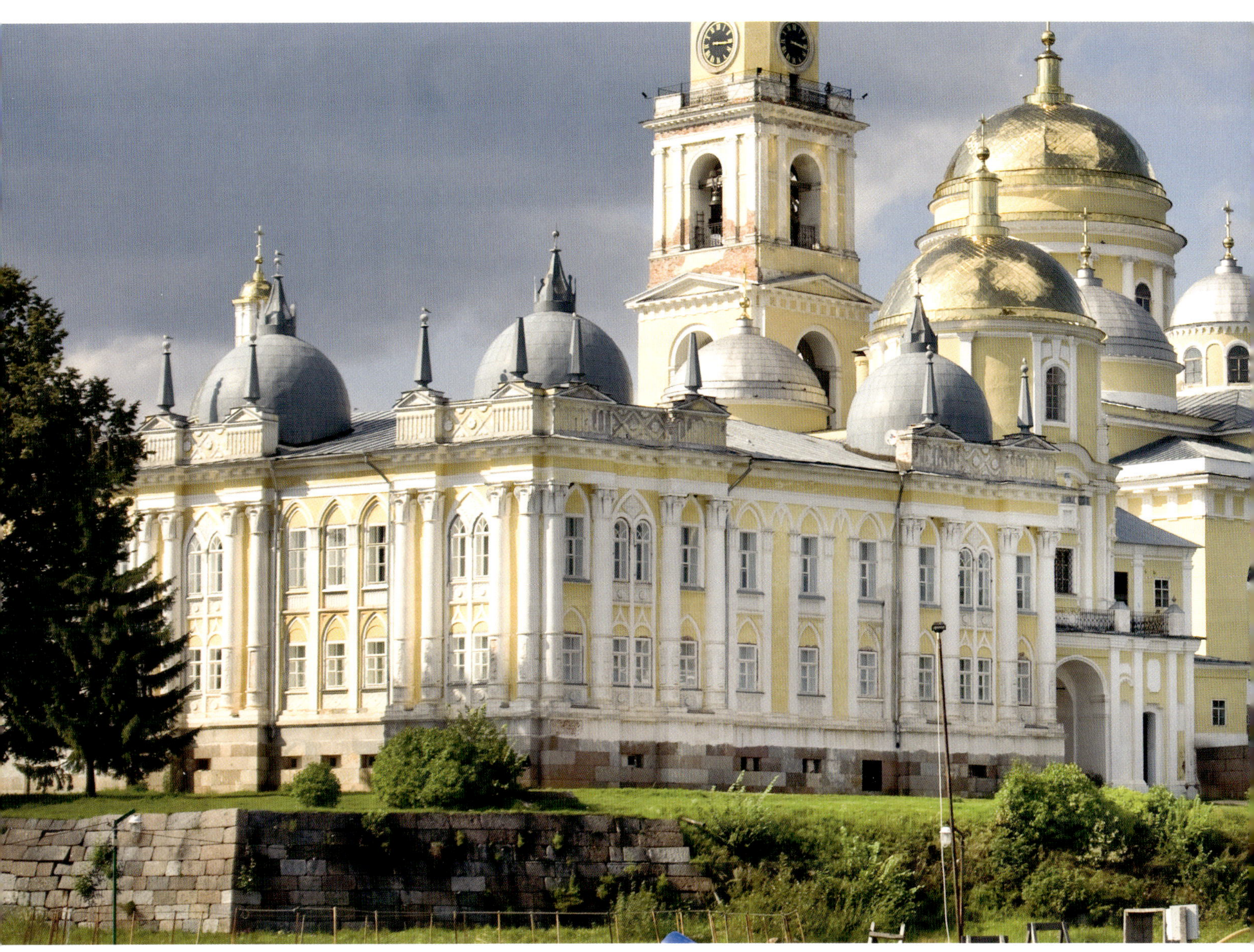

SAINT NILUS STOLOBENSKY MONASTERY

Archbishop's Chambers and cloisters. East view.

BRUMFIELD, AUGUST 23, 2016.

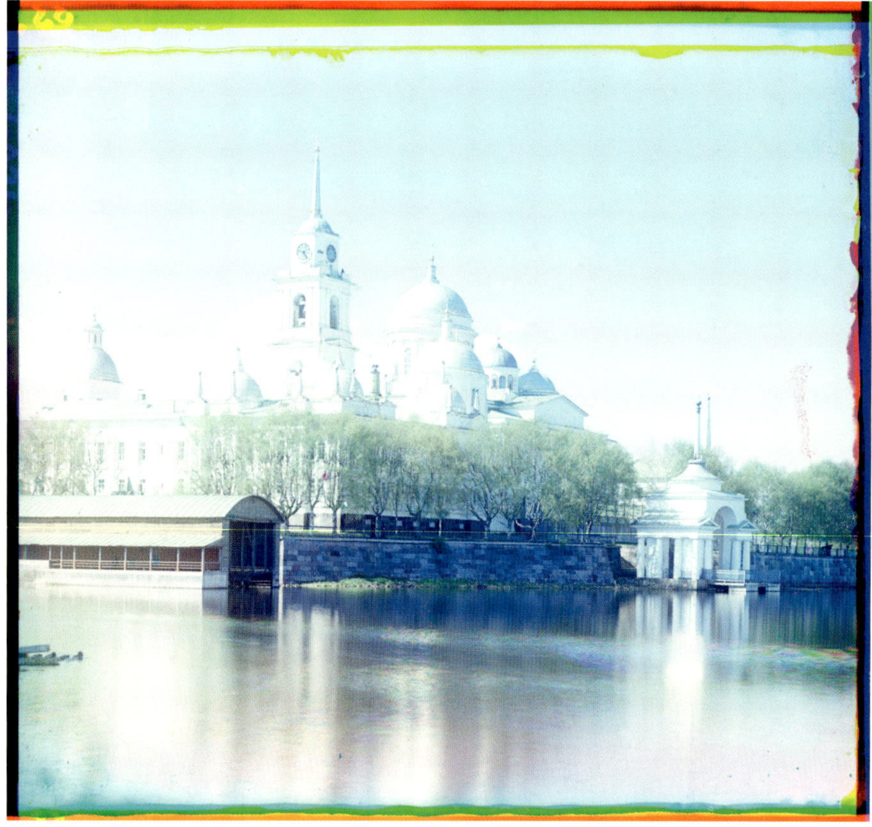

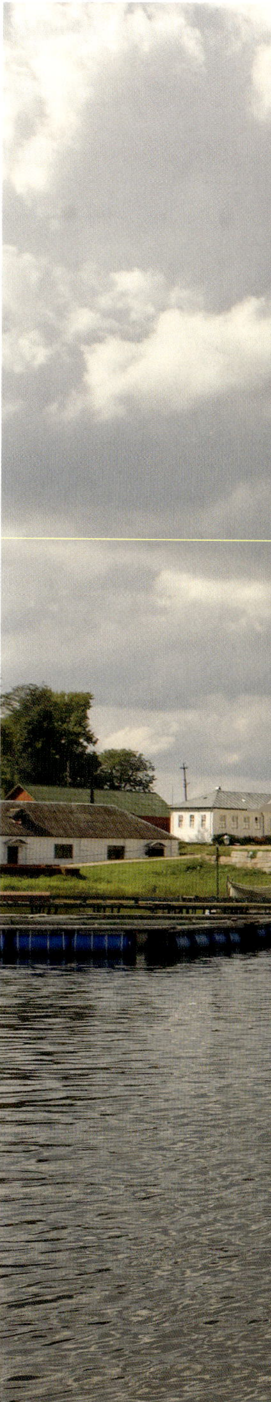

rod to the northwest and the Volga River basin led at the end of the seventeenth century to economic growth reflected in the construction of two masonry cathedrals.

Prokudin-Gorsky's several photographs of Ostashkov include a southwest view of the Trinity Cathedral, begun in 1685 and consecrated in 1697. During the eighteenth and nineteenth centuries the cathedral was frequently modified and gained the neoclassical pediments seen in his photograph. The structure also gained a one-story gallery with four secondary chapels (partially visible in his photograph) dedicated to the Saint Paraskeva Piatnitsa, the Okovetsky Icon, Saint George, and Saint Nicholas. After the war, the exterior was restored to what was considered its original form, with a roofline culminating in semicircular decorative gables (*zakomary*) supporting the five cupolas seen in my photograph.

Granted formal status as a town in 1770, Ostashkov also gained a new, regular plan from the architect Ivan Starov as part of Catherine the Great's extensive reforms of provincial centers. The new plan required the demolition of the remains of medieval earthen ramparts. Residents chose to memorialize the fortress with a Rampart Pillar (Valskii Stolp) that served

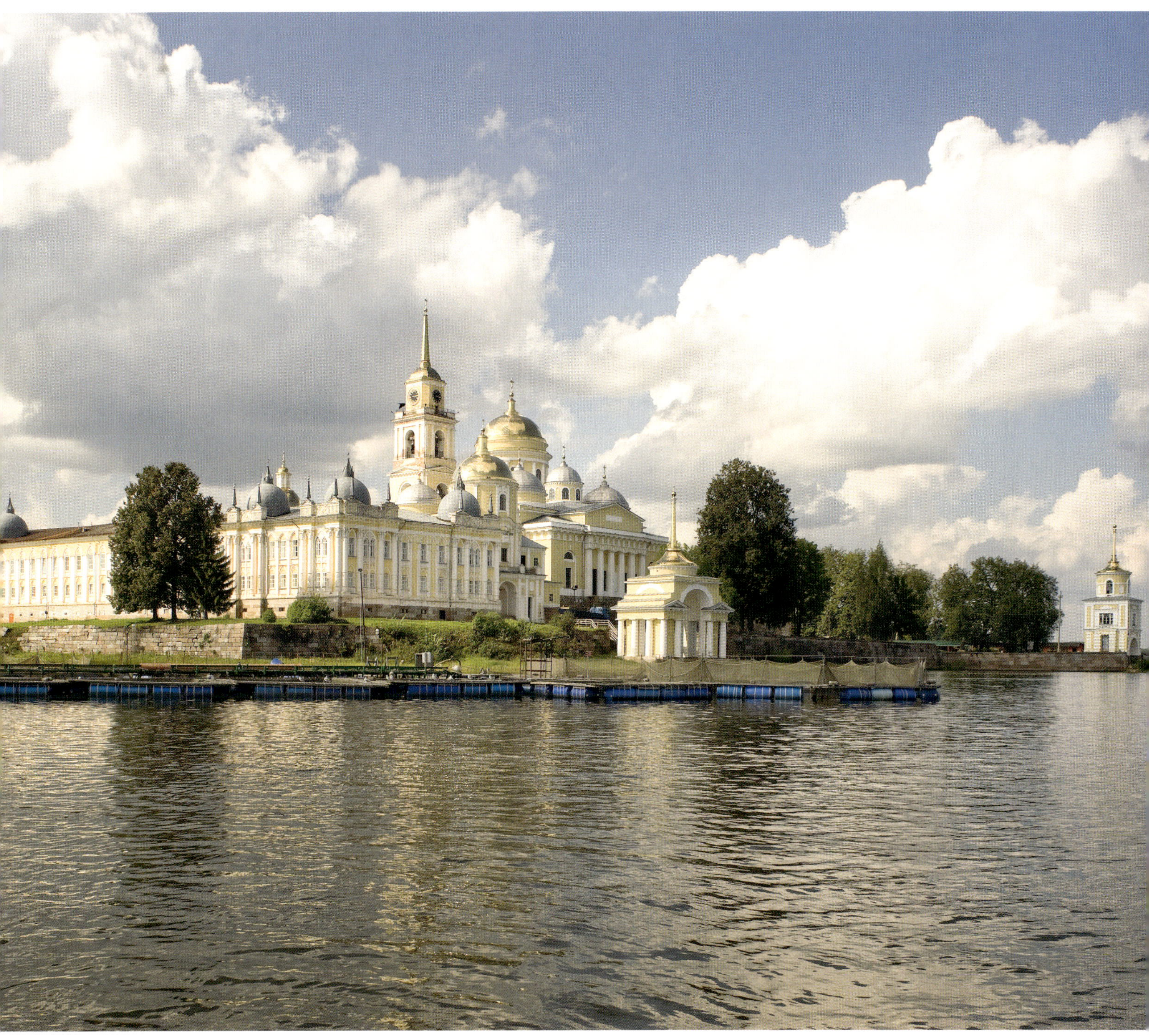

SAINT NILUS STOLOBENSKY MONASTERY

Southeast view from east cape of Stolobny Island.
From left: Church of Saints Peter and Paul over West
Gate, south cloisters and Archbishop's Chambers, bell
tower and Epiphany Cathedral, Church of Saint Nilus
over East Gate, Archbishop's Landing. PROKUDIN-
GORSKY 21110. SUMMER 1910.

SAINT NILUS STOLOBENSKY MONASTERY

Southeast view from Lake Seliger. *From left*: bakery,
south cloisters and Archbishop's Chambers, bell tower
and Epiphany Cathedral, Church of Saint Nilus over
East Gate, Archbishop's Landing. BRUMFIELD, AUGUST
23, 2016.

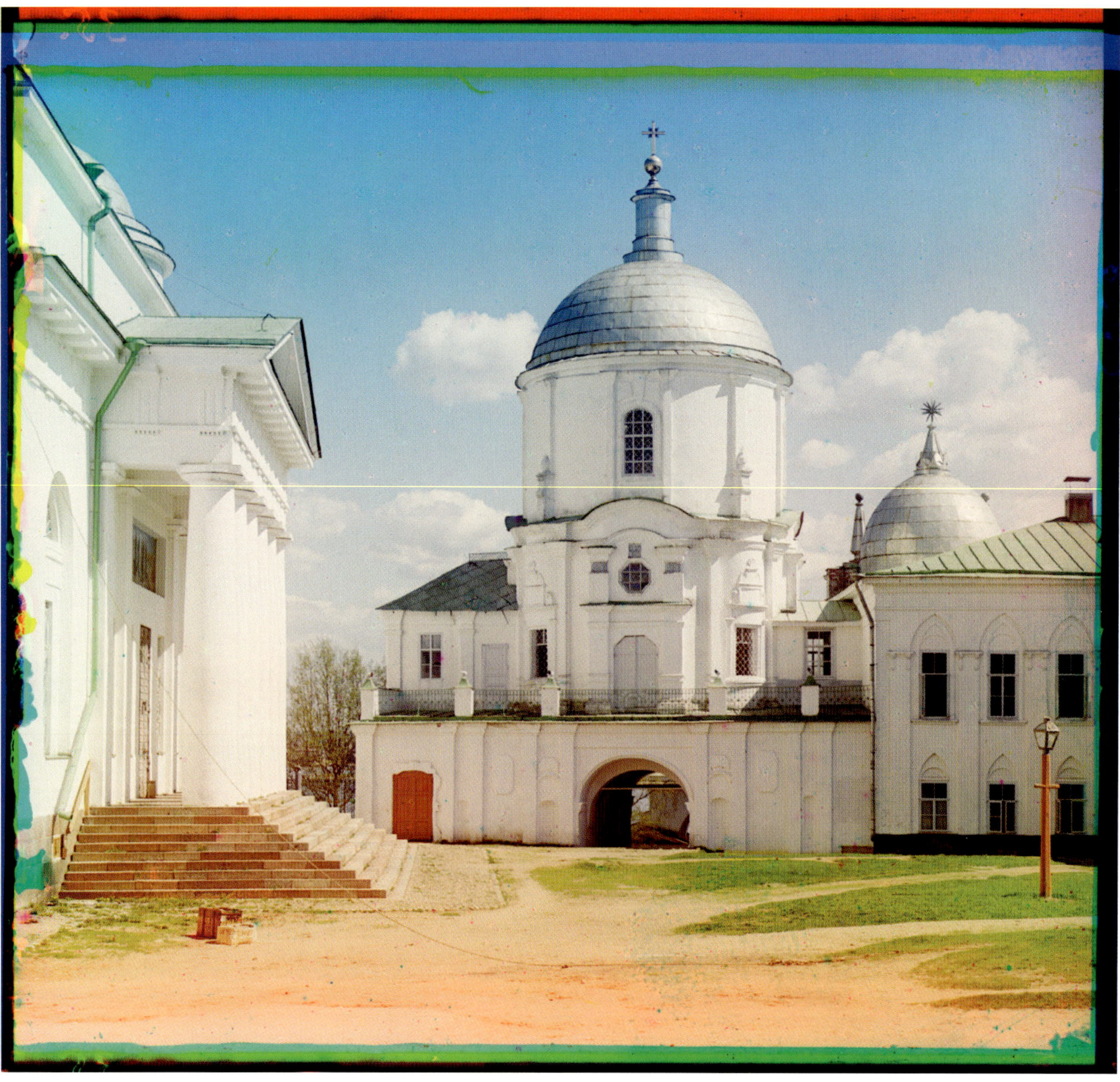

as a chapel with icons on the facade. Three others soon followed, the first of which, seen in Prokudin-Gorsky's photograph on former Kamennaia Street, was erected in 1785 and dedicated to the Smolensk Icon of the Virgin. (Until 1711 the main town gate stood on this site.) The pillar, in a baroque style, rests on a fieldstone base. In the shadows on the far right is the photographer's son Mikhail. My photograph shows little apparent change, apart from the intrusion of a light pole and electric wires.

Seen here is a south view of the Zhitenny Smolensk Icon Monastery, situated on an island in Lake Seliger just to the

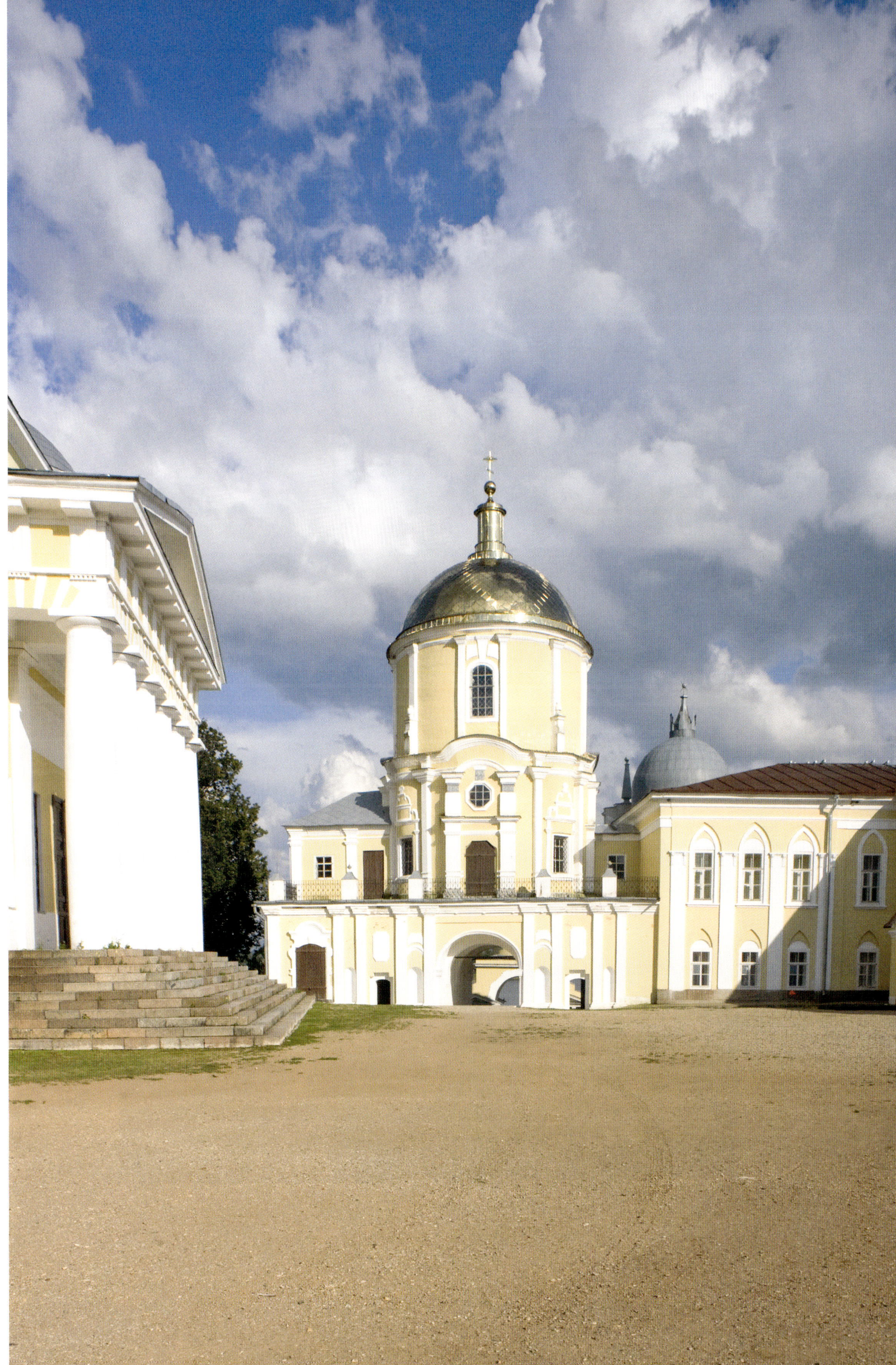

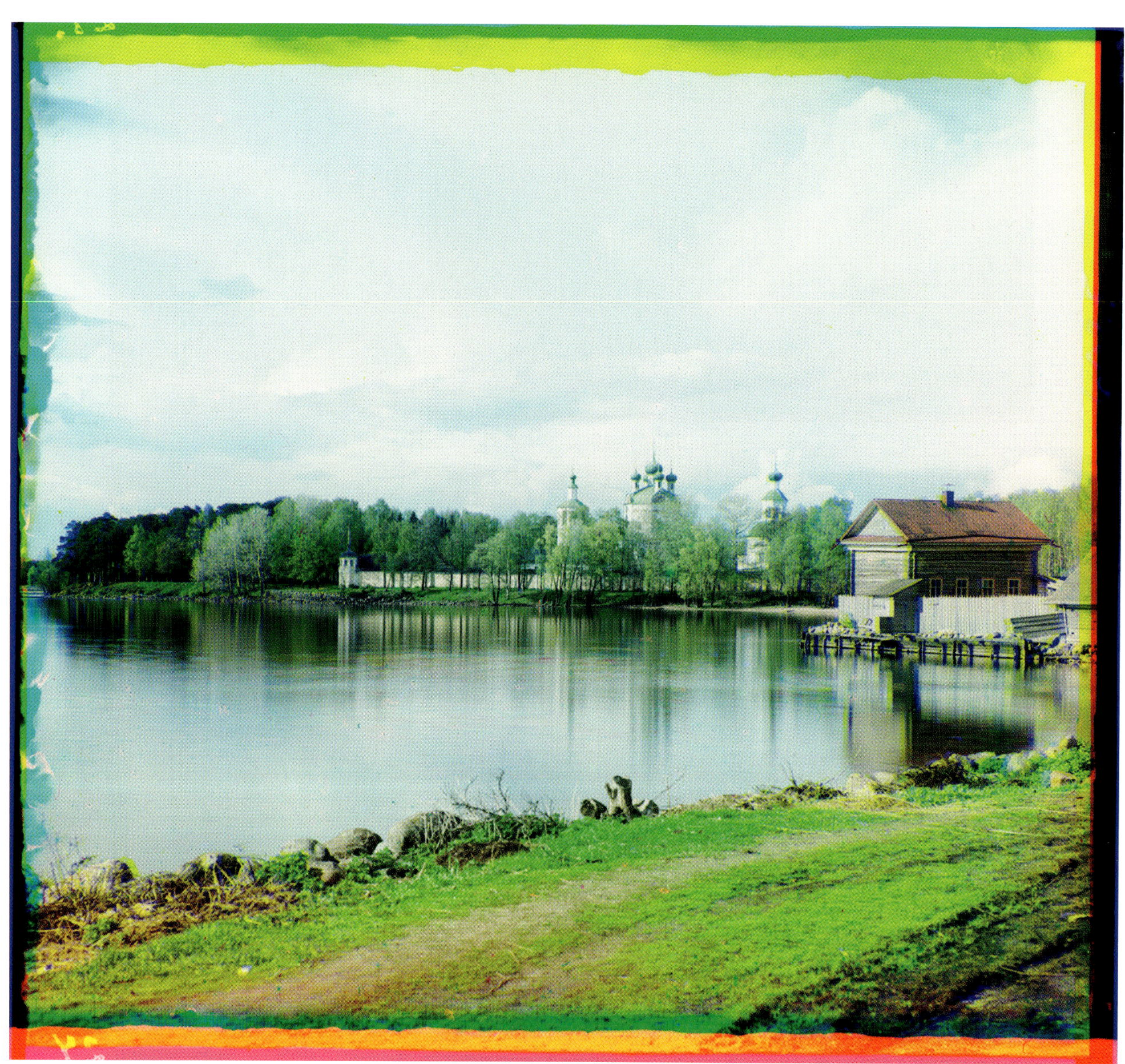

OSTASHKOV Zhitenny-Smolensk Icon of the Virgin Monastery. Northeast view with Lake Seliger. *From left*: southeast corner tower, east wall, bell tower, Cathedral of the Smolensk Icon, Church of Saints John the Divine and Andrew over Holy Gate. PROKUDIN-GORSKY 21103. MAY 1910.

OSTASHKOV Zhitenny-Smolensk Icon of the Virgin Convent. Church of Saints John the Divine and Andrew over Holy Gate. West view. BRUMFIELD, AUGUST 24, 2016.

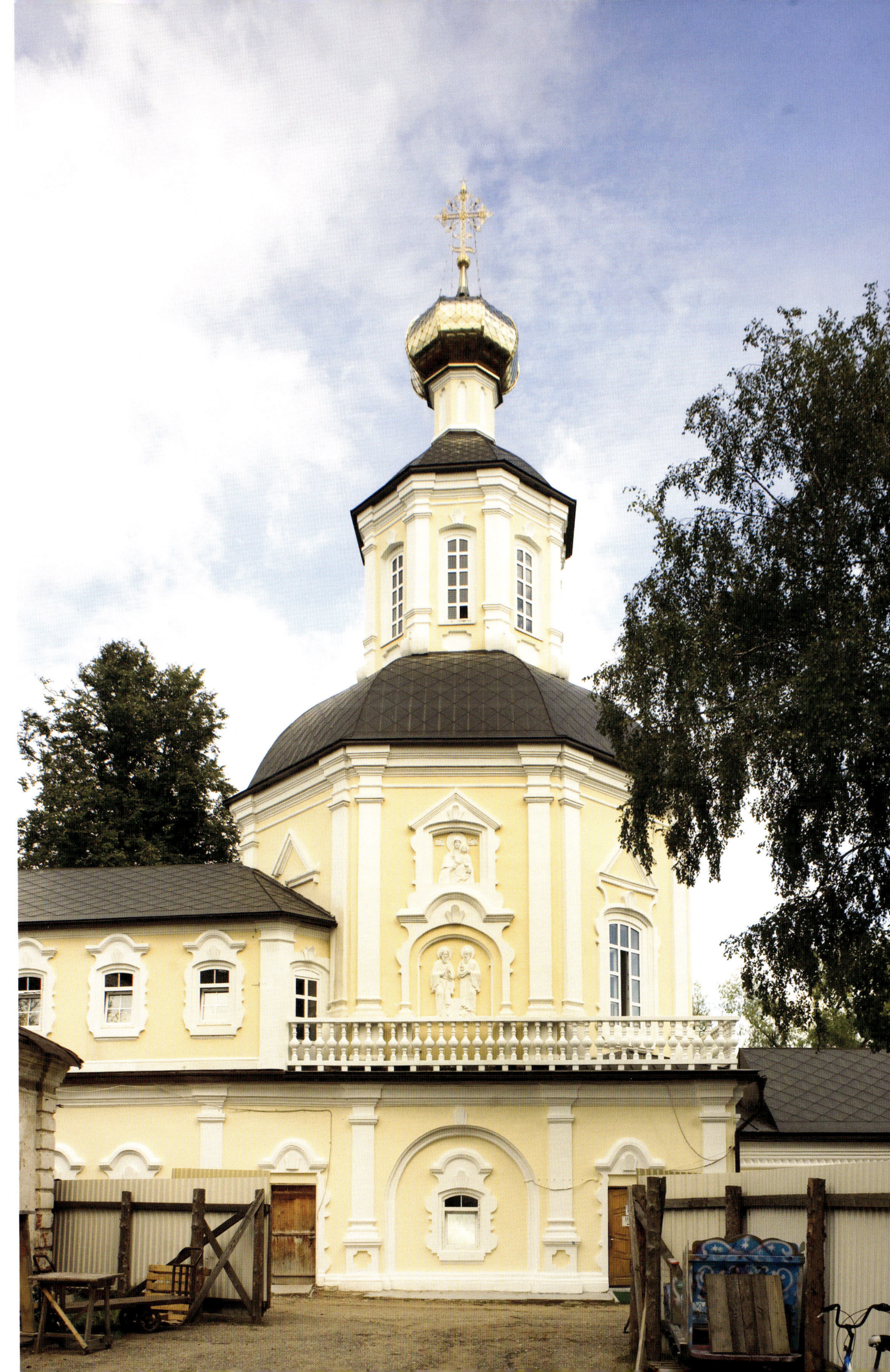

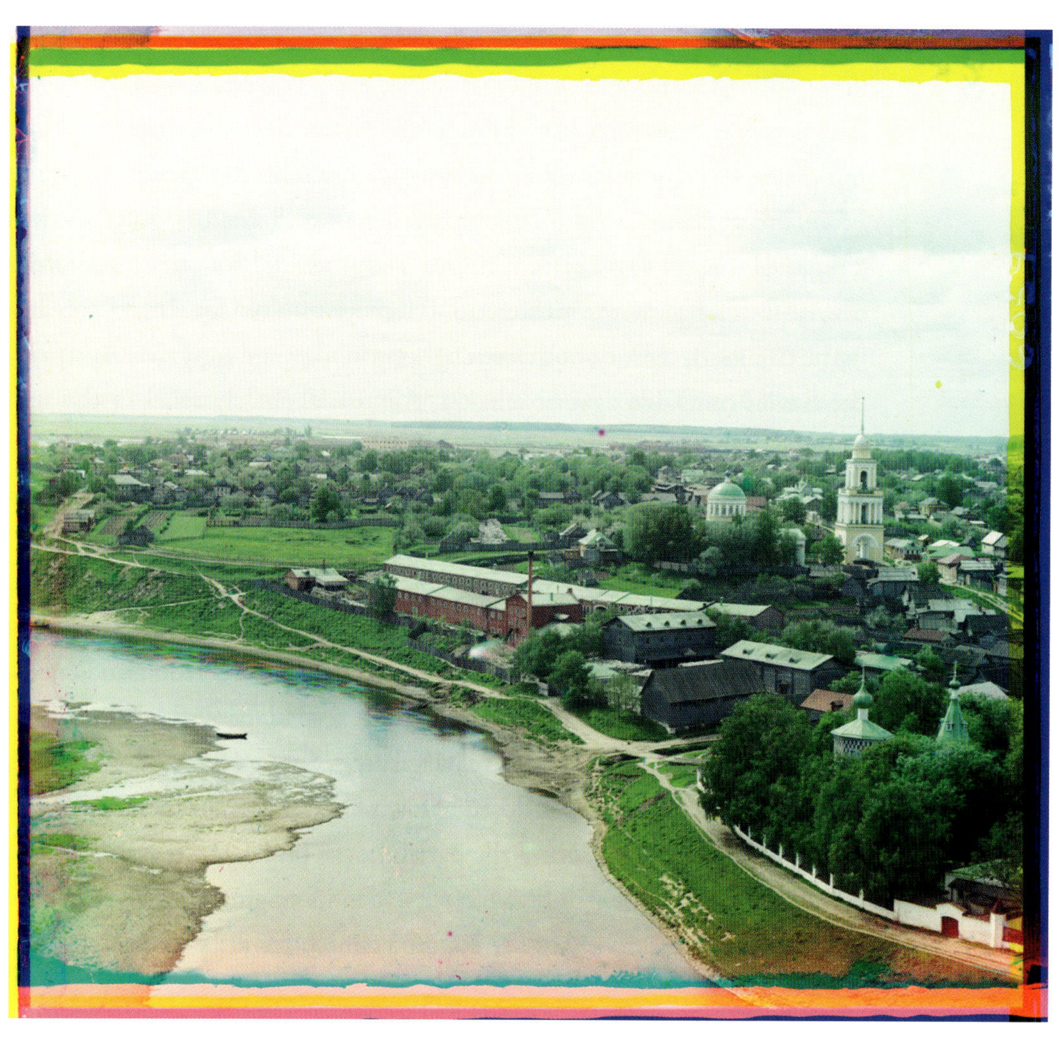

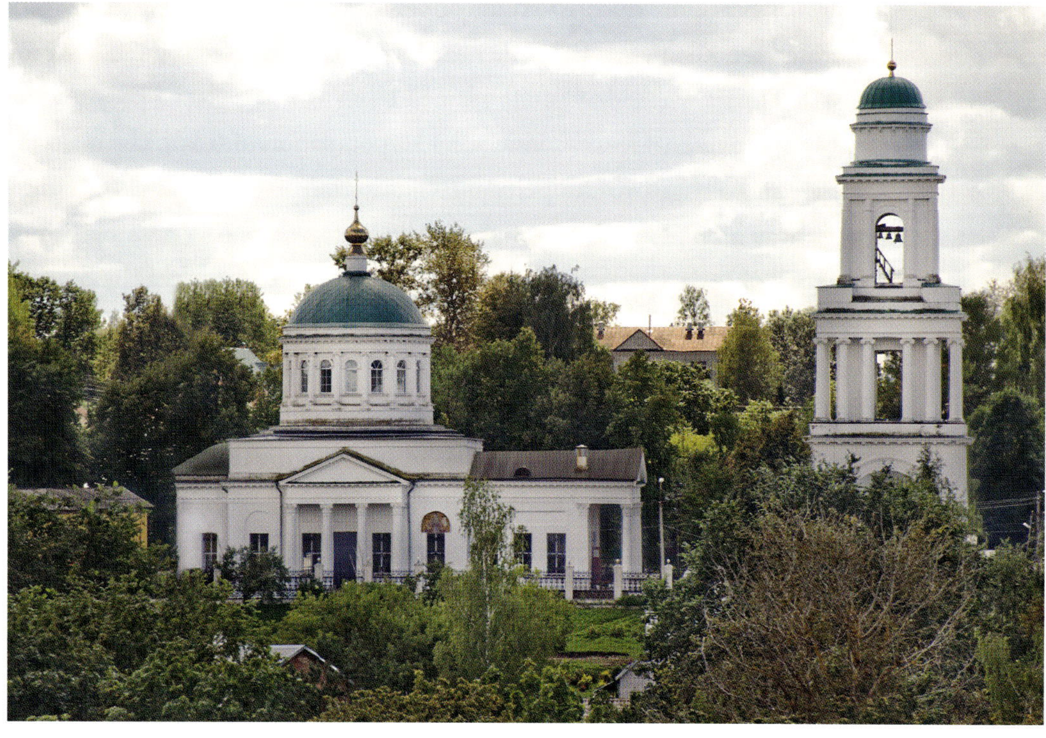

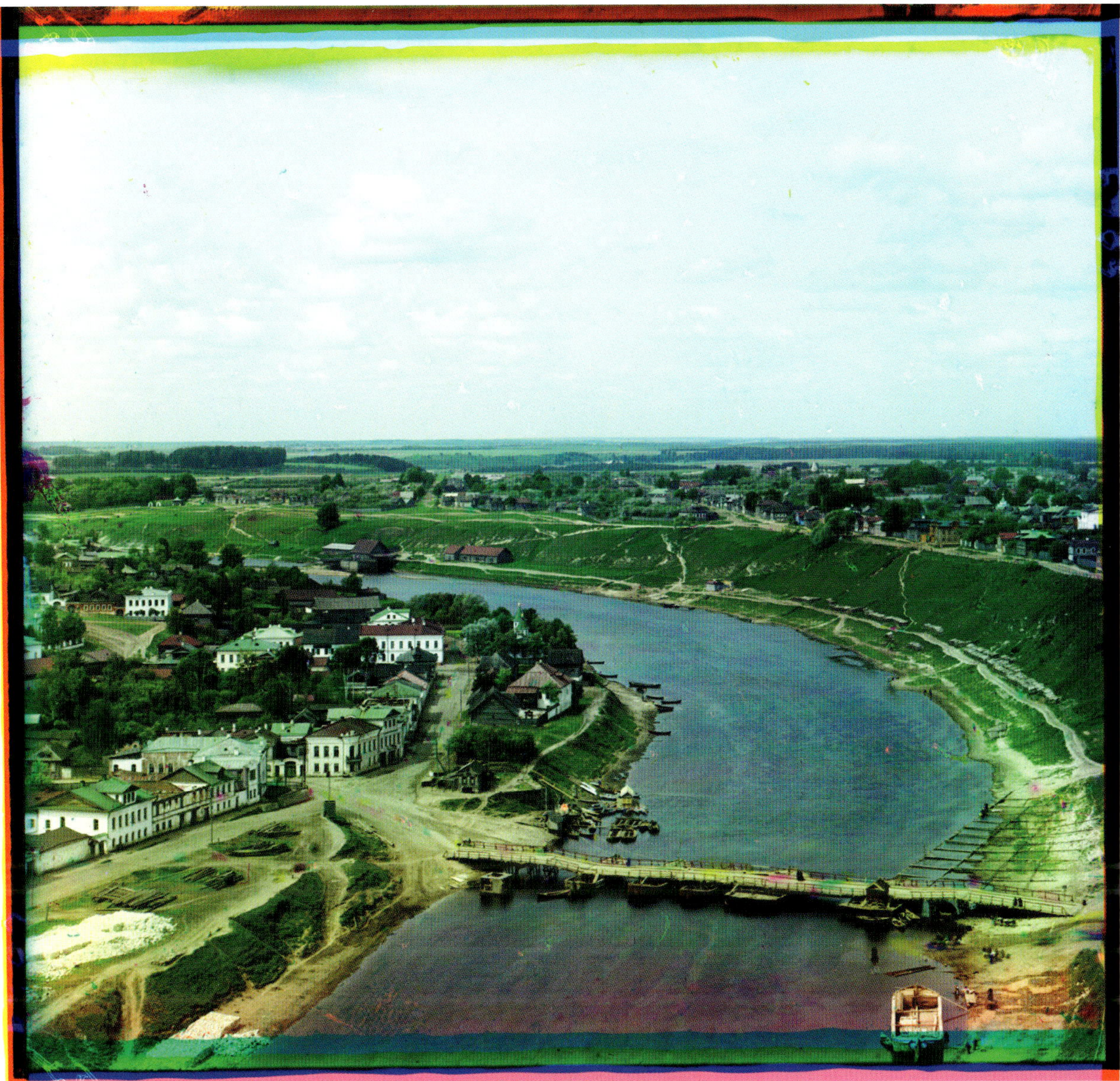

RZHEV View south across Volga River toward Prince Dmitry side and the Cathedral of the Okovetsky Icon of the Virgin. PROKUDIN-GORSKY 21130. SUMMER 1910.

RZHEV View south across Volga River toward Prince Dmitry side and the Cathedral of the Okovetsky Icon of the Virgin. BRUMFIELD, AUGUST 13, 2016.

RZHEV View northwest up the Volga River with the Prince Dmitry side (right bank) and the Prince Fyodor side (*on right*). Most of the buildings were destroyed during protracted battles primarily in 1942. The small house with a four-sloped roof at the river bend was one of the few that survived the war (compare with illustration on the following page). PROKUDIN-GORSKY 21137. SUMMER 1910.

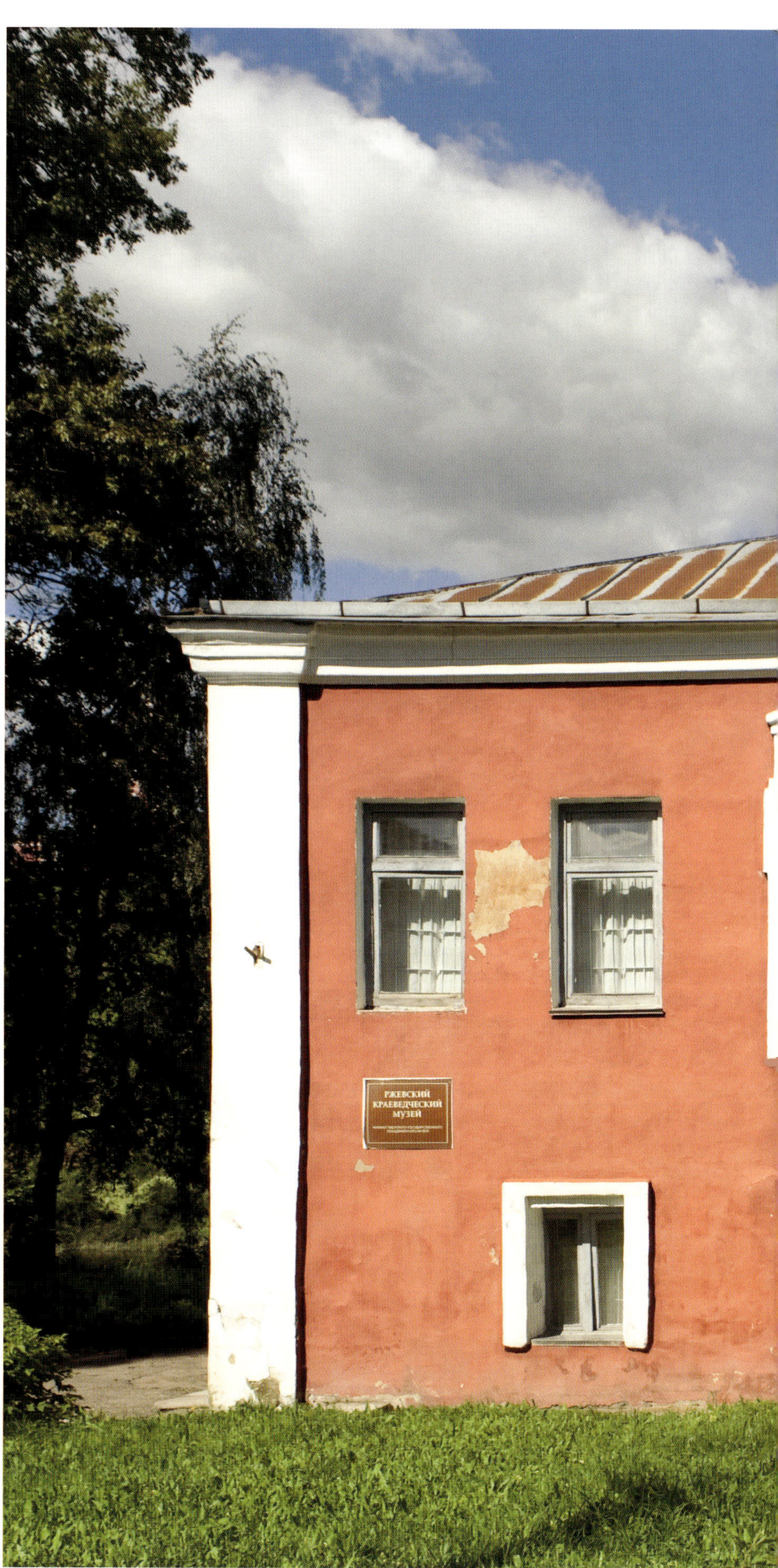

RZHEV House built in eighteenth century for Nemilov merchant family. Restored after World War II and now part of the Rzhev Local History Museum. BRUMFIELD, AUGUST 13, 2016.

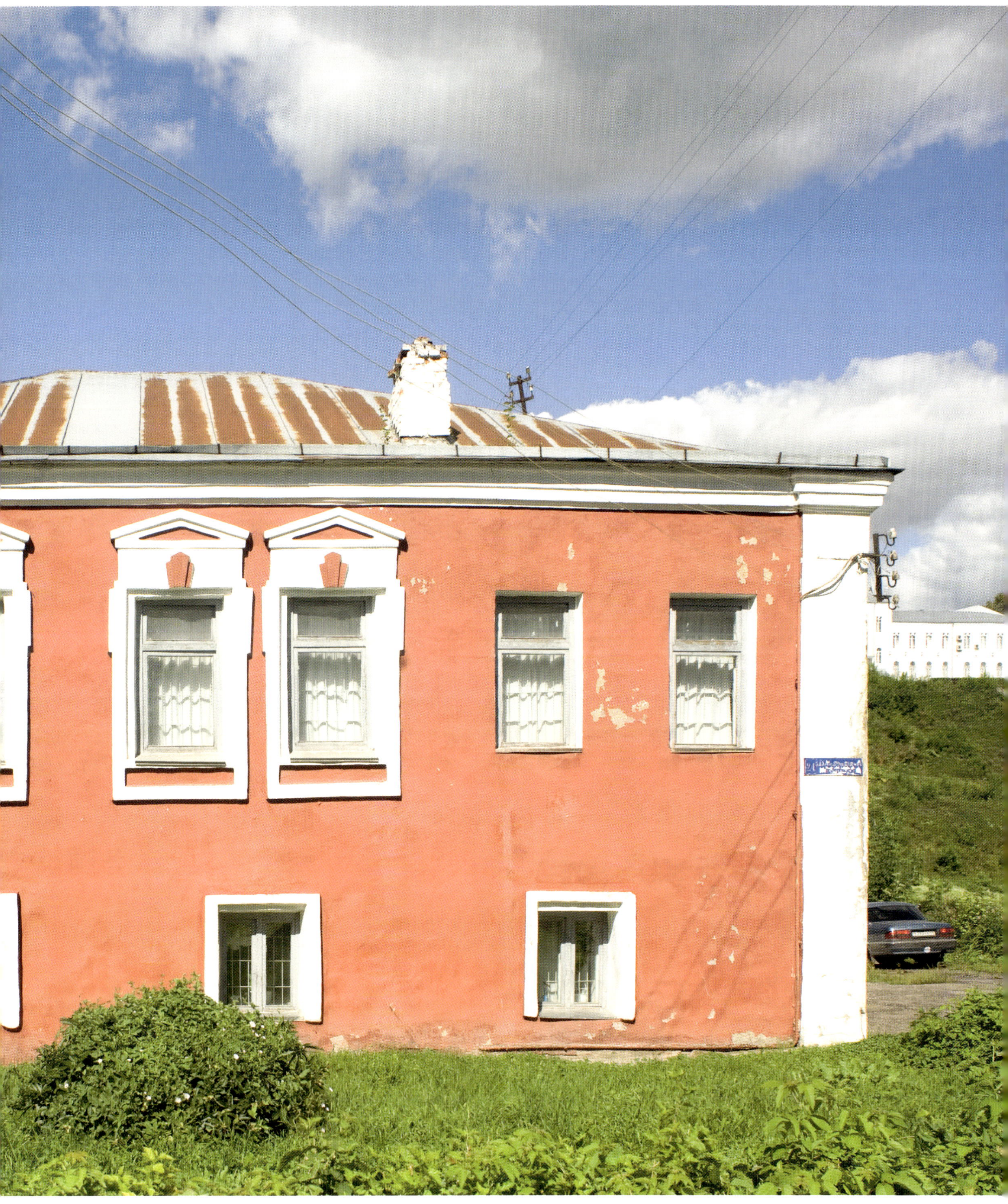

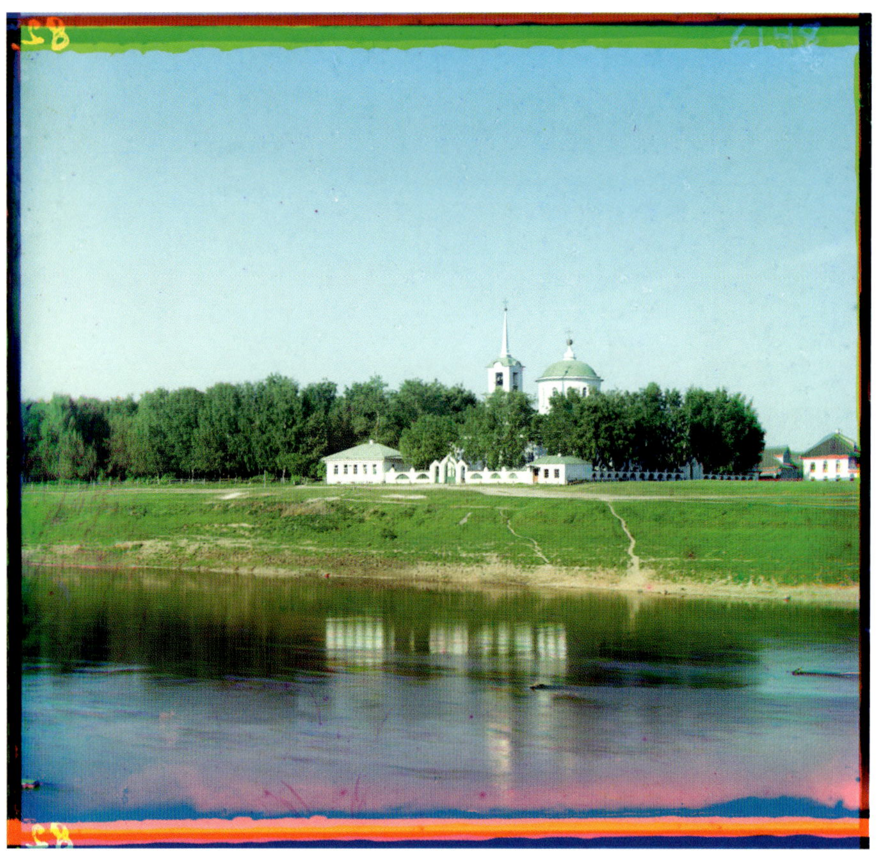

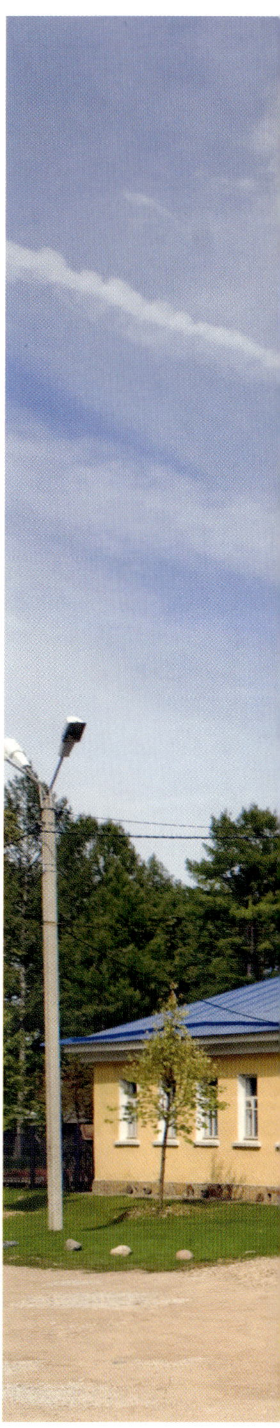

ZUBTSOV View northeast across
Volga River toward the Cathe-
dral of the Dormition (*right*).
PROKUDIN-GORSKY 21183.
SUMMER 1910.

ZUBTSOV Cathedral of the Dormition. West view. BRUMFIELD,
AUGUST 14, 2016.

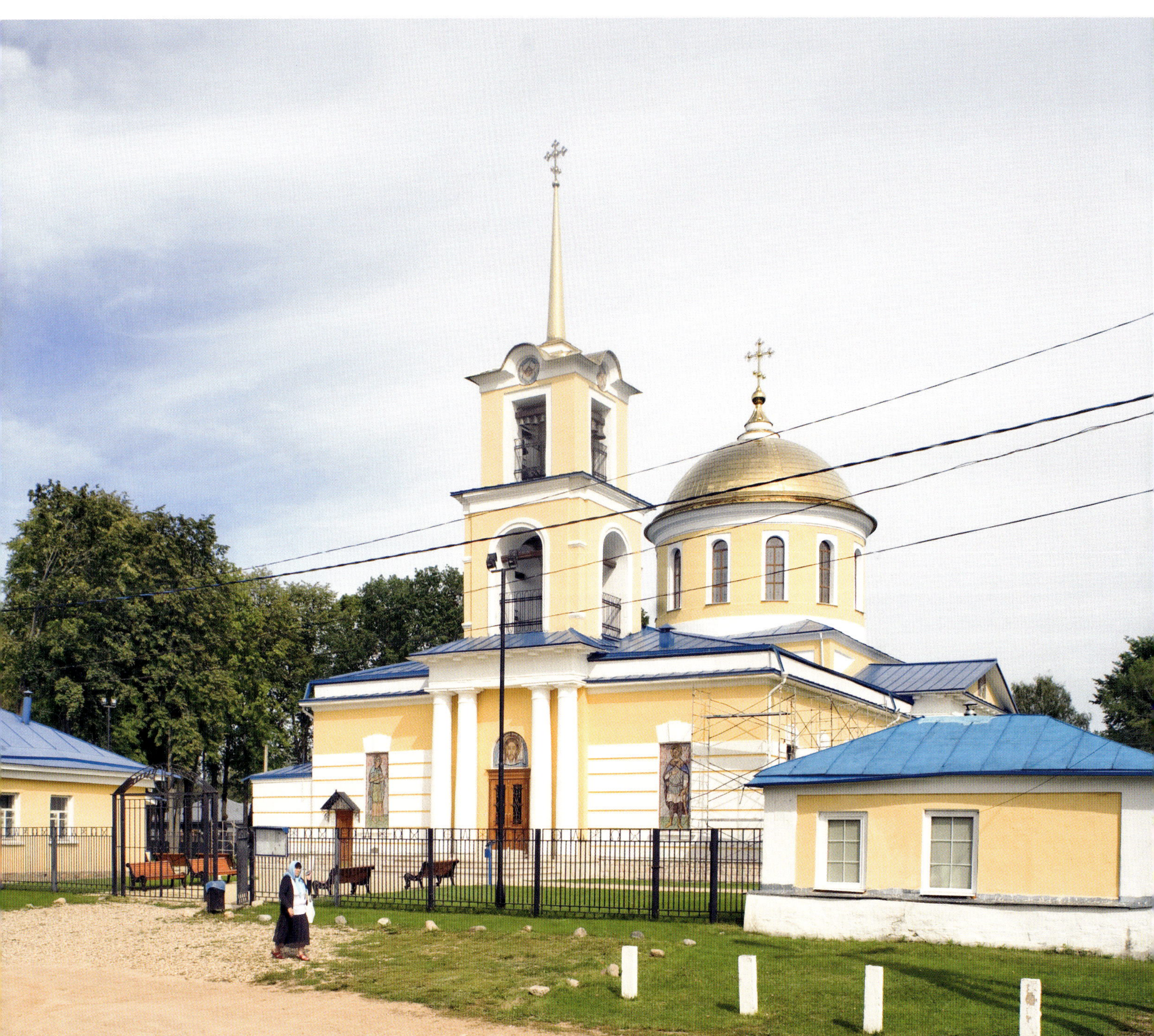

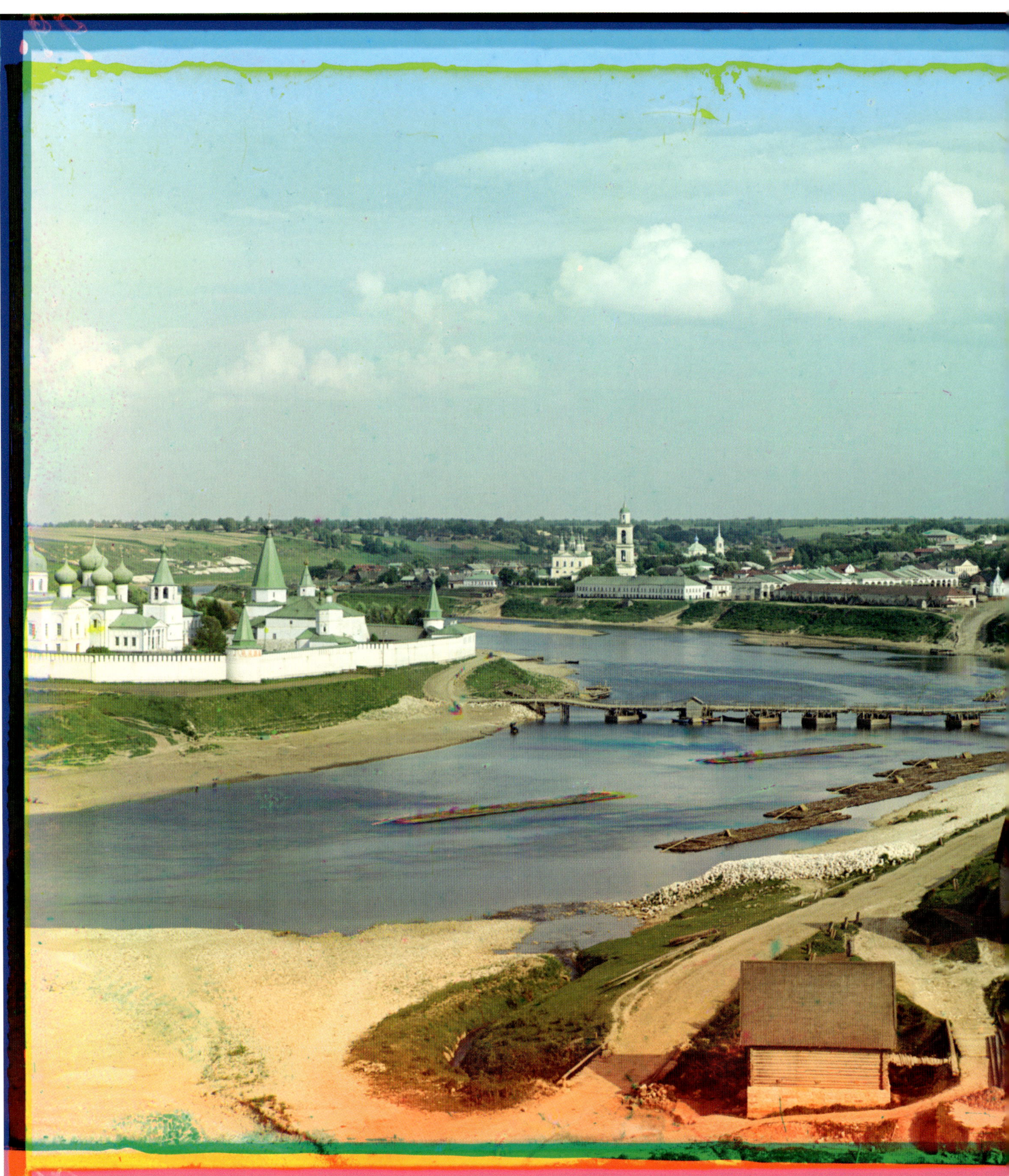

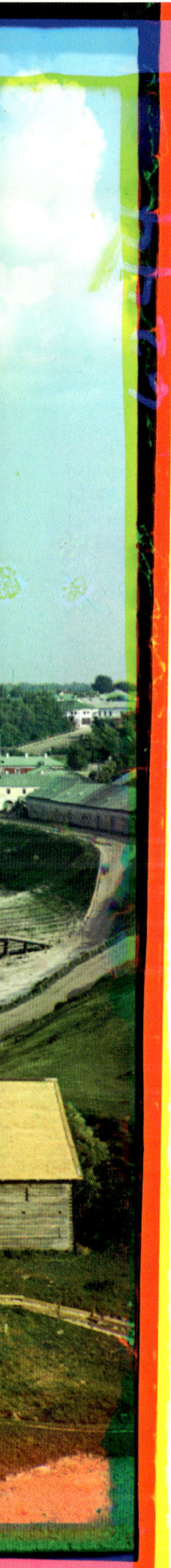

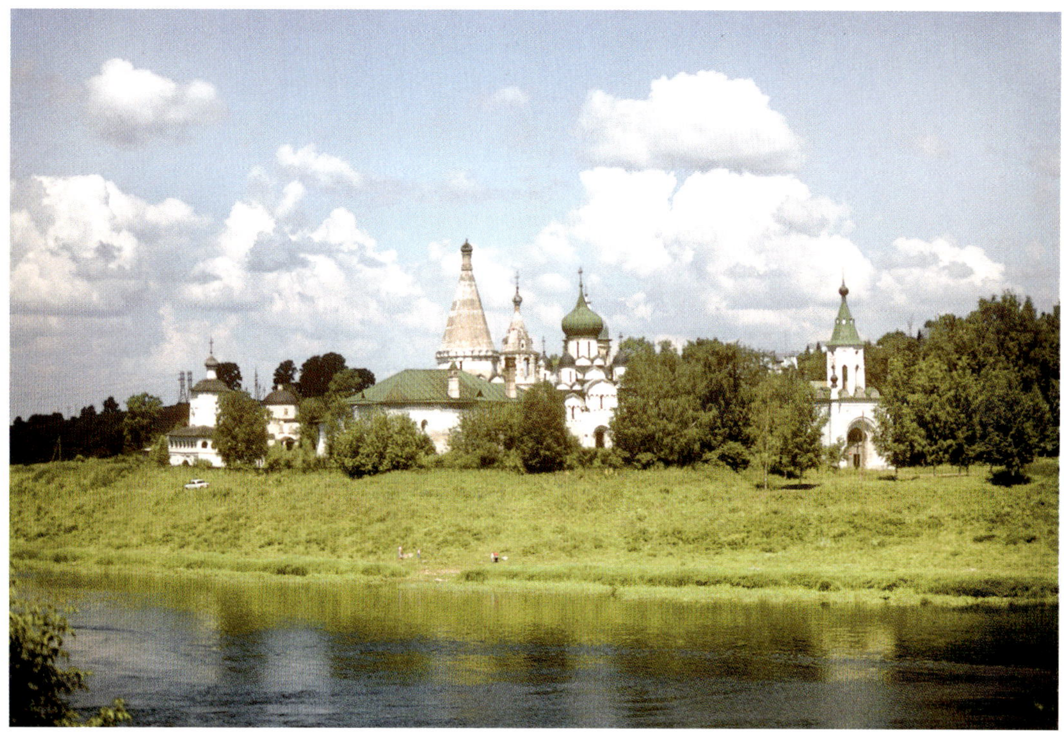

The town's most prominent landmark was the Dormition Monastery, founded around 1100, destroyed during a
Tatar raid in 1292, and revived in the early sixteenth century by Prince Andrei Ioannovich of Staritsa. His clearest
photograph of the Dormition Monastery is a northeast view
across the Volga. Seen from right is the Dormition Tower
over the Holy Gates (1885), the southwest corner tower,
the limestone Dormition Cathedral (1530s), the refectory
Church of the Presentation (1570), and the Church of Saint
John the Divine over the west gate. My 1997 photograph
(above) shows a similar perspective, while another view
shows the cathedral ensemble in detail. Within the monastery Prokudin-Gorsky photographed treasures in the
Dormition Cathedral but took no exterior photographs of
the structure itself. During the Soviet period, the structure
remained, but the cathedral interior was thoroughly ransacked.

Although much of the market square that Prokudin-
Gorsky photographed has vanished, a few parish churches
remain. Among them is the Church of the Transfiguration
(also known as Saint Nicholas in honor of a secondary altar),

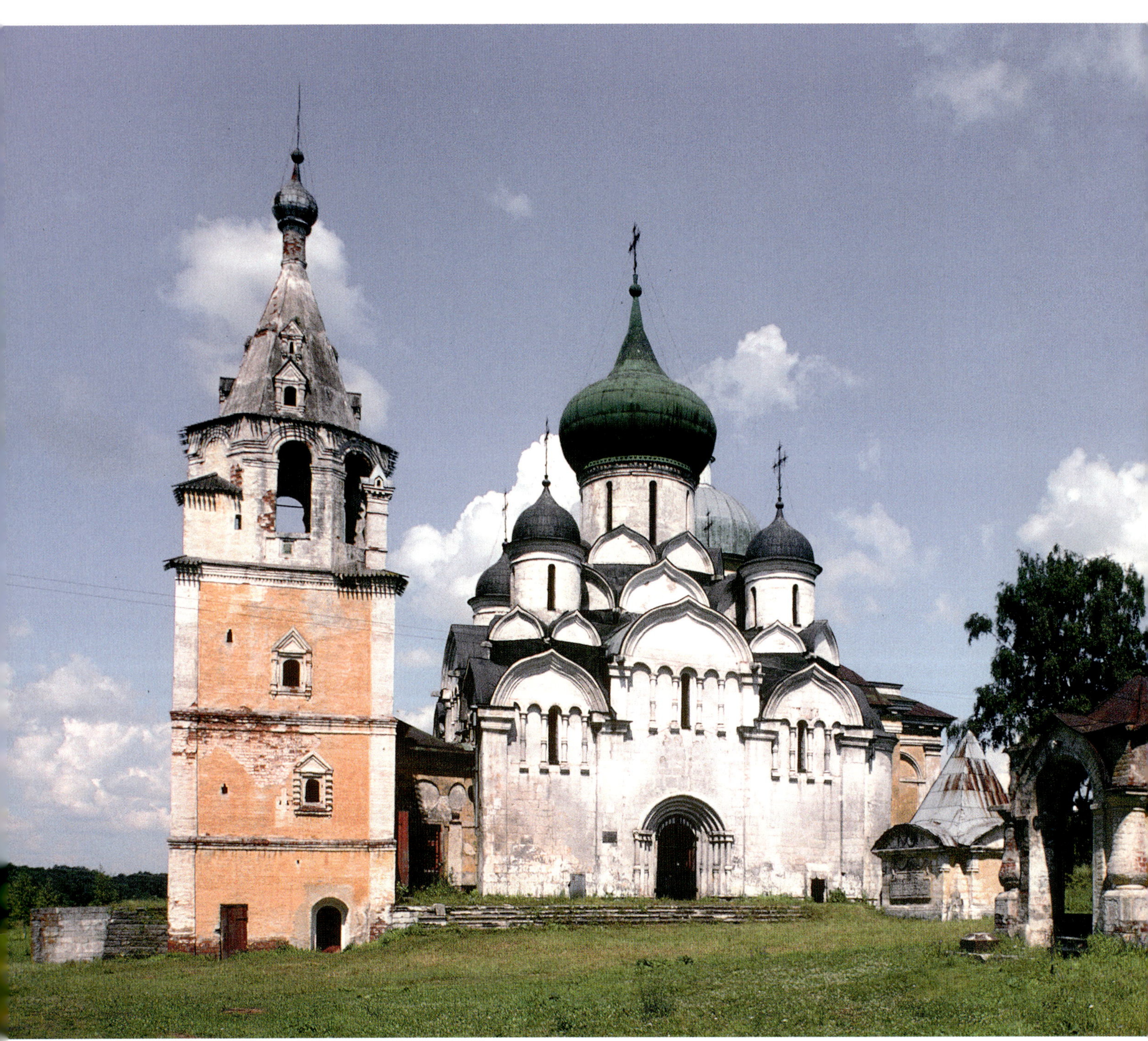

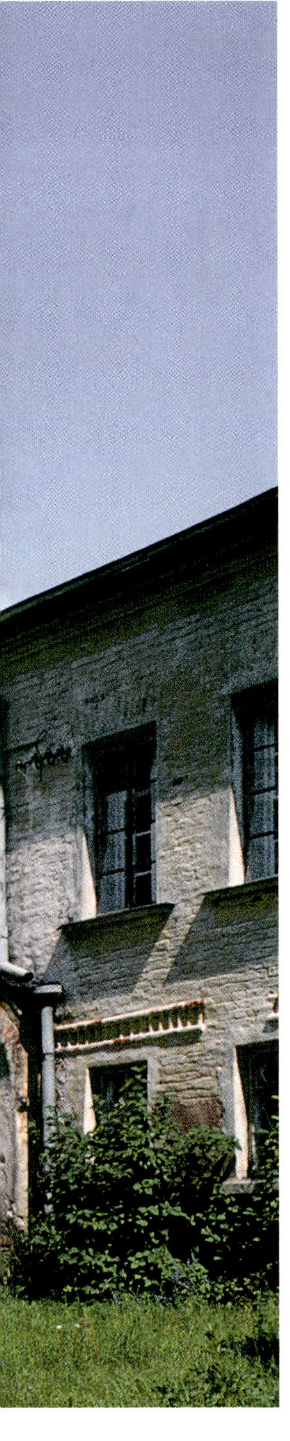

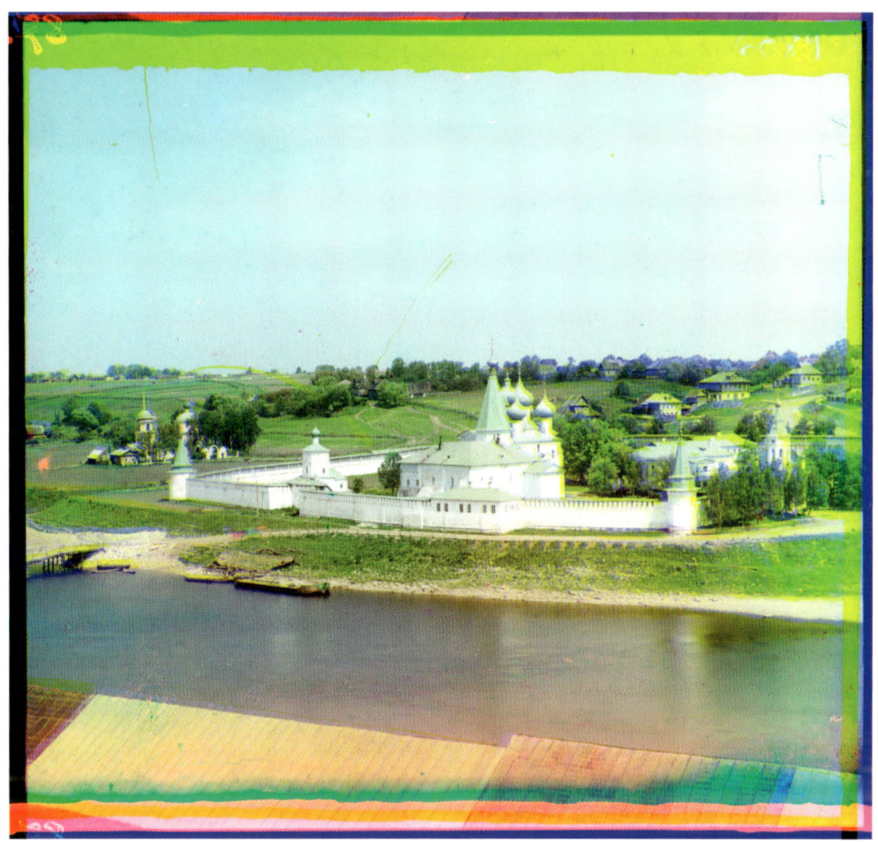

STARITSA Dormition Monastery. *From left*: bell tower, Dormition Cathedral, burial chamber of general Ivan Glebov. South view. BRUMFIELD, JULY 21, 1997.

STARITSA View northeast across Volga River with Dormition Monastery on east bank. *From left*: northwest corner tower, Church of Saint John the Divine, refectory Church of the Presentation, Dormition Cathedral, southwest corner tower, Holy Gate. PROKUDIN-GORSKY 21153. SUMMER 1910.

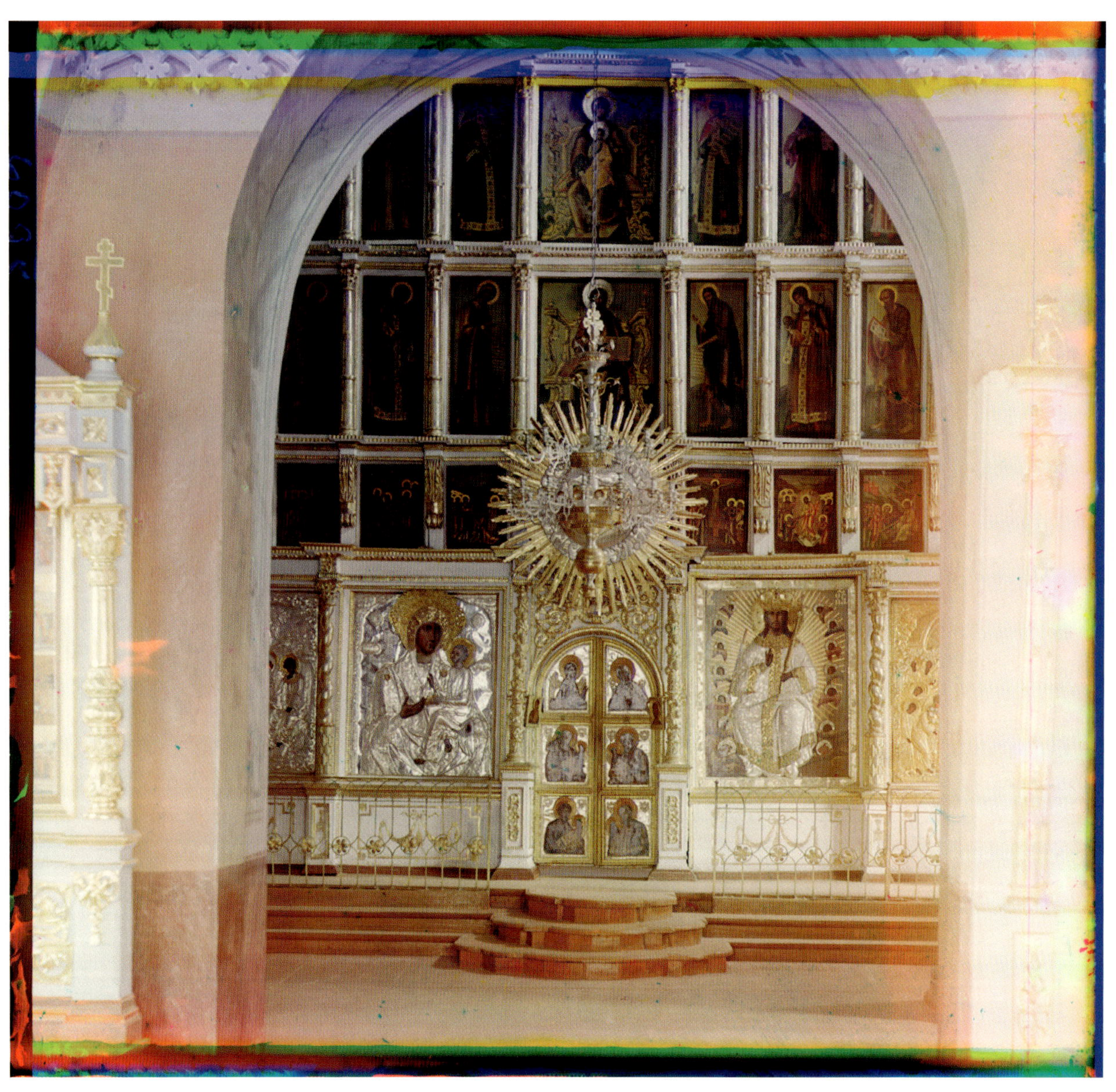

STARITSA Dormition Monastery. Dormition Cathedral. Interior, view east toward iconostasis. PROKUDIN-GORSKY 21156. SUMMER 1910.

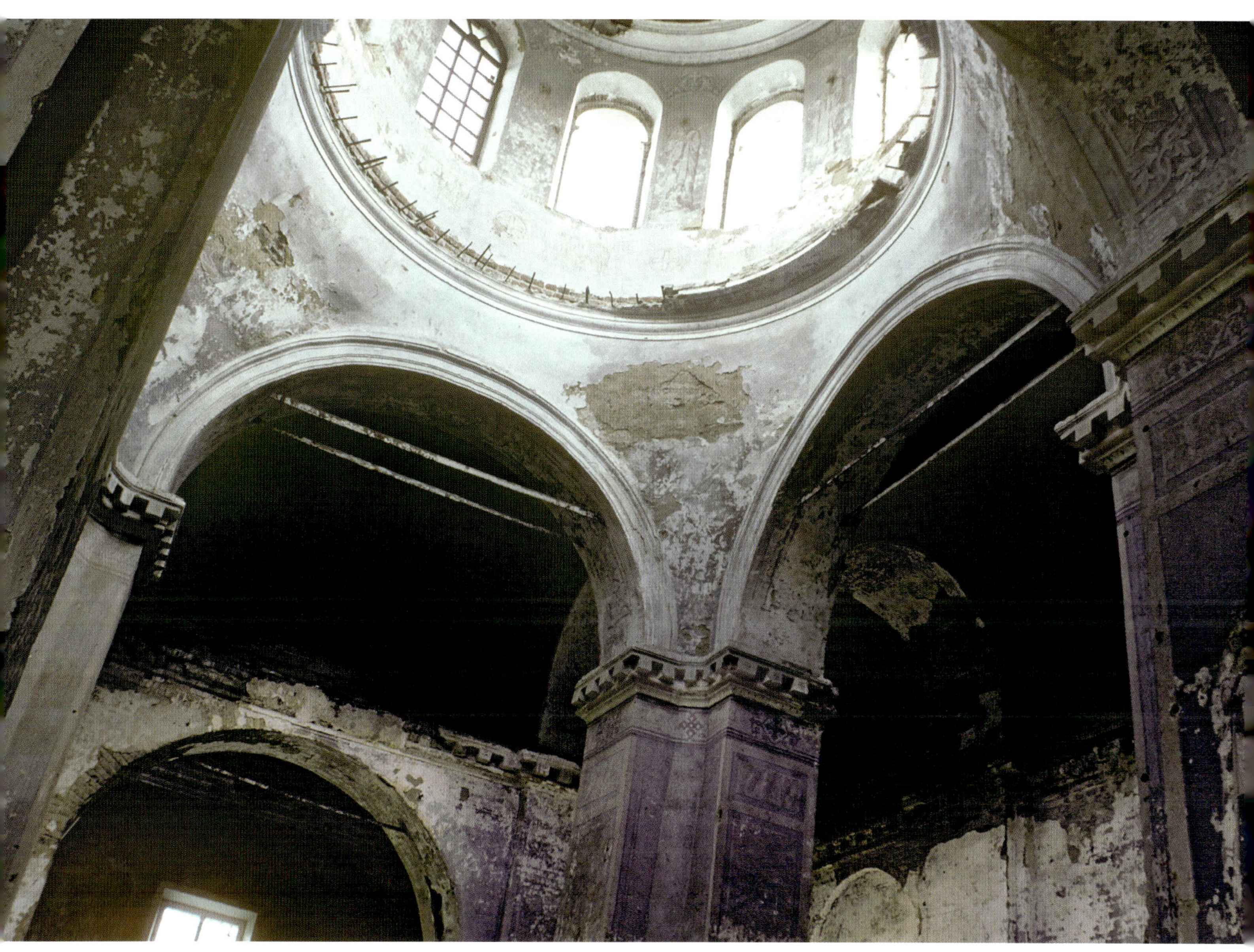

STARITSA Dormition Monastery. Dormition Cathedral. Interior, view southeast. BRUMFIELD, JULY 21, 1997.

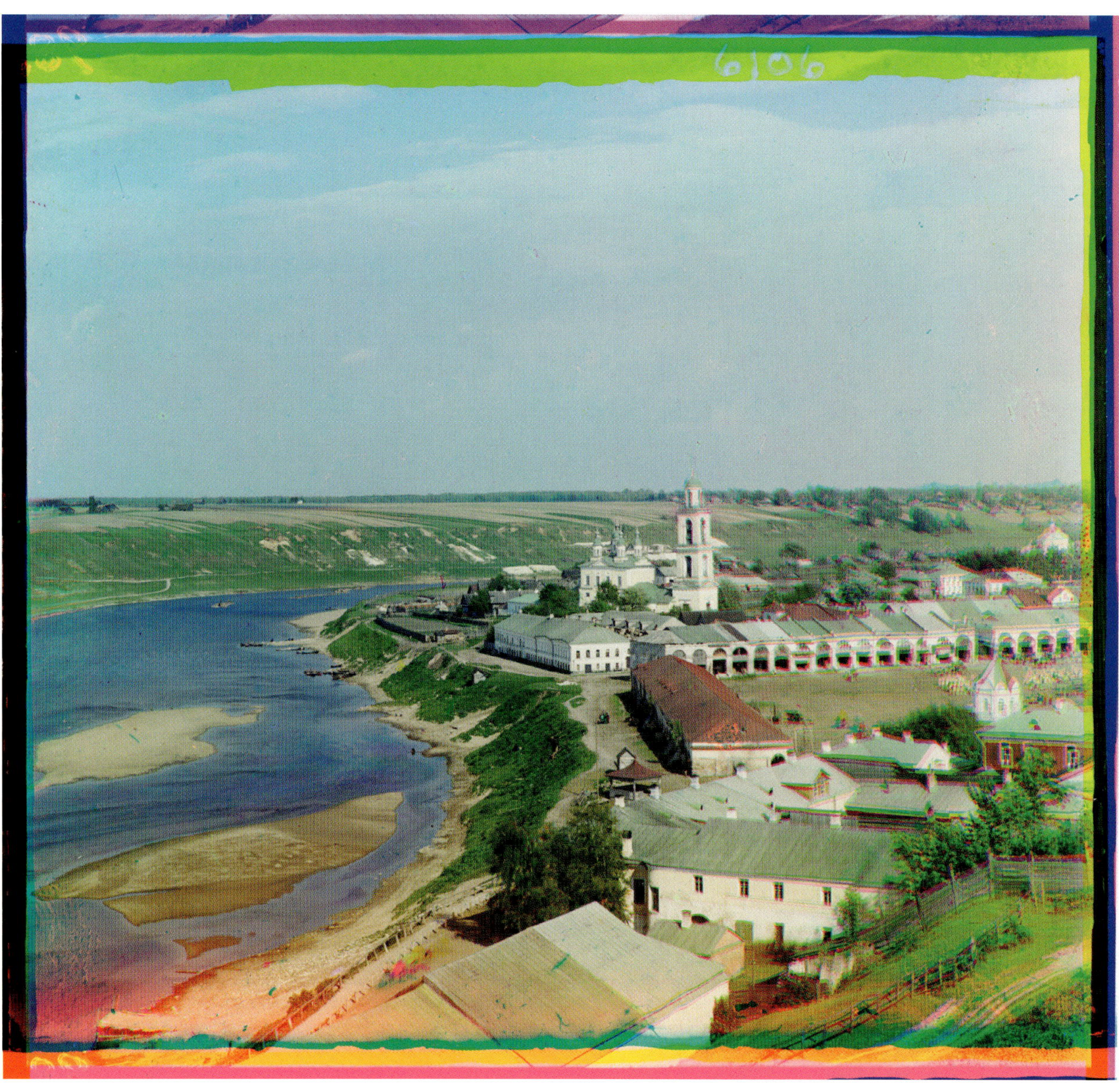

built in stages between 1784 and 1814 with the bell tower added in 1843. During the Soviet period, the church was deformed, but its core—including the bell tower—remained, as seen in a photograph from 1997. Delightfully idiosyncratic in design is the Church of the Nativity of the Virgin, also known as the Church of Saint Paraskeva from the dedication of its secondary altar. Although the surroundings have changed beyond recognition, the church has survived. Prokudin-Gorsky's distant view gives a clearer sense of those surrounding, including the massive bell tower of the Cathedral of Saints Boris and Gleb. He did not photo-

STARITSA View south up left (west) bank of Volga River, with Trading Rows and Church of the Transfiguration (Saint Nicholas). PROKUDIN-GORSKY 21164. SUMMER 1910.

STARITSA Church of the Transfiguration (Saint Nicholas) and bell tower. Northwest view. BRUMFIELD, JULY 21, 1997.

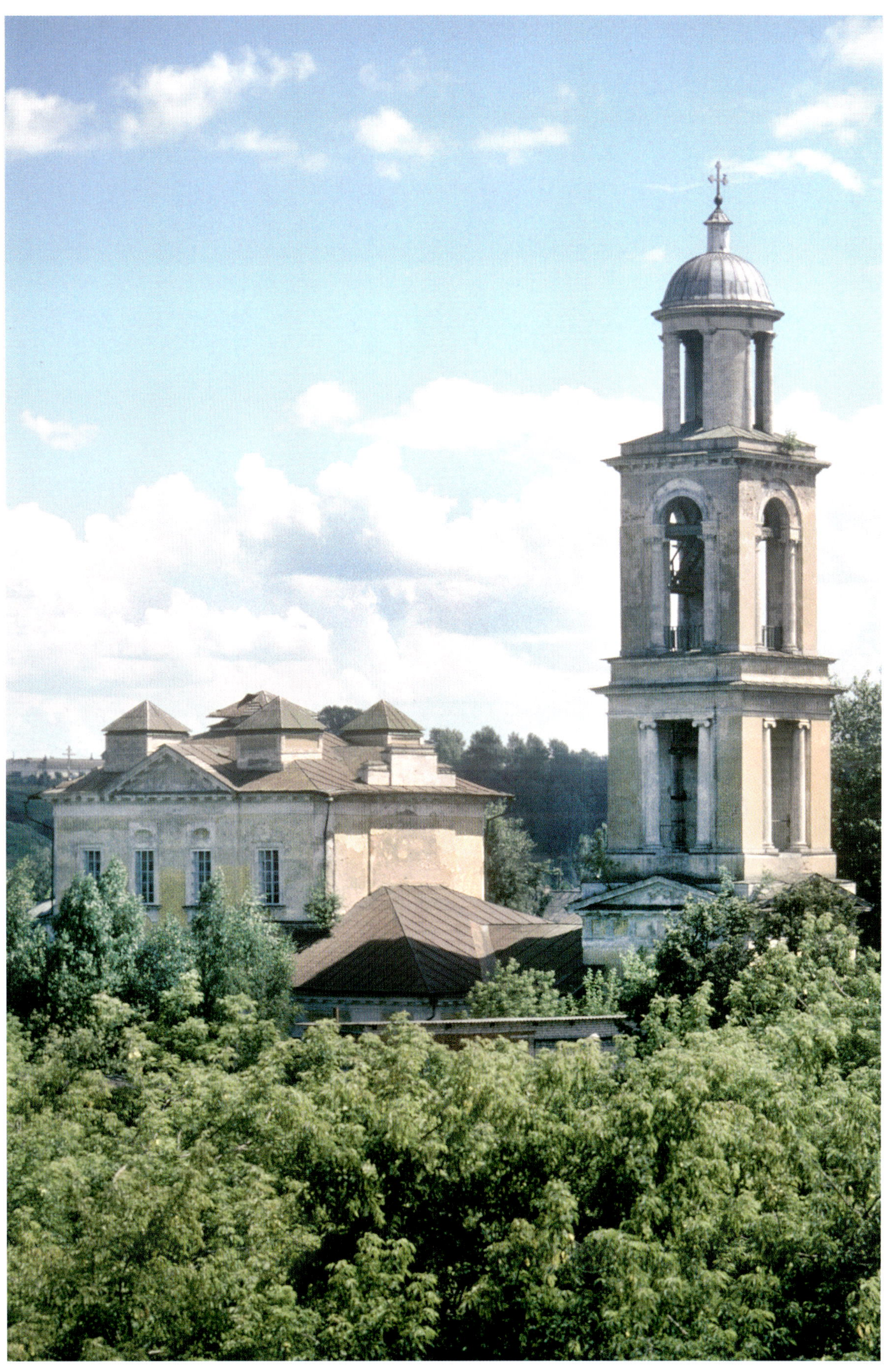

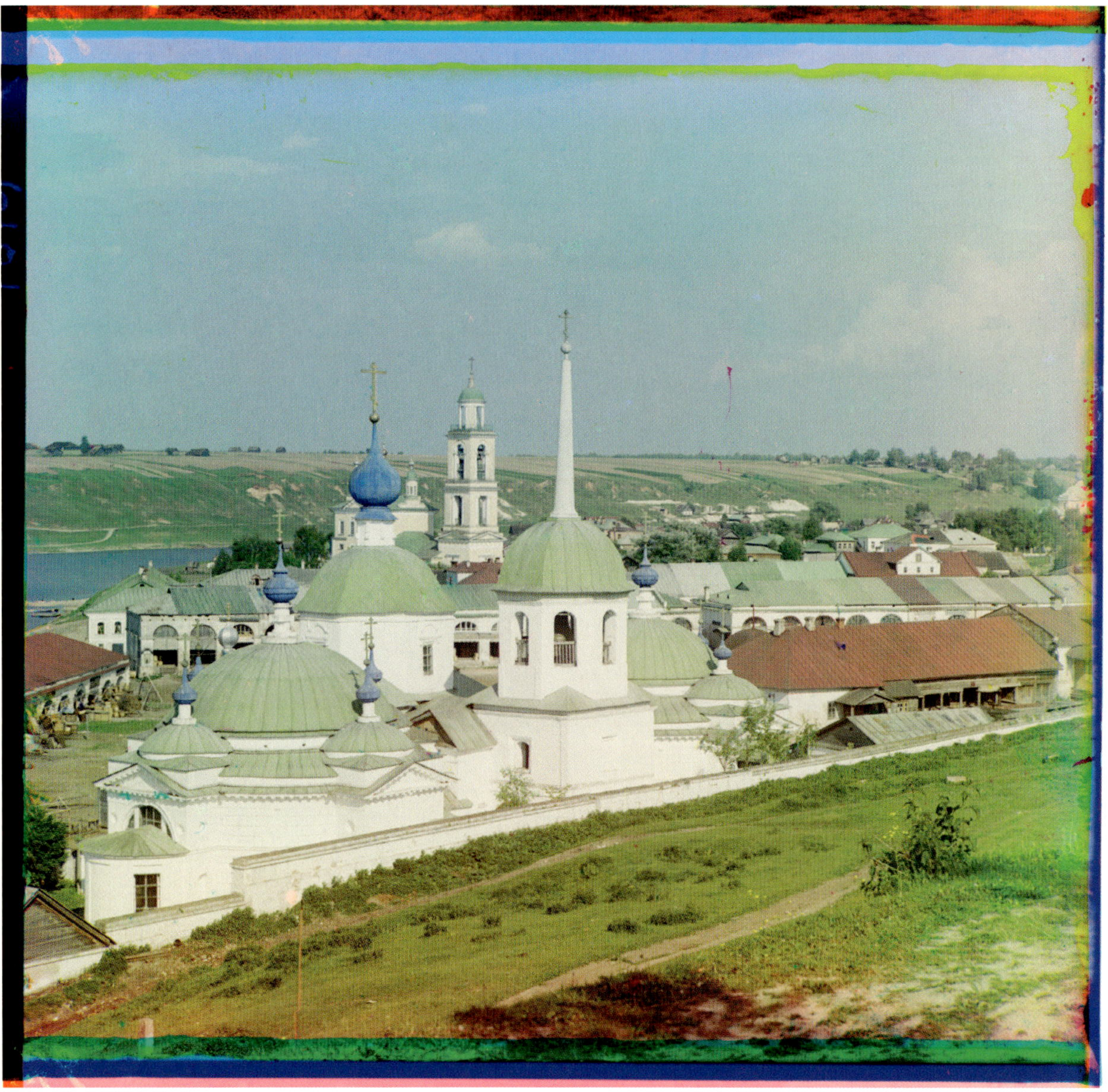

STARITSA Church of the Nativity of the Virgin (Church of Saint Paraskeva). Northwest view. PROKUDIN-GORSKY 21160. SUMMER 1910.

graph the cathedral itself, which is considered among the masterpieces of late neoclassicism. The cathedral has survived; the bell tower has not.

In the course of his journeys on the upper Volga area, Prokudin-Gorsky was particularly active in the town of Torzhok, justly renowned for its ensembles of neoclassical architecture. Its favorable location on the Tvertsa River just above its confluence with the Volga made it one of the oldest trading centers in the upper Volga region. (The name "Torzhok" derives from the word *torg*, or "trade.") The first reference to the town in writing is in 1138, but the settlement

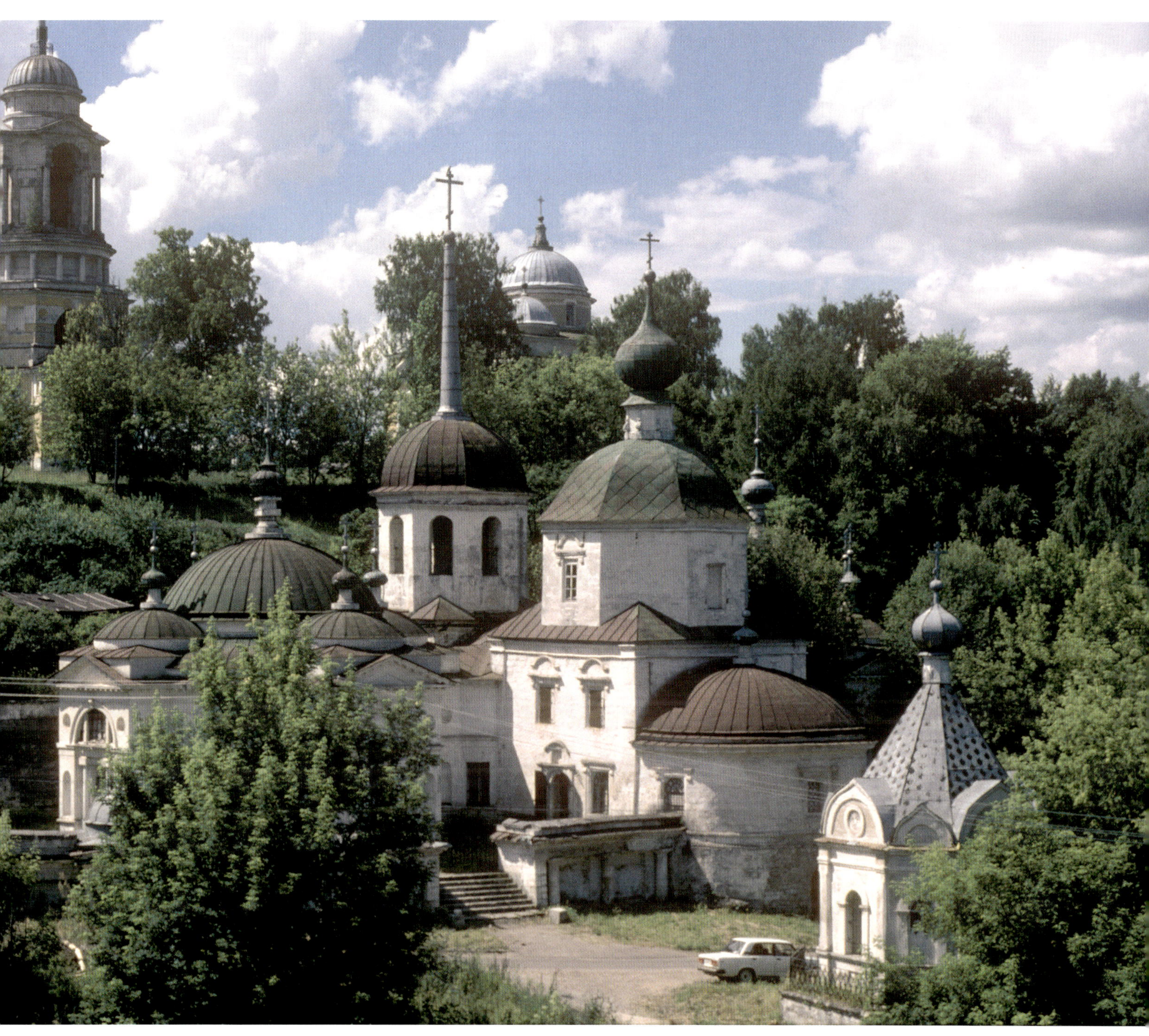

STARITSA Church of the Nativity of the Virgin
(Church of Saint Paraskeva). Southeast view.
Left: bell tower of Cathedral of Saints Boris and Gleb.
Right: Chapel of Saint Alexander Nevsky. BRUMFIELD,
JULY 21, 1997.

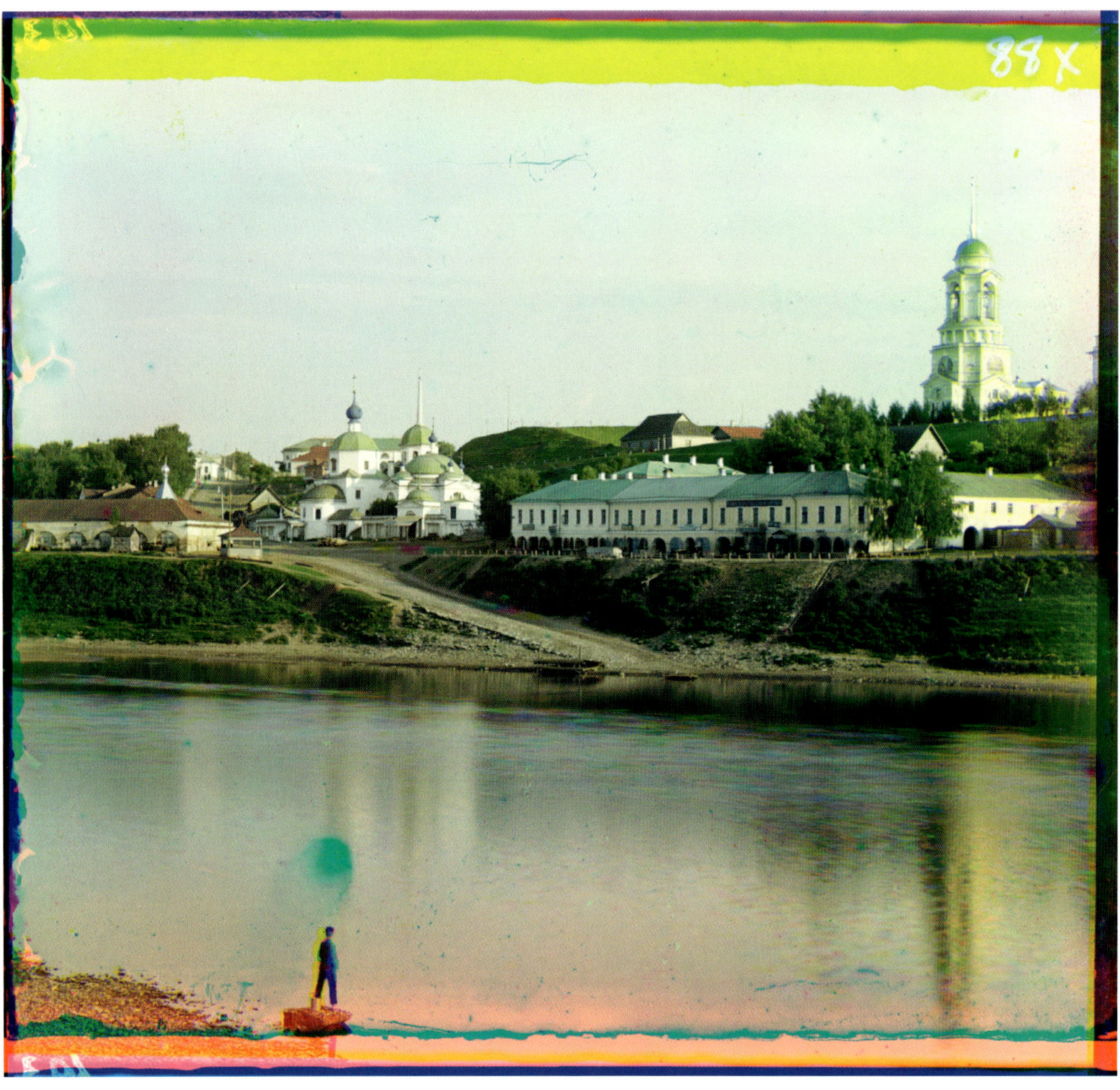

STARITSA View toward left bank of Volga from Dormition Monastery. *From left*: Trading Rows (back facade), Church of the Nativity of the Virgin (Church of Saint Paraskeva), bell tower of Cathedral of Saints Boris and Gleb. PROKUDIN-GORSKY 20070. SUMMER 1910.

may have existed as early as the tenth century. As an outpost of the medieval commercial center of Novgorod, the town was frequently contested. During the first three centuries of its recorded history, Torzhok was sacked no fewer than twenty times—usually by feuding Russian princes. The rise of Muscovite power in the fifteenth century brought an end to Novgorod's independence in the 1480s, and in 1478 Torzhok entered the domains of Moscow's ruler Ivan III (the Great).

After the founding of Saint Petersburg in 1703, Torzhok experienced a revival of its fortunes, as the town became

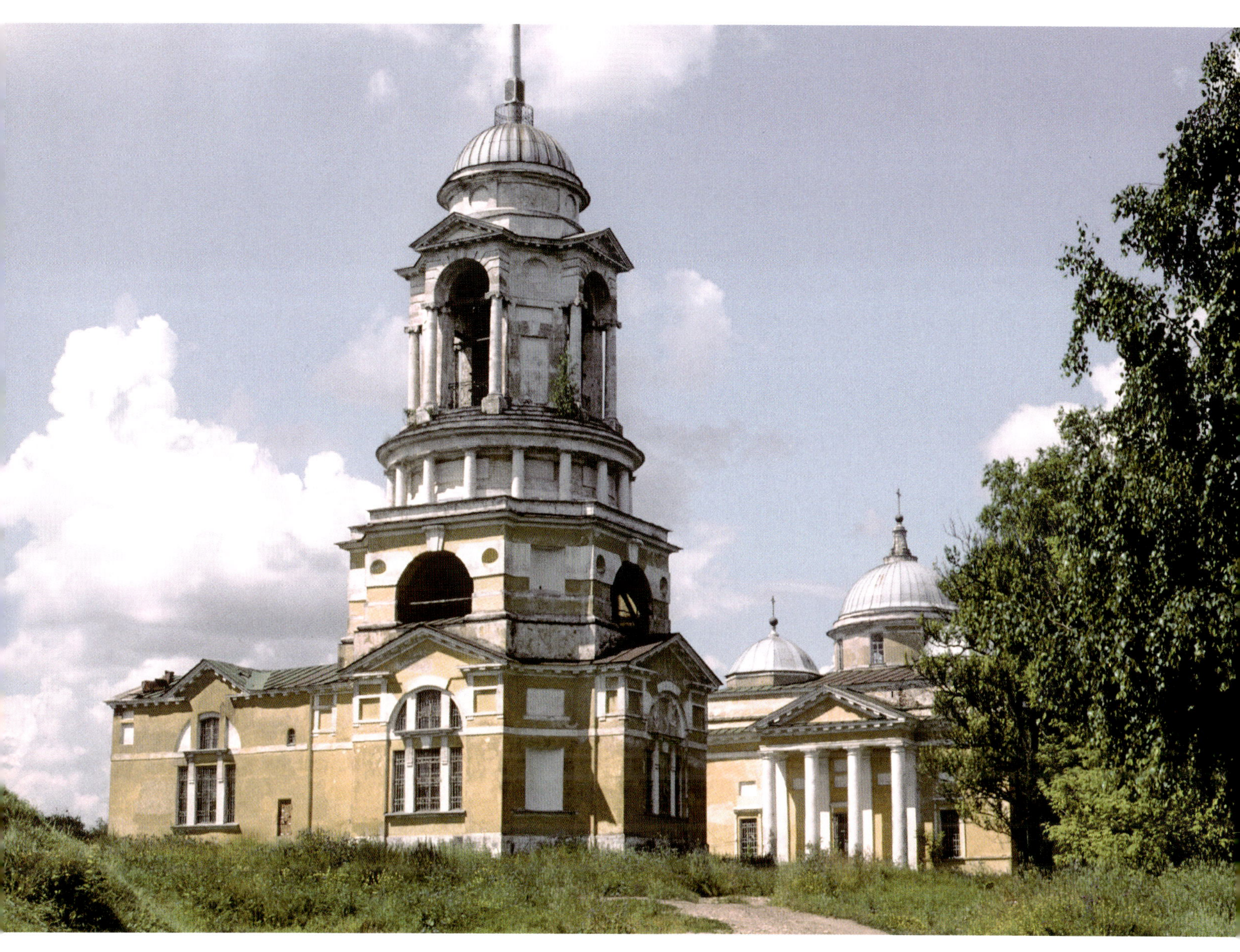

a shipment point for supplies moving to the new imperial capital. The post road between Moscow and Petersburg brought eminent visitors, including Russia's greatest writers: Alexander Pushkin, Nikolai Gogol, Ivan Turgenev, and Leo Tolstoy, and in the 1770s Catherine the Great commissioned the architect Matvei Kazakov to build a small "Transit Palace." Like many regional centers, Torzhok was rebuilt in the late eighteenth century, when Catherine the Great undertook the transformation of Russian provincial life by bringing order into city plans. Torzhok benefited from these ideas of classical harmony with the design of a

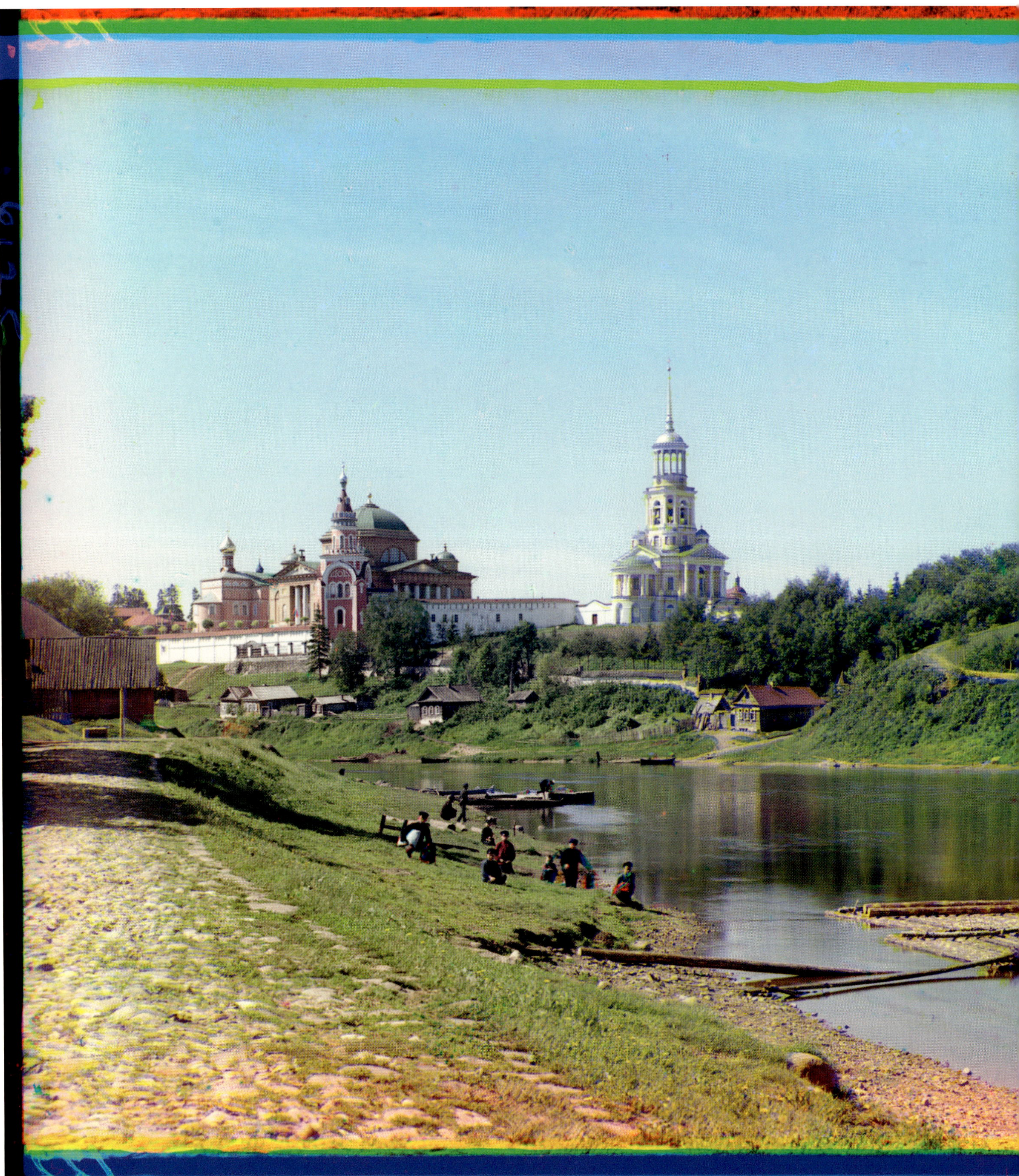

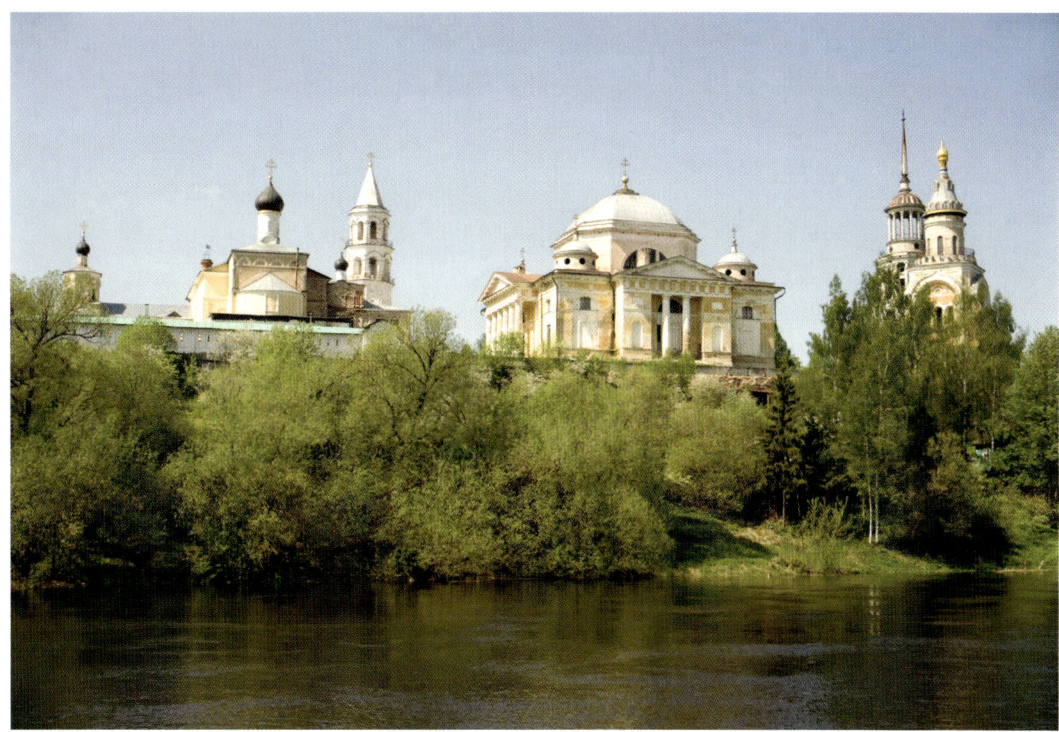

TORZHOK Monastery of Saints Boris and Gleb. Northeast view from left bank of Tvertsa River. *From left*: Church of the Presentation, Cathedral of Saints Boris and Gleb, "Candle" (northeast) Tower, Holy Gate with bell tower and Church of Miraculous Icon of the Savior. PROKUDIN-GORSKY 21181. SUMMER 1910.

TORZHOK Monastery of Saints Boris and Gleb. East view from left bank of Tvertsa River. *From left*: Church of the Entry into Jerusalem, Church of the Presentation and bell tower, Cathedral of Saints Boris and Gleb, Church of Miraculous Icon of the Savior and bell tower over Holy Gate, "Candle" (northeast) Tower. BRUMFIELD, MAY 14, 2010.

new central square and arcaded market buildings. In addition, the town's prosperous residents rebuilt their houses according to model neoclassical designs that contribute to the attractive ambience of Torzhok.

The dominant feature in the landscape of Torzhok is the Monastery of Saints Boris and Gleb, reputed to have been founded in 1083 and dedicated to the earliest martyrs of the Russian Orthodox Church. Originally built of logs, the monastery was gradually rebuilt in brick during the seventeenth century. In 1785 work began on a new Cathedral of Saints Boris and Gleb, designed by Nikolai Lvov and considered one of the greatest monuments of Russian neoclassicism. Prokudin-Gorsky photographed the monastery from various perspectives in relation to the Tvertsa River, including an evocative distant view. From my numerous photographs of the monastery, I have chosen a view directly across the Tvertsa with the monastery rising in all its splendor. Prokudin-Gorsky's closer view illuminates the central cathedral ensemble. My closer perspective shows the ensemble rising from fresh spring foliage. None of these photographs, however, reveals the ruination of the church

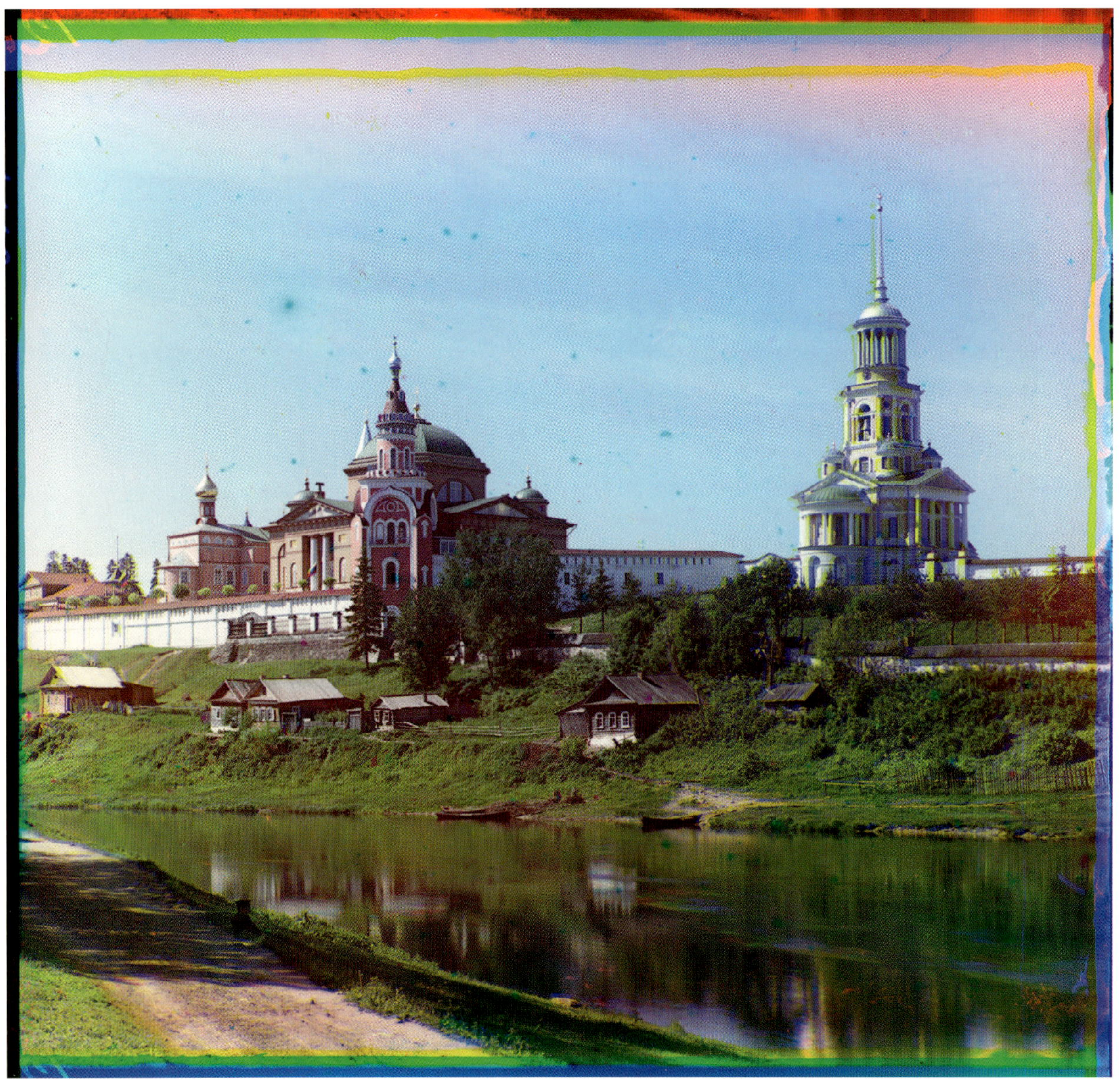

interiors through the Soviet decades, when the monastery was, among other things, used as a prison.

The monastery's most visible landmark is the high bell tower above the Church of the Mandylian Icon of the Savior, attributed at least in part to Nikolai Lvov and constructed in 1804–11 over the Holy Gate (main entrance). Prokudin-Gorsky captured the immediate surroundings with impressive clarity, although the upper part of the spire extended beyond the range of his lens. Although the basic structure has survived, my photographs show widespread degradation of the exterior.

TORZHOK Monastery of Saints Boris and Gleb. Northeast view from left bank of Tvertsa River. *From left*: Church of the Presentation, Cathedral of Saints Boris and Gleb, "Candle" (northeast) Tower, Holy Gate with bell tower and Church of Miraculous Icon of the Savior. PROKUDIN-GORSKY 21168. SUMMER 1910.

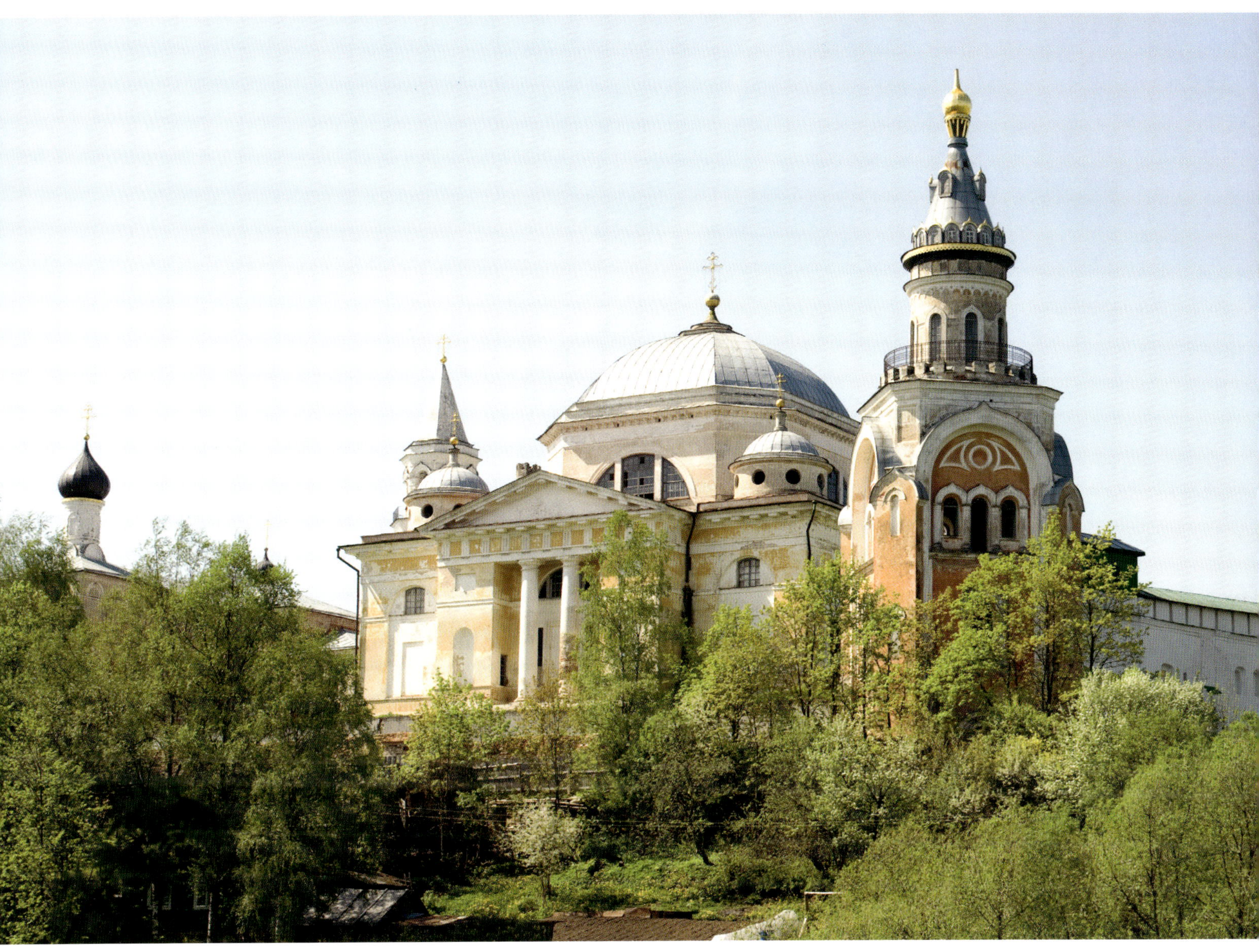

The architectural transformation of Torzhok in the early nineteenth century was accompanied by the construction of new churches in the neoclassical style. In 1815–22 Torzhok's major cathedral, the Transfiguration of the Savior, was rebuilt to a plan by the eminent architect Carlo Rossi. Some two decades later the Transfiguration Cathedral was joined by a late neoclassical structure, the Cathedral of the Entry into Jerusalem, built in 1841–42 to a design by Ivan Lvov, architect of Tver Province (no relation to the architect Nikolai Lvov). Prokudin-Gorsky photographed the ensemble of both churches in brilliant light from the opposite

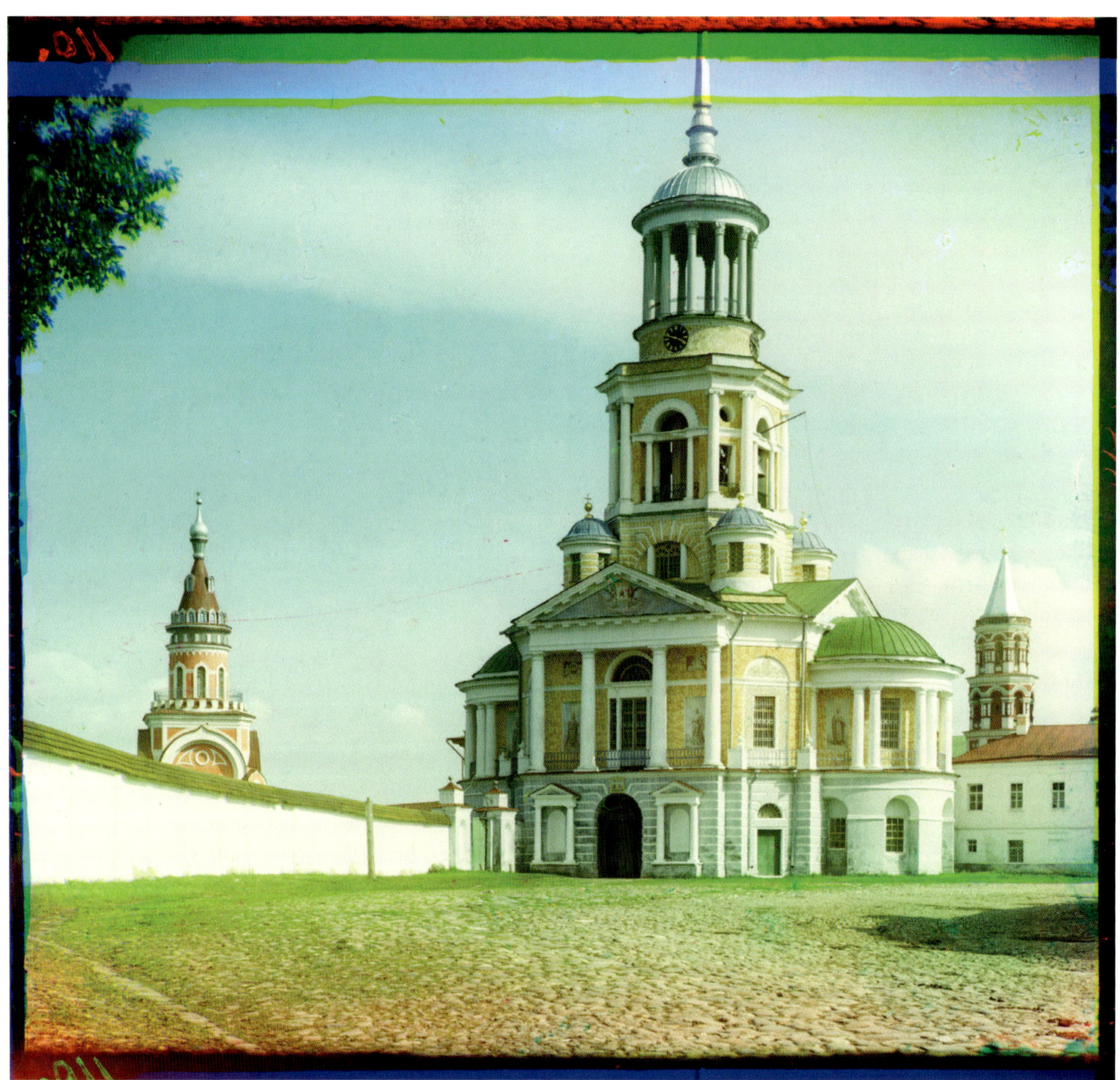

TORZHOK Monastery of Saints Boris and Gleb. Holy Gate with bell tower and Church of Miraculous Icon of the Savior. Northwest view. *Left*: "Candle" Tower. PROKUDIN-GORSKY 21174. SUMMER 1910.

TORZHOK Monastery of Saints Boris and Gleb. Holy Gate with bell tower and Church of Miraculous Icon of the Savior. Southeast view. BRUMFIELD, MAY 14, 2010.

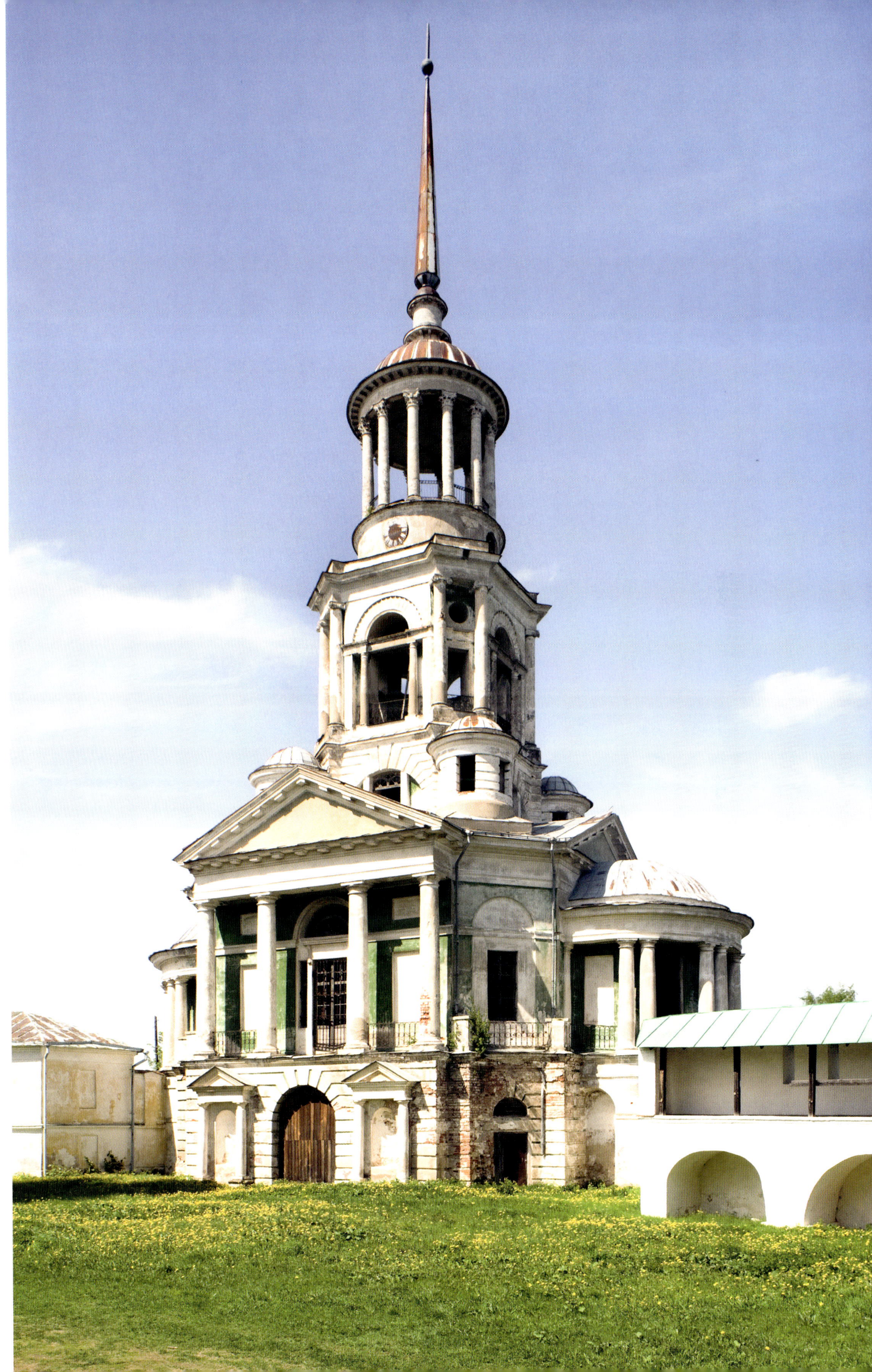

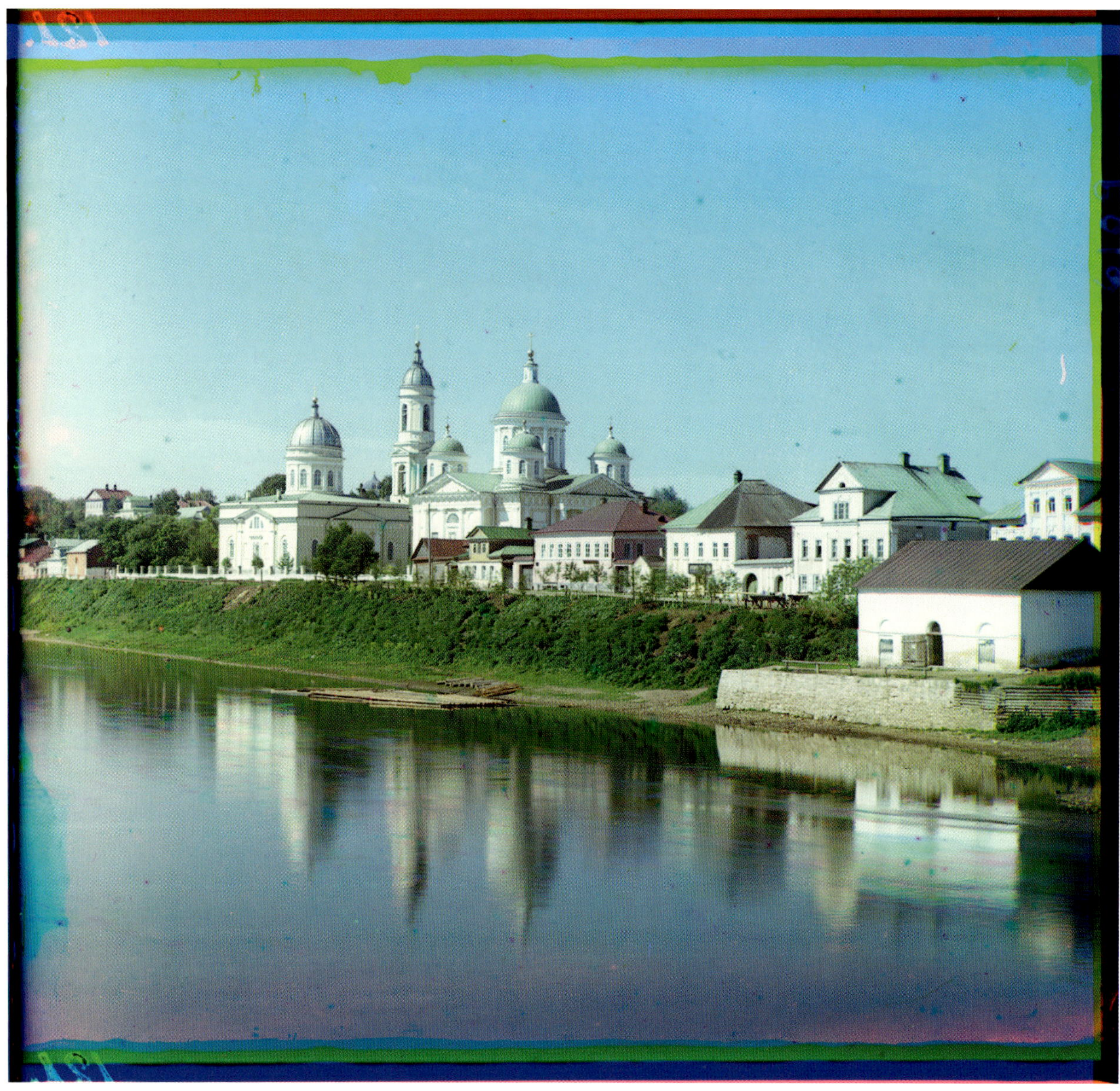

(left) bank of the Tvertsa, thus giving his camera the proper
space for rendering the east facades of the large structures.
Recent photographs from a similar perspective show damage to the exterior. Little remains of the original interiors.

Neoclassical parish churches on the right bank appear
distantly in Prokudin-Gorsky's other photographs. The incursion of mid-nineteenth-century eclecticism is evident in
the Church of the Annunciation, also known as Archangel
Michael, constructed of brick in 1758 and rebuilt in 1864,
with a bell tower added in 1887. Its elevated location near

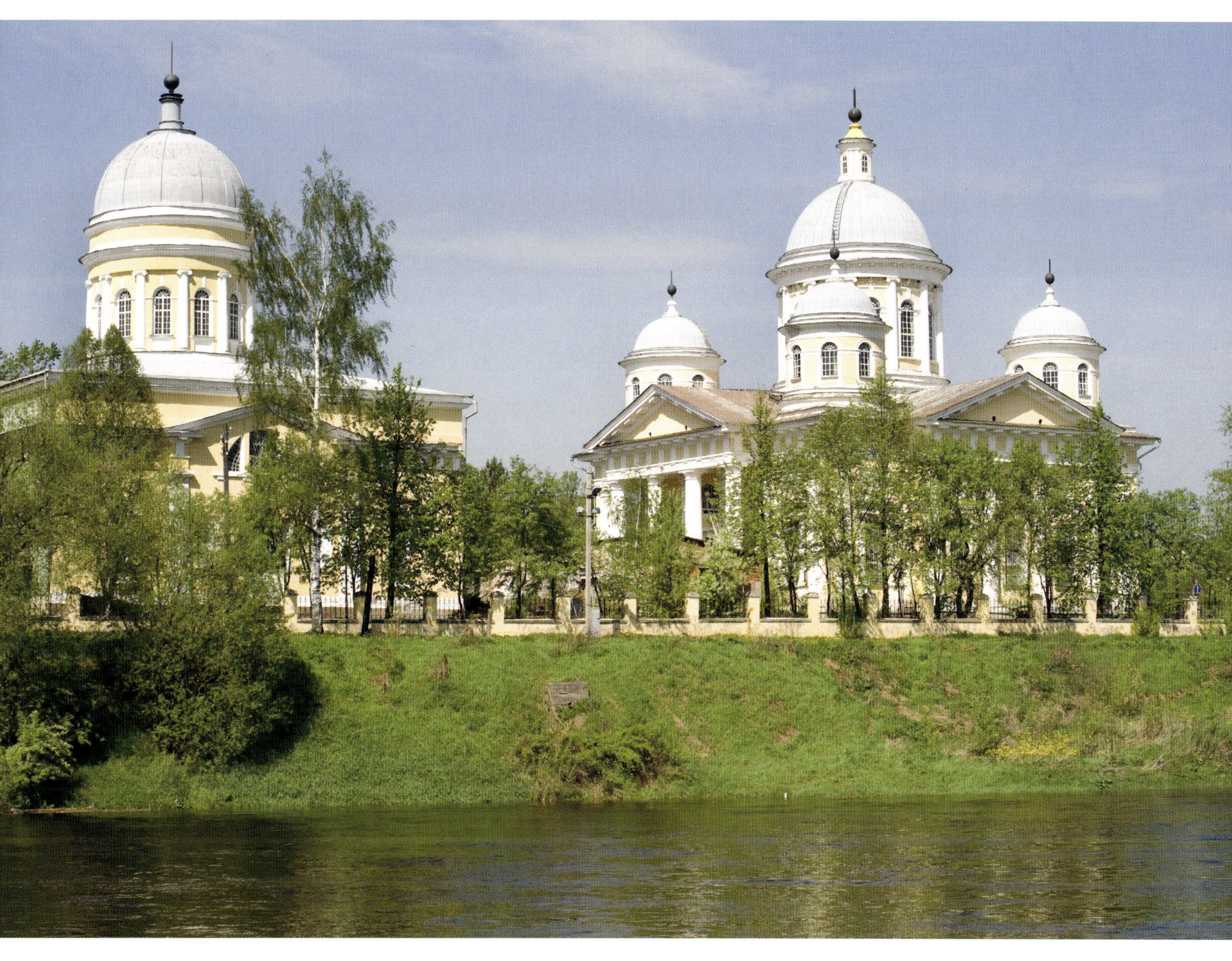

the Monastery of Saints Boris and Gleb make it one of the
most visible of the town's parish churches.

On the opposite (left) bank of the Tvertsa, the primary
ensemble was the Resurrection Convent, whose monumental rotunda Church of the Decapitation of John the Baptist, built in 1833–40 to a design by Ivan Lvov, is an impressive work of Roman-style late neoclassicism in Russia.
Prokudin-Gorsky's beautifully illuminated view from the
right bank across the river reveals the dominant position
of this church, while including the merchant houses along

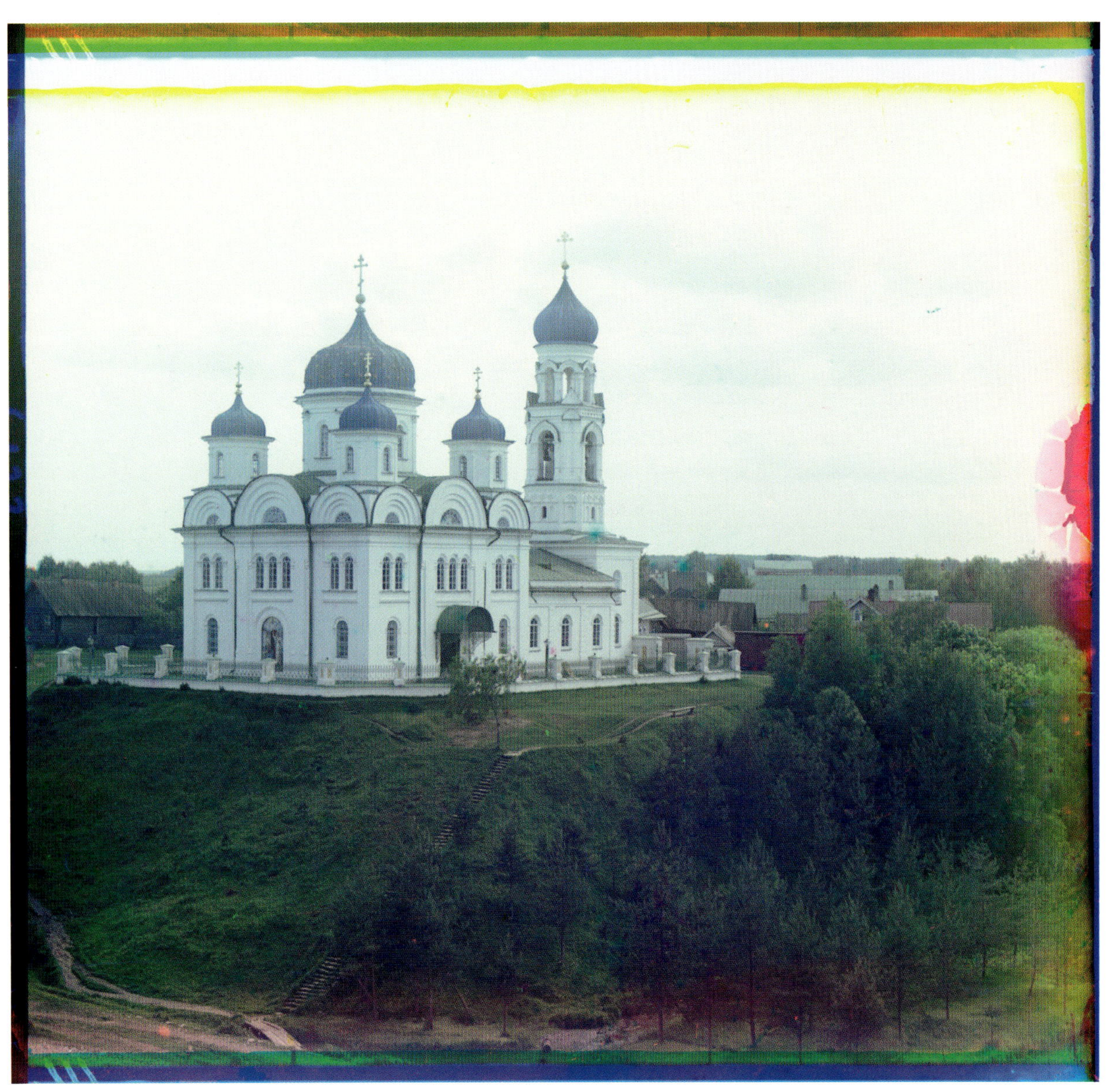

TORZHOK Church of the Annunciation (Archangel
Michael). Northeast view. PROKUDIN-GORSKY 21179.
SUMMER 1910.

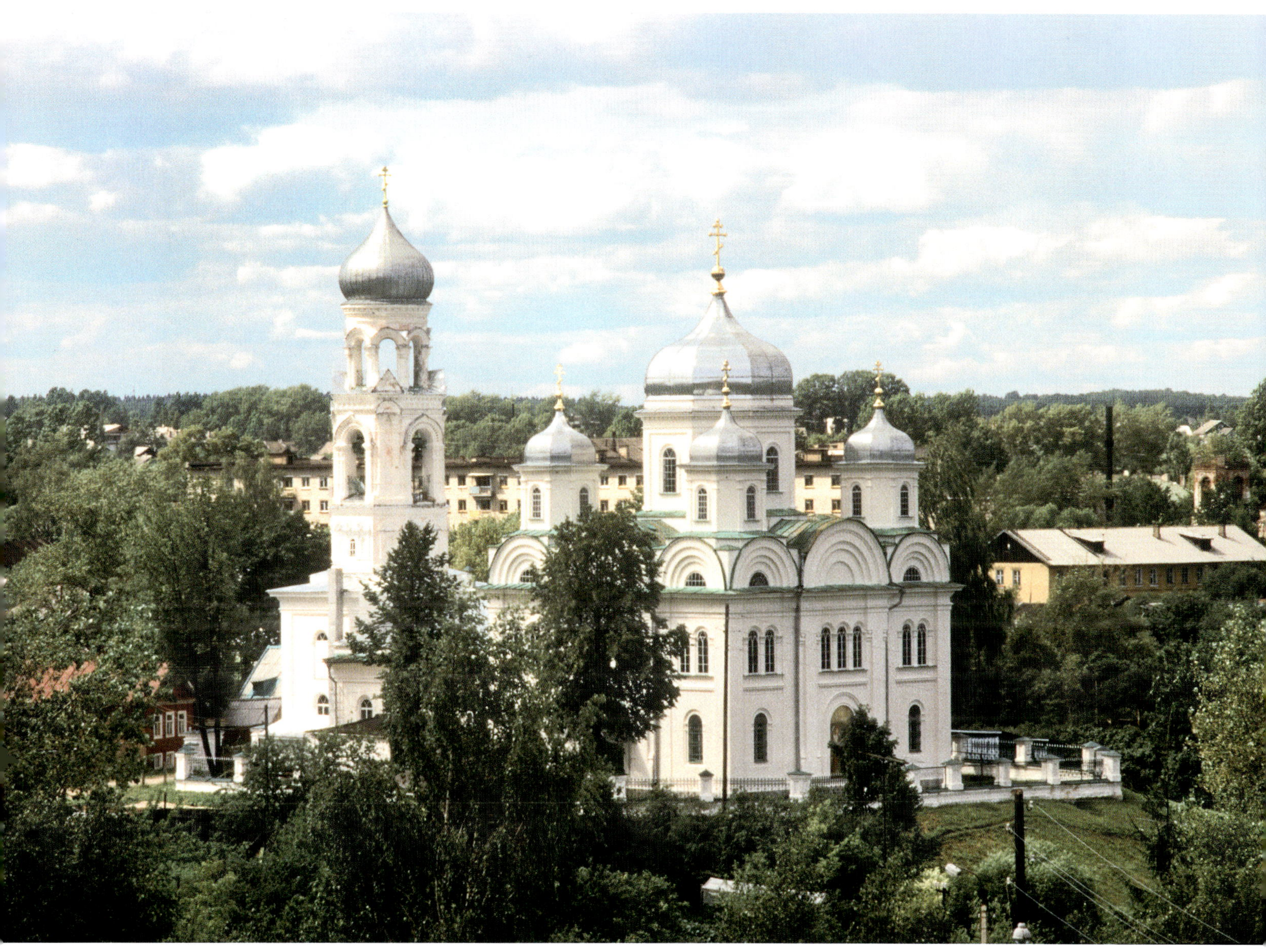

TORZHOK Church of the Annunciation (Archangel
Michael). Southeast view from Monastery of Saints
Boris and Gleb. BRUMFIELD, JULY 3, 1995.

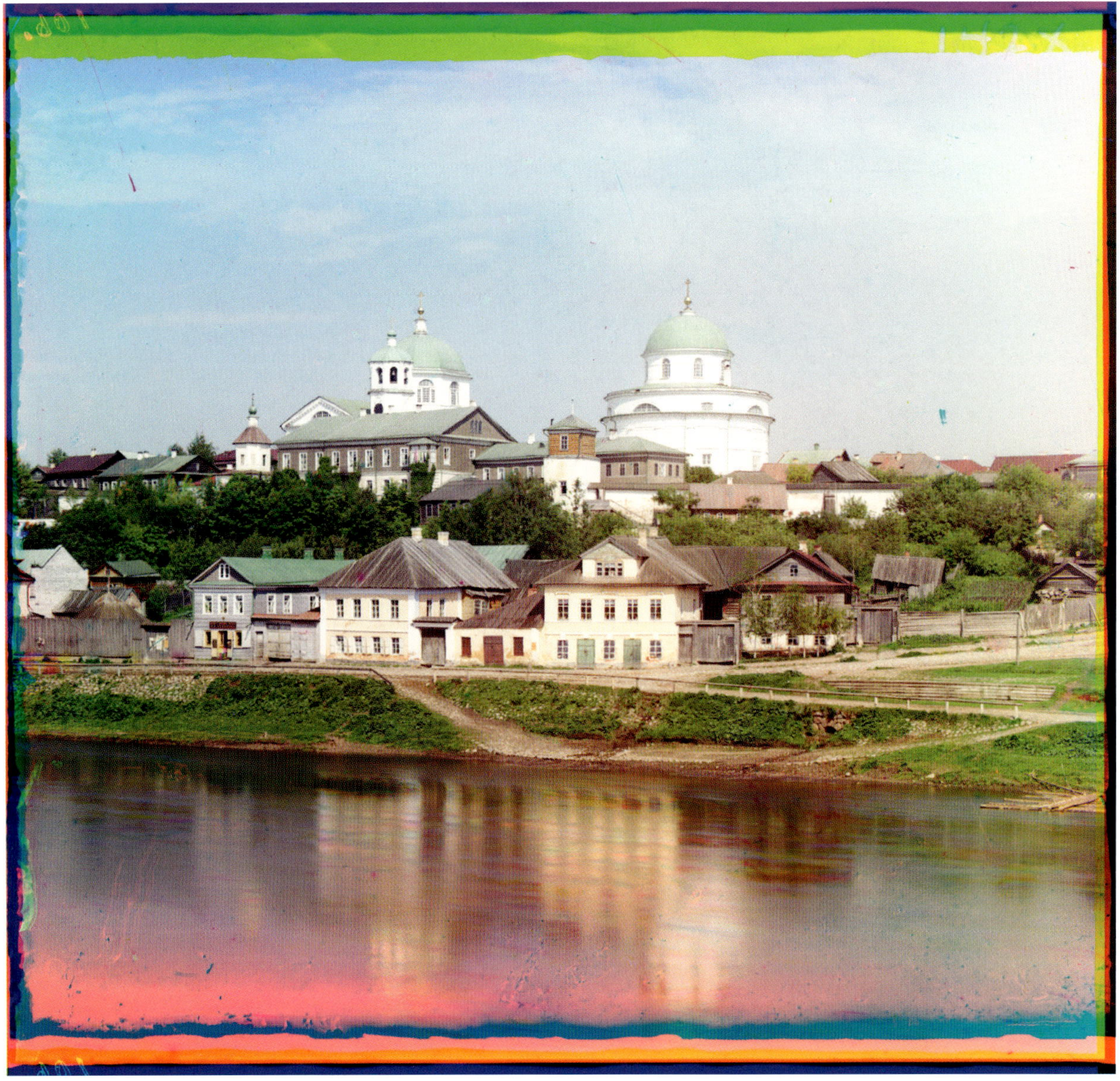

the embankment below. Closed in the early 1920s, the convent was used to house facilities for a sewing factory. My photographs of the convent show deterioration resulting from decades of neglect. For comparison with the Prokudin-Gorsky photograph, I have chosen a broad perspective to the north that includes both sides of the Tvertsa before a thunderstorm.

By the time Prokudin-Gorsky visited Torzhok, it was an important grain center of some thirteen thousand souls, with flour mills and eight tanneries. Its most famous product was an intricate form of embroidery that included decorative patterns in gold and silver thread. In view of the destructive events that swept through Torzhok in the twentieth century (including its position on the front line in the fall of 1941), it is remarkable that the town has an

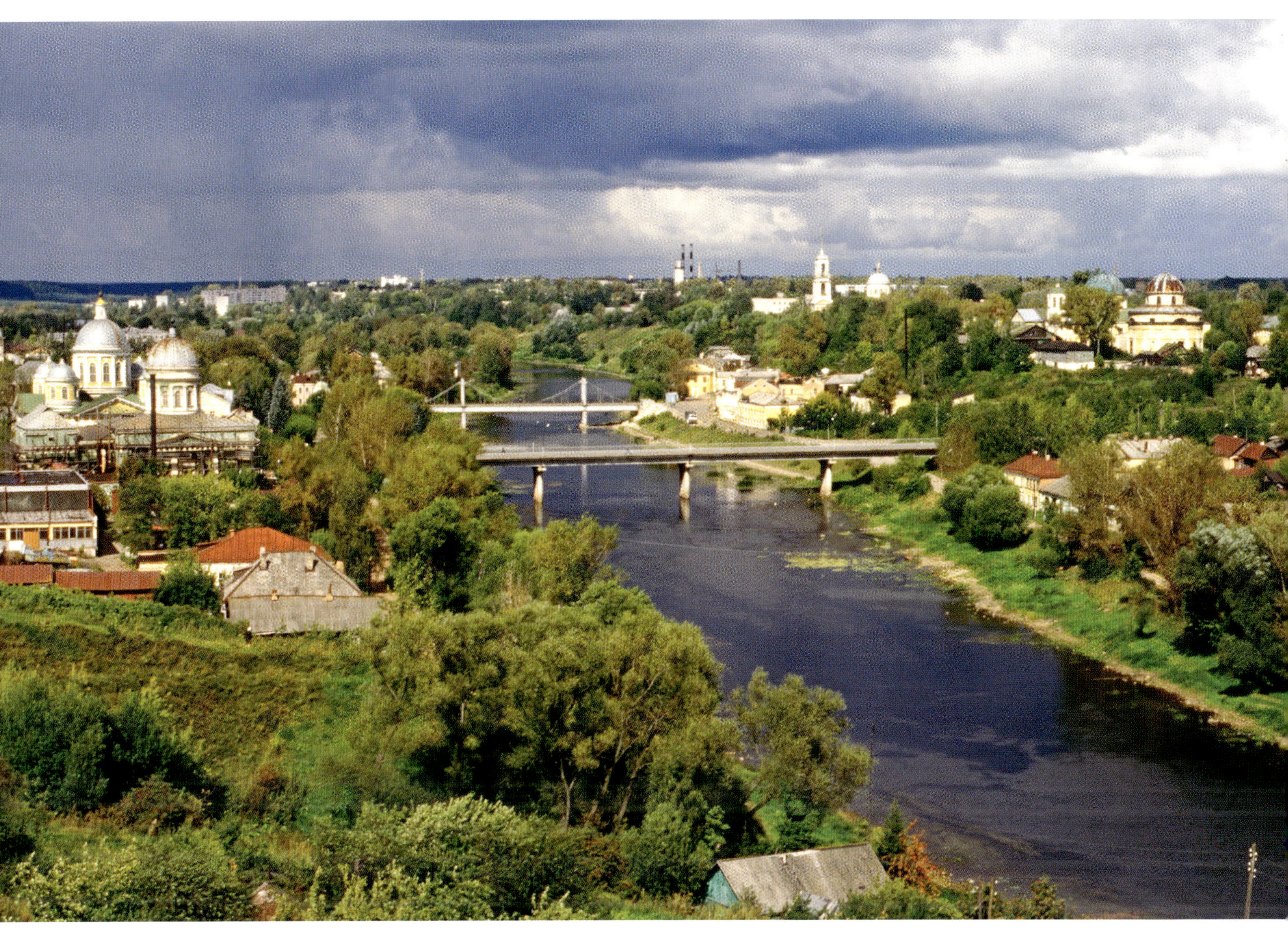

TORZHOK Resurrection Convent with houses along left bank. Southwest view from right bank of Tvertsa River. PROKUDIN-GORSKY 20122. SUMMER 1910.

TORZHOK View north up Tvertsa River from bell tower of Monastery of Saints Boris and Gleb. *From left*: Church of Saint Clement, Cathedral of the Transfiguration, Church of the Entry into Jerusalem, houses and shops on left bank of Tvertsa, Church of Elijah the Prophet, Resurrection Convent. BRUMFIELD, AUGUST 13, 1995.

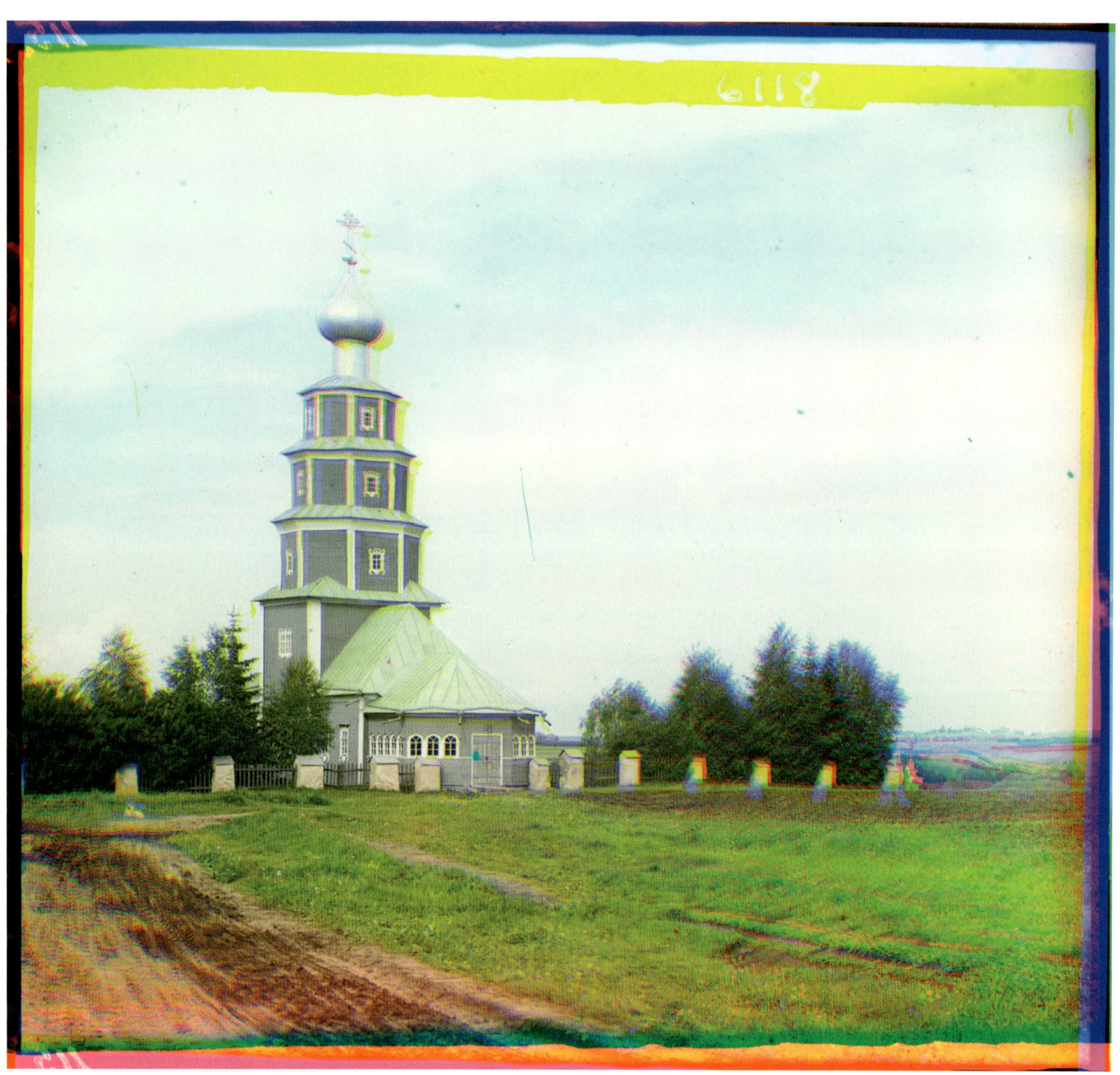

TORZHOK Church of the Tikhvin Icon of the Virgin (Old Church of the Ascension). Northwest view.
PROKUDIN-GORSKY 21175. SUMMER 1910.

TORZHOK Wooden Church of the Tikhvin Icon of the Virgin (Old Church of the Ascension). Southwest view.
BRUMFIELD, AUGUST 13, 1995.

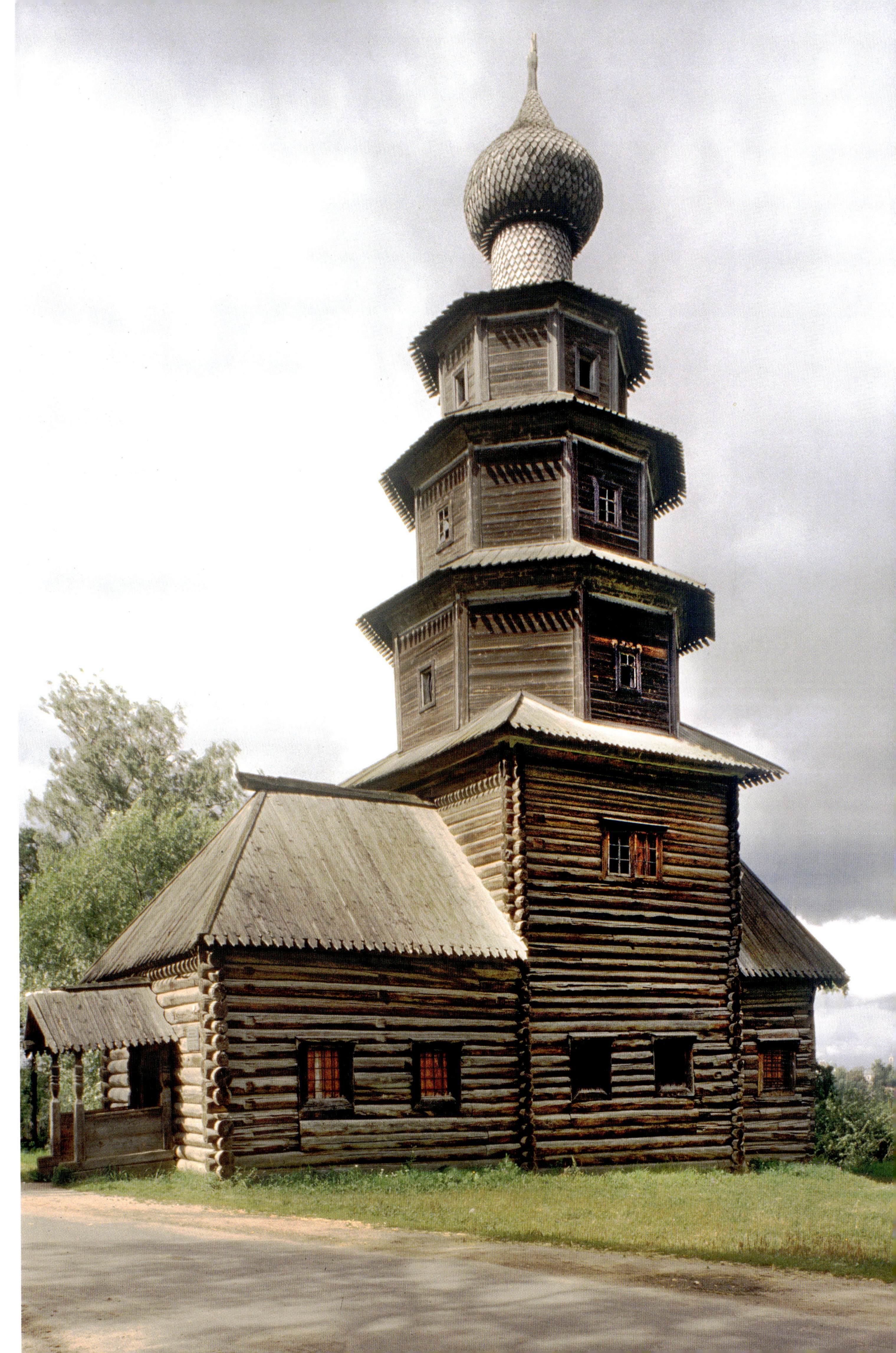

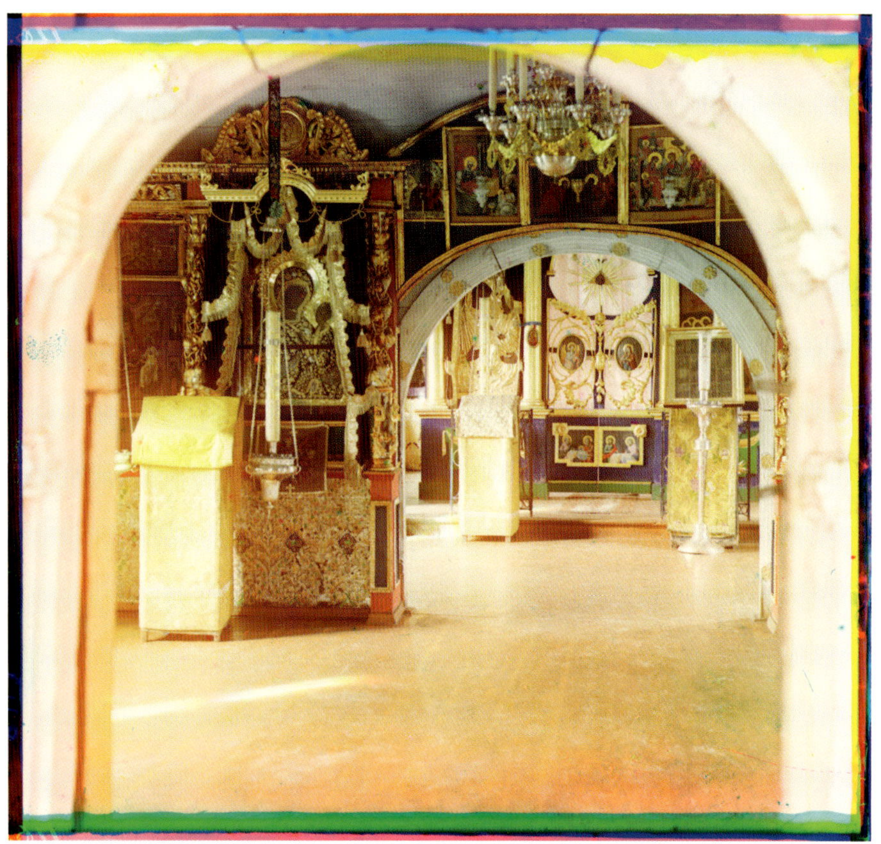

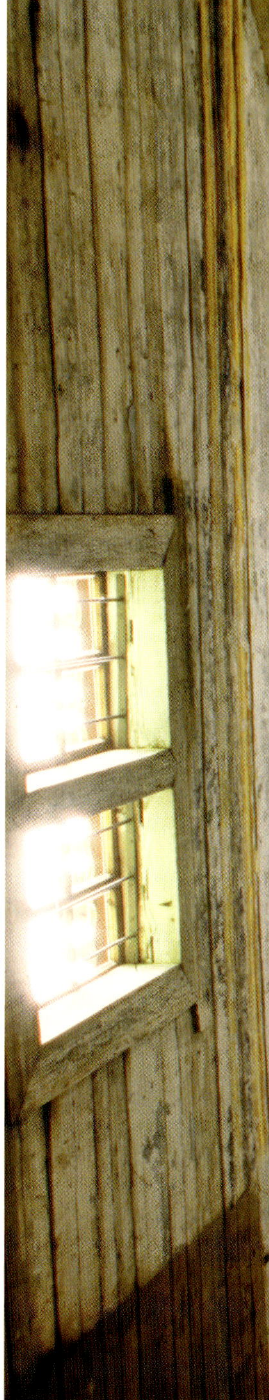

extraordinary example of wooden church architecture. Frequently repaired since its construction in the mid-seventeenth century, the log Church of the Ascension is a gravity-defying tower of ascending octagons overlooking the steep bank of the Tvertsa River. Prokudin-Gorsky's photograph, taken from the northwest, shows an attached vestibule leading to a later semicircular structure that served as an exonarthex. Photographs from 1995 and later show unobstructed views of the monument. For the past several years this distinctive form has been obscured by scaffolding in a prolonged restoration effort. Prokudin-Gorsky also photographed the interior, little of which now remains. My photographs from 2006 show painted decorative motifs on the upper part of the interior.

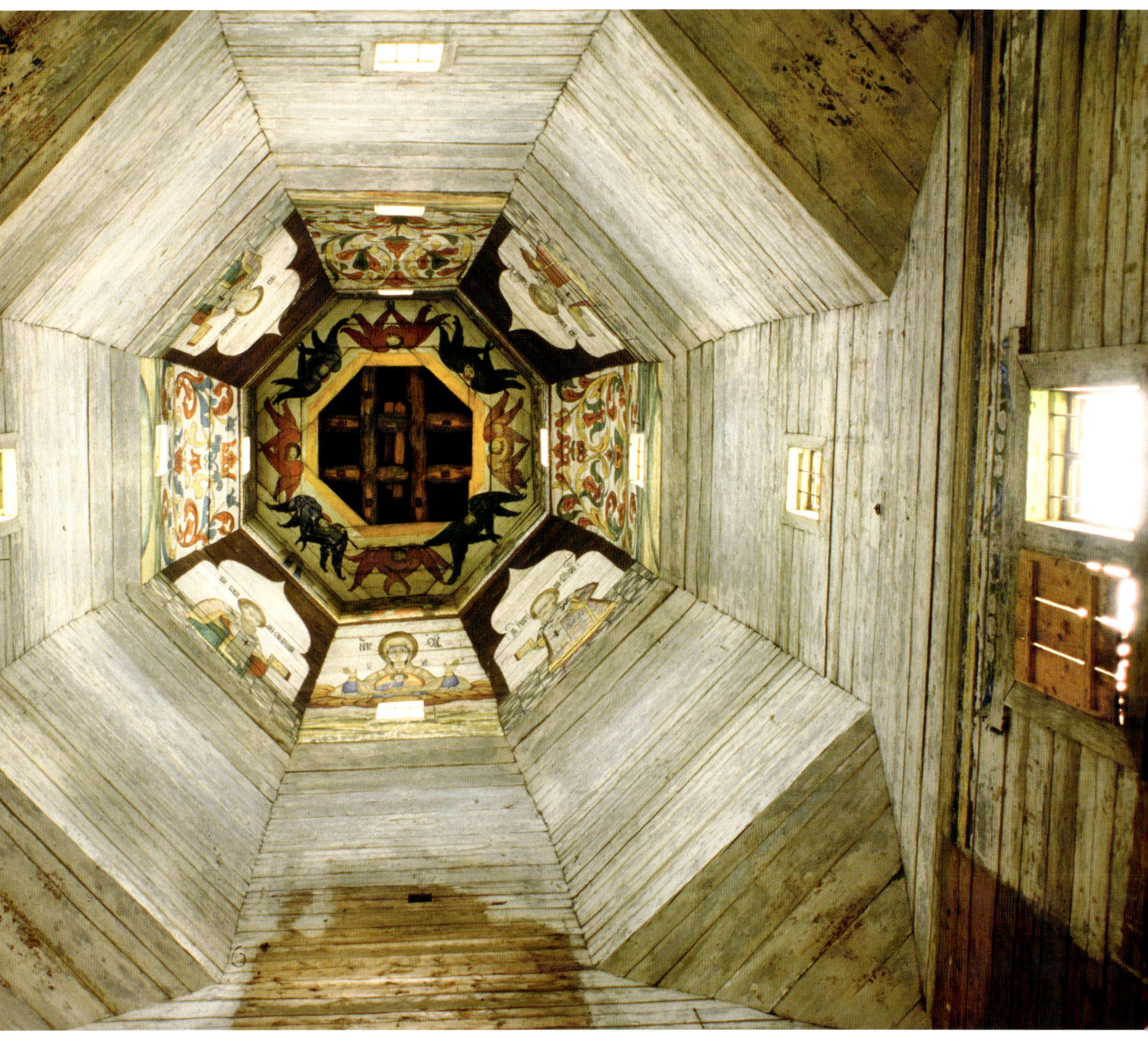

TORZHOK Church of the Tikhvin Icon of the Virgin. Interior, view east toward iconostasis (not extant). PROKUDIN-GORSKY 21176. SUMMER 1910.

TORZHOK Church of the Tikhvin Icon of the Virgin. Interior. View upward into tower with wall paintings. *Center*: Mary Theotokos of the Sign, located above position of lost iconostasis. BRUMFIELD, AUGUST 18, 2006.

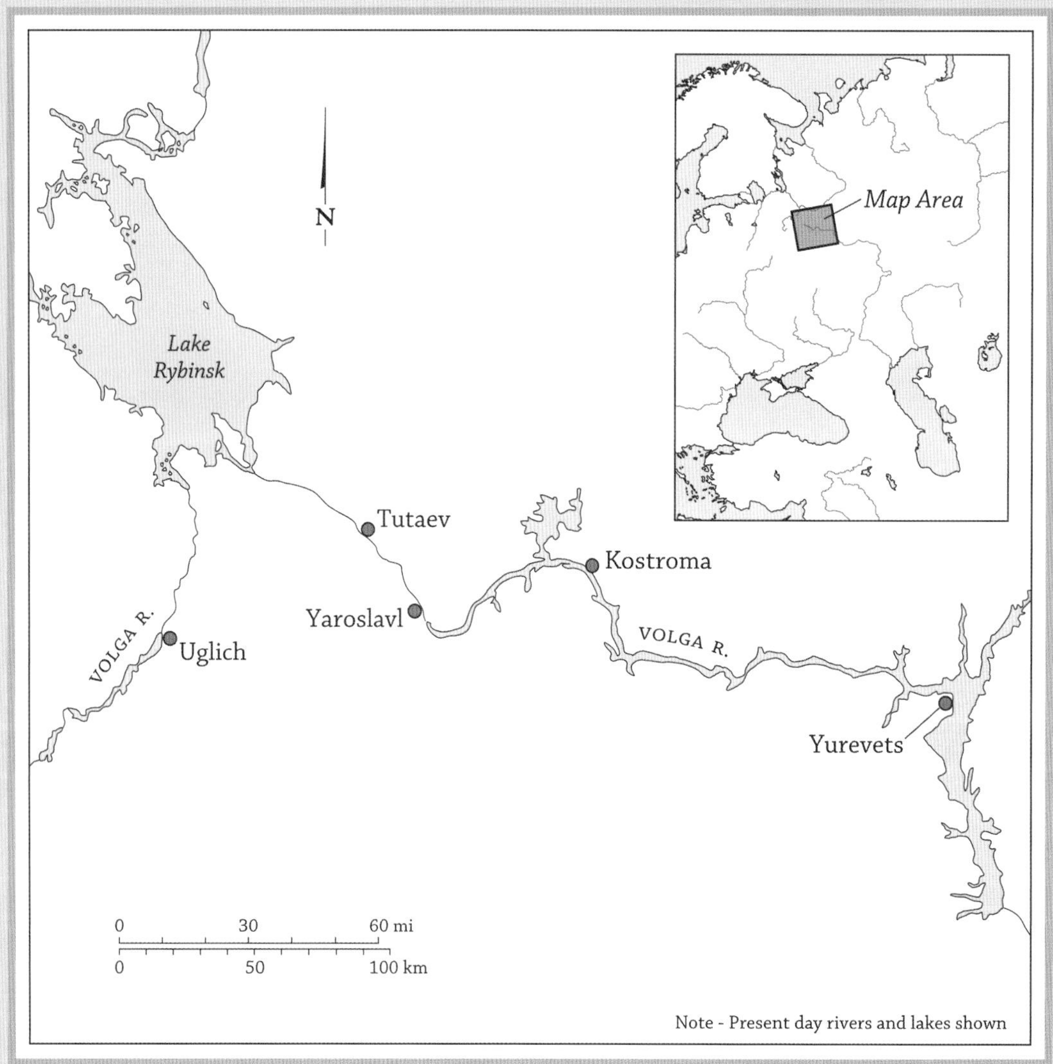

N
Lake Rybinsk
Tutaev
Kostroma
Yaroslavl
VOLGA R.
Uglich
VOLGA R.
Yurevets
Map Area
0   30   60 mi
0   50   100 km
Note - Present day rivers and lakes shown

Of all the provincial towns photographed by Sergey Prokudin-Gorsky in the upper Volga basin, none possesses a more dramatic reputation than Uglich, founded probably in the tenth century. It was here that Ivan the Terrible's ten-year-old son Dmitry (by his noncanonical marriage to Maria Nagaya) met a violent death in May 1591. Historians now consider the fatal knife wound an accident, perhaps associated with an epileptic fit; but popular and enduring legend assumed that the tsarevitch was murdered at the instigation of Boris Godunov (1551?–1605), who held de facto power in Russia during the final years of the reign of Tsar Feodor (1557–98), the last of the Ryurikovich dynasty. Godunov's formal accession to the throne in 1598 gave cause to hope that policies of this vigorous and intelligent ruler would continue to work to the benefit of Russia, as they had during his regency. Yet persistent rumors of his guilt in the murder of the tsarevitch, together with rival political interests and a series of natural disasters, undermined his power; and after his death in 1605 there began a period of social chaos and incessant fighting known as the Time of Troubles. Only with the accession to power in 1613 of Michael, first of the Romanov tsars, was a modicum of order restored to a devastated Muscovite state.

Because of the traumatic memories associated with the death of the tsarevitch — and the need for healing and reconciliation — Uglich was filled with churches and chapels. By one count there were thirty churches, in addition to the churches in three monastic institutions. Approximately half of these

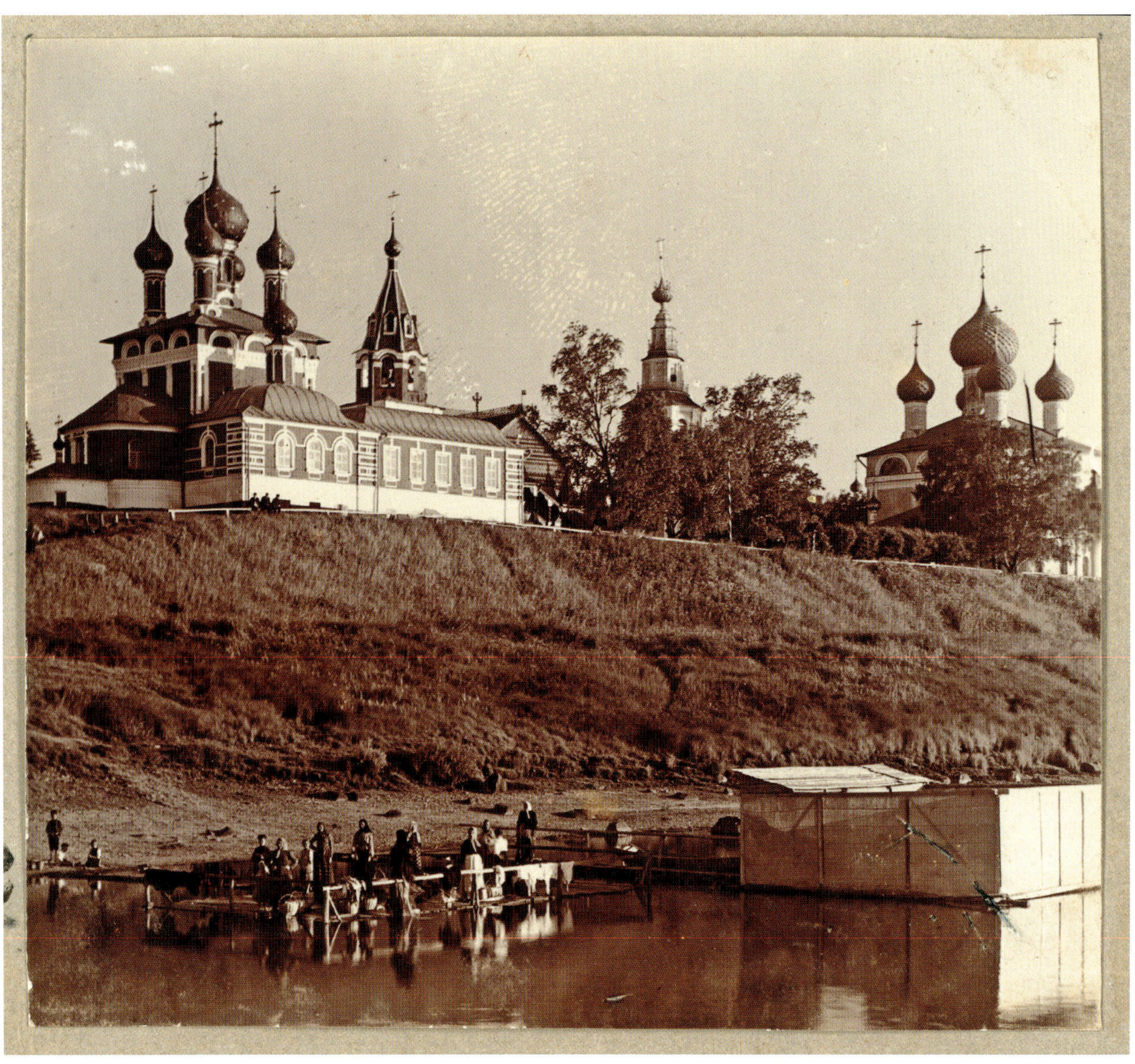

churches were demolished during the Soviet period. One of
Russia's pioneering architectural photographers, Ivan Barshchevsky, had already recorded much of the architecture
of Uglich—as well as that of other Volga towns—in the late
1880s and 1890s, but Prokudin-Gorsky returned with his
color process and the perception of an artist, evident in his
composition of women washing laundry on the banks of the
Volga with the Church of Saint Dmitry in the background.
Unfortunately, Prokudin-Gorsky's glass negatives of Uglich
have not survived, yet images made from his contact prints
give valuable information about the architecture of the his-

UGLICH North view from Volga
River, with Church of Saint Tsarevitch Dmitry on the Blood. *Background*: Cathedral bell tower.
BRUMFIELD, AUGUST 9, 1991.

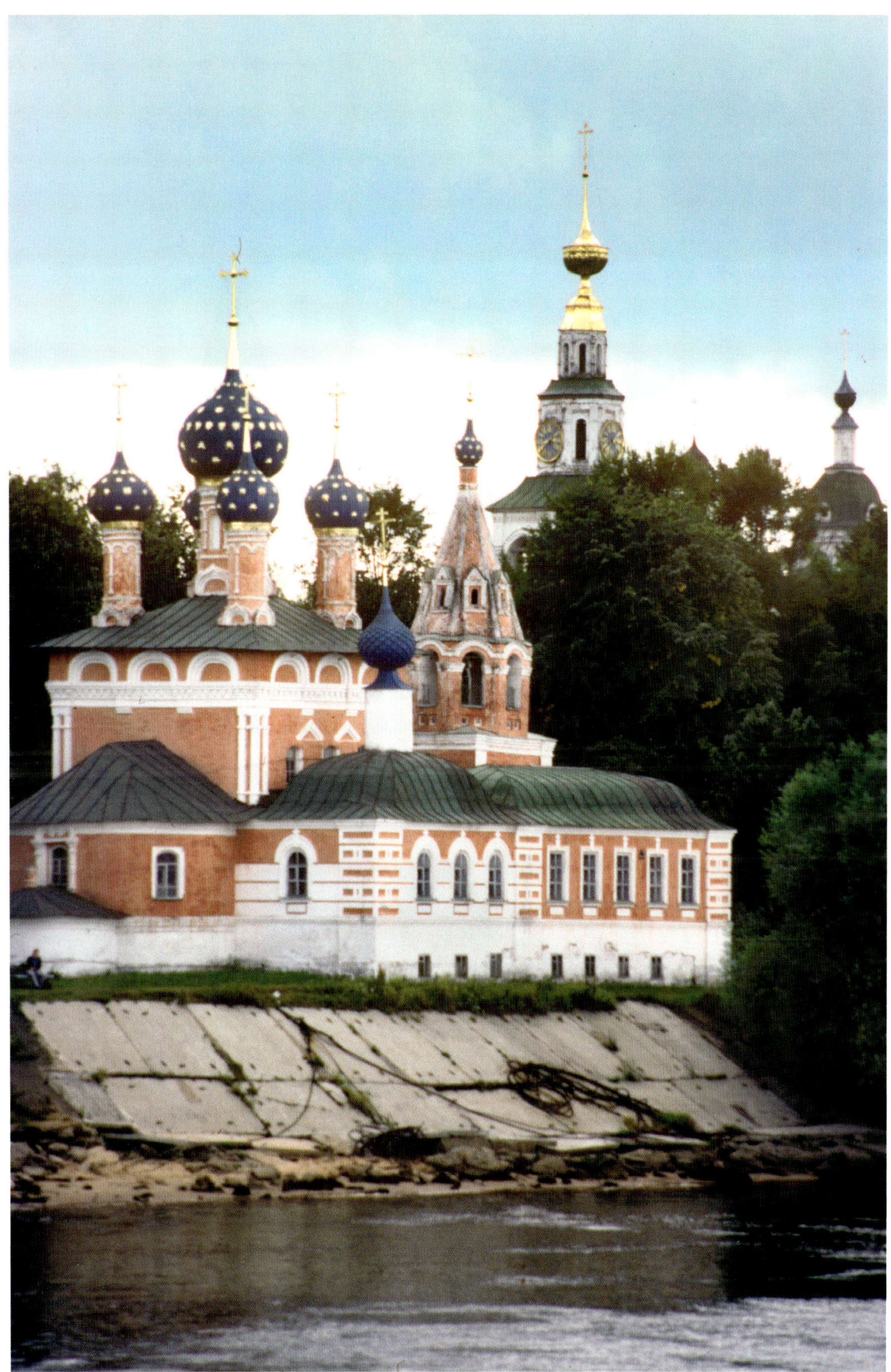

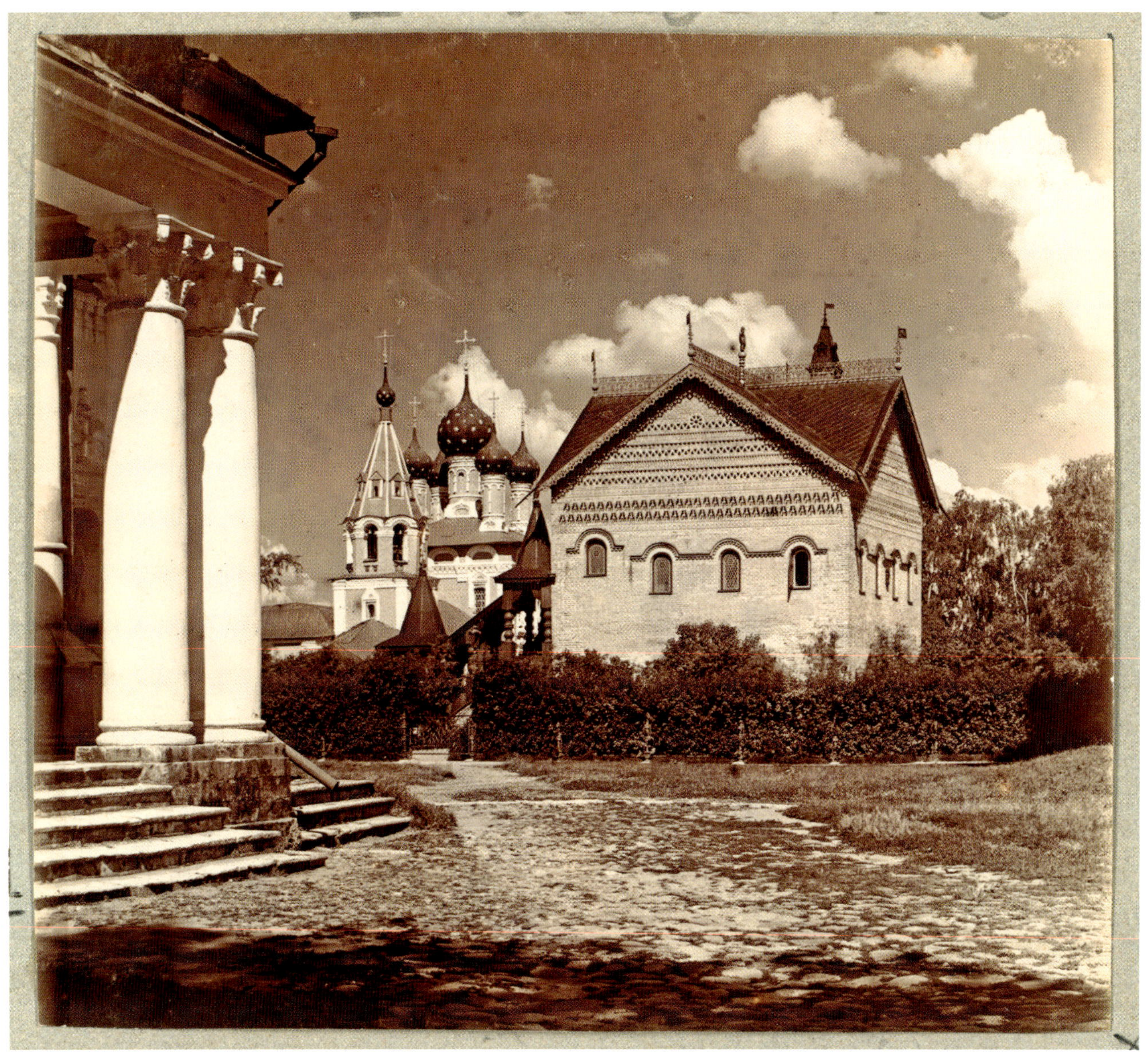

torical town and its condition before the revolution. Several general views were taken from the Volga River. Photographs from 1991 show changes to the river embankment but many of the structures intact.

Prominent among Prokudin-Gorsky's photographs are monuments associated with Tsarevitch Dmitry in Uglich and above all his residence, known as the Palace of the Appanage Princes, dating from the 1480s and extensively renovated as a museum in 1890–92 by Nikolai Sultanov. My photographs show the structure in excellent condition. Nearby is the Church of Saint Dmitry "on the Blood," built

UGLICH Palace of Appanage Princes (Palace of Tsarevitch Dmitry). Southwest view. PROKUDIN-GORSKY 02363. SUMMER 1910.

UGLICH Palace of Appanage Princes (Palace of Tsarevitch Dmitry). Southwest view. BRUMFIELD, JULY 30, 1997.

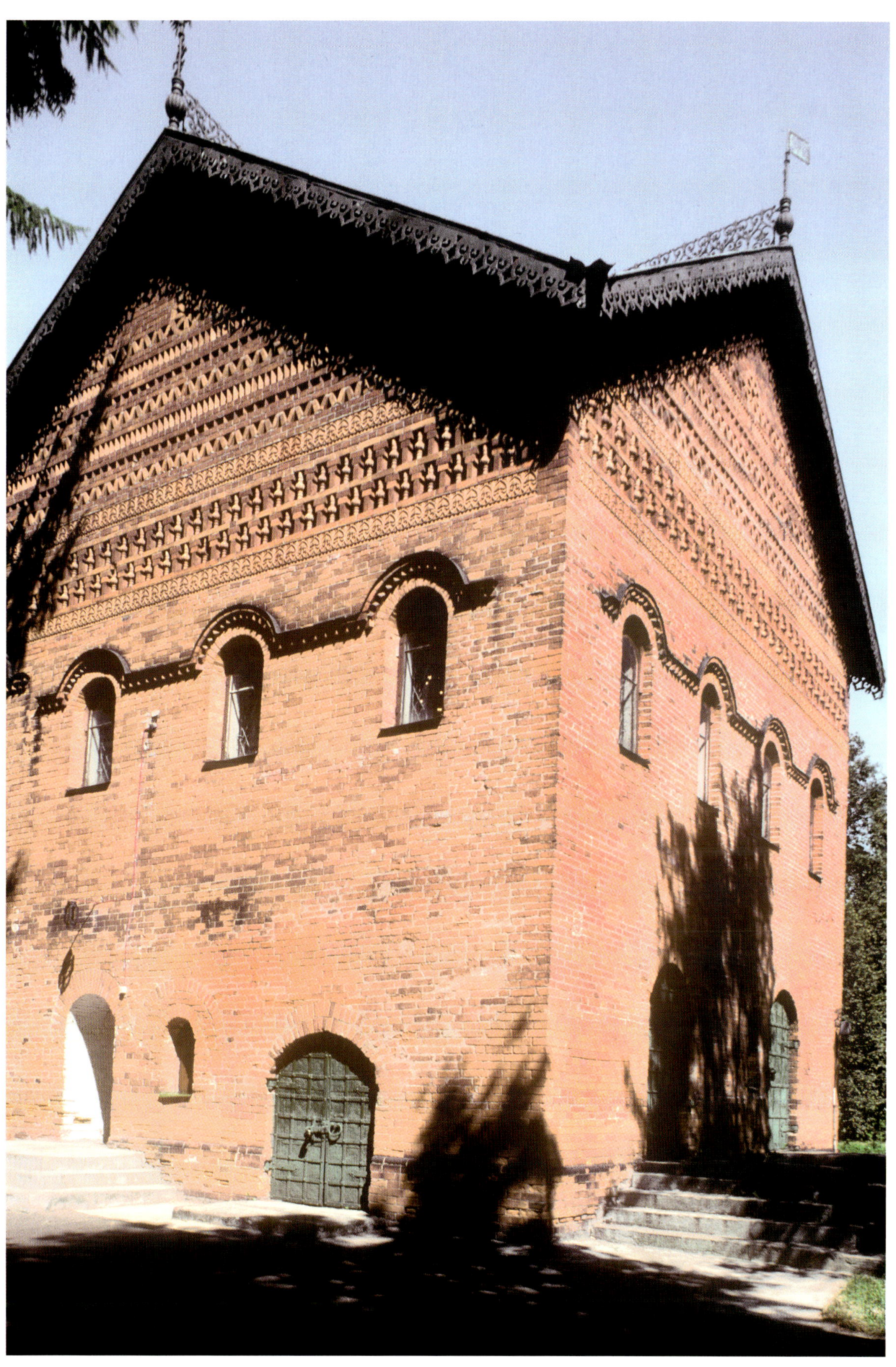

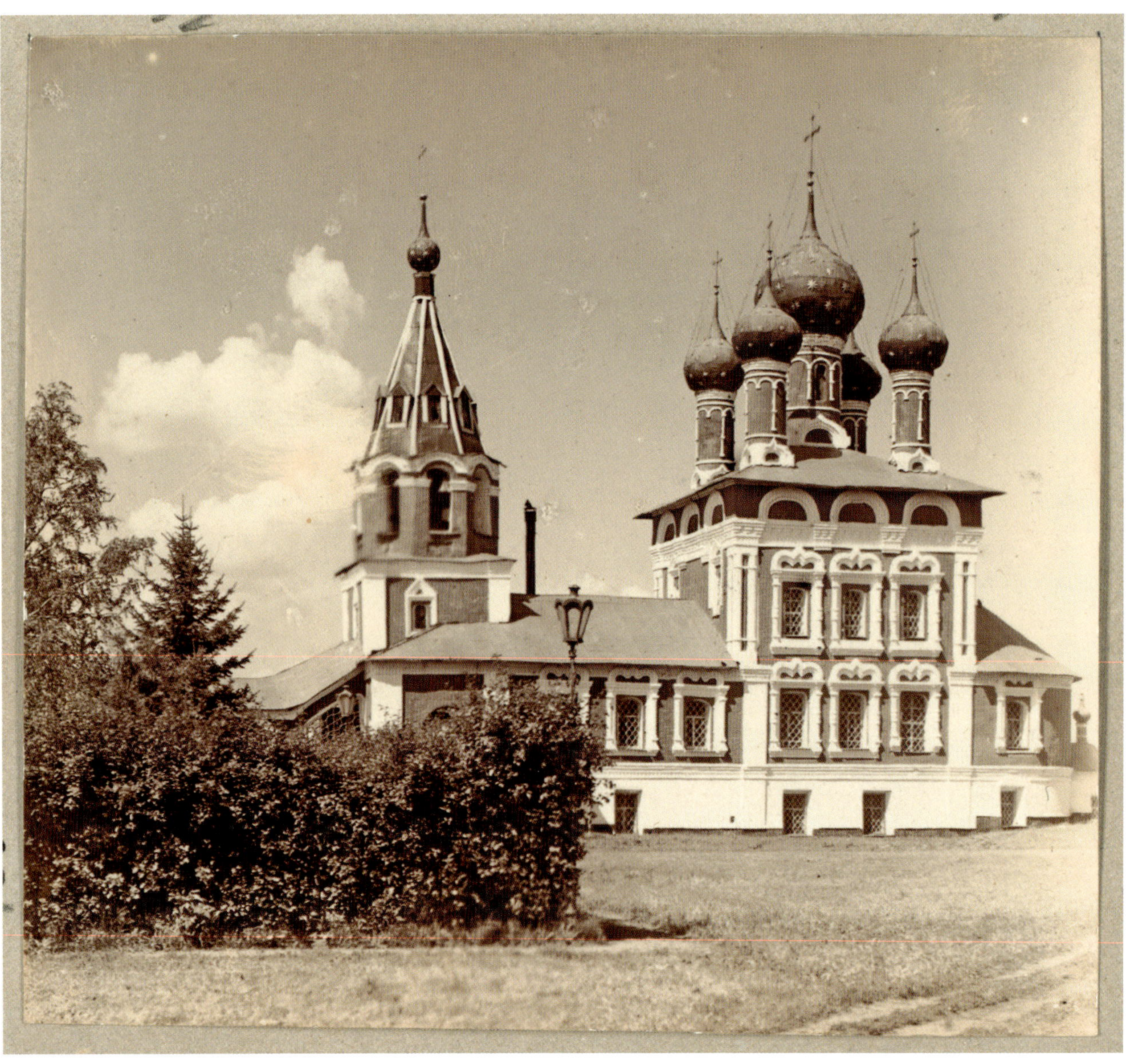

in 1692 on the presumed site of the child's death. The bright colors of the church are missing in Prokudin-Gorsky's surviving contact print, yet that record allows a clear view of the highly ornamented south facade. My photographs show a typical seventeenth-century style: five blue cupolas with golden stars, facades painted red with white trim, and a bell tower in the west.

From an architectural perspective the most distinctive monument in Uglich is the elegant ensemble of the Resurrection Monastery, located on the edge of town. Prokudin-Gorsky's photographs of the monastery include the main

UGLICH Church of Saint Tsarevitch Dmitry on the Blood. South view. PROKUDIN-GORSKY 02356. SUMMER 1910.

UGLICH Church of Saint Tsarevitch Dmitry on the Blood. South view. BRUMFIELD, JULY 16, 2007.

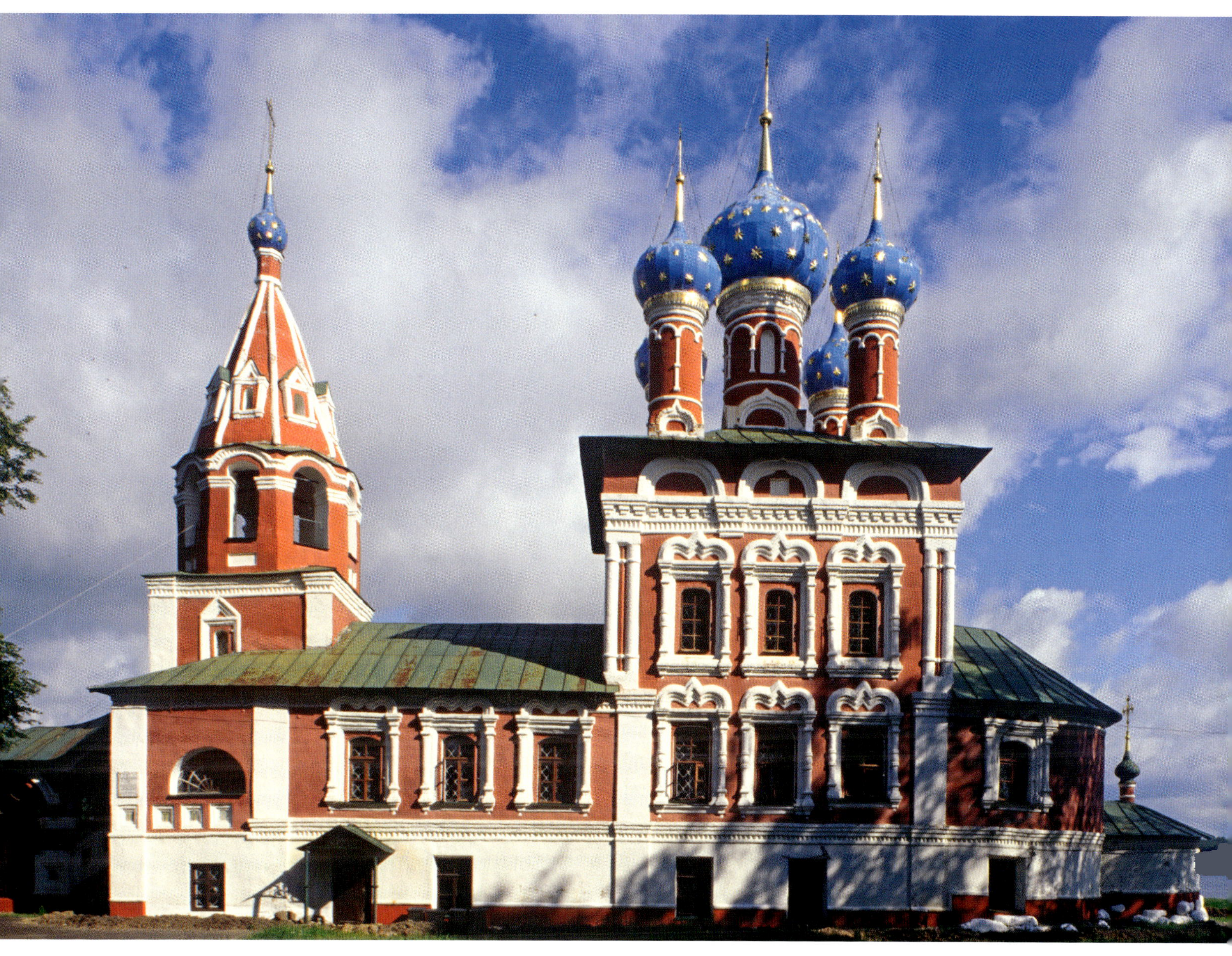

Cathedral of the Resurrection, rebuilt in 1674–77 with the support of metropolitan Jonah Sysoevich, builder of the Archbishop's Court in Rostov. Monumental yet austere in design, the two-story building had five elongated onion domes in the manner of Rostov's great churches. As part of the project, a large belfry in the Rostov style was attached to the cathedral's south facade, visible in Prokudin-Gorsky's view from the northwest. The third level of the four-story belfry contained the miniature Church of Saint Mary of Egypt. Attached to the south of the bell gable and built in the same period is the Church of Smolensk Icon of the Virgin, which also contained the monastery refectory. For comparison, I have chosen a west view taken

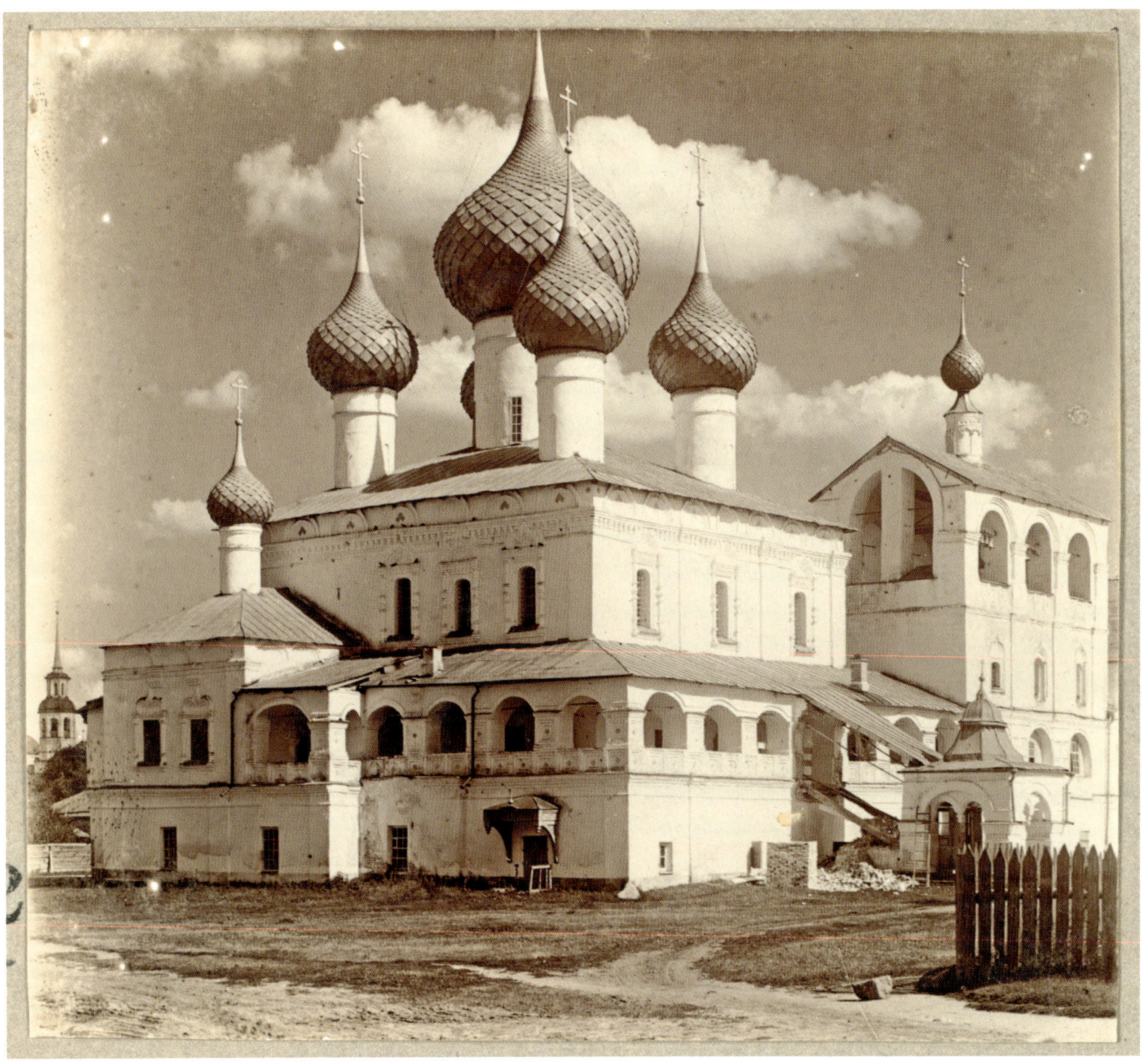

in 1997 that shows the entire ensemble, a unique example of monastic buildings linked in a single integrated whole.

Several parish churches that Prokudin-Gorsky recorded were demolished during the Soviet period, but others survived, including the Church of the Nativity of John the Baptist on the Volga (also known as the Mandylian Icon of the Savior), one of the most beautiful in Uglich. Like the structure itself, the origins of the church are complex. It was built in the late seventeenth century by the merchant Nikifor Chepolosov as a memorial to his six-year-old son Ivan (John), who was killed under mysterious circumstances in

UGLICH Resurrection Monastery. Cathedral of the Resurrection and bell gable. Northwest view. PROKUDIN-GORSKY 02372. SUMMER 1910.

UGLICH Resurrection Monastery. West view. *From left*: Cathedral of the Resurrection, bell gable with Church of Saint Mary of Egypt, Church of the Smolensk Icon of the Virgin. BRUMFIELD, JULY 30, 1997.

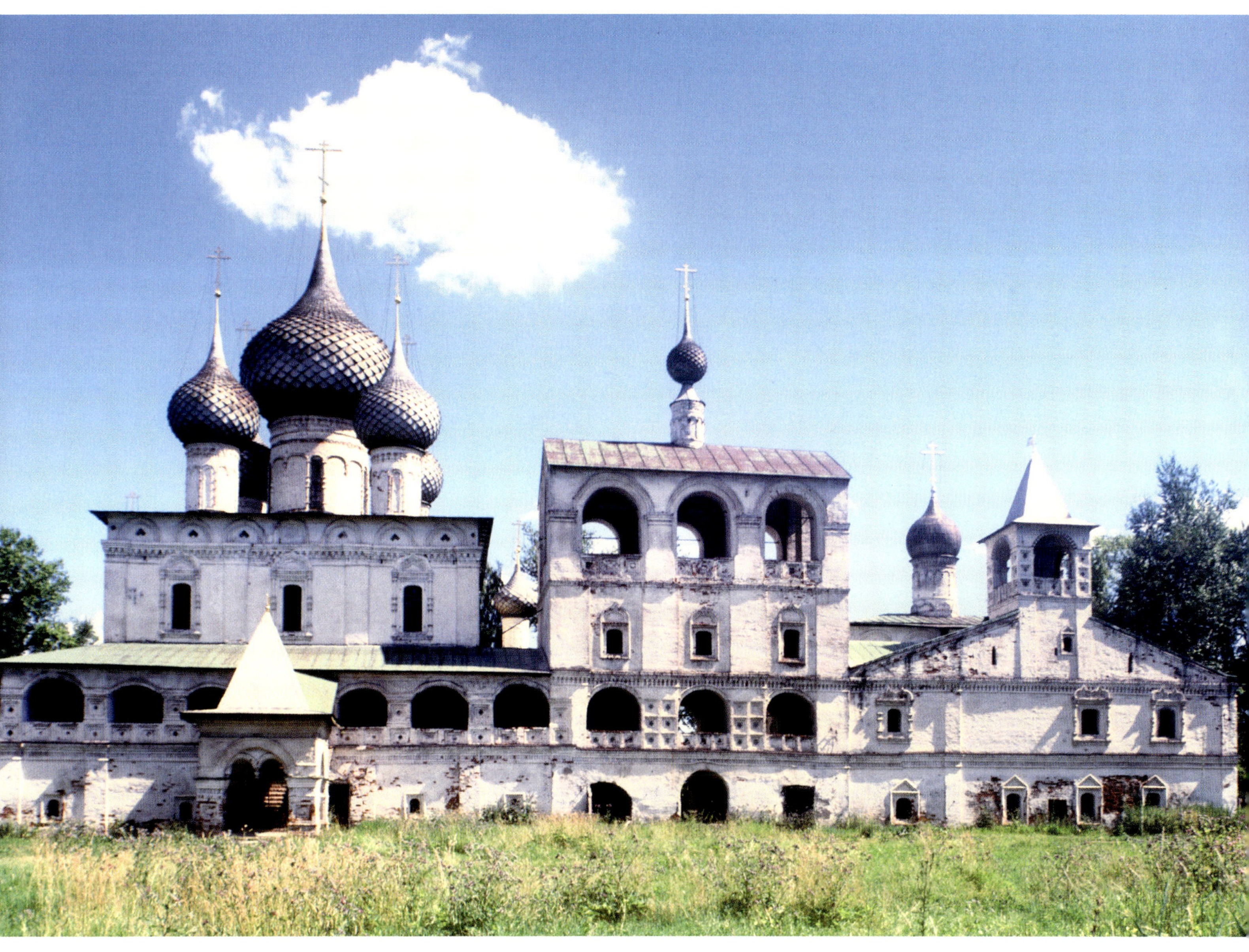

June 1663 by one of his father's workers. The child was buried next to a wooden Church of the Nativity of John the Baptist, and in 1689 Chepolosov initiated the construction of a masonry church as a memorial. The son's remains were reburied in the new church, and monks in the nearby Resurrection Monastery gathered information that ultimately led to the sanctification of the boy as the Blessed Ivan. (Metropolitan Jonah played a significant role in this process.)

The core of the church consists of a cuboid structure with five cupolas common in seventeenth-century parish architecture. The apse extending from the east contains the main altar dedicated to the Mandylian Icon of the Savior. It is flanked by two chapels dedicated to Simeon the Stylite

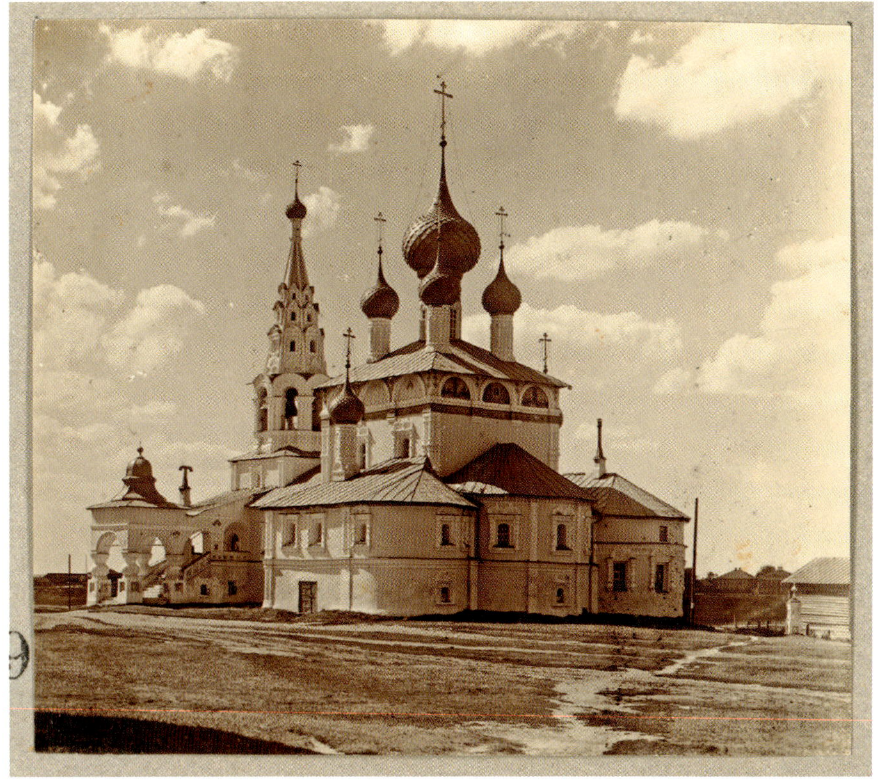

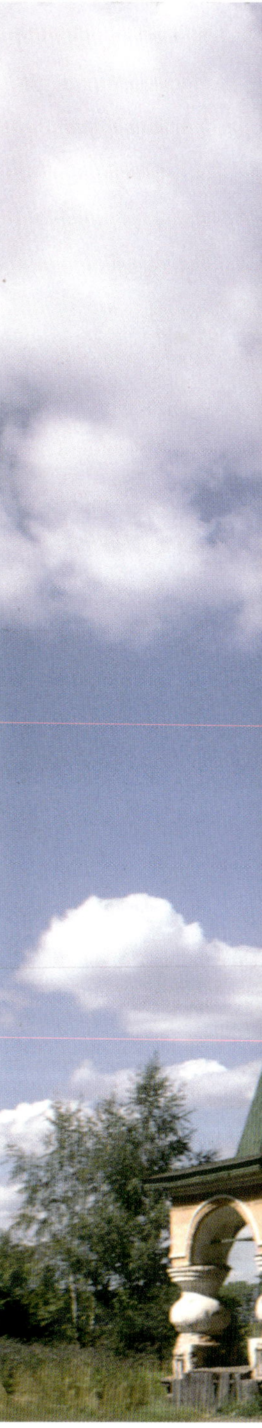

(on the south) and the Nativity of John the Baptist (north). A refectory
vestibule on the west leads to a bell tower with "tent" tower, and a covered
staircase descends at right angles from the upper level. Prokudin-Gorsky's
late afternoon view from the southeast displays these elements with rich
shadow emphasis. In 1935 the church was closed and used as a warehouse.
Although it was restored in 1961–70 as a cultural object, I witnessed its continued use as a warehouse in the late 1980s. The chiaroscuro effect created
by the afternoon sun enhances the form of the church in my 1997 view from
the southeast.

Farther down the Volga on the approaches to Yaroslavl is the town of Tutaev, composed of two settlements, one on each side of the Volga. On the
right bank is Borisoglebsk, whose origins evidently predate the Mongol sack
of Yaroslavl in 1238. By the fifteenth century the settlement was referred to as
the Borisoglebsk Fishing Quarter, and in 1777, during the reign of Catherine
the Great, it became officially known as Borisoglebsk. In 1822 the two settlements were merged with the name Romanov-Borisoglebsk, changed to Tutaev in 1918 to avoid any association with the Romanov dynasty.

Although sacked during the Time of Troubles, Borisoglebsk prospered
during the latter half of the seventeenth century, as witnessed by the com-

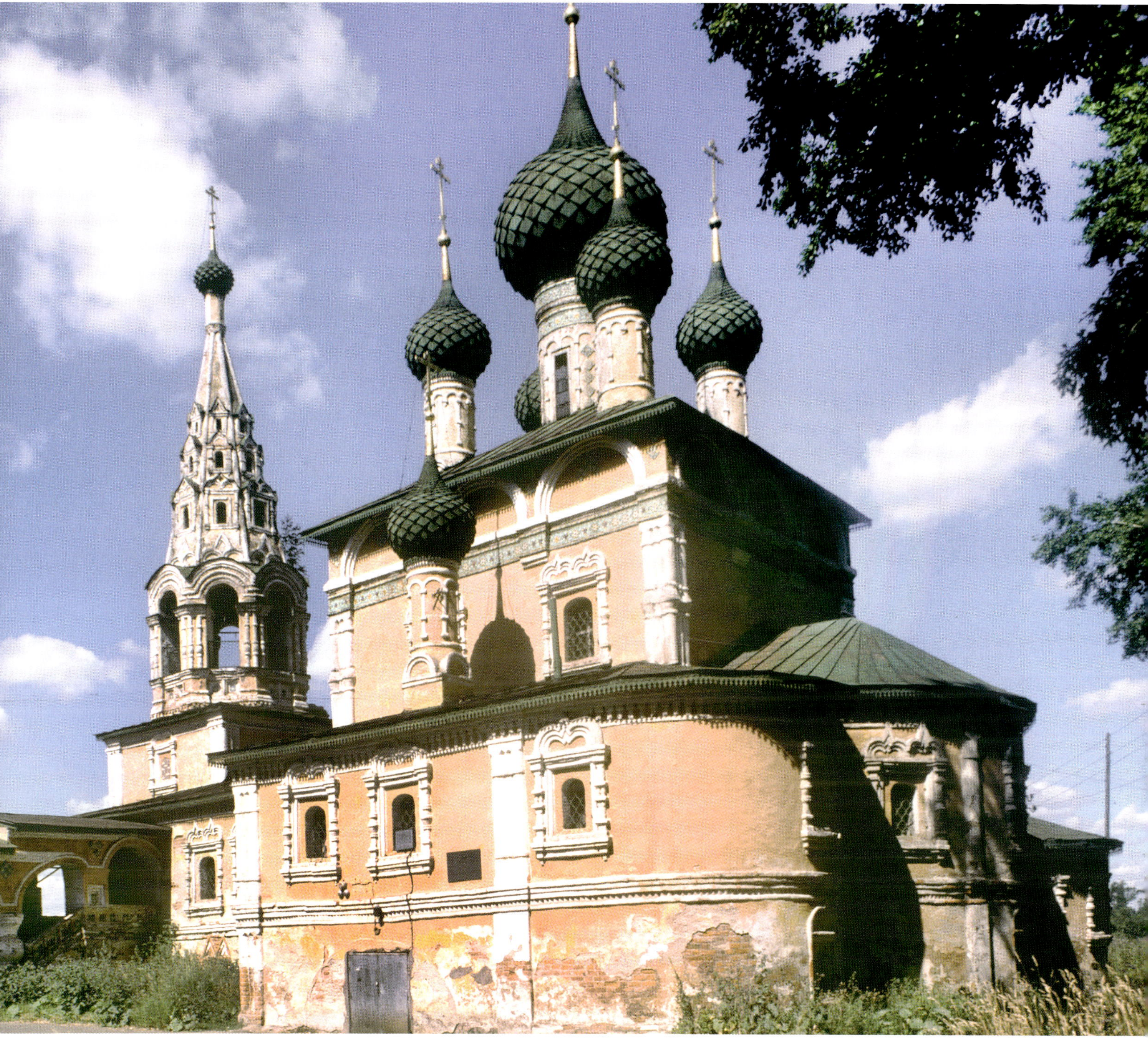

UGLICH Church of Nativity of John the Baptist.
Southeast view. PROKUDIN-GORSKY 02378. SUMMER 1910.

UGLICH Church of Nativity of John the Baptist on the
Volga. Southeast view. BRUMFIELD, JULY 30, 1997.

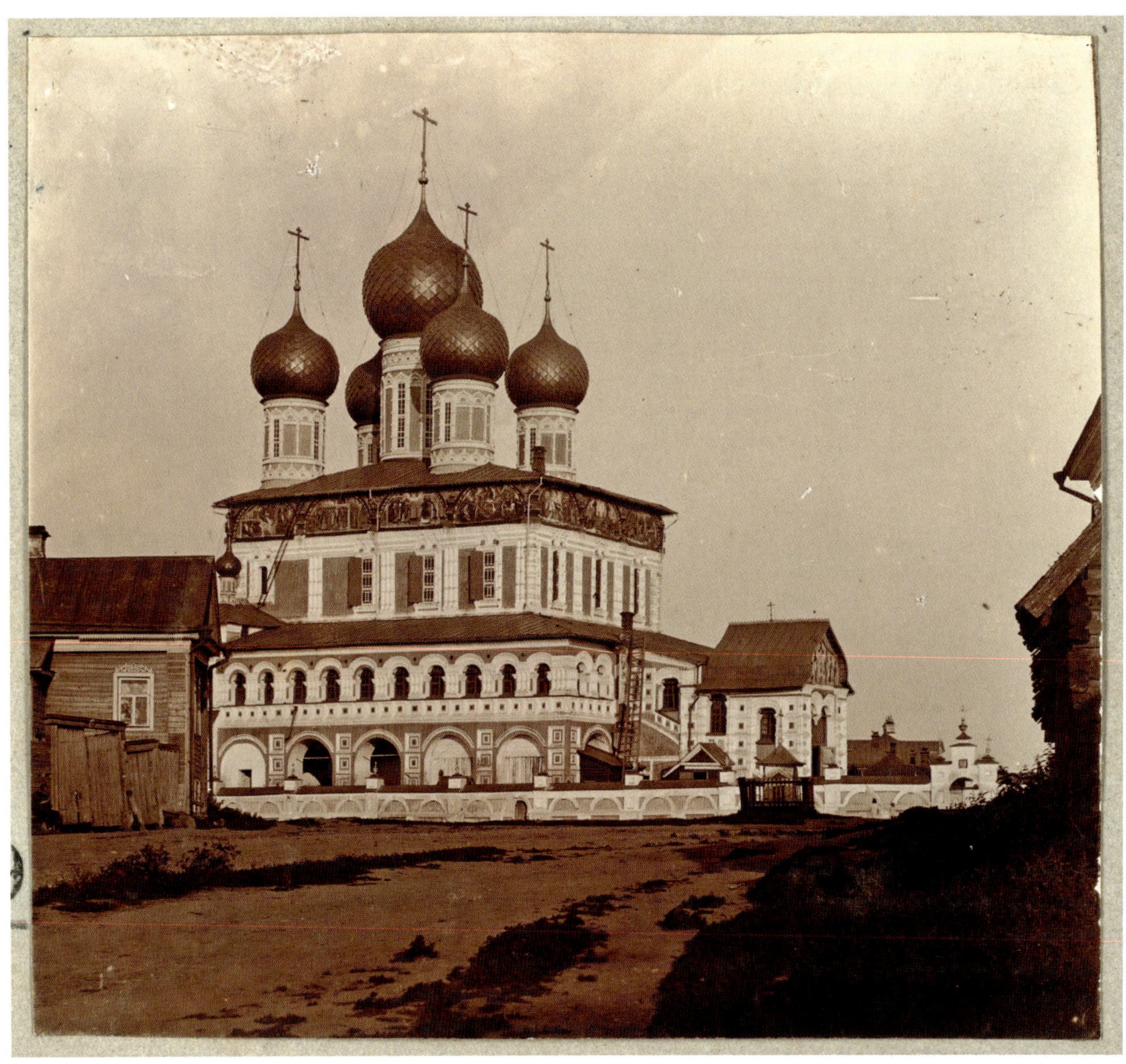

pletion in 1678 of the magnificent Cathedral of the Resurrection. This was also the time of spiritual and political crisis stemming from an Orthodox Church schism that originated in the 1650s. The dissenters, known as Old Believers, had a large presence in the Borisoglebsk area, and the official church no doubt wished to make an architectural statement that proclaimed the glory of Orthodoxy. Although the original negatives are missing, we have Prokudin-Gorsky's contact prints of this grand edifice with its intricate facade ornamentation.

TUTAEV (BORISOGLEBSK)
Cathedral of the Resurrection. Northwest view. PROKUDIN-GORSKY 02405. SUMMER 1910.

TUTAEV (BORISOGLEBSK)
Cathedral of the Resurrection. Southeast view. BRUMFIELD, JULY 25, 1997.

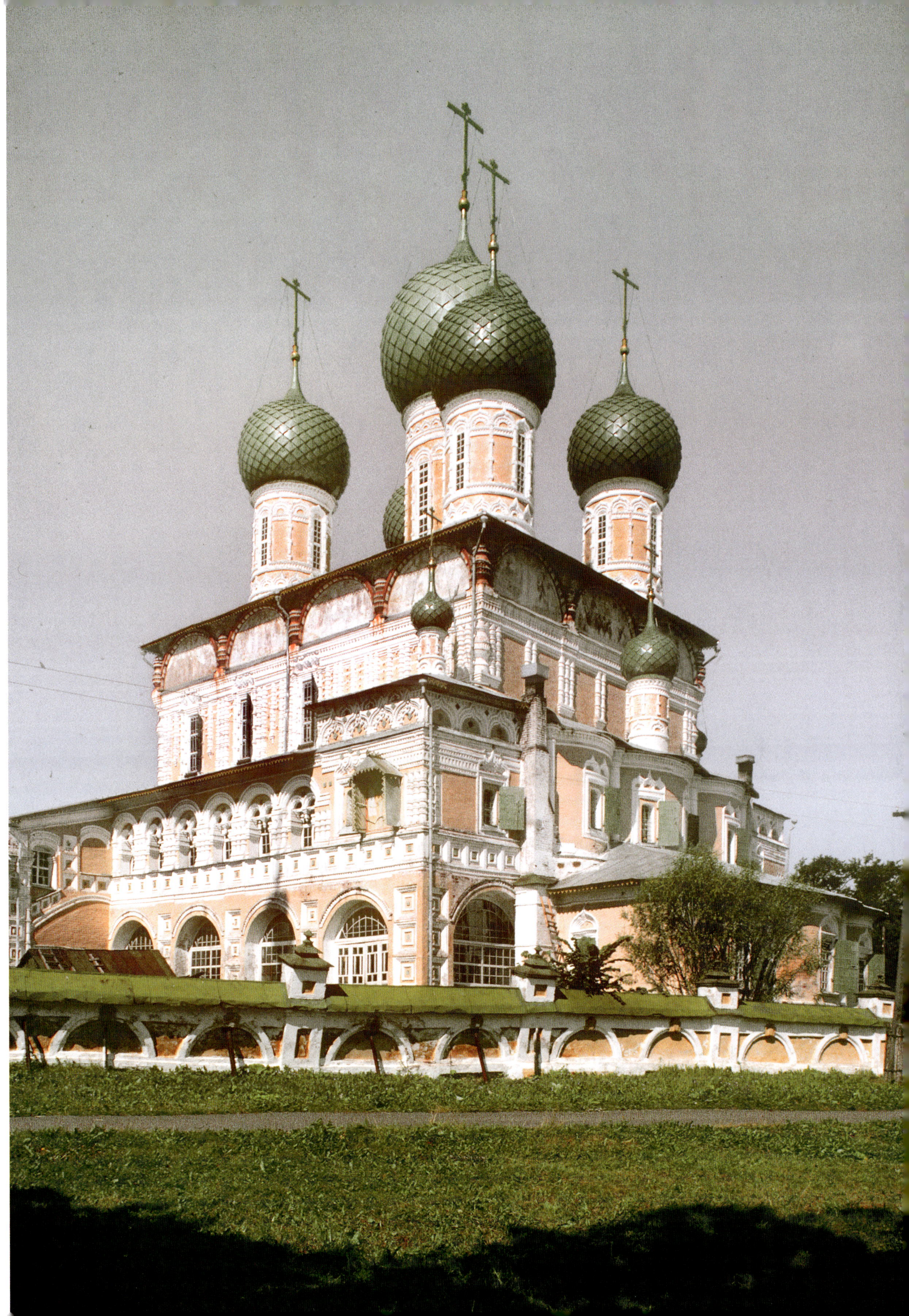

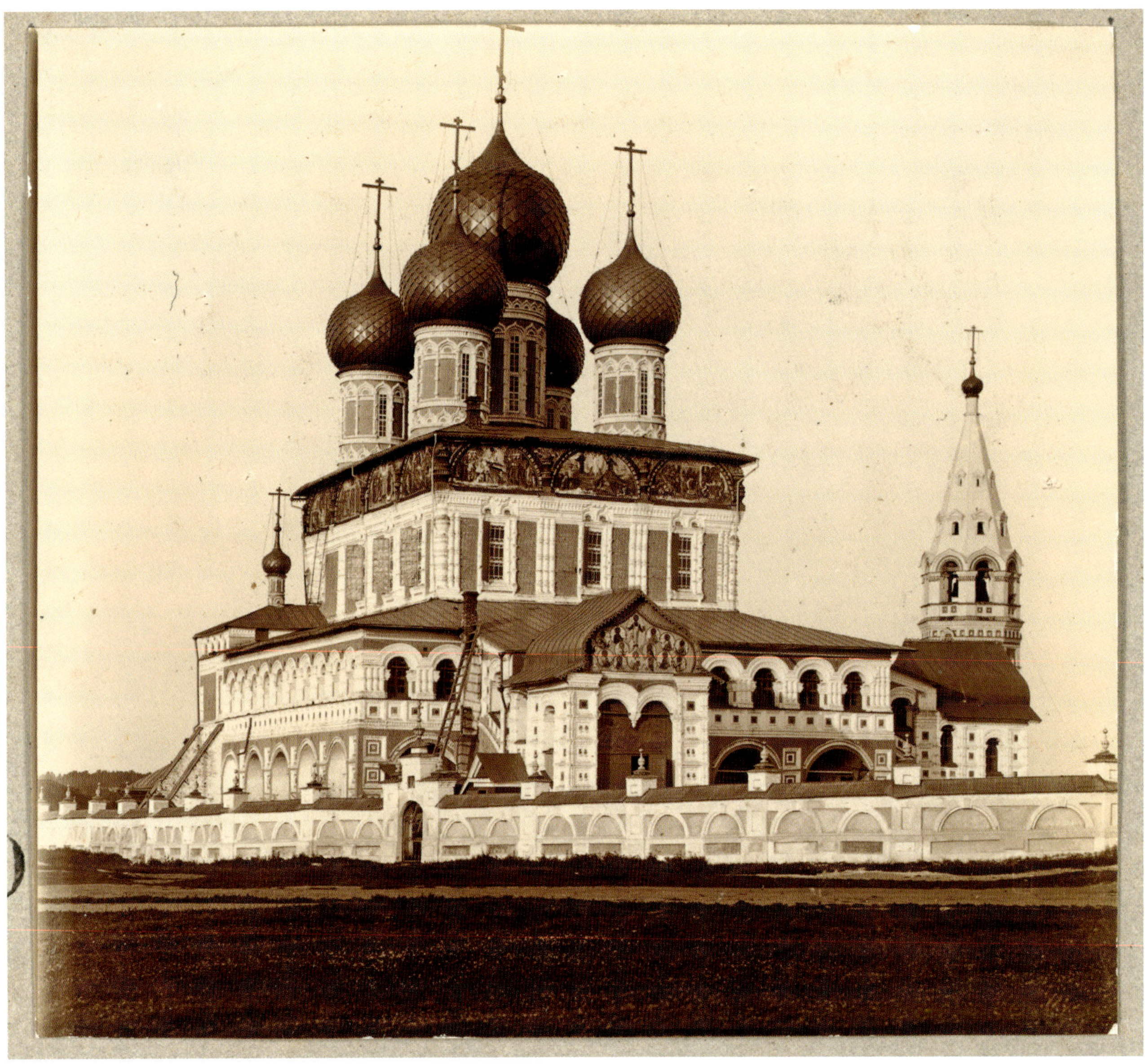

The cathedral's complex structure had its origins in a brick church built in 1652 on the site of wooden Church of Saints Boris and Gleb and dedicated to the revered Smolensk Icon of the Virgin (the Hodegetria Icon). In 1670 the partial collapse of that structure led to the rebuilding of a vastly larger shrine dedicated to the Resurrection. Its ground level included of walls from the earlier church, along with the altar dedicated to the Smolensk Icon. (Russian churches often have multiple altars, each with its own dedication.) This lower level served for worship while the rebuilding was under way. It had secondary altars dedicated

TUTAEV (BORISOGLEBSK)
Cathedral of the Resurection. Northwest view. PROKUDIN-GORSKY 02406. SUMMER 1910.

TUTAEV (BORISOGLEBSK)
Cathedral of the Resurrection and bell tower. East view from Volga River. BRUMFIELD, JULY 15, 2007.

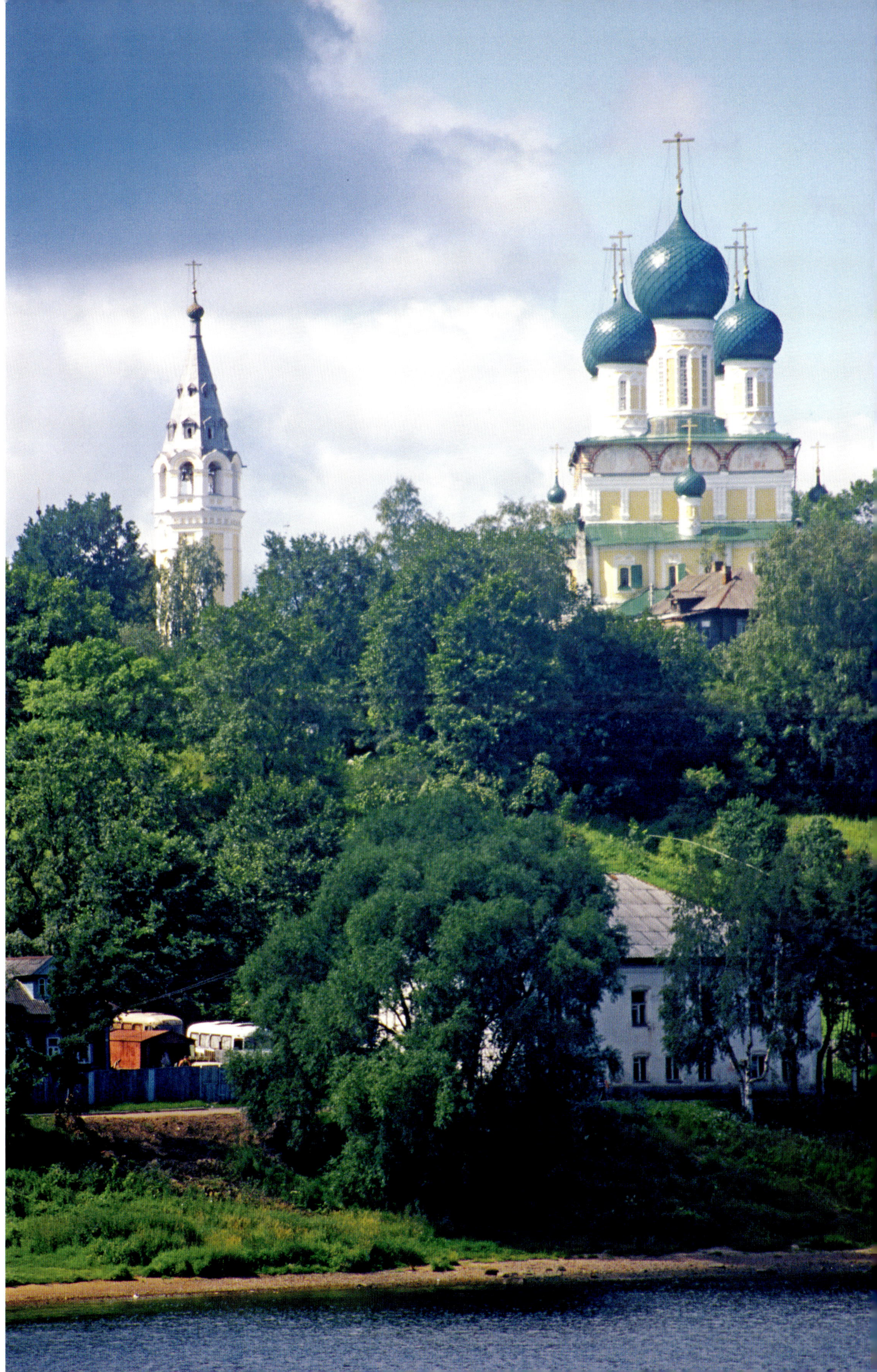

to John the Baptist (in the north) and Saint Charalambos of Magnesia, martyred apparently during the reign of Septimius Severus (193–211).

Completed in 1678, the structure represents a mixture of late seventeenth-century decorative architectural styles from Rostov and Yaroslavl—logical in view of the patronage of metropolitan Jonah Sysoevich. The lower level, which could be more easily heated, continued in use for winter services. The upper level—known as a "summer" (i.e., unheated) church—contained the main altar, dedicated to the Resurrection of Christ, and a secondary altar to Saints Boris and Gleb in remembrance of the early wooden church. The walls of the main structure are enhanced by galleries attached on the north, west, and south facades. At the east end of the north and south galleries are chapels dedicated to Saint Nicholas and to Saints Peter and Paul (north). The latter is prominent in Prokudin-Gorsky's north view. The cathedral compound includes a bell tower and decorated Holy Gate. My east view from the river in 2007 shows the cathedral and its lofty cupolas visible above summer foliage.

The settlement of Romanov, on the Volga left bank opposite Borisoglebsk, was established in the late thirteenth century following the sanctification of Roman Vladimirovich, a feudal prince based in Uglich. Vulnerable to Tatar raids, Romanov was formally absorbed into Muscovy by the end of the fifteenth century. Its fate thereafter was checkered until a revival in the seventeenth century. In the 1650s, the Cathedral of the Elevation of the Cross was rebuilt of brick in an early sixteenth-century style, with five large cupolas, attached chapels, and a tall bell tower attached to the northwest corner. Prokudin-Gorsky's photograph from the northeast sharply captures these components. Although the cathedral was closed for much of the Soviet period and its iconostasis pilfered, its seventeenth-century frescoes were largely preserved. My photographs from 1997 show bright whitewashed walls after its return to religious use in 1992.

Nearby is a church with a dual dedication to the Kazan Icon of the Virgin and the Transfiguration of the Savior. Built in 1758 in an archaic seventeenth-century parish style, the colorful, idiosyncratic structure has been beloved by generations of artists. Painted bright red with white trim, its forms seem to cascade down the steep left bank of the Volga. Above all is a slender free-standing bell tower at the east crest above the church. Although the original glass negative is not extant, Prokudin-Gorsky's view conveys the church components in relation to the river. My photographs from the river give a sense of this "stairway to heaven" ascending the steep bank.

Just to the north of Yaroslavl and rising above the east bank of the Volga

River near the small Tolga River is one of the most revered of Russia's monastic institutions: the Tolg Yaroslavl Presentation Monastery (now Convent). The array of its towers, spires, and cupolas at the river's edge gives it the appearance of a miraculous apparition. Indeed, the monastery was founded in 1314 at the site where Archbishop Prokhor (Trifon) of Rostov is said to have miraculously seen an icon of the Virgin Mary. Subsequently known as the Tolg Icon of the Virgin, this image of Mary is considered the protectress of the Yaroslavl lands and is frequently reproduced in Russian churches. Prokhor dedicated the monastery to the Presentation of the Virgin Mary in the Temple. He was acquainted with Moscow's princes and played an important role in the consolidation of Moscow's spiritual authority.

Prokudin-Gorsky photographed the monastery in the summer of 1910 as part of a trip along the middle Volga from Uglich to Kineshma. Although the original glass plates are missing, his contact prints provide valuable information about the state of the monastery. Many of the monastic buildings that he saw dated to the seventeenth century, including the central Cathedral of the Presentation (1681–83), a large structure encased in a raised gallery and crowned with five cupolas. Prokudin-Gorsky's photographs from the Volga center on the cathedral as well as the adjacent bell tower, originally built in 1683–85 and expanded in a neoclassical style in 1826 by Petr Pankov, chief architect of Yaroslavl Province. Also visible are the Church of Saint Nicholas over West Gate (1672) with adjacent structures completed in the 1680s. My 1997 view, illuminated by evening sun, is slightly downriver. Close inspection reveals changes to the exteriors of the churches, built in a more traditional style than that created in Rostov by Metropolitan Jonah during the same period. In particular there were significant losses to the interior in the late Soviet period, when the monastery was used to house juvenile delinquents.

From inside the monastery Prokudin-Gorsky photographed the east facade of the Church of Saint Nicholas over the Holy Gate, the main monastery entrance in the west. Built in the early 1670s with the support of the merchant brothers Semyon and Ivan Sverchkov, the church was consecrated by Hegumen Gordian, whose efforts gave the monastery much of its ultimate form. The facade displays figures of Russian saints. My 1997 photograph shows the restored gate church and cloisters.

The city of Yaroslavl, some five hours by steamer down the Volga River from Rybinsk (according the 1914 Baedeker), claimed much of Prokudin-Gorsky's attention in the summer of 1911, and with good reason. Not only was it a major provincial capital (population then over 110,000) and a gate-

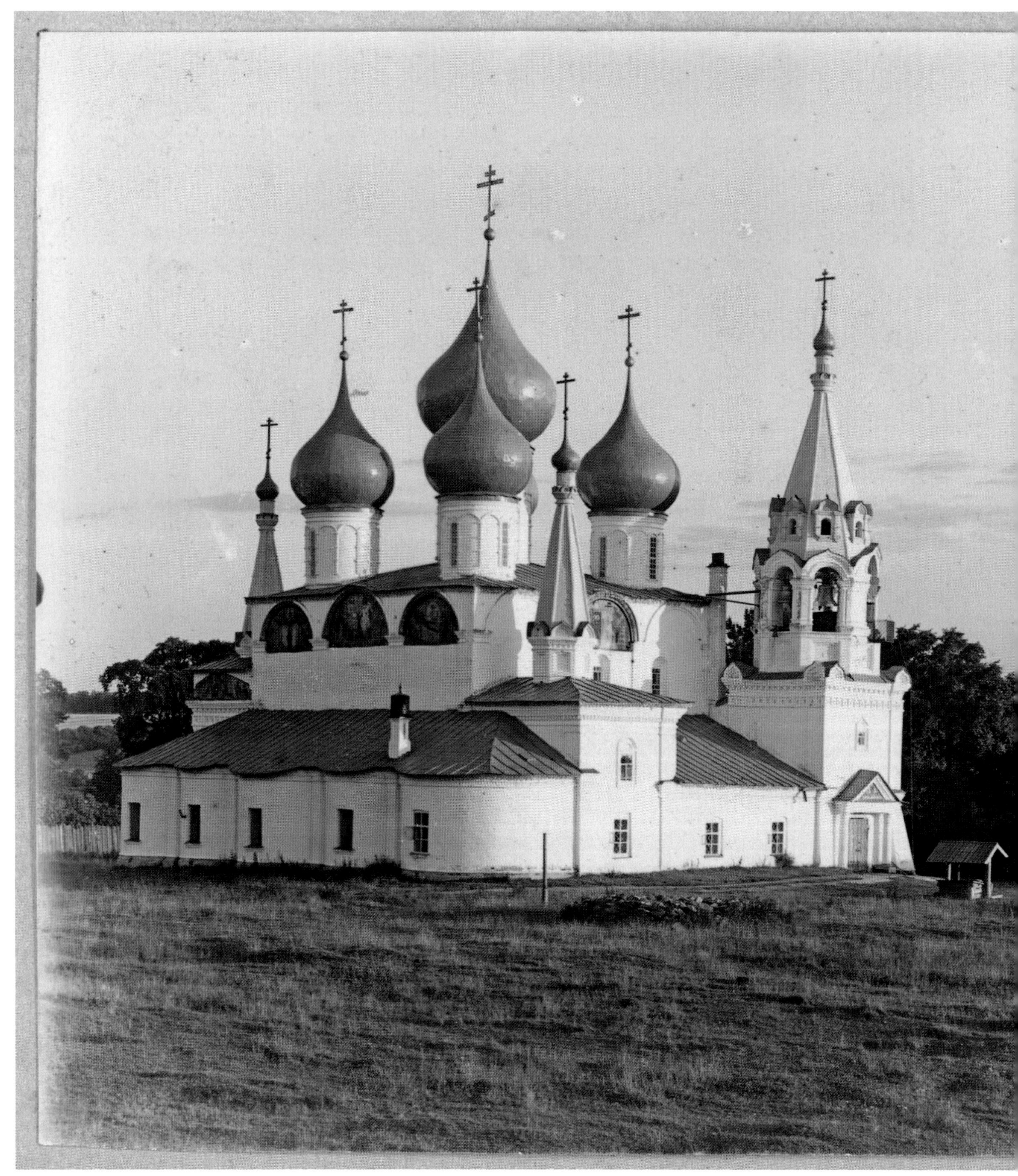

TUTAEV (ROMANOV) Cathedral of Elevation of the Cross. Northeast view.

PROKUDIN-GORSKY 02408. SUMMER 1910.

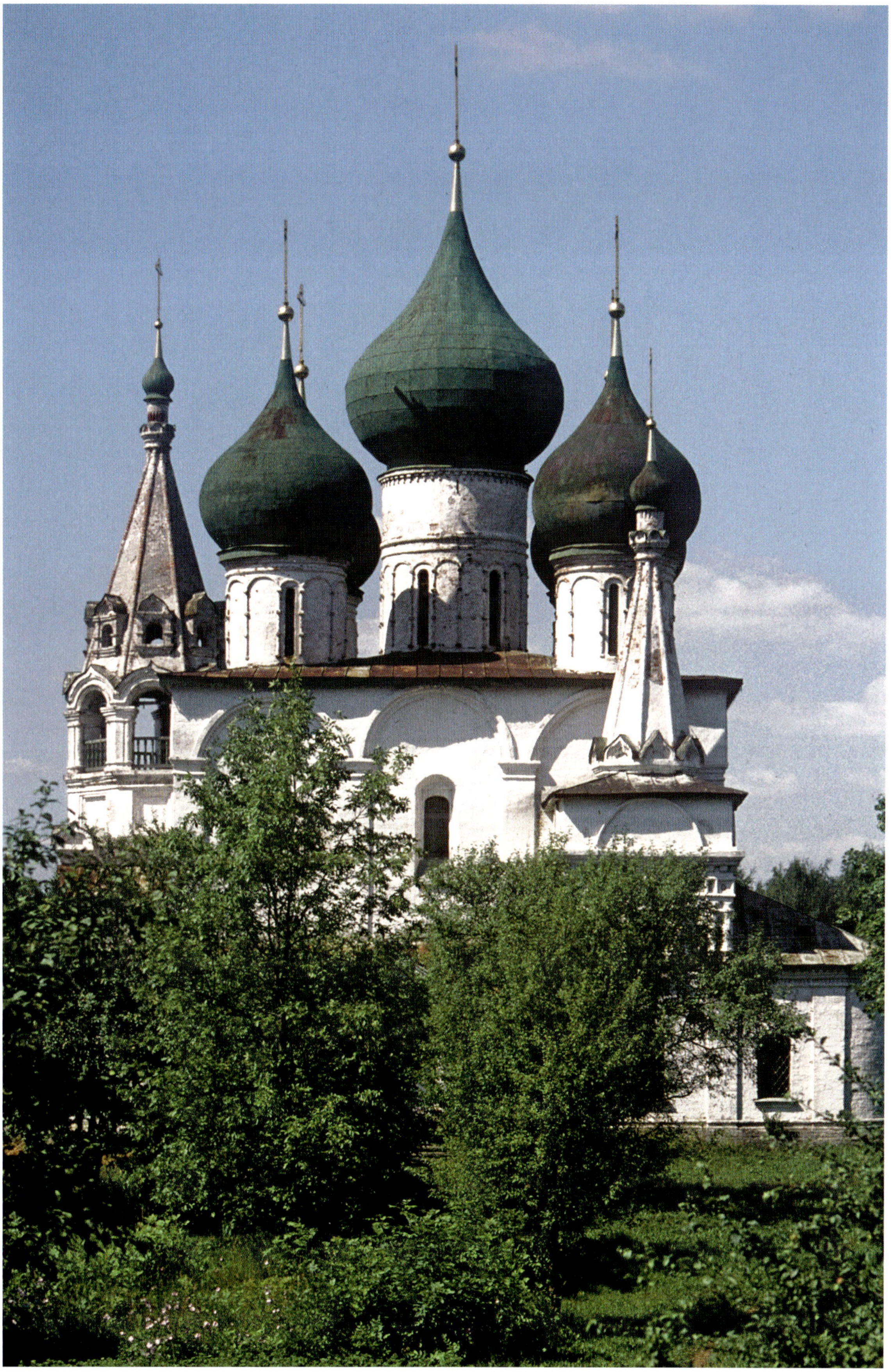

TUTAEV (ROMANOV) Cathedral of Elevation of the Cross. South view.
BRUMFIELD, JULY 26, 1997.

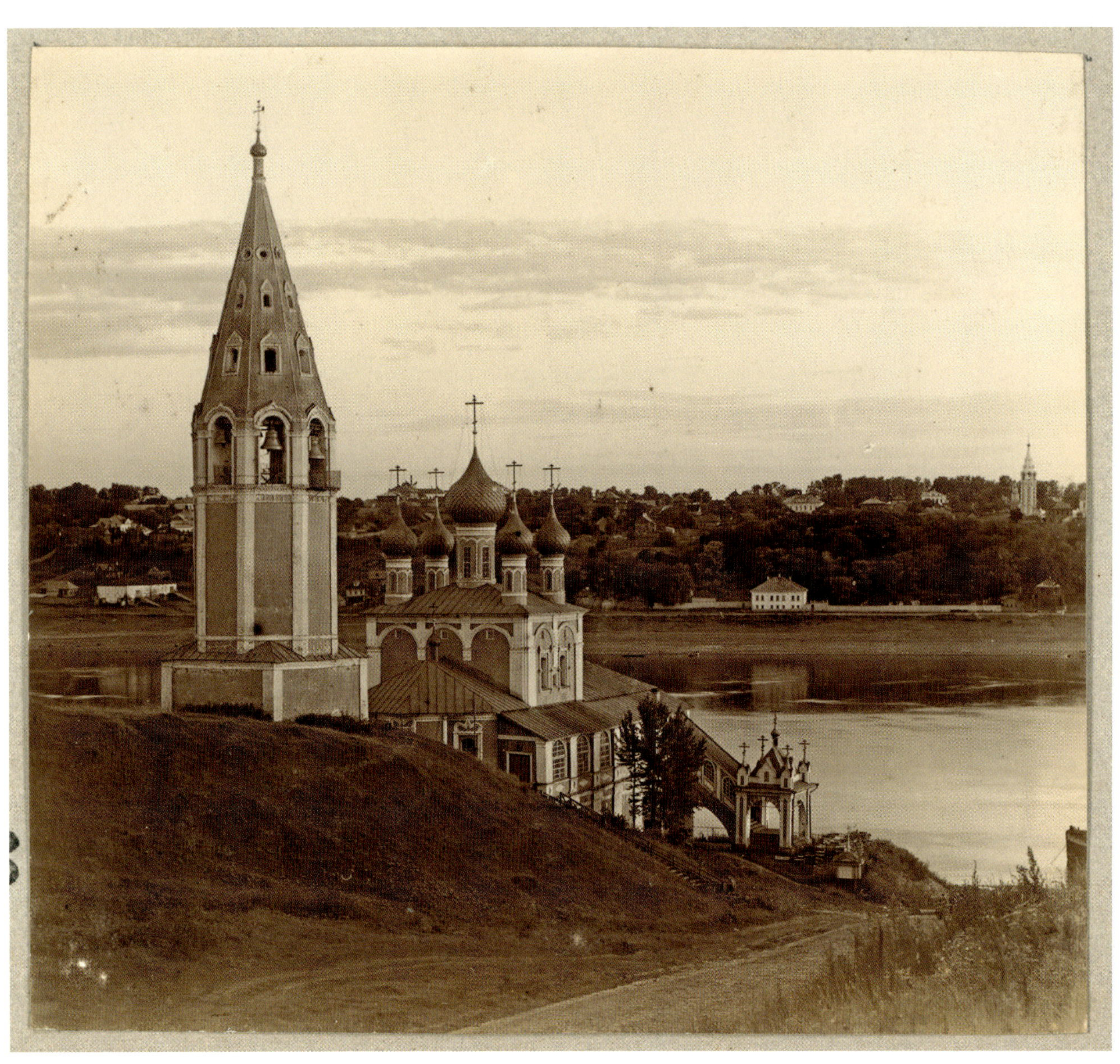

TUTAEV (ROMANOV) Church of Kazan Icon of the
Virgin and bell tower. Northeast view. PROKUDIN-
GORSKY 02409. SUMMER 1910.

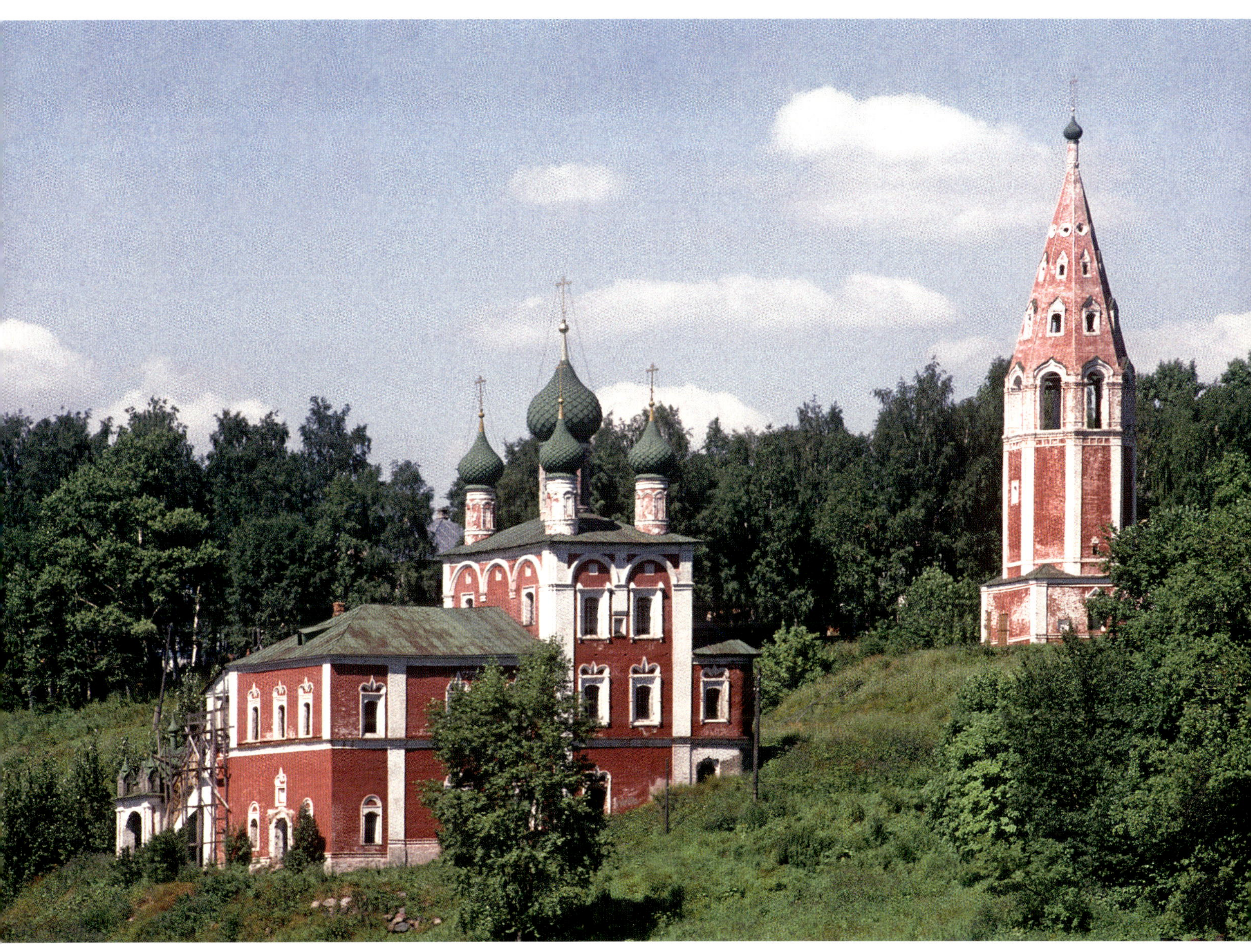

TUTAEV (ROMANOV) Church of Kazan Icon of the
Virgin and bell tower. Southwest view from Volga
River. BRUMFIELD, JULY 25, 1997.

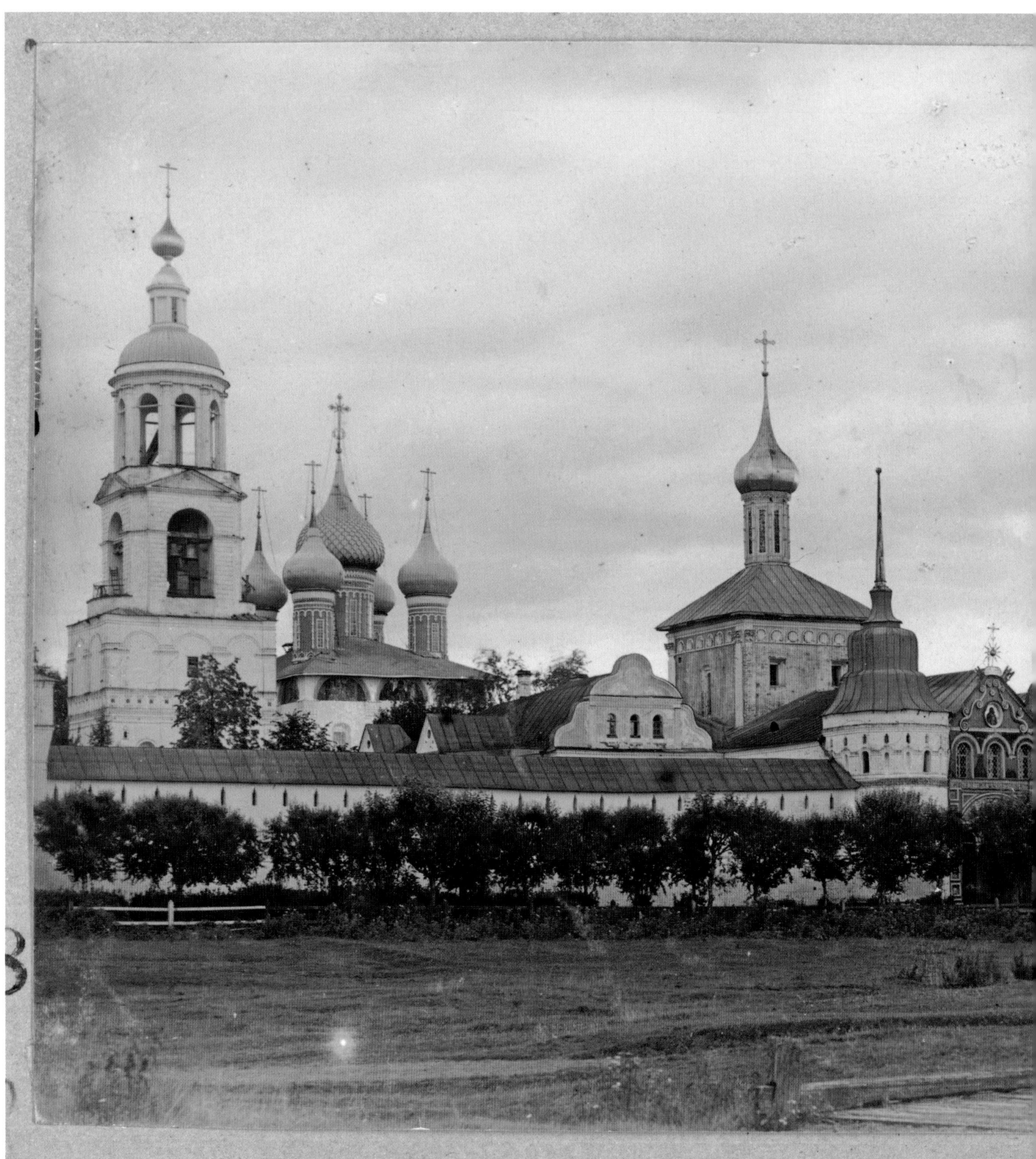

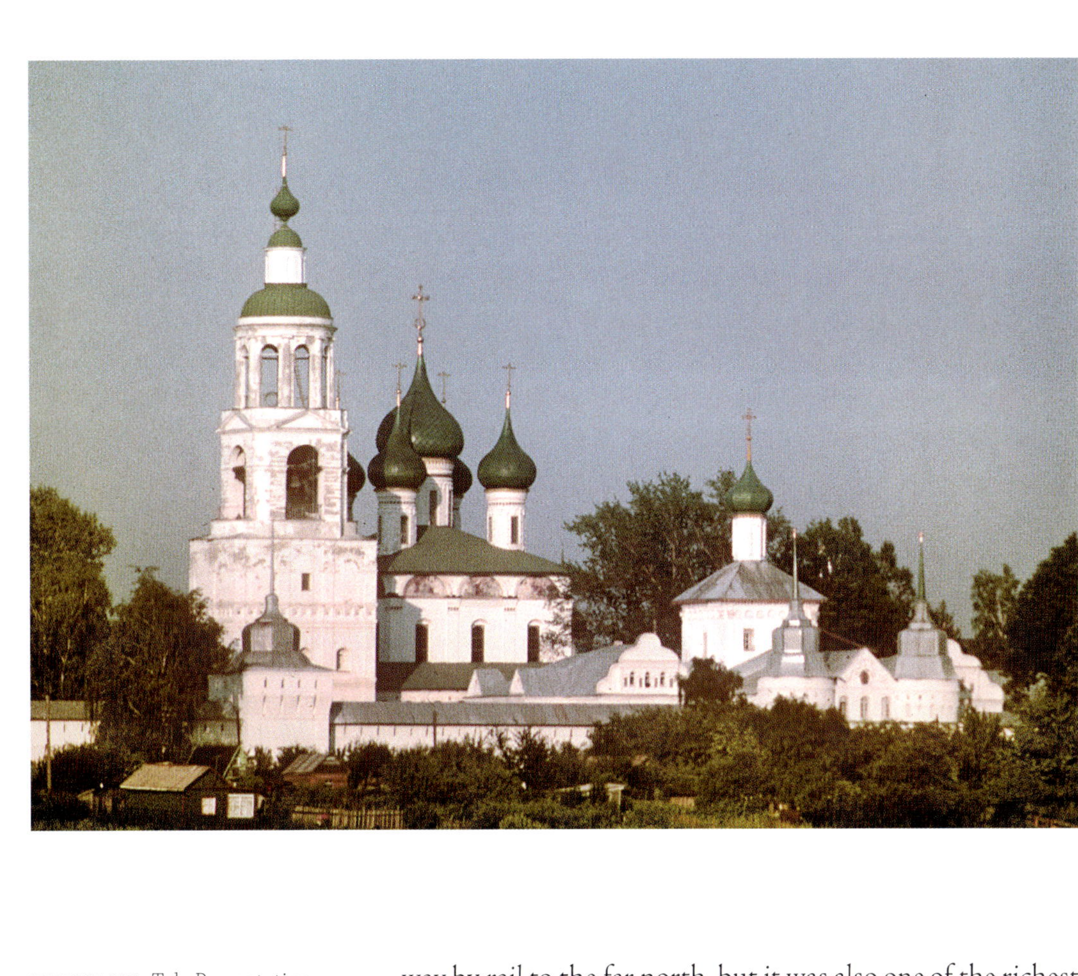

way by rail to the far north, but it was also one of the richest cultural centers of late medieval Russia. Among the centers of medieval Russian culture—Vladimir, Pskov, Novgorod, and Moscow itself—none has a greater concentration of religious art than the city of Yaroslavl, located some 250 kilometers northeast of Moscow.

The Russian settlement was founded probably in the early eleventh century by Yaroslav, the Prince of Rostov, who subsequently ruled as grand prince in Kiev from 1037 to 1054. According to popular legend Yaroslav and his troops seized an existing site of pagan worship, and with his axe he personally destroyed a wooden statue of the Great Bear. In the seventeenth century Yaroslavl adopted as its heraldic symbol a standing bear holding a poleaxe. Although Yaroslavl flourished in the early thirteenth century, its strategic location made it the target of many raids by the Volga Bulgars and, from 1238, the Tatars.

At the same time, Yaroslavl benefited from its location to serve as a center not only for trade within the extensive

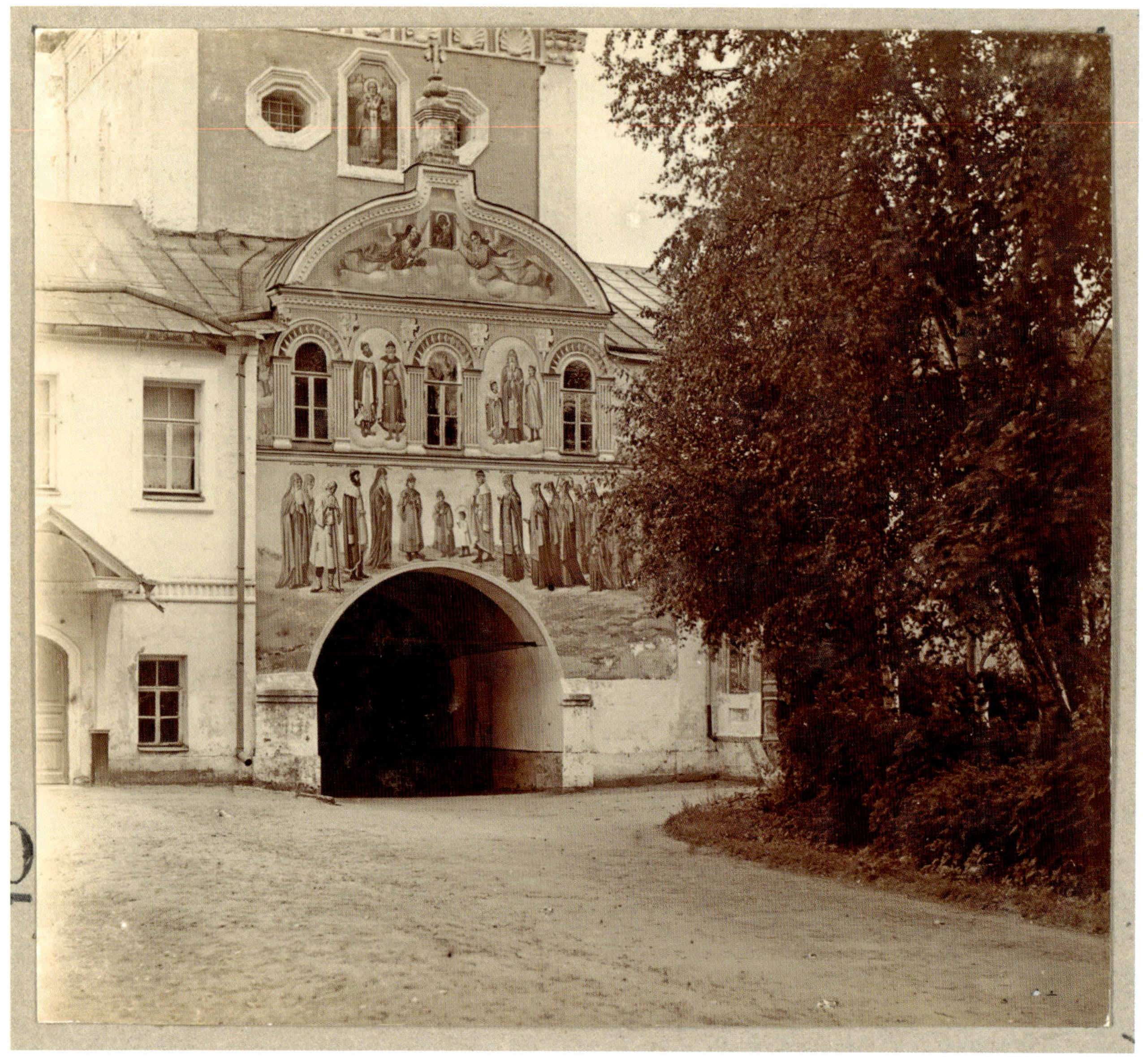

Volga River basin but also for exploitation of the forested expanses of the Russian north. In the latter part of the sixteenth century, Ivan the Terrible established a port at the Archangel Monastery on the Northern Dvina River near the White Sea and thus opened Moscow for commerce with western Europe. This in turn enhanced Yaroslavl's strategic position within a mercantile network that stretched from the White Sea to Siberia and the Orient. With new trading possibilities, Yaroslavl attracted colonies of Russian and foreign merchants (English, Dutch, and German).

Spared the worst of the disorder inflicted on Russia in

YAROSLAVL Tolg Presentation Monastery. Church of Saint Nicholas over Holy Gate. East view. PROKUDIN-GORSKY 02415. SUMMER 1910.

YAROSLAVL Tolg Presentation Monastery. Church of Saint Nicholas over Holy Gate. East view with cloisters. BRUMFIELD, JULY 24, 1997.

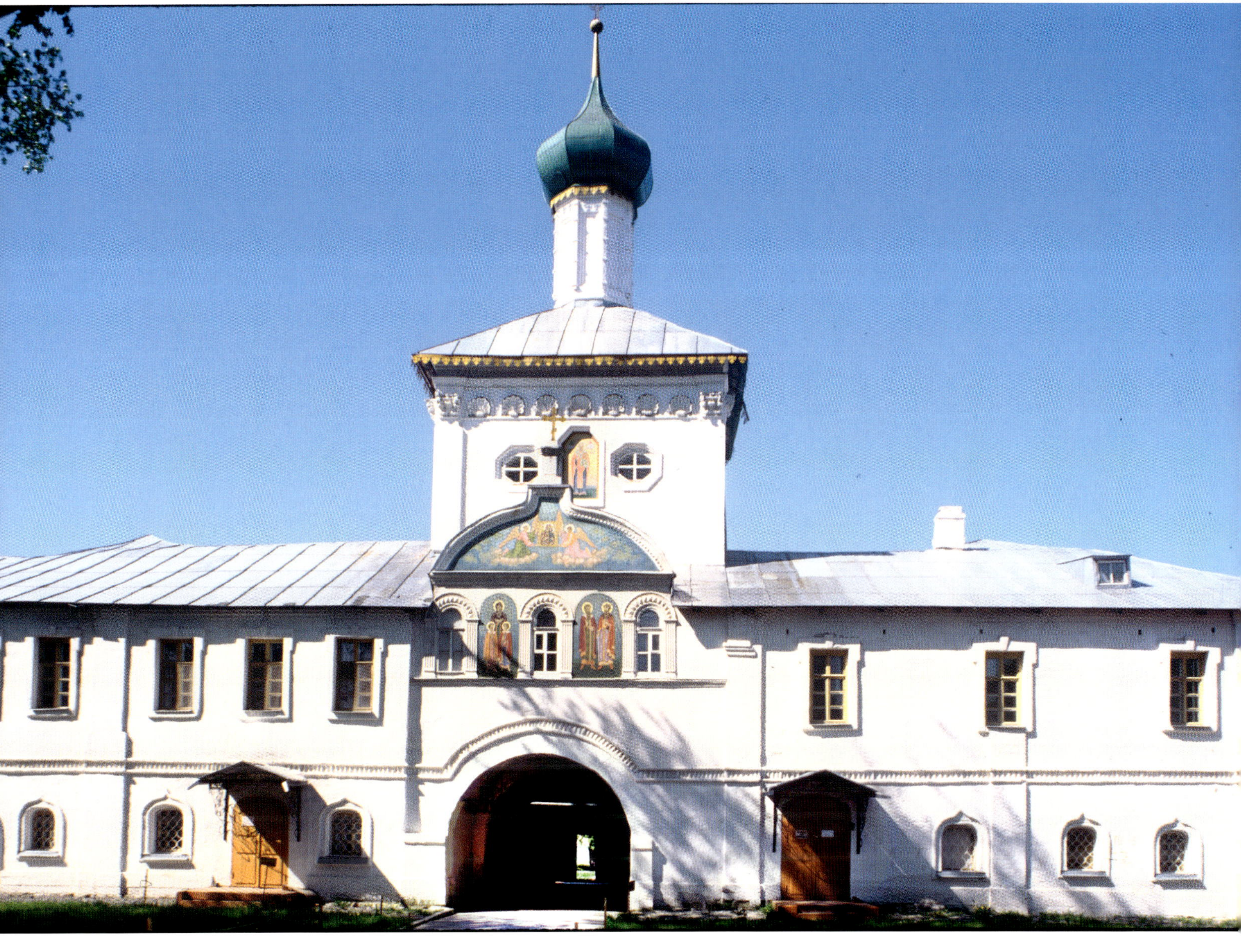

the latter part of Ivan the Terrible's reign, Yaroslavl eluded the devastation of the Time of Troubles. During the occupation of Moscow by Polish forces, Yaroslavl in 1612 became the center of national resistance to the Poles as well as the Swedes. The participation of Yaroslavl's merchants in this national resistance brought them extensive privileges from the government of the new ruler, Mikhail Fyodorovich (1596–1645), first tsar of the Romanov dynasty. With the relative stability of the seventeenth century, Yaroslavl's wealth increased through its position as an essential trading link between Moscow and the north, as well as Siberia. During this period its ensembles of brick churches, superbly proportioned and ornamented with ceramic tiles, made Yaroslavl an object of wonder for Western as well as Russian travelers. Only

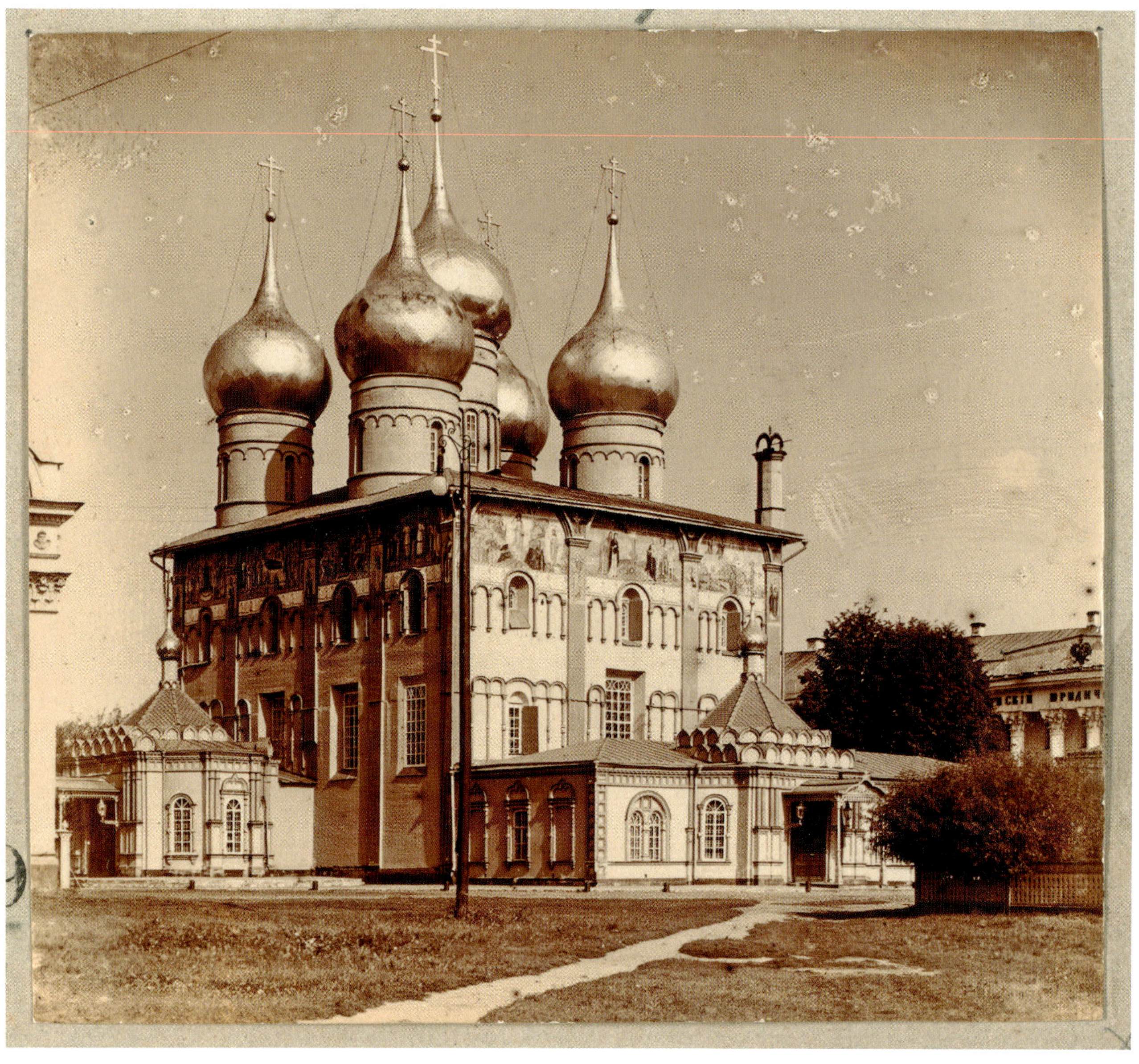

Moscow could rival Yaroslavl in its concentration of new churches, sponsored by a combination of wealthy merchants, city districts, and trade associations. In the seventeenth century, forty-four masonry churches were erected within the area's thirty-five parishes. Despite damage inflicted during the Soviet era, many of these churches have survived.

Yaroslavl has become a large provincial center (population around 600,000), with extensive industry anchored by petrochemicals. Fortunately, the city's industrial development has taken place to the west, away from the river,

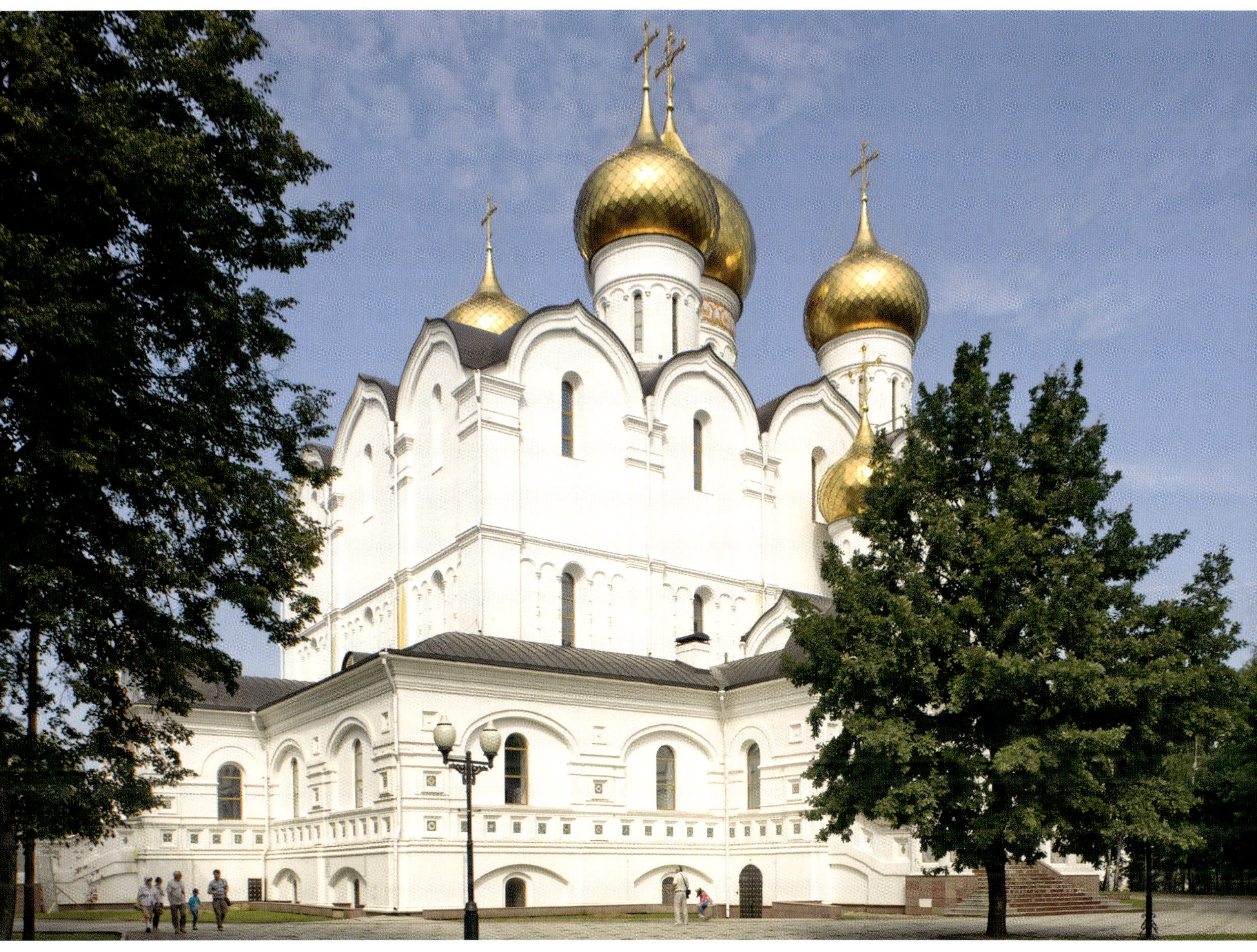

and Yaroslavl has thus preserved some of the loveliest corners of traditional Russia. Situated on the high right bank of the Volga at its confluence with the Kotorosl River, Yaroslavl has retained much of its beauty, enhanced by a tree-lined boulevard overlooking the Volga.

The embankment centers on the town's main cathedral, dedicated to the Dormition of the Virgin. The fourth version to be built on the site, the cathedral that Prokudin-Gorsky photographed was erected in the 1660s and painted with frescoes shortly thereafter. A four-tiered bell tower in the Russo-Byzantine style was built in 1836. During a two-week uprising against the Bolsheviks in July 1918, the cathedral was heavily shelled. Partially repaired, the cathedral was closed in 1929, with a removal of all later addi-

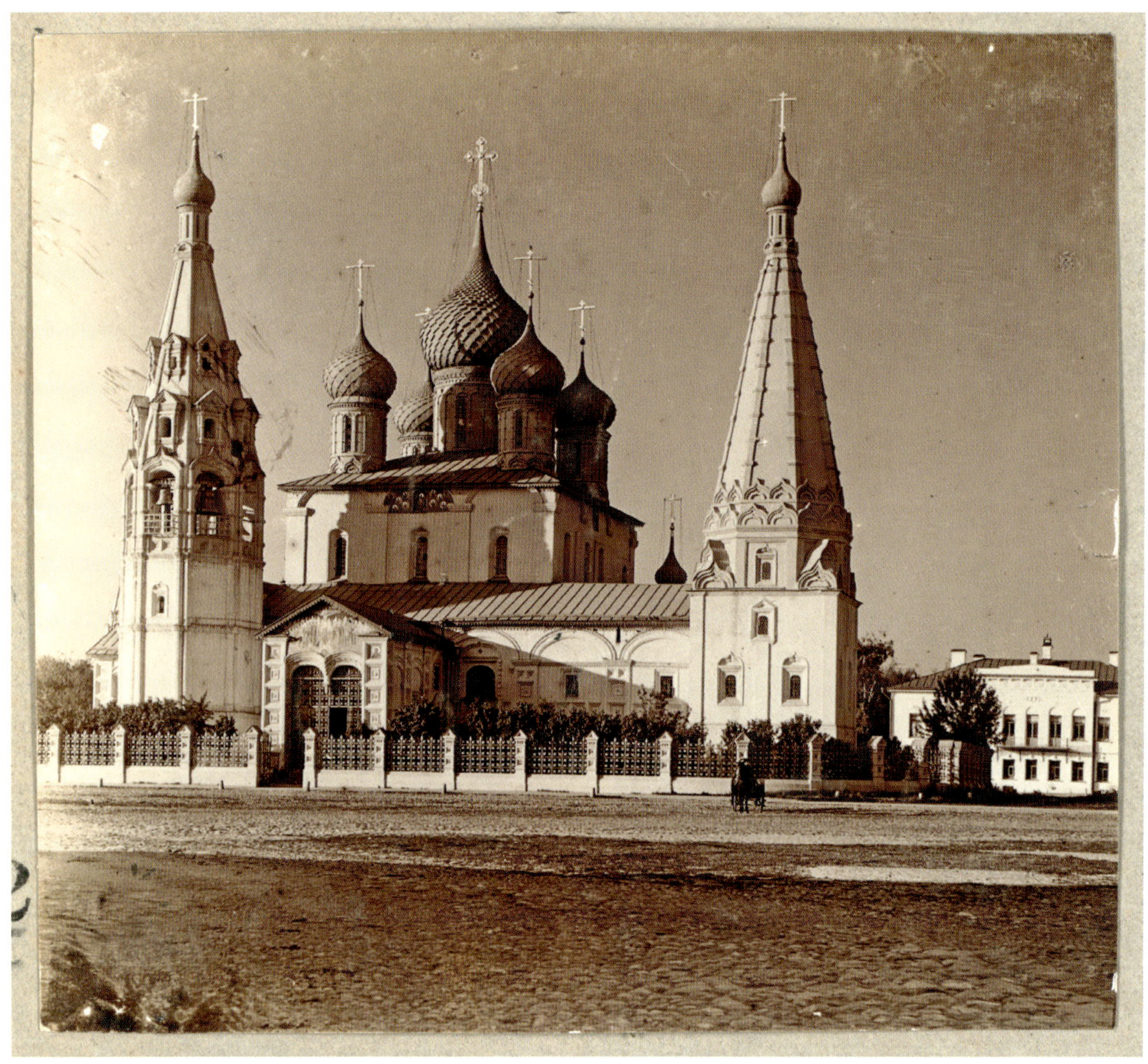

tions—perhaps a prelude to museification. Instead, it was demolished at the height of the Stalinist terror in 1937. My photographs from 2017 show the new cathedral, rebuilt in 2006–12 with substantially different proportions.

Among the most graceful of Yaroslavl's seventeenth-century monuments is the Church of Elijah the Prophet (1647–50), located on the city's central square of the city. Unfortunately, the Elijah Church is represented in the Prokudin-Gorsky Collection only by the contact print. Yet this image is sufficient to demonstrate a rare degree of preservation as measured in my photographs of various years. The donors of the Elijah Church, the Skripin brothers, be-

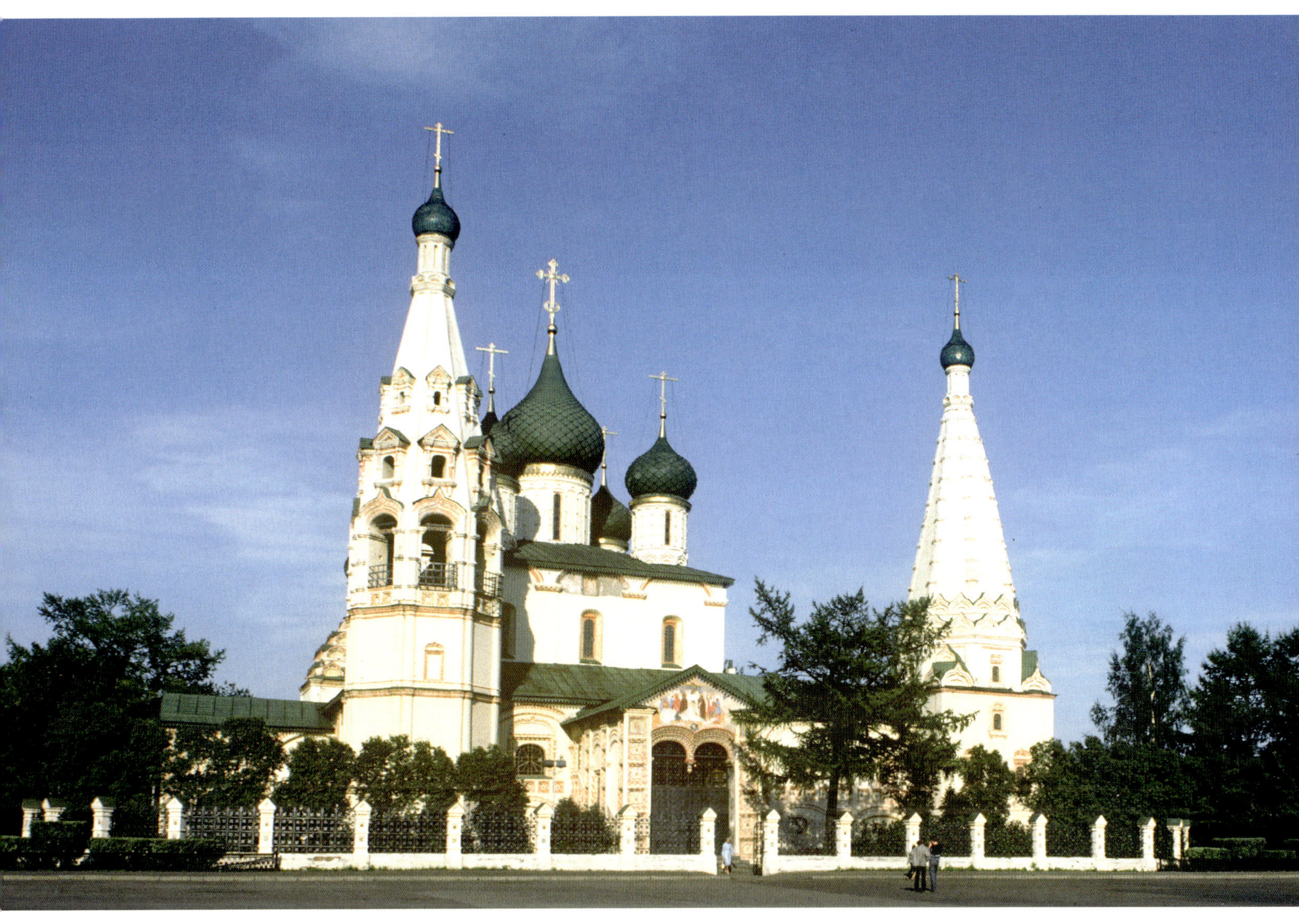

came wealthy from the Siberian fur trade. Their magnificent church consists of a central component raised on a high base that supported an enclosed gallery. The structure is crowned with five cupolas. Its corners are adorned by attached chapels, as well as a soaring bell tower, with a chapel at the southwest corner.

During the seventeenth century, the districts beyond the Kotorosl River witnessed the construction of several distinctive architectural ensembles. The largest and most elaborate of these structures is the Church of the Decapitation of John the Baptist, located in the Tolchkovo district near the Kotorosl, a small tributary of the Volga. Prokudin-Gorsky photographed this superb monument only from the west in afternoon light. Unfortunately, his original negative is lost, but the surviving print from his contact album gives

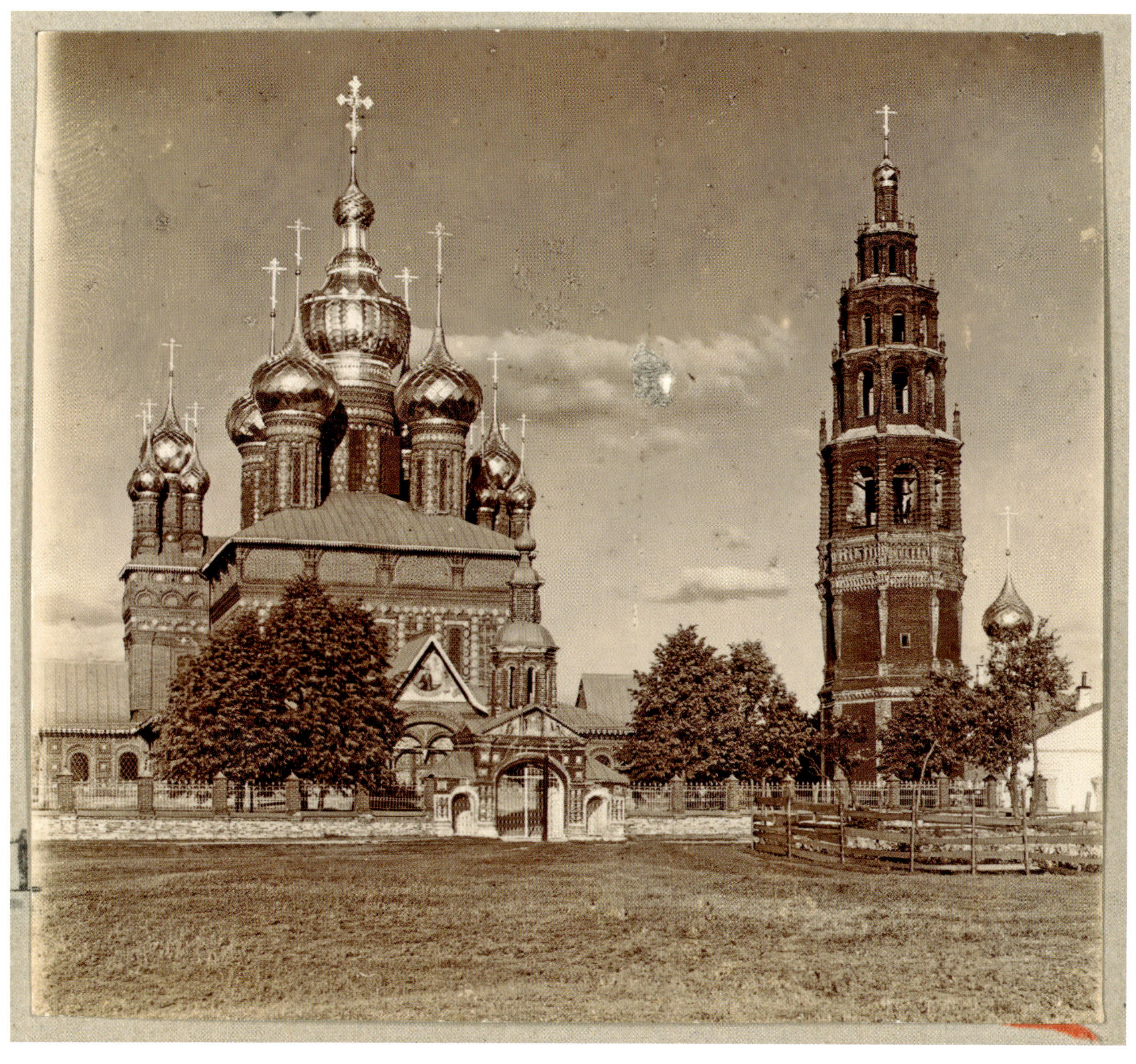

a unique view of the entire church ensemble from an open field. That view was closed by the construction during the Soviet period of a large chemical plant next to the church.

The Tolchkovo church was constructed between 1671 and 1687 with funds provided by parishioners and by the entrepreneurs Rodion and Leonty Yeremin, whose wealth derived from leather workshops located in the district. The plan of the church included an enclosed gallery on three sides of the rectangular structure and two symmetrical chapels at each eastern corner. Entrance porches with steeply pitched roofs mark the center of the north, west, and south galleries. The brick facades (not stuccoed) are decorated by clusters of attached columns with a mélange of decorative elements such as

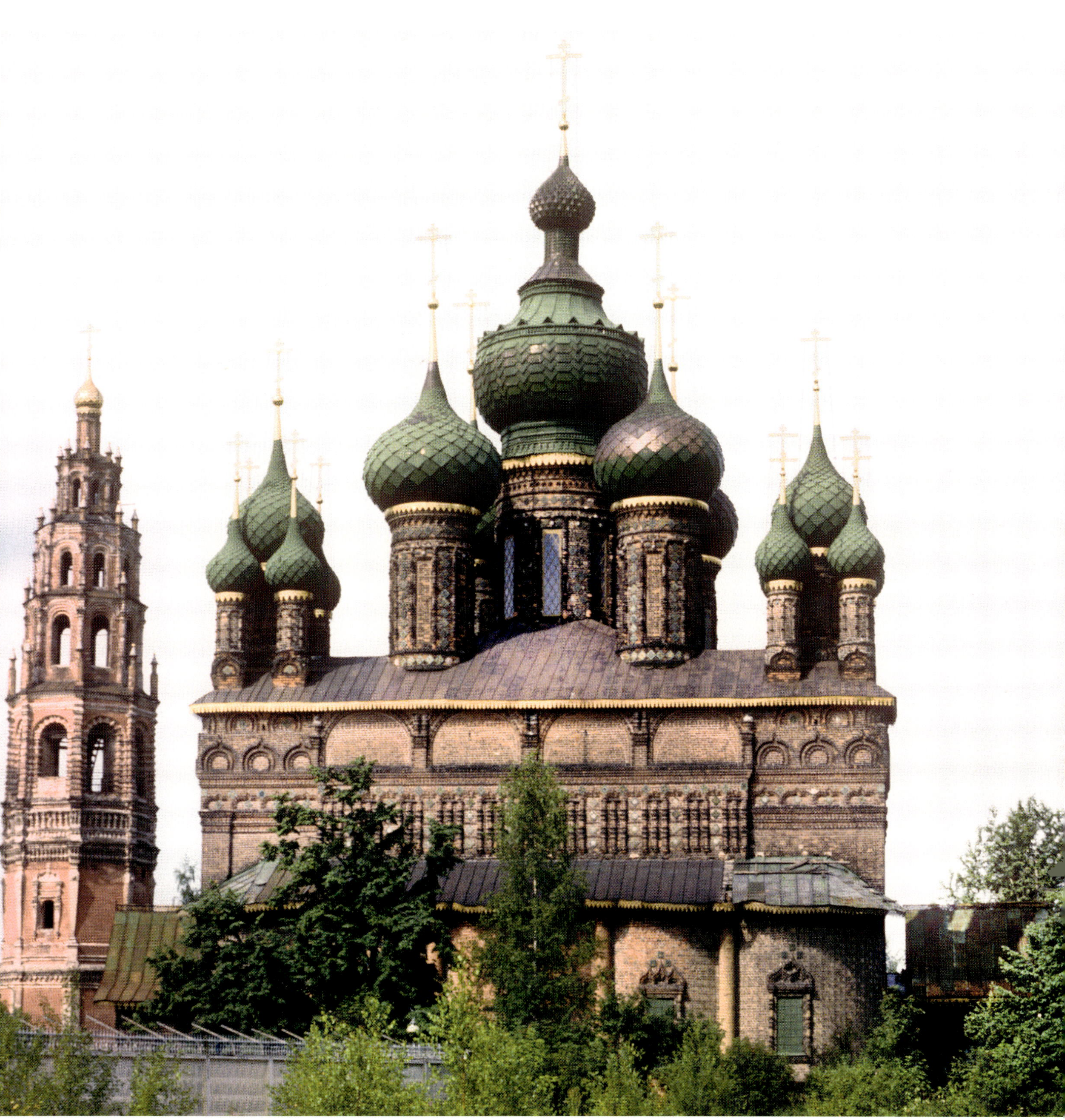

YAROSLAVL Church of the Decapitation of John the Baptist at Tolchkovo. West view. PROKUDIN-GORSKY 02436. SUMMER 1910.

YAROSLAVL Church of the Decapitation of John the Baptist at Tolchkovo. East view with bell tower. BRUMFIELD, JUNE 29, 1995.

miniature pointed arches over paired columns of molded patterned brick. The elaborate brick forms are enhanced by bright polychrome tiles visible in my detailed photographs.

Great ingenuity was demonstrated by the anonymous master builders in the design of the two east chapels, which are dedicated to the Three Prelates (Saints Basil the Great, Gregory the Theologian, and John Chrysostom) and to the Kazan miracle workers Saints Gury and Varsonofy. In an unusual solution, the chapel cornices are elevated to the height of the main structure. The result is a uniform roof level that creates an impressive visual effect from the west. The chapel structures also create a monumental unity on the east facade, with accent points provided by each chapel's cluster of five miniature cupolas on elongated drums. The decorative relief work on the upper tiers of the east facade is complemented by colorful trompe l'oeil rustication on the lower apsidal structure, divided into five segments. My photographs over the years show that the painted pattern has faded, yet the east facade is no less impressive.

The Church of John the Baptist had ancillary structures, including a modest winter church dedicated to the Ascension, built in 1659–65 and demolished by the factory in the early 1950s. The main approach to the church from the west was framed by a Holy Gate, which has survived at the factory boundary. The dominant feature of the ensemble is the bell tower, built at the turn of the eighteenth century in the florid style known as "Moscow baroque." Forty-five meters in height, this grand campanile is decorated with limestone elements, including balusters and pinnacles that emphasize the ascending octagons—an amalgam of Russian and Dutch design.

Prokudin-Gorsky also photographed the interior of this remarkable church, whose walls are covered with frescoes. It is something of a miracle that the Tolchkovo ensemble and the frescoes have, for the most part, survived. During the 1930s the chemical plant that produced paints on the adjacent territory used the church for storage of harsh chemicals. Fortunately, the Yaroslavl museum regained control of the church.

There is basic information about the masters whose work covers the walls of this large interior, from the galleries and side chapels to the altar. The main space was painted from June 1694 to July 1695 by a group of sixteen artists under the guidance of Yaroslavl masters Dmitry Grigorev Plekhanov and Fedor Ignatyev, who also did frescoes for the side chapels in 1700. Plekhanov was already renowned for his work at the Archangel Cathedral in the Moscow Kremlin, and at other major churches in Rostov, Yaroslavl, and Vologda. Ivan and Andrei Yeremin provided major support for the vast project, which included over five hundred segments with some two thousand motifs — the largest such ensemble in Yaroslavl and, by some calculations, in the Orthodox world.

The north and south walls are divided horizontally into nine registers. The three registers at the top illustrate the life and teachings of Christ. The fourth level from the top displays the Passion of Christ. Closer to the viewer's eye level, the fifth and sixth registers from the top illustrate the life of John the Baptist, with emphasis on the Beheading and the Finding of the Head of John the Baptist. (In addition to the Beheading, the Orthodox Church observes three holidays dedicated to the Finding of the Head of John the Baptist.) The seventh register from the top displays an unusual rendering of scores of Orthodox saints arranged by the days of the calendar. The bottom two levels of the north and south walls consist of an inscription band about the church and a decorative border. At the very top, the ceiling vaults show major festivals such as the Dormition. As usual, the central dome contains a portrayal of Christ Pantocrator.

Of the four massive piers that support the ceiling vaults, only the two west piers are visible in the main space. The east piers are concealed behind an elaborately carved six-tiered icon screen originally made over a period from 1687 to 1701. After the closing of the parish in the early 1930s, the icons were removed for conservation. Prokudin-Gorsky photographed vivid details on the lower part of the south face of the northwest pier. The two scenes depict the Apostle Peter escaping from prison and the baptism of the Ethiopian Eunuch by the Apostle Philip. My view with a wide lens gives a sense of the space around the pier, including the north wall and the frame of the icon screen. Prokudin-Gorsky also photographed a portion of the lower left side of the north wall, including images of the miraculous discovery of the head of John the Baptist. These frescoes have been well preserved.

However impressive the main space, the frescoes that cover the enclosed galleries (*papert* in Russian) seem more lively and accessible because of the lower ceiling vaults. They were completed in 1703–4 with the support of metropolitan Dmitry of Rostov, a leading prelate during the reign of Peter the Great. The curved ceiling vaults of the gallery display episodes from the Old Testament, such as the Fall of Jericho and the Six Days of Creation. The walls include depictions of the Seven Sacraments, the Last Judgment, and the Fruits of the Paschal Mystery as well as scenes from edifying literary works such as *The Great Mirror* (*Speculum maius*), a thirteenth-century encyclopedic compendium whose fragments appeared in Russian during the seventeenth century. The didactic nature of these scenes — often accompa-

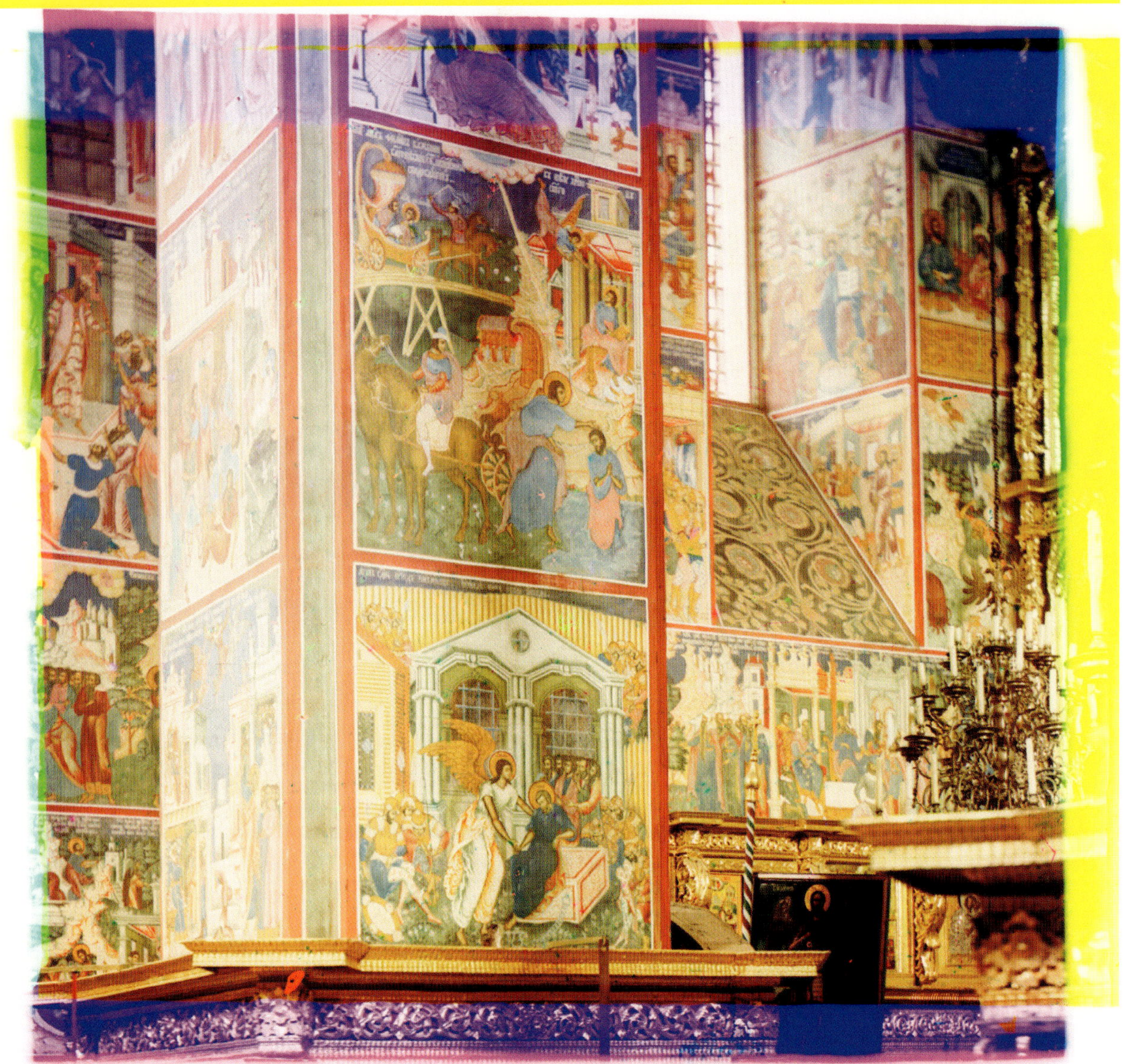

YAROSLAVL Church of the Decapitation of John the Baptist at Tolchkovo. Interior, northwest pier with scenes from Acts of the Apostles. PROKUDIN-GORSKY 21257. SUMMER 1911.

YAROSLAVL Church of the Decapitation of John the Baptist at Tolchkovo. Interior, northwest pier with north wall (*left*) and icon screen. BRUMFIELD, AUGUST 15, 2017.

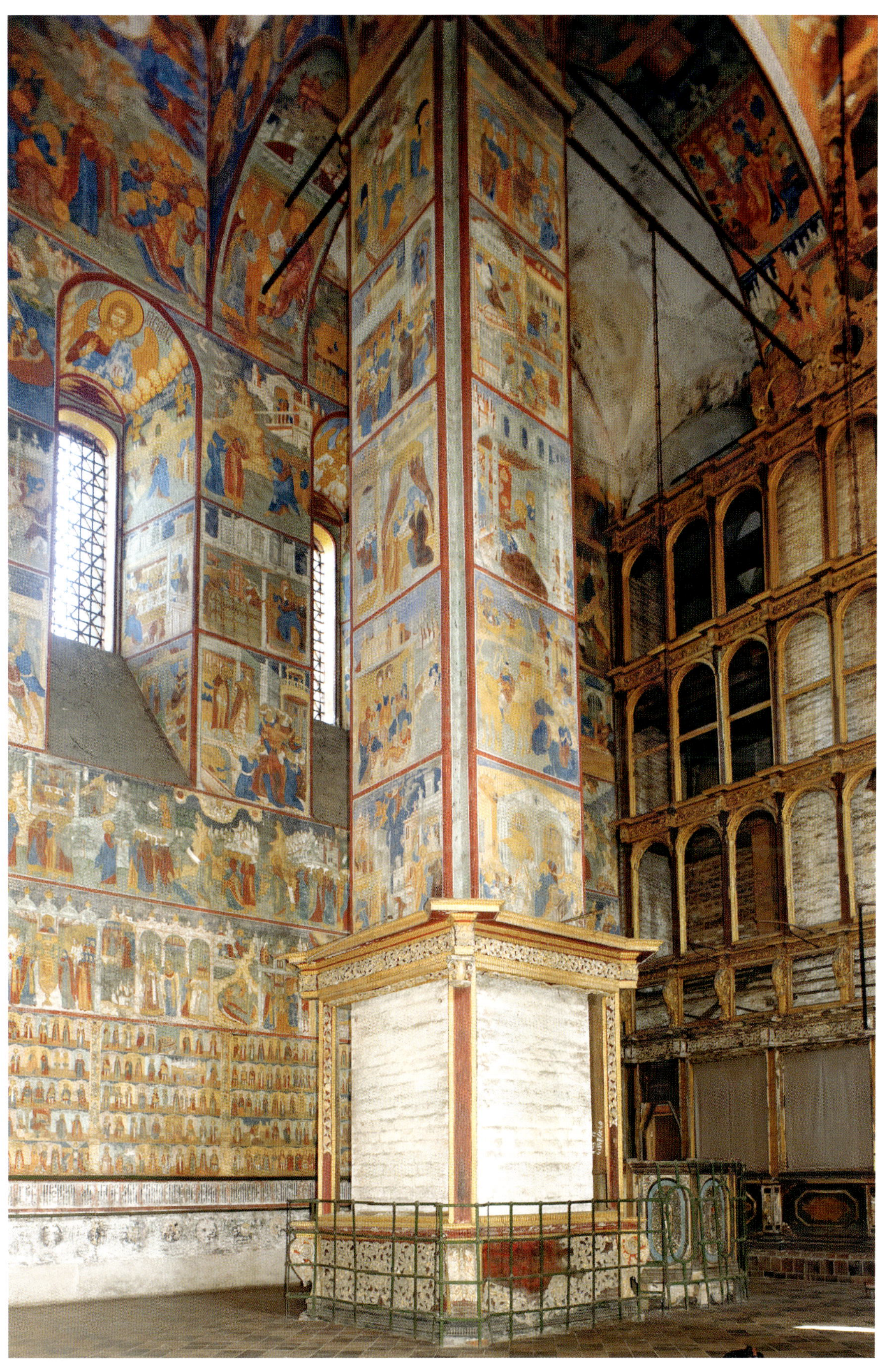

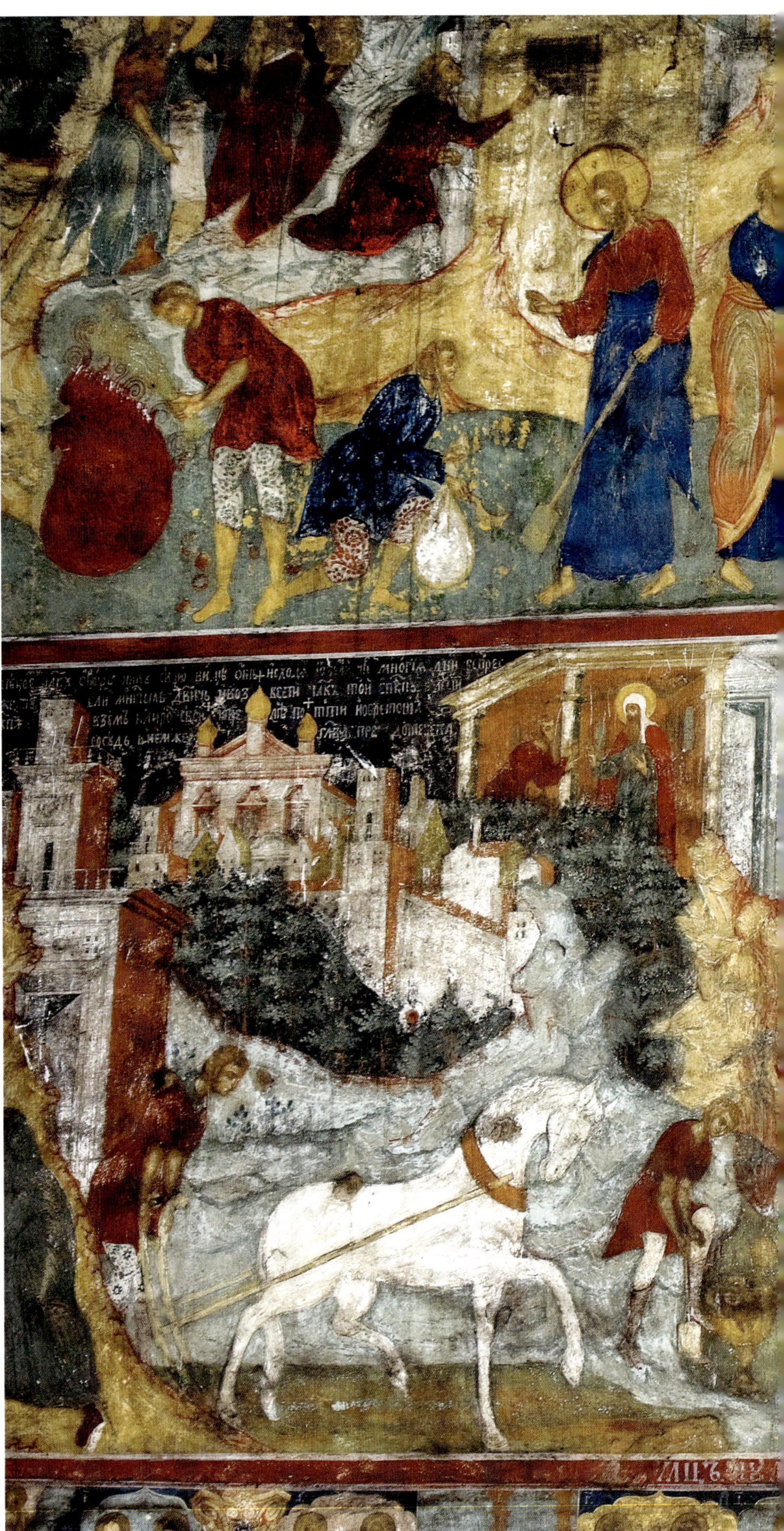

YAROSLAVL Church of the Decapitation of John the Baptist at Tolchkovo. Interior, northwest corner. Frescoes on north wall depicting Finding of the Head of John the Baptist. BRUMFIELD, AUGUST 15, 2017.

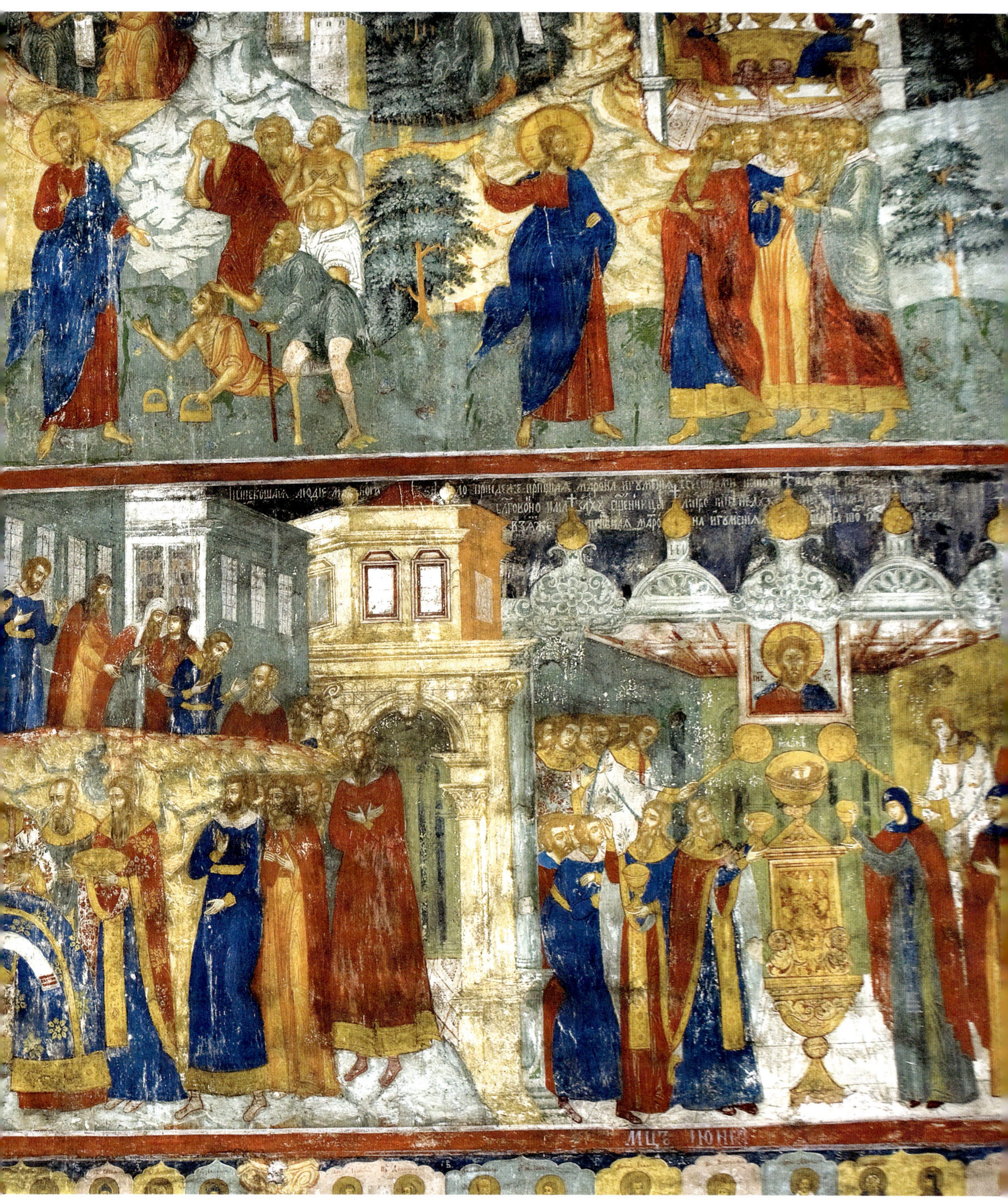

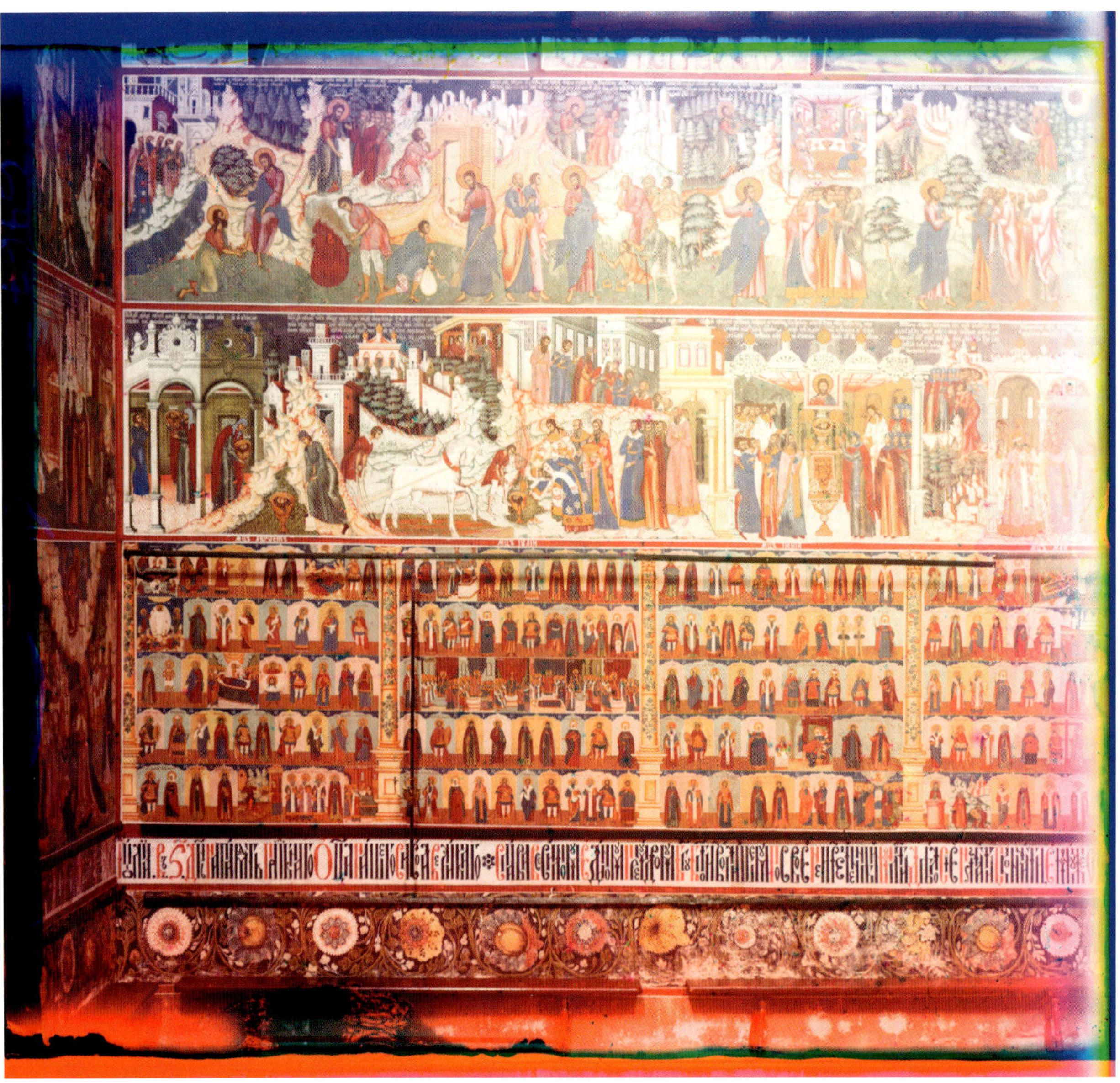

YAROSLAVL Church of the Decapitation of John the Baptist at Tolchkovo. Interior, northwest corner. Frescoes on north wall depicting Finding of the Head of John the Baptist. PROKUDIN-GORSKY 21259. SUMMER 1911.

YAROSLAVL Church of the Decapitation of John the Baptist at Tolchkovo. Interior, west gallery, main portal. PROKUDIN-GORSKY 21273. SUMMER 1911.

YAROSLAVL Church of the Decapitation of John the Baptist at Tolchkovo. Interior, west gallery, view north with right side of main portal. BRUMFIELD, AUGUST 15, 2017.

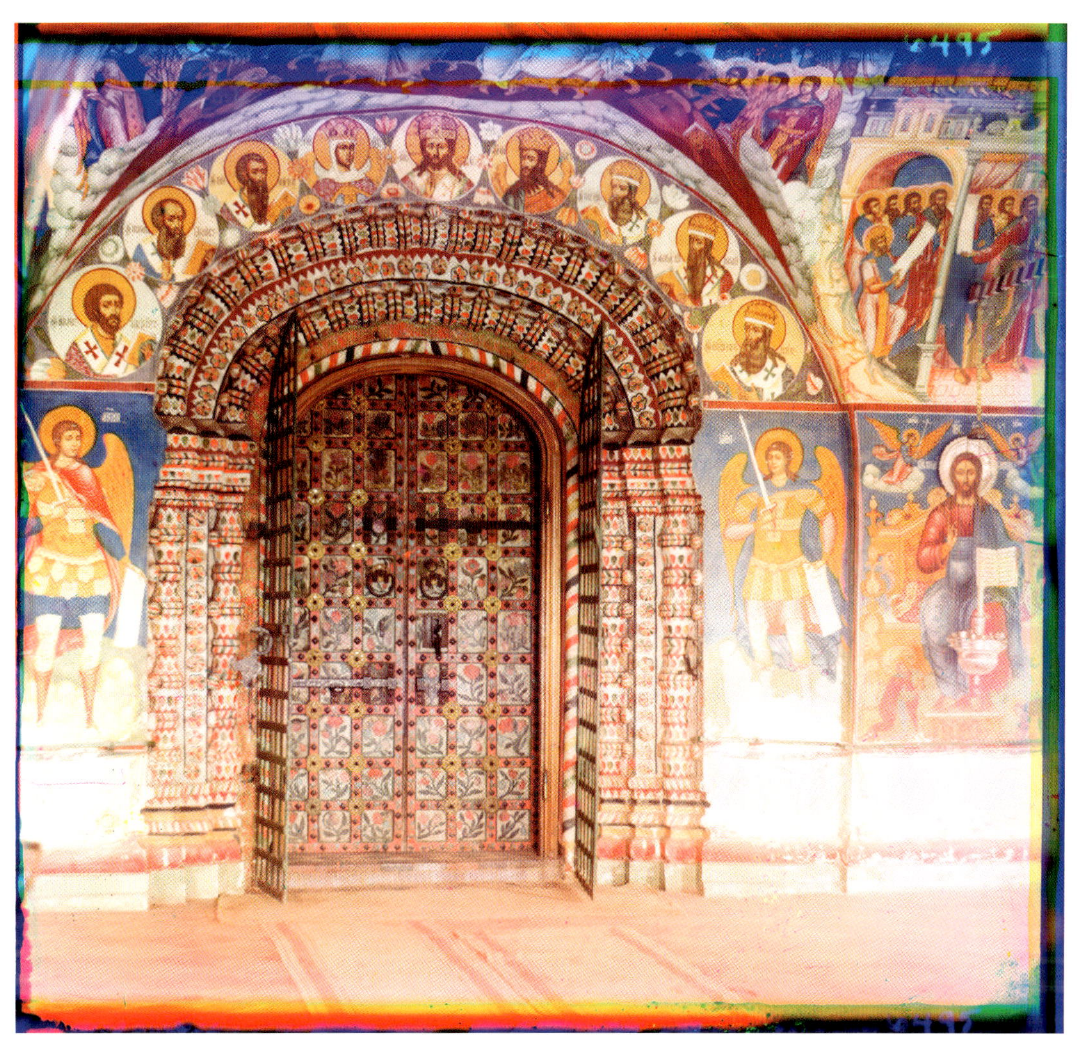

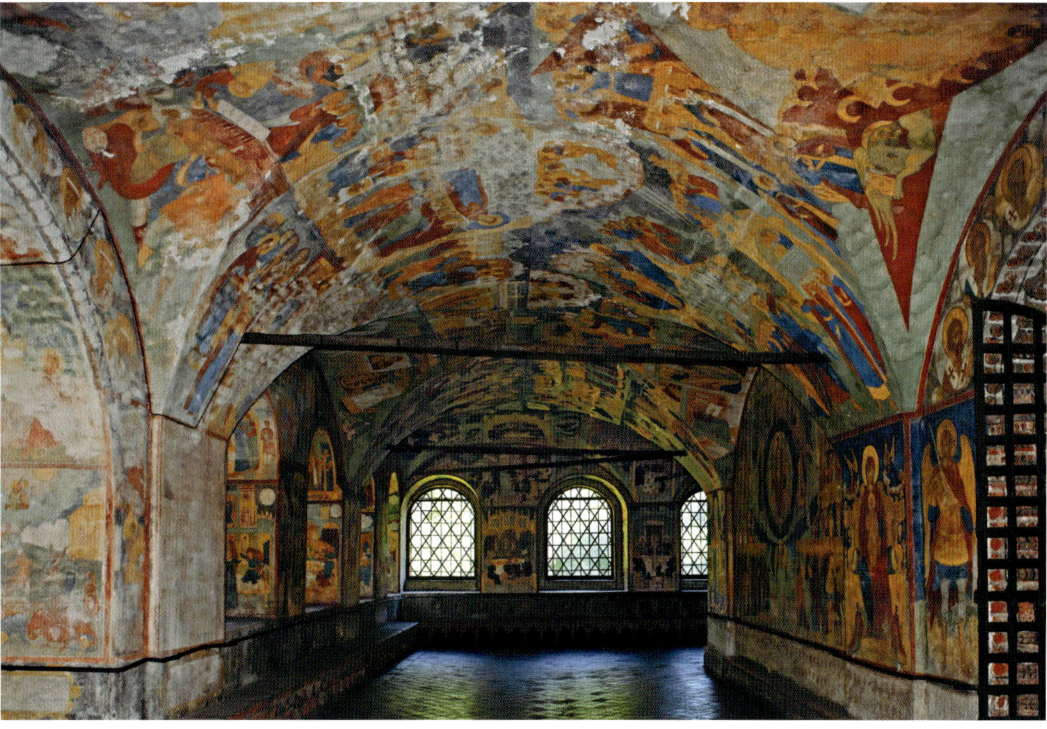

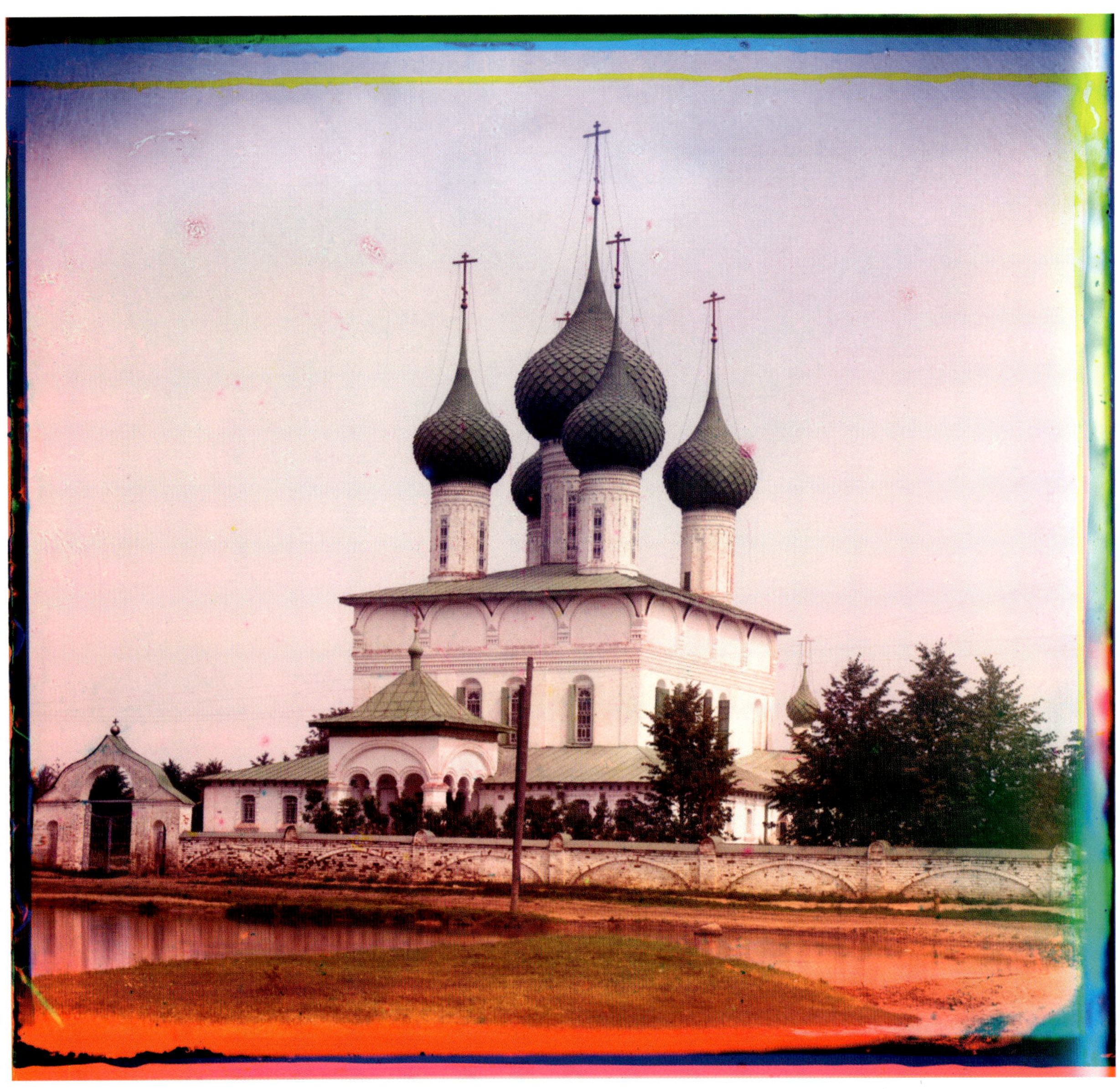

nied by texts—can be related to the use of the gallery as a
resting place for pilgrims who visited the church, as well as
a space for parishioners and others who came to the church
for confession and to speak with the priests. In this space
Prokudin-Gorsky photographed the main portal to the interior. My photograph shows an edge of the portal within
the context of the west gallery.

A distinctive feature of Yaroslavl church architecture is
the pairing of "summer" and "winter" churches, the smaller
of which would be heated, while the larger, more imposing church would be reserved for use primarily in the sum-

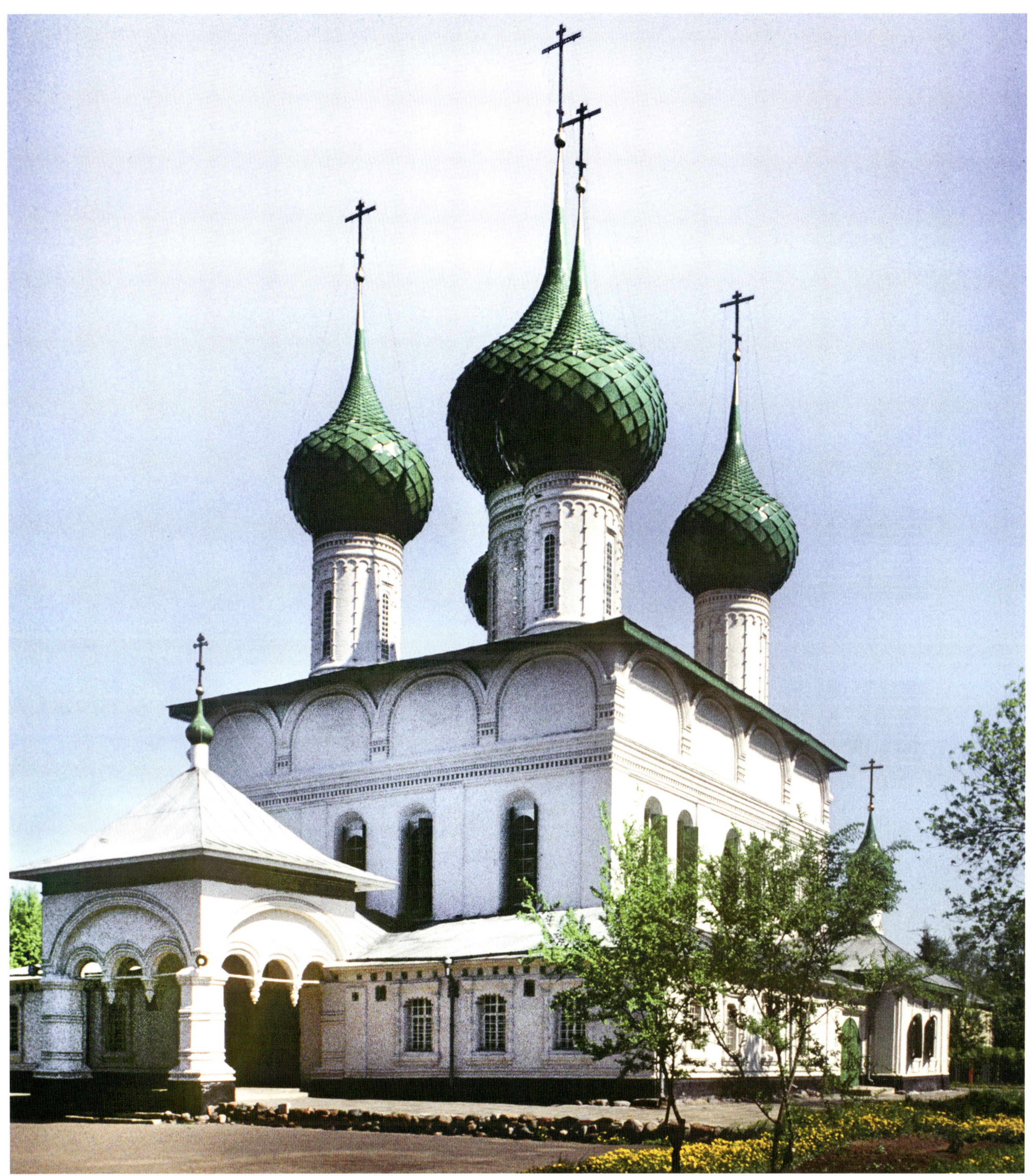

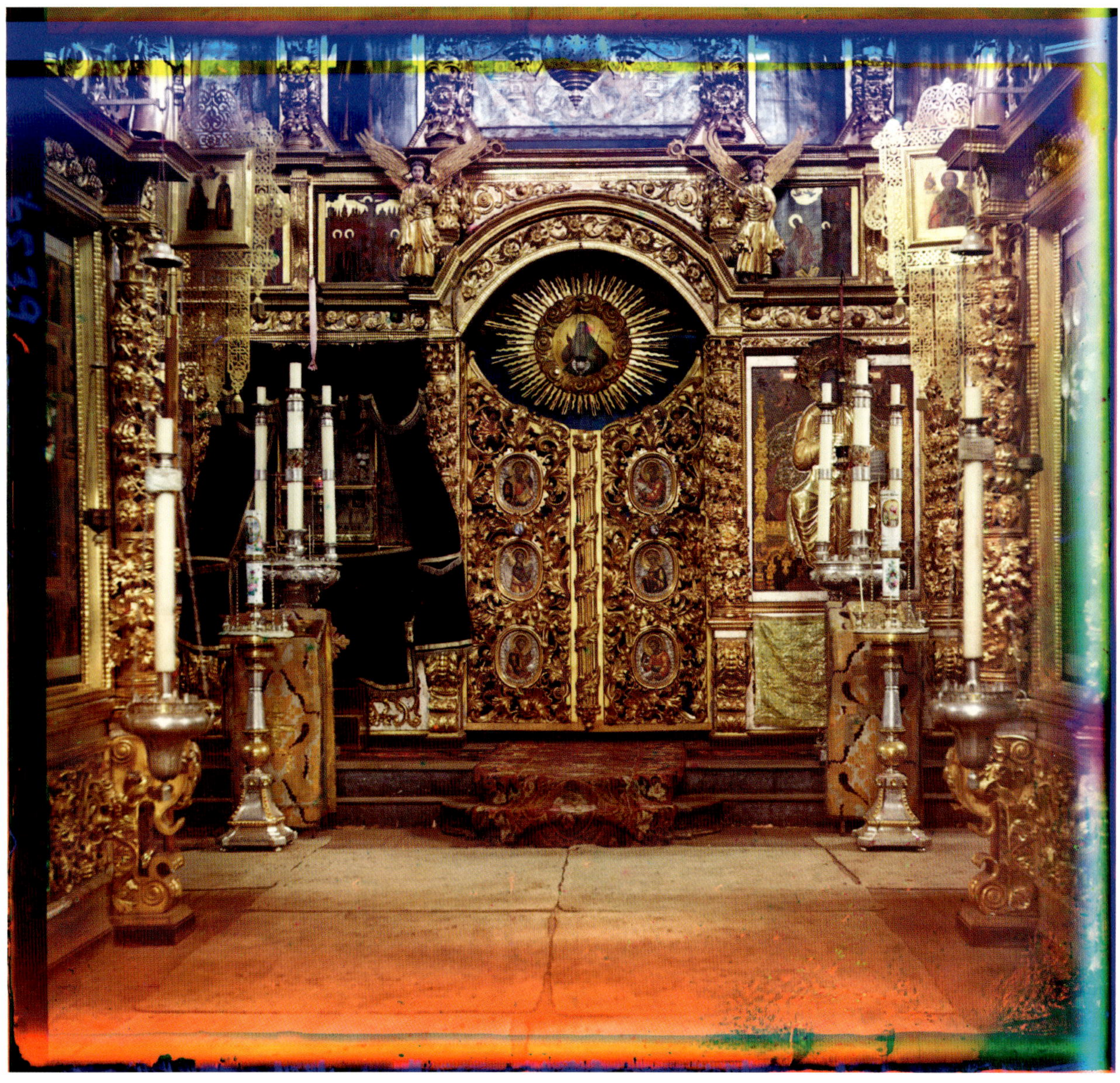

mer. These structures were completed at different times, and even large churches had chapels that could be heated for use throughout the year. An example is the ensemble of churches associated with the Saint Theodore Icon of the Virgin, built in 1681–87 with the financial assistance of Rodion Yeremin. Closed in 1930 and used as a workshop, it reverted to the Orthodox Church in 1987 and served as the city's main cathedral.

Prokudin-Gorsky's photographs of the cathedral interior and the iconostasis are especially valuable documents. (They are misidentified as belonging to the winter church.) The

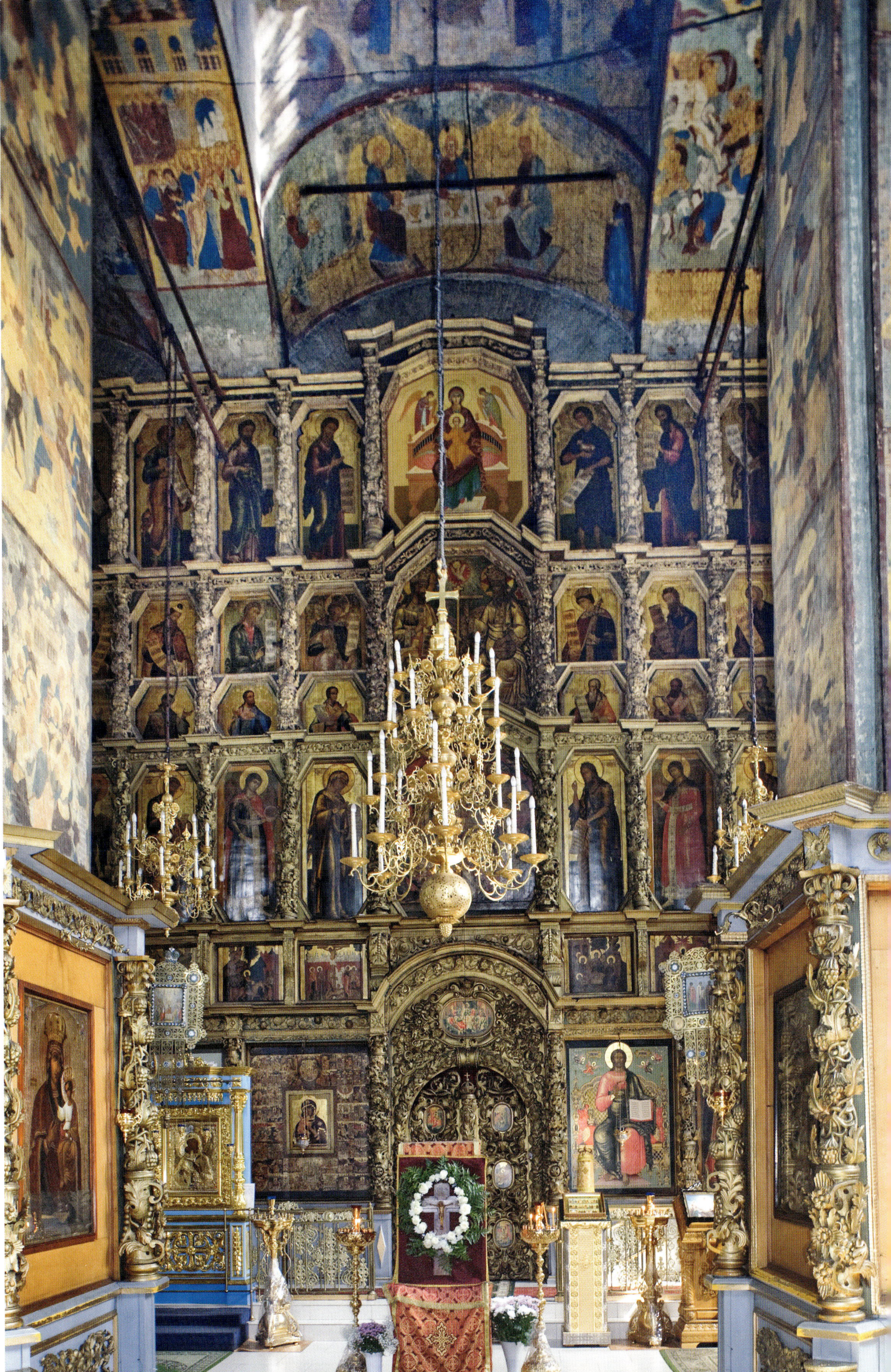

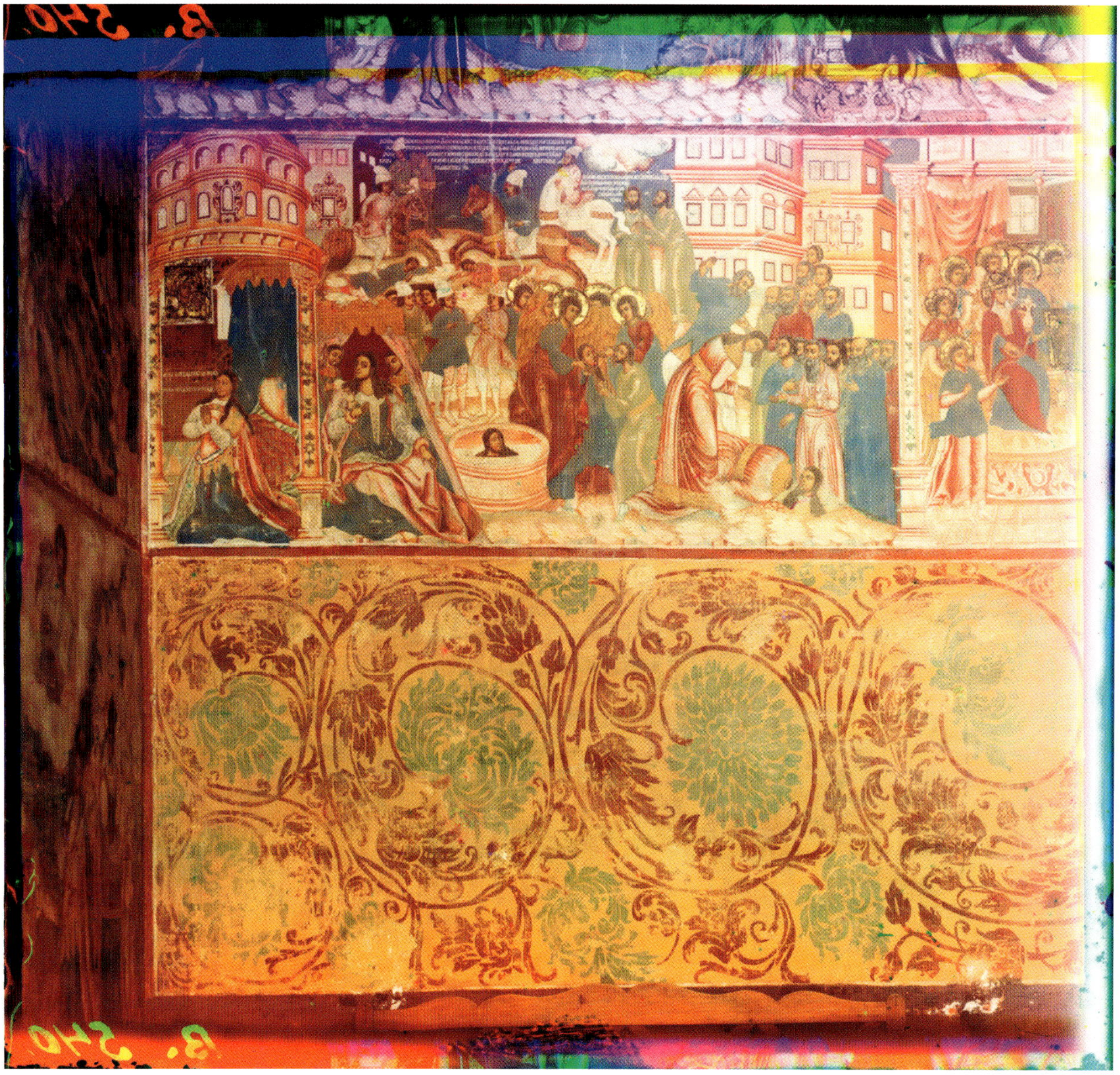

use of the church as a workshop during the Soviet period caused losses to the interior. Fortunately, the frescoes are relatively well preserved. Prokudin-Gorsky photographed a fresco detail on the lower left side of the north wall. My photograph of the same fresco from a different angle shows accurate colors.

Yaroslavl's consummate architectural ensemble belongs to the Korovniki district, near the confluence of the Kotorosl River with the Volga. The area takes its name from the Russian word *korova* (cow) and was used as pasturage, but its inhabitants also engaged in ceramic crafts, brick making, and pottery, all of which play a major role in the structure and decoration of this ensemble of two churches, with a large freestanding bell tower between

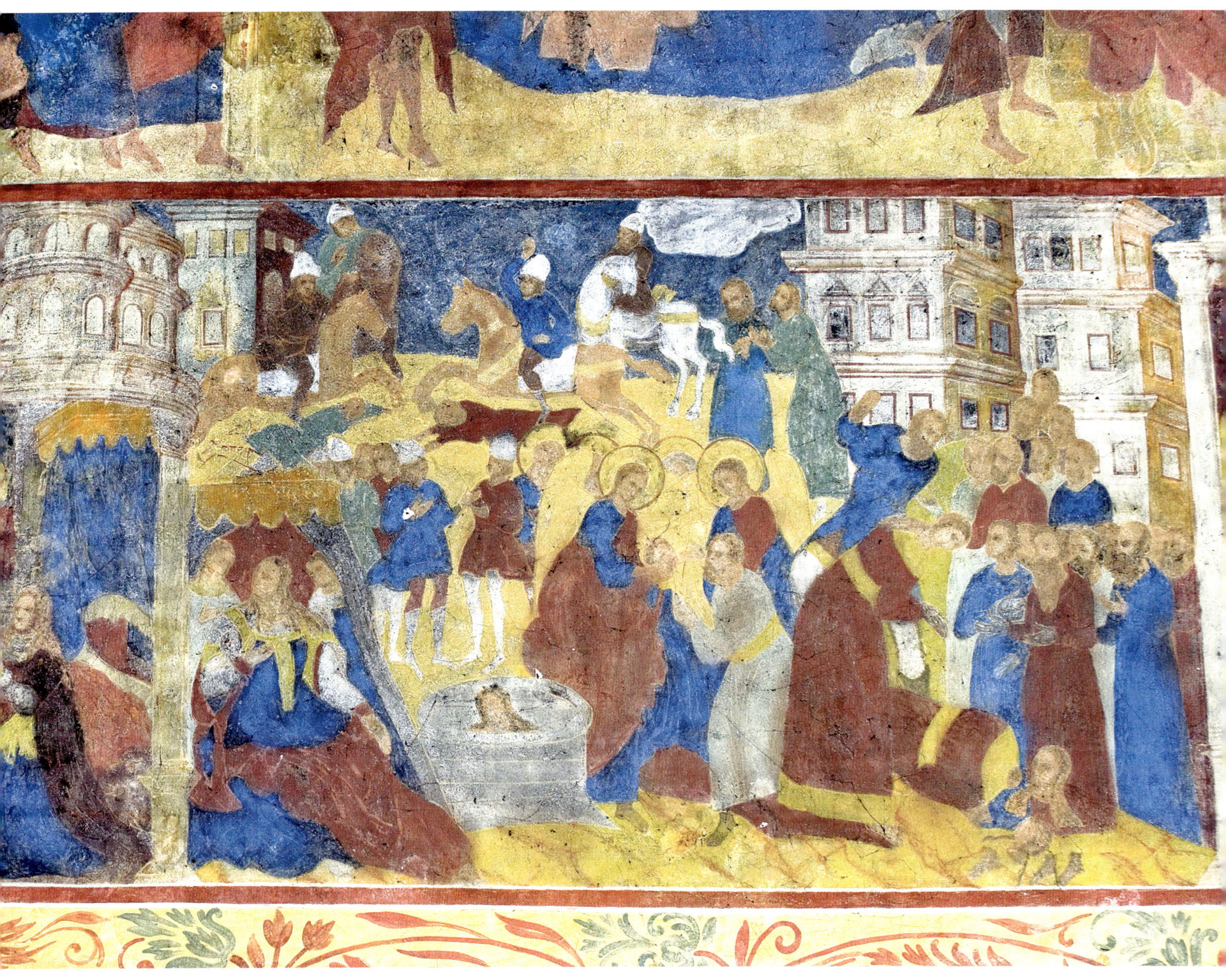

YAROSLAVL Church of the Saint Theodore Icon of the Virgin. Interior, northwest corner, fresco on north wall depicting Finding of the Head of John the Baptist.
PROKUDIN-GORSKY 21310. SUMMER 1911.

YAROSLAVL Church of the Saint Theodore Icon of the Virgin. Interior, northwest corner, fresco on north wall depicting Finding of the Head of John the Baptist.
BRUMFIELD, AUGUST 14, 2017.

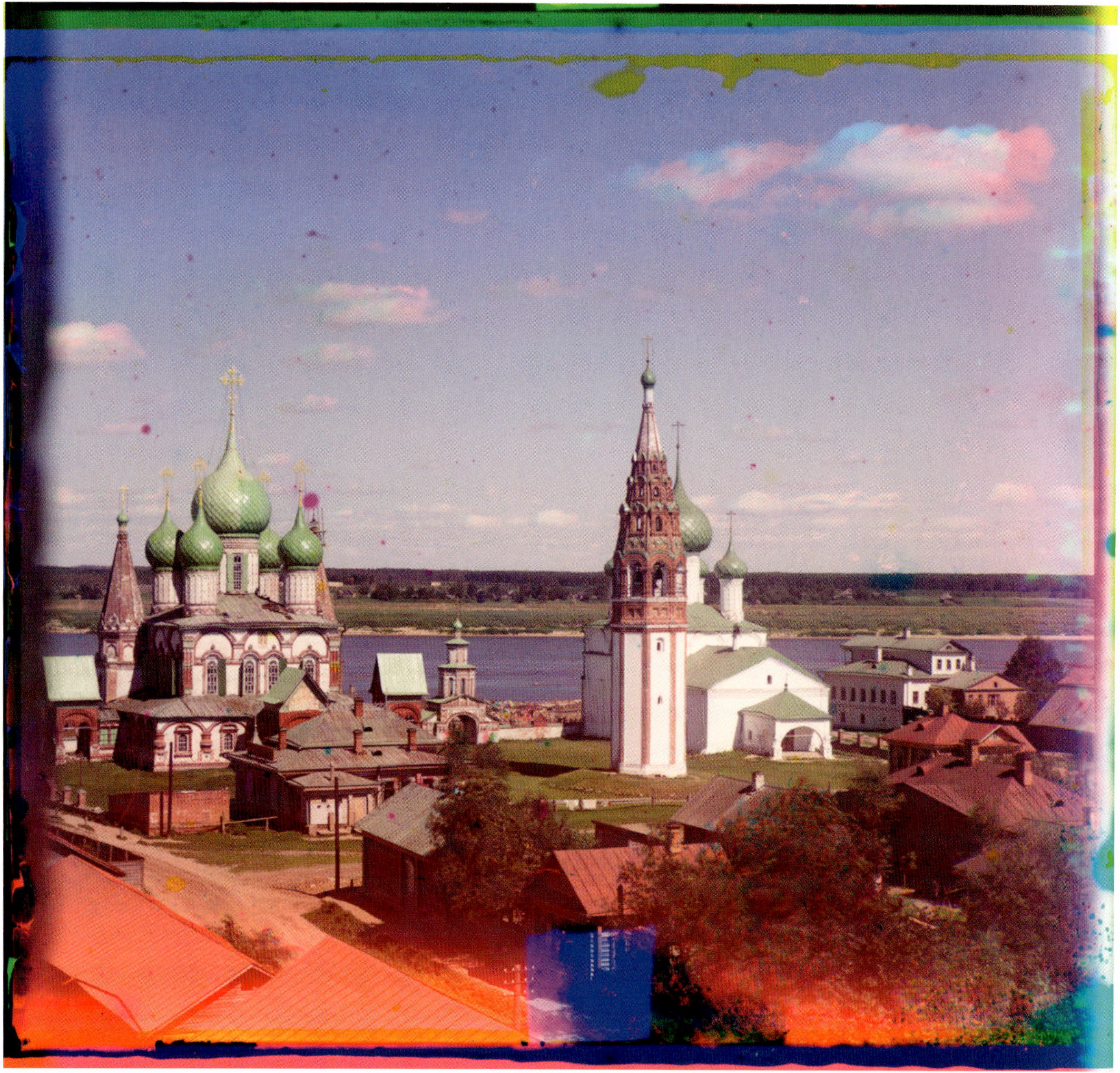

them, all superbly photographed by Prokudin-Gorsky from the upper story of a distant building. Over the decades I have recorded many changes to this ensemble, but I am particularly taken by a view form the Volga embankment.

The main structure of the Korovniki ensemble is the Church of Saint John Chrysostom, built in 1649–54 by the merchants Ivan and Fedor Nezhdanov, who were buried in its south gallery. Its central plan has the traditional four interior piers, but both the east and west piers are shifted away from the center, thus creating an extended rectangle under the central drum and extending the length of the church.

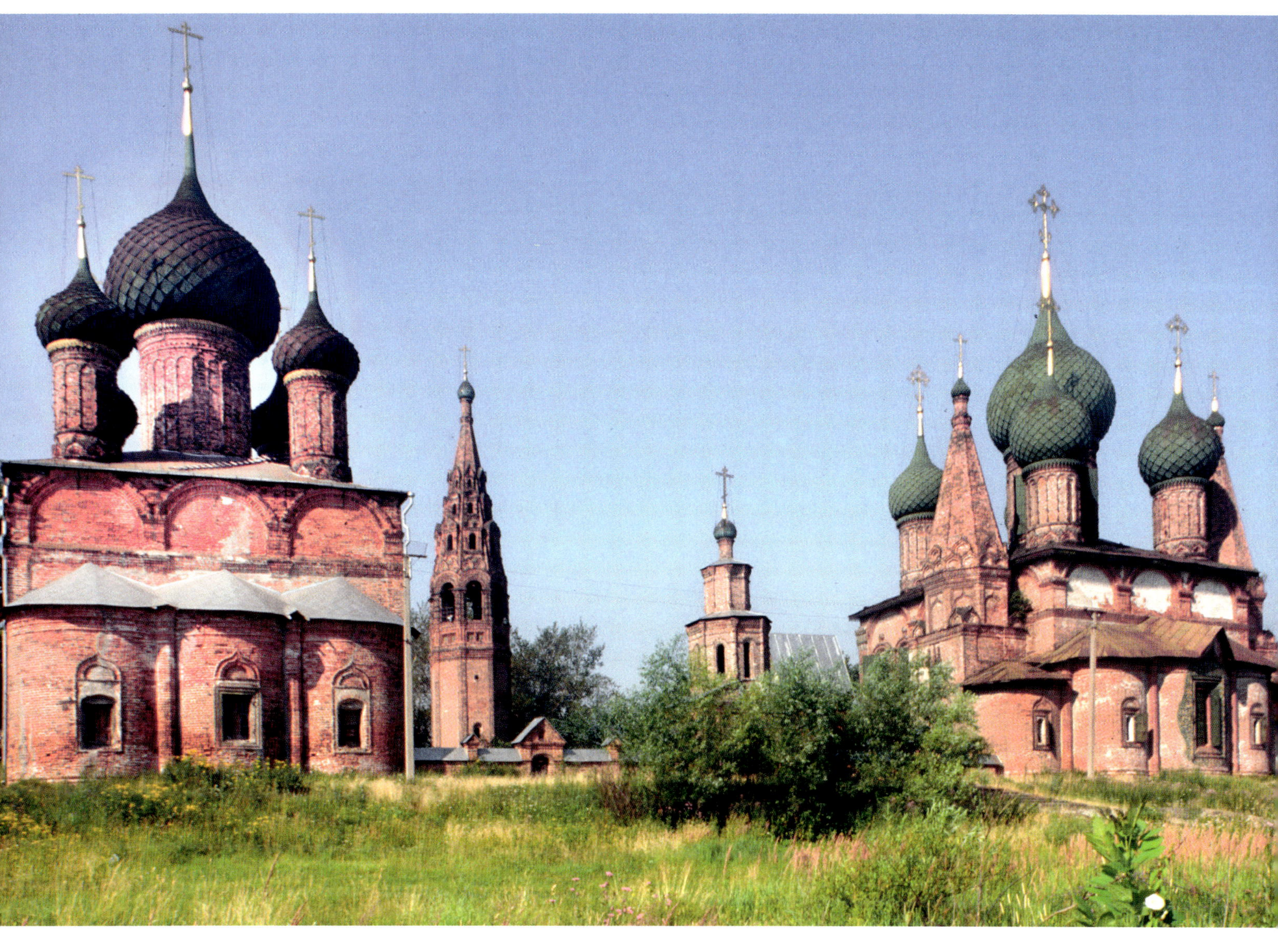

This extension of a four-piered structure would in turn give rise to changes in the tectonic system, particularly in the construction of the roof. Innovative systems of reinforced vaulting obviated the structural purpose of curved gables, which were merged into a highly decorated cornice beneath a sloped roof. The church was remodeled with more elaborate decoration in the 1680s, including a large ceramic tile border for the window in the center of the apse, which faces the Volga.

The Chrysostom Church is flanked by galleries on the north, west, and south facades, and at their east end the enclosed galleries lead to attached chapels (with tower roofs),

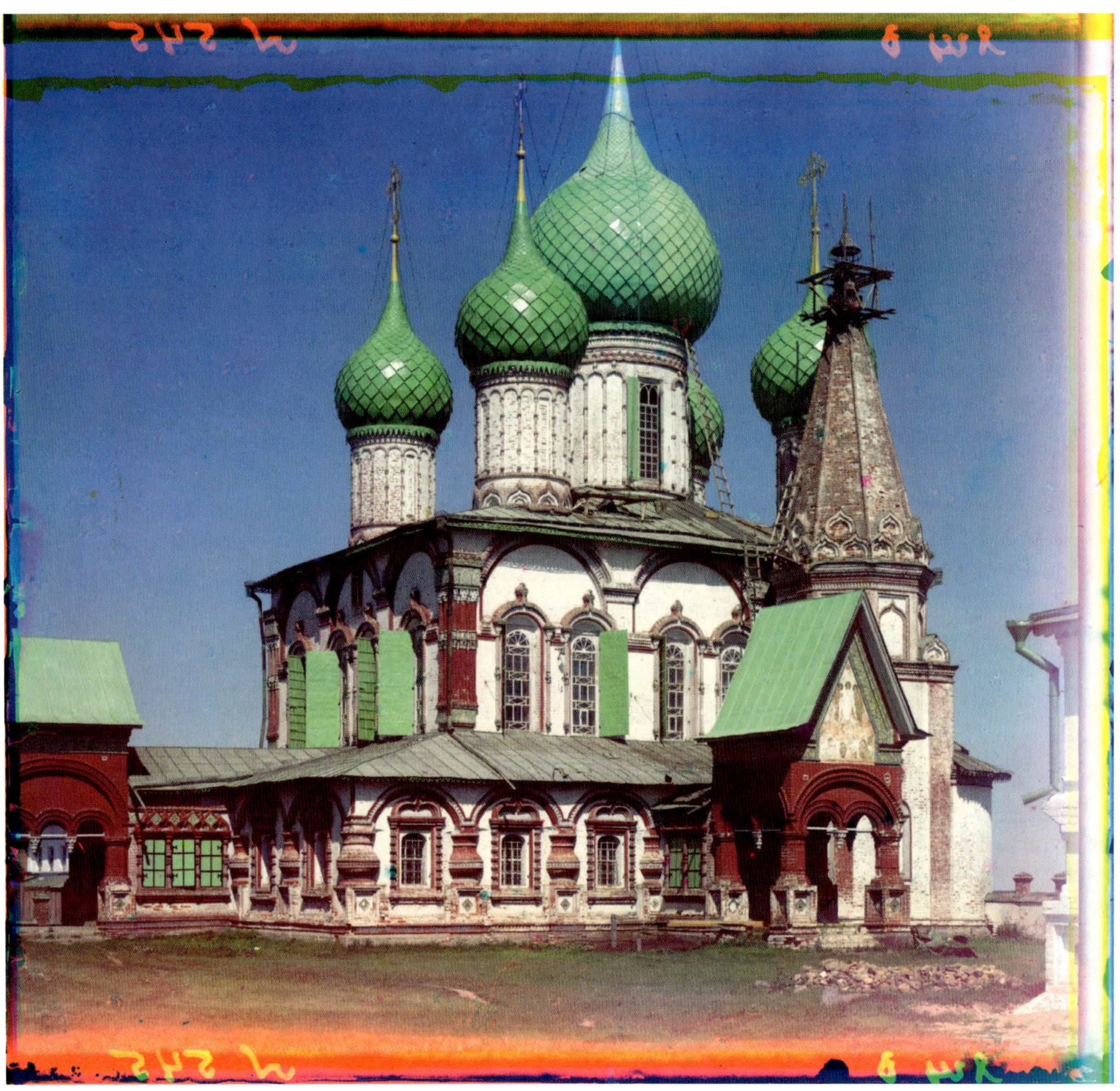

whose apses merge into a five-part apsidal structure. (Many large Yaroslavl churches integrated their attached chapels within the main structure through this design.) Each point of entry to the gallery has a semidetached porch (added in the 1680s) with a sloped roof, and when seen from the west or east they initiate the pyramidal ascent to the great ensemble of drums and cupolas, whose height exceeds that of the main structure.

In its final iteration the Korovniki monument is a consummate example of the intricate use of polychrome ceramic ornament that symbolized wealth and artistry in Rus-

YAROSLAVL Church of Saint John Chrysostom. Southwest view. PROKUDIN-GORSKY 21410. SUMMER 1911.

YAROSLAVL Church of Saint John Chrysostom. Southwest view. BRUMFIELD, AUGUST 15, 2017.

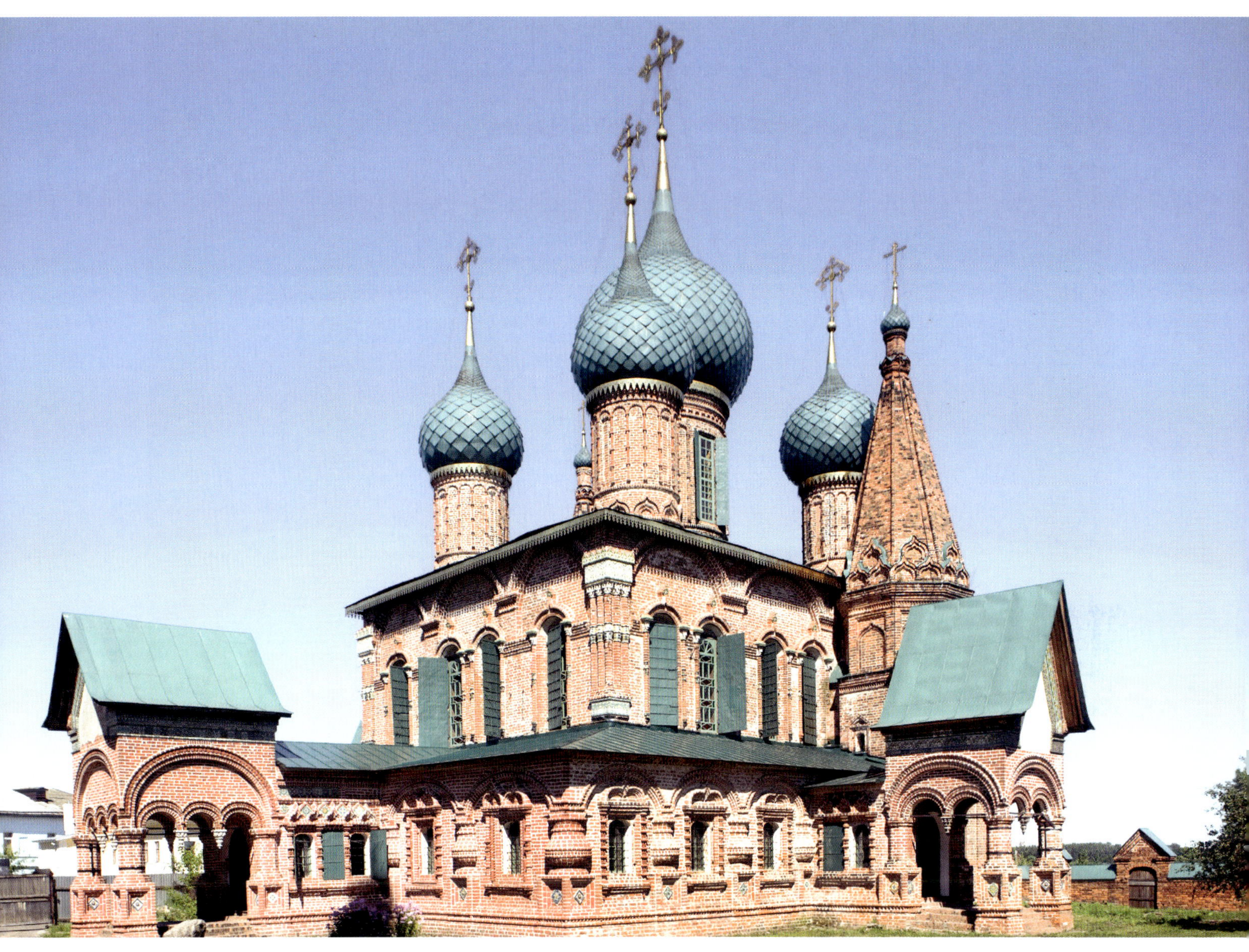

sian church decoration during the latter half of the seventeenth century. In Yaroslavl it served also to enrich the conservative limits of the four-piered structural design. Yaroslavl builders countered the possibility of monotony with the soaring cupola superstructure and with polychrome ornament at key structural points. During the Soviet period the interior, including the great iconostasis, suffered significant damage, but most of the frescoes have been preserved. Among his interior work, Prokudin-Gorsky photographed frescoes in the lower registers on the left side of the north wall, with scenes from the life of Saint John Chrysostom. My photographs of the same space show adequate conservation.

The second church of the Korovniki ensemble is dedicated to the Vladi-

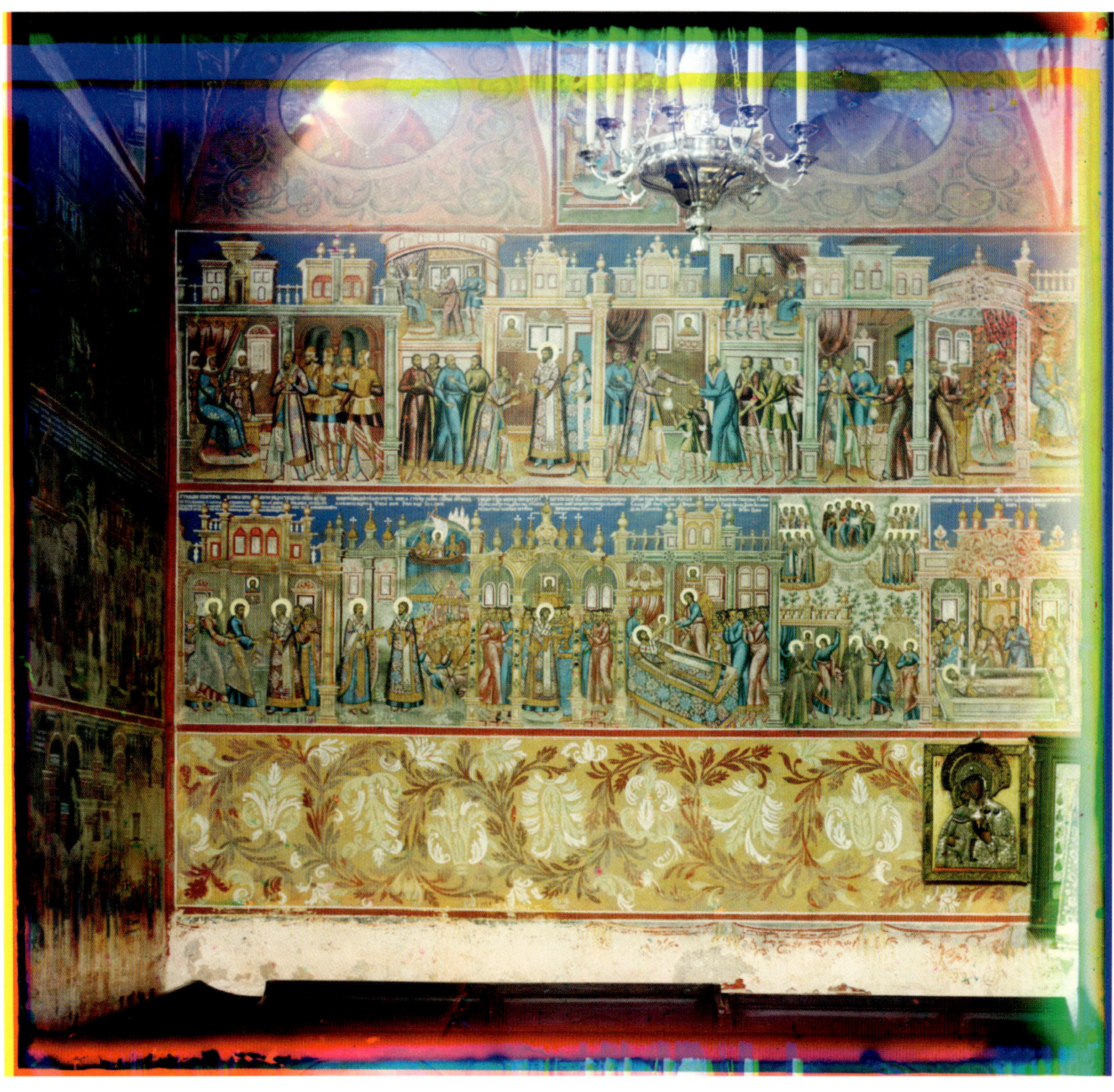

mir Icon of the Virgin, visible in Prokudin-Gorsky's general view of the ensemble. Built in 1669 as a "winter" church, it has a more modest appearance that complements the main church, particularly when seen from the Volga. In 1992 the Korovniki ensemble was transferred to the local community of Russian Orthodox Old Believers, which uses the Vladimir Church as a place of worship.

Although smaller than Yaroslavl, Kostroma (six hours down river by steamer in Prokudin-Gorsky's day) once rivaled its neighbor for the beauty of its churches and the fame of its Trinity-Ipatiev Monastery, one of the great cen-

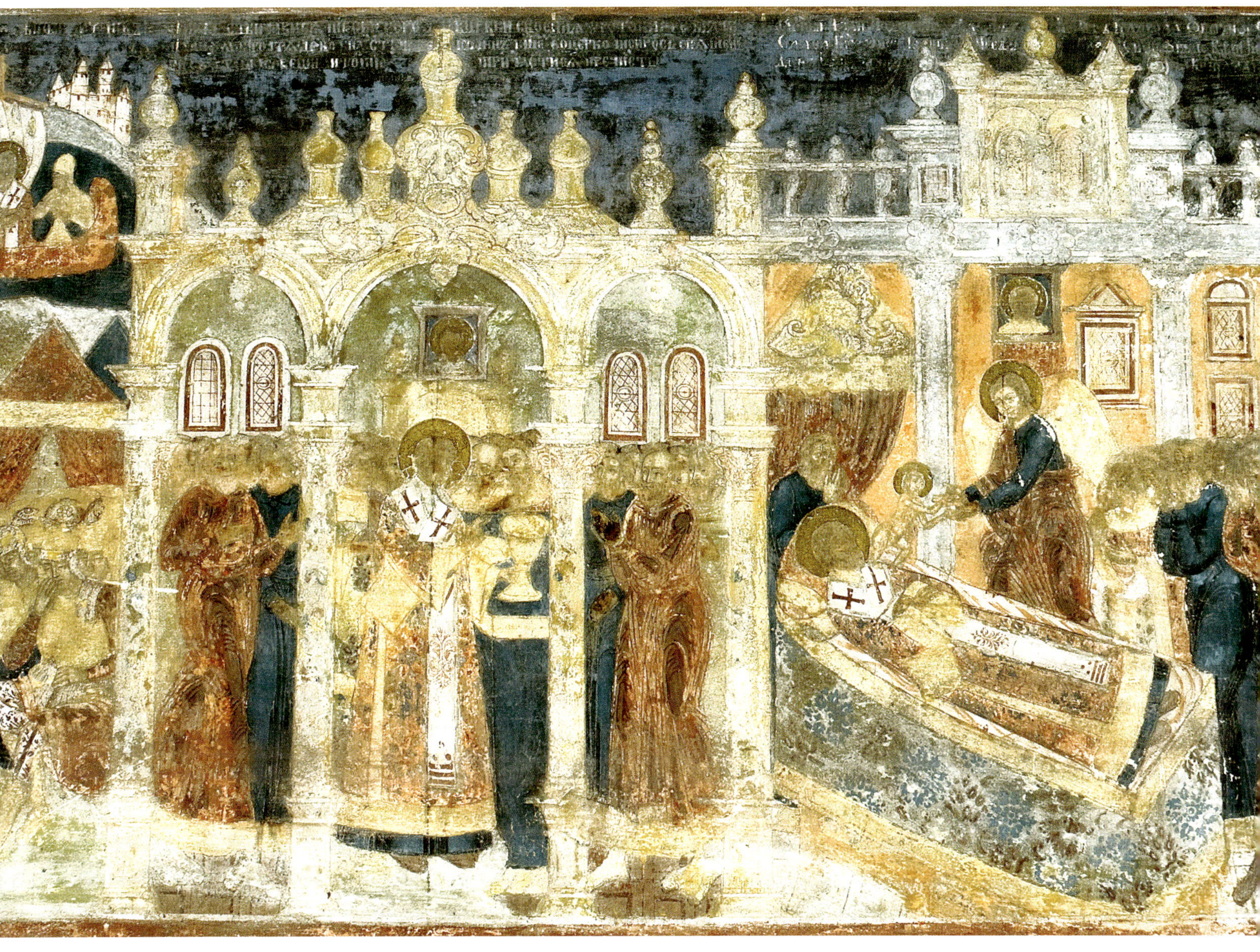

ters of medieval Russian chronicle writing. The Ipatiev Monastery also played an important role in the founding of the Romanov dynasty in 1613. Acquainted with the imperial family, Prokudin-Gorsky was drawn to the monastery in advance of the Romanov dynasty tercentenary in 1913. During his second visit, in 1911, he photographed several relics associated with the solemn events of March 1613.

During the sixteenth century, the Ipatiev Monastery's main benefactors were Dmitry Godunov and his nephew—and future tsar—Boris Godunov (1552–1605). The Godunovs considered the monastery to have been founded by their legendary Tatar ancestor Murza Chet, who in 1330 left the Golden Horde for the court of Muscovite Prince Ivan Kalita (1288–1341). Once in Moscow, he accepted Christianity and the Christian name Zakhary (Zacharius). As a sign of favor, Ivan Kalita gave him extensive lands near Kostroma. According to this version, Zakhary/Chet was cured of an illness by a vision of the Virgin Mary flanked by Saint Philip and Saint Hypatius, the early fourth-century bishop of the diocese of Gangra in Asia Minor and a strong supporter of the Trinitarian doctrine at the First Ecumenical Council (325). In gratitude, Zakhary provided support at the site of his vision for the establishment of a monastery dedicated to the Holy Trinity and its defender, Saint Hypatius (Ipaty, in Russian).

According to another version, the monastery was founded in 1275 by Prince Vasily Yaroslavich (1236?–1276), brother of Grand Prince Alexander Nevsky (1220?–63). Although legally the grand prince of Vladimir from 1272 to 1276, Vasily continued to live in his home domain of Kostroma. In this case it is possible that with the waning of the Kostroma principality after Vasily's death, the small monastery, bereft of support, might have formed the nucleus of the monastic institution established by the wealthy Zakhary.

By irony of fate, the Trinity-Ipatiev Monastery was closely tied to Boris Godunov's nemesis, the Romanovs. After the death of Ivan the Terrible's son Feodor in 1598, Russia's first dynasty, the Ryurikids, was extinguished. Boris Godunov, an able administrator who had been the guiding force in affairs of state, achieved the throne and intended to create a new dynasty. Godunov, however, had alienated many in his rise to power and was aware that much of the elite favored the Romanovs, who were related to Ivan the Terrible through his first marriage to the widely admired Anastasia Romanovna Zakharina-Yureva (1530?–1560).

In his vendetta against the Romanovs, Godunov in 1600 sent Mikhail Nikitich to an agonizing death in Nyrob (see Journey 6). That same year he not only exiled Mikhail's brother, Fyodor Nikitich (1533?–1633), but also compelled him and his wife, Ksenia, to take monastic vows as Filaret and Marfa. Godunov's premature death in 1605 led to the killing of his family by an enraged mob and ushered in a dynastic interregnum known as the Time of Troubles. In 1610 Filaret—now a prelate in the Orthodox Church—was imprisoned by the Polish King Sigismund III for refusing to sign a treaty legitimizing the accession of his son Władysław IV to the Muscovite throne. (Filaret would return to Moscow only in 1619.) With the fervent support of the Orthodox Church, Moscow in late 1612 was recaptured from supporters of the Polish claimant to the throne, but the country remained in the throes of fighting and chaos. Among those freed from the Kremlin was the small Romanov family, including Filaret's wife (now known by her monastic name Marfa) and their sixteen-year-old son Mikhail.

Russia remained in the throes of fighting and chaos, as armed bands of troops and marauders pillaged the country. In late 1612 Marfa and Mikhail—in effect fugitives in their own land—retreated to a Romanov estate near Kostroma and soon thereafter sought more secure shelter behind the walls of the Ipatiev Monastery. Shortly after arriving at the monastery, the sixteen-year-old Mikhail Romanov (1596–1645) was elected by a national assembly (*zemsky sobor*) to the tsar's throne on February 21 / March 3, 1613, thus laying the foundation for the Romanov dynasty. On March 14/24, a delegation from the assembly arrived at the monastery to persuade a reluctant Mikhail to accept the crown.

Prokudin-Gorsky's photographs on the monastery include the east wall viewed across the Kostroma River near its confluence with the Volga. My photographs over a century later show a largely unchanged view. On the left is the upper part of the Trinity Cathedral, the monastery's central shrine, rebuilt in 1650–52 and crowned with five gilded domes. The center of this view is occupied by the large Archbishop's Cloisters, part of which dates to the seventeenth century. An expansion of the building was completed in the late 1850s over the monastery's east gate. Designed by Konstantin Ton, the leading proponent of the Russo-Byzantine style, the building culminates in a twelve-sided "tent" tower over the Church of Saints Chrysanthus and Daria, third-century Roman martyrs. The Water Gate was built between 1586 and 1597, but after several rebuildings of the wall, the gate's location was conjectural by the time of this photograph. On the left is an east view of the upper part of the mid-seventeenth-century Trinity Cathedral. On the right is the Powder Tower in the wall's northeast corner.

As stability returned under Romanov rule in the seventeenth century, the Ipatiev Monastery received substantial donations acknowledging its role in the dynasty's accession. Central among its buildings was the Cathedral of the Holy Trinity, rebuilt in 1650–52. The original monastery structures were of wood, including the main church (*sobor*), dedicated in this case to the Holy Trinity. In the mid-sixteenth century Dmitry Godunov built the first masonry version, which was severely damaged in 1649 from an explosion of gunpowder stored in the cellar. Tsar Aleksei Mikhailovich (son of Mikhail Romanov) promptly assented to a rebuilding in 1650. The design of the cathedral is traditional, with a crown of five cupolas. Yet its form is unusual in having the main facade on the north, with an ornately decorated

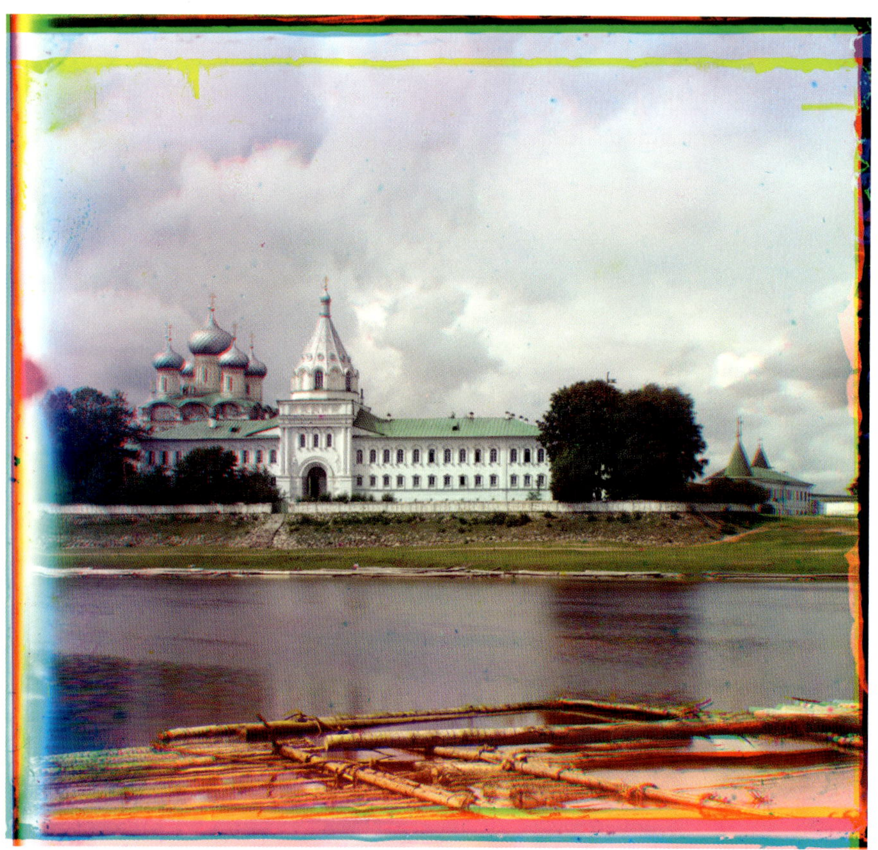

KOSTROMA Trinity-Ipatiev Monastery. East view across Kostroma River. *From left*: Trinity Cathedral, bell tower, Archbishop's Cloisters with tower and Church of Saints Chrysanthus and Daria. PROKUDIN-GORSKY 21304. SUMMER 1911.

KOSTROMA Trinity-Ipatiev Monastery. East view across Kostroma River. *From left*: Cathedral of Nativity of the Virgin; Trinity Cathedral; bell tower; Archbishop's Cloisters with Gate Church of Saints Chrysanthus and Daria. BRUMFIELD, AUGUST 13, 2017.

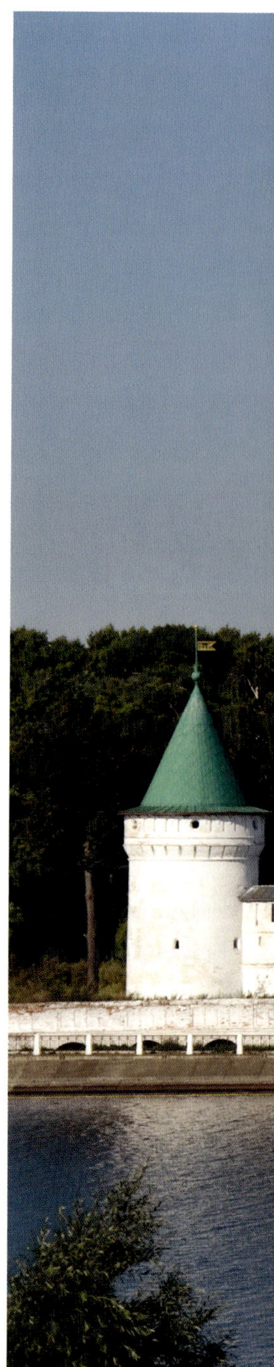

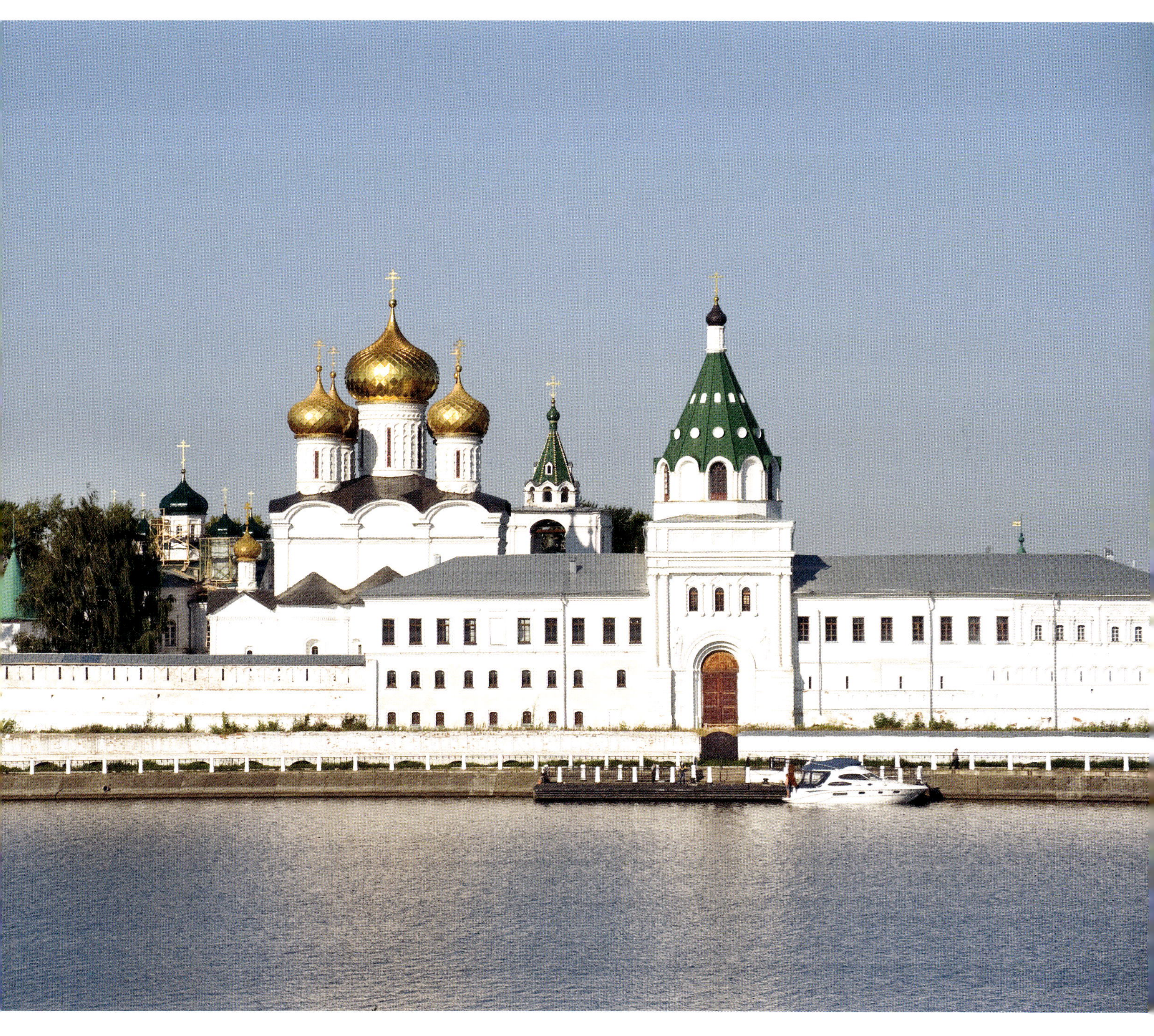

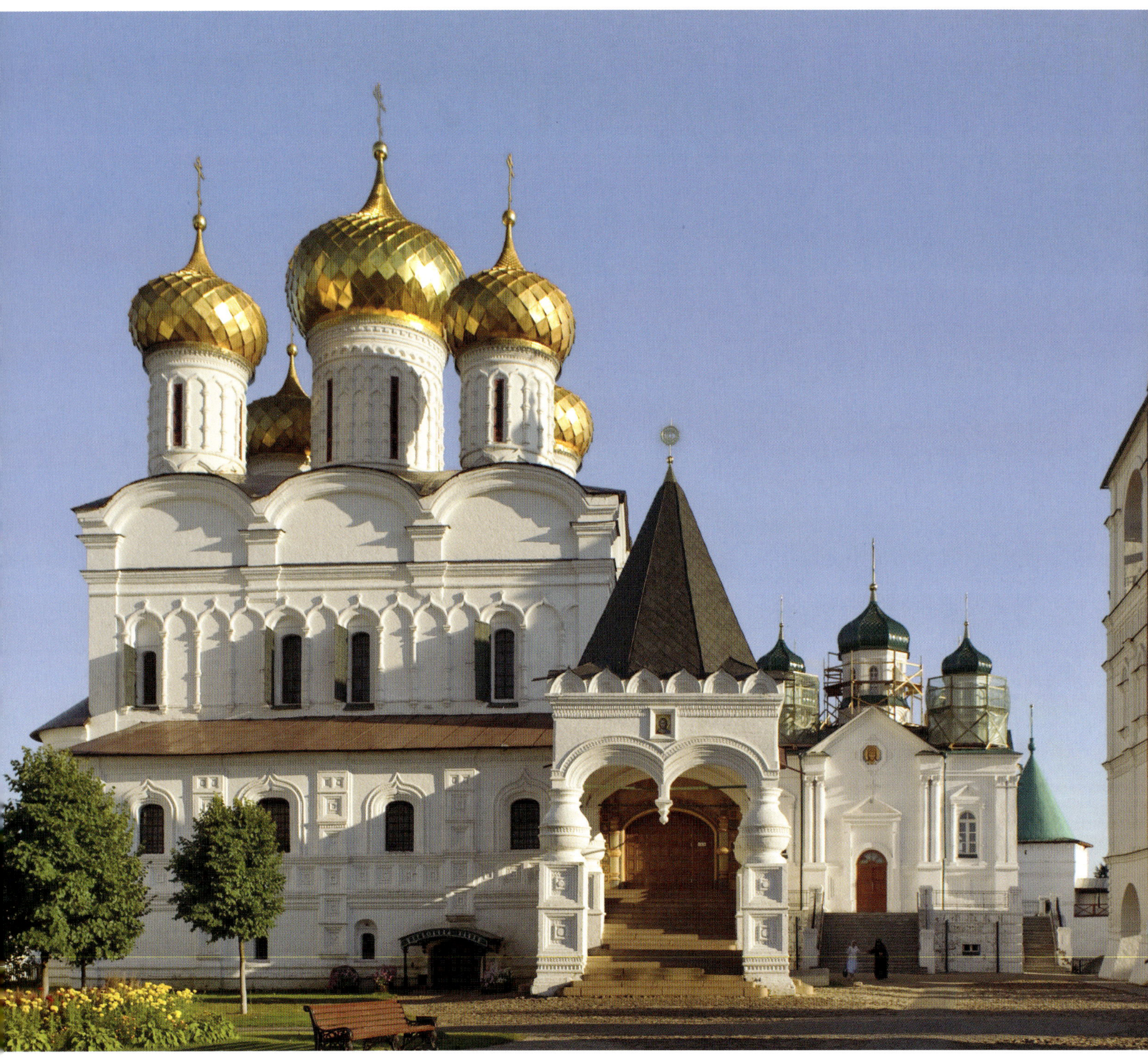

KOSTROMA Trinity-Ipatiev Monastery. *From left*:
Trinity Cathedral; Cathedral of Nativity of the Virgin;
bell tower. North view. BRUMFIELD, AUGUST 13, 2017.

KOSTROMA Trinity-Ipatiev Monastery. Cathedral of
the Trinity. North view. Main staircase at northwest
corner. PROKUDIN-GORSKY 02472. SUMMER 1910.

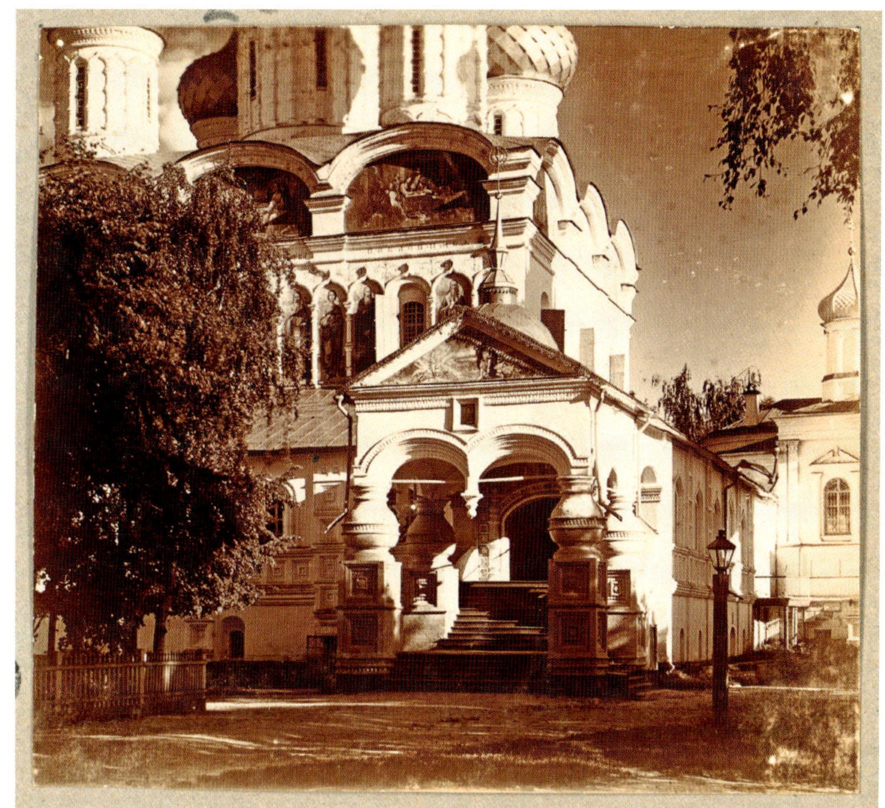

porch at the northwest corner containing a stone staircase that ascends to an enclosed gallery. Although the original glass negative is missing in the Library of Congress collection, Prokudin-Gorsky's contact print shows the northwest porch and staircase, which would be used by Nicholas II during his 1913 visit. My photograph from August 2017 shows the cathedral ensemble from the north.

After the completion of construction in 1652, work commenced on the interior and its large iconostasis. Two years later, in 1654, master artists from Kostroma began the frescoes, but work came to a halt in 1656 due to an outbreak of plague that decimated the town. The interior was finally painted in the summer of 1685 by a group of court artists that included Gury Nikitin and Sila Savin. Within the gallery space, the main portal is on the west so that one faces the iconostasis upon entering the cathedral proper. Prokudin-Gorsky photographed the portal, but there is no glass negative for this view with its frescoes. My recent photograph of the portal displays the color range and the restoration of the fresco of the Feodor Image of the Virgin.

Attached to the southwest corner of the Trinity Cathedral gallery is the Cathedral of the Nativity of the Virgin. An earlier church, built of logs in 1564, served as a burial place for the Tatar eminence Chet and his descen-

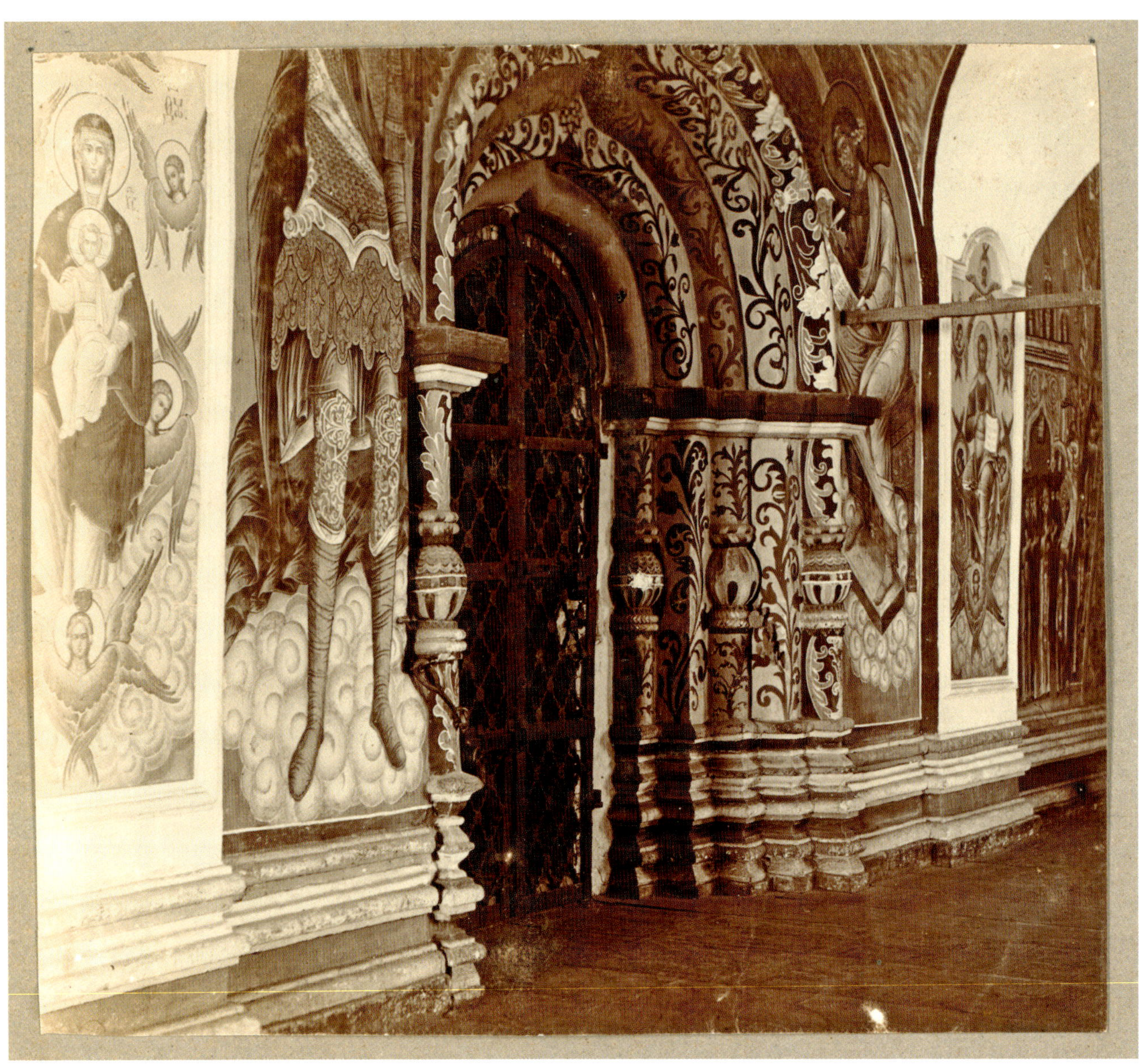

KOSTROMA Trinity-Ipatiev Monastery. Cathedral of the Trinity, interior. West gallery, main portal. PROKUDIN-GORSKY 02473. SUMMER 1910.

KOSTROMA Trinity-Ipatiev Monastery. Cathedral of the Trinity, interior. West gallery, bay to left of main portal. *Frescoes from left*: fragment of Last Judgment, Feodor Icon of the Virgin (an image especially venerated by the Romanovs), Archangel Michael with raised sword. BRUMFIELD, AUGUST 13, 2017.

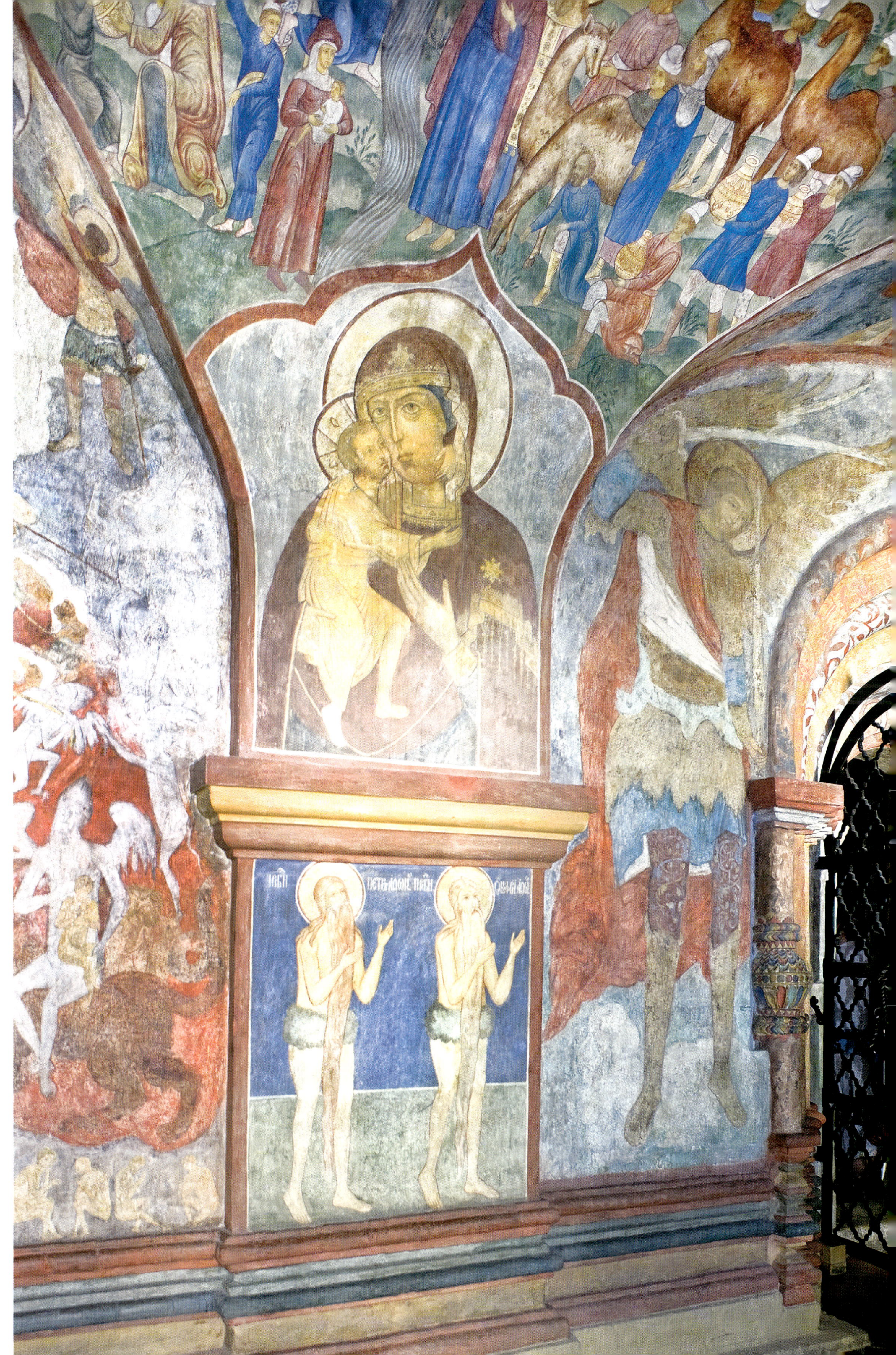

dants. In 1859–63 an eighteenth-century brick version of the church was replaced by the architect Konstantin Ton, who designed the Russo-Byzantine church photographed by Prokudin-Gorsky. The new Nativity Cathedral was commissioned by Alexander II in commemoration of the 250th anniversary of the founding of the Romanov dynasty. The Nativity Cathedral has had a turbulent history. After the closure of the monastery in 1922, its buildings were converted to other uses. In the 1932 the Nativity Cathedral was demolished as a nineteenth-century excrescence honoring the detested Romanovs by a court architect who disfigured the adjacent seventeenth-century landmark. In 2008 a decision was taken at the highest state level to rebuild the Nativity Cathedral in Konstantin Ton's Russo-Byzantine design. The basic structural work was completed by 2013 to commemorate the four hundredth anniversary of the reestablishment of Russian statehood in 1613. Work on the interior continues.

Facing the Trinity Cathedral is the main bell tower, whose basic open-gable form was begun in 1603 by the boyar Dmitry Godunov, uncle of Tsar Boris Godunov. Expanded during the subsequent half century, the archaic structure gained a decorative cap in the nineteenth century. As Prokudin-Gorsky's photographs demonstrate, many medieval monuments were painted with frescoes on the exterior, primarily during the nineteenth century. But the Ipatiev Monastery bell tower was exceptional in the degree to which the surface is covered with devotional paintings of scenes from the life of Christ. During the Soviet period these paintings were effaced as a nineteenth-century addition in a Western academic style that promoted Christianity and disfigured the earlier form. Another view of the campanile through the north courtyard arch shows its painted form even more clearly. My 2017 photograph of the restored bell tower shows a whitewashed monolithic structure, clean of line and with an impressive display of light and shadow.

During the nineteenth century, the memorialization of the monastery's connections to the Romanovs assumed a national character. One of the main components of the commemoration was the renovation of the cloister space where Mikhail Romanov and his mother stayed. This project was initiated after a visit by Tsar Alexander II in 1858, who commanded that the modest structure be re-created in a seventeenth-century style. The substantial reconstruction of what became known as the Boyar Romanov Chambers was undertaken by the architect Fyodor (Friedrich) Rikhter, who was at that time involved in a similar Romanov Chambers project near the Moscow Kremlin. Although the Library of Congress collection lacks Prokudin-Gorsky's original glass negative, his sepia contact print shows details of the structure. A recent photograph shows the results of a restoration after the monastery's return to the Orthodox Church.

Among the most appealing of Prokudin-Gorsky's Kostroma photographs are colorful views of the Church of the Resurrection in the Grove, whose secondary name, "na Debrakh" (in the grove or thicket), refers to a dense growth of trees in this low area near the Volga. Its original creation is dated to the late thirteenth century and attributed to Prince Vasily Yaroslavich, who liked to hunt in this area. With the support of an expanded parish and a major donation from the wealthy merchant Kirill Grigorev (who traded with England), the church was rebuilt in brick in 1649–52. The central cuboid structure is elevated on a high ground story and crowned with five cupolas overlooking the Volga. The tall windows are framed by florid ornamental brick surrounds. Vertical and horizontal decorative strips lead to an ornamental cornice, above which are semicircular zakomary containing religious paintings. As usual, these paintings were effaced as nineteenth-century excrescences during the Soviet period, but they are faintly visible in Prokudin-Gorsky's photographs.

The north, west, and south facades of the church have an attached, enclosed gallery elevated on an arcade. Each side of the gallery has a staircase descending to an elaborately decorated porch, seen in Prokudin-Gorsky's view from the southeast. The brick walls were painted with bright trompe l'oeil diamond rustication (a typical decorative device in seventeenth-century Russian churches). Although much of the earlier painted decoration on the main structure faded during the Soviet period, the pattern is clearly visible on the walls of the apsidal structure in the east. Prokudin-Gorsky also photographed the Holy Gate, or main entrance. Visible on the right in his photograph is the dome of the companion Church of the Icon of the Virgin of the Sign, rebuilt in 1801 to serve as a "winter" church for the parish. My view of the west facade and Holy Gate is taken from the Volga embankment.

After Kostroma the Volga River dips and bends before heading due east, past Kineshma to Yurevets, where it turns sharply to the south in the direction of Nizhny Novgorod. This bend, or pivot, on the high right bank of the Volga formed an ideal point to survey the river for a great distance. It also accounts for the beauty of the landscape within which the town is situated—high forested bluffs marked by ravines that descend to the main part

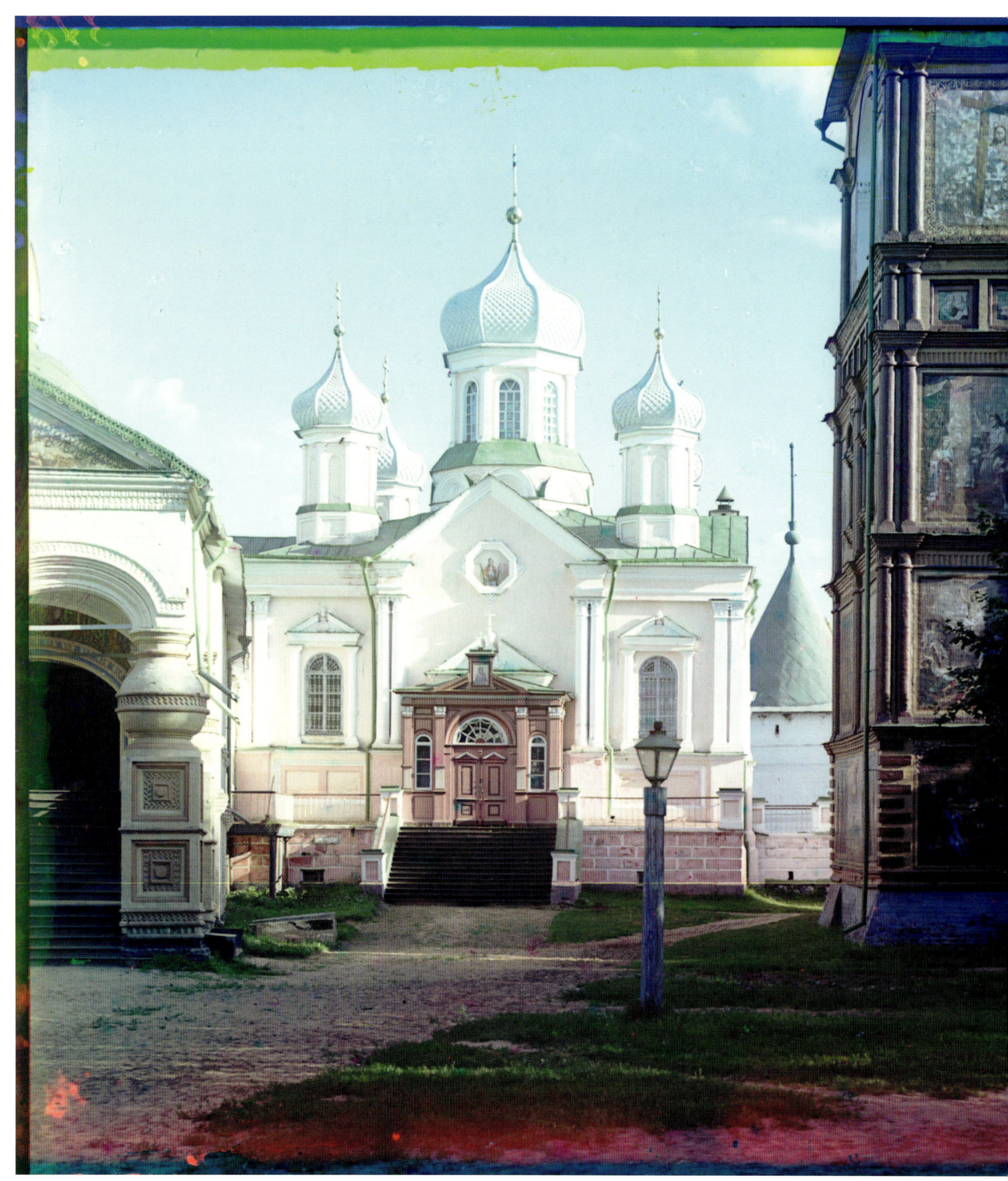

KOSTROMA Trinity-Ipatiev Monastery. Cathedral of the Nativity of the Virgin. North view.
Right: bell tower. PROKUDIN-GORSKY 21223. SUMMER 1910.

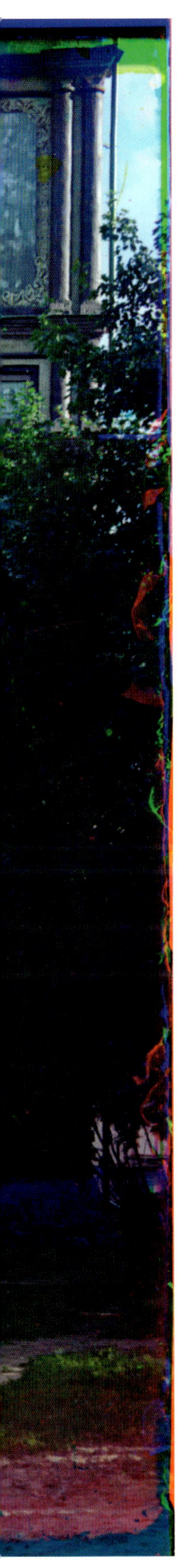

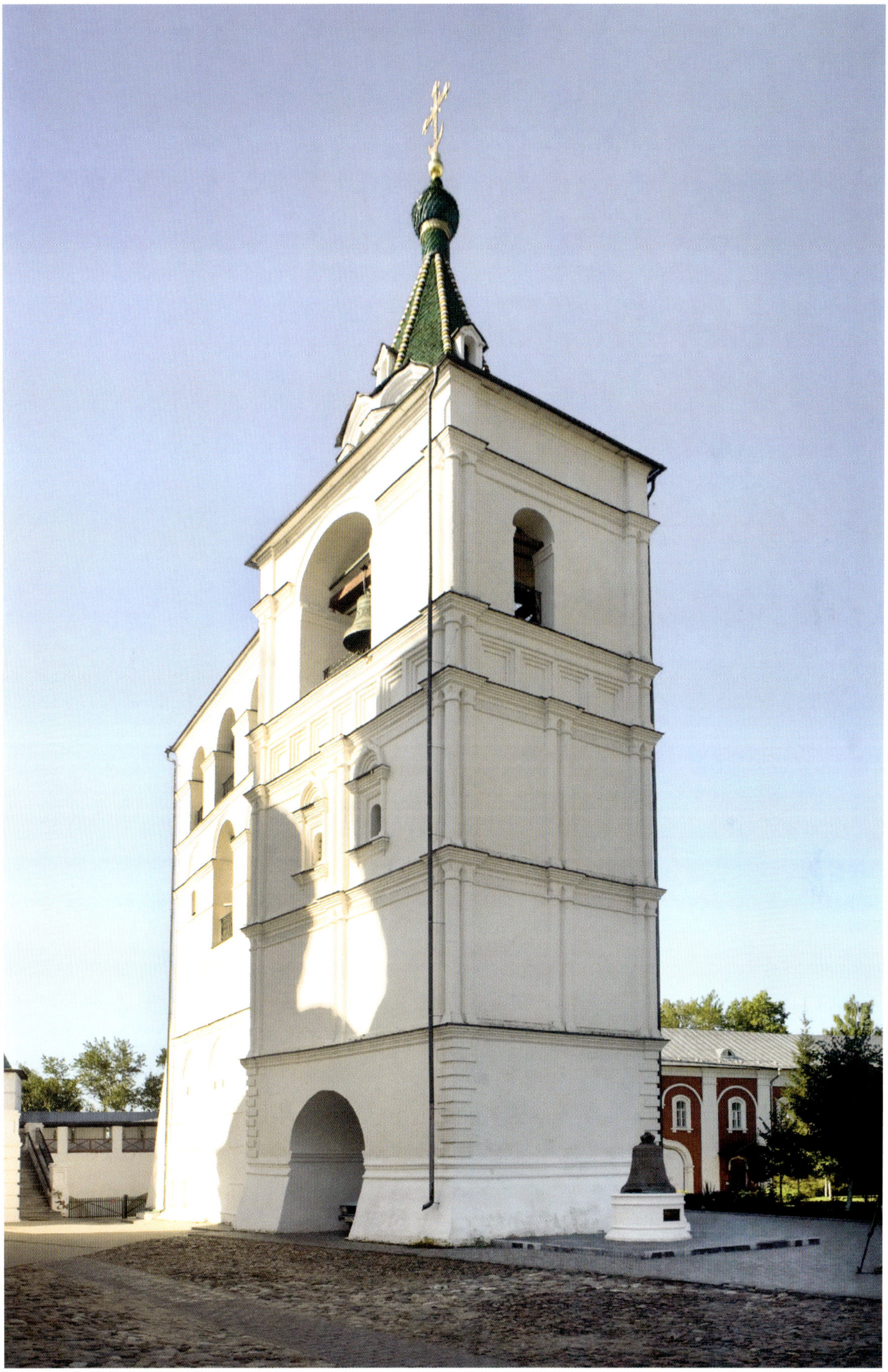

KOSTROMA Trinity-Ipatiev Monastery. Bell tower (*zvonnitsa*). Northeast view.
BRUMFIELD, AUGUST 13, 2017.

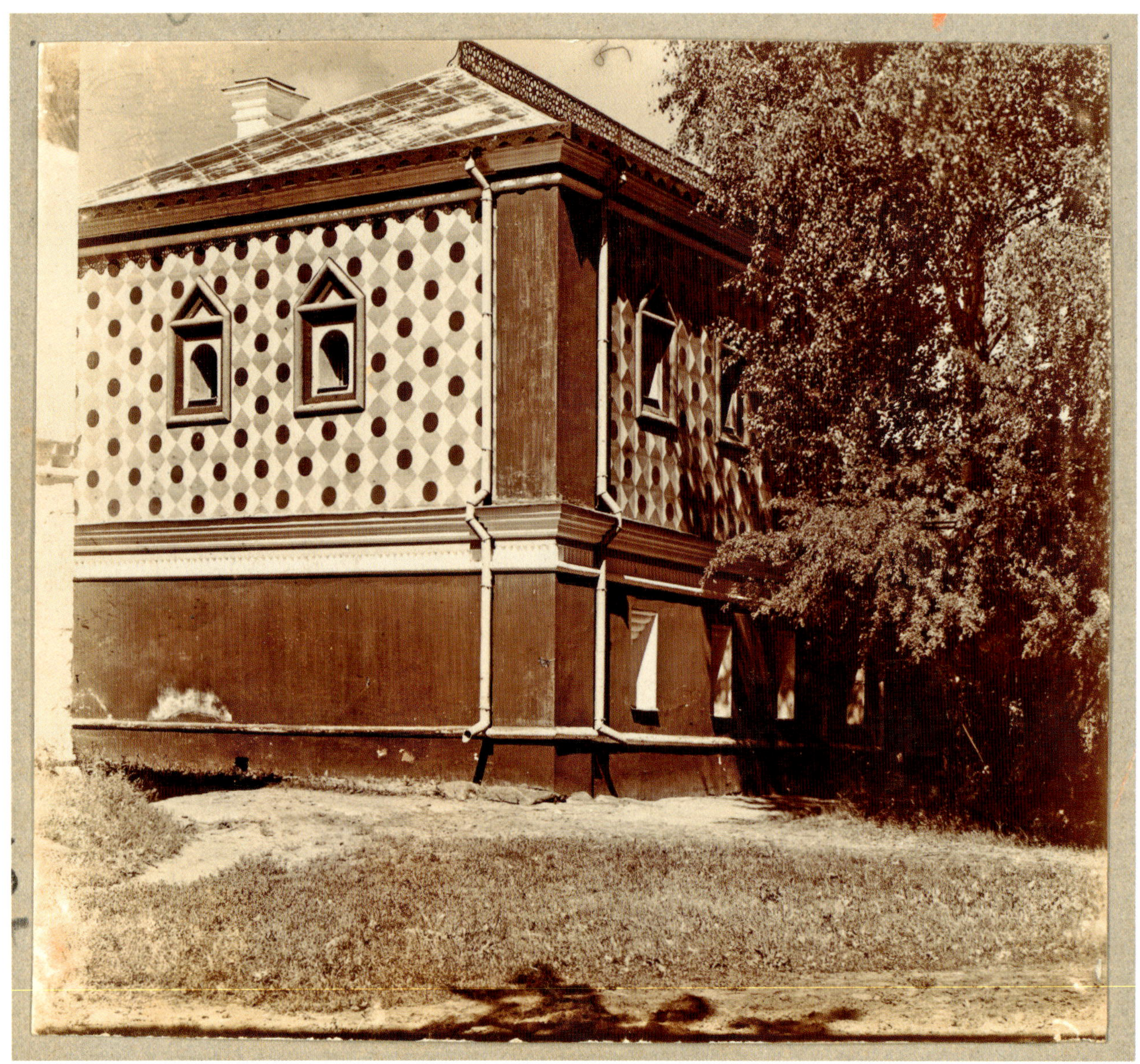

KOSTROMA Trinity-Ipatiev Monastery. Romanov
Chambers. Southeast corner. PROKUDIN-GORSKY 02484.
SUMMER 1910.

KOSTROMA Trinity-Ipatiev Monastery. Romanov
Chambers. East view. BRUMFIELD, AUGUST 13, 2017.

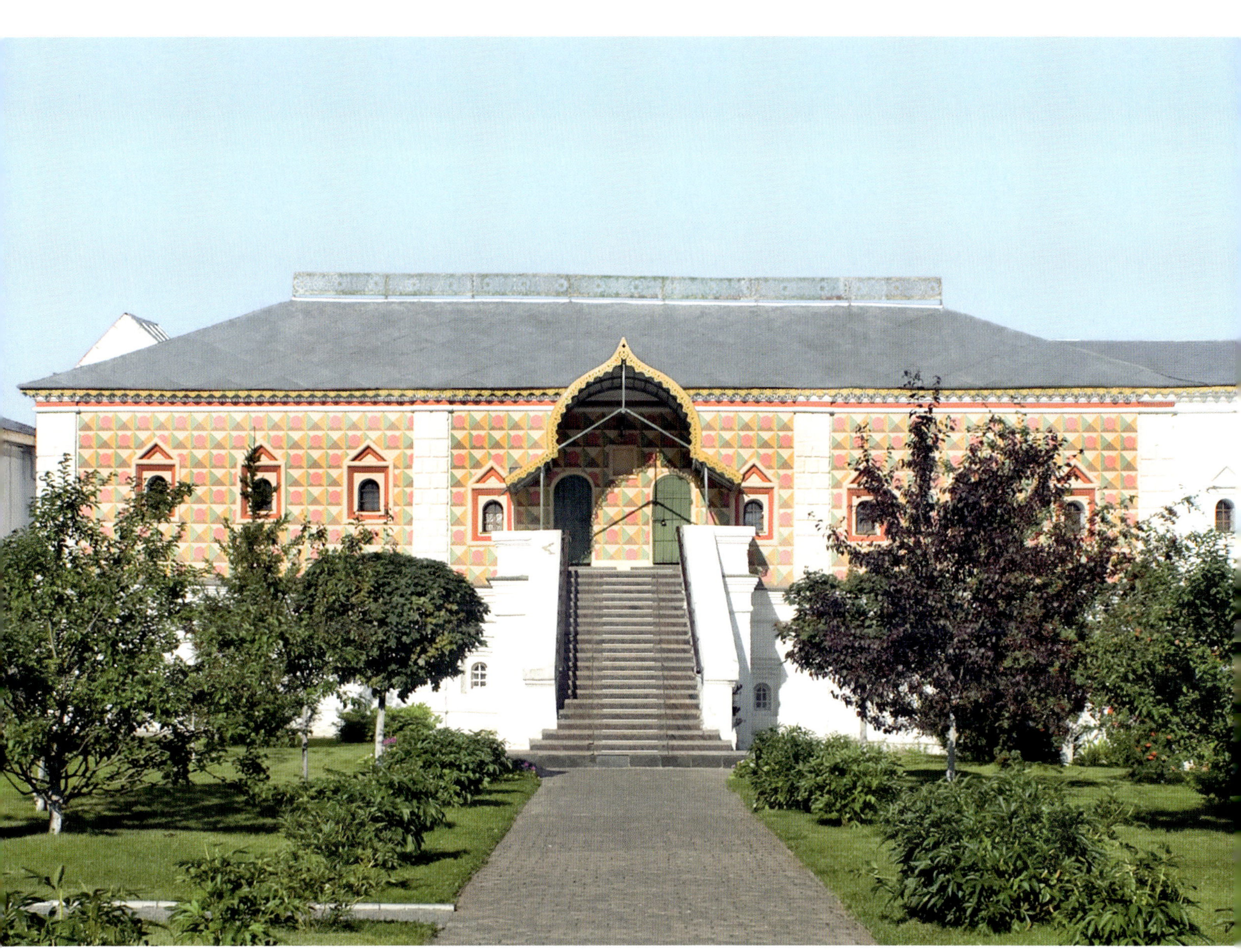

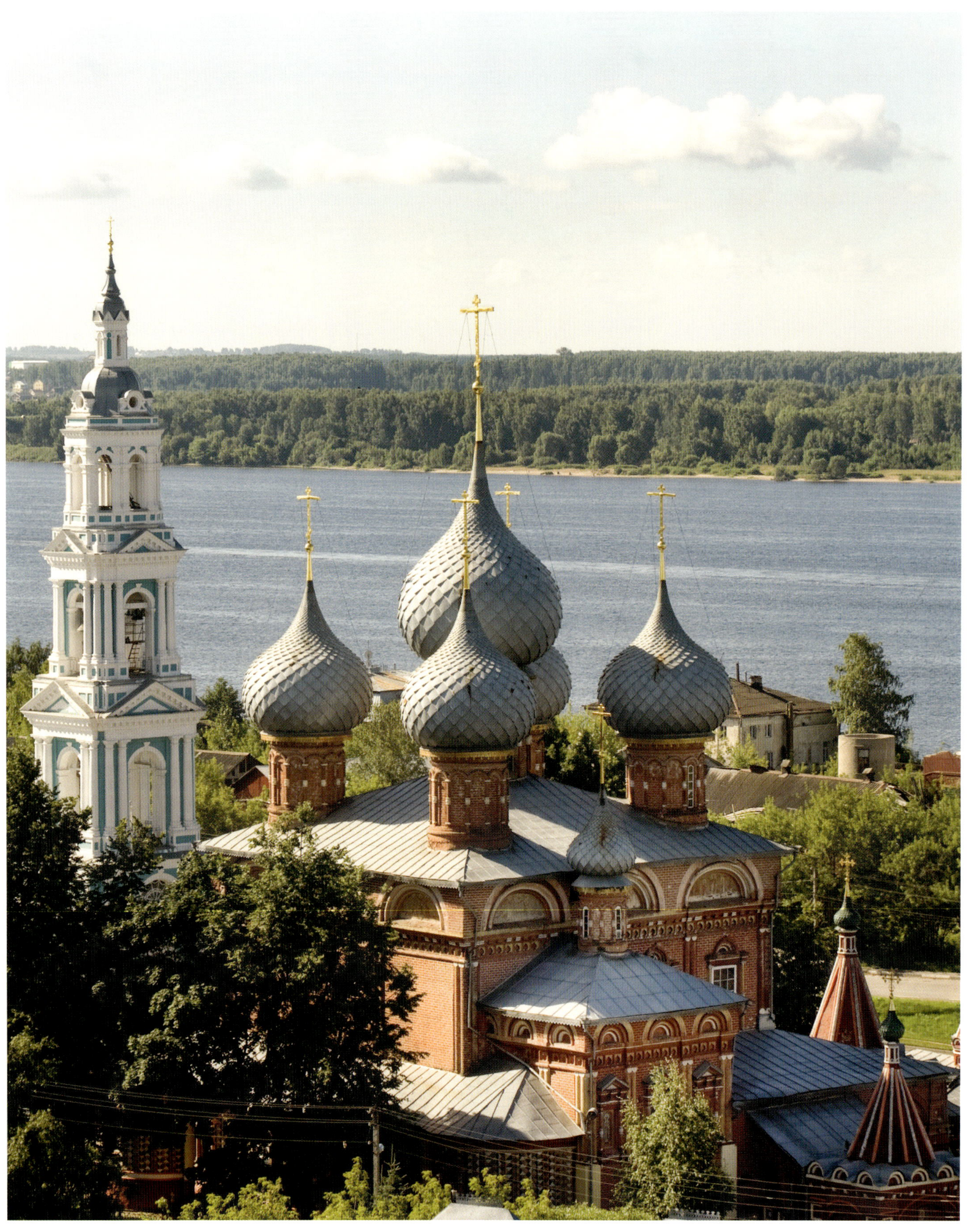

KOSTROMA Church of the Resurrection in the Thicket. Northeast view with Chapel of the
Three Prelates. *Background*: bell tower and Volga River. BRUMFIELD, AUGUST 12, 2017.

of town along the river. Perhaps this beauty imprinted itself in some mysterious way on the imagination of the town's most famous son, the filmmaker Andrei Tarkovsky.

The year 1225 is the generally accepted date of the founding of the town, formally known as Yurevets Povolzhsky (on the Volga) to distinguish it from other towns with the same name. According to ancient accounts, it was founded by Prince Yury (a Slavic form of George), son of Prince Vsevolod the Great Nest, the last major ruler of Vladimir before the Mongol invasion of 1237. Legend has it that during a river journey from Yaroslavl to Vladimir, Yury camped on the site and had a vision of an icon, or sacred image, of Saint George. Responding to the heavenly sign, Yury built a log fort and a wooden church dedicated to Saint George. Such legends typically served to sanctify what was a pragmatic decision — in this case to guard and fortify a strategic river bend.

Just over a decade after Prince Yury's vision, the settlement suffered from the Mongol invasion in the winter of 1237–38 — the same catastrophe that led to Yury's death during the Battle on the Seet (Sit') River (March 4, 1238). The town revived under the authority of regional princes, and in 1452 it was absorbed into the holdings of Basil II (the Blind), Grand Prince of Moscow. During this period Yurevets was frequently attacked by Tatar raiders from the south, a threat eliminated in 1552 with Ivan the Terrible's conquest of Kazan. Despite its prominent geographical position, enhanced by a location opposite the mouth of the Unzha River, Yurevets was overshadowed by other towns along the Volga such as Nizhny Novgorod, some 190 kilometers to the south. Nonetheless, the Volga River provided the town with a transportation artery that was used in the nineteenth and early twentieth centuries by local entrepreneurs.

The prosperity of Yurevets was reflected in several churches, including a central complex formed by the Cathedrals of the Entry into Jerusalem (early eighteenth century) and the Dormition, completed in the mid-nineteenth century. Adjacent to the two cathedrals is one of the Volga River's tallest bell towers, also built in the mid-nineteenth century and containing a small Church of Saint George — a reference to the town's first church. Prokudin-Gorsky's broad view shows the tower and surrounding area, part of which was submerged by the postwar hydroelectric development of the Volga. Despite damage during the Soviet period, the bell tower is still the dominant landmark. These photographs of the expanse of the Volga convey a sense of a land on the boundary of two ages.

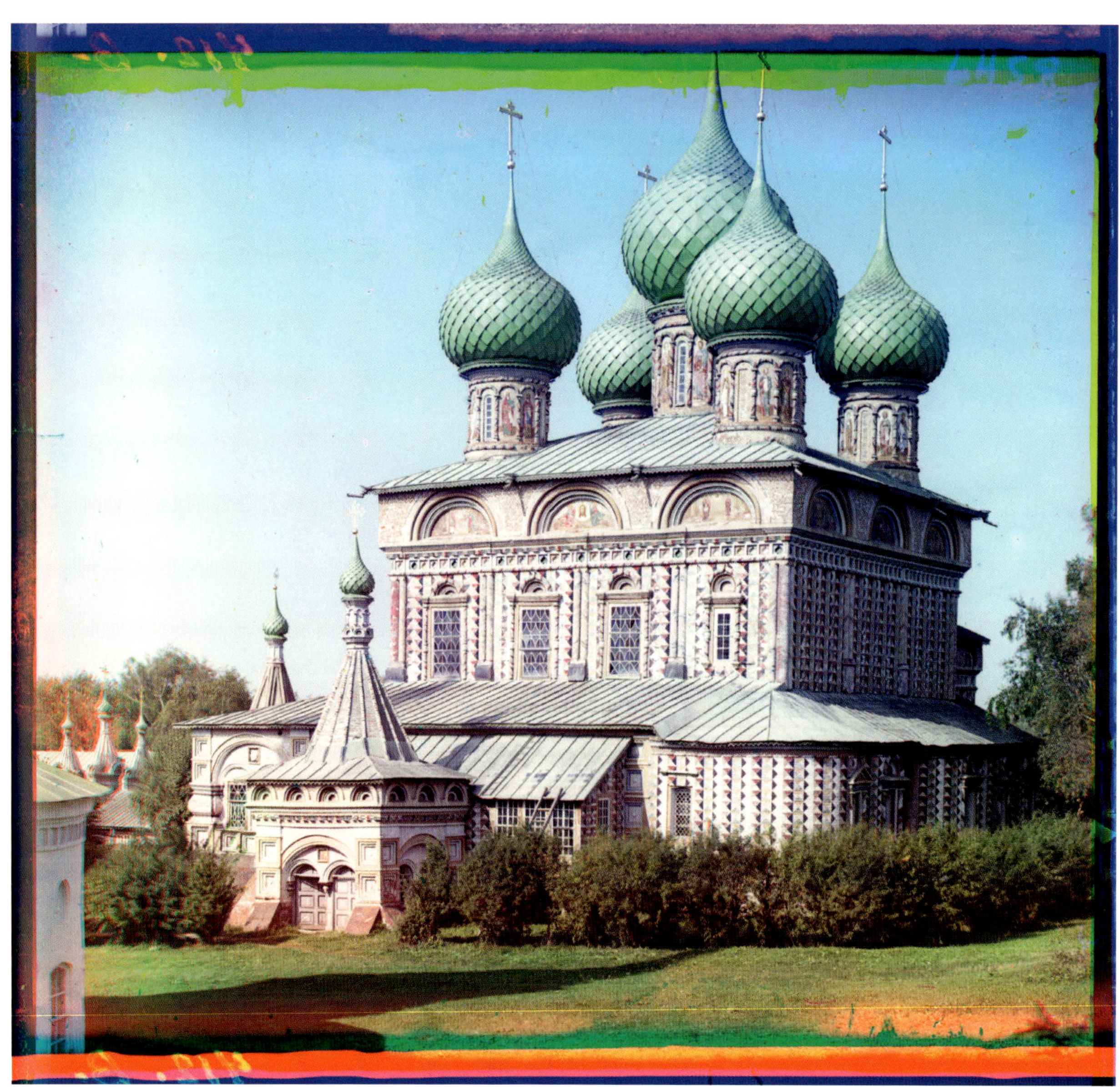

KOSTROMA Church of the Resurrection in the Thicket.
Southeast view. PROKUDIN-GORSKY 21251. SUMMER 1910.

KOSTROMA Church of the Resurrection in the Thicket.
Southeast view. BRUMFIELD, AUGUST 13, 2017.

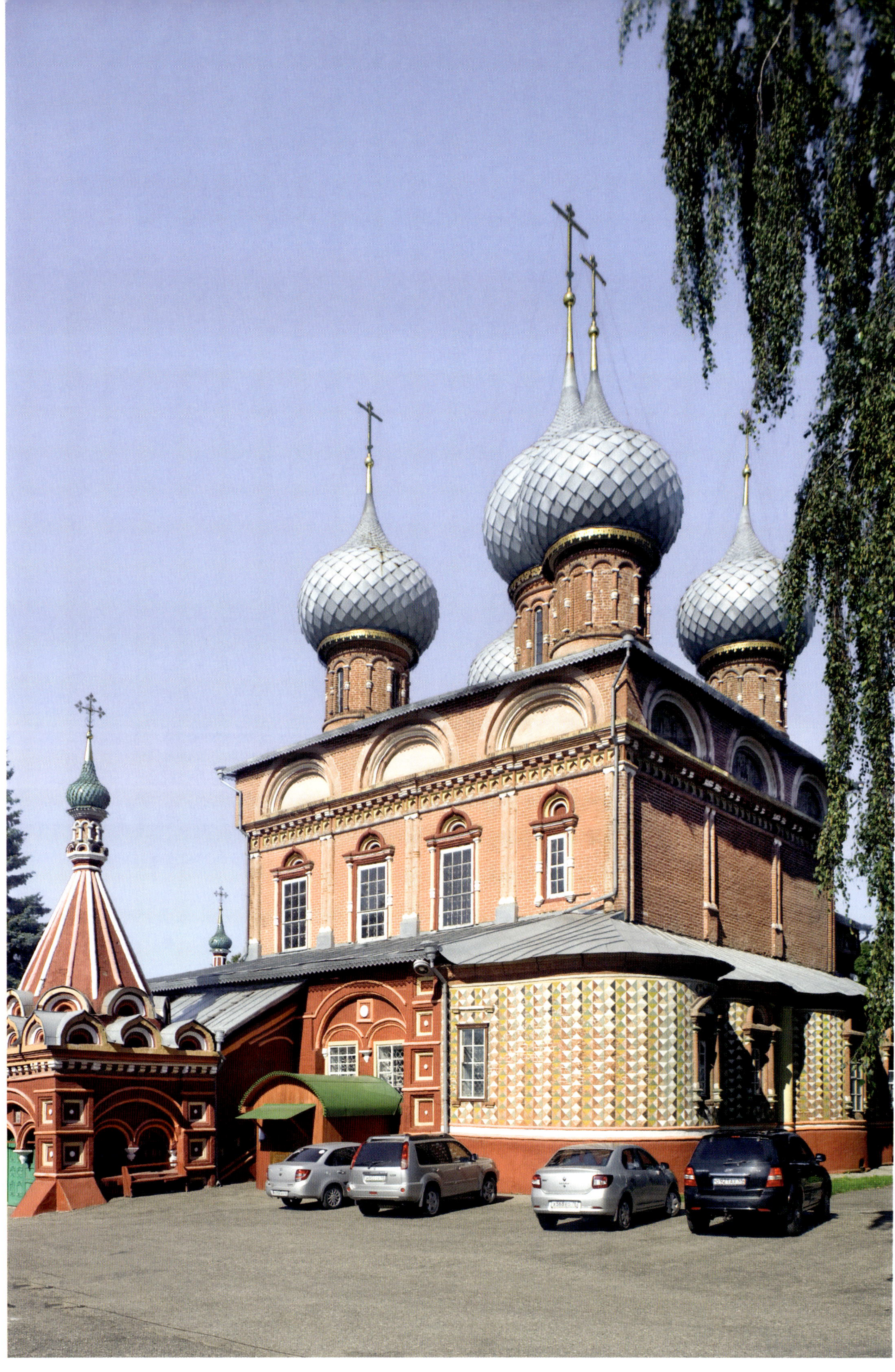

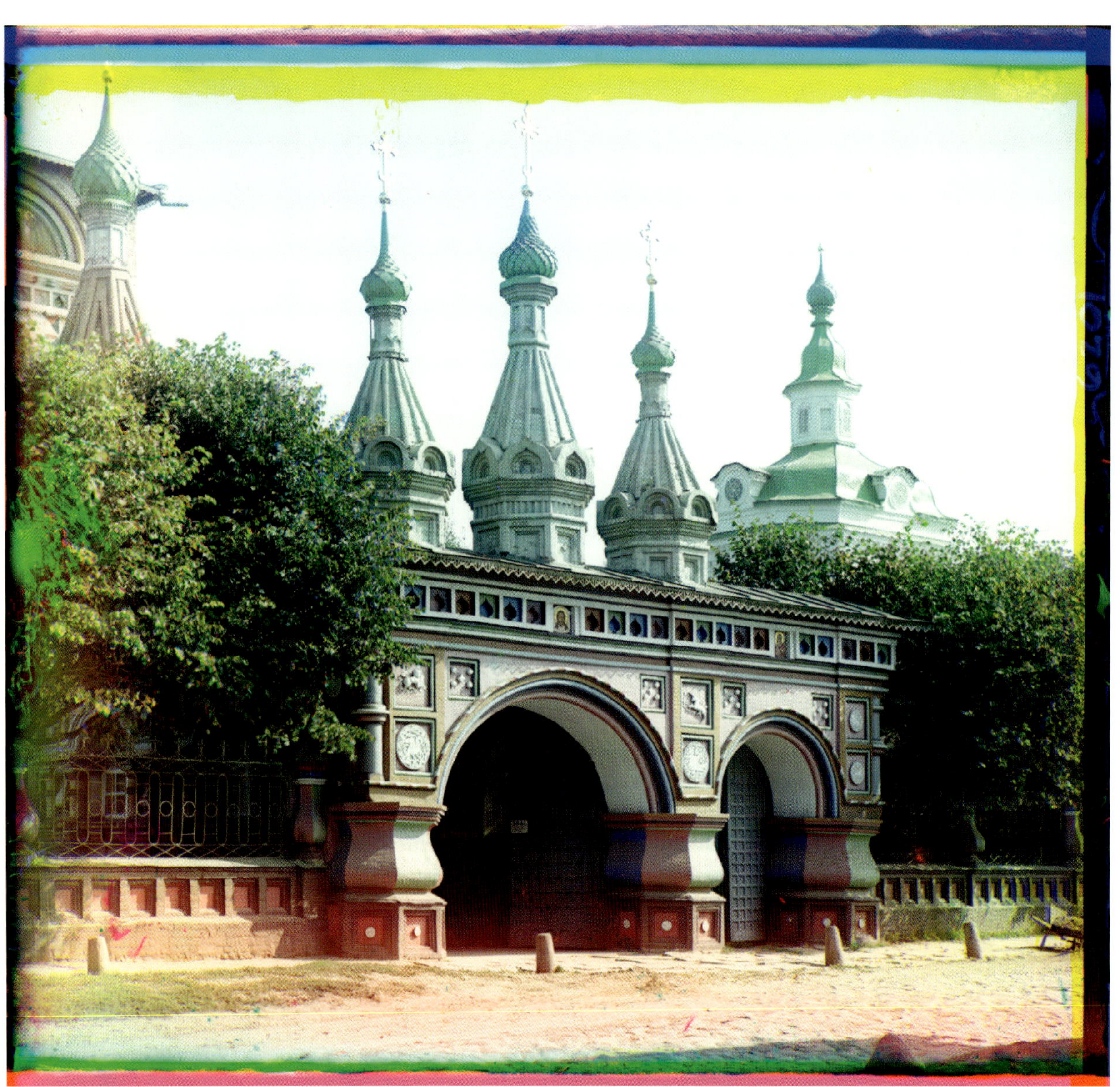

KOSTROMA Church of the Resurrection in the Thicket. West view with Holy Gate. *Right*: dome of Church of the Icon of the Virgin of the Sign. PROKUDIN-GORSKY 21213. SUMMER 1910.

KOSTROMA Church of the Resurrection in the Thicket. West view with Holy Gate. BRUMFIELD, AUGUST 12, 2017.

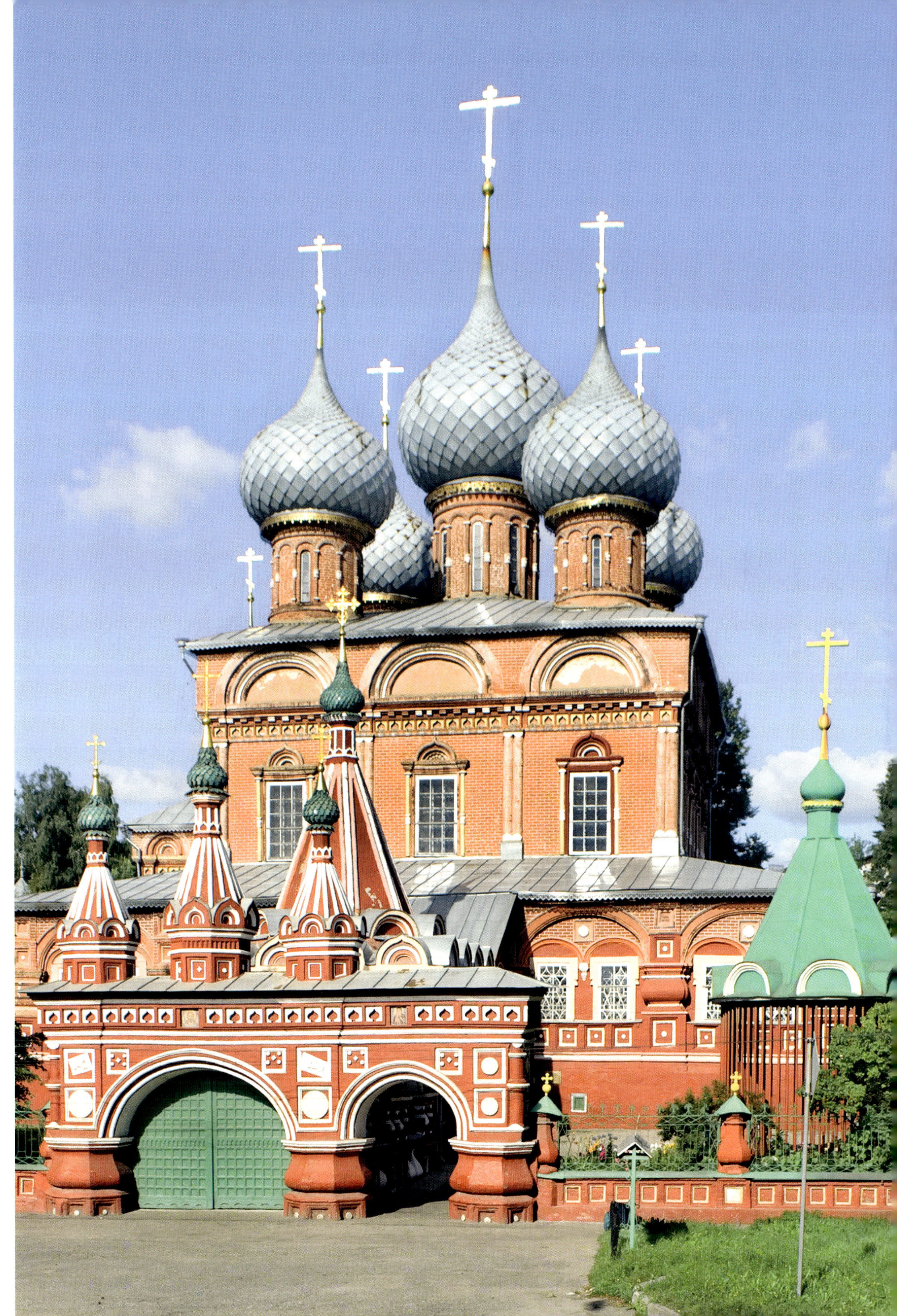

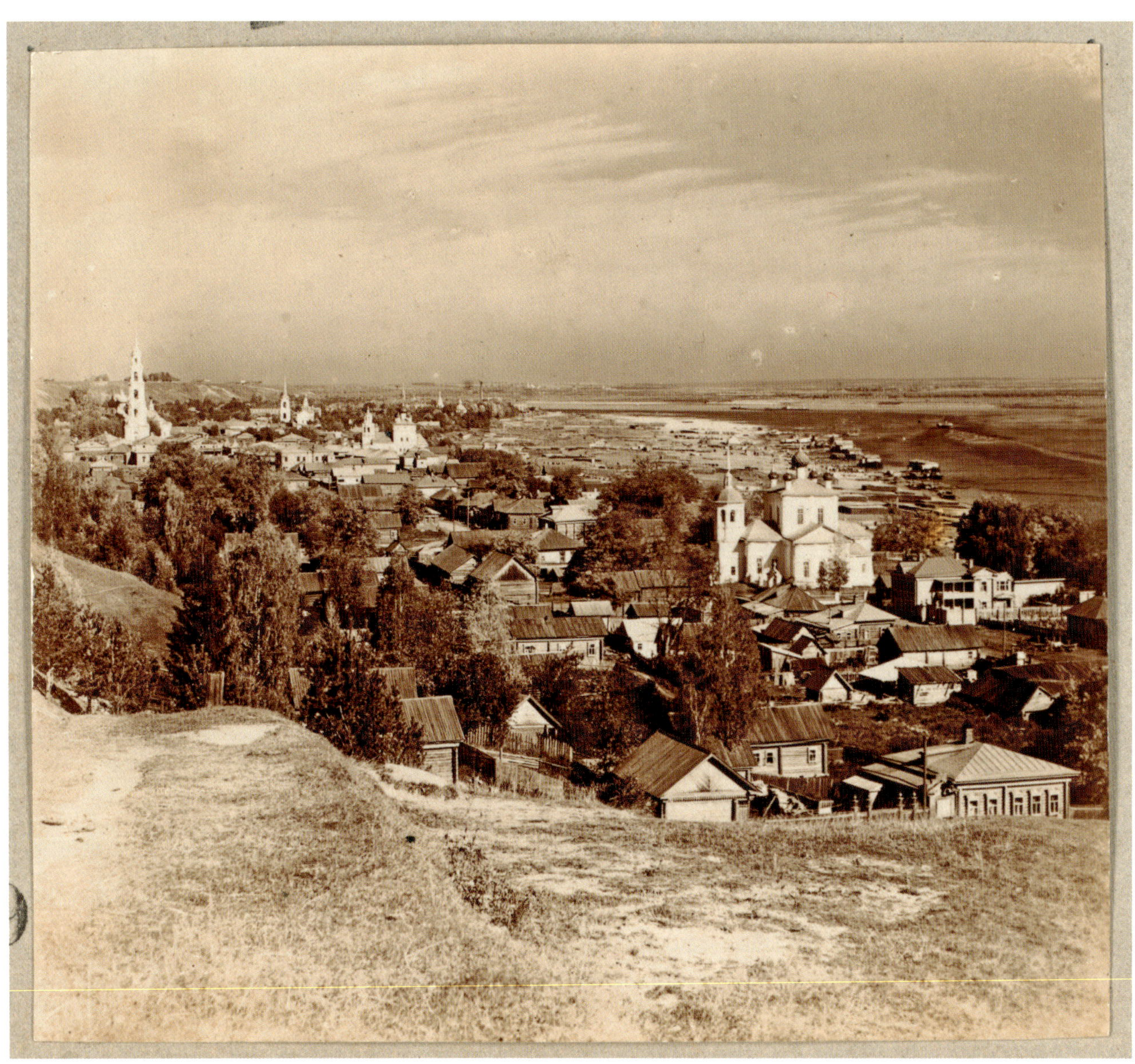

YUREVETS View north from fortress hill. *From left*:
bell tower and Church of Saint George, Church of the
Transfiguration, Church of the Annunciation, Church
of the Ascension (*right foreground*). Only the five-
tiered bell tower survived the Soviet period. PROKUDIN-
GORSKY 02525. SUMMER 1910.

YUREVETS View north from fortress hill. *From left*:
bell tower and Church of Saint George, Old Cathedral
of the Entry into Jerusalem, Soviet Street, Church of
the Purification. BRUMFIELD, JULY 15, 2012.

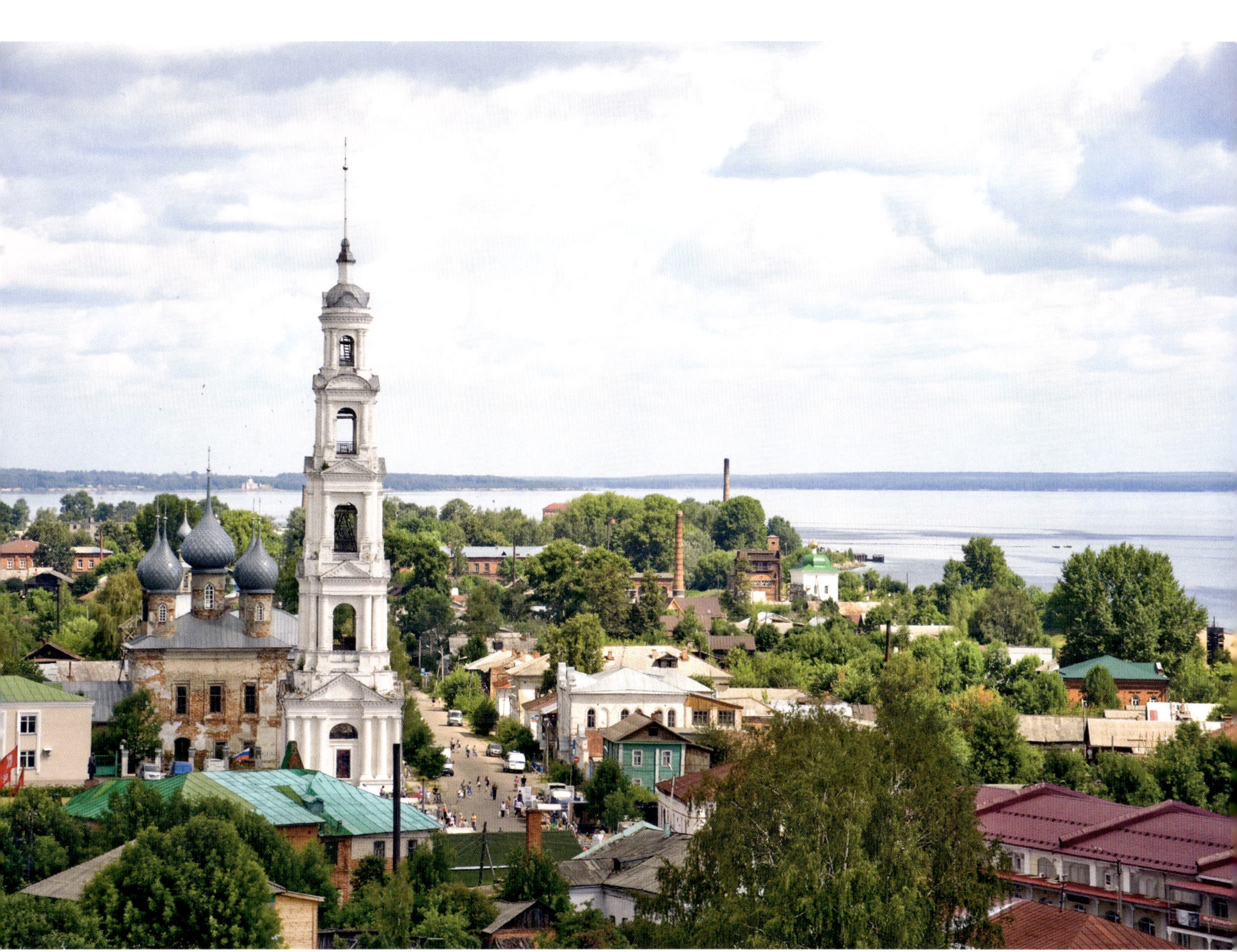

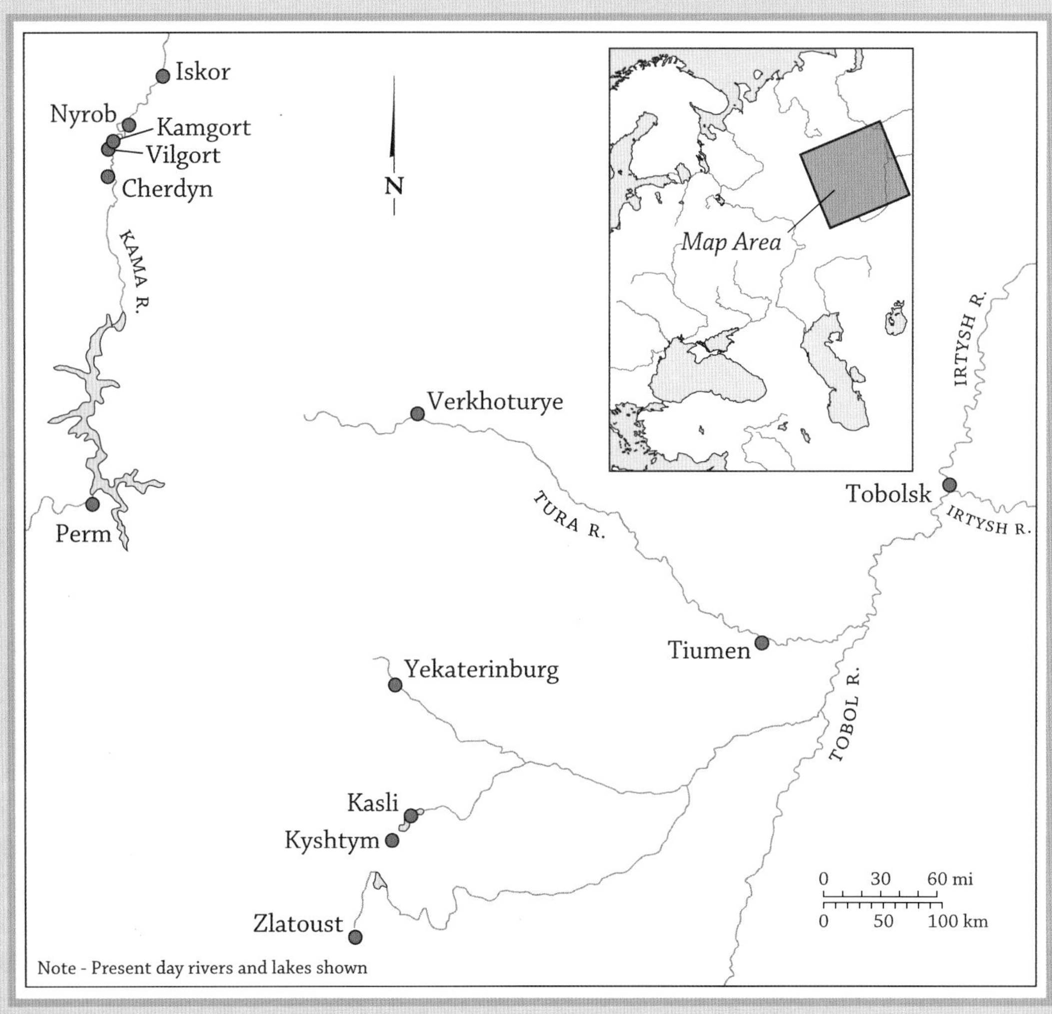

Iskor
Nyrob
Kamgort
Vilgort
Cherdyn
KAMA R.
Perm
N
Verkhoturye
TURA R.
Map Area
IRTYSH R.
Tobolsk
IRTYSH R.
Tiumen
TOBOL R.
Yekaterinburg
Kasli
Kyshtym
Zlatoust
0   30   60 mi
0   50   100 km
Note - Present day rivers and lakes shown

SIX · From the Ural Mountains
into Siberia

The Ural Mountains, the boundary between the European and Asian parts of Russia, form one of the country's most intensively developed industrial areas. In the summer of 1909 Sergey Prokudin-Gorsky traveled to this region in a railway car equipped with a photographic laboratory. His photographs from that trip and a later one in 1912 show not only industrial settlements nestled in the Urals but also the beauty of the mountain landscape even in the process of its exploitation. As part of his commission from the Ministry of Transportation, Prokudin-Gorsky photographed the area's expanding network of railroads, which provided a dramatic contrast to the rugged terrain over which they were built.

A major point in this network was the city of Perm, situated along the high east bank of the Kama River, with sweeping vistas across the river to the west. As a center of the Urals metalworking industry and headquarters for the Perm Railway (the major link between Siberia and Arkhangelsk), the city grew steadily and had a population of some sixty thousand by 1910 (current population around 1,000,000). In addition to its nineteen Orthodox churches and a convent, Perm had a Catholic and a Lutheran church, and two synagogues. The toponym "Perm"—apparently derived from Finno-Ugric words *pera ma*, meaning "distant land"—is documented as early as the twelfth-century chronicle "Tale of Bygone Years." At that time "Perm" was variously used to mean lands extending from the Vychegda River basin in the north to the Pechora and Izhma River networks in the east and south to the Vishera and Kama Rivers (part of the Volga basin). Until the fifteenth century, this territory was nominally controlled by the economic power of Novgorod, whose hunters and traders exploited its supply of valuable furs.

The city now known as Perm had its origins in the quest by Peter the Great to utilize the rich ore deposits of the Urals and secure sources of high-quality industrial metals. As was the case for other towns in the Urals (including Yekaterinburg), the guiding force in developing the area was Vasily Tatishchev (1686–1750), one of Russia's early professional historians. A scholar with a gift for practical activity, Tatishchev had boundless admiration for Peter the Great and was an influential proponent of the central role of autocrat and state in Russian history, of the view that Russians are a "state people." During the 1720s Tatishchev opened mines, smelters, and metalworking factories throughout the Ural Mountains. In 1720 Tatishchev established a settlement at the village of Egoshikha, located near the small Egoshikha River, a tributary of the Kama. With nearby sources of copper ore, the site was considered ideal for a large smelter. The project was then entrusted to Georg Wilhelm Hennin (de Gennin; 1676–1750), a military engineer of German origins who worked closely with Tatishchev. Construction began on the main Egoshikha factory on May 4, 1723, which is considered the city's founding date. The name Perm was officially adopted only in 1781 after a command by Catherine the Great that transformed the large factory settlement into an administrative center for the Urals.

Since its origins Perm has been associated with heavy industry, and by the 1860s it became one of the most important arms-producing areas in Russia. Because of its favorable location on the Kama River, Perm during the nineteenth century developed into a transportation center for salt and other minerals, as well as metal ore and the products of metal factories throughout the western Ural Mountains. In 1846 regular steamboat service was established on the Kama. In 1863 Perm was included in the main Siberian Highway, and in 1878 construction was completed on the first phase of the Urals Railroad from Perm to Yekaterinburg, part of a railroad construction boom that culminated in the early twentieth century with the completion of the Trans-Siberian Railway.

Of the many urban panoramas that Prokudin-Gorsky took in the Ural region, his view of Perm is particularly evocative of the industrialization of Russia. The Kama River, with its steamers and barges, stretches toward the railroad bridge, while in the foreground plumes of smoke rise from one of

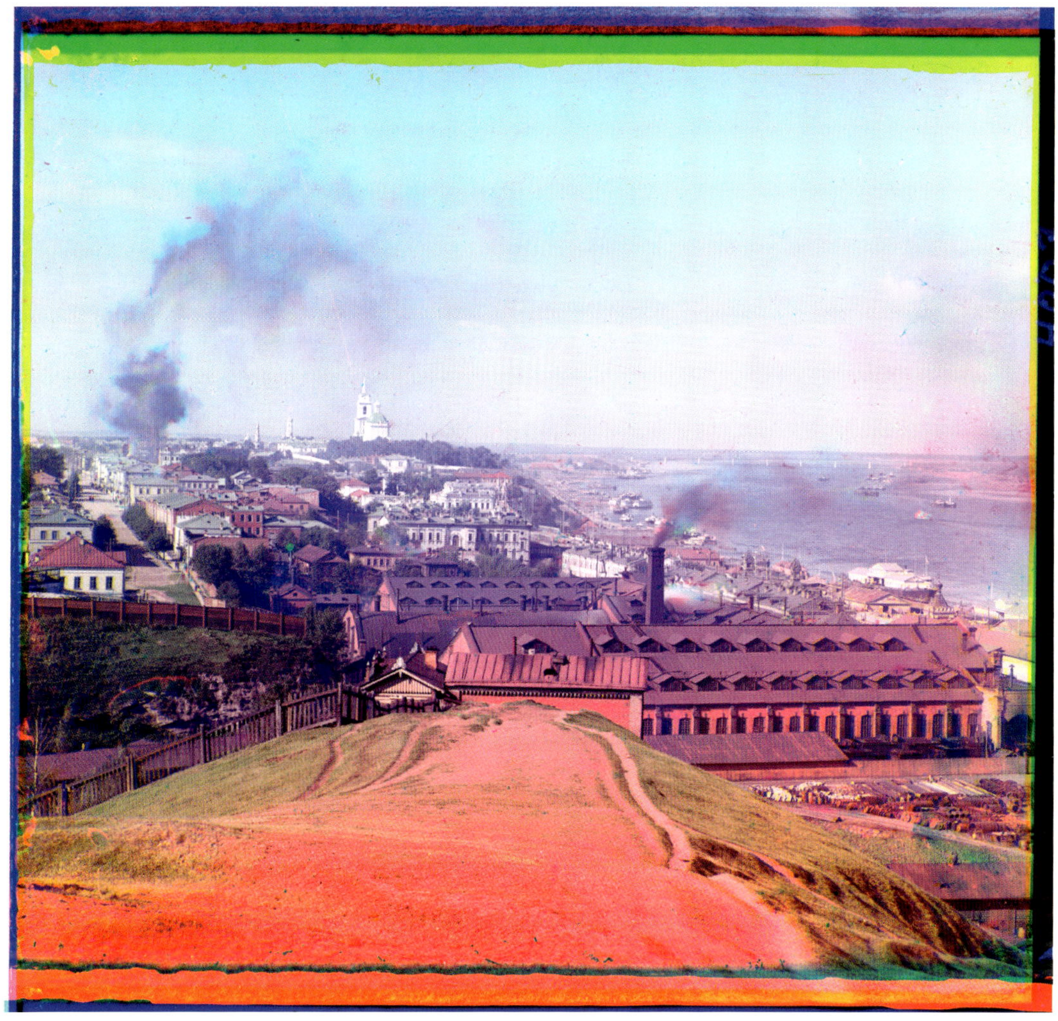

PERM View west down left bank of Kama River, with workshops and administration of Urals Railroad. Towers in distance (*from right*): Cathedral of the Transfiguration, Trinity Cathedral, mosque. PROKUDIN-GORSKY 20451. SUMMER 1909.

the city's foundries, many of which supplied the railroad. The well-kept streets with commercial and industrial enterprises are punctuated by the verticals of the Transfiguration Cathedral bell tower and the minaret of the main mosque.

The city's most visible historical landmark is the Cathedral of the Transfiguration of the Savior, overlooking the Kama River. The cathedral was the center of the Transfiguration Monastery, founded in 1560 by the Stroganovs at their settlement up the Kama River at Pyskor. Transferred to Perm in 1781, the monastery became a bishop's residence. Construction of the cathedral lasted several decades until 1819, at which time work began on its neoclassical bell tower, designed by Ivan Sviyazev and finally completed in

1832. During the Soviet period the interior was disfigured by the conversion of the cathedral and adjacent monastery buildings to house both the art museum—with its excellent collection of regional religious art—and the history museum.

Much of Perm burned during a fire in 1842, but the town quickly recovered. During the half century before World War I the expansion of Perm led to the construction of brick buildings in decorative eclectic styles for commercial, private, and religious use. Of particular interest near the Kama River is the imposing mosque, built in 1902–3 in an eclectic "Moorish" design by the Perm architect Alexander Ozhegov. Supported by local merchant dynasties such as the Timkins and Ibatullins, the mosque was closed in the Soviet period and converted to the local Communist Party archive. In 1990 it was restored to religious use.

Prokudin-Gorsky was indefatigable in traveling to remote locations to the north of Perm, journeys that were arduous despite improvements in rail and river transportation. To reach the historical settlements of Cherdyn and Nyrob on the Kolva River (a northern tributary of the Kama), he relied on a river steamer. Cherdyn was settled perhaps as early as the ninth century, and by the fourteenth century Russians (and Orthodox missionaries) had moved into the area. Not until the 1470s did Moscow assume control of the Cherdyn region, which was subjected to Nogai raids until the conquest of Kazan by Ivan the Terrible in 1552. During the sixteenth century Cherdyn was a gateway for Russian settlers crossing the Ural Mountains to the east. Situated on the right bank of the Kolva River, near its confluence with the Vishera, Cherdyn controlled river passage in several directions: north to the Pechora basin, via the Kolva River; south to the Volga and Moscow via the Kama River; and east to the Ob River basin and Siberia via the Vishera. At the turn of the seventeenth century, a more direct Siberian route through Solikamsk undercut Cherdyn's strategic position.

In 1467 a monastery dedicated to Saint John the Divine was established in Cherdyn, the oldest monastic institution in the Urals. After a fire in 1700, the log structures were replaced with this brick church, seen from the northwest. Square in plan, the church rises to a tiered octagonal tower supporting a single cupola. Although the monastery was closed in 1784, the church continued to be used and its territory was enclosed by a brick and iron fence. In the early twentieth century it was reestablished as a convent, with a need for additional structures—hence the stacks of bricks and flagstone. Visible in the left background is a cemetery around a lone pine, beyond which is the

Kolva River. Despite minor changes, the church has been well preserved on both exterior and interior.

Prokudin-Gorsky's general views of Cherdyn from the newly built brick water tower show a regular plan lined with solidly built houses of brick and wood. This view to the northeast, taken from the town water tower, shows a tidy street with brick and wooden houses, most of which have four-sloped roofs. Attached to the houses are enclosed yards with large sheds, some of which serve as stables. The well-maintained structures reflect the prosperity of this merchant town, situated on the Kolva River (in background). In the distance is an array of churches that stretches from the dimly visible Church of Saint John the Divine on the left to the Churches of the Epiphany, the Dormition, and the Transfiguration. On the right is the red brick bell tower of the Cathedral of the Resurrection, which consists of two parts. My photograph from the same water tower (after a special security clearance) shows some of the same orientation points, but also many losses.

Surrounding Cherdyn are villages whose names are rich with consonants: Pokcha, Vilgort, Iskor, Kamgort, and Pianteg on the Kama River. Each settlement has its architectural heritage, preserved in Prokudin-Gorsky's photographs. To the northeast of Cherdyn on the road to Nyrob is the village of Vilgort, with Church of the Trinity. In the fifteenth century Russian settlers made their way to this area, which had long been inhabited by Komi-Permiak ethnic groups. The dominant feature in this view from the road to the south is the bell tower of the Church of the Trinity, whose basic structure was built in 1777 in a decorated archaic manner. In 1902 the church gained a large refectory and bell tower built of red brick in a "Russian Revival" style. Farther on the same road is Iskor, which Prokudin-Gorsky captured in a panoramic view north. The village is located near the small Iskorka River, a tributary of the Kolva. The dominant feature is the whitewashed brick Church of the Nativity of Christ, built in an archaic style in 1783 with a tiered bell tower added in 1786.

Prokudin-Gorsky's visit to the northern Urals (presumably in the spring of 1913 in connection with the Romanov tercentenary) included the small settlement of Nyrob, forty kilometers to the north of the regional center of Cherdyn. Referred to in written sources as early as 1579, isolated Nyrob soon became a place of tsarist punishment at the turn of the seventeenth century. References to the agony of the Romanov dynasty are usually associated with Yekaterinburg and the Ipatiev house, where Nicholas and his family were murdered in July 1918. Yet the Romanovs had another sacrifice

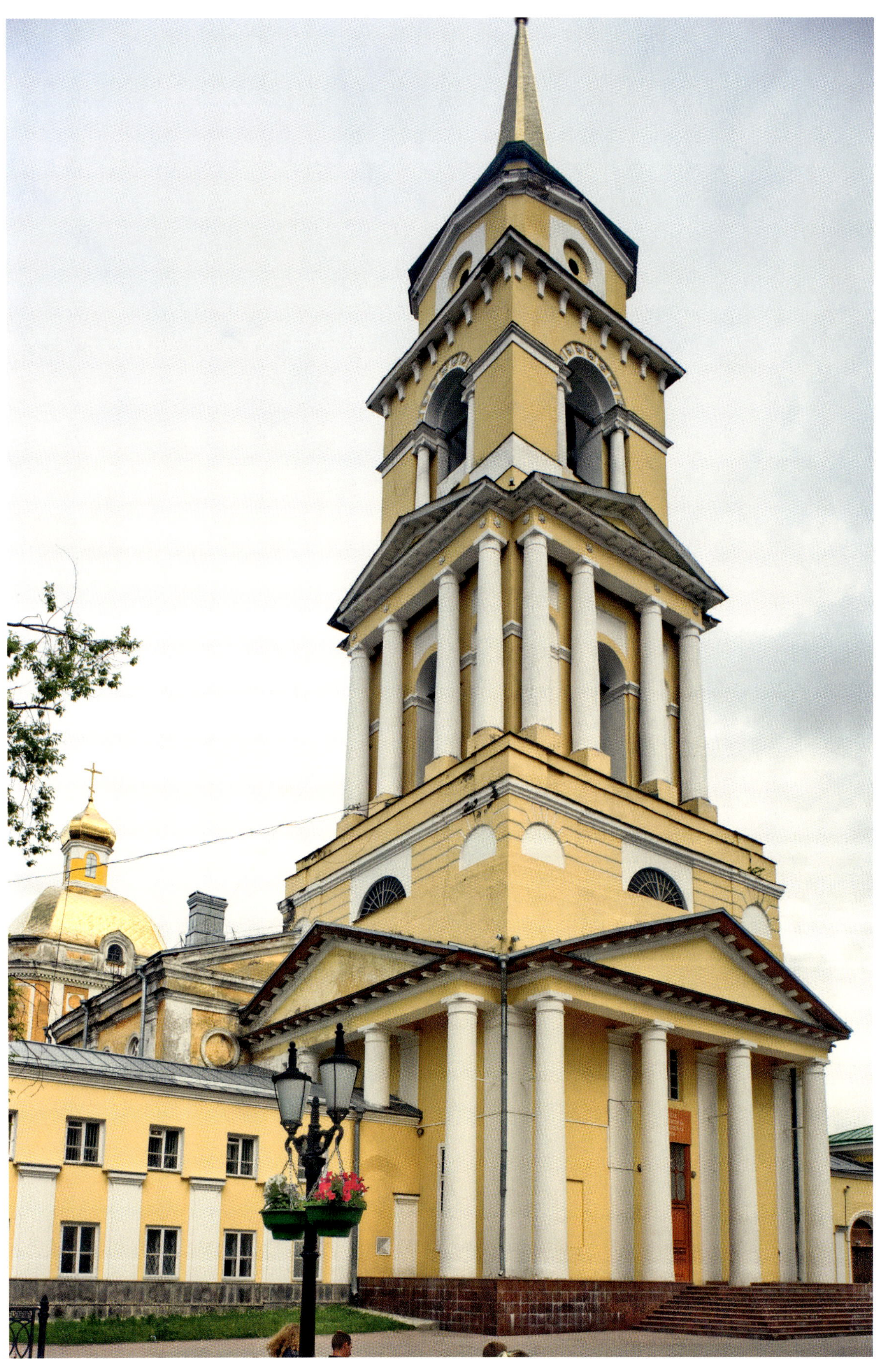

PERM Bell tower and Cathedral of the Transfiguration. Northwest view. BRUMFIELD, JUNE 15, 2014.

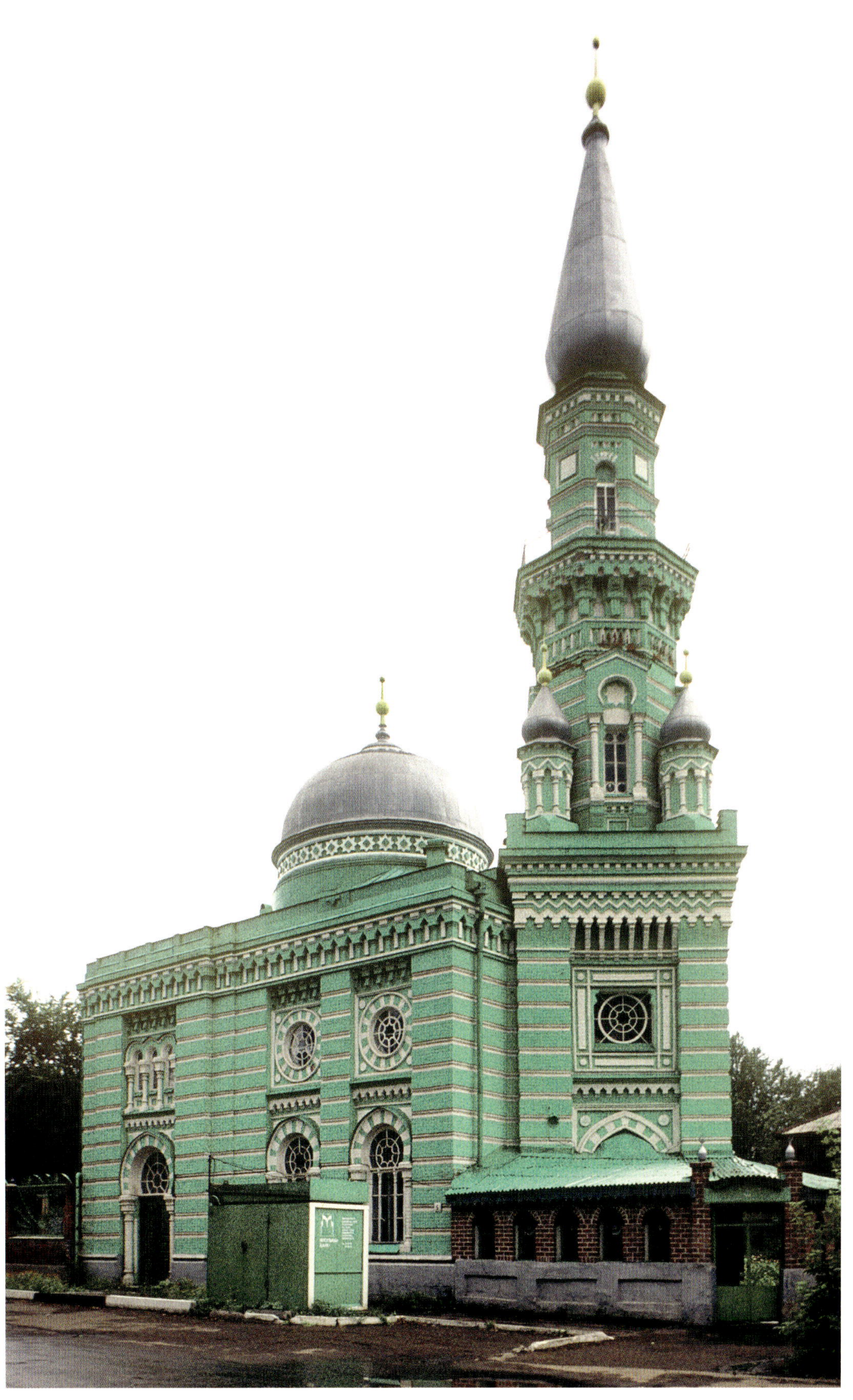

PERM Mosque. BRUMFIELD, AUGUST 22, 1999.

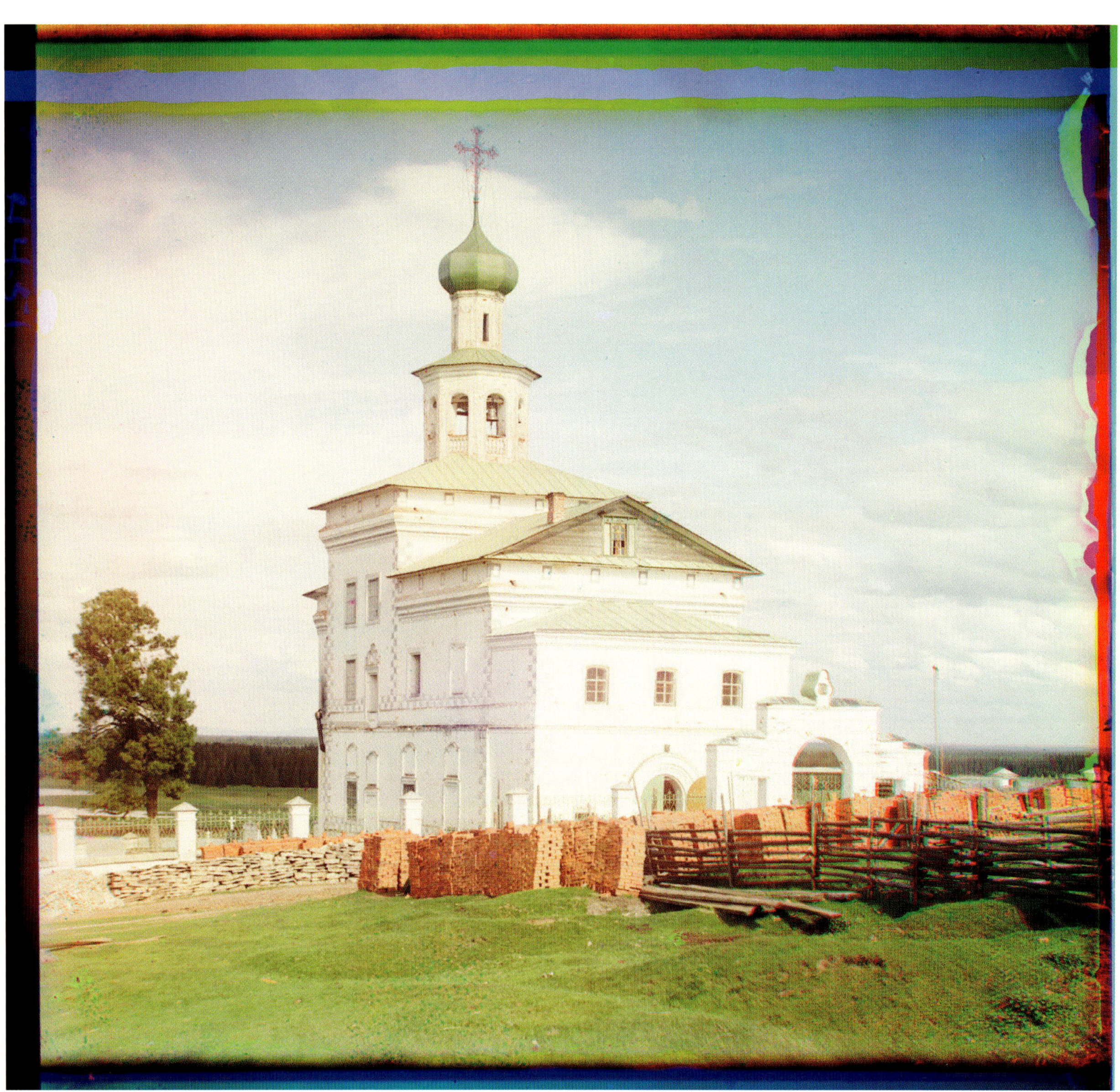

CHERDYN Church of Saint John the Divine. Northwest view. PROKUDIN-GORSKY 20698. SPRING 1913.

CHERDYN Church of Saint John the Divine. Southeast view. BRUMFIELD, AUGUST 13, 2000.

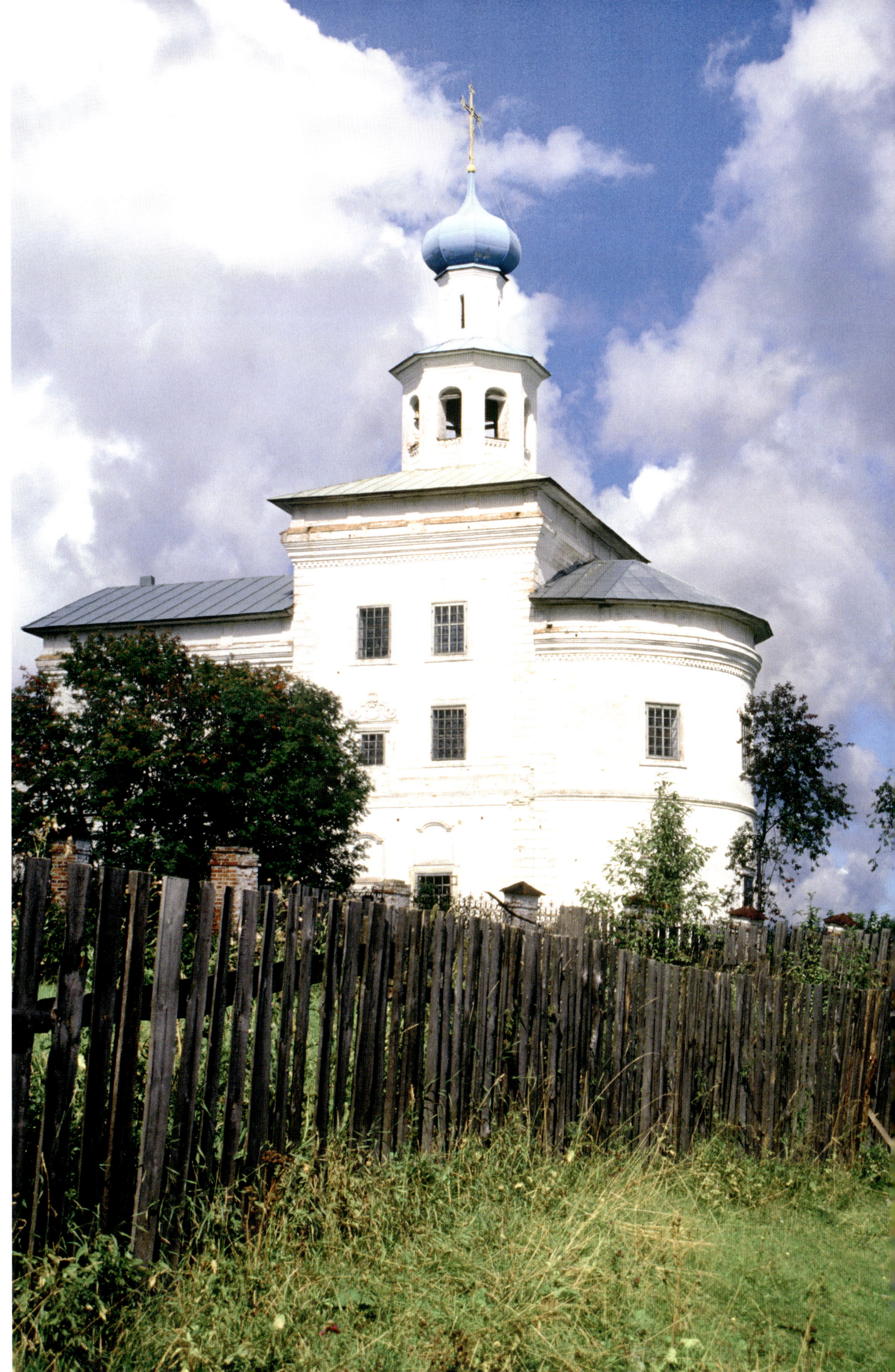

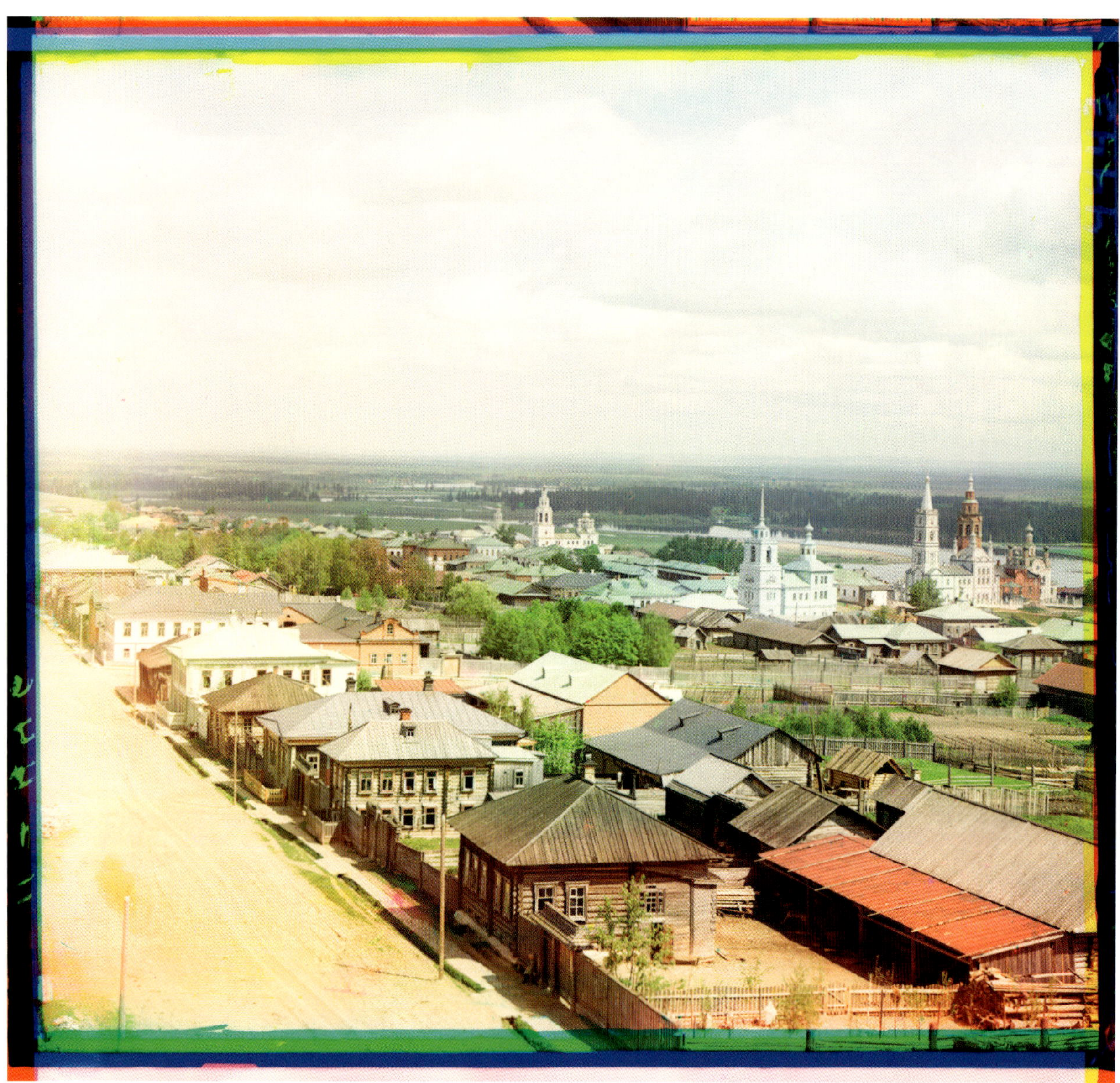

CHERDYN View northeast from water tower toward Kolva River. *From left*: Church of Saint John the Divine; Church of the Epiphany; Church of the Dormition; Church of the Transfiguration; bell tower (red brick) and Cathedral of the Resurrection. PROKUDIN-GORSKY 20690. SPRING 1913.

CHERDYN View northeast from water tower toward Kolva River. *From left*: Church of Saint John the Divine; Church of the Transfiguration (without cupolas), bell tower and Cathedral of the Resurrection. BRUMFIELD, AUGUST 14, 2000.

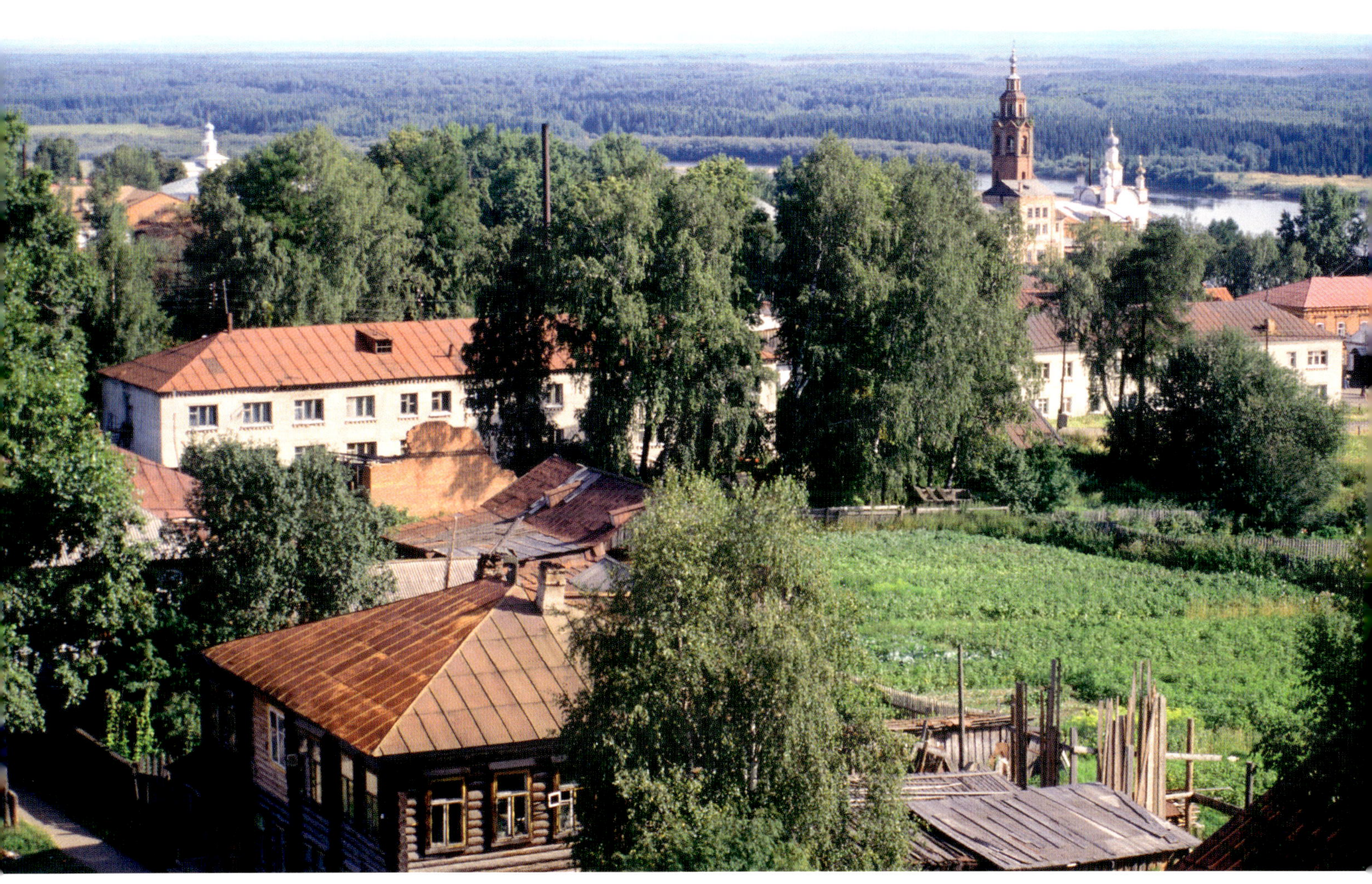

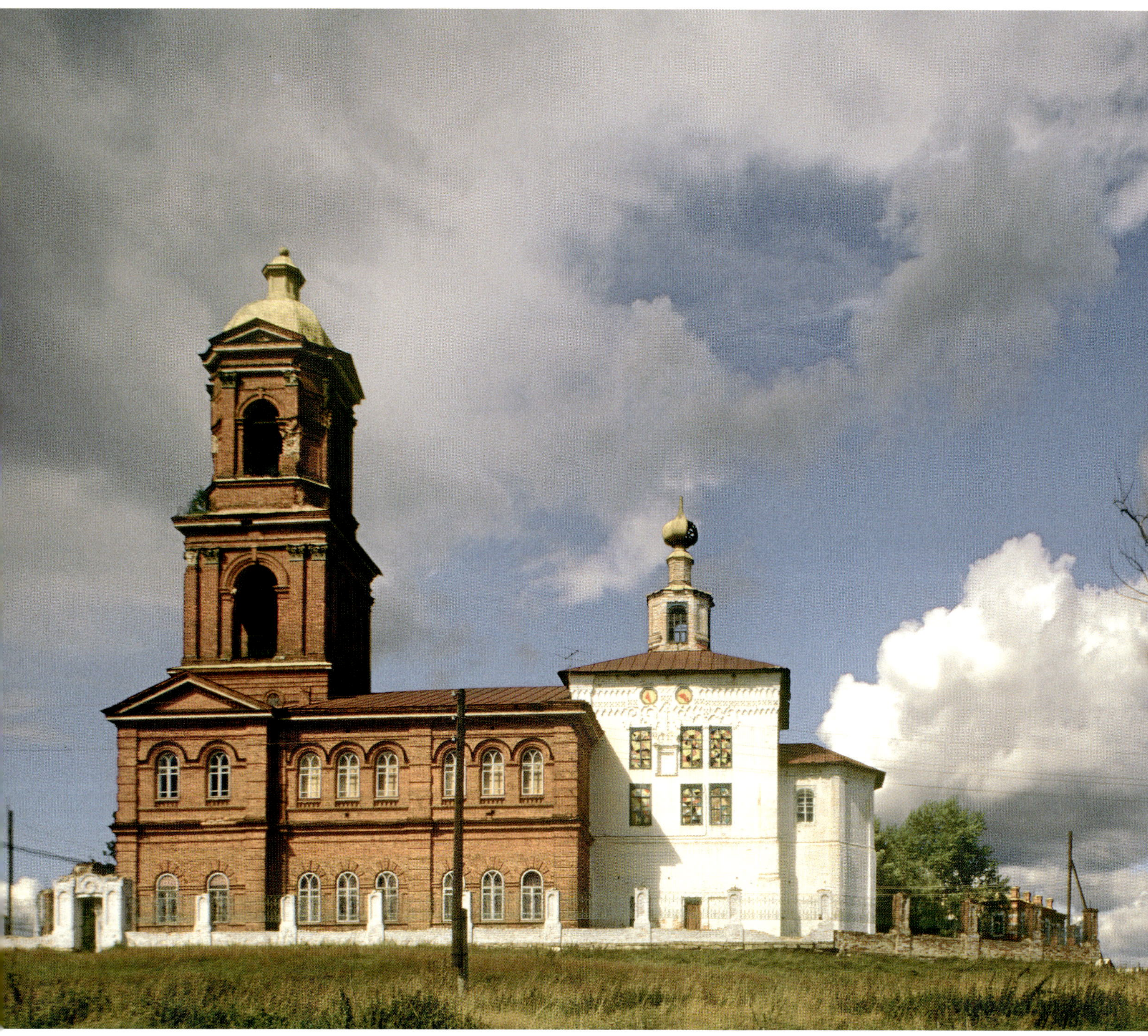

VILGORT Church of the Trinity. South view.
BRUMFIELD, AUGUST 14, 2000.

VILGORT View northeast on road to Nyrob, with
Church of the Trinity. PROKUDIN-GORSKY 20689.
SPRING 1913.

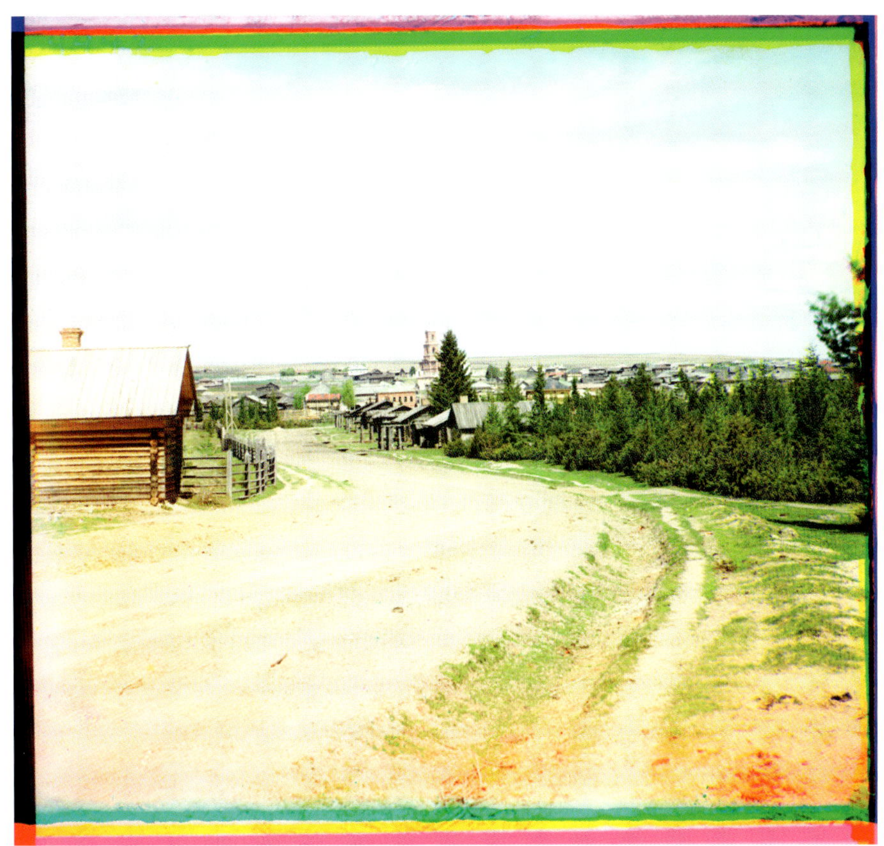

in the Urals area, that of the boyar Mikhail Nikitch Romanov. It was here, in 1601, that Tsar Boris Godunov exiled Mikhail Nikitich, whose aunt was the much-beloved first wife of Ivan the Terrible, Anastasia. The ambitious Godunov had reasons for concern about his own unsteady claims to the Muscovite throne after the end of the Riurikovich dynasty in 1598. To eliminate a rival, Godunov subjected Mikhail to harsh treatment in Nyrob. Kept in fetters and thrown into a deep pit, Mikhail died the following year.

However, Godunov's own days were numbered, and after his death in 1605, Russia was plunged into the Time of Troubles. Although its consequences lingered for decades, that crisis formally ended in 1613 with the accession to the throne of Mikhail Fedorovich Romanov, nephew of Mikhail Nikitich and son of Fyodor Nikitich Romanov, who led the Russian Orthodox Church as Metropolitan (subsequently Patriarch) Filaret. Nyrob thus had impressive claims as a significant place in the sacralization of the Romanov ascent to dynastic authority. After the founding of the Romanov dynasty in 1613, the site of Mikhail Nikitich's death was commemorated by two log churches dedicated to the Epiphany and to Saint Nicholas. Indeed, the log Church of Saint Nicholas was built near the original burial place

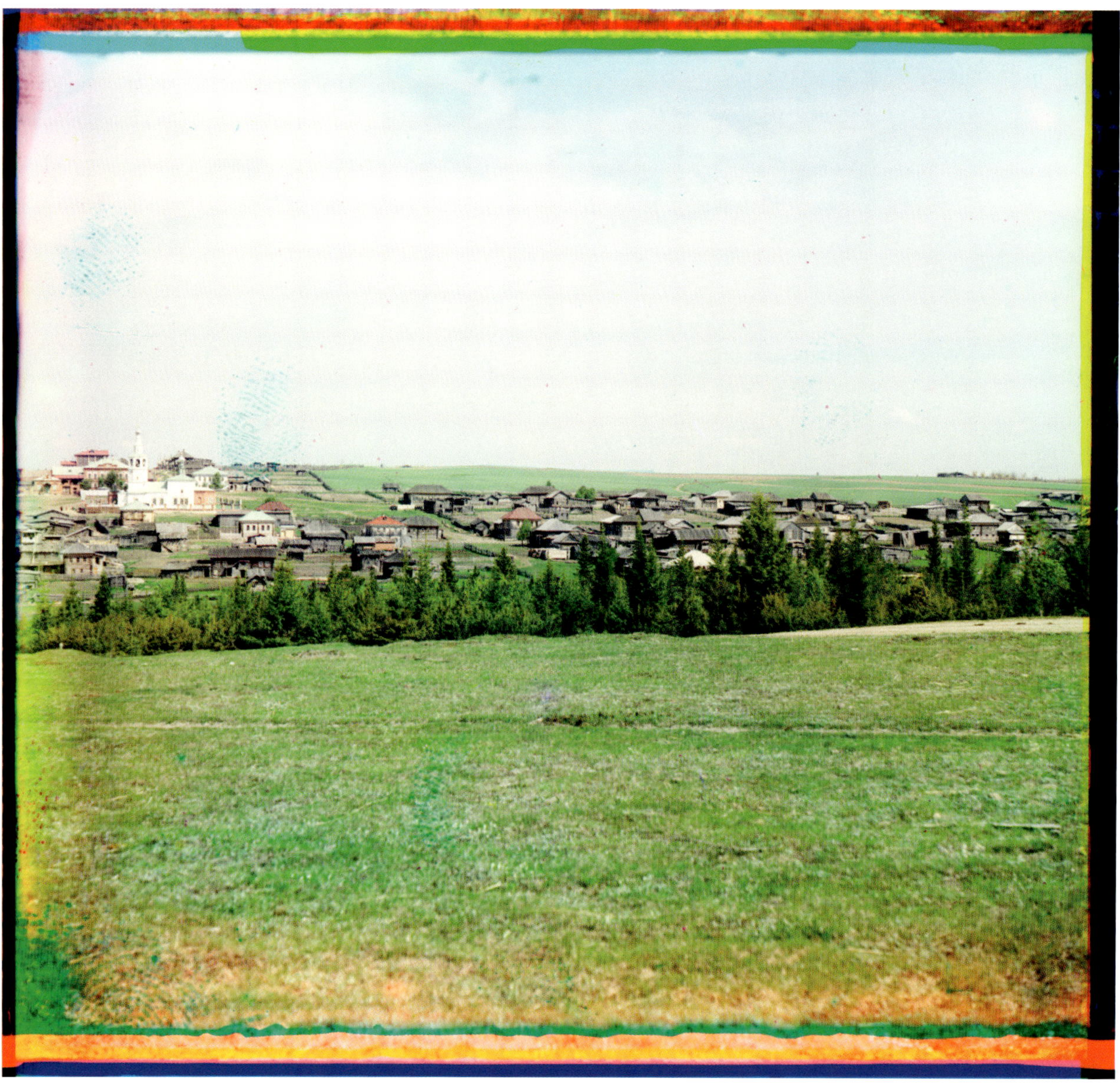

of Mikhail Nikitich almost immediately after the establishment of the dynasty in 1613.

At the beginning of the eighteenth century, the small
settlement gained an ensemble of two masonry churches:
the Church of Saint Nicholas (1704–5), an unheated structure used for worship in the summer, and the adjacent winter church of the Epiphany (1736)—both of which were
photographed by Prokudin-Gorsky. The church ensemble
was completed by a tall octagonal bell tower (demolished in
1934). The interiors of both churches were richly painted,
particularly the Epiphany Church, which held the casket

ISKOR View north with Church of
the Nativity of Christ. PROKUDIN-
GORSKY 20687. SPRING 1913.

ISKOR Church of the Nativity
of Christ. Southwest view.
BRUMFIELD, AUGUST 14, 2000.

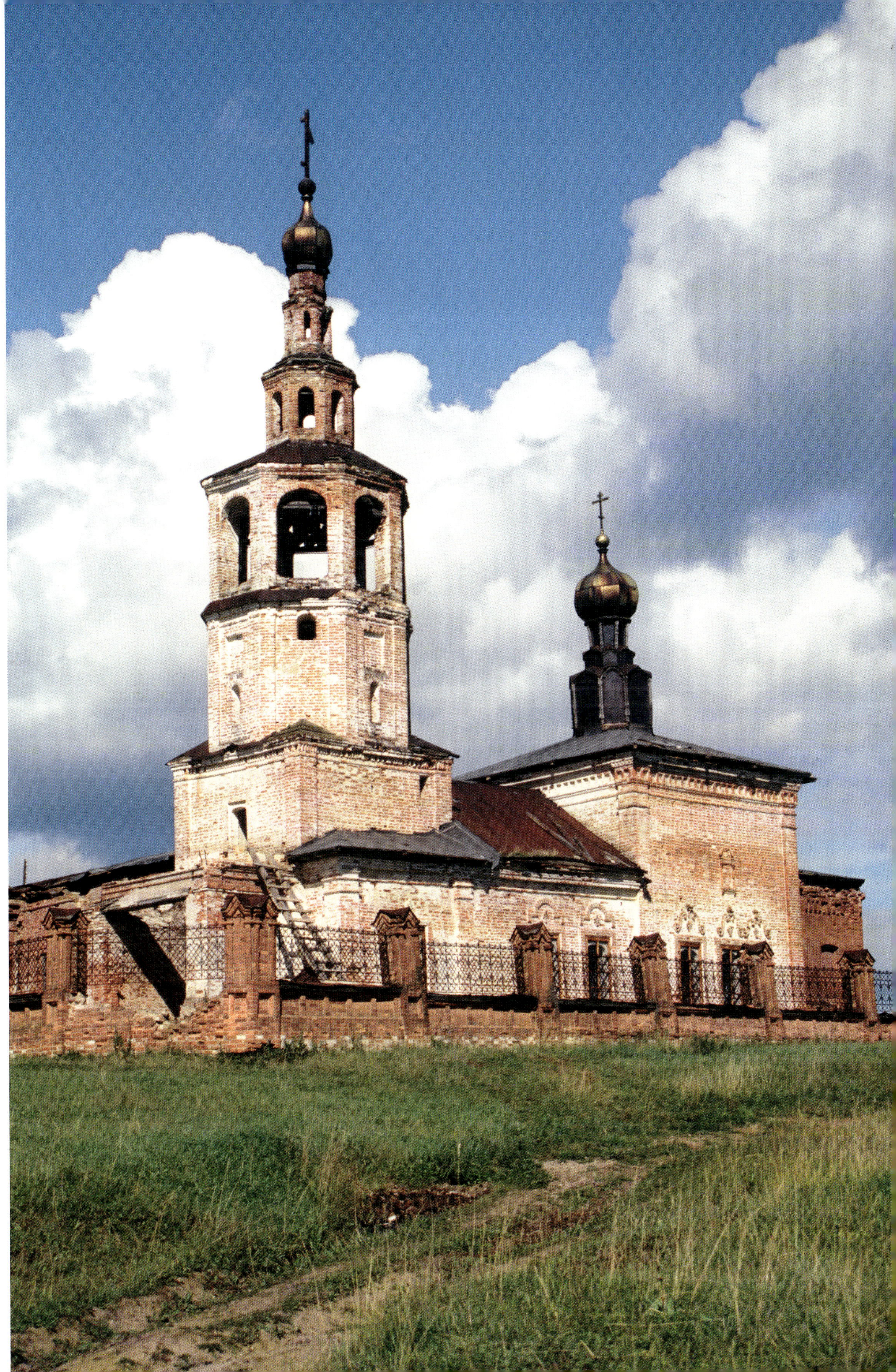

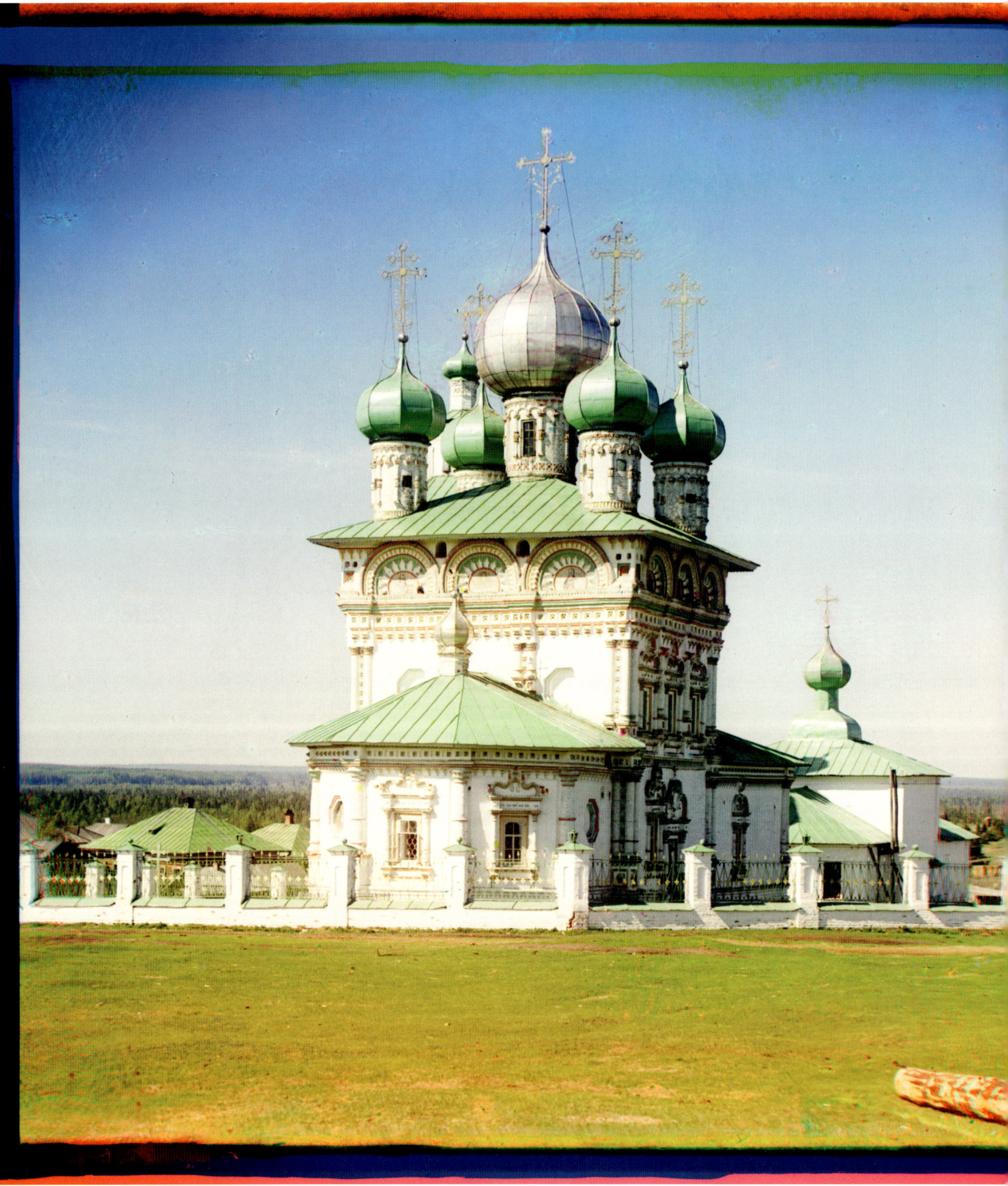

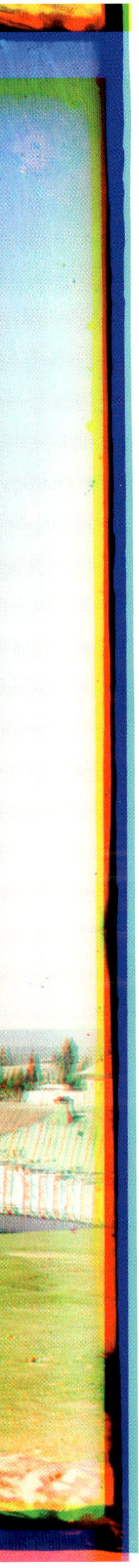

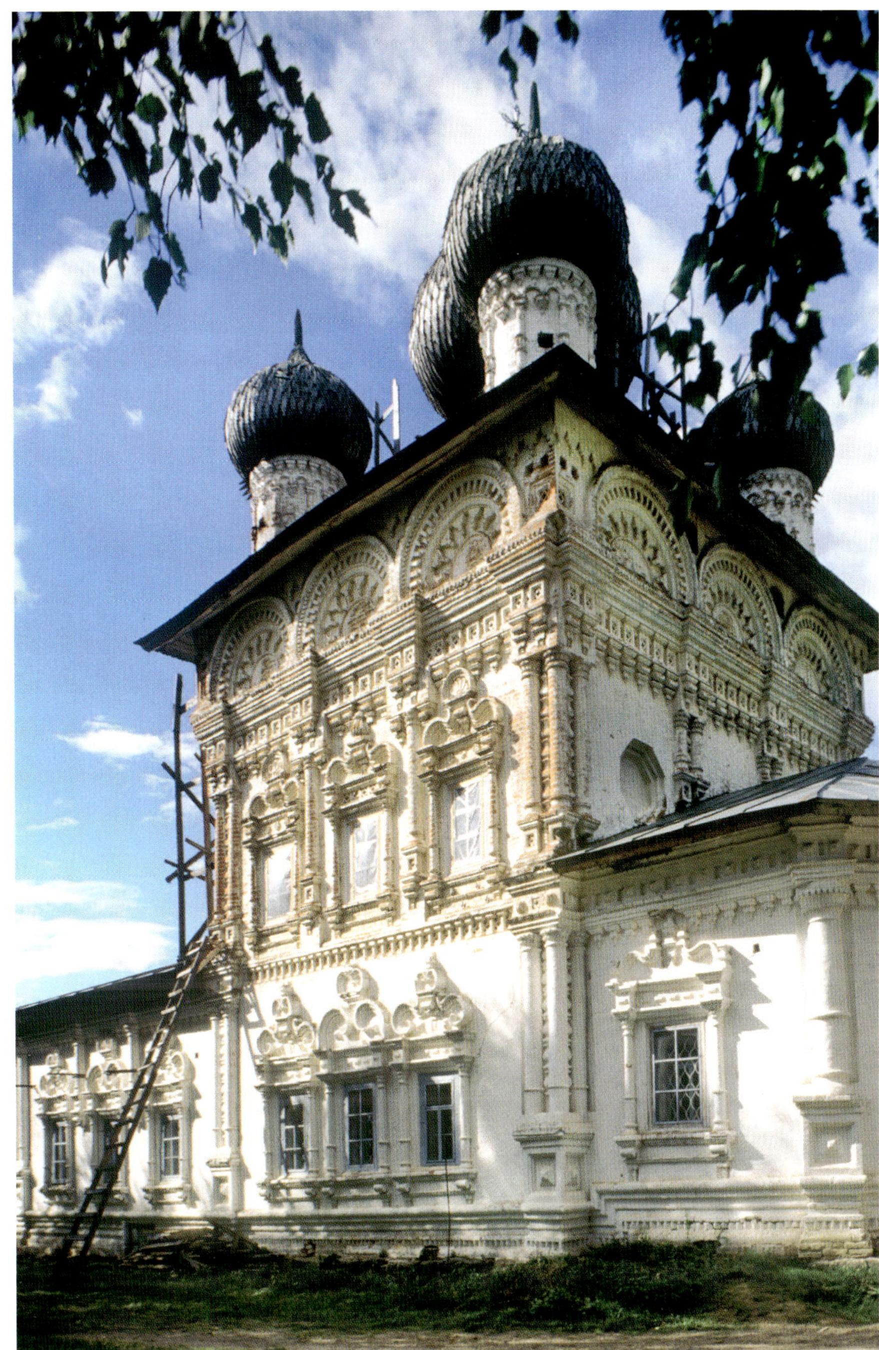

NYROB Church of Saint Nicholas. Northeast view. PROKUDIN-GORSKY 20670. SPRING 1913.

NYROB Church of Saint Nicholas. Southeast view. BRUMFIELD, AUGUST 14, 2000.

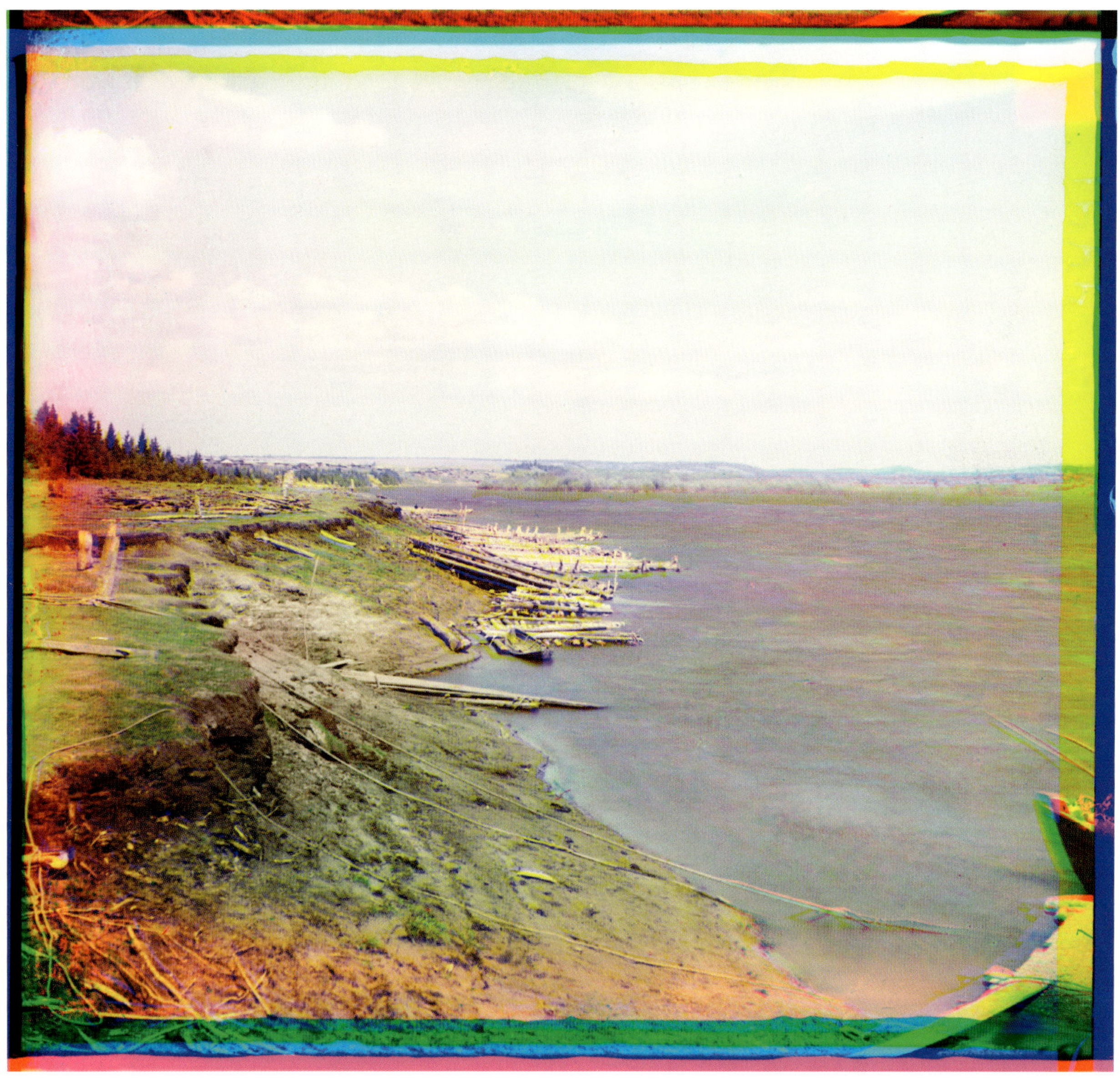

of Mikhail Nikitich Romanov. Prokudin-Gorsky's photographs are an essential record, particularly since most components of the Romanov memorial, including the interior of the Epiphany Church, were destroyed during the Soviet period. Fortunately, the distinctive Saint Nicholas Church survived as a structure. The church's facade ornamentation — from the window surrounds and the arcaded cornice to the drums beneath the onion cupolas — are unusual even by seventeenth-century Russian standards. In a crowning touch, the shingles of the wooden cupolas contribute to the play of texture and shadow on the surface of this idiosyn-

KAMGORT Kolva River and ferry on road to Nyrob. PROKUDIN-GORSKY 20688. SPRING 1913.

KAMGORT Ferry across Kolva River. BRUMFIELD, AUGUST 14, 2000.

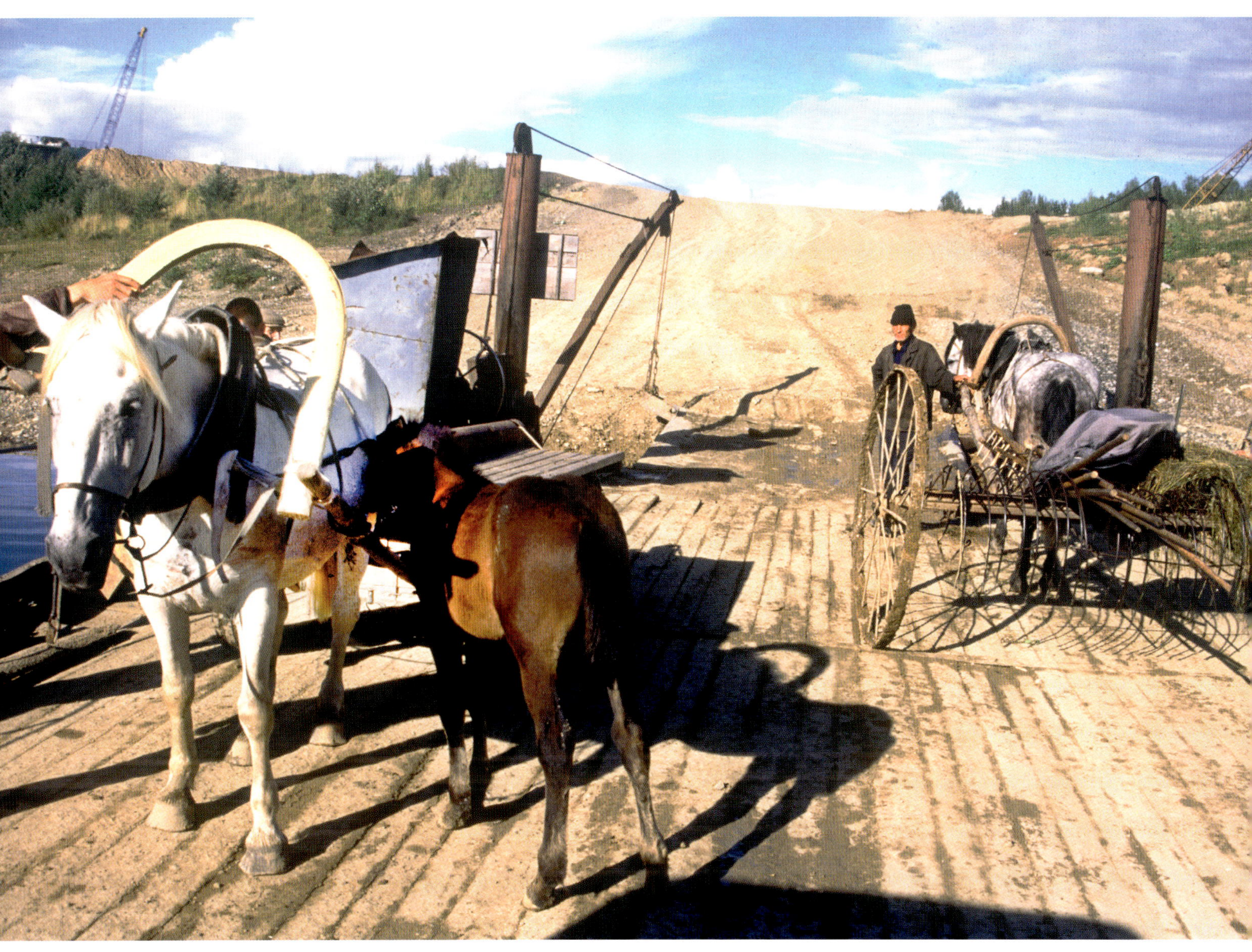

cratic structure. The road back from Nyrob to Cherdyn included a ferry over the Kolva River, photographed by Prokudin-Gorsky. At the time of my visit in August 2000, passage by ferry was still required—a timeless charm.

One of the most dramatic settings in the Urals is the town of Verkhoturye, located on the upper reaches of the Tura River three hundred kilometers to the north of Yekaterinburg. With its ornamental walls spectacularly situated on a sheer stone cliff above the rocky Tura, Verkhoturye (its name means "Upper Tura") played a critical role in extending Russian authority to the east during the seventeenth century. Although the Tura River, one thousand kilometers in length, is not particularly large by Russian standards, it is a crucial link from the eastern watershed of the Urals to the

Siberian river networks. With a current population of around nine thousand, its small size belies the fact that for much of the seventeenth and eighteenth centuries Verkhoturye was the primary point of transit from European Russia across the Ural Mountains into the vast Siberian domains.

With the founding of Tobolsk in 1585 Russia had a strategic anchor in Western Siberia at the confluence of the Tobol and Irtysh Rivers. In 1595 Tsar Feodor, son of Ivan the Terrible, announced a search for new paths to Siberia. The challenge was to find a more direct way across the Urals to the Tobol basin. The Tura, which flows into the Tobol River south of Tobolsk, proved the logical choice. Shortly thereafter Artemy Babinov, a free peasant from Solikamsk, blazed a trail across the Urals from Solikamsk to the Tura River. Within a remarkably short period of two years the almost three-hundred-kilometer path was improved to a state road that led to the fortified settlement of Verkhoturye, founded in 1598. In the same year a log church was built and dedicated to the Trinity.

Shortly thereafter Verkhoturye was designated the primary customs point for passage to Siberia. This tight control on movement to and from Siberia allowed the state to maintain its revenues through taxes on goods such as fur pelts—most especially the highly valued sable. Indeed, the ancient town shield, officially confirmed in 1783, contains a standing black sable. The Verkhoturye area also became a center of boat building. Throughout the seventeenth century Verkhoturye bustled with activity as salt, manufactured goods, and other essential items were shipped to new settlements in Siberia, while a flow of fur pelts made its way back toward Moscow. This "black gold" was so valuable that a separate fur treasury was created, which enabled the pelts to be carefully guarded and assessed.

For the first century of its existence Verkhoturye consisted of log buildings, but by the beginning of the eighteenth century, the fortress, or kremlin, ensemble was rebuilt in brick as a symbol of authority high above the Tura River on Trinity Rock. The centerpiece of the ensemble was the Trinity Cathedral, so designated after the church's reconstruction in brick between 1703 and 1709. The cathedral, with its soaring bell tower, is unique not only for its spectacular location but also for a design accented with elements from the Italian renaissance, medieval Muscovy, and the Ukrainian baroque. The Russian flair for ornament is especially evident in the ceramic work on the facade, including figures of radiating tiles. The structure was completed just before Peter redirected Russia's brick masons to the building of his new capital, Saint Petersburg. Ransacked during the Soviet era, the Trinity Cathedral has recently been the object of thorough restoration work, visible in photographs from 1999. The Russian move into Siberia was closely connected with the Orthodox Church, which promptly established its presence in new settlements. In 1604—less than a decade after its founding—Verkhoturye gained one of the first monasteries in Russia's Asian territory. Dedicated to Saint Nicholas and to the Transfiguration of the Savior, this monastery was followed in 1621 with the establishment of the Convent of the Intercession of the Virgin, also one of the earliest in Asian Russia. Despite its decline when the main route over the Urals to Siberia shifted southward to Yekaterinburg in the 1760s, Verkhoturye remained an important religious center attracting many pilgrims. Central to its status as a pilgrimage destination was the veneration of the local Saint Simeon of Verkhoturye (ca. 1607–1642). His parents apparently perished from the chaos during the Time of Troubles in central Russia, and the youth fled to the Urals, where he found refuge in the forests near Verkhoturye. According to the account of his life compiled at the end of the seventeenth century, Simeon devoted himself to a prayerful, ascetic existence helping the peasants in the neighboring villages. He also worked among the indigenous Mansi people. In 1704 Simeon's relics were transferred to the Monastery of Saint Nicholas, which eventually attracted thousands of pilgrims annually.

By the early twentieth century the number of pilgrims had become so great that the monastery constructed the enormous Cathedral of the Elevation of the Cross—considered the second-largest church in Russia. Nicholas II took a personal interest in this project, which was dedicated with much fervor in 1913. An experienced climber of church towers, Prokudin-Gorsky used the Trinity Cathedral bell tower for a camera perch to photograph the monastery (original glass negatives missing). Closed in 1925, the monastery's church interiors suffered extensive interior damage when the walled territory was converted to a place of incarceration for juvenile delinquents. The structures survived, and in 1990 the monastery was returned to the Orthodox Church. My distant view of 1999 shows restoration scaffolding around the Cathedral of the Elevation of the Cross.

The "capital" of the Urals is Yekaterinburg. Although it was administratively a district center within Perm Province, its population in 1910 (over seventy thousand) exceeded that of Perm itself. Located on the upper reaches of the Iset River, Yekaterinburg was founded in 1721 by Peter the Great's energetic colonizer of Siberia, Vasily Tatishchev, and named after Peter's second wife, Catherine I. By the beginning of the twentieth century, Yekaterinburg had become a major educational and research center, with several government agencies and institutions engaged in the study of mining

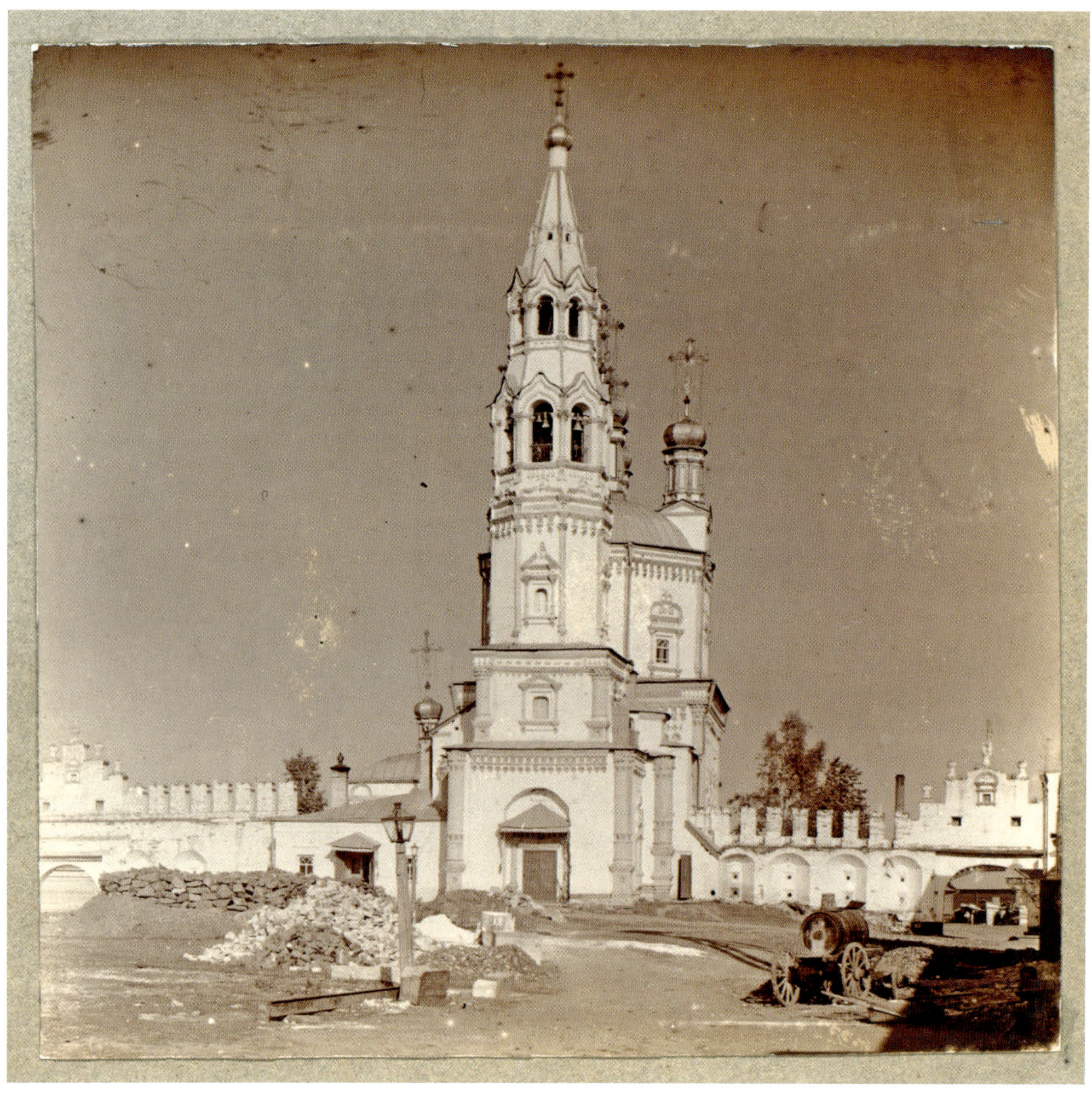

(gold as well as ore), chemical research, natural history, and meteorology. It was also an important railroad junction. According to the *Great Siberian Railway Guide*, the best hotel in town was the "American," with rooms ranging in price from one to four rubles per night.

Prokudin-Gorsky's panoramas show the city's environment to have been relatively clean in comparison with other Ural settlements more heavily engaged in metalworking. Together with fifteen Orthodox churches, Yekaterinburg contained a Jewish prayer house, a mosque, a Lutheran church, a Catholic church, and three Old Believer chapels.

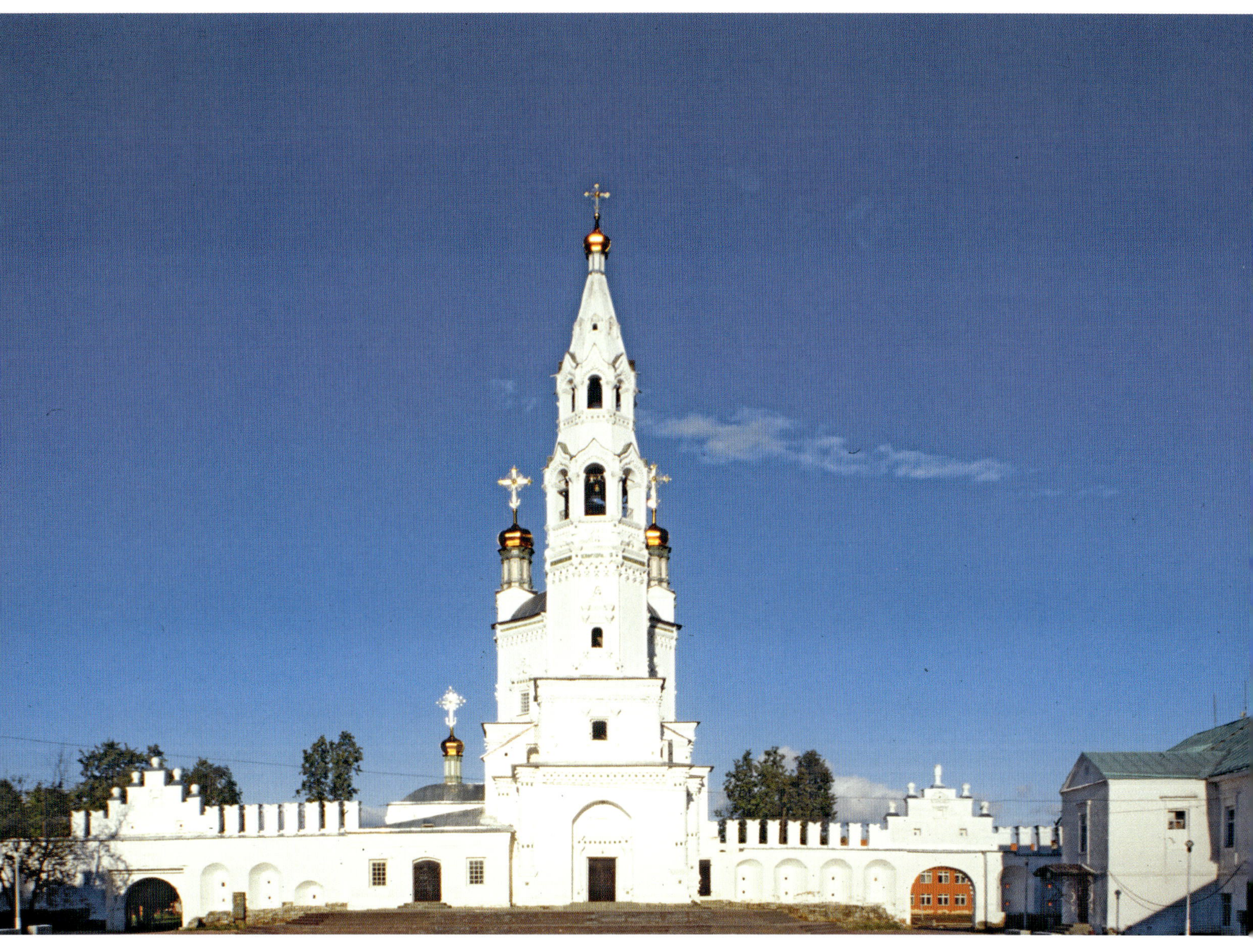

Prokudin-Gorsky took several wide views across City Pond, and while many of the negatives show damage, a contact print contains detailed information. The pond was created in 1724 when the engineer Georg Wilhelm de Gennin (Hennin) dammed the Iset River to create a source of energy for an iron factory established by Peter the Great in 1723. This photograph shows the main embankment at the southern end of City Pond in Yekaterinburg. Of special interest is the view of the Cathedral of Saint Catherine, built in 1758–68 in an early baroque style with a bell tower and spire at the west end. Its demolition in 1930 was a major blow to the city's architectural heritage. To the left is the main town fire tower. On the corner to the left is the Sevastyanov house, built in 1860–66 in a gothic revival style by the

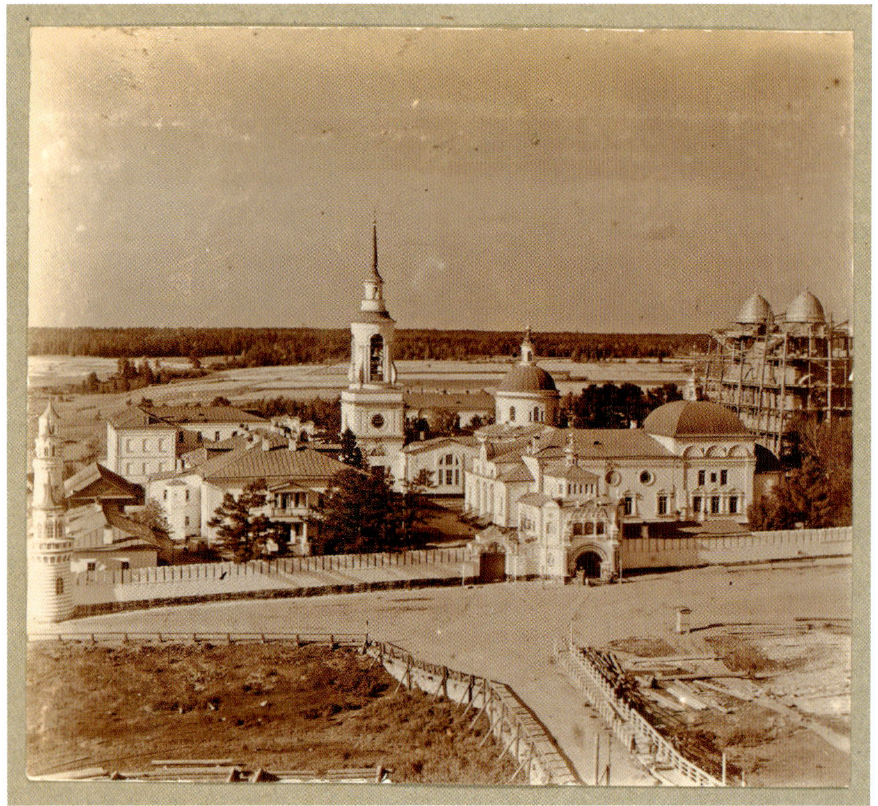

architect A. I. Paduchev. My contemporary view of the same area shows dramatic changes to the city skyline including one of Russia's tallest skyscrapers, named after the poet and bard Vladimir Vysotsky.

Within a few years of Prokudin-Gorsky's visit, Yekaterinburg and the other cities of the Urals would be engulfed by the struggle between the Red and White forces during the civil war. Control of the Urals was vital to both sides, and some of the most severe fighting occurred there in 1918 and 1919. In the summer of 1918, when the town was on the verge of capture by the Whites and their allies from the Czech legion, Bolsheviks executed Nicholas and Alexandra, their son, and four daughters, who had been held in a house belonging to the military engineer N. N. Ipatiev. Remarkably, the house is barely visible in one of Prokudin-Gorsky's best photographs of Ascension Hill and the south embankment of City Pond. The house was razed in September 1977. The site is now occupied by the massive Church of All Russian Saints, begun in 2000 and consecrated in 2003. In 1924 the city was renamed for Yakov Sverdlov, who had done much to consolidate Bolshevik power in the Urals. In 1991 the name "Yekaterinburg" was restored.

In the summer of 1909 Prokudin-Gorsky ascended Ascension Hill in the town center and photographed its eponymous Church of the Ascension,

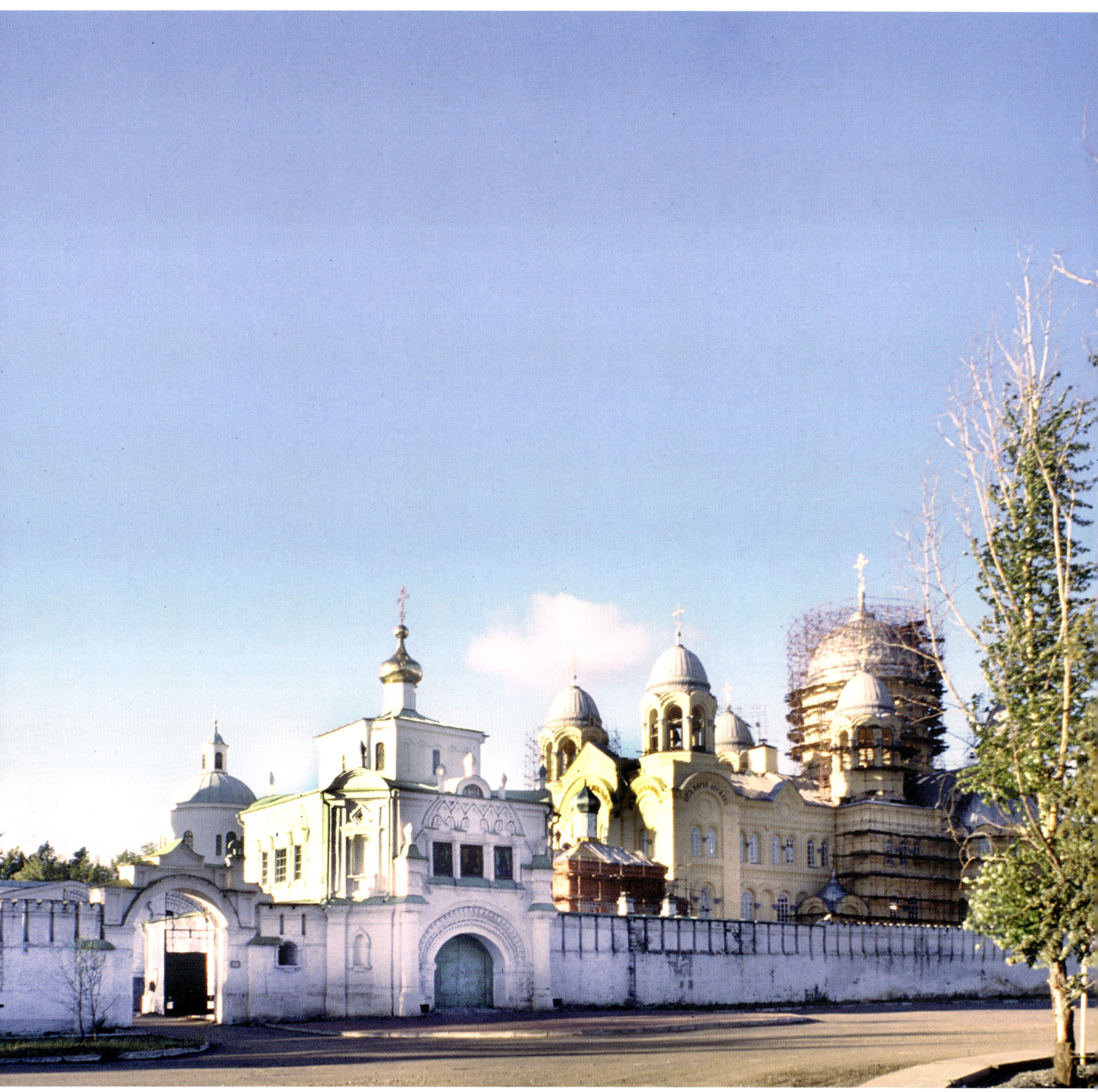

VERKHOTURYE Monastery of Saint Nicholas. View north from Trinity Cathedral bell tower. PROKUDIN-GORSKY 02099. SUMMER 1909.

VERKHOTURYE Monastery of Saint Nicholas, south-west view. *From left*: bell tower, Transfiguration Cathedral (dome), south wall and Gate Church of Saints Simeon and Anna, Cathedral of the Elevation of the Cross. BRUMFIELD, AUGUST 26, 1999.

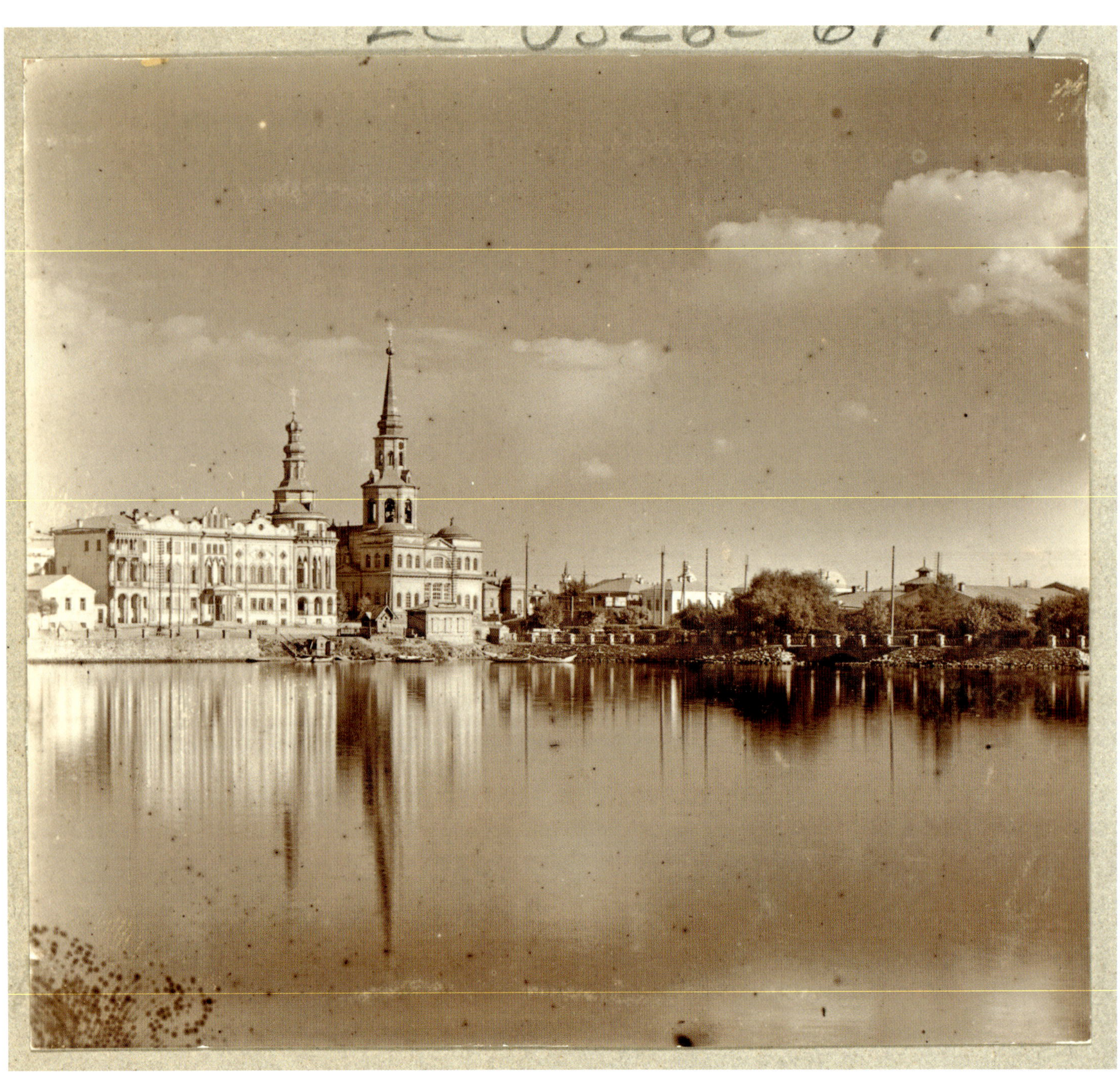

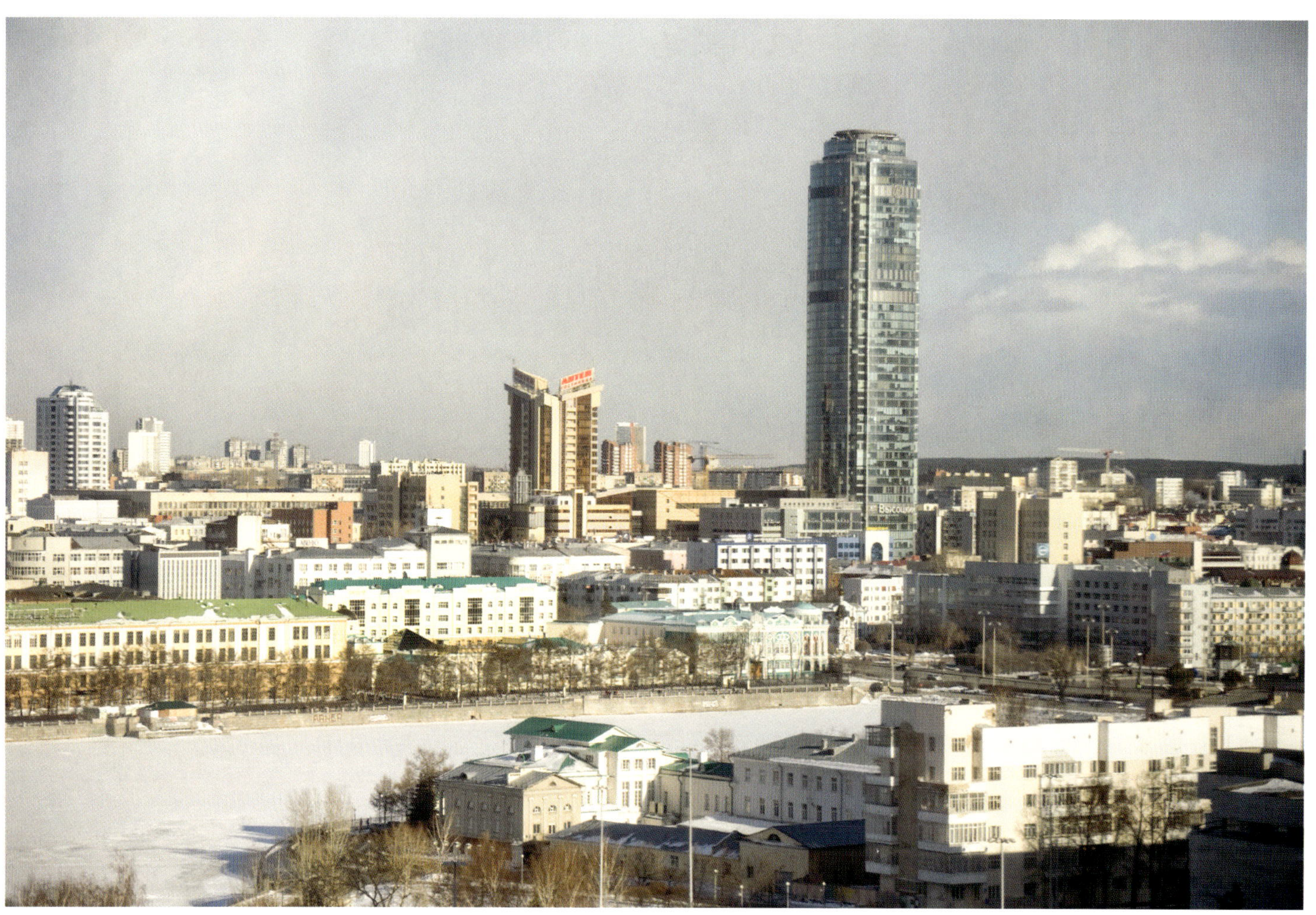

YEKATERINBURG View southeast across City Pond, with Cathedral of Saint Catherine (not extant) and Sevastyanov House (District Court). PROKUDIN-GORSKY 02043. SUMMER 1909.

YEKATERINBURG View southeast across City Pond, with Sevastyanov House and Vysotsky Tower. *Foreground*: House of the Mining Region Director. BRUMFIELD, APRIL 1, 2017.

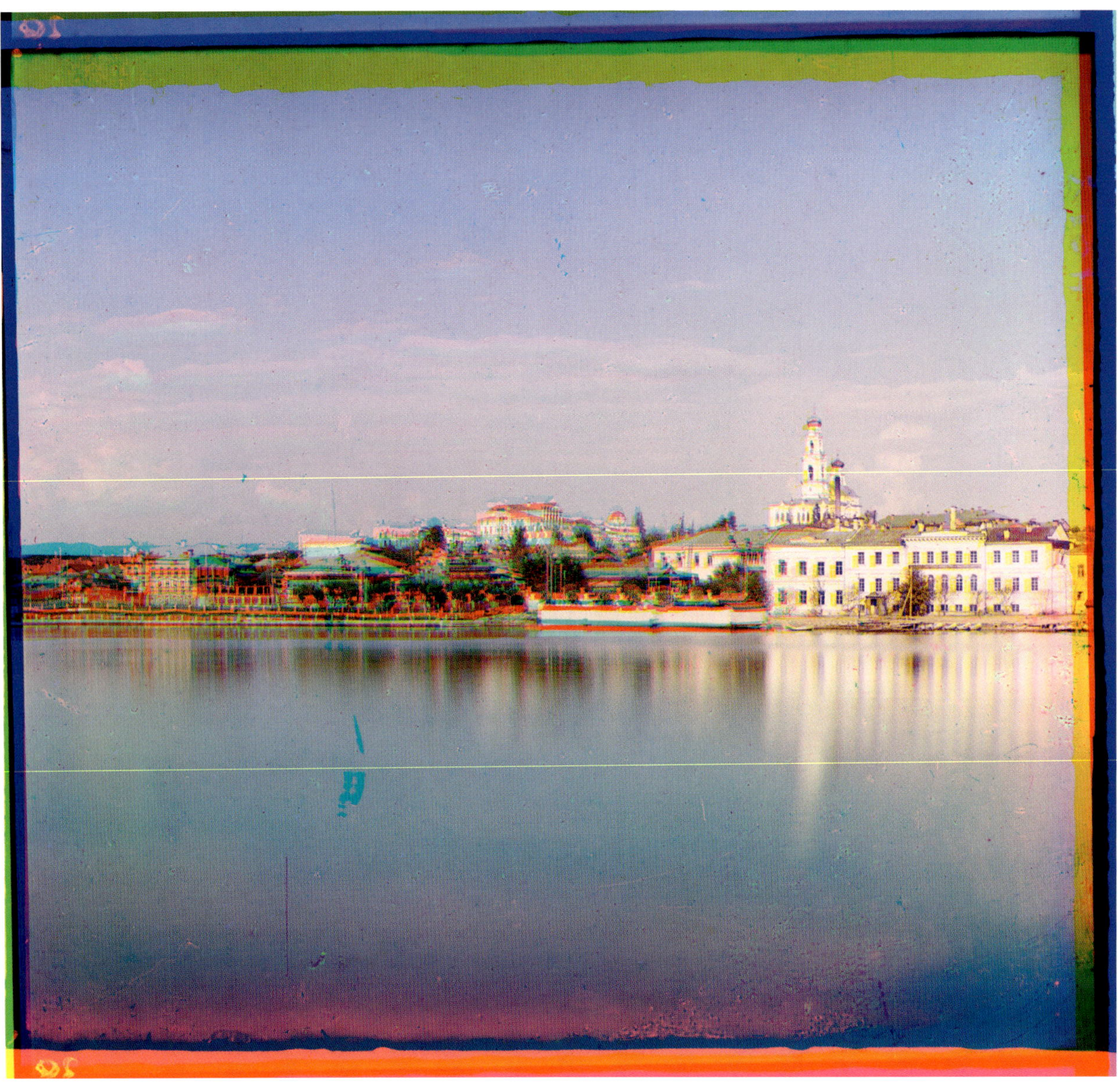

framed by trees in the Kharitonov Garden. My photograph of the Ascension Church from a closer perspective shows it to be a rare survivor of Soviet-era church destruction. Nearby Prokudin-Gorsky photographed the monumental Rastorguev-Kharitonov Mansion on Ascension Hill. The area was developed in the late 1820s by Peter Yakovlevich Kharitonov (1794–1838), who married Maria Rastorgueva in 1816. Both families were prominent owners of metal-working factories in the Urals. Accused of cruelty toward workers at his Kyshtym factory, Kharitonov was exiled to Finland in 1837. The initial design of the mansion, built in

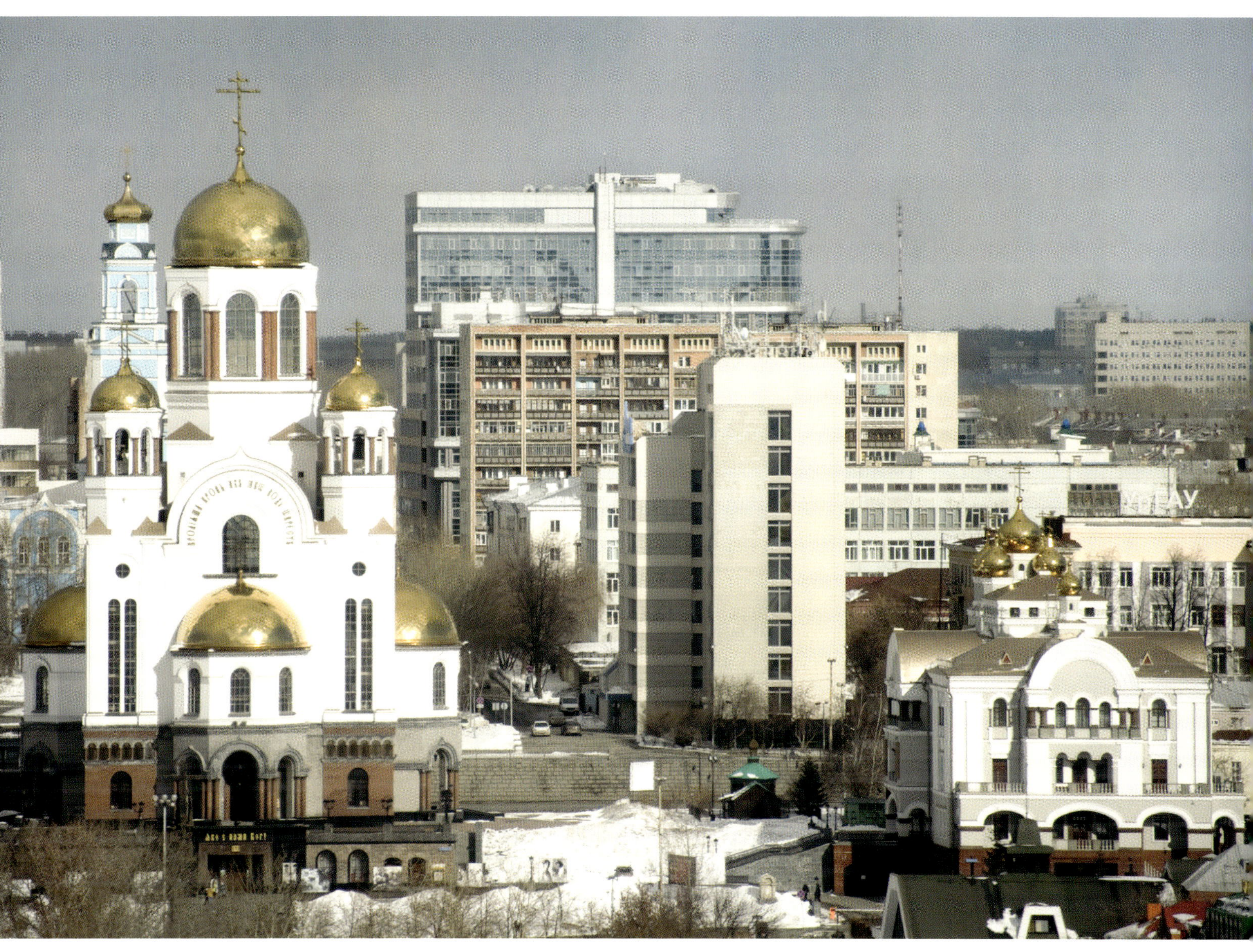

YEKATERINBURG View east across City Pond toward Church of All Saints Resplendent in the Russian Land. *Left background*: bell tower of Church of the Ascension. *Right*: Church of Saint Nicholas at the Patriarchal Legation. BRUMFIELD, APRIL 1, 2017.

stages from 1794 to 1824, has been attributed to the Swiss architect Tommaso Adamini (1764–1828), but additional work on the ensemble was done by Mikhail Malakhov, the leading practitioner of neoclassicism in Yekaterinburg. Its main facade, with a Corinthian portico, overlooks Ascension Square, which extended to the bell tower of the Church of the Ascension. Imposing even in terms of Moscow and Saint Petersburg, this palatial structure was the subject of a number of my photographs.

In Prokudin-Gorsky's Yekaterinburg work, religious architecture is represented primarily by the New Convent of

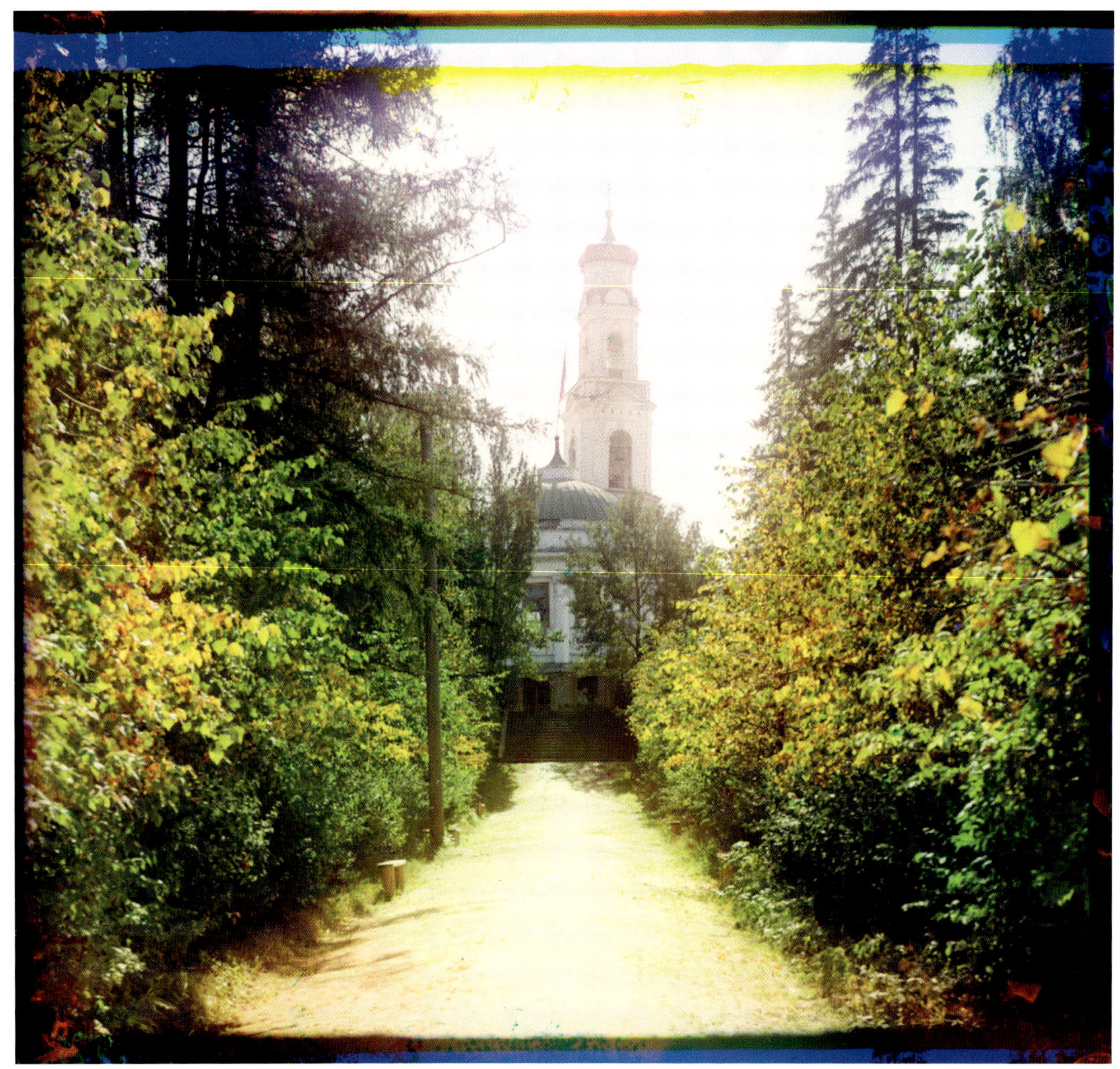

YEKATERINBURG Church of the Ascension bell tower.
View from Kharitonov Garden. PROKUDIN-GORSKY
20473. SUMMER 1909.

YEKATERINBURG Church of the Ascension. Southeast
view. BRUMFIELD, AUGUST 26, 1999.

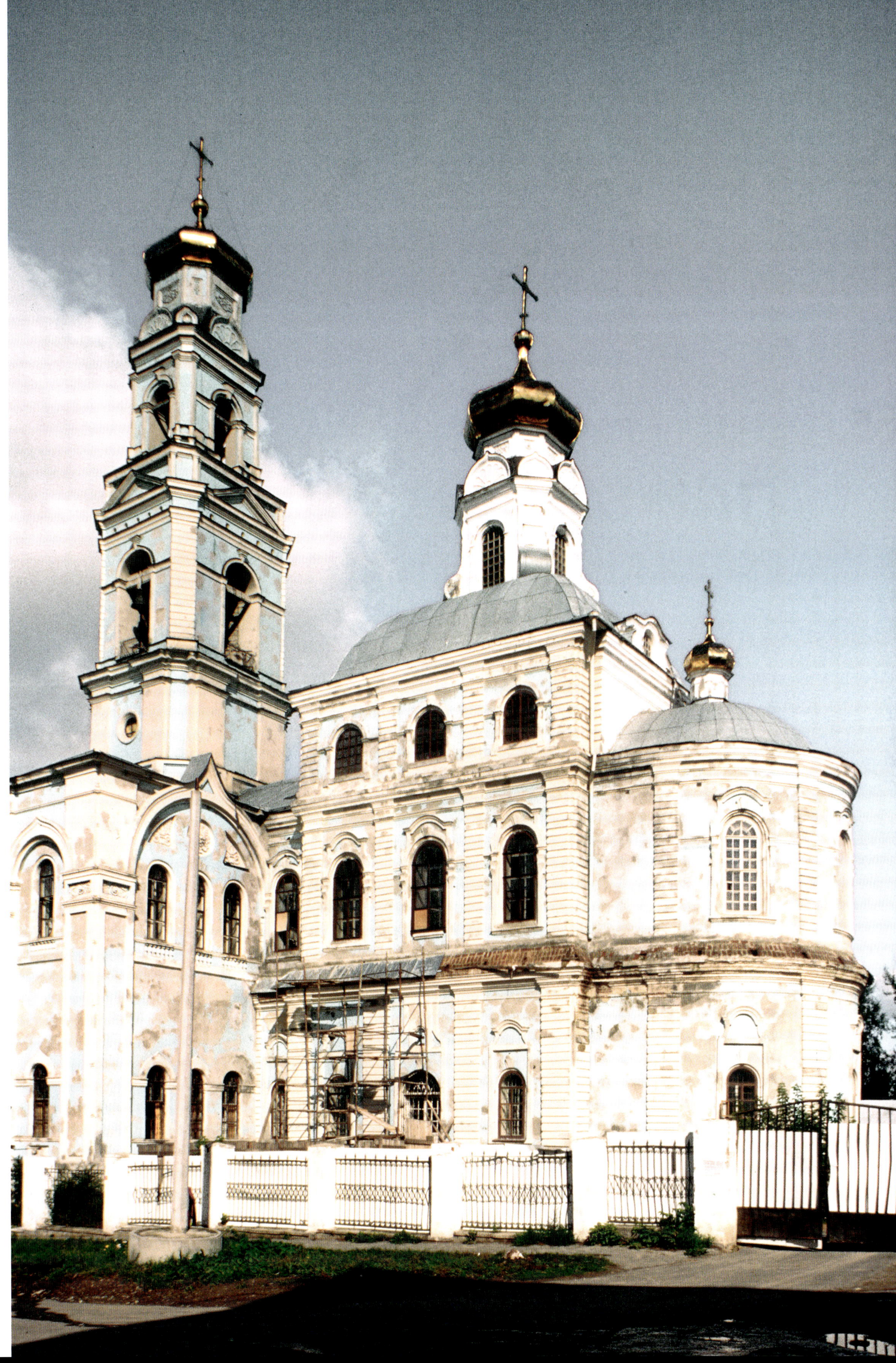

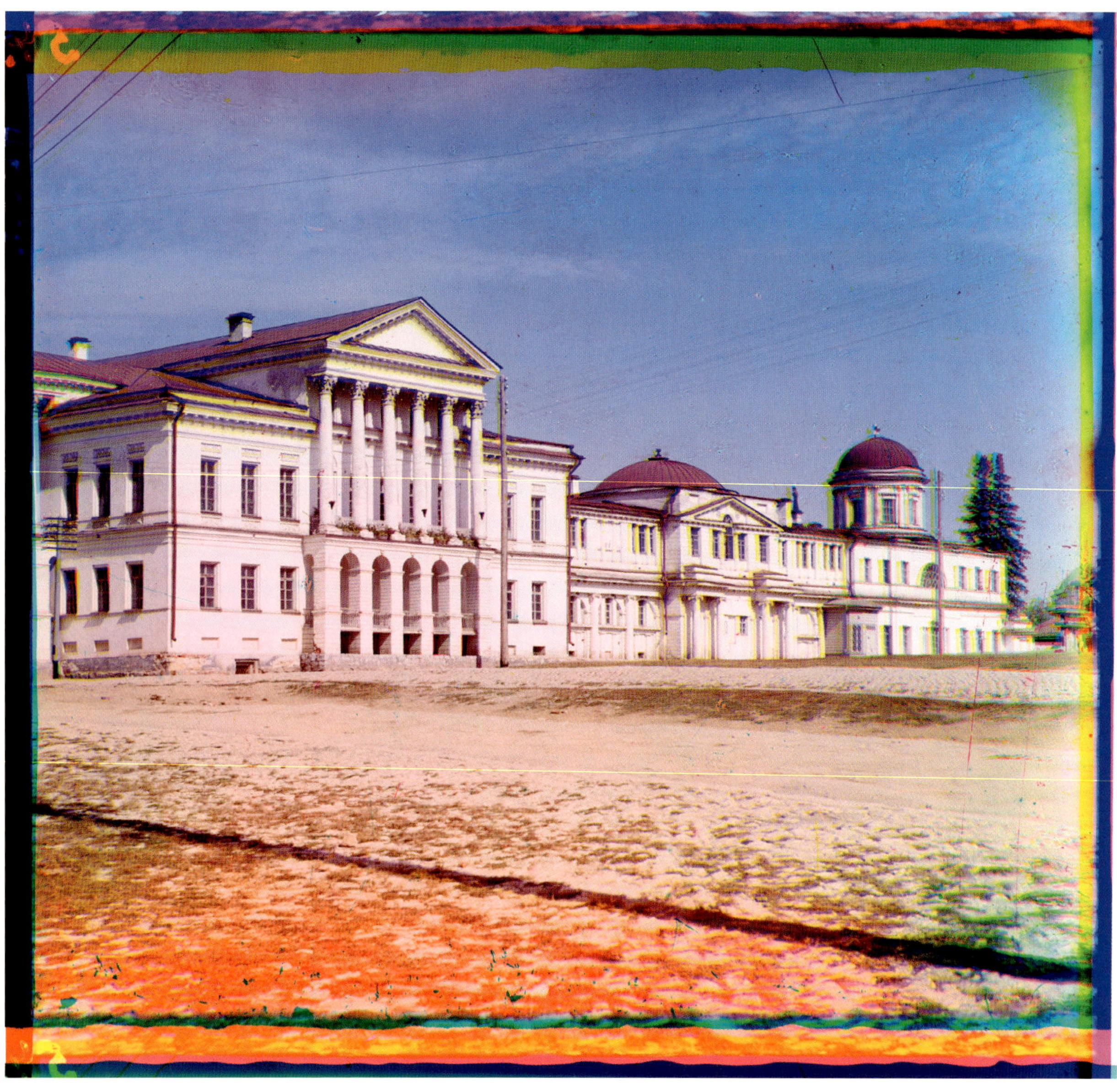

the Tikhvin Icon of the Virgin, which Prokudin-Gorsky photographed from multiple perspectives. Established in 1809, the convent became one of the largest in Russia by the beginning of the twentieth century. Its center was dominated by the capacious Cathedral of Saint Alexander Nevskii, built in 1838–52 to a project design by the Saint Petersburg architects David Visconti and Ludwig Charlemagne II. Construction was supervised by the local architect Mikhail Malakhov, who essentially created neoclassical Yekaterinburg in the first half of the century. Although the original negative is missing, Prokudin-Gorsky's contact

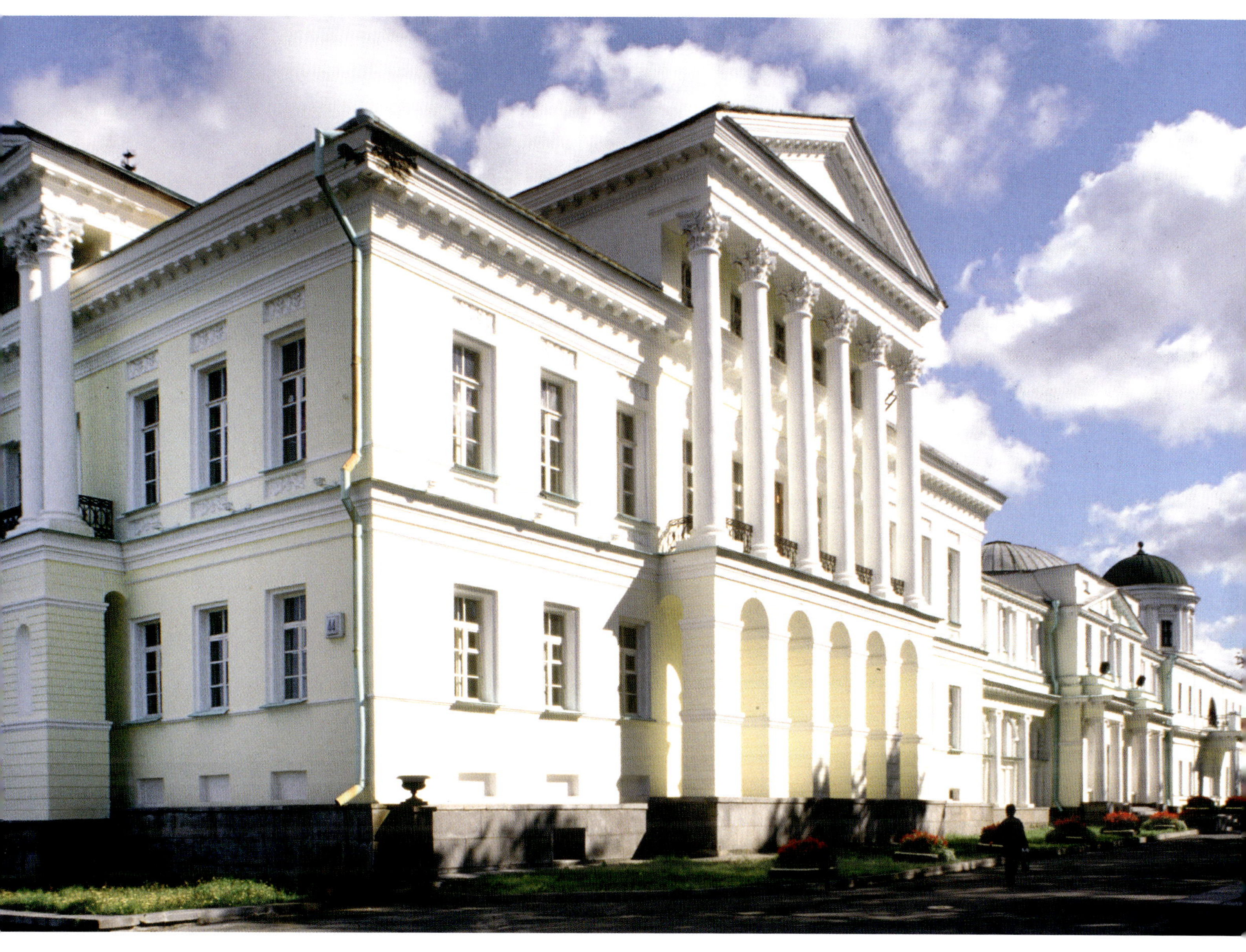

print illuminates the late neoclassical design, with its large rotunda supporting the central dome. Disfigured and used for various purposes during the
Soviet period, the cathedral was returned to the Orthodox Church in 1992
and has now been restored.

In the mountainous region between Perm and Yekaterinburg there existed
settlements whose sole purpose was the mining and working of metal ore.
Near Yekaterinburg were the settlements of Kym, where Prokudin-Gorsky
photographed the ruins of one of the Stroganov factories, and Tagil, which
contained one of the Demidov copper smelters. The Stroganovs were among
the first to exploit the wealth of the Urals, as early as the sixteenth century,
while the Demidovs pioneered the large-scale development of the area's de-

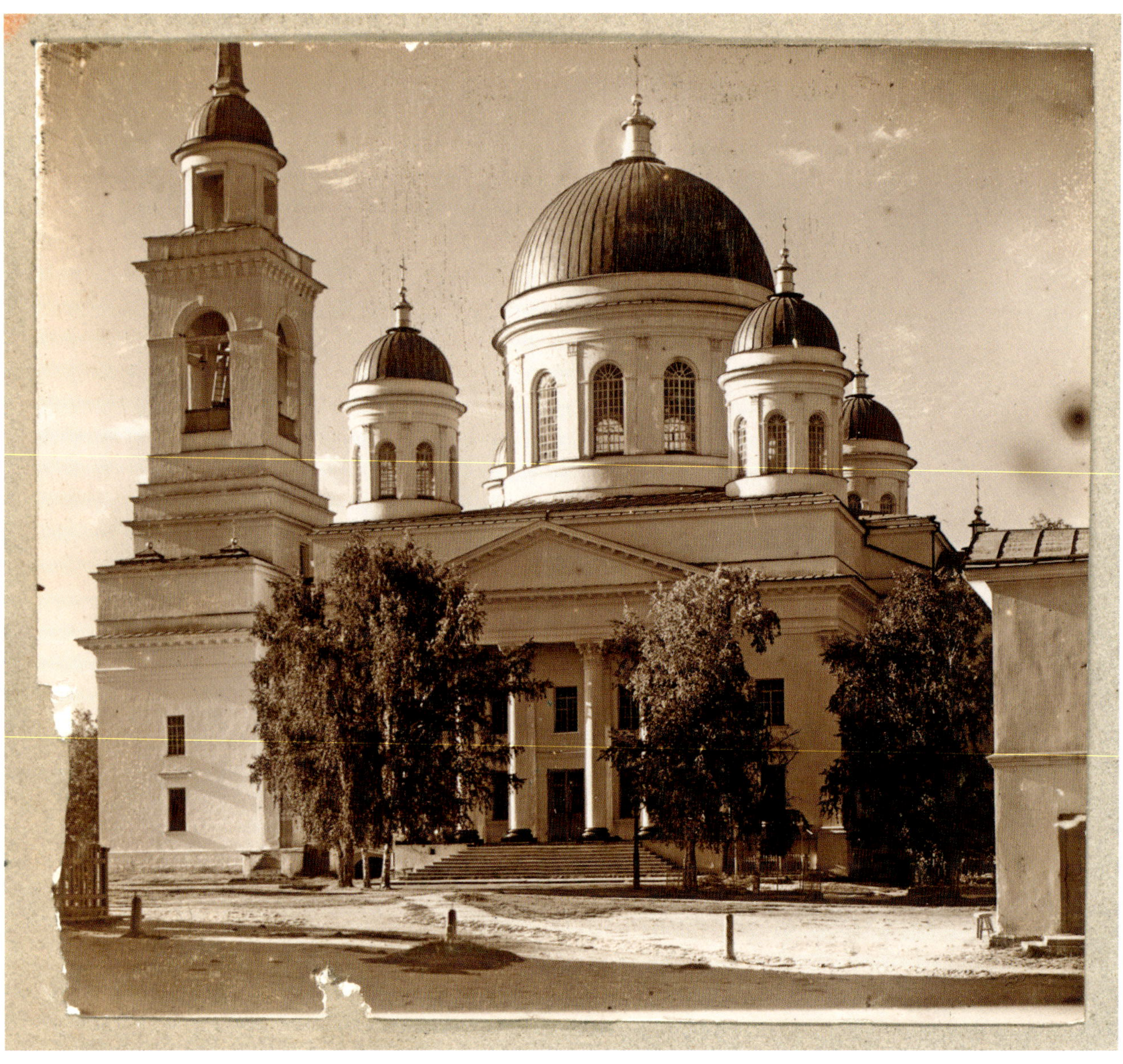

posits of iron and copper ore during the reign of Peter the Great. It was in the region surrounding the Tagil River that the Urals iron industry took its origins in meeting Peter's insatiable need for armaments.

From a historical perspective, the most interesting of these factory settlements is Zlatoust, a town on the Ai River to the east of Ust-Katav with a population of some 34,000 by 1910. The Zlatoust factory was established in 1754 by a merchant from Tula (a metalworking center and armory near Moscow), who bought a large tract of land from the Bashkirs and in typical Russian fashion built not only an iron

YEKATERINBURG New Convent of the Tikhvin Icon of the Virgin. Cathedral of Saint Alexander Nevsky. South view. PROKUDIN-GORSKY 02048. SUMMER 1909.

YEKATERINBURG New Convent of the Tikhvin Icon of the Virgin. Cathedral of Saint Alexander Nevsky. South view. BRUMFIELD, APRIL 1, 2017.

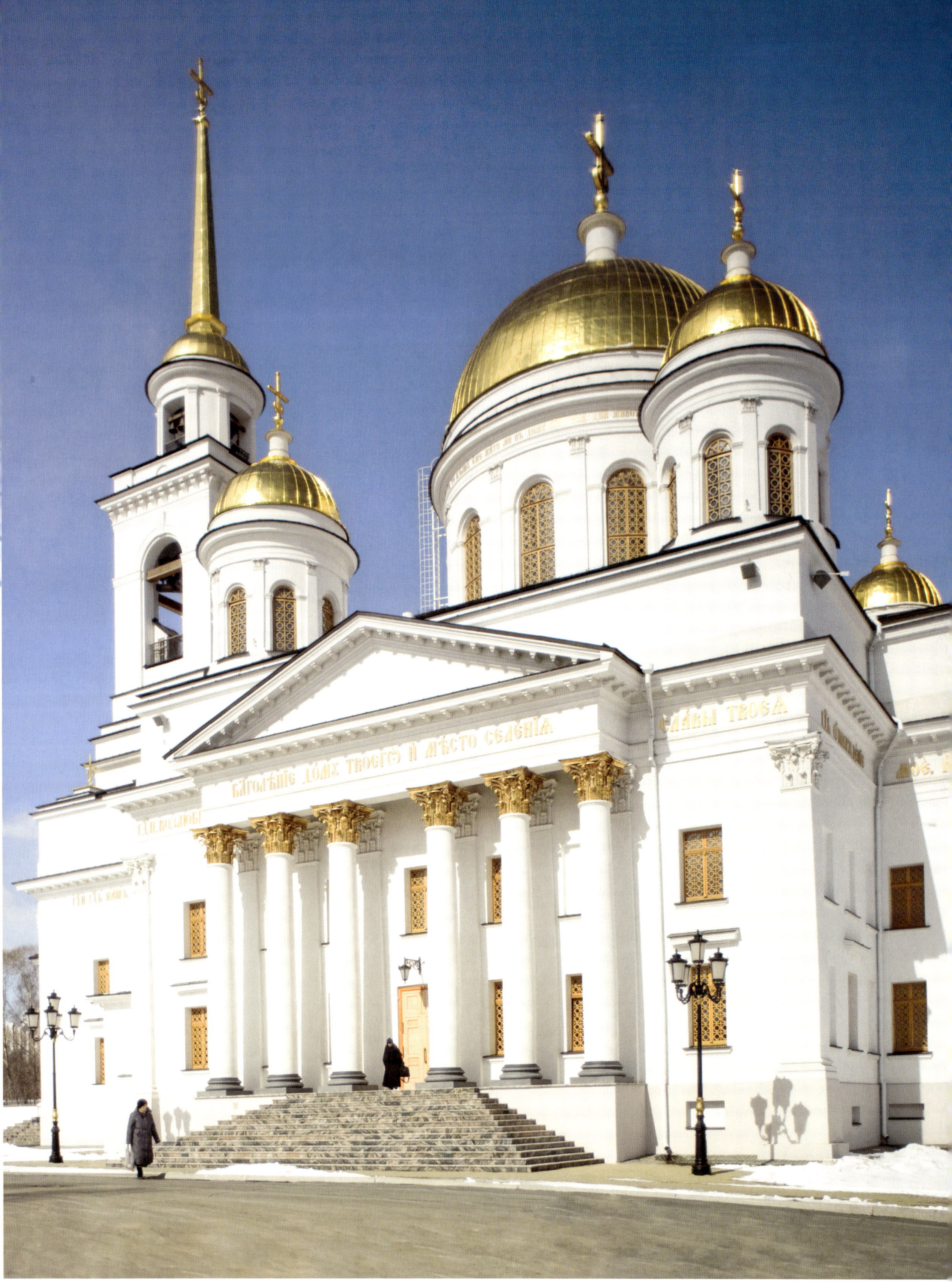

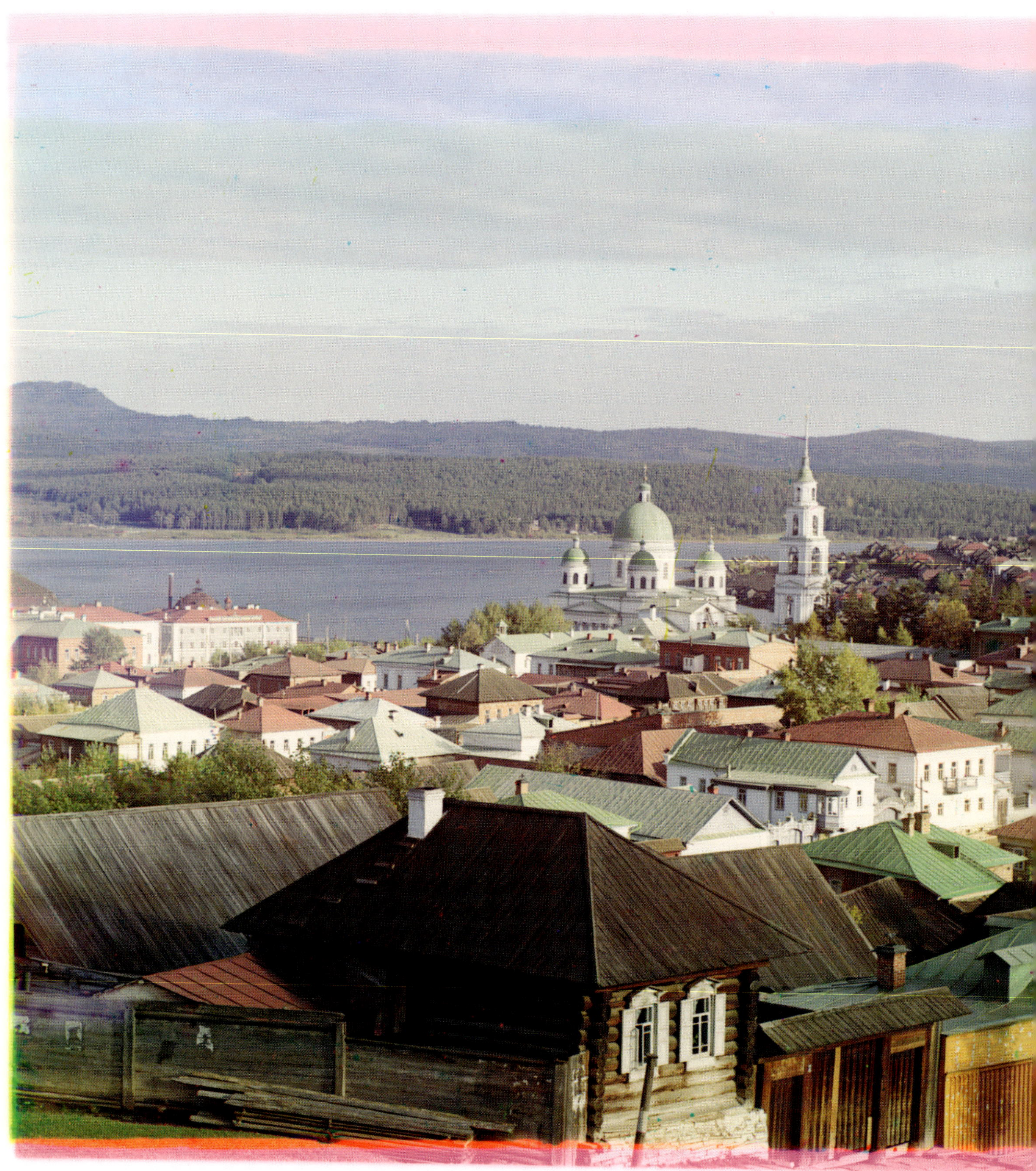

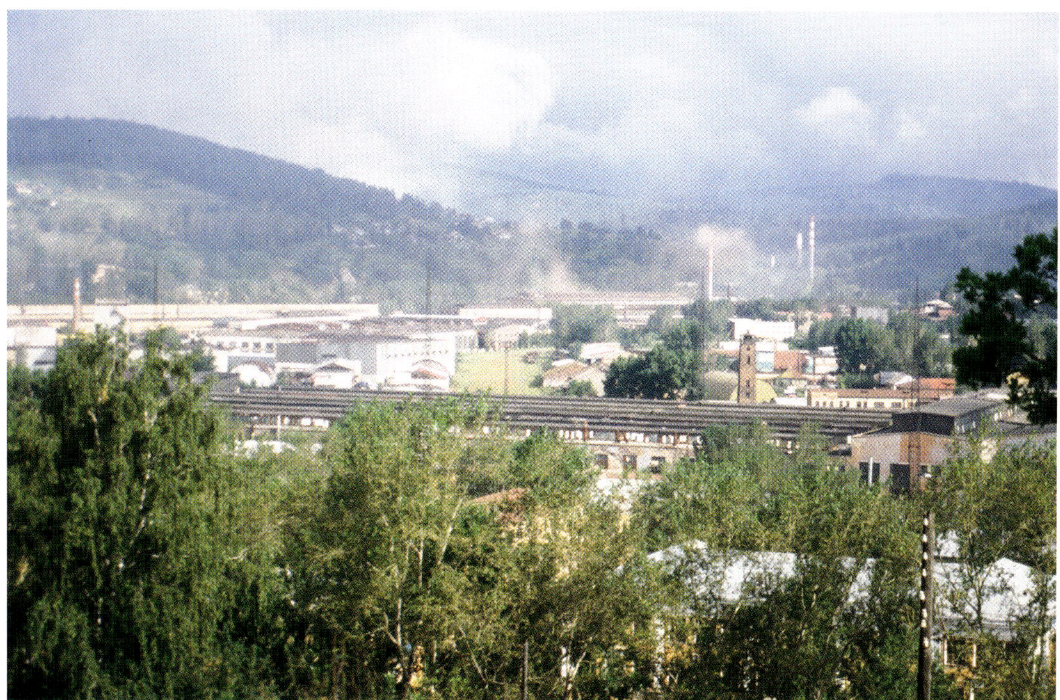

works but also a church, dedicated to three Byzantine theologians: Basil the Great, Gregory the Theologian, and John Chrysostom (the Golden Mouth, or, in Russian, Zlatoust). Two decades later the factory was sacked and burned by Yemelyan Pugachev, a renegade Don Cossack who in the fall of 1773 raised a revolt among Cossacks in the Urals. Their cause gained support from discontent among Urals factory workers, many of whom were serfs, as well as among ethnic groups such as the Bashkirs who were increasingly exploited by Russian colonization. Pugachev's charismatic leadership, compounded by surprise and disorganization among local authorities, spread the revolt over a large area that reached to the agricultural lands of the Volga and posed a threat to Moscow before the army succeeded in crushing the rebels at the end of 1774. Although Catherine the Great and her government had restored order, the memory of Pugachev achieved a legendary status that survived into the twentieth century, particularly in the Urals.

The Zlatoust factory was reestablished, and in 1811 the state acquired it as a center for the production of cold steel weapons. Its workshops were renowned for their swords

(Alexander I visited the factory in 1824, as did the future Alexander II in 1837). Prokudin-Gorsky took dramatic panoramas from the two hills, Koso-tur and Urenga, that flank the town on the shores of the millpond formed by damming the Ai River. One view shows the Cathedral of Three Saints (de-molished during the Soviet period) on the background of the factory pond. The arsenal buildings—between the church and the factory—exemplify the functional neoclassical government architecture that spread from Peters-burg throughout the empire. My panorama from Urenga Hill shows a smoke-filled valley of factories—and no churches.

Just beyond Zlatoust is the boundary between Europe and Asia (marked by a small pyramid of white stone) on the way to Chelyabinsk, which was a major transit point on the Trans-Siberian for the large numbers of peasants encouraged by the government to resettle on the fertile west Siberian plains at the beginning of this century. A connecting rail line from Chelyabinsk leads due north to Yekaterinburg, from which Prokudin-Gorsky began the eastern phase of his Urals expedition. Among the factory towns that he photographed in the area is Kyshtym, where Peter Kharitonov had a factory. Prokudin-Gorsky's view includes the Church of the Descent of the Holy Spirit, which I photographed across the main factory pond in 2003.

Approximately midway between Chelyabinsk and Yekaterinburg lay an-other remote factory town, Kasli, founded in 1747 on the shores of Lake Irtyash, which feeds the Techa, a tributary of the Iset. Prokudin-Gorsky's stunningly clear panorama, taken from the bell tower of the Dormition Church (shadow visible) shows solid houses with spacious garden plots. The view centers on the west facades of two churches: the Church of Saint Nicholas (1858–61) and, just to the south, the Church of the Ascension (1848–52), which towers over the settlement. My photograph offers a closer view of this fine example of the Russo-Byzantine style. All five of the Kasli churches were closed in 1930. Fortunately, the Ascension Church suffered no structural damage and was reopened in 1944 as part of the wartime rap-prochement between the Soviet regime and the Church. (The Orthodox Church was supportive of the war effort, and it was noted that a functioning church led to an increase in worker productivity.)

The Kasli panorama is one of Prokudin-Gorsky's richest. Taken in later afternoon light with deep shadows, it has endless detail. For example, the wooden house on a whitewashed brick foundation in the foreground is a fortress, with its four-sloped red metal roof and yard enclosed with sheds for every need, including the animals that sustained the household. The bright green of vegetable plots shows the careful tending of cabbage and pota-

KYSHTYM Factory view. *From left*: Church of the Descent of the Holy Spirit, factory Church of the Trinity (severely damaged in the Soviet period). PROKUDIN-GORSKY 02163. FALL 1909.

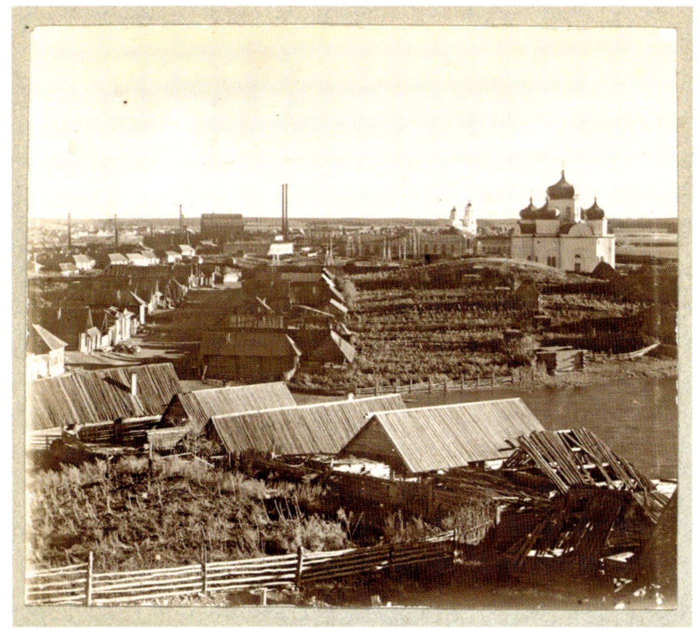

KYSHTYM Church of the Descent of the Holy Spirit. Southeast view across factory pond. BRUMFIELD, JULY 14, 2003.

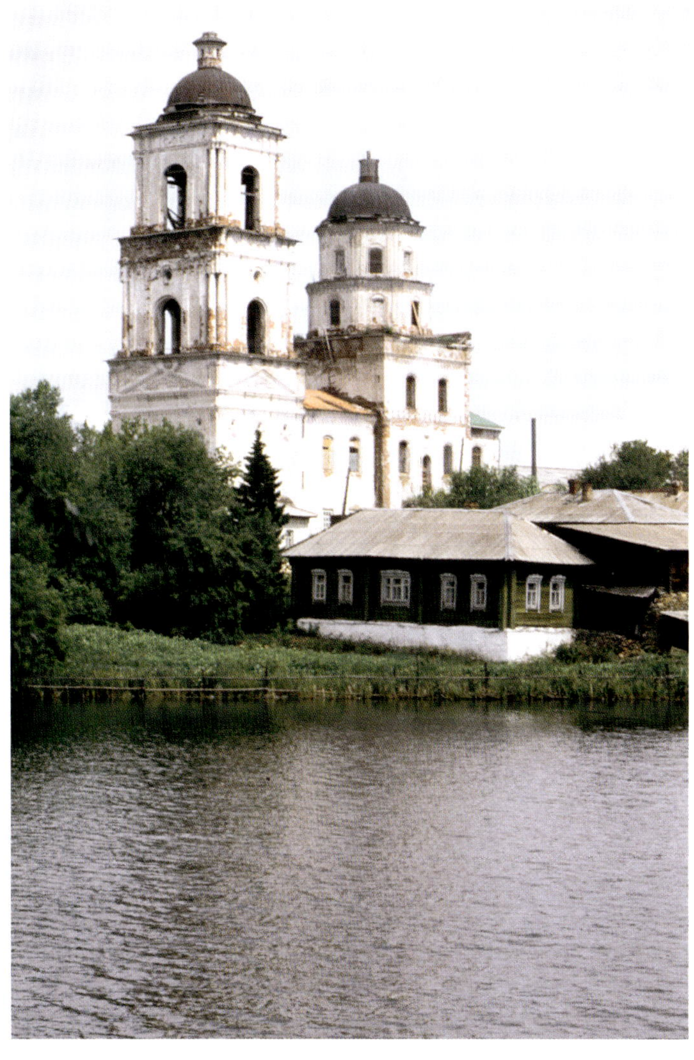

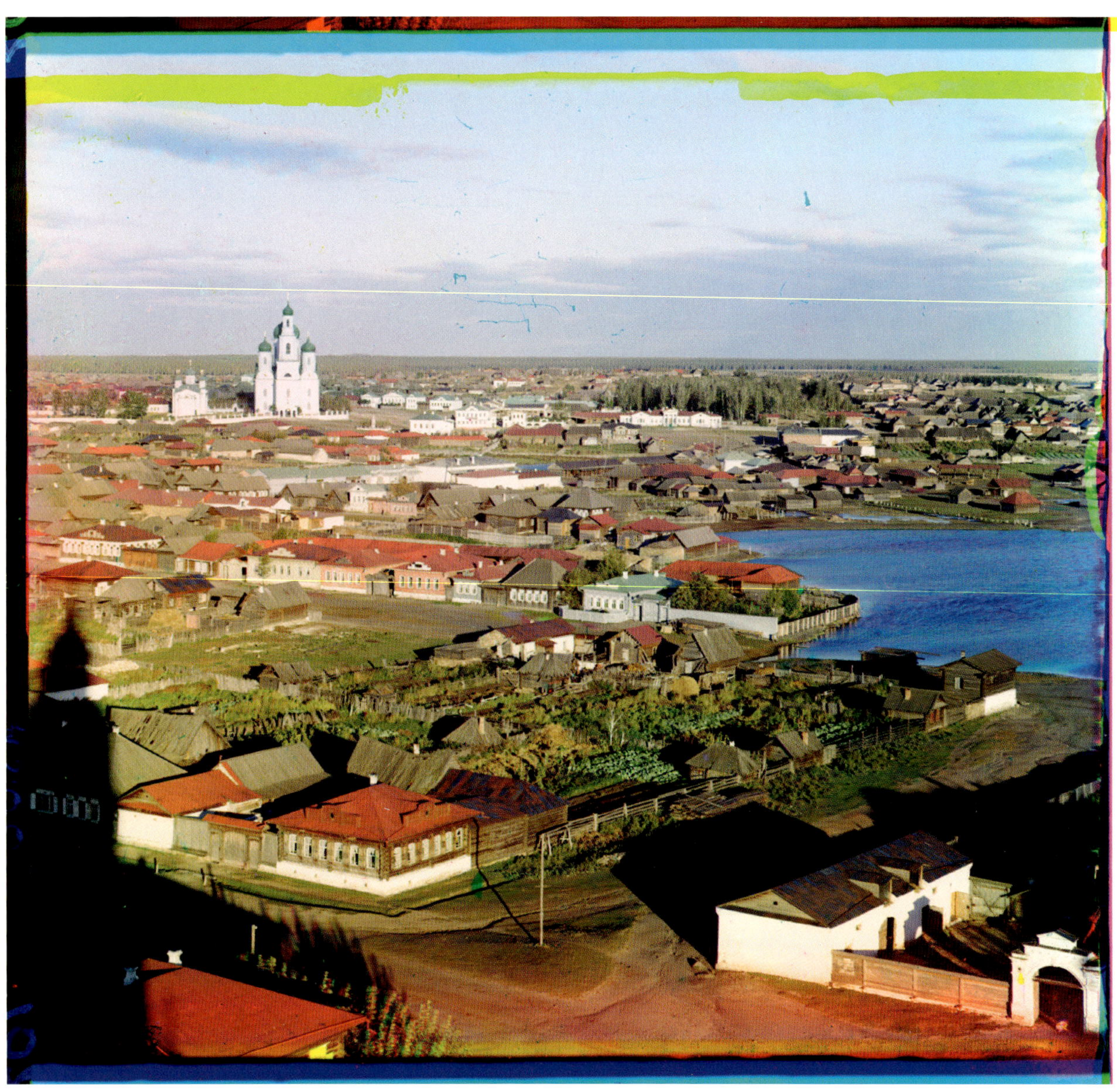

KASLI View east from bell tower of Church of the
Dormition toward Church of the Ascension. PROKUDIN-
GORSKY 20500. SUMMER 1909.

KASLI Church of the Ascension. Southwest view.
BRUMFIELD, JULY 14, 2003.

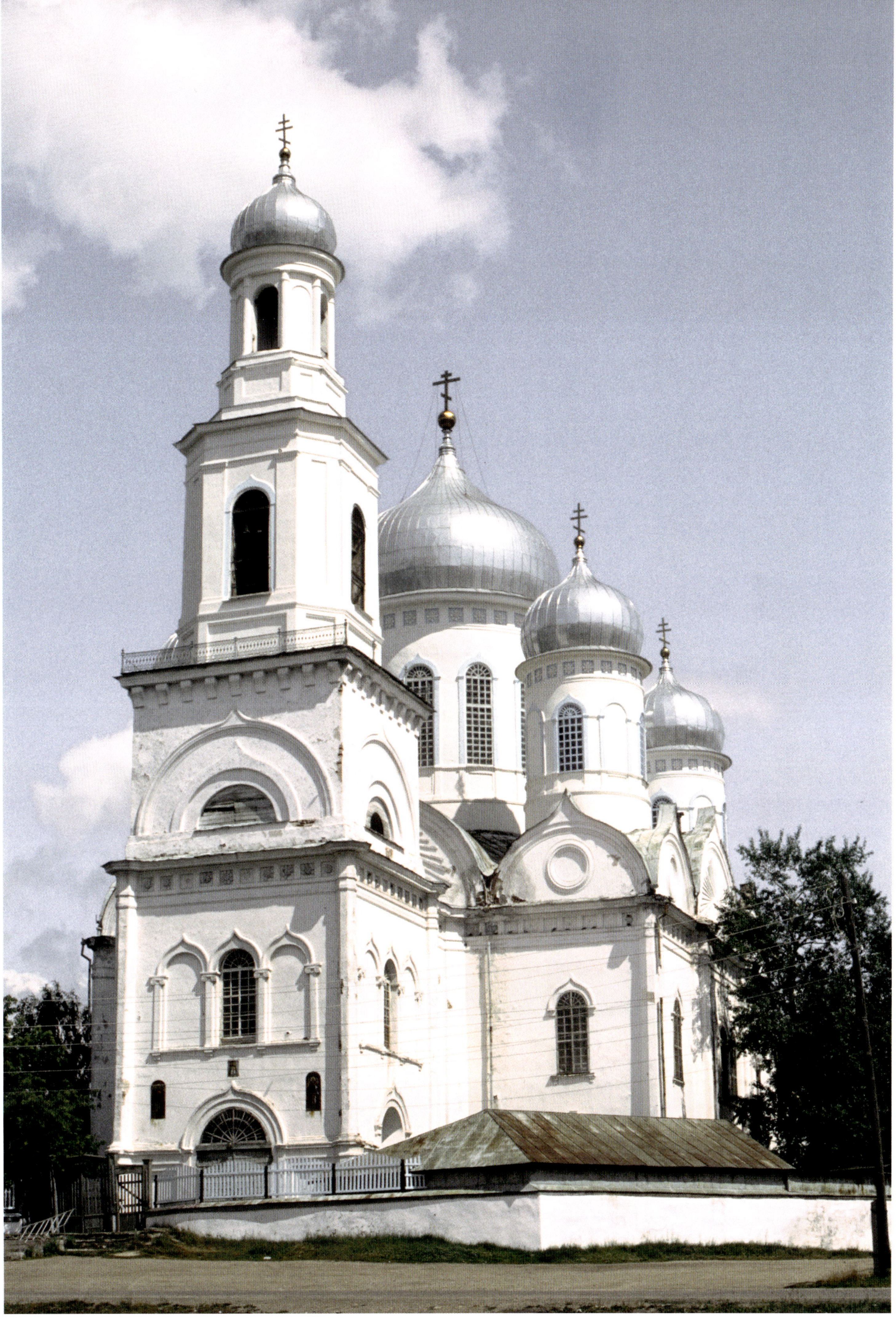

toes, essential staples. In the distance, many other houses, some painted in a variety of colors, follow a similar courtyard layout. The photograph offers a microcosm of life in such factory settlements, surrounded with fields, forests, and boundless space.

By the time of Prokudin-Gorsky's trip the railway from Yekaterinburg continued to Omsk, where it linked with the Trans-Siberian. Of the main cities along the northern route from Perm to Omsk, Tyumen was among the oldest, founded in 1581 by emissaries from Ivan the Terrible. Its location on the banks of the Tura River is supposed to have been the site of the Tatar settlement Chingi-Tura at the confluence of the Tura and Tyumenka Rivers. The area had been conquered a few years earlier by the Cossack leader Yermak, the beginning step of an epochal Russian move across the Ural Mountains into the enormous north Asian land mass. Although its rivers were only tributaries of the Irtysh (itself a tributary of the great Ob River), Tyumen was well situated to utilize Siberia's vast water network.

Like most early Russian towns in Siberia, Tyumen originally served as a fortified settlement for Cossacks and other troops, who in the seventeenth century protected developing trade routes, particularly with China. When the southern boundary of Moscow's Asian territory became more settled during the eighteenth century, Tyumen's importance increased for transportation as well as small commercial and industrial enterprises. Before the construction of the Trans-Siberian Railway, Tyumen was an important transit point on the main Siberian road for those exiled to penal colonies and mines. In its entry on Tyumen, the 1914 Baedeker guide notes that between 1823 and 1898 "a melancholy procession of 908,266 persons" passed through the town. George Kennan's *Siberia and the Exile System*, frequently republished at the end of the nineteenth century, remains the best account of that ordeal.

As a regional administrative point for Western Siberia, Tyumen also became a center of the Russian Orthodox Church. Its Trinity Monastery, founded in 1616 on the high right bank of the Tura River and originally dedicated to the Transfiguration, was a modest collection of log buildings until its transformation in the early part of the eighteenth century by an energetic Ukrainian prelate, Bishop Fedor Leshchinskii. An ally of Peter the Great, Bishop Fedor saw architecture as a reflection of a broad cultural transformation, and the Trinity Cathedral that he built at the monastery in 1709–15 is Tyumen's earliest surviving building. Prokudin-Gorsky's photographs of the monastery in 1912 show an ensemble that had changed little since the eighteenth century. My photographs almost nine decades later suggest a similar stability—but only from the exterior. In the mid-eighteenth century Trinity Cathedral was joined by the Church of Saints Peter and Paul (1741–55), built to honor the memory of Peter the Great. Gutted during the Soviet era, both churches are now being restored. These early examples of a provincial baroque style with Ukrainian features served as a model for other eighteenth-century churches in Tyumen, culminating with the ornate Cathedral of the Icon of the Sign.

Prokudin-Gorsky's photographs of Tyumen emphasize its relation to the Tura River, a tributary of the Tobol. One of his river views includes the Church of Saint George (also dedicated to the Ascension). My closer view from 1999 shows this fine baroque structure disfigured during the Soviet period. Even after the coming of the railway, much of Tyumen's commerce continued to derive from the Tura and its access to the Tobol and the Irtysh—even though the Tura was fully navigable only in the spring. The daunting vastness of Siberia's reaches gradually submitted in the nineteenth century to new forms of transportation. The first steamboat to ply a Siberian river was constructed here in 1838. The greatest impetus for economic growth came with the completion of a railroad from Yekaterinburg, on the east slope of the Ural Mountains. This line ultimately became an important segment of the Trans-Siberian Railroad, transporting the wealth of Siberia's forests, mines, and new grain farms, as well as leather and other products of local factories. Furthermore, at the turn of the twentieth century over half a million settlers passed through Tyumen en route to Siberia's open agricultural lands.

Water level permitting, one could take a steamer 412 versts (440 kilometers) from Tyumen down the Tura and Irtysh Rivers to Tobolsk, the last city on Prokudin-Gorsky's eastward itinerary. Tobolsk is now served by a rail line from Tyumen, but in 1910—and for long thereafter—it thrived as one of the main Siberian river ports, situated at the confluence of the Tobol River with the wide Irtysh. Tobolsk was founded in 1587, and because of its strategic location had its own kremlin, or fortress. It had one of the oldest monasteries in Russia and administered a vast area in north central Siberia. Yet even by Siberian standards getting to Tobolsk required much time and patience (the most reliable steamer route, along the Irtysh from Omsk, took four to five days), and with the shift of the main transportation routes to

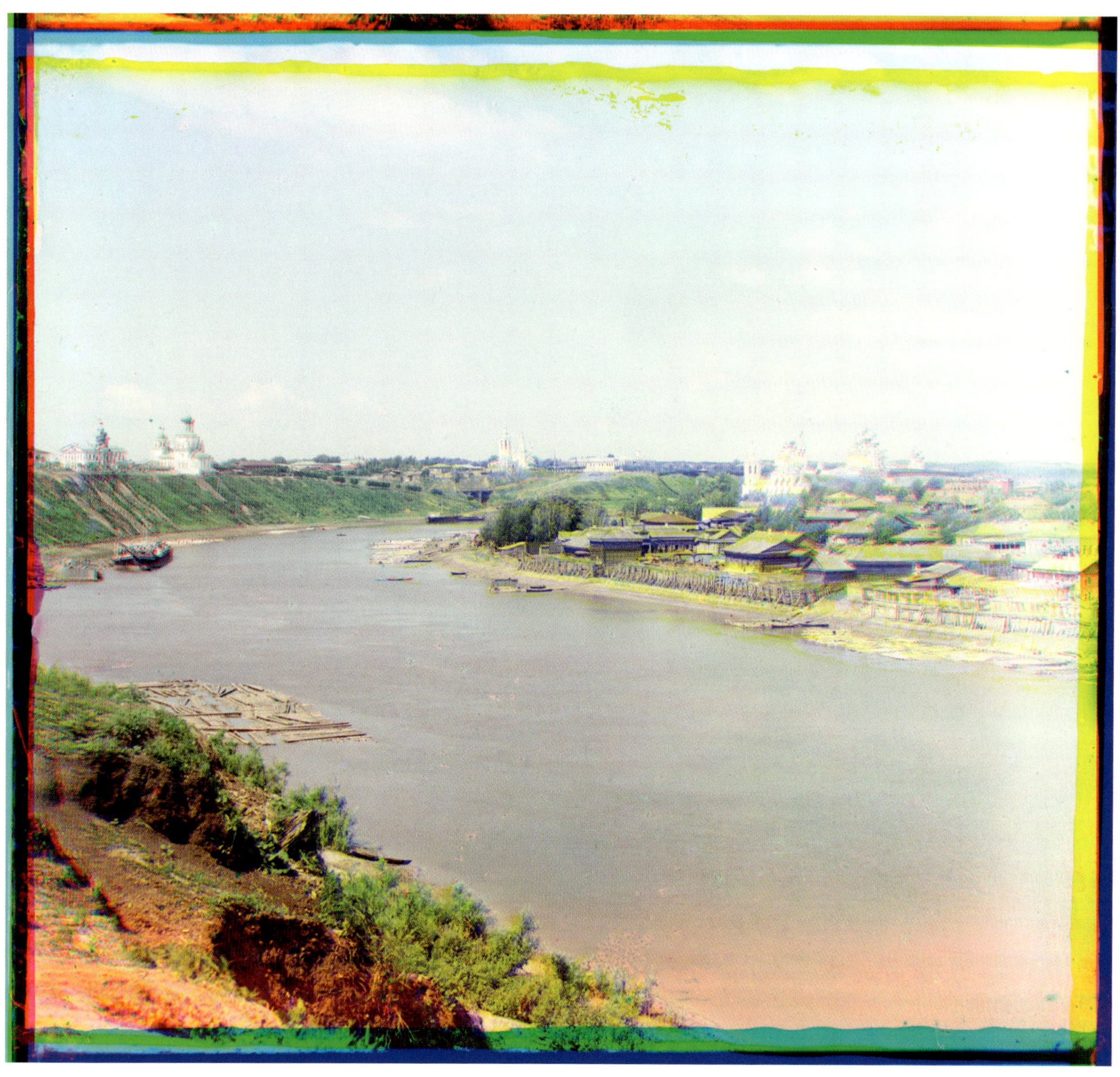

the south, Tobolsk remained a small town (population approximately twenty thousand in 1910). The built environment exists precariously on the edge of the shimmering expanse of the Siberian rivers.

Although Tyumen is now the capital of the vast territory that bears its name, this region was for much of its history ruled from Tobolsk, whose citadel overlooked the high right bank of the Irtysh River. Of the many rivers that run through Siberia, none has more historical and emotional resonance than the Irtysh, a tributary of the mighty Ob River and a critical artery for Russian movement into

TYUMEN View northwest up right bank of Tura River, with Trinity Monastery (*right*). PROKUDIN-GORSKY 20846. 1912.

TYUMEN Trinity Monastery. East view across Tura River. BRUMFIELD, SEPTEMBER 4, 1999.

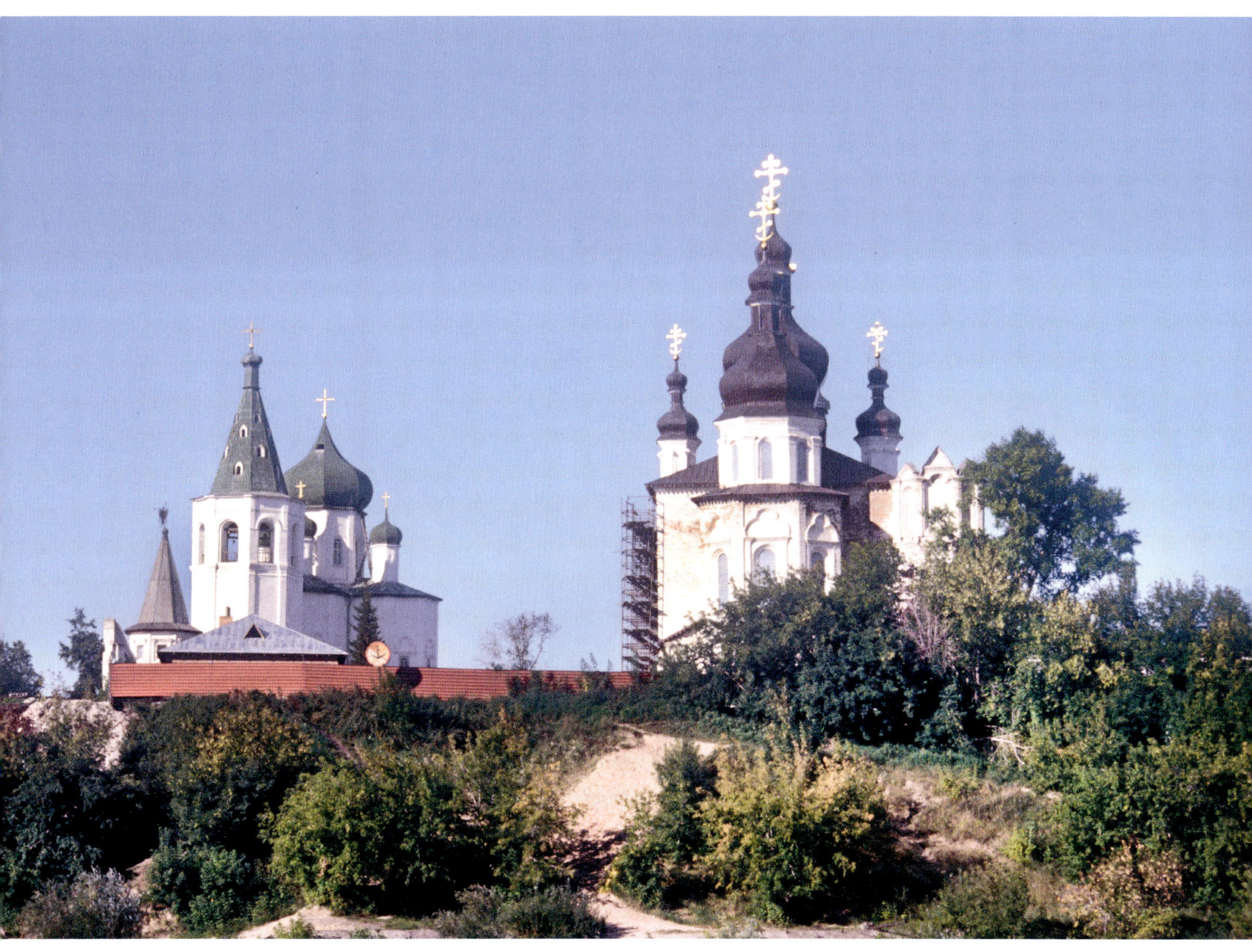

Siberia. It was near the Irtysh that a band of Cossacks, led by the legendary Yermak and supported by the Stroganovs from their citadel in Solvychegodsk, defeated the Tatar forces of Kuchum Khan in 1582. Although the precise dates are questioned by historians, Yermak captured Chingi-Tura (later Tyumen) in the fall of 1581 but abandoned his conquest in order to proceed straight to Kashlyk, capital of Kuchum Khan, where there occurred the epochal battle memorialized in a painting by Ivan Surikov. Yermak was killed in a surprise raid in 1584, and his conquests remained temporarily unconsolidated; but Tsar Boris Godunov was aware of the significance of Siberia and launched an aggressive campaign to establish settlements.

Tobolsk was founded in 1587 by the Cossack leader Daniel Chulkov at the

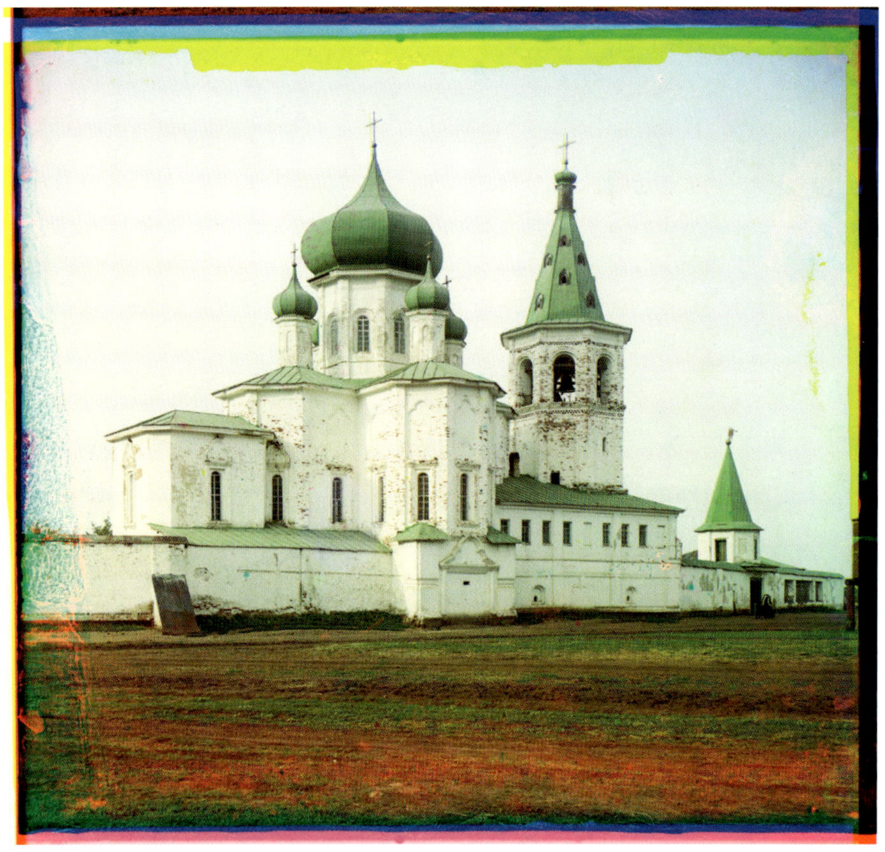

confluence of the Tobol and Irtysh Rivers, near the site of Ermak's victory. The town (current population around 100,000) is sharply divided by the landscape into two sections, upper and lower. The lower part, being closer to the Irtysh River, was the most intensively developed in the eighteenth and nineteenth centuries. Here lived the merchants—some of them in grand mansions—as well as the tradesmen and craftsmen. The lower town was marked by churches that defined various sections of the town. Most of the churches were Russian Orthodox, many built in a florid "Siberian baroque" style. But Tobolsk also had a Tartar district, with a mosque in the lower town near the river, as seen in Prokudin-Gorsky's detailed view. My 1999 view from a similar perspective shows the same landmarks, including the mosque, which has been renovated in good condition. There was also a significant Polish diaspora, originally sent to the region in exile. Their presence led to the building of the magnificent late nineteenth-century Catholic Church of the Holy Trinity, visible just below the kremlin in Prokudin-Gorsky's sweeping perspective. My 1999 photograph shows the results of a recent restoration. The upper part of the town was reserved primarily for institutions of power, the territorial administration, and the treasury, as

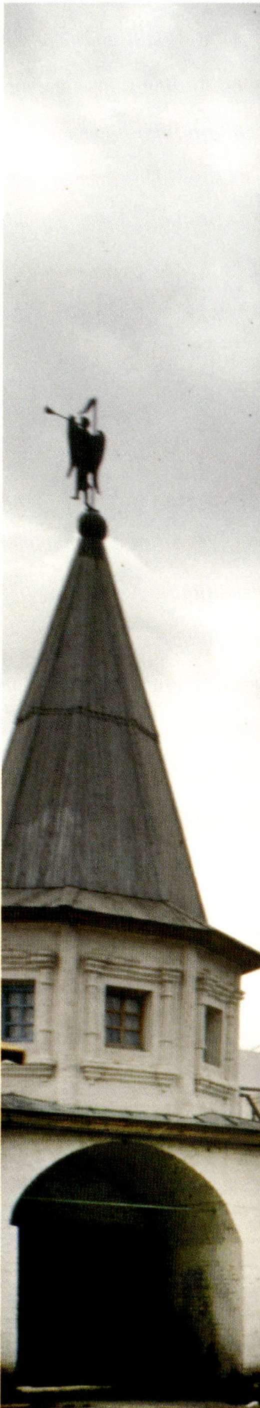

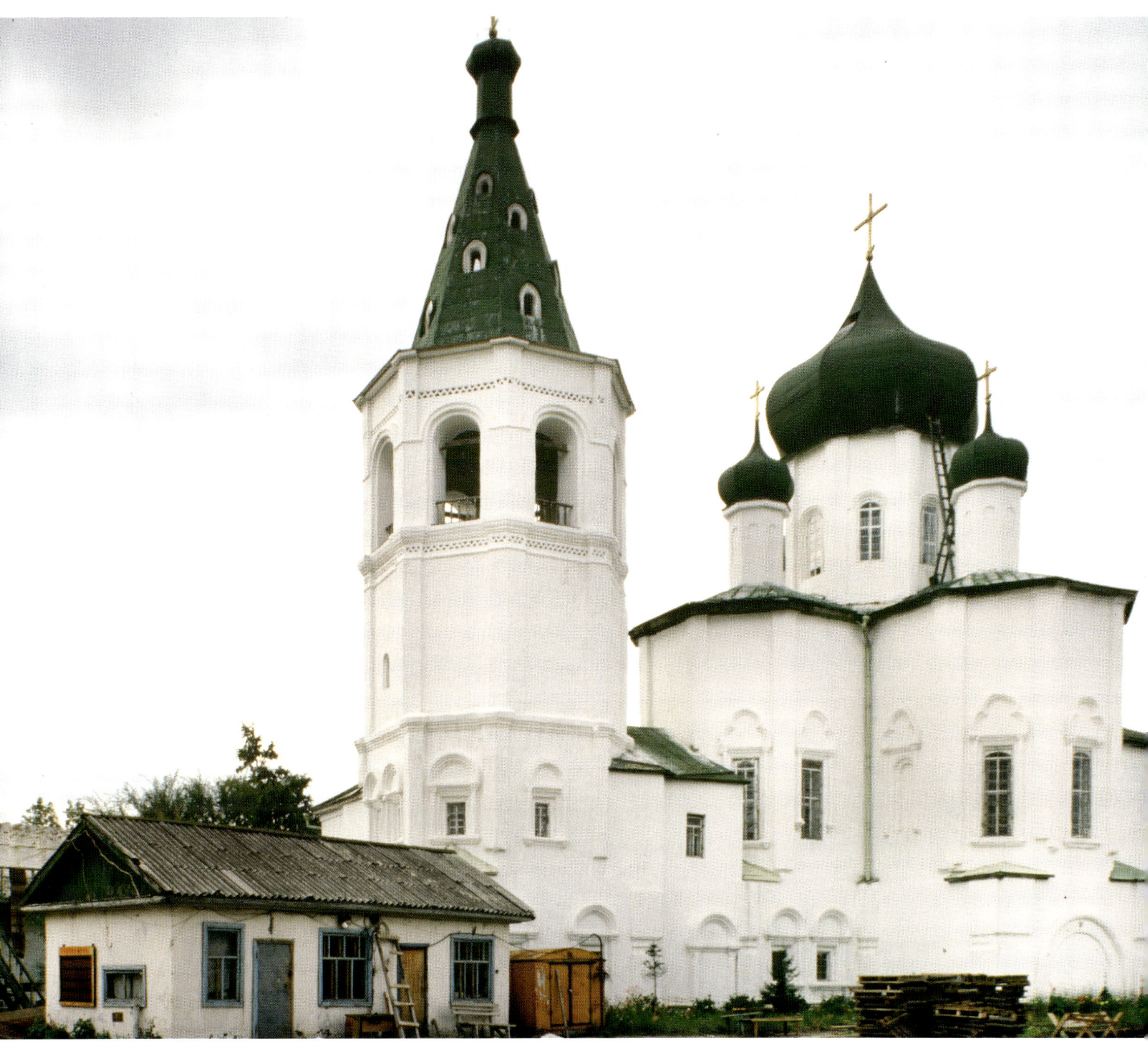

TYUMEN Monastery of the Trinity. Church of Saints Peter and Paul. Southwest view. PROKUDIN-GORSKY 20848. 1912.

TYUMEN Monastery of the Trinity. South Gate, bell tower, Church of Saints Peter and Paul. Northeast view. BRUMFIELD, AUGUST 29, 1999.

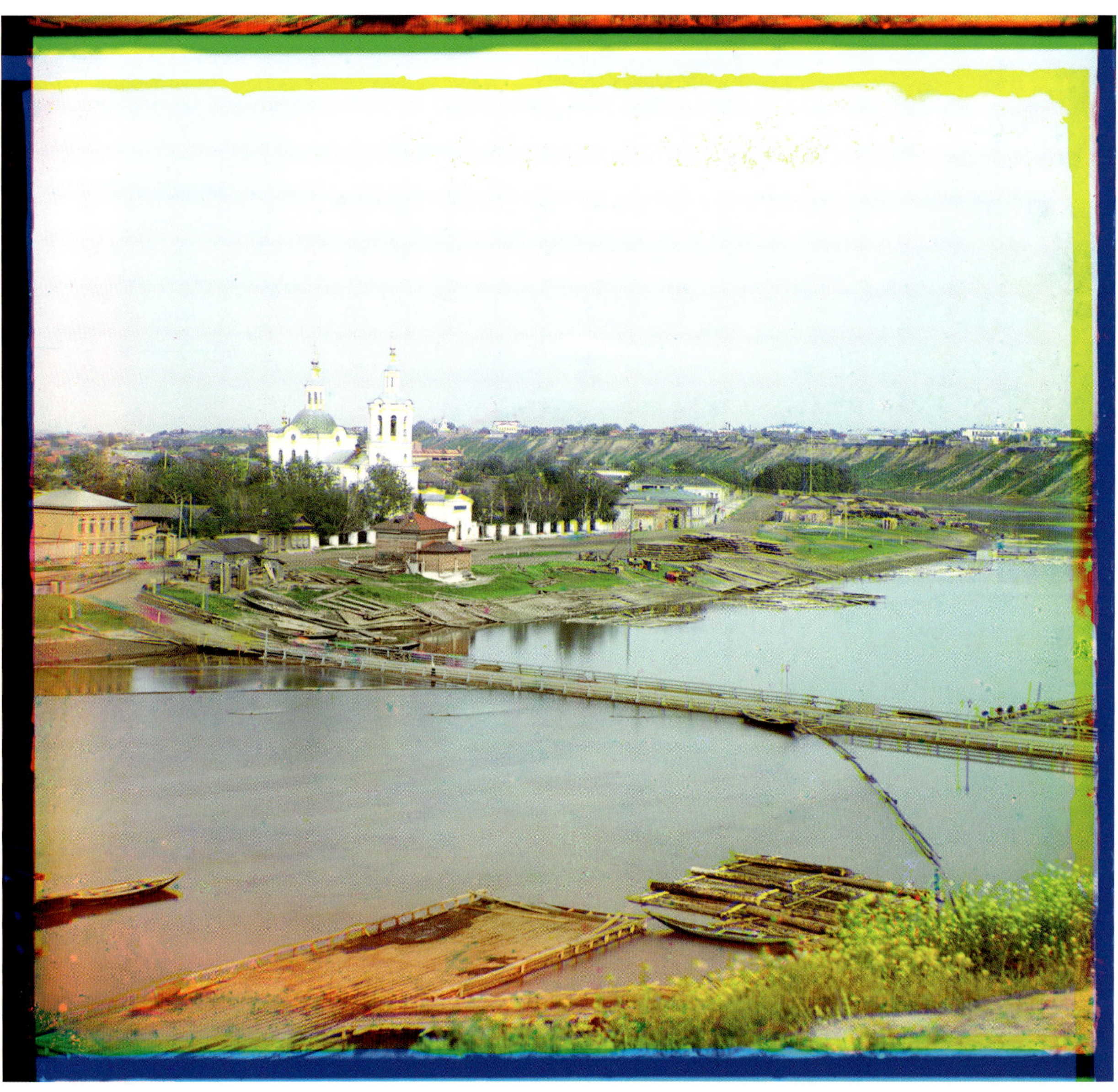

well as the central prison. The earliest ensemble of historical buildings, frequently referred to as the Tobolsk kremlin,
is located on a high bluff overlooking the lower town. Extensive restoration efforts have returned to this ensemble
much of its former monumentality. Primary among these
buildings is Siberia's first cathedral, built in the 1680s with
a dual dedication to Saint Sophia and to the Dormition.

The presence of the Orthodox Church was particularly
strong in Tobolsk, and by 1621 it had become the seat of the
vast eparchy of Siberia, with a wooden cathedral was dedi-

TYUMEN View southeast from
Trinity Monastery toward right
bank of Tura River, with Church
of Saint George (Ascension).
PROKUDIN-GORSKY 20849. 1912.

TYUMEN Church of Saint
George (Ascension). South view.
BRUMFIELD, SEPTEMBER 4, 1999.

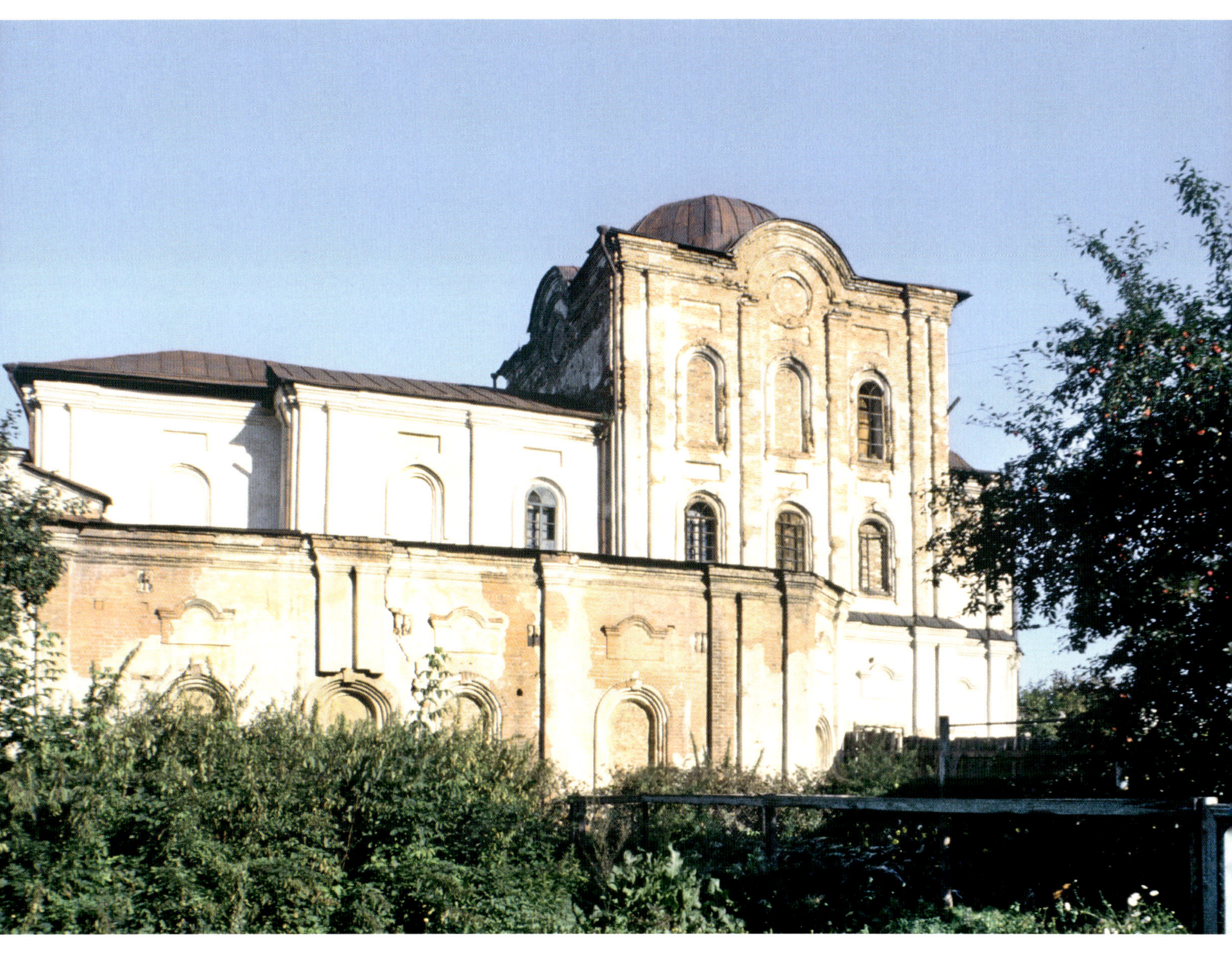

cated to Saint Sophia (Divine Wisdom). The Sophia dedication linked it to the primary cathedrals of ancient Rus in Kiev and Novgorod, as well as to the sixteenth-century Saint Sophia Cathedral in Vologda. (Until 1620 Tobolsk and Siberia were part of the Vologda eparchy.) Fires periodically consumed the wooden cathedral, and after a lightning strike in May 1677, Metropolitan Pavel, prelate of Siberia, obtained support from Moscow to build Siberia's first brick temple in the manner of Moscow Kremlin shrines. Foundation work began in 1681, yet the construction required skills not available in Siberia, and in 1683 a group of experienced masons was sent from Veliky Ustiug in the Russian north. The cathedral project was super-

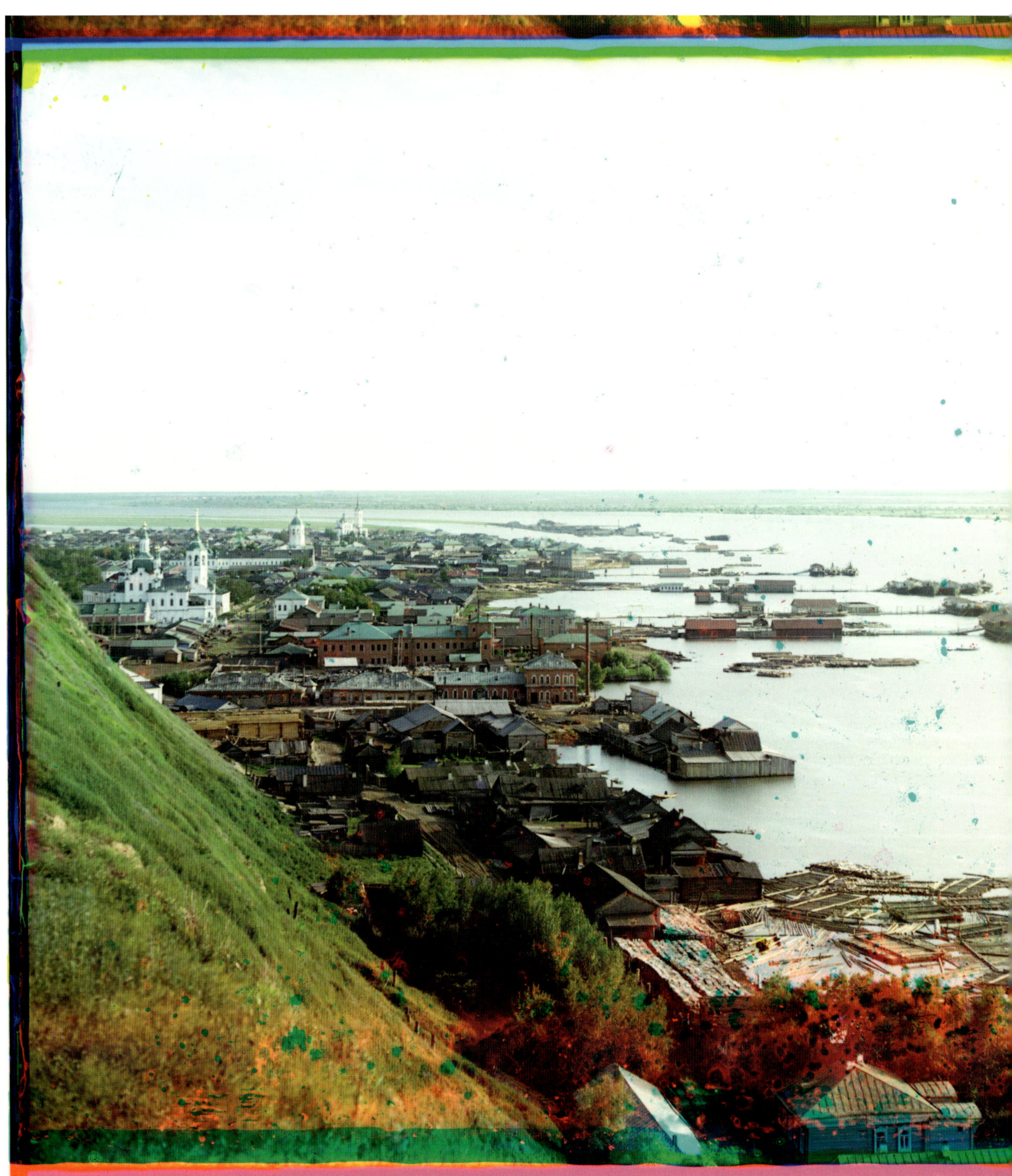

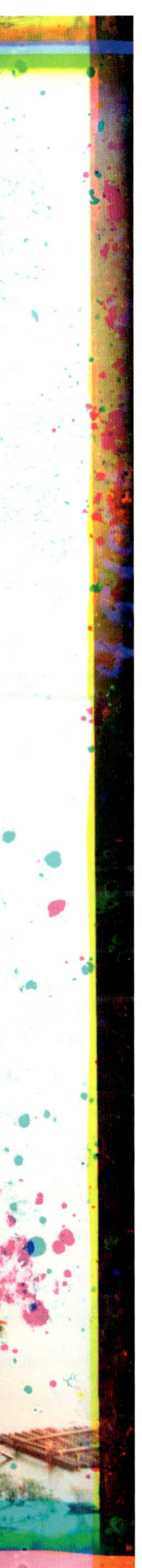

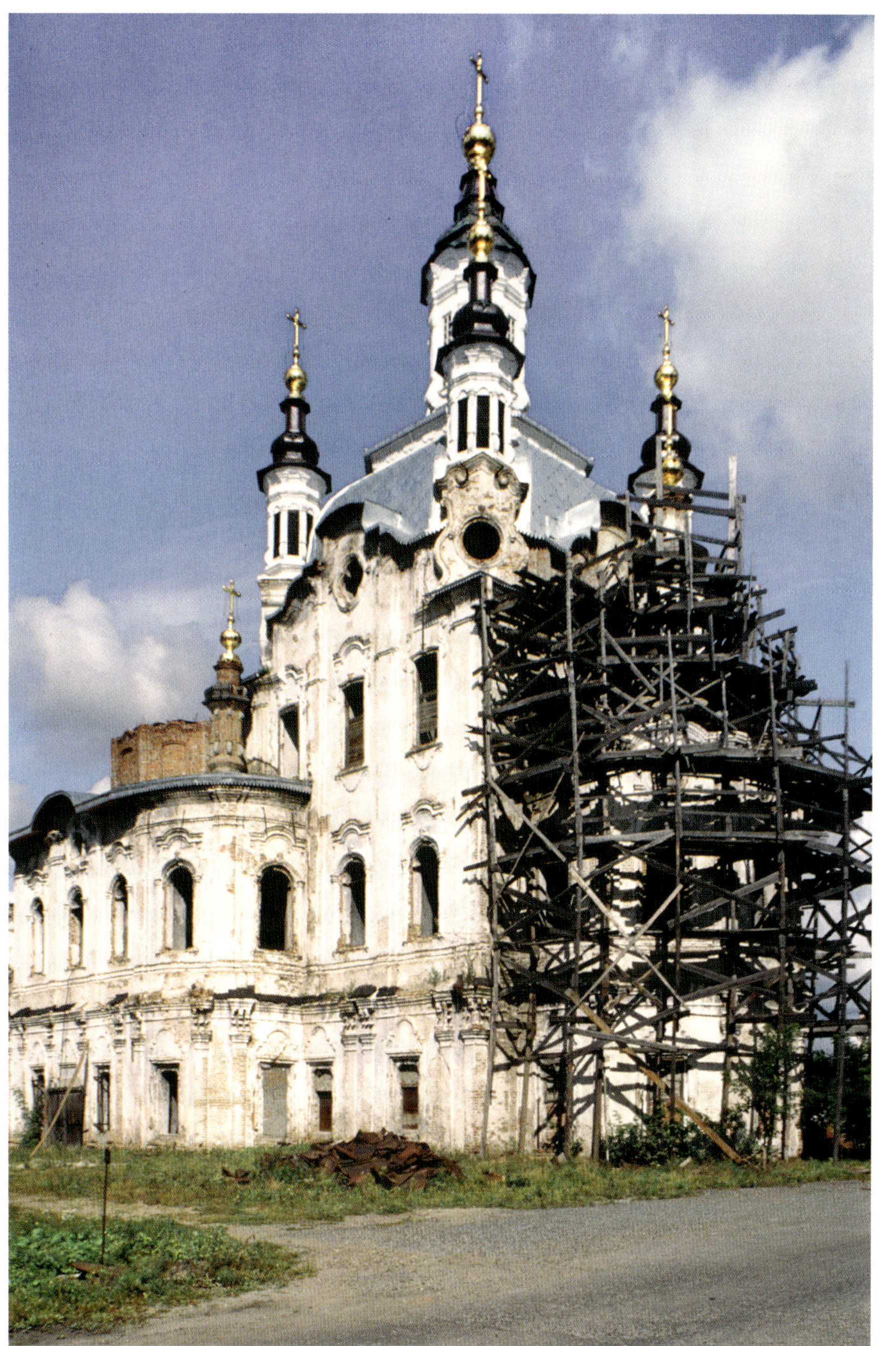

  View south from the
Kremlin down Irtysh River, with
Church of the Resurrection (Saint
Zacharius), Church of the Trans-
figuration and bell tower and
Church of Elevation of the Cross.
PROKUDIN-GORSKY 20758. SUMMER
1912.

  Church of Saint Zacha-
rius and Elizabeth (Resurrection).
Southeast view. BRUMFIELD,
AUGUST 31, 1999.

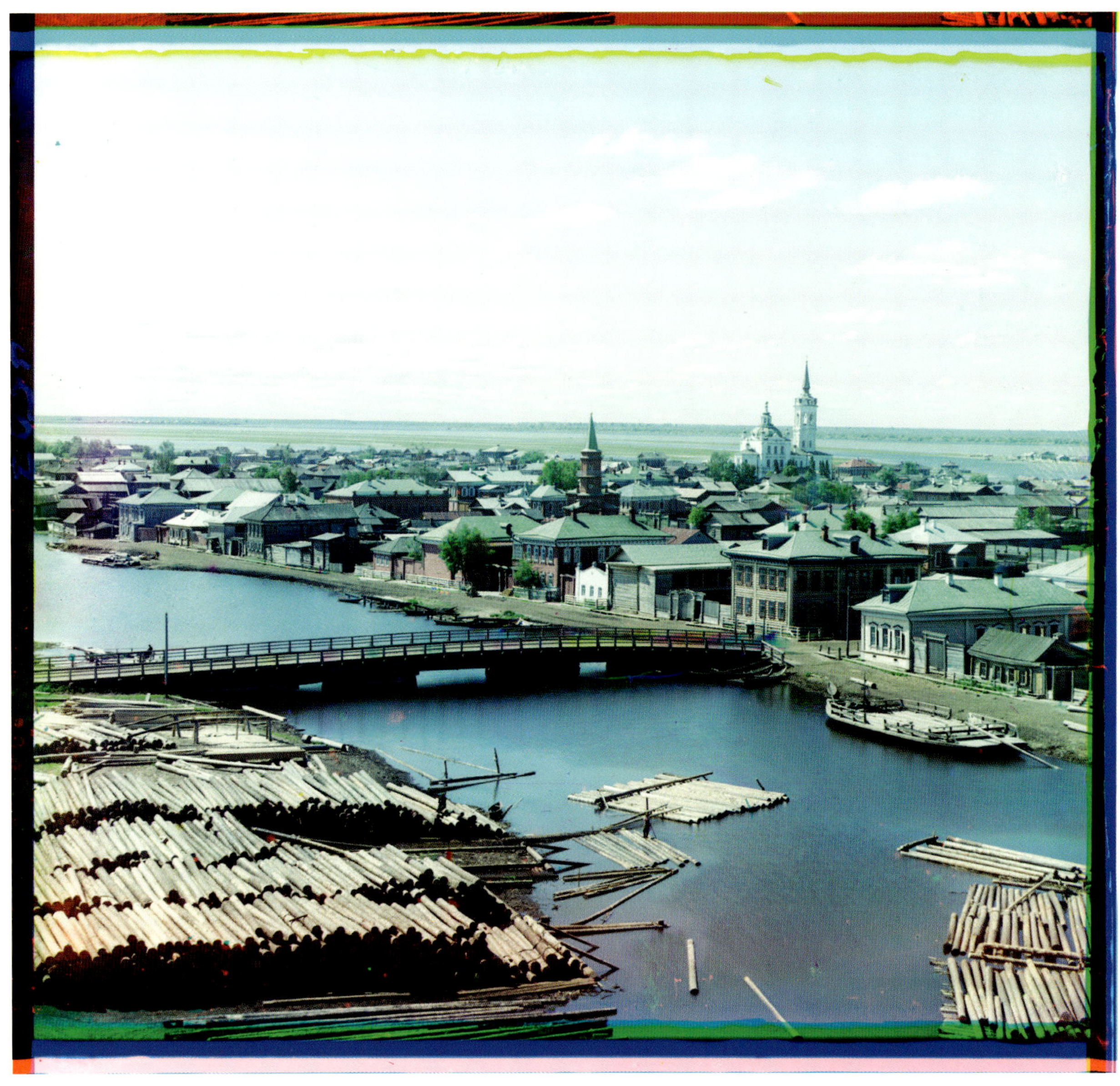

vised by Vasily Larionov, a master builder from Moscow, who brought with him specialized materials, as well as a plan of the recently renovated Ascension Cathedral in the Moscow Kremlin.

Despite construction difficulties—including the collapse of part of the structure—the cathedral was finally consecrated in 1686 to the Dormition of the Virgin, thus giving it two main altars—the Dormition and Saint Sophia. The Dormition echoed the dedication of the central cathedrals of Vladimir and the Moscow Kremlin. (The Kremlin cathedrals often served as prototypes for large churches through-

TOBOLSK View southwest from Transfiguration Church bell tower across Monastyrka and Irtysh Rivers. Mosque and Church of Elevation of the Cross. PROKUDIN-GORSKY 20755. SUMMER 1912.

TOBOLSK Church of Elevation of the Cross. Southeast view. BRUMFIELD, AUGUST 31, 1999.

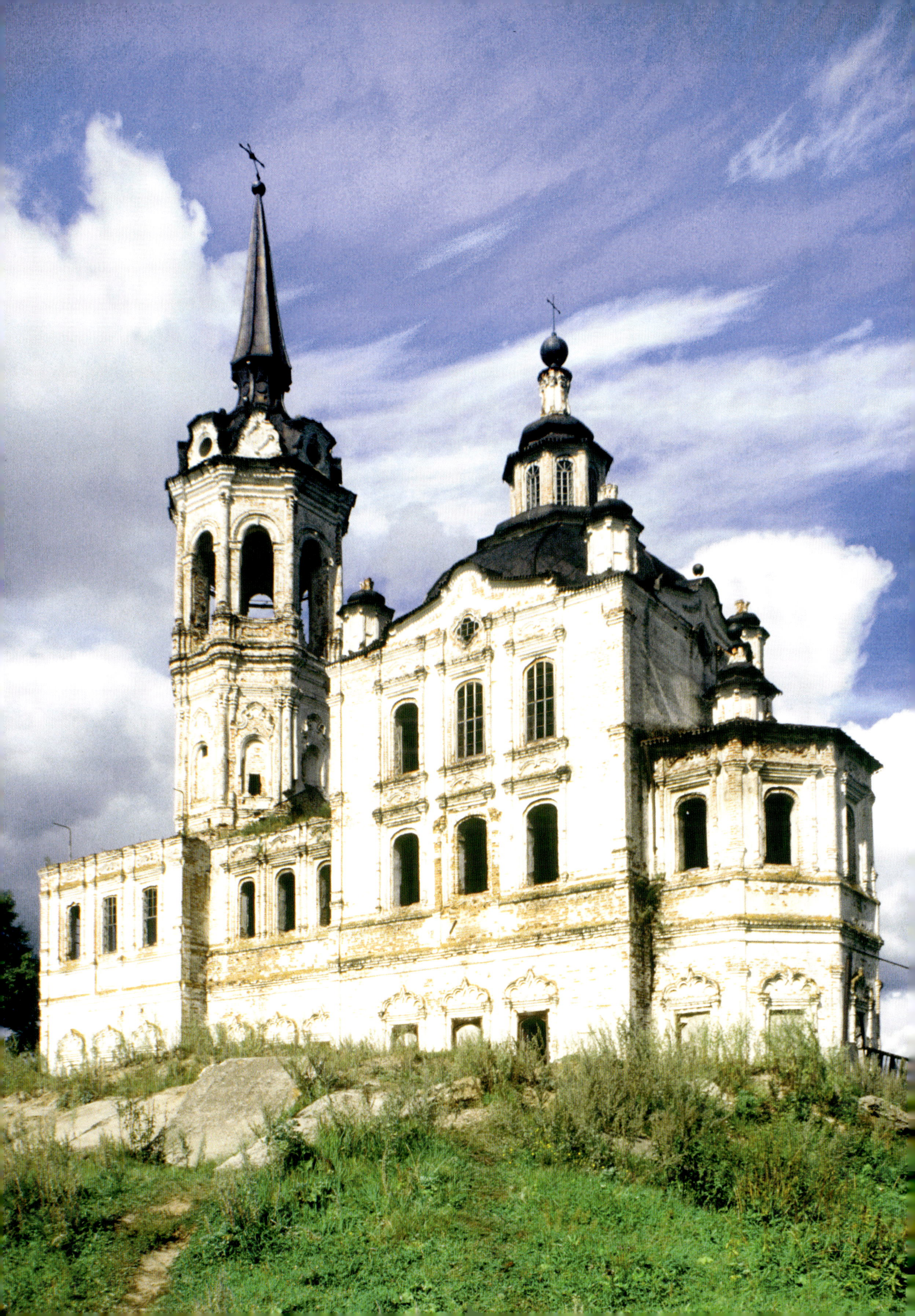

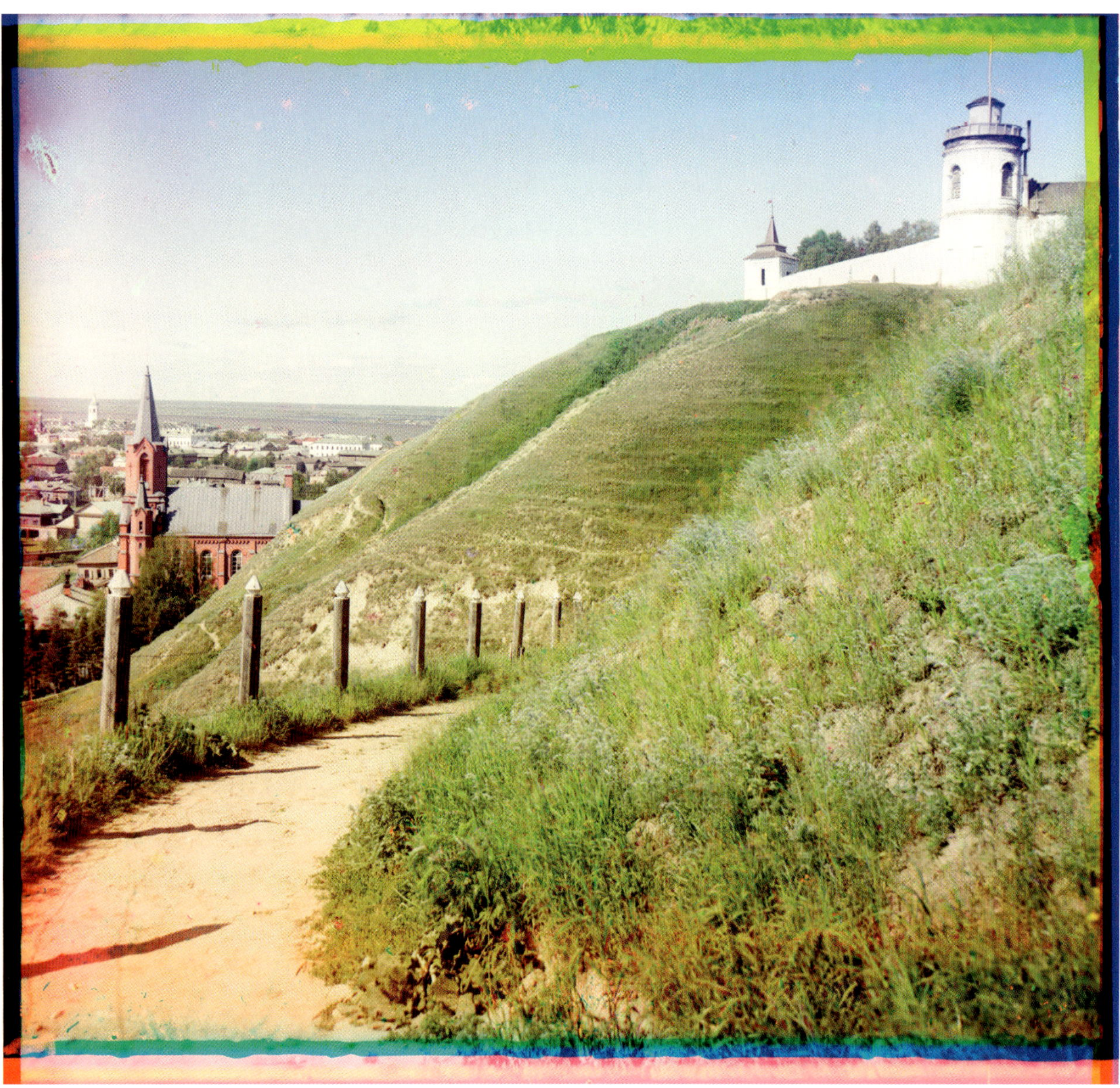

out Russia, thus symbolizing the spiritual and political connections with the capital.) In the mid-eighteenth century, the Sophia Cathedral domes were replaced with the current baroque cupolas, and the roofline was modified from a curved form on top of semicircular gables (*zakomary*) to a flat roof. During the same period a chapel dedicated to Saint John Chrysostom was added on the north facade, visible in Prokudin-Gorsky's view from the northwest. The small narthex on the west facade dates to 1851.

The Sophia-Dormition Cathedral was closed in 1920 and its interior ransacked. Used in the 1930s for grain storage,

TOBOLSK View of kremlin west wall. *Below*: Catholic Church of the Trinity. PROKUDIN-GORSKY 20868. SUMMER 1912.

TOBOLSK Catholic Church of the Trinity. BRUMFIELD, AUGUST 31, 1999.

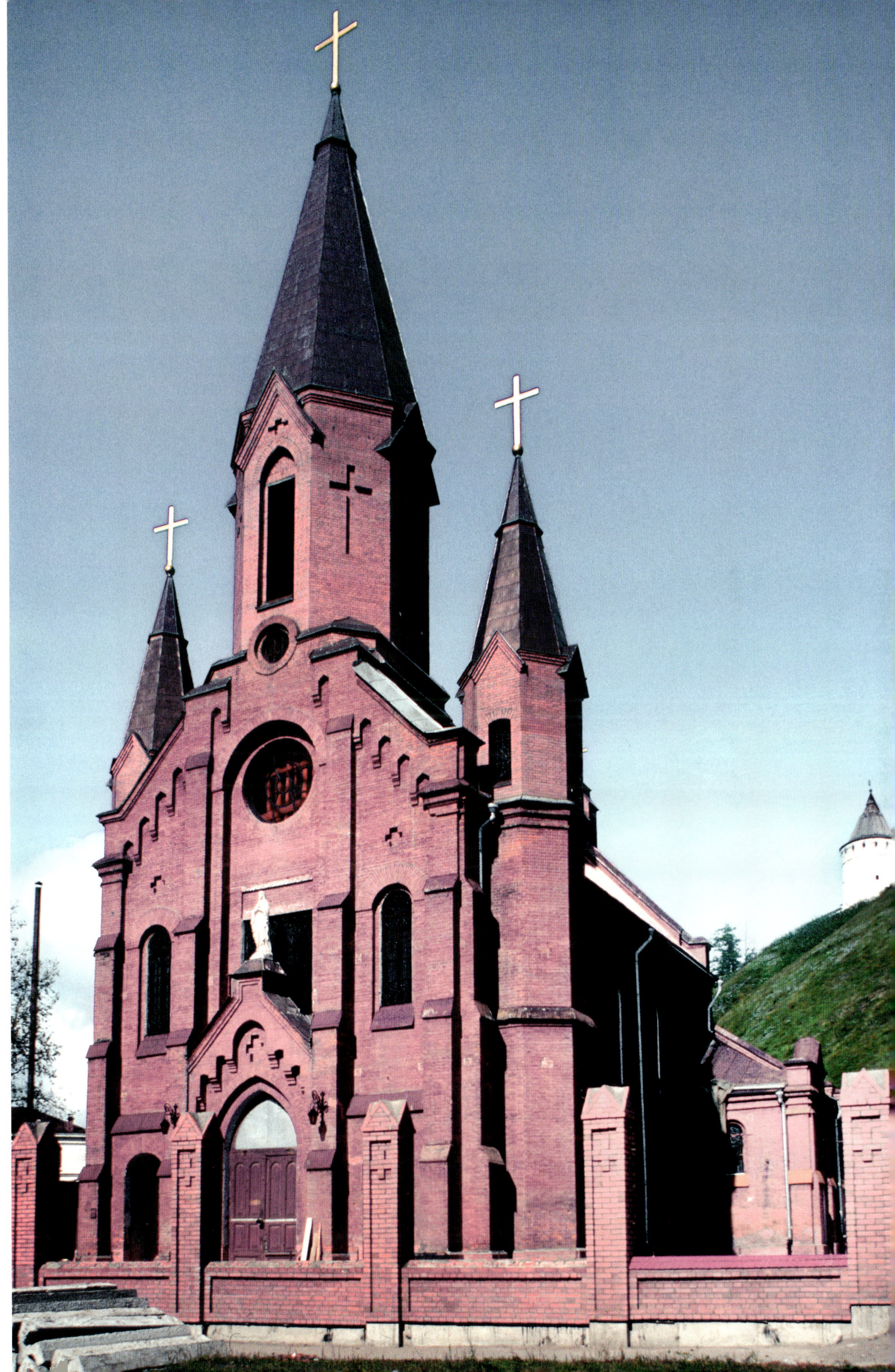

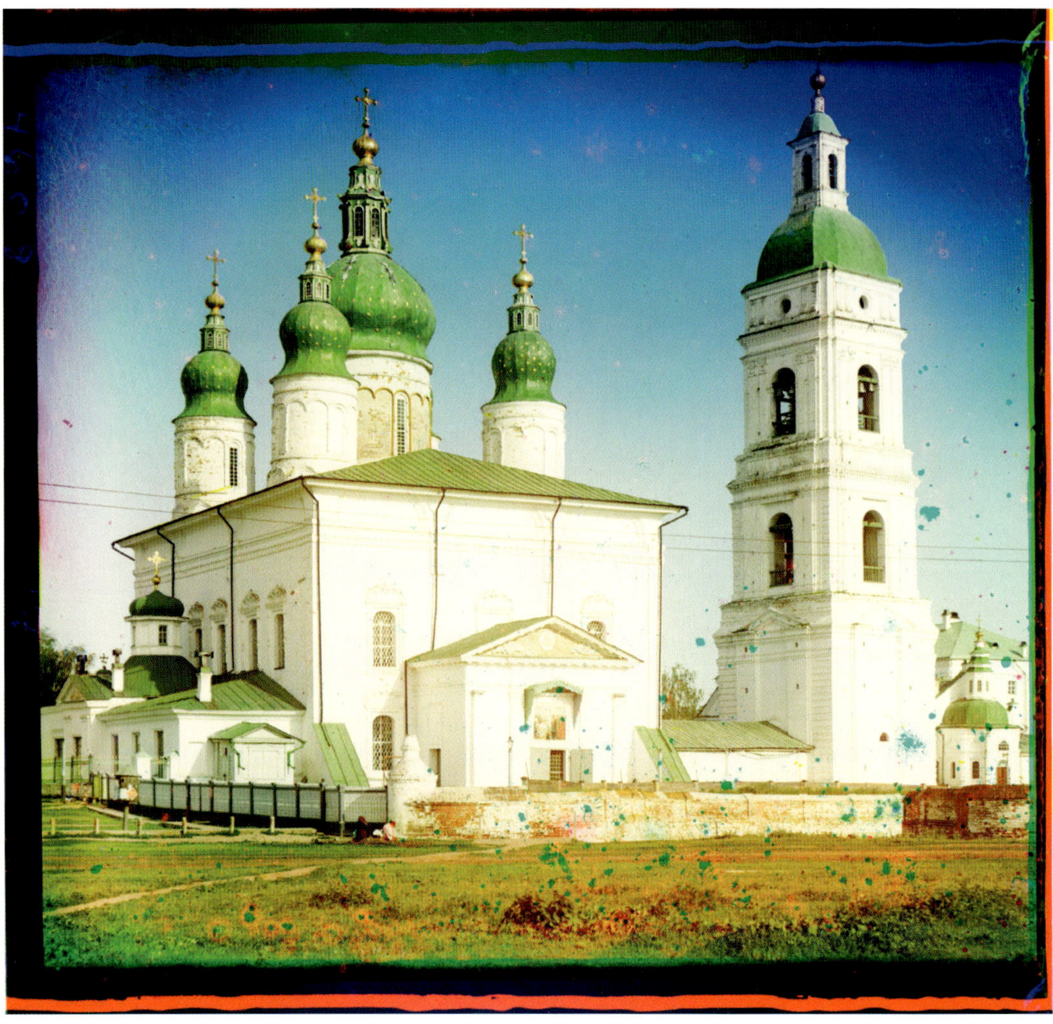

the structure was granted to the Tobolsk museum in 1961. As often occurred in late Soviet restoration work, the roofline was returned to the original curvilinear form over the zakomary gables. The difference is visible in a comparison of Prokudin-Gorsky's photograph with mine from 1999. In 1993 the cathedral reverted to the Orthodox Church, which embarked on a prolonged process of renovating the interior. Other buildings of the cathedral ensemble in the Tobolsk kremlin include a seventy-five-meter-tall neoclassical bell tower (1794–97), a church sacristy of the same period (on the site of a Gate Church of Saint Sergius of Radonezh from the 1680s), and the Cathedral of the Intercession of the Virgin, built in 1743–46 as a "winter church" for the Sophia Cathedral with a secondary altar to Saints Antony

TOBOLSK Cathedral of Saint Sophia and the Dormition, with Chapel of Saint John Chrysostom (*left*) and bell tower. Northwest view. PROKUDIN-GORSKY 20857. SUMMER 1912.

TOBOLSK Cathedral of Saint Sophia and the Dormition, with Chapel of Saint John Chrysostom (*left*). Northwest view. BRUMFIELD, AUGUST 31, 1999.

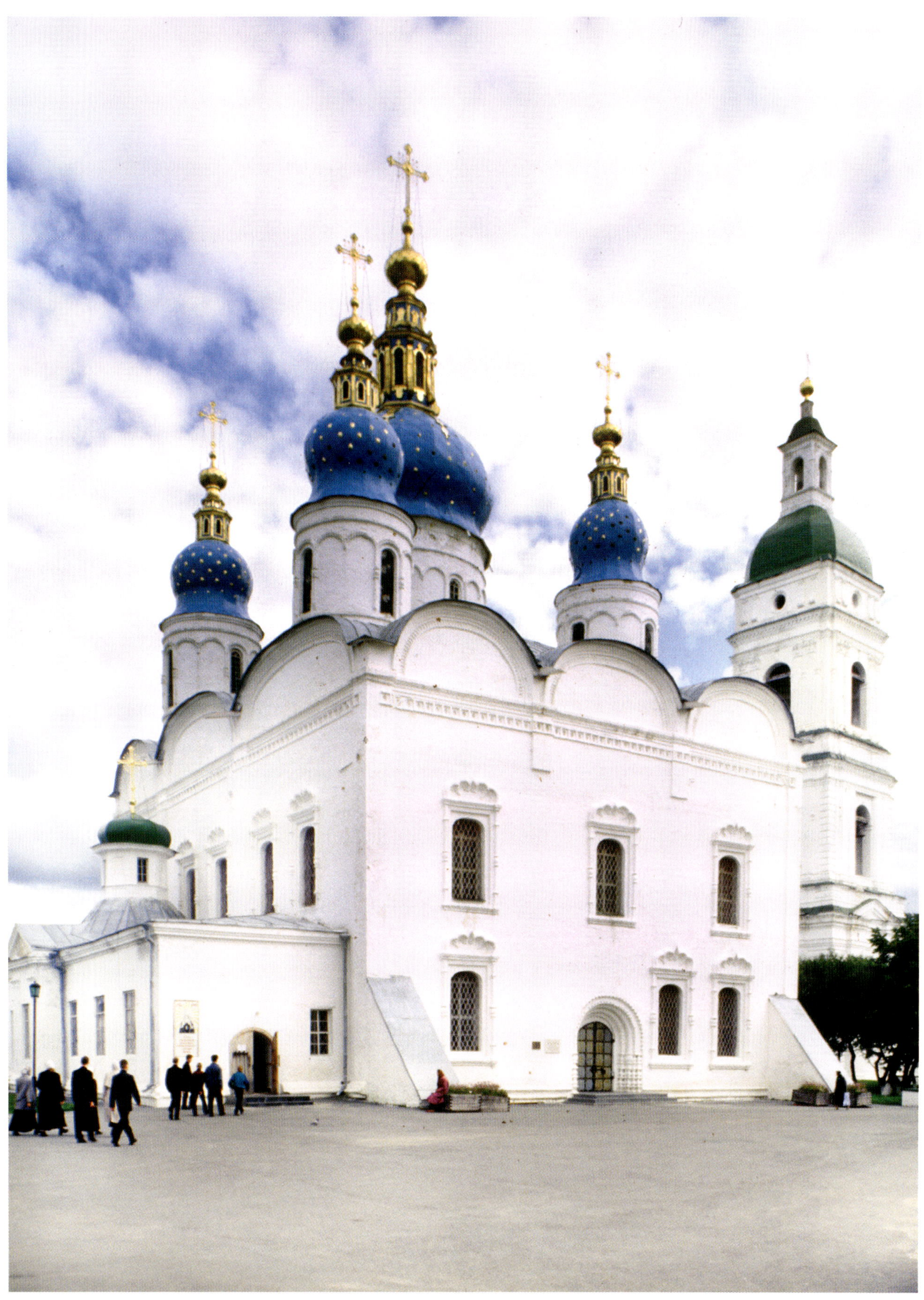

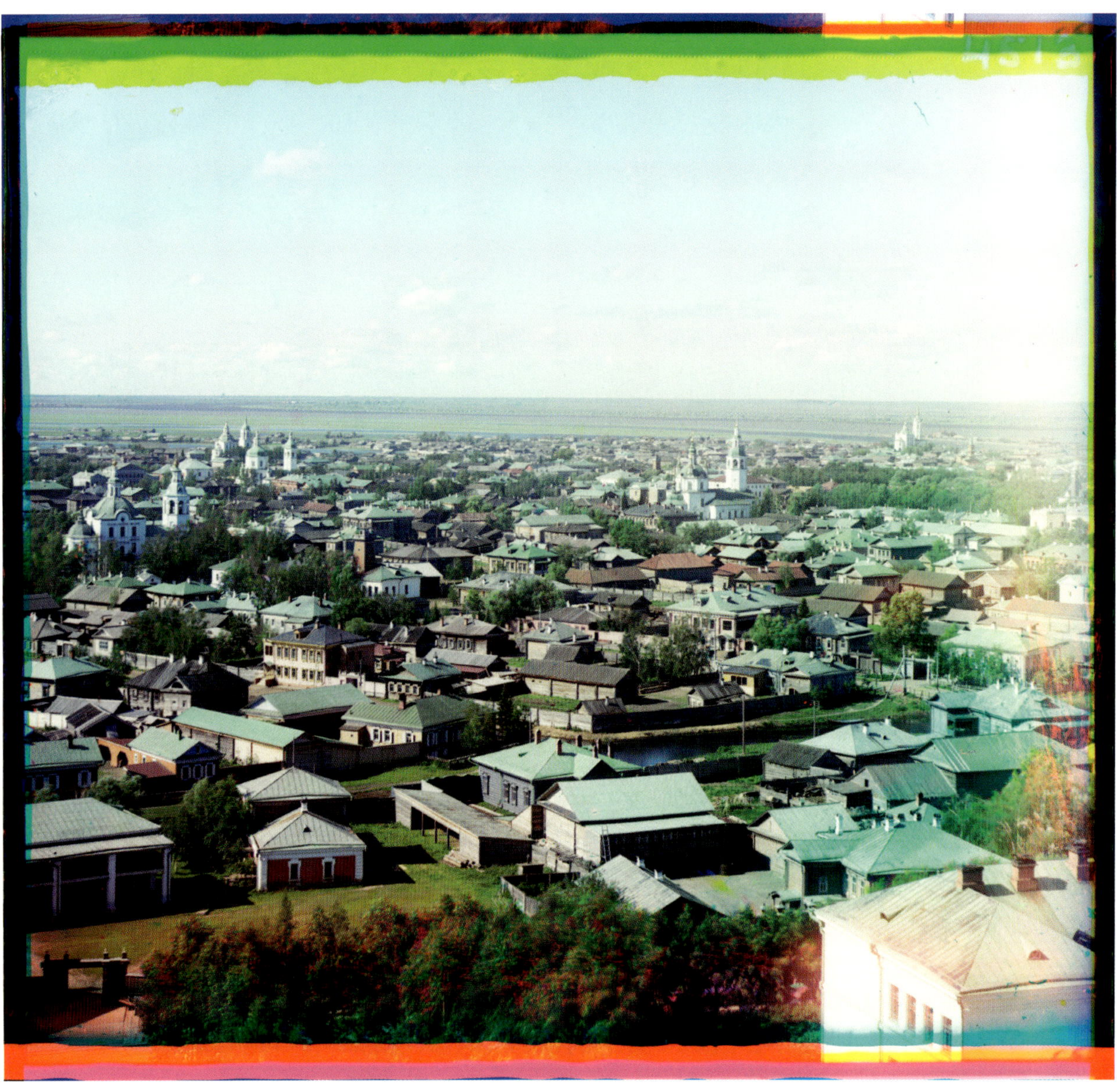

and Feodosy of Kiev. Closed in 1937, it was revived for worship in 1945.

Eighteenth-century Tobolsk parish churches were constructed and decorated in a "Siberian baroque" style. Deformed during the Soviet era, some are being restored in the lower town. Notable examples include the Church of the Archangel Michael, the Church of Saints Zacharias and Elizabeth, and the Church of the Elevation of the Cross, located near the Irtysh River, all built in the middle and latter part of the eighteenth century. Although Prokudin-Gorsky did not photograph the churches in detail, they are

TOBOLSK View southwest from Kremlin toward Irtysh River, with Church of Archangel Michael, Church of Saint Paraskeva (Purification), Church of the Nativity of Christ, Church of the Annunciation, and Church of Elevation of the Cross. PROKUDIN-GORSKY 20761. SUMMER 1912.

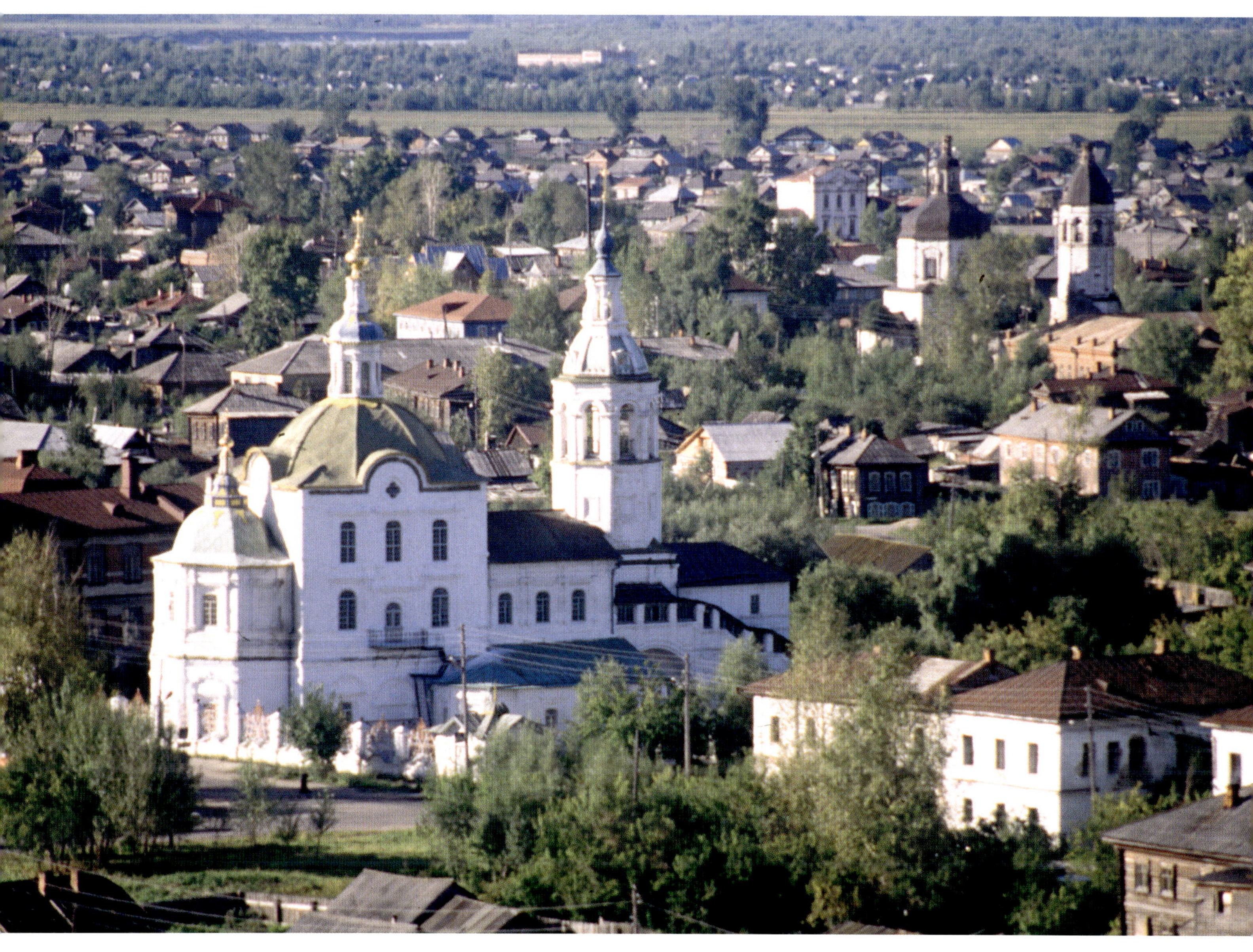

visible in his panoramic view southwest from the kremlin. From a distance the view seems little changed almost
a century later. Much the same could be said of Prokudin-
Gorsky's view north from the lower town with the exuberant Church of Saints Zacharias and Elizabeth and the
magisterial kremlin ensemble in the background. The revival of the Sophia Cathedral ensemble in the kremlin is a
major cultural development.

Among the few secular buildings to be well maintained in
the lower town is the mansion built after the 1788 fire for the
merchant and tax farmer Kuklin. This example of provincial

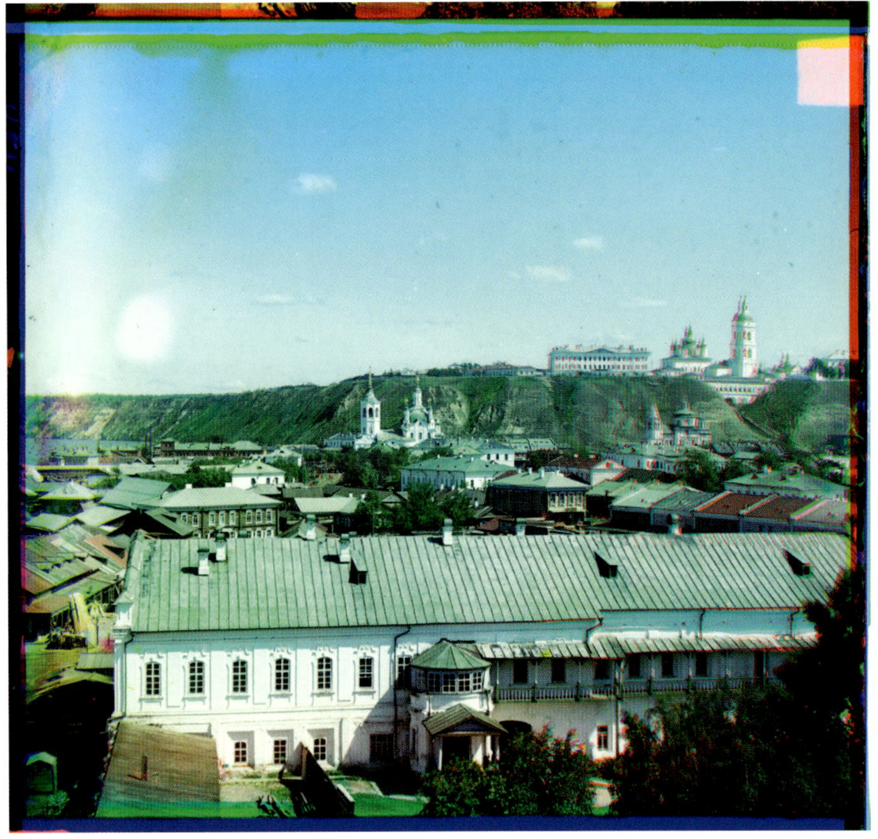

TOBOLSK View northeast toward Kremlin with bell tower and Cathedral of Saint Sophia and the Dormition. *Foreground*: Church of Saint Zacharius and Elizabeth (Resurrection). PROKUDIN-GORSKY 20759. SUMMER 1912.

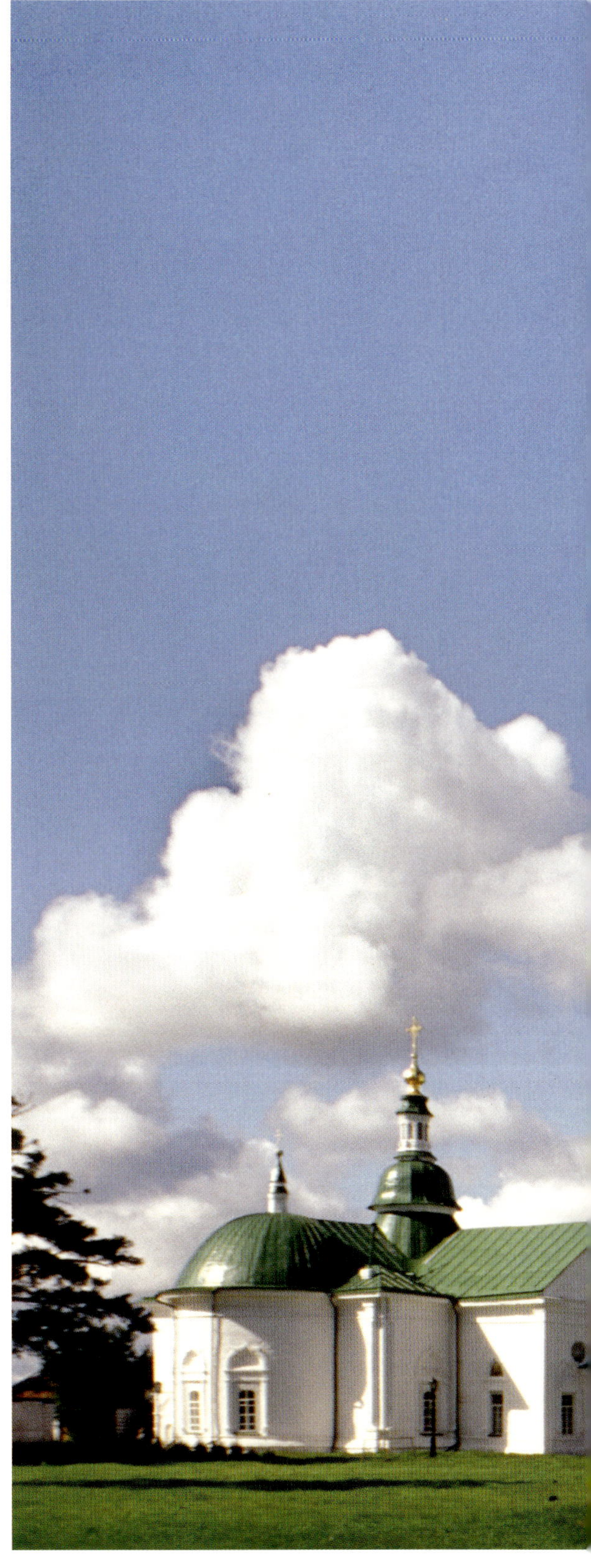

TOBOLSK KREMLIN *Right*: Cathedral of Saint Sophia and the Dormition, with sacristy. *Left*: bell tower and Intercession Cathedral. East view. BRUMFIELD, AUGUST 31, 1999.

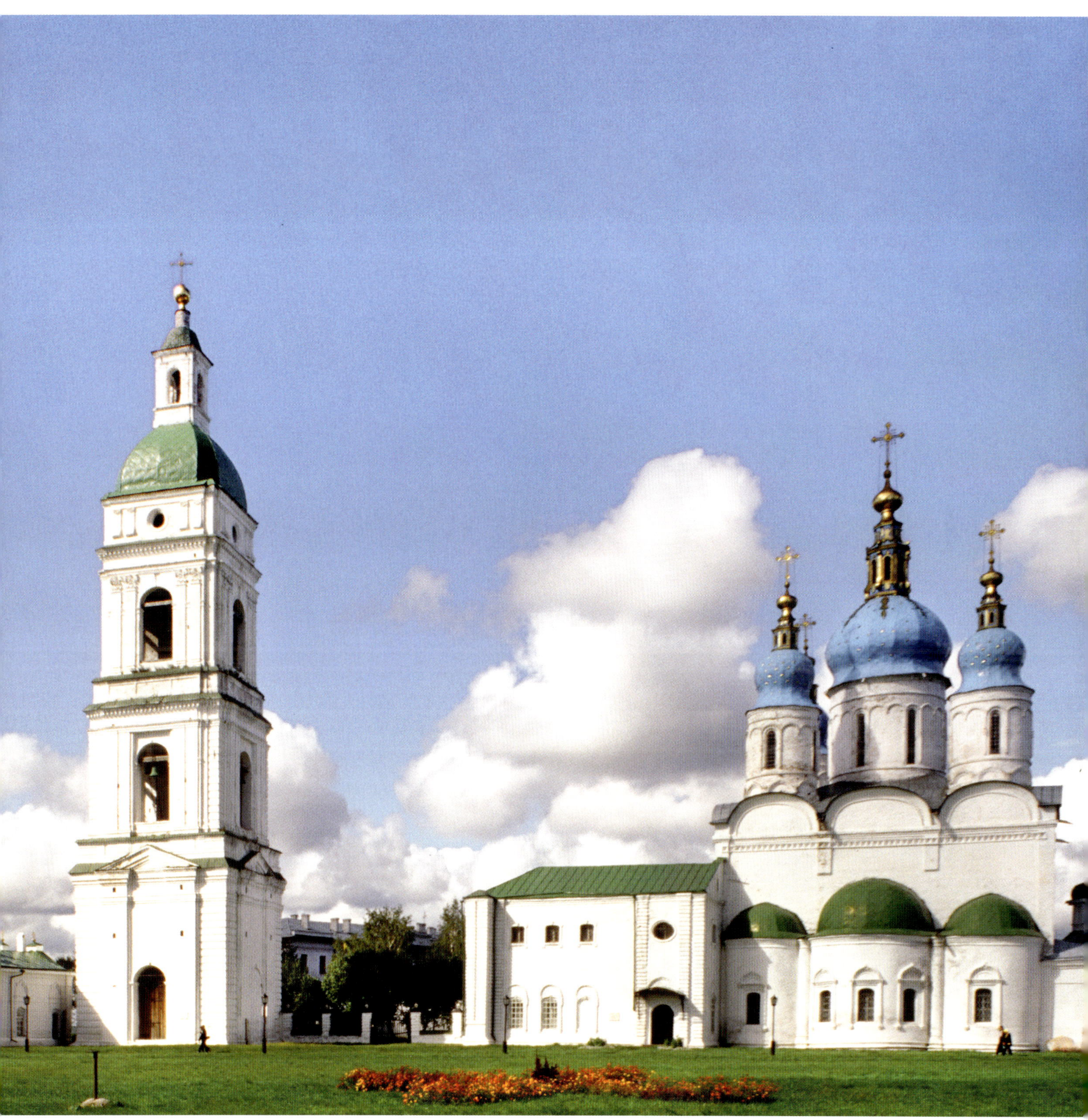

neoclassicism was taken over by the government after Kuklin's bankruptcy in 1817 and converted into a residence for the provincial governor-general. It was here that Nicholas II and his family spent a period from August 1917 through April 1918 before their transfer to Yekaterinburg, where they were murdered in July 1918. The interior of the mansion has been partially restored, including the study used by Nicholas. The lower town has other imposing brick buildings from the late eighteenth to the early twentieth century. Among these monuments is the high school attended for eight years by the renowned chemist Dmitry Mendeleev. Tobolsk also had districts with large wooden houses, many with carved decorative detail. With the passing years the number of these buildings declined for lack of resources to maintain them. Nonetheless, it is still possible to stand on the bluff of the upper city, at the edge of the Sophia Court, and survey the grand vista that beckoned the Russians into Siberia.

The country that Prokudin-Gorsky photographed in his travels through the Urals and Western Siberia continued, like the rest of Russia, to live in the ways of the nineteenth century, even as it faced increasing change in its major industrial centers. The railway, for all its inefficiencies, expedited that process of change as it plunged into the untamed landscape. In 1914 Baedeker still recommended that intrepid travelers to Siberia carry a pistol ("in trips away from the railway"), warned against endemic thievery, and noted that the hotels are "almost invariably costly and indifferent. Bed-linen, soap, etc., should always be taken. A disturbing feature is the inevitable concert or 'sing-song' in the dining room, which usually lasts far into the night." This is not the sort of information that the Ministry of Transportation would have wanted from Prokudin-Gorsky. Within a few years of his visit, the boisterous development of capitalism in Siberia would be replaced by a radically different approach toward modernization.

Among Sergey Prokudin-Gorsky's special interests were Central Asian territories recently absorbed into the Russian Empire. He was not the first Russian to photograph Turkestan, as it was then called. Among the treasures of the Library of Congress is the *Turkestan Album*, one of the richest sources of visual information on the culture of Central Asia. This lavish edition (four parts, with a total of six volumes) was produced in 1871–72 under the patronage of Konstantin P. von Kaufmann, a Russian army general and the first governor-general of Turkestan, as the Russian Empire's Central Asian holdings were called. Kaufmann held that position from 1867 to 1886 and played a major role in establishing Russia's dominant position in Central Asia. The forces of conquest were followed by scholars interested in documenting the region's cultural heritage. The primary photographic compilers for the *Turkestan Album* were Aleksandr L. Kun (1840–1888), an orientalist attached to the army, and Nikolai V. Bogaevskii (1843–1912), a military engineer. One of their tasks was to compile a visual survey of the newly acquired territories, the center of which was Samarkand.

Samarkand—"Radiant Center of the Earth," city of Tamerlane, and now an administrative center in Uzbekistan—is among the oldest settled points in Central Asia. Archaeological excavations in the heart of Samarkand have uncovered a Paleolithic campsite, and artifacts from the Bronze Age have been discovered near the city. Evidence suggests that by the sixth century BCE Samarkand—or Maracanda, as it was then known—served as the capital of Sogdiana, which was ruled by the Persian Achaemenid dynasty from the sixth to the fourth centuries BCE.

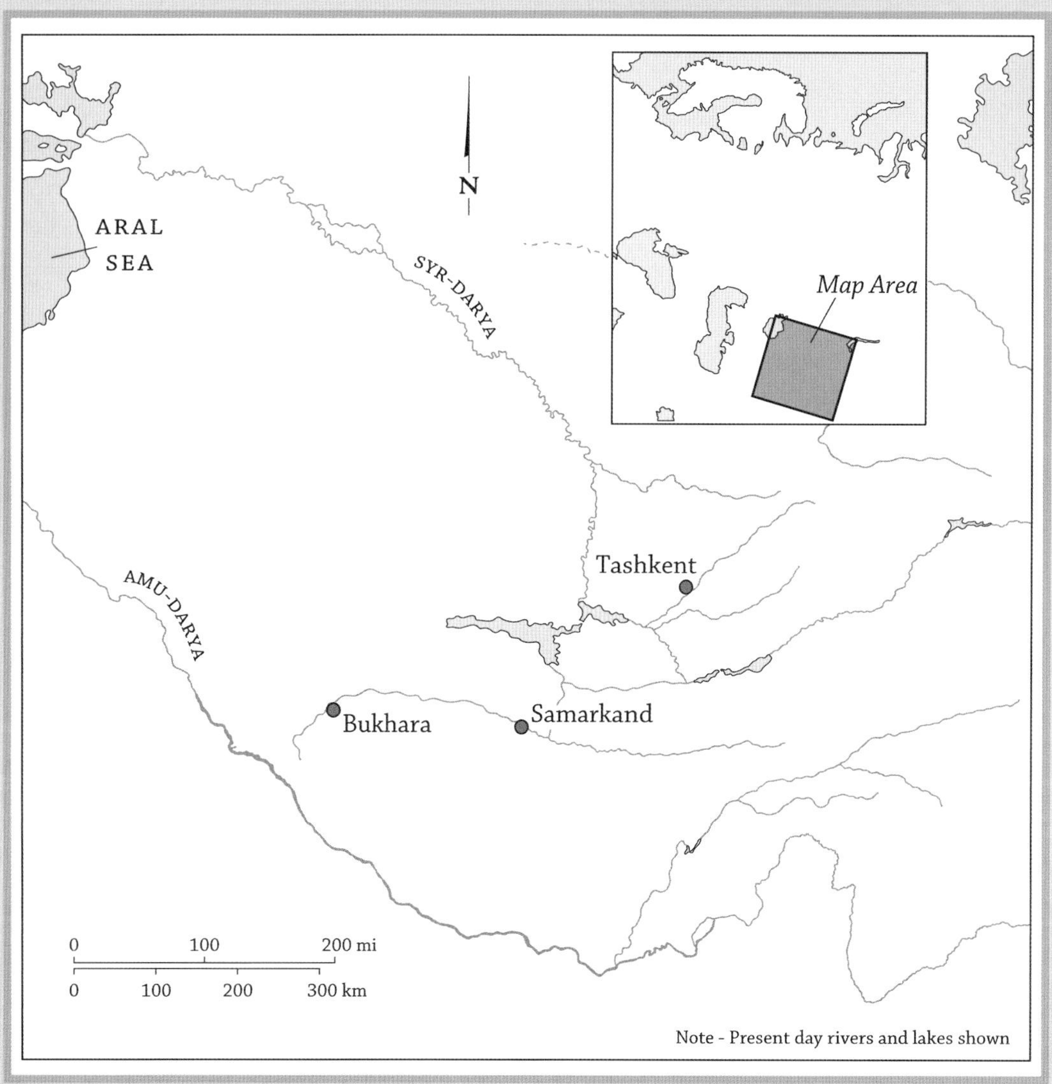

ARAL
SEA
SYR-DARYA
AMU-DARYA
N
Map Area
Tashkent
Bukhara
Samarkand
0   100   200 mi
0   100   200   300 km
Note - Present day rivers and lakes shown

The first historical reference to Maracanda relates to Alexander the Great's conquest of Central Asia, a campaign that led him to the walls of the Maracanda citadel. After a siege in the spring of 327 BCE, Alexander took the fortress and placated the populace by marrying the daughter (Roxana) of a local ruler. Hellenic control continued under Seleucus I (358–281 BCE), a general who had accompanied Alexander on his conquest of Bactria and Sogdiana; but the Seleucids were unable to maintain their power in the area. Soon after the death of Seleucus, a revolt by Bactrian Greeks established a Bactrian kingdom, which flourished until the first century BCE, when the area was taken by the Chinese. The eventual formation of the Kushan kingdom, about the beginning of the Christian era, led to a period of considerable prosperity, as the trade route from India and China—the "Silk Road"—passed through Samarkand on the way to Byzantium. The Kushan kingdom fell in its turn to the Turks, who established a khanate in Sogdiana during the fifth century.

Each of these eras left its imprint on the culture of Samarkand and the surrounding area—in coins, pottery, and statuary—but none had so profound an effect as the introduction of Islam by Arab conquest at the beginning of the eighth century. Arab incursions into Transoxiana (the area beyond the Oxus River, including Sogdiana) began at the end of the seventh century, but Samarkand was not occupied by the Arabs until 712—the year they took Cordova. The conquest was undoubtedly motivated more by greed than by a desire to spread the word of the Prophet, and bitter resistance to the Arabs' harsh rule flared in Central Asia for several decades.

In fact, Arab caliphates in the area lasted only until the ninth century. But the conquest established Islam as the dominant religion—although others were tolerated—and in so doing defined the cultural basis from which the arts in Central Asia subsequently derived. Within this framework, Arab, Persian, Mongol, and Uzbek would create in Samarkand and Bukhara an architectural legacy that is one of the major accomplishments of Islamic civilization.

With the assumption of power by local Central Asian dynasties—the Tahirids and the Samanids—Samarkand and Bukhara continued to flourish as centers of trade and culture. Bukhara, an ancient settlement whose oasis is first mentioned in the seventh century, was particularly noted for its achievements in the sciences during the reign of the Samanids. Having chosen the city as their capital, the Samanids not only supported extensive construction but also put into practice a singularly fine architectural sense. The earliest extant monument in the area—the mausoleum of Ismail Samani—dates from this period, and it displays so sure a command of form that one wonders what else must have existed in the city at that time.

The fall of the Samanids, in 999, introduced a period of rapidly changing dynasties and fragmentation, but the commercial significance of both cities continued to support their prosperity—until the thirteenth century. It was then that Samarkand and Bukhara were inundated by the first wave of a Mongol invasion that would eventually reach Vladimir, Kiev, and the Adriatic.

"They had pity on none, for they slew women, men, infants, tore open the wombs of those with child and slaughtered the unborn. The flames of this destruction swept in all directions, and evil spread over the land, like a cloud driven by the wind." In Central Asia, as in central Russia a few years later, the havoc caused by the invasion of the Mongols under Genghis Khan and his immediate successors seemed beyond the power of human comprehension or expression. Chroniclers, whether the Muslim author of the above passage (Ibn Al-Asr) or a Russian monk from Novgorod, record essentially the same details of slaughter and pillage, the same sequence of siege, resistance, and destruction.

Both Samarkand and Bukhara attempted resistance, and both were taken in 1220, with the predictable consequences, and were given over to pillage. Futile rebellions occurred during the decades following the conquest, but no effective challenge was offered to the Mongols, who occasionally returned to sack the cities in their domain. As in Russia, the nomadic Mongols in Central Asia preferred to establish their own large encampments—some of which became thriving, if short-lived, trading centers—rather than occupy the cities they had conquered.

Bukhara, although sacked again in 1273 and 1316, apparently suffered less than Samarkand, for in his book *Il Milione* (also known as *The Travels*; late thirteenth century) Marco Polo described it as a large city. (His father and uncle had been merchants there at the beginning of the 1260s, and he himself traveled in the area between 1271 and 1295.) As late as the mid-fourteenth century, Samarkand, beset by internal dissension and prey to the exactions of the Mongols, stood largely in ruin, while Timur, the man who would eventually make it the capital of an empire, was still engaged in petty brigandage. By the end of the century, however, the entire civilized world, from China to England, from Cairo to Moscow, would know his name—Timur i Lenk, or Tamerlane, "Scourge of God and terror of the world."

From the time of his first major victory, near Samarkand in 1370, until his death during a march against China in 1405, Timur directed a series of campaigns as brilliant as they were destructive. No force—Ottoman, Crusader, Egyptian, Indian, or rival Mongol horde—could withstand the might of his armies, whose organization and tactics were based on principles inherited from the Great Khan, and whose mobility overwhelmed attempts at resistance. No fortress, however massive or remote, was impregnable to his siege equipment, his artillery, his engineers, and his shock troops. Minarets built of severed heads attested to his victories in Afghanistan, Isfahan, Aleppo, Baghdad, Damascus, Delhi, and Armenia, while trains of booty and slaves, scholars and craftsmen converged on Samarkand and his palaces, situated on the surrounding plain.

Born in 1336 near the town of Shakhrisabz (forty miles south of Samarkand), Timur was raised in the Chagatai *ulus*, least stable of the four Mongol empires distributed among the sons of Genghis Khan. The Chagatai lands suffered from a continuing tension between seminomadic Mongols and the settled Muslim population, as well as border warfare with the Il-Khanate, or Mongol state in Persia. By the fourteenth century this vast area had disintegrated into a collection of smaller, often hostile, dynasties and Mongol clans (such as the one to which Timur's father owed allegiance), and their feuds were very much a part of Timur's youth. During one early skirmish he received the wounds that crippled both his right arm and right leg, giving rise to the Persian epithet "Timur i Lenk" (Timur the Lame)—whence our Tamerlane, or Christopher Marlowe's Tamburlaine.

Through a combination of military skill and diplomatic cunning, Timur proved eminently capable of exploiting the weaknesses of those he opposed in the struggle for domination of Samarkand—most notably, Hussein, whom he defeated in 1370. At the same time he appeased the settled population, weary of disorder, and rendered homage to Muslim religious leaders as well as to the ineffectual descendants of Chagatai (to whom he was related by one of his marriages). Above all, he was generous with the men who followed him, a well-organized horde of warriors that embarked from Central Asia with families, tradesmen, craftsmen, and camp followers in campaigns of conquest and pillage lasting several years.

Despite his mobile existence, Timur intended to establish a stable political and dynastic order based in Samarkand, and to this end he spared no expense in the adornment of the city. Remnants of two of his greatest projects—the Bibi Khanym mosque and Gur Emir, the mausoleum built in 1404 for Timur's descendants—allow one to grasp something of the capital's splendor, the combination of heroic scale with the exquisite detail of ceramic ornamentation. But Timur, characteristically, spent little time in the city whose monuments served as a record of his conquests and a repository for loot from three continents. Even during his return to Samarkand, he preferred to remain in grand encampment on the outskirts of the city.

After his death, in 1405, the ephemeral order Timur had imposed gave way to another period of internal struggle and invasion, culminating in the Uzbek expulsion of his dynasty early in the sixteenth century. In 1504 Babur, the last of Samarkand's Timurid rulers, was driven from the area by the Uzbek Shaybani Khan after a four-year struggle that saw the city change hands several times. The young Babur, twenty-one years old at the time of his exodus, subsequently founded the Moghul dynasty in India, and his account of defeat, treachery, and poverty, as well as the great victories in Hindustan, is vividly told in his remarkable autobiography, the *Bubur-nama*.

But the Ferghana Valley, heartland of Timur's empire, remained in the hands of the Shaybanid dynasty, who shifted their capital from Samarkand to Bukhara in the middle of the sixteenth century. Samarkand's brief revival in the middle of the seventeenth century resulted in the completion of the imposing Registan complex, but thereafter the city entered another period of decline, which left it virtually depopulated by the eighteenth century. Although Bukhara continued to serve as the capital of various Uzbek dynasties (the Shaybanids and, after 1599, the Astrakhanids) as well as an important center of Islamic studies, it too steadily declined in power and vitality. By the 1860s the Russian Empire had perceived its manifest destiny in Central Asia.

The conquest was swift, and by local standards painless. By 1868 Russian troops under the redoubtable general Konstantin Kaufmann had conquered most of Turkestan (including Tashkent and Samarkand), and reduced the emirate of Bukhara to a state of dependency. Samarkand became an administrative center, a new Russian town arose, and the Trans-Caspian Railway reached the city in 1888. Colonial expansion not only revived commerce in Samarkand (cotton was among its most valuable commodities) but also stimulated interest in Central Asia among Russian scholars—and American travelers, such as Eugene Schuyler—who began to study the monuments of Samarkand. Bukhara, however, maintained its fictive autonomy under a series of despotic emirs, until their overthrow in an uprising supported by the Red Army in 1920.

In 1924 the Turkestan and Bukhara Soviet Republics merged to form the Uzbek Soviet Socialist Republic, whose capital, until 1929, was Samarkand (thereafter, it was Tashkent). The Soviet government suppressed Islam but attempted to establish a sense of cultural identity among the Uzbeks: their vernacular language was given an alphabet (initially Latin, and then, from 1940, Cyrillic), and a national theater and several education institutes were established. Emphasis has been placed on the restoration of architectural monuments, most of which had fallen into considerable neglect. In both Samarkand and Bukhara numerous mosques, mausoleums, and madrasas (religious schools) were restored or rebuilt, while special workshops preserved the skills necessary for the restoration of the ceramic ornamentation that covers so many of the city's remarkable structures. Through the efforts of the contemporary master (*usto* in Uzbek), the achievement of artists and craftsmen who lived centuries ago is gradually being regained.

BUKHARA

The "Holy City," as it came to be known in the eighteenth century with the great number of its mosques, Bukhara has preserved far more of its Eastern appearance than has Samarkand, whose Timurid mosques are surrounded by Russian colonial and Soviet architecture. Despite the invasions and destruction that have marked the city's history, Bukhara contains architectural monuments built as early as the tenth century. Samarkand, by contrast, has nothing from before the fourteenth century. Bukhara has a new city, but old Bukhara is still composed of a maze of streets dominated by the citadel (*ark* in Uzbek), and the minaret and dome of the twelfth-century Kalyan Mosque. Between 1785 and 1920 Bukhara was ruled by eight emirs in the Manghit dynasty. After the Russian capture of Samarkand (1868), the Emirate of Bukhara became a Russian protectorate.

Prokudin-Gorsky's travels in Turkestan included trips in January 1907 and 1911 to the ancient city of Bukhara. Among the ancient monuments photographed is a bright winter view of the main entrance to the citadel, or ark, Bukhara's oldest archeological site, with layers going back at least to the sixth century CE. The ark in its present form originated in the sixteenth century under the Shaybanid dynasty, who reconstructed the platform on the ruins of earlier citadels. In the eighteenth and nineteenth centuries the palace was rebuilt. The towers flanking the entrance were erected in the eighteenth century. Honeycomb windows adorn the upper tier, and the loggia contains a large clock between two carved wooden columns.

For a sense of the scale on which the Karakhanids built during the twelfth century in Bukhara, one need only look, from almost any part in the central city, to see the great mass of the Kalyan Minaret, some fifty meters in

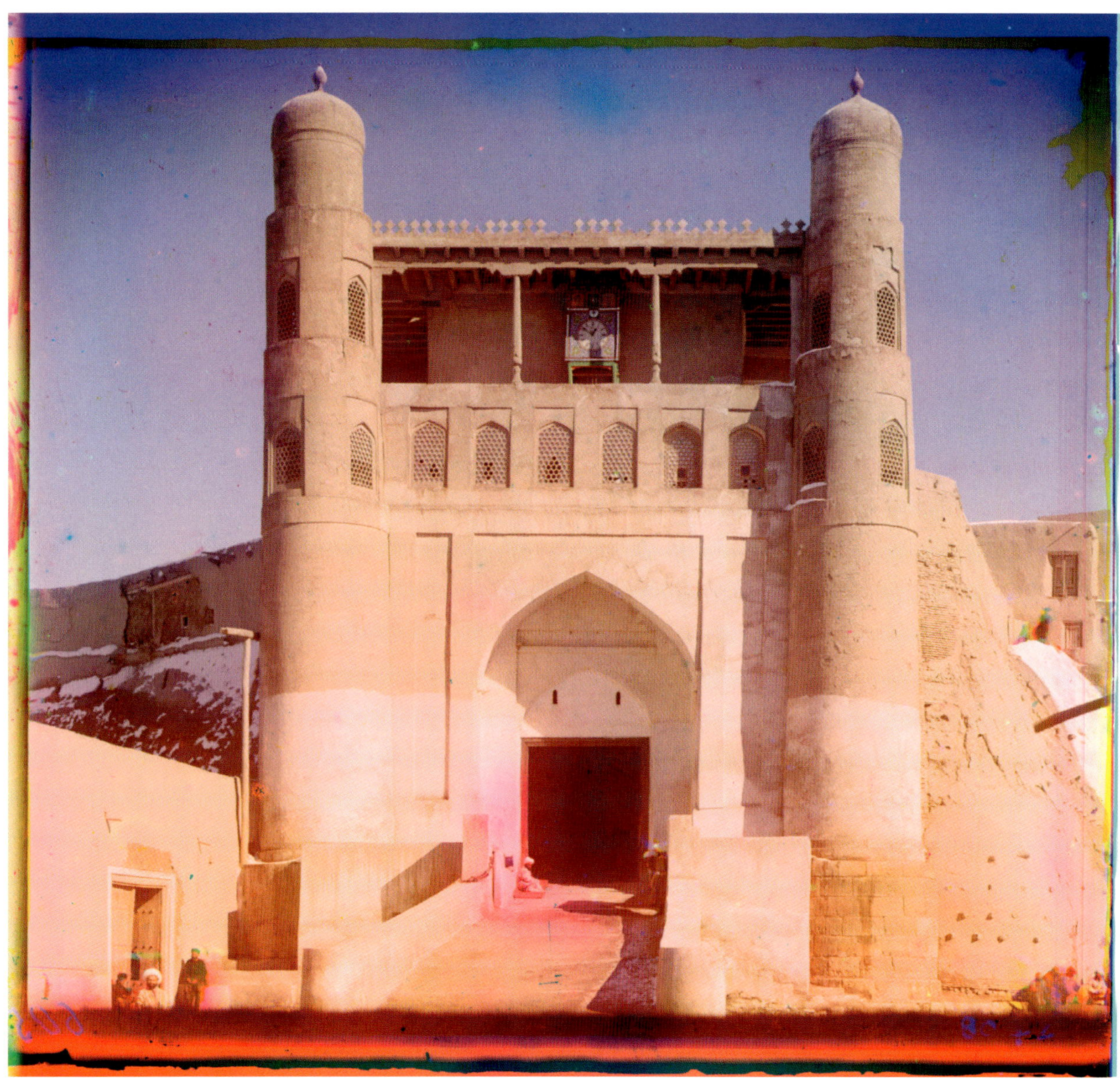

height. (This does not include the stork's nest that graces this and most other minarets in Bukhara. Tradition considers the nest to be a mark of Allah's favor.) Prokudin-Gorsky photographed this monument from the perspective of a nearby alley, which gives a sense of the tower's scale. My photographs include a view from another alley with the adjacent Miri Arab Madrasa. The minaret is the one part of the great Poi-Kalyan ensemble (see below) to have survived from the twelfth century. After considerable technical difficulties that led to the collapse of the first version, the minaret was completed in 1127 during the reign of Arslankhan.

BUKHARA Ark (citadel). Main entrance. PROKUDIN-GORSKY 21871. JANUARY 1907.

BUKHARA Ark. Main entrance and south wall. BRUMFIELD, MAY 12, 1972.

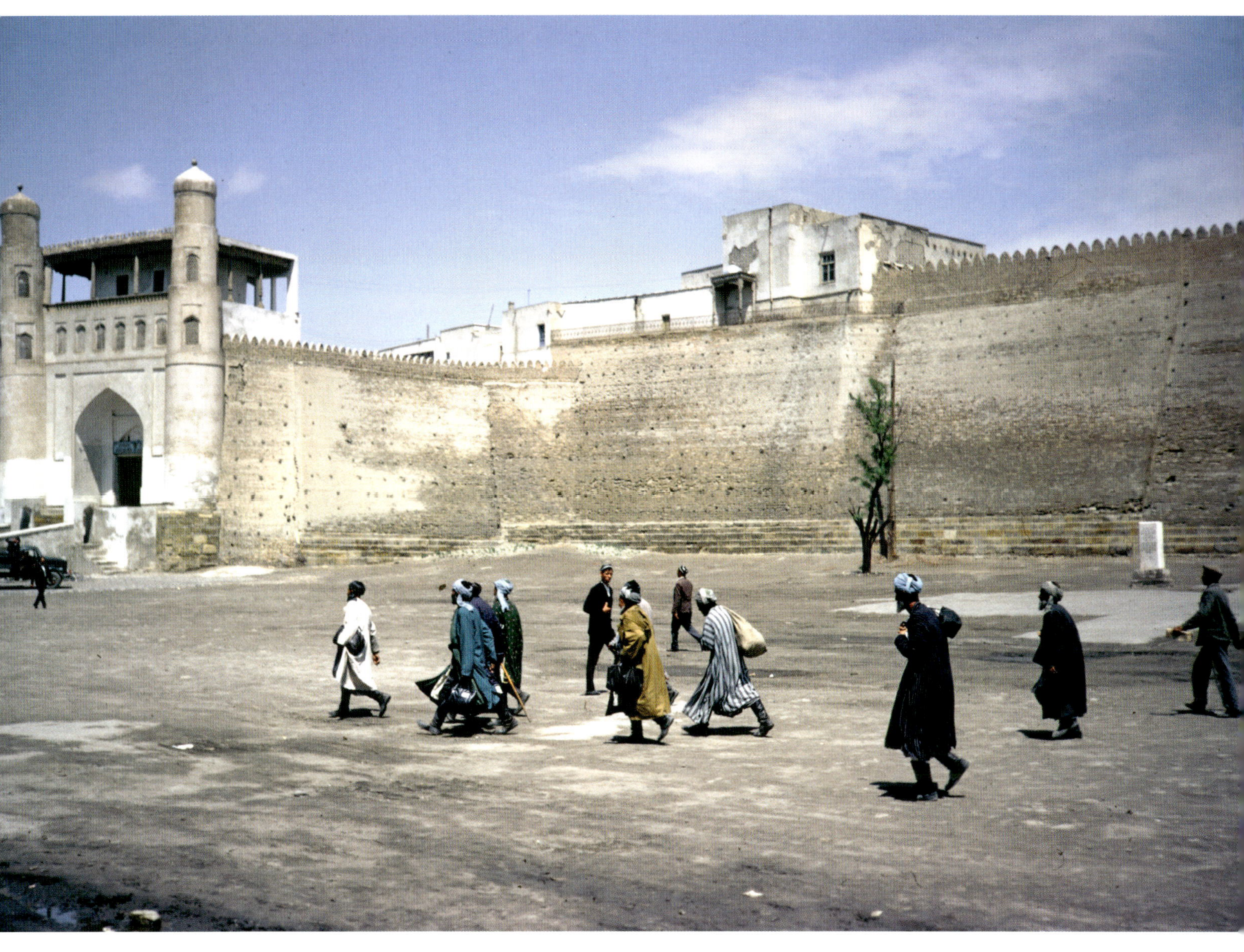

The successive rings of decorative brick courses, some of which show traces of blue ceramic glaze, taper sharply from a massive base to the lantern, with its sixteen window niches. The structure culminates in a well-preserved "stalactite" cornice.

The Kalyan Minaret is part of a monumental ensemble known as the Poi-Kalyan ("Footrest of the Great One"). Adjacent to the minaret is the city's main place of worship, the Kalyan Mosque, an open court structure completed in 1514 on the site of a twelfth-century mosque. Within these walls, which contain an area of one hectare, as many as ten thousand worshippers could gather for prayers at the call of the muezzin. After decades of neglect, the mosque is now restored. The Poi-Kalyan complex is completed

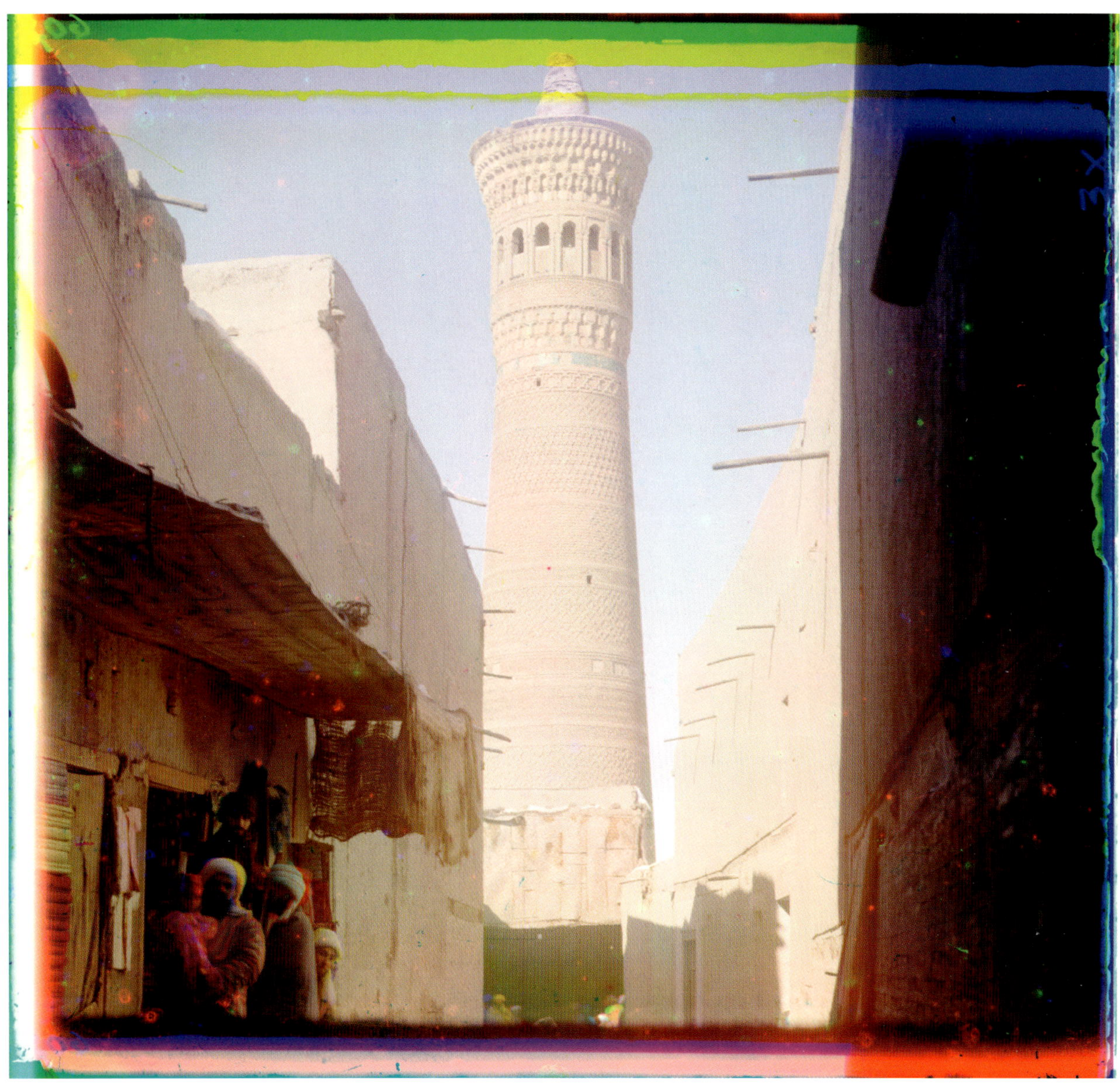

by the Miri Arab Madrasa, whose main portal faces that of the Kalyan Mosque. Commissioned in the early sixteenth century by sheikh Miri-Arab Yemani, a spiritual adviser to Ubaidulla-khan, the madrasa was apparently financed by the sale of some three thousand Persian Moslems of the Shiite sect into slavery. (In the sixteenth-century conflict between the Shiite and Sunni sects intensified both in Persia, where Shi'a triumphed with the Safavid dynasty, and in Central Asia.). The Miri Arab was arranged according to the traditional plan for the madrasa: a rectangular court with four iwan (main or entrance arch) structures on the axes, sur-

BUKHARA Kalyan Minaret. Poi Kolian ensemble. PROKUDIN-GORSKY 20003. JANUARY 1907.

BUKHARA Kalyan Minaret. *Left*: Miri-Arab Madrasa. BRUMFIELD, MAY 12, 1972.

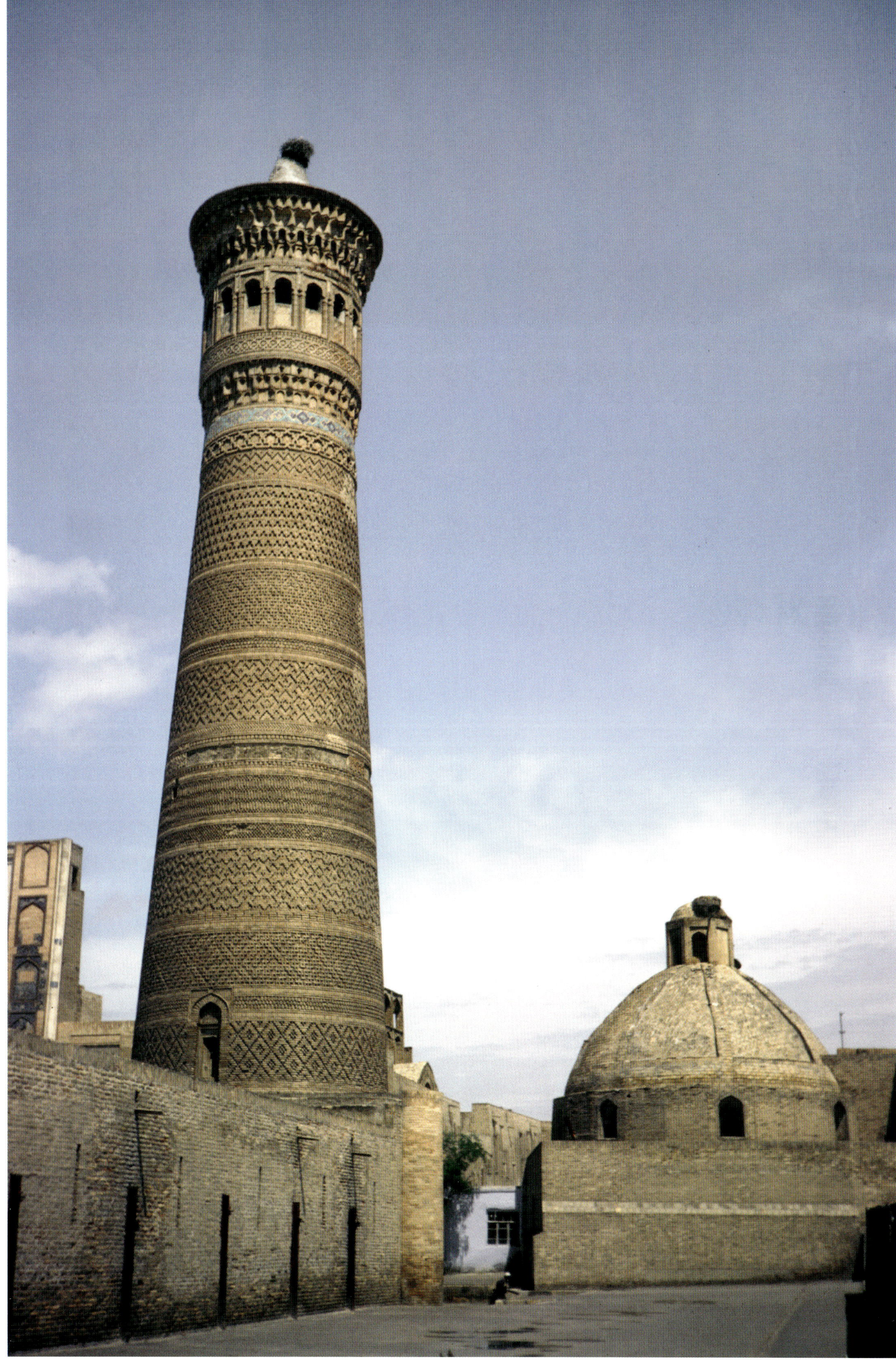

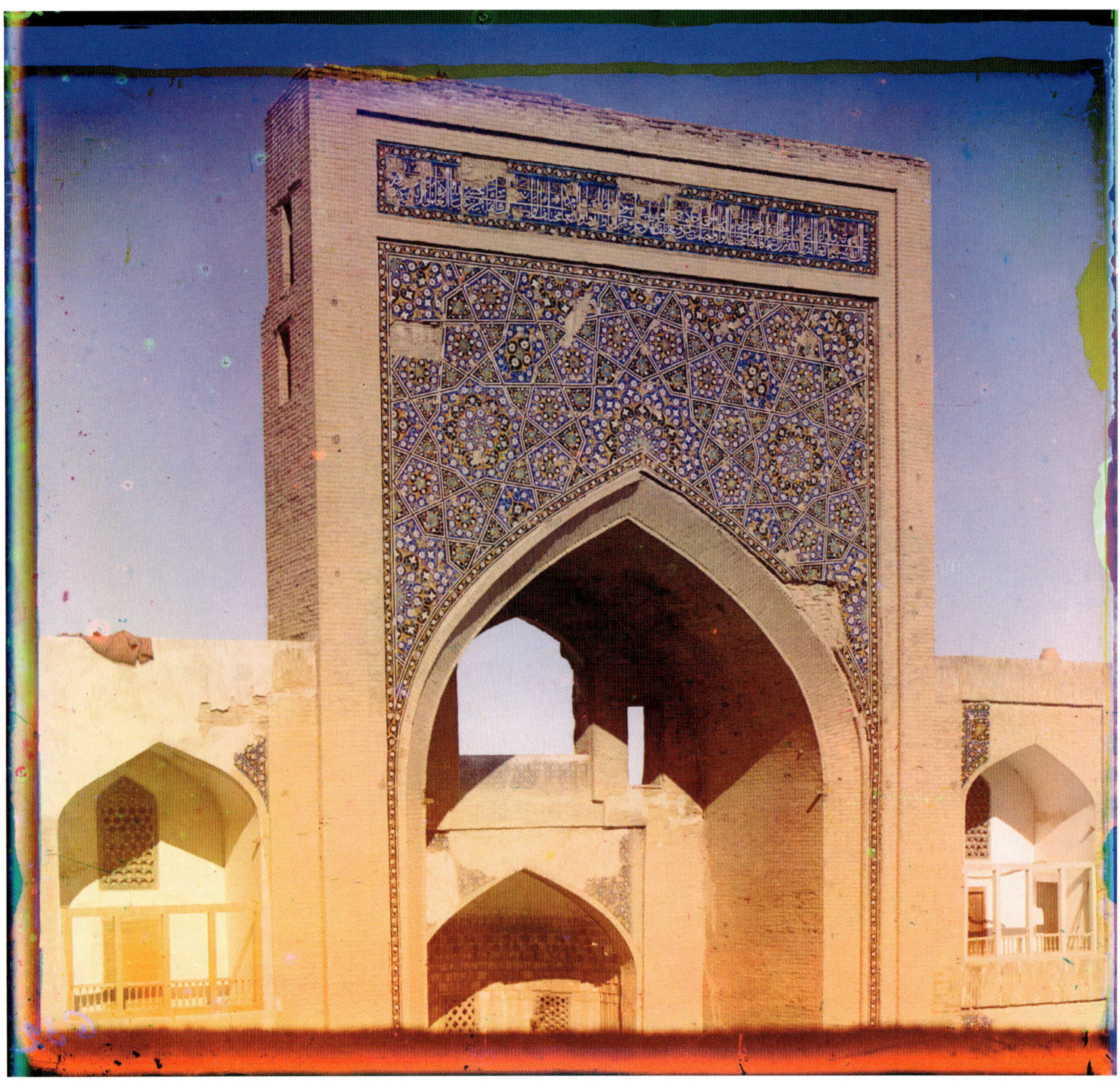

rounded by two stories of cells (*khudzhri*) connected by an open arcade decorated with ceramic tile. Prokudin-Gorsky photographed the best-preserved iwan, with its magnificent ceramic facade. My 1972 photograph shows a remarkable similarity, even to the areas of loss. However impressive the exterior decoration, the interior of the cells provided little in the way of comfort: a small, poorly ventilated space used for study, meals, and sleep. During the late Soviet period, the Miri Arab Madrasa was restored and served as the region's sole institution for the study of Islam.

The most impressive accomplishment of the Astrakha-

BUKHARA Miri Arab Madrasa. Poi Kolian ensemble. Courtyard. Iwan arch. PROKUDIN-GORSKY 21876. JANUARY 1907.

BUKHARA Miri Arab Madrasa. Courtyard. Iwan arch, flanked by rooms (*hujra*) for scholars. BRUMFIELD, MAY 12, 1972.

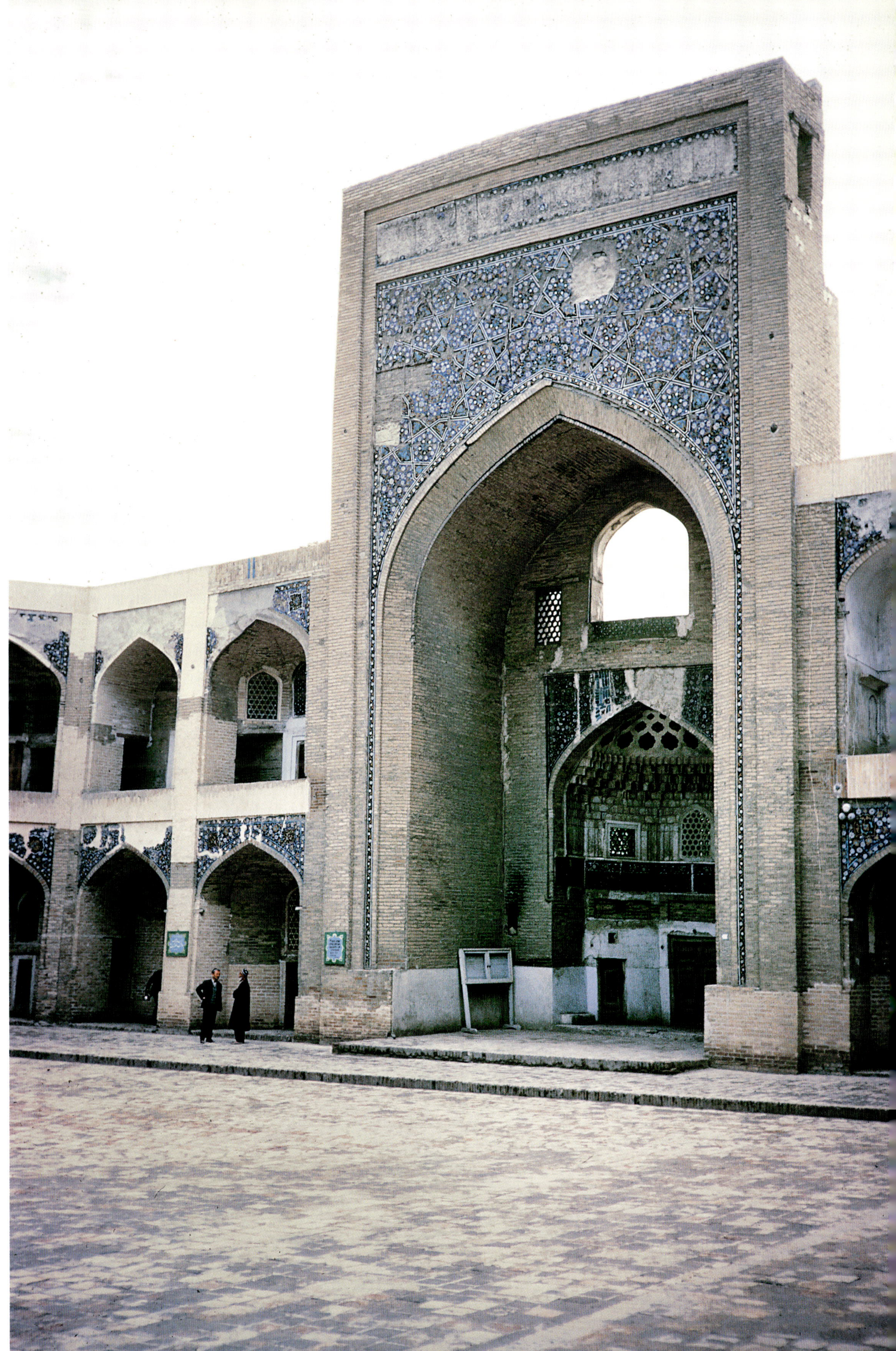

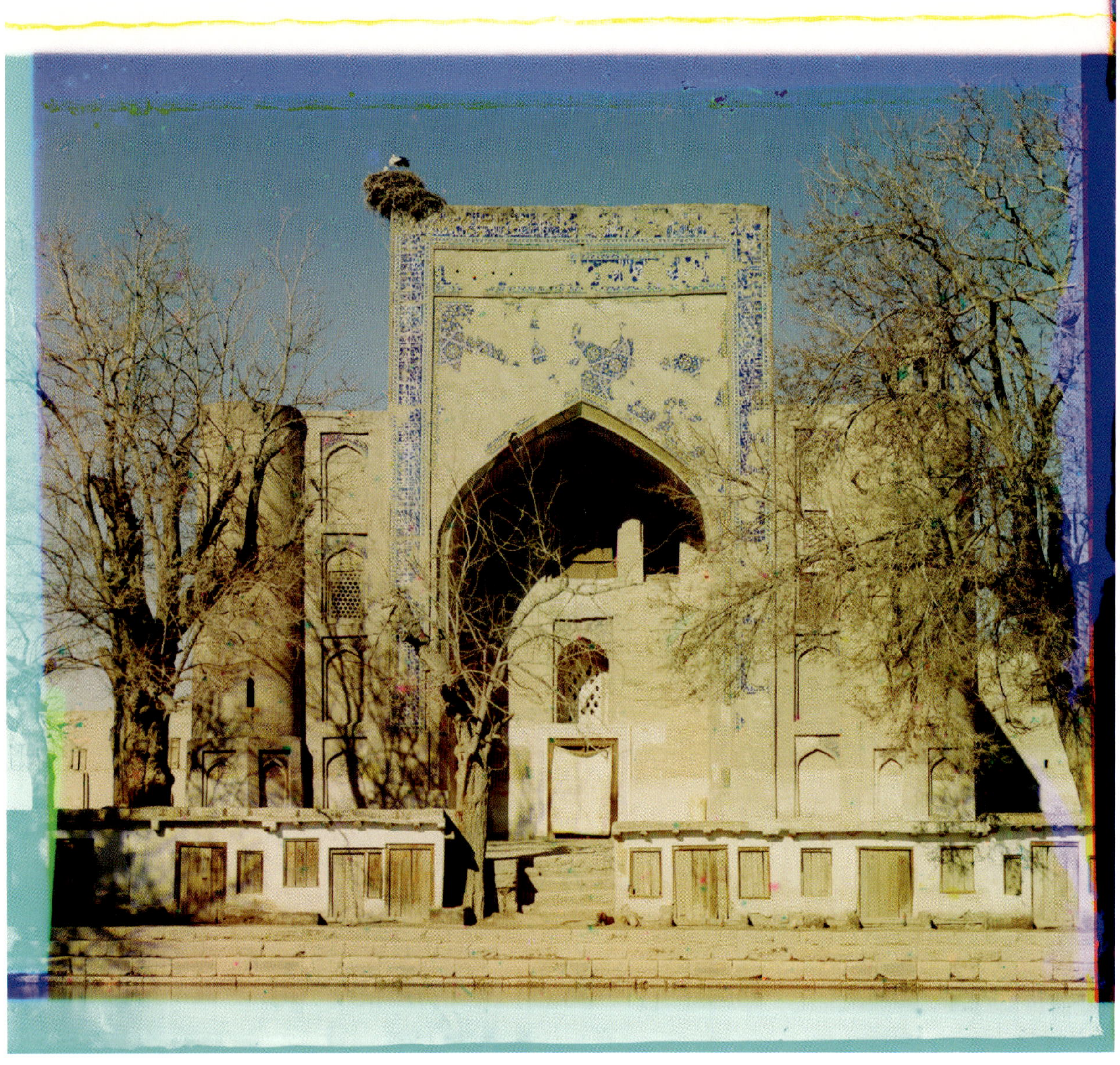

nid dynasty in the seventeenth century lay not in the construction and decoration of mosques but in its organization of urban space. The best example, combining both aesthetic and practical considerations, is the Liabi-Khauz ensemble, a trading area containing a large square reservoir that not only provided a source of water but also served as a reflecting pool for the surrounding buildings. The oldest of these, the Kukeldash Madrasa (1578), was constructed during the reign of Sahibanid Abdulla-khan (1557–1598). The reservoir and the two other buildings in the complex—the Madrasa and the Khanaka of Nadir Divan-begi—were built in the

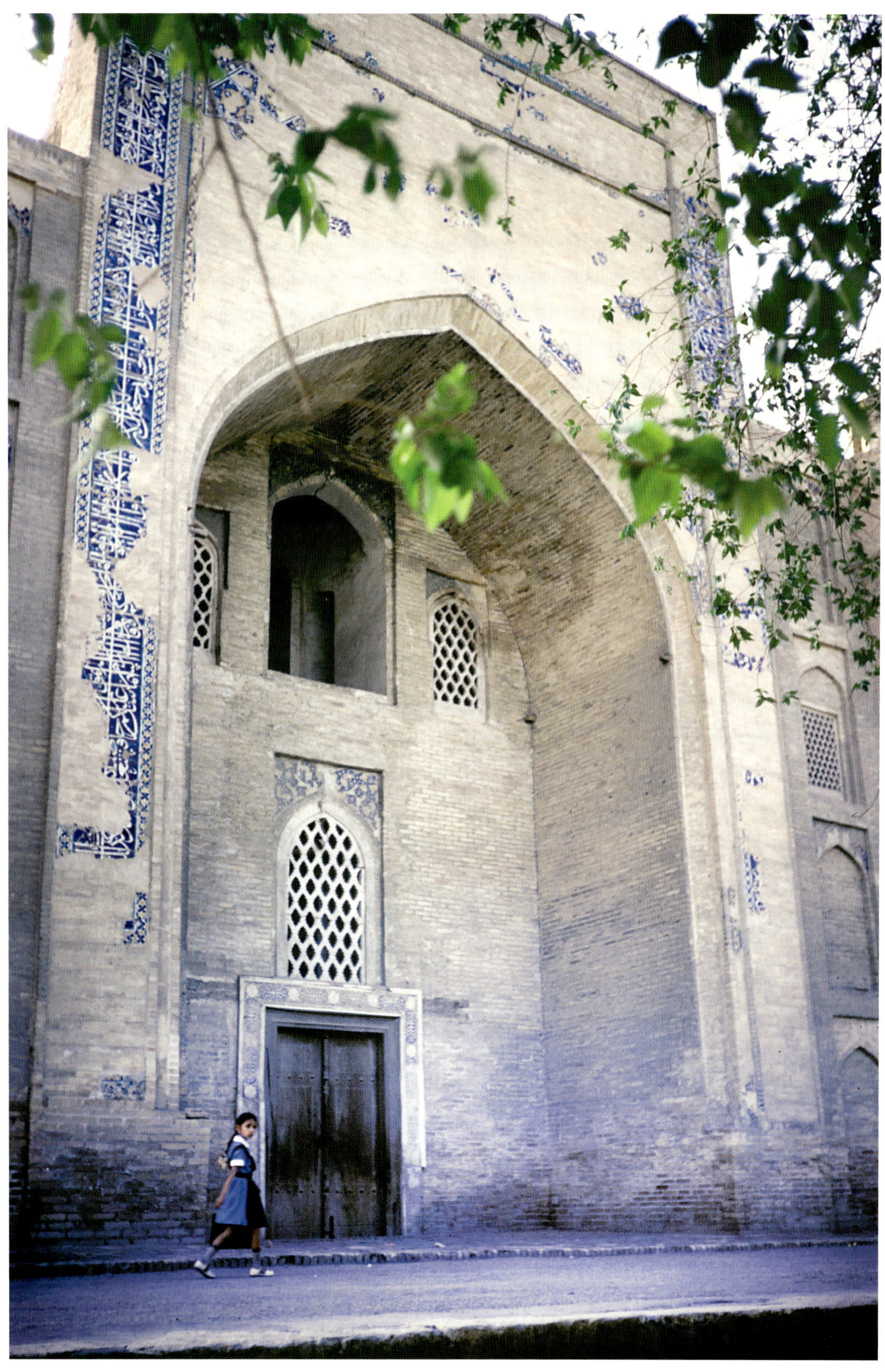

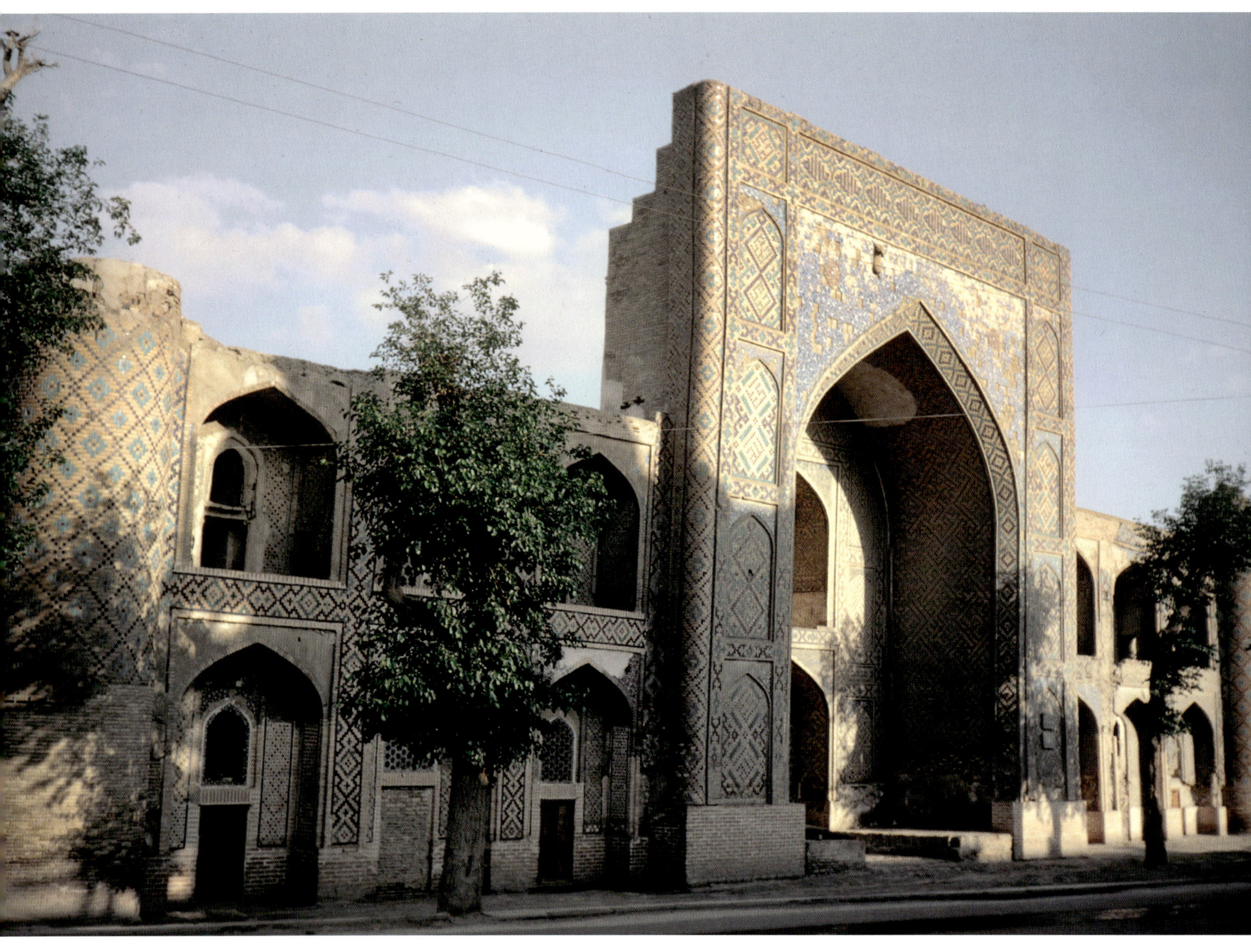

1620s by Nadir Divan-begi, vizier (minister) of Imam Kuli-khan. The *khanaka* (roughly equivalent to a monastery) and the madrasa face each other across the pool.

In addition to a view of the Madrasa of Nadir Divan-begi, Prokudin-Gorsky took a clear view of the Khanaka of Nadir Divan-begi across the pool. My photographs include a close view with a young girl in Soviet-era school uniform. Although the Madrasa and Khanaka of Nadir Divan-begi are typical examples of Astrakhanid architecture, they form an exquisite ensemble. With the restoration of the reservoir, its stepped embankment, and the adjacent park, Liabi-

BUKHARA Modari-khan Madrasa. Main facade with peshtak and entrance arch. BRUMFIELD, MAY 13, 1972.

BUKHARA Modari-khan Madrasa. Courtyard facade. PROKUDIN-GORSKY 21881. JANUARY 1907.

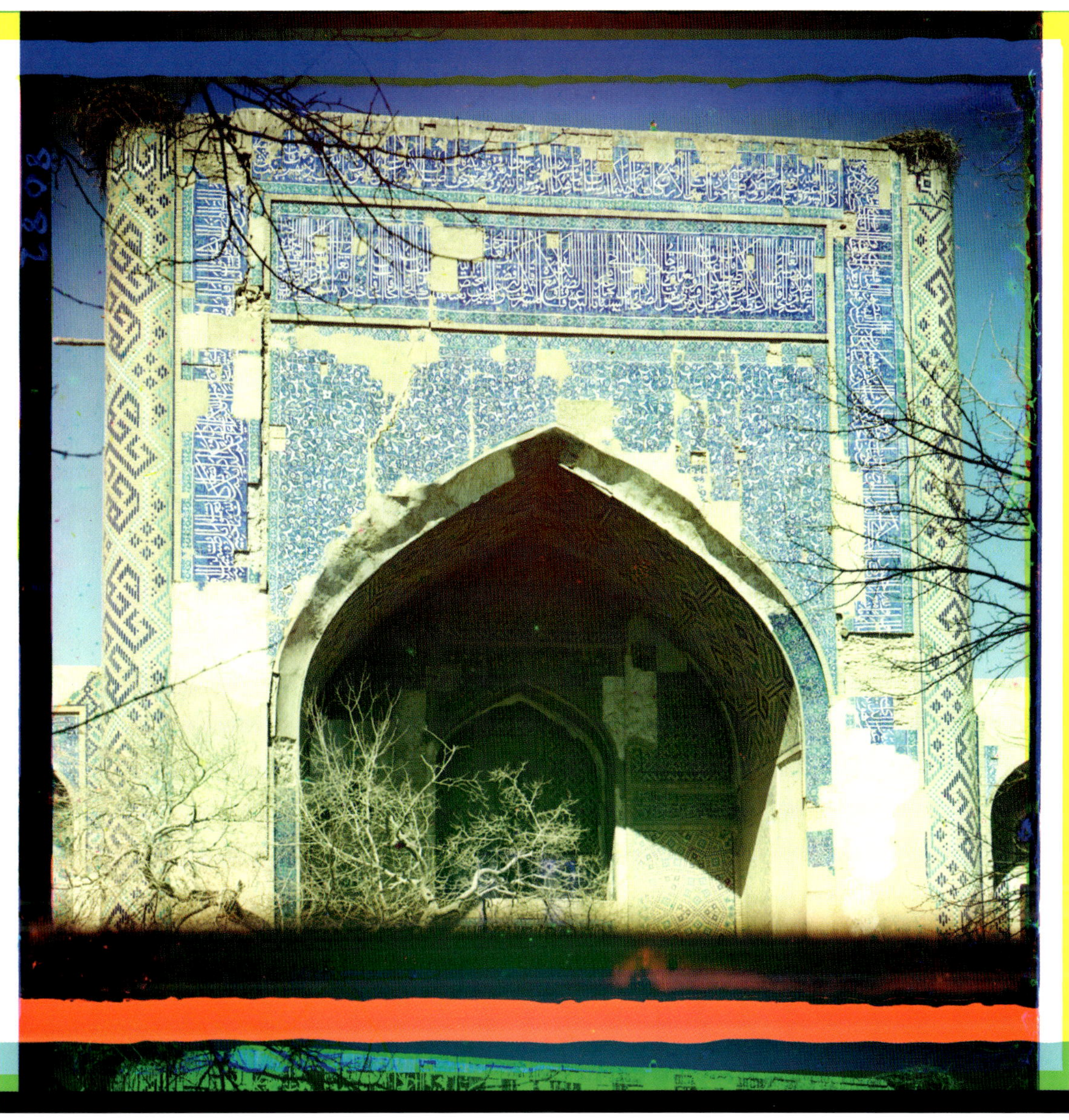

Khauz once again provides the residents of Bukhara with a respite from the searing heat of summer.

A distinctive feature of Bukhara's Islamic architecture is the *kosh medrese*, consisting of two religious schools facing each other. One is the Madori-khan Madrasa, built in 1566–67 to honor the mother of Abdulla-khan II (1534–98), the last effective ruler of the Sheibanid dynasty. In 1972 I photographed the magnificent street facade of the Modari-khan peshtak (entrance arch). Despite significant losses, the facade and iwan show an elaborate array of ceramic work, including intricate geometric and floral patterns with intertwining tendrils. On the sides and top are remnants of large Perso-Arabic inscription bands in the Thuluth cursive style. The facade is flanked

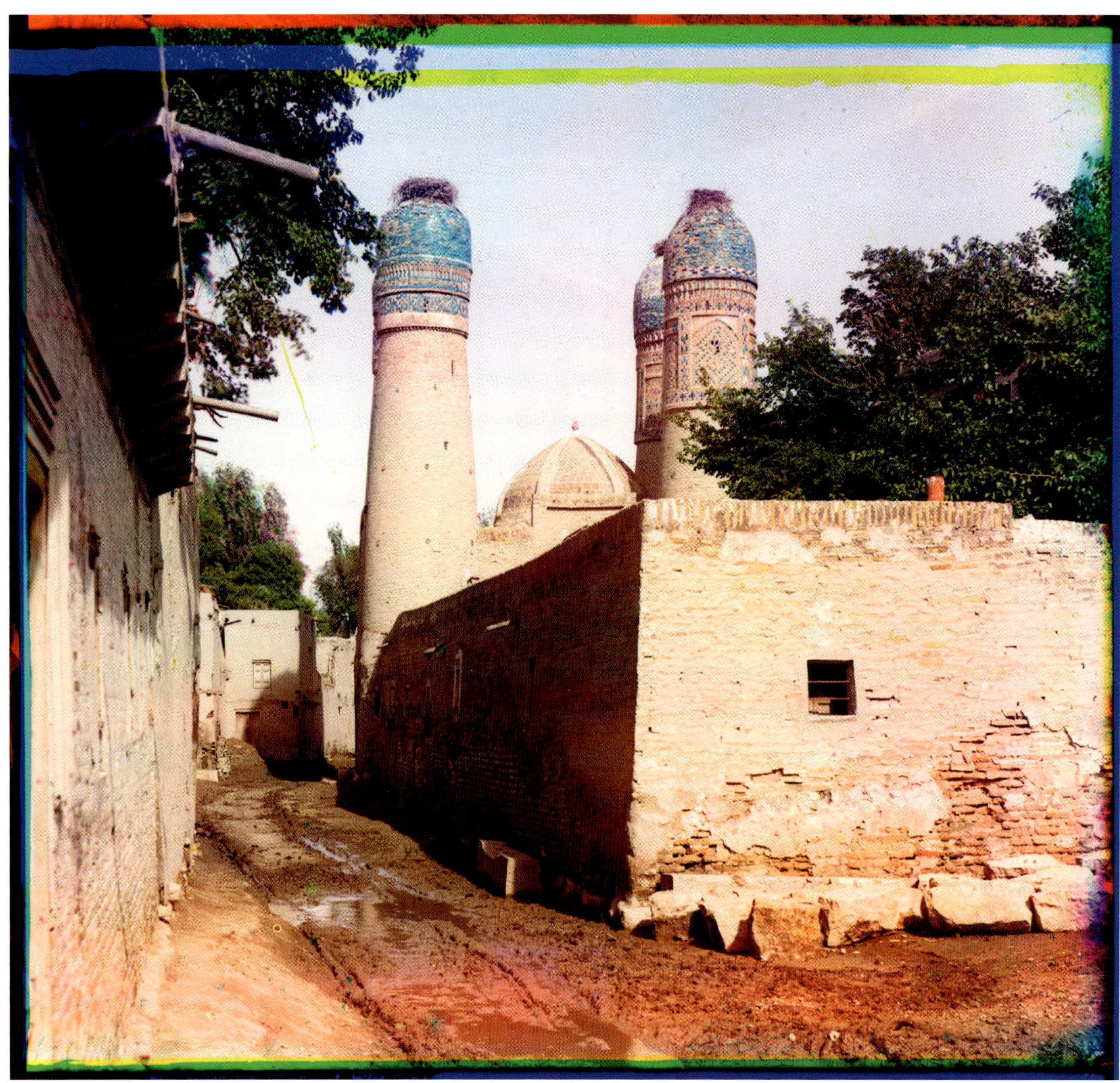

by columns with geometric tile patterns composed of Kufic letters that form words from the Kalima, the basis of the Shahada, or Islamic declaration of faith. Prokudin-Gorsky photographed the courtyard facade of the same structure.

With the decline of Astrakhanid power and a concomitant increase in feudal disorder and oppression during the eighteenth century, Bukhara entered a period of stagnation that would extend into the twentieth century. The effects of this decline were noticeable in architecture. During a period of some two centuries, there were few buildings of any architectural significance. One of them, the Char Minar

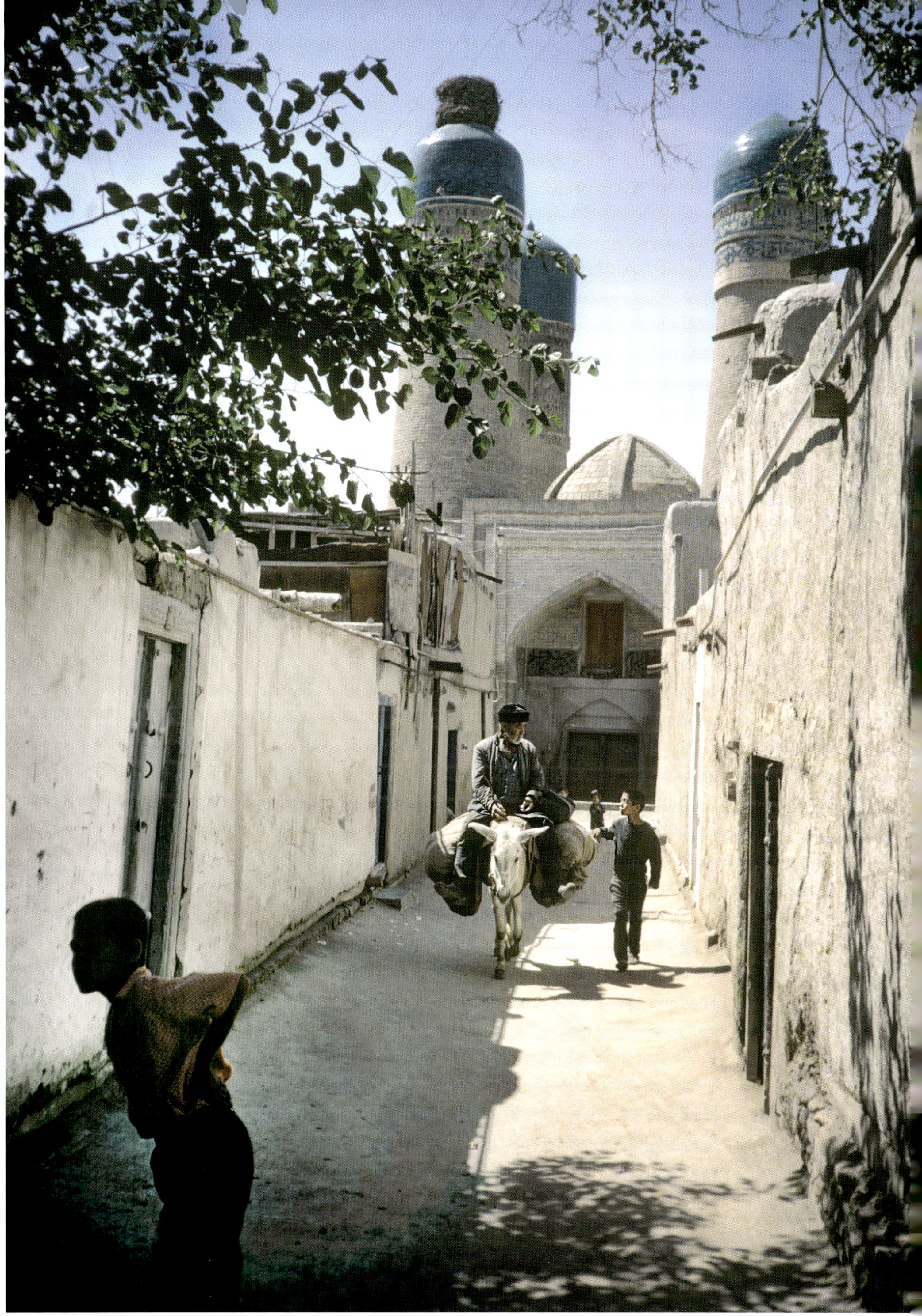

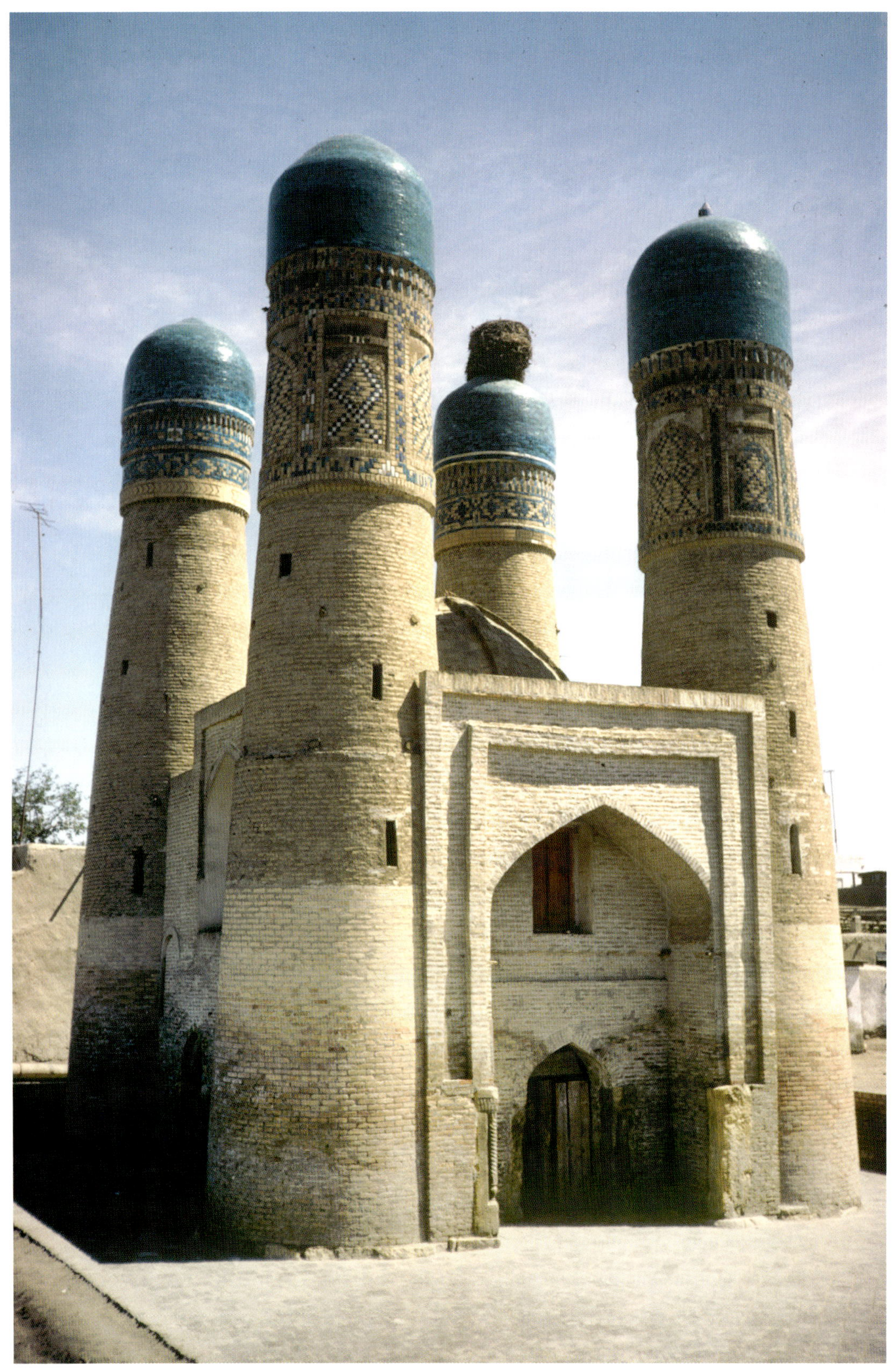

BUKHARA Char Minar Mosque. Main facade after excavation and conservation work.

BRUMFIELD, MAY 14, 1972.

("Four Minarets") Mosque is among the most appealing monuments in the city, despite its modest size. Built in 1807 as part of a *khauz*, or reservoir, ensemble, the domed structure with four towers (not, in fact, minarets) served as a covered entrance to the madrasa of Caliph Niiazkul. Prokudin-Gorsky took two views from the street, of which the closer is included here. I photographed the mosque from the opposite alleyway and in a close view that shows the preservation efforts undertaken during the Soviet period.

SAMARKAND

During a trip in 1911 Prokudin-Gorsky gave special attention to the Islamic architecture of Samarkand—the city of Tamerlane, the "Radiant Center of the Earth," captured by Alexander the Great, sacked by Genghis Khan, and now administrative center of Samarkand oblast in contemporary Uzbekistan. Samarkand contains some of the greatest landmarks of Islamic architecture, including Gur Emir ("Tomb of the Ruler"), the burial place of the Timur (Tamerlane). The monument was begun by Timur in 1403 in memory of his grandson Muhammed Sultan, who had founded a madrasa on this site in the late fourteenth century. Following Timur's unexpected death from pneumonia in 1405, his body was also placed in the structure, which became the mausoleum of the Timurids. It was completed by another of Timur's grandsons, the astronomer-king Ulugh Beg.

Prokudin-Gorsky's view from the east side shows severe damage to the ceramic ornamentation of the ribbed dome. The cylinder beneath the dome as well as the facades of the structure are adorned with sacred inscriptions. Prokudin-Gorsky's photographs of this monument are an indispensable documentary record of their condition. They also reflect Russian interest in the cultural monuments of Turkestan and their preservation. The photograph from 1972 shows the results of Soviet-era restoration work, including the ceramic tiles that cover the ribs of the dome. My photographs include a west view of the structure after a May rain shower.

The defining Timurid mosque was Bibi Khanim, among the greatest in Central Asia. Built in 1399–1405 with the spoils of Tamerlane's campaign in India in 1398, Bibi Khanym was named in homage to Tamerlane's senior wife, Sarai Mulk Khanym. Among Prokudin-Gorsky's photographs of the monuments is a general view of the rectangular courtyard, which centers on the Main, or Friday, Mosque (on right). The photograph from 1972 offers a similar spectacle of grand ruin. Prokudin-Gorsky's closer views reveal con-

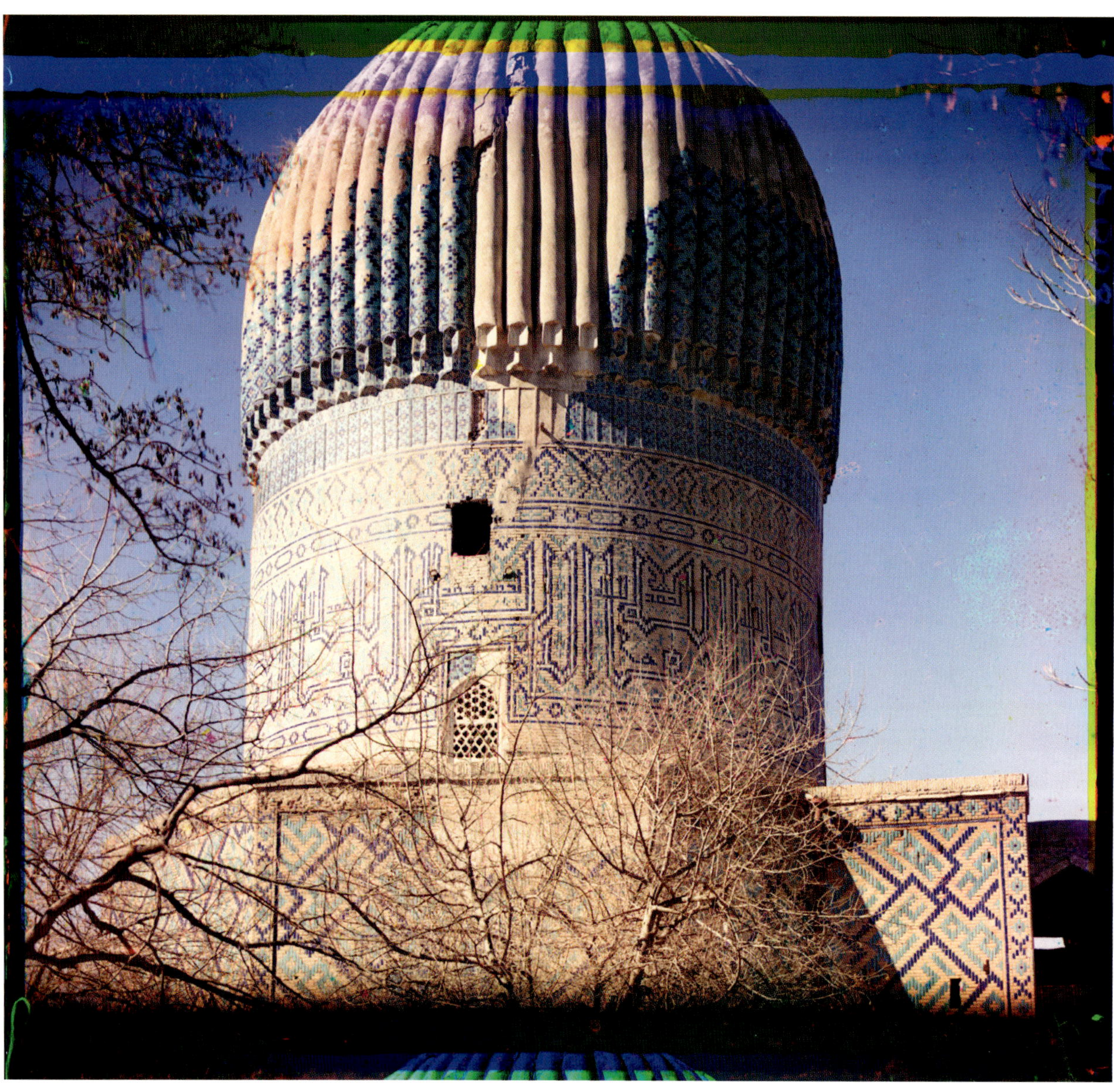

SAMARKAND Gur Emir (Timurid mausoleum). Burial place of Tamerlane. East view. PROKUDIN-GORSKY 21731. JANUARY 1907.

SAMARKAND Gur Emir (Timurid mausoleum). West view after thunderstorm. BRUMFIELD, MAY 16, 1972.

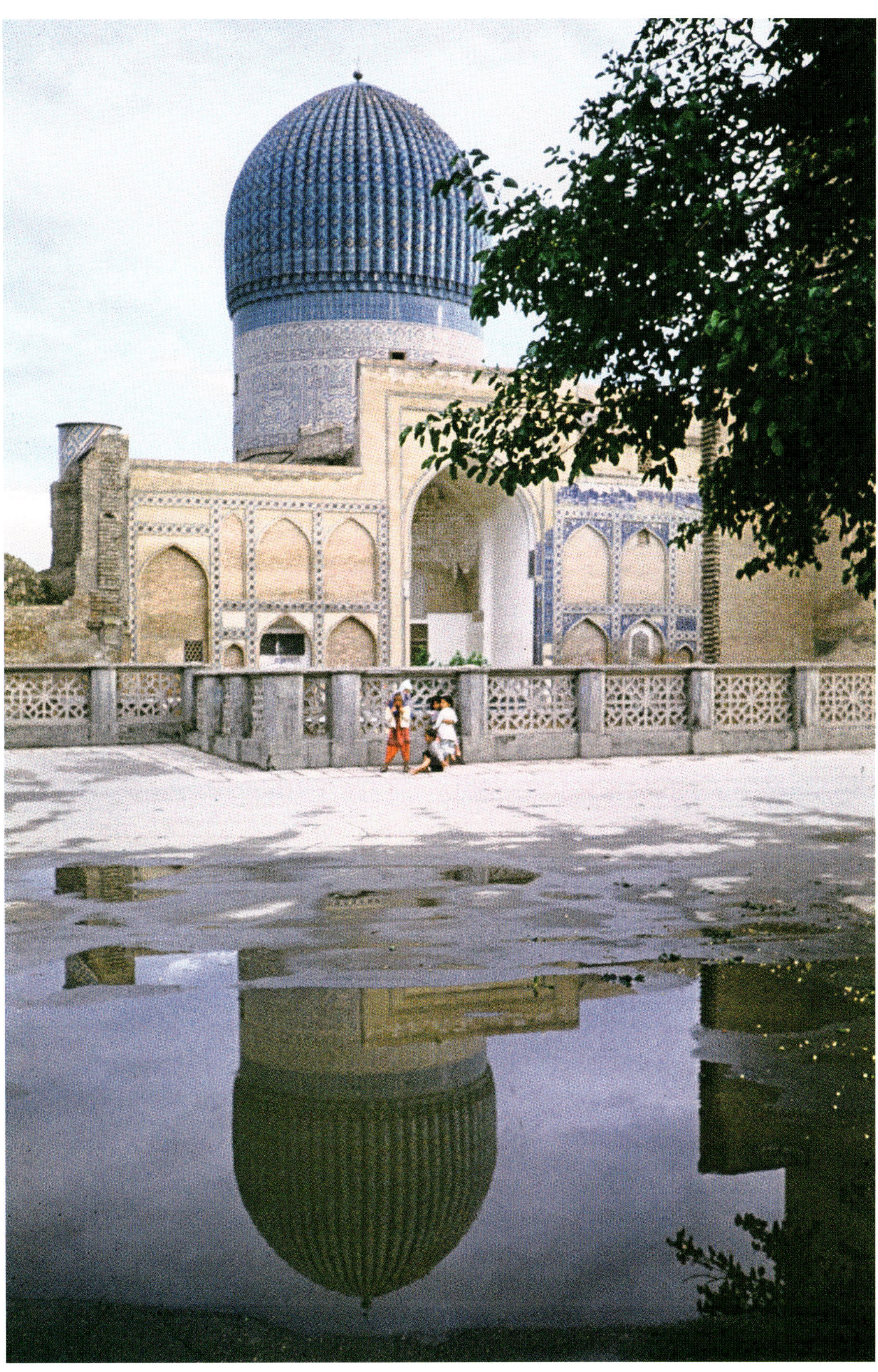

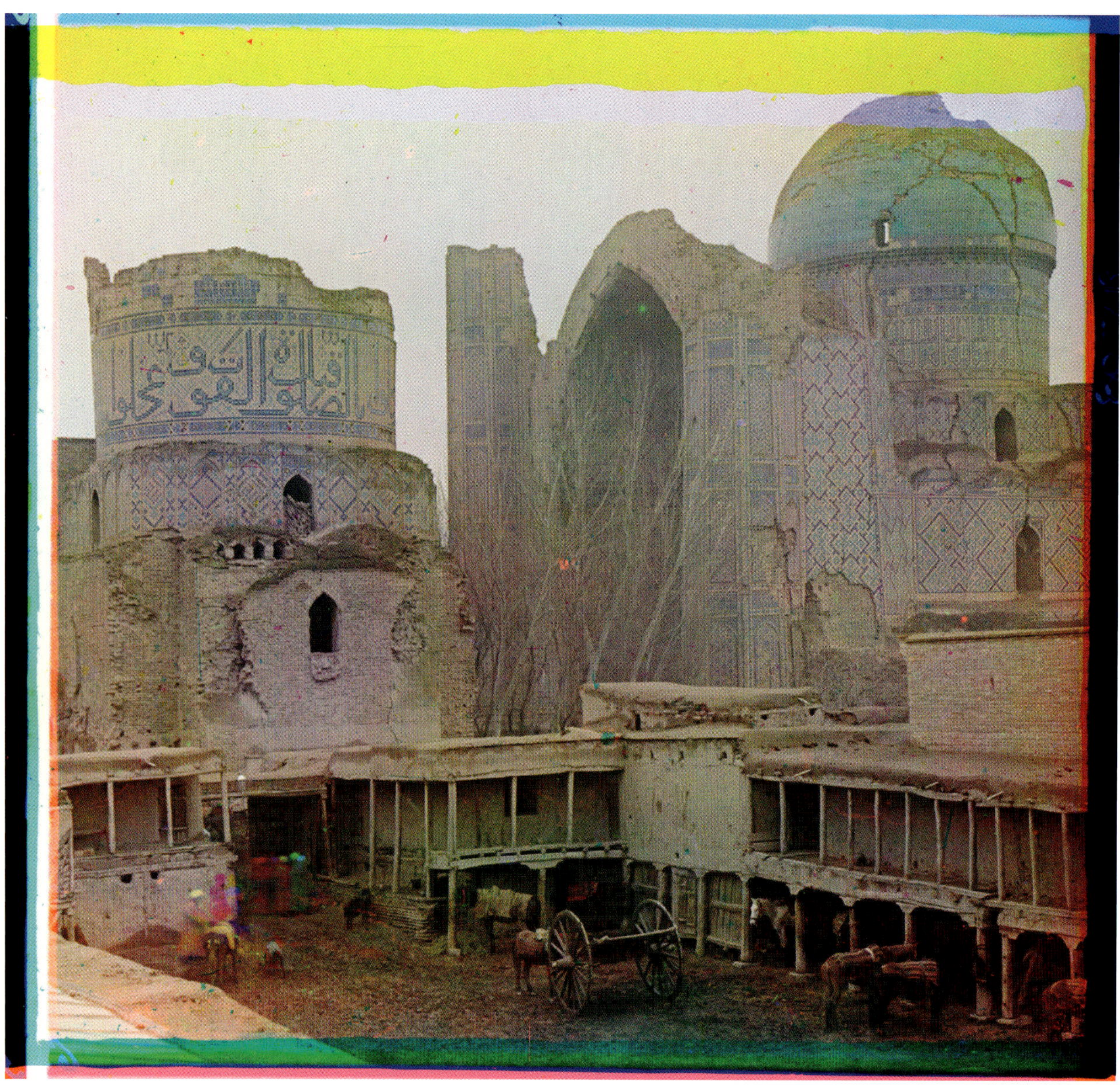

siderable damage, particularly after an earthquake in 1897. Yet much of the ceramic ornamentation remained, as my photograph reveals. One of Prokudin-Gorsky's detailed views shows elaborate ceramic work on the right minaret (mistakenly identified as "left" in his original note) that flanks the entrance arch. Although the walls show severe damage, much is visible of the original ceramic ornamentation, including interlocking star patterns and faience panels on the polygonal minaret.

The center of Samarkand is graced by the exquisite Registan ensemble, consisting of three religious schools (*ma-*

SAMARKAND Bibi Khanym architectural ensemble. PROKUDIN-GORSKY 21835. JANUARY 1907.

SAMARKAND Bibi Khanym ensemble. Ruins of main entrance structure. BRUMFIELD, MAY 15, 1972.

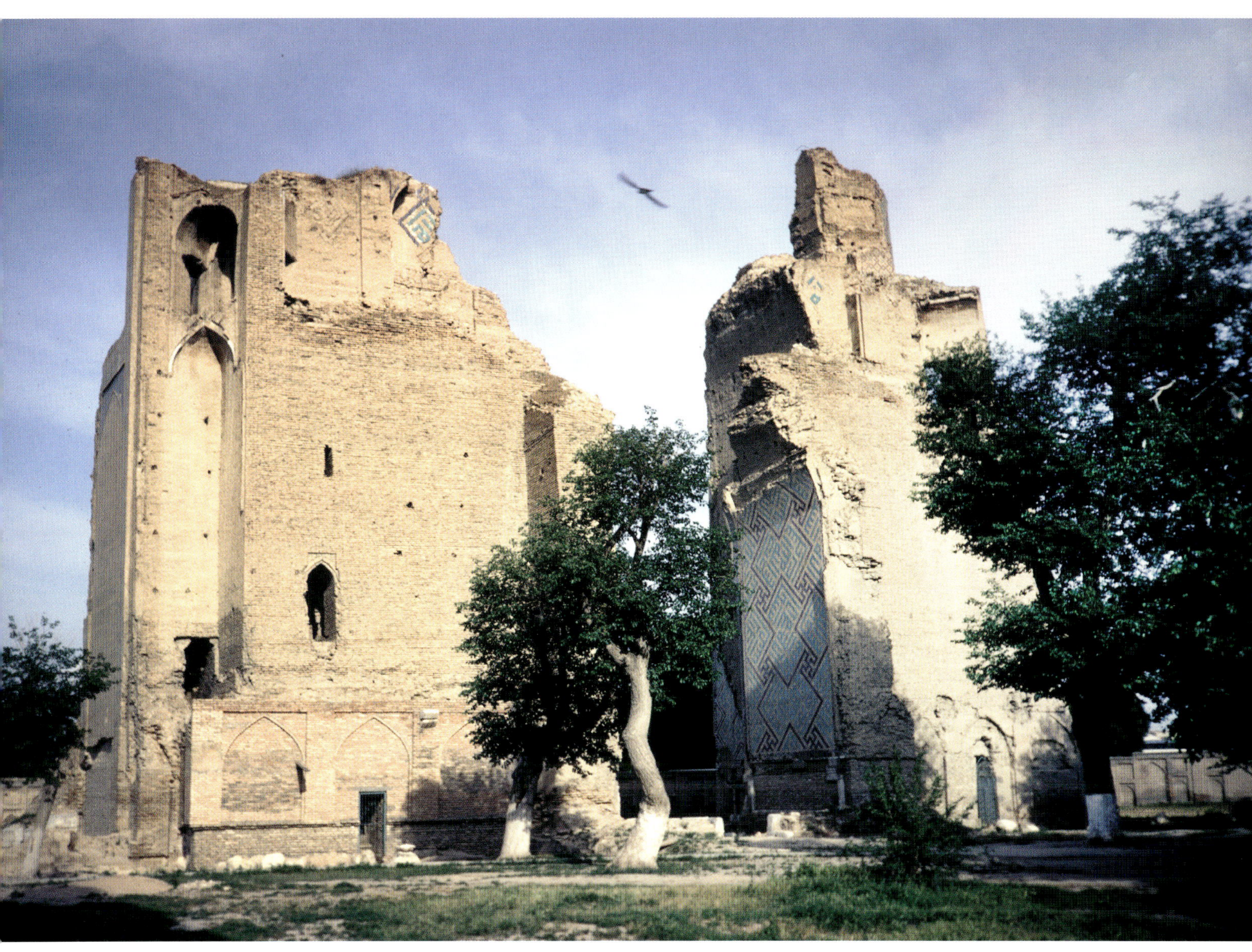

drasa) that were among the most distinguished in Islam. The square is framed by two surpassing structures of similar design—the Ulugh Beg Madrasa and the Shir Dor Madrasa. The oldest component is the Ulugh Beg Madrasa, built in 1417–20 by the scholar-king Ulugh Beg (1393?–1449), grandson of Timur. Shown here is the main facade with the great iwan arch at the entrance. The facade displays remnants of polychrome ceramic ornamentation, including panels of geometric and botanical motifs, and a vertical Perso-Arabic inscription band. The walls also display monumental geometric tile figures, within which are patterns of block Kufic script that form words from the Kalima. The lens of Prokudin-Gorsky's camera captured only a portion of the grand facade. My wider lens conveys the entire facade.

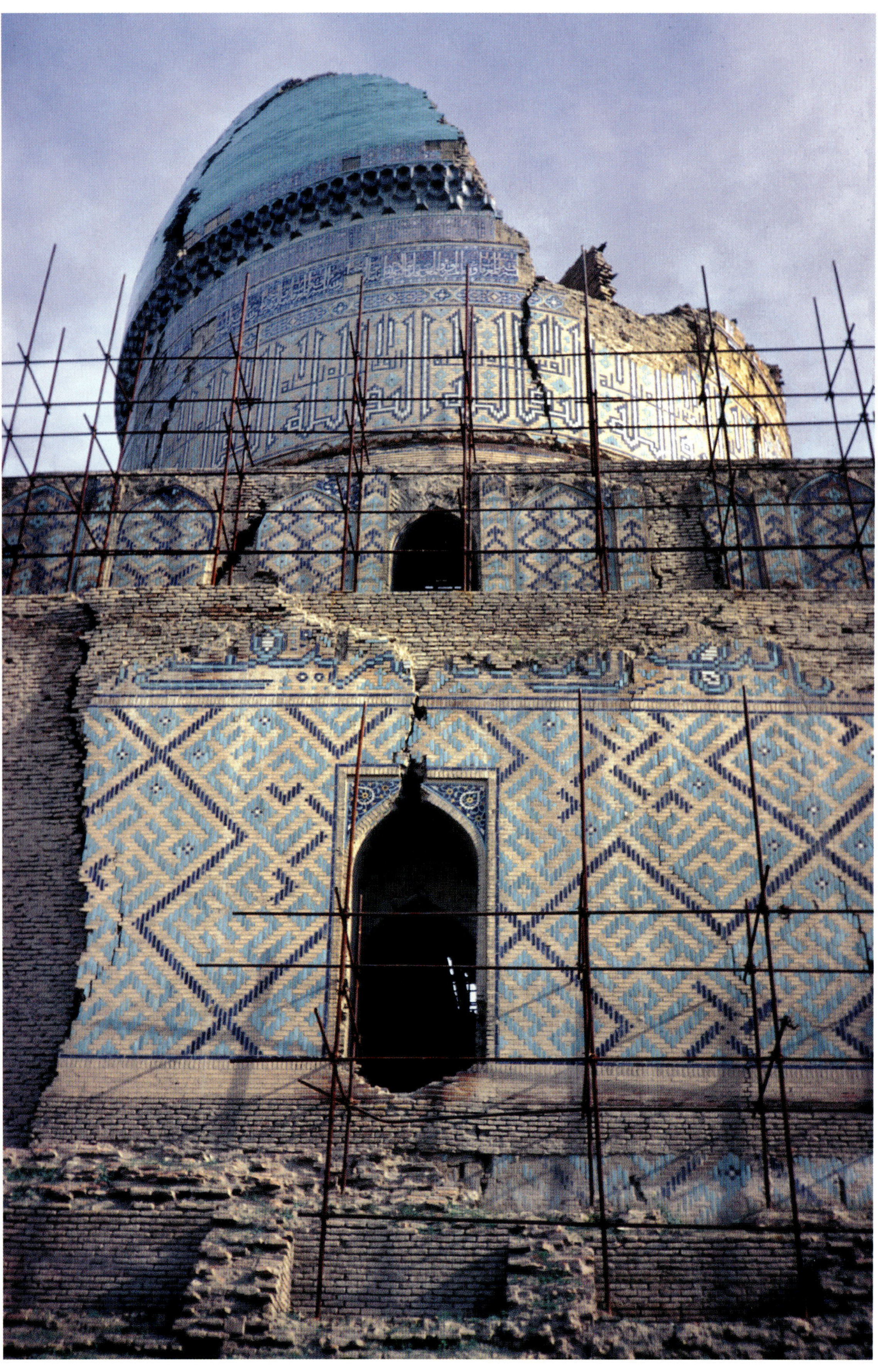

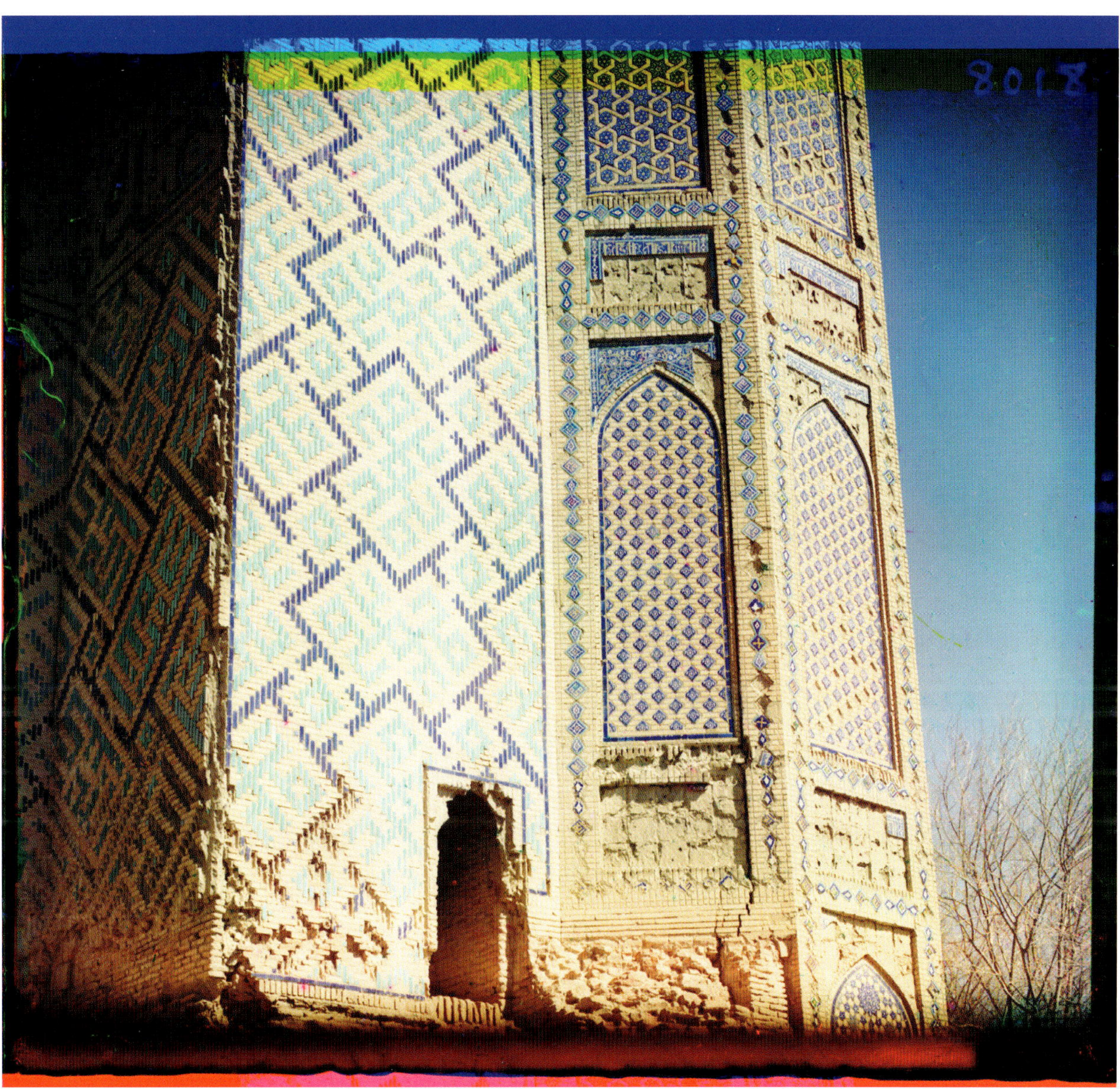

SAMARKAND Ruins of Bibi Khanym Mosque. Northwest facade. BRUMFIELD, MAY 15, 1972.

SAMARKAND Bibi Khanym Mosque. Left minaret flanking the main entrance peshtak. PROKUDIN-GORSKY 21759. JANUARY 1907.

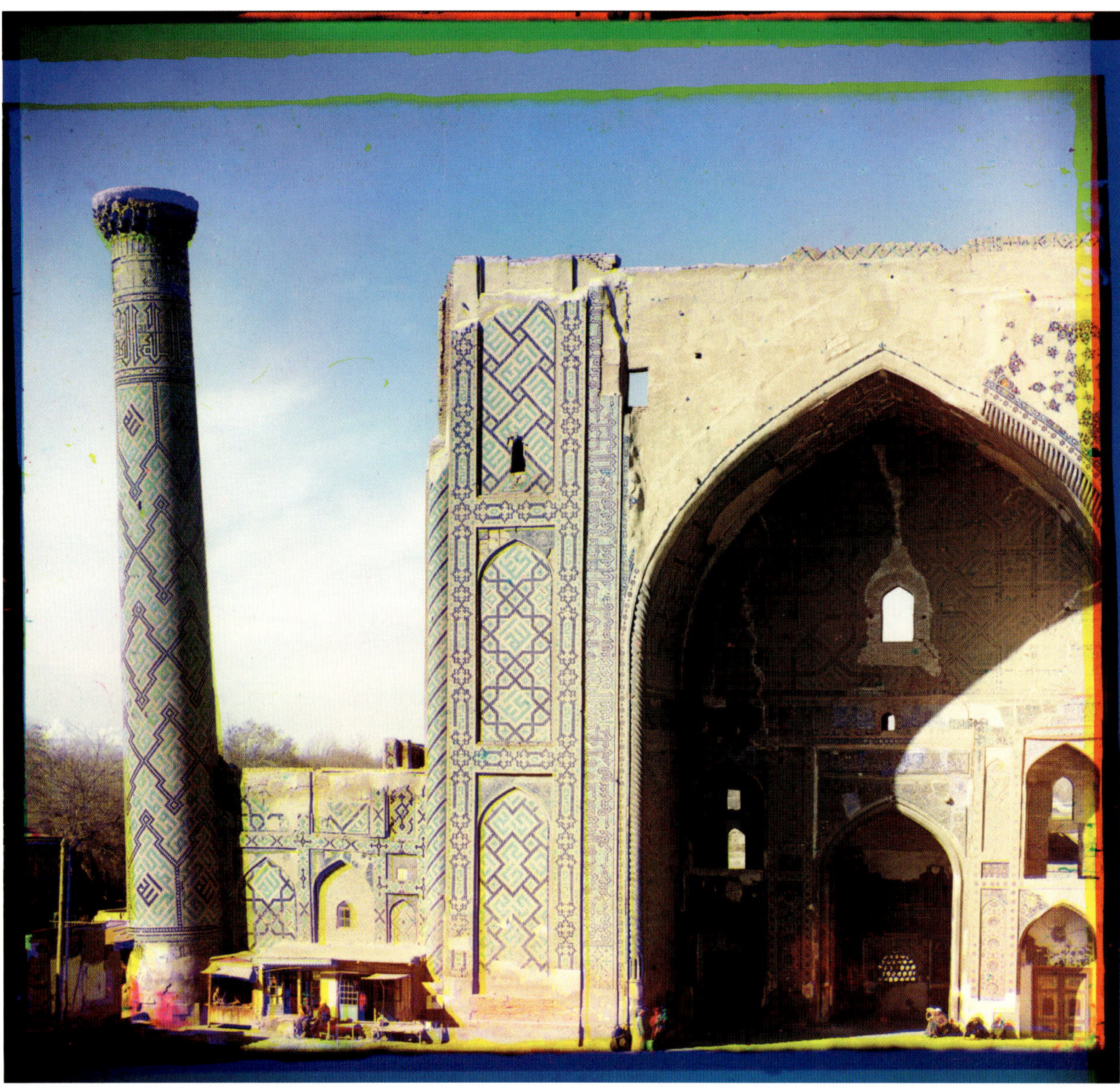

The Shir Dor Madrasa was built in 1619–36 during the Bukhara Astrakhanid dynasty. Prokudin-Gorsky's original glass negative of the spectacular polychrome facade is lost, but the contact print provides the best view of the main facade. Shown here is part of the main facade and imposing entrance iwan (on right), with a flanking minaret behind which is a ribbed dome over an instruction hall. Despite structural damage, the remarkable ceramic work is relatively well preserved. The minaret displays geometric figures integrated with words in block Kufic script from the Kalima, or Islamic declaration of faith. The cylinder supporting the

SAMARKAND Ulugh-Beg Madrasa. Left side of main facade. View across Registan Square from Shir-Dor madrasa. Noticeable lean of minaret. PROKUDIN-GORSKY 21724. JANUARY 1907.

SAMARKAND Ulugh-Beg Madrasa. Main facade. View across Registan Square from Shir-Dor Madrasa. BRUMFIELD, MAY 15, 1972.

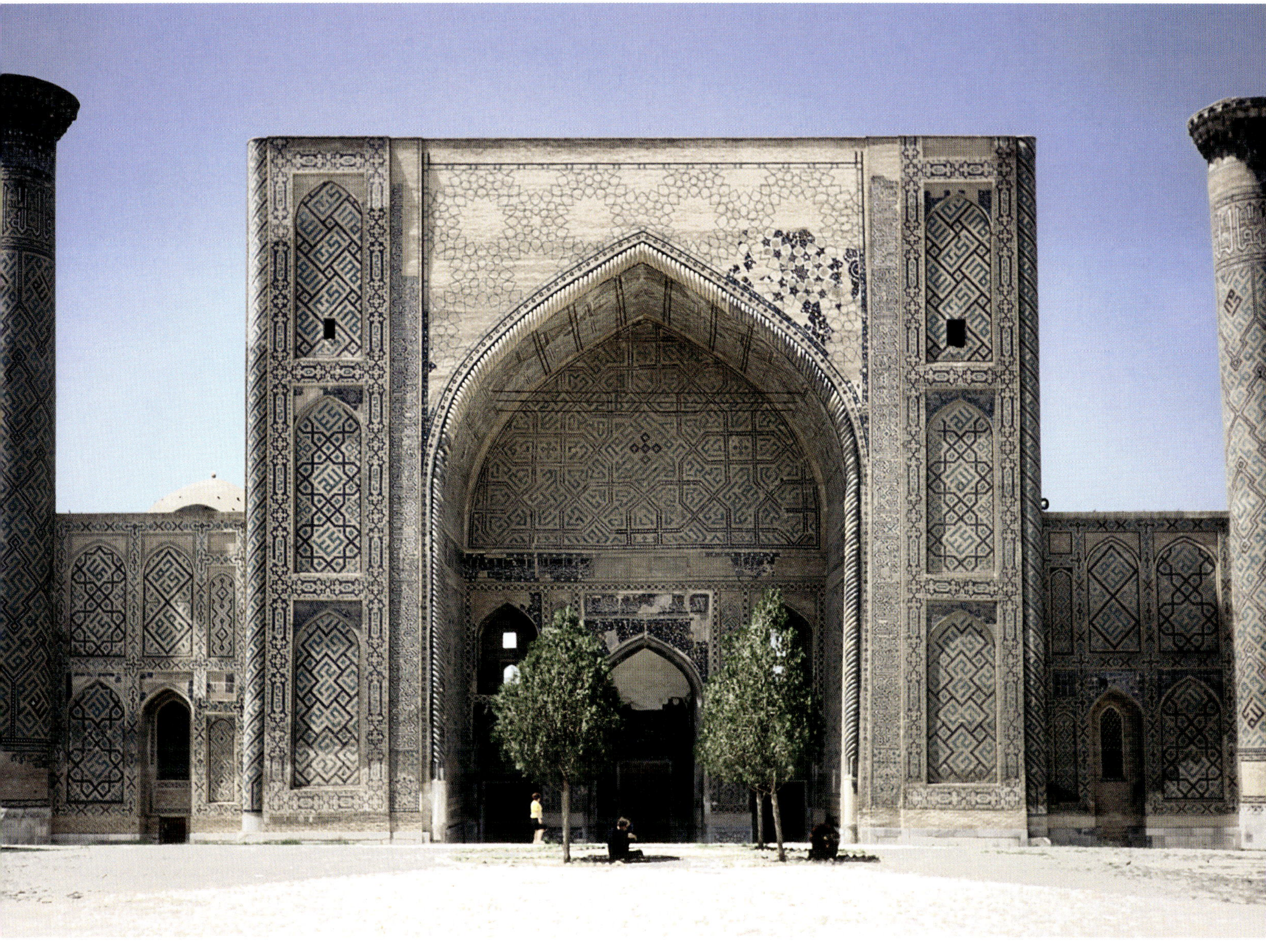

dome contains intricate inscription bands as well as faience panels. My views through a wide lens show the extent of the main facade.

Fortunately, the original negatives of Prokudin-Gorsky's detailed photographs of the main facade have survived. One view shows the left side of the main facade and iwan (on right). At the corner is an attached minaret, behind which is a ribbed dome over an instruction hall. Despite structural damage, the profuse ceramic work is relatively well preserved. The minaret displays geometric figures integrated with words in block Kufic script from the Kalima. The cylinder supporting the dome contains inscription bands as well as faience panels. In my decades of photographic work, I have never been more impressed than by the moment when the entire monumental

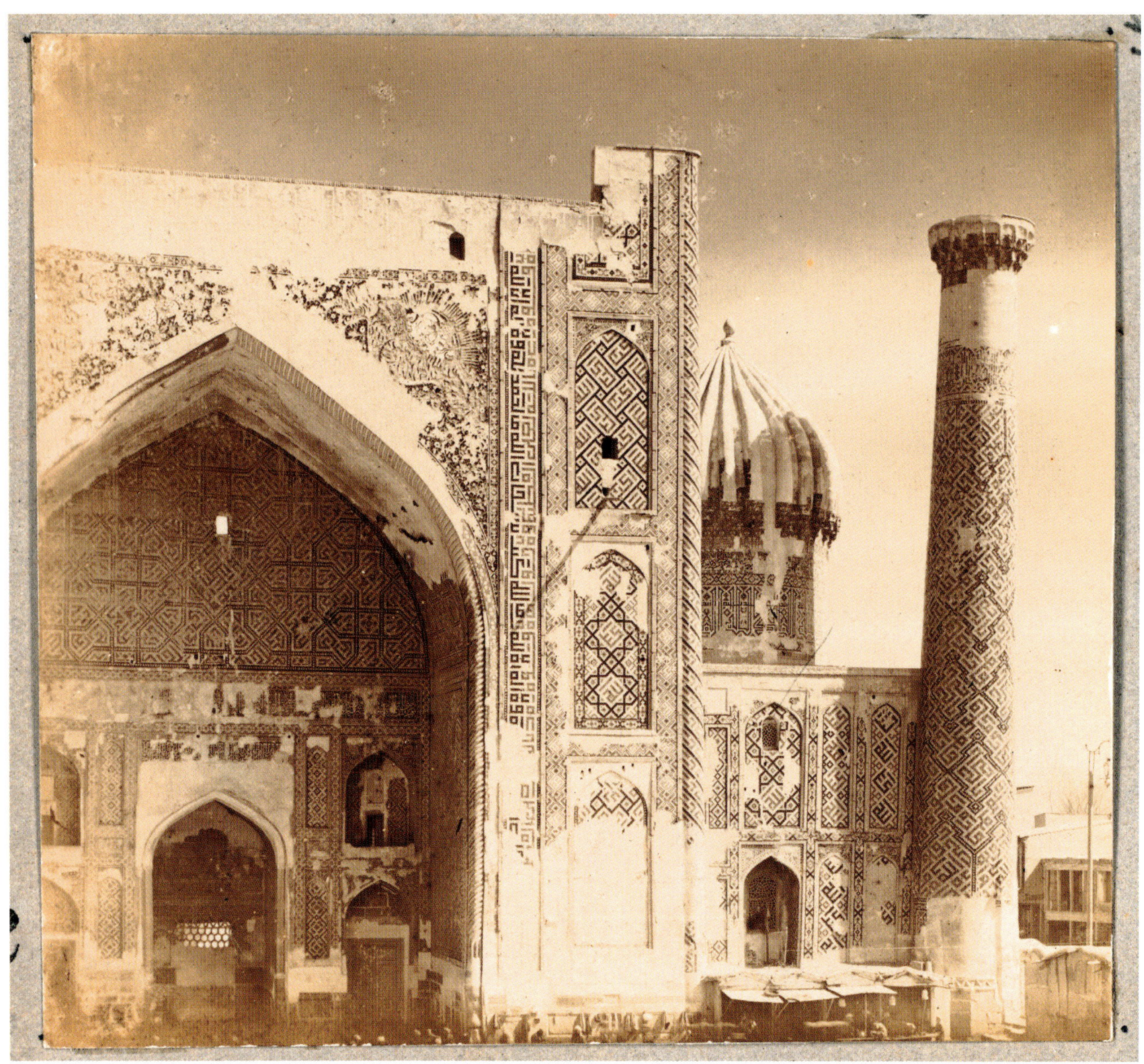

SAMARKAND Shir-Dor Madrasa. Right side of main facade. View across Registan Square from Ulugh-Beg Madrasa. PROKUDIN-GORSKY 02261. JANUARY 1907.

SAMARKAND Shir-Dor Madrasa. Main facade. Southwest view. BRUMFIELD, MAY 15, 1972.

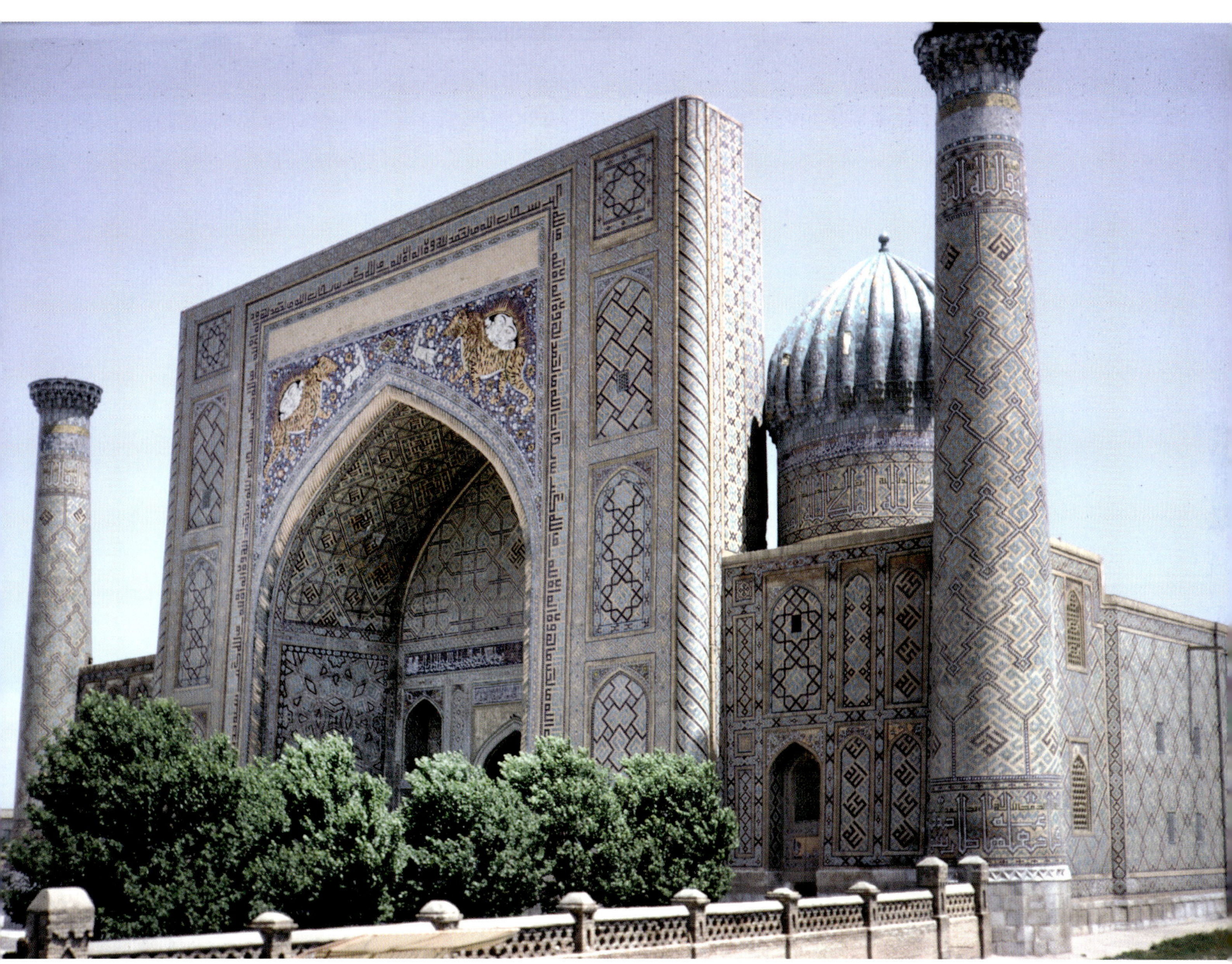

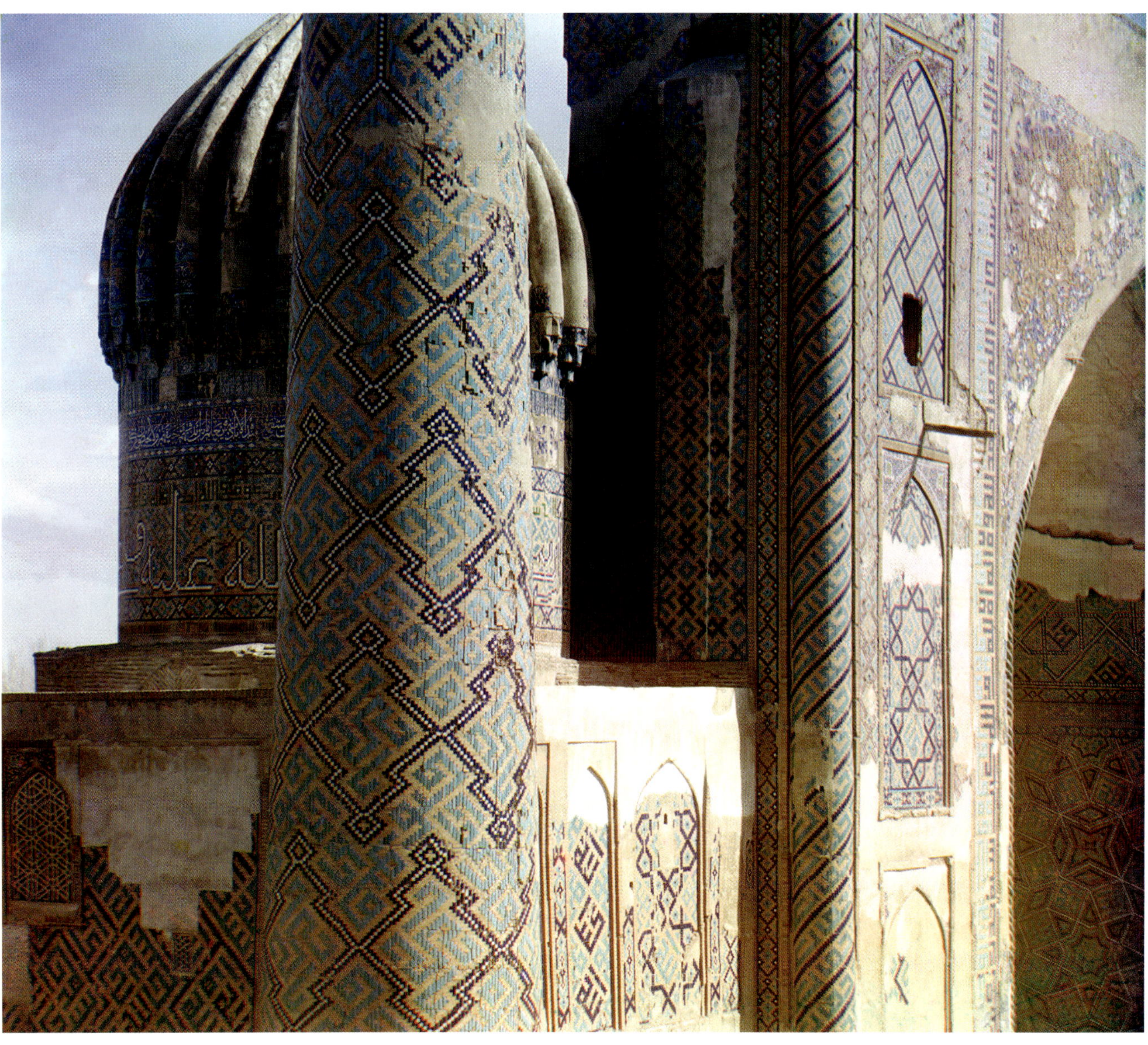

ceramic facade was transformed — transfigured — by the setting sun after a May rainstorm.

The interior courtyard of the Shir Dor Madrasa is no less astonishing. Prokudin-Gorsky's view from the interior courtyard parapet shows the ribbed dome over an instruction hall at the southwest corner. Despite losses in this active seismic zone, the surface displays intricate ceramic decoration that includes geometric and botanical motifs, as well as a horizontal Perso-Arabic inscription band. Restoration of the ceramic tiles on the dome ribs was implemented by Uzbek craftsmen during the Soviet period. The mina-

SAMARKAND Shir-Dor Madrasa. Left side of main facade. View from Tilla-Kari madrasa. PROKUDIN-GORSKY 21736. JANUARY 1907.

SAMARKAND Shir-Dor Madrasa. Main facade in setting sun. Northwest view. BRUMFIELD, MAY 16, 1972.

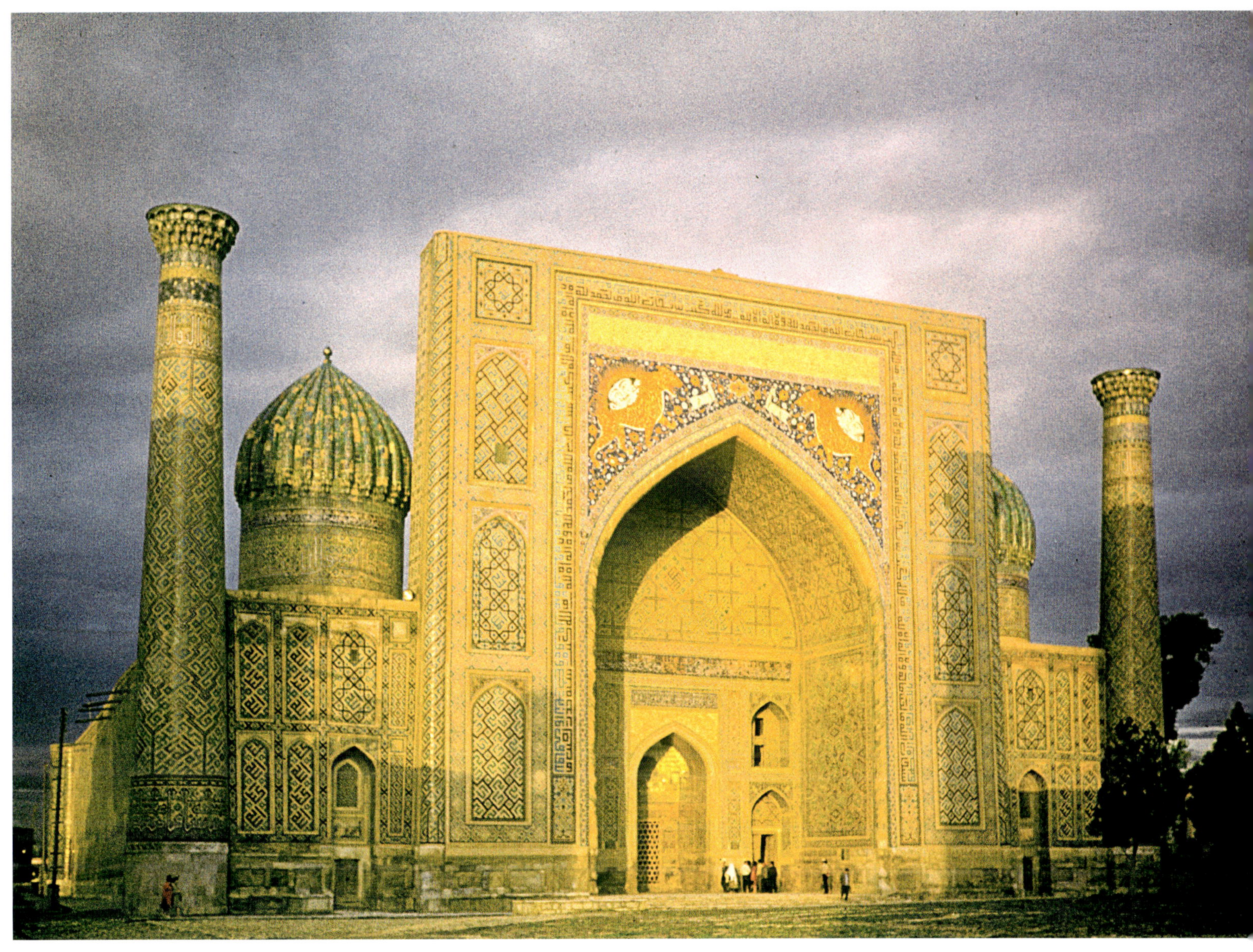

ret is covered in geometric tile figures with patterns of block Kufic script forming words from the Kalima. My photograph shows little difference in this well-preserved structural segment. The open interior of the madrasa is rectangular in plan, with a two-story arcade containing scholars' cells overlooking the courtyard. Despite losses in this active seismic zone, much of the surface is covered with ceramic decoration that includes geometric and botanical motifs, as well as a vertical Perso-Arabic inscription band. Visible within the arches are geometric tile figures with patterns of block Kufic script forming words from the Kalima.

The remarkably intricate ceramic work and plasticity are evident in my photograph of the courtyard side of the main iwan arch. In the center is a

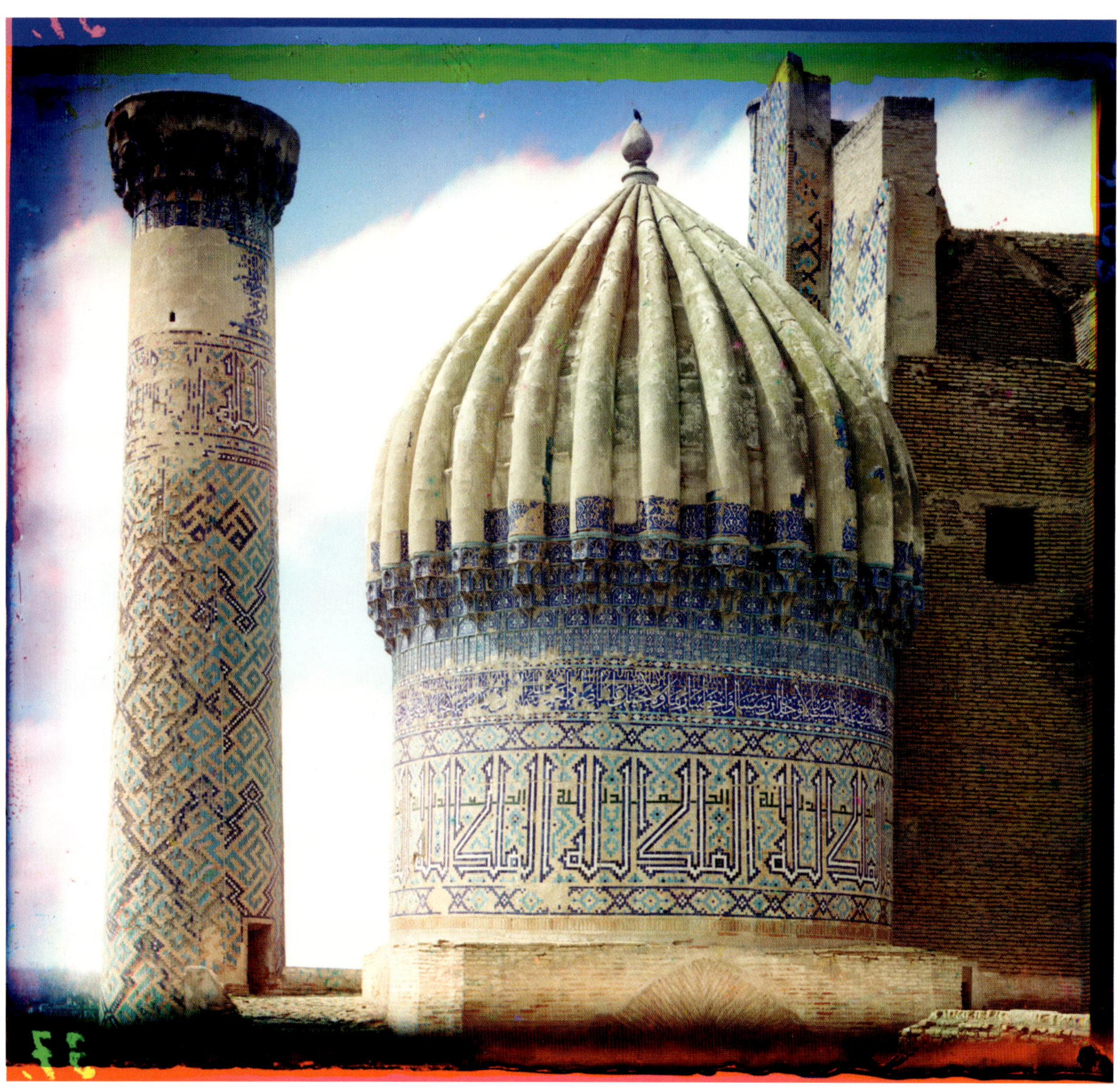

lattice window, with decorative panels containing floral and geometric figures on either side. Above the window is an inscription in the Thuluth cursive style. The niche culminates in a curved vault composed of ceramic components in a manner known as *mocárabe*—also referred to as a "stalactite" vault because of the appearance of the suspended decorative elements. Prokudin-Gorsky also photographed intricate ornamental details within this arch. Panels of Perso-Arabic inscriptions in the cursive Naskh manner are set within strips of floral motifs. Especially notable is the faience mosaic in the center, with a vase supporting the in-

SAMARKAND Registan. Shir-Dor Madrasa. Minaret and dome over instruction hall at southwest corner. View from courtyard. PROKUDIN-GORSKY 21755. JANUARY 1907.

———

SAMARKAND Shir-Dor Madrasa. Courtyard view toward iwan arch of main entrance. BRUMFIELD, MAY 15, 1972.

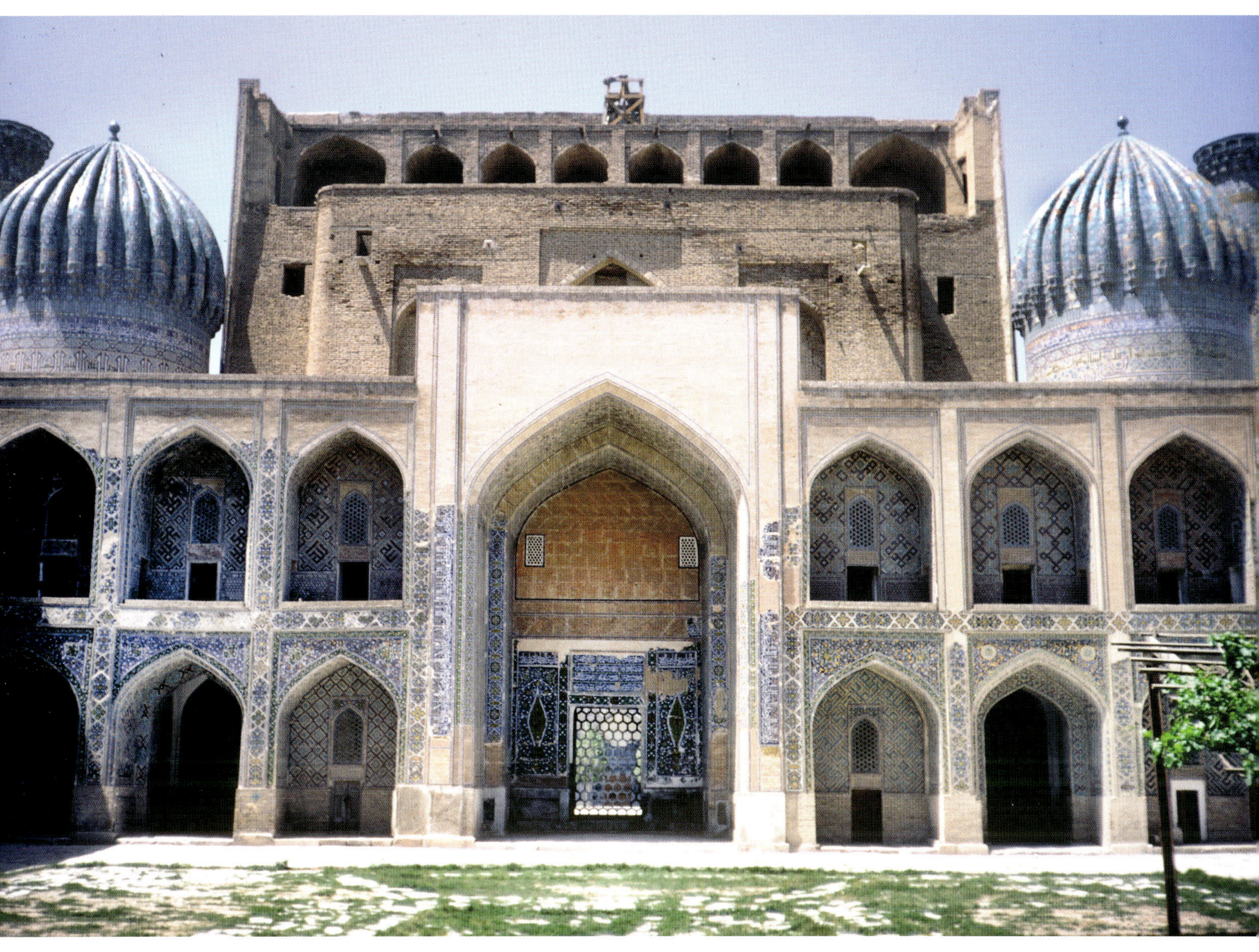

tricate figure of a bush, or Tree of Life. Remnants of a similar figure are visible on the inner face of the arch (on left). All the figures are surrounded by intertwined tendrils.

The third component of Registan is the Tilla Kari Madrasa, built in 1646–60 on the site of a former caravanserai. The glass negative for Prokudin-Gorsky's most effective view of the structure is missing from the collection, but the contact print nonetheless provides essential information about the cylinder that once supported the great main dome. The colors that would have suffused his original photograph are visible in the photograph from 1972, taken in the setting sun after that perfect rainstorm.

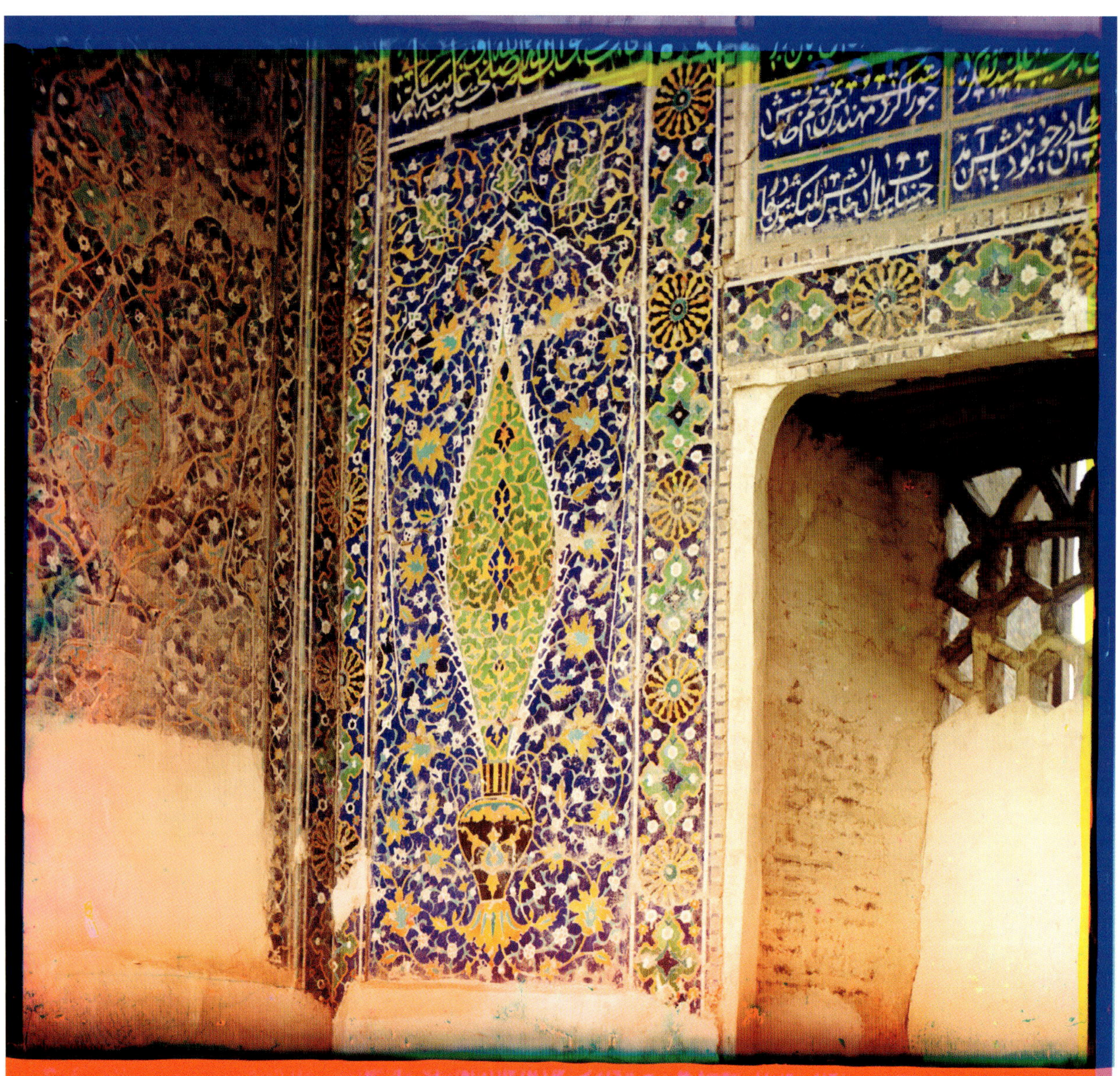

SAMARKAND Registan. Shir-Dor Madrasa. Ceramic decoration on courtyard side of the main iwan arch. PROKUDIN-GORSKY 21810. JANUARY 1907.

SAMARKAND Shir-Dor Madrasa. Main iwan arch in courtyard. BRUMFIELD, MAY 15, 1972.

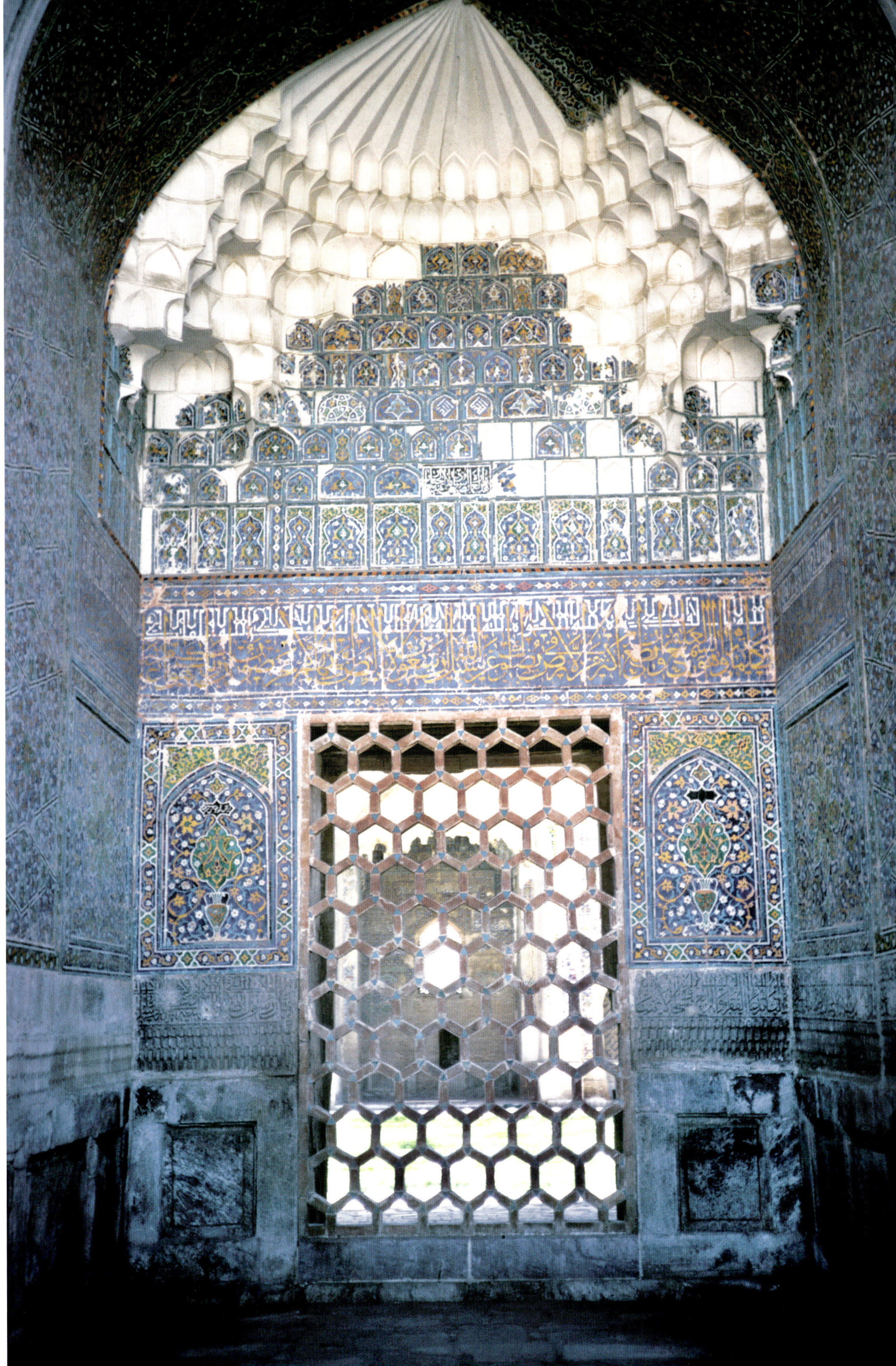

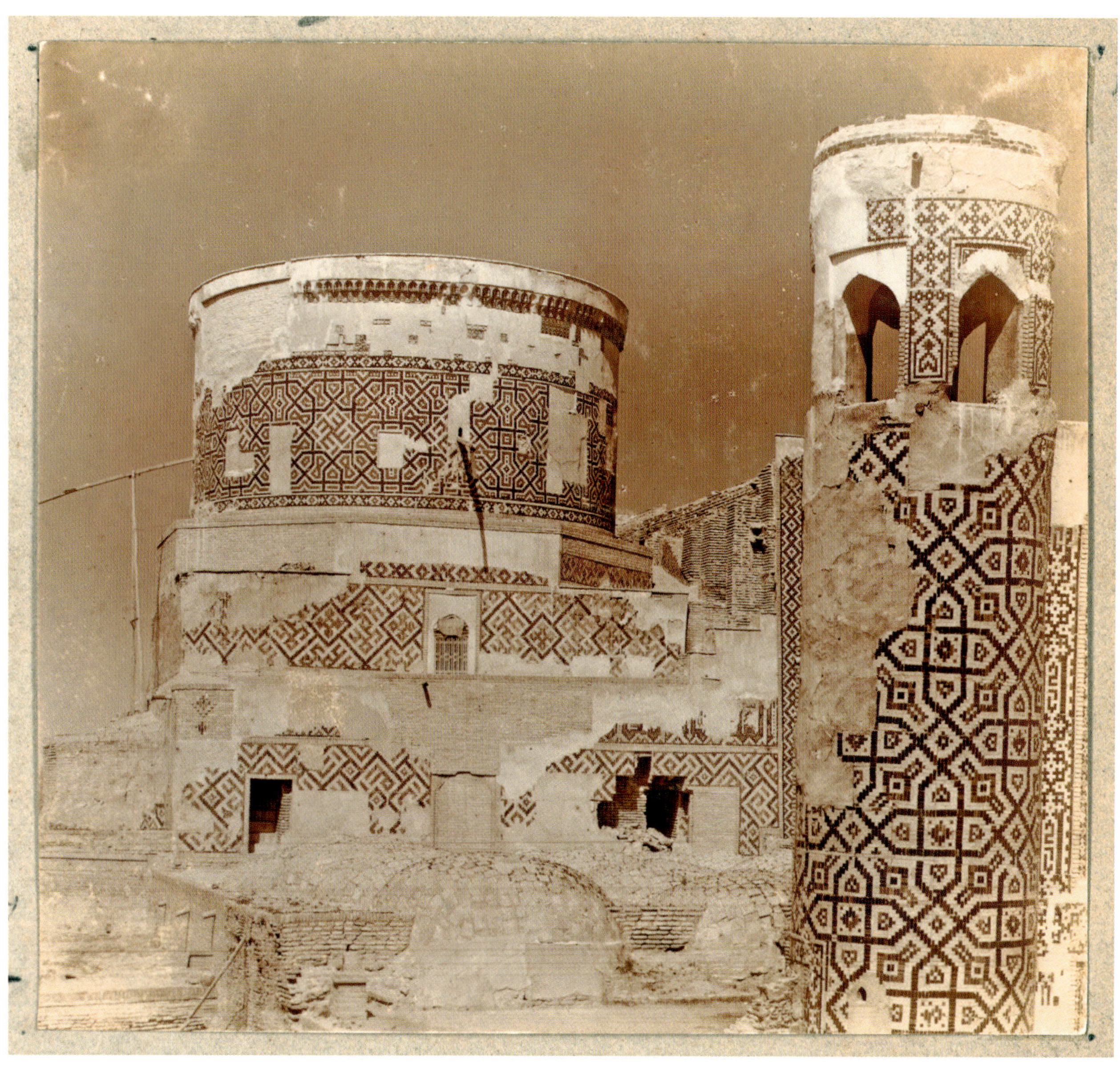

SAMARKAND Tilla Kari Madrasa. Southwest corner with minaret and cylinder that supported main dome of mosque. PROKUDIN-GORSKY 02262. JANUARY 1907.

SAMARKAND Tilla Kari Madrasa. West facade in setting sun, with cylinder that supported main dome of mosque. BRUMFIELD, MAY 16, 1972.

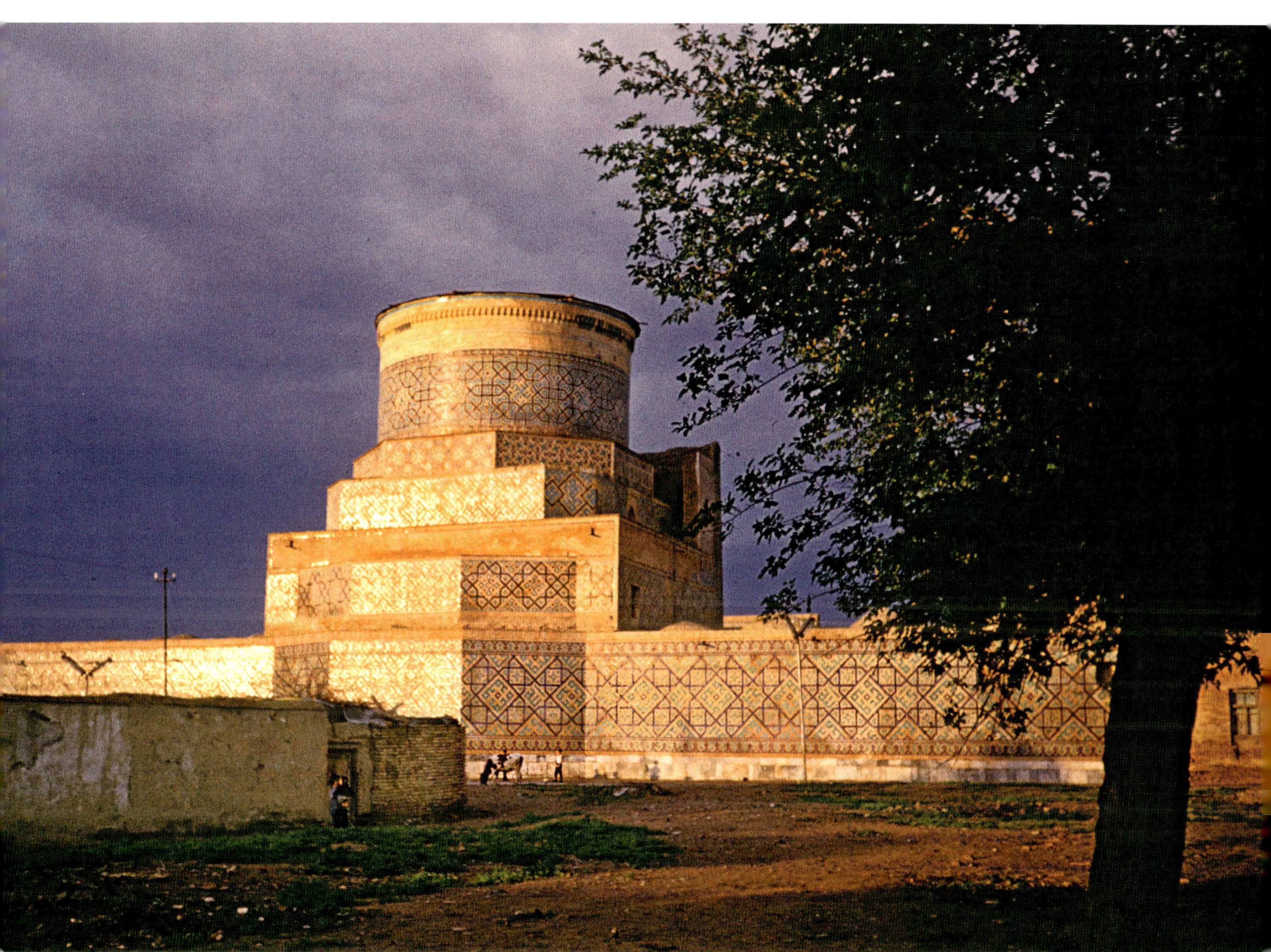

Each of the Samarkand ensembles photographed by Prokudin-Gorsky is uniquely remarkable, yet the city has another supreme example of Islamic art—a necropolis known as Shakhi Zinda, located beyond the central city on a small hillside used from time immemorial as a cemetery. The main ensemble consists of mausoleums from the fourteenth and fifteenth centuries, with blue domes, high ceramic portals, patterned stone vaults, and rich polychrome ornamentation. Several of some two dozen mausoleums and shrines were commissioned by Tamerlane and by his grandson Ulugh Beg, the astronomer-king. Most of the tombs contain either members of the ruling family or various high officials.

There is more than one legend surrounding the name (which means "the living king"), but all agree that it refers to Kussam Ibn Abbas, who is supposed to have brought Islam to the area in the latter part of the seventh century and who, according to one story, was decapitated for preaching the true faith. Following the execution, he took up his head and walked away, presumably to the site on which his mausoleum now rests. The motif of the decapitated but living saint is present in pre-Islamic sources from Central Asia, as well as in Russian and Western hagiography. One Soviet source states that Kussam Ibn Abbas, a nephew of the Prophet, participated in an Arab attack on Samarkand in 673 and was killed in the course of battle, but even this is open to doubt. Samarkand was not occupied by the Arabs until 712 (the year they took Cordova), and bitter resistance to their rule continued for several decades thereafter. Shakhi Zinda marks the traditional place of his burial and is considered sacred ground. The topography of the graveyard was been well preserved.

Archeological excavations have revealed that as early as the eleventh century mausoleums and mosques existed on the site, but none survived the city's conquest in 1220 by the Mongol hordes of Genghis Khan. As Galina Pugachenkova notes, "The superstitious Mongols could not bring themselves to destroy the tomb of Kussam Ibn Abbas, but with the other mausolea they did not stand on ceremony." As a consequence of this lack of ceremony, the earliest extant buildings within the complex date from the first part of the fourteenth century, some decades before Tamerlane made Samarkand his capital in 1369–70. The major monuments at Shakhi Zinda date from the time of the Timurids.

Among Prokudin-Gorsky's most striking photographs of Shakhi Zinda is a northwest view of a middle group of mausoleums taken in the light of the setting sun across the hummocks of the ancient burial ground. In the background are the snow-covered peaks of the Turkestan Range to the southeast. Arrayed from the left is the Octahedron mausoleum, the Shirin Beka Aka mausoleum, the Shadi Mulk Aga mausoleum, the Emir Zade mausoleum, and the two domes of the Kazy-Zade Rumi mausoleum, built in 1437 by Ulugh Beg, grandson of Tamerlane—all visible in my photographs. Also evident are remnants of the ceramic tile decoration (including patterned script), much of which has since been restored or replicated.

Prokudin-Gorsky's work at Shakhi Zinda shows not only great artistry but also a methodical approach to architectural documentation. The ensemble begins at the bottom of the hill with the main entrance structure, or *darvozakhana*. His view of the monument shows an entrance chamber, or *chartak*, and a mosque (on left) built in 1434–35 to provide an appropriate frame for the beginning of the necropolis passageway. The large entrance arch, or *peshtak*, contains the chartak portal that is framed by its own pointed arch. Near the portal are turbaned pilgrims seated on carpets that serve as prayer rugs. Although damaged, the facade displays a profusion of ceramic decoration, including geometric and floral designs as well as patterned Arabic script. In May 1972, I photographed the brick stairway beyond the darvozakhana. The stairway leads dramatically to groups of ceramic-covered mausoleums. The most imposing structures at Shakhi Zinda frame this steep ascent.

The ascent's dominant structure, with two domes, is thought to have been built in 1437 by the astronomer king Ulugh Beg. Identified in some sources as the mausoleums of Tamerlane's benefactress and her daughter (Uldzk Inak and Bibi Zinet), the structure is also considered the tomb of Ulugh Beg's fellow astronomer, Kazy-Zade Rumi. This view shows extensive damage to the ceramic decoration (including patterned Arabic script), which has since been restored.

The top of the ascent is marked by another portal structure, which leads to the middle group of mausoleums. Although the original glass negative is not extant, Prokudin-Gorsky's contact print gives an excellent sense of the middle ensemble in relation to the larger setting, seen from the hillside to the northeast. My photograph of the ensemble was taken within the middle passage on an overcast day, which reduced the shadow contrast. Prokudin-Gorsky photographed several of the monuments in this middle group, including the Shirin Beka Aka mausoleum, built in 1385–86 for Tamerlane's younger sister. Prokudin-Gorsky's photograph shows the facade of the entrance arch. Despite significant damage, the surface displays

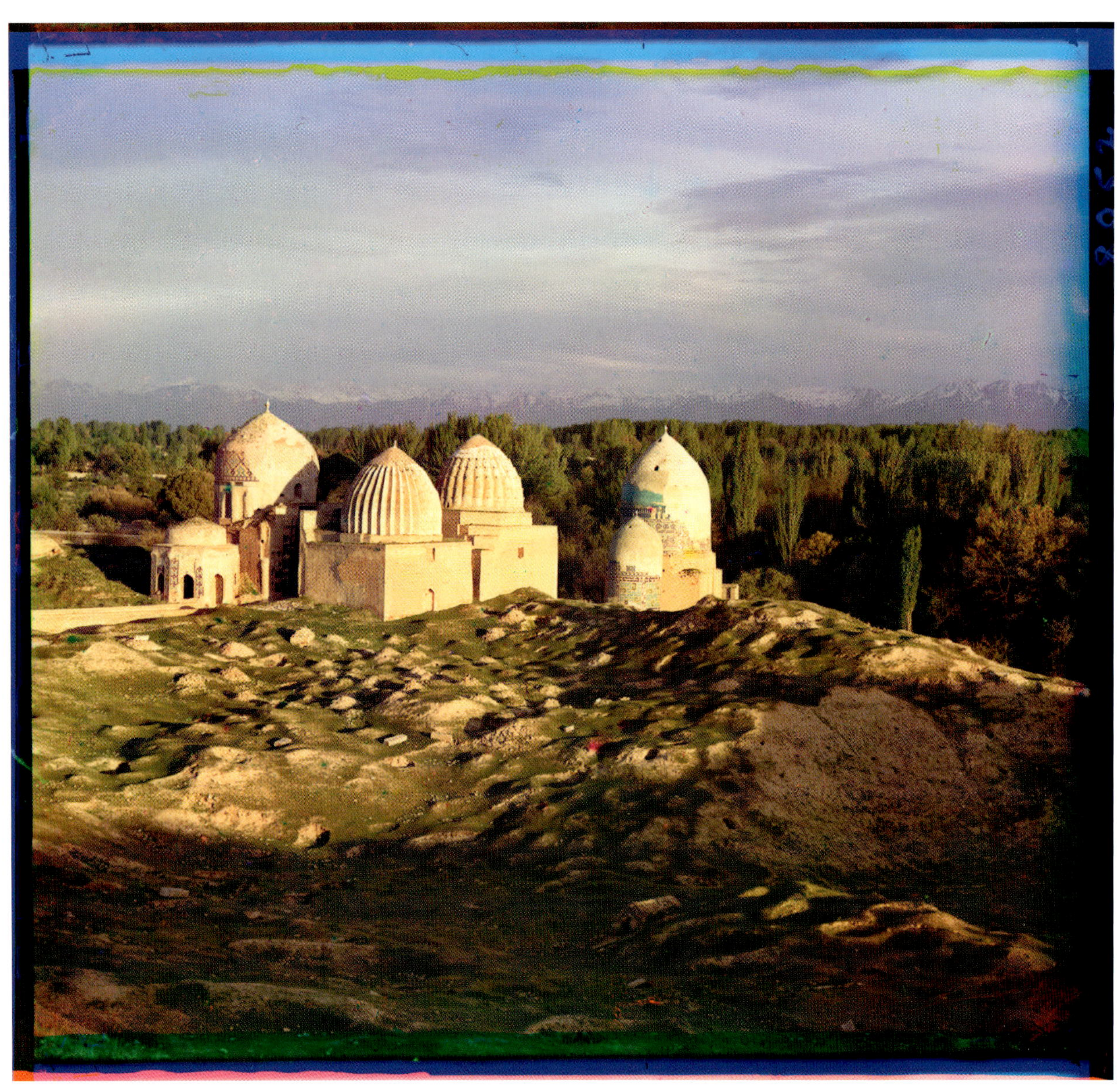

SAMARKAND Shakhi Zinda. Northwest view of central ensemble. *From left*: Octahedron mausoleum; Shirin Beka Aka mausoleum; Shadi Mulk Aka mausoleum; Emir Zade mausoleum; double domes of the Kazy-Zade Rumi mausoleum. *In background*: Turkestan Range to the southeast. *Foreground*: cemetery mounds. PROKUDIN-GORSKY 21833. 1911.

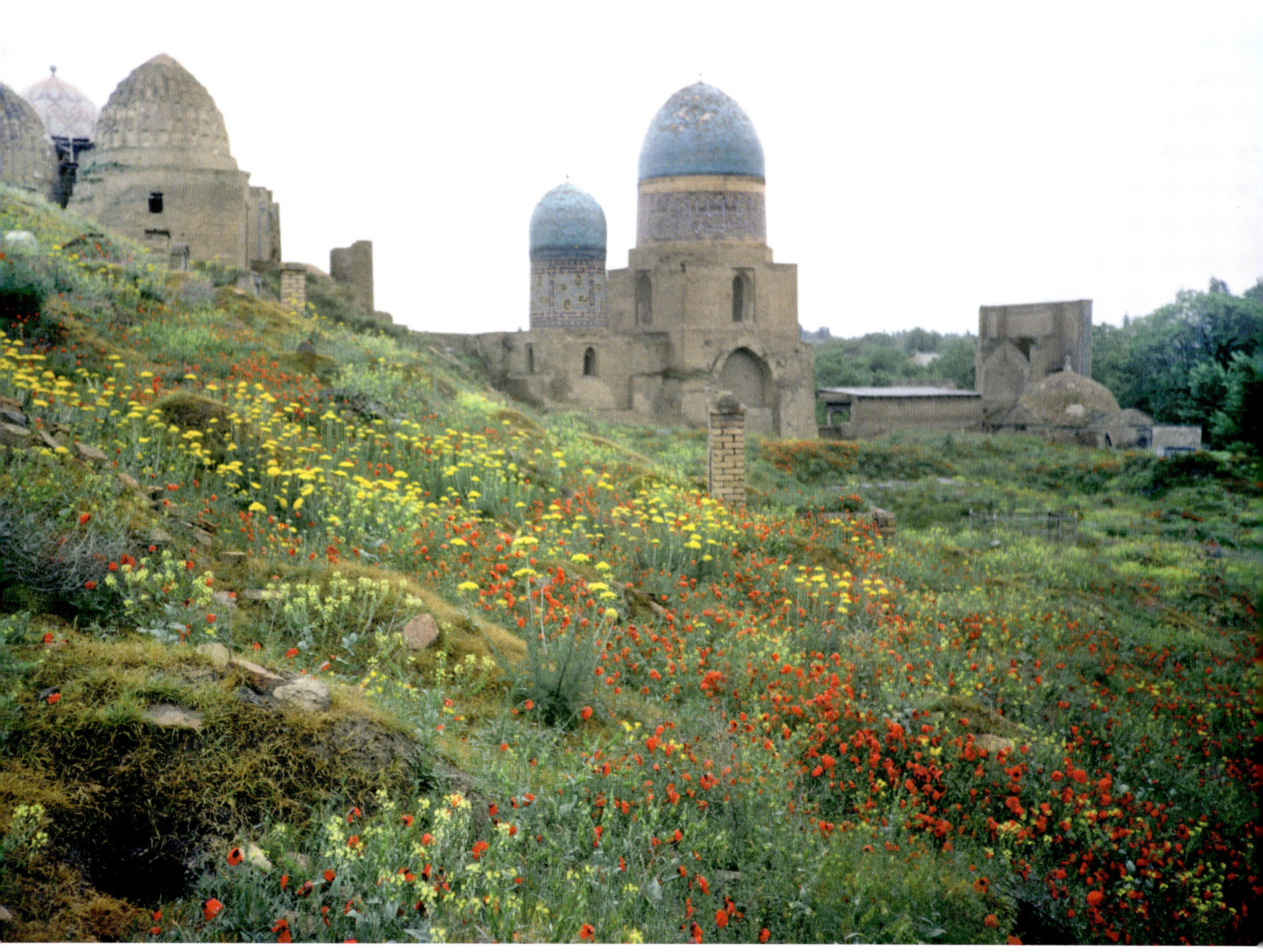

SAMARKAND Shakhi Zinda. West view from cemetery.
From left: the Shadi Mulk Aga and Emir Zade mausoleums, with ribbed domes; the Shirin Beka Aga mausoleum; and the two domes of the mausoleum built
in 1437 by Ulugh Beg and traditionally associated with
the astronomer Kazy-Zade Rumi. Much of the profuse
ceramic tile decoration, partially visible here, has been
restored. On the cemetery slope are remnants of burial
mounds and brick tombs. BRUMFIELD, MAY 16, 1972.

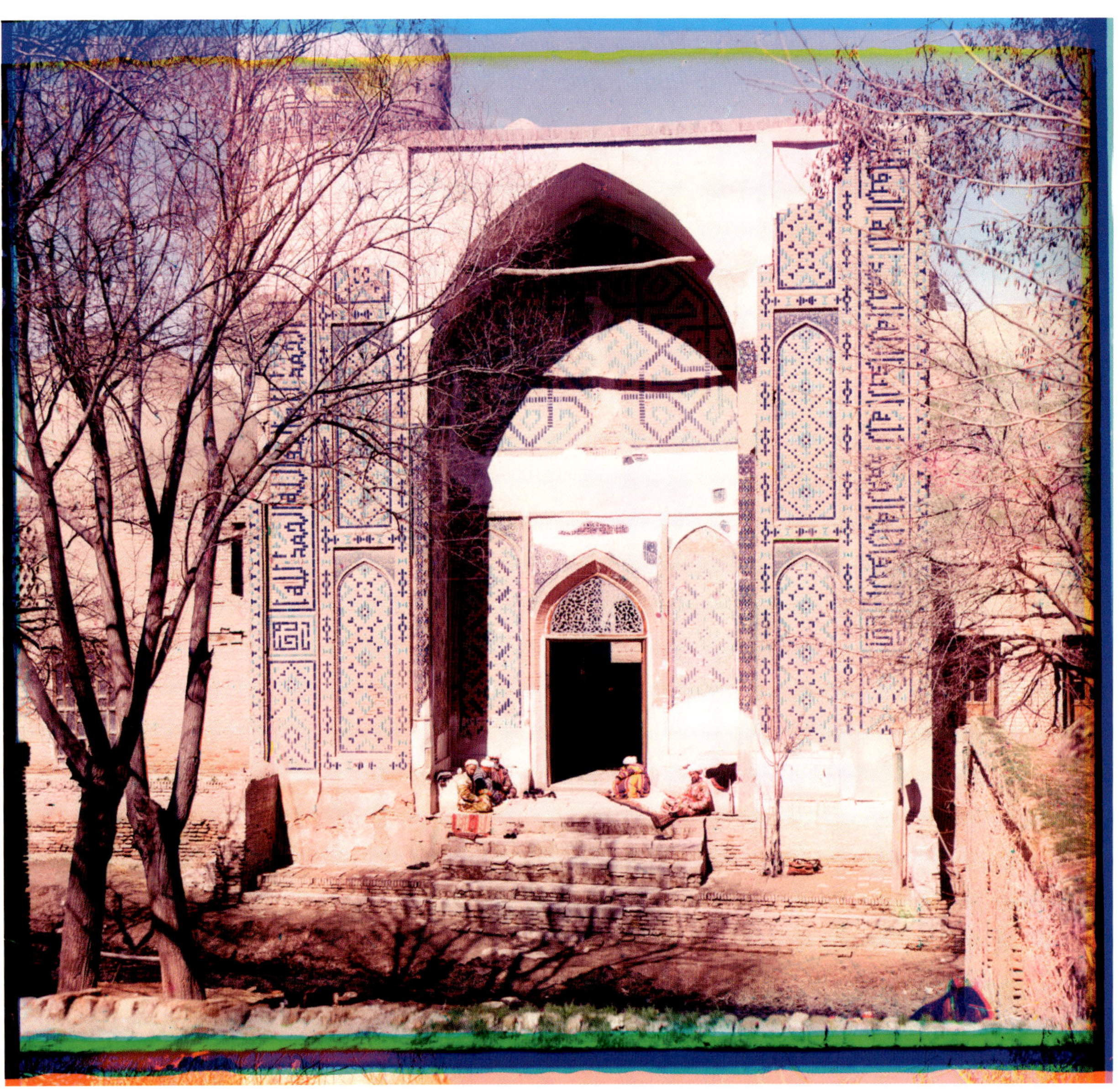

SAMARKAND Shakhi Zinda. Main entrance, or *darvo-zakhana*. PROKUDIN-GORSKY 21817. 1911.

SAMARKAND Shakhi Zinda. Stairway from main entrance to lower ensemble. BRUMFIELD, MAY 17, 1972.

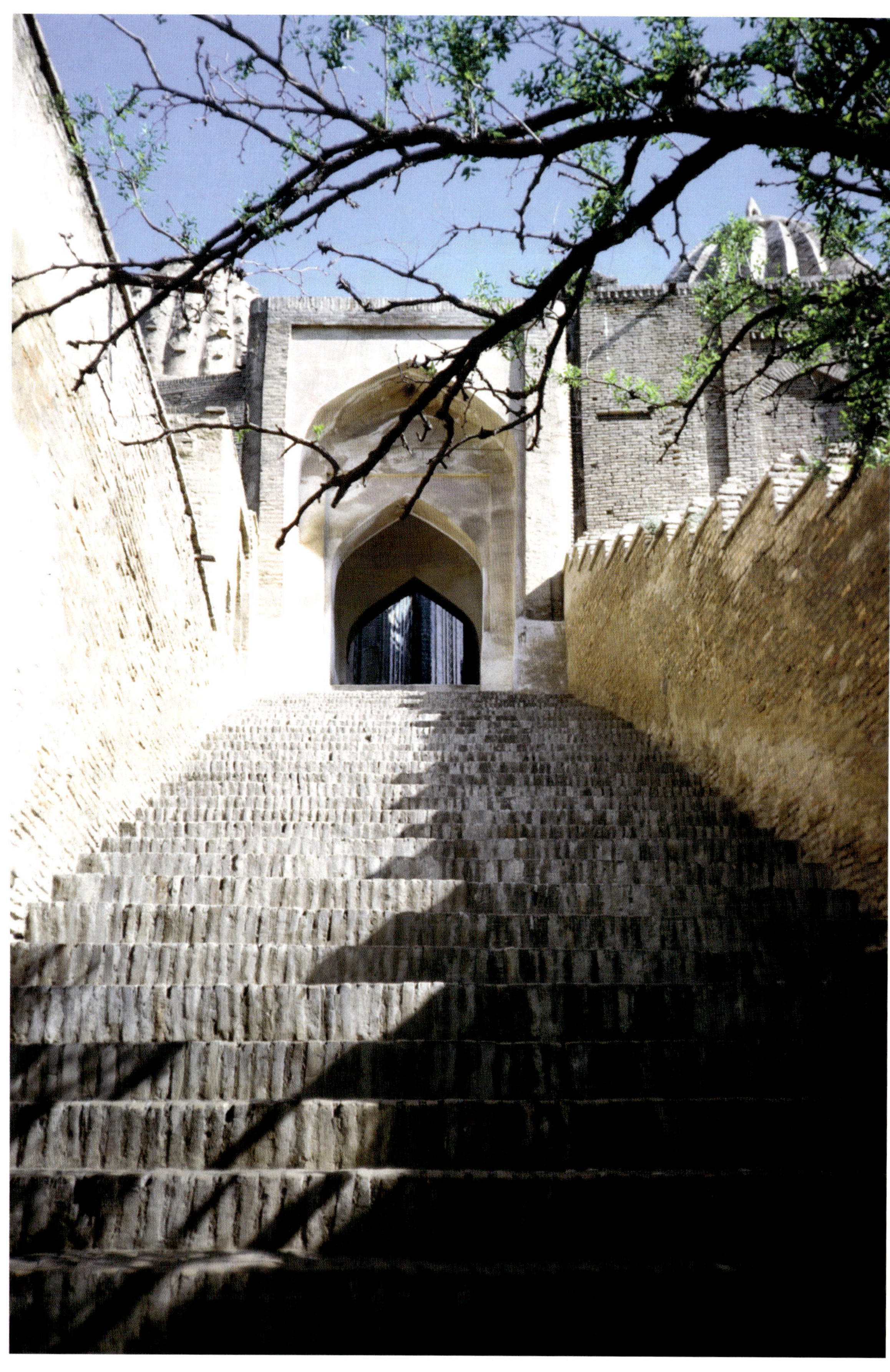

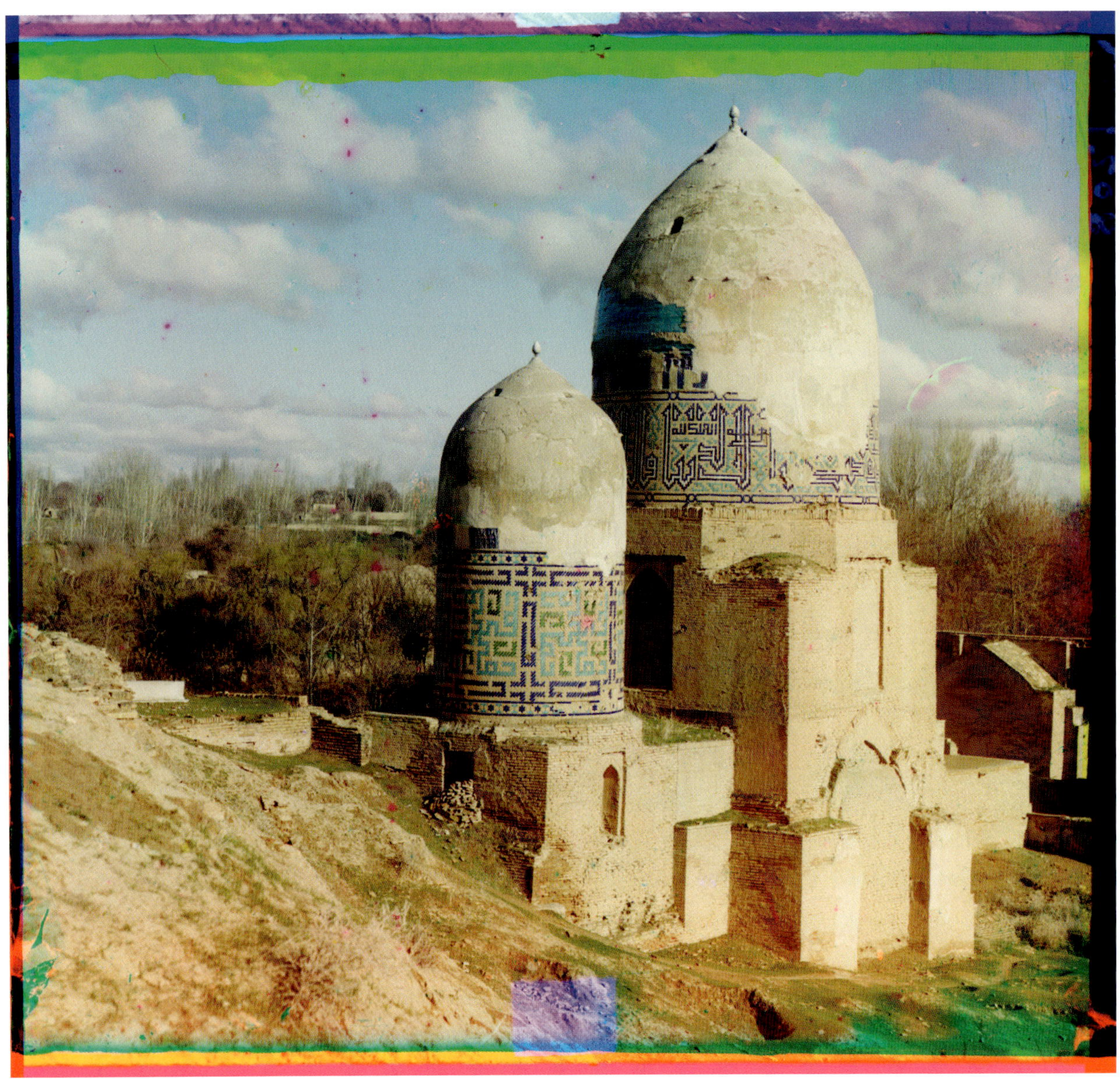

profuse ceramic ornamentation with Persian influence, including early examples of composite mosaics. Above the
portal is an inscriptional panel in Thuluth cursive letters
intertwined with floral motifs. Some of the facade inscriptions have been attributed to Socrates. Visible at the top is
the lower part of the ceramic "honeycomb" vaulting at the
peak of the entrance arch.

Prokudin-Gorsky's photographs of the middle group
conclude with the Emir-Zade mausoleum, built in 1386 by
a member of Tamerlane's court. Despite losses to its polychrome ornament, the facade is a fundamental display of

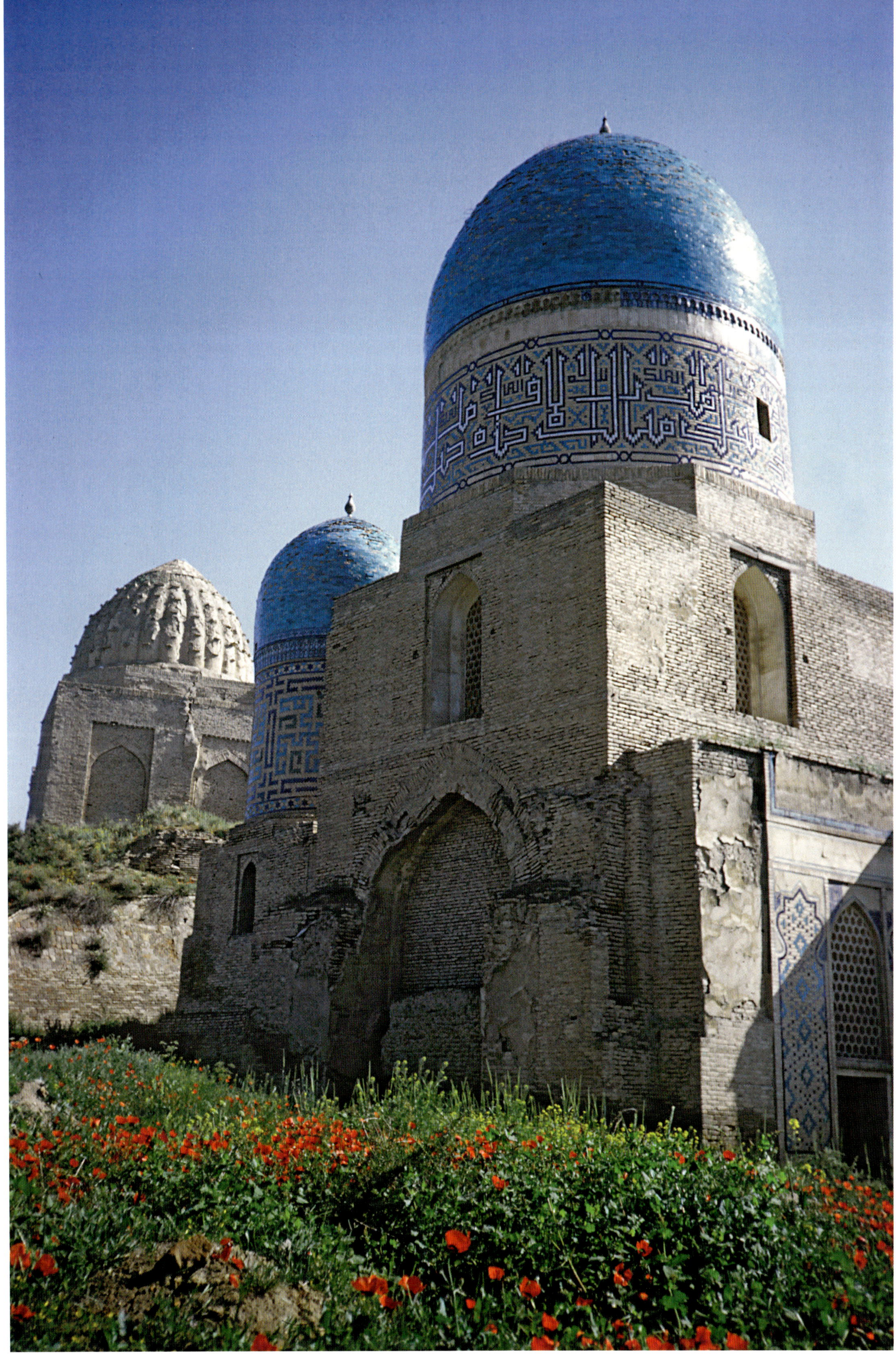

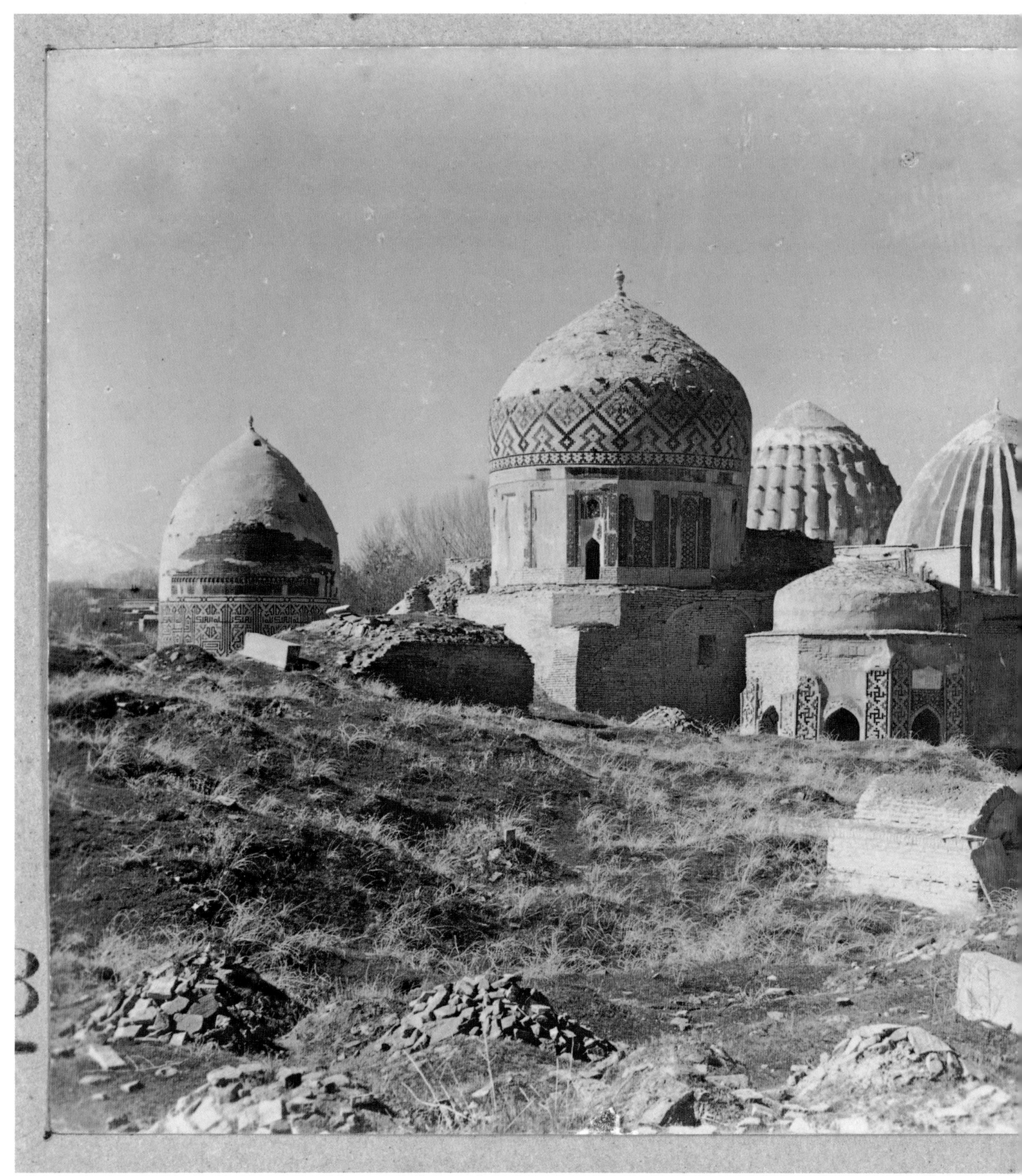

SAMARKAND Shakhi Zinda. Northeast view of central ensemble. *From left*: Mausoleum of
Kazy-Zade Rumi, Shirin Beka Aga mausoleum, Emir Zade mausoleum, Octahedron mausoleum,
Shadi Mulk Aga mausoleum. PROKUDIN-GORSKY 02280. 1911.

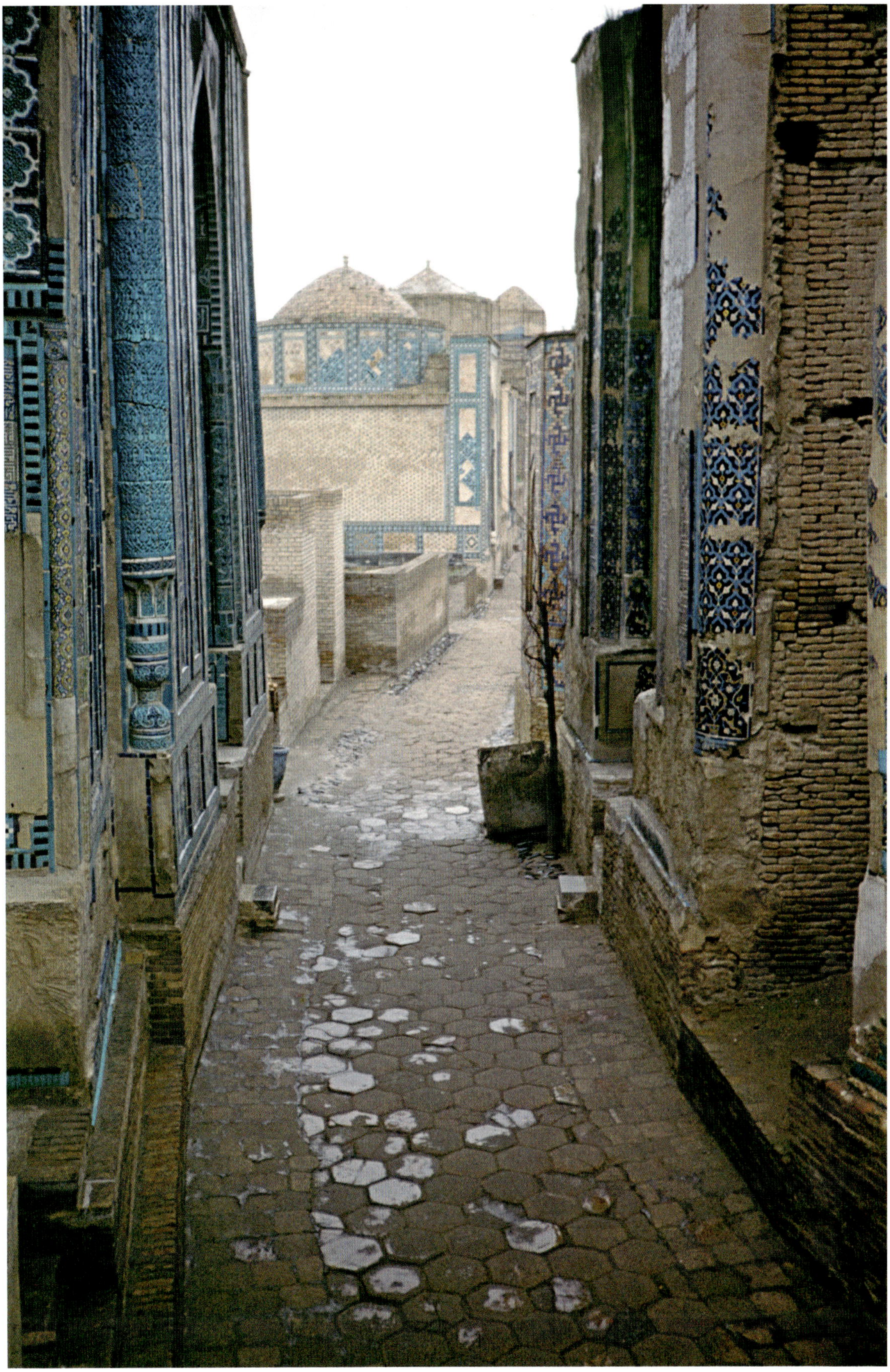

SAMARKAND Shakhi Zinda. View toward middle passage. *From left*: Shadi Mulk Aka Mauso-leum, Usto Ali Nesefi mausoleum, octahedron mausoleum, Shirin Beka Aga mausoleum, Tuglu-Tekin mausoleum. BRUMFIELD, MAY 16, 1972.

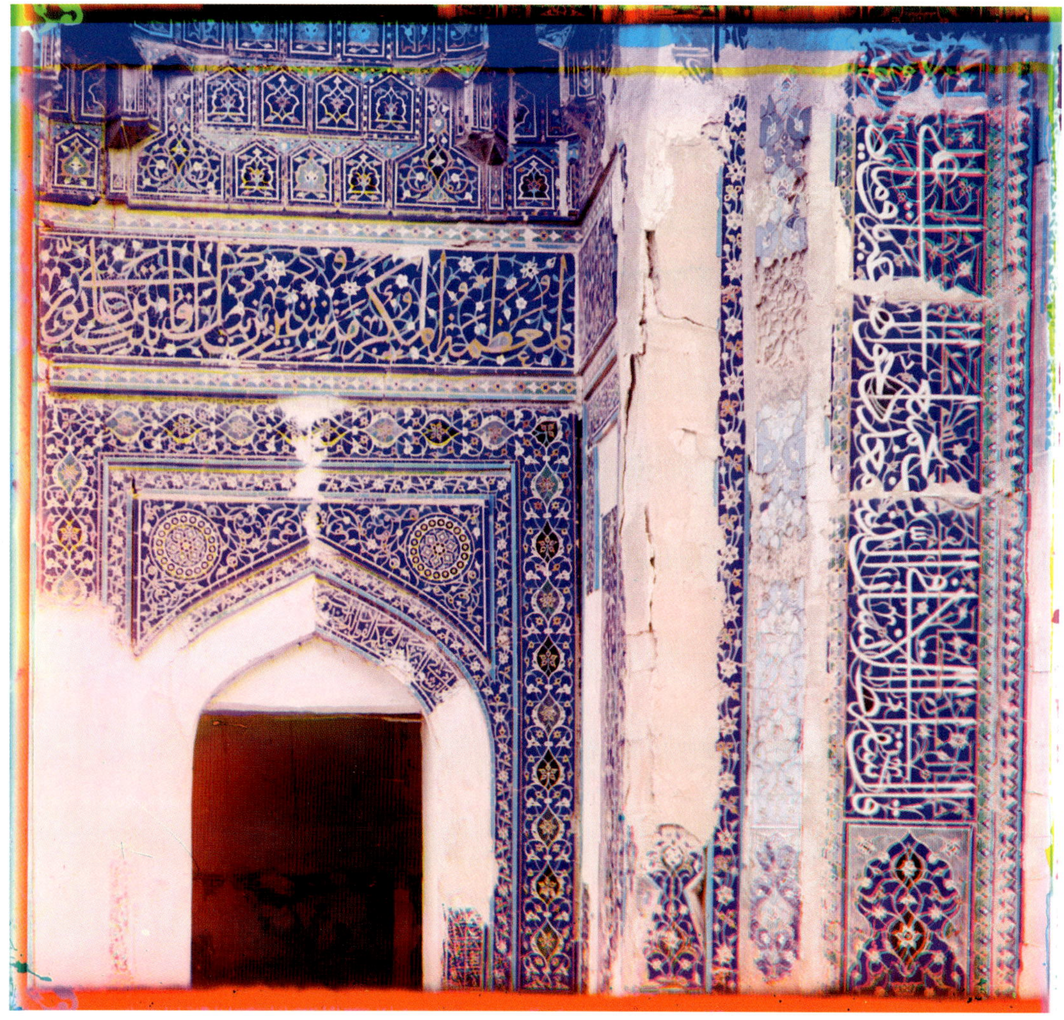

Central Asian decorative art. The entrance arch contains a variety of ceramic tiles (including majolica), as well as glazed carved terra cotta and mosaic work. In addition to geometric designs and eight-lobed rosettes, the flanks of the arch contain panels with patterns formed of block Kufic script.

Because of the narrow confines of the Shakhi Zinda passageway and the limits of Prokudin-Gorsky's lens, his photographs are usually facade details. An exception is his view of the culminating mausoleum in the middle group. Although the patron of this mausoleum, built around 1380, is unknown, it is referred to by the name of its master builder, Usto Ali Nesefi. Despite severe losses to the main facade, surviving ornamentation reveals one of the most elaborate decorative programs in the entire necropolis. The

SAMARKAND Shakhi Zinda. Shirin Beka Aga mausoleum. Ceramic work in portal arch. PROKUDIN-GORSKY 21816. 1911.

SAMARKAND Shakhi Zinda. Shirin Beka Aga mausoleum. Ceramic work around portal. BRUMFIELD, MAY 16, 1972.

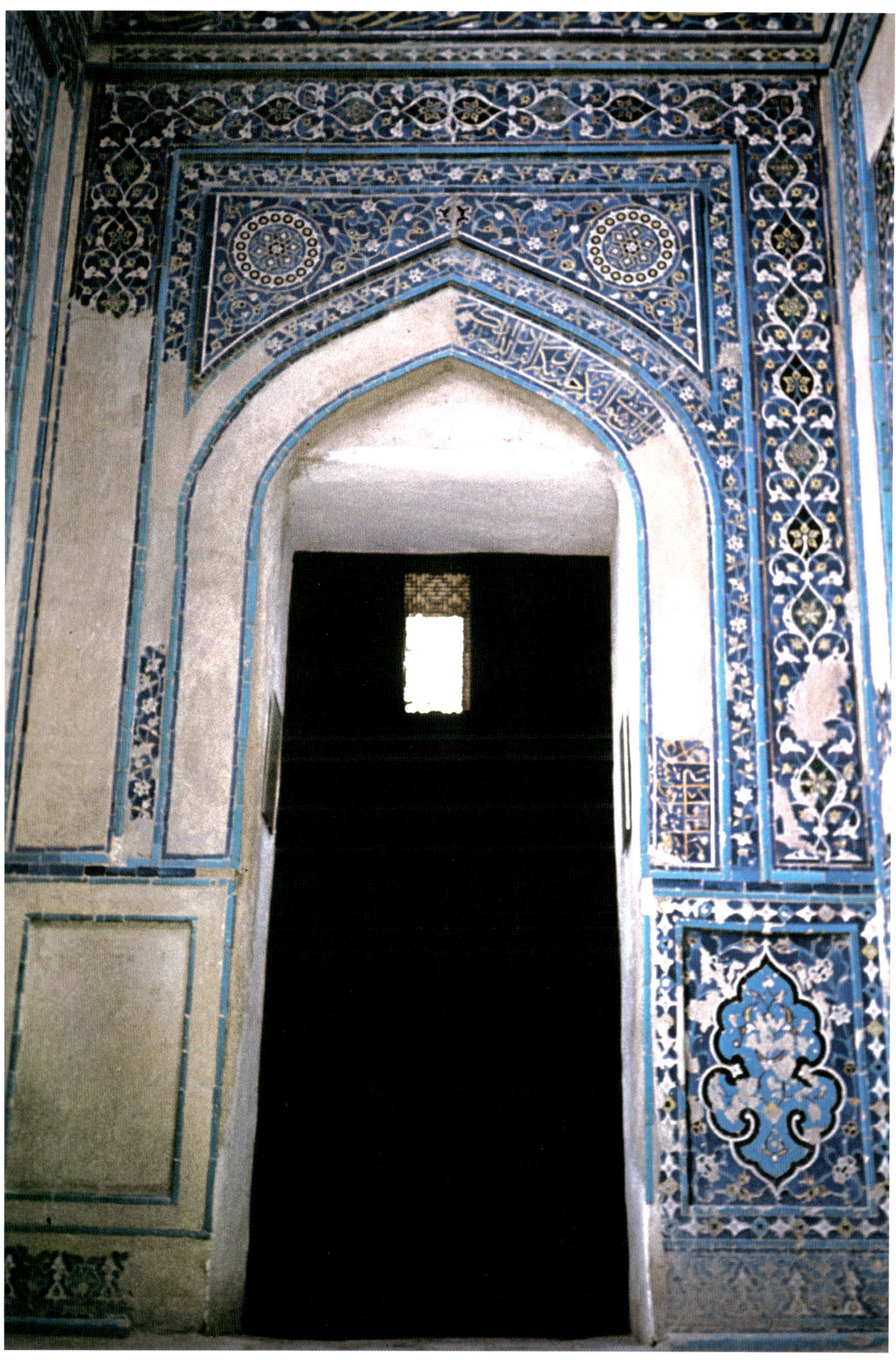

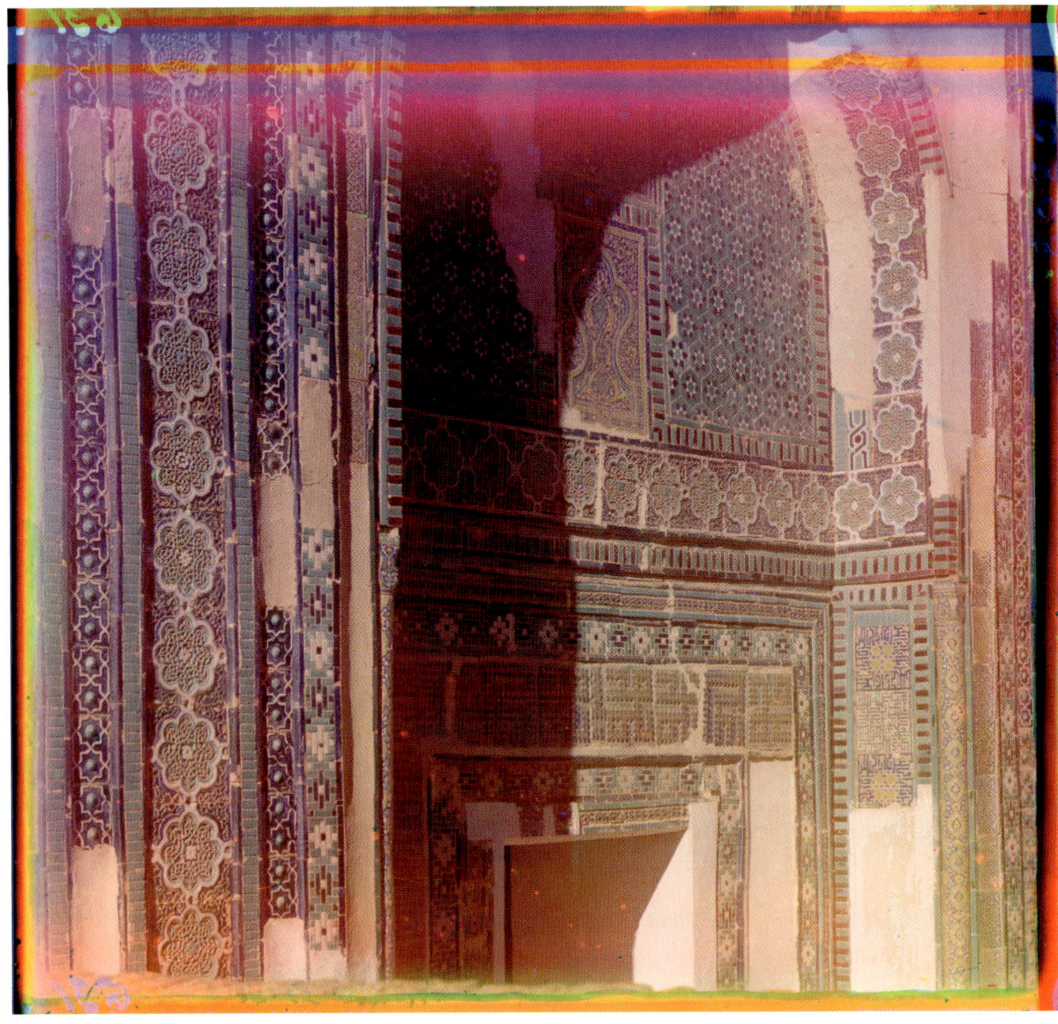

ceramic work includes polychrome majolica tiles in geometric patterns, faience panels, and Arabic script. These forms are framed by interlocking bands of intricate design. The arched entrance niche is flanked by carved terra cotta columns. The side of the structure displays geometric patterns with Kufic script.

Beyond this central portal and its cluster of mausoleums, the passage veers slightly to the right and continues some one hundred meters to the final group of mausoleums and mosques, including the mosque devoted to Kussam Ibn Abbas. This cluster is framed by another (the third) chartak, or portal structure—the northernmost within the necropolis passageway, built around 1405 adjacent to the

SAMARKAND Shakhi Zinda. Emir-Zade mausoleum. PROKUDIN-GORSKY 21879. 1911.

SAMARKAND Shakhi Zinda. Emir-Zade mausoleum. Ceramic work around portal. BRUMFIELD, MAY 16, 1972.

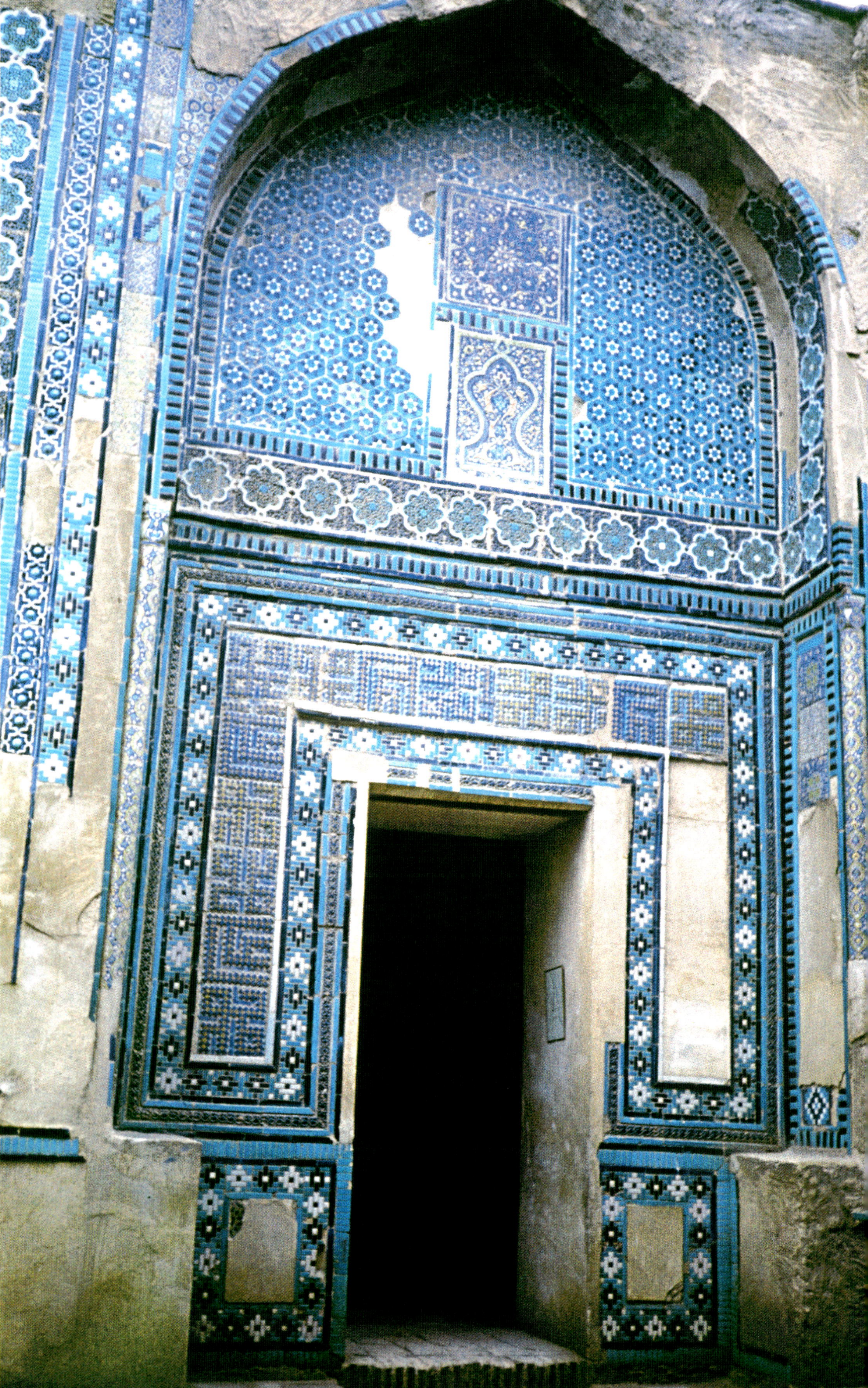

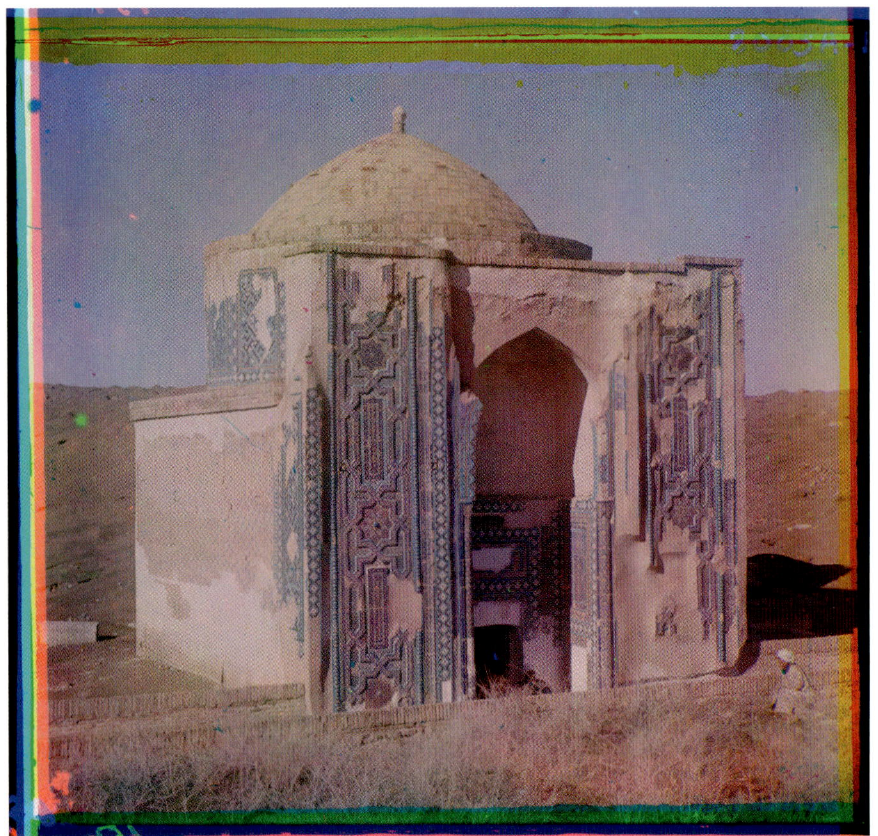

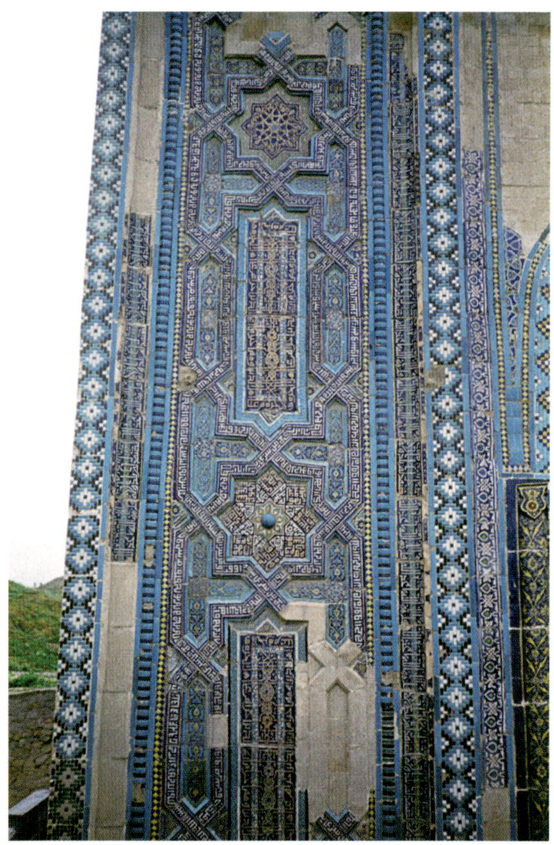

Kussam Ibn Abbas shrine. My photograph from a perch above the chartak shows the monuments in context.

Near the chartak portal at the end of the northern cluster, Prokudin-Gorsky photographed the main facade arch of the Hodja Ahmad mausoleum, built in the mid-fourteenth century for a local spiritual leader. In addition to ceramic mosaics, the Hodja Ahmad mausoleum has glazed carved terra cotta columns and panels with intricate floral, geometric, and inscriptional designs. Curving tendrils link floral patterns, including the lotus blossom. Above the bricked portal is an inscription panel, and the arch niche culminates in a complex geometric design. My photographs captured a poignant moment when a young woman and a boy with a crutch came to pray at the shrine, whose portal was unblocked during a Soviet-era restoration. The Hodja Ahmad mausoleum is situated at right angles to another mausoleum, built in 1361 adjacent to the Kussam Ibn Abbas shrine. Identified in some sources as the Kutlug Aka mau-

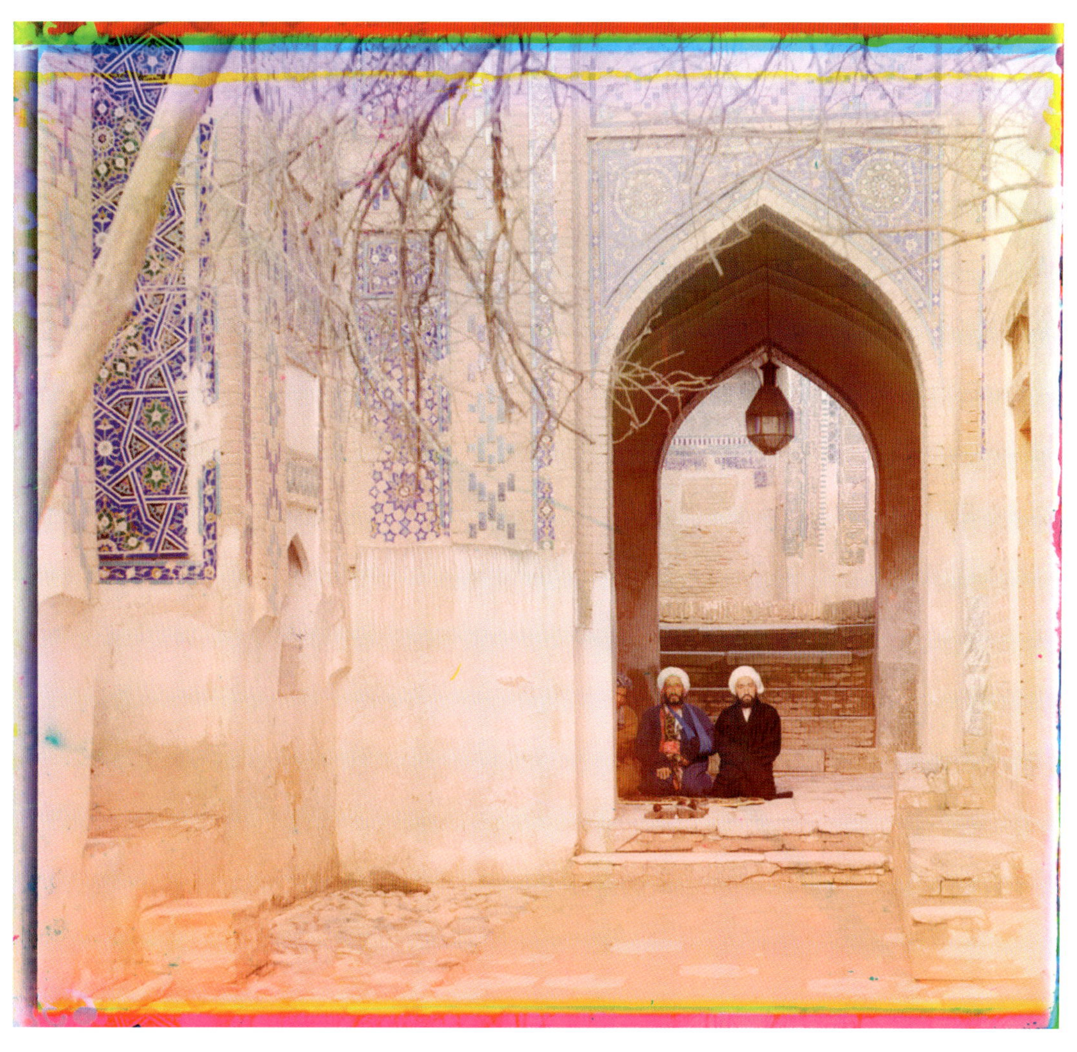

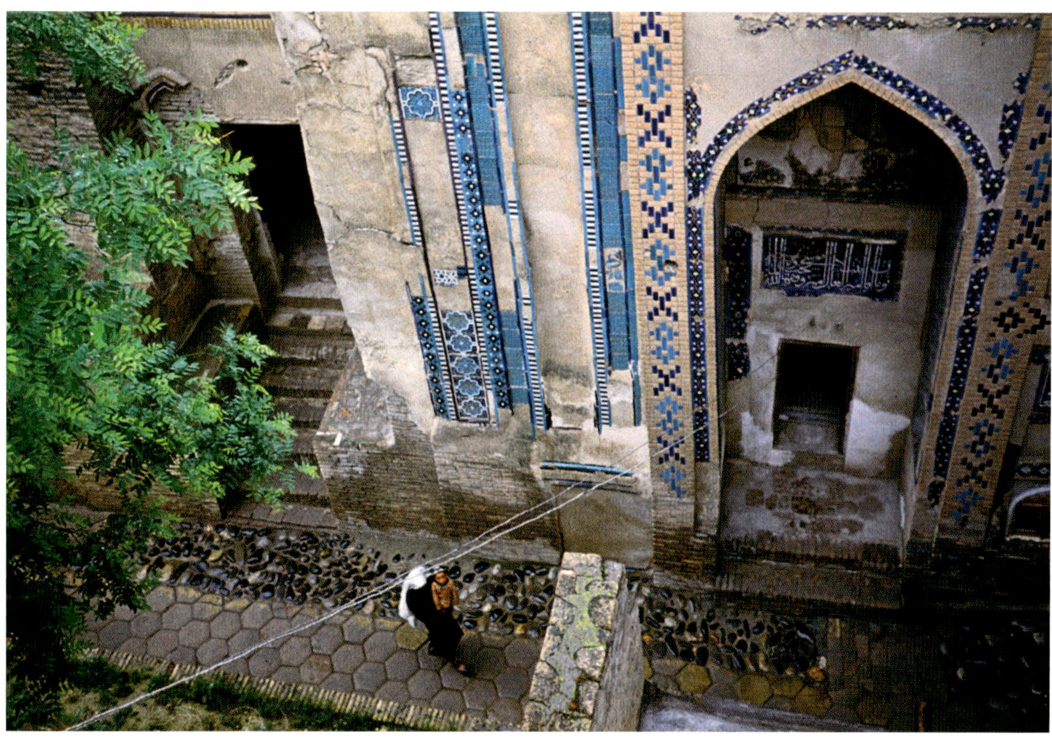

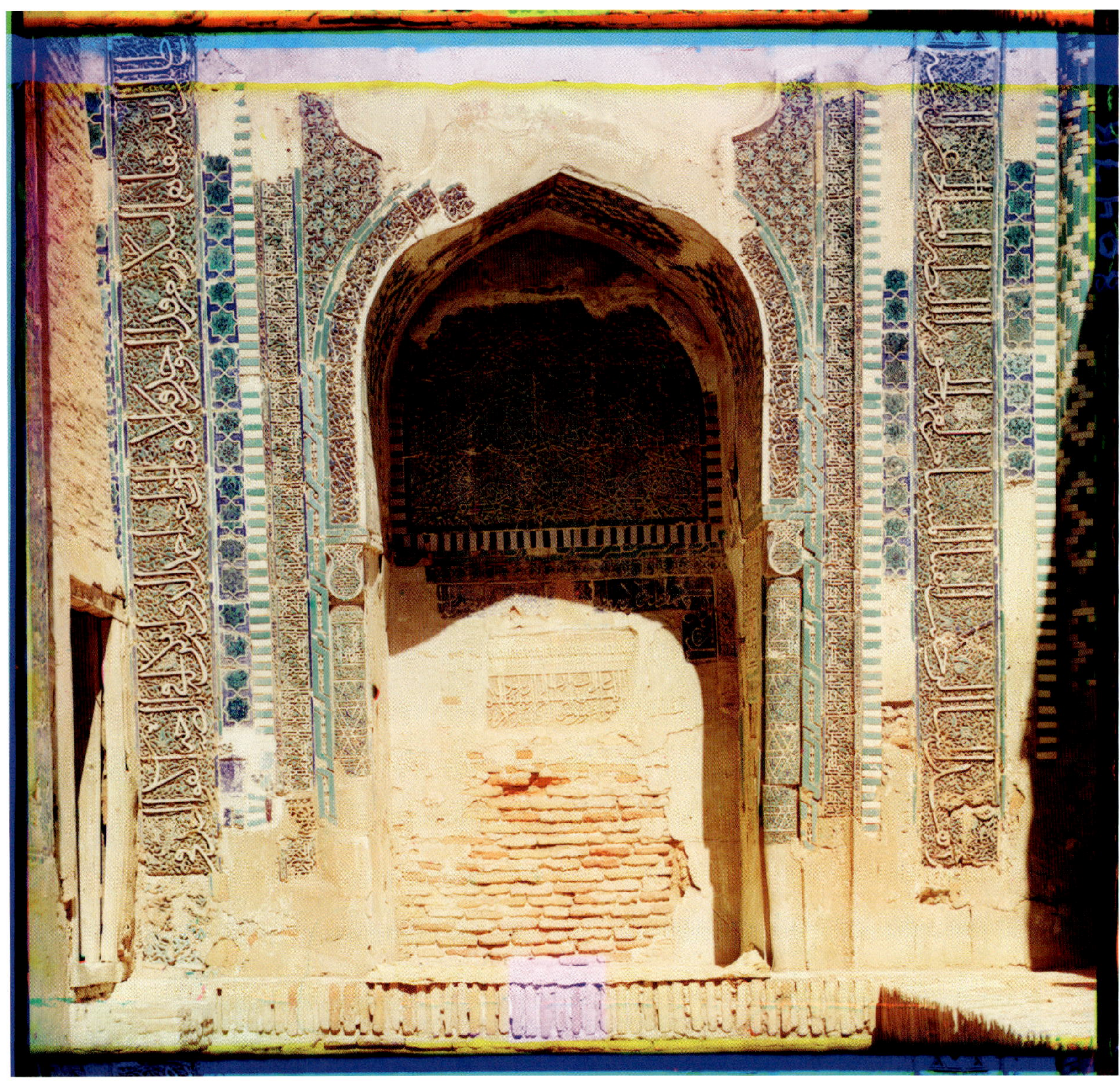

SAMARKAND Shakhi Zinda. Hodja Ahmad mausoleum. PROKUDIN-GORSKY 21820. 1911.

soleum, its patron has not been identified, although it was apparently intended for a prominent noblewoman.

The memorial burial shrines at Shakhi Zinda show limited structural diversity—usually one cuboid chamber with an elaborately decorated portal and a cupola that is either mounted on a drum or placed directly over the chamber. Although the scale of the monuments cannot compare with the vast dimensions of Bibi Khanym and Gur Emir—both contemporaneous with Shakhi Zinda—the architectural details of the necropolis show considerable sophistication, and the sense of ensemble is exquisitely maintained.

SAMARKAND Shakhi Zinda. Supplicants at Hodja Ahmad mausoleum. The boy on the left walked with a wooden crutch. The woman with small child removes her outer veil before kneeling in prayer. BRUMFIELD, MAY 16, 1972.

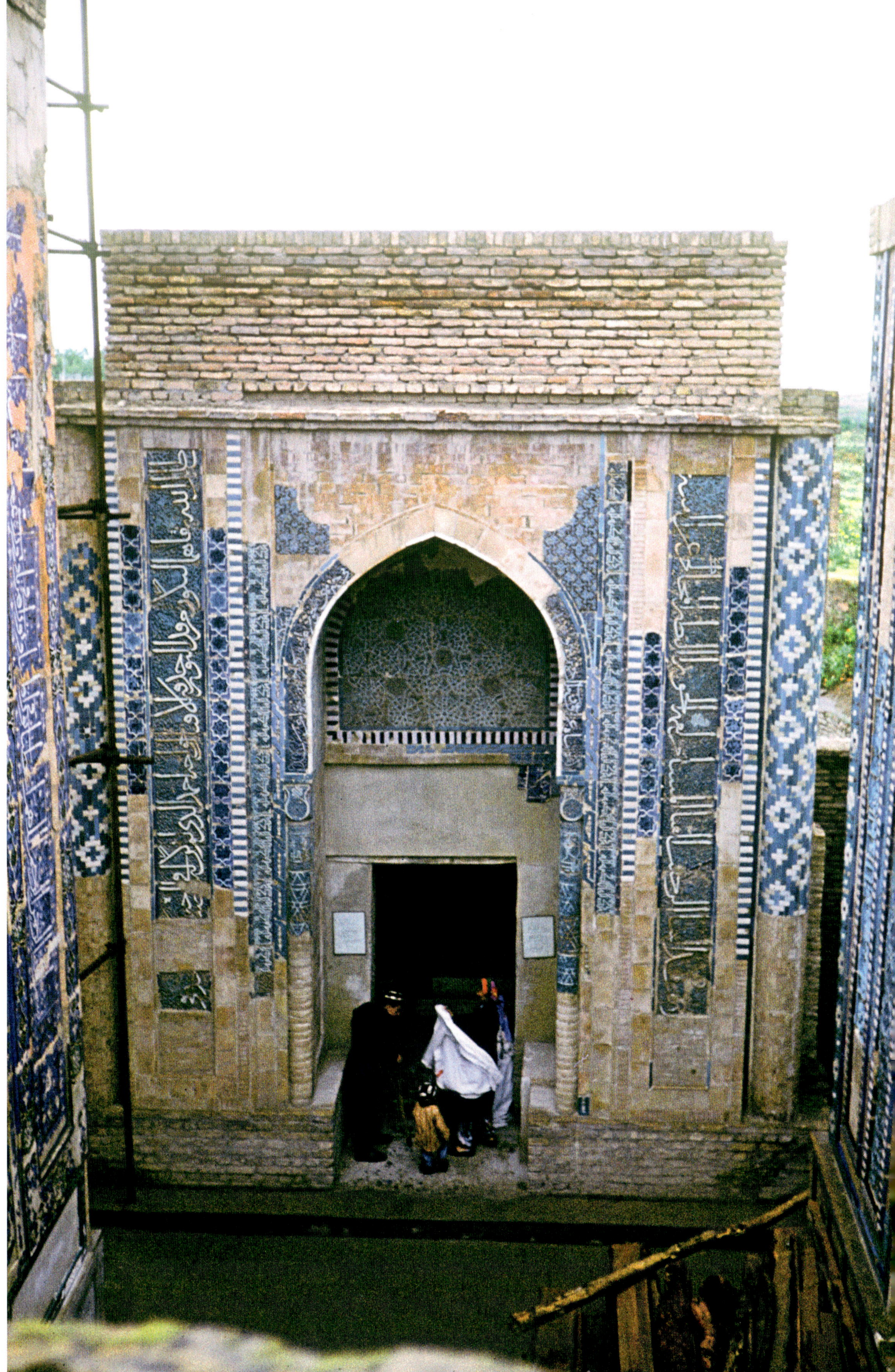

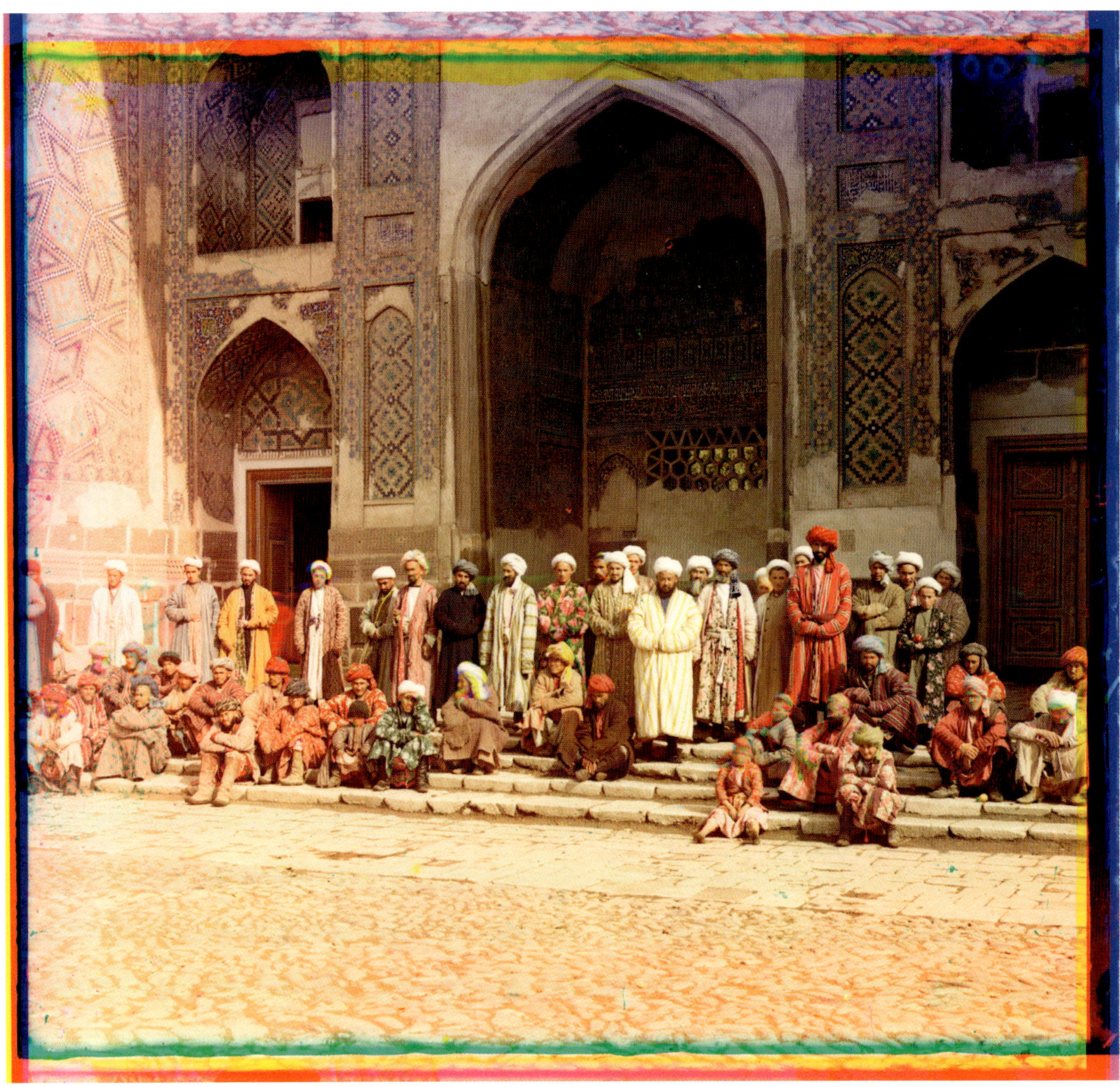

The most striking feature of Shakhi Zinda, however, is its ceramic decoration, which some specialists consider to be unsurpassed in the Moslem world. Close inspection reveals different color glazes and ceramic paints in white, red, orange, and green, but the dominant tonality is blue: sky blue, dark blue, blue-violet, blue-green—the gradation of hues seems infinite. When the entire facade—or a large part of it—has been preserved, one gains an idea of the impression Shakhi Zinda must have produced on those who saw it in the fifteenth century: a narrow passage flanked by structures whose surface, inside as well as out, was covered by

SAMARKAND Shir-Dor Madrasa. Lower part of main facade. View across Registan Square from Ulugh-Beg Madrasa. PROKUDIN-GORSKY 21726. JANUARY 1907.

NEAR TAILAK (on road from Samarkand) Shearing sheep at the Zeravshan River. BRUMFIELD, MAY 17, 1972.

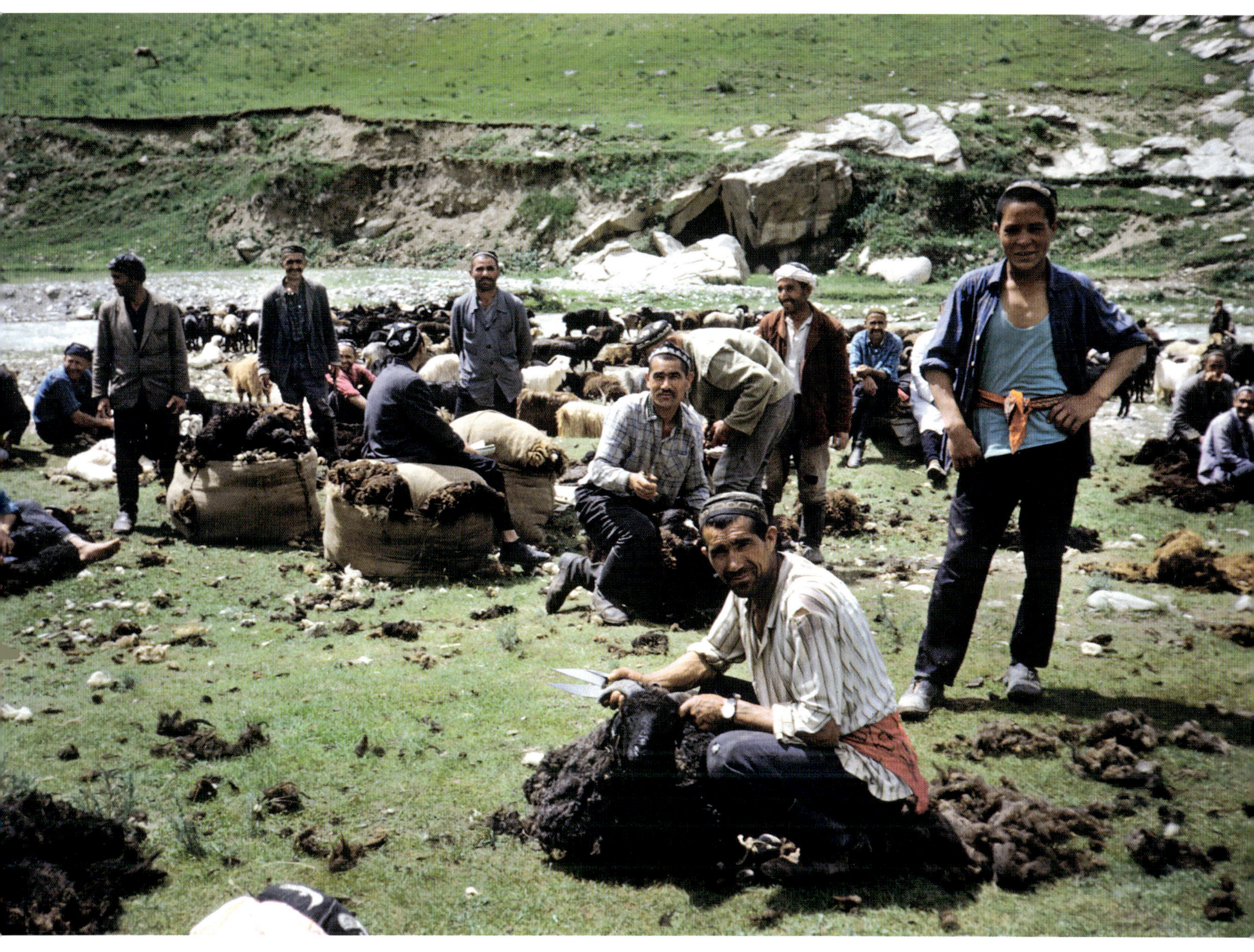

polychrome patterns set within this celestial blue. The designs themselves—carved, molded, in glazed ceramic patterns, in faience mosaics—are derived from floral and geometric motifs frequently overlaid by epigraphs in a delicate Arabic script of the cursive, or *Nashk*, variety, in contrast to the Kufic inscriptions that typically encircle the drums.

While walking through Shakhi Zinda—as Prokudin-Gorsky had six decades earlier—I was struck not only by its beauty but also by its fragility, its vulnerability to the effects of time and the elements (including seismic activity). Fortunately, the mid-twentieth century witnessed a painstaking program of restoration, with master craftsmen gathered in workshops that have preserved the art of architectural ceramic decoration. Through their efforts the vision of artists and craftsmen who lived five centuries ago is gradually being regained. A necropolis whose name signifies eternal life, Shakhi Zinda has achieved its own form of immortality.

As a coda to the Central Asian journey, I have decided to summon a different chord. Although this volume has examined photography as a means of conveying architectural form, the people who live in the shadow of monuments have been a constant presence in my work as well as Prokudin-Gorsky's. (Indeed, one could write a separate study of his photographs of the peoples among whom he traveled.) I am therefore concluding this journey with two photographs in which the human presence is immediately in view. The first is Prokudin-Gorsky's superb photograph of a gathering of turbaned mullahs and youths on the steps in front of the main facade beneath the glorious iwan arch of the Shir-Dor Madrasa. The counterpart is my photograph of a group of men—Uzbeks, Tadzhiks—shearing sheep in the almost blindingly clear May sunlight with the Zeravshan River and a verdant slope in the background. Sheep's wool has been a central part of human existence for countless millennia (and none is richer than the wool in this view), and a view of this arduous work would itself distinguish the photograph. But to this is added the good spirit and openness with which these people accepted my presence.

In terms of its circumstances, Sergey Prokudin-Gorsky's final expedition was also his grimmest. With the outbreak of World War I on July 28, 1914, Russia underwent a draconian transition to war footing. For Prokudin-Gorsky this would mean an increase in travel restrictions and a lessening of financial and logistical support. Yet unexpectedly, support was renewed in 1916 when he received a commission to photograph construction during the summer along the new railroad to the northern ice-free port of Romanov-on-Murman (now Murmansk), which was to serve as a depot for allied war materiel shipped to Russia forces. The strategic project lasted from 1914 to the spring of 1917, when the rail link was connected to Petrograd. Several of the photographs (not reproduced in this book) showed prisoners-of-war from the Austro-Hungarian and German armies. Kept in primitive conditions, the prisoners suffered from health problems exacerbated by the heavy labor.

Although Prokudin-Gorsky's primary purpose was to photograph construction related to the railroad, he also photographed the area's few towns and their churches. Among the towns was Petrozavodsk ("Peter's factory"), founded in September 1703, just four months after Saint Petersburg. In the first image in this chapter, the panoramic view toward the northeast, taken from Golikovka Station, includes the white churches and administrative buildings of the central part of town, as well as the area of wooden houses to the southwest of the Aleksandrovsky Factory, whose red metal roofs are

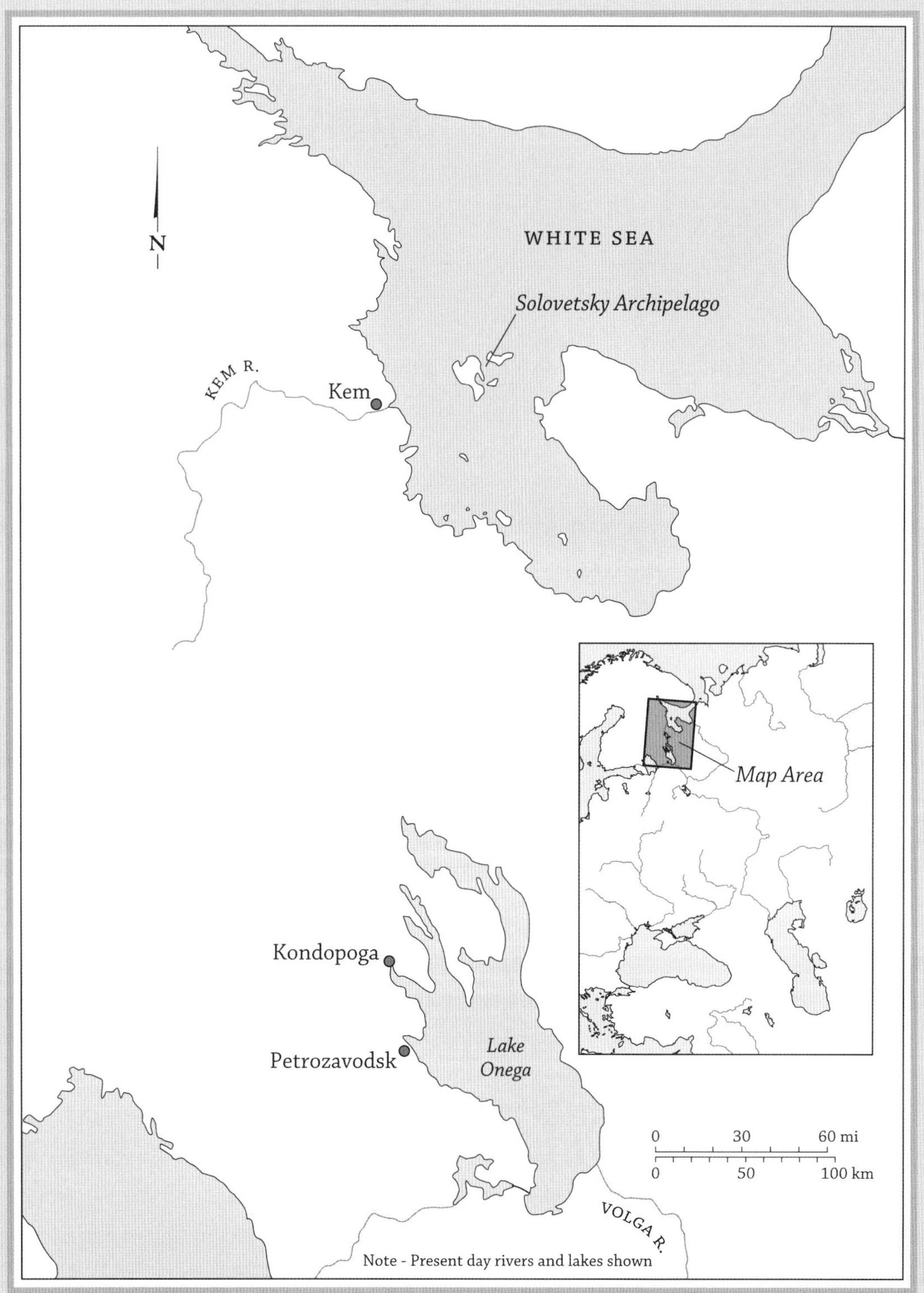

N
WHITE SEA
Solovetsky Archipelago
KEM R.
Kem
Kondopoga
Petrozavodsk
Lake Onega
VOLGA R.
Map Area
0   30   60 mi
0   50   100 km
Note - Present day rivers and lakes shown

just visible. The largest church (on left) is the Cathedral of the Descent of the Holy Spirit. To its right is the factory Church of Saint Alexander Nevsky. Beyond are the towers of the Resurrection Cathedral and the Church of Saints Peter and Paul. In the background is the view across to the other side of Petrozavodsk. Most of the historical architecture that Prokudin-Gorsky photographed was destroyed in the Soviet period and during battles in 1944. An exception is the Church of Saint Alexander Nevsky, built in a simple but monumental neoclassical style with a Doric portico and a central dome flanked by square belfries. Closed in 1929, the church was converted to a museum in 1931. Returned to the Orthodox Church in 1990s, the structure underwent a prolonged restoration and in June 2000 was consecrated as the primary cathedral of the Petrozavodsk and Karelia eparchy (bishopric). My photograph was taken a month after this momentous event.

Some four hundred kilometers to the north of Petrozavodsk is Kem, a small regional center and White Sea port in the Republic of Karelia. Known as a major route to the Solovetsky Archipelago and its Solovetsky-Transfiguration Monastery, the town has a dramatic history, which, like that of the Solovetsky islands, combines elements of the spiritual with human tragedy. The setting of Kem is dramatic, with a rocky coastline bounded by dense forest that reaches the west shore of the White Sea. The town is located primarily on an island known as Lepostrov ("Läppäsaari" in Karelian), which is flanked by the arms of the small Kem River near its confluence with the White Sea. During the medieval period these northern lands were held by the commercial power of Novgorod. In 1450 Novgorod granted the settlement at the mouth of the Kem River to the Solovetsky Transfiguration Monastery, which had been established in 1436 on a group of islands in the southwestern White Sea. Through this grant the Solovetsky Monastery, protected on its archipelago, acquired a land base and port some sixty kilometers over water to the west.

Because of its strategic location, Kem gained the attentions of hostile neighbors in the late sixteenth century. Ivan the Terrible was at that time mired in the Livonian War (1558–83), a protracted conflict that in its latter phase involved a struggle with Sweden for control of the eastern Baltic region. In 1589 Kem was raided by Finnic forces, and in 1590 the region was attacked by the Swedes. The following year Moscow reaffirmed Solovetsky Monastery's title to the Kem territory. The power of the monastery allowed it to function as a surrogate for an exhausted Muscovy, and during the next century Kem was defended and fortified under the monastery's direction.

Kem briefly returned to state control from 1704 to 1711 during the early

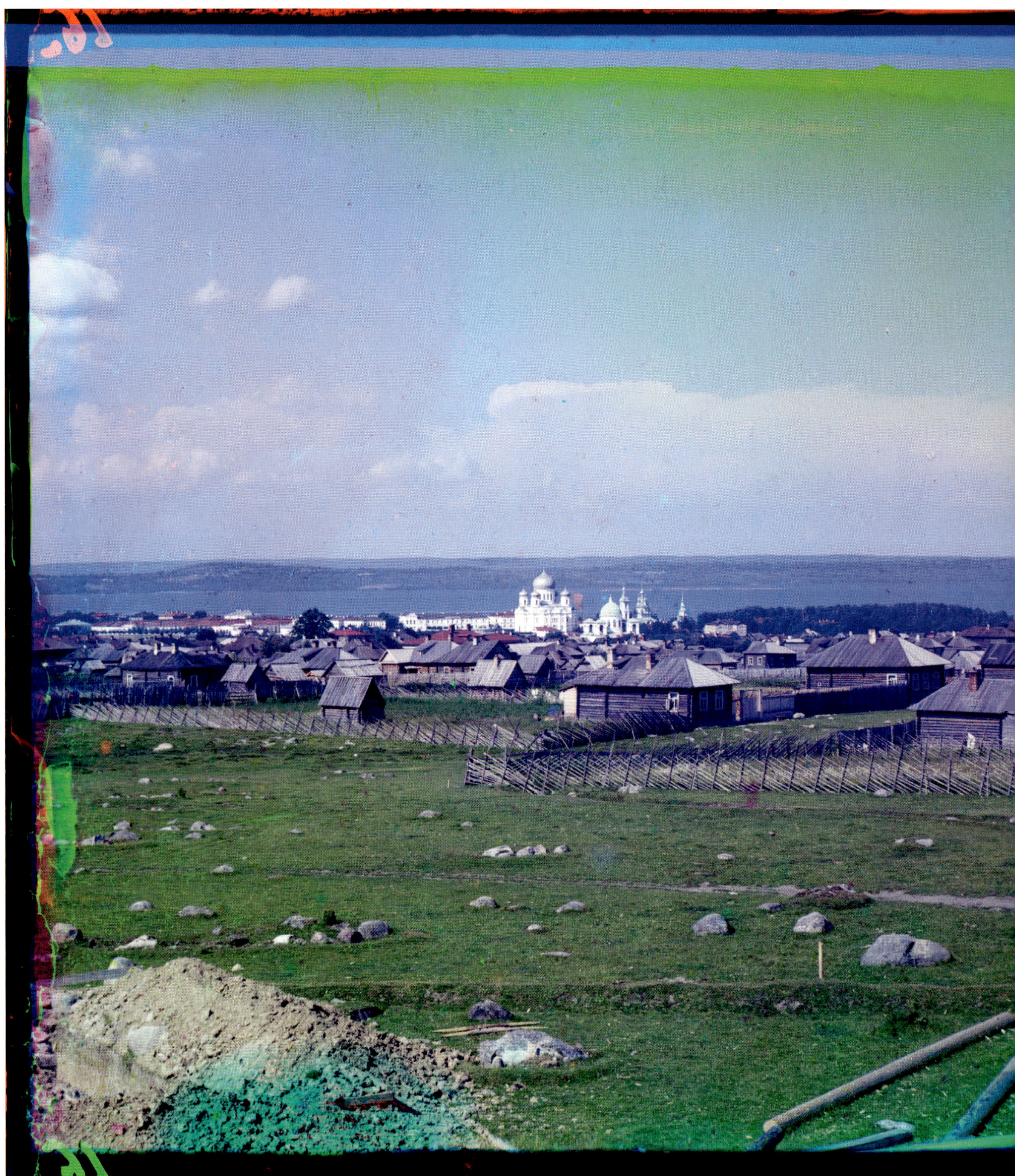

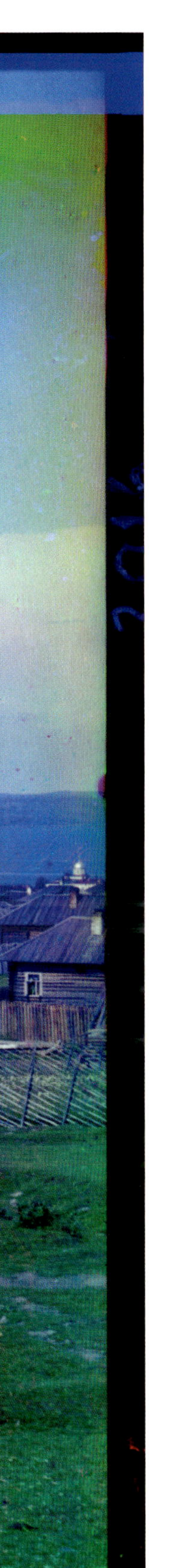

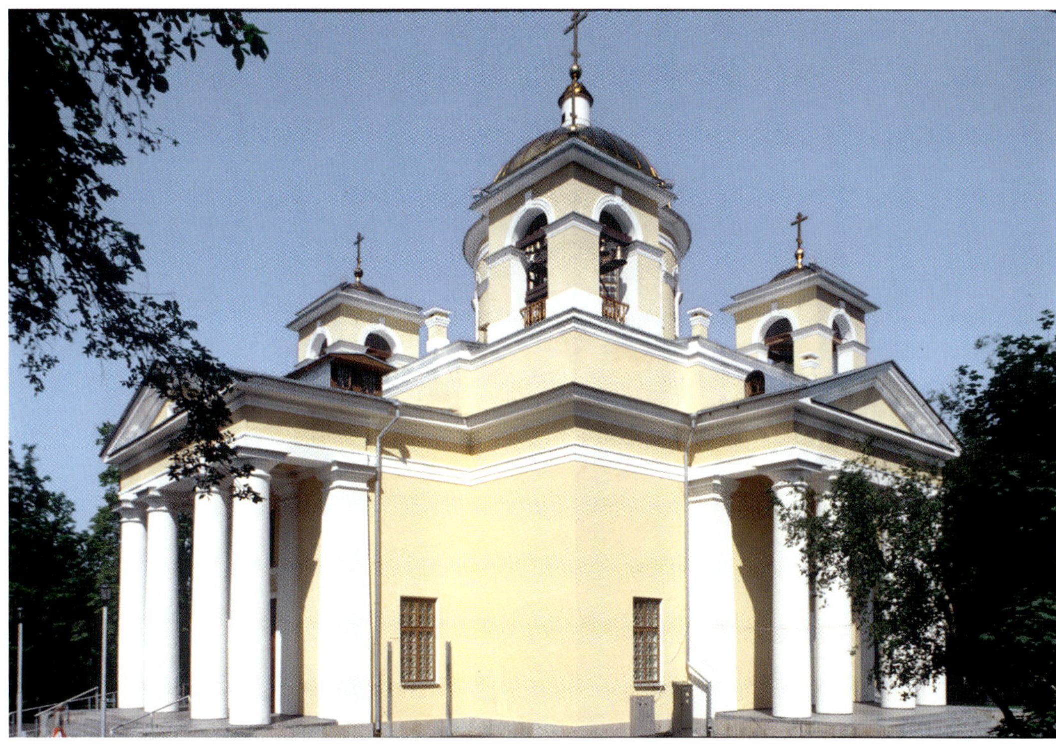

phase of Peter the Great's struggle with Sweden in the Great Northern War (1700–21). With Peter's victory over King Charles XII at Poltava (July 1709), pressure on Russia's White Sea territory diminished. During the nineteenth century the town existed primarily on fishing. In 1903 Kem gained a large masonry church, the Cathedral of the Annunciation, visible in Prokudin-Gorsky's photograph. During the Soviet period, the cathedral was modified for use by the administration of the penal camp established by the Cheka (the Soviet political police) in 1919 on the territory of the former Solovetsky Monastery. The Annunciation Cathedral is now being restored as part of the recently established Monastery of the New Russian Martyrs and Confessors. My photograph almost a century later shows the damage inflicted upon building.

The port of Kem served as the gateway to the Solovetsky Transfiguration Monastery, one of Russia's most renowned monastic institutions. The monastery is located primarily on Great Solovetsky Island, part of an archipelago in the

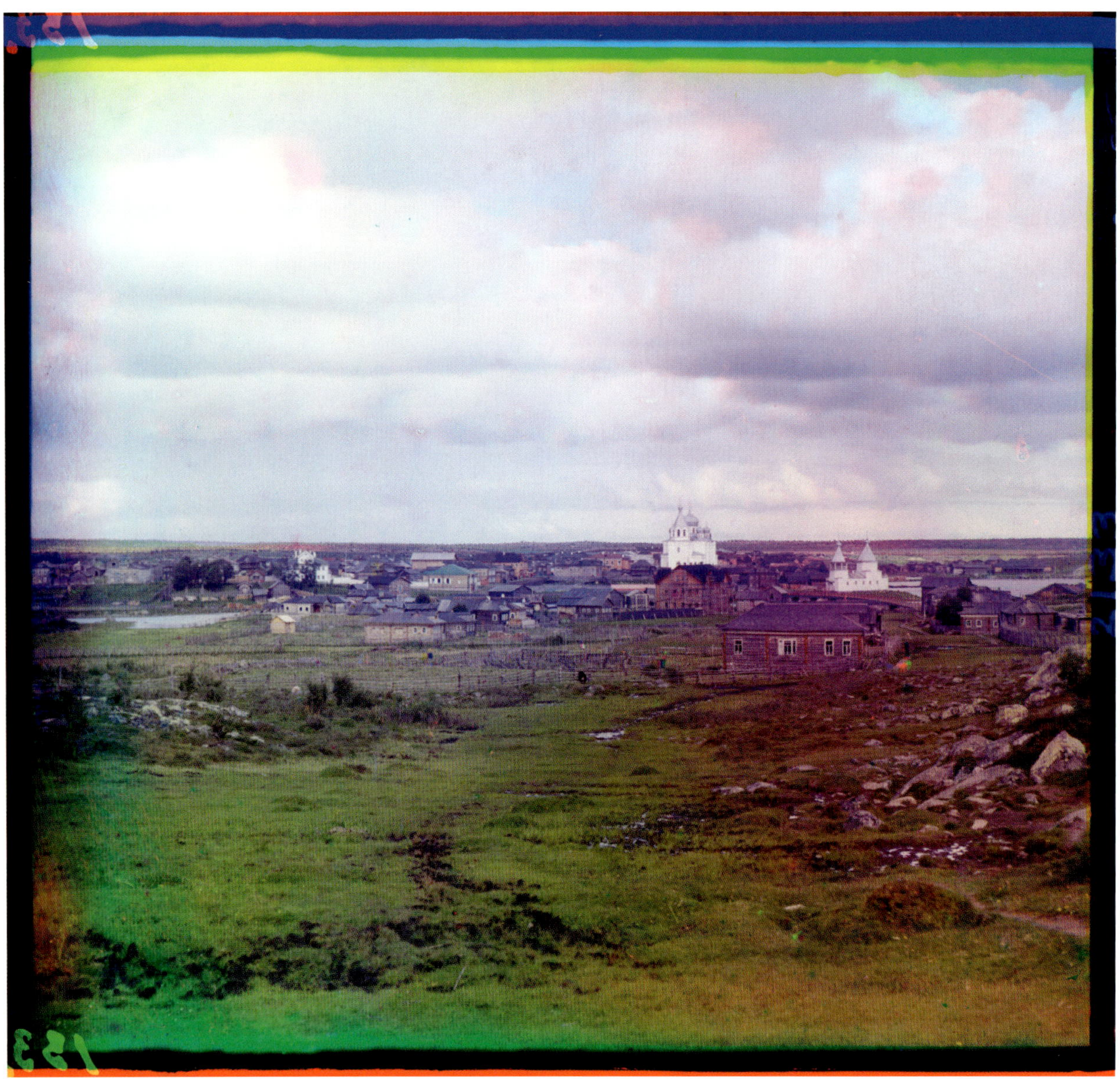

southwestern part of the White Sea. The archipelago's first known Russian settlement dated from 1429 when the monk Zosima joined forces with Herman, a hermit who had periodically visited Solovetsky Island. The elderly Zosima died in 1435, but the following year another monk, Zavvaty, returned to the island and founded a retreat dedicated to the Transfiguration of the Savior. During this early period, the monastery belonged to the domains of the Russian city-state of Novgorod. After Novgorod's subjugation to Moscow in 1478 the Muscovite grand princes reaffirmed the strategic importance of this remote monastic outpost.

KEM General view toward the northeast with Cathedral of the Annunciation. PROKUDIN-GORSKY 20334. SUMMER 1916.

KEM Cathedral of the Annunciation. Southwest view. BRUMFIELD, JULY 25, 2001.

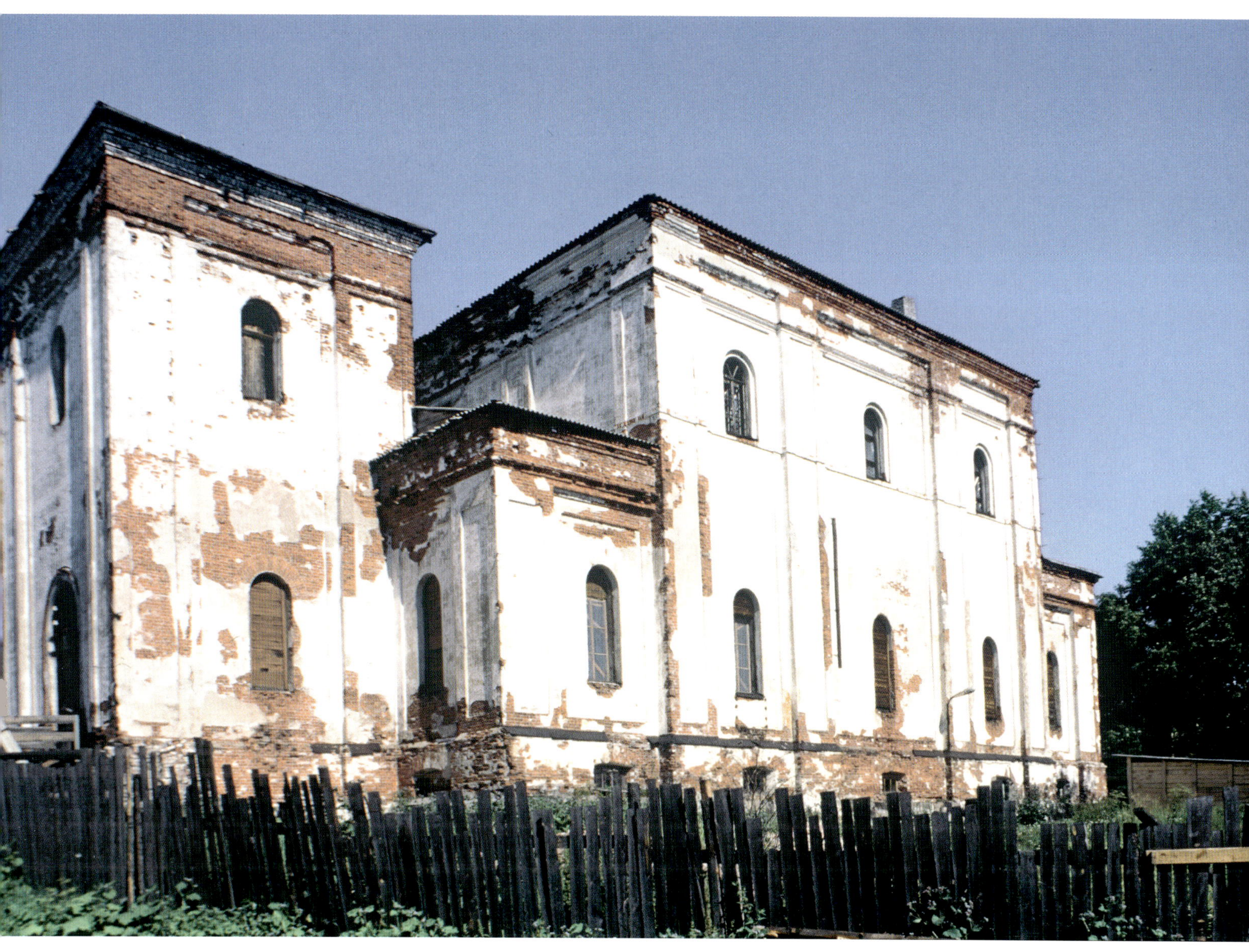

The great flourishing of the monastery occurred in the sixteenth century under the direction of Philip Kolychev, a Moscovite monk of noble origins who left his privileged existence in 1537, joined the Solovetsky monastic community, and in 1547 became its spiritual leader (*hegumen*). During the next eighteen years Philip guided a program of construction that transformed the monastery and created monumental buildings of stone and brick such as the Cathedral of the Transfiguration of the Savior (1558–66) and the Refectory Church of the Dormition (1552–57), among the most impressive manifestations of late medieval Russian architecture. These structures are visible above the monastery walls in Prokudin-Gorsky's west view from the harbor. My photographs taken from a similar west perspective in

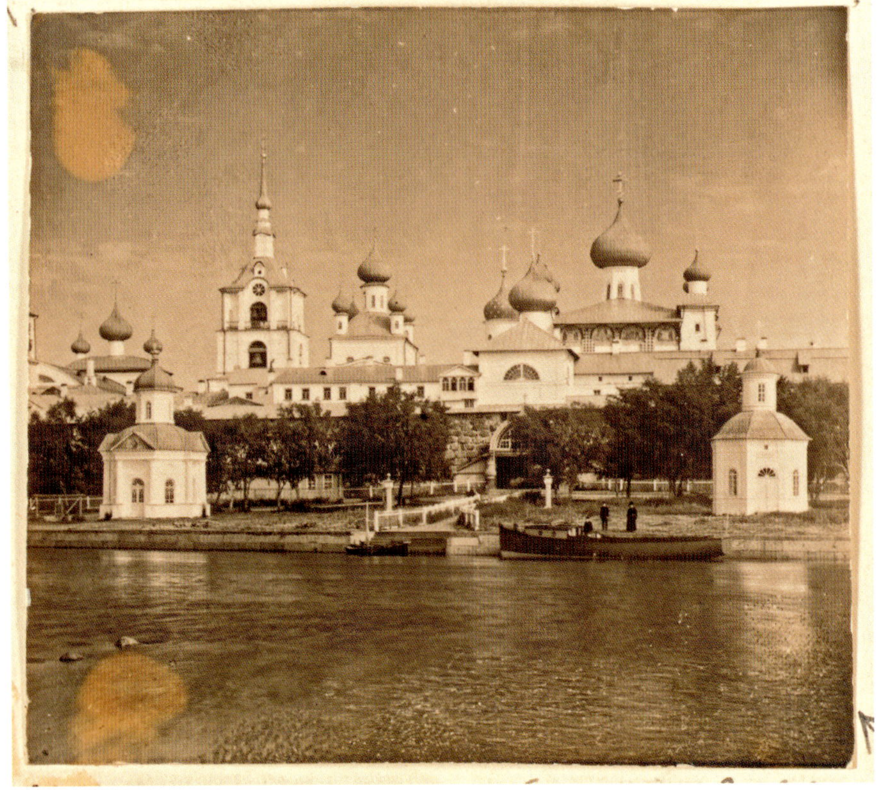

1998 and 1999 show limited damage but preservation of the exterior of the main ensemble. In the summer of 1566, Philip was called back to Moscow by Ivan the Terrible, who supported Philip's appointment as metropolitan of the Russian Church. Philip's resistance to Ivan's misrule led to his exile and death in 1569.

Despite the turbulence of the late sixteenth century, construction at the monastery continued. Late sixteenth-century churches in the monastery include the Church of Saint Nicholas (1577; razed and rebuilt in 1830–34) and the Gate Church of the Annunciation, built in 1596–1601 over the west gate and much modified in the nineteenth century. Prokudin-Gorsky photographed the Annunciation Church and adjacent walls from the west. The Annunciation Church plays a central role in defining the west face of the monastery, which I photographed from the northwest on a late midsummer's evening in 1998. Prokudin-Gorsky took a close view of the entrance arch and the Church of the Annunciation. The massive boulders of the walls stand in vivid contrast to the whitewashed surface and Italianate window of the church.

Between 1582 and 1594 monks and hired labor manhandled thousands of granite boulders into place as the walls and round towers of the monas-

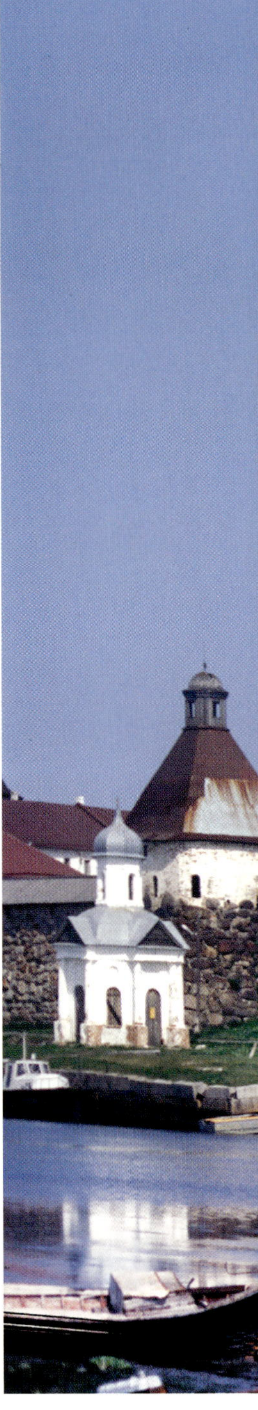

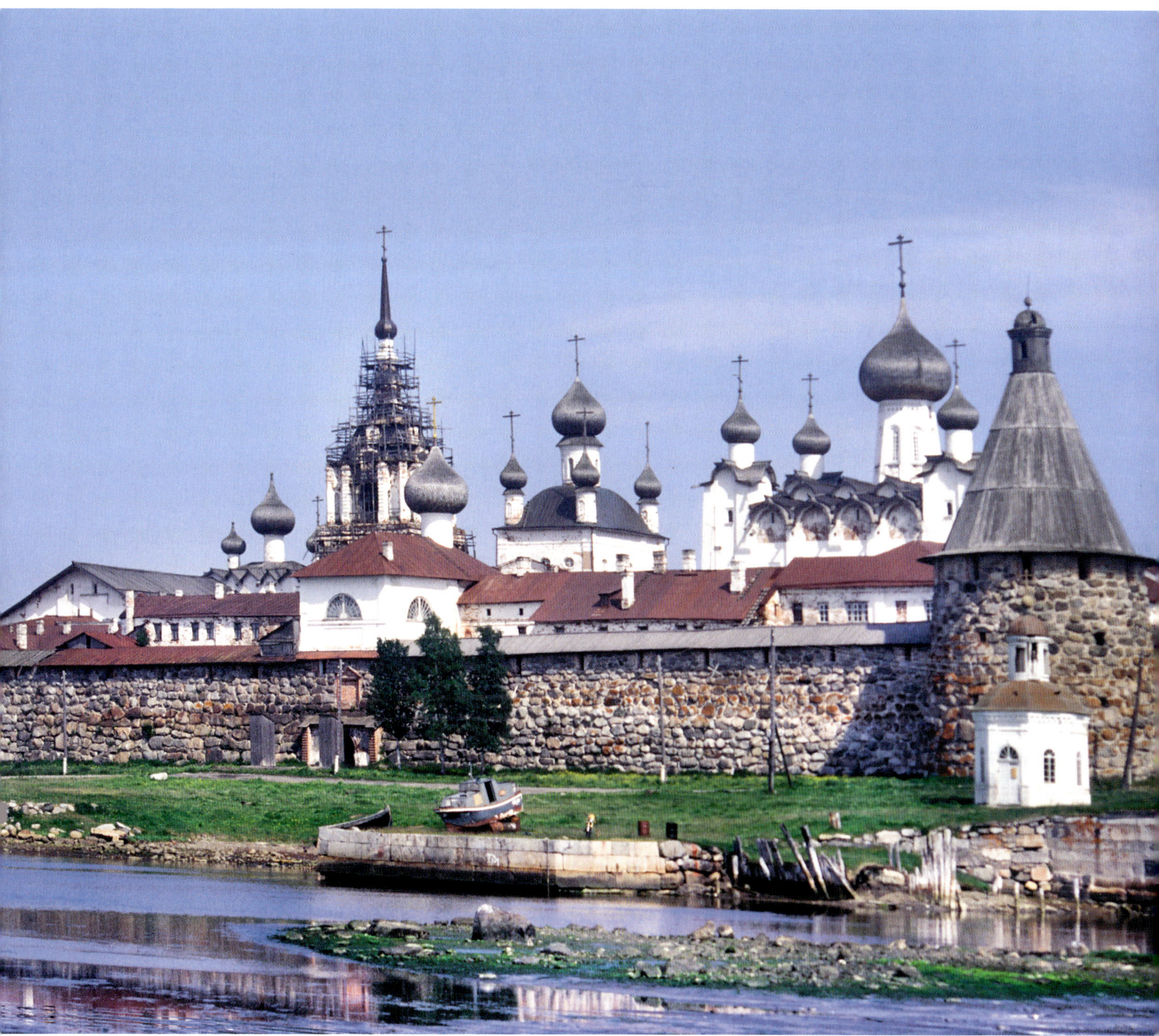

SOLOVETSKY TRANSFIGURATION MONASTERY

West view from harbor. *From left*: Refectory Church of the Dormition; Chapel of Saint Alexander Nevsky; bell tower; Church of Saint Nicholas; Church of Annunciation; west wall and Holy Gate; Transfiguration Cathedral; Chapel of Saints Peter and Paul. PROKUDIN-GORSKY 02039. SUMMER 1916.

SOLOVETSKY TRANSFIGURATION MONASTERY

Southwest view at harbor. *From left*: Chapel of Saint Alexander Nevsky; west wall; Refectory Church of Dormition; bell tower; Church of Annunciation over Holy Gate; Church of Saint Nicholas; Transfiguration Cathedral; Chapel of Saints Peter and Paul. BRUMFIELD, JUNE 29, 1999.

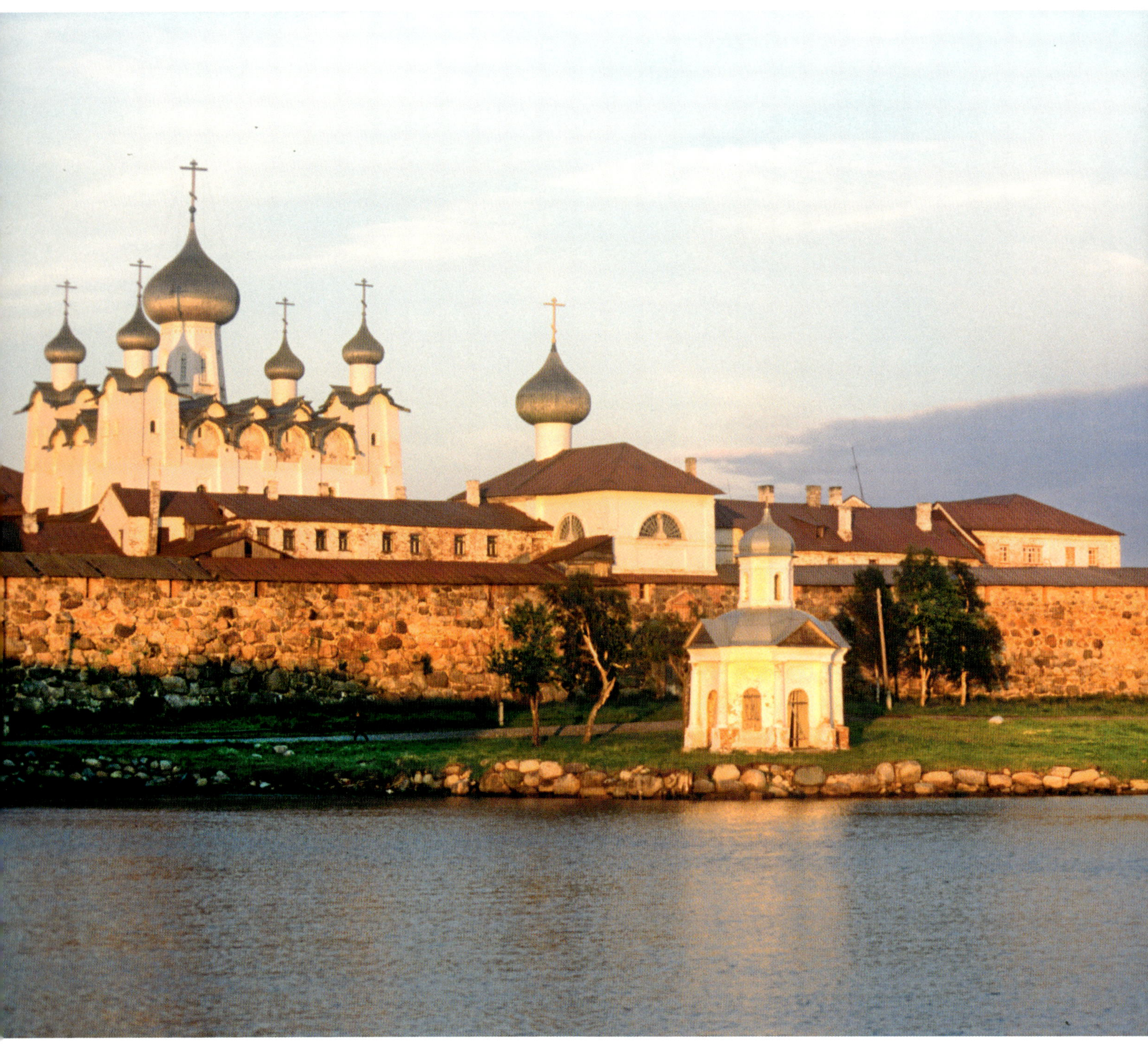

SOLOVETSKY TRANSFIGURATION MONASTERY
Northwest view. *From left*: Transfiguration Cathedral,
west wall with Annunciation Church over Holy Gate,
Chapel of Saint Alexander Nevsky, White Tower (*background*), Spinning Tower. BRUMFIELD, JULY 25, 1998.

SOLOVETSKY TRANSFIGURATION MONASTERY
West wall with Spinning Tower and Annunciation
Church over Holy Gate. Northwest view. PROKUDIN-
GORSKY 20345. SUMMER 1916.

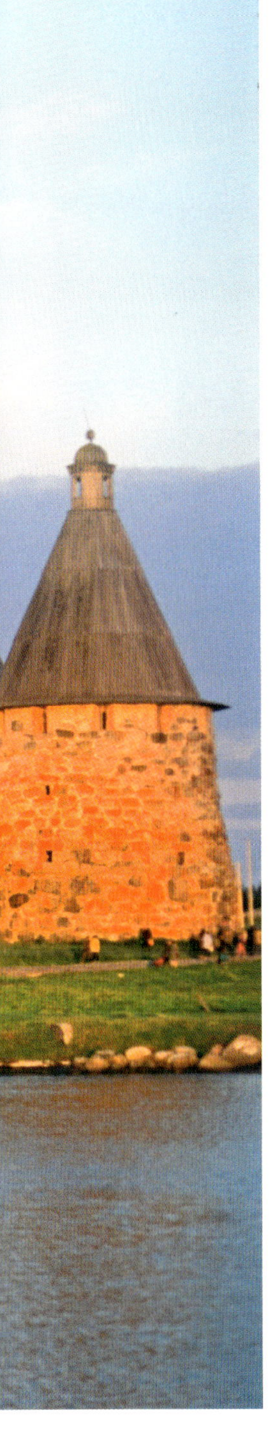

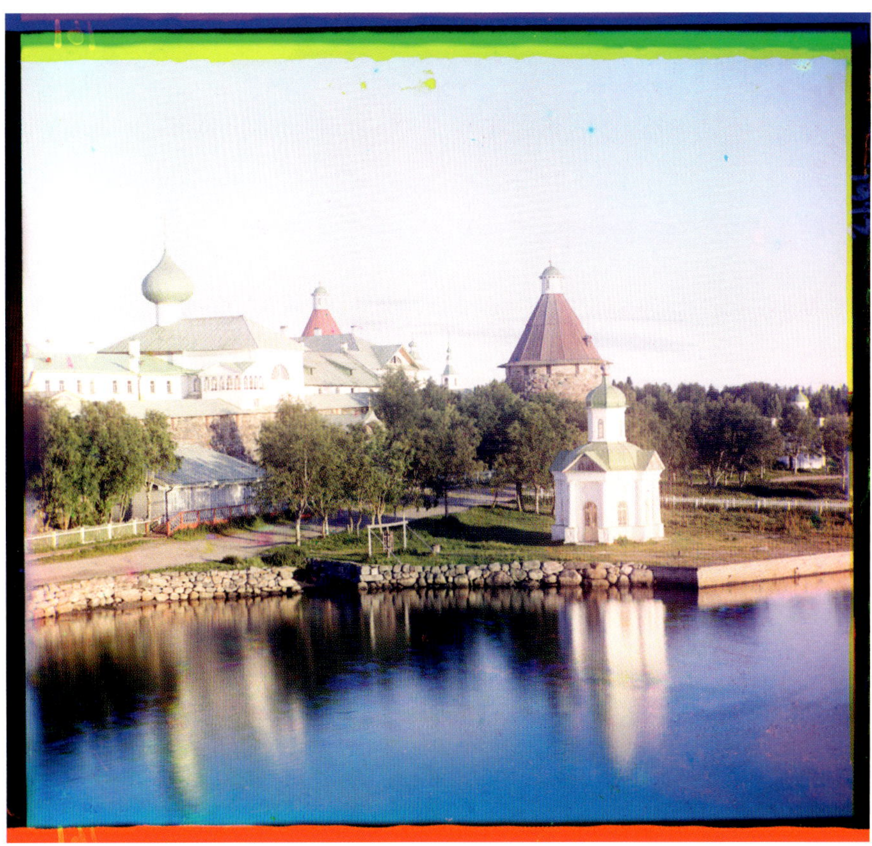

tery arose from the marshy ground. The massive structures drew Prokudin-Gorsky's attention in photographs that include a striking view of the Korozhnaya Tower at the north corner of the west wall. A comparison with photographs taken in 1998 shows significant losses, particularly to the Church of the Icon of the Virgin, Succor to All Who Grieve. On the north wall Prokudin-Gorsky photographed the Saint Nicholas Tower, which has been well preserved. His widest view is of the east wall, with minor square towers associated with brewing operations (*kvas*, beer), as well as east views of the main church ensemble. Photographs taken from a similar perspective in 1998 show Soviet-era modifications and damage to the upper parts of the churches.

Despite the conflicts of the seventeenth century, the Solovetsky Monastery remained one of Muscovy's most prestigious among the privileged religious centers, closely connected to the court. It received many donations, the churches were repaired, and other buildings were added in the eighteenth century. During the nineteenth century, the monastery became a major pilgrimage site, with its own steamship and hotel. At the beginning of the twentieth century, the monastery built an electric generating station with

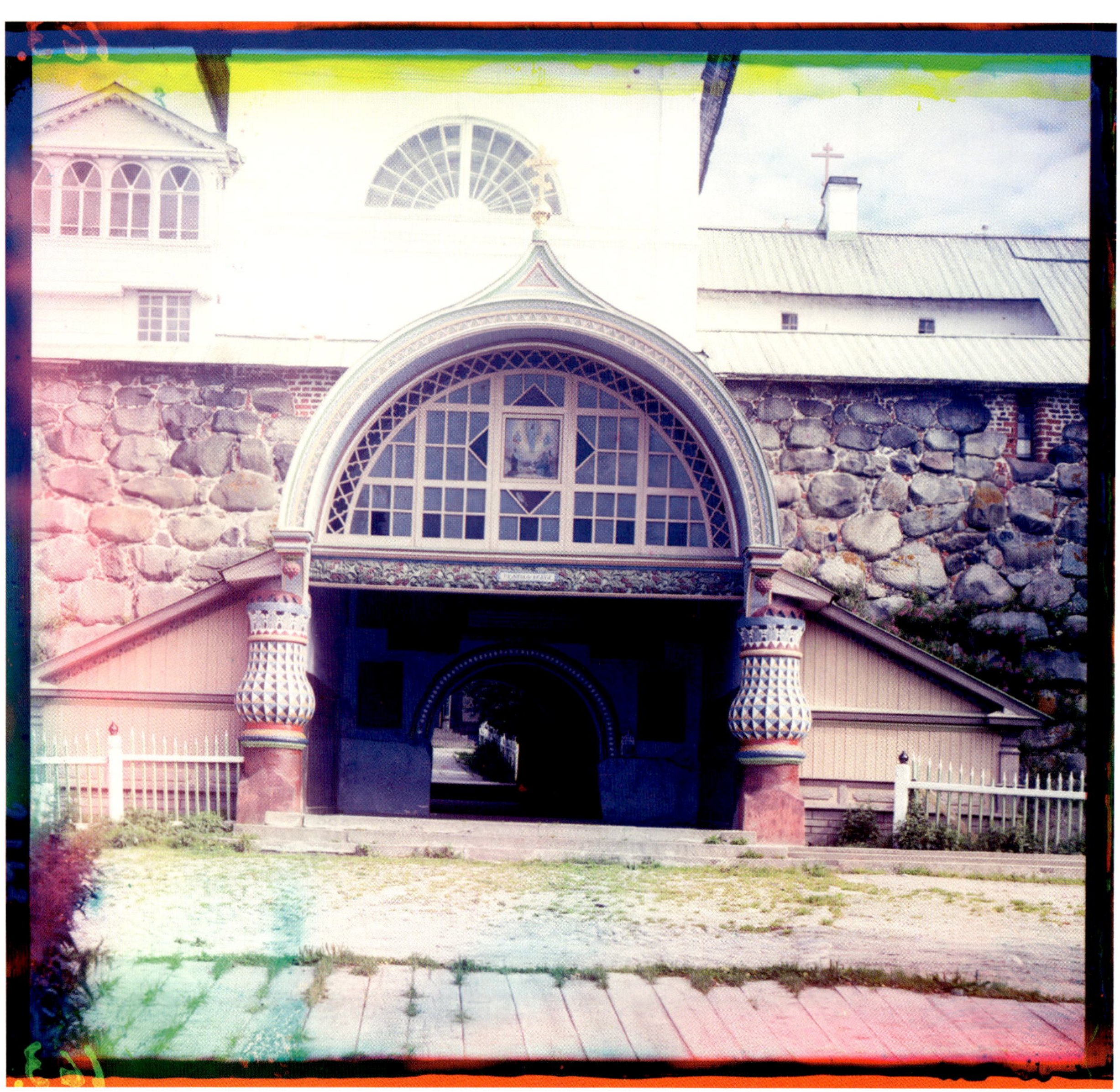

SOLOVETSKY TRANSFIGURATION MONASTERY
Annunciation Church over Holy Gate. West view.
PROKUDIN-GORSKY 20346. SUMMER 1916.

SOLOVETSKY TRANSFIGURATION MONASTERY
Annunciation Church over Holy Gate. West view.
BRUMFIELD, JULY 25, 1998.

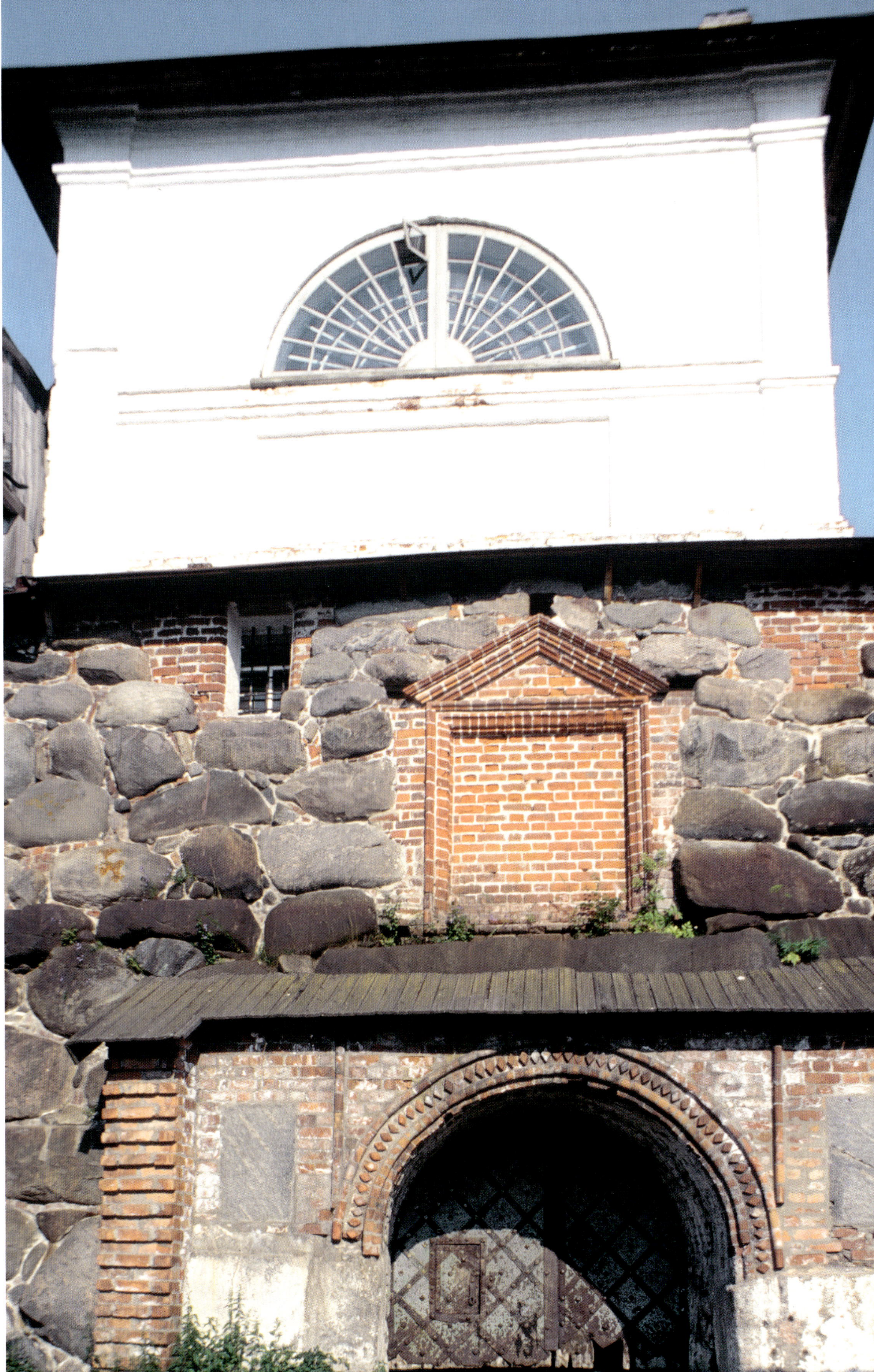

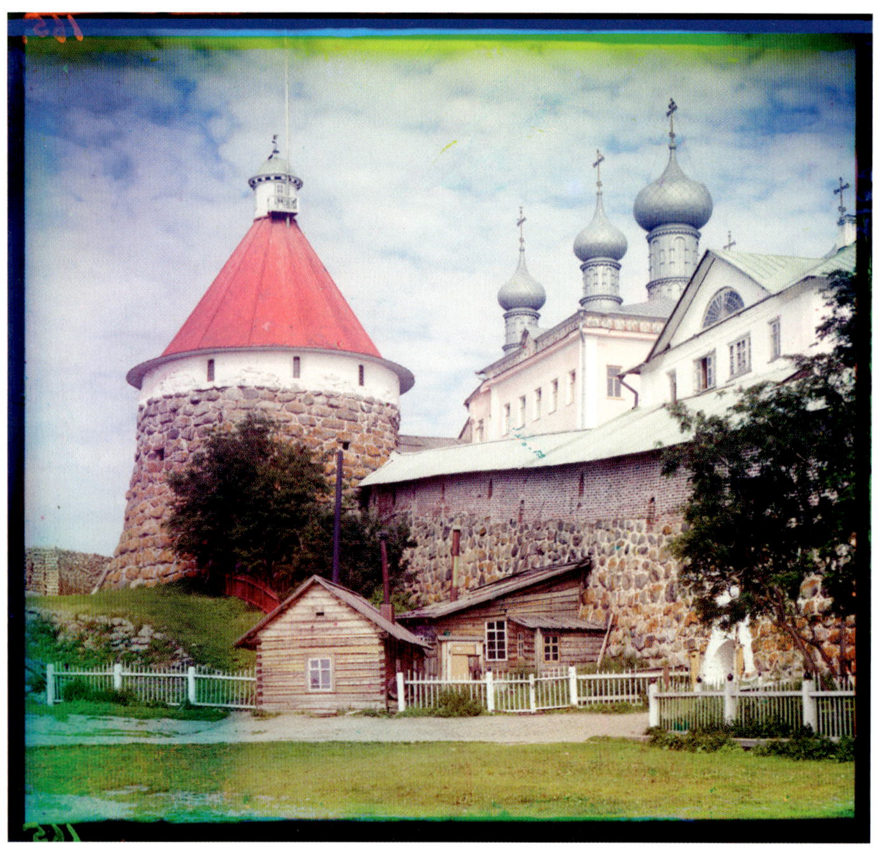

SOLOVETSKY TRANSFIGURA-TION MONASTERY West wall with Korozhnaya Tower and Church of the Icon of the Virgin, Succor to All Who Grieve. Southwest view. PROKUDIN-GORSKY 20348. SUMMER 1916.

SOLOVETSKY TRANSFIGURA-TION MONASTERY West wall. *From left*: Korozhnaya Tower, icon workshop and Church of the Icon of the Virgin, Succor to all Who Grieve (cupolas removed in Soviet period), Superior's Building, Chapel of Saint Alexander Nevsky, Dormition Tower. Southwest view. BRUMFIELD, JUNE 29, 1999.

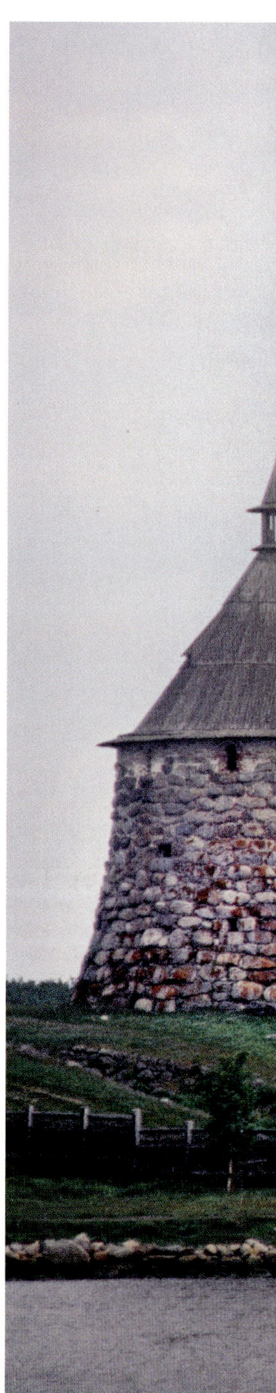

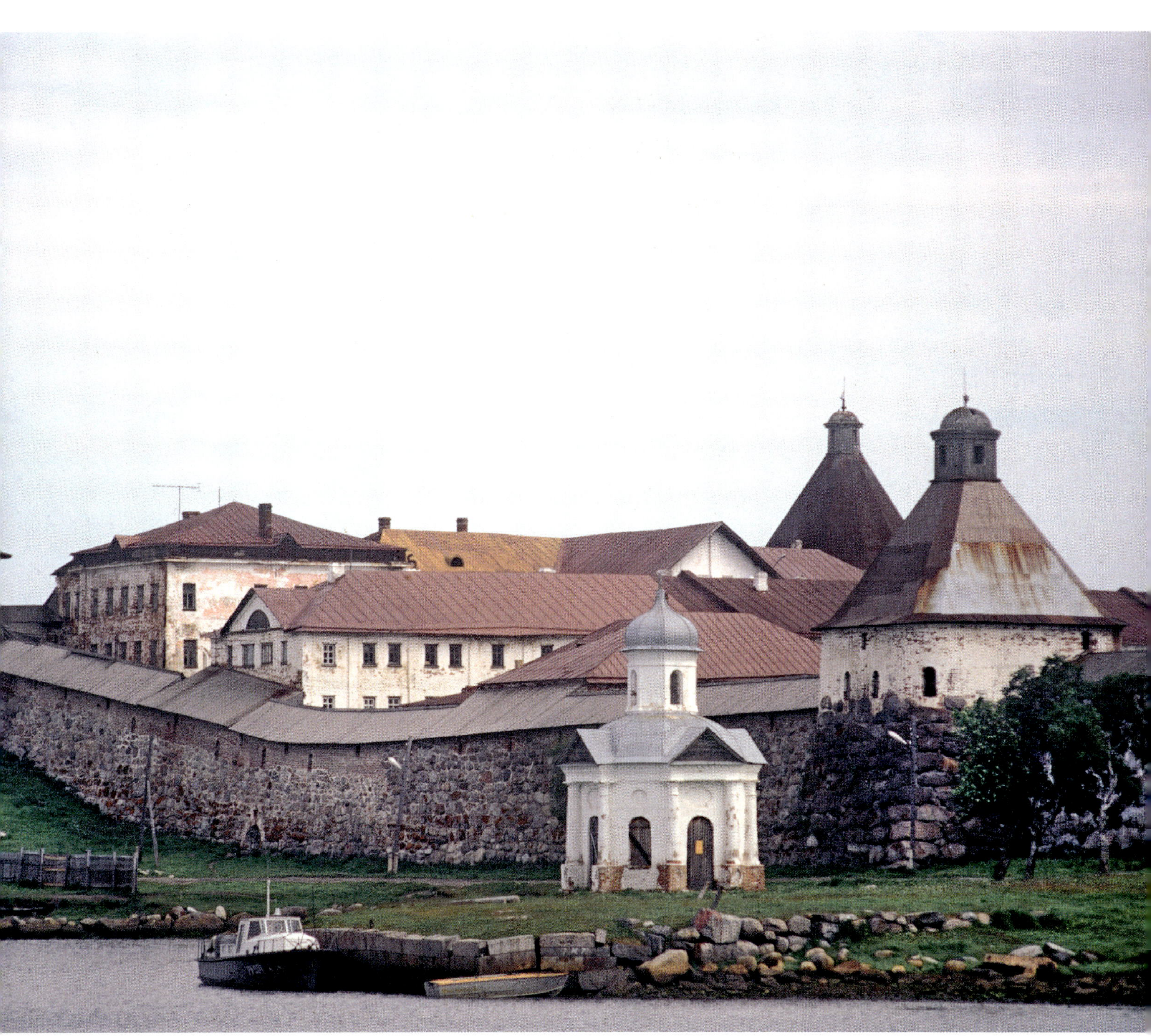

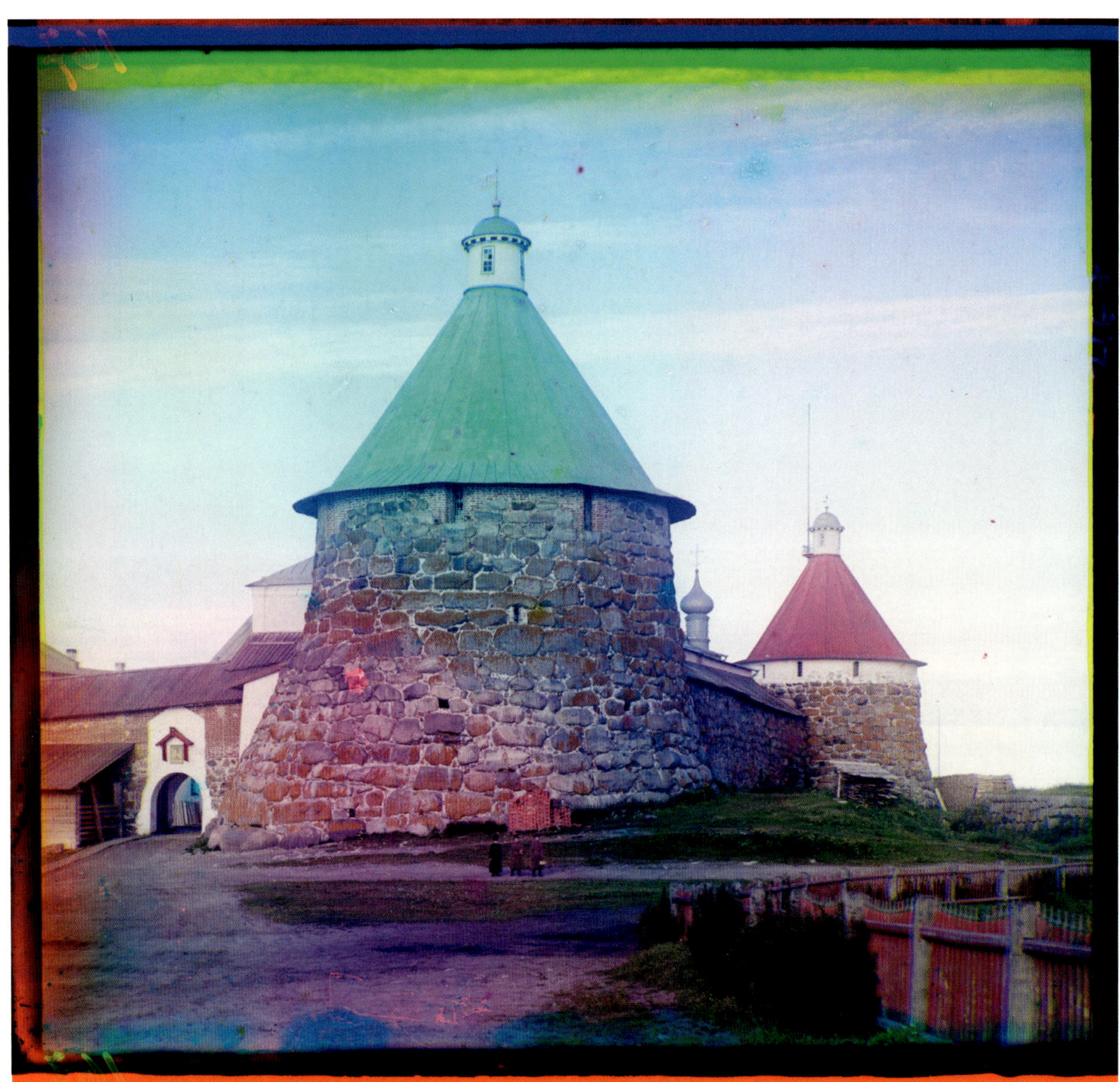

SOLOVETSKY TRANSFIGURATION MONASTERY
North wall with Saint Nicholas Tower and Gate. East
view. *Right*: Korozhnaya Tower. PROKUDIN-GORSKY
20350. SUMMER 1916.

SOLOVETSKY TRANSFIGURATION MONASTERY
Saint Nicholas Tower and Gate. Southeast view.
BRUMFIELD, JULY 25, 1998.

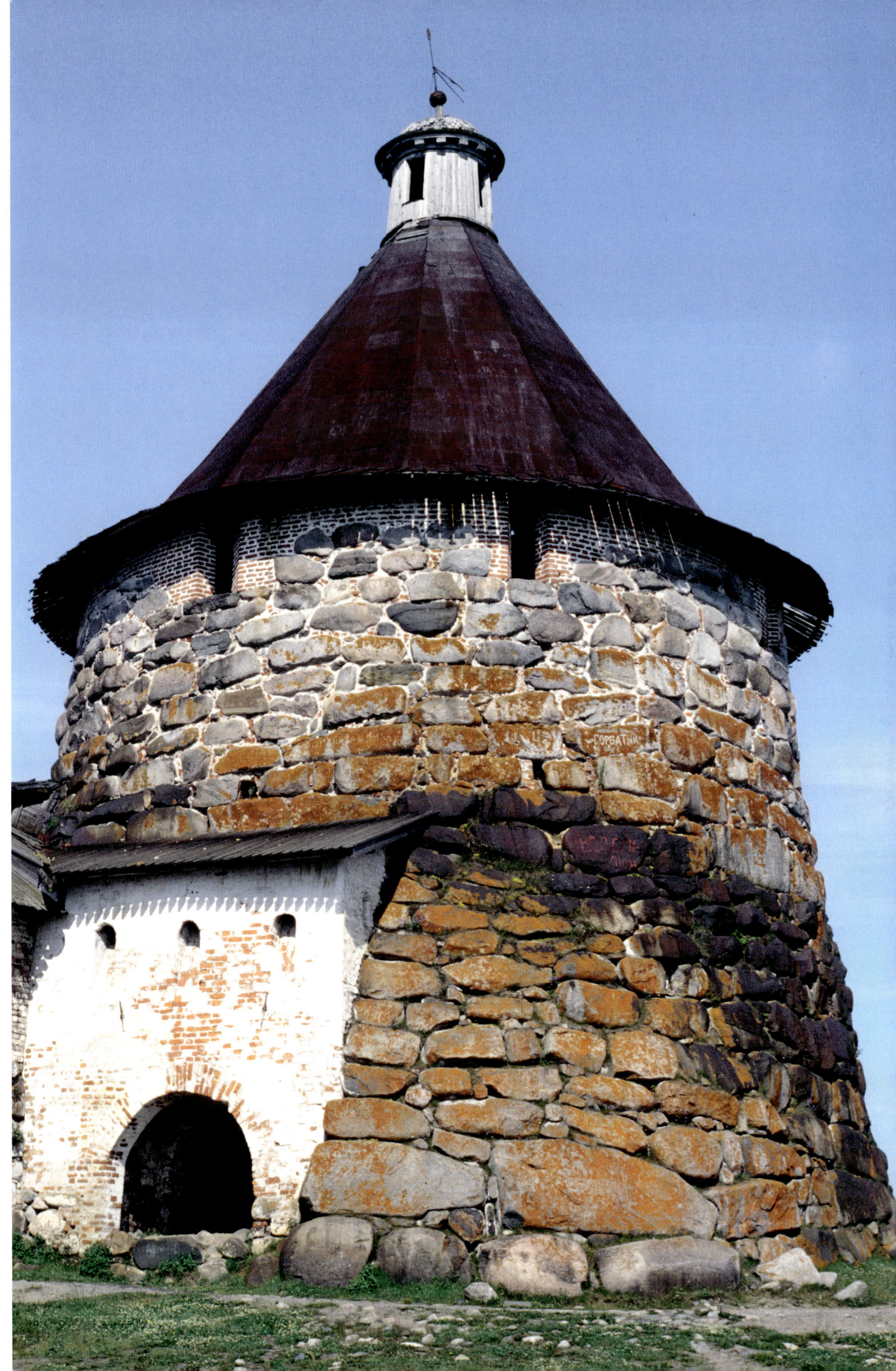

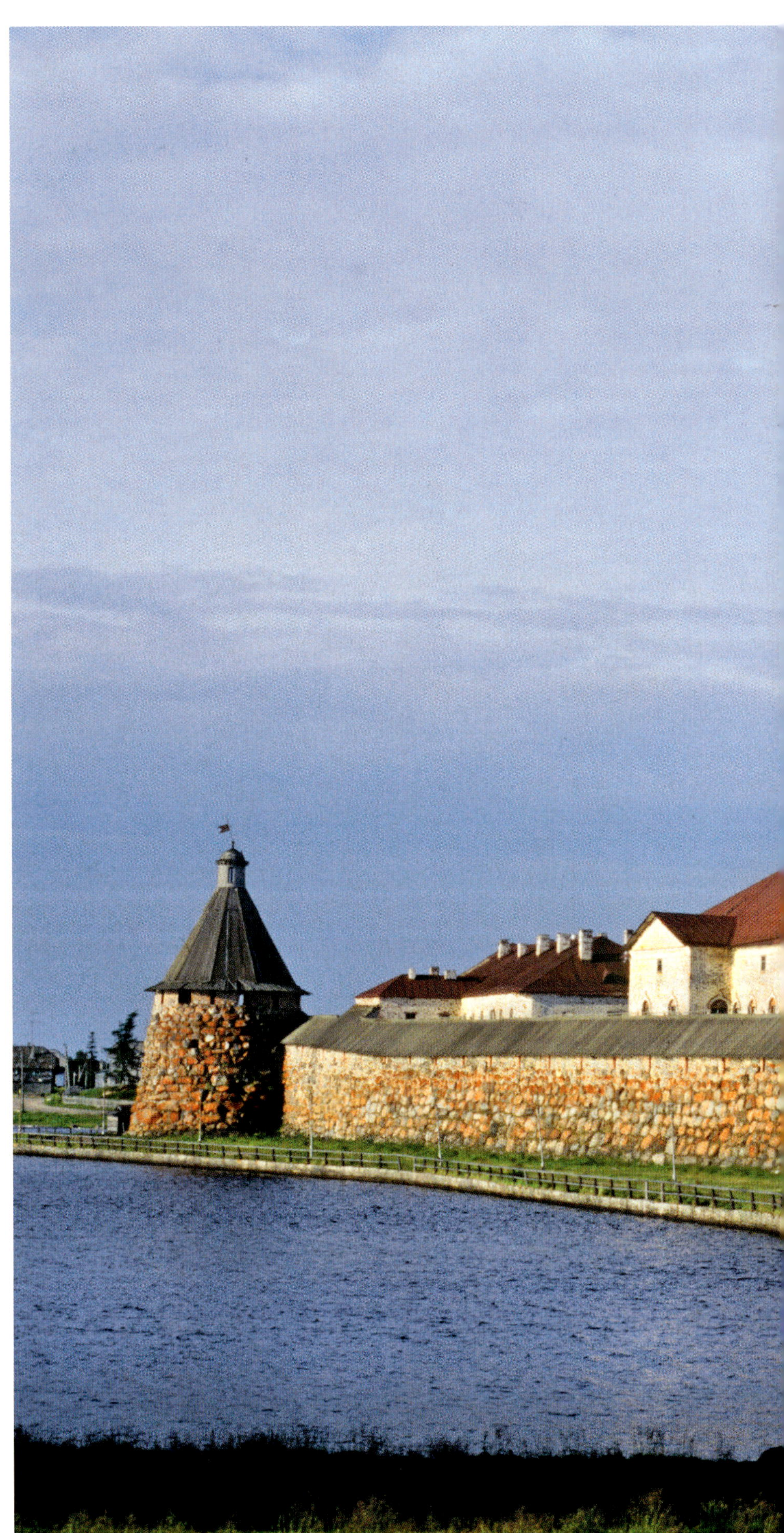

SOLOVETSKY TRANSFIGURA-
TION MONASTERY East wall.
From left: Archangel Tower, New
Cloisters, Church of Trinity and
Saints Zosima and Savvaty (cupo-
las removed in Soviet period),
Transfiguration Cathedral, Cook
Tower, Church of Saint Nicholas,
refectory and Dormition Church.
Northeast view. BRUMFIELD,
JULY 26, 1998.

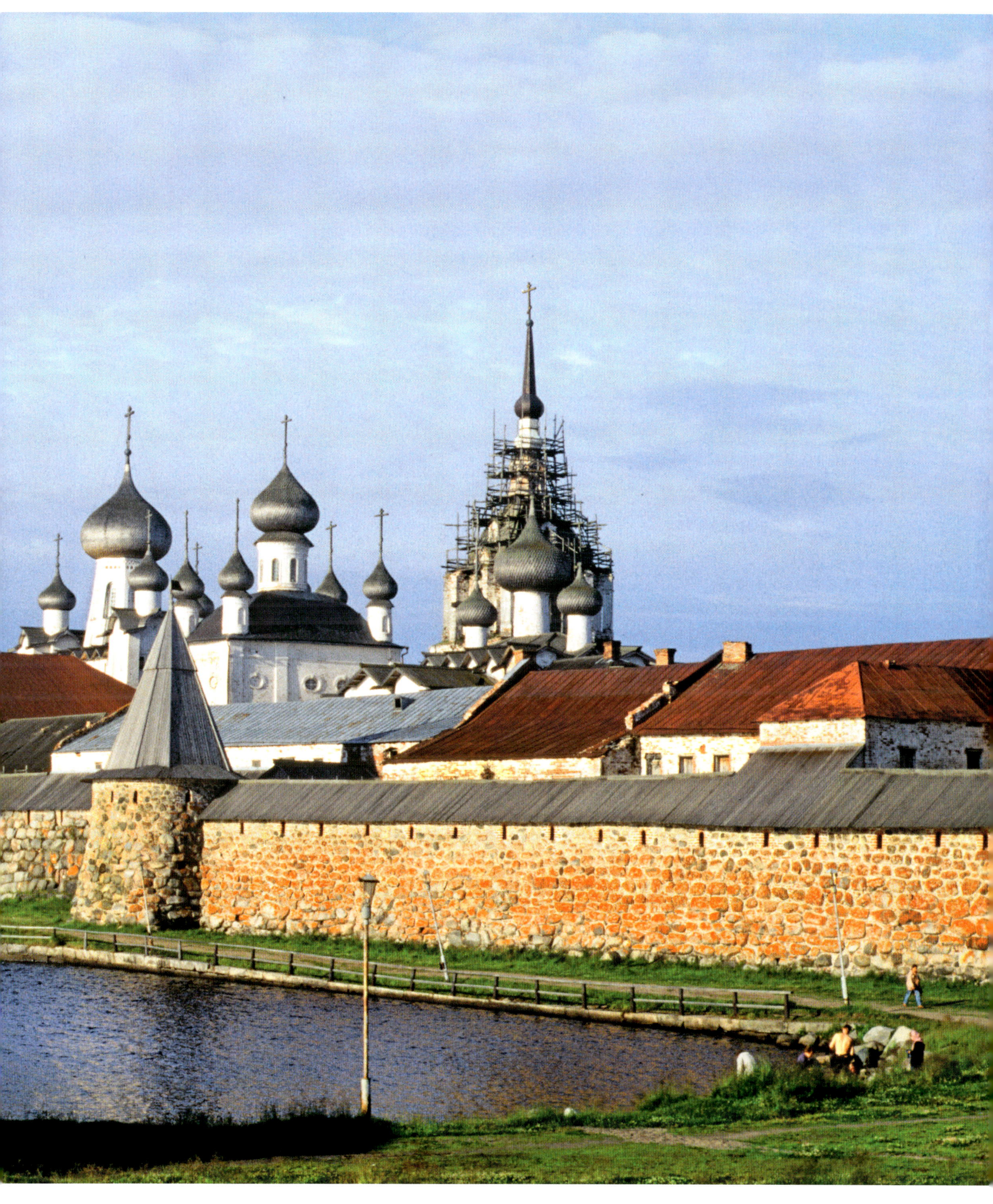

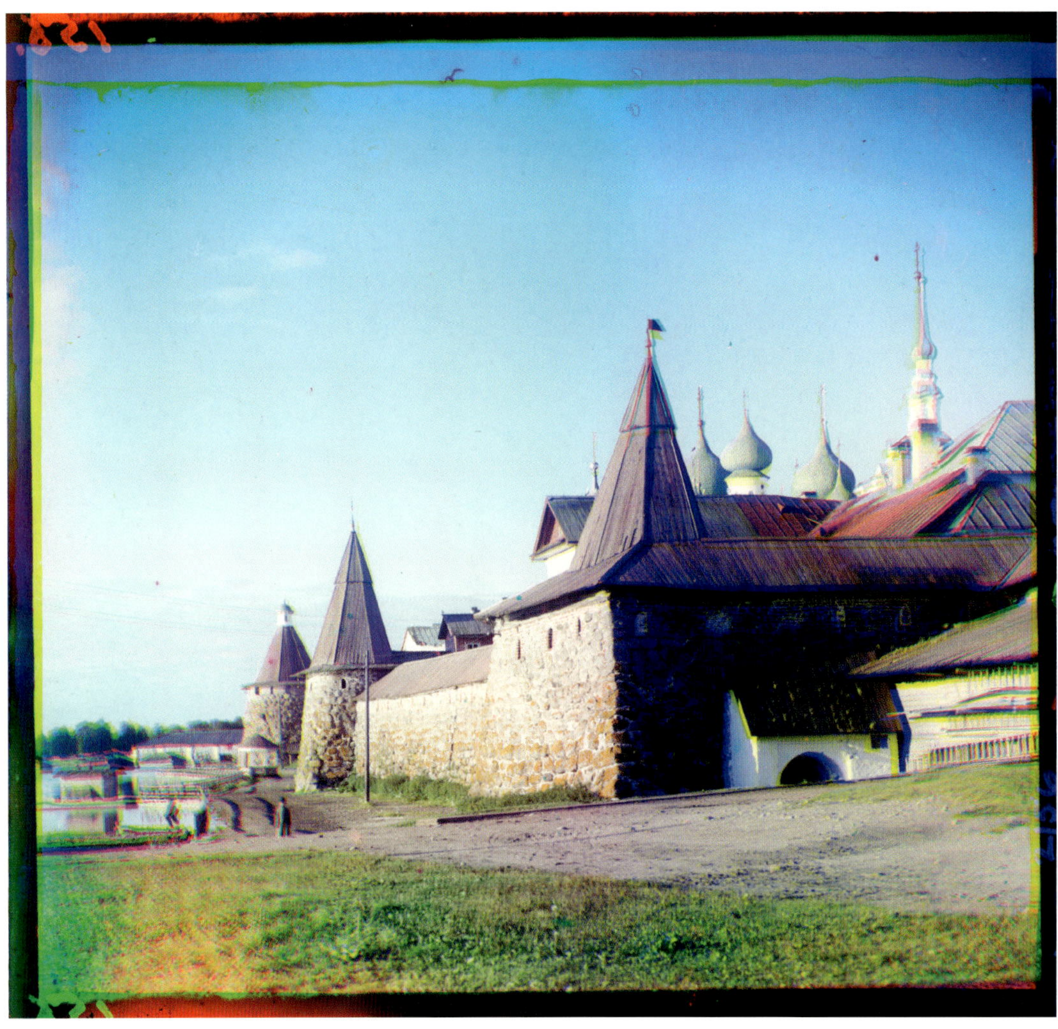

equipment provided by the Saint Petersburg affiliate of the Siemens Company. These improvements were very much in the spirit of Philip, who maintained a steady view of practical aspects necessary for the monastery's existence as a self-sustaining community. In that vein he initiated a system of canals to improve transportation through the boggy terrain. Expanded throughout the nineteenth century, the canal system continued to be developed, as photographed by Prokudin-Gorsky. Although no longer essential to the economic position of the monastery, the canals are still used.

The highest point on the main island — and the entire archipelago — is Sekirnaya Gora (Poleaxe Hill), almost eighty meters in height. In the nineteenth century a special monastic retreat (*skete*) was founded here and dedicated to the As-

SOLOVETSKY TRANSFIGURATION MONASTERY East wall. *From left*: Archangel Tower, Cooks Tower and Kvas Brewing Tower. Northeast view. PROKUDIN-GORSKY 20344. SUMMER 1916.

GREAT SOLOVETSKY ISLAND Work on boat canal. PROKUDIN-GORSKY 20353. SUMMER 1916.

GREAT SOLOVETSKY ISLAND Monastery boat canal. BRUMFIELD, JULY 26, 1998.

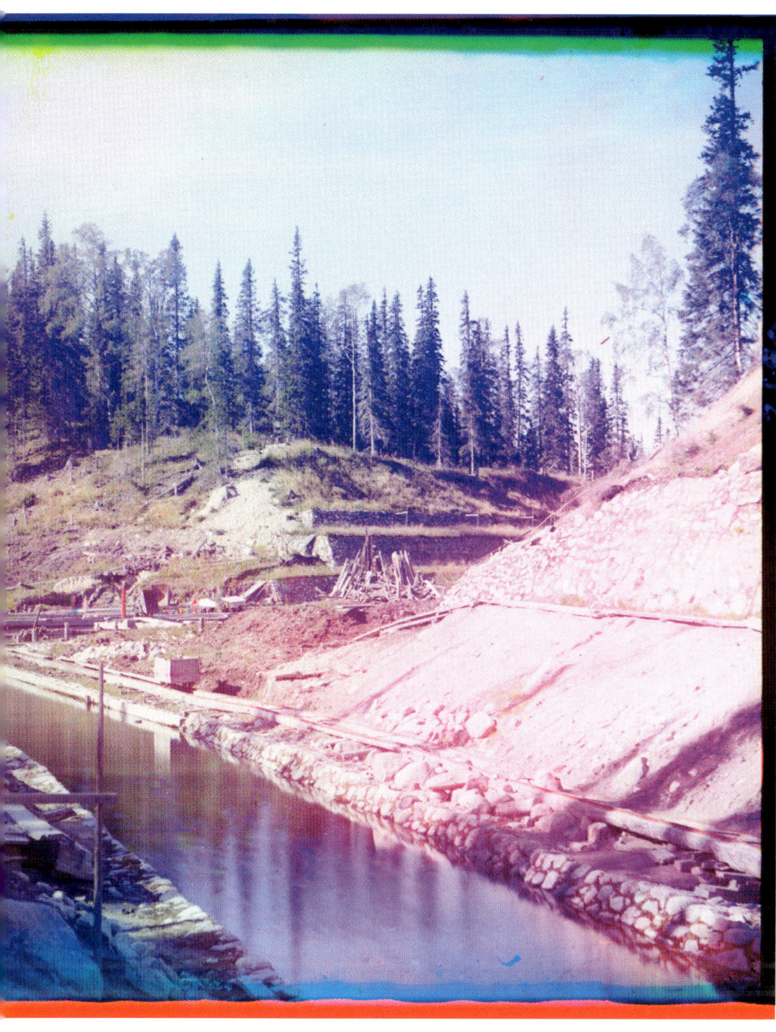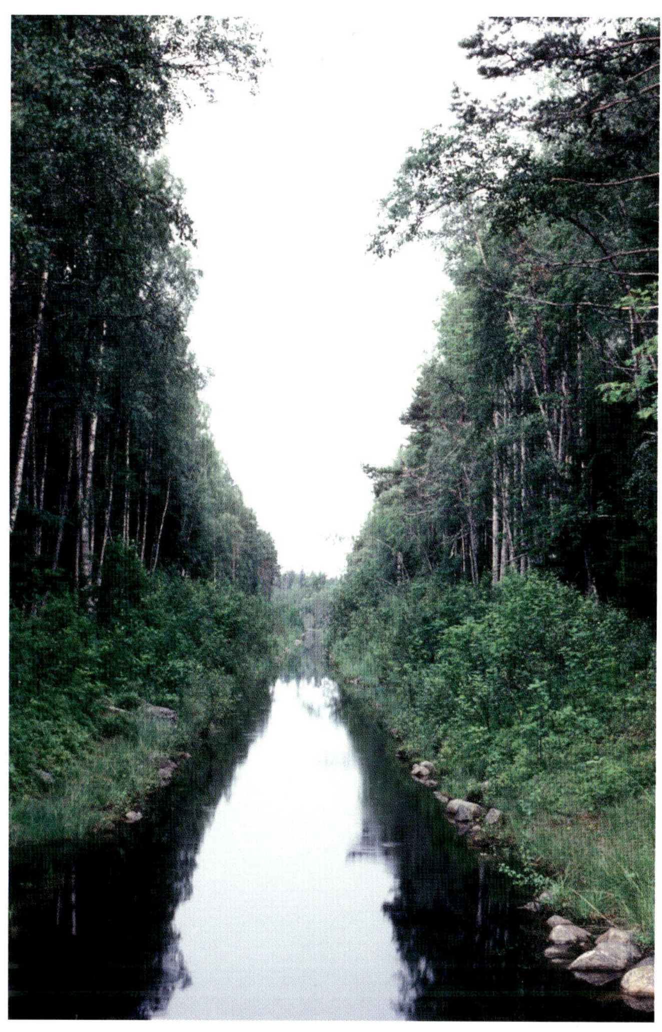

cension. A simple but sturdy two-story brick church of the same dedication was erected in 1860–62 to a design by A. I. Shakhlarev. Because of its commanding height and the dangerous waters surrounding the island, state authorities decided to place a small lighthouse above the cupola—a unique case in Russian church architecture. Its light can reach a distance of ten miles. Prokudin-Gorsky placed his camera in a hayfield and took a distant view of the entire hill, with the church jutting at the crown. I made a closer study of the church itself before its interior restoration.

Indeed, there is a haunting, strangely prophetic aura surrounding these photographs taken in the midst of a cataclysmic world struggle. Five years later, toward the end of the Russian civil war in 1921, the Bolsheviks expropriated the monastery. Two years later, a fire of mysterious origins spread throughout the central stone churches and reduced their interiors to ashes. It was here, in 1923, that the Soviet regime established a prototypical con-

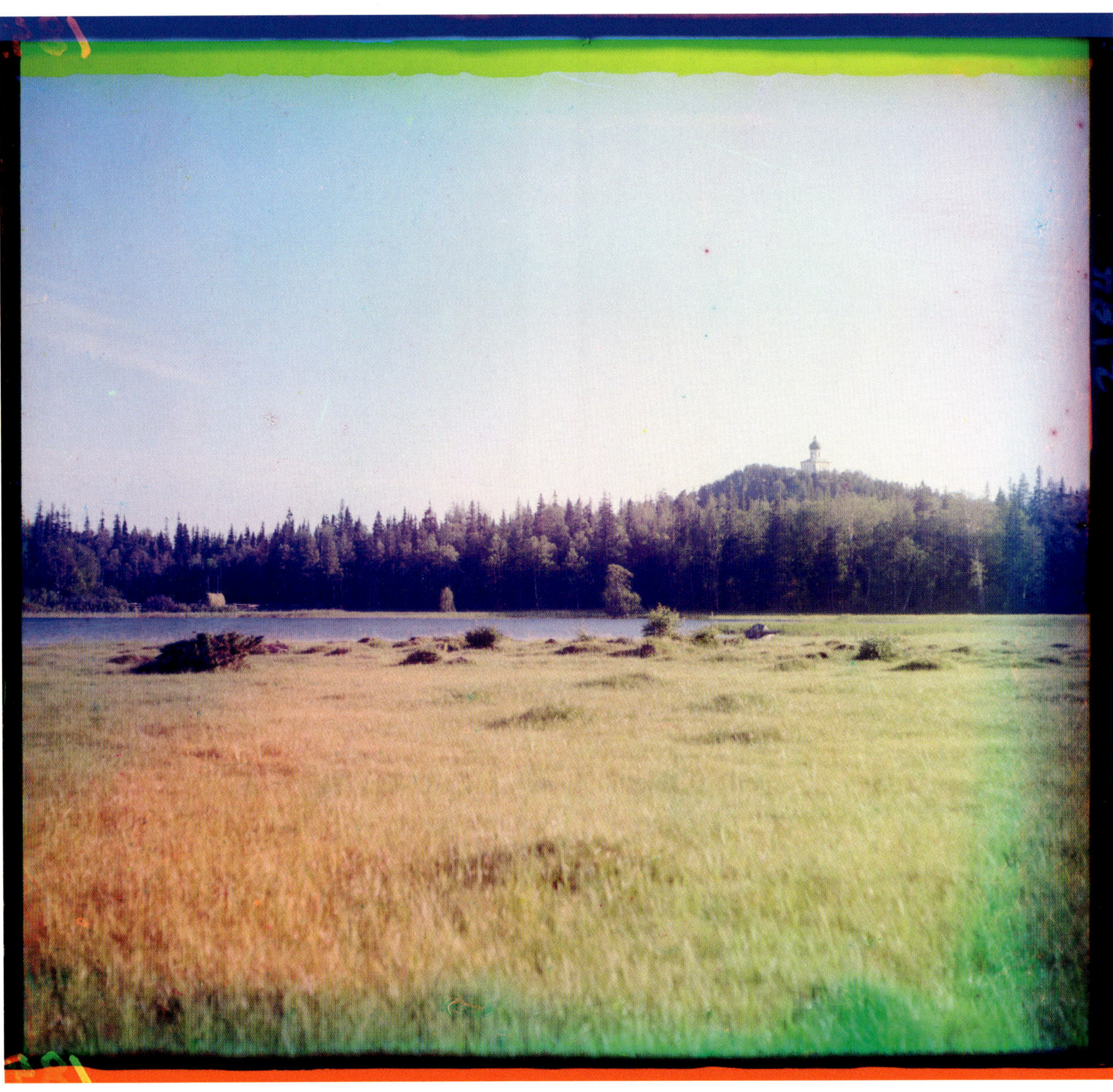

centration camp, named the Solovetsky Camp of Special Designation (SLON), described by Alexander Solzhenitsyn in his book *The Gulag Archipelago*. Superseded by larger camps, the Solovetsky camp closed in 1939, and the territory became a military base. Attempts to restore the monumental Transfiguration Monastery began in the 1960s. In 1992, Patriarch Aleksy reconsecrated the relics of the monastery's founders with solemn ceremony, and worship began on a regular basis. Much of the monastery has now been returned to the Orthodox Church.

GREAT SOLOVETSKY ISLAND
Sekirnaya (Poleaxe) Hill with Church of the Ascension. PROKUDIN-GORSKY 20356. SUMMER 1916.

GREAT SOLOVETSKY ISLAND
Church of the Ascension on Sekirnaya Hill. East view. BRUMFIELD, JULY 26, 1998.

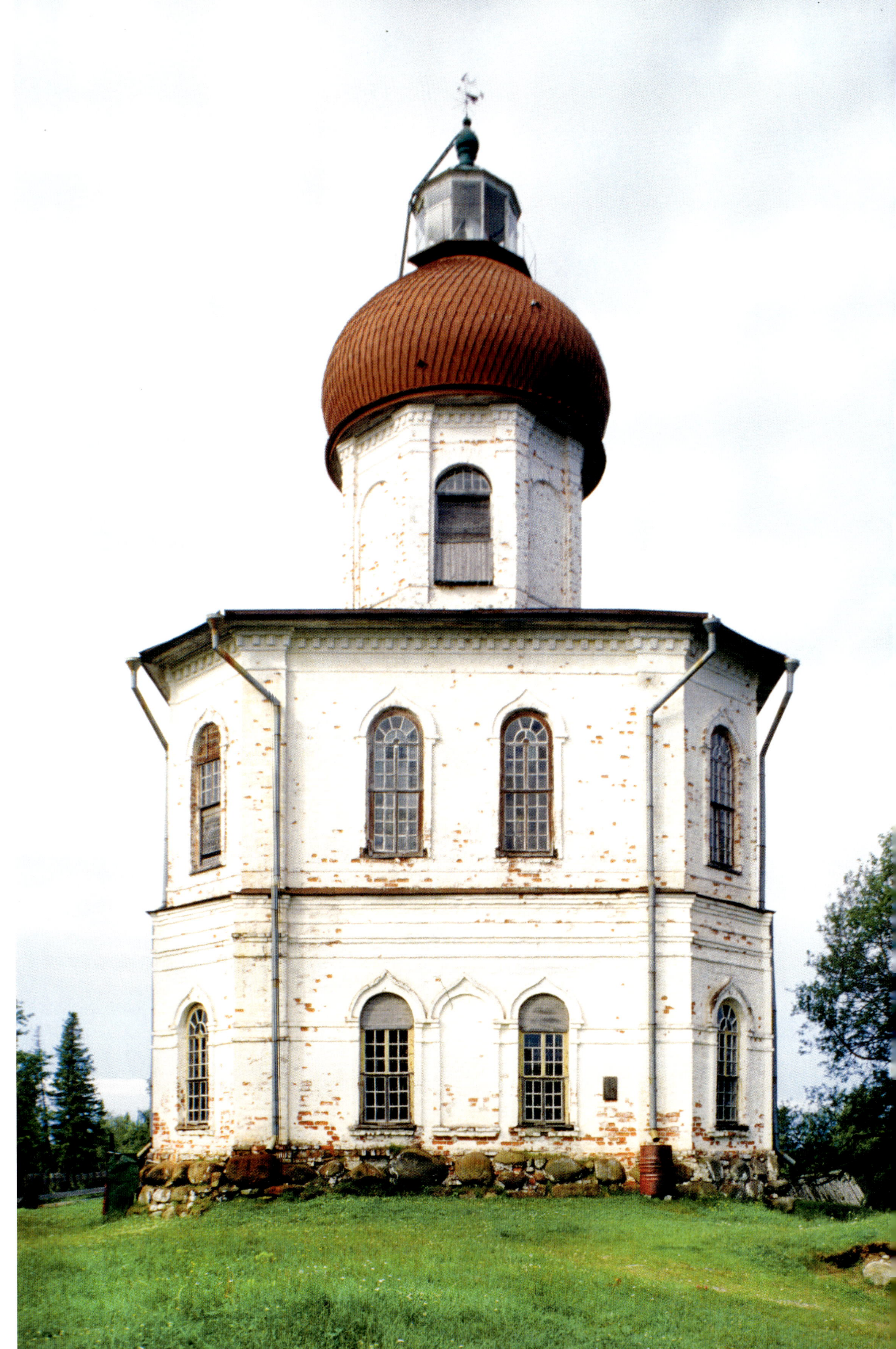

Above the Abyss

*A Reflection on Photography
as an Instrument of Memory*

Time and memory are two of the broadest categories in human thought, fundamentals of philosophy, and of thought about thought. Interpretations of Prokudin-Gorsky's photographic project—now universally available through the digitization of his collection at the Library of Congress—have often focused on their technical brilliance and the nostalgic appeal of a lost world vividly rediscovered in brilliant color. These photographs transport us back in time and create an illusion of memory. The images seem so tactile and so close. Such interpretations and glosses on Prokudin-Gorsky's work tell us much, but what do they neglect?

In Prokudin-Gorsky's idealistic project, photography, like the railroads that he rode and documented, served as a means of uniting a vast, culturally diverse empire through a vision that would enlighten those who saw the images. To behold the regions of the empire in bright colors would be to comprehend not only its diversity but also the role the empire played in uniting the peoples of an immeasurable Eurasian territory. In addition to documenting the medley of diverse cultures, he also recorded evidence of the empire's development. Commissioned to photograph the expansion of Russia's transportation network—seen as the engine of economic growth and progress—Prokudin-Gorsky paradoxically used that network as a means of recovering Russia's past. Yet his vibrant images portray an order that would collapse in almost unimaginable violence within a decade or less of the photographing. It would be unreasonable to fault Prokudin-Gorsky for lack of foresight, although as a resident of Saint Petersburg he was aware of the possibility of terror attacks: One of them killed a potential patron, prime minster Peter Stolypin, in 1911. And when he photographed Leo Tolstoy at his Yasnaya Polyana estate in 1908, he surely knew of the great writer's fulminations against the imperial regime and the Orthodox Church.

Nonetheless, with the eventual patronage of Nicholas II, Prokudin-Gorsky embarked on a heroic enterprise to record the empire as none before him had done, an enterprise that continues to enrich our knowledge and vision decades later. The question is not what eluded his vision but how do we respond to that vision? What are the levels on which we can respond? These are by no means simple questions, and attempts to address them often have an ideological bent. "The Russia that we have lost"—who are "we" and what was "lost" after 1917?

The answers could well depend on the specific group considering the question. Among Prokudin-Gorsky's photographs of splendid Islamic monuments in Bukhara, there are portraits of haggard prisoners held under barbaric conditions. Some might argue that these portraits, together with those of ample local potentates, play into a European, orientalist narrative of Central Asian societies as semibarbaric. But such an interpretation is out of character for Prokudin-Gorsky and does not correspond to the direct humanity of his photographs. In any event few would regret the loss of the Emirate of Bukhara, a harshly repressive regime that at the time of Prokudin-Gorsky's visit had the status of a Russian protectorate. But should we contemplate Prokudin-Gorsky's specifically Russian photographs without an awareness of the other parts of the empire that was Russia?

A contemplation of the Prokudin-Gorsky photographs raises challenging questions of social and political history. Several of his photographs show Russian settlers and enterprises in the southern areas of the empire, but to whom had that land belonged? The perspective that Prokudin-Gorsky implicitly endorses in his photographs is that of Russians as bringers of progress and amelioration. This approach became especially pervasive after widespread peasant uprisings in 1905–6 that led to the "Stolypin reforms" of 1906. For the next half decade Peter Stolypin initiated policies for the resettlement of hundreds of thousands of land-poor peasants from the Russian heartland to the empire's peripheral areas—a process facilitated by railroad construction. Prokudin-Gorsky's photographs show evidence of this new Russian presence.

However, it was one thing when peasants were steered to uninhabited tracts in Siberia, and another when they were given plots in southern areas (particularly Turkestan) that were inhabited by non-Russian peoples. Already exposed to wealthy, extensively irrigated cotton estates (which Prokudin-Gorsky also photographed) in the Syr-Darya basin, significant elements of the non-Russia population harbored a festering resentment that contributed to the explosive Central Asian revolt of 1916. This uprising, exacerbated by wartime conscription of Muslims, spread through much of Turkestan (including the Samarkand region) in the latter half of 1916 and led to a staggering carnage that is referred to in contemporary Kyrgyzstan as "genocide." Among other victims were Kazakhs and Russian settlers. The area that Prokudin-Gorsky had calmly photographed five years earlier was now torn by violence, while the photographer himself was at the other end of the empire at work on his last Russian expedition, to document construction of the strategic railroad to the new Arctic port of Murman (Murmansk). This urgent military project involved the forced labor of Central Powers prisoners-of-war, whom Prokudin-Gorsky also photographed.

The preceding comments should persuade us that nostalgic interpretations of Prokudin-Gorsky's photography ("the Russia we have lost," a sense of the lost idyll) may be superficially appealing, but they ignore a larger, at times devastating, context. We allow these photographs to transport us to reveries of the past, yet a knowledge of Russian history compels us to think about the future (now past) of the subjects portrayed. For example, to look at a group of children on a White Lake levee in Belozersk is to wonder what became of them in the next decade, after suffering years of war, social collapse, hunger, and savage violence. How many of them survived? The church in the background has long been a ruin, but what happened to the children?

The appealing, innocent faces of these and other children in Prokudin-Gorsky's work remind us of the opening words of Vladimir Nabokov's *Speak, Memory*: "The cradle rocks above the abyss, and common sense tells us that our existence is but a brief crack of light between two eternities of darkness." Photography is "light writing," and with an awareness of history Prokudin-Gorsky's photographs illuminate that Nabokovian moment. It might be added that *Speak, Memory*, first published as a single volume in 1951, is primarily devoted to a time and milieu that also nurtured Prokudin-Gorsky and was both forever lost and preserved through the writer's memory.

The enduring appeal of Prokudin-Gorsky's images suggests a further paradox: without a fundamental, destructive break caused by the Bolshevik revolution, the prerevolutionary past summoned in his photographs might have been viewed more critically, devoid of the pathos that enshrouds a violently destroyed ancien régime. The collapse of the Russian Empire was not simply the result of military defeat. As we have noted, the empire that Prokudin-Gorsky photographed encompassed traditional cultures of extraordinary beauty, and yet that empire was riven with apparently intractable social contradictions, violent political dissension, uneven economic development, illiteracy, and desperate poverty. Traces of those fractures and contradictions can be detected through a careful analysis of his photographs, yet there is some comforting impulse that draws us to interpret the photographs with an elegiac glow.

Literature can provide a cautionary note to idyllic reimagining. Andrei Belyi's novel *Petersburg* (first published in 1913, a productive year in Prokudin-Gorsky's work) and Alexander Zinoviev's satirical novel *Yawning Heights* (first published in Switzerland in 1976) both acerbically dissect Russian regimes in the process of dissolution. Yet in the aftermath of 1991 Zinoviev expressed regret for the collapse of the Soviet Union and vehemently criticized the immediate post-Soviet order. Neither Belyi nor Zinoviev would have recognized the rerevolutionary "Russia we have lost" as conceived by Stanislav Govorukhin (see introduction). And both would likely have been skeptical of Leonid Parfyonov's "flower of a nation."

Part of the conundrum is that Prokudin-Gorsky largely neglected the urban centers—Moscow and Saint Petersburg in particular—where urban social and political conflict was most obvious. This focus on the regions was the logical result of his agreement with the Ministry of Transportation. But did he have other motives in this decision? Did the regions seem (misleadingly) to provide a calmer, more stable representation of empire? Even so, there are elements of discord, such as the photograph with a Black Hundreds banner next to one of the most sacred Russian icons, the Smolensk Virgin. To speak of these hovering ambiguities is not to deny the profound cultural worth and beauty of Prokudin-Gorsky's photographs. They are not deceptions, but as complex works of art they expand under our gaze and cannot be reduced to simple interpretations.

Prokudin-Gorsky's work has now achieved a monumental status comparable to the architectural monuments that he recorded. His photographs not only evoke the past but also contribute to the bridge between past and future that we call "historical preservation." (In Russian the root of the term for "monument"—architectural or otherwise—is *pamyatnik*, related to the word for memory, *pamyat*.) Memory and preservation are inevitably linked to the past, but they are equally concerned with the creation of the future of our memory. What should we remember, and what should be preserved in order that we should remember the essential things? Recent discussions of collective memory and the creation of heritage symbols have focused on the work of Pierre Nora and his concept of *lieux de mémoire*. These "places of memory" need not be physical places but can refer to various modes of cultural expression that achieve a generally acknowledged position in a collective's consciousness of itself and memory of itself. I would suggest that Russian responses to Prokudin-Gorsky's collected photographs—which portray specific places—have themselves become a "place of memory." This complex and evolving process shows no signs of waning in the assimilation of his work.

However firmly cultural preservation and memory are embedded in society, the historian should be aware of the intricate nuances and ironies of preservation. Preservation by whom of what and for what reason? The Soviet period, for example, combined widespread destruction of religious art and architecture with the careful study and, at times, preservation of historical monuments—for the most part, Orthodox churches. In the Marxist concept of humanistic development, the secular enterprise of scholarship was to recast religious art as an episode within the history of artistic expression devoid of religious content and context. In a display of cyclical history, the Orthodox Church during the post-Soviet era has reclaimed for religious use many structures that were preserved through the vigorous efforts of museum specialists. The cycle continues as religion replaces secular agency, monuments are restored, and memory is recalibrated.

A comparison of Prokudin-Gorsky's photographs with mine provides examples of this evolving process and its many nuances in the Soviet and post-Soviet eras. Many of the churches that he photographed still stand, whatever the modifications and whatever the reasons for those modifications. There are areas, however, in which no comparison is possible. A large part of my photographic work has documented the architecture of Moscow and Saint Petersburg. Although Prokudin-Gorsky did limited commercial work in these two centers—the dual capitals of Russia—they are not represented in his collection as it has survived at the Library of Congress. Indeed, his mission was to present to Russia's capital cities images of the far-flung regions of the empire. Yet Moscow was the city in which the tumult of the twentieth century was most visibly transformative.

A few of the larger provincial cities, such as Smolensk, Yaroslavl, Perm, and Yekaterinburg, have their place in the Prokudin-Gorsky Collection. In the case of the first two, my photographs show the preservation benefits of city planning mindful of prerevolutionary patterns. The historical centers of Smolensk, Yaroslavl, and Tobolsk have survived in a form that Prokudin-Gorsky would quickly recognize. Yet in the major cities of Yekaterinburg and Perm, my views of sites photographed by Prokudin-Gorsky reveal a cityscape massively transformed by the Stalin-era industrialization drive and the concomitant antireligious campaigns, as well as the post-Soviet building boom. It is a dark caprice of fate that both sites connected with the final agony of the Romanovs—the Governor's House in Tobolsk, where Nicholas and his family were held from August 1917 until April 1918—and the Ipatiev House in Yekaterinburg—where they were murdered in July 1918—are visible (just barely) in Prokudin-Gorsky panoramas. The former, now a memorial museum to the Romanovs, appears in my photographs, while the latter, famously razed by Boris Yeltsin in 1977, is now occupied by the grand memorial Church on the Blood in Honor of All Saints Resplendent in the Russian Land, which incorporates the cellar of the Ipatiev house.

A significant part of my photographic collection is devoted to country estate houses, which suffered enormous damage during the twentieth century beginning with the revolutionary violence of 1905. Such estate houses played a pervasive role in Russian culture, from Pushkin, Tolstoy, and Turgenev to Chekhov and the works of numerous painters. Indeed, Prokudin-Gorsky came from a country estate (near Kirzhach), yet estate houses are absent in his collection—probably because they were remote from the transportation arteries that formed his official mission, At the same time, his photographs of Torzhok, Rzhev, and Staritsa give an idea of the regional market towns that sustained the surrounding estates. In Rzhev, largely destroyed in 1942 during some most savage battles on the Eastern Front, only isolated points of comparison remain. In contrast, my photographs of Torzhok and Staritsa reveal the paradoxical benefits of economic stagnation for preserving a provincial architectural environment.

Russia's wooden architecture—particularly its churches—has been loudly and rightly proclaimed as a consummate expression of the national culture. Yet the record of preservation in this area, as I have observed it over the past few decades, is not encouraging. The Prokudin-Gorsky Collection contains a few outstanding examples of wooden structures, such as the Church of the Intercession at Ankhimovo (Vytegra region), which before its destruction by a careless fire in 1960 rivaled the famous Transfiguration Church at Kizhi in its complexity and plentitude of domes. I photographed its recent reproduction overlooking the Neva River in the Saint Petersburg suburbs — a location that says as much about tourist cruise traffic as it does about preservation priorities.

Curiously, Prokudin-Gorsky did not photograph the wooden tower Church of the Dormition in Kondopoga (Republic of Karelia), even though he took a few technical photographs of the Kondopoga docks in 1916 as part of the Murman railway project. He must have seen this remarkable, soaring church that seemed to defy gravity on the shore of an inlet in the White Sea. In the summer of 2002 I photographed the interior as well as the exterior of the Kondopoga church, and it is prominently featured in the first chapter of my *Architecture at the End of the Earth: Photographing the Russian North*. As I write these lines in Moscow (August 2018), a colleague informs me that this surpassing landmark has just fallen to fire, an irreparable loss inflicted on Russia's architectural heritage — by an arsonist, in this case.

In surveying the paths of Prokudin-Gorsky's work and my own, I have found fortuitous congruencies, such as my trip to Central Asia in May 1972. Yet the most disturbing impression occurred during my trip to Rzhev in July 2016. I knew that the Rzhev so beautifully photographed by Prokudin-Gorsky had been pulverized during one of the most prolonged, destructive campaigns on the Eastern Front, but it was difficult to comprehend the extent of the carnage. Captured by the Wehrmacht in October 1941, Rzhev became the focus of a series of Soviet counteroffensives that extended from early January 1942 until March 1943, when the Red Army retook the town. Following their defeat in front of Moscow in late 1941, German forces were determined to hold the Rzhev salient as "a dagger toward Moscow," and Soviet forces were equally determined to take it. The struggle for Rzhev thus became a rare example on the Eastern Front of the lethal positional fighting that characterized the Western Front during World War I. As usual in such massive battles, casualty figures are debated, but both sides lost hundreds of thousands, with Soviet losses at least double those of the Germans.

Toward the end of my Rzhev visit in July 2016 — seventy-five years after the battle — I walked to a recently created war memorial cemetery on the north side of Rzhev. A joint Russian and German project, the memorial is located next to a large brick works. In the twilight I saw an open field. The German section, framed by replicas of statues by Käthe Kollwitz, consisted of rows of grey granite stones with thousands of names etched by computer-driven machines. In contrast, the Soviet side consisted primarily of covered pits edged with simple white concrete borders extending to a distant tree line — over ten thousand bodies in common graves (or, as Russians call them, "brotherly graves"). And this is only one of many anonymous graves in the Rzhev area. The exception to anonymity is at the entrance to the memorial, where thousands of Kazakh and Russian names are etched in red granite to commemorate the dead from the 100th and 101st Independent Infantry Brigades formed in the Soviet Republic of Kazakhstan—a reminder of the many nationalities that fought in the Red Army. There is also near the entrance a memorial to the hundreds of Jews from the Rzhev area massacred during the German occupation. It is unlikely that Prokudin-Gorsky—at that time living in German-occupied France—knew of the fate of the town he had photographed four decades earlier.

The presence of the Prokudin-Gorsky Collection at the Library of Congress is now a given, a jewel that has inspired decades of scholarship. And yet the very fact of the collection's survival remains an object of astonishment: Prokudin-Gorsky's frenetic activity before and during the Great War—and even during the first revolutionary year; the slaughter of Nicholas and his family; Prokudin-Gorsky's abrupt departure from Russia and wanderings in Europe between two world wars; the mysterious appearance of the bulk of his collection, enormous in its weight; his existence in Nazi-occupied France; his quiet death in late September 1944; and the visit of a representative from the Library of Congress a few years thereafter. What logic could possibly have predicated such a peripatetic course of events?

In many ways my own path is no less improbable. The idea to document and study Russia's architectural heritage took shape in the late 1970s while I was still lecturing on Russian literature in the Slavic Department at Harvard. Most said that the project I envisioned was not feasible, not appropriate. Some suggested that I become a professional photographer. How, they reasoned, was it possible to pursue a career that combined Slavic studies and photography? I believed, however, that in this specific case photography could serve as an inextricable element in the study of a neglected area of Russia's cultural history. Lacking the usual academic support, I found allies among those who responded to the photographs while understanding that I had the means to place them in a scholarly context. Encouragement came from a series of fortuitous meetings with discerning editors and publishers, but the ultimate validation of this overarching project came with the establishment of my collection at the Photographic Archives of the National Gallery of Art. With this support I was able to structure the photographic fieldwork as part of a fundamental archive that both preserved what I had done and allowed the documentary project to evolve.

The current volume is the manifestation of this evolving process. It takes its place as the continuation of work with Duke University Press that began with the publication in 1995 of *Lost Russia: Photographing the Ruins of Russian Architecture*, which has recently been republished in a twentieth-anniversary edition. Written in the wake of the Soviet Union's collapse, the book and its photographs provided a personal, aestheticized view of monuments and monumental ruins as I photographed them in that transitional period from the late 1980s to the early 1990s.

I was deliberate about the aestheticization because I found the monuments, even in ruined state, to be hauntingly beautiful. I wished to convey that. (Now that some of the monuments have been restored, I find them of less interest from an aesthetic perspective.) Copies of the book made their way to Russia, and I found that some colleagues there were puzzled by the title. In what sense did I think that Russia was "lost"? To an extent the intention of my title had been "lost in translation," yet their reaction led to a reexamination of the questionable use of the term "loss" in referring to a nation's culture.

My representation of Russia's architectural heritage in a changing social environment continued with the publication in 2015 of *Architecture at the End of the Earth: Photographing the Russian North*. Devoted to decades of fieldwork in the historical regions surrounding the White Sea, the volume provided a view of preservation and loss in a boundless area that continues to experience a negative demographic shift. Both Prokudin-Gorsky and I photographed monuments in the north, such as wooden churches, that no longer exist. Population loss is followed by loss of memory, yet photographs, properly recorded, provide a means for memory recovery in one of Russia's most distinctive regions. This current, third volume represents the capstone of my documentary project with Duke University Press. Combining my photographic work with that of Prokudin-Gorsky creates a depth of perception that illuminates, monument by monument, questions of conservation and restoration.

Architectural heritage is only one component of a nation's cultural history, yet this heritage acutely reflects the balance of cultural past with contemporary social and economic priorities. Historical buildings are a form of real estate, and as such are subject to competing interests. The survival or destruction of architectural landmarks—and specifically those photographed by Prokudin-Gorsky—may reflect many, seemingly contradictory impulses. We have noted the important role played by the Russian Orthodox Church in the process of restoration, yet the Church has often been criticized by preservationists for renovations taken after the restitution of church property.

Some observers would interpret the state of heritage preservation as a reflection of larger social and political issues. Without denying the existence of such issues, I have, during almost a half century of work in Russia, become increasingly wary of such extrapolations. To live in Russia and know its culture is to realize the nuances lost in stereotypes and facile generalizations. Photographs—existing beyond their original context—seem to invite such generalizations, and we assume responsibility for such myths when interpreting the work of Prokudin-Gorsky ("lost Russia"). Fortunately, his photographs are always accessible for reexamination. They not only provide an inexhaustible source of detail for Russia at a specific time but also a sense of time collapsed in our contemplation of each image.

I am reluctant to draw overarching conclusions based on my decades of field experience in the Soviet Union and in post-Soviet Russia. It is not my intention, nor is it the purpose of this book, to offer generalizations on the current condition of Russia, of Russian culture, or of Russian heritage preservation. These are broad topics that require separate and quite different studies. My comparative approach is based on the specifics of documenting architectural heritage in two photographic collections—Prokudin-Gorsky's and my own. This approach touches upon social and historical nuances, as I have indicated in my introductory and concluding comments on Prokudin-Gorsky's work. Beyond that, however, I do not wish to make general extrapolations based on fieldwork in complicated times in a very complex country.

In Russia, where I am considered a preservationist as well as photographer and historian, I am asked in public discussions whether my documentary project plays a constructive role in the preservation of architectural monuments. We (the audience and I) would like to think that it does. Russian colleagues have worked with great ingenuity to create digital archives for my photographs, and I am deeply grateful for these efforts. They have presented my record of their monuments to a public both in and beyond Russia. Many institutions have collaborated to create a durable, properly archived structure for Prokudin-Gorsky's photographs and for my own. These archival structures enable us to remember not just Russia's architectural heritage but also its reflection in history. Whatever the complexities of interpreting Prokudin-Gorsky's photographs of an empire on the brink of cataclysm, his dedication to documenting the land that he explored has given us an astonishing revelation of the power of photography.

INDEX